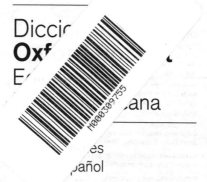

Diccio
Oxf
E

ana

es

pañol

OXFORD
UNIVERSITY PRESS

OXFORD
UNIVERSITY PRESS

Great Clarendon Street, Oxford OX2 6DP

Oxford University Press is a department of the University of Oxford.
It furthers the University's objective of excellence in research, scholarship,
and education by publishing worldwide in

Oxford New York

Auckland Cape Town Dar es Salaam Hong Kong Karachi
Kuala Lumpur Madrid Melbourne Mexico City Nairobi
New Delhi Shanghai Taipei Toronto

With offices in

Argentina Austria Brazil Chile Czech Republic France Greece
Guatemala Hungary Italy Japan Poland Portugal Singapore
South Korea Switzerland Thailand Turkey Ukraine Vietnam

OXFORD and OXFORD ENGLISH are registered trade marks of
Oxford University Press in the UK and in certain other countries

© Oxford University Press 2003
Database right Oxford University Press (maker)
First published 2003
2010 2009
10 9 8 7 6

This dictionary includes some words which have or are asserted to
have proprietary status as trade marks or otherwise. Their inclusion
does not imply that they have acquired for legal purposes a
non-proprietary or general significance nor any other judgement
concerning their legal status. In cases where the editorial staff have
some evidence that a word has proprietary status this is indicated in
the entry for that word but no judgement concerning the legal status
of such words is made or implied thereby

ISBN-13: 978 0 19 431600 2

Printed in China

Índice

Cómo utilizar el *Oxford Pocket*

palabras que se escriben igual pero tienen diferente significado	**bomba**[1] *nf* **1** (*Mil*) bomb **2** (*noticia*) bombshell ▶ **carro/paquete ~** car/parcel bomb
los distintos sentidos de una palabra	**bomba**[2] *nf* **1** (*Mec*) pump **2** (*And, gasolinera*) gas station, petrol station (*GB*) **3** (*And, elástica*) balloon ▶ **~ de aire** (air) pump
notas gramaticales, culturales y de uso	**computadora** *nf* (*tb* computador *nm*) computer **NOTA** Al empezar a trabajar en computador(a), se entra en el sistema (**log in/ on**). A veces hay que introducir una contraseña (**key in/enter your password**). Se puede navegar por internet (**surf the Net**) o mandar emails a los amigos (**email your friends**). Al terminar, se sale del sistema (**log off/out**). ▶ **~ personal** personal computer (*abrev* **PC**)
categorías gramaticales (verbo, sustantivo, etc.)	**dulce** *adj* **1** sweet **2** (*persona, voz*) gentle • *nm* candy [*pl* -ies], sweet (*GB*) → **CANDY** ▶ **~ de leche** soft fudge
remisiones a notas relacionadas	
ejemplos de uso	**reventar(se)** *vt, vi, vp* burst: *Si comes más, vas a ~.* If you eat any more you'll burst. ▶ **me revienta** I, you, etc. hate *sth*
información sobre el uso geográfico de una palabra	**reventón** *nm* (*Mx*) party [*pl* -ies]
plural irregular de los sustantivos	

información sobre el uso geográfico de una palabra	**baby carriage** n (USA) coche (de niño) (estilo moisés)
formas verbales irregulares	**babysit** /'beɪbɪsɪt/ vi (-tt-) (pt/pp -sat) ~ (for sb) cuidar a un niño (de algn) **babysitter** n babysitter
palabras estrechamente relacionadas con la principal	
otras formas posibles de escribir una palabra	**campground** (tb **campsite** GB) /'kæmpgraʊnd/-saɪt/ n camping (lugar) → CAMPING
pronunciación y acento	
adjetivos comparativos y superlativos	**cool** /kuːl/ adj (-er/-est) **1** fresco → FRÍO **2** (coloq) chévere, padre (Mx): "I'll meet you at three." "Cool." —Quedamos a las tres. —Vale. **3** (coloq) impasible
palabras que se utilizan en determinadas situaciones	**4** ~ (about sth/towards sb) indiferente (a algo/algn) **5** (acogida) frío ▶ keep/stay cool no perder la calma: Keep ~! ¡Tranquilo! •
estructuras gramaticales	vt, vi **1** ~ (sth) (down/off) enfriar(se) (algo) **2** ~ (sb) (down/off) refrescar(se) (a algn) ■ cool (sb)
phrasal verbs y expresiones	down/off calmar(se) (a algn) • the cool n [U] el fresco ▶ keep/ lose your cool (coloq) mantener/ perder la calma

A a

a prep
• **dirección** to: *Se acercó a mi.* She came up to me.
• **posición** on: *a la izquierda* on the left ◊ *a este lado* on this side ◊ *sentarse a la mesa* sit at the table
• **distancia**: *a 10m de aquí* ten meters from here
• **tiempo** (*hora, edad*) at: *a las doce* at twelve o'clock ◊ *a los sesenta años* at (the age of) sixty ◊ *Estamos a dos de mayo.* It's the second of May. **2** (*después de*): *al año de su llegada* a year after his arrival ◊ *Volvió a las dos horas.* He returned two hours later.
• **finalidad**: *Me agaché a recogerlo.* I bent down to pick it up.
• **modo o manera**: *ir a pie* go on foot ◊ *Hazlo a tu manera.* Do it your way. ◊ *vestir a lo hippy* dress like a hippy
• **complemento directo**: *No conozco a tu tía.* I don't know your aunt.
• **complemento indirecto 1** to: *Dáselo a tu hermano.* Give it to your brother. **2** (*para*) for: *Le compré un regalo a mi hijo.* I bought a present for my son. **3** (*de*) from: *No le copies a Juan.* Don't copy from Juan.
• **otras construcciones 1** (*medida, reparto*) at: *Salen a tres por persona.* **2** (*tarifa, precio*) a, per (*más fml*): *diez dólares al mes* ten dollars a month ◊ *Están a 200 el kilo.* They're 200 a kilo. **3** (*Dep*): *Ganaron dos a cero.* They won two to nothing. **4** (*órdenes*): *¡A trabajar!* Let's do some work! ◊ *¡Sal a buscarla!* Go out and look for her. ▸ **¿a qué...?** what...for? *¿A qué fuiste?* What did you go for?

abadía *nf* abbey

abajo *adv* **1** (*posición*) below **2** ~ **de** under **3** (*edificio*) downstairs: *el vecino de ~* the man who lives downstairs **4** (*dirección*) down: *calle/escaleras ~* down the street/stairs ● *interj* down with *sth/sb* ▸ **echar** ~ **1** (*edificio*) knock *sth* down **2** (*gobierno*) bring *sth* down **el/la de** ~ the bottom one **hacia** ~ downwards **más** ~ **1** (*más lejos*) further down **2** (*en sentido vertical*) lower down

abalanzarse *vp* **1** ~ **sobre** pounce on *sth/sb* **2** ~ **hacia** rush towards *sth/sb*

abanderado *nm* **1** (*Pol*) leader **2** (*representante*) representative

abandonado *adj* **1** abandoned **2** (*edificio*) derelict

abandonar *vt* **1** abandon: ~ *a una criatura/un proyecto* abandon a child/a project **2** (*lugar*) leave ● *vi* **1** (*desistir*) give up **2** (*Dep*) withdraw

abanicar(se) *vt, vp* fan (yourself)

abanico *nm* **1** fan **2** (*gama*) range

abarrotado *adj* crammed (with *sth*) ▸ ~ **de gente** crowded

abarrotar *vt* pack

abarrotería *nf* grocery store, grocer's (*GB*)

abarrotero/a *nm-nf* grocer

abarrotes *nm* groceries

abastecer *vt* supply *sb* (with *sth*): *La granja abastece de huevos a todo el pueblo.* The farm supplies the whole village with eggs. ● **abastecerse** *vp* stock up (on *sth*)

abastecimiento *nm* **1** (*acción*) supplying: *¿Quién se encarga del ~ de las tropas?* Who is in charge of supplying the troops? **2** (*suministro*) supply: *el ~ de agua* the water supply

abasto *nm* ▸ **no dar** ~: *Con tanto que hacer no doy* ~. I have far too much to do.

abdicar *vt, vi* abdicate

abdomen *nm* abdomen

abdominal *adj* abdominal ● **abdominales** *nm* **1** (*músculos*) stomach muscles **2** (*ejercicios*) sit-ups: *hacer* ~*es* do sit-ups

abecedario *nm* alphabet

abedul *nm* birch (tree)

abeja *nf* bee

abejorro *nm* bumblebee

abertura *nf* **1** (*hueco*) gap **2** (*grieta*) crack

abeto *nm* fir (tree)

abierto *adj* **1** open: *Deje la puerta abierta.* Leave the door open. ◊ ~ *al público* open to the public **2** (*llave*) running: *dejar una llave abierta* leave a faucet running **3** (*cierre*) undone **4** (*persona*) sociable

abismo *nm* **1** abyss **2** (*fig*) gulf

ablandar(se) *vt, vp* soften

ablusado *adj* loose-fitting

abobado/a *adj* = ATONTADO/A

abofetear *vt* slap

abogacía *nf* legal profession ▸ **ejercer la** ~ practice law

abogado/a *nm-nf* lawyer
NOTA Lawyer es un término general. En Gran Bretaña se

distingue entre **barrister**, que actúa en todos los tribunales, y **solicitor**, que normalmente se encarga de preparar los documentos legales y de asesorar a los clientes. En EE.UU. se usa **attorney** para hablar de los diferentes tipos de abogado: **criminal, tax attorney**, etc. ▶ **~ defensor** defense counsel **~ del diablo** devil's advocate

abolición *nf* abolition

abolir *vt* abolish

abolladura *nf* dent

abollar *vt* dent

abombado *adj* convex

abonar *vt* 1 *(tierra)* fertilize 2 *(pagar)* pay ● **abonarse** *vp* 1 *(publicación, servicio)* buy a subscription *(to sth)* 2 *(Dep, Teat)* buy a season ticket *(for sth)*

abono *nm* 1 *(fertilizante)* fertilizer 2 *(pago)* payment 3 *(Dep, Teat, transporte)* season ticket

abordaje *nm (barco)* boarding

abordar *vt* 1 *(barco)* board 2 *(asunto)* approach

aborigen *nmf* native

aborrecer *vt* 1 *(detestar)* detest 2 *(animal)* abandon

abortar *vi* 1 *(espontáneamente)* have a miscarriage 2 *(voluntariamente)* have an abortion ● *vt, vi (Comp)* abort

aborto *nm* 1 *(espontáneo)* miscarriage 2 *(provocado)* abortion

abotonar *vt* button *sth (up)*

abovedado *adj* vaulted

abrasador *adj* burning

abrasar *vt* burn ● *vi* 1 *(be* boiling hot 2 *(sol)* beat down ● **abrasarse** *vp* 1 burn yourself 2 *(al sol)* get sunburnt

abrasivo *adj, nm* abrasive

abrazar *vt* hug, embrace *(más fml)*

abrazo *nm* hug, embrace *(más fml)* ▶ **un (fuerte) ~** love/lots of love: *Dales un ~ a tus padres.* Give my love to your parents.

abrebotellas *nm* bottle-opener

abrecartas *nm* letter opener

abrelatas *nm* can-opener

abreviación *nf* shortening

abreviar *vt (palabra)* abbreviate

abreviatura *nf* abbreviation

abridor *nm* opener

abrigado/a *adj* 1 *(lugar)* sheltered 2 *(tb* **abrigador***)* *(ropa)* warm 3 *(persona)* well wrapped up: *Vas demasiado ~.* You've too many clothes on.

abrigar *vt* 1 *(prenda)* keep *sb* warm 2 *(arropar)* wrap *sb* up ●

vi be warm: *Este suéter abriga mucho.* This sweater's very warm. ● **abrigarse** *vp* wrap up

abrigo *nm* coat ▶ **al ~ de** sheltered from *sth* **de ~**: warm: *ropa de ~* warm clothes

abril *nm* April *(abrev* **Apr.***)* →MAYO

abrir *vt* 1 open: *~ la puerta* open the door ◊ *~ fuego* open fire 2 *(llave, gas)* turn *sth* on 3 *(túnel)* bore 4 *(agujero, camino)* make ● *vi (puerta)* open up ● **abrirse** *vp* 1 open 2 *(tierra)* crack ▶ **~se camino en la vida** get on in life **~se la cabeza** split your head open **en un ~ y cerrar de ojos** in the twinkling of an eye **no ~ el pico/la boca** not say a word

abrochar(se) *vt, vp* 1 do *sth* up *(for sb)* 2 *(broche, etc.)* fasten

abrupto *adj (terreno)* rugged

absceso *nm* abscess

absolución *nf* 1 *(Rel)* absolution 2 *(Jur)* acquittal

absoluto *adj* absolute ▶ **en ~**: *nada en ~* nothing at all ◊ —*¿Te importa?* —*En ~.* "Do you mind?" "Not at all."

absolver *vt* 1 *(Rel)* absolve *sb* 2 *(Jur)* acquit *sb (of sth)*

absorbente *adj* absorbent

absorber *vt* absorb

abstención *nf* abstention

abstenerse *vp* abstain *(from sth)*: *~ de fumar* abstain from smoking ◊ *El senador se abstuvo.* The senator abstained.

abstinencia *nf* abstinence

abstracto *adj* abstract

abstraído *adj* preoccupied

absurdo *adj* absurd

abuchear *vt* boo

abuelo/a *nm-nf* 1 grandfather *[fem* grandmother*]*, grandad *[fem* granny*]* *(coloq)* 2 **abuelos** grandparents

abultar *vi* be bulky: *¿Abulta mucho?* Does it take up much room?

aburrido/a *adj (que aburre)* boring ● *nm-nf* bore ▶ **estar ~** be bored →BE

aburrimiento *nm (tb* **aburrición** *nf)* boredom: *¡Qué ~ de película!* What a boring film!

aburrir *vt* 1 bore: *¿Te estoy aburriendo?* Am I boring you? ◊ *Me aburre este libro.* This book is boring. 2 *(hartar)* be sick of: *Me aburres con tus quejas.* I'm sick of your moaning. ● **aburrirse** *vp* get bored ▶ **~se como una ostra** be bored stiff

A

abusar *vi* ~ **(de) 1** abuse *sth/sb*: ~ *de la confianza de algn* abuse sb's trust ◇ *Abusaron de ella.* She was sexually abused. **2** (*alcohol, tabaco*) drink/smoke too much

abusivo *adj* (*aprovechado*) freeloader, scrounger (*GB*): *¡Mira que eres* ~! You're a real freeloader!

abuso *nm* **1** abuse: ~ *de drogas* drug abuse **2** (*alcohol, tabaco*) excessive drinking/smoking ● **es un** ~ that's outrageous

acá *adv* here: *Ven* ~. Come here. ◇ *Ponlo más (para)* ~. Bring it nearer. ◇ ~ **para allá** *Llevo todo el día de* ~ *para allá.* I've been running around all day. ◇ *He andado de* ~ *para allá buscándote.* I've been looking for you everywhere.

acabado *adj* finished

acabar *vt, vi* ~ **(de)** finish (*sth*): *Tengo que* ~ *de lavar el carro.* I have to finish washing the car. ● *vi* **1** ~ **(en/por)** end up: *El vaso acabará por romperse.* The glass will end up broken. ◇ ~ **en la ruina** end up penniless **2** **de hacer algo** have just done sth: *Acabo de verlo.* I've just seen him. **3** ~ **en** end in *sth*: *Acaba en "d".* It ends in "d". **4** ~ **con** (a) (*persona*) be the death of *sb* (b) (*poner fin*) put an end to *sth* ● **acabarse** *vp* run out (*of sth*) ▸ ~ **mal**: *Esto tiene que* ~ *mal.* No good can come that's it! ◇ *Ése acabará mal.* He'll come to no good. **¡se acabó!** that's it!

acabose *nm* ▸ **ser el** ~ be the limit

academia *nf* **1** academy [*pl* -ies]: ~ *militar* military academy **2** (*escuela*) school: ~ *de idiomas* language school

académico *adj* academic

acampada *nf* ▸ **ir de** ~ go camping

acampar *vi* camp

acantilado *nm* cliff

acariciar *vt* **1** (*persona*) caress **2** (*animal*) stroke

acarrear *vt* **1** (*transportar*) transport **2** (*causar*) bring *sth* about

acaso *adv* **1** (*quizás*) perhaps **2** (*preguntas*): *¿* ~ *dije yo eso?* Did I say that? ▸ **por si** ~ (just) in case

acatar *vt* (*ley, orden*) obey

acatarrarse *vp* catch a cold

acceder *vi* **1** (*estar de acuerdo*) agree (*to do*) *sth* **2** (*institución*) be admitted (*to sth*): *Las mujeres podrán* ~ *al ejército.* Women will

be admitted to the army. **3** (*Comp*) access *sth*

accesible *adj* accessible (*to sb*)

acceso *nm* **1** access **2** (*vía de entrada*) approach **3** ~ **de** (*ataque*) fit: *un* ~ *de tos* a coughing fit

accesorio *nm* accessory [*pl* -ies]

accidentado/a *adj* **1** (*terreno*) rugged **2** (*difícil*) difficult ● *nm-nf* casualty [*pl* -ies]

accidental *adj* accidental

accidente *nm* **1** accident: ~ *de tráfico* road accident ◇ *sufrir un* ~ have an accident **2** (*Geog*) (*geographical*) feature ▸ ~ **aéreo/de carro** plane/car crash

acción *nf* **1** action: *entrar en* ~ go into action ◇ ~ *legal* legal action **2** (*obra*) act: *una buena/mala* ~ a good/bad deed **3** (*Fin*) share

accionar *vt* work

accionista *nmf* shareholder

acebo *nm* holly bush/tree

acechar *vt, vi* lie in wait (*for sth/sb*)

acecho *nm* ▸ **estar al** ~ lie in wait (*for sth/sb*)

aceite *nm* oil

aceituna *nf* olive: ~*s rellenas/sin hueso* stuffed/pitted olives

aceleración *nf* acceleration

acelerador *nm* gas pedal, accelerator (*GB*)

acelerar *vt, vi* accelerate ▸ ~ **el paso** walk faster

acelerón *nm* ▸ **dar un** ~ (*Aut*) put your foot down

acelga *nf* chard [*U*]

acento *nm* accent: *con* ~ *cubano* with a Cuban accent

acentuar *vt* **1** (*poner tilde*) put the accent on *sth* **2** (*resaltar, agravar*) accentuate ● **acentuarse** *vp* (*llevar tilde*) have an accent

aceptable *adj* acceptable

aceptar *vt* **1** accept **2** (*acceder a*) agree (*to do sth*): *Aceptó irse.* He agreed to leave.

acera *nf* sidewalk, pavement (*GB*)

acerca *adv* ▸ ~ **de** about, concerning (*más fml*)

acercar *vt* **1** (*aproximar*) bring *sth* closer (*to sth/sb*) **2** (*dar*) pass: *Acércame el cuchillo.* Pass me the knife. **3** (*en carro*) give *sb* a lift ● **acercarse** *vp* get closer (*to sth/sb*), approach (*sth/sb*) (*más fml*): *Acércate a mí.* Come closer to me.

acero *nm* steel

acertado/a *adj* **1** (*correcto*) right **2** (*inteligente*) clever

acertante *nmf* winner

acertar vt guess ● vi 1 ~ (en/con) (al elegir) get sth right 2 (al obrar) be right to do sth 3 ~ (a/en) (al disparar) hit sth

acertijo nm riddle

achantado adj (And) down

achaque nm ailment

achatar vt flatten ● **achatarse** vp get flattened

achicar vt 1 (empequeñecer) make sth smaller 2 (agua) bail sth out

achicharrar vt 1 (quemar) burn 2 (color) scorch ● **achicharrarse** vp (pasar calor) burn

achís interj achoo NOTA Al estornudar, uno se disculpa con **excuse me!** La gente puede decir **bless you!**

acholado adj (And) mestizo [pl -s]

acidez nf acidity ▶ ~ **estomacal** heartburn

ácido adj (sabor) sharp ● nm acid

acierto nm 1 (respuesta correcta) correct answer 2 (buena idea) good idea

aclamar vt acclaim

aclarar vt 1 (explicar) clarify 2 (enjuagar) rinse 3 (color) lighten ● vi (cielo) clear up

acné nm acne

acobardar vt intimidate ● **acobardarse** vp feel intimidated

acogedor/a adj (lugar) cozy

acoger vt 1 (invitado, idea, noticia) welcome 2 (refugiado, huérfano) take sb in

acolitar vt (And) cover for sb

acomedido adj helpful

acomedirse vp (Mx) offer to help

acomodado adj (con dinero) well off

acomodador/a nm-nf usher [fem usherette]

acomodarse vp 1 (instalarse) settle down: ~ en el sofá settle down on the couch 2 (adaptarse) adjust (to sth)

acompañante nmf

acompañar vt 1 go/come with sth/sb, accompany (más fml): ¿Me acompañas? Are you coming (with me)? 2 (Mús) accompany sb (on sth)

acomplejarse vp get a complex

aconsejable adj advisable

aconsejar vt advise sb (to do sth): —¿Lo compro? —No se lo aconsejo. "Shall I buy it?" "I wouldn't advise you to."

acontecimiento nm event

acoplarse vp fit in (with sth/sb)

acorazado adj armor-plated ● nm battleship

acordar vt agree (to do sth) ● **acordarse** vp ~ (de) remember: Acuérdate de mandar la carta. Remember to mail the letter. ◇ Me acuerdo de haberlo visto. I remember seeing it. ◇ No me acuerdo de él. I can't remember him. →REMEMBER ▶ ¡te acordarás! you'll regret it!

acorde nm (Mús) chord

acordeón nm accordion

acordonar vt (lugar) cordon sth off

acorralar vt (persona) corner

acortar vt shorten ● **acortarse** vp get shorter

acostado adj 1 (tumbado) lying down 2 (en la cama) in bed

acostar vt put sb to bed ● **acostarse** vp 1 (ir a la cama) go to bed: Es hora de ~. Time for bed. 2 (tumbarse) lie down →LIE²

acostumbrado adj ▶ estar ~ a be used to sth/sb/doing sth

acostumbrarse vp get used to sth/sb/doing sth

acotamiento nm (Mx) breakdown lane, hard shoulder (GB)

acreedor/a nm-nf creditor ▶ ser ~ de be worthy of sth

acribillar vt 1 riddle: ~ a algn a balazos riddle sb with bullets 2 (mosquitos) bite sb to death

acrobacia nf acrobatics [pl]

acróbata nmf acrobat

acta nf 1 (reunión) minutes [pl] 2 (certificado) certificate

actitud nf attitude

activar vt 1 (poner en marcha) activate 2 (acelerar) accelerate

actividad nf activity [pl -ies]

activo adj active

acto nm 1 (acción, Teat) act: un ~ violento an act of violence 2 (ceremonia) ceremony [pl -ies]: el ~ de clausura the closing ceremony ▶ ~ seguido immediately afterward(s) en el ~ right away

actor, /actriz nm-nf actor [fem actress] →ACTRESS ▶ ~ principal male/female lead

actuación nf performance

actual adj 1 (del momento presente) current: el estado ~ de las obras the current state of the building work 2 (de hoy en día) present-day: la ciencia ~ present-day science NOTA La palabra inglesa **actual** significa "exacto", "verdadero": What's the actual date of the wedding? ¿Cuál es la fecha exacta de la boda?

actualidad nf present situation
▶ de ~ topical: temas de ~ topical issues

actualizar vt update

actualmente adv (ahora) at the moment **NOTA** La palabra inglesa actually significa "en realidad", "de hecho": It was actually quite cheap. En realidad fue bastante barato.

actuar vi 1 (artista) perform 2 ~ de act as sth

acuarela nf watercolor

acuario nm aquarium ● (tb Acuario) nm, nmf Aquarius

acuático adj 1 (Biol) aquatic 2 (Dep) water: deportes ~s water sports

acudiente nmf (And) guardian

acudir vi 1 (ir) go (to sth/sb): ~ en ayuda de algn go to sb's aid 2 (venir) come (to sth/sb): Los recuerdos acudían a mi memoria. The memories came flooding back. 3 (recurrir) turn to sb: No sé a quién ~. I don't know who to turn to.

acueducto nm aqueduct

acuerdo nm agreement ▶ de ~ all right, OK (más coloq) estar de ~ agree (with sb) ponerse de ~ agree (to do sth)

acuerpado adj (Am) muscly

acumular(se) vt, vp accumulate

acunar vt rock

acupuntura nf acupuncture

acurrucarse vp curl up

acusación nf accusation: hacer una ~ make an accusation

acusado/a nm-nf accused: los ~s the accused

acusar vt 1 accuse sb (of sth) 2 (Jur) charge sb (with sth) 3 (mostrar) show signs of sth: ~ el cansancio show signs of tiredness

acusetas nmf (tb acusón/ona nm-nf) tattletale, telltale (GB)

acústica nf acoustics [pl]

adaptador nm (Elec) adaptor

adaptar vt adapt ● adaptarse vp 1 (aclimatarse) adapt (to sth) 2 (ajustarse) fit

adecuado adj right: el momento ~ the right time

adelantado adj 1 (aventajado) advanced: Está muy ~ para su edad. He's very advanced for his age. 2 (que se ha hecho mucho): Llevo el ensayo muy ~. I'm coming along well with my essay. 3 (en comparaciones) ahead: Vamos muy ~s con respecto a la otra clase. We're way ahead of the other class. 4 (reloj) fast:

Llevo el reloj cinco minutos ~. My watch is five minutes fast.
▶ por ~ in advance

adelantar vt 1 (objeto) move sth forward 2 (fecha, etc.) bring sth forward 3 (reloj) put sth forward 4 (sobrepasar) pass, overtake (GB) 5 (cassette) fast forward ● adelantar(se) vi, vp (reloj) gain

adelante adv forward: un paso ~ a step forward ● interj (¡entre!) come in 2 (¡siga!) go ahead ▶ hacia/para ~ forwards más ~ 1 (espacio) further on 2 (tiempo) later

adelanto nm advance: los ~s de la ciencia advances in science ◊ pedir un ~ ask for an advance

adelgazar vi, vp lose weight: ~ un kilo lose a kilo

además adv 1 (también) also: Se lo acusa ~ de estafa. He's also accused of fraud. →TAMBIÉN 2 (lo que es más) (and) what's more: ~, no creo que venga. What's more, I don't think he'll come.
▶ ~ de as well as

adentro adv ~ (de) inside: Está muy ~. It's right inside. ▶ más ~ further in para mis ~s to myself, yourself, etc.: reír para sus ~s laugh to yourself

aderezar vt (ensalada) dress

aderezo nm (ensalada) dressing

adhesivo adj adhesive ● nm sticker

adicional adj (cama, etc.) extra

adicto/a adj addicted (to sth) ● nm-nf addict

adiestrar vt train

adiós interj 1 (despedida) goodbye, bye (coloq): decir ~ con la mano wave goodbye 2 (saludo al pasar) hello

adivinanza nf riddle

adivinar vt guess ▶ ~ el pensamiento read sb's mind

adivino/a nm-nf fortune-teller

adjetivo nm adjective

administración nf administration ▶ ~ de empresas business studies [sing] ~ de lotería lottery agency [pl -ies]

administrador/a nm-nf administrator

administrar vt 1 (gestionar) run: ~ un negocio run a business 2 (dar) administer sth (to sb): ~ justicia/un medicamento administer justice/a medicine ● administrarse vp manage your money

administrativo/a adj administrative ● nm-nf administrative assistant

admirable adj admirable

admiración nf (signo de puntuación) exclamation point, exclamation mark (GB)

admirador/a nm-nf admirer

admirar vt 1 (apreciar) admire 2 (asombrar) astonish

admisión nf admission ▸ examen/prueba de ~ entrance exam

admitir vt 1 (aceptar) accept 2 (culpa, error) admit 3 (dejar entrar) admit sth/sb (to sth) ▸ no se admite(n)...: No se admiten perros/menores de 18 años.. No dogs./No entrance to under-18s. ◇ No se admiten tarjetas de crédito. We do not accept credit cards.

adolescencia nf adolescence

adolescente nmf teenager, adolescent (más fml)

adolorido/a adj sore

adonde adv where

adónde adv interr where

adoptar vt adopt

adoptivo/a adj 1 (hijo, país) adopted 2 (padres) adoptive

adoquín nm paving stone

adorar vt adore

adormecerse vp doze off

adormecido/a adj sleepy

adornar vt decorate

adorno nm 1 decoration: ~s de Navidad Christmas decorations 2 (objeto) ornament

adosar vt (Mx, documento) attach

adquirir vt 1 acquire 2 (comprar) buy

adquisición nf acquisition

adrede adv on purpose

aduana nf 1 (oficina) customs [pl]: pasar la ~ go through customs 2 (derechos) customs duty

adulterio nm adultery

adúltero/a adj adulterous ● nm-nf adulterer

adulto/a adj, nm-nf adult: las personas adultas adults

adverbio nm adverb

adversario/a nm-nf adversary [pl -ies]

advertir vt 1 (avisar) warn sb (about/of sth) 2 (decir) tell: Se lo advertí. I told you so!

aéreo adj 1 air: tráfico ~ air traffic 2 (vista, foto) aerial

aeróbics (tb aeróbicos) nm aerobics [sing]: hacer ~ do aerobics

aeromoza nf stewardess

aeronave nf aircraft [pl aircraft] ▸ ~ espacial spacecraft [pl spacecraft]

aeropuerto nm airport

aerosol nm aerosol

afán nm (And) hurry [U]: No hay ~. There's no hurry. ▸ estar de/tener ~ be in a hurry

afanado adj (And) 1 (con prisa) in a hurry 2 (preocupado) worried

afanador/a nm-nf (Mx) cleaner

afanar vt (And) rush ● afanarse vp 1 ~ (en/por) try your hardest (to do sth) 2 (And, preocuparse) worry 3 (And, apurarse) hurry up

afectar vt affect

afecto nm affection ▸ tener/tomar ~ be/become fond of sth/sb

afeitar(se) vp shave: ~ la barba/la cabeza shave your beard off/shave your head ▸ cuchilla/hoja de ~ razor blade

afeminado adj effeminate

aferrarse vp cling to sth/sb

afiche nm poster

afición nf 1 interest (in sth) 2 (pasatiempo) hobby [pl -ies]

aficionado/a adj 1 (entusiasta) keen (on sth) 2 (amateur) amateur ● nm-nf 1 (a) (Dep, música pop) fan (b) (Cine, Teat, música clásica) lover: un ~ a la ópera an opera lover 2 (amateur) amateur

aficionarse vp 1 (pasatiempo) get into sth 2 (placeres, vicios) acquire a taste for sth

afilado adj sharp

afilar vt sharpen

afiliarse vp ~ (a) join (sth)

afinar vt (Mús) tune ▸ ~ la puntería take better aim

afirmar vt state, say (más coloq): Afirmó sentirse preocupado. He said he was worried. ▸ ~ con la cabeza nod (your head)

afirmativo adj affirmative

aflojar vt loosen ● aflojarse vp 1 loosen 2 (tornillo, nudo) come loose

afluente nm tributary [pl -ies]

afónico adj ▸ estar/quedarse ~ have lost/lose your voice

afortunado adj lucky

África nf Africa

africano/a adj, nm-nf African

afrontar vt face up to sth

afuera adv outside ● afueras nf outskirts: en las ~s on the outskirts

agachar vt lower: ~ la cabeza lower your head ● agacharse vp bend down

agallinarse vp lose your nerve

agalludo adj (And) stingy

agarrar vt 1 (asir) grab: ~ a algn del brazo grab sb by the arm 2 (sujetar) hold 3 (atrapar, contraer) catch: ~ una gripa catch flu ● **agarrarse** *vp* hold on (to *sth/sb*)

agazaparse *vp* crouch (down)

agencia *nf* agency [*pl* -ies] ▶ ~ **de viajes** travel agency [*pl* -ies]

agenda *nf* 1 (*calendario*) datebook, diary [*pl* -ies] (*GB*) 2 (*direcciones, teléfonos*) address book

agente *nmf* 1 (*representante*) agent 2 (*policía*) police officer

ágil *adj* (*persona*) agile

agilidad *nf* agility

agitado *adj* 1 (*vida, día*) hectic 2 (*mar*) rough

agitar *vt* 1 (*botella*) shake 2 (*pañuelo, brazos*) wave 3 (*alas*) flap ● **agitarse** *vp* get worked up

agobiante *adj* 1 (*persona*) tiresome 2 (*calor*) stifling

agobiar *vt* overwhelm ● **agobiarse** *vp* be weighed down with *sth*

agobio *nm* 1 (*calor*): ¡*Qué* ~! *Abre la ventana.* Phew! Open the window. 2 (*preocupación*): *Estoy con el* ~ *de los exámenes.* I'm in a sweat about the exams.

agonía *nf* agony [*pl* -ies] ● **agonías** *nmf* misery [*pl* -ies]: *Eres una verdadera* ~. You're a real misery.

agonizar *vi* be dying

agosto *nm* August (*abrev* **Aug.**) → MAYO ▶ **hacer el/su** ~ make a fortune

agotado *adj* 1 (*cansado*) worn out, exhausted (*más fml*) 2 (*existencias*) sold out 3 (*libros*) out of print

agotador *adj* exhausting

agotamiento *nm* exhaustion

agotar *vt* 1 exhaust 2 ~ *un tema* exhaust a subject 2 (*existencias*) use *sth* up 3 (*cansar*) wear *sb* out ● **agotarse** *vp* 1 run out: *Se me agota la paciencia.* My patience is running out. 2 (*libro, entradas*) sell out

agraciado *adj* 1 (*físico*) attractive 2 (*número*) winning

agradable *adj* pleasant ▶ ~ **a la vista/al oído** pleasing to the eye/ear

agradar *vi* please *sb*: *Intenta* ~ *a todo el mundo.* He tries to please everyone.

agradecer *vt* 1 (*dar las gracias*) thank *sb* (for *sth*): *Agradezco que hayas venido.* Thank you for coming. 2 (*sentir gratitud*) be grateful to *sb* (for *sth*)

agradecido *adj* grateful: *Le quedo muy* ~. I am very grateful to you.

agradecimiento *nm* gratitude: *unas palabras de* ~ a few words of thanks

agrandar *vt* enlarge

agrario *adj* (*ley, etc.*) land: *reforma agraria* land reform

agravar *vt* make *sth* worse ● **agravarse** *vp* get worse

agredir *vt* attack

agregar *vt* add (*sth* to *sth*)

agresión *nf* aggression

agresivo *adj* aggressive

agrícola *adj* agricultural

agricultor/a *nm-nf* farmer

agricultura *nf* farming, agriculture (*más fml*)

agridulce *adj* sweet and sour

agriera *nf* acidity

agrietar(se) *vt, vp* 1 crack 2 (*piel*) chap

agrio *adj* 1 (*leche, carácter*) sour 2 (*limón, experiencia*) bitter

agriparse *vp* catch a cold

agronomía *nf* agronomy

agrónomo *adj* agricultural

agrupar *vt* put *sth/sb* in a group ● **agruparse** *vp* get into groups: ~ *de tres en tres* get into groups of three

agua *nf* water ▶ ~ **corriente** running water ▶ ~ **de la llave** tap water ▶ ~ **de limón** (*real*) lemonade ▶ ~ **dulce/salada** fresh/salt water: *peces de* ~ *dulce* freshwater fish ▶ ~ **mineral (con/sin gas)** (fizzy/still) mineral water ▶ ~ **oxigenada** hydrogen peroxide ▶ ~ **potable** drinking water ▶ ~**s negras** sewage [*U*] ▶ **con el** ~ **al cuello** in deep water

aguacate *nm* avocado [*pl* -s]

aguacero *nm* (heavy) shower: *Ayer cayó un buen* ~. It really poured down yesterday.

aguafiestas *nmf* spoilsport

aguamala *nf* jellyfish [*pl* jellyfish]

aguanieve *nf* sleet

aguantar *vt* 1 put up with *sth/sb*: ~ *el dolor* put up with the pain **NOTA** En negaciones se usa mucho **stand**: *No aguanto este calor.* I can't stand this heat. ◊ ¡*No hay quien te aguante!* You're unbearable! 2 (*peso*) take: *El puente no aguantó el peso.* The bridge couldn't take the weight. 3 (*respiración*) hold ● *vi* 1 (*durar*) last 2 (*esperar*) hold on 3 (*resistir*) hold ● **aguantarse** *vp* put up with it: *Yo también tengo hambre, pero me aguanto.* I'm hungry too, but I put up with it. ◊ *Si no te gusta, te aguantas.* If you don't like it, tough!

aguante nm **1** (físico) stamina **2** (paciencia) patience: ¡Tienes un ~! You're so patient!

aguardiente nm eau-de-vie

aguarrás nm white spirit

aguas interj (Mx) watch out

agudo adj **1** (inteligencia, etc.) sharp **2** (ángulo, dolor) acute **3** (sonido, voz) high-pitched **4** (comentario) witty **5** Es una palabra aguda. The accent is on the last syllable. ● **agudos** nm (Mús) treble [U]

aguijón nm (insecto) sting ▸ **clavar el ~** sting

águila nf eagle ▸ **~ o sol** (Mx) heads or tails

aguja nf **1** needle: enhebrar una ~ thread a needle ◇ ~s de pino pine needles **2** (reloj) hand **3** (tocadiscos) stylus

agujero nm hole: hacer un ~ make a hole ▸ **~ negro** black hole

agujetas nf (Mx) shoelaces ▸ **tener ~** be stiff: Tengo ~ en las piernas. My legs are stiff.

ahí adv **1** there: Ahí lo tienes. There it is. **2** (más o menos) not bad: –¿Cómo andas? –Ahí. "How are you?""Not too bad." ▸ **~ abajo/arriba** down/up there ~ **dentro/fuera** in/out there ~ **mismo** right there ¡~ va! (jagárrala!) catch! ¡~ voy! coming! **por ~ 1** (lugar determinado) over there **2** (lugar no determinado): He estado por ~. I've been out. ◇ ir por ~ dar una vuelta go out for a walk **3** (tiempo) around: por ~ a la una at around one

ahijado/a nm-nf godchild [pl godchildren] [masc godson] [fem god-daughter]

ahogador nm (Mx) choke

ahogar vt **1** (asfixiar) suffocate **2** (en agua) drown ● **ahogarse** vp **1** (asfixiarse) suffocate **2** (en agua) drown **3** (respirar mal): Cuando me da el asma me ahogo. When I have an asthma attack, I can't breathe. **4** (al atragantarse) choke ▸ **~se en un vaso de agua** be get worked up over nothing

ahora adv now: hasta ~ up until now ◇ ~ voy. I'm coming. ▸ **~ mismo 1** (en este momento) right now **2** (enseguida) right away **de ~ en adelante** from now on ¡hasta ~! see you soon!

ahorcado nm (juego) hangman

ahorcar(se) vt, vp (oneself) NOTA En el sentido de "ahorcar", el verbo hang forma el pasado con -ed.

ahorita adv right away

ahorrador/a adj thrifty: ser poco ~ be bad with money ● nm-nf saver

ahorrar vt, vi save: ~ tiempo/dinero save time/money

ahorro nm saving: mis ~s de toda la vida my life savings

ahumado adj smoked ● **ahumados** nm smoked fish [U]

ahumar vt **1** (alimentos) smoke **2** (habitación) fill sth with smoke ● **ahumarse** vp **1** (habitación) fill with smoke **2** (ennegrecerse) blacken

ahuyentar vt frighten sth/sb away

aire nm **1** air: ~ puro fresh air **2** (viento) wind: Hace mucho ~. It's very windy. ▸ **~ acondicionado** air conditioning **al ~:** con el pecho al ~ barechested ◇ un vestido con la espalda al ~ a backless dress **al ~ libre** in the open air: un concierto al ~ libre an open-air concert **a mi ~:** estar a su ~ do your own thing ◇ hacer algo a mi ~ do sth my way **darse ~s de superioridad** put on airs **saltar/volar por los ~s** blow up **tomar el ~** get some fresh air

airear vt air ● **airearse** vp get some fresh air

aislado adj isolated

aislante adj insulating ● nm insulator

aislar vt **1** (separar) isolate sth/sb (from sth/sb) **2** (incomunicar) cut sth/sb off (from sth/sb) **3** (con aislante) insulate

ajedrez nm **1** (juego) chess **2** (tablero y piezas) chess set

ajeno adj **1** (de otro) somebody else's **2** (de otros) other people's: meterse en los problemas ~s interfere in other people's lives

ajetreado adj busy

ají nm chili [pl -ies]

ajo nm garlic

ajuar nm trousseau

ajustado adj tight

ajustar vt **1** adjust **2** (apretar) tighten **3** (puerta) leave sth ajar ● vi fit: La puerta no ajusta. The door doesn't fit. ▸ **~ las cuentas** settle accounts with sb

al prep + inf **1** when: Se echó a reír al verme. He burst out laughing when he saw me. **2** (simultaneidad) as: Lo vi al salir. I saw him as I was leaving.

ala nf **1** wing: las ~s de un avión the wings of a plane ◇ el ~ radical del partido the radical wing of the party **2** (sombrero) brim

▶ **~ delta 1** (*aparato*) hang-glider **2** (*deporte*) hang-gliding

alabanza nf praise [U]

alabar vt praise sth/sb (for sth)

alacrán nm scorpion

alambrada nf wire fence

alambre nm wire

álamo nm poplar

alarde nm ▶ **hacer ~ de** show off about sth

alardear vi boast (about/of sth)

alargado adj long

alargar vt **1** extend: *~ una carretera* extend a road **2** (*ropa*) lengthen **3** (*duración*) prolong **4** (*estirar, brazo, mano*) stretch sth out ● **alargarse** vp **1** get longer **2** (*prolongarse demasiado*) drag on **3** (*al hablar*) go on for too long

alarma nf alarm: *dar la (voz de) ~* raise the alarm ◊ *Saltó la ~.* The alarm went off. ▶ **~ antirrobo/de incendios** burglar/fire alarm

alarmante adj alarming

alarmarse vp **~ (por)** be alarmed (at sth)

alba nf dawn: *al ~* at dawn

albañil nmf **1** builder **2** (*que sólo pone ladrillos*) bricklayer

albaricoque nm apricot

alberca nf (*Mx*) swimming pool ▶ **~ cubierta** indoor pool

albergar vt house ● **albergarse** vp shelter

albergue nm **1** (*residencia*) hostel: *un ~ juvenil* a youth hostel **2** (*de montaña*) shelter

albóndiga nf meatball

alborotado adj **1** (*excitado*) in a state of excitement: *Los ánimos están ~s.* Feelings are running high. **2** (*con confusión*) in confusion

alborotar vt **1** (*desordenar*) mess sth up **2** (*revolucionar*) stir sth up ● vi (*hacer ruido*) make a racket ● **alborotarse** vp get excited

alboroto nm **1** (*barullo*) racket **2** (*disturbar*) disturbance

álbum nm album

albur nm (*Mx*) pun

alburear vi (*Mx*) play with words

alcachofa nf artichoke

alcalde/esa nm-nf mayor

alcance nm **1** reach: *al ~ de la mano* within reach **2** (*arma, emisora*) range: *misiles de medio ~* medium-range missiles

alcancía nf money box

alcantarilla nf sewer

alcantarillado nm sewage system

alcanzar vt **1** reach: *~ un acuerdo* reach an agreement **2** (*conseguir*) achieve **3** (*atrapar*) catch sb up ● vi **1** (*ser suficiente*) be enough **2** (*llegar*) reach: *No alcanzo.* I can't reach.

alcaparra nf caper

alcoba nf bedroom

alcohol nm alcohol ▶ **sin ~** non-alcoholic

alcohólico/a adj, nm-nf alcoholic

alcoholismo nm alcoholism

aldea nf small village

aldeano/a adj, nm-nf villager

alebrestarse vp (*And*) **1** get worked up **2** (*caballo*) rear up

alegar vt **1** claim: *Alegan que existió fraude.* They're claiming fraud. **2** (*razones, motivos*) cite

alegrar vt **1** (*hacer feliz*) make sb happy **2** (*animar*) (a) (*persona*) cheer sb up (b) (*fiesta*) liven sth up **3** (*casa, etc.*) brighten sth up ● **alegrarse** vp **1** (*estar contento*) (a) be pleased (about sth/to do sth): *Me alegro de saberlo.* I am pleased to hear it. (b) be delighted for sb **2** ▶ **por algo** (*cara, ojos*) light up

alegre adj **1** (*feliz*) happy **2** (*de buen humor*) cheerful **3** (*música, espectáculo*) lively **4** (*color, habitación*) bright

alegría nf joy: *gritar/saltar de ~* shout/jump for joy ▶ **¡qué ~!** that's great! *¡Qué ~ verte!* It's great to see you!

alejar vt **1** (*retirar*) move sth/sb away (from sth/sb) **2** (*distanciar*) distance sth/sb (from sth/sb) ● **alejarse** vp **1** (*apartarse*) move away (from sth/sb): *~ de un objetivo* move away from a goal ◊ *No se alejen mucho.* Don't go too far away. **2** (*camino*) leave

alemán/ana adj, nm-nf, nm German

alergia nf allergy [pl -ies] (to sth): *tener ~ a algo* be allergic to sth ▶ **~ al polen** hay fever

alérgico/a adj allergic (to sth)

alero nm (*tejado*) eaves [pl]

alerta adj, nf alert: *en estado de ~* on the alert ◊ *Dieron la (voz de) ~.* They sounded the alert.

alertar vt alert sb (to sth)

aleta nf **1** (*pez*) fin **2** (*buceador, foca*) flipper **3** (*Aut*) fender, wing (GB)

alfabético adj alphabetical

alfabeto nm alphabet

alfalfa nf alfalfa

alféizar nm (*ventana*) window sill

alfiler nm pin

alfombra nf **1** (*grande*) carpet **2** (*más pequeña*) rug

alfombrilla nf mat

alga nf **1** (*agua dulce*) weed [U] **2** (*agua salada*) seaweed [U] **NOTA** También existe la palabra científica **algae**.

álgebra nf algebra

algo pron something, anything **NOTA** La diferencia entre **something** y **anything** es la misma que hay entre **some** y **any**. →SOME ● adv **1** + adj rather: ~ *ingenuo* rather naive → FAIRLY **2** + verbo a little: *Mi hija me ayuda* ~. My daughter helps me a little. ▶ ~ **así** something like that *¿~ más?* (*en tienda*) anything else? **en** ~ in any way: *Si en* ~ *puedo ayudarles...* If I can help you in any way... **por** ~ **será** there must be a reason

algodón nm **1** (*planta, fibra*) cotton **2** (*bola de algodón*) cotton wool [U] (*GB*) ▶ ~ **de azúcar/dulce** cotton candy, candyfloss (*GB*)

alguien pron somebody, anybody **NOTA** La diferencia entre **somebody** y **anybody** es la misma que hay entre **some** y **any**. **Somebody** y **anybody** llevan el verbo en singular, pero suelen ir seguidos de **they**, **them** y **their**: ~ *dejó el abrigo*. Somebody left their coat behind. →SOME

alguno/a adj some, any: *Compré* ~s *libros*. I bought some books. ◊ *¿Algún problema?* Any problems? → SOME **2** (*con número*) several: ~s *centenares de personas* several hundred people **3** (*uno que otro*) the odd: *Alguna mala nota sacarás*. You're bound to get the odd bad grade. ● pron: ~s *protestaron*. Some (people) protested. ◊ *Seguro que fue* ~ *de ustedes*. It must have been one of you. ▶ **alguna cosa** something, anything **algún día** some day **en algún lugar/sitio/en alguna parte** somewhere, anywhere **NOTA** La diferencia entre **something** y **anything**, y **somewhere** y **anywhere** es la misma que hay entre **some** y **any**. →SOME

aliado/a adj allied ● nm-nf ally [pl -ies]

alianza nf **1** (*unión*) alliance **2** (*anillo*) wedding ring

aliarse vp form an alliance (*with/against sth/sb*)

alicates nm wire-cutters [pl] →PAIR

aliento nm breath: *mal* ~ bad breath ▶ **sin** ~ out of breath

alimaña nf pest

alimentación nf **1** (*acción*) feeding **2** (*dieta*) diet **3** (*comida*) food

alimentar vt feed *sth/sb* (*on/with sth*) ● vi be nourishing ● **alimentarse** vp live on sth

alimenticio adj **1** (*tb* **alimentario**) food: *productos* ~s foodstuffs **2** (*nutritivo*) nutritious

alimento nm **1** (*comida*) food: ~s *enlatados* canned food(s) **2** (*valor nutritivo*) nourishment: *Son de mucho* ~. They're very nourishing.

alineación nf **1** (*Dep*) line-up [pl -ups] **2** (*Mec*) alignment

alinear vt **1** (*poner en hilera*) line *sth/sb* up **2** (*Dep*) field

aliñar vt **1** season **2** (*ensalada*) dress

aliño nm **1** seasoning **2** (*ensalada*) dressing

alisar vt smooth

alistar vt get *sb* ready ● **alistarse** vp (*prepararse*) get ready **2** (*enrolarse*) enlist (*in sth*)

alivianarse vp loosen up

aliviar vt relieve: ~ *el dolor* relieve pain ◊ *El masaje me alivió un poco*. The massage made me feel a little better. ● **aliviarse** vp recover (*from sth*)

alivio nm relief

allá adv **1** (*lugar*) (over) there: *Déjalo* ~. Leave it (over) there. ◊ *a 30 km de* ~ 30 kilometers from there ◊ *de León para* ~ from León on **2** (*tiempo*) back in...: ~ *por los años 60* back in the 60s ▶ ~ **abajo/arriba** down/up there ● ~ **adentro/afuera** in/out there ● ~ **mismo** right there ● ~ **tú** it's your, his, etc. problem **¡**~ **voy!** here I come! **más** ~ **de** (*hacia un lado*) further over **más** ~ **de** beyond

allanamiento nm raid ▶ ~ **de morada** breaking and entering

allanar vt **1** (*suelo*) level **2** (*policía*) raid

allí adv there: *¡*~ *está!* There he is! ◊ *una chica que pasaba por* ~ a girl who was passing by ▶ ~ **abajo/arriba** down/up there ● ~ **adentro/afuera** in/out there ● ~ **mismo** right there **es** ~ **donde...** that's where...

alma nf soul: *No había ni un* ~. There wasn't a soul. ◊ *un* ~ *noble* a noble soul

almacén nm **1** (*tienda*) store, shop (*GB*) **2** (*bodega*) warehouse **3** (*habitación*) storeroom

▶ **grandes almacenes** department store [*sing*]

almacenar *vt* store

almeja *nf* clam

almendra *nf* almond

almendro *nm* almond (tree)

almíbar *nm* syrup

almirante *nmf* admiral

almohada *nf* pillow

almorzar *vi* **1** (*al mediodía*) have lunch **2** (*refrigerio*) have a (mid-morning) snack ● *vt* **1** (*al mediodía*) have *sth* for lunch **2** (*refrigerio*) have *sth* mid-morning

almuerzo *nm* **1** (*al mediodía*) lunch: *¿Qué hay de ~?* What's for lunch? →DINNER **2** (*refrigerio*) mid-morning snack

aló *interj* (*teléfono*) hello

alocado *adj* **1** (*persona*) crazy **2** (*decisión, etc.*) rash

alojamiento [*pl*] *nm* accommodations [*pl*], accommodation (*GB*) ▶ **dar/proporcionar ~ 1** (*cobrando*) provide *sb* with accommodations **2** (*sin cobrar*) put *sb* up

alojar *vt* **1** (*cobrando*) accommodate **2** (*sin cobrar*) put *sb* up ● **alojarse** *vp* stay

alpinismo *nm* mountaineering: *hacer ~* go mountaineering

alpiste *nm* birdseed

alquilar *vt* **1** (*tomar*) rent, hire **2** (*ceder*) rent *sth* (out), let *sth* (out), hire *sth* (out) **NOTA** En EE.UU. **rent** equivale a "alquilar", "arrendar" o "rentar": *~ un traje/una casa* rent a suit/a house ◇ *una empresa que alquila televisores* a company that rents out TVs. En Gran Bretaña, se usa **hire** cuando se trata de alquilar algo por un período corto: *~ una bici* hire a bike ◇ *Alquilan caballos a los turistas.* They hire (out) horses to tourists., y **rent** para períodos más largos: *~ un cuarto* rent a room. **Let** *sth* (out) se refiere sólo a locales o casas: *Se alquila una oficina.* There's an office to let.

alquiler *nm* **1** (*acción de alquilar*) rental, hire: *una compañía de ~ de coches/carros* a car rental company **2** (*precio*) (a) rental charge (b) (*casa, habitación*) rent → ALQUILAR ▶ **carro/coche de ~** rental car, hire car (*GB*)

alquitrán *nm* tar

alrededor *adv* **1 ~ (de)** (*en torno a*) around: *las personas a mi ~* the people around me **2 ~ de** (*aproximadamente*) about: *~ de las diez* (at) about ten ● **alrededores** *nm* (*ciudad*) outskirts

alta *nf* ◇ **dar de/el ~ a algn** discharge *sb* (from hospital)

altanero *adj* cocky

altar *nm* altar

altavoz *nm* loudspeaker

alterar *vt* alter ● **alterarse** *vp* **1** (*enojarse*) get angry **2** (*ponerse nervioso*) get nervous ▶ **~ el orden público** cause a breach of the peace ¡no te alteres! keep calm!

alternar *vt, vi* alternate ● *vi* (*con gente*) socialize

alternativa *nf* alternative

alterno *adj* alternate

altibajos *nm* ups and downs

altitud *nf* height, altitude (*más fml*): *a 3.000 m de ~* at an altitude of 3,000 meters

alto *adj* **1** tall, high **NOTA Tall** describe a personas, árboles y edificios que suelen ser estrechos además de altos: *un hombre/edificio ~* a tall man/building. **High** se usa mucho con sustantivos abstractos: *~s niveles de contaminación* high levels of pollution ◇ *~s tipos de interés* high interest rates, y para referirnos a la altura sobre el nivel del mar: *la ciudad más alta del mundo* the highest city in the world. Los antónimos de **tall** son **short** y **small**, y el antónimo de **high** es **low**. Las dos palabras tienen en común el sustantivo **height**. **2** (*mando, funcionario*) high-ranking **3** (*clase social, región*) upper: *el ~ Cauca* the upper Cauca **4** (*sonido*) loud ● *adv* **1** (*poner, subir*) high: *Ese cuadro está muy ~.* That picture is too high up. ▶ **2** (*hablar, tocar*) loudly ● *nm* height: *Tiene 2m de ~.* It's two meters high. ● *interj* stop ▶ **~ el fuego** ceasefire **pasar por ~** overlook

altura *nf* height: *Tiene 2m de ~.* It's two meters high/tall. ▶ **a estas ~s** at this stage **a la ~ de...** near: *un corte a la ~ del codo* a cut near the elbow **~ máxima** maximum headroom **de gran/poca ~** high/low

alucinación *nf* hallucination

alucinante *adj* amazing

alucinar *vi* (*delirar*) hallucinate

alud *nm* avalanche

aludido *adj* ◇ **darse por ~**: *No se dio por ~.* He didn't take the hint. ◇ **Siempre te das por ~.** You always take things personally.

alumbrado *nm* lighting

alumbrar *vt* light *sth* (up) ● *vi* give off light: *Alumbra debajo de* *la cama.* Shine a light under the bed.

aluminio *nm* aluminum

alumnado *nm* students [pl]

alumno/a *nm-nf* student
NOTA En la educación primaria, también se usa **pupil**.

alzar *vt* raise ● **alzarse** *vp* rebel (*against sth/sb*)

ama *nf* ▶ **~ de casa** housewife [pl -wives] **~ de llaves** housekeeper

amable *adj* **~ (con)** kind (*to sb*) ▶ **si es tan ~ (de...)** if you would be so kind (as to...)

amaestrar *vt* train ▶ **sin ~** untrained

amamantar *vt* **1** (*persona*) breastfeed **2** (*animal*) suckle

amanecer *vt* **1** (*alba*) dawn: *al ~* at dawn (*salida del sol*) sunrise ● *vi* **1** dawn: *Estaba amaneciendo.* Day was dawning. ◊ *Amaneció soleado.* It was sunny in the morning. **2** (*despertarse*) wake up

amanerado *adj* **1** (*rebuscado*) affected **2** (*afeminado*) effeminate

amante *adj* loving: *~ de la música* music-loving ● *nmf* lover

amañado *adj* comfortable

amañador *adj* pleasant

amapola *nf* poppy [pl -ies]

amar *vt* love

amargado/a *adj* bitter (*about sth*) ● *nm-nf* killjoy

amargar *vt* **1** (*persona*) make *sb* bitter **2** (*ocasión*) ruin ● **amargarse** *vp* get upset ▶ **amargarle la vida a algn** make sb's life a misery

amargo *adj* bitter

amarillento *adj* yellowish

amarillo *adj, nm* **1** (*color*) yellow: *ir de ~* wear yellow ◊ *pintar algo de ~* paint sth yellow **2** (*semáforo*) amber

amarra *nf* (*Náut*) mooring rope: *soltar ~s* cast off

amarrado *adj* stingy

amarrar *vt* **1** tie *sth/sb* up **2** (*Náut*) moor ● **amarrar(se)** *vt, vp* (*zapatos, etc.*) do *sth* up

amasar *vt* **1** (*Cocina*) knead **2** (*fortuna*) amass

amateur *adj, nmf* amateur

amazona *nf* (*jinete*) horsewoman [pl -women]

ámbar *nm* amber

ambición *nf* ambition

ambicionar *vt* (*desear*) want

ambicioso *adj* ambitious

ambientación *nf* (*Cine, Teat*) setting

ambientador *nm* air freshener

ambiental *adj* **1** background: *música ~* background music **2** (*del medio ambiente*) environmental **3** (*del aire*) atmospheric

ambientar *vt* (*novela, película*) set *sth in...*

ambiente *nm* **1** atmosphere: *un ~ contaminado* a polluted atmosphere ◊ *El bar tiene buen ~.* The bar has a good atmosphere. ◊ *No hay ~ en la calle.* The streets are dead. **2** (*entorno*) environment: *el ~ familiar* the family environment ▶ **estar/no estar en su ~** be in your element/be like a fish out of water

ambiguo *adj* ambiguous

ambos *pron* both (of us, you, them): *Me llevo bien con ~.* I get on well with both of them. ◊ *A ~ nos gusta bailar.* Both of us like dancing./We both like dancing.

ambulancia *nf* ambulance

ambulante *adj* traveling

ambulatorio *adj* outpatient: *un paciente ~* an outpatient

amén *nm* amen

amenaza *nf* threat

amenazador (*tb* **amenazante**) *adj* threatening

amenazar *vt, vi* **~ (con)** threaten (*to do sth*): *Amenazaron con matarlo./Lo amenazaron de muerte.* They threatened to kill him. ◊ *Amenaza lluvia.* It looks like (it's going to) rain.

ameno *adj* **1** (*entretenido*) entertaining **2** (*agradable*) pleasant

América *nf* America
NOTA America o American en inglés suelen referirse a EE.UU.

americano/a *adj, nm-nf* American

ametralladora *nf* machine gun

amígdala *nf* tonsil: *Me operaron de las ~s.* I had my tonsils out.

amigdalitis *nf* tonsillitis

amigo/a *adj* **1** (*voz*) friendly **2** (*mano*) helping ● *nm-nf* friend ▶ **ser muy ~(s)** be good friends (*with sb*): *Soy muy ~ suyo.* We're good friends.

amiguismo *nm* favoritism

amistad *nf* **1** (*relación*) friendship **2** amistades friends: *~es influyentes* friends in high places ▶ **entablar/hacer ~** become friends

amistoso *adj* friendly

amnesia *nf* amnesia

amnistía *nf* amnesty [pl -ies]

amo/a *nm-nf* owner

amoblar = AMUEBLAR

amoniaco *nm* ammonia

amontonar vt 1 (*apilar*) pile sth up 2 (*acumular*) amass • **amontonarse** vp 1 (*apiñarse*) cram (into sth)

amor nm love: *una historia de ~ a love story* ◇ *con ~* lovingly ▶ *~ propio* pride **hacer el ~** make love (to/with sb)

amoratado adj 1 (*de frío*) blue 2 (*con moretones*) black and blue 3 (*ojo*) black

amordazar vt gag

amorío nm (love) affair

amoroso adj 1 (*relativo al amor*) love: *vida amorosa* love life 2 (*cariñoso*) loving

amortiguador nm shock absorber

amotinarse vp 1 (*preso, masas*) riot 2 (*Náut, Mil*) mutiny

amparar vt protect sth/sb (*against/from sth/sb*) • **ampararse** vp 1 (*refugiarse*) shelter (*from sth/sb*) 2 **~ en** (*apoyarse*) seek the protection of sth/sb

amparo nm 1 (*protección*) protection 2 (*lugar de abrigo*) shelter 3 (*apoyo*) support

amperio nm amp

ampliación nf 1 (*cantidad*) increase 2 (*local, negocio, información*) expansion 3 (*plazo, acuerdo*) extension 4 (*Fot*) enlargement

ampliar vt 1 (*dimensiones, tiempo*) extend 2 (*cantidad*) increase: *La revista amplió su difusión.* The magazine increased its circulation. 3 (*negocio, imperio*) expand 4 (*Fot*) enlarge

amplificador nm amplifier

amplio adj 1 (*gama, margen*) wide 2 (*lugar*) spacious 3 (*ropa*) baggy

ampolla nf blister

amputar vt amputate

amueblar vt furnish ▶ **sin ~** unfurnished

amuleto nm charm

amurallado adj walled

analfabeto/a adj, nm-nf illiterate: *ser un ~* be illiterate

analgésico nm painkiller

análisis nm [pl -lyses] ▶ **~ de sangre** blood test

analizar vt analyze

anaranjado adj, nm orange

anarquía nf anarchy

anarquismo nm anarchism

anarquista adj, nmf anarchist

anatomía nf anatomy [pl -ies]

ancheta nf (And) Christmas hamper

ancho adj 1 (*de gran anchura*) wide 2 (*ropa*) baggy: *El pantalón me queda ~.* These pants are too

big. 3 (*sonrisa, hombros*) broad: *Es muy ~ de espaldas.* He has broad shoulders. → BROAD • nm width: *¿Cuánto mide de ~?* How wide is it? ◇ *Tiene 2m de ~.* It's two meters wide. ▶ **a mis anchas** 1 (*como en casa*) at home: *Ponte a tus anchas.* Make yourself at home. 2 (*con libertad*) quite happily: *Aquí pueden jugar a sus anchas.* They can play here quite happily.

anchoa nf anchovy [pl -ies]

anchura nf (*medida*) width: *No tiene suficiente ~.* It isn't wide enough.

anciano/a adj 1 elderly • nm-nf elderly man/woman [pl men/women]: *los ~s* the elderly → AGED ▶ **asilo/residencia de ~s** retirement home

ancla nf anchor ▶ **echar el ~/levar ~s** drop/weigh anchor

andamio nm scaffolding [U]

andar¹ vi 1 (*caminar*) walk 2 (*funcionar*) work 3 (*estar*) be: *¿Quién anda ahí?* Who's there? ◇ *~ ocupado* be busy ◇ *¿Qué andas buscando?* What are you looking for? 4 (*salir*) **~ con** go out with sb 5 **~ por** be about sth: *Debe ~ por los 50.* He must be about 50. • **andarse** vp **~ con**: *No te andes con bromas.* Stop fooling around. ◇ *Habrá que ~ con cuidado.* We'll have to be careful. ▶ **¡ándale!** 1 come on!: *¡Ándale, no exageres!* Come on, don't exaggerate! 2 (*sorpresa*) hey!: *¡Ándale, si está lloviendo!* Hey, it's raining! **NOTA** Para otras expresiones con andar, ver el sustantivo, adjetivo, etc., p. ej. **andar a gatas** en GATO.

andar² (*tb* **andado** nm And) walk [*sing*]

andén nm 1 (*tren, etc.*) platform 2 (*acera*) sidewalk, pavement (GB)

andrajoso/a adj ragged • nm-nf scruff

anécdota nf anecdote

anemia nf anemia ▶ **tener ~** be anemic

anémico adj anemic

anestesia nf anesthetic: *Me pusieron ~.* They gave me an anesthetic.

anestesiar vt anesthetize

anestesista nmf anesthetist

anfetamina nf amphetamine

anfibio adj amphibious • nm amphibian

anfiteatro nm 1 (*romano*) amphitheatre 2 (And, morgue) morgue

anfitrión/ona *nm-nf* host [*fem* hostess] ▶ **equipo** = home team

ángel *nm* angel: ~ *de la guarda* guardian angel

angina *nf* 1 (*tb* **anginas**) tonsillitis [*U*] 2 ~ *de pecho* angina

anglicano/a *adj, nm-nf* Anglican

anglosajón/ona *adj, nm-nf* Anglo-Saxon: *los países anglosajones* English-speaking countries

angosto *adj* narrow

anguila *nf* eel

ángulo *nm* angle: ~ *recto/agudo* right/acute angle ◇ *Veo las cosas desde otro* ~. I see things from a different angle.

angustia *nf* anguish

angustiado *adj* anxious: *esperar* ~ wait anxiously

angustiar *vt* worry ● **angustiarse** *vp* 1 (*inquietarse*) worry (*about sth/sb*) 2 (*apenarse*) get upset (*about sth*)

anidar *vi* (*aves*) nest

anillo *nm* ring ▶ **venir como** ~ **al dedo** be just right

animado *adj* 1 lively 2 (*dispuesto*) keen (*to do sth*)

animal *adj, nm* animal: ~ *doméstico/salvaje* domestic/wild animal ◇ *el reino* ~ the animal kingdom

animar *vt* 1 (*persona*) cheer *sb* up 2 (*conversación, partido*) liven *sth* up 3 (*apoyar*) cheer *sb* on 4 ~ **a algn a que haga algo** encourage *sb* to do sth ● **animarse** *vp* 1 (*persona*) cheer up: *¡Anímate!* Cheer up! 2 (*decidirse*) decide (*to do sth*)

ánimo *nm* spirits [*pl*]: *Estaba bajo de* ~. Her spirits were low. ● *interj* cheer up!

aniquilar *vt* annihilate

anís *nm* (*semilla*) aniseed

aniversario *nm* anniversary [*pl* -ies]

ano *nm* anus

anoche *adv* last night

anochecer *vi* get dark ● *nm* dusk: *al* ~ at dusk ▶ **antes/después del** ~ before/after dark

anónimo *adj* anonymous ● *nm* (*mensaje*) anonymous message

anorexia *nf* anorexia

anoréxico/a *adj, nm-nf* anorexic

anormal *adj* abnormal

anotar *vt* 1 (*apuntar*) note *sth* down 2 (*triunfo*) score

ansia *nf* 1 ~ **(de)** longing (for *sth*): ~ *de cambio* a longing for change 2 ~ **(por)** desire (for *sth/to do sth*): ~ *por mejorar* a desire to improve

ansiedad *nf* anxiety [*pl* -ies]

antártico *adj* Antarctic ● **el Antártico** *nm* the Antarctic (Ocean)

ante[1] *prep* 1 before: ~ *las cámaras* before the cameras 2 (*enfrentado con*) in the face of *sth*

ante[2] *nm* suede

anteanoche = ANTENOCHE

anteayer *adv* the day before yesterday

antebrazo *nm* forearm

antecomedor *nm* (*Mx*) breakfast nook

antelación *nf* ▶ **con** ~ in advance: *con un año de* ~ a year in advance

antemano *adv* ▶ **de** ~ in advance

antena *nf* 1 (*TV, etc.*) antenna [*pl* -s], aerial (*GB*) 2 (*Zool*) antenna [*pl* -nae] ▶ ~ **parabólica** satellite dish

antenoche *adv* the night before last

anteojos *nm* glasses

antepasado/a *nm-nf* ancestor

anteponer *vt* (*poner delante*) put *sth* before *sth*

anterior *adj* previous

antes *adv* 1 (*previamente*) before → AGO 2 (*más temprano*) earlier ▶ ~ **de** before: ~ *de ir a la cama* before going to bed ▶ ~ **que nada** above all **de** ~ previous: *en la casa de* ~ in my previous house **lo** ~ **posible** as soon as possible

antiaéreo *adj* anti-aircraft

antibalas *adj* bulletproof

antibiótico *nm* antibiotic

anticipación *nf* ▶ **con** ~ in advance

anticipado/a *adj* ▶ **por** ~ in advance

anticipar *vt* 1 (*adelantar*) bring *sth* forward 2 (*dinero*) advance *sth* (*to sb*) 3 (*sueldo, alquiler*) pay *sth* in advance

anticipo *nm* (*dinero*) advance

anticonceptivo *adj, nm* contraceptive

anticuado/a *adj, nm-nf* old-fashioned: *¡Eres un* ~! You're so old-fashioned!

anticuario *nm* (*tb* **anticuaria** *nf*) antique shop

anticuerpo *nm* antibody [*pl* -ies]

antidisturbios *adj* riot: *policía* ~ riot police

antidoping *adj* ▶ **control/prueba** ~ drug test: *Dio positivo en la prueba* ~. He tested positive.

antídoto *nm* antidote (*to sth*)

antidroga *adj* anti-drug

antier = ANTEAYER

antifaz *nm* mask

antiguamente *adv* in the olden days

antigüedad *nf* 1 (*cualidad*) age 2 (*en trabajo*) seniority 3 (*época*) ancient times [*pl*] 4 (*objeto*) antique: *tienda de ~es* antique shop

antiguo *adj* 1 (*viejo*) old 2 (*anterior*) former, old (*más coloq*) 3 (*Hist*) ancient

antílope *nm* antelope

antimotines (*And*) = ANTIDISTUR-BIOS

antipático *adj* nasty

antirrobo *adj* anti-theft: *sistema ~* anti-theft device

antojarse *vp*: *Iré cuando se me antoje*. I'll go when I feel like it. ◇ *Al niño se le antojó*. The child took a fancy to it.

antojitos *nm* (*Mx*) snacks

antojo *nm* (*capricho*) whim ▶ **tener ~ de** have a craving for *sth*

antónimo *adj, nm* opposite

antorcha *nf* torch

antro *nm* (*local*) dive

anual *adj* annual

anulación *nf* 1 cancellation 2 (*matrimonio*) annulment

anular¹ *vt* 1 cancel 2 (*matrimonio*) annull 3 (*gol, etc.*) disallow 4 (*votación*) declare *sth* invalid

anular² *nm* (*dedo*) ring finger

anunciar *vt* 1 (*informar*) announce 2 (*publicidad*) advertise ● **anunciarse** *vp* (*publicidad*) advertise

anuncio *nm* 1 (*TV, prensa*) advertisement, ad (*coloq*) 2 (*cartel*) poster 3 (*declaración*) announcement ▶ **~ luminoso** neon sign

anzuelo *nm* hook

añadir *vt* add

año *nm* year: *todo el ~* all year ◇ *todos los ~s* every year ◇ *¡Feliz ~!* Happy New Year! ● *~s* leap year **~(s) luz** light year(s) **Año Nuevo** 1 (*noche*) New Year's Eve 2 (*día*) New Year's Day **de dos, etc. ~s**: *una chica de veinte ~s* a girl of twenty/a twenty-year-old girl ◇ *A Ana, de 12 ~s, le gusta el cine*. Ana, aged 12, likes movies. **los ~s 50, 60, etc.** the fifties, sixties, etc. **quitarse ~s** (*al hablar*) lie about your age **tener dos, etc. ~s** be two, etc. (years old): *Tengo diez ~s*. I'm ten (years old). ◇ *¿Cuántos ~s tienes?* How old are you? ➔ OLD **un ~ sí y otro no** every other year

añorar *vt* (*extrañar*) miss

apachurrar *vt* (*gente, ropa*) squash 2 (*botón, etc.*) press

apaciguar *vt* appease ● **apaciguarse** *vp* calm down

apagado *adj* 1 (*persona*) listless 2 (*color*) dull 3 (*volcán*) extinct ▶ **estar ~** (*luz, aparato*) be off 2 (*fuego*) be out

apagar *vt* 1 (*fuego, cigarrillo*) put *sth* out 2 (*vela, etc.*) blow *sth* out 3 (*luz, aparato*) switch *sth* off ● **apagarse** *vp* go out

apagón *nm* power outage, power cut (*GB*)

apanado (*And*) = EMPANADO

apanar (*And*) = EMPANAR

apantallar *vt* impress

apapachar *vt* (*Mx*) cuddle

apapacho *nm* (*Mx*) cuddle

aparador *nm* 1 (*mueble*) sideboard 2 (*vitrina*) store window, shop window (*GB*)

aparato *nm* 1 (*máquina*) machine 2 (*doméstico*) appliance 3 (*TV, radio*) set 4 (*dental*) braces [*pl*], brace (*GB*) 5 (*gimnasia*) apparatus [*U*] 6 (*Med*) ~ *digestivo* the digestive system

aparatoso *adj* spectacular

aparecer *vi* 1 appear 2 (*algo/algn perdido*) turn up 3 (*figurar*) be: *Mi nombre no aparece*. My name isn't in. 4 (*llegar*) show up ● **aparecerse** *vp* appear (*to sb*)

aparejador/a *nm-nf* quantity surveyor

aparentar *vt* 1 (*fingir*) pretend: *Tuve que ~ alegría*. I had to pretend I was happy. 2 (*edad*) look: *Aparenta unos 50 años*. He looks about 50. ● *vi* show off

aparente *adj* apparent

aparición *nf* 1 appearance 2 (*Rel*) vision 3 (*fantasma*) apparition ▶ **hacer ~** appear

apariencia *nf* appearance

apartado *adj* remote ● *nm* 1 section 2 (*párrafo*) paragraph ▶ **~ postal/de correos** PO box

apartamento *nm* apartment, flat (*GB*)

apartar *vt* 1 (*obstáculo*) move *sth* (out of the way) 2 (*alejar*) separate *sth/sb* from *sth/sb* ● **apartarse** *vp* move (over) ▶ **~ la vista** look away

aparte *adv* 1 (*a un lado*) aside 2 (*separadamente*) separately ● *adj* 1 (*diferente*) apart: *un mundo ~* a world apart 2 (*separado*) separate: *una cuenta ~* a separate bill ▶ **~ de** 1 (*excepto*) apart from *sth/sb* 2 (*además de*) as well as

apasionado/a *adj* passionate ● *nm-nf* lover of *sth*

apasionante *adj* exciting

apasionar *vi* love: ¡Me apasiona! I love it! ● **apasionarse** *vp* be crazy *about* sth/sb

apedrear *vt* stone

apego *nm* affection (*for* sth/sb)
▶ tener ~ be attached *to* sth/sb

apelación *nf* appeal

apelar *vi* appeal

apellidarse *vp*: Se apellida Morán. Her surname is Morán.

apellido *nm* surname →SURNAME

apenado *adj* **1** sad (*about* sth) **2** (*con vergüenza*) embarrassed (*about* sth)

apenar *vt* **1** sadden **2** (*con vergüenza*) embarrass ● **apenarse** *vp* **1** be sad (*about* sth) **2** (*con vergüenza*) be embarrassed (*about* sth)

apenas *adv* **1** (*casi no*) hardly: ~ había cola. There was hardly any line. ◊ ~ lo veo. I hardly ever see him. ◊ ~ lo veo. I hardly ever see him. ◊ ~ (*escasamente*) scarcely **3** (*en cuanto*) as soon as

apéndice *nm* appendix [*pl* -dices]

apendicitis *nf* appendicitis

apeñuscar *vt* (*And*) stuff sth into sth

aperitivo *nm* **1** (*bebida*) aperitif **2** (*comida*) appetizer

apertura *nf* **1** opening: la ceremonia de ~ the opening ceremony **2** (*comienzo*) beginning

apestar *vi* stink (*of* sth) ● **apestarse** *vp* **1** (*persona*) catch flu **2** (*planta*) become blighted

apetecer *vi* fancy: ¿Te apetece un café? Do you fancy a coffee?

apetito *nm* appetite: El paseo te abrirá el ~. The walk will give you an appetite.

apiadarse *vp* take pity *on* sb

apicultura *nf* bee-keeping

apilar *vt* stack

apiñarse *vp* crowd (together)

apiñonado *adj* olive-skinned

apio *nm* celery

aplanadora *nf* steamroller

aplastante *adj* overwhelming

aplastar *vt* **1** (*cosa hueca, persona*) crush **2** (*cosa blanda, insecto*) squash **3** (*derrotar*) crush **4** (*peinado*) flatten

aplaudir *vt, vi* applaud

aplauso *nm* applause [*U*]

aplazar *vt* **1** put sth off, postpone (*más fml*) **2** (*pago*) defer

aplicable *adj* applicable

aplicación *nf* application

aplicado *adj* **1** applied (*to* sth) **2** (*persona*) hard-working

aplicar *vt* **1** apply sth (*to* sth): ~ una regla/una crema apply a rule/a cream **2** (*poner en práctica*) put sth to use ● *vi* (*And*) ~ (*para*) apply (*for* sth) ● **aplicarse** *vp* apply yourself (*to* sth)

apoderarse *vp* ~ **de** take sth

apodo *nm* nickname

apolítico *adj* apolitical

apología *nf* defense (*of* sth/sb)

aporrear *vt* **1** (*puerta*) bang on sth **2** (*piano*) bang away on sth ● **aporrearse** *vp* (*And*) hit yourself: ~ en la mano hit your hand

aportación *nf* (*tb* **aporte** *nm*) contribution (*to* sth)

aportar *vt* contribute

aposta *adv* on purpose

apostar(se) *vt, vi, vp* ~ (*por*) bet (*on* sth/sb): ~ por un caballo bet on a horse ◊ ~ Apuesto a que no viene. I bet he won't come.

apóstol *nm* apostle

apoyado *adj* **1** (*inclinado*) leaning *against* sth: ~ contra la pared leaning against the wall **2** (*descansando*) resting *on/against* sth: Tenía el brazo ~ en el respaldo. I was resting my arm on the back of the chair.

apoyar *vt* **1** lean sth on/against sth **2** (*descansar*) rest sth on/against sth: Apoya la cabeza en mi hombro. Rest your head on my shoulder. **3** (*defender*) support ● **apoyarse** *vp* lean on/against sth: ~ en un bastón/contra una pared lean on a stick/against a wall

apoyo *nm* support

apreciado *adj* (*cartas*) dear

apreciar *vt* **1** (*cosa*) value **2** (*persona*) think highly of sb **3** (*percibir*) see

aprecio *nm* regard (*for* sth/sb)
▶ tener ~ be fond of sb

aprender(se) *vt, vi, vp* learn: ~ francés learn French ◊ ~ a manejar learn to drive

aprendiz/a *nm-nf* apprentice: ~ de cocinero apprentice chef

aprendizaje *nm* learning: el ~ de un idioma learning a language

apresurarse *vp* hasten to do sth
▶ ¡apresúrate! hurry up!

apretado *adj* **1** (*ajustado*) tight **2** (*gente*) squashed together

apretar *vt* **1** (*botón, pedal*) press **2** (*tuerca, tapa, nudo*) tighten **3** (*gatillo*) pull **4** (*exigir*) be strict with sb **5** (*mano*) squeeze ● *vi* be too small (*for* sb) ● **apretarse** *vp* squeeze up (*against* sth) ▶ ~se cinturón tighten your belt

aprieto nm ▶ **estar en ~s/un** ~ be in a fix **poner en un** ~ put sb in a tight spot

aprisa adv fast ● interj hurry up

aprobación nf approval ▶ **dar su** ~ give your consent (to sth)

aprobar vt **1** (examen, ley) pass: Aprobé en el primer intento. I passed first time. **2** (aceptar) approve of sth/sb

apropiado adj appropriate

apropiarse vp ~ **de** take sth

aprovechado/a nm-nf freeloader, sponger (GB)

aprovechar vt **1** (utilizar) use **2** (recursos naturales) exploit **3** (oportunidad, abusar) take advantage of sth/sb ● vi: Aprovecha ahora que no está el jefe. Seize the chance now the boss isn't here. ● **aprovecharse** vp take advantage (of sth/sb) ▶ **¡que (le) aproveche!** enjoy your meal!

aproximadamente adv more or less, approximately (más fml)

aproximado adj approximate

aproximarse vp get close (to sth/sb), approach (más fml)

aptitud nf **1** aptitude (for sth) **2** aptitudes (sing): tener ~ es musicales have a gift for music

apto adj suitable (for sth)

apuesta nf bet: hacer una ~ make a bet

apuntar vt **1** (anotar) note sth down **2** (inscribir) put sb's name down ● vt, vi aim (sth) (at sth/sb): Me apuntó con la pistola. He aimed his gun at me. ● **apuntarse** vp **1** (inscribirse) put your name down, enroll (más fml) (on sth) **2** (Dep, triunfo) score **3** (participar): Si van a la playa, me apunto. If you're going to the beach, I'll come along. ◊ Se apunta a todo. She joins in with everything. **4** (rifa): ~ a una rifa buy a raffle ticket

apunte nm note

apuñalar vt stab

apurarse vp (darse prisa) get a move on **2** (preocuparse) worry

apuro nm **1** (aprieto) fix **2** apuros trouble [U] **3** (prisa) rush [U]

aquel/aquella adj [pl those] (tb **aquél/aquélla**) pron **1** (cosa) that one [pl those (ones)]: Prefiero aquellos. I prefer those (ones). **2** (persona): ¿Conoces a aquellos? Do you know those people?

aquello pron: ¿Ves ~ de allá? Can you see that thing over there? ◊ No te imaginas lo que fue ~. You can't imagine what it was like. ◊ ~ de tu jefe that business with

your boss ▶ ~ **que...** what...: ~ que tu madre dijo what your mother said

aquí adv **1** (lugar) here: ~ mismo/ cerca right/near here ◊ Por ~, por favor. This way, please. **2** (ahora) now: de ~ **en adelante** from now on ◊ hasta ~ up till now

árabe adj **1** Arab: el mundo ~ the Arab world **2** (arte, literatura) Arabic ● nmf Arab: los ~s the Arabs ● nm (lengua) Arabic

aracha nf cockroach

arado nm plow

arancel nm tariff

arandela nf **1** (aro) metal ring **2** (para tornillo) washer

araña nf spider

arañar(se) vt, vp scratch (yourself): ~se los brazos scratch your arms

arañazo nm scratch

arar vt plow

arbitrar vt **1** (fútbol, boxeo) referee **2** (tenis) umpire

arbitrario adj arbitrary

árbitro/a nm-nf (fútbol, boxeo) referee **2** (tenis) umpire **3** (mediador) arbitrator

árbol nm tree: ~ frutal fruit tree ▶ ~ **genealógico** family tree

arboleda nf grove

arbusto nm bush

arcada nf ▶ **dar** ~s retch

archipiélago nm archipelago [pl -s/-es]

archivador nm **1** (mueble) filing cabinet **2** (carpeta) file

archivar vt **1** (clasificar) file **2** (Comp) store: ~ datos store data **3** (asunto) shelve

archivo nm **1** (policía, Comp) file **2** (Hist) archive(s): un ~ histórico historical archives

arcilla nf clay

arco nm **1** (edificio) arch **2** (Geom) arc **3** (Dep, Mús) bow **4** (fútbol) goal ▶ ~ **iris** rainbow

arcón nm large chest

arder vi **1** (quemarse) burn **2** (estar muy caliente) be boiling hot ▶ **estar que arde** (persona) be fuming

ardilla nf squirrel

ardor nm (entusiasmo) enthusiasm ▶ ~ **de estómago** heartburn

área nf area

arena nf sand ▶ ~s **movedizas** quicksands

arepa nf corn pancake

arequipe nm (And) fudge

arete nm earring

Argentina nf Argentina

argentino/a adj, nm-nf Argentinian

argolla nf ring

argot nm **1** (coloquial) slang **2** (profesional) jargon

argumento nm **1** (razón) argument **2** (Cine, Teat) plot

árido adj (terreno, tema) dry

Aries nm, nmf Aries

arisco adj unfriendly

arista nf (Geom) edge

aristocracia nf aristocracy

aristócrata nmf aristocrat .

aritmética nf arithmetic

arma nf **1** weapon: ~s nucleares nuclear weapons **2** armas ▸ ~ blanca knife [pl knives] ~ de doble filo double-edged sword ~ de fuego firearm

armada nf navy [pl -ies]

armadillo nm armadillo [pl -s]

armadura nf armor [U]: una ~ a suit of armor

armamento nm arms [pl]

armar vt **1** (entregar armas) arm sb (with sth) **2** (ensamblar) assemble **3** (carpa, etc.) put sth up ▸ ~ barullo/jaleo (ruido) make a racket **~se de paciencia** be patient **~se de valor** pluck up courage **~se un lío** get confused **~ un lío** kick up a fuss

armario nm **1** cupboard **2** (para ropa) closet, wardrobe (GB)

armazón nm (lentes) frames [pl]

armisticio nm armistice

armonía nf harmony [pl -ies]

armónica nf harmonica

arneses nm harness [sing]

aro nm **1** ring **2** (gimnasia) hoop

aroma nm aroma

aromático adj aromatic

arpa nf harp

arpón nm harpoon

arqueología nf archeology

arqueólogo/a nm-nf archeologist

arquero nm goalkeeper

arquitecto/a nm-nf architect

arquitectura nf architecture

arrabal nm slum

arraigado adj deep-rooted

arraigar(se) vi, vp take root

arrancar vt **1** (sacar) pull sth out **2** (planta) pull sth up **3** (página) tear sth out **4** (quitar) pull sth off ● vt, vi (motor) start

arranque nm **1** (motor) starting: Tengo problemas con el ~. I have problems starting the car. **2** (persona) go: Tiene poco ~. He doesn't have much go. **3** ~ de fit of sth

arrasar vt destroy ● vi (ganar) win hands down

arrastrar vt **1** (por el suelo) drag: ~ los pies drag your feet ◊ sacar a algn arrastrado drag sb away **2** (problema, enfermedad): Viene arrastrando la gripa desde hace un mes. He's had the flu for over a month. ● **arrastrarse** vp **1** (gatear) crawl **2** (humillarse) grovel (to sb)

arre interj giddy up

arrear vt (ganado) drive

arrebato nm ▸ dar le ~ take it into your head (to do sth)

arrecife nm reef

arreglado adj **1** (persona) dressed up: una señora muy arreglada a smartly dressed lady **2** (ordenado) tidy **3** (asunto) sorted out

arreglar vt **1** (reparar) fix **2** (hacer obras) do sth up: ~ el baño do up the bathroom **3** (ordenar) tidy sth (up) **4** (asunto) sort sth out ● **arreglarse** vp **1** (acicalarse) get ready **2** (mejorar) get better **3** (salir bien) work out ▸ **arreglárselas** manage

arreglo nm **1** (reparación) repair: hacer ~s do repairs **2** (acuerdo) agreement ▸ **no tiene ~ 1** (objeto) it can't be fixed **2** (problema) it can't be solved **3** (persona) (s) he's a hopeless case

arrendador/a nm-nf landlord [fem landlady]

arrendar vt **1** (ceder) rent sth out **2** (tomar) rent →ALQUILAR

arrepentido adj sorry (for/about sth) →SORRY

arrepentimiento nm **1** (pesar) regret **2** (Rel) repentance

arrepentirse vp **1** (lamentar) regret: Me arrepiento de haberlo hecho. I regret doing it. **2** (pecado) repent (of sth)

arrestar vt **1** (detener) arrest **2** (encarcelar) imprison

arresto nm **1** (detención) arrest **2** (prisión) imprisonment

arrevesado = ENREVESADO

arriar vt lower

arriba adv **1** up: aquel castillo allá ~ that castle up there ◊ de la cintura para ~ from the waist up **2** (piso) upstairs: los vecinos de ~ our upstairs neighbors ● interj come on: ¡~ el América! Come on América! ▸ ~ **del todo** at the very top ¡~ **las manos!** hands up! de ~ **abajo 1** up and down: mirar a algn/mover algo de ~ abajo look sb/move sth up and down **2** (completamente) completely hacia ~ upwards **más ~ 1** (más *lejos*) further up **2** (*en sentido vertical*) higher up

arriesgado *adj* **1** (*peligroso*) risky **2** (*audaz*) daring

arriesgar *vt* risk ● **arriesgarse** *vp* take a risk/risks: *Si fuera tú, no me arriesgaría*. If I were you, I wouldn't risk it.

arrimar *vt* bring sth closer (*to sth*) ● **arrimarse** *vp* go/come near sth

arrinconar *vt* **1** (*cosa*) put sth in a corner **2** (*acorralar*) corner **3** (*marginar*) exclude

arroba *nf* (*Comp*) at **NOTA** El símbolo @ se lee at: *juan@rednet.mx* se lee "juan at rednet dot mx".

arrodillarse *vp* kneel (down)

arrogante *adj* arrogant

arrojar *vt* throw

arrollar *vt* **1** (*peatón*) run sb over **2** (*viento, agua*) carry sth away **3** (*vencer*) thrash

arropar(se) *vt, vp* wrap (sb) up: *Arrópate bien.* Wrap up well.

arroyo *nm* stream

arroz *nm* rice ► ~ **con leche** rice pudding

arrozal *nm* rice field

arruga *nf* **1** (*piel*) wrinkle **2** (*papel, ropa*) crease

arrugar(se) *vt, vp* **1** (*piel*) wrinkle **2** (*ropa*) crease **3** (*papel*) crumple

arruinar *vt* ruin ● **arruinarse** *vp* go bankrupt

arsenal *nm* (*armas*) arsenal

arsénico *nm* arsenic

arte *nm* **1** art: *una obra de* ~ a work of art **2** (*habilidad*) skill (*at sth*) ► **como por ~ de magia** as if by magic

artefacto *nm* **1** (*dispositivo*) device **2** (*aparato extraño*) contraption

artefacto *nm* **1** (*dispositivo*) device **2** (*aparato extraño*) contraption

arteria *nf* artery [*pl* -ies]

artesanal *adj* (*producto*) handmade: *una tradición* ~ a craft tradition

artesanía *nf* **1** (*productos*) handicrafts [*pl*] **2** (*habilidad*) craftsmanship ► **de ~** handmade

artesano/a *nm-nf* craftsman/woman [*pl* -men/-women]

ártico *adj* Arctic ● **el Ártico** *nm* the Arctic (Ocean)

articulación *nf* **1** (*Anat, Mec*) joint **2** (*pronunciación*) articulation

artículo *nm* **1** article: *un ~ sobre Perú* an article about Peru ◊ *el ~ definido* the definite article

2 *artículos* (*productos*) goods: *~s para el hogar* household goods

artificial *adj* artificial

artillería *nf* artillery

artista *nmf* **1** artist **2** (*Cine, Teat*) actor [*fem* actress] →ACTRESS

arveja *nf* pea

arzobispo *nm* archbishop

as *nm* **1** (*cartas*) ace → BARAJA **2** (*persona*) top: *un as del deporte* a top sportsman

asa *nf* handle

asado *adj* roast: *bien* ~ well done ● *nm* **1** (*alimento*) roast: *un ~ de res* roast beef **2** (*parrillada*) barbecue: *hacer un* ~ have a barbecue

asalariado/a *nm-nf* wage earner

asaltante *nmf* **1** (*agresor*) attacker **2** (*ladrón*) raider

asaltar *vt* **1** (*lugar*) raid **2** (*persona*) mug

asalto *nm* **1** (*lugar*) raid (*on sth*) **2** (*persona*) attack (*on sb*) **3** (*boxeo*) round

asamblea *nf* **1** (*reunión*) meeting **2** (*parlamento*) assembly [*pl* -ies]

asar *vt* **1** (*carne, etc.*) roast **2** (*papa entera*) bake ● **asarse** *vp* roast: *Me estoy asando vivo.* I'm roasting.

ascendente *nm* ascendant

ascender *vt* promote sb (*to sth*) ● *vi* **1** (*elevarse*) go up, rise (*más fml*) **2** (*montaña*) climb (up) sth **3** (*empleado*) be promoted (*to sth*)

ascenso *nm* **1** (*aumento*) rise (*in sth*) **2** (*montaña*) ascent **3** (*empleado, Dep*) promotion

ascensor *nm* elevator, lift (*GB*)

asco *nm* ► **dar ~**: *El hígado me da ~.* I can't stand liver. ◊ *Este país da* ~. This country makes me sick. **estar hecho un ~ 1** (*sitio*) be filthy **2** (*persona*) feel terrible **hacer ~s** turn your nose up (*at sth*) *¡qué ~!* **1** (*qué repugnante*) how disgusting! **2** (*qué fastidio*) what a pain!: *¡Qué ~ de tiempo!* What lousy weather!

ascua *nf* ► **en ~s** on tenterhooks

aseado *adj* **1** (*persona*) clean **2** (*lugar*) tidy

asearse *vp* **1** (*lavarse*) wash up, have a wash (*GB*) **2** (*arreglarse*) tidy yourself up

asegurar *vt* **1** (*garantizar*) ensure **2** (*afirmar*) assure **3** (*seguros*) insure sth/sb ● **asegurarse** *vp* (*comprobar*) make sure (*of sth*): *Asegúrate de cerrar la puerta.* Make sure you close the door.

asentir vi ▶ ~ **con la cabeza** nod

aseo nm 1 (cualidad) cleanliness 2 (acción) cleaning ▶ ~ **personal** personal hygiene

aserrín nm sawdust

asesinar vt murder →ASESINATO

asesinato nm murder
NOTA Assassinate, assassination y assassin sólo se usan al hablar de un personaje importante: un intento de ~ contra el Presidente an assassination attempt on the President ◊ un asesino a sueldo a hired assassin.

asesino/a nm-nf murderer →ASESINATO ● adj (mirada) murderous

asfaltar vt asphalt

asfalto nm asphalt

asfixia nf suffocation

asfixiar(se) vt, vp suffocate

así adv, adj 1 (de este modo, como este) like this: Sujétalo ~. Hold it like this. 2 (de ese modo, como ese) like that: La gente ~ me gusta. I like people like that. ◊ Yo soy ~. That's the way I am. ▶ **así, así** so-so ~ **de grande,** **gordo, etc.** this big, fat, etc. ~ **que** so: No llegó, ~ que me fui. He didn't come so I left. ◊ ¡~ que se muda! So you're moving, are you? ¡~ **se habla/hace!** well said/done! **o** ~ **or so:** unos diez o ~ about ten or so y ~ **sucesivamente** and so on (and so forth)

Asia nf Asia

asiático/a adj, nm-nf Asian

asiento nm seat

asignar vt assign

asignatura nf subject

asilo nm 1 (residencia) home 2 (Pol) asylum

asimilar vt assimilate

asistencia nf 1 (presencia) attendance 2 (a enfermos) care: ~ sanitaria health care

asistente adj present (at sth): los ~s a la reunión those present at the meeting ● nmf (And, Educ) unregistered student ▶ ~ **social** social worker

asistir vi (acudir) attend: ~ a una clase attend a class ● vt (médico) treat

asma nf asthma

asmático/a adj, nm-nf asthmatic

asno/a nm-nf ass

asociación nf association

asociar vt, vp associate sth/sb (with sth/sb) ● **asociarse** vp form a partnership

asomar(se) vt, vp put your head out of, around, etc. sth: ~ la

ventana/puerta put your head out of the window/around the door ◊ Asómate al balcón. Come out onto the balcony.

asombrarse vp be amazed (by sth): Se asombró al verme. He was amazed to see me.

asombro nm amazement: poner cara de ~ look amazed

aspa nf (molino) sail

aspecto nm 1 (apariencia) look: No puedo salir con este ~. I can't go out looking like this. ◊ No tienes buen ~. You don't look well. 2 (faceta) aspect

áspero adj rough

aspiradora nf (tb aspirador nm) vacuum cleaner: pasar la ~ vacuum

aspirante nmf candidate (for sth)

aspirar vt 1 (respirar) breathe sth in 2 (máquina) suck sth up 3 (cocaína) snort ● vi aspire to sth

aspirina nf aspirin

asqueroso/a adj 1 (sucio) filthy 2 (repugnante) disgusting

asta nf 1 (bandera) flagpole 2 (toro, etc.) horn ▶ **a media** ~ at half mast

asterisco nm asterisk

astilla nf splinter

astillero nm shipyard

astro nm star

astrología nf astrology

astrólogo/a nm-nf astrologer

astronauta nmf astronaut

astronomía nf astronomy

astrónomo/a nm-nf astronomer

astucia nf 1 (habilidad) shrewdness: tener ~ be shrewd 2 (malicia) cunning 3 (ardid) trick

astuto adj 1 (hábil) shrewd 2 (malicioso) cunning

asunto nm 1 (tema) matter 2 (Pol) affair ▶ **no es** ~ **mío** it's none of my, your, etc. business

asustar vt scare ● **asustarse** vp be scared (of sth)

atacar vt attack

atajar vt 1 (agarrar) catch 2 (detener) stop 3 (enfermedad) stop the spread of sth

atajo nm short cut

ataque nm 1 attack (on sth/sb): un ~ al corazón a heart attack 2 (risa, tos) fit: Le dio un ~ de tos. He had a coughing fit. ▶ ~ **de** **nervios** nervous breakdown **de** ~ (And) great: Lo estamos pasando de ~. We're having a great time.

atar vt 1 tie sth/sb (up) 2 (zapatos) do sth up

atardecer nm dusk: al ~ at dusk ● vi get dark

atareado adj busy

atascamiento (tb atasco) nm (Aut) traffic jam

atascar vt block sth (up) ● **atascarse** vp 1 get stuck 2 (mecanismo) jam

ataúd nm casket, coffin (GB)

atención nf attention ▶ **con ~** attentively **llamar la ~ 1** (sobresalir) attract attention 2 (sorprender) surprise 3 (atraer) like sth/sb: No me llama la atención trabajar. I really don't like working. **4** (reprender) tell sb off

atender vt 1 (recibir) see: ~ a un paciente see a patient 2 (tienda) serve: ¿Lo atendieron? Are you being served? 3 (tarea, problema, solicitud) deal with sth **4** (contestar) answer: ~ el teléfono answer the phone ● vi pay attention to sth/sb

atenerse vp 1 (reglas, órdenes) abide by sth 2 (consecuencias) face ▶ **(no) saber a qué ~** (not) know what to expect

atentado nm 1 (ataque) attack (on sth/sb) 2 (intento de asesinato) attempt on sb's life

atentamente adv (fórmula de despedida) Sincerely, Yours sincerely (GB) **NOTA** En Gran Bretaña se usa **Yours faithfully** cuando la carta empieza con *Dear Sir* o *Dear Madam*. Si empieza con *Dear Mr Jones, Dear Mrs Smith*, etc., se usa **Yours sincerely** para despedirse.

atentar vi **~ contra** make an attempt on sb's life

atento adj 1 (prestando atención) attentive: Escuchó ~. He listened attentively. 2 (amable) kind ▶ **estar ~ a algo** 1 (mirar) watch out for sth 2 (prestar atención) pay attention to sth

ateo/a nm-nf atheist: ser ~ be an atheist

aterrador adj terrifying

aterrizaje nm landing: ~ forzoso emergency landing

aterrizar vi land

aterrorizar vt 1 (dar miedo) terrify 2 (con violencia) terrorize

atestado adj packed (with sth/sb)

atestar vt fill sth to overflowing

atiborrarse vp stuff yourself (with sth)

ático nm 1 (desván) attic 2 (apartamento) top-floor apartment

atizar vt (fuego) poke

atlántico adj Atlantic ● **el Atlántico** nm the Atlantic (Ocean)

atlas nm atlas

atleta nmf athlete

atlético adj athletic

atletismo nm athletics [sing]

atmósfera nf atmosphere: ~ cargada/de malestar stuffy/uneasy atmosphere

atole nm (Mx) hot corn drink

atómico adj atomic

átomo nm atom

atontado/a adj groggy ● nm-nf dimwit

atontar vt 1 (marear) make sb groggy 2 (volver tonto) dull your senses

atorado adj stuck

atorarse vp get stuck

atormentar vt torment

atornillar vt screw sth down/in/on: ~ la última pieza screw on the last part

atracador/a nm-nf 1 (ladrón) robber 2 (en la calle) mugger

atracar vt 1 (banco, etc.) hold sth/sb up 2 (en la calle) mug ● vt, vi (barco) dock

atracción nf attraction: una ~ turística a tourist attraction ▶ **sentir ~ por** be attracted to sb

atraco nm 1 (robo) hold-up [pl -ups]: Cometió un ~ en una joyería. He held up a jewelry store. **2** (en la calle) mugging

atracón nm ▶ **darse un ~** stuff yourself (with sth)

atractivo adj attractive ● nm 1 (cosa que atrae) attraction: los ~s de la ciudad the city's attractions 2 (interés) appeal [U] 3 (persona) charm

atraer vt 1 attract: ~ a los turistas attract tourists ◇ Me atrae mucho. I'm very attracted to him. 2 (idea) appeal to sb

atragantarse vp 1 choke (on sth) 2 (objeto) get stuck in sb's throat: Se le atragantó una espina. A bone got stuck in his throat.

atrancarse vp 1 (tubería) get blocked 2 (mecanismo, persona) get stuck

atrapado adj trapped

atrapar vt catch

atrás adv back: más ~ further back ◇ sentarse ~ sit at the back ▶ **dejar ~** leave sth/sb behind **echarse/volverse ~** (desdecirse) go back on your word **hacia/para ~** backwards

atrasado/a adj 1 (publicación, sueldo) back: los números ~s de una revista the back issues of a magazine 2 (país, etc.) backward 3 (reloj) slow: Tu reloj va ~. Your watch is slow. ▶ **tener ~** (trabajo, etc.) be behind with sth

atrasar vt 1 (aplazar) put sth off, postpone (más fml) 2 (reloj) put sth back ● **atrasar(se)** vi, vp (reloj) be slow: (Se) atrasa diez minutos. It's ten minutes slow.

atraso nm 1 (demora) delay 2 (subdesarrollo) backwardness

atravesar vt 1 (cruzar) cross 2 (perforar, experimentar) go through sth ● **atravesarse** vp 1 (en el camino) block sb's path 2 (en la garganta) get sth stuck in your throat

atreverse vp ~ (a) dare (do sth): No me atrevo a pedírselo. I daren't ask him. ◇ ¿Cómo te atreves? How dare you? →DARE

atrevido/a adj 1 daring: un vestido/acto ~ a daring dress/act 2 (insolente) sassy, cheeky (GB)

atributo nm attribute

atropellado/a adj (por vehículo): Murió ~. He died after being run over.

atropellar vt run sb over: Me atropelló un carro. I was run over by a car.

atufar vt make sth stink (of sth) ● vi stink (of sth) ● **atufarse** vp get annoyed

atún nm tuna [pl tuna]

audaz adj bold

audición nf 1 (oído) hearing: perder ~ lose your hearing 2 (prueba) audition

audiencia nf audience

audífonos nm headphones

auditorio nm 1 (audiencia) audience 2 (edificio) concert hall

aula nf 1 (escuela) classroom 2 (universidad) lecture room

aullar vi howl

aullido nm howl

aumentar vt 1 increase 2 (lupa, etc.) magnify ● vi increase

aumento nm rise (in sth)

aun adv even: ~ así no lo haría. Even so, I wouldn't do it.

aún adv 1 (afirmativo/interrogativo) still: ~ falta una hora. There's still an hour to go. ◇ ¿~ estás aquí? Are you still here? 2 (negativo) yet: ¿~ no te han contestado? —No, ~ no. "Didn't they write back yet?" "No, not yet." → STILL 3 (comparativo) even: Ésta me gusta ~ más. I like this one even better.

aunque conj 1 (a pesar de que) although, though (más coloq) **NOTA** Para más énfasis se puede usar **even though**. 2 (incluso si) even if: Ven, ~ sea tarde. Come even if it's late.

auricular nm 1 (teléfono) receiver 2 auriculares headphones

aurora nf dawn

ausencia nf absence

ausentarse vp 1 (no ir) stay off: ~ de la escuela stay off school 2 (estar fuera) be away (from...)

ausente adj absent (from sth) ● nmf absentee

austeridad nf austerity

austero adj austere

Australia nf Australia

australiano/a adj, nm-nf Australian

Austria nf Austria

austríaco/a (tb austriaco/a) adj, nm-nf Austrian

auténtico adj genuine

auto nm (carro) car

autoadhesivo nm sticker

autobiografía nf autobiography [pl -ies]

autobiográfico adj autobiographical

autobús nm bus

autodefensa nf self-defense

autodidacta adj, nmf self-taught: Es un ~. He's self-taught.

autoescuela nf driving school

autogol nm own goal: meter un ~ score an own goal

autógrafo nm autograph

automático adj automatic ● nm (costura) snap, press stud (GB)

automóvil nm car

automovilismo nm motor racing

automovilista nmf motorist

autonomía nf 1 (autogobierno) autonomy 2 (independencia) independence

autónomo/a adj 1 autonomous 2 (trabajador) self-employed

autopista nf freeway, motorway (GB) ▸ ~ de cuota (Mx) turnpike, toll road (GB)

autopsia nf post-mortem

autor/a nm-nf 1 (escritor) author 2 (Mús) composer 3 (crimen) perpetrator

autoridad nf authority [pl -ies]

autorización nf permission

autorizar vt 1 (acción) authorize 2 (dar derecho) give sb the right (to do sth)

autorretrato nm self-portrait

autoservicio nm 1 (restaurante) self-service restaurant 2 (supermercado) supermarket 3 (gasolinera) self-service gas/petrol (GB) station

auxiliar adj auxiliary ● nmf assistant ▸ ~ de vuelo flight attendant

auxilio *nm* help: *un grito de* ~ a cry for help

auyama *nf* (And) pumpkin

avalancha *nf* avalanche

avanzar *vi* advance

avaricia *nf* greed

avaricioso/a *adj, nm-nf* greedy: *Es un* ~. He's greedy.

avaro/a *adj* miserly ● *nm-nf* miser

ave *nf* bird

avellana *nf* hazelnut ● *adj, nm* (color) hazel

avellano *nm* hazel

avemaría *nf* Hail Mary

avena *nf* (cereal) oats [pl]

avenida *nf* avenue (abrev **Ave.**)

aventar *vt* throw

aventón *nm* ride ▸ *pedir* ~ hitch a ride

aventura *nf* 1 (peripecia) adventure 2 (amorío) fling

aventurero/a *adj* adventurous ● *nm-nf* adventurer

avergonzar *vt* 1 (humillar) make *sb* feel ashamed 2 (abochornar) embarrass ● **avergonzarse** *vp* 1 (arrepentirse) be ashamed (of *sth*) 2 (estar incómodo) be embarrassed (at *sth*)

avería *nf* 1 (Aut, mecanismo) breakdown 2 (falla) fault

averiarse *vp* (Mec) break down

averiguar *vt* find *sth* out

avestruz *nm* ostrich

aviación *nf* 1 aviation 2 (fuerzas aéreas) air force

avinagrado *adj* sour

avión *nm* plane ▸ *ir/viajar en* ~ fly por ~ (correo) airmail

avioneta *nf* light aircraft [pl light aircraft]

avisar *vt* 1 (informar) let *sb* know (about *sth*) 2 (advertir) warn ▸ *sin* ~ unexpectedly: *Se fue sin* ~. He left without saying anything.

aviso *nm* 1 notice: *hasta nuevo* ~ until further notice 2 (advertencia) warning 3 (anuncio) advertisement, ad (coloq) ▸ ~ *luminoso* 1 (señal) neon sign 2 (para avisar) warning light

avispa *nf* wasp

avispado *adj* bright

avispero *nm* (nido) wasps' nest

axila *nf* armpit

ayer *adv* yesterday: ~ *en/por la mañana/tarde* yesterday morning/afternoon ◊ ~ *en/por la noche* last night ◊ *el periódico de* ~ yesterday's paper ▸ *antes de* ~ the day before yesterday

ayuda *nf* help [U]

ayudante *adj, nmf* assistant

ayudar *vt, vi* help

ayunar *vi* fast

ayunas ▸ *en* ~: *Estoy en* ~. I've had nothing to eat or drink.

ayuno *nm* fast: *3 días de* ~ 3 days of fasting

ayuntamiento *nm* 1 (concejo) council 2 (edificio) city hall, town hall (GB)

azabache *nm* jet

azada *nf* (tb **azadón** *nm*) hoe

azafata *nf* (avión) stewardess

azafrán *nm* saffron

azahar *nm* orange blossom

azar *nm* 1 (casualidad) chance 2 (destino) fate ▸ *al* ~ at random

azotador *nm* caterpillar

azotar *vt* whip ● *vi* fall on the ground

azote *nm* smack

azotea *nf* (flat) roof

azúcar *nm* sugar

azucarero *nm* (tb **azucarera** *nf*) sugar bowl

azucena *nf* lily [pl -ies]

azufre *nm* sulphur

azul *adj, nm* blue ▸ ~ *celeste/marino* sky/navy blue ~ *turquesa* turquoise

azulado (tb **azuloso**) *adj* bluish

azulejo *nm* tile

B b

baba *nf* 1 (persona) dribble 2 (animal) foam ▸ *caerse la* ~ dote on *sb*: *Se le cae la* ~ *por su sobrina.* She dotes on her niece.

babear *vi* dribble

babero *nm* bib

babor *nm* port: *a* ~ to port

babosa *nf* slug

bacalao *nm* cod [pl cod]

bacano *adj, adv* (And) great: *Estuvo muy* ~. It was great.

bache *nm* 1 (hoyo) pothole 2 (dificultad) tough time

bachillerato *nm* high school

bacteria *nf* bacterium [pl -ria]

bafle *nm* (loud)speaker

bahía *nf* bay

bailar *vt, vi* 1 (danza) dance 2 (trompo) spin ● *vi* 1 (estar suelto) be loose 2 (quedar grande) be too big (for *sb*) ▸ ~ *pegado/agarrado* have a slow dance ~ *con la más fea* draw the short straw **sacar a** ~ ask *sb* to dance

bailarín/ina *nm-nf* dancer

baile *nm* **1** (*fiesta, danza*) dance **2** (*acción*) dancing: *Me gusta el ~.* I like dancing. ▸ **~ de disfraces** costume ball, fancy dress ball (GB)

baja *nf* **1** (*Econ*) fall (in sth): *Continúa la ~ de la inflación.* Inflation continues to fall. **2** (*Mil*) casualty [pl -ies] ▸ **darse de ~** drop out of sth

bajada *nf* **1** (*descenso*) descent **2** (*pendiente*) slope: *La calle tiene mucha ~.* The street slopes steeply. **3** (*Econ*) fall (in sth) **4** (*parada*) stop

bajamar *nf* low tide

bajar *vt* **1** get *sth* down: *~ la maleta* get your suitcase down **2** (*traer, poner más abajo*) bring *sth* down: *Bájalo un poco.* Bring it down a little. **3** (*llevar*) take *sth* down: *¿Hay que ~ esto al sótano?* Do we have to take this down to the basement? **4** (*ir/venir abajo*) go/come down: *~ la cuesta* go down the hill **5** (*vista, voz*) lower **6** (*volumen*) turn *sth* down **7** (*cabeza*) bow **8** (*precio*) bring *sth* down **9** (*Comp*) download: *~ algo de internet* download sth from the Internet ● *vi* **1** (*ir/venir abajo*) go/come down **2** (*temperatura, río*) fall **3** (*hinchazón*) go down **4** (*marea*) go out **5** (*precios*) come down ● **bajar(se)** *vi, vp* **1** (*carro*) get out (of sth) **2** (*transporte público, caballo, bicicleta*) get off (sth)

bajo¹ *nm* **1** (*voz, instrumento*) bass **2** (*vivienda*) first-floor apartment

bajo² *prep* under: *la lluvia* in the rain

bajo³ *adv* low ● *adj* **1** (*persona*) short **2** **~ (en)** low (in sth): *una sopa baja en calorías* a low-calorie soup ◊ *El volumen está muy ~.* The volume's too low. **3** (*zapato*) flat **4** (*voz*) quiet: *hablar en voz baja* speak quietly **5** (*barrio*) poor

bala *nf* (*arma*) bullet ▸ **como una ~** like a shot

balaca *nf* (*And*) **1** (*accesorio*) hairband **2** (*Dep*) sweatband

balacear *vt* (*Mx*) riddle *sth/sb* with bullets

balacera *nf* shoot-out

balance *nm* **1** balance **2** (*número de víctimas*) toll

balancear(se) *vt, vp* **1** swing **2** (*cuna, mecedora*) rock

balanza *nf* **1** (*instrumento*) scales [pl] **2** (*Com*) balance

balar *vi* bleat

balazo *nm* **1** (*disparo*) shot **2** (*herida*) bullet wound

balbucear (*tb* **balbucir**) *vt, vi* (*adulto*) stammer ● *vi* (*bebé*) babble

balcón *nm* balcony [pl -ies]

balde¹ *nm* bucket

balde² ▸ **en ~** in vain

baldosa *nf* **1** (*interior*) floor tile **2** (*exterior*) paving stone

balero *nm* **1** (*Mx, juguete*) cup and ball toy **2** (*Mec*) ball bearing

baliza *nf* **1** (*Náut*) buoy. **2** (*aviación*) beacon

ballena *nf* whale

ballet *nm* ballet

balneario *nm* **1** (*termales*) spa **2** (*en costa*) seaside resort

balón *nm* **1** (*gas, etc.*) bag

balonmano *nm* handball

balsa *nf* (*embarcación*) raft

bambolearse *vp* sway

bambú *nm* bamboo

banano *nm* banana

banca *nf* **1** (*bancos*) banks [pl]: *la ~ suiza* Swiss banks **2** (*sector*) banking

bancarrota *nf* bankruptcy ▸ **en ~** bankrupt

banco *nm* **1** (*Fin, etc.*) bank: *~ de datos/sangre* data/blood bank **2** (*asiento*) bench **3** (*iglesia*) pew **4** (*peces*) shoal ▸ **~ de arena** sandbank

banda¹ *nf* band: *una ~ para el pelo* a hairband ▸ **~ sonora** soundtrack

banda² *nf* **1** (*pandilla*) gang **2** (*Mús*) band ▸ **~ terrorista** terrorist group

bandada *nf* **1** (*aves*) flock **2** (*peces*) shoal

bandear *vp* get by

bandeja *nf* tray ▸ **poner/servir en ~** hand *sb* sth on a plate

bandera *nf* **1** flag **2** (*Mil*) colors [pl] ▸ **~ blanca** white flag

banderín *nm* pennant

bandido/a *nm-nf* bandit

bando *nm* **1** (*Mil, Pol*) faction **2** (*en juegos*) side

banquero/a *nm-nf* banker

banqueta *nf* **1** (*Mx, acera*) sidewalk, pavement (GB) **2** (*mueble*) stool

banquete *nm* dinner, banquet (*más fml*) ▸ **~ de bodas** wedding reception →MATRIMONIO

banquillo *nm* **1** (*Dep*) bench **2** (*Jur*) dock

bañado *adj* bathed ▸ **~ en oro/plata** gold-plated/silver-plated

bañar *vt* **1** bathe **2** (*en metal*) plate *sth* (*with sth*) **3** (*Cocina*) coat *sth* (in/with sth) ● **bañarse** vp 1 (en tina) take a bath 2 (en ducha) take a shower 3 (nadar) go for a swim 4 (lavarse) wash up, wash (GB)

bañera nf bath

baño nm 1 (cuarto de baño, w.c.) bathroom →TOILET 2 (en bañera) bath 3 (en ducha) shower 4 (mar, etc.) swim: darse un ~ go for a swim ▸ ~ **María** double boiler, bain marie (GB)

baqueta nf drumstick

bar nm 1 (bebidas alcohólicas) bar 2 (cafetería) snack bar

baraja nf deck/pack (GB) of cards **NOTA** Los palos de la baraja española no tienen traducción porque en EE.UU. y Gran Bretaña se usa la baraja francesa, que consta de 52 cartas divididas en cuatro palos o suits: hearts (corazones), diamonds (diamantes), clubs (tréboles) y spades (picas). Cada palo tiene un ace (as), king (rey), queen (reina), y un jack (joto/a). Al empezar a jugar, se baraja (shuffle), se corta (cut) y se reparten (deal) las cartas.

baranda (tb barandilla) nf (tb barandal nm) 1 (escalera) banister(s): bajar por la ~ slide down the banisters 2 (balcón) railing(s)

barata nf (Mx, saldo) sale

barato, -a adj cheap ● adv cheaply: Aquí se vende ~ Prices are low here.

barba nf beard: dejarse crecer la ~ grow a beard ◊ un hombre con ~ a bearded man ▸ **hacer la ~** (Mx) suck up to sb

barbacoa nf 1 (Mx) meat roasted in a pit 2 (fiesta) barbecue

barbaridad nf 1 barbarity 2 (disparate) nonsense [U] ▸ **¡qué ~!** good heavens!

bárbaro, -a adj 1 barbarian 2 (estupendo) terrific 3 Hace un frío/calor ~. It's freezing cold/boiling hot. ● nm-nf barbarian ▸ **¡qué ~!** good Lord!

barbecho nm fallow land ▸ **dejar en ~** leave sth fallow

barbilla nf chin

barca nf (small) boat: dar un paseo en ~ go out in a boat →BOAT ▸ ~ **de remos** rowboat, rowing boat (GB)

barco nm 1 (buque) ship 2 (más pequeño) boat →BOAT ▸ ~ **de vapor/vela** steamship/sailboat ir en ~ go by boat/ship

barda nf (Mx) 1 (pared) (high) wall 2 (cerca) (high) fence

bareta nf (And) marijuana

bareto nm (And) joint

barítono nm baritone

barniz nm 1 (madera) varnish 2 (cerámica) glaze

barnizar vt 1 (madera) varnish 2 (cerámica) glaze

barómetro nm barometer

barquillo nm ice cream cone

barra nf 1 bar 2 (pan) baguette 3 (pandilla) gang

barranco nm (tb barranca nf) ravine

barrendero/a nm-nf road sweeper

barrer vt 1 (limpiar, arrasar) sweep 2 (derrotar) thrash ● vi sweep up

barrera nf 1 barrier 2 (fútbol) wall

barricada nf barricade

barriga nf 1 (estómago) belly [pl -ies] 2 (panza) paunch: echar ~ get a paunch

barril nm barrel

barrio nm 1 area: Se criaron en este ~. They grew up in this area. 2 (en las afueras) suburb 3 (zona típica) quarter ▸ **el ~ antiguo** the old quarter ▸ **del ~** local: el panadero del ~ the local baker

barro nm 1 (lodo) mud 2 (arcilla) clay ▸ **de ~** earthenware

barroco adj, nm baroque

barrote nm iron bar

barullo nm 1 (ruido) racket 2 (confusión) muddle

basar vt base sth on sth ● **basarse** vp en 1 (persona) have grounds (for sth) 2 (teoría, película) be based on sth

báscula nf scales [pl]

base nf 1 base: un jarrón con poca ~ a vase with a small base ◊ ~ militar military base 2 (fundamento) basis [pl bases] ▸ ~ **de datos** database ~ **espacial** space station

básico, -a adj basic

basquetbol (tb básquetbol, basket) nm basketball

bastante adj 1 (mucho): Hace ~ tiempo que no la veo. It's quite a long time since I last saw her. ◊ Tengo ~s cosas que hacer. I have quite a lot of things to do. 2 (suficiente) enough ● pron 1 (mucho) quite a lot 2 (suficiente) enough ● adv 1 + adj/adv pretty: Está ~ bien. It's pretty good. →FAIRLY 2 (lo suficiente) enough 3 (mucho) a lot

bastar vi be enough: Bastará con 5.000 pesos. 5,000 pesos will be enough. ▸ **¡basta (ya)!** that's enough!

bastilla nf hem

basto adj 1 (persona, tejido, etc.) coarse 2 (superficie) rough

bastón nm walking stick

bastos nm (cartas) →BARAJA

basura nf garbage [U], rubbish [U] (GB) ▸ tirar a la ~ throw sth away

basurero/a nm-nf garbage collector, dustman [pl -men] (GB) ● nm 1 (vertedero) garbage dump, tip (GB) 2 (contenedor) trash can, bin (GB) 3 (para papel) wastebasket, bin (GB)

bata nf 1 (de baño) robe, dressing gown (GB) 2 (trabajo, colegio) overall 3 (laboratorio) lab coat 4 (hospital) white coat

batalla nf battle ▸ de ~ everyday: mis botas de ~ my everyday boots

batallón nm battalion

bate (tb bat) nm bat

batería nf 1 (Elec, Mil) battery [pl -ies]: Se quedó sin ~. The battery is dead. 2 (Mús) drums [pl] ● nmf drummer ▸ ~ de cocina set of saucepans

batidora nf mixer

batir vt 1 beat: ~ huevos beat eggs ◇ ~ al contincante beat your opponent 2 (crema) whip 3 (récord) break

batuta nf baton

baúl nm 1 (equipaje) trunk 2 (Aut) trunk, boot (GB)

bautismal adj baptismal

bautismo nm 1 (sacramento) baptism 2 (acto de poner un nombre) christening

bautizar vt 1 (sacramento) baptize 2 (poner un nombre) (a) (persona) christen: ~ el bebé con el nombre de Ana christen the baby Ana (b) (barco, invento) name

bautizo nm christening

baya nf (Bot) berry [pl -ies]

baza nf 1 (cartas) trick 2 (recurso) asset

bazo nm spleen

bebé nm baby [pl -ies]

bebedor/a nm-nf (heavy) drinker

beber(se) vt, vi, vp drink: Bébaselo todo. Drink it up. ▸ ~ a la salud de drink to sb's health ~ (a pico) de (la) botella drink straight from the bottle ~ a sorbos sip ~ como un caballo/cosaco drink like a fish ~ en vaso drink from a glass ~se algo de un trago drink sth in one go

bebida nf drink

bebido adj 1 (ligeramente) tipsy 2 (borracho) drunk

beca nf 1 (del Estado) grant 2 (privada) scholarship

bechamel nf white sauce

beige adj, nm beige

béisbol (beisbol Mx) nm baseball

bélico adj 1 (belicoso) warlike 2 (armas, juguetes) war: películas bélicas war movies

belleza nf beauty [pl -ies]

bemol adj (Mús) flat: si ~ B flat

bendecir vt bless ▸ ~ la mesa say grace

bendición nf blessing ▸ dar/echar la ~ bless sth/sb

bendito adj blessed

beneficiar vt benefit sth/sb ▸ beneficiarse vp benefit (from sth)

beneficio nm 1 (bien) benefit 2 (Com, Fin) profit: dar/obtener ~s produce/make a profit ▸ en ~ de to the advantage of sth/sb: en ~ suyo to your advantage

beneficioso adj beneficial

benéfico adj charity: obras benéficas charity work ◇ una institución benéfica a charity

bengala nf 1 flare 2 (de mano) sparkler

benigno/a adj 1 (tumor) benign 2 (clima) mild

berenjena nf eggplant, aubergine (GB)

bermudas nm o nf Bermuda shorts →PANTALÓN

berrinche nm tantrum: estar con ~ have a tantrum

berro nm watercress [U]

besar vt kiss

beso nm kiss: Nos dimos un ~. We kissed. ▸ tirar un ~ blow (sb) a kiss

bestia nf beast ● adj, nmf brute: ¡Qué ~ eres! You're such a brute! ▸ a lo ~/como una ~ like crazy: Trabaja como una ~. He works like crazy. ◇ Come como una ~. He eats a huge amount.

bestial adj 1 (enorme) huge: Tengo un hambre ~. I'm famished. 2 (genial) great

bestialidad nf 1 (brutalidad): Hizo muchas ~es. He did a lot of disgusting things. 2 (estupidez) stupid thing 3 (grosería): decir ~es be rude

besugo nm bream [pl bream]

betabel nm (Mx) beet, beetroot (GB)

betún nm 1 (calzado) shoe) polish: ponerles ~ a los zapatos give your shoes a polish 2 (pastel) frosting, icing (GB)

biberón nm bottle

Biblia nf Bible

bíblico adj biblical

bibliografía nf bibliography [pl -ies]

biblioteca nf 1 (edificio, conjunto de libros) library [pl -ies] 2 (mueble) bookcase

bibliotecario/a nm-nf librarian

bicarbonato nm bicarbonate

biceps nm biceps [pl biceps]

bicho nm 1 (insecto) bug 2 (cualquier animal) animal 3 (persona) nasty guy: un ~ raro a weirdo ▶ ¿qué te picó? what's bugging you, him, her, etc.?

bicicleta (tb bici) nf bicycle, bike (coloq): ¿Sabes montar en ~? Can you ride a bike? ◊ ir en ~ al trabajo cycle to work ◊ dar un paseo en ~ go for a bike ride ▶ ~ de carreras/montaña racing/mountain bike

bicimoto nm (Mx) moped

bidé nm bidet

bidón nm drum

bien¹ adv 1 well: portarse ~ behave well ◊ estar/ponerse ~ be/get well ◊ —¿Cómo estás? —Muy ~, gracias. "How are you?" "Very well, thanks." 2 (de acuerdo, adecuado) OK: Les pareció ~. They thought it was OK. ◊ —¿Me lo presta? —Está ~. "Can I borrow it?" "OK." 3 (calidad, aspecto, olor, sabor) good: La escuela está ~. The school is good. ◊ ¡Qué ~ huele! That smells really good! 4 (correctamente): Contesté ~ la pregunta. I got the right answer. ◊ hablar ~ el español speak good Spanish ▶ andar/estar ~ de have plenty of sth ¡(muy) ~! (very) good! **NOTA** Para otras expresiones con bien, ver el adjetivo, verbo, etc., p. ej. llevarse bien en LLEVAR.

bien² conj ▶ bien... bien... either... or...: Voy a ir ~ en tren, o ~ en carro. I'll go either by train or by car.

bien³ nm 1 good: el ~ y el mal good and evil 2 bienes possessions ▶ ~es de consumo consumer goods por el ~ de for the good of sth/sb por tu ~ for your, his, her, etc. own good ¡qué ~! great!

bien⁴ adj well-to-do: Son de familia ~. They're from a well-to-do family.

bienestar nm well-being

bienvenida nf welcome ▶ dar la ~ welcome sb

bienvenido adj welcome

bigote nm 1 (persona) mustache: un hombre con ~ a man with a mustache 2 (gato) whiskers [pl]

bikini nm bikini [pl -s]

bilingüe adj bilingual

bilis nf bile

billar nm 1 (juego) pool 2 (mesa) pool table 3 billares (local) pool hall

billete nm 1 (Fin) bill, (bank)note (GB): ~s de $100 hundred dollar bills 2 (dinero) money ▶ ~ de lotería lottery ticket

billetera nf wallet

billón nm (un millón de millones) trillion →BILLION

binario adj binary

bingo nm 1 (juego) bingo 2 (sala) bingo hall

binoculares (tb binóculos And) nm binoculars

biodegradable adj biodegradable

biografía nf biography [pl -ies]

biología nf biology

biólogo/a nm-nf biologist

biombo nm screen

bisabuelo/a nm-nf 1 great-grandfather [fem great-grandmother] 2 bisabuelos great-grandparents

bisagra nf hinge

bisnieto/a 1 great-grandson [fem great-granddaughter] 2 bisnietos great-grandchildren

bisonte nm bison [pl bison]

bistec nm steak

bisturí nm scalpel

bisutería nf costume jewelry

bit nm bit

bizco adj cross-eyed

bizcocho nm 1 (galleta) cookie, biscuit (GB) 2 (pastel) (sponge) cake

biznieto/a nm-nf = BISNIETO

blanco/a adj white ● nm-nf (persona) white man/woman [pl men/women] ● nm 1 (color) white 2 (diana) target: dar en el ~ hit the target ▶ en ~ blank: un cheque/página en ~ a blank check/page en ~ y negro black and white más ~ que la nieve as white as snow quedarse en ~ go blank

blando adj 1 soft: un queso/profesor ~ a soft cheese/teacher 2 (carne) tender

blanqueador nm bleach

blanquear vt 1 whiten 2 (echar cal) whitewash 3 (dinero) launder

blasfemar vi blaspheme

blasfemia nf blasphemy [U]: decir ~s blaspheme

blindado adj 1 (vehículo) armored 2 (puerta) reinforced

bloc *nm* writing pad

bloque *nm* 1 block: *un ~ de mármol* a marble block ◊ *un ~ de viviendas* an apartment building 2 (*Pol*) bloc

bloquear *vt* 1 (*obstruir*) block: *~ el paso* block access 2 (*Mil*) blockade ● **bloquearse** *vp* (*persona*) freeze

bloqueo *nm* 1 (*Dep*) block 2 (*Mil*) blockade

blusa *nf* blouse

bluyín *nm* (*And*) 1 (*tb* bluyínes) jeans [*pl*] 2 (*tela*) denim

bobada *nf* 1 nonsense [*U*]: *decir ~s* talk nonsense ◊ *Deja de hacer ~s.* Stop being silly. 2 (*tb* bobadita) (*cosita*) (little) thing: *Compré unas ~s.* I bought a couple of things.

bobina *nf* 1 (*hilo*) reel 2 (*Elec, alambre*) coil

bobo/a *adj, nm-nf* 1 (*tonto*) stupid 2 (*ingenuo*) naive: *Eres un ~.* You're so naive. ▸ **hacerse el ~** play the fool

boca *nf* (*Anat*) mouth → MY 2 (*entrada*) entrance ▸ **~ abajo/arriba** (*recostado*) face down/up ▸ **~ de incendio** hydrant ▸ **el a ~** mouth-to-mouth resuscitation **quedarse con la ~ abierta** (*por sorpresa*) to be dumbfounded

bocacalle *nf* side street: *una ~ de la calle 3* a side street off Third Street

bocadillo *nm* (*And, jalea*) guava jelly

bocado *nm* bite: *Se lo comió de un ~.* He ate it all in one bite.

boceto *nm* 1 (*Arte*) sketch 2 (*idea general*) outline

bochinche (*tb* bonche) *nm* 1 (*alboroto*) racket: *armar un ~* cause a racket 2 (*discusión*) fight

bochorno *nm* 1 (*calor*) Hace ~. It's muggy. ◊ *un día de ~* a stiflingly hot day 2 (*vergüenza*) embarrassment: *¡Qué ~!* How embarrassing!

bocina *nf* 1 (*Aut*) horn: *tocar la ~* sound your horn 2 (*Mús*) speaker 3 (*teléfono*) mouthpiece

bocón/ona *adj* big-mouthed: *¡Qué ~ eres!* You and your big mouth! ● *nm-nf* big mouth

boda *nf* wedding → MATRIMONIO ▸ **~s de oro/plata** golden/silver wedding [*sing*]

bodega *nf* 1 (*edificio*) warehouse 2 (*cuarto*) storeroom 3 (*para vino*) wine cellar 4 (*barco, avión*) hold

bodegón *nm* (*Arte*) still life [*pl* still lifes]

body *nm* bodysuit, body [*pl* -ies] (*GB*)

bofetada *nf* (*tb* bofetón *nm*) slap (in the face): *Me dio una ~.* She slapped me (in the face).

boicot *nm* boycott

boicotear *vt* boycott

boina *nf* beret

bola *nf* 1 ball 2 *una ~* (*Mx, mucho*) a lot ▸ **~ de nieve** snowball **~s de alcanfor** mothballs **en ~(s)** stark naked

bolear *vt* (*Mx, zapatos*) polish

bolera *nf* bowling alley

bolero *nm* frill: *una falda de ~s* a frilly skirt

boleta *nf* 1 ticket 2 (*Educ*) report

boletín *nm* bulletin: *~ informativo* news bulletin

boleto *nm* 1 ticket 2 (*quiniela*) coupon

boliche *nm* 1 (*Dep*) bowling 2 (*local*) bowling alley

bolígrafo *nm* (ballpoint) pen

bolillo *nm* 1 (*Mx, pan*) roll 2 (*And, de policía*) truncheon

Bolivia *nf* Bolivia

boliviano/a *adj, nm-nf* Bolivian

bollo *nm* 1 (*dulce*) bun 2 (*pan*) roll

bolo *nm* skittle: *jugar a ~s* play skittles

bolsa¹ *nf* 1 bag: *una ~ de deportes/papas* a sports bag/bag of chips ◊ *una ~ de plástico* a plastic bag 2 (*Mx, bolso*) purse, handbag (*GB*) 3 (*Mx, en prenda*) pocket 4 (*de aire*) (air) pocket ▸ **~ de agua caliente** hot-water bottle **~ de trabajo/empleo** job openings [*pl*]

bolsa² *nf* stock exchange

bolsillo *nm* pocket ▸ **de ~** pocket: *guía de ~* pocket guide

bolso *nm* purse, handbag (*GB*) ▸ **~ de viaje** travel bag

bomba¹ *nf* 1 (*Mil*) bomb 2 (*noticia*) bombshell ▸ **carro/paquete ~** car/parcel bomb

bomba² *nf* 1 (*Mec*) pump 2 (*And, gasolinera*) gas station, petrol station (*GB*) 3 (*And, elástica*) balloon ▸ **~ de aire** (air) pump

bombacho/a *adj* loose ● **bombachos** *nm* (*de deporte*) sweatpants, tracksuit bottoms (*GB*)

bombardear *vt* bombard

bombazo *nm* 1 (*explosión*) bomb blast 2 (*noticia*) bombshell

bombero *nmf* firefighter ▸ **carro/coche de ~s** fire engine **los ~s** the fire department [*sing*], the fire brigade [*sing*] (*GB*)

bombillo *nm* light bulb

bombo *nm* 1 (*Mús*) bass drum 2 (*lotería*) lottery drum ▸ **a ~ y**

platillo: *Lo anunció a ~ y platillo.* He made a great song and dance about it. **dar** ~ make a fuss (*about sth/sb*)

bombón *nm* **1** (*Mx*) marshmallow **2** (*And*) lollipop

bombona *nf* cylinder

bómper *nm* (*And*) bumper

bonachón/ona *adj* good-natured

bondad *nf* goodness ▶ **tener la ~ de** be so good as to do sth: *¿Tiene la ~ de ayudarme?* Would you be so good as to help me?

bondadoso *adj* kind (*to sth/sb*)

bonito *adj* **1** nice: *una casa/voz bonita* a nice house/voice **2** (*aspecto físico*) pretty

bono *nm* voucher ▶ **~ del ahorro** savings bond

boquiabierto *adj* (*sorprendido*) speechless

boquilla *nf* (*Mús*) mouthpiece

borda *nf* side of the ship ▶ **echar/tirar por la ~** (*fig*) throw sth away

bordado *adj* embroidered ● *nm* embroidery [*U*]

bordar *vt* embroider

borde *nm* **1** edge: *al ~ de la mesa* on the edge of the table **2** (*vaso, plato, etc.*) rim ▶ **al ~ de** (*fig*) on the verge of sth

bordo *nm* ▶ **a ~** on board: *subir a ~ del avión* get on board the plane

borrachera *nf* ▶ **agarrar/ponerse una ~** get drunk on sth

borracho/a *adj, nm-nf* drunk

borrador *nm* **1** (*de borrar*) eraser **2** (*texto*) draft

borrar *vt* **1** erase **2** (*pizarrón*) clean **3** (*Comp*) delete ● **borrarse** *vp* withdraw (*from sth*)

borrasca *nf* storm

borrascoso *adj* stormy

borrego/a *nm-nf* lamb

borrón *nm* smudge (*on sth*): *hacer un ~* make a smudge

borroso *adj* **1** (*impreciso*) blurred: *Lo veo todo ~.* Everything's blurred. **2** (*escritura*) illegible

bosque *nm* wood

bostezar *vi* yawn

bostezo *nm* yawn

bota *nf* boot: *~s de caminar* walking boots

botánica *nf* botany

botar *vt* **1** (*pelota*) bounce **2** (*buque*) launch **3** (*desechar*) throw sth away **4** (*expulsar*) throw sb out (*of sth*) ● *vi* bounce ▶ **hasta para ~**: *Hay comida hasta para ~.* There's enough food to feed an army.

bote[1] *nm* boat ▶ **~ de pedal** pedal boat **~ salvavidas** lifeboat

bote[2] *nm* **1** (*lata*) can **2** (*Mx, basura*) trash can, bin (*GB*)

bote[3] *nm* (*pelota*) bounce ▶ **dar/pegar ~s** bounce

botella *nf* bottle ▶ **de/en ~** bottled: *leche en ~* bottled milk

botín[1] *nm* (*bota*) ankle boot

botín[2] *nm* (*dinero*) loot

botiquín *nm* **1** (*maletín*) first-aid kit **2** (*armario*) medicine chest **3** (*habitación*) sickroom

botón *nm* **1** (*ropa*) button **2** (*control*) knob **3** (*Bot*) bud **4 botones** (*en hotel*) bellhop, bellboy (*GB*)

bóveda *nf* vault

boxeador *nm* boxer

boxear *vi* box

boxeo *nm* boxing

bozal *nm* muzzle

braga *nf* fly, flies [*pl*] (*GB*): *Llevas la ~ abierta.* Your fly is undone.

brasa *nf* ember ▶ **a la(s) ~(s)** grilled: *carne a la ~* grilled meat

brasero *nm* **1** (*small*) brazier **2** (*eléctrico*) electric heater

brasier *nm* bra

Brasil *nm* Brazil

brasileño/a *adj, nm-nf* Brazilian

bravo *adj* **1** (*animal*) fierce **2** (*persona*) angry (*with sb*) (*at/about sth*) ● *interj* bravo

braza *nf* **1** (*Náut*) fathom **2** (*natación*) breaststroke: *nadar (de) ~* do (the) breaststroke

brazada *nf* **1** stroke **2** (*natación*) breaststroke

brazalete *nm* armband

brazo *nm* **1** arm ▶ **MY ~** (*lámpara*) bracket **3** (*río*) branch ▶ **~ de gitano/reina** Swiss roll **del ~** arm in arm **ponerse con los ~s en cruz** stretch your arms out to the side **quedarse de ~s cruzados**: *No se quee ahí de ~s cruzados.* Don't just stand there!

brea *nf* tar

brecha *nf* track ▶ **camino de ~** dirt road

breve *adj* short ▶ **en ~** shortly **en ~s palabras** in a few wordsemsp; **ser ~** (*hablando*) be brief

bricolaje *nm* do it yourself

brigada *nf* **1** (*Mil*) brigade **2** (*policía*) squad: *la ~ antidroga* the drug squad ● *nmf* sergeant major

brillante *adj* **1** (*luz, color*) bright **2** (*superficie*) shiny **3** (*fenomenal*) brilliant ● *nm* diamond

brillar *vi* shine: *Sus ojos brillaban de alegría.* Their eyes shone with

brillo

joy. ◇ ¡Cómo brilla! Look how shiny it is!

brillo nm gleam ▶ sacar ~ make sth shine

brincar vi jump: ~ la reata (Mx) jump rope/skip (GB)

brinco nm jump ▶ ¡~s dieras! (Mx) you wish! **dar/pegar un ~** jump: dar ~s de alegría jump for joy

brindar vi drink (a toast) (to sth/sb) ● vt **1** (dedicar) dedicate sth to sb **2** (proporcionar) provide ● **brindarse** vp offer to do sth

brindis nm toast ▶ hacer un ~ drink a toast (to sth/sb)

brisa nf breeze

británico/a adj British ● nm-nf Briton: los ~s the British

brocha nf brush ▶ ~ de afeitar/ rasurar shaving brush

broche nm **1** (costura) fastener **2** (joya) brooch ▶ ~ a presión snap, press stud (GB)

broma nf joke: hacer/gastar ~s a algn play jokes on sb ▶ ~ pesada practical joke **de/en** ~ jokingly: Lo digo en ~. I'm only joking. ¡ni en ~(s)! no way!

bromear vi joke

bromista adj, nmf joker: Es muy ~. He's a real joker.

bronca nf **1** (pelea) row **2** (reprimenda) telling-off [pl tellings-off]: Me echaron una ~. I was told off. ▶ armar/montar una ~ kick up a fuss

bronce nm bronze

bronceado nm (sun)tan

bronceador nm suntan lotion

broncearse vp get a suntan

bronquitis nf bronchitis

brotar vi **1** (plantas) sprout **2** (flor) bud **3** (líquido) gush (out)

brote nm **1** shoot **2** (flor) bud **3** (epidemia, violencia) outbreak

bruces ▶ caerse de ~ fall flat on your face

bruja nf witch

brujería nf witchcraft

brujo nm **1** (hechicero) wizard **2** (tribus primitivas) witch doctor

brújula nf compass

bruma nf mist

brusco/a adj **1** (repentino) sudden **2** (persona) abrupt

brutal adj (violento) brutal

bruto/a adj **1** (torpe) dense **2** (grosero) crude **3** (peso, ingresos) gross ● nm-nf **1** (torpe) idiot **2** (grosero) slob

buceador/a nm-nf diver

bucear vi dive

buceo nm diving: practicar el ~ go diving

budismo nm Buddhism

budista adj, nmf Buddhist

buen mozo adj good-looking

bueno adj **1** good: Es una buena noticia. That's good news. **2** (amable) kind: Fue muy ~ conmigo. He was very kind to me. **3** (comida) tasty **4** (correcto) right **5** (menudo): ¡Buena la hizo! You really screwed up this time! ◇ ¡Buena se va a poner su mamá! Your mother'll get in a terrible state! ● nm-nf good guy: Ganó el ~. The good guy won. ● adv: —¿Quiere ir al cine? —Bueno. "Would you like to go to the movies?" "OK." ◇ ~, yo pienso que... Well, I think that... ● interj (Mx, teléfono) hello ▶ ~ de... good old...: el ~ de Juan good old Juan estar ~ be a stunner ¡(muy) buenas! good day! pasar ~ have fun por las buenas: Es mejor que lo hagas por las buenas. It would be better if you did it willingly. ◇ Se lo pido por las buenas. I'm asking you nicely. por las buenas o por las malas whether you like, he likes, etc. it or not **NOTA** Para otras expresiones con bueno, ver la sustantivo, p. ej. ¡buen provecho! en PROVECHO.

buey nm ox [pl oxen]

búfalo nm buffalo [pl buffalo o -es]

bufanda nf scarf [pl -s o scarves]

bufet (tb bufé) nm buffet

bufete nm (Jur) legal practise

buhardilla nf **1** (ático) attic **2** (ventana) dormer window

búho nm owl

buitre nm vulture

bujía nf (Mec) spark plug

bulimia nf bulimia

bulímico/a adj bulimic

bulla nf racket: hacer/armar ~ make a racket

bullicio nm **1** (ruido) racket **2** (actividad) hustle and bustle

bulto nm **1** shape **2** (paquete) package ▶ a ~ roughly: A ~, calculo 50. There are roughly 50. hacer ~ be bulky: Hace muy poco ~. It hardly takes up any room.

buñuelo nm fritter

buque nm ship ▶ ~ de guerra warship

burbuja nf bubble ▶ con ~s carbonated, sparkling (GB) hacer ~s bubble sin ~s non-carbonated, still (GB) tener ~s (bebida) be fizzy

burgués/esa adj middle-class

burguesía nf middle class

burla nf 1 (mofa) mockery [U]: un tono de ~ a mocking tone 2 (broma) joke: Déjate de ~s. Stop joking. ▶ hacer ~ make fun of sth/sb

burlar vt (eludir) evade ● **burlarse** vp make fun of sth/sb

burlón adj mockng

burocracia nf (papeleo) red tape

burócrata nmf 1 (pey) bureaucrat 2 (Mx, funcionario) civil servant

burrada nf stupid thing: decir ~s talk nonsense

burro/a adj 1 (estúpido) dense 2 (terco) pig-headed ● nm-nf 1 (animal) donkey 2 (persona) idiot ▶ ~ de carga (persona) dogsbody [pl -ies] **~ de planchar** (Mx) ironing board

bus nm bus

busca¹ nf ▶ **en ~ de** in search of sth/sb

busca² (tb **buscapersonas**) nm pager

buscador nm (Comp) search engine

buscador/a nm-nf ▶ **~ de oro** gold prospector **~ de tesoros** treasure hunter

buscar vt 1 look for sth/sb 2 (sistemáticamente) search for sth/sb 3 (en libro, lista) look sth up 4 (recoger a algn) (a) (en carro) pick sb up (b) (a pie) meet 5 (conseguir y traer) get: Fui a ~ al médico. I went to get the doctor. ◇ ¿Quepo? Is there room for me? **2 ~ por** go through sth: La cama no cabía por la puerta. The bed wouldn't go through the door. ● **no cabe duda** there is no doubt **no ~ en sí de contento/alegría** be overjoyed

buseta nf (And) small bus

búsqueda nf search (for sth) ▶ **a la ~ de** in search of sth

busto nm bust

butaca nf 1 (sillón) armchair 2 (Cine, Teat) seat

buzo nm 1 (buceador) diver 2 (And) sweater →SWEATER

buzón nm mailbox, postbox (GB) ▶ **~ de voz** voicemail **echar al ~** mail, post (GB)

C c

cabal adj (persona) upright ▶ **en sus ~es** in your right mind

cabalgar vi ride: ~ en mula ride (on) a mule

caballerango nm (Mx) groom

caballería nf 1 (animal) mount 2 (Mil) cavalry

caballeriza nf stable

caballero nm 1 gentleman [pl -men] 2 (Hist) knight ▶ **de ~(s)**: sección de ~s men's clothing department

caballete nm 1 (Arte) easel 2 (soporte) trestle 3 (gimnasia) horse

caballitos nm merry-go-round [sing]

caballo nm 1 (animal, gimnasia) horse 2 (ajedrez) knight 3 (Mec) horsepower (abrev hp): un motor de diez ~s a ten horsepower engine ▶ **a ~ entre...** halfway between... **~ de carrera(s)** racehorse **~ de mar** sea horse

cabaña nf (choza) hut

cabecear vi 1 (afirmar, de sueño) nod 2 (caballo) toss its head 3 (fútbol) head

cabecera nf 1 head: en la ~ de la mesa at the head of the table 2 (cama) headboard ▶ **~ municipal** town

cabecilla nmf ringleader

cabello nm hair

caber vi 1 fit (in/into sth): No cabe en la maleta. It won't fit in the suitcase.

cabezal nm headrest

cabezazo nm 1 (golpe) butt 2 (Dep) header ▶ **dar un ~** head the ball

cabezón adj, nmf ▶ **ser (un) ~** (terco) be pig-headed

cabina nf 1 (avión) cockpit 2 (barco) cabin 3 (camión) cab

cabizbajo adj downcast

cabeza nf 1 head: tener buena/mala ~ para las cifras have a good head/no head for figures 2 (lista, liga) top 3 (juicio) sense ▶ **~ abajo** upside down **~ de ajo** head of garlic **de ~ de familia** head of the household **de ~** headlong: tirarse al mar de ~ dive headlong into the sea **ir a la ~** be in the lead **irse la ~ a algn** feel dizzy **mal de la ~** crazy **metérsele algo a algn en la ~** take it into your head to do sth **perder la ~** go crazy **por ~** a/per head **ser un ~ dura** be stubborn **tener la ~ en otro planeta** have your head in the clouds

cable nm cable

cabo nm 1 (extremo) end 2 (Náut) rope 3 (Geog) cape ● nmf (Mil) corporal ▶ al ~ de after: al ~ de un año after a year **de ~ a rabo** from beginning to end **llevar a ~** carry sth out

cabra nf goat ▶ **loco como/más loco que una ~** off your rocker

cabrito nm (animal) kid

caca nf poop, poo (GB) ▶ **hacer ~** poop, poo (GB)

cacahuate nm peanut

cacao nm 1 cocoa 2 (de labios) lip balm

cacarear vi 1 (gallo) crow 2 (gallina) cackle

cacería nf ▶ **ir de ~** go hunting

cacerola nf casserole

cachar vt 1 catch 2 (And, entender) understand

cacharro nm 1 (vasija) pot 2 (cachivache) thing: una casa llena de ~s a house full of junk

cachear vt frisk

cachetada nf slap ▶ **dar una ~** slap

cachete nm cheek

cacho nm 1 (pedazo) piece 2 (cuerno) horn

cachorro/a nm-nf 1 (perro) puppy [pl -ies] 2 (león, tigre) cub

cachucha nf peaked cap

caco nm burglar →THIEF

cactus (tb **cacto**) nm cactus [pl -es o cacti]

cada adj 1 each 2 (con expresiones numéricas o de tiempo) every: ~ semana/vez every week/time ◇ ~ diez días every ten days → EVERY 3 (con valor exclamativo): ¡Dices ~ cosa! The things you come up with! ▶ ~ **cosa a su tiempo** all in good time ~ **cual** everyone ¿~ **cuánto?** how often? ~ **dos días, semanas, etc.** ~ día, semana, etc. de por medio every other day, week, etc. ~ **dos por tres** constantly ~ **loco con su tema** each to his own ~ **uno** each (one): ~ uno valía 5 euros. Each one cost 5 euros. ◇ Nos dieron una bolsa a ~ uno. They gave each of us a bag./They gave us a bag each. **para cada...** between: un libro para ~ dos alumnos one book between two students

cadáver nm corpse

cadena nf 1 chain 2 (Radio) station 3 (TV) channel ▶ ~ **perpetua** life imprisonment

cadera nf hip

cadete nmf cadet

caducar vi 1 (documento, plazo) expire 2 (alimento) go past its expiration/expiry (GB) date 3 (medicamento) be out of date: ¿Cuándo caduca? When does it have to be used by?

caducidad nf ▶ **fecha de ~** expiration date, expiry date (GB)

caer vi 1 fall: El vaso cayó del balcón. The glass fell off the balcony. ◇ ~ **en la trampa** fall into the trap ◇ Caía la noche. Night was falling. 2 ~ **(en)** (entender) get sth: Ya caigo. Now I get it. 3 (persona): Me cae bien/mal. I like him/can't stand him. ◇ ¿Qué tal te cayó su novia? What did you think of his girlfriend? ● **caerse** vp 1 (diente, pelo) fall out ▶ **caérsele algo a algn** drop sth: Se me cayó el helado. I dropped my ice cream. →DROP **NOTA** Para otras expresiones con **caer**, ver el sustantivo, adjetivo, etc., p. ej. **caer gordo** en GORDO.

café nm 1 coffee: ¿Quieres un ~? Would you like a (cup of) coffee? 2 (establecimiento) cafe ● adj, nm (color) brown ▶ ~ **expreso/exprés** espresso [pl -s]

cafeína nf caffeine: sin ~ caffeine free

cafetal nm coffee plantation

cafetera nf coffee pot ▶ ~ **eléctrica** coffee maker

cafetería nf snack bar

cafetero/a adj 1 coffee: la industria cafetera the coffee industry 2 (persona): ser muy ~ be very fond of coffee ● adj (caficultor/a) nm-nf coffee grower

caída nf 1 fall: una ~ de 3m a three-meter fall ◇ la ~ del gobierno the fall of the government 2 (descenso) fall in sth: una ~ de los precios a fall in prices 3 (pelo) loss: la ~ del pelo hair loss ▶ **a la ~ de la tarde/noche** at dusk/nightfall ~ **libre** free fall

caído/a adj fallen ● nm: los ~s en la guerra those who died in the war ▶ ~ **del cielo** 1 (inesperado) out of the blue 2 (oportuno): Nos llega ~ del cielo. It's a real godsend.

caimán nm alligator

caja nf 1 box: una ~ de cartón a cardboard box ◇ una ~ de pañuelos a box of tissues 2 (botellas) (a) crate (b) (vino) case 3 (ataúd) coffin 4 (supermercado) checkout 5 (otras tiendas) cash desk 6 (banco) teller's window ▶ ~ **de ahorros** savings bank ~ **de cambios/velocidades** gearbox ~ **de herramientas** toolbox ~ **fuer-**

te/de seguridad safe ~ **negra** black box ~ **registradora** till

cajero/a *nm-nf* cashier ▶ **~ automático** ATM, cash machine (GB)

cajetilla *nf* pack

cajón *nm* 1 (*mueble*) drawer 2 (*de madera*) crate

cajuela *nf* (*Mx*) trunk, boot (GB)

cal *nf* lime

calabacita *nf* (*tb* **calabacín** *nm*) zucchini, courgette (GB)

calabaza *nf* pumpkin

calabozo *nm* 1 (*mazmorra*) dungeon 2 (*celda*) cell

calamar *nm* squid [*pl* squid]

calambre *nm* cramp: *Me dio un ~*. I got cramp.

calamidad *nf* (*desgracia*) disaster: *pasar ~es* suffer misfortune

calar *vt* 1 **~ hasta los huesos**: *Hace un frío que cala hasta los huesos.* It's bitterly cold.

calavera *nf* 1 skull 2 (*Mx, Aut*) tail light

calcar *vt* trace

calcetín *nm* sock

calcinado *adj* charred

calcinar *vt* burn *sth* down

calcio *nm* calcium

calcomanía *nf* sticker

calculadora *nf* calculator

calcular *vt* 1 work *sth* out, calculate (*más fml*) 2 (*suponer*) reckon

cálculo *nm* calculation: *hacer unos ~s* make some calculations ▶ **hacer un ~ aproximado** make a rough estimate

caldera *nf* boiler

calderilla *nf* small change

caldero *nm* cauldron

caldo *nm* 1 (*para cocinar*) stock 2 (*sopa*) broth [*U*]

calefacción *nf* heating

calendario *nm* calendar

calentador *nm* heater: *~ de agua* water heater

calentamiento *nm* warm-up: *hacer un poco de ~* warm up ▶ **~ global** global warming

calentar *vt* 1 heat *sth* up 2 (*templar*) warm *sth/sb* up ● **calentarse** *vp* 1 get very hot: *El motor se calentó demasiado.* The engine overheated. 2 (*templarse*, *Dep*) warm up

caleta *nf* (*And*, *escondite*) cache

calibre *nm* caliber

calidad *nf* quality [*pl* -ies]: *fruta de ~* quality fruit ▶ **en ~ de** as: *en ~ de portavoz* as a spokesperson

cálido *adj* warm

caliente *adj* 1 hot: *agua ~* hot water 2 (*templado*) warm →FRÍO

calificación *nf* 1 (*nota escolar*) grade 2 (*descripción*) description: *No merece otra ~*. It cannot be described in any other way.

calificar *vt* 1 (*corregir*) grade 2 (*a un alumno*) give *sb* a grade 3 (*describir*) label *sb* (*as sth*)

caligrafía *nf* handwriting

callado *adj* 1 quiet 2 (*en silencio*) silent: *Permaneció ~*. He remained silent.

callar *vt* 1 (*persona*) get *sb* to be quiet 2 (*información*) keep quiet about *sth* ● **callar(se)** *vi, vp* 1 (*no hablar*) say nothing 2 (*dejar de hablar/hacer ruido*) go quiet, shut up (*coloq*): ¡*calla!* ¡cállate (la boca)! be quiet!, shut up! (*coloq*)

calle *nf* street (*abrev* St): *Está en la ~ 3*. It's in Third Street. **NOTA** Al nombrar la casa o portal se usa *at*: *Vivo en la ~ Goya 49-10*. We live at 49-10 Goya Street. →STREET ▶ **~ arriba/abajo** up/down the street ~ **cerrada/ciega** cul-de-sac **quedarse en la ~** (*sin trabajo*) lose your job

callejero *adj* ▶ **perro ~** stray (dog)

callejón *nm* alleyway ▶ **~ sin salida** dead end

callejuela *nf* side street

callo *nm* 1 (*dedo del pie*) corn 2 (*mano, planta del pie*) callus ▶ **~ de hacha** (*Mx*) scallop

calma *nf* calm: *mantener la ~* keep calm ▶ ¡(con) ~! calm down! **perder la ~** lose your temper **tomar con ~** take *sth* easy

calmante *nm* 1 (*dolor*) painkiller 2 (*nervios*) tranquilizer

calmar *vt* 1 (*nervios*) calm 2 (*dolor*) relieve 3 (*hambre, sed*) satisfy ● **calmarse** *vp* calm down

calor *nm* heat ▶ **entrar en ~** warm up **hacer ~** be hot: *Hace ~*. It's hot. **tener ~** be/feel hot: *Tengo ~*. I'm hot. →FRÍO

caloría *nf* calorie: *una dieta baja en ~s* a low-calorie diet

caluroso *adj* 1 (*muy caliente*) hot 2 (*tibio, fig*) warm: *una noche/bienvenida calurosa* a warm night/welcome

calva *nf* bald patch

calvo *adj* bald: *quedarse ~* go bald

calza *nf* (*diente*) filling

calzada *nf* road

calzado *nm* footwear

calzar *vt* 1 (*zapato*) wear: *Calzo zapato plano.* I wear flat shoes. 2 (*número*) take: ¿*Qué número calzas*? What size do you take? 3 (*persona*) put *sb's* shoes on: ¿*Puede ~ al niño*? Can you put the boy's shoes on for him?

4 (*And, diente*) fill: *Me tienen que ~ una muela.* I have to have a tooth filled. ● **calzarse** *vp* put your shoes on

calzón (*tb* **calzones**) *nm* **1** (*mujer*) panties [*pl*] **2** (*tb* **calzoncillo(s)**) (*hombre*) underpants [*pl*] →PANTALÓN

cama *nf* bed: *irse a la ~* go to bed ◊ *meterse en/salir de la ~* get into/out of bed ▸ **~ camarote** bunk bed **~ individual/de matrimonio** single/double bed **estar/quedar de ~** be shattered

camada *nf* litter

camaleón *nm* chameleon

cámara *nf* **1** chamber: *la ~ de comercio* the chamber of commerce ◊ *música de ~* chamber music **2** **~ (de fotos/fotográfica)** (*Cine, Fot*) camera ▸ **~ de Senadores/Diputados** Senate/Chamber of Deputies **~ lenta** in slow motion

camarada *nmf* **1** (*Pol*) comrade **2** (*colega*) buddy [*pl* -ies]

camarógrafo/a *nm-nf* cameraman/woman [*pl* -men/-women]

camarón *nm* shrimp

camarote *nm* cabin

cambiante *adj* changing

cambiar *vt* **1** change *sth* (*for sth*): *~ el carro por otro* trade in your car for another one **2** (*dinero*) change (*into sth*): *~ pesos por dólares* change pesos into dollars **3** (*intercambiar*) exchange *sth* (*for sth*): *Si no le gusta lo puede ~.* You can exchange it if you don't like it. ● *vi* change: *~ de* change jobs/trains/the subject ● **cambiarse** *vp* **1** change: *~ de zapatos* change your shoes **2** (*persona*) get changed ▸ **~ de opinión** change your mind **~ de velocidad** shift/change (*GB*) gear **~(se) de casa** move house

cambio *nm* **1** change (*in/of sth*): *un ~ de temperatura/planes* a change in temperature/of plan **2** (*intercambio*) exchange: *un ~ de impresiones* an exchange of views **3** (*dinero suelto*) change: *Me dieron mal el ~.* They gave me the wrong change. ◊ *¿Tiene ~ de $100?* Do you have change for 100 dollars? **4** (*Fin*) exchange rate **5** (*carro, bicicleta*) gear: *hacer un ~* shift gear ▸ **a ~ (de/de que)** in return (*for sth*): *a ~ de que usted me ayude en matemáticas* in return for you helping me with my math **~ de sentido** U-turn **en ~** on the other hand

camello/a *nm-nf* camel ● *nm* work: *¡Qué ~!* What hard work!

camellón *nm* (*Mx*) central reservation

camerino *nm* **1** (*Teat*) dressing room **2** (*Dep*) locker room

camilla *nf* (*Med*) stretcher

caminante *nmf* hiker

caminar *vt, vi* walk ▸ **ir caminando** go on foot

caminata *nf* trek ▸ **darse una ~** go on a long walk

camino *nm* **1** (*carretera no asfaltada*) track **2** (*ruta, medio*) way: *No me acuerdo del ~.* I can't remember the way. ◊ *La encontré en el ~.* I met her on the way. **3** (*senda*) path (*to sth*): *el ~ a la fama* the path to fame ▸ **agarrar ~** clear off **a medio ~** halfway: *A medio ~ paré a descansar.* I stopped to rest halfway. **andar/ir por buen/mal ~** be on the right/wrong track **~ vecinal** minor road (**estar/ir**) **~ de...** (be) on the/your way to... **ponerse en ~** set off

camión *nm* **1** (*carga*) truck **2** (*autobús*) bus ▸ **~ cisterna** tanker **~ de la basura** garbage truck, dustcart (*GB*) **~ de mudanzas/trasteos** moving van, removal van (*GB*)

camionero/a *nm-nf* **1** truck driver **2** (*autobús*) bus driver

camioneta *nf* **1** (*carga*) van **2** (*pasajeros*) station wagon, estate car (*GB*)

camisa *nf* shirt ▸ **~ de fuerza** straitjacket **meterse en ~ de once varas** get yourself into a mess

camiseta *nf* **1** T-shirt **2** (*Dep*) shirt **3** (*ropa interior*) undershirt, vest (*GB*)

camisón *nm* nightie

camorra *nf* **1** (*jaleo*) ruckus: *armar/montar ~* have/throw a fit **2** (*pelea*) fight

camorrero/a *nm-nf* troublemaker

camote *nm* sweet potato [*pl* -es] ▸ **poner como ~** tell *sb* off

campamento *nm* camp: *ir de ~* go to a camp

campana *nf* **1** bell **2** (*extractor*) extractor hood

campanada *nf* **1** (*campana*): *Sonaron las ~s.* The bells rang out. **2** (*reloj*) stroke ▸ **dar dos, etc. ~s** strike two, etc.: *El reloj dio seis ~s.* The clock struck six.

campanario *nm* belfry [*pl* -ies]

campaña *nf* (*Com, Pol, Mil*) campaign

campeón/ona nm-nf champion: *el ~ del mundo* the world champion

campeonato nm championship

campesino/a nm-nf **1** (*agricultor*) farmworker **NOTA** También se dice peasant, pero tiene connotaciones de pobreza. **2** (*aldeano*) countryman/woman [pl -men/-women]: *los ~s* country people

campestre adj ● *comida ~* picnic

camping nm campground, campsite (GB) ▸ *ir de ~* go camping

campo nm **1** (*naturaleza*) country: *en el ~* in the country **2** (*tierra de cultivo*) field: *~s de maíz* corn fields **3** (*paisaje*) countryside: *El ~ es precioso en mayo.* The countryside looks nice in May. **4** (*ámbito, Fís, Comp*) field: *~ magnético* magnetic field ◊ *el ~ del arte* the field of art **5** (*Dep*) field: *salir al ~* come out onto the field **6** (*campamento*) camp: *~ de concentración* concentration camp ▸ *~ de batalla* battlefield *~ de golf* golf course *~ de juego* ground en *~ contrario* (*Dep*) away: *jugar en ~ contrario* play an away game

camuflaje nm camouflage

camuflar vt camouflage

cana¹ nf gray hair: *tener ~s* have gray hair

cana² nf (*cárcel*) jail

canal nm **1** (a) (*artificial, de riego*) canal: *el ~ de Panamá* the Panama Canal (b) (*natural*) channel **2** (*TV, Comp*) channel

canario nm (*pájaro*) canary [pl -ies]

canasta nf basket: *meter una ~* score a basket ▸ *~ familiar* family shopping basket

cancelar vt **1** cancel **2** (*deuda*) settle

cáncer nm cancer [U]: *~ de pulmón* lung cancer

Cáncer nm, nmf (*Astrol*) Cancer

cancha nf **1** (*tenis, basquetbol, etc.*) court: *Los jugadores ya están en la ~.* The players are on court. **2** (*fútbol*) field **3** (*desenvoltura*) self-confidence: *Tiene mucha ~.* He's very self-assured. ▸ *tener ~* have a way with sth/sb: *Tiene mucha ~.* He's very experienced.

canción nf **1** song **2** (*excusa*) story [pl -ies] ▸ *~ de cuna* lullaby [pl -ies]

candado nm padlock: *cerrado con ~* padlocked

candela nf lighter: *¿Tienes ~?* Do you have a light?

candelero nm (*para velas*) candlestick

candidato/a nm-nf candidate (*for sth*)

candidatura nf candidacy (*for sth*): *presentar su ~ al senado* run for the senate

caneca nf **1** (*And*) (*cocina*) trash can, bin (GB) **2** (*oficina*) wastebasket, bin (GB) **3** (*calle*) litter basket, litter bin (GB) **4** (*tambor*) oildrum

canela nf cinnamon

cangrejo nm **1** (*de mar*) crab **2** (*de río*) crayfish (GB) crayfish

canguro nm kangaroo

caníbal nmf cannibal

canibalismo nm cannibalism

canica nf marble

canjear vt exchange sth (*for sth*)

canoa nf canoe

canoso adj gray

canotaje nm canoeing: *hacer ~* go canoeing

cansado adj **1** (*fatigado*) tired (*from sth*): *Estoy ~ de tanto correr.* I'm tired from all that running. **2** (*harto*) tired of sth/sb **3** (*que fatiga*) tiring →BE

cansancio nm tiredness

cansar vt **1** (*fatigar*) tire sth/sb (*out*) **2** (*hartar*): *Me cansa tener que hacerlo todo.* I get tired of having to do everything. ● vi be tiring: *El trabajo cansa mucho.* The work is very tiring. ● **cansarse** vp get tired (*of sth/sb*)

cansón adj **1** (*agotador*) tiring **2** (*molesto*) tiresome: *¡Qué tipo más ~!* That guy is such a pain!

cantaleta nf: *Esa es la ~ de toda su vida.* That's been the story of his life. ▸ *echar ~* be a nuisance

cantante nmf singer

cantar vt, vi sing ● vi **1** (*cigarra, pájaro*) chirp **2** (*gallo*) crow ▸ *~ las verdades/las cuarenta* tell sb a few home truths *~ victoria* celebrate

cántaro nm pitcher

cantautor/a nm-nf singer-songwriter

cantera nf **1** (*de piedra*) quarry [pl -ies] **2** (*Dep*) youth squad

cantidad nf **1** amount: *¿Cuánta ~ necesita?* How much do you need? **2** (*personas, objetos*) number: *¡Qué ~ de carros!* What a lot of cars! ◊ *Había ~ de gente.* There were a lot of people. **3** (*dinero*) sum **4** (*magnitud*) quantity: ● adv a lot: *Habla ~(es).* He talks a lot.

cantimplora nf water bottle

canto¹ nm **1** (*arte*) singing **2** (*canción, poema*) song

canto² nm (borde) edge ▸ **de ~** on its/their side

canto³ nm (piedra) pebble

canturrear vt, vi hum

caña nf 1 (junco) reed 2 (bambú, etc.) cane: ~ **de azúcar** sugar cane ▸ ~ **(de pescar)** fishing rod

cañería nf pipe: la ~ **de desagüe** the drainpipe

cañón nm 1 (artillería) cannon 2 (fusil) barrel: una escopeta de dos cañones a double-barreled shotgun 3 (Geog) canyon

caoba nf mahogany

caos nm chaos [U]: Fue un ~ total. It was total chaos.

capa nf 1 layer: la ~ **de ozono** the ozone layer 2 (pintura, barniz) coat 3 (prenda) (a) (larga) cloak (b) (corta) cape

capacidad nf 1 capacity (for sth): una gran ~ **de trabajo** a great capacity for work ◊ Tiene ~ **para 300 personas.** It has capacity for 300 guests. 2 (aptitud) ability [pl -ies] (to do sth)

capar vt castrate ▸ ~ **clase** (And) skip class

caparazón nm shell

capataz nmf foreman/woman [pl -men/-women]

capaz adj capable (of sth) ▸ **ser ~ de** be able to do sth: No sé cómo fue ~ de decírselo. I don't know how he could tell her. ◊ No soy ~ de hacerlo. I just can't do it.

capellán nm chaplain

capilla nf chapel ▸ ~ **ardiente** chapel of rest

capital nm, nf capital

capitalismo nm capitalism

capitalista adj, nmf capitalist

capitán/ana nm-nf, nm-nf captain

capítulo nm 1 (libro) chapter 2 (Radio, TV) episode

capó nm (carro) hood, bonnet (GB)

caporal nm foreman [pl -men]

capote nm cape

capricho nm (antojo) whim ▸ **dar un ~** give sb a treat

caprichoso adj 1 (que quiere cosas): ¡Qué niño más ~! That child's never satisfied! 2 (que cambia de idea): Es muy ~. He's always changing his mind. ◊ un cliente ~ a fussy customer

Capricornio nm Capricorn

captura nf 1 (fugitivo) capture 2 (armas, drogas) seizure

capturar vt 1 (fugitivo) capture 2 (armas, drogas) seize

capucha nf (capuchón) hood

capullo nm 1 (flor) bud 2 (insecto) cocoon

caqui nm khaki

cara nf 1 (rostro) face 2 (disco, papel, Geom) side ▸ ~ **a ~** face to face ~ **dura**: Es un ~ dura. What a jerk! ~ **o sello** (And) heads or tails **dar la ~** face the music **partir/romper la ~** smash sb's face in **poner ~ de asco** make a face **tener buena/mala ~** (persona) look well/sick **volver/voltear la ~** look the other way

caracol nm 1 (de tierra) snail 2 (tb caracola nf) (de mar) conch, winkle (GB)

carácter nm 1 character 2 (índole) nature ▸ **tener buen/mal ~** be good-natured/ill-tempered **tener mucho/poco ~** be strong-minded/weak-minded

característica nf characteristic

característico adj characteristic

caracterizar vt characterize

carambola nm starfruit

caramelo nm 1 (golosina) candy [pl -ies], sweet (GB) 2 (azúcar quemado) caramel

carantoña nf ▸ **hacer ~s** caress

carátula nf 1 (CD, etc.) jacket, sleeve (GB) 2 (Mx, reloj) dial 3 (libro, revista) cover

caravana nf 1 (expedición) caravan 2 (tráfico) backup, tailback (GB) 3 (Mx, reverencia) bow

carbón nm coal ▸ ~ **vegetal** charcoal

carboncillo nm charcoal

carbonizar(se) vt, vp burn

carbono nm carbon

carburante nm fuel

carca adj, nmf old fogey: ¡Qué gente más ~! What a bunch of old fogeys!

carcacha nf (carro) old banger

carcajada nf roar of laughter ▸ **reír(se) a ~s** split your sides (laughing) **soltar una ~** burst out laughing

cárcel nf prison: ir a la ~ go to prison ◊ Fue condenado a un año de ~. He was sentenced to a year's imprisonment.

carcelero/a nm-nf jailer

cardenal nm cardinal

cardíaco (tb cardiaco) adj ▸ **ataque/paro ~** cardiac arrest

cardinal adj cardinal

cardo nm thistle

carecer vi ~ **de** lack sth ▸ **carece de sentido** it doesn't make sense

careta nf mask

carga nf 1 (tb cargada) (acción) loading: La ~ del buque llevó un día. It took a day to load the ship. **2** (*peso*) load: ~ *máxima* maximum load **3** (*mercancía*) (a) (*avión, barco*) cargo [*pl* -s/-es] (b) (*camión*) load **4** (*explosivo, Elec*) charge **5** (*obligación*) burden ▸ **¡a la ~!** charge!

cargadera *nf* **1** (*vestido, brasier*) shoulder strap **2 cargaderas** (*pantalones*) suspenders, braces (*GB*)

cargado *adj* **1** loaded (*with sth*): *Venían ~s de maletas.* They were loaded down with suitcases. ◇ *un fusil ~* a loaded rifle **2** (*responsabilidades*) burdened *with sth* **3** (*atmósfera*) stuffy **4** (*bebida*) strong (*comida*) big

cargador *nm* (*Elec*) charger

cargamento *nm* **1** (*avión, barco*) cargo [*pl* -s/-es] **2** (*camión*) load

cargar *vt* **1** load: *Cargaron el camión de cajas.* They loaded the truck with boxes. ◇ *un arma* load a weapon (*pluma, encendedor*) fill **3** (*pila, batería*) charge ● *vi* **1** ~ **con** (a) (*llevar*) carry *sth*: *Siempre me toca ~ con todo.* I always end up carrying everything. (b) (*responsabilidad*) shoulder *sth* **2** (*Mil*) charge (*at sb*)

cargo *nm* **1** position: *un ~ importante* an important position **2** (*Pol*) office **3 cargos** (*Jur*) charges ▸ **dar/tener ~ de conciencia** feel guilty **hacerse ~ de 1** (*responsabilizarse*) take charge of *sth* **2** (*cuidar de algn*) look after *sb*

cargue *nm* (*And*) loading

caribeño/a *adj, nm-nf* Caribbean

caricatura *nf* caricature: *hacer una ~* draw a caricature

caricia *nf* caress ▸ **hacer ~s** caress

caridad *nf* charity: *vivir de la ~* live on charity

caries *nf* **1** (*enfermedad*) tooth decay [*U*] **2** (*hueco*) cavity [*pl* -ies]

cariño *nm* **1** (*afecto*) affection **2** (*delicadeza*) loving care **3** (*apelativo*) sweetheart ▸ **con ~** (*cartas*) with love **tener/agarrar ~** be/become fond of *sth/sb*

cariñoso *adj* **1** affectionate (*towards sth/sb*) **2** (*abrazo, saludo*) warm

caritativo *adj* charitable (*to/ towards sb*)

carnada *nf* bait

carnal *adj* (*sensual*) carnal ● *nm* (*Mx*) buddy [*pl* -ies]

carnaval *nm* carnival

carne *nf* **1** (*Anat, Rel, fruta*) flesh **2** (*alimento*) meat **NOTA** En inglés se usan distintas palabras para referirse al animal y a la carne que se obtiene de ellos. Del cerdo (**pig**) se obtiene **pork**, de la vaca (**cow**), **beef** y del ternero (**calf**), **veal**. Mutton es la carne de la oveja (**sheep**), y del cordero (**lamb**) se obtiene la carne de cordero o **lamb**. ▸ **~ de res** beef ~ **molida** ground meat, mince (*GB*) **~s frías** cold meat [*U*] **en ~ viva** raw: *Tienes la rodilla en ~ viva.* Your knee is red and raw. **ser de ~ y hueso** be only human **tener ~ de gallina** have goose bumps

carné (*tb* **carnet**) *nm* card ▸ **~ de afiliado** membership card

carnero *nm* ram

carnicería *nf* **1** (*tienda*) butcher shop, butcher's (*GB*) **2** (*matanza*) massacre

carnicero/a *nm-nf* butcher

carnívoro/a *adj* carnivorous

caro *adj* expensive ● *adv*: *comprar/pagar algo muy ~* pay a lot for *sth* ▸ **costar/pagar ~** (*fig*) cost *sb* dearly: *Pagará ~ su error.* His mistake will cost him dearly.

carpa¹ *nf* (*pez*) carp [*pl* carp]

carpa² *nf* (*para acampar, etc.*) tent

carpeta *nf* **1** folder **2** (*tejido*) mat

carpintería *nf* carpentry

carpintero/a *nm-nf* carpenter

carraspear *vi* clear your throat

carraspera *nf* hoarseness ▸ **tener ~** be hoarse

carreola *nf* (*Mx*) stroller, push-chair (*GB*)

carrera *nf* **1** (*corrida*) run: *Ya no estoy para ~s.* I'm not up to running any more. **2** (*Dep*) race: *~ de relevos* relay race **3** (*licenciatura*) degree: *¿Qué ~ hizo?* What did you major in? **4** (*profesión*) career **5** (*vía*) street **6** (*en pelo*) part, parting (*GB*) ▸ **~ a campo traviesa** cross-country race **~ de armamentos** arms race **~ de caballos** horse race **carro/coche de ~s** racing car

carreta *nf* cart ▸ **echar ~** (*And*) pad *sth* out

carrete *nm* (*hilo*) spool

carretera *nf* road: *por ~* by road ▸ **~ circunvalar/de circunvalación** outer belt, ring road (*GB*) **~ de doble vía** divided highway, dual carriageway (*GB*) **~ intermunicipal/secundaria** back road, B-road (*GB*) **~ nacional/principal** highway, A-road (*GB*) **por ~** by road

carretilla nf wheelbarrow

carril nm 1 (*Dep, carretera*) lane 2 (*riel*) rail

carrilera nf (*And*) track

carrillo nm cheek

carro nm 1 (*Aut*) car: en ~ by car 2 (*de caballos*) cart 3 (*vagón, carruaje*) carriage 4 (*tb carrito*) (*aeropuerto, etc.*) cart, trolley (*GB*): ~ de compras/del mercado shopping car ▶ **~ cama** sleeping car **~ de la basura** (*And*) garbage truck, dustcart (*GB*)

carrocería nf bodywork [U]

carroña nf carrion

carrotanque nm tanker

carroza nf 1 (*de caballos*) carriage 2 (*en desfile*) float

carruaje nm carriage

carrusel nm merry-go-round

carta nf 1 (*misiva*) letter: poner una ~ mail a letter ◊ una ~ certificada/recomendada a certified/registered (*GB*) letter 2 (*naipe*) card: jugar a las ~s play cards →BARAJA 3 (*menú*) menu 4 (*documento*) charter ▶ **~ de navegación** chart **echar las ~s** tell sb's fortune

cartearse vp write to sb

cartel[1] nm 1 (*afiche*) poster: poner un ~ put up a poster 2 (*letrero*) sign

cartel[2] nm (*mafia*) cartel

cartelera nf 1 (*periódico*) listings [pl] 2 (*avisos*) bulletin board, noticeboard (*GB*) ▶ **en ~ on**: Lleva un mes en ~. It has been on for a month.

cartera nf 1 (*billetera*) wallet 2 (*maletín*) briefcase

carterista nmf pickpocket

cartero/a nm-nf letter carrier, postman/woman [pl -men/-women] (*GB*)

cartilla nf 1 (*Educ*) reader 2 (*Mx, Mil*) identity card

cartón nm 1 (*material*) cardboard 2 (*cigarrillos, leche*) carton

cartucho nm (*proyectil, recambio*) cartridge

cartulina nf card

casa nf 1 (*vivienda*) (a) house (b) (*apartamento*) apartment (c) (*edificio*) apartment building 2 (*hogar*) home: No hay nada como estar en la ~. There's no place like home. 3 (*empresa*) company [pl -ies] ▶ **~ de empeños** pawnshop **~ rodante/móvil** trailer, caravan (*GB*) **como una ~** huge: una mentira como una ~ a huge lie **en la ~** home: quedarse en la ~ stay home ◊ ¿Está tu mamá en la ~? Is your mother

in? **en (la) ~ de** at sb's (house)
NOTA En lenguaje coloquial se omite la palabra house: Estaré en la ~ de Ana. I'll be at Ana's. **ir a (la) ~ de** go home **ir a (la) ~ de** go to sb's (house) **pasar por la ~ de** drop by sb's (house): Pasaré por su ~ mañana. I'll drop by tomorrow.

casaca nf (*blusón*) smock

casado/a adj married (to sb) • nm-nf married man/woman [pl men/women] ▶ **los recién ~s** the newly-weds

casar vi balance (with sth): Las cuentas no casaban. The accounts didn't balance. • **casarse** vp (~ con) get married (to sb) ▶ **~se por la Iglesia/por lo civil** get married in church/a civil ceremony →MATRIMONIO

cascabel nm bell ▶ **serpiente/víbora de ~** rattlesnake

cascada nf waterfall

cascajo nm 1 (*escombros*) rubble [U] 2 (*And*) piece of gravel

cascanueces nm nutcracker

cáscara nf 1 (*huevo, nuez*) shell: ~ de huevo eggshell 2 (*limón, naranja*) peel 3 (*plátano*) skin 4 (*cereal*) husk

cascarón nm eggshell

cascarrabias nmf grouch

casco nm 1 (*cabeza*) helmet 2 (*botella*) empty bottle 3 (*animal*) hoof [pl -s o hooves] 4 (*barco*) hull ▶ **~ antiguo** old town

caserío nm 1 (*aldea*) hamlet 2 (*casa*) farmhouse

casero/a adj 1 home-made 2 (*persona*) home-loving • nm-nf landlord [fem landlady] [pl -ies]

caseta nf 1 (*casa pequeña*) hut 2 (*en feria*) stand ▶ **~ de peaje** toll booth **~ electoral** voting booth **~ telefónica** (*Mx*) phone booth

casi adv 1 (*frases afirmativas*) almost, nearly: ~ me caigo. I almost/nearly fell. ◊ Está ~ lleno. It's almost/nearly full. ◊ Yo ~ diría que... I would almost say... →NEARLY 2 (*frases negativas*) hardly: No la veo ~ nunca. I hardly ever see her. ◊ No vino ~ nadie. Hardly anybody came. ◊ No queda ~ nada. There's hardly anything left. ▶ **casi, casi** very nearly: ~. ~ llegaban a mil personas. There were very nearly a thousand people.

casilla nf 1 (*ajedrez, etc.*) square 2 (*formulario, etc.*) box: marcar la ~ con una cruz put a cross mark in the box 3 (*cartas, llaves*) pigeon-hole 4 (*electoral*) voting booth ▸ **sacar de sus ~s** drive sb up the wall

casillero nm 1 (con candado) locker 2 (sin puerta) pigeonholes [pl] 3 (Comp) mailbox

casino nm 1 (juego) casino [pl -s] 2 (de socios) club

caso nm case: en cualquier ~ in any case ▸ **el ~ es que...** 1 (el hecho es que...) the fact is (that)... 2 (lo que importa) the main thing is that... **en ~ de** in the event of sth, **en ~ de que** if... En ~ de que le pregunte... If he asks you... **en el mejor/peor de los ~s** at best/worst **en tal ~** in that case **en todo ~** in any case **hacer ~ a/de** take notice of sth/sb **hacer/venir al ~** be relevant **ser un ~ a** be a right one **ser un ~ aparte** be something else **yo en tu ~** if I were you

caspa nf dandruff

cassette nf cassette, tape (más coloq)

casta nf 1 (animal) breed 2 (grupo social) caste ▸ **de ~** thoroughbred

castaño nm brown

castañuelas nf castanets

castidad nf chastity

castigar vt punish sb (for sth) 2 (Dep) penalize

castigo nm punishment: Habrá que ponerles un ~. They'll have to be punished.

castillo nm castle ▸ **~ de arena** sandcastle

casto adj chaste

castor nm beaver

castrar vt castrate

casual adj chance: un encuentro ~ a chance meeting

casualidad nf chance: de/por pura ~ by sheer chance ◇ ¿No tendrás por ~ su teléfono? You wouldn't have their number by any chance? ▸ **da la ~ (de) que...** it so happens that... **¡qué ~!** what a coincidence!

catálogo nm catalog

catar vt taste

catarata nf 1 (cascada) waterfall 2 (Med) cataract

catarina nf (Mx) ladybug, ladybird (GB)

catarro nm cold: Tengo ~. I have a cold.

catástrofe nf catastrophe

catear vt, vi (registrar) search

catecismo nm catechism

catedral nf cathedral

catedrático/a nm-nf head of department

categoría nf 1 (sección) category [pl -ies] 2 (nivel) level: un torneo de ~ juvenil a youth tournament 3 (estatus) status ▸ **de primera, segunda, etc.** ~ first-rate, second-rate, etc.

categórico adj categorical

cateo nm (policía) search

catolicismo nm Catholicism

católico/a adj, nm-nf Catholic: ser ~ be a Catholic

catorce adj, nm, pron 1 fourteen 2 (fecha) fourteenth

catsup nm ketchup

cauce nm 1 (río) river bed 2 (vía) channel

caucho nm 1 (sustancia) rubber 2 (And, banda elástica) rubber band

caudal nm (agua) flow

caudaloso adj large: un río muy ~ a very large river

caudillo nm 1 (líder) leader 2 (jefe militar) commander

causa nf 1 (origen, ideal) cause: la ~ principal the main cause ◇ Lo abandonó todo por la ~. He left everything for the cause. 2 (motivo) reason: sin ~ aparente for no apparent reason ▸ **a/por ~ de** because of sth/sb

causar vt 1 (ser la causa de) cause 2 (alegría, pena): Me causó una gran alegría/tristeza. It made me very happy/sad.

cautela nf ▸ **con ~** cautiously

cauteloso adj cautious

cautivador adj captivating

cautivar vt (atraer) captivate

cautiverio nm captivity

cautivo/a adj, nm-nf captive

cavar vt, vi dig

caverna nf cavern

caviar nm caviar

cavilar vi think deeply (about sth): después de mucho ~ after much thought

caza nf 1 (a) (caza mayor): ir de ~ go hunting (b) (caza menor) shooting 2 (Cocina) game ▸ **ir a la ~ de** be after sth/sb

cazabombardero (tb caza) nm fighter-bomber

cazador/a nm-nf hunter

cazar vt 1 hunt 2 (con escopeta) shoot 3 (capturar) catch 4 (conseguir) land ● vi 1 hunt 2 (con escopeta) shoot

cazuela nf casserole

CD nm CD

CD-ROM nm CD-ROM

cebada nf barley

cebar vt 1 (engordar) fatten sth/sb up 2 (atiborrar) fill sth/sb up

cebo nm bait

cebolla nf onion

cebollín nm (tb cebolla larga nf) (de tallo verde) scallion, spring onion (GB)

cebra nf zebra

ceder vt hand sth over (to sb) ● vi 1 (transigir) give in (to sth/sb) 2 (intensidad, fuerza) ease off 3 (romperse) give way ▸ **ceder el paso** (señal) yield, give way (GB) ~ **la palabra** hand over to sb

cedro nm cedar

cédula nf (finanzas) bond ▸ ~ **de ciudadanía** (abrev ID card)

cegar vt blind

ceguera nf blindness

ceja nf eyebrow

celador nm nightwatchman [pl -men]

celda nf cell

celebración nf 1 (fiesta, aniversario) celebration 2 (acontecimiento): La ~ de los juegos será en junio. The games will be held in June.

celebrar vt 1 (festejar) celebrate 2 (llevar a cabo) hold ● **celebrarse** vp take place

celeste adj heavenly

celo (tb **celos**) nm jealousy [U]: No son más que ~s. That's just jealousy. ◊ Sentía ~s. He felt jealousy. ▸ **dar ~s** make sb jealous **en** ~ 1 (hembra) on heat 2 (macho) in rut **tener ~s (de)** be jealous (of sb)

celofán nm Cellophane®

celosía nf lattice

celoso/a adj, nm-nf jealous: Es un ~. He's very jealous.

célula nf cell

celular adj cellular ● nm cellphone, mobile phone (GB)

celulitis nf cellulite

cementerio nm 1 cemetery [pl -ies] 2 (de iglesia) graveyard ▸ ~ **de carros/coches** salvage yard, scrapyard (GB)

cemento nm cement

cena nf dinner

cenar vi have dinner ● vt have sth for dinner

cencerro nm bell

cenicero nm ashtray

cenit nm zenith

ceniza nf ash

censo nm census ▸ ~ **electoral** electoral register

censor/a nm-nf censor

censura nf censorship

censurar vt 1 (libro, película) censor 2 (reprobar) censure

centavo nm (moneda) cent →Ver pág. 224 ▸ **estar sin un/no tener ni un** ~ be flat broke

centella nf spark

centellear vi 1 (estrellas) twinkle 2 (luz) flash

centena nf hundred

centenar nm a hundred or so: un ~ de carros a hundred or so cars ▸ ~es **de...** hundreds of...

centenario nm centennial, centenary (GB): el sexto ~ de su nacimiento the 600th anniversary of his birth

centeno nm rye

centésimo/a adj, nm-nf, pron hundredth: una centésima de segundo a hundredth of a second

centígrado adj centigrade (abrev C)

centímetro nm centimeter (abrev cm) →Ver pág. 222

centinela nmf 1 (Mil) sentry [pl -ies] 2 (vigía) lookout

centrado adj 1 (en el centro) centered 2 (persona) settled

central adj central ● nf 1 (energía) power plant: una ~ nuclear a nuclear power plant 2 (oficina principal) head office ▸ ~ **telefónica** telephone exchange

centrar vt 1 (poner en el centro) center 2 (atención, mirada) focus sth on sth 3 (esfuerzos) concentrate (sth) (on sth) ● vi (Dep) cross ● **centrarse** vp 1 (girar en torno) center on/around sth: Su vida se centra en sus hijos. She centers her whole life around her children. 2 (adaptarse) settle down

céntrico adj: un apartamento ~ an apartment in the center of town ◊ las calles céntricas downtown

centro nm center: el ~ de la ciudad downtown ◊ el ~ de atención the center of attention ▸ ~ **cultural** arts center ~ **escolar** school **ir al** ~ go downtown

centrocampista nmf (Dep) midfielder

ceño nm frown

cepa nf 1 (vid) vine 2 (árbol) stump

cepillar vt 1 (ropa, pelo) brush 2 (madera) plane ● **cepillarse** vp 1 (ropa, pelo) brush 2 (And, adular) butter sb up

cepillo nm 1 brush 2 (madera) plane ▸ ~ **de dientes/pelo** toothbrush/hairbrush ~ **de uñas** nail brush **echar** ~ **a** (And) butter sb up

cepo nm 1 (*trampa*) trap 2 (*Aut*) clamp

cera nf wax

cerámica nf pottery

cerca¹ nf (*valla*) fence

cerca² adv nearby ▶ **~ de** 1 (*a poca distancia*) near 2 (*casi*) nearly: *El avión se retrasó ~ de una hora.* The plane was nearly an hour late. **de ~** close up: *Deja que lo vea de ~.* Let me see it close up.

cercanías nf outskirts

cercano adj 1 close (*to sth*): *un pariente ~* a close relative 2 (*distancia*) near (*sth/sb*) →NEAR

cercar vt 1 (*poner una valla*) fence sth in 2 (*rodear*) surround

cerdo/a nm-nf pig **NOTA** Pig es el sustantivo genérico. El macho es **boar** y la hembra **sow**. Piglet es la cría del cerdo. ● nm (*carne*) pork →CARNE

cereal nm cereal: *Desayuno ~es.* I have cereal for breakfast.

cerebral adj (*Med*) brain: *un tumor ~* a brain tumor

cerebro nm 1 (*Anat*) brain 2 (*persona*) brains [*sing*]: *el ~ de la banda* the brains behind the gang

ceremonia nf ceremony [*pl* -ies]

cereza nf cherry [*pl* -ies]

cerezo nm cherry (tree)

cerillo nm (*tb* **cerilla** nf) match: *encender el ~* strike a match

cero nm 1 zero: *~ punto/coma cinco* zero point five 2 *a diez grados bajo ~.* It's ten below (zero). 2 (*Dep*) nothing, nil (*GB*) ◊ *uno a ~* one to nothing/one nil (*GB*) ◊ *Empataron a ~.* It was a scoreless tie/a goalless draw (*GB*). (b) (*tenis*) love: *quince a ~* fifteen love ▶ **empezar/partir de ~** start from scratch **un ~ a la izquierda** a nobody →*Ver pág. 221*

cerrado/a adj 1 closed, shut (*más coloq*) 2 (*con llave*) locked 3 (*espacio*) enclosed 4 (*noche*) dark 5 (*curva*) sharp

cerradura nf lock

cerrajero/a nm-nf locksmith

cerrar vt 1 close, shut (*más coloq*): *~ la puerta/los ojos* shut the door/close your eyes 2 (*gas, llave*) turn sth off 3 (*sobre*) seal 4 (*botella*) put the top on sth ● vi close, shut (*más coloq*) ● **cerrarse** vp close, shut (*más coloq*): *Se me cerró la puerta.* The door closed on me. ▶ **~ con llave** lock **~(se) de un golpe/portazo** slam **¡cierra el pico!** shut up!

cerro nm hill

cerrojo nm bolt ▶ **poner el/cerrar con ~** bolt sth **quitar el ~** unbolt sth

certeza (*tb* **certidumbre**) nf certainty [*pl* -ies] ▶ **tener la ~ de que...** be certain that...

certificado adj certified: *por correo ~* by registered mail ● nm certificate ▶ **~ escolar** school leaving certificate

certificar vt 1 (*dar por cierto*) certify 2 (*carta, etc.*) register

cerveza nf beer: *tomar unas ~s* have a few beers ▶ **~ de barril** beer on tap, draught beer (*GB*) **~ negra** stout **~ sin alcohol** alcohol-free beer

césped nm 1 grass: *No pisar el ~.* Keep off the grass. 2 (*jardín privado*) lawn

cesta nf basket

cesto nm (big) basket ▶ **~ de la ropa sucia** laundry basket

chabacano adj vulgar ● nm (*Mx, fruta*) apricot

chacal nm jackal

chacha nf 1 (*sirvienta*) maid 2 (*niñera*) nanny [*pl* -ies]

cháchara nf 1 (*conversación*) chatter [*U*]: *¡Déjate de ~!* Stop chattering! 2 (*Mx, objeto*) knickknack ▶ **estar de ~** chatter away

chafa adj (*Mx*) useless

chal nm shawl

chaleco nm vest, waistcoat (*GB*) ▶ **~ antibalas** bulletproof vest **~ salvavidas** life vest, life jacket (*GB*)

chalet (*tb* **chalé**) nm 1 (*en ciudad*) house 2 (*en costa*) villa 3 (*en campo*) cottage

chalupa nf (*barco*) boat

chamaco/a nm-nf (*Mx*) kid

chamarra nf jacket

chamba nf job

chambonada nf screw-up [*pl* -ups]: *Ese dibujo es una ~.* You really screwed up that drawing.

champán (*tb* **champaña**) nm champagne

champiñón nm mushroom

champú nm shampoo: *~ anticaspa* dandruff shampoo

chamuscar vt singe

chancho/a adj filthy ● nm-nf pig →CERDO

chanchullo nm swindle ▶ **hacer ~** a trick **sb hacer ~** be involved in a racket

chancla (*tb* **chancleta**) nf 1 (*pantufla*) slipper 2 (a) (*sandalia*) sandal (b) (*de caucho*) flip-flop

changarro nm (Mx) small store, small shop (GB)

chango nm (Mx) monkey

chantaje nm blackmail ▶ **hacer ~** blackmail

chantajear vt blackmail sb (into doing sth)

chantajista nmf blackmailer

chantar vt 1 (golpe, etc.) give: ~ una paliza a algn give sb a beating 2 (trabajo) land sth on sb

chapa nf 1 (cerradura) lock 2 (insignia) badge 3 (madera) veneer

chapado adj (metal) plated: ~ en oro gold-plated ▶ ~ a la antigua old-fashioned

chaparro adj short

chaparrón nm downpour

chapola nf (And) moth

chapopote nm (Mx) Tarmac®

chapotear vi splash around

chapucero/a adj, nm-nf (persona) slapdash: Ese plomero es un ~. That plumber is really slapdash.

chapurrear (chapucear And) vt have a smattering of sth: ~ el italiano have a smattering of Italian

chapuza nf (Mx, trampa) trick ▶ **hacer ~ trick de**

chapuzón nm dip ▶ **darse un ~** go for a dip

chaqueta nf jacket

charanga nf brass band

charco nm 1 (de lluvia) puddle 2 (bañadero) pool

charcutería nf (tienda) delicatessen

charla nf 1 (conversación) chat 2 (conferencia) talk (on sth/sb)

charlar vi chat (to sb) (about sth)

charlatán/ana adj talkative ● nm-nf 1 (hablador) chatterbox 2 (indiscreto) gossip

charol nm patent leather

charola nf tray

charro nm (Mx, jinete) horseman [pl -men]

chárter adj, nm charter: un vuelo ~ a charter flight

chasco nm (decepción) let-down, disappointment (más fml): ¡Vaya ~! What a let-down! ▶ **llevarse un ~** be disappointed

chasis nm chassis [pl chassis]

chasquear (tb **chascar**) vt 1 (lengua) click 2 (látigo) crack 3 (dedos) snap ● vi 1 (látigo) crack 2 (madera) crackle 3 (dientes) chatter

chasquido nm 1 (látigo) crack 2 (madera) crackle 3 (lengua) click: dar un ~ con la lengua click your tongue 4 (dedos) snap

chat nm (Comp) chat room

chatarra nf scrap [U]: El carro es una ~. The car's only fit for scrap.

chatarrero/a nm-nf scrap merchant

chatear vi (Comp) chat

chato adj 1 (persona) snub-nosed 2 (nariz) snub 3 (edificio, árbol) low

chaval/a nm-nf 1 boy [fem girl] 2 chavales (chicos y chicas) kids ▶ **estar hecho un ~** look very young

chavo/a nm-nf guy [fem girl]

chécheres nm stuff [U]

chepa nf 1 hump 2 (And, suerte) stroke of luck

cheque nm check: un ~ por valor de... a check for... ◇ cobrar un ~ pay a check in ▶ ~ **de viajero** traveler's check ▶ ~ **en blanco/sin fondos** blank/bad check

chequear (**checar** Mx) vt check ▶ **¡checa eso!** (Mx) check this out!

chequeo nm check-up [pl -ups]: hacerse un ~ have a check-up

chequera nf checkbook

chévere adj great

chicanear vi 1 (engañar): ¡Deja de ~! Stop trying to con me/us! 2 (And, presumir) show off

chicha nf alcoholic drink made from fermented corn, rice, pineapple, etc. ▶ **ni ~ ni limonada** neither one thing nor the other

chícharo nm pea

chicharra nf 1 (insecto) cicada 2 (timbre) buzzer

chicharrón nm crackling [U]

chichón nm lump

chicle nm (de mascar) chewing gum [U]: Cómprame un ~. Buy me some chewing gum. 2 chicles (And, prenda) leggings

chico/a adj small ● nm-nf 1 boy [fem girl] 2 chicos (niños y niñas) children, kids (coloq) 3 (joven) young man/woman [pl men/women]

chicote nm whip

chiflado/a adj (loco) crazy (about sth/sb) ● nm-nf crackpot

chifladura nf 1 (locura) madness 2 (idea) wild notion

chiflar vi 1 whistle 2 (encantar) love sth: Me chifla el pescado. I love fish. ● vt 1 (con la boca) whistle 2 (instrumento) blow ● **chiflarse** vp 1 (enloquecer) go crazy 2 (entusiasmarse) be crazy about sth/sb

chile nm chili [pl -ies]

Chile nm Chile

chileno/a *adj, nm-nf* Chilean

chillar *vi* **1** (*gritar*) yell (*at sb*) **2** (*berrear*) bawl **3** (*aves, frenos*) screech **4** (*cerdo*) squeal **5** (*ratón, colores*) clash

chillido *nm* **1** (*persona*) shriek **2** (*ave, frenos*) screech **3** (*cerdo*) squeal **4** (*ratón*) squeak

chillón *adj* loud

chimenea *nf* **1** (*hogar*) fireplace: *al lado de la ~* by the fireplace ◊ *Enciende la ~.* Light the fire. **2** (*conducto*) chimney **3** (*barco*) funnel

chimpancé *nm* chimpanzee

chimuelo *adj* (*Mx*) toothless

chinche *nf* **1** (*bicho*) bedbug **2** (*tachuela*) thumbtack, drawing pin (*GB*)

chinchín *nm* (*brindis*) cheers

chino *adj* (*Mx, pelo*) curly

chino/a *adj, nm-nf* Chinese ● *nm-nf* Chinese man/woman [*pl* men/women]: *los ~s* the Chinese

chip *nm* (*Comp*) chip

chipi chipi *nm* **1** (*Mx*) drizzle **2** (*And, marisco*) baby clam

chipote *nm* (*Mx*) bump

chiquero *nm* pigsty [*pl* -ies]

chiquillo/a *nm-nf* kid

chiquito/a *adj* small ● *nm-nf* (*tb* chiquillo) kid: *cuando yo era ~* when I was a kid

chirimoya *nf* custard apple

chiripa *nf* stroke of luck ▶ **de ~** by sheer luck

chirriar *vi* **1** (*bicicleta*) squeak **2** (*puerta*) creak **3** (*frenos*) screech **4** (*ave*) squawk

chirrido *nm* **1** (*bicicleta*) squeak **2** (*puerta*) creak **3** (*frenos*) screech **4** (*ave*) squawk

chisme *nm* **1** (*hablado*) gossip [*U*]: *contar ~s* gossip **2** (*cosa*) thing

chismear (*tb* chismorrear, chismosear) *vi* gossip

chismorreo (*tb* chismoseo *And*) *nm* gossip [*U*]

chismoso/a *adj* gossipy ● *nm-nf* gossip: *¡Es un ~!* He's such a gossip!

chispa *nf* spark ▶ **estar ~** be rather merry **estar que echa ~s** be hopping mad **tener ~** be witty

chispazo *nm* spark

chispear *vi* (*llover*) spit

chistar *vi* ▶ **sin ~** without saying a word

chiste *nm* **1** (*hablado*) joke: *entender/agarrar el ~* get the joke **2** (*dibujo*) cartoon

chistoso *adj* funny ▶ **hacerse el ~** play the fool

chito *interj* (*¡silencio!*) sh

chiva *nf* (*And*) **1** (*bus*) bus **2** (*primicia*) exclusive

chivato/a *nm-nf* **1** tattletale, telltale (*GB*) **2** (*de la policía*) informer

chivo *nm* **1** (*And, cabra*) goat **2** (*cría*) kid

chocante *adj* (*desagradable*) unpleasant

chocar *vi* **1** (*estrellarse*) crash: *El carro chocó contra una pared.* The car crashed into a wall. **2** (*sorprender*) surprise **3** (*molestar*) annoy ● *vt*: *¡Choca esos cinco!/¡Chócala!* Put it there! ● **chocarse** *vp* (*And*) crash

chochear *vi* go senile

chocolate *nm* **1** chocolate: *una caja de ~s* a box of chocolates **2** (*líquido*) hot chocolate

chocolatina *nf* candy bar, chocolate bar (*GB*)

chofer *nmf* **1** driver **2** (*carro privado*) chauffeur

choke *nm* choke

cholo/a *adj, nm-nf* (*And*) mestizo [*pl* -s]

chompa *nf* (*And*) jacket

chongo *nm* (*pelo*) bun

chopo *nm* poplar

choque *nm* **1** (*colisión, ruido*) crash **2** (*enfrentamiento*) clash

chorcha *nf* (*Mx*) get-together ▶ **estar en la/una ~** party

chorizo *nm* chorizo [*pl* -s]

chorlito *nm* ▶ **ser un cabeza de ~** be a scatterbrain

chorrear *vi* **1** (*gotear*) drip **2** (*estar empapado*) be dripping wet

chorro *nm* **1** jet **2** (*abundante*) gush **3** (*Cocina*) dash ▶ **a ~s**: *salir a ~s* gush out

chotear *vt* make fun of *sb*

choza *nf* hut

chubasco *nm* shower

chuchería *nf* **1** (*golosina*) sweet **2** (*alhaja*) trinket

chueco *adj* crooked

chulear *vt* **1** (*Mx, piropear*) compliment **2** (*And, marcar*) check, tick (*GB*)

chuleta *nf* chop

chulo *adj* lovely ● *nm* (*tb* chulito *And*) check, tick (*GB*)

chupada *nf* **1** suck: *El niño le daba ~s a su paleta.* The boy was sucking his Popsicle. **2** (*cigarrillo*) puff: *dar una ~ a un cigarrillo* have a puff of a cigarette

chupado *adj* (*persona*) skinny
→DELGADO

chupar vt 1 suck 2 (absorber) soak sth up ▶ ~ **del bote** freeload ~**se el dedo** 1 suck your thumb 2 ¿Crees que me chupo el dedo? Do you think I'm stupid? ~**se los dedos** lick your fingers: Estaba para ~se los dedos. It was delicious.

chupete nm 1 (tb **chupón, chupo**) (de bébé) pacifier, dummy [pl -ies] (GB) 2 (golosina) lollipop ▶ ~ **helado** (And) Popsicle®, ice lolly [pl -ies] (GB)

churro nm 1 kind of doughnut 2 (marihuana) joint 3 (Mx, Cine) bad movie ▶ **de** ~ by sheer luck

chutar vt shoot ● **chutarse** vp shoot sth up ▶ **ir que chuta** go really well

chuzar vt 1 prick 2 (apuñalar) knife

cibercafé nm Internet cafe

cicatriz nf scar: Me quedó una ~. I was left with a scar.

cicatrizar vi heal

ciclismo nm cycling: hacer ~ cycle

ciclista nmf cyclist

ciclo nm cycle

ciclón nm cyclone

ciego/a adj blind: quedarse ~ go blind ◇ ~ **de rabia** blind with rage ● nm-nf blind man/woman [pl men/women]: los ~s the blind ● **a ciegas**: Lo hice a ciegas. I did it without thinking.

cielo nm 1 sky [pl skies] 2 (Rel) heaven: ir al ~ go to heaven ▶ **¡cielos!** interj good heavens! ▶ **ser un** ~ be an angel

ciempiés nm centipede

cien adj, nm, pron 1 a hundred: ~ **mil** a hundred thousand 2 (centésimo) hundredth →Ver pág. 221 ▶ ~ **mil veces** hundreds of times

ciencia nf 1 science 2 **ciencias** (Educ) science [sing] ▶ ~**s empresariales** business studies [sing] ▶ ~**s naturales** natural science [sing]

ciencia-ficción nf science fiction

científico/a adj scientific ● nm-nf scientist

ciento nm, adj (a) hundred [pl hundred]: ~ **tres** a hundred and three ◇ varios ~s several hundred →Ver pág. 221 ▶ **(al)** ~ **por** ~ a hundred percent ~**s de a...** hundreds of... ▶ **por** ~ percent: un/el 50 por ~ 50 percent

cierre nm 1 (acto de cerrar) closure 2 (collar, bolso) clasp 3 (cremallera) zipper

cierto adj 1 certain: con ~ anhelo with a certain desire ◇ a ciertas horas at certain times 2 (verdadero) true ▶ **¿cierto?**: Estás cansada, ¿cierto? You're tired, aren't you? ◇ No han venido, ¿~ que no? They haven't come, have they? ▶ **hasta** ~ **punto** up to a point ▶ **por** ~ by the way

ciervo/a nm-nf deer [pl deer] **NOTA** Deer es el sustantivo genérico. El macho es **stag** (o **buck**) y la hembra **doe**. Fawn es el cervatillo.

cifra nf 1 (número, dinero) figure: un número de dos ~s a two-figure number 2 (teléfono) digit

cigarrillo nm cigarette

cigüeña nf stork

cilantro nm cilantro, coriander (GB)

cilíndrico adj cylindrical

cilindro nm cylinder

cima nf top

cimientos nm foundations

cinc nm zinc

cincel nm chisel

cinco adj, nm, pron 1 five 2 (fecha) fifth

cincuenta adj, nm, pron 1 fifty 2 (cincuentavo) fiftieth

cine nm movie theater, cinema (GB): ir a ~ go to the movies ▶ **de** ~ (festival, director, etc.) movie, film (GB): un actor de ~ a movie/film actor

cinematográfico adj movie, film (GB): su debut ~ his movie/film debut

cínico/a adj hypocritical ● nm-nf hypocrite

cinta nf 1 (lazo) ribbon 2 (cassette) tape ▶ ~ **adhesiva/pegante** (And) Scotch® tape, Sellotape® (GB) ~ **aislante** insulating tape ▶ ~ **para el pelo** hairband

cintura nf waist: Tengo 60cm de ~. I have a 24inch waist.

cinturón (tb **cinto**) nm belt: ser ~ negro be a black belt ▶ ~ **(de seguridad)** seat belt

circo nm 1 (espectáculo) circus 2 (anfiteatro) amphitheater

circuito nm 1 (Dep) track 2 (Elec) circuit

circulación nf 1 circulation: mala ~ de la sangre poor circulation 2 (tráfico) traffic

circular¹ adj round ● nf (comunicado) circular

circular² vt, vi circulate ● vi 1 (carro) drive 2 (tren, autobús) run 3 (rumor) go around ▶ **¡circulen!** move along!

círculo nm 1 circle 2 (asociación) society [pl -ies] ▶ ~ **polar ártico/**

antártico Arctic/Antarctic Circle ~ **vicioso** vicious circle

circunferencia nf 1 (círculo) circle 2 (perímetro) circumference

circunstancia nf circumstance

cirio nm candle

ciruela nf plum ▸ ~ **pasa** prune

ciruelo nm plum (tree)

cirugía nf surgery: ~ **estética/plástica** cosmetic/plastic surgery

cirujano/a nm-nf surgeon

cisne nm swan

cisterna nf 1 (depósito) tank 2 (baño) cistern

cita nf 1 (amigos, pareja) date 2 (médico, abogado) appointment: pedir ~ **con el dentista** make a dental appointment 3 (frase) quotation

citadino/a adj city ● nm-nf city dweller

citar vt 1 (convocar) arrange to meet sb 2 (Jur) summons 3 (hacer referencia) quote (from sth/sb) ● **citarse** vp (con) arrange to meet (sb)

citófono nm (And) intercom

cítricos nm citrus fruits

ciudad nf town, city [pl **-ies**] **NOTA** Town es la palabra general para referirse a una ciudad: Me voy a la ~ a hacer unas compras. I'm going into town to do some shopping. City se refiere a una ciudad grande o importante. ▸ ~ **natal** home town

ciudadanía nf citizenship

ciudadano/a adj: la seguridad ciudadana public safety ◇ El alcalde pidió la colaboración ciudadana. The mayor asked everyone to work together. ● nm-nf citizen

cívico adj public-spirited: sentido ~ public-spiritedness

civil adj civil ● nmf civilian ▸ **de** ~ 1 (militar) in civilian dress 2 (policía) in plain clothes

civilización nf civilization

civilizado adj civilized

civismo nm community spirit

clamar vt (exigir) demand ● vi (gritar) shout

clamor nm 1 (gritos) shouts [pl] 2 (en show) cheers [pl]: el ~ **del público** the cheers of the audience

clan nm clan

clandestino adj clandestine

clara nf egg white

claraboya nf skylight

clarear vi 1 (despejarse) clear up 2 (amanecer) get light

claridad nf 1 clarity 2 (luz) light

clarificar vt clarify

clarín nm bugle

clarinete nm clarinet

claro adj 1 clear 2 (color) light: azul ~ light blue 3 (luminoso) bright 4 (pelo) fair 5 (poco espeso) thin ● nm 1 (bosque) clearing 2 (clima) sunny spell ● adv clearly ● interj of course: ~ **que sí/no** of course/of course not ▸ **dejar/poner en** ~ make sth clear **más** ~ **que el agua** crystal clear

clásico adj 1 (Arte, Hist, Mús) classical 2 (típico) classic: el ~ **comentario** the classic remark ● nm classic

clasificación nf 1 classification 2 (Dep): partido de ~ qualifying game ◇ Italia encabeza la ~ mundial. Italy is number one in the world rankings. ◇ la ~ **general de la liga** the league table

clasificado adj classified ▸ **anuncios/avisos** ~**s** classified ads

clasificar vt, vi classify ● **clasificarse** vp qualify (for sth) ● ~**se en segundo, tercer, etc. lugar** come second, third, etc.

clasificatorio adj qualifying

clasista adj class-conscious ● nmf snob

claudicar vi surrender

claustro nm 1 (edificio) cloister 2 (conjunto de profesores) faculty 3 (reunión) faculty meeting

claustrofobia nf claustrophobia: tener ~ suffer from claustrophobia

claustrofóbico adj claustrophobic

cláusula nf clause

clausura nf (cierre) closure ▸ **de** ~ closing: acto de ~ closing ceremony

clausurar(se) vt, vp end

clavado nm dive: hacer un ~ dive ● adj fixed ▸ **estar** ~ **con** be devoted to sb

clavar vt 1 (clavo, estaca) hammer sth into sth 2 (cuchillo, puñal) stick sth into sth/sb 3 (sujetar con clavos) nail 4 (estafar) rip sb off ● **clavarse** vp 1 **me clavé una espina en el dedo.** I have a thorn in my finger. ◇ Cuidado, te vas a *clavar el alfiler.* Be careful you don't hurt yourself with that pin. **2** (*Mx*, *robar*) swipe ▶ ~**se a estudiar** (*And*) study really hard

clave *nf* **1** key (*to sth*): *la ~ de su éxito* the key to their success ◇ *factor ~* key factor **2** (*código*) code **3** (*Mús*) clef: *~ de sol/fa* treble/bass clef ▶ **ser ~** be central *to sth*

clavel *nm* carnation

clavícula *nf* collarbone

clavo *nm* **1** nail **2** (*Cocina*) clove ▶ **dar en el ~** hit the nail on the head

claxon *nm* horn: *tocar el ~* sound your horn

clero *nm* clergy [*pl*]

clic *nm* click ▶ **hacer ~** click: *hacer doble ~* double-click

cliché *nm* (*tópico*) cliché

cliente/a *nm-nf* **1** (*tienda, restaurante*) customer **2** (*empresa*) client

clima *nm* **1** climate **2** (*fig*) atmosphere: *un ~ de tensión* a tense atmosphere ▶ **al ~** (*And*) at room temperature

climatizado *adj* air-conditioned

clímax *nm* climax

clínica *nf* clinic

clip *nm* **1** (*papel*) paper clip **2** (*pelo*) bobby pin, hairgrip (*GB*) **3** (*vídeo*) video [*pl* -s]

cloaca *nf* sewer

clónico *adj* (*Biol*) cloned ● *nm* (*tb* **clon**) clone

cloro *nm* chlorine

club *nm* club

clutch (*tb* **cloch, cloche**) *nm* clutch

coacción *nf* coercion

coaccionar *vt* coerce *sb* (*into sth*)

coagular(se) *vt, vp* clot

coágulo *nm* clot

coalición *nf* coalition

coartada *nf* alibi [*pl* -s]

coba *nf* ▶ **dar ~** soft-soap *sb*

cobarde *adj* cowardly ● *nmf* coward

cobardía *nf* cowardice [*U*]: *Es una ~.* It's an act of cowardice.

cobayo/a *nf* guinea pig

cobertizo *nm* shed

cobertura *nf* **1** coverage: *la ~ de un acontecimiento en la prensa* press coverage of an event ◇ *Estos teléfonos celulares dan una ~ amplia.* These cellphones have a wide coverage. ◇ *tener ~* get a signal **2** (*de seguro*) cover

cobija *nf* blanket

cobijar *vt, vp* shelter (*from sth*)

cobra *nf* cobra

cobrador/a *nm-nf* **1** (*autobús*) (bus) conductor **2** (*deudas, recibos*) collector

cobrar *vt, vi* **1** charge (*sb*) (*for sth*): *¿Me cobra, por favor?* Can I have the check, please? **2** (*salario*): *Todavía no he cobrado las clases.* I still haven't been paid for those classes. ◇ *¡Hoy cobramos!* Today is pay day! ● *vt* **1** (*cheque*) cash **2** (*adquirir*) gain: *~ fuerza* gain momentum ● *vi* (*golpe*) get a smack ● **cobrarse** *vp* **1** *Cóbrese, por favor.* Here you are. ◇ *¿Se cobra las bebidas?* How much are the drinks? **2** (*costar*) cost: *La guerra se cobró muchas vidas.* The war cost many lives. ▶ **~ de más/menos** overcharge/undercharge

cobre *nm* copper

cobro *nm* **1** (*pago*) payment **2** (*recaudación*) charging

Coca-Cola® *nf* Coke®

cocaína *nf* cocaine

cocción *nf* cooking: *tiempo de ~* cooking time

cocear *vi* kick

cocer *vt* **1** (*hervir*) boil **2** (*pan*) bake **3** (*cerámica*) fire ● *vi* (*alimento*) cook ● **cocerse** *vp* **1** (*alimento*) cook **2** (*tener calor*) boil: *Me estoy cociendo con este suéter.* I'm boiling in this sweater.

coche *nm* **1** (*Aut*) car: *en ~* by car **2** (*vagón, carruaje*) carriage **3** (*para bebé*) baby carriage, pram (*GB*) ▶ **~ cama** sleeping car

cochera *nf* **1** (*carro*) garage **2** (*autobús*) depot

cochinada *nf* **1** (*cosa sucia*): *¡Qué ~ de casa!* This house is disgusting! **2** (*mala jugada*) dirty trick: *hacerle una ~ a algn* play a dirty trick on *sb* ▶ **hacer ~s** make a mess

cochino/a *nm-nf* (*animal, persona*) pig ● *adj* **1** (*sucio*) dirty **2** (*tramposo*) cheat: *Los del equipo contrario fueron muy ~s.* The other team were terrible cheats. **3** (*indecoroso*) offensive **4** (*despreciable*) rotten

cocido (*tb* **cocinado** *And*) *nm* stew

cocina *nf* **1** (*lugar*) kitchen **2** (*arte de cocinar*) cookery: *un libro de ~* a cookery book **3** (*gastronomía*) cooking: *la ~ china* Chinese cooking

cocinar *vt, vi* cook: *No sé ~.* I can't cook. ● **cocinarse** *vp* **1** (*alimento*) cook **2** (*tener calor*) boil

cocinero/a *nm-nf* cook

coco *nm* **1** (*fruto*) coconut **2** (*cabeza*) head **3** (*ser fantástico*) boogeyman, bogeyman (GB) [pl -men] **4** (persona fea) fright ▸ **comerle el ~ a algn** brainwash sb **comerse el ~** worry yourself (about sth/sb) tener mucho ~ be very brainy

cocodrilo nm crocodile

cocotero nm coconut palm

coctel nm **1** (bebida) cocktail **2** (fiesta) cocktail party [pl -ies]

cocuyo nm **1** (insecto) glowfly [pl -ies], glow-worm (GB) (And, Aut) parking light

codazo nm **1** (violento, para abrirse paso): abrirse paso a ~s elbow your way through the crowd **2** (para llamar la atención) nudge

codearse vp rub shoulders with sb

codicia nf **1** (avaricia) greed **2** ~ de lust for sth: su ~ de poder their lust for power

codiciar vt (ambicionar) covet

codificar vt encode

código nm code ▸ ~ de (la) circulación Traffic Laws ▸ postal ZIP code, postcode (GB)

codo nm elbow ▸MY

codorniz nf quail

coeficiente nm coefficient ▸ ~ intelectual intelligence quotient (abrev IQ)

coexistencia nf coexistence

cofradía nf brotherhood

cofre nm **1** (caja) box **2** (Mx, Aut) hood, bonnet (GB)

coger vt **1** (tomar) take: Coge los que quieras. Take as many as you like. ◇ Lo cogí del brazo. I took him by the arm. **2** (agarrar) catch: ~ una pelota catch a ball ◇ Lo cogió robando. He was caught stealing. ◇ un resfriado catch a cold **3** (fruta, flores) pick **4** (tomar prestado) borrow **5** (entender) get: No lo cojo. I don't get it. **6** (atropellar) run ● **cogerse** vp hold: Cójase de mi mano. Hold my hand. ▸ ~ y... up and do sth: Cogí y me fui. I upped and left. **NOTA** Para otras expresiones con coger, ver el sustantivo, p.ej. **coger camino** en CAMINO.

cogido adj ▸ ~s del brazo/de la mano arm in arm/holding hands

cogote nm neck

coherencia nf coherence

cohete nm rocket

cohibir vt inhibit ● **cohibirse** vp feel inhibited

coincidencia nf coincidence ▸ **da la ~ de que...** it just so happens (that)...

coincidir vi **1** (estar de acuerdo) agree (with sb) (on/about sth): Coinciden en que es un tipo estupendo. They agree that he's a great guy. ◇ ~ en todo agree on everything **2** (en un lugar): Coincidimos en el congreso. We were both at the conference. **3** (acontecimientos, resultados) coincide (with sth)

cojear vi **1** (ser cojo) be lame: Cojeo del pie derecho. I'm lame in my right foot. **2** (por lesión) limp **3** (mueble) be wobbly ▸ ~ del mismo pie have the same faults (as sb)

cojera nf limp

cojín nm cushion

cojo/a adj **1** (persona): estar ~ (de un pie) have a limp ◇ Se quedó ~ después del accidente. The accident left him with a limp. **2** (animal) lame **3** (mueble) wobbly ● nm-nf cripple ▸ andar/ir ~ limp

col nf cabbage ▸ ~es de Bruselas Brussels sprouts

cola¹ nf **1** (animal) tail **2** (fila) line, queue (GB): hacer/ponerse en la ~ stand in line/join the line ◇ Había mucha ~. There was a long line. **3** (trasero) bottom **4** (vestido) train ▸ ¡a la ~! get in line! ~ de caballo ponytail

cola² nf (pegamento) glue

colaboración nf collaboration

colaborador/a nm-nf collaborator

colaborar vi collaborate (on sth)

colador nm **1** strainer **2** (verduras, etc.) colander

colar vt **1** (infusión) strain **2** (café) filter **3** (verduras, etc.) drain ● **colarse** vp **1** (líquido) seep through sth **2** (persona) (a) sneak in: Me colé en el bus sin pagar. I sneaked onto the bus without paying. (b) (en cola) cut in: ¡Oiga, no se cuele! Hey! No cutting in! ▸ ~se en una fiesta crash a party

colcha nf bedspread

colchón nm mattress

colchoneta nf **1** (camping, playa) air bed **2** (gimnasio) mat

colección nf collection

coleccionar vt collect

coleccionista nmf collector

colecta nf collection ▸ hacer una ~ (de caridad) collect for charity

colectivo adj, nm collective

colega nmf **1** (compañero) colleague **2** (amigo) friend

colegial/a nm-nf schoolboy/girl [pl schoolchildren]

colegiatura nf (Mx) school fees [pl]

colegio nm 1 (Educ) school: ir al ~ go to school →SCHOOL 2 (asociación) association ▶ ~ de curas/monjas Catholic school ~ electoral electoral college ~ privado private school ~ público public school, state school (GB) →ESCUELA

cólera nm (enfermedad) cholera

colesterol nm cholesterol

coleta nf pigtail

colgado adj hanging on/from sth ▶ ~ del/al teléfono on the phone dejar a algn ~ leave sb in the lurch estar ~ (And) be behind mal ~: Tiene el teléfono mal ~. He left the phone off the hook.

colgante nm pendant

colgar vt 1 hang sth from/on sth 2 (ropa) hang sth up 3 (ahorcar) hang →AHORCAR(SE) ● vi hang (from/on sth) ▶ ~ (el teléfono) hang up: Me colgó el teléfono. He hung up (on me). ◊ No cuelgue, por favor. Please hold. ~ las botas/los guantes retire

cólico nm colic [U]

coliflor nf cauliflower

colilla nf cigarette butt

colina nf hill

colirio nm eye drops [pl]

colisión nf collision (with sth): una ~ de frente a head-on collision

colitis nf diarrhea [U]

collage nm collage: hacer un ~ make a collage

collar nm 1 (adorno) necklace 2 (perro, gato) collar

collarín nm (surgical) collar

colmena nf beehive

colmillo nm (persona) canine (tooth) 2 (animal) tusk

colmo nm ▶ para ~ to make matters worse ser el ~ be the limit

colocado adj ▶ estar ~ be employed: estar bien ~ have a good job

colocar vt 1 place 2 (bomba) plant 3 (emplear) find sb a job (with sb) ● colocarse vp get a job (as sth)

Colombia nf Colombia

colombiano/a adj, nm-nf Colombian

colombina® nf lollipop

colon nm colon

colonia¹ nf 1 colony [pl -ies] 2 (grupo de viviendas) housing development 3 (barrio) area

colonia² nf (perfume) cologne [U]: echarse ~ put cologne on

colonial adj colonial

colonización nf colonization

colonizador/a adj colonizing ● nm-nf settler

colonizar vt colonize

coloquial adj colloquial

coloquio nm discussion

color nm color ▶ de colores colored: lápices de ~es colored pencils en/a ~: un televisor en/a ~ a color TV

colorado adj 1 red 2 (Mx, chiste, etc.) dirty ▶ como un tomate as red as a beet ponerse ~ blush

colorante adj, nm coloring ▶ sin ~s no artificial colorings

colorear vt color sth (in)

colorete nm blusher

colorido nm coloring: una ceremonia de gran ~ a very colorful ceremony

colorín nm ▶ ~ colorado... and that's the end of the story

columna nf 1 column 2 (Anat) spine ▶ ~ vertebral backbone

columpiar vt give sb a swing ● columpiarse vp have a swing

columpio nm swing

coma¹ nf (Med) coma: en (estado de) ~ in a coma

coma² nf 1 comma 2 (Mat) point: diez ~ cinco (10,5) ten point five (10·5) →Ver pág. 221

comadrona nf midwife [pl -wives]

comal nm (Mx) griddle

comandante nmf major

comando nm 1 (Mil) commando [pl -s] 2 (terrorista) cell

comarca nf area

combate nm 1 combat [U]: Hubo feroces ~s. There was fierce fighting. 2 (boxeo) bout ▶ de ~ fighter: avión de ~ fighter plane fuera de ~ 1 out of action 2 (boxeo) knocked out: dejar a algn fuera de ~ knock sb out

combatiente nmf combatant

combatir vt combat ● vi fight (for/against sth/sb): ~ contra los rebeldes fight (against) the rebels

combinación nf 1 combination 2 (prenda) slip

combinar vt 1 combine 2 (ropa) match sth (with sth) ● vi (colores) go with sth 2 (ropa) match: La falda no combina con la blusa. The skirt doesn't match the blouse.

combustible adj combustible ● nm fuel

combustión nf combustion

comedia nf comedy [pl -ies] ▶ ~ musical musical

comedor nm 1 (casa, hotel) dining room 2 (colegio, fábrica) cafeteria 3 (muebles) dining room suite

comelón/ona = COMILÓN/ONA

comentar vt 1 (decir) say 2 (tema) discuss

comentario nm remark: hacer un ~ make a remark ▶ ~ de texto textual criticism **hacer ~s** comment (on sth/sb) **sin ~** no comment

comentarista nmf commentator

comenzar vt, vi start (sth/to do sth/doing sth)

comer vt 1 eat 2 (insectos) esb eat alive: Me comieron los mosquitos. I was eaten alive by the mosquitoes. 3 (ajedrez, etc.) take ● vi 1 eat 2 (al mediodía) have lunch 3 (en la noche) have dinner ▶ ~ a besos smother sb with kisses ~ **como pelón de hospicio/como una fiera/vaca** eat like a horse **comérsele la lengua los ratones:** ¿Se te comieron la lengua los ratones? Have you lost your tongue? **dar/echar de ~** feed

comercial adj commercial ● nm (TV, etc.) advertisement, ad (coloq) ▶ **centro/galería ~** shopping mall

comercializar vt market

comerciante nmf (dueño de tienda) storekeeper, shopkeeper (GB)

comerciar vi 1 (producto) trade (in sth) 2 (persona) do business (with sb)

comercio nm 1 (negocio) trade: ~ exterior foreign trade 2 (tienda) store, shop (GB)

comestible adj edible

cometa nm (astro) comet ● nf (juguete) kite

cometer vt 1 (delito) commit 2 (error) make

cometido nm 1 (encargo) assignment 2 (obligación) duty [pl -ies]

cómic nm comic

comicios nm elections

cómico/a adj 1 (gracioso) funny 2 (de comedia) comedy: actor ~ comedy actor ● nm-nf comedian

comida nf 1 (alimento) food 2 (ocasión en la que se come) meal 3 (al mediodía) lunch 4 (en la noche) dinner

comidilla nf ▶ **ser la ~** be the talk of sth

comido adj: Ya vinieron ~s. They had already eaten. ▶ ~ **por la** envidia/la rabia/los celos eaten up with envy/anger/jealousy

comienzo nm beginning ▶ **a ~s de...** at the beginning of... ▶ **dar ~** begin **en sus ~s** in its early stages

comillas nf quotation marks ▶ **entre ~** in quotation marks

comilón/ona adj greedy ● nm-nf big eater

comilona nf feast ▶ **darse/pegarse una ~** stuff yourself (with sth)

comisaría nf 1 (police) police station 2 (And, región) province

comisario nm superintendent

comisión nf commission: una ~ del 5% a 5% commission ▶ **a ~** on commission

comité nm committee →JURADO

como adv 1 (modo, en calidad de, según) as: Respondí ~ pude. I answered as best I could. ◇ Me lo llevé ~ recuerdo. I took it home as a souvenir. ◇ ~ te decía... As I was saying... 2 (comparación, ejemplo) like: Tiene un carro ~ el nuestro. He has a car like ours. ◇ suave ~ la seda smooth as silk 3 (aproximadamente) around: Llamé ~ a diez personas. I called around ten people. ● conj 1 (condición) if: ~ venga tarde, no podremos ir. If he's late, we won't be able to go. 2 (causa) as: ~ era temprano, me hice un café. As it was early, I made a cup of coffee. ◇ ~ **que/si** as if: Me trata ~ si fuera su hijo. He treats me as if I were his son. ~ **sea** (a cualquier precio) at all costs 2 (no importa): ~ **quieres el té?** —Como sea. "How do you like your tea?" "I don't care."

cómo adv 1 (interrogación) how: ¿~ se traduce esta palabra? How do you translate this word? 2 (¿por qué?) why: ¿~ no me lo dijiste? Why didn't you tell me? 3 (al no oír o entender) excuse me?: ¿Cómo? ¿Puedes repetir? Excuse me? Can you say that again? 4 (exclamación): ¡~ te pareces a tu papá! You're just like your father! ● interj (enfado, asombro) what: ¡Cómo! ¿No estás vestido todavía? What! Aren't you dressed yet? ▶ **¿a ~ están?** how much is it/are they? **¿~ es?** (descripción) what is he, she, it, etc. like? **¿~ es eso?** **¿~ es que...?** how come?: ¿~ es que no fuiste? How come you didn't go? **¿~ estás?** how are you? **¿~ no!** of course! **¿~ que...?** (asombro, enfado) **¿~ que no lo sabía?** What do you mean, you

C

didn't know? ¡~ **voy a...**! how am I, are you, etc. to...!: ¡~ **lo iba a saber**! How was I to know!

cómoda nf dresser

comodidad nf **1** (confort) comfort **2** (conveniencia) convenience

comodín nm joker

cómodo adj **1** (confortable) comfortable **2** (conveniente) convenient ▶ **ponerse ~** make yourself comfortable

compact disc nm **1** (disco) CD **2** (aparato) CD player

compacto adj compact

compadecer(se) vt, vp feel sorry for sb

compaginar vt combine sth (with sth)

compañerismo nm comradeship

compañero/a nm-nf **1** (amigo) companion **2** (pareja) partner **3** (trabajo) colleague ▶ **~ de apartamento/departamento** roommate, flatmate (GB) **~ de clase** classmate **~ de equipo** teammate

compañía nf company [pl -ies] ▶ **~ aérea** airline **hacer ~** keep sb company

comparable adj comparable

comparación nf comparison: *Esta casa no tiene ~ con la anterior.* There's no comparison between this house and the old one. ▶ **en ~ con** compared to/with sth/sb

comparar vt compare sth/sb (to/with sth/sb)

compartimento (tb **compartimiento**) nm compartment

compartir vt share

compás nm **1** (Mat, Náut) compass **2** (Mús) (a) (tiempo) time: el **~ de tres por cuatro** three four time (b) (división de pentagrama) measure, bar (GB)

compasión nf pity, compassion (más fml) ▶ **tener ~ de** take pity on sb

compasivo adj compassionate (towards sb)

compatible adj compatible

compatriota nmf fellow countryman/woman [pl -men/-women]

compenetrarse vp **1** ~ con algo identify with sth **2** ~ con algn get along well with sb

compensación nf compensation

compensar vt **1** (dos cosas) make up for sth **2** (persona) repay sb (for sth) ● vi: *No me compensa ir sólo una hora.* It's not worth going for an hour. ◇ *A la larga compensa.* It's worth it in the long run.

competencia nf **1** (rivalidad, certamen) competition **2** (eficacia, habilidad) competence: *falta de ~* incompetence ▶ **hacer la ~** compete with sth/sb

competente adj competent

competir vi compete

compinche nmf buddy [pl -ies]

complacer vt please

complejo adj, nm complex: *un ~ de oficinas* an office complex ◇ *tener ~ de gordo/superioridad* have a complex about being fat/a superiority complex

complemento nm **1** (suplemento) supplement **2** (accesorio) accessory [pl -ies] **3** (Gram) object

completamente adv completely

completar vt complete

completo adj **1** complete **2** (jornada, tiempo) full: *trabajar tiempo ~* work full-time ▶ **por ~** completely

complicado adj complicated

complicar vt **1** (liar) complicate **2** (implicar) implicate sb in sth ● **complicarse** vp become complicated ▶ **~se la vida** make life hard for yourself

cómplice nmf accomplice (in/to sth)

complot nm plot

componer vt **1** (formar) make sth up **2** (Mús) compose ● **componerse** vp consist of sth

comportamiento nm behavior [U]

comportarse vp behave

composición nf composition

compositor/a nm-nf composer

compota nf compote

compra nf purchase: *una buena ~* a good buy ▶ **ir/salir de ~s** go shopping

comprar vt buy: *¿Me lo compras?* Will you buy it for me? ◇ *Le compré el carro a un amigo.* I bought the car from a friend.

comprender vt, vi (entender) understand ● vt **1** (darse cuenta) realize ● vt **2** (incluir) include

comprendido adj: *niños de edades comprendidas entre los 11 y 13 años* children aged between 11 and 13

comprensión nf understanding ▶ **mostrar ~** be understanding towards sb

comprensivo adj understanding (towards sb)

compresa nf sanitary napkin, sanitary towel (GB)

comprimido nm (pastilla) tablet

comprobar vt check

comprometedor adj comprometiendo

comprometer vt 1 (obligar) commit sb to sth 2 (poner en un compromiso) put sb in an awkward position ● **comprometerse** vp 1 promise (to do sth): No me comprometo a ir. I'm not promising to go. 2 (matrimonio) get engaged (to sb)

comprometido adj (situación) awkward

compromiso nm 1 (obligación) commitment 2 (acuerdo) agreement 3 (cita, matrimonial) engagement: argolla de ~ engagement ring 4 (aprieto) awkward position ▶ **por** ~ out of a sense of duty **sin** ~ without obligation

compuesto adj 1 compound: palabras compuestas compound words 2 ~ **de/por** consisting of sth ● nm compound

computadora nf (tb **computador** nm) computer **NOTA** Al empezar a trabajar en computador(a), se entra en el sistema (**log in/on**). A veces hay que introducir una contraseña (**key in/enter your password**). Se puede navegar por internet (**surf the Net**) o mandar emails a los amigos (**email your friends**). Al terminar, se sale del sistema (**log off/out**). ▶ ~ **personal** personal computer (abrev **PC**)

comulgar vi (Rel) take communion

común adj 1 common 2 (compartido) joint: un esfuerzo ~ a joint effort ▶ ~ **y corriente** ordinary **poner en** ~ discuss sth **tener en** ~ 1 (aficiones) share sth 2 (parecerse) have sth in common

comunicación nf 1 communication 2 (teléfono): Se cortó la ~. We were cut off.

comunicado adj (transporte): El pueblo está mal ~. The village is poorly served by public transportation. ● nm announcement

comunicar vt communicate sth (to sb) ● **comunicarse** vp 1 communicate with sth/sb: Mi habitación se comunica con la tuya. My room communicates with yours. ◊ Le cuesta ~ con la gente. It's hard for him to communicate with people. 2 (ponerse en contacto) get in touch with sb

comunidad nf community [pl -ies]

comunión nf communion ▶ **hacer la (primera)** ~ take (your) first communion

comunismo nm communism

comunista adj, nmf communist

con prep 1 with: Vivo ~ mis papás. I live with my parents. ◊ ¿~ qué lo limpia? What do you clean it with? **NOTA** A veces se traduce por **and**: pan ~ mantequilla bread and butter. También se puede traducir por **to**: ¿~ quién hablabas? Who were you talking to? ◊ Es muy simpática ~ todos. She is very nice to everybody. 2 (contenido) of: una maleta ~ ropa a suitcase (full) of clothes 3 (a pesar de): ~ lo duro que trabaja y no lo va a acabar. He's working so hard but he won't get it done. ◊ ¡Pero ~ lo que te gusta el café! But you're so fond of coffee! 4 + inf: ~ estudiar poco, pasará el examen. You'll pass if you study now. ◊ Será suficiente ~ llamarla. All you need to do is call her. ▶ ~ **(tal de) que...** as long as...: ~ tal de que me avises as long as you tell me

cóncavo adj concave

concebir vt 1 (idea, plan, novela) conceive 2 (entender) understand ● vt, vi (quedar embarazada) conceive

conceder vt give: ~ un préstamo a algn give sb a loan ◊ ¿Me concede unos minutos, por favor? Could you spare me a couple of minutes, please? 2 (premio, beca) award 3 (reconocer) acknowledge

concejal/a nm-nf (city) councilor

concejo nm 1 (cabildo) (city) council 2 (edificio) city hall, town hall (GB)

concentración nf concentration

concentrado adj (persona) immersed (in sth) 2 (sustancia) concentrated ● nm concentrate: ~ de mango mango juice concentrate

concentrar(se) vt, vp concentrate (on sth)

concepto nm 1 (idea) concept 2 (opinión) opinion: No sé qué ~ tienes de mí. I don't know what you think of me.

concha nf shell

conchudo/a adj, nm-nf: Es un ~. He has a nerve.

conciencia nf 1 (sentido moral) conscience: tener la ~ limpia/tranquila have a clear conscience 2 (conocimiento) consciousness: ~ de clase class consciousness ▶ **a** ~ thoroughly

concientizar vt make sb aware (of sth) ● **concientizarse** vp become aware (of sth)

concierto nm 1 (recital) concert 2 (obra) concerto [pl -s]

concilio nm council

concisoconciso adj concise

conciudadano/a nm-nf fellow citizen

concluir vt, vi (terminar) complete ● vt (deducir) conclude sth (from sth)

conclusión nf conclusion: llegar a/sacar una ~ reach/draw a conclusion

concordar vi agree (with sth/sb): Todos concuerdan en que fue un éxito. Everyone agrees it was a success.

concretar vt 1 (precisar) specify 2 (fecha) fix

concreto adj 1 (específico) specific 2 (preciso) definite ● nm concrete

concurrido adj 1 (lleno de gente) crowded 2 (popular) popular

concursante nmf contestant

concursar vi 1 (concurso) take part (in sth) 2 (para puesto) compete

concurso nm 1 (juego, Dep) competition 2 (Radio, TV) (a) (de preguntas) quiz show (b) (de juegos) game show 3 (para puesto) process of exams and interviews ▶ ~ de belleza beauty pageant, beauty contest (GB)

condecoración nf medal

condecorar vt award sb a medal (for sth)

condena nf sentence ▶ poner una ~ give sb a sentence

condenado adj 1 (maldito) wretched 2 (predestinado) doomed (to sth)

condenar vt 1 (desaprobar) condemn 2 (Jur) (a) (a una pena) sentence sb (to sth) (b) (por delito) convict sb (of sth) ● condenarse vp go to hell

condensar(se) vt, vp condense

condescendiente adj 1 (amable) kind (to sth) 2 (tolerante) tolerant (of/towards sb) 3 (con prepotencia) condescending: una sonrisita ~ a condescending smile

condición nf 1 condition: Lo hago con la ~ de que me ayudes. I'll do it on condition that you help me. ◇ poner las condiciones lay down the conditions ◇ en perfectas condiciones in perfect condition 2 (social) background ▶ en condiciones de 1 (físicamente) fit to do sth 2 (tener la posibilidad) in a position to do sth sin condiciones unconditional: aceptar sin condiciones accept unconditionally

condicional adj conditional

condicionar vt condition

condimentar vt season sth (with sth)

condimento nm seasoning

condominio nm condominium

condón nm condom

cóndor nm condor

conducir vt, vi 1 (llevar) lead sb (to sth/sb) 2 (carro, etc) drive 3 (moto) ride

conducta nf behavior [U]

conducto nm 1 (tubo) pipe 2 (Med) duct

conductor/a nm-nf driver

conectar vt 1 (unir) connect: ~ la impresora a la computadora connect the printer to the computer 2 (enchufar) plug sth in

conejillo nm ▶ ~ de Indias guinea pig

conejo/a nm-nf rabbit NOTA Rabbit es el sustantivo genérico. El macho es **buck**, y la hembra **doe**.

conexión nf connection (to/with sth; between...)

confeccionar vt make

conferencia nf 1 (charla) lecture 2 (congreso) conference

conferencista (tb conferenciante) nmf lecturer

confesar vt, vi 1 confess (to sth): ~ un crimen/haber robado un banco confess to a crime/to robbing a bank 2 (cura) hear (sb's) confession: Los domingos no confiesan. They don't hear confession on Sundays. ● confesarse vp 1 (Rel) (a) go to confession (b) ~ de confess sth, confess (to doing sth) 2 (declararse) confess ▶ ~ la verdad tell the truth

confesión nf confession

confesionario nm confessional

confesor nm confessor

confeti nm confetti

confianza nf 1 confidence (in sth/sb): No tienen ~ en él. They don't have confidence in him. 2 (naturalidad, amistad): tratar a algn con ~ treat sb in a friendly way ◇ Te lo digo porque tenemos ~. I can tell you because we're friends. ▶ ~ en uno mismo self-confidence **de ~** trustworthy: un empleado de ~ a trustworthy employee **en ~** in confidence

confiar vi 1 (fiarse) trust sth/sb: Confíe en mí. Trust me. 2 (esperar) hope: Confío en que no llueva. I hope it doesn't rain. ● vt entrust sth/sb with sth: Le confié la organización de la fiesta. I entrusted him with the

C

arrangements for the party. ● **confiarse** *vp* be overconfident

confidencial *adj* confidential

confirmar *vt* confirm

confiscar *vt* confiscate

confite *nm* candy [*pl* -ies]

confitería *nf* **1** (*tienda*) confectioner's [*pl* confectioners] **2** (*ramo comercial*) confectionery

conflicto *nm* conflict ▸ **~ de intereses** clash of interests

conformarse *vp* **1** be happy (*with sth*): *Me conformo con un seis.* I'll be happy with a pass. ◇ *~ con poco* be easily pleased **2** (*resignarse*): *No le gusta, pero tendrá que ~.* He doesn't like it, but he'll have to get used to the idea.

conforme *conj* se ● *adj* ▸ **estar ~ 1** (*de acuerdo*) agree (*with sth*) **2** (*contento*) be satisfied (*with sth/sb*)

conformista *adj, nmf* conformist

confundir *vt* **1** (*mezclar*) mix sth up **2** (*dejar perplejo*) confuse **3** (*equivocar*) mistake *sth/sb for sth/sb*: *~ la sal con el azúcar* mistake the salt for the sugar ● **confundirse** *vp* (*equivocarse*): *~ de puerta* knock/ring at the wrong door ◇ *e confundirse de casa.* You have the wrong house. ◇ *Todos se pueden ~.* We all make mistakes.

confusión *nf* **1** (*falta de claridad*) confusion **2** (*equivocación*) mistake

confuso *adj* **1** (*poco claro*) confusing **2** (*desconcertado*) confused

congelador *nm* freezer

congelar(se) *vt, vp* freeze: *El lago se congeló.* The lake froze over. ◇ *Me estoy congelando.* I'm freezing.

congénito *adj* congenital

congestionado *adj* **1** (*calles*) congested **2** (*nariz*) blocked up **3** (*cara*) flushed

congestionar *vt*: *El accidente congestionó el tráfico.* The accident caused traffic congestion. ● **congestionarse** *vp* (*enrojecer*) get red in the face

congreso *nm* congress

cónico *adj* conical

conífera *nf* conifer

conjugar *vt* conjugate

conjunción *nf* conjunction

conjuntivitis *nf* conjunctivitis

conjunto *nm* **1** (*objetos, obras*) collection **2** (*totalidad*) whole: *el ~ de la industria* industry as a

whole **3** (*Mús*) group **4** (*ropa*) outfit **5** (*Mat*) set

conjuro *nm* spell

conmigo *pron pers* with me ▸ **~ mismo** with myself

conmoción *nf* shock ▸ **~ cerebral** concussion

conmovedor *adj* moving

conmover *vt* move

conmutador *nm* switchboard

cono *nm* cone

conocer *vt* **1** know **2** (*persona, por primera vez*) meet **3** (*saber de la existencia*) know of *sth/sb*: *¿Conoce un buen hotel?* Do you know of a good hotel? ▸ **~ algo como la palma de la mano** know sth like the back of your hand **se conoce que...** it seems (that)...

conocido/a *adj* (*famoso*) well known ● *nm-nf* acquaintance

conocimiento *nm* knowledge [U] ▸ **perder/recobrar el ~** lose/ regain conciousness **sin ~** unconscious

conque *conj* so

conquista *nf* conquest

conquistador *adj* conquering ● *nm-nf* **1** conqueror **2** (*de América*) conquistador

conquistar *vt* **1** (*Mil*) conquer **2** (*enamorar*) win sb's heart

consagrar *vt* **1** (*Rel*) consecrate **2** (*dedicar*) devote sth (*to sth*) **3** (*lograr fama*) establish *sth/sb* (*as sth*)

consciente *adj* **1** aware (*of sth*) **2** (*Med*) conscious

consecuencia *nf* **1** (*secuela*) consequence: *pagar las ~s* suffer the consequences **2** (*resultado*) result: *como ~* as a result

conseguir *vt* **1** (*obtener*) obtain, get (*más coloq*): *~ una visa* obtain a visa ◇ *~ que algn haga algo* get sb to do sth **2** (*lograr*) achieve: *para ~ nuestros objetivos* to achieve our aims **3** (*ganar*) win

consejo *nm* **1** (*recomendación*) advice [U] **NOTA** Hay palabras en español ("consejo", "noticia", etc.) que tienen traducción incontable en inglés (**advice**, **news**, etc.). "Un consejo/una noticia" se dice **some advice/news** o **a piece of advice/news**: *Le voy a dar un ~.* I'm going to give you some advice/a piece of advice. Si se usa el plural ("consejos", "noticias", etc.) se traduce por el sustantivo incontable: *Tengo buenas noticias.* I have some good news. **2** (*organismo*) council ▸ **~ de administración** board of directors **el ~ de ministros** the Cabinet

consentimiento nm consent

consentir vt 1 (tolerar) allow: No consentiré que me trates así. I won't allow you to treat me like this. ◊ No se lo consientas. Don't let him get away with it. 2 (mimar) spoil

conserje nmf 1 janitor, porter (GB) 2 (escuela, etc.) custodian, caretaker (GB)

conserjería nf 1 janitor's quarters, porter's lodge (GB) 2 (escuela, etc.) custodian's quarters, caretaker's lodge (GB)

conserva nf 1 (en lata) canned food: atún en ~ canned tuna 2 (en vidrio) food in jars

conservador/a adj, nm-nf conservative

conservante nm preservative

conservar vt 1 (comida) preserve 2 (cosas) keep 3 (calor) retain

conservatorio nm school of music

consideración nf 1 (reflexión, cuidado) consideration: tomar algo en ~ take sth into consideration 2 (respeto) respect (for sb) ▶ con/sin ~ considerately/inconsiderately

considerado adj (respetuoso) considerate ▶ bien/mal ~ highly regarded/frowned upon

considerar vt 1 (sopesar) consider 2 (ver, apreciar) regard sth/sb (as sth): La considero nuestra mejor jugadora. I regard her as our best player.

consigna nf 1 (eslogan) slogan 2 (orden) orders [pl] 3 (para equipaje) baggage room, left luggage office (GB)

consignación nf (dinero) deposit

consignar vt (And, dinero, etc.) pay sth in: ~ dinero en una cuenta pay money into a bank account

consigo pron pers 1 (él, ella) with him/her 2 (usted(es)) with you 3 (ellos, ellas) with them ▶ ~ mismo with himself, herself, etc.

consistir vi consist of sth: Mi trabajo consiste en atender al público. My work consists of dealing with the public.

consola nf control panel

consolación nf consolation

consolar vt console

consonante nf consonant

conspiración nf conspiracy [pl -ies]

constancia nf (perseverancia) perseverance

constante adj 1 (continuo) constant 2 (perseverante) hard-

working: ser ~ en los estudios work hard at your studies

constar vi 1 (ser cierto) be sure (of sth): Me consta que él lo hizo. I'm sure he did it. 2 ~ de consist of sth: La obra consta de tres actos. The play consists of three acts.

constelación nf constellation

constitución nf constitution

constitucional adj constitutional

constituir vt be, constitute (fml)

construcción nf construction: en ~ under construction ◊ Trabajan en la ~. They're construction workers.

constructor/a nm-nf building contractor ● nf construction company [pl -ies]

construir vt, vi build

consuelo nm consolation

cónsul nmf consul

consulado nm consulate

consulta nf 1 (pregunta) question: ¿Le puedo hacer una ~? Could I ask you something? 2 (Med) office hours [pl], surgery (GB) ▶ de ~ reference: libros de ~ reference books

consultar vt 1 consult sth/sb (about sth) 2 (palabra, dato) look sth up ▶ ~ con la almohada sleep on sth

consultorio nm (Med) doctor's office, surgery [pl -ies] (GB) ▶ ~ sentimental 1 (Period) problem page 2 (Radio) phone-in

consumidor/a nm-nf consumer ● adj consuming: países ~es de petróleo oil-consuming countries

consumir vt 1 consume 2 (energía) use ▶ ~ preferentemente antes de... best before...

consumo nm consumption ▶ ~ mínimo (And) minimum charge

contabilidad nf 1 (cuentas) accounts [pl] 2 (profesión) accounting, accountancy (GB) ▶ llevar la ~ do the accounts

contactar vt contact

contacto nm contact ▶ mantenerse/ponerse en ~ con keep/get in touch with sb poner a algn en ~ con put sb in touch with sb

contado ▶ al ~ cash: pagar algo al/de ~ pay cash for sth

contador/a nm-nf accountant ● nm (luz, etc.) meter

contagiar vt pass sth on to sb ● **contagiarse** vp be contagious

contagioso adj contagious

contaminación nf **1** pollution **2** (*radiactiva, alimenticia*) contamination

contaminar vt, vi **1** pollute **2** (*radiactividad, alimentos*) contaminate

contante adj ▸ **dinero ~ y sonante** hard cash

contar vt **1** count **2** (*cuento, etc.*) tell: *Cuénteme lo de ayer.* Tell me about yesterday. ◊ *Es largo de ~.* It's a long story. ● vi **1** count: *Cuenta hasta 50.* Count to 50. **2 ~ con** (*confiar*) count on sth/sb ▸ **¿qué (me) cuenta(s)?** how are things?

contemplar vt contemplate: *~ un cuadro/una posibilidad* contemplate a painting/possibility

contemporáneo/a adj, nm-nf contemporary [*pl* -ies]

contenedor nm **1** (*basura*) trash can, bin (GB) **2** (*mercancías*) container

contener vt **1** contain **2** (*aguantarse*) hold sth back: *~ el llanto* hold back your tears

contenido nm contents [*pl*]

contentarse vp **~ con** be satisfied with sth: *Se contenta con poco.* He's easily pleased.

contento adj **1** (*feliz*) happy **2** (*satisfecho*) pleased (with sth/sb)

contestación nf reply [*pl* -ies]: *Espero ~.* I await your reply.

contestador nm ▸ **~ (automático)** answering machine

contestar vt answer ● vi **1** answer **2** (*replicar*) answer back: *¡No me contestes!* Don't mouth off to me!

contigo pron prep with you: *Quiero hablar ~.* I want to talk to you. ▸ **~ mismo** with yourself

continente nm continent

continuación nf continuation ▸ **a ~** (*ahora*) next

continuar vi **1** go on (with sth/doing sth), continue (with sth/to do sth) (*más fml*) **2** (*estar todavía*) be still...: *Continúa haciendo calor.* It's still hot. ▸ **continuará...** to be continued...

continuo adj continuous, continual →CONTINUAL

contorno nm **1** (*perfil*) outline **2** (*medida*) measurement

contra prep **1** against **2** (*con verbos como tirar, disparar*) at: *lanzar piedras ~ las ventanas* throw stones at the windows **3** (*con verbos como chocar, arremeter*) into: *Se estrelló ~ un árbol.* He hit a tree. **4** (*golpe, ataque*) on: *Se dio un buen golpe ~ el asfalto.* She fell down on the concrete. ◊ *un atentado ~ su vida* an attempt on

his life **5** (*tratamiento, vacuna*) for: *una cura ~ el cáncer* a cure for cancer **6** (*resultado*) to: *Ganó por diez votos ~ seis.* He won by ten votes to six. **7** (*Dep*) versus (*abrev* **v, vs**): *Francia ~ Brazil* France v Brazil ▸ **en ~ (de)** against ◊ *¿Estás a favor o en ~?* Are you for or against?

contraatacar vi fight back

contraataque nm counter-attack

contrabajo nm (*instrumento*) double bass

contrabandista nmf smuggler ▸ **~ de armas** gunrunner

contrabando nm **1** (*actividad*) smuggling **2** (*mercancía*) contraband ▸ **comprar/vender de ~** buy/sell sth on the black market **~ de armas** gunrunning **pasar de ~** smuggle sth in

contradecir vt contradict

contradicción nf contradiction

contradictorio adj contradictory

contraer vt **1** contract: *~ deudas/la malaria* contract debts/malaria **2** (*compromisos, obligaciones*) take sth on ● **contraerse** vp (*materiales, músculos*) contract ▸ **~ matrimonio** get married (to sb)

contraluz nm o nf ▸ **a ~** against the light

contrapeso nm counterweight

contrapié ▸ **a ~** on the wrong foot

contraportada nf **1** (*libro*) back cover **2** (*Period*) back page

contrariedad nf setback

contrario/a adj **1** (*equipo, opinión, teoría*) opposing **2** (*dirección, lado*) opposite **3** (*persona*) opposed (to sth) ● nm-nf opponent ▸ **al/por el ~** on the contrary **de lo ~** otherwise **llevar la contraria** disagree (*todo*) **lo ~** (quite) the opposite

contrarreloj adj timed: *una carrera ~* a time trial ● nf (*Dep*) time trial ▸ **a ~** against the clock

contraseña nf password →COMPUTADORA

contrastar vt, vi contrast (sth) (with sth)

contraste nm contrast

contratar vt **1** take sb on **2** (*deportista, artista*) sign

contratiempo nm **1** (*problema*) setback **2** (*accidente*) mishap

contrato nm contract

contraventana nf shutter

contravía nm: *ir en ~* drive the wrong way (down the road) ◊ *Por ahí no, que es ~.* Not down there, it's one way.

contribuir vi **1** contribute (sth) (to/towards sth): Contribuyó con mil euros a la campaña. He contributed a thousand euros to the campaign. **2 ~ a hacer algo** help (to) do sth

contribuyente nmf taxpayer

contrincante nmf rival

control nm **1** control: ~ de natalidad birth control ◊ perder el ~ lose control **2** (policía) checkpoint ▶ **bajo/fuera de ~** under/out of control **~ remoto** remote control

controlar vt control

convalidar vt recognize: ~ un título have a degree recognized

convencer vt **1** convince sb (of sth/to do sth): Me convenció de que estaba bien. He convinced me (that) it was right. **2** (persuadir) persuade sb (to do sth): A ver si lo convence para que venga. See if you can persuade him to come. ● vi be convincing ● **convencerse** vp get sth into your head: Tiene que ~ de que se acabó. You must get it into your head that it's over.

conveniente adj convenient ▶ **ser ~**: Es ~ que salgamos de madrugada. It's a good idea to leave early.

convenio nm agreement

convenir vi **1** (ser conveniente) suit: Haz lo que más te convenga. Do whatever suits you best. **2** (ser aconsejable): No le conviene trabajar tanto. You shouldn't work so hard. ● vt, vi agree on sth/to do sth: Hay que ~ la fecha de la reunión. We must agree on the date of the meeting.

convento nm **1** (monjas) convent **2** (monjes) monastery [pl -ies]

conversación nf conversation

conversar vi talk (to/with sb) (about sth/sb)

convertir vt **1** turn sth/sb into sth **2** (Rel) convert sb (to sth) ● **convertirse** vp **1** (llegar a ser) become sth **2** (transformarse) turn into sth: El príncipe se convirtió en rana. The prince turned into a frog. **3** (Rel) convert (to sth) ▶ **~se en realidad** come true

convexo adj convex

convivir vi live together, live with sb

convocar vt **1** (huelga, elecciones, reunión) call **2** (citar) summon

convocatoria nf **1** call: una ~ de huelga/elecciones a strike call/a call for elections **2** (inscripción): Pasé en la ~ de junio. I passed in

June. ◊ presentarse para la ~ apply for the post

coñac nm brandy [pl -ies]

cooperar vi cooperate (with sb) (on sth)

coordinar vt coordinate

copa nf **1** (vaso) (wine) glass **2** (bebida) drink **3** (árbol) top **4 Copa** (Dep) Cup **5 copas** (cartas) →BARAJA

copia nf copy [pl -ies]: hacer/sacar una ~ make a copy

copiar vt, vi copy sth (from sth/sb)

copiloto nmf **1** (avión) copilot **2** (automóvil) co-driver

copión/ona nm-nf copycat

copo nm flake: ~ de nieve snowflake

coquetear vi flirt (with sb)

coqueto/a adj (que coquetea) flirtatious ● nm-nf flirt: Es un ~. He's a flirt.

coral¹ nm (Zool) coral

coral² adj choral ● nf (coro) choir

corazón nm **1** heart: en pleno ~ de la ciudad in the very heart of the city ◊ en el fondo de su ~ deep down **2** (fruta) core **3** (dedo) middle finger **4 corazones** (cartas) hearts →BARAJA ▶ **de todo ~** from the heart **tener buen ~** be kind-hearted

corazonada nf hunch

corbata nf tie: ir con ~ wear a tie ▶ **~ de moño** bow tie

corbatín nm bow tie

corcho nm **1** cork **2** (pesca) float

corcholata nf (Mx) bottle top

cordel nm string

cordero/a nm-nf lamb →CARNE

cordillera nf (mountain) range

cordón nm **1** (cuerda) cord (zapato) (shoe)lace **3** (Elec) lead ▶ **~ policial** police cordon **~ umbilical** umbilical cord

córnea nf cornea

córner nm corner

corneta nf bugle

coro nm (en iglesia, coral) choir

corona nf **1** (de rey, monarquía, diente) crown **2** (de flores) wreath

coronación nf (de rey) coronation

coronar vt crown

coronel nmf colonel

coronilla nf crown (of the head) ▶ **hasta la ~** sick to death of sth/sb

corporal adj **1** body: lenguaje ~ body language **2** (contacto, funciones, etc.) bodily: las necesidades -es bodily needs

corpulento adj hefty

C

corral nm 1 yard 2 (de niño) playpen

correa nf 1 strap: ~ del reloj watch strap 2 (cinturón) belt 3 (para perro) leash

corrección nf correction: hacer una ~ make a correction

correcto adj correct

corrector nm ▶ ~ ortográfico spellchecker

corredor/a nm-nf 1 (atleta) runner 2 (ciclista) cyclist ● nm (pasillo) corridor

corregimiento nm (And) small village

corregir vt correct

correo nm 1 mail, post (GB) → MAIL 2 (oficina) post office ▶ ~aéreo airmail del ~/de ~s postal: huelga de ~s postal strike echar al ~ mail, post (GB)

correr vi 1 run: Salí corriendo detrás de él. I ran out after him. ◇ Echó a ~. He ran off. 2 (apurarse) hurry: ¡Corre! Hurry up! 3 (vehículo) go fast 4 (manejar deprisa) drive fast 5 (líquidos) flow: El agua corría por la calle. Water flowed down the street. ● vt 1 (mover) move sth (along/down/over/up): Corre un poco la silla. Move your chair over a little. 2 (cortina) draw 3 (Dep) compete in sth: ~ los 100m compete in the 100 meters 4 (echar) kick sb out ■ **correrse** vp (moverse una persona) move up/over 2 (tinta, maquillaje) run ▶ salir corriendo rush off

correspondencia nf (correo) correspondence

corresponder vi 1 (tener derecho) be entitled to sth 2 (pertenecer, ser adecuado): Pon una cruz donde corresponda. Check as appropriate. ◇ Ese texto corresponde a otra foto. That text goes with another photograph. 3 (premio) go to sth/sb: El premio le correspondió a mi grupo. The prize went to my group.

correspondiente adj 1 corresponding (to sth) 2 (propio) own: Cada estudiante tendrá su título. Each student will have their own diploma. 3 (adecuado) relevant: presentar la documentación ~ produce the relevant documents ~ a for: temas ~s al primer año subjects for the first grade

corresponsal nmf correspondent

corrida nf ▶ ~ de toros bullfight

corriente adj 1 (normal) ordinary: gente ~ ordinary people 2 (común) common: un árbol ~ a common tree ● nf 1 (agua, luz) current 2 (aire) draft ▶ ponerse al ~ get up to date seguir la ~ a algn humor sb

corroer(se) vt, vp (metales) corrode

corromper vt corrupt

corrugado adj corrugated

corrupción nf corruption

cortacésped nm lawnmower

cortada nf cut

cortado adj embarrassed

cortar vt 1 cut: Córtalo en seis pedazos. Cut it into six pieces. 2 (agua, luz, parte del cuerpo, rama) cut sth off: Cortaron el gas. The gas has been cut off. 3 (con tijeras) cut sth ● vi cut: Esas tijeras cortan mucho. Those scissors are very sharp. ■ **cortarse** vp (herirse) cut: Me corté la mano con los vidrios. I cut my hand on the glass. 2 (leche, etc.) curdle 3 (teléfono): Estábamos hablando y de repente se cortó. We were talking and then suddenly we got cut off. 4 (turbarse) get embarrassed ▶ ~ el pasto/césped mow the lawn ~se el pelo 1 (uno mismo) cut your hair 2 (en peluquería) have your hair cut

cortaúñas nm nail clippers [pl]

corte¹ nm cut: Sufrió varios ~s en el brazo. He got several cuts on his arm. ▶ ~ de luz power outage, power cut (GB) ~ de pelo haircut ~ y confección dressmaking

corte² nf court

cortesía nf courtesy [pl -ies]: por ~ out of courtesy

corteza nf 1 (árbol) bark 2 (pan) crust 3 (queso) rind ▶ la ~ terrestre the earth's crust

cortina nf curtain: abrir/cerrar las ~s draw the curtains

corto adj short: El pantalón le queda ~. The pants are too short for you. ◇ de manga corta short-sleeved ● nm (Cine) 1 (tb cortometraje) short 2 cortos (And) [sing] ▶ ~ de vista near-sighted ni ~ ni perezoso without thinking twice

cortocircuito nm short-circuit

cosa nf 1 thing 2 (algo): Le quería preguntar una ~. I wanted to ask you something. 3 (nada) nothing: No hay ~ más linda que el amor. There's nothing more wonderful than love. 4 cosas (asuntos) affairs: Quiero solucionar primero mis ~s. I want to sort out my own affairs first. ◇ Nunca habla de sus ~s.

He never talks about his personal life. ▸ ¡~s de la vida! that's life! **entre una ~ y otra** what with one thing and another **¡lo que son las ~s!** would you believe it! **¡qué ~ más rara!** how odd! **ser ~ de algn**: Esta broma es ~ tuya. This joke must be your doing. **ser poca ~ 1** (herida) not be serious **2** (persona) be a poor little thing **ver ~ igual/semejante**: ¿Habráse visto ~ igual? Did you ever see anything like it?

cosecha nf **1** harvest **2** (vino) vintage

cosechar vt, vi harvest

coser vt, vi sew: ~ un botón sew a button on

cosmético adj, nm cosmetic

cósmico adj cosmic

cosmos nm cosmos

cosquillas nf ▸ **hacer ~** tickle **tener ~** be ticklish: Tengo muchas ~ en los pies. My feet are very ticklish.

costa¹ nf coast: en la ~ sur on the south coast

costa² ▸ **a ~ de** at sb's expense **a ~ de lo que sea/a toda ~** at all costs **vivir a ~ de** live off sb

costado nm side: Duermo de ~. I sleep on my side.

costal nm sack

costar vi **1** cost: Cuesta $30. It costs 30 dollars. ◇ El accidente costó la vida a cien personas. The accident cost the lives of a hundred people. **2** (tiempo) take: Leerme el libro me costó un mes. It took me a month to read the book. **3** (resultar difícil) find it hard (to do sth) ▸ **~ mucho/poco 1** (dinero) be expensive/cheap **2** (esfuerzo) be hard/easy **~ trabajo**: Me cuesta trabajo madrugar. I find it hard to get up early. ◇ El vestido me costó mucho trabajo. The dress was a lot of work. **~ un riñón/un ojo de la cara** cost an arm and a leg

Costa Rica nf Costa Rica

costarricense adj, nmf Costa Rican

costilla nf rib

costo nm cost: el ~ de la vida the cost of living

costra nf scab

costumbre nf **1** (persona) habit: Lo hago por ~. I do it out of habit. **2** (país) custom: una ~ mexicana a Mexican custom ▸ **agarrar la ~** get into the habit (of sth) **de ~** usual: más simpático que de ~ nicer than usual

costura nf **1** (labor) sewing **2** (puntadas) seam: Se descosió de/por la ~. The seam has come undone.

costurera nf seamstress

costurero nm sewing kit

cotidiano adj daily

cotorra nf parrot

coyote nm coyote

coz nf kick: dar/pegar coces kick

crack nm (droga) crack

cranear(se) vt, vp (planear) figure sth out

cráneo nm skull

cráter nm crater

creación nf creation

creador/a nm-nf creator

crear vt **1** create: ~ problemas create problems **2** (empresa) set sth up ▸ **crearse** vp: ~ enemigos make enemies

creatividad nf creativity

creativo adj creative

crecer vi **1** grow **2** (criarse) grow up **3** (río) rise ▸ **dejarse ~ el pelo, la barba, etc.** grow your hair, a beard, etc.

creciente adj increasing

crecimiento nm growth

credencial nm (Mx, club, sociedad) (membership) card

crédito nm **1** (préstamo) loan **2** (forma de pago) credit: comprar algo a ~ buy sth on credit

credo nm creed

crédulo adj gullible

creencia nf belief

creer vt, vi **1** (aceptar como verdad, tener fe) believe (in sth/sb): ~ en la justicia believe in justice ◇ Nadie me cree. Nobody believes me. **2** (pensar) think: —¿Lloverá? —No creo. "Will it rain?" "I don't think so." ● **creerse** vp **1** believe: No me lo creo. I don't believe it. **2** (uno mismo) think you are sth/sb: Se cree muy listo. He thinks he's very clever. ◇ ¿Qué se habrá creído? Who does he think he is? ▸ **creo que sí/no** I think so/I don't think so

creído/a adj, nm-nf (engreído) conceited: ser un ~ be conceited

crema nf **1** cream: ~ (de leche) cream ◇ Ponte ~ en la cara. Put some cream on your face. ◇ una bufanda (color) ~ a cream (colored) scarf **2** (pastelería) confectioner's custard ▸ **~ de afeitar/rasurar** shaving cream **~ dental** toothpaste

cremallera nf **1** zipper, zip (GB): subir la ~ do your zipper up ◇ Bájame la ~ (del vestido). Unzip my dress for me. **2** (del pantalón) fly, flies [pl] (GB): Tienes la ~ abajo. Your fly is open.

crematorio *nm* crematorium

crepe (*tb* **crepa** *Mx*) *nf* crêpe

crepúsculo *nm* twilight

crespo *adj* curly ▸ *nm* (*pelo*) curl

cresta *nf* 1 (*gallo*) comb 2 (*otras aves, montaña, ola*) crest

creyente *nmf* believer ▸ **no ~** non-believer

cría *nf* 1 (*animal recién nacido*) baby [*pl* -ies]: *una ~ de conejo* a baby rabbit 2 (*crianza*) breeding: *la ~ de perros* dog breeding

criadero *nm* farm ▸ **~ de perros** kennels [*pl*]

criado/a *nm-nf* servant

criar *vt* 1 (*educar*) bring *sb* up 2 (*animal*) rear ● **criarse** *vp* grow up

crimen *nm* 1 crime 2 (*asesinato*) murder

criminal *adj, nmf* criminal

crin (*tb* **crines**) *nf* mane [*sing*]

crisis *nf* crisis [*pl* crises]

crispetas *nf* (*And*) popcorn [*U*]

cristal *nm* 1 piece of glass: *un ~ roto* a piece of broken glass 2 (*vidrio fino, mineral*) crystal 3 (*lámina*) pane: *el ~ de la ventana* the windowpane

cristalero/a *nm-nf* glazier

cristalino *adj* (*agua*) crystal clear

cristianismo *nm* Christianity

cristiano/a *adj, nm-nf* Christian

Cristo *nm* Christ ▸ **antes/después de ~** BC/AD

criterio *nm* 1 (*principio*) criterion [*pl* -ria] 2 (*capacidad de juzgar, Jur*) judgement: *tener buen ~* have good judgement 3 (*opinión*) opinion: *según nuestro ~* in our opinion

crítica *nf* 1 criticism 2 (*Period*) review 3 (*conjunto de críticos*) critics [*pl*]

criticar *vt, vi* criticize

crítico/a *adj* critical ● *nm-nf* critic

croissant *nm* croissant

crol *nm* crawl: *nadar (de) ~* do the crawl

cromo *nm* 1 (*de colección*) picture card 2 (*Quím*) chromium

crónico *adj* chronic

cronológico *adj* chronological

cronometrar *vt* time

cronómetro *nm* (*Dep*) stopwatch

croqueta *nf* croquette

cruce *nm* 1 (*tb* **crucero** *Mx*) (*carreteras*) intersection, junction (*GB*) 2 (*para peatones*) crosswalk, pedestrian crossing (*GB*) 3 (*híbrido*) cross: *un ~ de bóxer y labrador* a cross between a boxer and a labrador

crucero *nm* (*viaje*) cruise: *hacer un ~* go on a cruise

crucificar *vt* crucify

crucifijo *nm* crucifix

crucigrama *nm* crossword: *hacer ~s* do crosswords

crudo *adj* 1 (*sin cocinar*) raw 2 (*poco cocido*) underdone 3 (*clima, realidad*) harsh 4 (*ofensivo*) shocking ● *nm* crude oil

cruel *adj* cruel

crueldad *nf* cruelty [*pl* -ies]

crujido *nm* 1 (*hojas secas, papel*) rustle 2 (*madera, huesos*) creak

crujiente *adj* (*madera, huesos*) crunchy

crujir *vi* 1 (*hojas secas*) rustle 2 (*madera, huesos*) creak 3 (*alimentos*) crunch 4 (*dientes*) grind

crustáceo *nm* crustacean

cruz *nf* cross ▸ **C~ Roja** Red Cross **ponerse con los brazos en ~** stretch your arms out to the side

cruzar *vt* 1 cross: *~ la calle corriendo* run across the street ◇ *~ el río a nado* swim across the river ◇ *~ las piernas* cross your legs 2 (*palabras, miradas*) exchange ● **cruzarse** *vp* meet (*sb*): *Nos cruzamos en el camino.* We met on the way. ▸ **~ los brazos** fold your arms

cuaderno *nm* 1 notebook 2 (*de ejercicios*) exercise book

cuadra *nf* 1 block: *Hay tres ~s de aquí hasta mi casa.* It's only three blocks to my house from here. 2 (*para caballos*) stable

cuadrado *adj, nm* square ▸ **estar ~** be stocky

cuadrar *vi* square (*with sth*) ● *vt* (*Com*) balance ● **cuadrarse** *vp* 1 (*Mil*) stand to attention 2 (*And, estacionarse*) park

cuadrilla *nf* gang

cuadro *nm* 1 (*Arte*) painting 2 **cuadros** (*tela*) plaid [*sing*], check [*sing*] (*GB*): *Los ~s te favorecen.* You look good in plaid. ▸ **a escocés** plaid, tartan (*GB*)

cuádruple *adj* quadruple ● *nm* four times: *¿Cuál es el ~ de cuatro?* What is four times four?

cuajar *vt* 1 (*leche*) curdle 2 (*yogurt*) set ● *vi* set off the ground: *El proyecto nunca cuajó.* The project never got off the ground. ● **cuajarse** *vp* 1 (*leche*) curdle 2 (*yogurt*) set

cual *pron* 1 (*persona*) whom: *Tengo diez alumnos, de los ~es dos son ingleses.* I have ten students, two of whom are English. ◇ *la familia para la ~ trabaja* the family he works for → WHOM 2 (*cosa*) which: *Le pegó, lo ~ no* *está nada bien.* He hit her, which just isn't right. ◇ *un trabajo en el* ~ *me siento cómodo* a job I feel comfortable in →WHICH

cuál *pron* **1** what: *¿* ~ *es la capital de Perú?* What's the capital of Peru? **2** *(entre varios)* which (one): *¿* ~ *prefieres?* Which one do you prefer? →WHAT

cualidad *nf* quality [*pl* -ies]

cualquier *(tb* **cualquiera)** *adj* **1** any: ~ *bus le sirve.* You can get any bus. ◇ *en* ~ *caso* in any case → SOME **2** *(uno cualquiera)* any old: *un trapo* ~ any old cloth
● **cualquiera** *pron* **1** *(cualquier persona)* anybody **2** *(entre dos)* either (one): ~ *de los dos me sirve.* Either (of them) will do. ◇ —*¿Cuál puedo usar?* —Cualquiera. "Which one can I use?" "Either one." **3** *(entre más de dos)* any (one): *en* ~ *de esos países* in any one of those countries
● **cualquiera** *nmf (don nadie)* nobody: *No es más que un* ~. He's just a nobody. ▶ ~ *cosa* anything → **cosa que...** whatever: ~ *cosa que pida,* se la compran. They buy her whatever she wants. **en** ~ **lugar/parte/sitio** anywhere **por** ~ **cosa** over the slightest thing

cuando *adv* when: ~ *venga Juan, nos vamos.* When Juan gets here, we'll go. ◇ *Me atacaron*—*volvía a la casa.* I was attacked as I was going home. ◇ *Pase por acá* ~ *quiera.* Pop in here whenever you want. ▶ ~ **mucho** at most ~ **sea grande** when I, you, etc. grow up **de** ~ **en** ~ from time to time

cuándo *adv* when ▶ **¿desde** ~? how long...?: *¿Desde* ~ *viven acá?* How long have you lived here? **¿hasta** ~? how long...: *¿Hasta* ~ *se queda?* How long are you staying?

cuanto *adj:* **Haz** *cuantas pruebas sean necesarias.* Do whatever tests are necessary. ◇ *Lo haré cuantas veces haga falta.* I will do it as many times as I have to. ● *pron:* *Llora* ~ *quieras.* Cry as much as you want. ▶ ~ **antes** as soon as possible → **más/menos...** the more/less...: ~ *más tiene, más quiere.* The more he has, the more he wants. **en** ~ as soon as: *En* ~ *me vio, salió corriendo.* As soon as he saw me, he ran off. **en** ~ **a...** as for... **unos** ~**s** a few: *Unos* ~*s llegaron tarde.* A few people were late.

cuánto *adj*
● *interrogativo* **1** *(+ sustantivo incontable)* how much **2** *(+ sustantivo contable)* how many
● *exclamativo:* *¡* ~ *vino tomó!* What a lot of wine he drank! ◇ *¡A cuántas personas ha ayudado!* He's helped so many people! ● *pron* how much [*pl* how many] ● *adv* **1** *(interrogativo)* how much **2** *(exclamativo):* *¡* ~ *los quiero!* I'm so fond of them! ▶ **¿** ~ **es/cuesta/vale?** how much is it? **¿** ~ **(tiempo)/** ~**s días, meses, etc?** how long...?: *¿* ~*s años llevas aquí?* How long have you been living here?

cuarenta *adj, nm, pron* **1** forty **2** *(cuadragésimo)* fortieth

cuaresma *nf* Lent ▶ **cada año por la** ~ once in a blue moon

cuarta *nf: Es una* ~ *más alto que yo.* He's several inches taller than me.

cuartel *nm* barracks ▶ ~ **general** headquarters

cuartilla *nf* sheet of paper

cuarto *nm* room ▶ ~ **de baño** bathroom ~ **de estar** living room ~ **de San Alejo/los trastos** junkroom **hacerle un** ~ **a algn** *(And)* cover for sb

cuarto/a *adj, nm-nf, pron* fourth *(abrev* **4th)** ● *nm* quarter: *un* ~ *de hora/kilo* a quarter of an hour/a kilo ● **cuarta** *nf (Aut)* fourth (gear) ▶ ~ **creciente/menguante** first/last quarter ~**s de final** quarter-finals **la dos, etc.** **y** ~ a quarter after/past *(GB)* two, etc. **un** ~ **para las dos, etc.** a quarter to two, etc.

cuate *nm (Mx)* **1** *(gemelo)* twin **2** *(amigo)* buddy [*pl* -ies]

cuatrimestre *nm (Educ)* term

cuatro *adj, nm, pron* **1** four **2** *(fecha)* fourth

cuatrocientos/as *adj, nm, pron* four hundred

cubertería *nf* cutlery set

cubeta *nf (Mx)* bucket

cúbico *adj* cubic

cubierta *nf (Náut)* deck: *subir a* ~ go up on deck

cubierto *adj* **1** covered *(in/with sth):* ~ *de manchas* covered in stains ◇ *La cama estaba cubierta con una sábana.* The bed was covered with a sheet. **2** *(tiempo)* overcast **3** *(instalación)* indoor: *una piscina cubierta* indoor swimming pool ● **cubiertos** *nm* silverware [U]: *poner los* ~*s* put out the silverware ◇ *aprender a usar los* ~*s* learn how to use a knife and fork ▶ **ponerse a** ~ take cover *from sth/sb*

cubo nm cube ► ~ **(de la basura)** trash can, bin (GB)

cubrecama nm bedspread

cubrir vt cover sth/sb (with sth): ~ *la pared de fotos* cover the wall with photos ◊ ~ *los gastos del viaje* cover traveling expenses

cuclillas ► **en** ~ squatting **ponerse en** ~ squat

cucú nm cuckoo

cucurucho nm (helado, papel) cone

cuello nm 1 neck: *Me duele el* ~. My neck hurts. ◊ *el* ~ *de una botella* the neck of a bottle → MY 2 (ropa) collar: *el* ~ *de la camisa* shirt collar ► **alto/de tortuga** turtleneck ~ **en V** V-neck ~ **ortopédico** (surgical) collar

cuenca nf (Geog) basin ► ~ **minera** (carbón) coalfield

cuenco nm (recipiente) bowl

cuenta nf 1 (Com, Fin) account: *una* ~ *corriente* a checking/current (GB) account 2 (factura) (a) (de servicios) bill: *la* ~ *del teléfono* the phone bill (b) (restaurante, etc.) check, bill (GB) 3 (Mat) sum: *No me salen las* ~s. I can't work this out. 4 (rosario) bead ► ~ **atrás/regresiva** countdown **darse** ~ **de** ~ realize (that...): *Me di* ~ *de que no había nadie.* I realized (that) no one was there. 2 (ver) notice sth/that... **echar/sacar la** ~ work sth out **hacer** ~ work sth out por la ~ **que me trae** for my, your, etc. own sake **tener/tomar en** ~ 1 (hacer caso) bear sth in mind 2 (reprochar) take sth to heart

cuentakilómetros nm odometer, milometer (GB)

cuentista nmf 1 short-story writer 2 (mentiroso) fibber

cuento nm 1 story [pl -ies]: ~s de hadas fairy stories 2 (mentira) fib ► ~ **chino** tall story **no venir a** ~ be irrelevant

cuerda nf 1 rope: *Amárralo con una* ~. Tie it with some rope. 2 (Mús) string: *instrumentos de* ~ stringed instruments ► ~s **vocales** vocal cords **dar** ~ **a algn** encourage sb (to talk) **dar** ~ **a un reloj** wind up a clock/watch

cuerdo adj sane

cuernito nm (Mx) croissant

cuerno nm horn ► **poner los** ~s (ser infiel) cheat on sb

cuero nm leather ► **en** ~s stark naked

cuerpo nm body [pl -ies] ► **a** ~ **de rey** like a king ~ **de bomberos** fire department, fire brigade (GB) **de** ~ **entero** full-length:

una foto de ~ *entero* a full-length photo **sacar el** ~ avoid sb

cuervo nm crow

cuesta nf slope ► **a** ~s on your back ~ **abajo/arriba** downhill/uphill

cuestión nf (asunto, problema) matter: *en* ~ *de horas* in a matter of hours ◊ *Es* ~ *de vida o muerte.* It's a matter of life or death. ► **en** ~ in question **la** ~ **es...** the thing is...

cuestionario nm questionnaire: *llenar un* ~ fill out a questionnaire

cueva nf cave

cuidado nm care ● interj 1 look out! 2 ~ **con**: *¡* ~ *con el perro/escalón!* Beware of the dog/Watch the step! ► **al** ~ **de** in charge of sth/sb **con (mucho)** ~ (very) carefully **tener** ~ be careful (with sth/sb)

cuidadoso adj careful

cuidar vt, vi look after sth/sb: ~ *las plantas/de los niños* look after the plants/the children ● **cuidarse** vp look after yourself: *No se cuida nada.* She doesn't look after herself at all.

culata nf (arma) butt

culebra nf 1 (Zool) snake 2 (And, deuda) debt

culebrón nm soap (opera)

culinario adj culinary

culpa nf fault ► **echar la** ~ blame sb (for sth) **por** ~ **de** because of sth/sb **tener la** ~ be to blame (for sth): *No tengo la* ~ *de lo que pasó.* I'm not to blame for what happened.

culpabilidad nf guilt

culpable adj guilty (of sth) ● nmf culprit

culpar vt blame sb (for sth)

cultivar vt grow

cultivo nm growing: *el* ~ *de tomates* tomato growing

culto adj 1 (persona) cultured 2 (expresión, etc.) formal ● nm 1 (veneración) worship (of sth/sb): *el* ~ *al sol* sun worship 2 (secta) cult 3 (misa) service

cultura nf culture

cultural adj cultural

cumbamba nf (And) jaw

cumbre nf summit

cumpleaños nm birthday: *¡Feliz* ~! Happy Birthday!

cumplido adj (puntual) punctual ● nm compliment ► **recién** ~s: *Tiene once años recién* ~s. He's just turned eleven. **sin** ~s without ceremony

cumplir vt 1 (años) be: *En mayo cumplirá 30.* She'll be 30 in May. ◇ *¿Cuántos años cumples?* How old are you? 2 (condena) serve ● vt, vi ~ (con) 1 (orden) carry sth out 2 (promesa, obligación) fulfill ● vi (hacer lo que corresponde) do your duty: *Yo he cumplido.* I've done my part. ● **cumplirse** vp 1 (predicción) come true 2 (plazo) expire ▸ **hacer algo por** ~ do sth just to be polite

cuna nf (bebé) crib, cot (GB)

cundir vi (extenderse) spread: *Que no cunda el pánico.* Don't panic.

cuneta nf ditch

cuña nf 1 (de puerta) wedge 2 (TV) advertisement, ad (coloq)

cuñado/a nm-nf brother-in-law [fem sister-in-law] [pl -ers-in-law]

cuota nf 1 fee: *la ~ de socio* the membership fee 2 (plazo) installment: *~ inicial* deposit 3 (Mx, Aut) toll

cupón nm 1 (vale) coupon 2 (para sorteo) ticket

cúpula nf dome

cura¹ nf 1 (curación, tratamiento) cure: *~ de reposo* rest cure 2 (vendaje) bandage 3 (And) = CURITA ▸ **tener/no tener** ~ be curable/incurable

cura² nm priest

curandero/a nm-nf 1 folk healer 2 (pey) quack

curar vt 1 (sanar) cure (sb) (of sth): *Esas pastillas me curaron la gripa.* Those pills cured my flu. 2 (herida) bandage 3 (alimentos) cure ● **curarse** vp 1 (ponerse bien) recover (from sth) 2 (herida) heal (over/up)

curiosidad nf curiosity ▸ **por** ~ out of curiosity **tener** ~ be curious (about sth): *Tengo ~ por saber.* I'm curious to find out.

curioso/a adj 1 (interesado) curious 2 (extraño) odd ● nm-nf 1 (mirón) onlooker 2 (indiscreto) busybody [pl -ies]

curita nf Band-Aid®, plaster (GB)

currículum nm 1 ~ vitae resumé, CV (GB) 2 (Educ) curriculum

cursi adj 1 (persona) affected 2 (cosa) cutesy, twee (GB)

cursillo nm short course

curso nm 1 course: *el ~ de un río* the course of a river ◇ *~s de idiomas* language courses 2 (año académico) (school) year ▸ **el año/mes en** ~ the current year/month

cursor nm cursor

curtir vt tan

curul nm seat

curva nf curve

curvo adj 1 (forma) curved 2 (doblado) bent

custodia nf custody

custodiar vt guard

cutícula nf cuticle

cutis nm skin

cuy nm guinea pig

cuyo adj rel whose

D d

dado nm die [pl dice]: *echar/tirar los ~s* roll the dice

daltónico adj color-blind

dama nf 1 (señora) lady [pl -ies] 2 **damas** checkers [sing], draughts [sing] (GB) 3 (en juego) king ▸ ~ **de honor** (en boda) bridesmaid →MATRIMONIO

danés/esa adj, nm Danish ● nm-nf Dane

danza nf dance

dañar vt 1 damage 2 (persona) hurt 3 (And, aparato) break ● **dañarse** vp 1 (And, comida) go bad 2 (aparato) break 3 (And, carro) break down

dañino adj harmful

daño nm damage (to sth) [U]: *El carro sufrió muchos ~s.* The car was badly damaged. ▸ ~**s y perjuicios** damages **hacer** ~ hurt: *Me haces ~.* You're hurting me. ◇ *Me hace ~ la comida picante.* Spicy food disagrees with me. **hacerse** ~ hurt yourself: *Me hice ~ en la mano.* I hurt my hand.

dar vt 1 give 2 (Educ) teach: *~ clases nocturnas para adultos* teach adults at night school 3 (reloj) strike: *El reloj dio las doce.* The clock struck twelve. 4 (fruto, flores) bear 5 (olor) give sth off ● vi 1 ~ **a** overlook sth: *La casa da al río.* The house overlooks the river. 2 (golpear) hit sth/sb: *El carro dio contra el árbol.* The car hit the tree. 3 (ataque) have: *Le dio un ataque/de tos.* He had a heart attack/a coughing fit. 4 (hora) be: *¿Ya dieron las dos?* Is it two o'clock yet? 5 (luz) shine: *La luz me daba en los ojos.* The light was shining in my eyes. ● **darse** vp 1 (tomarse) take: *~ un baño* take a bath/shower 2 (golpear) hit: *Se dio con la rodilla en la mesa.* He hit his knee against the table. ▸ ~ **las dos, etc.** strike two, etc.: *Dieron las seis en el reloj.* The clock struck six. **dárselas de** act: *dárselas de listo* act smart ▪ **no doy ni una** I, you, etc. can't do anything right ▪ **NOTA** Para otras expresiones con **dar**, ver el sustantivo, adjetivo, etc., p. ej. **dar la cara** en CARA.

dátil *nm* date

dato *nm* **1** (*información*) information [U]: *un ~ importante* an important piece of information **2 datos** (*Comp*) data [U]: *procesamiento de ~s* data processing ▸ **~s personales** personal details

de *prep*

● **posesión 1** (*de algn*): *el libro de Pedro* Pedro's book ◇ *el perro de mis amigos* my friends' dog ◇ *Es de ella.* It's hers. **2** (*de algo*): *una página del libro* a page of the book ◇ *las habitaciones de la casa* the rooms in the house ◇ *la catedral de Puebla* Puebla cathedral

● **origen, procedencia** from: *Soy de Cali.* I'm from Cali. ◇ *de León a México* from León to Mexico City

● **descripciones de personas 1** (*cualidades físicas*) (a) with: *una niña de pelo rubio* a girl with fair hair (b) (*ropa, colores*) in: *la chica del vestido rojo* the girl in the red dress **2** (*cualidades no físicas*) of: *una persona de carácter* a person of character ◇ *una mujer de 30 años* a woman of 30

● **descripciones de cosas** of: *un vaso de leche* a glass of milk ◇ *un libro de gran interés* a book of great interest ◇ *un vestido de lino* a linen dress

● **tema, asignatura**: *un libro/profesor de física* a physics book/ teacher ◇ *No entiendo de política.* I don't understand about politics.

● **números y expresiones de tiempo**: *más/menos de diez* more/ less than ten ◇ *un billete de $10* a ten dollar bill ◇ *un cuarto de kilo* a quarter of a kilo ◇ *de noche/día* at night/during the day ◇ *a las diez de la mañana* at ten in the morning

● **agente** by: *un libro de Fuentes* a book by Fuentes ◇ *seguido de tres jóvenes* followed by three young people

● **causa**: *morirse de hambre* die of hunger ◇ *saltar de alegría* jump for joy

● **otras construcciones**: *el mejor actor del mundo* the best actor in the world ◇ *de un golpe/trago* with one blow/in one gulp ◇ *¿Qué hay de postre?* What's for dessert? ▸ **de a** (*And*) each: *Tocan de a tres.* There are three each.

debajo *adv* **1** underneath: *Llevo una camiseta ~.* I'm wearing a T-shirt underneath. ◇ *el de ~* the bottom one **2 ~ de** under: *~ de la mesa* under the table ▸ **por ~ de** below *sth*

debate *nm* debate: *hacer un ~* have a debate

deber[1] *vt* **1** + *sustantivo* owe: *Le debo 2.000 pesos/una explicación.* I owe you 2,000 pesos/an explanation. **2** + *inf* (a) (*presente, futuro*) must: *Debes estudiar.* You must study. ◇ *La ley deberá ser anulada.* The law must be abolished. →MUST (b) (*pasado, condicional*) should: *Hace una hora que debías estar aquí.* You should have been here an hour ago. ◇ *No deberías salir.* You shouldn't go out. ▸ **v aux ~ de 1** (*afirmativo*) must: *Ya debe de estar en la casa.* She must be home by now. **2** (*negativo*): *No debe de ser fácil.* It can't be easy. ● **deberse** *vp* be due to *sth*: *Esto se debe a la falta de fondos.* This is due to lack of funds.

deber[2] *nm* duty [*pl* -ies]: *cumplir con un ~* do your duty

debido *adj* proper ▸ **~ a** because of *sth/sb*

débil *adj* weak

debilidad *nf* weakness

debilitar(se) *vt, vi* weaken

década *nf* decade ▸ **la ~ de los ochenta, noventa, etc.** the eighties, nineties, etc. [*pl*]

decadente *adj* decadent

decano/a *nm-nf* dean

decapitar *vt* behead

decena *nf* **1** (*Mat*) ten **2** (*aproximadamente*) about ten: *una ~ de veces* about ten times

decente *adj* decent

decepción *nf* disappointment: *llevarse una ~* be disappointed

decepcionante *adj* disappointing

decepcionar *vt* **1** (*desilusionar*) disappoint: *Me decepcionó la película.* The movie was disappointing. **2** (*fallar*) let *sb* down

decidir(se) *vt, vi, vp* decide: *~ hacer algo* decide to do *sth* ◇ *Nos decidimos por el rojo.* We decided on the red one. ▸ **¡decídete!** make up your mind!

décima *nf* tenth ▸ **tener unas ~s (de fiebre)** have a slight fever

decimal *adj, nm* decimal

décimo/a *adj, pron* tenth

decimotercero/a *adj, pron* thirteenth **NOTA** Para "decimocuarto", "decimoquinto", etc., ver pág. 221

decir¹ *vt* say, tell **NOTA** *Decir* se suele traducir por **say**: —*Es la una, dijo Rosa.* "It's one o'clock," said Rosa. ◇ *¿Qué dijo?* What did he say? Al especificar la persona con la que hablamos, es más común usar **tell**: *Me dijo que llegaría tarde.* He told me he'd be late. ◇ *¿Quién te lo dijo?* Who told you? **Tell** se utiliza también para dar órdenes: *Me dijo que me lavara las manos.* She told me to wash my hands. → SAY. ▸ **digamos...** let's say... **digo...** I mean...: *Cuesta dos, digo tres euros.* It costs two, I mean three, euros. **el qué dirán** what people will say **no me diga (s)!** you don't say! **se dice que...** they say that... **sin ~ nada** without a word **NOTA** Para otras expresiones con **decir**, ver el sustantivo, adjetivo, etc., p. ej. **no decir ni jota** en JOTA.

decir² *nm* saying ▸ **es un ~ you** know what I mean

decisión *nf* **1** decision **2** (*determinación*) determination ▸ **tomar una ~** make/take a decision

decisivo *adj* decisive

declaración *nf* **1** declaration: *una ~ de amor* a declaration of love **2** (*manifestación pública, Jur*) statement: *hacer una ~* make a statement ◇ *La policía le tomó (la) ~.* The police took his statement. ▸ **dar ~** give evidence **~ de (la) renta** tax return

declarar *vt, vi* **1** declare: *¿Algo que ~?* Anything to declare? **2** (*en público*) state: *según declaró el senador* according to the senator's statement **3** (*Jur*) testify ● **declararse** *vp* **1** announce: *~ a favor/en contra de algo* announce (that) you are in favor of/against **2** (*incendio, epidemia*) break out **3** (*confesar amor*): *Se me declaró.* He told me he loved me. ▸ **~se culpable/inocente** plead guilty/not guilty

decodificador *nm* decoder

decodificar *vt* decode

decomisar *vt* seize

decoración *nf* **1** (*acción, adorno*) decoration **2** (*estilo*) décor

decorado *nm* set

decorar *vt* decorate

dedal *nm* thimble

dedicación *nf* dedication

dedicar *vt* **1** devote *sth* to *sth/sb*: *¿A qué dedicas el tiempo libre?* How do you spend your free time? **2** (*canción, poema*) dedicate *sth* (*to sb*) **3** (*libro, etc.*) autograph ● **dedicarse** *vp*: *¿A qué te dedicas?* What do you do for a living? ◇ *Se dedica a las ventas.* He's in marketing.

dedicatoria *nf* dedication

dedillo *nm* ▸ **al ~** by heart

dedo *nm* **1** (*mano*) finger **2** (*pie*) toe ▸ **MY ~ anular/corazón/índice** ring/middle/index finger **~ meñique 1** (*mano*) little finger **2** (*pie*) little toe **~ pulgar/gordo 1** (*mano*) thumb **2** (*pie*) big toe **echar ~** (*And*) hitch-hike **no tener dos ~s de frente** be as dumb as a post, be as thick as two short planks (*GB*)

deducir *vt* **1** (*concluir*) deduce *sth* (*from sth*) **2** (*restar*) deduct *sth* (*from sth*)

defecto *nm* **1** defect: *un ~ en el habla* a speech defect **2** (*moral*) fault **3** (*ropa, etc.*) flaw → MISTAKE ▸ **encontrar/sacar ~s a todo** find fault with everything

defectuoso *adj* faulty

defender *vt* defend *sth/sb* (*against sth/sb*) ● **defenderse** *vp* get by: *No sé mucho pero me defiendo.* I don't know much but I get by.

defendido/a *nm-nf* defendant

defensa *nf* **1** defense: *las ~s del cuerpo* the body's defenses ◇ *un equipo con buena ~* a team with a good defense **2** (*Aut*) bumper ● *nmf* (*Dep*) defender ▸ **en ~ propia** in self-defense

defensivo *adj* defensive ▸ **estar/ponerse a la defensiva** be/go on the defensive

deficiencia *nf* deficiency [*pl* -ies]

deficiente *adj, nmf* mentally deficient **NOTA** Hoy en día es más común decir **mentally ill**.

definición *nf* definition

definir *vt* define

definitivamente *adv* **1** (*para siempre*) for good: *Volvió ~ a su país.* He returned home for good. **2** (*de forma determinante*) definitely

definitivo *adj* final **2** (*solución*) definitive ▸ **en definitiva** in short

deforestación *nf* deforestation

deformado *adj* (*ropa*) out of shape

deformar *vt* **1** (*cuerpo*) deform **2** (*ropa*) pull *sth* out of shape **3** (*imagen, realidad*) distort ●

D

demostrar

deformarse *vp* 1 (*cuerpo*) become deformed 2 (*ropa*) lose its shape

deforme *adj* deformed

defraudar *vt* 1 (*decepcionar*) disappoint 2 (*estafar*) defraud

degeneración *nf* degeneration

degenerado/a *adj, nm-nf* degenerate

degenerar(se) *vi, vp* degenerate

degradar *vt* degrade

dejar *vt* leave: *¿Dónde dejaste las llaves?* Where did you leave the keys? ◊ *¡Déjame en paz!* Leave me alone! 2 (*abandonar*) give sth up: ~ *el trabajo* give up work 3 (*permitir*) let sb (do sth) ● *vi* ~ **de** 1 (*parar*) stop doing sth: *Dejó de llover.* It's stopped raining. 2 (*abandonar una costumbre*) give up doing sth: ~ *de fumar* give up smoking ● *v aux* + **participio**: *La noticia me dejó preocupado.* I was worried by the news. **NOTA** Para expresiones con **dejar**, ver el sustantivo, adjetivo, etc., p. ej. **dejar colgado** en COLGADO.

del Ver DE

delantal *nm* 1 (*cocina*) apron 2 (*de niño*) overall

delante *adv* in front (of sth/sb): *Si no ves la pizarra, ponte ~.* Sit at the front if you can't see the board. ◊ *Me lo contó ~ de otros.* She told me in front of other people. ● ~ **de** *los asientos de* ~ the front seats **hacia** ~ forward

delantero/a *adj* front ● *nm-nf* (*Dep*) forward: *jugar de centro* ~ play center forward ▶ **llevar la delantera** be in the lead

delatar *vt* inform on sb

delegación *nf* 1 (*comisión*) delegation: *una* ~ *de paz* a peace delegation 2 (*Mx, distrito*) district 3 (*Mx, estación de policía*) police station

delegado/a *nm-nf* (*Pol*) delegate

deletrear *vt* spell

delfín *nm* dolphin

delgado *adj* thin, slim **NOTA** Thin es la palabra más general, y se usa para personas, animales o cosas. **Slim** se refiere a una persona delgada y con buen tipo, y **skinny** significa "delgaducho".

deliberado *adj* deliberate

delicadeza *nf* (*tacto*) tact: *Podías haberlo dicho con más* ~. You could have put it more tactfully. ◊ *Es una falta de* ~. It's very tactless. ▶ **tener la** ~ **de** have the courtesy *to do sth*

delicado *adj* delicate

delicioso *adj* delicious ▶ **pasar** ~ (*And*) have a great time

delincuencia *nf* crime ▶ ~ **juvenil** juvenile delinquency

delincuente *nmf* criminal

delineante *nmf* draftsman/woman [*pl* -men/-women]

delinquir *vi* commit an offense

delirar *vi* 1 (*Med*) be delirious 2 (*decir bobadas*) talk nonsense

delito *nm* crime

delta *nm* delta

demanda *nf* 1 (*Com*) demand: *la oferta y la* ~ supply and demand 2 (*Jur*) claim: *presentar/poner una* ~ *por algo* submit a claim for sth

demandar *vt* 1 (*exigir*) demand 2 (*Jur*) sue sb (*for sth*)

demás *adj* other: *los* ~ *niños* (the) other kids ● *pron* (the) others: *Los* ~ *se quedaron en la casa.* The others stayed home. ◊ *ayudar a los* ~ help others ▶ **lo** ~ the rest: *Lo* ~ *no importa.* Nothing else matters. **y** ~ and so on

demasiado *adj* 1 (+ *sustantivo incontable*) too much 2 (+ *sustantivo contable*) too many ● *pron* too much [*pl* too many] ● *adv* 1 (*modificando a un verbo*) too much: *Fumas* ~. You smoke too much. 2 (*modificando a adj o adv*) too: *Vas* ~ *rápido.* You're going too fast.

demo *nf* demo [*pl* -s]

democracia *nf* democracy [*pl* -ies]

demócrata *nmf* democrat

democrático *adj* democratic

demonio *nm* 1 (*diablo*) devil 2 (*espíritu*) demon 3 (*niño*) little devil ▶ **¿cómo, dónde...** ~**s?** how, where, etc. on earth? **de mil/de todos los** ~**s**: *Hace un frío de mil* ~. It's freezing. **saber a** ~**s** taste foul

demorar *vt* 1 (*tardar*) take (time) *to do sth*: *La operación demoró una hora.* The operation took an hour. 2 (*retrasar*) hold sth/sb up ● **demorarse** *vp*: *No te demores.* Don't be long. ◊ *¡Cómo te demoras!* You're taking a long time! ◊ *Se demoró mucho en contestar.* It took him a long time to reply. ◊ *Eso no se demora nada.* It won't take a minute. ▶ **no** ~ **en...**: *¡Rápido, que no demora en llegar el avión!* Quick! The plane will be here soon. **se demora... in** *it takes...*: *En tren se demora dos horas.* It takes two hours by train.

demostrar *vt* 1 (*probar*) prove 2 (*mostrar*) show

denegar vt refuse

densidad nf 1 density [pl -ies] 2 (niebla) thickness

denso adj dense

dentadura nf teeth [pl]: ~ postiza false teeth

dentífrico nm toothpaste

dentista nmf dentist

dentro adv 1 in, inside: El gato está ~. The cat is inside. ◇ allá/acá ~. in there/here 2 (edificio) indoors: quedarse ~ stay indoors 3 ~ de in: ~ del sobre in/inside the envelope ◇ ~ de un rato/mes in a little while/in a month's time ▸ **de/desde ~** from (the) inside ▸ **de lo que cabe** all things considered ▸ **de nada** very soon ▸ **hacia ~** in: Mete la panza hacia ~. Pull your tummy in. ▸ **por ~** (on the) inside: pintado por ~ painted on the inside

denuncia nf 1 (accidente, delito) report: presentar una ~ report sth to the police 2 (contra una persona) complaint: presentar una ~ contra algn make a formal complaint against sb

denunciar vt 1 report sth/sb (to sb) 2 (criticar) denounce

departamento nm 1 (sección) department 2 (apartamento) apartment, flat (GB)

depender vi 1 ~ (de que/de que/de si...) depend on sth/on whether...: Depende del tiempo que haga. It depends on the weather. ◇ Depende de que me traigas el dinero. It depends on whether you bring me the money. 2 ~ **de algn (que...)** be up to sb (whether...): Depende de mi jefe que pueda tener un día libre. It's up to my boss whether I can have a day off. 3 ~ **de** (económicamente) be dependent on sth/sb

dependiente/a nm-nf sales clerk, shop assistant (GB)

depilar(se) vt, vp 1 (cejas) pluck 2 (piernas, axilas) (a) (con cera) wax: Me tengo que ~. I must have my legs waxed. (b) (con máquina) shave

deporte nm sport: ¿Practica algún ~? Do you play any sports? **NOTA** En inglés se utilizan tres verbos al hablar de deportes. Para los deportes con pelota, se usa play, p. ej. play soccer/tennis. Con aerobics, athletics, judo etc. se dice do, p. ej. do karate, y para los deportes como natación, ciclismo, etc., se usa go. p. ej. go swimming, cycling, etc. ▸ **hacer ~** get some exercise

deportista nmf sportsman/woman [pl -men/-women] ● adj athletic

deportivo adj 1 sports: club ~ sports club 2 (conducta) sporting: una conducta poco deportiva unsporting behavior ● nm (carro) sports car

depósito nm 1 (Fin, Geol, Quím) deposit 2 (almacén) warehouse ▸ ~ **de cadáveres** morgue

depresión nf depression

deprimente adj depressing

deprimir vt depress ● **deprimirse** vp get depressed

deprisa adv quickly ● interj hurry up!

derecha nf 1 right: Siga por/Voltee a la ~. Keep/turn right. ◇ la casa de la ~ the house on the right 2 **la Derecha** (Pol) the Right 3 (mano) right hand: escribir con la ~ be right-handed 4 (pie) right foot ▸ **de ~** (Pol) right-wing

derecho adj 1 (diestro) right 2 (recto) straight: Póngase ~. Sit up straight. 3 (erguido) upright ● adv straight: Vete ~ a la casa. Go straight home. ◇ Siga ~ hasta el final de la calle. Go straight on to the end of the road. ● nm 1 (anverso) right side 2 (facultad legal o moral) right: ¿Con qué ~ entras? What right do you have to come in? ◇ los ~s humanos human rights ◇ el ~ de voto the right to vote 3 (estudios) law ▸ **en su ~** within my, your, etc. rights **¡no hay ~!** it's not fair!

deriva nf ▸ **a la ~** adrift

derivar(se) vi, vp 1 (palabra, etc.) derive from sth 2 (proceder) stem from sth

derramamiento nm ▸ ~ **de sangre** bloodshed

derramar(se) vt, vp spill ▸ ~ **sangre/lágrimas** shed blood/tears

derrame nm hemorrhage

derrapar vi skid

derretir(se) vt, vp melt

derribar vt 1 (edificio) demolish 2 (puerta) batter sth down 3 (persona) knock sb down 4 (avión, pájaro) bring sth down

derrochador/a adj wasteful ● nm-nf squanderer

derrochar vt 1 (dinero) squander 2 (rebosar) be bursting with sth

derrota nf defeat

derrotar vt defeat

derruir vt demolish

derrumbar vt demolish ● **derrumbarse** vp collapse

derrumbe (*tb* **derrumbamiento**) *nm* **1** (*hundimiento*) collapse **2** (*demolición*) demolition

desabrigado *adj*: *Vas muy ~.* You're not very warmly dressed.

desabrochar *vt* undo: *Me desabroché la blusa.* I undid my blouse. ● **desabrocharse** *vp* come undone

desactivar *vt* defuse

desafiar *vi* **1** (*retar*) challenge *sb* (*to sth*) **2** (*peligro*) brave

desafilado *adj* blunt

desafinado *adj* out of tune

desafinar *vi* **1** (*cantando*) sing out of tune **2** (*instrumento*) be out of tune **3** (*instrumentista*) play out of tune

desafío *nm* challenge

desafortunado *adj* unfortunate

desagradable *adj* unpleasant

desagradar *vi* dislike *sth*: *No me desagrada.* I don't dislike it.

desagradecido *adj* ungrateful

desagüe *nm* waste pipe

desahogarse *vp* **1** let off steam **2** ~ **con algn** confide in sb

desalentador *adj* discouraging

desaliñado *adj* scruffy

desalmado *adj* heartless

desalojar *vt* clear

desamarrar(se) = DESATAR

desamparado *adj* helpless

desangrarse *vp* bleed to death

desanimado *adj* (*deprimido*) depressed

desanimar *vt* discourage ● **desanimarse** *vp* lose heart

desaparecer *vi* disappear ▸ ~ **del mapa** vanish off the face of the earth

desaparición *nf* disappearance

desapegado = DESPEGADO(2)

desapercibido *adj* unnoticed: *pasar* ~ go unnoticed

desaprovechar *vt* waste

desarmador *nm* (*Mx*) screwdriver

desarmar *vt* **1** (*persona, ejército*) disarm **2** (*desmontar*) take *sth* to pieces

desarme *nm* disarmament

desarrollado *adj* developed ▸ **poco** ~ undeveloped

desarrollar(se) *vt*, *vp* develop

desarrollo *nm* development

desastre *nm* disaster

desastroso *adj* disastrous

desatar *vt* (*nudo, cuerda, animal*) untie ● **desatarse** *vp* **1** (*animal*) get loose **2** (*paquete, cuerda*) come undone: *Se me desató el zapato.* One of my laces has come undone.

desatascar *vt* unblock

desatender *vt* (*descuidar*) neglect

desatornillar *vt* unscrew

desatrancar *vt* **1** (*desatascar*) unblock **2** (*puerta*) unbolt

desautorizado *adj* unauthorized

desayunar *vi* have breakfast: *antes de* ~ before breakfast ● *vt* have *sth* for breakfast: *¿Qué quieres* ~? What would you like for breakfast?

desayuno *nm* breakfast: *¿Le preparo el* ~? Can I get you some breakfast?

desbandada *nf* ▸ **salir en** ~ scatter in all directions

desbarajuste *nm* mess: *¡Qué* ~! What a mess!

desbaratar *vt* **1** (*planes, papeles, etc.*) mess *sth* up **2** (*Mx, nudo, tejido*) undo **3** (*destrozar*) ruin

desbocado *adj* (*caballo*) runaway

desbocarse *vp* (*caballo*) bolt

desbordamiento *nm* flood

desbordar *vt*: *La basura desbordaba la bolsa.* The bag is overflowing with trash. ● **desbordarse** *vp* (*río*) burst its banks

descafeinado *adj* decaffeinated

descalificación *nf* (*Dep*) disqualification

descalificar *vt* (*Dep*) disqualify

descalzarse *vp* take your shoes off

descalzo *adj* barefoot: *andar* ~ walk barefoot ◇ *No andes* ~. Don't go around in your bare feet.

descampado *nm* area of open ground

descansado *adj* refreshed

descansar *vt*, *vi* rest (*sth*) (*on sth*): ~ *la vista* rest your eyes ● *vi* take a break: *Descansemos un rato.* Let's have a break for a while. ▸ **¡que descanse(s)!** have a good rest!

descansillo *nm* landing

descanso *nm* **1** (*reposo*) rest **2** (*en el trabajo*) break: *trabajar sin* ~ work without a break

descapotable *adj*, *nm* convertible

descarado *adj* impudent

descarga *nf* **1** (*mercancía*) unloading **2** (*Elec*) discharge

descargado *adj* (*pila, batería*) dead, flat (*GB*)

descargar *vt* unload: ~ *un camión/una pistola* unload a truck/gun ● **descargarse** *vp* (*pila, batería*) go dead, go flat (*GB*)

descaro *nm* nerve

descarriarse *vp* go off the straight and narrow

descarrilamiento *nm* derailment

descarriarse *vp* be derailed

descartar *vt* rule sth/sb out

descendencia *nf* descendants [*pl*]

descender *vi* 1 (*ir/venir abajo*) go/come down 2 (*temperatura, precios, nivel*) fall 3 ~ **de** (*familia*) be descended from sb 4 (*Dep*) be relegated

descendiente *nmf* descendant

descenso *nm* 1 (*bajada*) descent 2 (*temperatura*) drop *in sth* 3 (*precios*) fall *in sth* 4 (*Dep*) relegation

deschavetado *adj* crazy

descifrar *vt* 1 (*mensaje*) decode 2 (*escritura*) decipher 3 (*enigma*) solve

descolgado *adj* (*teléfono*) off the hook

descolgar *vt* 1 (*algo colgado*) take sth down 2 (*teléfono*) pick sth up

descolorido *adj* faded

descomponer *vt* 1 break sth down (*into sth*) 2 (*aparato, máquina*) break ● **descomponer(se)** *vt, vp* (*pudrirse*) rot

descompuesto *adj* ▸ **estar ~** be out of order

desconcertado *adj* ▸ **estar/quedar ~** be taken aback: *Quedó ~ ante mi negativa.* He was taken aback by my refusal.

desconcertar *vt* disconcert

desconectar *vt* 1 disconnect 2 (*apagar*) turn sth off 3 (*desenchufar*) unplug ● **desconectarse** *vp* 1 (*aparato*) switch off 2 (*persona*) cut yourself off (*from sth/sb*)

desconfiado *adj* wary

desconfiar *vi* not trust sth/sb: *Desconfía hasta de su sombra.* He doesn't trust anyone.

descongelar *vt* (*refrigerador, alimento*) defrost

desconocer *vt* not know: *Desconozco el porqué.* I don't know the reason why.

desconocido/a *adj* unknown ● *nm-nf* stranger

desconsiderado *adj* inconsiderate

descontado *adj* ▸ **dar por ~ que...** take it for granted that...

descontar *vt* 1 (*hacer descuento*) give a discount (*on sth*): ~ *el 10% en algo* give a 10% discount on sth 2 (*restar*) deduct 3 (*no contar*) not count: *Si descontar-*

mos *las vacaciones...* If we don't count the vacation...

descontento *adj* dissatisfied (*with sth/sb*)

descorchar *vt* uncork

descortés *adj* rude

descoser *vt* unpick ● **descoserse** *vp* come apart at the seams

describir *vt* describe

descripción *nf* description

descuartizar *vt* 1 (*carnicero*) carve sth up 2 (*asesino*) chop sth/sb up

descubierto *adj* uncovered: *el pecho ~* bare-chested ◊ *un vestido con la espalda descubierta* a backless dress ▸ **al ~** (*al aire libre*) in the open air

descubridor/a *nm-nf* discoverer

descubrimiento *nm* discovery [*pl* -ies]

descubrir *vt* 1 (*encontrar, darse cuenta*) discover 2 (*averiguar*) find sth (out) 3 (*estatua, placa*) unveil ▸ **se descubrió todo** (*el asunto*) it all came out

descuento *nm* discount: *Me hicieron un 5% de ~.* They gave me a five percent discount. ◊ *Son 5.000 menos el ~.* It's 5,000 before the discount.

descuidado *adj* 1 (*desatendido*) neglected 2 (*poco cuidadoso*) careless 3 (*persona*) scruffy

descuidar *vt* neglect ● **descuidarse** *vp*: *Si me descuido, pierdo el tren.* I nearly missed the train.

descuido *nm*: *El accidente ocurrió por un ~ del conductor.* The driver lost his concentration and caused an accident. ◊ *El perro se le escapó en un ~.* The dog ran off while he wasn't paying attention.

desde *prep* 1 (*tiempo*) since: *Vivo aquí ~ 1986.* I've been living here since 1986. →**FROM** 2 (*lugar, cantidad*) from: ~ *abajo* from below ◊ ~ *acá se ve la playa.* You can see the beach from here. ▸ **desde... hasta...** from... to...: *desde el 8 hasta el 15* from the 8th to the 15th

desear *vt* 1 (*suerte*) wish sb sth: *Te deseo suerte.* I wish you luck. 2 (*anhelar*) wish for sth

desechable *adj* disposable

desembarcar *vt* 1 (*mercancía*) unload 2 (*persona*) set sb ashore ● *vi* disembark

desembocadura *nf* 1 (*río*) mouth 2 (*calle*) end

desembocar *vi* ~ **en** 1 (*río*) flow into sth 2 (*calle, túnel*) lead to sth

desembolsar *vt* pay sth (out)

desempacar vt unpack

desempatar vi 1 (Dep) break a tie, play off [pl -offs] (GB) 2 (Pol) break the deadlock

desempate nm tiebreaker, play-off (GB)

desempeñar vt 1 (cargo) hold 2 (papel) play

desempleado/a adj, nm-nf unemployed: los ~s the unemployed

desempleo nm unemployment

desencajado adj 1 (cara) contorted 2 (hueso) dislocated

desenchufar vt unplug

desenfadado adj 1 (informal) casual 2 (sin inhibiciones) uninhibited

desenfocado adj out of focus

desenfundar vt pull sth out

desenganchar vt unhook • **desengancharse** vp (droga) come off drugs

desengaño nm disappointment ▶ **llevarse/sufrir un ~ amoroso** be disappointed in love

desenredarse vp ~ **el pelo** get the tangles out of your hair

desenrollar(se) vt, vp 1 (papel) unroll 2 (cable) unwind

desenroscar vt unscrew

desenterrar vt dig sth up

desentonar vi clash (with sth)

desenvolver vt unwrap • **desenvolverse** vp get along: Se desenvuelve bien en el trabajo. He's getting along well at work.

deseo nm wish: Pida un ~. Make a wish.

desértico adj 1 (zona) desert: un terreno ~ desert terrain 2 (clima) arid

desertificación nf desertification

desertor/a nm-nf deserter

desesperación nf (tb desespero nm) despair: para ~ mía to my despair

desesperado adj 1 desperate: Estoy ~ por verla. I'm desperate to see her. 2 (situación, caso) hopeless ▶ **a la desesperada** in desperation

desesperar vt drive sb crazy • vi despair (of sth): ¡No desesperes! Don't despair! • **desesperarse** vp become exasperated

desfasado adj out of date

desfavorable adj unfavorable

desfigurar vt 1 (persona) disfigure 2 (imagen, hechos, etc.) distort

desfiladero nm gorge

desfilar vi 1 march 2 (modelos) parade

desfile nm parade ▶ ~ **de modas** fashion show

desgarrar(se) vt, vp tear

desgastar(se) vt, vp 1 (ropa, zapatos) wear (sth) out: Se me desgastó el suéter por los codos. My sweater's worn at the elbows. 2 (rocas) wear (sth) away, erode (más fml)

desgaste nm 1 (por uso) wear: Esta alfombra sufre mucho ~. This rug gets very heavy wear. 2 (rocas) erosion

desgracia nf misfortune ▶ **por ~** unfortunately **tener la ~ de** be unlucky enough to do sth

desgraciado/a adj 1 (sin suerte) unlucky 2 (infeliz) unhappy • nm-nf 1 (pobre) wretch 2 (mala persona) swine

deshabitado adj deserted

deshacer vt 1 (nudo, paquete) undo 2 (desmontar) take sth apart 3 (cama) strip 4 (derretir) melt • **deshacerse** vp 1 (nudo, costura) come undone 2 (derretirse) melt 3 ~ **de** get rid of sth/sb

deshelar(se) (tb deshielar(se)) vt, vp thaw

deshinchar vt = DESINFLAR • **deshincharse** vp go down: Ya se me deshinchó el tobillo. The swelling in my ankle has gone down.

deshonesto adj dishonest

desierto adj deserted • nm desert

designar vt 1 (persona) appoint sb (sth/to sth): Fue designado (como) presidente/para el puesto. He was appointed chairman/to the post. 2 (sitio) designate sth (as sth)

desigual adj (irregular) uneven

desigualdad nf inequality [pl -ies]

desilusión nf disappointment ▶ **llevarse una ~** be disappointed

desilusionar vt disappoint

desinfectante nm disinfectant

desinfectar vt disinfect

desinflar vt let the air out of sth • **desinflarse** vp (objeto inflado) deflate

desinhibirse vp let your hair down

desintegración nf disintegration

desintegrarse vp disintegrate

desinterés nm lack of interest

desistir vi ~ **(de)** give up (doing sth)

desleal adj disloyal

deslizador nm (playa) surfboard

deslizamiento nm ▶ ~ **de tierra(s)** landslide

deslizar vt 1 slide 2 (con disimulo) slip: ~ la carta en el bolsillo slip the letter into your pocket ● **deslizarse** vp slide

deslumbrante adj dazzling

deslumbrar vt dazzle

desmantelar vt dismantle

desmaquillador adj ▶ **crema/loción desmaquilladora** make-up remover

desmayarse vp faint

desmayo nm fainting fit ▶ **darle a algn un ~** faint

desmedido adj excessive

desmejorado adj: Lo encontré un poco ~. He wasn't looking too well. ◊ Está muy ~ últimamente. He's gone rapidly downhill recently.

desmentir vt deny

desmenuzar vt 1 break sth into small pieces 2 (pan, galletas) crumble sth (up)

desmontar vt 1 take sth apart 2 (andamio, estantería, tienda de campaña) take sth down ● vi (caballo) dismount

desmoralizarse vp lose heart

desnivel nm: el ~ entre casa y jardín the difference in level between house and garden

desnivelado adj not level

desnudar(se) vt, vp undress

desnudo adj 1 (persona) naked: medio ~ half-naked 2 (parte del cuerpo, vacío) bare: brazos ~s/ paredes desnudas bare arms/ walls →NAKED

desnutrido adj undernourished

desobedecer vt disobey

desobediencia nf disobedience

desobediente adj, nmf disobedient: ¡Eres una ~! You're a very disobedient girl!

desodorante nm deodorant

desolador adj devastating

desolar vt devastate: La noticia nos desoló. We were devastated by the news.

desorden nm mess: Tenía la casa en ~. The house was (in) a mess.

desordenado/a adj, nm-nf messy: ¡Eres un ~! You're so messy! ▶ **dejar algo ~** mess sth up

desordenar vt mess sth up: Me desordenaste el armario. You've made a mess of my closet.

desorganizado/a adj, nm-nf disorganized: Soy un ~. I'm disorganized.

desorganizar vt 1 disrupt 2 (desordenar) mess sth up

desorientar vt (desconcertar) confuse ● **desorientarse** vp get disoriented: Me desorienté. I'm lost.

despachar vt 1 (atender) serve 2 (solucionar) settle 3 (librarse de algn) get rid of sb

despacho nm 1 (oficina) office 2 (en casa) study [pl -ies]

despacio adv 1 (lentamente) slowly 2 (largo y tendido) at length ● interj slow down

despampanante adj stunning

despatarrarse vp sprawl

despectivo adj 1 (tono, etc.) disparaging 2 (término) pejorative

despedida nf 1 goodbye, farewell (más fml): cena de ~ farewell dinner 2 (celebración) leaving party [pl -ies] ▶ **~ de soltero/a** bachelor party [pl -ies], stag/hen night (GB)

despedir vt 1 (decir adiós) see sb off 2 (empleado) fire 3 (calor, luz, olor) give sth off ● **despedirse** vp say goodbye (to sth/sb)

despegado adj 1 (separado) unstuck 2 (persona) distant

despegar vt pull sth off ● vi (avión) take off ● **despegarse** vp come off

despegue nm take-off [pl -offs]

despeinado adj messy: Estás ~. Your hair's messy.

despeinar(se) vt, vp mess sb's/ your hair up

despejado adj clear: un cielo ~/ una mente despejada a clear sky/ mind

despejar vt clear ● vi (cielo) clear up ● **despejarse** vp 1 (nubes) clear 2 (despertarse) wake up

despensa nf pantry

desperdiciar vt waste

desperdicio nm 1 waste 2 **desperdicios** scraps

desperezarse vp stretch

desperfecto nm 1 (deterioro) damage [U] 2 (imperfección) flaw

despertador nm alarm (clock): poner el ~ set the alarm

despertar vt 1 (persona) wake sb up 2 (interés, sospecha) arouse ● **despertar(se)** vi, vp wake up ▶ **tener (un) buen/mal ~** wake up in a good/bad mood

despido nm dismissal

despierto adj 1 (no dormido) awake 2 (espabilado) bright

despistado adj 1 (por naturaleza) absent-minded 2 (distraído) miles away: Iba ~. I was miles away. ▶ **hacerse el ~**: Nos vio pero se hizo el ~. He saw us but pretended not to.

despistar vt 1 (desorientar) confuse 2 (a un perseguidor) shake sb off

despiste nm absent-mindedness [U]: ¡Qué ~ el suyo! He's so absent-minded!

desplazado adj out of place

desplazar vt (sustituir) take the place of sth/sb ● **desplazarse** vp go: ~ en taxi go by taxi

desplegar vt 1 (mapa, papel) unfold 2 (velas) unfurl 3 (tropas, etc.) deploy

despliegue nm deployment

desplomarse vp collapse

despoblación nf depopulation

despoblado adj (sin habitantes) uninhabited

déspota nmf tyrant

despreciable adj despicable

despreciar vt 1 (menospreciar) look down on sb 2 (rechazar) reject

desprecio nm contempt (for sth/sb)

desprender vt 1 (separar) take sth off 2 (emanar) give sth off ● **desprenderse** vp 1 (separarse) come off 2 ~ de get rid of sth

desprendimiento nm ▸ ~ de tie-rra(s) landslide

desprestigiar vt discredit

desprevenido adj ▸ agarrar/pillar ~ catch sb unawares

desproporcionado adj dispro-portionate (to sth)

desprovisto adj lacking in sth

después adv 1 (más tarde) after-ward(s), later (más coloq): Vino poco ~. He came shortly after-ward(s). ◇ Si estudias ahora, ~ puedes ver la tele. If you do your homework now, you can watch TV later. 2 (a continua-ción) next: ¿Qué pasó ~? What happened next? ▸ ~ de after sth: ~ de hablar con él after talking to him ◇ El café está ~ del banco. The cafe is after the bank. ~ de que when: ~ de que acabes, pon la mesa. When you've finished, set the table. ~ de todo after all

despuntar vi 1 (alba, día) break 2 (plantas) bud 3 (persona) stand out

destacar vi point sth out ● **desta-car(se)** vi, vp stand out: El rojo destaca sobre el verde. Red stands out against green.

destapador nm bottle-opener

destapar vt 1 (quitar la tapa) take the lid off sth 2 (en cama) pull the covers off sb ● **destaparse** vp (en cama) throw the covers off

destaponar(se) vt, vp unblock

destartalado adj dilapidated

destemplar vt 1 (dientes) set sb's teeth on edge 2 (aflojar) loosen ●

destemplarse vp (Mús) go out of tune: Se destiempla cada vez que canta. She always sings out of tune. ▸ ~se los dientes: Se me destiemplan los dientes comiendo mango verde. Eating green man-goes sets my teeth on edge.

destender vt ▸ ~ la cama (para acostarse) pull the covers back

desteñir(se) vt, vp fade ● vi fade: Esa camisa roja destiñe. The color runs in that red shirt.

destinar vt (persona) post

destinatario/a nm-nf addressee

destino nm 1 (sino) fate 2 (avión, tren, etc., pasajero) destination 3 (lugar de trabajo): Me van a cambiar de ~. I'm going to be transferred somewhere else. ▸ con ~ a... for...: el ferry con ~ a Cozumel the ferry for Cozumel

destornillador nm screwdriver

destrozado adj (abatido) devas-tated (at/by sth)

destrozar vt 1 destroy 2 (hacer trozos) smash 3 (arruinar) ruin

destrucción nf destruction

destructivo adj destructive

destructor nm (Náut) destroyer

destruir vt destroy

desvalido adj helpless

desvalijar vt 1 (casa, etc.) ran-sack 2 (posesiones): Me desvali-jaron el carro. Everything was stolen from my car. 3 (persona) rob sb of all they have

desván nm loft

desvanecerse vp 1 (desmayarse) faint 2 (desaparecer) disappear

desvariar vi 1 (delirar) be deliri-ous 2 (decir disparates) talk non-sense

desvelar vt 1 (espabilar) keep sb awake 2 (revelar) reveal ● **des-velarse** vp 1 (espabilarse) wake up 2 (desvivirse) do your utmost for sb

desventaja nf disadvantage ▸ en ~ at a disadvantage

desvergonzado adj 1 (que no tiene vergüenza) shameless: ser un ~ have no shame 2 (insolente) impudent

desvestir vt undress ● **desvestir-se** vp get undressed

desviación nf 1 (tráfico) detour 2 (irregularidad) deviation (from sth)

desviar vt divert: ~ el tráfico/los fondos de una sociedad divert traffic/company funds ● **desviar-se** vp 1 (carretera) branch off 2 (carro) turn off ▸ ~ la mirada avert your eyes ~se del tema wander off the subject

desvío nm detour

desvivirse vp live for sth/sb: Se desviven por sus hijos. They live for their children.

detalladamente adv in detail

detallado adj detailed

detallar vt 1 (contar con detalle) give details of sth 2 (especificar) specify

detalle nm 1 (pormenor) detail 2 (atención) gesture ▸ ¡qué ~! how thoughtful! tener muchos ~s (con algn) be very considerate (to sb)

detallista adj thoughtful

detectar vt detect

detective nmf detective

detector nm detector: un ~ de mentiras/metales a lie/metal detector

detención nf 1 (arresto) arrest 2 (paralización) halt: La falta de material motivó la ~ de las obras. Lack of materials brought the building work to a halt.

detener vt 1 stop 2 (arrestar) arrest ● **detenerse** vp stop

detenidamente adv carefully

detenido/a adj: estar/quedar ~ be under arrest ● nm-nf detainee

detergente nm detergent

deteriorar vt damage ● **deteriorarse** vp deteriorate

determinado/a adj 1 (cierto) certain: en ~s casos in certain cases 2 (artículo) definite

determinar vt determine

detestar vt detest

detrás adv 1 behind: Los otros vienen ~. The others are coming behind. 2 (atrás) at/on the back: El mercado/precio está ~. The market is at the back./The price is at the back. ▸ ~ de 1 behind 2 (después de) after: Fuma un cigarrillo ~ de otro. He smokes one cigarette after another. **estar ~ de algn** be after sb **por ~** from behind

deuda nf debt ▸ **tener una ~** be in debt (to sth/sb)

devaluar vt devalue

devastador adj devastating

devolución nf 1 (artículo) return 2 (dinero) refund

devolver vt 1 return sth (to sth/sb) 2 (dinero) refund: Se le devolverá el importe. You will have your money refunded. 3 (vomitar) bring sth up

devorar vt devour

devoto adj (piadoso) devout

devuelta nf (And) change: Quédese con la ~. Keep the change.

día nm 1 day: al ~ siguiente the following day 2 (fechas): Llegó el ~ 3 de mayo. He arrived on 3 May. →MAYO 1 al/por ~ a day: dos veces al ~ twice a day ¡buenos ~s! good morning! **dar los buenos ~s** say good morning **de ~/durante el ~** in/during the daytime **Día de la madre/del padre** Mother's/Father's Day **Día de los enamorados** Valentine's Day **Día de los inocentes** April Fool's Day **NOTA** En EE.UU. y Gran Bretaña el equivalente de este día es April Fool's Day, el 1 de abril. **Día de los Muertos/Todos los Santos** All Saints' Day →HALLOWEEN **Día de (los) Reyes (Magos)** January 6 **Día de Navidad** Christmas Day → NAVIDAD **~ libre 1** (no ocupado) free day 2 (sin ir a trabajar) day off **~ de mañana** in the future **estar al ~** be up to date **hacer buen ~** be a nice day **hacerse de ~** get light **poner al ~** bring sth/sb up to date **ser de ~** be light **todos los ~s** every day →EVERYDAY

diabetes nf diabetes [U]

diabético/a adj, nm-nf diabetic

diablo nm devil

diadema nf Alice band

diagnóstico nm diagnosis [pl -noses]

diagonal adj, nf diagonal

diagrama nm diagram

dialecto nm dialect

diálogo nm conversation

diamante nm 1 (piedra) diamond 2 diamantes (cartas) diamonds →BARAJA

diámetro nm diameter

diapositiva nf slide: una ~ en color a color slide

diariamente adv every day

diario adj daily ● nm 1 (periódico) newspaper 2 (personal) diary [pl -ies] ▸ **a ~** every day **de/para ~** everyday: ropa de ~ everyday clothes →EVERYDAY

diarrea nf diarrhea [U]

dibujante nmf 1 draftsman/woman [pl -men/-women] 2 (humor) cartoonist

dibujar vt draw

dibujo nm 1 (Arte) drawing: estudiar ~ study drawing ◊ un ~ a drawing 2 (motivo) pattern ▸ ~ lineal technical drawing **~s animados** cartoons

diccionario nm dictionary [pl -ies]

dicho adj that [pl those]: ~ año that year ● nm (refrán) saying ▸ ~ de otra forma/manera in

D

other words **~ y hecho** no sooner said than done

diciembre nm December (abrev Dec.) →MAYO

dictado nm dictation

dictador/a nm-nf dictator

dictadura nf dictatorship

dictar vt, vi dictate ▶ **~ clase** teach **~ sentencia** pass sentence

diecinueve adj, nm, pron **1** nineteen **2** (fecha) nineteenth

dieciocho adj, nm, pron **1** eighteen **2** (fecha) eighteenth

dieciséis adj, nm, pron **1** sixteen **2** (fecha) sixteenth

diecisiete adj, nm, pron **1** seventeen **2** (fecha) seventeenth

diente nm tooth [pl teeth] → MY ▶ **~ de ajo** clove of garlic **~ de leche** milk tooth [pl milk teeth]

diesel nm (motor) diesel engine

diestro adj (persona) right-handed ▶ **a diestra y siniestra** left, right and center

dieta nf diet: estar a ~ be on a diet

dietético adj (refresco, etc.) diet →LOW-CALORIE

diez adj, nm, pron **1** ten **2** (fecha) tenth ▶ **sacar un ~** get top grades/marks (GB)

difamar vt **1** (de palabra) slander **2** (por escrito) libel

diferencia nf difference: Venezuela tiene una hora de ~ con Colombia. There's an hour's difference between Venezuela and Colombia. ◇ No hay ~ de precio. There's no difference in price. ◇ ~ de opiniones difference of opinion ▶ **a ~ de** unlike **con ~** by far: Es el mejor con ~. It's by far the best.

diferenciar vt differentiate sth (from sth) ● **diferenciarse** vp: No se diferencian en nada. There's no difference between them. ◇ ¿En qué se diferencia? What's the difference?

diferente adj different (from sth/sb) ● adv differently: Pensamos ~. We think differently.

diferido adj ▶ **en ~** pre-recorded

difícil adj difficult

dificultad nf difficulty [pl -ies]

difuminar vt blur

difundir vt **1** (Radio, TV) broadcast **2** (publicar) publish **3** (oralmente) spread ● **difundirse** vp (noticia, luz) spread

difunto/a adj late: el ~ presidente the late president ● nm-nf deceased: los familiares del ~ the family of the deceased

difusión nf **1** (ideas) dissemination **2** (programas) broadcasting **3** (diario, etc.) circulation

digerir vt digest

digestión nf digestion ▶ **hacer la ~**: Todavía estoy haciendo la ~. I just ate. ◇ Hay que hacer la ~ antes de nadar. You shouldn't go swimming right after meals.

digestivo adj digestive

digital adj digital

dignarse vp deign to do sth

dignidad nf dignity

digno adj **1** decent: un trabajo ~ a decent job **2** **~ de** worthy of sth: ~ de atención worthy of attention ▶ **~ de confianza** reliable

dije nm charm

dilatar(se) vt, vp **1** (ampliar) expand **2** (poros, pupilas) dilate

dilema nm dilemma

diluir(se) vt, vp **1** (sólido) dissolve **2** (líquido) dilute

diluvio nm flood ▶ **el ~ Universal** the Flood

dimensión nf dimension ▶ **de grandes/enormes dimensiones** huge

diminutivo adj, nm diminutive

diminuto adj tiny

dimisión nf resignation: Presentó su ~. He handed in his resignation.

dimitir vi resign (from sth)

Dinamarca nf Denmark

dinámico adj dynamic ● **dinámica** nf dynamics [sing]

dinamita nf dynamite

dínamo (tb **dinamo**) nf dynamo [pl -s]

dinastía nf dynasty [pl -ies]

dineral nm fortune

dinero nm money [U]: ¿Tienes ~? Do you have any money?

dinosaurio nm dinosaur

dioptría nf: ¿Cuántas ~s tienes? How strong are your glasses?

dios nm god ▶ **como D~ manda** right: un carro como ~ manda a real car ◇ hacer algo como ~ manda do sth right **¡D~ me libre!** God forbid! **¡D~ mío!** my God! **D~ sabe/sabrá** D~ God knows **¡por (amor de) D~!** for God's sake!

diosa nf goddess

dióxido nm dioxide: ~ de carbono carbon dioxide

diploma nm **1** diploma **2** (universidad) degree certificate

diplomacia nf diplomacy

diplomático/a adj diplomatic ● nm-nf diplomat

diputado/a nm-nf deputy [pl -ies], congressman [fem congresswoman]

dique nm dyke ▶ ~ **seco** dry dock

dirección nf 1 (rumbo) direction: Iba en ~ contraria. I was going in the opposite direction. ◊ salir con ~ al sur set off for the south 2 (datos) address

direccional nf (vehículo) turn signal, indicator (GB) ▶ poner las ~es signal

directamente adv (derecho) straight: volver ~ go straight back

directivo/a adj management: el equipo ~ the management team ● nm-nf director

directo adj direct ▶ en ~ live: una transmisión en ~ a live broadcast

director/a nm-nf 1 director 2 (colegio) principal 3 (banco) manager 4 (Period) editor 5 (orquesta) conductor ▶ ~ **gerente** chief executive officer (abrev CEO), managing director (GB)

directorio nm telephone directory [pl -ies]

dirigente adj (Pol) ruling ● nmf 1 (Pol) leader: máximo ~ leader 2 (empresa) manager

dirigir vt 1 (Cine, Teat, tráfico) direct 2 (carta, mensaje) address sth to sth/sb 3 (arma, manguera, telescopio) point sth at sth/sb 4 (debate, campaña, expedición, partido) lead 5 (negocio) run ● **dirigirse** vp 1 (ir) head for...: ~ hacia la ciudad head for town 2 (hablar) speak to sb 3 (por carta) write to sb

discapacitado/a adj, nm-nf disabled: los ~s the disabled

disciplina nf 1 discipline 2 (asignatura) subject

discípulo/a nm-nf disciple

disc jockey nmf disc jockey (abrev DJ)

disco nm 1 (Mús) record: grabar/poner un ~ make/play a record 2 (Comp) disk: el ~ duro the hard disk 3 (Dep) discus 4 (objeto circular) disc ▶ ~ **compacto** compact CD

discográfico adj record: un sello ~ a record label

discoteca nf club

discreción nf discretion

discreto adj 1 (persona) discreet 2 (mediocre) modest

discriminación nf discrimination (against sb): la ~ racial/de la mujer racial discrimination/discrimination against women

discriminar vt discriminate against sb

disculpa nf 1 (excusa) excuse: Esto no tiene ~. There's no excuse for this. 2 (pidiendo perdón) apology [pl -ies]

disculpar vt forgive: Disculpa que llegue tarde. Sorry I'm late. ● **disculparse** vp apologize (to sb) (for sth)

discurso nm speech: pronunciar un ~ give a speech

discusión nf 1 (debate) discussion 2 (disputa) argument

discutido adj (polémico) controversial

discutir vt 1 (debatir) discuss 2 (cuestionar) question ● vi 1 (hablar) discuss sth: ~ de arte discuss art 2 (desacuerdo) argue (with sb) (about sth)

disecar vt 1 (animal) stuff 2 (flor) press 3 (hacer la disección) dissect

diseñador/a nm-nf designer

diseñar vt 1 design 2 (plan) draw sth up

diseño nm design: ~ gráfico graphic design

disfraz nm costume

disfrazarse vp (para fiesta) dress up (as sth/sb)

disfrutar vi, vt enjoy sth: Disfruto bailando/con el fútbol. I enjoy dancing/soccer. ◊ ~ de buena salud enjoy good health ● vi (pasarla bien) enjoy yourself

disgustado adj upset

disgustar vi upset sb

disgusto nm 1 (tristeza) sorrow 2 (desgracia) accident ▶ **a ~** 1 (con pesar) upset 2 (de mala gana) unwillingly **dar ~s** upset: Me da muchos ~s. He's always upsetting me. **llevarse un ~** be upset **matar a ~s** make sb's life a misery

disimular vt hide ● vi pretend: ¡Ahí viene! ¡Disimula! There she is! Pretend you haven't seen her.

disimulo nm ▶ **con/sin ~** surreptitiously/openly

dislexia nf dyslexia

disléxico/a adj, nm-nf dyslexic

dislocar(se) vt, vp dislocate

disminución nf drop (in sth)

disminuido/a adj, nm-nf disabled: los ~s físicos people with a physical disability

disminuir vt reduce ● vi drop

disolver(se) vt, vp 1 (en líquido) dissolve 2 (manifestación) break (sth) up

disparado adj ▶ salir ~ shoot out: Salieron ~ del banco. They shot out of the bank.

disparar *vt, vi* shoot: *Disparaban contra todos.* They were shooting at everyone. ● **dispararse** *vp* **1** (*arma, alarma, alegría*) go off **2** (*aumentar*) shoot up

disparate *nm* **1** (*dicho*) nonsense [U]: *¡No digas ~s!* Don't talk nonsense! **2** (*hecho*) stupid thing

disparo *nm* shot: *morir a raíz de un ~* die from a gunshot wound

dispersar(se) *vt, vp* disperse

disponer *vi* **~ de 1** (*tener*) have sth **2** (*utilizar*) use sth ● **disponerse** *vp* get ready for sth/to do sth

disponible *adj* available

dispositivo *nm* device

dispuesto *adj* **1** (*ordenado*) arranged **2** (*preparado*) ready (*for sth*) **3** (*servicial*) willing **4** (*decidido*) prepared to do sth: *No estoy ~ a renunciar.* I'm not prepared to resign.

disputado *adj* hard-fought

disputar *vt* (*Dep*) play ● **disputarse** *vp* compete for sth

disquete (*tb* **diskette**) *nm* floppy disk

disquetera *nf* (*Comp*) disk drive

distancia *nf* distance: *¿A qué ~ está el centro?* How far is it to downtown? ▶ **a mucha/poca ~ de...** a long way/not far from...

distante *adj* distant

distinción *nf* **1** distinction: *hacer una ~* make a distinction **2** (*premio*) award ▶ **sin ~ de...** regardless of...

distinguido *adj* distinguished

distinguir *vt* **1** distinguish sth/sb (*from sth/sb*): *No puedo ~ a los dos hermanos.* I can't tell the difference between the two brothers. **2** (*divisar*) make sth out ● **distinguirse** *vp* be known *for sth*

distinto *adj* **1** different (*from/to sth/sb*) **2 distintos** (*diversos*) various: *los ~s aspectos del tema* the various aspects of the matter

distorsionar *vt* distort

distracción *nf* (*pasatiempo*) pastime

distraer *vt* **1** (*entretener*) keep sb amused **2** (*apartar la atención*) distract sb (*from sth*) ● **distraerse** *vp* **1** (*pasar el tiempo*) pass your time *doing sth* **2** (*despistarse*) be distracted

distraído *adj* absent-minded ▶ **estar/ir ~** be in a fog, be miles away (*GB*)

distribución *nf* **1** distribution **2** (*casa, etc.*) layout

distribuir *vt* distribute

distrito *nm* district ▶ **~ electoral** (*Pol*) congressional district, constituency [*pl* -ies] (*GB*)

disturbio *nm* riot

disuadir *vt* dissuade sb (*from sth*)

diversión *nf* **1** (*pasatiempo*) pastime **2** (*placer*) fun **3** (*espectáculo*) entertainment

diverso *adj* **1** (*variado*) different: *gente de ~ origen* people from different backgrounds **2 diversos** (*varios*) various: *El libro abarca ~s aspectos.* The book covers various aspects.

divertido *adj* **1** (*gracioso*) funny **2** (*agradable*) enjoyable ▶ **estar/ser (muy) ~** be (great) fun

divertir *vt* amuse ● **divertirse** *vp* have fun ▶ **~se en grande** have a great time *¡que te diviertas!* have a good time!

dividir *vt* divide: *~ el trabajo/el pastel* divide (up) the work/cake ◊ *~ ocho entre/por dos* divide eight by two ● **dividir(se)** *vt, vp* split (*into sth*): *~se en dos facciones* split into two factions

divino *adj* divine

divisa *nf* (*dinero*) (foreign) currency: *pagar en ~s* pay in foreign currency

divisar *vt* make sth/sb out

división *nf* **1** division **2** (*Dep*) league: *un equipo de primera ~* a major-league/first division (*GB*) team **3** (*pared*) partition

divorciado/a *adj* divorced ● *nm-nf* divorcé [*fem* divorcée]

divorciarse *vp* get divorced (*from sb*)

divorcio *nm* divorce

divulgar(se) *vt, vp* spread

do *nm* C: *do mayor* C major

dobladillo *nm* hem

doblaje *nm* (*Cine*) dubbing

doblar *vt* **1** (*plegar*) fold **2** (*torcer, flexionar*) bend **3** (*duplicar*) double **4** (*esquina*) turn **5** (*Cine*) dub: *~ una película al español* dub a film into Spanish ● *vi* **1** (*girar*) turn: *~ a la derecha* turn right **2** (*campanas*) toll ● **doblarse** *vp* **1** (*cantidad*) double **2** (*torcerse*) bend

doble *adj* double ● *nm* **1** (*cantidad*) twice as much/many: *Gana el ~ que yo.* She earns twice as much as me. ◊ *Había el ~ de gente.* There were twice as many people. **2 + de adj** twice as...: *el ~ de ancho* twice as wide **3 dobles** (*tenis*) doubles ● *nmf* (*persona parecida, Cine*) double

doblez *nm* fold

doce adj, nm, pron **1** twelve **2** (fecha) twelfth

doceavo adj, nm twelfth

docena nf dozen: una ~ de huevos a dozen eggs ◊ **por/a ~s** by the dozen

doctor/a nm-nf doctor (abrev Dr.)

doctorado nm Ph.D.: estudiantes de ~ Ph.D. students

doctrina nf doctrine

documentación nf **1** (persona) (identity) papers [pl] **2** (vehículo) documents [pl]

documental nm documentary [pl -ies]

documento nm document ▸ **~ de identidad** identity card

dólar nm dollar →Ver pág. 224

doler vi **1** hurt: Me duele la pierna. My leg hurts. ◊ Me dolió que no me apoyaran. I was hurt by their lack of support. **2** (cabeza, muela) ache: Me duele la cabeza. I have a headache. ▸ **el bazo** get a stitch

dolido adj **1** hurt: Está ~ por lo que dijo. He's hurt at what you said. **2** ~ **con** upset with sb

dolor nm **1** (físico) pain **2** (pena) grief ▸ **~ de cabeza, muelas, estómago,** etc. headache, toothache, stomach ache, etc.

dolorido adj sore

doloroso adj painful

domador/a nm-nf tamer

domar vt **1** tame **2** (caballo) break sth in

domesticar vt domesticate

doméstico adj **1** household: tareas domésticas household chores **2** (animal) domestic

domicilio nm: cambio de ~ change of address ◊ servicio a ~ delivery service

dominante adj dominant

dominar vt **1** dominate **2** (idioma) be fluent in sth **3** (materia, técnica) be good at sth

domingo nm Sunday (abrev Sun.) → LUNES ▸ **D~ de Ramos/Resurrección** Palm/Easter Sunday

dominio nm **1** (control) control: ~ del balón ball control **2** (lengua) command **3** (técnica) mastery ▸ **ser del ~ público** be common knowledge

dominó nm (juego) dominoes [sing]

don/doña nm-nf Mr. [fem Mrs.] ▸ **un ~ nadie** a nobody

dona nf donut

donante nmf (tb donador/a nm-nf) donor

donar vt donate

donativo nm donation

donde adv **1** where: la ciudad ~ nací the city where I was born ◊ Déjalo ~ pueda. Leave it over there somewhere. ◊ un lugar ~ vivir a place to live **2** (con prep): la ciudad a/hacia ~ se dirigen the city they're heading for ◊ un alto de/desde ~ se ve el mar a hill you can see the sea from ◊ la calle por ~ pasan los taxis the street the taxis go along

dónde adv where: ¿De ~ eres? Where are you from? ▸ **¿hacia ~?** which way? **¿por ~ se va a...?** how do you get to...?

dorado adj **1** gold: un bolso ~ a gold bag **2** (época, pelo) golden

dormido adj **quedarse ~ 1** (dormirse) fall asleep **2** (despertarse tarde) oversleep

dormir vi **1** sleep: No dormí nada. I didn't sleep a wink. **2** (estar dormido) be asleep: mientras dormía while I was asleep ● vt (niño) put sb to sleep ● **dormirse** vp **1** (conciliar el sueño) fall asleep **2** (despertarse tarde) oversleep **3** (parte del cuerpo) go to sleep: Se me durmió la pierna. My leg's gone to sleep. ▸ **¡a ~!** time for bed! ● **como un lirón/tronco** sleep like a log

dormitorio nm bedroom

dorso nm back: al ~ de la tarjeta on the back of the card

dos adj, nm, pron **1** two **2** (fecha) second ▸ **~?** puntos colon **en un ~ por tres** in a flash **las/los ~** both: las ~ manos both hands ◊ Fuimos los ~. Both of us went./ We both went.

doscientos/as adj, nm, pron two hundred

dosis nf dose

dotado adj ~ **de** (cualidad) endowed with sth **2** (equipado) equipped with sth

dote nf **1** (de mujer) dowry [pl -ies] **2** **dotes** talent (for sth) [sing]: tener ~s de cómico have a talent for comedy

dragón nm dragon

drama nm drama

dramático adj dramatic

driblar vt, vi (Dep) dribble (past sb)

droga nf **1** drug: una ~ blanda/dura a soft/hard drug **2 la droga** drugs [pl]: la lucha contra la ~ the fight against drugs

drogadicto/a nm-nf drug addict

drogar vt drug ● **drogarse** vp take drugs

droguería nf (And, farmacia) drugstore, chemist's (GB)

ducha nf shower: *darse un ~* take a shower

ducharse vp take a shower

ducho adj ▶ **estar ~ en** know a lot about sth

duda nf doubt: *fuera de/sin ~* (*alguna*) beyond/without (any) doubt ◇ *¿Tienen alguna ~?* Are there any questions? ▶ **sacar de ~s** dispel sb's doubts

dudar vt, vi doubt: *Lo dudo.* I doubt it. ◇ *¿Dudas de mi palabra?* Do you doubt my word? • vi 1 (*persona*) mistrust sb: *Duda de todos.* She mistrusts everyone. 2 **~ en** hesitate *to do sth*: *No dudes en preguntar.* Don't hesitate to ask. 3 **~ entre**: *Dudo entre los dos.* I can't make up my mind between the two.

dudoso/a adj 1 (*incierto*) doubtful: *Estoy algo ~.* I'm rather doubtful. 2 (*sospechoso*) dubious: *un penalty ~* a dubious penalty

duelo nm (*enfrentamiento*) duel

duende nm elf [pl elves]

dueño/a nm-nf 1 owner 2 (*bar, pensión*) landlord [*fem* landlady [pl -ies]]

dulce adj 1 sweet (*persona, voz*) gentle • nm candy [pl -ies], sweet (GB) →CANDY ▶ **~ de leche** soft fudge

duna nf dune

dúo nm 1 (*composición*) duet 2 (*pareja*) duo [pl -s]

duodécimo/a adj, nm-nf, pron twelfth

dúplex nm duplex apartment

duque/esa nm-nf duke [*fem* duchess] NOTA Para "los duques", refiriéndonos a un duque y duquesa, se dice **the duke and duchess**.

duración nf 1 length 2 (*pila, etc.*) life: *pilas de larga ~* long-life batteries

durante prep during, for: *~ la cena* during dinner ◇ *~ un año* for a year NOTA During se refiere al momento en que se desarrolla una acción, y **for** al especificarse la duración de esta acción: *Me sentí mal ~ la reunión.* I felt sick during the meeting. ◇ *Anoche llovió ~ dos horas.* Last night it rained for two hours.

durar vi last: *~ mucho/poco* last a long time/not last long

durazno nm 1 peach 2 (*árbol*) peach (tree)

duro adj 1 hard: *El queso está ~.* The cheese is hard. ◇ *ser ~ con algn* be hard on sb 2 (*castigo, clima, crítica, disciplina*) harsh 3 (*fuerte, resistente, carne*) tough

• adv 1 (*mucho*) hard: *trabajar ~* work hard 2 (*firmemente*) tight: *¡Agárrese ~!* Hold on tight! 3 (*And, sonido*) loud: *¡Hable más ~!* Speak up! ◇ *Ponlo más ~.* Turn it up. ▶ **darle ~** hit sth hard • **de oído** hard of hearing **~ y parejo** flat out

E e

e conj and

ébano nm ebony

ebullición nf ▶ **punto de ~** boiling point

echado adj ▶ **estar ~** be lying down

echar vt 1 (*tirar*) throw 2 (*dar*) give: *Échame un poco de agua.* Give me some water. 3 (*poner*) put sth in/on sth: *~ leña al fuego* put some wood on the fire 4 (*humo, olor*) give sth off 5 (*expulsar*) (a) kick sb out: *Me echaron del bar.* I was kicked out of the bar. (b) (*escuela*) expel (c) (*trabajo*) fire • vi start *doing sth/to do sth*: *Eché a correr.* I started to run. • **echarse** vp 1 (*tumbarse*) lie down 2 (*comenzar*) start *doing sth/to do sth* NOTA Para expresiones con **echar**, ver el sustantivo, adjetivo, etc., p. ej. **echarse la siesta** en SIESTA.

eclesiástico adj ecclesiastical

eclipse nm eclipse

eco nm echo [pl -es]: *Había ~ en la cueva.* The cave had an echo.

ecografía nf scan: *hacerse una ~* have a scan

ecología nf ecology

ecológico adj ecological

ecologismo nm environmentalism

ecologista adj environmental • nmf environmentalist

economía nf economy [pl -ies]

económico adj 1 (*que gasta poco*) economical 2 (*Econ*) economic

economista nmf economist

ecosistema nm ecosystem

ecoturismo nm ecotourism

ecuación nf equation

Ecuador nm Ecuador

ecuador nm equator

ecuatorial adj equatorial

ecuatoriano/a adj, nm-nf Ecuadorian

edad nf age: *¿Qué ~ tiene?* How old is he? ▶ **de mi ~** my, your, etc.

age: *No había ninguno de mi ~.* There wasn't anybody my age. la **E~ Media** the Middle Ages [pl] **no tener ~** be too young/old (for sth/to do sth) **tener ~** be old enough (for sth/to do sth)

edecán *nf* (Mx) hostess

edición *nf* **1** (*publicación*) publication **2** (*tirada, versión, TV, etc.*) edition: *~ pirata/semanal* pirate/ weekly edition

edificar *vt, vi* (*construir*) build

edificio *nm* building

editar *vt* **1** (*publicar*) publish **2** (*preparar texto*) edit

editor/a *nm-nf* **1** (*empresario*) publisher **2** (*textos, Period, TV, etc.*) editor

editorial *adj* (*sector*) publishing ● *nm* (*periódico*) editorial ● *nf* publishing house: *¿De qué ~ es?* Who are the publishers?

edredón *nm* comforter, quilt (GB)

educación *nf* **1** (*enseñanza*) education: *~ sanitaria/sexual* health/ sex education **2** (*crianza*) upbringing: *Tuve una buena ~.* I was well brought up. **▶ ~ física** physical education (*abrev* P.E.) **ser de buena/mala ~** be good/bad manners (*to do sth*)

educado *adj* polite **▶ bien/mal ~** well mannered/rude

educar *vt* **1** (*enseñar*) educate **2** (*criar*) bring sb up **▶ ~ el oído** train your ear

educativo *adj* **1** educational **2** (*sistema*) education: *el sistema ~* the education system

efectivamente *adv* (*respuesta*) that's right: *—¿Lo vendió ayer?* *—Efectivamente.* "Did you sell it yesterday?" "That's right."

efectivo *adj* effective ● *nm* cash **▶ pagar en ~** pay (for sth) in cash

efecto *nm* **1** effect: *hacer/no hacer ~* have an effect/no effect **2** (*pelota*) spin: *La pelota iba con ~.* The ball had a spin on it. **▶ ~s (personales)** belongings **en ~** indeed

efectuar *vt* carry sth out

efervescente *adj* effervescent

eficaz *adj* **1** (*efectivo*) effective **2** (*eficiente*) efficient

eficiente *adj* efficient

egoísta *adj, nmf* selfish: *Es un ~.* He's really selfish.

egresado/a *nm-nf* graduate

egresar *vi* graduate

eje *nm* **1** (*ruedas*) axle **2** (*Mat, Geog, Pol*) axis [pl axes]: *~ de coordenadas* x and y axes

ejecutar *vt* **1** (*realizar*) carry sth out **2** (*pena de muerte, Jur*) execute **3** (*Comp*) run

ejecutivo/a *adj, nm-nf* executive: *órgano ~* executive body ◊ *un ~ importante* an important executive

ejemplar *adj* exemplary ● *nm* (*texto, CD, etc.*) copy [pl -ies]

ejemplo *nm* example: *Espero que les sirva de ~.* Let this be an example to you. **▶ dar ~** set an example **por ~** for example (*abrev* e.g.)

ejercer *vt* **1** (*profesión*) practice **2** (*autoridad, poder, derechos*) exercise ● *vi* practice

ejercicio *nm* **1** exercise: *hacer un ~ de matemáticas* do a math exercise ◊ *hacer más ~* get more exercise **2** (*profesión*) practice

ejército *nm* army [pl -ies]

ejote *nm* (Mx) green bean

el/la *art def* the → THE **▶ el/la de...** **1** (*posesión*): *La de Ana es mejor.* Ana's (one) is better. **2** (*característica*) the one (with...): *el de la barba* the one with the beard ◊ *Quiero la de lunares.* I want the spotted one. **3** (*ropa*) the one in...: *la de rojo/del abrigo rojo* the one in red/in the red coat **4** (*procedencia*) the one from...: *el de La Paz* the one from La Paz **el/la de/que...** **1** (*persona*) the one (who/that)...: *Ese no es el que vi.* He isn't the one I saw. **2** (*cosa*) the one (which/that)...: *La que compramos era mejor.* The one (that) we bought was nicer. ◊ *el de ayer* yesterday's one **3** (*quienquiera*) whoever: *El que llegue primero que haga café.* Whoever gets there first makes the coffee.

él *pron pers* **1** (*persona*) (a) (*sujeto*) he: *José y él son primos.* José and he are cousins. (b) (*complemento, en comparaciones*) him: *Es para él.* It's for him. ◊ *Soy más alto que él.* I'm taller than him. **2** (*cosa*) it **▶ de ~** (*posesivo*) his: *el carro de él* his car ◊ *Son de él.* They're his. **es ~** it's him

elaborar *vt* **1** (*producto*) produce **2** (*preparar*) prepare

elástico *adj* **1** elastic **2** (*atleta*) supple

elección *nf* **1** choice: *no tener ~* have no choice **2 elecciones** election(s): *convocar elecciones* call an election **▶ elecciones generales/legislativas** general election(s) **elecciones municipales** local election(s)

elector/a *nm-nf* voter

electorado *nm* electorate

electoral *adj* electoral: *lista ~* list (of (election) candidates

electricidad *nf* electricity

electricista *nmf* electrician

eléctrico *adj* electric, electrical **NOTA** Electric se usa para electrodomésticos y aparatos eléctricos concretos, p. ej.: *an electric razor/fence*, y en frases hechas como: *an electric shock*, y en expresiones como: *The atmosphere was electric*. Electrical se refiere a la electricidad en sentido más general: *electrical engineering/appliances*.

electrocutarse *vp* be electrocuted

electrodo *nm* electrode

electrodoméstico *nm* electrical appliance

electrónica *nf* electronics [*sing*]

electrónico *adj* electronic

elefante/a *nm-nf* elephant

elegante *adj* elegant

elegir *vt* 1 (*votar*) elect 2 (*optar*) choose: *No me dieron a ~.* They didn't let me choose.

elemental *adj* elementary

elemento *nm* element

elevado *adj* high ▸ **~ a cuatro, etc.** (raised) to the fourth, etc. power **~ al cuadrado/cubo** squared/cubed

elevador *nm* elevator, lift (*GB*)

elevar *vt* raise

eliminación *nf* elimination

eliminar *vt* eliminate

eliminatoria *nf* heat

ella *pron pers* 1 (*persona*) (a) (*sujeto*) she: *Ana y ~ son primas.* She and Ana are cousins. (b) (*complemento, en comparaciones*) her: *Es para ~.* It's for her. ◇ *Soy más alta que ~.* I'm taller than her. 2 (*cosa*) it ▸ **de ~** (*posesivo*) her(s): *la tía de ~* her aunt ◇ *El collar era de ~.* The necklace was hers. **es ~** it's her

ello *pron* (*complemento*) it

ellos/as *pron pers* 1 (*sujeto*) they 2 (*complemento, en comparaciones*) them: *Dígaselo a ~.* Tell them. ▸ **de ~** (*posesivo*) their(s): *la casa de ~* their house **son ~** it's them

elogiar *vt* praise

elote *nm* 1 (*mazorca*) corn on the cob: *Me comí un ~.* I had corn (on the cob). 2 (*Mx, granos*) corn [*U*]

El Salvador *nm* El Salvador

email *nm* email →COMPUTADORA

emanciparse *vp* become independent

embadurnarse *vp* get covered in *sth*

embajada *nf* embassy [*pl* -ies]

embajador/a *nm-nf* ambassador

embalse *nm* (*represa*) reservoir

embarazada *adj, nf* pregnant (woman): *estar ~ de dos meses* be two months pregnant

embarazo *nm* pregnancy [*pl* -ies]: *Tiene seis meses de ~.* She's six months pregnant.

embarcación *nf* boat →BOAT

embarcadero *nm* pier

embarcar *vt* 1 (*pasajeros*) embark 2 (*mercancías*) load ● *vi* board

embargo *nm* (*bloqueo*) embargo [*pl* -es] ▸ **sin ~** however y **sin ~** and yet...

embarrado *adj* muddy

embarrar(se) *vt, vp* (*sth*) muddy ▸ **embarrarla** mess things up

embestida *nf* (*toro*) charge

embestir *vt, vi* (*toro*) charge (at *sth/sb*)

emblema *nm* emblem

embolsar(se) *vt, vp* pocket

emborracharse *vp* get drunk (*on sth*)

emboscada *nf* ambush: *tender una ~ a algn* lay an ambush for *sb*

embotellamiento *nm* (*tráfico*) traffic jam

embrión *nm* embryo [*pl* -s]

embrujado *adj* 1 (*persona*) bewitched 2 (*lugar*) haunted

embrujo *nm* spell

embudo *nm* funnel

embustero/a *nm-nf* (*mentiroso*) liar

embutido *nm* cold meats [*pl*]

emergencia *nf* emergency [*pl* -ies]

emigración *nf* emigration

emigrante *adj, nmf* emigrant: *trabajadores ~s* migrant workers

emigrar *vi* 1 emigrate 2 (*dentro de un país, animales*) migrate

eminencia *nf* 1 (*persona*) leading figure 2 **Eminencia** Eminence

emisión *nf* 1 (*emanación*) emission 2 (*Radio, TV*) (a) (*programa*) broadcast (b) (*señal*) transmission: *problemas con la ~* transmission problems

emisora *nf* (*Radio*) radio station

emitir *vt* (*Radio, TV*) broadcast

emoción *nf* emotion

emocionante *adj* 1 (*conmovedor*) moving 2 (*apasionante*) exciting

emocionar *vt* 1 (*conmover*) move 2 (*apasionar*) thrill ● emocionar-

se *vp* **1** (*conmoverse*) be moved (by *sth*) **2** (*apasionarse*) get excited (about *sth*)

empacar *vt* pack

empachado *adj* • **estar ~** have indigestion

empacho *nm* indigestion [U]

empalagar *vt, vi* be too sweet (for *sb*)

empalagoso *adj* **1** (*alimento*) sickly sweet **2** (*persona*) smarmy

empalmar *vt* **1** connect (*sth*) (with *sth*)

empalme *nm* **1** connection **2** (*tren, carreteras*) junction

empanada *nf* pie

empanado (*tb* empanizado) *adj* breaded

empanar (*tb* empanizar) *vt* **1** (*pan rallado*) cover *sth* in breadcrumbs **2** (*harina*) dip *sth* in batter

empañar *vt* (*vapor*) cloud • **empañarse** *vp* steam up

empapado *adj* soaked through

empapar *vt* **1** soak **2** (*absorber*) soak *sth* up • **empaparse** *vp* get soaked ▸ **~se hasta los huesos** get soaked to the skin

empapelar *vt* paper

empaquetar *vt* pack

emparejar *vt* **1** (a) (*personas*) pair *sb* off (with *sb*) (b) (*cosas*) match *sth* (with *sth*) **2** (*pelo, muro, etc.*) make *sth* even • **emparejarse** *vp* pair off (with *sb*)

empatado *adj* • **ir ~s:** *Cuando me fui iban ~s. Van ~s dos-dos.* It's tied at two/two all (GB).

empatar *vi* **1** (*Dep*) (a) (*resultado final*) tie, draw (GB) (with *sb*) (b) (*en marcador*) catch up **2** (*votación, concurso*) tie (with *sb*) ▸ **~ a cero, uno, etc.** tie at zero, one, etc., draw nil nil, one all, etc. (GB)

empate *nm* tie, draw (GB): *un ~ a dos/dos-dos* a two-two tie/draw ▸ **el gol del ~** the equalizer

empedrado *nm* cobbles [*pl*]

empeine *nm* instep

empelotar *vt* undress • **empelotarse** *vp* get undressed

empeloto *adj* (*And*) naked

empeñado *adj* determined (to do *sth*)

empeñar *vt* pawn • **empeñarse** *vp* insist (on doing *sth*)

empeño *nm* determination (to do *sth*) ▸ **casa de ~** pawnshop **poner ~** take pains with/to do *sth*

empeorar *vt* make *sth* worse • *vi* get worse

emperador/triz *nm-nf* emperor [*fem* empress]

empezar *vt, vi* start (*sth/doing sth/to do sth*) ▸ **para ~** start with

empinado *adj* (*cuesta*) steep

empírico *adj* empirical

empleado/a *nm-nf* **1** employee **2** (*oficina*) clerk

emplear *vt* **1** (*dar trabajo*) employ **2** (*utilizar*) use **3** (*tiempo, dinero*) spend: *~ mal el tiempo* waste your time

empleo *nm* (*puesto*) job → WORK **2** (*trabajo*) employment ▸ **sin ~** unemployed

empollar *vi* (*ave*) sit (on *sth*)

empotrado *adj* built-in

emprendedor/a *adj* enterprising

emprender *vt* **1** (*iniciar*) begin **2** (*negocio*) start *sth* (up) **3** (*viaje*) set off on *sth* ▸ **~ la marcha/viaje (hacia)** set out (for...)

empresa *nf* **1** (*Com*) company [*pl* -ies] **2** (*proyecto*) enterprise ▸ **~ estatal/pública** state-owned company **~ privada** private company

empresarial *adj* business: *sentido ~* business sense

empresariales *nf* business studies [*sing*]

empresario/a *nm-nf* **1** businessman/woman [*pl* -men/-women] **2** (*espectáculo*) impresario [*pl* -s]

empujar *vt* **1** push **2** (*bicicleta, etc.*) wheel **3** (*obligar*) push *sb* into *sth*: *Su familia la empujó a que estudiara derecho.* Her family pushed her into studying law.

empujón *nm* shove • **a empujones:** *Salió a empujones.* He pushed his way out.

empuñar *vt* **1** (*arma, palo, etc.*) brandish **2** (*tener en la mano*) hold

en *prep*
● lugar **1** (*dentro*) in, inside: *Las llaves están en el cajón.* The keys are in the drawer. **2** (*dentro, con movimiento*) into: *Entró en la casa.* He went into the house. **3** (*sobre*) on **4** (*sobre, con movimiento*) onto: *Está goteando agua en el suelo.* Water is dripping onto the floor. **5** (*ciudad, país, campo*) in: *Trabaja en la capital.* He works in the capital. **6** (*punto de referencia*) at **NOTA** Al hablar de un lugar como punto de referencia, se usa **at:** *Espérame en la esquina.* Wait for me at the corner. ◊ *Nos vemos en la estación.* We'll meet at the station. También se utiliza **at** para edificios donde la gente trabaja, estudia o se divierte:

Está en el colegio. He's at school. ◊ *Mis papás están en el teatro.* My parents are at the theater.

• **expresiones de tiempo 1** (*meses, años, siglos, estaciones*) in: *en verano/el siglo XII* in the summer/the twelfth century **2** (*día*) on: *en Nochebuena* on Christmas Eve **3** (*Navidad, Semana Santa, momento*) at: *Voy a mi casa en Navidad.* I go home at Christmas. ◊ *en ese momento* at that moment **4** (*dentro de*) in: *Te veo en una hora.* I'll see you in an hour.

• **otras construcciones 1** (*transporte*) by: *en avión/carro* by plane/car **2** + *inf*: *Fui la primera en llegar.* I was the first to arrive.

enamorado/a *adj* in love (*with sb*) ► *nm-nf* (*aficionado*) lover: *un ~ del arte* an art lover

enamorar *vt* win sb's heart ► **enamorarse** *vp* fall in love (*with sth/sb*)

enano/a *adj* **1** tiny **2** (*Bot, Zool*) dwarf: *un pino ~ a* dwarf pine ► *nm-nf* dwarf [*pl* -s o dwarves]

encabezado *nm* (*Period*) headline **2** (*tb* **encabezamiento**) (*página, documento*) heading

encabezar *vt* head

encadenar *vt* **1** (*atar*) chain *sth/sb* (to *sth*) **2** (*ideas*) link

encajar *vt* **1** (*colocar, meter*) fit *sth* (into *sth*) **2** (*juntar*) fit *sth* together: *~ las piezas del rompecabezas* fit the pieces of the jigsaw together ► *vi* fit

encaje *nm* lace

encallar *vi* (*barco*) run aground

encaminarse *vp* head (*for/to...*): *~ hacia la casa* head for home

encanar *vt* lock *sb* up

encantado *adj* **1** (*very*) pleased (*with sth/sb; to do sth*): *Estoy ~ de que haya venido.* I'm very pleased (that) you've come. **2** (*hechizado*) (a) enchanted (b) (*edificio*) haunted ► *~ (de conocerlo/la)* pleased to meet you

encantador *adj* lovely

encantamiento *nm* spell

encantar *vt* cast a spell on *sth/sb* ► *vi* love sth: *Me encanta ir al cine.* I love going to the movies.

encanto *nm* charm ► **como por ~** as if by magic **ser un ~** be delightful

encapricharse *vp* take a fancy to *sth/sb*

encapuchado *adj* hooded

encarcelar *vt* imprison

encargado/a *adj, nm-nf* in charge (*of sth*): *¿Quién es el ~?*

Who's in charge? ◊ *Eres el ~ de recoger el dinero.* You're in charge of collecting the money.

encargar *vt* **1** (*mandar*) ask *sb* to do *sth*: *Me encargaron que regara el jardín.* They asked me to water the garden. **2** (*producto*) order: *~ un sofá a la tienda* order a couch from the store ● **encargarse** *vp* ~ **de 1** (*cuidar*) look after *sth/sb* **2** (*ser responsable*) be in charge of *sth*

encargo *nm* **1** (*recado*) errand: *hacer un ~* run an errand **2** (*Com*) order: *hacer un ~* place an order

encariñado *adj* fond of *sth/sb*

encariñarse *vp* get attached to *sth/sb*

encarretarse *vp* (*And*) **1** (*hablar*) get talking **2** ~ **con** make out with *sb*, get off with *sb* (GB)

encarrilar *vt* (*tren*) put *sth* on the rails

encartar *vt* (*And*) land *sb* with *sth* ● **encartarse** *vp* (*And*) get landed with *sth/sb*

encauzar *vt* **1** (*agua*) channel **2** (*asunto*) conduct

encendedor *nm* lighter

encender *vt* **1** (*con llama*) light **2** (*aparato, luz*) turn *sth* on ● **encenderse** *vp* (*aparato, luz*) come on

encendido *adj* **1** (*con llama*) lighted **2** (*aparato, luz*) on: *Tenían la luz encendida.* The light was on. ► **estar ~** be lit: *El fuego está ~.* The fire is lit.

encerrar *vt* **1** shut *sth/sb* up **2** (*con llave, encarcelar*) lock *sth/sb* up ● **encerrarse** *vp* **1** shut yourself in **2** (*con llave*) lock yourself in

encestar *vi* score (a basket)

enchapado (*enchape And*) *nm* veneer

enchilado *adj* (*Mx*) hot

enchinar *vt* (*Mx*) perm ► **~se el cuero/la piel** get goose bumps

enchufar *vt* (*aparato*) plug *sth* in

enchufe *nm* **1** (*macho*) plug **2** (*hembra*) socket

encía *nf* gum

enciclopedia *nf* encyclopedia

encima *adv* **1** (*en*) on: *~ de la mesa* on the table **2** (*sobre*) on top of (*sth/sb*): *~ de los libros* on top of the books ◊ *el/la de ~* the top one **3** (*cubriendo algo*) over: *poner una tela ~ del sofá* put a cloth over the couch **4** (*además*) on top of everything ► **estar ~ de algn** be on sb's back **hacer por ~** do *sth* superficially **llevar ~** have *sth* on you **mirar por ~ del**

hombro look down your nose at *sb* **por ~ de** above: *El agua nos llegaba por ~ de las rodillas.* The water came above our knees. ◇ *Está por ~ de los demás.* He is above the rest. **quitarse de ~ a algn** get rid of sth/sb **venirse ~** *(estar cerca)*: *La Navidad se nos viene ~.* Christmas is just around the corner.

encoger(se) *vi, vp* shrink ▶ **~se de hombros** shrug your shoulders

encontrar *vt* find: *No encuentro mi reloj.* I can't find my watch. ● **encontrarse** *vp* **1 ~ (con)** a *(citarse)* meet: *Decidimos encontrarnos aquí.* We decided to meet here. (b) *(por casualidad)* run into *sb*: *Me la encontré en la calle.* I ran into her in the street. **2** *(sentirse)* feel: *Me encuentro mal* I don't feel well. ◇ *¿Se encuentra bien?* Are you all right?

encorvarse *vp (persona)* become stooped

encrespar *vt (pelo)* curl ● **encresparse** *vp* go curly

encuadernar *vt* bind

encubrir *vt* **1** conceal **2** *(delincuente)* harbor

encuentro *nm* **1** *(reunión)* meeting **2** *(Dep)* game

encuesta *nf* **1** survey: *hacer una ~* do a survey **2** *(sondeo)* opinion) poll

encurtido *adj* pickled

enderezar *vt* **1** *(poner derecho)* straighten **2** *(persona)* correct ● **enderezarse** *vp* straighten (up): *¡Enderézate!* Stand up straight!

endeudarse *vp* get into debt

endulzar *vp* sweeten

endurecer(se) *vt, vp* harden

enemigo/a *adj, nm-nf* enemy [*pl* -ies]: *el ejército ~* the enemy army

enemistar = ENFRENTAR (2) ● **enemistarse** *vp* fall out (with *sb*)

energía *nf* energy: *No tengo ~s ni para levantarme.* I don't even have the energy to get up. ▶ **~ eléctrica/nuclear** electric/nuclear power

enero *nm* January *(abrev* **Jan.**)
→MAYO

enésimo *adj (Mat)* nth ▶ **por enésima vez** for the umpteenth time

enfadado *adj* angry *(with sb)* *(at/ about sth)*

enfadar *vt* make *sb* angry ● **enfadarse** *vp* get angry *(at/with sb)* *(at/about sth)*

énfasis *nm* emphasis [*pl* emphases]

enfermar(se) *vi, vp* fall ill *(with sth)*

enfermedad *nf* **1** illness: *salir de una ~ grave* recover from a serious illness **2** *(contagiosa)* disease: *~ hereditaria/de Parkinson* hereditary/Parkinson's disease
→DISEASE

enfermería *nf* **1** infirmary [*pl* -ies] **2** *(carrera)* nursing

enfermero/a *nm-nf* nurse

enfermo/a *adj* sick, ill (*GB*) **NOTA** En Gran Bretaña, **ill** se usa solamente detrás de un verbo: *estar/caer ~.* ill delante y **sick** va delante de un sustantivo: *un animal ~* a sick animal ◇ *Hay 15 niños ~s.* There are 15 children off sick. Pero **si sick** va con un verbo como *be* o *feel*, significa "con ganas de vomitar": *Tengo ganas de vomitar.* I feel sick. ● *nm-nf* **1** sick person: *los ~s* the sick **2** *(paciente)* patient

enfocar *vt* **1** *(ajustar)* focus *sth (on sth/sb)* **2** *(iluminar)* shine a light *on sth* **3** *(asunto)* approach

enfoque *nm (Fot)* focus

enfrentamiento *nm* confrontation

enfrentar *vt* **1** bring *sb* face to face *with sth/sb* **2** *(enemistar)* set *sb* at odds *(with sb)* ● **enfrentarse** *vp* **1 ~ a** face *sth/sb*: *El país se enfrenta a una crisis.* The country is facing a crisis. ◇ *Perú se enfrenta a Chile hoy.* Peru face Chile today. **2 ~ (con)** argue (with *sb*)

enfrente *adv* opposite: *el señor que estaba ~* the man sitting opposite ▶ **~ de** across from, opposite (*GB*)

enfriar *vt* cool *sth* (down) ● **enfriarse** *vp* get cold

enfurecer *vt* infuriate ● **enfurecerse** *vp* become furious *(with sb)* (*at sth*)

enganchar *vt* **1** *(acoplar)* attach **2** *(engarzar And)* *(anzuelo, cable, etc.)* hook ● **engancharse** *vp* **1** *(atascarse)* get caught **2** *(rasgarse)* get snagged

enganche *nm (Mx, Fin)* down payment

engañar *vt* **1** *(mentir)* lie to *sb*: *No me engañes.* Don't lie to me. ▶ LIE[2] **2** *(ser infiel)* cheat on *sb* ● **engañarse** *vp* fool yourself

engaño *nm (estafa)* con

engatusar *vt* sweet-talk *sb (into sth)*

engendrar *vt* **1** *(concebir)* conceive **2** *(causar)* generate

engordar *vt (cebar)* fatten *sth/sb* (up) ● *vi* **1** *(persona)* put on

weight: ~ *mucho* put on a lot of weight **2** (*alimento*) be fattening

engrapadora *nf* stapler

engrapar *vt* staple

engrasar *vt* **1** (*con grasa*) grease **2** (*con aceite*) oil

engreído/a *adj, nm-nf* conceited: *Es un* ~. He's conceited.

engullir *vt* gobble *sth* (up/down)

enhebrar *vt* thread

enigma *nm* enigma

enjabonar(se) *vt, vp* soap

enjambre *nm* swarm

enjaular *vt* cage

enjuagar *vt* rinse ● **enjuagarse** *vp* rinse (out) your mouth

enjugarse *vp* (*sudor, lágrimas*) wipe *sth* (away)

enlace *nm* link **2** (*transportes*) connection

enlatar *vt* can

enlazar *vt, vi* connect (*sth*) (*to/ with sth*)

enloquecedor *adj* infuriating

enloquecer *vi* **1** (*volverse loco*) go crazy: ~ *de alegría* go wild with joy **2** (*gustar mucho*) be crazy *about sth* ● *vt* drive *sb* crazy

enmarcar *vt* frame

enmascarar *vt* mask ● **enmascararse** *vp* put on a mask

enmendar *vt* **1** (*errores, defectos*) correct **2** (*daños*) repair **3** (*ley*) amend ● **enmendarse** *vp* mend your ways

enmienda *nf* (*ley*) amendment (*to sth*)

enmohecerse *vp* go moldy

enmudecer *vi* **1** (*perder el habla*) lose your voice **2** (*callar*) get quiet

ennegrecer *vt* blacken ● **ennegrecerse** *vp* go black

enojado *adj* angry (*at/with sb*) (*at/about sth*)

enojar *vt* make *sb* angry ● **enojarse** *vp* get angry (*at/with sb*) (*at/about sth*): *No se enoje con ellos*. Don't get mad at them.

enorgullecer *vt* make *sb* proud: *Su labor nos enorgullece.* We're proud of his achievements. ● **enorgullecerse** *vp* be proud of *sth/sb*

enorme *adj* enormous

enredadera *nf* creeper

enredado *adj* (*involucrado*) involved (*with sth*)

enredar *vt* **1** (*pelo, cuerdas*) get *sth* tangled (up) **2** (*involucrar*) involve *sb* (*in sth*) **3** (*complicar*) complicate ● **enredarse** *vp* **1** (*pelo, cuerdas*) get tangled (up) **2** (*amorío, disputa, etc.*) get involved (*with sb*) (*in sth*) **3** (*con-*

fundirse) get confused (*about/ over sth*)

enredo *nm* mess

enrejado *nm* **1** (*jaula, ventana*) bars [*pl*] **2** (*para plantas*) trellis

enrevesado *adj* **1** complicated **2** (*persona*) awkward

enriquecer *vt* enrich ● **enriquecerse** *vp* get rich

enrojecer *vt* redden ● **enrojecer(se)** *vi, vp* go red (*with sth*): ~ *de ira* get red with anger

enrolarse *vp* enlist (*in sth*)

enrollar *vt* roll *sth* up

enroscar *vt* **1** (*tapón*) screw *sth* on **2** (*piezas, tuercas*) screw *sth* together

ensalada *nf* salad ▶ ~ *de frutas* fruit salad ~ *mixta* mixed salad

ensaladera *nf* salad bowl

ensamblar *vt* assemble

ensanchar *vt* widen ● **ensancharse** *vp* **1** (*extenderse*) widen **2** (*dar de sí*) stretch

ensangrentado *adj* bloodstained

ensangrentar *vt* (*manchar*) get blood on *sth*

ensayar *vt, vi* **1** practice **2** (*Mús, Teat*) rehearse

ensayo *nm* **1** (*experimento*) test: *un tubo de* ~ a test tube **2** (*Mús, Teat*) rehearsal: ~ *general* dress rehearsal **3** (*texto*) essay

enseguida *adv* straightaway

ensenada *nf* inlet

enseñado *adj* ▶ *bien* ~ well trained *tener mal* ~: *Lo tiene muy mal* ~. You spoil him.

enseñanza *nf* **1** teaching **2** (*sistema nacional*) education

enseñar *vt* **1** teach *sth*, teach *sb* to do *sth* **2** (*mostrar*) show

ensillar *vt* saddle *sth* (up)

ensimismado *adj* **1** (*pensativo*) lost in thought **2** (*embebido*) engrossed (*in sth*): *estar* ~ *leyendo un libro* be deeply engrossed in a book

ensordecedor *adj* deafening

ensordecer *vt* deafen ● *vi* go deaf

ensuciar(se) *vt, vp* get (*sth*) dirty: *Te ensuciaste el vestido de aceite.* You have oil on your dress.

ensueño *nm* ▶ *de* ~ dream: *una casa de* ~ a dream home

entablar *vt* **1** (*comenzar*) start *sth* (up): ~ *una conversación* start up a conversation **2** (*Jur*): ~ *una demanda contra algn* take proceedings against *sb*

entapetar *vt* (*And*) carpet

entender *vt* understand ● *vi* **1** understand: *fácil de* ~ easy to understand **2** ~ **de** know a lot about sth • **entenderse** get along (with sb) ▸ **dar a** ~ imply ~ **mal** misunderstand

entendido/a nm-nf expert • interj: ¡Entendido! Right! ◇ ¿Entendido? All right?

enterado adj ▸ **estar** ~ know (about sth) ▸ **no darse por** ~ turn a deaf ear (to sth)

enterarse vp (suceso) hear (about sth) ▸ **te vas a enterar** (amenaza) you, he, they, etc. will get what for

entero adj **1** (completo, leche) whole **2** (intacto) intact

enterrador/a nm-nf gravedigger

enterrar vt bury ▸ ~**se en vida** shut yourself away

entierro nm **1** funeral **2** (sepelio) burial

entonación nf intonation

entonar vt (cantar) sing • vi **1** sing in tune **2** (combinar) go (with sth) • **entonarse** vp perk up

entonces adv then ▸ **en/por aquel** ~ at that time

entornado adj (puerta) ajar

entornar vt half-close

entorno nm **1** (ambiente) environment **2** (círculo) circle: ~ familiar family circle **3** (alrededores): en el ~ de la ciudad in and around the city

entrada nf **1** (acción de entrar) (a) entry (into sth): Prohibida la ~. No entry. (b) (club, asociación) admission (to sth): No cobran ~ a los socios. Admission is free for members. **2** (boleto/tiquete) ticket: No hay ~s. Sold out. **3** (puerta) entrance (to sth) **4 entradas** (pelo) receding hairline: Cada vez tiene más ~s. His hairline is receding fast. ▸ ~ **gratuita/ libre** free admission

entrañable adj (querido) much-loved

entrañas nf (Anat) entrails

entrar vi **1** (a) go in/inside: No me atreví a ~. I didn't dare to go in. ◇ El clavo no entró bien. The nail didn't go in right. (b) (pasar) come in/inside: Hágalo ~. Ask him to come in. **2** ~ **en/a** (a) go into...: ~ al/en el banco go into the bank ◇ ~ en detalles go into detail (b) (pasar) come into...: No entre en/a mi habitación sin llamar. Knock before you come into my room. **3** ~ **a/en** (ingresar) (a) (profesión, esfera social) enter sth (b) (institución, club) join sth **4** (caber) (a) (ropa) fit: Esta falda no me entra. This skirt doesn't fit (me). (b) ~ (**en**) fit (in/

into sth): No entra en la maleta. It won't fit in the trunk. **5** (velocidades) engage: La primera nunca entra bien. First never seems to engage right. ▸ **no me entra (en la cabeza)...** I, you, etc. just don't understand...

entre prep **1** (dos cosas, personas) between **2** (más de dos cosas, personas) among **3** (en medio) somewhere between: Tiene los ojos ~ agrisados y azules. Her eyes are somewhere between gray and blue. ▸ ~ **sí 1** (dos personas) to each other: Hablaban ~ sí. They were talking to each other. **2** (varias personas) among themselves: Lo discutieron ~ sí. They discussed it among themselves. ▸ ~ **todos** together

entreabierto adj half open

entrecejo nm space between the eyebrows

entrecortado adj **1** (voz) faltering **2** (frases) broken

entrecot nm fillet steak

entredicho nm ▸ **poner en** ~ call sth into question

entrega nf **1** handing over **2** (mercancía) delivery [pl -ies] **3** (fascículo) installment: Se va a publicar por ~s. It will be published in installments. ▸ ~ **de medallas/ premios** medal ceremony/prize-giving ~ **inmediata** express delivery: mandar una carta por ~ inmediata send a letter express

entregado adj devoted (to sth/sb)

entregar vt **1** hand sth/sb over (to sb) **2** (premio, etc.) present sth (to sb) **3** (mercancía) deliver • **entregarse** vp **1** (rendirse) give yourself up (to sb) **2** (dedicarse) devote yourself to sth/sb

entrenador/a nm-nf **1** trainer **2** (Dep) coach

entrenamiento nm training

entrenar(se) vt, vp train

entrepierna nf crotch

entretanto adv in the meantime

entretener vt **1** (demorar) keep: No lo voy a ~ mucho. I won't keep you long. **2** (divertir) entertain **3** (distraer) keep sb busy • **entretenerse** vp **1** (disfrutar): Lo hace por ~. He does it to pass the time. ◇ Me entretengo con cualquier cosa. I'm easily amused. **2** (distraerse) hang around (doing sth)

entretenido adj entertaining ▸ **estar** ~ be busy (doing sth)

entretenimiento nm **1** (diversión) entertainment **2** (pasatiempo) pastime

entrevista nf 1 (reunión) meeting 2 (trabajo, Period) interview

entrevistador/a nm-nf interviewer

entrevistar vt interview ● **entrevistarse** vp ~ (con) meet sb

entristecer vt sadden ● **entristecerse** vp be sad (because of/about sth)

entrometerse vp interfere (in sth)

entrometido/a adj meddlesome ● nm-nf meddler

enturbiar vt 1 (líquido) make sth cloudy 2 (relaciones, asunto) cloud ● **enturbiarse** vp 1 (líquido) become cloudy 2 (relaciones, asunto) become muddled

entusiasmado adj excited (at/about sth)

entusiasmar vt thrill ● **entusiasmarse** vp get excited (about/over sth)

entusiasmo nm enthusiasm (for sth) ▶ **con** ~ enthusiastically

entusiasta adj enthusiastic ● nmf enthusiast

enumerar vt list

enunciado nm (problema, teoría) statement

enunciar vt enunciate

envasado adj ▶ ~ **al vacío** vacuum-packed

envasar vt 1 (embotellar) bottle 2 (enlatar) can

envase nm 1 (botella) bottle 2 (lata) can 3 (caja) package

envejecer(se) vt, vi (persona, vino) age

envenenar(se) vt, vp poison (yourself): ~se comiendo hongos eat poisonous mushrooms

enviado/a nm-nf 1 (emisario) envoy 2 (Period) correspondent

enviar vt send

enviciarse vp get hooked (on sth)

envidia nf envy: hacer algo por ~ do sth out of envy ◇ ¡Qué ~! I really envy you! ▶ **dar** ~ make sb jealous **tener** ~ be jealous (of sth/sb)

envidiar vt envy

envidioso/a adj, nm-nf envious: Es un ~. He's so envious.

envío nm 1 (acción) sending 2 (paquete) package 3 (Com) consignment

enviudar vi be widowed

envoltorio nm wrapper

envolver vt wrap sth/sb (up) (in sth): ¿Se lo envolvemos? Would you like it wrapped? ▶ ~ **para regalo** gift-wrap

envuelto adj ▶ **verse** ~ **en** find yourself involved in sth

enyesado adj in a cast

enyesar vt put sth in plaster

epa interj 1 (para animar) hey 2 (cuidado) careful

epicentro nm epicentre

epidemia nf epidemic

epilepsia nf epilepsy

episodio nm episode

época nf 1 time: en aquella ~ at that time 2 (era) age ▶ **de** ~ period: mobiliario de ~ period furniture

equilibrio nm 1 balance: mantener/perder el ~ keep/lose your balance ◇ ~ **de fuerzas** balance of power 2 (Fís) equilibrium

equilibrista nmf 1 (acróbata) acrobat 2 (en cuerda floja) tightrope walker

equipaje nm 1 baggage [U]: ~ **de mano** hand baggage ▶ **hacer el** ~ pack

equipar vt 1 equip sth/sb (with sth) 2 (ropa, Náut) fit sth/sb out (with sth)

equipo nm 1 (personas) team: un ~ **de voleibol/expertos** a volleyball team/team of experts → JURADO 2 (equipamiento) (a) equipment [U]: un ~ **de laboratorio** laboratory equipment (b) (Dep) gear: ~ **de pesca** fishing gear ▶ ~ **de sonido/música** hi-fi (system)

equitación nf horseback riding, horse riding (GB)

equivaler vi (valer) be equivalent to sth

equivocación nf 1 (error) mistake: cometer una ~ make a mistake 2 (malentendido) misunderstanding

equivocado adj wrong

equivocarse vp 1 (confundirse) be wrong (about sth) 2 ~ (de): Se equivocó de número. You have the wrong number. ◇ ~ **de carretera** take the wrong road

era nf (período) era

erección nf erection

erguir vt (cabeza) hold sth up

erizo nm hedgehog ▶ ~ **de mar** sea urchin

ermita nf hermitage

ermitaño nf hermit

erosión nf erosion

erosionar vt erode

erótico adj erotic

errar vt miss: ~ **el tiro** miss (with) your shot ● vi (vagar) wander

errata nf mistake

erróneo adj wrong

error nm mistake: cometer un ~ make a mistake →MISTAKE

eructar vi burp

eructo nm burp

erupción nf 1 eruption 2 (Med) rash

esbelto adj 1 (delgado) slender 2 (elegante) graceful

escabeche nm ▸ **en** ~ in brine

escabullirse vp 1 (irse) slip away 2 ~ **de** (entre) slip out of sth

escafandra nf diving suit

escala nf 1 scale: en una ~ de uno a diez on a scale of one to ten 2 (viajes) stopover ▸ ~ **musical** scale **hacer** ~ stop (over) in...

escalada nf (montaña) climb

escalador/a nm-nf climber

escalar vt, vi climb

escalera nf (edificio) stairs [pl]: Me caí por las ~s. I fell down the stairs. **NOTA** Si se refiere a toda la estructura de la escalera, se dice staircase: La casa tiene una ~ antigua. The house has an antique staircase. ▸ **bajar/subir las ~s** go downstairs/upstairs ~ **de caracol** spiral staircase ~ **de incendios** fire escape ~ **eléctrica/mecánica** escalator

escalofrío nm shiver ▸ **dar** ~ send shivers down your spine **tener/sentir ~s** shiver

escalón nm step

escalope nm cutlet

escama nf scale

escampar vi clear up

escandalizar vt shock

escándalo nm 1 (asunto) scandal 2 (ruido) racket ▸ **armar/hacer un** ~ make a scene

escandaloso adj (risa, color) loud

escáner nm (aparato) scanner

escapada nf 1 (fuga) escape 2 (viaje) short break: una ~ de fin de semana a weekend break 3 (Dep) breakaway

escaparate nm 1 (tienda) store window, shop window (GB) 2 (And, aparador) sideboard 3 (And, de ropa) wardrobe

escapar(se) vi, vp 1 (lograr salir) escape (from sth/sb) 2 (evitar) escape sth: ~ de la justicia escape arrest ● **escaparse** vp 1 (gas, líquido) leak 2 (detalles, oportunidad, medio de transporte) miss: No se te escapa nada. You don't miss a thing. 3 (involuntariamente) let sth slip: Se me escapó que estaba embarazada. I let (it) slip that she was pregnant. ◊ Se le escapó una grosería. He accidentally swore. 4 ~ **de** (obligación) get out of sth ▸ **dejar** ~ 1 (persona) let sb get away 2 (oportunidad) miss

escapatoria nf way out

escape nm 1 (gas, líquido) leak 2 (Aut) exhaust (pipe)

escarabajo nm beetle

escarbar vi, vt (tierra) dig

escarcha nf frost

escarmentado adj ▸ **estar** ~ have learned your lesson

escarmentar vt teach sb a lesson ● vi learn your lesson

escarpines nm bootees

escasear vi be scarce

escasez nf shortage: Hay ~ de agua/profesorado. There is a water shortage/shortage of teachers.

escaso adj 1 (+ sustantivo contable en plural) few: a ~s metros de distancia a few meters away 2 (+ sustantivo incontable) little: La ayuda que recibieron fue escasa. They received very little help. ◊ debido a/ ~ interés due to lack of interest ◊ productos de escasa calidad poor quality products 3 (apenas) barely: Tiene dos años ~s. She's barely two. ▸ **andar** ~ **de** be short of sth

escena nf scene ▸ **poner en** ~ stage sth

escenario nm 1 (Teat, etc.) stage: salir al ~ come onto the stage 2 (lugar) scene: el ~ del crimen the scene of the crime

escenificar vt 1 (representar) stage 2 (adaptar) dramatize

esclarecer vt 1 (explicar) clarify 2 (delito) clear sth up

esclavitud nf slavery

esclavizado adj ▸ **tener** ~ **a algn** treat sb like a slave

esclavizar vt enslave

esclavo/a adj, nm-nf slave: ser ~ del dinero be a slave to money

esclusa nf lock

escoba nf 1 broom 2 (de bruja) broomstick

escobilla nf (cuarto de baño) toilet brush

escocer vi sting

escocés/esa adj Scottish ● nm-nf Scotsman/woman [pl -men/ -women]: los escoceses the Scots

Escocia nf Scotland

escoger vt, vi choose

escolar adj 1 school: año ~ school year 2 (sistema) education: el sistema ~ the education system ● nmf schoolboy [fem schoolgirl] [pl schoolchildren]

escolta nf, nmf escort

escoltar vt escort

escombros nm rubble [U]: reducir algo a ~s reduce sth to rubble

esconder(se) *vt, vp* hide (*sth*) (*from sth/sb*)

escondido *adj* (*recóndito*) secluded ▶ **a escondidas** in secret

escondite *nm* 1 (*escondrijo*) hiding place 2 (*tb* **escondidas** *nf*) (*juego*) hide-and-seek

escopeta *nf* shotgun

Escorpión (*tb* Escorpio) *nm, nmf* (*Astrol*) Scorpio [*pl* -s]

escorpión *nm* (*alacrán*) scorpion

escotado *adj* low-cut: *un vestido ~ por detrás* a dress with a low back

escote *nm* 1 (*prenda*) neckline 2 (*pecho*) chest ▶ **en pico/V** V-neck

escotilla *nf* hatch

escozor *nm* sting

escribir *vt* 1 write 2 (*ortografía*) spell: *¿Cómo se escribe?* How do you spell it? ● *vi* write: *Aún no sabe ~*. He can't write yet. ● **escribirse** *vp* — *con: ~ con un inglés* have an English pen pal ▶ **~ a mano** write *sth* (out) by hand

escrito *nm* 1 (*carta*) letter 2 (*documento*) document ▶ **poner por ~** put *sth* in writing

escritor/a *nm-nf* writer

escritorio *nm* desk

escritura *nf* 1 writing 2 Escritura(s) Scripture: *las (Sagradas) Escrituras* the Holy Scripture(s)/the Scriptures

escrupuloso *adj* 1 (*aprensivo*) fussy 2 (*honrado*) scrupulous

escrutinio *nm* 1 (*recuento*) count 2 (*inspección*) scrutiny

escuadra *nf* 1 (*regla*) set square 2 (*Mil*) squad

escuadrón *nm* squadron

escuchar *vt, vi* listen (*to sth/sb*): *Nunca me escuchas*. You never listen to me.

escudo *nm* 1 shield: *~ protector* protective shield 2 (*insignia*) emblem ▶ **~ de armas** coat of arms

escuela *nf* 1 school: *Iré después de la ~*. I'll go after school. ◇ *Mañana voy a ir a la ~ para hablar con tu profesor.* Tomorrow I'm going to go to the school to talk to your teacher. →SCHOOL 2 (*academia*) academy [*pl* -ies]: *~ de policía* police academy ▶ **~ de manejo/conducción** driving school ● **primaria** elementary school, primary school (*GB*) ● **~ secundaria** high school, secondary school (*GB*) **NOTA** Una escuela pública se dice **public school** en EE.UU., y **state school** en Gran Bretaña, donde un **public**

school es un tipo de escuela privada tradicional.

escular *vt, vi* go through *sth*: *¡No me esculques!* Don't go through my things. ◇ *~ es de muy mala educación.* It's very rude to go through other peoples' things.

esculpir *vt, vi* sculpt

escultor/a *nm-nf* sculptor

escultura *nf* sculpture

escupir *vt* 1 (*expectorar*) spit *sth* (out) 2 (*a algn*) spit at *sb* ● *vi* spit

escupitajo *nm* spit [*U*]: *Había un ~ en el suelo.* There was some spit on the ground. ◇ *soltar un ~* spit

escurridor *nm* 1 (*verduras*) colander 2 (*para platos*) dishrack

escurrir *vt* 1 (*ropa*) wring *sth* (out) 2 (*platos, verduras, etc.*) drain ● *vi* 1 (*ropa*) drain 2 (*ropa*) drip ● **escurrirse** *vp* slip (*out of/from sth*)

ese/a *adj* that [*pl* those]: *a partir de ~ momento* from that moment on ● (*tb* **ése/a**) *pron* 1 (*cosa*) that one [*pl* those (ones)]: *Yo no quiero ésos.* I don't want those ones. 2 (*persona*): *¡Fue ésa!* It was her! ◇ *Yo no voy con ésos.* I'm not going with them.

esencia *nf* essence

esencial *adj* essential (*to/for sth*)

esfera *nf* 1 (*Geom, ámbito*) sphere 2 (*reloj*) face

esférico *adj* spherical

esfero *nm* (*And*) (ballpoint) pen

esfinge *nf* sphinx

esforzarse *vp* try (hard) (*to do sth*): *~ mucho* try very hard

esfuerzo *nm* 1 effort: *Haga un ~ y coma algo.* Make an effort to eat something. ◇ *No debes hacer ~s, aún no estás recuperado.* Don't overdo it, you're still recovering. 2 (*intento*) attempt (*at doing sth/to do sth*) ▶ **sin ~** effortlessly

esfumarse *vp* vanish ▶ **¡esfúmate!** get lost!

esgrima *nf* (*Dep*) fencing

esgrimir *vt* (*arma*) wield

esguince *nm* (*Med*) sprain: *hacerse un ~ en el tobillo* sprain your ankle

eslogan *nm* slogan

esmaltar *vt* enamel

esmalte *nm* enamel ▶ **~ de uñas** nail varnish

esmeralda *nf* emerald

esmerarse *vp* try very hard (*to do sth*): *Esmérate un poco más.* Try a little harder.

esmero *nm* ▶ **con ~** (very) carefully

esmoquin nm tuxedo [pl -s], dinner jacket (GB)

esnob = SNOB

eso pron that: ¡~ es! That's right! ▸ a ~ de at about: a ~ de la una at about one o'clock ▸ AROUND ¡de eso nada!, ¡eso sí que no! no way! por ~ (por esa razón) so, therefore (más fml)

esófago nm esophagus

esos/as, ésos/as Ver ESE/A

espabilado adj bright ▸ estar ~ be wide awake

espabilar vt wake sb up ● vi 1 (avivarse) get with it 2 (apresurarse) get a move on

espacial adj space: misión ~ space mission

espacio nm 1 space 2 (sitio) room: Aquí hay ~ para tu suéter. There's room here for your sweater. 3 (Radio, TV) program

espada nf 1 (arma) sword 2 espadas (cartas) spades → BARAJA ▸ entre la ~ y la pared between a rock and a hard place

espagueti nm spaghetti [U]: Me encantan los ~s. I love spaghetti.

espalda nf 1 back ▸ MY 2 (natación) backstroke: nadar (de) ~ do the backstroke ▸ dar la ~ turn your back on sth/sb ● de ~s: Póngase de ~s a la pared. Stand with your back to the wall. ◇ ver a algn de ~s see sb from behind ▸ hacer algo a ~s de do sth behind sb's back

espantapájaros nm scarecrow

espantar vt 1 (asustar) terrify 2 (ahuyentar) drive sth/sb away ● vi 1 (horrorizar) appall 2 (detestar) hate sth: Me espanta la idea de viajar sola. I hate the idea of traveling alone.

espanto nm 1 (miedo) fear 2 (And, fantasma) ghost: Se me apareció un ~ I saw a ghost.

espantoso adj terrible: Está haciendo un calor ~. It's terribly hot.

España nf Spain

español/a adj, nm Spanish ● nm-nf Spaniard: los ~es the Spanish

esparadrapo nm Band-Aid®, plaster (GB)

esparcimiento nm recreation

esparcir vt scatter

espárrago nm asparagus [U]

esparto nm esparto

espátula nf spatula

especia nf spice

especial adj special ▸ en ~ 1 (sobre todo) especially →SPECIAL 2 (en concreto) in particular

especialidad nf specialty [pl -ies]

especialista nmf specialist (in sth): un ~ en suelos a soil specialist

especializarse vp specialize (in sth)

especialmente adv 1 (sobre todo) especially: Me encantan los animales, ~ los gatos. I love animals, especially cats. 2 (en particular) particularly: Estoy ~ preocupada por el abuelo. I'm particularly concerned about grandpa. 3 (expresamente) specially: ~ diseñado para niños specially designed for children →SPECIAL

especie nf 1 (Biol) species [pl species] 2 (clase) kind

especificar vt specify

específico adj specific

espécimen nm specimen

espectacular adj spectacular

espectáculo nm 1 spectacle 2 (función) show ▸ dar un ~ make a scene el mundo del ~ show business

espectador/a nm-nf 1 (Teat, Mús) member of the audience 2 (Dep) spectator

espejismo nm mirage

espejo nm mirror ▸ ~ retrovisor rear-view mirror

espera nf wait

esperanza nf hope ▸ ~ de vida life expectancy

esperar vt wait for sth/sb, expect, hope **NOTA** Wait indica que una persona espera, sin hacer otra cosa, a que algn llegue o a que algo suceda por fin: Estoy esperando a que deje de llover. I'm waiting for it to stop raining. Expect se usa cuando lo esperado es lógico y muy probable: Había más tráfico de lo que yo esperaba. There was more traffic than I had expected. ◇ Esperaba carta suya ayer. I was expecting a letter from him yesterday. También se dice **expect** para una mujer embarazada: ~ un bebé expect a baby. Hope expresa el deseo de que algo suceda o haya sucedido: Espero verte pronto. I hope to see you soon. ◇ Espero que sí/no. I hope so/not. ● vi wait: Estoy harta de ~. I'm fed up of waiting.

esperma nf sperm

espesar(se) vt, vp thicken

espeso adj thick

espía nmf spy [pl spies]

espiar vt, vi spy (on sb)

espichar vt (And) **1** press **2** (fruta, insecto) squash

espiga nf (cereal) ear

espigado adj tall and slim

espina nf **1** (Bot) thorn **2** (pez) bone ▶ **darle a algn mala ~** have a bad feeling about sth: Ese asunto me da mala ~. I have a bad feeling about it. **~ dorsal** spine

espinaca nf spinach [U]

espinilla nf **1** (pierna) shin **2** (grano) blackhead

espionaje nm spying: Se dedica al ~. He's a spy.

espiral adj, nf spiral

espiritismo nm spiritualism ▶ **hacer ~** attend a seance

espíritu nm spirit: ~ de equipo team spirit **2** (alma) soul ▶ **E~ Santo** Holy Spirit

espiritual adj spiritual

espléndido adj **1** (magnífico) splendid **2** (generoso) generous

espolvorear vt sprinkle sth (with sth)

esponja nf sponge

esponjoso adj **1** (pastel) light **2** (lana, pan) soft

espontáneo adj **1** (impulsivo) spontaneous **2** (natural) natural

esporádico adj sporadic

esposar vt handcuff

esposas nf handcuffs ▶ **poner las ~** handcuff sb

esposo/a nm-nf husband [fem wife] [pl wives]

espuma nf **1** foam **2** (cerveza, huevo) froth **3** (jabón, etc.) lather **4** (pelo) mousse ▶ **hacer ~ 1** (olas) foam **2** (jabón, etc.) lather

espumoso adj (vino) sparkling

esqueje nm cutting

esquela nf notelet

esquelético adj (flaco) skinny →DELGADO

esqueleto nm **1** (Anat) skeleton **2** (estructura) framework

esquema nm **1** (diagrama) diagram **2** (resumen) outline

esquí nm **1** (tabla) ski [pl skis] **2** (Dep) skiing ▶ **~ acuático** waterskiing: hacer ~ acuático go waterskiing

esquiador/a nm-nf skier

esquiar vi ski: Me gusta ~. I like skiing. ◊ Esquío cada domingo. I go skiing every Sunday.

esquilar vt shear

esquimal nmf Eskimo [pl Eskimo o -os]

esquina nf corner: la casa que hace ~ con la plaza the house on the corner of the square

esquirol nmf strikebreaker

esquivar vt **1** dodge **2** (persona) avoid

esquizofrenia nf schizophrenia

esquizofrénico/a adj, nm-nf schizophrenic

esta, ésta adj Ver ESTE/A

estabilidad nf stability

estabilizar(se) vt, vp stabilize: El enfermo se estabilizó. The patient's condition has stabilized.

estable adj stable

establecer vt **1** (crear) set sth up **2** (determinar, ordenar) establish **3** (récord) set ● **establecerse** vp **1** (afincarse) settle **2** (Com) set up: ~ por su cuenta set up your own business

establo nm **1** (vacas) barn **2** (caballos) stable

estación nf **1** station: ~ de metro/policía subway/police station **2** (del año) season ▶ **~ de bomberos** fire station **~ de servicio** service station

estacionamiento nm parking

estacionar vi park

estadero nm (And) small restaurant

estadio nm (Dep) stadium

estadística nf **1** (ciencia) statistics [sing] **2** (cifra) statistic

estado nm **1** state: la seguridad del ~ state security **2** (físico) condition ▶ **en mal ~ 1** (alimento) bad: agua en mal ~ contaminated water **2** (objeto, carretera) in poor condition **~ civil** marital status **los E~s Unidos** the United States (abrev USA/US)

estafa nf swindle

estafar vt swindle sb (out of sth)

estalactita nf stalactite

estalagmita nf stalagmite

estallar vi **1** (bomba explosiva) explode **2** (globo, bomba inflable) burst **3** (guerra, epidemia) break out **4** (escándalo, tormenta) break

estallido nm **1** (bomba) explosion **2** (guerra) outbreak

estampa nf (dibujo) picture

estampado adj (tela) patterned ● nm (tela) pattern

estampar vt **1** (imprimir) print **2** (arrojar) hurl sth/sb (against sth) ● **estamparse** vp smash into sth

estampida nf stampede

estampilla nf stamp

estancado adj (agua) stagnant

estancarse vp **1** (agua) stagnate **2** (negociación) come to a standstill

estancia nf **1** stay **2** (hacienda) ranch

estanco nm **1** tobacconist's **2** (And) liquor store, off-licence (GB)

estándar adj, nm standard

estandarte nm banner

estanque nm (jardín, parque) pond

estanquillo nm (Mx) general store

estante nm **1** (repisa) shelf [pl shelves] **2** (mueble de entrepaños) set of shelves

estantería nf **1** shelves [pl] **2** (libros) bookcase

estaño nm tin

estar v copul, vi **1** be: ¿Está Ana? Is Ana in? ◇ ~ enfermo/cansado be ill/tired **2** (aspecto) look: Hoy estás muy bonita. You look very nice today. ● v aux + gerundio be doing sth: Estaba jugando. I was playing. ● **estarse** vp be: ~ callado/quieto be quiet/still ▶ **está bien** (de acuerdo) OK: —¿Me lo prestas? —Está bien. "Can I borrow it?" "OK." ¿**estamos?** all right? ~ **a 1** (fecha): Estamos a tres de mayo. It's May third. **2** (temperatura): En Cancún está a 30ºC. It's 30ºC in Cancún. **3** (precio): ¿A cuánto/cómo están las papas? How much are the potatoes? ~ **con** (apoyar) be behind sb: ¡Animo, estamos contigo! Go for it, we're behind you! ~ **que...**: Estoy que me caigo de sueño. I'm dead on my feet. ~ **sin** manage without sth/sb: No puedo ~ sin carro. I can't manage without a car. **no ~ para** not be in the mood for sth **NOTA** Para otras expresiones con estar, ver el sustantivo, adjetivo, etc., p.ej. estar al día en DÍA.

estatal adj state: un organismo ~ a state organization

estático adj static

estatua nf statue

estatura nf height: de mediana ~ of average height ◇ Es bajo de ~. He's short.

estatuto nm statute

este nm east

este adj this [pl these] ● (tb **éste/a**) pron **1** (cosa) this one [pl these (ones)]: ¿Prefieres éstos? Do you prefer these ones? **2** (persona): ¿Quién es ~? Who's this? ◇ El dinero se lo di a ésta. I gave the money to her.

estela nf **1** (barco) wake **2** (avión) vapor trail

estelar adj **1** starring: un papel ~ a starring role **2** (de las estrellas) stellar

estelarizar vt (Mx) star in sth

estera nf mat

estercolero nm dunghill

estéreo adj, nm stereo

estéril adj sterile

esterilizar vt sterilize

esterlina adj sterling: libras ~s pounds sterling

estética nf aesthetics [sing]

esteticista nmf beautician

estético adj aesthetic

estiércol nm manure

estilista nmf stylist

estilizar vt (hacer delgado): Esa falda te estiliza la figura. That skirt makes you look very slim.

estilo nm **1** (natación) stroke: ~ mariposa butterfly (stroke) ▶ **algo por el ~** something like that **con ~** stylish

estiloso adj stylish

estima nf esteem ▶ **tener ~ a/por** think highly of sb

estimado adj (cartas) dear

estimulante adj stimulating ● nm stimulant

estimular vt stimulate

estímulo nm stimulus [pl -li]

estirado adj (altivo) snooty

estirar vt **1** stretch: ~ una cuerda stretch a rope tight **2** (brazo, pierna) stretch sth out **3** (dinero) spin sth out **4** (alisar) smooth ● **estirarse** vp **1** (desperezarse) stretch **2** (crecer) shoot up ▶ **la pata** kick the bucket

estirón nm ▶ **dar/pegar un ~** (crecer) shoot up

esto pron this: Hay que terminar con ~. We have to put a stop to this. **2** (vacilación) er: Quería decirle que, ~... I wanted to tell you... er...

estofado nm stew

estómago nm stomach →MY

estorbar vi be in the way: ¿Estorbo? Am I in the way? ● vt be in sb's way: ¿Le estorban esas cajas? Are those boxes in your way?

estornudar vi sneeze →ACHÍS

estos/as ver ESTE/A

éstos/as ver ÉSTE/A

estrago nm ▶ **hacer ~s** create havoc

estrangular vt strangle

estrategia nf strategy [pl -ies]

estratégico adj strategic

estrato nm stratum [pl -ta]

estrechar vt (ropa) take sth in ● **estrechar(se)** vt, vp (carretera, etc.) narrow [pl straits] **2** (abrazar) embrace

estrecho adj **1** narrow **2** (ropa) tight: Te queda estrecha. It's too tight (for you). ● nm straits [pl]

estrella nf star: un hotel de dos ~s a two-star hotel ◊ una ~ de cine a movie star ▸ ~ **fugaz** shooting star ~ **invitada** celebrity guest **ver (las) ~s** see stars

estrellado adj 1 (noche, cielo) starry 2 (figura) star-shaped

estrellar vt smash sth (into/against sth): Estrelló el carro contra un árbol. He smashed the car into a tree. ● **estrellarse** vp 1 (chocar) crash (into sth) 2 (fracasar) founder

estremecer(se) vt, vp shake ▸ ~**se de dolor** wince with pain

estrenar vt 1 ~ zapatos wear new shoes ◊ ¿Estás estrenando carro? Is that a new car you're driving? 2 (Cine) premiere 3 (Teat) stage sth for the first time

estreno nm 1 (Cine) première 2 (Teat) first night

estrés nm stress ▸ **tener** ~ **be** suffering from stress

estresado adj stressed (out): Está muy ~. He's really stressed.

estresante adj stressful

estreñido adj constipated

estreñimiento nm constipation

estreñir vt make sb constipated ● **estreñirse** vp become constipated

estría nf 1 groove 2 (piel) stretch mark

estribillo nm 1 (canción) chorus 2 (poema) refrain

estribo nm stirrup

estribor nm starboard: a ~ to starboard

estricto adj strict

estridente adj 1 (sonido) shrill 2 (color) gaudy

estrofa nf verse

estropajo nm 1 scourer 2 (Mx) loofah

estropear vt 1 spoil 2 (aparato) break ● **estropearse** vp 1 (averiarse) break down 2 (comida) go bad

estructura nf structure

estruendo nm racket

estuario nm estuary [pl -ies]

estuche nm 1 (pinturas, maquillaje, joyas) box 2 (lápices, instrumento musical) case

estudiante nmf student: un ~ de medicina a medical student

estudiar vt, vi study ▸ ~ **de memoria** learn sth by heart

estudio nm 1 study [pl -ies]: realizar un ~ do a study ◊ Tiene los libros en el ~. Her books are in the study. 2 (apartamento) studio apartment 3 (Fot, TV)

studio [pl -s] 4 **estudios** education [sing]: ~s primarios elementary education

estudioso adj studious

estufa nf stove

estupendo adj fantastic

estúpido/a adj stupid ● nm-nf idiot

etapa nf stage ▸ **por** ~**s** in stages

etcétera nm etcetera (abrev **etc.**)

eternidad nf eternity ▸ **una** ~ forever: Esperé una ~ I waited forever.

eterno adj eternal

ética nf ethics

ético adj ethical

etiqueta nf 1 label: la ~ de un paquete the label on a package 2 (precio) price tag ▸ **de** ~ formal: traje de ~ formal dress

etiquetar vt label

etnia nf ethnic group

étnico adj ethnic

eucalipto nm eucalyptus

euforia nf euphoria

eufórico/a adj euphoric

euro nm euro [pl -s]

Europa nf Europe

europeo/a adj, nm-nf European

eutanasia nf euthanasia

evacuación nf evacuation

evacuar vt 1 (desalojar) vacate 2 (trasladar) evacuate

evadido/a nm-nf escapee

evadir vt (eludir) evade ● **evadirse** vp escape (from sth)

evaluación nf assessment

evaluar vt assess

evangelio nm gospel

evaporación nf evaporation

evaporar(se) vt, vp evaporate

evasión nf 1 (fuga) escape 2 (distracción) distraction ▸ ~ **de impuestos** tax evasion

evasiva nf: Siempre está con ~s. He's always avoiding the issue.

eventual adj 1 (hipotético) possible: en caso de un ~ incendio in case of fire 2 (temporal) temporary

evidencia nf evidence ▸ **poner en** ~ show sb up

evidente adj obvious

evitar vt 1 (impedir) prevent 2 (rehuir) avoid sth/sb: Me evita a toda costa. He does everything he can to avoid me. ▸ **no lo puedo** ~ I, you, etc. can't help it **si puedo evitarlo** if I, you, etc. can help it

evocar vt evoke

evolución nf **1** (Biol) evolution **2** (desarrollo) development

evolucionar vi **1** (Biol) evolve **2** (desarrollarse) develop

exactitud nf exactness **2** (descripción, reloj) accuracy ▸ **con ~** exactly

exacto adj **1** (no aproximado) exact: Dos kilos ~s. Exactly two kilos. **2** (descripción, reloj) accurate **3** (idéntico) identical ● interj exactly

exageración nf exaggeration

exagerado adj **1** exaggerated: No seas ~. Don't exaggerate. **2** (excesivo) excessive

exagerar vt, vi exaggerate

exaltado/a adj angry (about sth) ● nm-nf hothead

exaltar vt (alabar) praise ● **exaltarse** vp get heated

examen nm exam: tomar/presentar un ~ take an exam ▸ **estar en/tener exámenes** be taking exams ~ **de manejo/conducción** driving test ~ **extraordinario** (Mx) retake ~ **final** finals [pl]

examinar vt examine ● **examinarse** vp take an exam ▸ **hacerse ~ los ojos, etc.** have your eyes, etc. tested

excavación nf excavation

excavadora nf digger

excavar vt **1** dig **2** (Arqueología) excavate ● vi dig

excelencia nf ▸ **por ~** par excellence **Su E~** His/Her/Your Excellency

excelente adj excellent

excepción nf exception ▸ **a/con ~ de** except (for) sth/sb

excepcional adj exceptional

excepto prep except (for) sth/sb: todos excepto yo everybody except me

exceptuar vt except: Exceptuando a uno, todos son jóvenes. Except for one, they're all young.

excesivo adj excessive: tener una excesiva afición por algo be much too keen on sth

exceso nm excess (of sth) ▸ **con/en ~** too much ~ **de equipaje** excess baggage

excitar vt **1** excite **2** (nervios) make sb nervous ● **excitarse** vp get excited (about/over sth)

exclamación nf (signo de puntuación) exclamation point, exclamation mark (GB)

exclamar vi, vt exclaim

excluir vt exclude sth/sb (from sth)

exclusiva nf (reportaje) exclusive

exclusivo adj exclusive

excursión nf excursion ▸ **ir/salir de ~** go on an excursion

excusa nf excuse (for sth): Siempre tiene ~s para no ir. He always finds an excuse not to go.

exento adj **1** (exonerado) exempt (from sth) **2** (libre) free (from sth)

exhalar vt **1** (gas, olor, etc.) give sth off **2** (suspiro, queja): un suspiro de alivio heave a sigh of relief ◇ un gemido de dolor groan with pain ● vi breathe out

exhaustivo adj thorough

exhausto adj exhausted

exhibición nf exhibition

exhibicionismo nm **1** exhibitionism **2** (sexual) indecent exposure

exhibicionista nmf **1** exhibitionist **2** (sexual) flasher (coloq)

exhibir vt **1** (exponer) exhibit **2** (película) show ● **exhibirse** vp (presumir) show off

exigencia nf **1** (requerimiento) requirement **2** (pretensión) demand (for sth)

exigente adj **1** (que pide mucho) demanding **2** (estricto) strict

exigir vt **1** (pedir) demand sth (from sb) **2** (requerir) require

exiliado/a adj exiled ● nm-nf exile

exiliar vt exile sb (from...) ● **exiliarse** vp go into exile (in...)

exilio nm exile

existencia nf **1** existence **2** existencias stock [sing]

existir vi **1** exist **2** (haber): No existe una voluntad de colaboración. There is no spirit of co-operation.

éxito nm **1** success **2** (canción, etc.) hit ▸ **tener ~** be successful

exorcismo nm exorcism

exótico adj exotic

expandir vt **1** expand **2** (incendio, rumor) spread ● **expandirse** vp spread

expansión nf expansion

expansionar vt expand

expatriado/a adj, nm-nf expatriate

expatriar vt exile ● **expatriarse** vp emigrate

expectación nf sense of expectancy

expectativa nf **1** (esperanza) expectation **2** (perspectiva) prospect: ~s electorales electoral prospects ▸ **estar a la ~** be on the lookout (for sth)

expedición nf (viaje) expedition

expediente nm **1** (documentación) file **2** (empleado, estu-

diante) record **3** (*Jur*) proceedings [*pl*] ▸ **abrir (un) ~** take proceedings (*against sb*)

expedir *vt* **1** issue: *~ una visa* issue a visa **2** (*enviar*) send

expensas *nf*: *a nuestras ~* at our expense

experiencia *nf* experience: *~ laboral* work experience ▸ **sin ~** inexperienced

experimentado *adj* (*persona*) experienced

experimental *adj* experimental: *con carácter ~* on an experimental basis

experimentar *vi* experiment (*with sth*) ● *vt* **1** (*aumento, mejoría*) show **2** (*cambio*) undergo

experimento *nm* experiment: *hacer un ~* carry out an experiment

experto/a *nm-nf* expert (*at/in sth*)

explanada *nf* open area

explicación *nf* explanation

explicar *vt* explain *sth* (*to sb*) ● **explicarse** *vp* (*entender*) understand ▸ **¿me explico?** do you see what I mean?

explorador/a *nm-nf* explorer

explorar *vt* **1** (*país, región*) explore **2** (*Med*) examine

explosión *nf* explosion: *~ una ~ nuclear/demográfica* a nuclear/population explosion ▸ **hacer ~** explode

explosivo *adj, nm* explosive

explotar *vi* (*hacer explosión*) explode

exponer *vt* **1** (*cuadro*) exhibit **2** (*ideas*) present **3** (*vida*) risk ● **exponerse** *vp* expose yourself *to sth*: *No se exponga demasiado al sol.* Don't stay out in the sun too long. ▸ **~se a que...** risk *sth*: *Te expones a que te multen.* You're risking a fine.

exportación *nf* export

exportador/a *nm-nf* exporter ● *adj* exporting: *un país ~ de petróleo* an oil-exporting country

exportar *vt* export

exposición *nf* **1** (*arte*) exhibition **2** (*de un tema*) presentation

exprés *adj* express

expresar *vt* express

expresión *nf* expression

expresivo *adj* **1** expressive **2** (*mirada*) meaningful **3** (*afectuoso*) affectionate

expreso *adj, nm* express

exprimidor *nm* juicer

exprimir *vt* (*fruta*) squeeze

expulsar *vt* **1** expel *sb* (*from...*) **2** (*Dep*) send *sb* off

expulsión *nf* expulsion

exquisito *adj* **1** (*comida, bebida*) delicious **2** (*gusto, objeto*) exquisite

éxtasis *nm* ecstasy [*pl* -ies]

extender *vt* **1** (*desdoblar*) spread *sth* (out): *~ un mapa sobre la mesa* spread a map out on the table **2** (*alargar*) extend: *~ una mesa* extend a table **3** (*brazo*) stretch out *sth* **4** (*alas, mantequilla, pintura*) spread ● **extenderse** *vp* **1** spread **2** (*espacio*) stretch: *El jardín se extiende hasta el lago.* The garden stretches down to the lake. **3** (*tiempo*) last: *El debate se extendió durante horas.* The debate lasted for hours.

extendido *adj* **1** widespread **2** (*brazos*) outstretched

extensión *nf* **1** (*superficie*) area **2** (*duración*): *una gran ~ de tiempo* a long period of time ◊ *¿Cuál es la ~ del contrato?* How long is the contract for? **3** (*teléfono*) extension

extenso *adj* **1** (*grande*) extensive **2** (*largo*) long

exterior *adj* outer: *la capa ~ de la Tierra* the outer layer of the earth **2** (*Com, Pol*) foreign: *política ~* foreign policy ● *nm* outside

exterminar *vt* exterminate

externo/a *adj* **1** external **2** (*capa, superficie*) outer: *la parte externa del muslo* the outer thigh ● *nm-nf* day student

extinción *nf* (*especie*) extinction

extinguidor (*tb* **extintor**) *nm* fire extinguisher

extinguir *vt* **1** (*fuego*) put *sth* out **2** (*especie*) wipe *sth* out ● **extinguirse** *vp* **1** (*fuego*) go out **2** (*especie*) become extinct

extirpar *vt* (*Med*) remove

extra *adj* **1** (*superior*) top quality **2** (*adicional*) extra ● *nmf* (*Cine, Teat*) extra ▸ **horas ~s** overtime [*U*]

extraer *vt* **1** extract *sth* from *sth/ sb* **2** (*sangre*) take *sth* from *sb*

extraescolar *adj* extra-curricular

extranjero/a *adj* foreign ● *nm-nf* foreigner ▸ **al/en el ~** abroad

extrañar *vt* **1** (*sorprender*) surprise **2** (*echar de menos*) miss ● **extrañarse** *vp* be surprised (*at sth/sb*) ▸ **ya me extrañaba a mí** I thought it was strange

extraño/a *adj* strange ● *nm-nf* stranger

extraordinario *adj* **1** (*excelente*) excellent **2** (*especial*) special ● *nm* (*Mx, examen*) retake

extraterrestre *adj* extraterrestrial ● *nmf* alien

extraviado *adj* **1** (*persona, cosa*) lost **2** (*animal*) stray

extraviar *vt* lose ● **extraviarse** *vp* **1** (*persona, objeto*) get lost **2** (*animal*) stray

extremar *vt* maximize: *~ las medidas de control* implement tight controls

extremidades *nf* (*cuerpo*) extremities

extremo *adj* extreme ● *nm* **1** (*punto más alto/bajo*) extreme: *ir de un ~ a otro* go from one extreme to another **2** (*punta*) end: *en el otro ~ de la ciudad* at the other end of town

extrovertido *adj* extrovert: *Es muy ~.* He's a real extrovert.

F f

fa *nm* F: *fa mayor* F major

fábrica *nf* **1** factory [*pl* -ies] **2** (*cemento, ladrillos, etc.*) works: *Va a cerrar la ~ de acero.* The steelworks is/are closing down. ▶ **~ de cerveza** brewery [*pl* -ies] ▶ **~ de papel** paper mill

fabricación *nf* manufacture ▶ **de ~ mexicana, colombiana, etc.** made in Mexico, Colombia, etc.

fabricante *nmf* manufacturer

fabricar *vt* manufacture, make (*más coloq*) ▶ **~ en serie** mass-produce

facha *nf* **1** (*aspecto*) look: *No me gusta su ~.* I don't like the look of him. **2** (*adefesio*) sight: *Esta chaqueta te hace ver con una ~ terrible.* You're a real sight in that jacket.

fachada *nf* (*edificio*) façade, front (*más coloq*)

fácil *adj* easy

factor *nm* factor

factura *nf* bill: *la ~ de la luz* the electric bill ◊ *Haga la ~.* Make out the bill.

facturación *nf* check-in

facturar *vt* bill

facultad *nf* **1** (*capacidad*) faculty [*pl* -ies] **2** (*Educ*) (a) (*universidad*) college: *un compañero de ~* a friend of mine from college (b) **Facultad** Faculty [*pl* -ies]: *~ de Derecho* Faculty of Law

faena *nf* (*tarea*) job: *No le dedique mucho tiempo a esa ~.* Don't spend a lot of time on that job.

▶ **~s agrícolas/del campo** farm work [*sing*]

faisán *nm* pheasant

faja *nf* **1** (*fajín*) sash **2** (*ropa interior*) girdle

fajo *nm* bundle

falda *nf* **1** (*ropa*) skirt **2** (*montaña*) lower slope ▶ **~ escocesa 1** plaid skirt **2** (*traje típico*) kilt ● **pantalón** culottes [*pl*] →PANTALÓN

falla *nf* **1** (*error*) mistake, error (*más fml*): *debido a una ~ humana* due to human error **2** (*defecto*) fault: *una ~ en los frenos* a fault in the brakes →MISTAKE

fallar *vi* **1** fail **2** (*a un amigo*) let sb down ● *vt* miss: *Falló el tiro.* He missed. ▶ **¡no fallar!** it, he, etc. is always the same: *Seguro que llega tarde, no falla nunca.* He's bound to be late; he's always the same.

falleba *nf* catch: *echar la ~* put the catch on

fallecer *vi* pass away

fallo *nm* ruling

falluca *nf* (*Mx*) smuggled goods [*pl*]

falsificación *nf* forgery [*pl* -ies]

falsificar *vt* forge

falso *adj* **1** false: *una falsa alarma* a false alarm **2** (*de imitación*) fake

falta *nf* **1** (*carencia*) lack of sth **2** (*error*) mistake **3** (*Dep*) foul: *hacer (una) ~* commit a foul ▶ **~ (de asistencia)** absence: *Ya tienes dos ~s este mes.* That's twice you've been absent this month. ◊ **ponerle ~ a algn** mark sb absent ▶ **de educación** rudeness: *¡Qué ~ de educación!* How rude! ▶ **hace(n) ~** need sth: *Me hace ~ un carro.* I need a car. ◊ *Te hace ~ estudiar más.* You need to study harder. ◊ *No hace ~ que venga.* You don't have to come. **sin ~** without fail

faltar *vi* **1** (*necesitar*) need sth/sb: *Les falta cariño.* They need affection. ◊ *Aquí falta un director.* This place needs a manager. **2** (*no estar*) be missing: *¿Falta alguien?* Is there anybody missing? ◊ *¿Falta algo?* Is anything missing? ◊ *sth: ~ a una clase* miss a class **4** (*quedar tiempo*): *Faltan diez minutos.* There are ten minutes to go. ◊ *¿Falta mucho para comer?* Is it long till lunch? ◊ *¿Te falta mucho?* Are you going to be long? **5** (*hora*): *Faltan cinco para las diez.* It's five to ten. ▶ **faltarle al respeto a algn** show no respect to sb **faltarle un tornillo a algn** have a screw loose

falta ver si... (*And*) what if...: *¡Falta ver si pasó algo!* What if something's happened? **¡lo que faltaba!** that's all I/we needed!

fama *nf* **1** (*celebridad*) fame **2** (*reputación*) reputation (*for sth*): *Tiene ~ de ser bueno.* He has a reputation for being good.

familia *nf* family [*pl* -ies]: *una ~ numerosa* a large family **NOTA** El apellido de la familia se puede expresar con la palabra **family**, o poniendo el apellido en plural: *the Mendoza family/the Mendozas*. ▸ **madre/padre de ~** mother/father **no ver ni por la ~** (*And*) be blind as a bat **venir de ~** run in the family

familiar *adj* **1** (*de la familia*) family: *lazos ~es* family ties **2** (*conocido*) familiar: *una cara ~* a familiar face ● *nmf* (*pariente*) relative

famoso *adj* **1** (*célebre*) famous (*for sth*) **2** (*de mala fama*) notorious (*for sth*)

fan *nmf* fan

fanático/a *nm-nf* fanatic

fandango *nm* (*fiesta*) party [*pl* -ies]

fanfarrón/ona *adj*, *nm-nf* show-off: *Es un ~ sin remedio.* He's a terrible show-off.

fanfarronear *vi* show off

fantasía *nf* fantasy [*pl* -ies]

fantasma *nm* ghost: *un relato de ~s* a ghost story

fantástico *adj* fantastic

farmacéutico/a *nm-nf* pharmacist

farmacia *nf* **1** (*tienda*) drugstore, chemist's (*GB*) **2** (*estudios*) pharmacy

faro *nm* **1** (*Náut*) lighthouse **2** (*Aut*) headlight

farol *nm* **1** (*lámpara*) lantern **2** (*alumbrado público*) streetlight

farola *nf* **1** streetlight **2** (*And, Aut*) headlight

fascículo *nm* installment

fascinante *adj* fascinating

fascinar *vi* love *sth*: *Me fascina bailar.* I love dancing.

fascismo *nm* fascism

fascista *adj*, *nmf* fascist

fase *nf* stage: *la ~ previa/clasificatoria* the preliminary/qualifying stage

fastidiar *vt*, *vi* **1** (*molestar*) annoy, bug (*coloq*): *Me fastidia tener que ir.* It really bugs me having to go. ◇ *No deja de ~ con eso.* He keeps pestering me about that. ◇ *Estos zapatos me van a ~.* These shoes are going to rub. ● **fastidiarse** *vp*

(*jorobarse*): *Tendrá que ~.* He'll just have to put up with it. ▸ **¡para que te fastidies!** so there! **¡te fastidias!** tough!

fastidio *nm* ▸ **dar ~**: *Los riñones me dan ~.* I can't stand kidney. **¡qué ~!** **1** (*qué repugnante*) how revolting! **2** (*qué molesto*) what a pain!

fatal *adj* fatal

fauna *nf* fauna

favor *nm* favor: *¿Me haces un ~?* Can you do me a favor? ▸ **a ~ de** in favor of *sth/sb*: *Estoy a ~ de actuar.* I'm in favor of taking action. **por ~** please

favorable *adj* favorable

favorecer *vt* **1** favor (*ropa, peinado*) suit: *Te favorece el rojo.* Red suits you.

favorecido *adj* winning: *el número ~* the winning number

favoritismo *nm* favoritism

favorito/a *adj*, *nm-nf* favorite

fax *nm* fax: *mandar un ~/algo por ~* send a fax/fax sth

fe *nf* faith (*in sth/sb*)

febrero *nm* February (*abrev* **Feb.**) →MAYO

fecha *nf* **1** date: *¿A qué ~ estamos?* What's the date today? ◇ *Tiene ~ del 3 de mayo.* It's dated May 3. **2** **fechas** (*época*) time [*sing*]: *en/por estas ~s* at/around this time (of the year) ▸ **~ límite/tope 1** (*solicitud*) closing date **2** (*proyecto*) deadline

fecundación *nf* fertilization

fecundar *vt* fertilize

federación *nf* federation

felicidad *nf* happiness: *cara de ~* a happy face ▸ **¡felicidades! 1** congratulations (*on sth*)!: *Te deseo muchas ~.* Best wishes. **2** (*cumpleaños*) happy birthday!

felicitaciones *nf* **1** congratulations (*on sth*): *¡~ por tus exámenes!* Congratulations on passing your exams. **2** (*cumpleaños*) happy birthday!

felicitar *vt* **1** congratulate *sb* (*on sth*): *¡Te felicito!* Congratulations! **2** (*fiestas*) wish *sb* (a) happy...: *~ a algn por las Navidades* wish sb a happy Christmas

feliz *adj* happy ▸ **¡~ cumpleaños/Navidad!** Happy birthday/Merry Christmas!

felpa *nf* plush

femenino *adj* **1** female **2** (*Dep, moda*) women's: *el equipo ~* the women's team **3** (*característico de la mujer, Gram*) feminine **NOTA** Female se aplica a las características físicas de las mujeres: *la figura femenina* the female figure, y **feminine** a las cualidades que consideramos típicas de una mujer: *Lleva ropa muy femenina.* She wears very feminine clothes.

feminista *adj, nmf* feminist

fenomenal *adj* fantastic

fenómeno *nm* **1** phenomenon [*pl* -mena] **2** (*prodigio*): *Es un* ~. He's fantastic.

feo *adj* **1** (*aspecto*) ugly **2** (*desagradable*) nasty: *una costumbre fea* a nasty habit

féretro *nm* casket, coffin (*GB*)

feria *nf* **1** fair ▶ ~ **de muestras** trade fair **irle a algn como en** ~ (*Mx*) go very badly

feriado *adj, nm* holiday: *días* ~s public holidays

fermentar *vt, vi* ferment

feroz *adj* fierce

ferretería *nf* **1** (*tienda*) hardware store **2** (*objetos*) hardware: *artículos de* ~ hardware

ferrocarril *nm* railroad, railway (*GB*): *estación de* ~ railway/train station

ferry *nm* ferry [*pl* -ies]

fértil *adj* (*tierra, persona*) fertile

festín *nm* feast

festival *nm* festival

festividad *nf* **1** (*celebración*) festivity [*pl* -ies] **2** (*Rel*) feast

festivo *adj* holiday ▶ **día** ~ holiday

fétido *adj* foul-smelling

feto *nm* fetus

fiable *adj* reliable

fiambre *nm* **1** (*carne*) cold meat **2** (*And*) picnic

fianza *nf* **1** (*Jur*) bail [*U*] **2** (*Com*) deposit

fiar *vt* let *sb* have *sth* on credit ● *vi* give credit ● **fiarse** *vp* trust *sb*: *No me fío de ella.* I don't trust her. ▶ **ser de** ~ be trustworthy

fibra *nf* fiber

ficción *nf* fiction

ficha *nf* **1** (*tarjeta*) (index) card **2** (*pieza de juego*) (playing) piece: *Se perdió una* ~. We've lost a piece. **3** (*que reemplaza el dinero*) token ▶ ~ **de dominó** domino [*pl* -es] ~ **médica/policial** medical/police record

fichaje *nm* (*Dep*) signing

fichar *vt* **1** (*policía*) open a file on *sb* **2** (*Dep*) sign

fichero *nm* **1** (*mueble*) filing cabinet **2** (*caja*) card index **3** (*conjunto de fichas, Comp*) file

ficho (*And*) = FICHA

fidelidad *nf* faithfulness ▶ **alta** ~ hi-fi

fideo *nm* noodle ▶ **como/hecho un** ~ as skinny as a rail, as thin as a rake (*GB*)

fiebre *nf* **1** fever: ~ *amarilla* yellow fever **2** (*temperatura anormal*) temperature: *Tiene 38° de* ~. He has a temperature of 38°.

fiel *adj* **1** (*leal*) faithful (*to sth/sb*) **2** (*creencias, palabra*) true to *sth*

fieltro *nm* felt

fiera *nf* wild animal ▶ **estar como/hecho una** ~ blow your stack, blow your top (*GB*)

fiero *adj* fierce

fierro *nm* (*hierro*) iron

fiesta *nf* **1** (*celebración*) party [*pl* -ies]: *dar/hacer una* ~ *de cumpleaños* hold a birthday party **2 fiestas**: *las* ~s *navideñas/del pueblo* the Christmas festivities/town festival ▶ **día (de)** ~ public holiday: *Hoy es* ~. Today's a public holiday.

figura *nf* figure: *una* ~ *de arcilla/política* a clay/political figure

figurar *vi* **1** be: *México figura entre los países de la NAFTA.* Mexico is one of the NAFTA countries. **2** (*destacar*) stand out from the crowd ● **figurarse** *vp* imagine

fijamente *adv* ▶ **mirar** ~ stare at *sth/sb*

fijar *vt* **1** fix **2** (*atención*) focus ● **fijarse** *vp* **1** (*darse cuenta*): *¿Se fijó si estaba?* Did you see if he was there? **2** (*prestar atención*) pay attention (*to sth*) **3** (*mirar*) look at *sth/sb*

fijo *adj* **1** fixed: *Las patas están fijas al suelo.* The legs are fixed to the ground. **2** (*permanente*) permanent ● *adv* (*sin duda*) definitely

fila *nf* **1** (*uno al lado de otro*) row: *en la primera/última* ~ in the front/back row **2** (*uno detrás de otro*) line: *Formen una* ~. Get in line. **3 filas** (*Mil, Pol*) ranks ▶ **(en)** ~ **india** (*en fila*) single file **estacionarse/parquear en doble** ~ double-park **hacer** ~ stand in line

filete *nm* **1** (*fino*) filet **2** (*grueso*) steak

filmadora *nf* video camera

filmar *vt* film

filo *nm* **1** (*navaja*) cutting edge **2** (*montaña*) ridge

filología *nf* philology ▶ ~ **hispánica, inglesa, etc.** Spanish, English, etc.: *Soy licenciado en F* ~ *Inglesa.* I have a degree in English.

filosofía *nf* philosophy [*pl* -ies]

filósofo/a *nm-nf* philosopher

filtrar vt filter ● **filtrarse** vp 1 filter (in/out) (through sth): *La luz se filtraba por las ranuras.* Light was filtering in through the cracks. 2 (*líquido*) leak (in/out) (through sth)

filtro nm filter

fin nm 1 end: *a ~ de mes* at the end of the month ◊ *No es el ~ del mundo.* It's the end of the world. 2 (*Cine, novela*) end 3 (*finalidad*) purpose ▶ **al ~ y al cabo** after all **al/por ~** at last **en ~ 1** (*bien*) well: *En ~, así es la vida.* Well, that's life. 2 (*en resumen*) in short **~ de semana** weekend: *Nos vemos los ~es de semana.* We see each other on weekends. →WEEKEND

final adj final ● nm 1 end: *a dos minutos del ~* two minutes from the end 2 (*Cine, novela*) ending ● nf final: *la ~ de la copa* the Cup Final ▶ **a finales de...** at the end of... **al ~** at/in the end **NOTA At the end** se usa en forma neutra, e **in the end** se usa al hablar de un período largo o con muchos cambios o problemas: *Al ~ todo va a salir bien.* It will all work out in the end. **al ~ de** at the end of

finalista adj, nmf finalist: *los equipos ~s* the finalists ◊ *Quedó ~.* He reached the final.

finca nf 1 (*casa de campo*) country estate 2 (*terreno*) (plot of) land

fingir vt, vi pretend: *Fingió no vernos.* He pretended he hadn't seen us.

finlandés/esa adj, nm Finnish ● nm-nf Finn

Finlandia nf Finland

fino adj 1 (*delgado*) fine 2 (*dedos, talle*) slender 3 (*elegante, de buena calidad*) posh (*coloq*) 4 (*educado*) polite 5 (*vista, oído*) keen

finta nf dummy [pl -ies]: *hacer una ~* dummy

firma nf 1 (*nombre*) signature 2 (*acto*) signing

firmar vt, vi sign

firme adj firm: *mostrarse ~* stand firm ▶ **¡firmes!** attention! **ponerse ~** stand to attention

fiscal adj tax: *los impuestos ~es* taxes ● nmf public prosecutor

fisgonear vt, vi snoop around (in sth): *No me fisgonees las cartas.* Don't snoop around in my letters.

física nf physics [sing]

físico/a adj physical ● nm-nf (*científico*) physicist ● nm (*aspecto*) appearance

fisicoculturismo (tb **fisiculturismo**) nm bodybuilding

flaco adj 1 (*delgado*) thin, skinny (*coloq*) →DELGADO 2 (*débil*) weak

flamante adj 1 (*espléndido*) smart 2 (*nuevo*) brand new

flamenco nm (*ave*) flamingo [pl -s/-es]

flan nm crème caramel

flaquear vi flag

flash nm flash

flauta nf flute

flautista nmf flautist

flecha nf arrow

flechazo nm love at first sight: *Fue un ~.* It was love at first sight.

flecos nm 1 (*adorno*) fringe [sing]: *una chaqueta con ~s* a fringed jacket **2** (*flequillo Mx*) (*pelo*) bangs [pl], fringe (*GB*) 3 (*borde deshilachado*) frayed edge ▶ **dejar hecho ~s** wear sb out

flexible adj flexible

flojera nf laziness ▶ **me da ~** I can't be bothered (to do sth) **¡qué ~!** what a drag!

flojo adj 1 (*poco apretado*) loose: *un tornillo ~* a loose screw (b) (*banda elástica, cuerda*) slack **2 ~ en** (*materia, etc.*) weak (at/in sth) 3 (*perezoso*) lazy 4 (*And, cobarde*) cowardly

flor nf 1 flower: *~es secas* dried flowers 2 (*árbol, arbusto*) blossom [U]: *las ~es del naranjo* orange blossom ▶ **en ~ in** bloom

flora nf flora

floreado adj flowery

florecer vi 1 (*planta*) flower 2 (*árbol, arbusto*) blossom 3 (*prosperar*) flourish

florero nm vase

floristería (tb **florería**) nf flower shop, florist's (*GB*)

flota nf fleet

flotar vi float

flote ▶ **a ~** afloat **sacar a ~ 1** (*barco*) refloat 2 (*negocio*) put sth back on its feet **salir a ~** pull through

fluido adj 1 (*circulación, diálogo*) free-flowing 2 (*lenguaje, estilo*) fluent ● nm fluid

flujo nm flow

flúor nm (*dentífrico*) fluoride

fluorescente adj fluorescent ● nm fluorescent light

fluvial adj river: *el transporte ~* river transport

foca nf seal

foco nm 1 focus 2 (a) (*bombilla*) light bulb (b) (*Teat, etc.*) spotlight (c) (*estadio*) floodlight

fogata nf bonfire

fogón nm burner

foguero nm ▶ de ~ blank

folclore (tb **folklore**) nm folklore

folio nm sheet (of paper)

follaje nm foliage

folleto nm 1 (*librito*) (a) (*publicidad*) brochure: un ~ de viajes a travel brochure (b) (*información, instrucciones*) booklet 2 (*hoja*) leaflet

fomentar vt promote

fomento nm promotion ▶ ~ de empleo job creation

fondo nm 1 bottom: llegar al ~ del asunto get to the bottom of things 2 (*mar, río*) bed 3 (*calle, pasillo*) end (b) (*habitación, escenario*) back: al ~ del bar at the back of the bar 4 (*recolecta*) kitty [pl -ies]: poner/hacer un ~ (*común*) have a kitty 5 fondos (*dinero*) funds: recaudar ~s raise funds ▶ a ~ 1 (+ sustantivo) thorough: una revisión a ~ a thorough review 2 (+ verbo) thoroughly: Límpialo a ~. Clean it thoroughly. de ~ 1 (*Dep*) distance: un corredor de ~ a distance runner 2 (*Mús*): música de ~ background music en el ~ 1 (a pesar de las apariencias) deep down: En el ~ sí que importa. Deep down you do care. 2 (en realidad) basically: En el ~ pensamos lo mismo. We basically agree. sin ~ bottomless

forastero/a nm-nf stranger

forcejear vi struggle

forense nmf forensic scientist

forestal adj forest: un guarda ~ a forest ranger

forjar vt forge ▶ ~se ilusiones get your hopes up

forma nf 1 (*contorno*) shape: en ~ de cruz in the shape of a cross ◇ La sala tiene ~ rectangular. The room is rectangular. 2 (*modo*) way: Es su ~ de ser. It's just the way he is. 3 (*Mx, formulario*) form ▶ de ~ espontánea, indefinida, etc. spontaneously, indefinitely, etc. de todas ~s anyway en plena forma in peak condition estar/ponerse/mantenerse en ~ be/get/keep in shape

formación nf 1 formation 2 (*preparación*) (a) (*educación*) education (b) (*trabajo*) training ▶ ~ profesional vocational training

formado adj ▶ estar ~ por be made up of sth/sb

formal adj 1 formal 2 (de fiar) reliable 3 (que se porta bien) well behaved

formar vt 1 (*crear*) form 2 (*educar*) educate ● vi (*Mil*) fall in ● **formarse** vp 1 (*hacerse*) form 2 (*educarse*) train

formatear vt (*Comp*) format

formato nm format

fórmula nf 1 formula [pl -s o formulae] 2 ▶ FORMULA 2 (*And, Med*) prescription

formulario nm form: llenar un ~ fill out a form

forrado adj ▶ estar ~ (tener dinero) be rolling in it

forrar vt 1 (*interior*) line sth (with sth): una caja de terciopelo line a box with velvet 2 (*exterior*) cover sth (with sth) ● **forrarse** vp (enriquecerse) make a killing

forro nm 1 (*interior*) lining 2 (*exterior*) cover

fortaleza nf 1 (*fuerza*) strength 2 (*fortificación*) fortress

fortuna nf fortune: probar ~ try your luck

forzar vt force

fosa nf 1 (*hoyo*) ditch 2 (*sepultura*) grave

fosforescente adj phosphorescent

fósforo nm 1 (*Quím*) phosphorus 2 (*cerillo*) match: prender un ~ strike a match

fósil nm fossil

foso nm 1 (*hoyo*) ditch 2 (de castillo) moat

foto nf photo [pl -s]: ~ tamaño cédula passport photo ◇ Me tomó una ~. He took my picture. ▶ tomarse/sacarse una ~ have your picture taken

fotocopia nf photocopy [pl -ies]: hacer/sacar una ~ de algo photocopy sth

fotocopiadora nf photocopier

fotocopiar vt photocopy

fotogénico adj photogenic

fotografía nf 1 (*actividad*) photography 2 (*foto*) photograph

fotografiar vt photograph

fotógrafo/a nm-nf photographer

fracasado/a nm-nf failure

fracasar vi 1 fail 2 (*planes*) fall through

fracaso nm failure

fracción nf 1 fraction 2 (*Pol*) faction

fraccionamiento nm (*Mx*) housing development

fractura nf fracture

fracturar(se) vt, vp fracture

frágil adj fragile

fragmento *nm* fragment

fraile *nm* monk

frambuesa *nf* raspberry [*pl* -ies]

francamente *adv* 1 frankly: ~, *no quería ir, pero me tocó.* Frankly, I didn't want to go, but I had to. 2 (*muy*) really: *Está ~ delicioso.* It's really delicious.

francés/esa *adj*, *nm* French ● *nm-nf* Frenchman/woman [*pl* -men/-women]: *los franceses* the French

Francia *nf* France

franco *adj* 1 (*sincero*) frank 2 (*claro*) marked: *un ~ deterioro* a marked decline

franela *nf* 1 (*material*) flannel 2 (*And, camiseta interior*) undershirt, vest (*GB*)

franja *nf* strip

franquear *vt* (*carta, paquete*) pay postage on *sth*

franqueza *nf* frankness: *Hablemos con ~.* Let's be frank.

frasco *nm* 1 (*colonia, medicina*) bottle 2 (*conservas, etc.*) jar

frase *nf* 1 (*oración*) sentence 2 (*locución*) phrase ▶ ~ **hecha** set phrase

fraterno (*tb* **fraternal**) *adj* brotherly

fraude *nm* fraud ▶ ~ **fiscal** tax evasion

fraudulento *adj* fraudulent

frecuencia *nf* frequency [*pl* -ies] ▶ **con** ~ often

frecuentar *vt* 1 (*lugar*) frequent 2 (*amigos*) hang around with *sb*

frecuente *adj* 1 (*reiterado*) frequent 2 (*habitual*) common: *Es una práctica ~ aquí.* It is (a) common practice here.

fregadero *nm* sink

fregar *vt* 1 (*lavar*) wash 2 (*molestar*) annoy 3 (*estropear*) ruin ● **fregarse** *vp* to be ruined: *Se nos fregó la fiesta.* Our party was ruined. ◊ *¡Me fregué!* I've really messed up! ▶ **¡no friegues!** you're kidding! **¡para que no friegue!** so there! **¡te fregaste!/¡se fregó!** tough!

freír(se) *vt*, *vp* fry

frenar *vi* brake: ~ *en seco* slam on the brakes

frenazo *nm*: *Se oyó un ~.* There was a screech of brakes. ▶ **dar un** ~ slam on the brakes

freno *nm* 1 (*Aut*) brake: ~ *de mano/emergencia* hand/emergency brake ◊ *poner/quitar el* ~ apply/release the brake(s) 2 (*reducción*) curb (*on sth*) 3 **frenos** (*tb* **frenillo**) (*dientes*) braces [*pl*], brace (*GB*)

frente *nf* (*Anat*) forehead ● *nm* front ▶ **a** ~ forward: *dar un paso al* ~ take a step forward **al** ~ **de** in charge of *sth* **de** ~ (*choque, etc.*) head-on **hacerle** ~ **a algo/algn** stand up to *sth/sb*

fresa *nf* 1 strawberry [*pl* -ies] 2 (*dentista*) drill

fresca *nf* (*insolencia*) cheeky remark: *¡Qué ~ tienes!* You have a nerve!

fresco/a *adj* 1 (*temperatura, ropa*) cool → **FRÍO** 2 (*comida*) fresh 3 *noticias frescas* the latest news 4 (*And, tranquilo, dejado*) laid-back ● *adj*, *nm-nf* (*descarado*) dirty so-and-so: *El muy ~ me estafó.* The dirty so-and-so swindled me. ● *nm* (*bebida*) soda ● *interj* (*And*) don't worry ▶ ~ **como una lechuga** (*as*) fresh as a daisy **hacer** ~ be chilly **tomar el** ~ get some fresh air

fresno *nm* ash (tree)

frijol (**frijol** *And*) *nm* bean ▶ ~ **rojo** red kidney bean ~**es refritos** refried beans

frío *adj*, *nm* cold **NOTA** Cold indica una temperatura más baja que **cool** y muchas veces desagradable: *Fue un invierno muy ~.* It was a terribly cold winter. Cool significa "fresco" más que "frío": *Aquí está fresquito.* It's nice and cool in here. **Hot** describe una temperatura bastante más caliente que **warm**. **Warm** es más bien "cálido", "templado", y muchas veces tiene connotaciones agradables: *No lo puedo tomar, está muy caliente.* I can't drink it, it's too hot. ◊ *¡Qué calor (el que) hace aquí!* It's too hot here! ◊ *Siéntate al lado del fuego, pronto entrarás en calor.* Sit by the fire, you'll soon get warm. ▶ **hacer** ~ be cold: *Hace ~.* It's cold. **tener** ~ be/feel cold: *Tengo ~ en las manos.* My hands are cold.

friolento *adj*, *nm-nf*: *Soy muy ~.* I feel the cold a lot.

fritar *vt* fry

frito/a *adj* fried ▶ **estar** ~ be finished **quedarse** ~ doze off

frondio *adj* 1 (*sucio*) filthy 2 (*feo*) ugly

frondoso *adj* leafy

frontal *adj* (*ataque*) frontal

frontera *nf* border →**BORDER**

fronterizo *adj* 1 border: *región fronteriza* border area 2 (*limítrofe*) neighboring: *dos países ~s* two neighboring countries

frontón *nm* 1 jai alai 2 (*cancha*) jai alai court

frotar(se) *vt, vp* rub: ~ *las manos* rub your hands together

fruncir *vt* (*costura*) gather ▸ ~ *el ceño* frown

frustración *nf* frustration

fruta *nf* fruit: *¿Quieres una* ~? Do you want some fruit? ◇ *un pedazo de* ~ a piece of fruit ◇ *¿Compramos* ~*s*? Shall we buy some fruit? ▸ ~*s secas* (*pasas, higos, etc.*) dried fruit [*U*]

frutal *adj* fruit: *un árbol* ~ a fruit tree

frutería *nf* fruit store, greengrocer's (*GB*)

frutero/a *nm-nf* fruit seller, greengrocer (*GB*) ● *nm* fruit bowl

fruto *nm* fruit ▸ ~*s secos* (*de cáscara dura*) nuts

fucsia *nm* fuchsia

fuego *nm* fire ▸ *a* ~ *lento/vivo* over a low/high heat: *cocer/cocinar a* ~ *lento* simmer ~*s artificiales* fireworks

fuente *nf* 1 (*en plaza, etc.*) fountain 2 (*manantial*) spring 3 (*bandeja*) dish 4 (*origen*) source: ~*s cercanas al gobierno* sources close to the government ▸ *saber algo de buena* ~ have sth on good authority

fuera *adv* 1 ~ (*de*) outside: *Hay grietas por* ~. There are cracks on the outside. 2 (*no en casa*) out: *comer* ~ eat out 3 (*de viaje*) away 4 ~ *de* out of sth: ~ *de alcance/de lo normal* out of reach/the ordinary ● *interj* get out ▸ ~ *de* (*broma/s*) joking apart ~ *de juego/lugar* offside ~ *de sí* beside himself, herself, etc. ~ *de tono* inappropriate

fuerte *adj* 1 strong: *un acento/olor* ~ a strong accent/smell 2 (*pesado, tráfico, lluvia, etc.*) heavy: *un* ~ *ritmo de trabajo* a heavy work schedule 3 (*dolor, crisis, descenso*) severe 4 (*abrazo, comida*) big ● *adv* 1 (*con fuerza, intensamente*) hard 2 (*firmemente*) tight: *¡Agárrate* ~! Hold on tight! 3 (*sonido*) loud: *Ponlo más* ~. Turn it up. ● *nm* (*fortaleza*) fort

fuerza *nf* 1 (*potencia, Fís, Mil, Pol*) force 2 (*energía física*) strength [*U*]: *recobrar las* ~*s* get your strength back ▸ *a la* ~ 1 (*forzando*) by force 2 (*por necesidad*): *Tengo que hacerlo a la* ~. I just have to do it. ~ *de voluntad* will power ~(*s*) *aérea(s)* air force [*sing*] *las* ~*s armadas* armed forces

fuga *nf* 1 (*huida*) flight: *emprender la* ~ take flight 2 (*gas, agua*) leak

fugarse *vp* 1 (*país*) flee sth: *Se fugó del país*. He fled the country. 2 (*cárcel*) escape (*from sth*) 3 (*casa, colegio*) run away (*from sth*)

fugaz *adj* fleeting

fugitivo/a *nm-nf* fugitive

ful *adj* ▸ *a* ~ at top speed

fulano/a *nm-nf* so-and-so [*pl* so-and-sos]: *Imagínate que viene* ~... Just suppose so-and-so comes... ▸ (*señor/don*) ~ *de tal* Mr. So-and-so

fulminante *adj* 1 (*instantáneo*) immediate 2 (*mirada*) withering 3 (*muerte*) sudden

fumador/a *nm-nf* smoker ▸ *¿fumador o no* ~? (*transportes, etc.*) smoking or non-smoking?

fumar *vt, vi* smoke

función *nf* 1 function 2 (*Teat*) performance

funcionamiento *nm* operation

funcionar *vi* 1 work: *¿Cómo funciona?* How does it work? 2 ~ (*con*) run (*on sth*): *Este carro funciona con diesel*. This car runs on diesel. ▸ *no funciona* (*en cartel*) out of order

funcionario/a *nm-nf* civil servant

funda *nf* 1 (*estuche*) case 2 (*almohada*) pillowcase 3 (*CD, etc.*) sleeve 4 (*cojín, edredón*) cover

fundación *nf* (*institución*) foundation

fundador/a *adj, nm-nf* founder

fundamental *adj* fundamental

fundar *vt* found

fundir(se) *vt, vp* 1 melt 2 (*fusible*) blow

fúnebre *adj* 1 funeral: *la marcha* ~ the funeral march 2 (*triste*) mournful ▸ *carro/coche* ~ hearse

funeral *nm* funeral (*tb funerales* [*pl*]) ● *nm* funeral [*sing*]

funeraria *nf* undertaker's [*pl* undertakers']

funicular *nm* 1 (*Ferrocarril*) funicular (railway) 2 (*teleférico*) cable car

furgoneta *nf* van

furia *nf* fury ▸ *con* ~ furiously *hecho una* ~ in a rage

furioso *adj* furious ▸ *ponerse* ~ fly into a rage

furtivo *adj* furtive ▸ *cazador/pescador* ~ poacher *caza/pesca furtiva* poaching

fusible *nm* fuse

fusil *nm* rifle

fusión *nf* 1 (*Fís*) fusion 2 (*hielo, metales*) melting: *punto de* ~

melting point 3 (*empresas*, *Pol*)
merger ▶ **punto de ~** melting
point

fusta *nf* riding crop

fútbol (**futbol** *Mx*) *nm* soccer,
football (*GB*) ▶ **~ americano** football, American football (*GB*)

futbolín *nm* 1 (*juego*) table football 2 **futbolines** (*local*) amusement arcade [*sing*]

futbolista *nmf* footballer

futuro *adj*, *nm* future

G g

gabacho/a *nm-nf* (*Mx*) Yank ●
adj (*Mx*) American →AMÉRICA

gabardina *nf* raincoat

gabinete *nm* 1 office 2 (*Pol*) Cabinet ▶ **~ de prensa** press office

gacela *nf* gazelle

gacho *adj* (*Mx*) unpleasant

gachupín/ina *nm-nf* (*Mx*) Spaniard

gafas *nf* 1 glasses: *No tengo las ~.*
I don't have my glasses on. 2 (*de
protección*) goggles

gaita *nf* 1 (*escocesa*, *gallega*) bagpipes [*pl*] 2 (*flauta*) flute

gaitero/a *nm-nf* piper

gajes *nm* ▶ **~ del oficio** part and
parcel of the job

gajo *nm* segment

gala *nf* 1 gala: *una cena de ~* a gala
dinner 2 **galas** best clothes ▶ **ir/
vestir(se) de ~** be dressed up

galáctico *adj* galactic

galán *nm* 1 attractive man 2 (*pre-
tendiente*) suitor

galante *adj* gallant

galápago *nm* turtle

galardón *nm* award

galardonado *adj* prizewinning

galardonar *vt* award sb a prize

galaxia *nf* galaxy [*pl* -ies]

galería *nf* 1 gallery [*pl* -ies]
→MUSEUM 2 (*balcón*) balcony [*pl*
-ies]

Gales *nm* Wales

galés/esa *adj*, *nm* Welsh ● *nm-nf*
Welshman/woman [*pl* -men/
-women]: *los galeses* the Welsh

galgo *nm* greyhound

gallada *nf* (*And*) crowd of people

galleta *nf* cookie, biscuit (*GB*)

gallina *nf* hen ● *adj*, *nmf* (*cobarde*) chicken: *¡No seas ~!* Don't be
a chicken! ▶ **la ~ ciega** blind
man's buff

gallinazo *nm* 1 (*pájaro*) black
vulture 2 (*And*, *hombre*) woman-
izer

gallinero *nm* 1 hen house 2 (*griterío*) madhouse 3 (*Teat*) gallery

gallo *nm* 1 (*ave*) rooster 2 (*Mús*)
wrong note

galón *nm* 1 (*medida*) gallon (*abrev
gal.*) ▶ *Ver pág. 222* 2 (*uniforme*)
stripe

galopar *vi* gallop

galope *nm* gallop: *Se fue al ~.* He
galloped off.

gama *nf* range

gambeta *nf* (*fútbol*) dribble

gambetear *vt*, *vi* (*fútbol*) dribble

gamín/ina *nm-nf* (*And*) street urchin

gamuza *nf* suede

gana *nf* ▶ **como me dé la ~** however I, you, etc. want **con/sin ~s**
enthusiastically/half-heartedly
darle a algn la ~ want to *do sth*:
Lo hago por que me da la ~. I'm
doing it because I want to. **de
buena/mala ~** willingly/reluc-
tantly **entrar ~s de feel like**
doing sth **hacer lo que me dé la
~** do what I, you, etc. like **¡las ~s!**
you wish! **quitarse las ~s** not feel
like (*sth anymore*): *Se me quitaron las ~s de salir.* I don't feel
like going out anymore. **tener/
sentir ~s (de) hacer algo** feel like
sth: *No tengo ~s.* I don't feel like
it.

ganadería *nf* 1 livestock farming
2 (*ganado*) livestock

ganadero/a *nm-nf* livestock
farmer

ganado *nm* 1 livestock 2 (*vacuno*)
cattle [*pl*] ▶ **~ equino/ovino/por-
cino** horses/sheep/pigs [*pl*]

ganador/a *adj* winning ● *nm-nf*
winner

ganancia *nf* profit

ganar *vt* 1 (*sueldo*, *etc.*) earn
2 (*premio*, *partido*, *guerra*) win
3 (*a un contrincante*) beat 4 (*conseguir*) gain (*by/from sth*): *¿Qué
gano yo con hacerlo?* What do I
gain by doing it? 5 (*tiempo*) save
● **ganarse** *vp* 1 (*dinero*, *respeto*)
earn: ~ *el pan/la vida* earn your
living 2 (*castigo*, *recompensa*)
deserve ▶ **salir ganando** do well
(*out of sth*)

gancho *nm* 1 hook 2 (*cebo*) bait
3 (*ropa*) (clothes) hanger 4 (*pelo*)
hairpin ▶ **~ de cosedora** (*And*)
staple **~ de nodriza** (*And*) safety
pin

ganga *nf* bargain

gangrena *nf* gangrene

gángster *nm* gangster

ganso/a nm-nf goose [pl geese]

garabatear vt, vi 1 (dibujar) doodle 2 (escribir) scribble

garabato nm 1 (dibujo) doodle 2 (escritura) scribble

garaje (tb **garage**) nm garage

garantía nf guarantee

garantizar vt 1 guarantee 2 (asegurar) assure

garbanzo nm garbanzo (bean), chickpea (GB)

garbo nm ▶ **andar con ~** walk gracefully **tener ~** be graceful

garfio nm hook

garganta nf 1 throat: Me duele la ~. I have a sore throat. 2 (Geog) gorge

gargantilla nf necklace

gárgaras nf ▶ **hacer ~** gargle

garita nf 1 (centinela) sentry box 2 (portería) lodge 3 (fronteriza) inspection booth

garra nf 1 (a) (uñas) claw (b) (mano, pie) paw 2 (ave) talon

garrafa nf carafe

garrafal adj monumental

garrapata nf tick

garrocha nf pole ▶ **salto con ~** pole vault

garrote nm 1 stick 2 (tortura) garrotte

garza nf heron

gas nm 1 gas 2 **gases** (Med) gas [U], wind [U] (GB)

gasa nf 1 (tejido) gauze 2 (vendaje) bandage

gaseosa nf soda, fizzy lemonade (GB)

gaseoso/a adj 1 (Quím) gaseous 2 (bebida) carbonated, fizzy (GB)

gasolina nf gas, petrol (GB) ▶ **~ sin plomo/verde** unleaded gas/petrol

gasolinera (tb **gasolinería**) nf gas station, petrol station (GB)

gastado adj (desgastado) worn out

gastar vt 1 (dinero) spend sth (on sth/sb) 2 (consumir) use 3 (agotar) use sth up

gasto nm 1 (dinero) expense: No gano ni para ~s. I don't earn enough to cover my expenses. 2 (energía, etc.) consumption ▶ **~s de envío** postage and handling [sing]

gastronomía nf cooking

gatear vi crawl

gatillo nm trigger

gato/a nm-nf cat **NOTA** Tomcat o **tom** es un gato macho, **kittens** son los gatitos. Los gatos ronronean (**purr**) y hacen miau (**miaow**). ● nm (Aut) jack

▶ **andar a gatas** crawl **dar ~ por liebre** take sb in **jugar al ~** (Mx) play tic-tac-toe, play noughts and crosses (GB)

gaviota nf seagull

gay adj, nm gay

gel nm gel ▶ **~ de baño/ducha** shower gel

gelatina nf 1 (sustancia) gelatine 2 (Cocina) Jell-O®, jelly [pl -ies] (GB) ▶ **estar como una ~** be shaking like a leaf

gemelo/a adj, nm-nf twin

gemido nm 1 (persona) groan 2 (animal) whine

Géminis nm, nmf Gemini

gemir vi 1 (persona) groan 2 (animal) whine

gen (tb **gene**) nm gene

genealógico adj genealogical

generación nf generation

general adj general ▶ **en ~/por lo ~** in general ● nmf (Mil) general

generalizar vt, vi generalize

generar vt generate

género nm 1 (tipo) kind 2 (Arte) genre: ~ policíaco crime writing 3 (Gram) gender 4 (tela) material: ~s de punto knitwear

generoso/a adj generous (to sb)

genética nf genetics [sing]

genético adj genetic

genial adj brilliant ● adv: pasarla ~ have a great time

genio nm 1 (lumbrera) genius [pl -es] (at sth) 2 (mal humor) temper ▶ **de mal ~** in a bad mood **tener mal ~** be bad-tempered

genital adj genital ● **genitales** nm genitals

gente nf people [pl]: Había mucha ~. There were a lot of people. ◇ La ~ lloraba. People were crying. ▶ **~ bien/normal y corriente** well-off/ordinary people [pl] **ser buena ~** be nice

geografía nf geography

geográfico adj geographical

geología nf geology

geológico adj geological

geometría nf geometry

geométrico adj geometric

geranio nm geranium

gerente nmf manager

germen nm germ

germinar vi germinate

gesticular vi 1 (manos) gesticulate 2 (cara) pull a face

gestión nf 1 (Com) management 2 (trámite) step: hacer gestiones para hacer algo take steps to do sth

gesto nm 1 gesture: un ~ simbólico a symbolic gesture ◇ hablar por

~s communicate by gesture 2 (cara) expression ▶ **hacer ~s 1** (mano) signal: *Me hizo un ~ para que entrara.* He signaled (to) me to come in. 2 (cara) pull a face/faces (at sb)

gigante/a adj, nm-nf giant

gigantesco adj enormous

gimnasia nf gymnastics [sing] 2 (educación física) physical education (abrev **P.E.**) ▶ **hacer ~** work out

gimnasio nm gym

ginebra nf gin

gira nf tour: *de ~* on tour

girar vt, vi 1 turn 2 **~ (alrededor de)** revolve (around sth/sb)

girasol nm sunflower

giro nm ▶ **~ bancario** bank draft **~ postal** postal (money) order

gitano/a adj, nm-nf gypsy [pl -ies]

glacial adj 1 (temperatura, etc.) freezing 2 (período) glacial

glaciar nm glacier ▶ **período/época ~** Ice Age

glándula nf gland

globo nm balloon ▶ **el ~ terráqueo** the globe

gloria nf glory [pl -ies] 2 (persona célebre) great name ▶ **estar en la ~:** *Aquí se está en la ~.* It's wonderful here. **huele/sabe a ~** it smells/tastes delicious

glorieta nf rotary [pl -ies], roundabout (GB)

glotón/ona adj greedy ● nm-nf glutton

glucosa nf glucose

gobernador/a nm-nf governor

gobernante adj governing ● nmf leader

gobernar vt 1 (país) govern 2 (barco) steer

gobierno nm government →JURADO

gol nm goal: *marcar/meter un ~* score a goal

golear vt thrash

golf nm golf

golfa nf hooker, tart (GB)

golfo nm 1 (Geog) gulf 2 (sinvergüenza) swine

golondrina nf swallow

golosina nf sweet

goloso/a adj, nm-nf: *ser muy/un ~* have a sweet tooth

golpe nm 1 blow: *Su muerte fue un duro ~.* Her death was a heavy blow. *◇ darse un ~ en la cabeza* bang your head *◇ Lo mataron a ~s.* They beat him to death. 2 (vehículo) accident: *dar un ~* have an accident 3 (moretón) bruise 4 (en la puerta) knock: *dar ~s en la puerta*

knock on the door 5 (Dep) stroke ▶ **de ~** suddenly **de ~ (y porrazo)** out of the blue **de un ~** in one go **~ de estado** coup **no dar (ni) ~** not do a stroke (of work) **tener buenos ~s** (humor) be very funny **un ~ bajo:** *Eso fue un ~ bajo.* That was below the belt.

golpear vt 1 hit 2 (puerta, etc.) bang 3 (repetidamente) beat (against/on sth)

goma nf 1 (de borrar, hule) eraser, rubber (GB) 2 (de pegar) glue 3 (banda elástica) rubber band ▶ **estar con (la) ~** (And) be keen on sth

gomina nf (hair) gel

gomoso adj (And) keen

gordo adj 1 fat 2 (grueso) thick 3 (grave) serious ● nm-nf fat man/woman [pl men/women] ● nm (lotería) first prize ▶ **caer ~:** *Me cae ~.* I can't stand him.

gorila nm 1 (animal) gorilla 2 (guardaespaldas) bodyguard

gorra nf cap ▶ **de ~** free: *entrar de ~* get in free

gorrión nm sparrow

gorro nm hat ▶ **~ de baño 1** (piscina) swimming cap 2 (ducha) shower cap **hasta el ~** fed up (with sth/sb)

gorrón/ona nm-nf scrounger

gotear vi 1 drip 2 (tubería) leak

gotera nf leak: *Cuando llueve tenemos ~s.* The roof leaks when it rains.

gótico adj, nm Gothic

gozar vi **~ (con/de)** enjoy sth: *Goza fastidiando a la gente.* He enjoys annoying people. *◇ ~ de buena salud* enjoy good health

grabación nf recording

grabado nm 1 engraving 2 (libro) illustration

grabadora nf tape recorder

grabar vt 1 (sonido, imagen) record 2 (metal, etc.) engrave

gracia nf 1 (encanto, simpatía) charm: *No es bonita pero tiene ~.* She's not pretty but there's something about her. 2 (Rel, elegancia) grace 3 (ocurrencia) witty remark ▶ **dar las ~s** thank sb (for sth) **¡gracias!** thank you, thanks (coloq): *muchas ~s* thank you very much **~s a...** thanks to sth/sb **hacer una ~** amuse sb: *Me hace una ~ oírla hablar.* The way she talks amuses me. **¡qué ~!** how funny! **tener ~** be funny

gracioso adj funny ▶ **hacerse el ~** play the fool

grada nf stand

grado nm 1 degree: *quemaduras de tercer ~* third-degree burns ◇ *Estamos a dos ~s bajo cero.* It's minus two. 2 **grados** (*alcohol*): *Este vino tiene muchos/13 ~s.* This wine is very strong/has 13% alcohol.

graduar vt (*regular*) adjust ● **graduarse** vp graduate ▸ **~se la vista** have your eyes tested

gráfico adj graphic ● nm (*tb* **gráfica** nf) graph

grafiti nm graffiti [U]

gramática nf grammar

gramo nm gram (*abrev* g) → *Ver pág.* 222

gran adj *Ver* GRANDE

granada nf 1 (*fruta*) pomegranate 2 (*Mil*) hand grenade

granaderos nm riot police [pl]

granate adj, nm maroon

Gran Bretaña nf Great Britain (*abrev* GB)

grande adj 1 (*tamaño*) big, large (*más fml*: *un gran problema* a big problem ◇ *¿~ o pequeño?* Large or small? →BIG 2 (*número, cantidad*) large: *una gran cantidad de gente* a large number of people 3 (*importante*) great ▸ **a ~s rasgos** in general terms (*la/una*) **gran parte de** most of **pasarla en ~** have a great time

granel ▸ **a ~ 1** (*en gran cantidad*) in bulk 2 (*sin envasar*) loose

granero nm barn

granito nm granite

granizada nf hailstorm

granizado nm crushed ice drink

granizar vi hail

granizo nm hail

granja nf farm

granjero/a nm-nf farmer

grano nm 1 grain: *un ~ de arena* a grain of sand 2 (*semilla*) seed 3 (*café*) bean 4 (*en la piel*) spot: *Me salieron ~s* I've come out in spots. ▸ **ir al ~** get to the point

grapa nf 1 (*para papel*) staple 2 (*Med*) stitch

grapadora nf stapler

grasa nf 1 fat 2 (*lubricante*) grease

grasiento adj greasy

graso adj greasy

gratis adj, adv free: *viajar/trabajar ~* travel free/work for nothing

grato adj pleasant: *~ al oído* pleasing to the ear

gratuito adj free

grava nf gravel

grave adj 1 serious 2 (*solemne*) solemn 3 (*sonido, nota*) low 4 (*voz*) deep

gravedad nf 1 (*Fís*) gravity 2 (*importancia*) seriousness: *herido de ~* seriously injured

gravemente adv seriously

graznar vi 1 (*cuervo*) caw 2 (*pato*) quack

Grecia nf Greece

gremio nm 1 (*oficio*) trade 2 (*artesanos, artistas*) guild

griego/a adj, nm-nf, nm Greek

grieta nf crack

grillo nm cricket

grima nf ▸ **dar ~** set your teeth on edge

gringo/a nm-nf gringo [pl -s]

gripa nf 1 (*con fiebre*) flu [U]: *Tengo ~.* I have the flu. 2 (*resfriado*) cold

gris adj, nm gray

gritar vt, vi shout (*at sb*): *~ de dolor* cry out in pain →SHOUT

grito nm 1 shout: *dar/pegar un ~* shout 2 (*auxilio, dolor, alegría*) cry [pl cries] ▸ **a ~s** at the top of your voice **el ~ de Dolores/independencia** (*Mx*) proclamation of independence

grosella nf redcurrant ▸ **~ negra** blackcurrant

grosería nf 1 (*palabrota*) swear word 2 (*acción*) rudeness

grosero/a adj, nm-nf rude: *Eres un ~.* You're so rude.

grosor nm thickness: *El muro tiene 1m de ~.* The wall is a meter thick.

grueso adj thick

grumo nm lump

gruñir vi 1 (*persona, cerdo*) grunt 2 (*perro, león*) growl 3 (*refunfuñar*) grumble

gruñón/ona adj, nm-nf grumpy: *Es un ~.* He's really grumpy.

grupo nm 1 group: *el trabajo en ~* group work 2 (*And, Educ*) grade, year (*GB*) ▸ **~ sanguíneo** blood group

gruta nf 1 (*natural*) cave 2 (*artificial*) grotto [pl -s/-es]

guácala interj ugh

guadaña nf scythe

guagua nf (*And*) baby [pl -ies]

guaje nm (*Mx*) gourd ● adj (*Mx*) stupid ▸ **hacerse ~** (*Mx*) pretend not to hear sb

guajolote nm turkey

guanábana nf soursop

guandoca nf (*And*) jail

guante nm glove ▸ **echar el ~** catch sb

guantera nf glove compartment

guapo adj 1 (hombre) good-looking 2 (mujer) pretty 3 (valiente) brave ▶ **estar/ir ~** look nice: Estás ~ con esa camisa. You look nice in that shirt.

guarda nmf 1 guard: ~ de seguridad security guard 2 (zoo) keeper

guardabarros nm fender, mudguard (GB)

guardaequipaje nm baggage room

guardaespaldas nmf bodyguard

guardar vt 1 keep: Guarda la entrada. Keep your ticket. ◊ ~ un secreto keep a secret 2 (recoger) put sth away 3 (custodiar) guard 4 (Comp) save ▶ **~ las apariencias** keep up appearances

guardarropa nm (local público) cloakroom

guardería nf day care center

guardia nf 1 police officer ● nf guard: hacer ~ mount guard ▶ **de ~** on duty: el médico de ~ the doctor on duty **en ~** on your guard

guardián/ana nm-nf guardian

guarecer vt shelter sb (from sth) ● **guarecerse** vp take shelter (from sth)

guarida nf 1 den 2 (ladrones) hideout

guarnición nf 1 (Cocina) garnish 2 (Mil) garrison

guarura nf (Mx) bodyguard

Guatemala nf Guatemala

guatemalteco/a adj, nm-nf Guatemalan

guateque nm party [pl -ies]

guau nm woof

guayaba nf guava

guayabo nm 1 (árbol) guava (tree) 2 (And, borrachera) hangover

guayo nm football shoe, football boot (GB)

gubernamental adj government

güero adj (Mx) blond(e) →RUBIO

guerra nf war: en ~ at war ◊ declarar la ~ a algn declare war on sb ▶ **dar ~** give sb trouble

guerrero/a adj warlike ● nm-nf warrior

guerrilla nf guerrillas [pl]

guerrillero/a adj, nm-nf guerrilla

gueto nm ghetto [pl -s/-es]

guía nmf (persona) guide ● nf 1 (libro) guide(book): ~ turística/del ocio tourist/listings guide 2 (estudios) prospectus ▶ **~ telefónica** telephone directory [pl -ies], phone book (coloq)

guiar vt guide ▶ **~se por** go by sth: ~se por las apariencias go by appearances

guijarro nm pebble

guinda nf cherry [pl -ies]

guiñar vt, vi wink (at sb): Me guiñó el ojo. He winked at me.

guiño nm wink

guiñol nm puppet show

guión nm 1 (Cine) script 2 (esquema) plan 3 (ortografía) (a) hyphen (b) (diálogo) dash

guisar vt, vi cook

guiso nm 1 (tb guisado) dish 2 (And, salsa) sauce

guitarra nf guitar

guitarrista nmf guitarist

gula nf greed

gusano nm 1 worm 2 (en alimentos) maggot 3 (de mariposa) caterpillar ▶ **~ de seda** silkworm

gustar vt 1 don't like it. **NOTA** Para decir "disfrutar haciendo algo", se usa **like doing sth**: ¿Te gusta pintar? Do you like painting?, y para "preferir hacer algo", se utiliza **like to do sth**: Me gusta ducharme antes de dormir. I like to take a shower before bed. 2 (atraer) like sb, fancy sb (GB): Creo que le gustas. I think he likes you. ▶ **me gusta más** I, you, etc. prefer sth

gusto nm taste: de mal ~ in bad taste ◊ para todos los ~s to suit all tastes ▶ **estar a ~** feel comfortable ¡mucho ~! pleased to meet you!

H h

haba nf lima bean

haber v aux 1 (tiempos compuestos) have: Me había dicho que vendría. He had told me he would come. 2 **~ que** must: Hay que ser valiente. You must be brave. ● **haber** vi there is/are **NOTA There is** se usa con sustantivos en singular e incontables: Hay un CD aquí. There's a CD here. ◊ No hay pan. There isn't any bread. ◊ No había nadie. There wasn't anybody there. **There are** se usa con sustantivos en plural: ¿Cuántas cervezas hay? How many beers are there? ▶ **de ~...** if...: De haberlo sabido... If I'd known... ¡haberlo dicho, hecho, etc.! you should have said so, done it, etc. ¿qué hay/hubo? how are things?

NOTA Para otras expresiones con **haber**, ver el sustantivo, adjetivo, etc., p.ej. **no hay derecho** en DERECHO.

habichuela nf (And) green bean

hábil adj 1 skillful 2 (astuto) clever

habilidad nf skill

habilidoso adj handy

habilitación nf (And, examen) retake

habilitar vt (local) convert

habitación nf 1 room: ~ doble/individual double/single room 2 (dormitorio) bedroom

habitante nmf inhabitant

habitar vt, vi live in sth

hábitat nm habitat

hábito nm habit

habitual adj 1 usual 2 (cliente, lector, visitante) regular

habituarse vp get used to sth

habla nf 1 (facultad) speech 2 (modo de hablar) way of speaking ▸ **de ~ inglesa, hispana, etc.** English-speaking, Spanish-speaking, etc. **sin ~** speechless

hablado adj spoken

hablador/a adj 1 talkative 2 (mentiroso) lying ● nm-nf chatterbox

hablante nmf speaker

hablar vt (idioma) speak ● vi 1 speak, talk (to sb) (about sth) **NOTA** Speak es más general: ~ en público speak in public ◇ ¿Puedo ~ con Ana? Can I speak to Ana?, y talk se usa más al referirnos a varios hablantes: ~ de arte talk about art ◇ Estuvimos hablando toda la noche. We talked all night. 2 ~ de (tratar) talk about sth ▸ ~ hasta por los codos/como loro mojado talk nineteen to the dozen ~ más alto/bajo speak up/lower your voice ¡ni ~! no way! no ~se con not be on speaking terms with sb

hacer vt
● Se traduce por **make** en los siguientes casos: 1 (fabricar): ~ aviones/una blusa make planes/a blouse 2 (dinero, ruido, cama): ~ ruido make a noise 3 (comentario, promesa, esfuerzo): ~ un esfuerzo make an effort 4 ~ el amor make love 5 (convertir en): El dolor te hace más fuerte. Pain makes you stronger.
● Se traduce por **do** en los siguientes casos: 1 (al hablar de una actividad sin decir de qué se trata): ¿Qué hacemos esta noche? What should we do tonight? ◇ Hago lo que puedo. I do what I can. 2 (al referirse a actividades como lavar, plan-char, limpiar y comprar): ~ las compras do the shopping 3 (estudios): ~ un curso do a course 4 ¿Me haces un favor? Will you do me a favor?

● **hacer (que...)** get sb to do sth: Me hacen venir cada día. They're getting me to come in every day.

● **otros usos:** 1 (escribir) write 2 (pintar, dibujar) paint, draw 3 (nudo) tie 4 (distancia) cover: Cada día hago 50 km. I cover 50kilometers a day. 5 (pregunta) ask 6 (papel) play: ~ el papel de Romeo play the part of Romeo 7 (deportes): ~ yoga do yoga ◇ ~ ciclismo go cycling →DEPORTE
● vi ~ de 1 work as sth: ~ de jardinero work as a gardener 2 (ejercer) act as sth: No hagas de padre conmigo. Don't act as if you were my father. 3 (cosa) serve as sth: La caja hacía de mesa. The box served as a table.
● v imp 1 (clima): Hace calor/sol. It's hot/sunny. ◇ Hizo buen tiempo ayer. We had nice weather yesterday. 2 (tiempo cronológico): hace un año a year ago ◇ hace poco recently ◇ ¡Hace mucho que estás aquí? Have you been here long? ◇ Se conocen desde hace años. They've known each other for ages. →AGO
● **hacerse** vp 1 + sustantivo become: Se hizo taxista. He became a taxi driver. 2 + adj: Me estoy haciendo viejo. I'm getting old. ◇ La clase se me hizo eterna. The lesson seemed to go on for ever. 3 ~ el/la + adj pretend to be sth: No te hagas el sordo. It's no good pretending to be deaf. 4 (cuando otra persona realiza la acción) have sth done: Se están haciendo una casa. They're having a house built. ◇ ~ tomar una foto have your photo taken ▸ ~ bien/mal be right/wrong (to do sth): ¿Hice bien en ir? Was I right to go? ~ como que/si... pretend: Hizo como que no me había visto. He pretended he hadn't seen me. ~se pasar por... pass yourself off as sth/sb ~ una de las suyas be up to your, his, her, etc. old tricks again ¿qué haces? 1 (profesión) what do you do? 2 (en este instante) what are you doing? **NOTA** Para otras expresiones con **hacer**, ver el sustantivo, adjetivo, etc., p. ej. **hacer frío** en FRÍO.

hacia prep 1 (dirección) towards: ~ abajo/arriba downwards/upwards 2 (tiempo) at about: ~ principios de mayo in early May ◇

Llego ~ las dos. I'll be there at about two. →AROUND

hacienda *nf* **1** Hacienda (Pol) the Treasury **2** (*finca*) estate

hada *nf* fairy [pl -ies]: *un cuento de ~s* a fairy story

halagar *vt* flatter

halar = JALAR

halcón *nm* falcon

hall *nm* hall

hallar *vt* find ● **hallarse** *vp* be

hallazgo *nm* discovery [pl -ies]

hamaca *nf* hammock

hambre *nf* hunger, starvation, famine **NOTA** Hunger es el término general y se usa en casos como: *hacer huelga de ~* go on (a) hunger strike, o para expresar un deseo: *de conocimiento/poder* hunger for knowledge/power. **Starvation** es el hambre sufrida durante un largo período: *morir de ~* die of starvation, y el verbo **starve** significa "morir de hambre" y se usa mucho en la expresión: *Me muero de ~.* I'm starving. **Famine** es hambre que afecta a un gran número de personas, normalmente después de una catástrofe natural: *A la larga sequía siguieron meses de ~.* The drought was followed by months of famine. ◊ *pasar/tener ~* go/be hungry *tener un ~ feroz* be starving

hambriento *adj* **1** hungry **2** (*muerto de hambre*) starving

hamburguesa *nf* hamburger, burger (*más coloq*)

hámster *nm* hamster

hara ~ *nf* spoon ▶ **~ de palo/madera** wooden spoon

harada *nf* spoonful

haradita *nf* teaspoonful

harapo *nm* rag

harilla (*tb* **harija**) *nf* teaspoon

harina *nf* flour

harón *nm* ladle

hartarse *vp* **1** (*cansarse*) be fed up (*with sth/sb*): *Ya me harté de él.* I'm fed up with him. **2** (*atiborrarse*) (a) be full (up): *Comió hasta ~.* He ate till he was full (up). (b) **~ de** stuff yourself with sth

harto *adj* **1** (*lleno*) full **2** (*cansado*) fed up (*with sth/sb*): *Me tienes ~.* I'm fed up with you. **3** (*mucho*) a lot of: *Hay ~ tráfico.* There's a lot of traffic.

hasta *prep*
● *tiempo* **1** until, till: *Me quedo ~ el lunes.* I'm staying until Monday. ◊ *¿~ cuándo te quedas?* How

long are you staying? **NOTA** Till es más informal y no suele ir al principio de la frase. **2** (*Mx, sentido negativo*): *Abren ~ las dos.* They only open at two/don't open till two. ◊ *Será terminado ~ fines del año.* It won't be finished till the end of the year.
● *lugar* **1** (*distancia*) as far as...: *Vino conmigo ~ Roma.* He came with me as far as Rome. **2** (*altura, cantidad*) up to...: *El agua llegó ~ aquí.* The water came up to here. **3** (*hacia abajo*) down to...: *La falda me llega ~ los tobillos.* The skirt comes down to my ankles.
● *saludos* use...: *¡~ mañana/el lunes!* See you tomorrow/on Monday! ◊ *¡~ luego!* Bye!
● *adv* even: *~ yo lo hice.* Even I did it.

haya *nf* beech (tree)

hazaña *nf* exploit ▶ **ser toda una ~** be quite a feat

hebilla *nf* **1** buckle **2** (*pelo*) slide

hebra *nf* (piece of) thread

hechicero/a *nm-nf* wizard [fem witch]

hechizar *vt* cast a spell on sb

hechizo *nm* spell

hecho *adj* **1** made: *¿De qué está ~?* What's it made of? ◊ *~ a mano* handmade **2** (*cocinado*) done: *un filete bien ~* a well done steak **NOTA** Una carne poco hecha se dice **rare** y en su punto **medium rare**. ● *nm* **1** fact **2** (*acontecimiento*) event ▶ **¡bien ~!** well done! **dar por ~** take sth for granted **de ~** in fact **~ y derecho** grown: *un hombre ~ y derecho* a grown man **mal ~** wrong: *Si se lo dijiste, mal ~.* You shouldn't have told him.

hectárea *nf* hectare (*abrev* ha)

helada *nf* frost

heladería *n* ice cream parlor

helado *adj* **1** (*congelado*) frozen **2** (*persona, lugar*) freezing ● *nm* ice cream

helar(se) *vt, vi, vp* freeze

helecho *nm* fern

hélice *nf* propeller

helicóptero *nm* helicopter

helio *nm* helium

hembra *nf* **1** female → FEMALE **2** (*enchufe*) socket

hemisferio *nm* hemisphere

hemorragia *nf* hemorrhage

heno *nm* hay

hepatitis *nf* hepatitis [U]

herbívoro *adj* herbivorous

herboristería nf health food store/shop (GB)

heredar vt inherit sth (from sb)

heredero/a nm-nf heir (to sth)

hereditario adj hereditary

herencia nf inheritance

herida nf 1 injury [pl -ies] 2 (bala, navaja) wound **NOTA** Wound se usa para heridas causadas por una arma de forma deliberada: ~s de bala gunshot wounds ◊ Lo hirieron en la guerra. He was wounded in the war. Si la herida es resultado de un accidente se usa injury/injure, que también se traduce por "lesión/lesionarse": sufrir ~s leves suffer minor injuries ◊ Los trozos de vidrio lo hirieron. He was injured by flying glass. ◊ lesiones cerebrales brain injuries.

herido/a nm-nf casualty [pl -ies]

herir vt 1 injure 2 (bala, navaja) wound

hermanastro/a nm-nf stepbrother [fem stepsister]

hermandad nf 1 (hombres) brotherhood 2 (mujeres) sisterhood 3 (gremio) association

hermano/a nm-nf brother [fem sister]: mi ~ mayor my older brother ◊ Son dos ~s y tres hermanas. There are two boys and three girls. **NOTA** Cuando "hermanos" se refiere a hermanos y hermanas, se dice brothers and sisters: Tengo cinco ~s. I have five brothers and sisters. ▶ ~ por parte de padre/madre, medio ~ half-brother/half-sister ~s siameses Siamese twins

herméticamente adv
▶ ~ cerrado hermetically sealed

hermético adj airtight

hermoso adj beautiful

hermosura nf beauty: ¡Qué ~! How beautiful!

hernia nf hernia

héroe, heroína nm-nf hero [pl -es] [fem heroine]

heroína nf (droga) heroin

herradura nf horseshoe

herramienta nf tool

herrar vt shoe

herrería nf forge

herrero/a nm-nf blacksmith

hervir vt, vi boil

heterosexual adj, nmf heterosexual

hexágono nm hexagon

hibernar vi hibernate

hichear vi whisper

hidratante adj ▶ crema/leche ~ moisturizer

hidratar vt (piel) moisturize

hidrato nm hydrate ▶ ~s de carbono carbohydrates

hidráulico adj hydraulic

hidroeléctrico adj hydroelectric

hidrógeno nm hydrogen

hiedra nf ivy

hielo nm ice [U]

hiena nf hyena

hierba nf 1 (Med, Cocina) herb 2 (pasto) grass 3 (marihuana) pot ▶ mala ~ weed

hierbabuena nf mint

hierro nm iron

hígado nm liver

higiene nf hygiene

higiénico adj hygienic

higo nm fig

higuera nf fig (tree)

hijastro/a nm-nf stepson [fem stepdaughter] [pl stepchildren]

hijo/a nm-nf son [fem daughter] [pl children]: No tenemos ~s. We don't have any children. ▶ ~ de papá rich kid

hijole interj nm ▶ wow

hilacha nf shred ▶ dar vuelo a la ~ (Mx) have a wild time

hilera nf 1 (a) (uno al lado de otro) row (b) (uno detrás de otro) line 2 (Mil, hormigas) column

hilla nf blade

hillo nm knife [pl knives]

hilo nm 1 thread: un carrete de ~ a spool of thread ◊ perder el ~ de la historia lose the thread of the story 2 (tela) linen 3 (metal) wire

himno nm hymn ▶ ~ nacional national anthem

hincapié nm ▶ hacer ~ stress sth

hincar vt 1 (diente) sink sth into sth 2 (estaca) drive sth into sth

hincha nmf fan

hinchado adj 1 swollen 2 (estómago) bloated

hincharse vp swell up

hinchazón nf (Med) swelling

hindú adj, nmf (Rel) Hindu

hinduismo nm Hinduism

hipermercado nm superstore

hipermétrope adj far-sighted, long-sighted (GB)

hipermetropía nf far-sightedness, long-sightedness (GB): tener ~ be far-sighted/long-sighted (GB)

hípica nf riding

hípico adj riding

hipnotizar vt hypnotize

hipo nm hiccups [pl]

hipócrita adj hypocritical ● nmf hypocrite

hipódromo nm racetrack, race-course (GB)

hipopótamo nm hippo [pl -s]

hipoteca nf mortgage

hipótesis nf hypothesis [pl -theses]

hippy (tb **hippie**) adj, nmf hippie

hispanohablante adj Spanish-speaking ● nmf Spanish speaker

histeria nf hysteria

histérico/a adj, nm-nf hysterical: ser un ~ get worked up about things ◇ ponerse ~ have hysterics

historia nf 1 history: ~ natural natural history ◇ pasar a la ~ go down in history 2 (relato) story [pl -ies] ▶ dejarse de ~s stop making excuses ~ médica medical history [pl -ies]

historiador/a nm-nf historian

historial nm record ▶ ~ profesional resumé, CV (GB)

histórico adj 1 historical 2 (importante) historic

historieta nf 1 (cómic) cartoon 2 (anécdota) story [pl -ies]

hobby nm hobby [pl -s]

hocico nm 1 muzzle 2 (cerdo) snout

hockey nm field hockey, hockey (GB) ▶ ~ sobre hielo hockey, ice hockey (GB)

hogar nm 1 (casa) home 2 (familia) home 3 (chimenea) fireplace

hogareño/a adj home-loving: ser muy ~ love being at home

hoguera nf bonfire: hacer una ~ make a bonfire

hoja nf 1 leaf [pl leaves] 2 (libro, etc.) page 3 (papel) sheet (of paper): una ~ en blanco a clean sheet of paper 4 (navaja, etc.) blade ▶ de ~ caduca/perenne deciduous/evergreen ~ de cálculo spreadsheet

hojalata nf tin (plate)

hojalatería nf sheet metal work

hojaldre nm puff pastry

hojear vt 1 (pasar hojas) flick through sth 2 (mirar por encima) glance at sth

hola interj hello, hi **NOTA** La palabra más general es **hello**, que también se usa al contestar el teléfono. **Hi** es más coloquial. Estas palabras suelen ir seguidos por **how are you?** o **how are you doing?** La respuesta suele ser **very well, thank you** o **fine, thanks** (más coloq).

Holanda nf Holland

holandés/esa adj, nm Dutch ● nm-nf Dutchman/woman [pl -men/-women]: los holandeses the Dutch

holgazán adj lazy ● nm-nf lazybones [pl lazybones]

holgazanear vi laze around

hollejo nm 1 skin 2 hollejos (And, hortalizas) peelings

hollín nm soot

holocausto nm holocaust

holograma nm hologram

hombre nm 1 man [pl men]: el ~ de la calle the man in the street 2 (humanidad) mankind → MAN ● interj: ¡~! ¡Qué bien que hayas venido. Great! You've come! ◇ ¡~! ¿qué haces aquí? Gee! What are you doing here? ▶ hacerse ~ grow up ~ de negocios businessman [pl -men] ~ lobo werewolf [pl -wolves] ~ rana frogman [pl -men]

hombrera nf shoulder pad

hombro nm shoulder ▶ llevar/sacar en ~s carry sth/sb on your shoulders

homenaje nm homage [U]: hacer un ~ a algn pay homage to sb ▶ en ~ a in honor of sth/sb

homicida nmf murderer

homicidio nm homicide

homogéneo adj homogeneous

homónimo nm homonym

homosexual adj, nmf homosexual

hondo adj deep

Honduras nf Honduras

hondureño/a adj, nm-nf Honduran

honestidad nf honesty

honesto adj honest

hongo nm 1 fungus [pl -gi] 2 (comestible) mushroom ▶ ~ venenoso toadstool

honor nm honor: el invitado de ~ the guest of honor 2 (buen nombre) good name ▶ tener el ~ de have the honor of sth

honra nf honor ▶ ¡a mucha ~! and proud of it!

honradez nf honesty

honrado adj honest

honrar vt 1 (mostrar respeto) honor 2 (ennoblecer) do sb credit

hora nf 1 hour: 90 km por ~ 90 kilometers an hour 2 (reloj, momento, horario) time: ¿Qué ~ es? What time is it? ◇ a cualquier ~ del día at any time of the day ◇ la ~ de dormir bedtime ▶ de última ~ last-minute entre ~s between meals ~ pico rush hour pasarse las ~s (muertas) haciendo algo do sth for hours on end ser ~ de be time to do sth: *Ya era ~ de que vinieras.* It was about time you came. **¡ya era ~!** about time too!

horario *nm* **1** (*clases, tren*) schedule, timetable (*GB*) **2** (*trabajo*) hours [*pl*]: *el ~ de atención al público* opening hours

horca *nf* (*cadalso*) gallows [*sing*]

horizontal *adj* horizontal

horizonte *nm* horizon

hormiga *nf* ant

hormigón *nm* concrete

hormigueo *nm* pins and needles [U]

hormiguero *nm* **1** (*agujero*) ants' nest **2** (*montículo*) anthill

hormona *nf* hormone

hornear *vt* bake

horno *nm* **1** *oven*: *encender el ~* turn the oven on ◊ *Esta sala es un ~.* It's like an oven in here. **2** (*industrial*) furnace **3** (*cerámica*) kiln ▶ **al ~** roast: *pollo al ~* roast chicken

horóscopo *nm* horoscope

horqueta *nf* fork

horquilla *nf* **1** (*para sujetar*) hairpin **2** (*And, puntas del pelo*) split ends [*pl*] **3** (*palo, bicicleta*) fork

horrible *adj* awful

horror *nm* **1** horror: *un grito de ~* a cry of horror ◊ *los ~es de la guerra* the horrors of war **2** (*mucho*) a lot: *Había un ~ de tráfico.* There was a lot of traffic. ▶ **¡qué ~!** how awful! **tenerle ~ a** hate sth

horrorizar *vt* **1** frighten: *Le horroriza la oscuridad.* He's frightened of the dark. **2** hate: *Me horroriza ese vestido.* I hate that dress.

horroroso *adj* **1** (*aterrador*) horrific **2** (*muy feo*) hideous **3** (*malo*) awful: *Hace un calor ~.* It's awfully hot.

hortaliza *nf* vegetable **2** (*Mx, huerta*) vegetable garden

hospedarse *vp* stay

hospital *nm* hospital → SCHOOL

hospitalidad *nf* hospitality

hospitalizar *vt* hospitalize

hostelería (*tb* **hotelería**) *nf* (*curso*) hotel and catering management

hostería *nf* hotel

hot cake *nm* (*Mx*) pancake

hotel *nm* hotel

hoy *adv* today: *el periódico de ~* today's paper ◊ *la música de ~* present-day music ▶ **de ~ en adelante** from now on **~ (en) día** nowadays **~ por ~** for the time being

hoyo *nm* hole: *cavar/hacer un ~* dig a hole

hoyuelo *nm* dimple

hoz *nf* sickle

huachinango *nm* (*Mx*) (red) snapper

huarache *nm* (*Mx*) sandal

hueco *adj* hollow: *sonar a ~* sound hollow ● *nm* **1** (*cavidad*) space **2** (*agujero*) hole **3** (*espacio en blanco*) gap: *Completa los ~s con verbos.* Fill in the gaps with verbs. **4** (*And, bache*) pothole **5** (*rato libre*) free time [U]: *Por la tarde tengo un ~.* I have some free time in the evening.

huelga *nf* strike: *en ~* on strike

huelguista *nmf* striker

huella *nf* **1** (*persona*) footprint **2** (*animal, vehículo*) track ▶ **~ (dactilar)** fingerprint **sin dejar ~** without trace

huérfano/a *adj, nm-nf* orphan: *quedarse ~ de madre* lose your mother

huerta *nf* (*huerto grande*) truck farm, market garden (*GB*)

huerto *nm* **1** vegetable garden **2** (*árboles frutales*) orchard

hueso *nm* **1** bone **2** (*fruta*) pit, stone (*GB*) **3** (*color*) ivory ▶ **en los ~s** nothing but skin and bone **ser un ~** (*ser malo*) be awful **un ~ duro (de roer)** a tough nut to crack

huésped/a *nm-nf* guest

huevas *nf* **1** (*Zool*) spawn [U] **2** (*Cocina*) roe [U]

huevo *nm* egg: *poner un ~* lay an egg ▶ **~ duro/tibio** hard-boiled/boiled egg **~ frito/estrellado** fried egg **~s rancheros** eggs on tortillas with chili sauce **~s revueltos/pericos** scrambled eggs **pensar en los ~s del gallo** (*And*) daydream

huida *nf* escape

huir *vi* escape ● *vt, vi* avoid *sth/sb*: *~ de la prensa* avoid the press

huitlacoche *nm* edible fungus

hule *nm* rubber: *~ espuma* foam rubber

humanidad *nf* humanity [*pl* -ies]

humanitario *adj* humanitarian

humano *adj* **1** human: *los derechos ~s* human rights **2** (*comprensivo, justo*) humane ● *nm* human being

humareda *nf* cloud of smoke

humedad *nf* **1** damp: *Esta pared tiene ~.* This wall is damp. **2** (*atmósfera*) humidity

humedecer *vt* dampen ● **humedecerse** *vp* get wet

húmedo *adj* 1 damp, moist **NOTA Damp** es el término más común y puede tener un matiz negativo: *paredes con humedad* damp walls ◊ *un trapo ~* a damp cloth ◊ *tiempo frío y ~* cold, damp weather ◊ *un pastel sabroso y esponjoso* a moist cake ◊ *cremas para mantener hidratada la piel* creams to keep your skin moist. **Humid** y **humidity** sólo se refieren al aire, a la humedad atmosférica. **2** (*aire, calor*) humid **3** (*lugar*) wet

humildad *nf* humility

humilde *adj* humble

humillante *adj* humiliating

humo *nm* **1** smoke **2** (*vehículo*) fumes [*pl*] **3 humos** airs: *darse muchos ~s* put on airs ▶ **bajarle los ~s a algn** take sb down a peg or two

humor *nm* **1** humor: *tener sentido del ~* have a sense of humor **2** (*TV, etc.*) comedy: *una serie de ~* a comedy series ▶ **de buen/mal ~** in a good/bad mood **estar de ~** be in the mood (*for sth*) **poner de mal ~** make sb angry **tener buen/mal ~** be good-tempered/bad-tempered

humorista *nmf* humorist

hundido *adj* **1** (*barco*) sunken **2** (*persona*) depressed

hundir *vt* **1** sink: *un barco* sink a boat ◊ *~ los pies en la arena* sink your feet into the sand **2** (*persona*) destroy ● **hundirse** *vp* **1** sink **2** (*derrumbarse*) collapse **3** (*negocio*) go under

huracán *nm* hurricane

hurgar *vi* rummage in/through sth: *No hurgues en mis cosas.* Don't rummage through my things. ▶ **~se la nariz** pick your nose

husmear *vi* sniff around ● *vt* (*olfatear*) sniff

I i

iceberg *nm* iceberg

icono *nm* (*Comp, Rel*) icon

ida *nf* outward journey: *durante la ~* on the way there ▶ **boleto/tiquete de ~** one-way ticket **boleto/tiquete de ~ y vuelta** round-trip ticket, return ticket (*GB*) ▶ **y vuelta** there and back: *Son dos horas de ~ y vuelta.* It's two hours there and back.

idea *nf* **1** (*ocurrencia*) idea **2** (*concepto*) concept **3** (*impresión*) impression: *Eso deja mala ~.* That creates a bad impression. **4 ideas** (*ideología*) convictions: *~s religiosas* religious convictions ▶ **¡ni ~!** I don't have a clue! **no tener la más remota/menor ~** not have the faintest idea

ideal *adj, nm* ideal: *Eso sería lo ~.* That would be ideal/the ideal thing. ◊ *un hombre sin ~es* a man without ideals

idealista *adj* idealistic ● *nmf* idealist

idealizar *vt* idealize

ídem *pron* (*lista*) ditto →DITTO

idéntico *adj* identical (*to sth/sb*)

identidad *nf* identity [*pl* -ies]

identificar(se) *vt, vp* identify (*sth; with sth/sb*) ▶ **sin ~** unidentified

ideología *nf* ideology [*pl* -ies]

idioma *nm* language

idiota *adj* stupid ● *nmf* idiot: *¡Qué ~!* What an idiot!

idiotez *nf* stupidity ▶ **decir idioteces** talk nonsense

ido *adj* **1** (*distraído*) absent-minded **2** (*loco*) crazy

ídolo *nm* idol

iglesia *nf* church: *la Iglesia católica* the Catholic Church →SCHOOL

iglú *nm* igloo [*pl* -s]

ignorante *adj, nmf* ignorant: *Es un ~.* He's an ignorant fool.

ignorar *vt* **1** (*desconocer*) not know: *Ignoro si se fue.* I don't know if he's already left. **2** (*hacer caso omiso*) ignore

igual *adj* **1** equal **2** (*idéntico*) the same (*as sth/sb*): *Esa falda es ~ a la suya.* That skirt is the same as yours. ● *nmf* equal ● *adv* **1** ~ **de** equally: *Son ~ de malos.* They're equally bad. **2** ~ **de... que** as... as: *Son ~ de culpables que nosotros.* They are as guilty as we are. **3** (*probablemente*) probably: *~ no vienen.* They probably won't come. **4** (*de todos modos*) anyway: *No le di permiso pero ~ salió.* I didn't give him permission but he went out anyway. ▶ **me da ~** it's all the same to me, you, etc.

igualar *vt* **1** (*Dep*) equalize **2** (*terreno*) level

igualmente *adv* equally ● *interj* the same to you

ilegal *adj* illegal

ileso *adj* unharmed

ilimitado *adj* unlimited

iluminado adj lit (up) (with sth)

iluminar vt light sth up

ilusión nf 1 (noción falsa) illusion 2 (sueño) dream: Era la ~ de su vida. It was her dream. 3 (esperanza) hope: lleno de ilusiones full of hope ▶ con la ~ de (que...) hoping to/that...: con la ~ de ganar hoping to win **hacerse ilusiones** build your hopes up

ilusionado adj 1 (esperanzado) enthusiastic 2 ~ con excited about sth

iluso/a adj gullible ● nm-nf mug

ilustración nf (dibujo) illustration

ilustrar vt illustrate

ilustre adj illustrious

imagen nf 1 image: cambiar de ~ change your image 2 (Cine, TV) picture

imaginación nf imagination

imaginario adj imaginary

imaginar(se) vt, vp imagine: Me imagino (que sí). I imagine so. ◊ Ya me lo imaginaba yo. I thought as much.

imán nm magnet

imbécil adj stupid ● nmf idiot

imitación nf imitation ▶ de ~ fake

imitar vt imitate

impacientar vt exasperate ● impacientarse vp get worked up (about sth)

impaciente adj impatient

impacto nm 1 (colisión, impresión, repercusión) impact: el ~ ambiental the impact on the environment 2 (huella) hole: un ~ de bala a bullet hole

impar adj odd: número ~ odd number

imparcial adj unbiased

impecable adj impeccable

impedido/a adj, nm-nf disabled: ser un ~ be disabled

impedimento nm 1 (obstáculo) obstacle 2 (Jur) impediment

impedir vt 1 (paso) block sth (up) 2 (imposibilitar) prevent sth/sb (from doing sth): La lluvia impidió que se celebrase la boda. The rain prevented the wedding from taking place. ◊ Nada te lo impide. There's nothing stopping you.

impenetrable adj impenetrable

imperativo adj, nm imperative

imperdible nm safety pin

imperfección nf 1 (tb imperfecto nm) flaw

imperialismo nm imperialism

imperio nm empire

impermeable adj, nm waterproof

impersonal adj impersonal

impertinente adj impertinent

implantar vt introduce

implicar vt 1 (involucrar) implicate: Lo implicaron en el asesinato. He was implicated in the murder. 2 (significar) imply

imponer vt impose ● **imponerse** vp prevail (over sth/sb)

importación nf import ▶ de ~ imported: un carro de ~ an imported car **de ~ y exportación** import-export: un negocio de ~ y exportación an import-export business

importador/a nm-nf importer ● adj importing: un país ~ de petróleo an oil-importing country

importancia nf importance ▶ adquirir/cobrar ~ become important **no tiene ~** it doesn't matter **quitar/restar ~** play sth down **sin ~** unimportant

importante adj 1 important 2 (considerable) considerable: un número ~ a considerable number

importar¹ vt import

importar² vi 1 (tener importancia) matter: No importa. It doesn't matter. 2 (preocupar) care (about sth/sb): No parecen importarle sus hijos. He doesn't seem to care about his children. ▶ ¿le/te importa...? do you mind...?: ¿Le importa venir acá? Do you mind coming here? ◊ ¿Te importa que abra la ventana? Do you mind if I open the window? **me importa un bledo, comino, etc.** I, you, etc. couldn't care less **no me importa** I, you, etc. don't mind (sth): No me importa esperar. I don't mind waiting.

importe nm 1 (cantidad) amount: el ~ de la deuda the amount of the debt 2 (costo) cost

imposible adj, nm impossible: No pida ~s. Don't ask (for) the impossible.

impotente adj impotent

imprenta nf 1 (taller) print shop 2 (máquina) printing press

imprescindible adj essential

impresión nf 1 (sensación) impression: hacer/causar ~ a algn make an impression on sb 2 (texto, etc.) printing ▶ me da la ~ de que... I get the feeling that...

impresionante adj 1 impressive: un logro ~ an impressive achievement 2 (espectacular) striking: una belleza ~ striking beauty

impresionar vt 1 impress: *Me impresiona su talento.* I am impressed by her talent. 2 (*emocionar*) move: *El final me impresionó mucho.* The ending was very moving. 3 (*desagradablemente*) shock

impreso adj printed ● *nm* form

impresora nf printer

imprevisto adj unforeseen ● *nm*: *Surgió un ~.* Something unexpected came up. ◇ *Tengo un dinero ahorrado para ~s.* I have some money put aside for a rainy day.

imprimir vt 1 (*imprenta*) print 2 (*huella*) imprint

improvisar vt improvise

imprudente adj 1 rash 2 (*conductor*) careless

impuesto nm tax: *libre de ~s* tax-free ▶ **I~ al Valor Agregado** sales tax, VAT (*GB*)

impulsar vt 1 drive 2 (*estimular*) stimulate

impulsivo adj impulsive

impulso nm 1 impulse: *actuar por ~ act on impulse* 2 (*empujón*) boost ▶ **tomar ~** get up speed

impuro adj impure

inaccesible adj inaccessible

inaceptable adj unacceptable

inadaptado adj maladjusted

inadecuado adj inappropriate

inadvertido adj unnoticed: *pasar ~* go unnoticed

inagotable adj 1 (*inacabable*) inexhaustible 2 (*incansable*) tireless

inaguantable adj unbearable

inalámbrico adj cordless

inapreciable adj (*valioso*) invaluable

inauguración nf opening, inauguration (*fml*): *la ceremonia de ~* the opening ceremony ◇ *Había unas cien personas en la ~.* There were a hundred people at the inauguration.

inaugurar vt open

incapacitado adj disabled

incapaz adj incapable *of sth*: *Es ~ de prestar atención.* He's incapable of paying attention.

incautar vt **~ de** seize *sth*

incendiar vt set fire to *sth* ● **incendiarse** vp catch fire

incendio nm fire ▶ **~ provocado** arson [*U*]

incidente nm incident

incinerar vt 1 incinerate 2 (*cadáver*) cremate

inclinar vt 1 tilt 2 (*cabeza para asentir o saludar*) nod ● **inclinarse** vp 1 lean: *El edificio se inclina*

hacia un lado. The building leans over to one side. 2 **~ por**: *Me inclino por el partido verde.* My sympathies lie with the Green Party.

incluido adj including: *con el IVA ~* including sales tax ▶ **todo ~** all-inclusive

incluir vt include

inclusive adv inclusive: *hasta el lunes ~* up to and including Monday ◇ *del 3 al 7 ambos ~* from the 3rd through the 7th

incluso adv even: *~ me dieron dinero.* They even gave me money.

incógnito adj ▶ **de ~** incognito: *viajar de ~* travel incognito

incoherente adj 1 (*confuso*) incoherent 2 (*ilógico*) inconsistent

incoloro adj colorless

incombustible adj fireproof

incomible adj inedible

incomodar vt make *sb* uncomfortable: *Él me incomoda.* He makes me feel uncomfortable.

incómodo adj 1 uncomfortable 2 (*penoso*) embarrassing

incompatible adj incompatible

incompetente adj, nmf incompetent

incompleto adj 1 incomplete 2 (*sin acabar*) unfinished

incomprensible adj incomprehensible

incomunicado adj 1 cut off: *Nos quedamos ~s por la nieve.* We were cut off by the snow. 2 (*preso*) in solitary confinement

inconfundible adj unmistakable

inconsciente adj unconscious: *un gesto/paciente ~* an unconscious gesture/patient ● adj, nmf (*irresponsable*) irresponsible: *Eres un ~.* You're so irresponsible.

incontable adj 1 countless 2 (*Gram*) uncountable

inconveniente adj 1 (*inoportuno, molesto*) inconvenient: *una hora ~* an inconvenient time 2 (*no apropiado*) inappropriate ● *nm* 1 (*dificultad, obstáculo*) problem 2 (*desventaja*) disadvantage

incorporación nf (*entrada*) entry (*into sth*)

incorporado adj 1 incorporated *into sth* 2 (*Mec*) built-in: *con antena incorporada* with a built-in antenna

incorporar vt 1 (*persona*) include *sb* (*in sth*) 2 (*territorio*) annex 3 (*persona acostada*) sit *sb* up ● **incorporarse** vp join *sth* 2 (*trabajo*) start *sth*: *El lunes me* *incorporo a mi nuevo empleo.* I start my new job on Monday.

incorrecto *adj* **1** *(erróneo)* incorrect **2** *(conducta)* impolite

increíble *adj* incredible

incrustarse *vp*: *La bala se incrustó en la pared.* The bullet embedded itself in the wall.

incubadora *nf* incubator

incubar(se) *vt, vp* incubate

inculto *adj, nm-nf* ignorant: *Es un ~.* He's so ignorant.

incultura *nf* lack of culture

incumplido *adj, nmf* unreliable: *Es un ~.* He's very unreliable.

incurable *adj* incurable

incursión *nf* (Mil) raid

indagación *nf* enquiry [*pl* -ies]

indecente *adj* **1** *(sucio)* filthy **2** *(espectáculo, gesto, lenguaje)* obscene **3** *(ropa)* indecent

indeciso/a *adj, nm-nf (carácter)* indecisive: *ser un ~* be indecisive

indefenso *adj* defenseless

indefinido *adj* **1** *(período, Gram)* indefinite **2** *(color, edad, forma)* indeterminate

indemnizar *vt* pay sb compensation *(for sth)*

independencia *nf* independence

independiente *adj* **1** independent **2** *(trabajador)* self-employed

independizarse *vp* **1** *(individuo)* leave home **2** *(país)* gain independence

indestructible *adj* indestructible

indeterminado *adj* **1** indeterminate **2** *(artículo)* indefinite

India *nf* India

indicación *nf* **1** sign **2** indicaciones (a) *(instrucciones)* instructions (b) *(camino)* directions

indicado *adj* **1** *(conveniente)* suitable **2** *(convenido)* specified **3** *(aconsejable)* advisable

indicador *nm* indicator ▶ ~ **de gasolina/presión** gas/pressure gauge

indicar *vt* **1** *(mostrar)* show: *~ el camino* show the way **2** *(señalar)* point sth out *(to sb)*: *Indicó que fue un error.* He pointed out that it was a mistake.

indicativo *nm* (teléfono) area code

índice *nm* **1** index **2** *(dedo)* index finger ▶ ~ **(de materias)** table of contents ~ **de natalidad** birth rate

índico *adj* Indian ● **el Índico** *nm* the Indian Ocean

indiferencia *nf* indifference *(to sth/sb)*

indiferente *adj* indifferent *(to sth/sb)*: *Es ~ a la moda.* She isn't interested in fashion. ▶ **me es ~** I, you, etc. don't care: *ser ~:* *Es ~ que sea blanco o negro.* It doesn't matter if it's black or white.

indígena *adj* indigenous ● *nmf* native

indigestión *nf* indigestion

indignado *adj* indignant *(at/about sth)*

indignante *adj* outrageous

indignar *vt* infuriate ● **indignarse** *vp* get angry *(with sb)* *(about sth)*

indigno *adj* **1** *(despreciable)* contemptible **2** ~ **de** unworthy of sth/sb: *una conducta indigna de un director* behavior unworthy of a director

indio/a *adj, nm-nf* Indian

indirecta *nf* hint ▶ **agarrar la ~** take the hint **echar/lanzar una ~** drop a hint

indirecto *adj* indirect

indiscreción *nf*: *Fue una ~ por su parte preguntarlo.* She shouldn't have asked. ◇ *si no es ~* if you don't mind my asking

indiscutible *adj* indisputable

indispensable *adj* essential ▶ **lo ~** the bare essentials [*pl*]

indispuesto *adj* *(enfermo)* not well

individual *adj* individual

individuo/a *nm-nf* individual

indudable *adj* undoubted ▶ **es ~ que...** there is no doubt that...

indulto *nm* pardon: *conceder el ~ a algn* pardon sb

industria *nf* industry [*pl* -ies]

industrial *adj* industrial ● *nmf* industrialist ▶ **en cantidades ~es** in huge amounts

industrialización *nf* industrialization

industrializar *vt* industrialize ● **industrializarse** *vp* become industrialized

inédito *adj* *(desconocido)* previously unknown

ineficaz *adj* **1** ineffective **2** *(persona)* inefficient

ineficiente *adj* *(persona)* inefficient

inercia *nf* inertia ▶ **por ~** through force of habit

inesperado *adj* unexpected

inestable *adj* **1** unstable **2** *(clima)* changeable

inevitable *adj* inevitable

inexperiencia *nf* inexperience

inexperto *adj* inexperienced

infancia *nf* childhood

infantería nf infantry ▶ ~ **de marina** marines [pl]

infantil adj 1 (de niño) children's: *literatura* ~ *a la de ustedes* children's books 2 (inocente) childlike: *una sonrisa* ~ *a childlike smile* 3 (pey) childish: *No sea* ~. Don't be childish.

infarto nm heart attack

infección nf infection

infeccioso adj infectious

infectar vt infect sth/sb (with sth) ● **infectarse** vp become infected

infeliz adj unhappy ◆ nmf wretch

inferior adj 1 inferior (to sth/sb): *de una calidad* ~ *a la de ustedes* inferior to yours 2 (por debajo) lower (than sth): *una cifra* ~ *a la del año pasado* a lower figure than last year

infidelidad nf infidelity [pl -ies]

infiel adj unfaithful (to sth/sb)

infierno nm hell: *ir al* ~ go to hell

infinidad nf (multitud) a great many: *una* ~ *de gente* a great many people

infinito adj infinite

inflación nf inflation

inflamación nf (Med) swelling, inflammation (más fml)

inflamarse vp 1 (encenderse) catch fire 2 (Med) swell: *Se me inflamó el tobillo.* My ankle is swollen.

inflar vt blow sth up, inflate (más fml)

influencia nf influence (on/over sth/sb)

influir vi ~ **en** influence sth/sb: *No quiero* ~ *en tu decisión.* I don't want to influence your decision.

información nf 1 information (on/about sth/sb) [U] → CONSEJO 2 (noticias) news [sing]: ~ *deportiva* sports news 3 (telefónica) directory assistance [U] 4 (recepción) information desk

informal adj (ropa, acto) casual

informar vt 1 (notificar) inform sb (of/about sth) 2 (anunciar) announce ◆ vi (dar un informe) report (on sth) ● **informarse** vp find out (about sth/sb): *Tengo que* ~*me de lo sucedido.* I have to find out what happened.

informática nf 1 computing 2 (Educ) information technology (abrev IT)

informático/a adj computer: *un centro* ~ *a computer centre* ◆ nm-nf IT specialist: *Mi hermano es* ~. My brother works in IT.

informe nm 1 (documento, presentación) report: *un* ~ *escolar a* school report 2 **informes** information [U]

infracción nf 1 offense: *una* ~ *de tráfico* a traffic offense 2 (acuerdo, contrato, regla) breach of sth

infrarrojo adj infrared

infundado adj unfounded

infundir vt 1 (miedo) instill (in/into sb) 2 (sospechas) arouse sb's suspicions 3 (respeto, confianza) inspire sth (in sb)

infusión nf herbal tea

ingeniar vt think sth up ▶ **ingeniárselas** find a way (to do sth/of doing sth): *Ingéniatelas como puedas.* You'll have to manage somehow.

ingeniería nf engineering ▶ ~ **genética** genetic engineering

ingeniero/a nm-nf engineer ▶ ~ **agrónomo/civil** agriculturist/civil engineer

ingenio nm 1 (inventiva) ingenuity 2 (humor) wit 3 (de azúcar) sugar mill

ingenioso adj 1 ingenious 2 (perspicaz) witty

ingenuo/a adj, nm-nf 1 (inocente) innocent 2 (crédulo) naive: *¡Eres un* ~! You're so naive!

ingerir vt consume

Inglaterra nf England

ingle nf groin

inglés/esa adj, nm English ◆ nm-nf Englishman/woman [pl -men/-women]: *los ingleses* the English

ingrato adj 1 (persona) ungrateful 2 (trabajo, tarea) thankless

ingrediente nm ingredient

ingresar vi 1 (Mil, club) join sth: ~ *en el ejército* join the army 2 (centro sanitario): *Ingreso mañana.* I'm going into hospital tomorrow. ◇ *Ingresó en el hospital a las 4.30.* He was admitted to hospital at 4.30.

ingreso nm 1 (entrada) (a) (ejército) enlistment (in sth) (b) (organización) entry (into sth) (c) (hospital, institución) admission (to sth) 2 **ingresos** (a) (persona, institución) income [sing] (b) (Estado, municipio) revenue [sing] ▶ **examen/prueba de** ~ entrance exam

inhabitado adj uninhabited

inhalador nm inhaler

inhalar vt inhale

inherente adj inherent (in sth/sb)

inhumano adj 1 (cruel) inhuman 2 (injusto) inhumane

iniciación nf 1 introduction (to sth) 2 (rito) initiation (into sth)

inicial adj, nf initial

iniciar vt begin

iniciativa nf initiative: tomar la/ tener ~ take the/show initiative ▶ **por ~ propia** on your own initiative

inicio nm 1 beginning: desde los ~s right from the beginning 2 (guerra, enfermedad) outbreak

injusticia nf injustice: Cometieron muchas ~s. Many injustices were done. ▶ **ser una ~**: Es una ~. It's not fair.

injusto adj unfair (on/to sb)

inmaduro/a adj, nm-nf (persona) immature: Es un ~. He's so immature.

inmediatamente adv immediately

inmediato adj immediate

inmejorable adj 1 (resultado, referencia, clima) excellent 2 (calidad, nivel) top 3 (precio, récord) unbeatable

inmenso adj 1 vast: la inmensa mayoría the vast majority 2 (sentimientos) great: una pena inmensa great sorrow

inmigración nf immigration

inmigrante nmf (tb inmigrado/a nm-nf) immigrant

inmigrar vi immigrate

inmobiliaria nf (tb agencia ~) real estate agent, estate agent (GB)

inmobiliario adj property: el mercado ~ the property market

inmoral adj immoral

inmortal adj, nmf immortal

inmóvil adj still: permanecer ~ stand still

inmunidad nf immunity

inmutarse vp: No se inmutó. He didn't bat an eye/eyelid (GB).

innato adj innate

innovador adj innovative

innumerable adj innumerable

inocente adj, nmf innocent: hacerse el ~ play the innocent →DÍA ● adj 1 (ingenuo) naive 2 (broma) harmless

inofensivo adj harmless

inolvidable adj unforgettable

inoportuno adj inopportune ▶ ¡qué ~! what a nuisance!

inoxidable adj (acero) stainless

inquieto adj 1 (agitado, activo) restless 2 (preocupado) worried (about sth/sb)

inquietud nf 1 (preocupación) anxiety [pl -ies] 2 inquietudes interest [sing]: Es una persoan sin ~es. He has no interest in anything.

inquilino/a nm-nf tenant

insatisfecho adj dissatisfied (with sth/sb)

inscribir vt 1 (en registro) register: ~ un nacimiento register a birth 2 (curso) enroll sb 3 (grabar) inscribe ● **inscribirse** vp 1 (curso) enroll (for/on sth) 2 (organización, partido) join 3 (concurso) enter

inscripción nf 1 (grabado) inscription 2 (a) (registro) registration (b) (curso, ejército) enrollment

insecticida nm insecticide

insecto nm insect

inseguridad nf 1 (falta de confianza) insecurity [pl -ies] 2 (tiempo, trabajo, etc.) uncertainty [pl -ies] ▶ **~ ciudadana** lack of safety on the streets

inseguro adj 1 (sin confianza) insecure 2 (peligroso) unsafe 3 (paso, voz) unsteady

insensible adj 1 insensitive (to sth) 2 (miembro, nervio) numb

inservible adj useless

insignia nf badge

insignificante adj insignificant

insinuación nf 1 (sugerencia) hint 2 (ofensiva) insinuation

insinuar vt 1 (sugerir) hint 2 (algo desagradable) insinuate ▶ **insinuársele a algn** make a pass at sb

insistente adj 1 (con palabras) insistent 2 (actitud) persistent

insistir vi insist (on sth): Insistió en que fuéramos. He insisted that we go.

insolación nf sunstroke [U]

insomnio nm insomnia

insonorizar vt soundproof

insoportable adj unbearable

inspeccionar vt inspect

inspector/a nm-nf inspector

inspiración nf inspiration

inspirado adj inspired

inspirar vt inspire (sb) (with sth): No me inspira ninguna confianza. He doesn't inspire me with confidence. ● **inspirarse** vp get inspiration (from sth)

instalación nf 1 installation 2 instalaciones facilities: instalaciones deportivas sports facilities ▶ **~ eléctrica** wiring

instalar vt install ● **instalarse** vp 1 (ciudad, país) settle (down) 2 (casa) move into sth: ~ en la nueva casa move into your new house

instantáneo adj instantaneous

instante nm moment: en ese ~ at that moment

instinto *nm* instinct ▸ **por ~** instinctively

institución *nf* (*organismo*) institution

instituto *nm* **1** institute **2** (*Educ*) secondary school ▸ **~ técnico/de formación profesional** technical college

instrucción *nf* **1** (*Mil*) training **2 instrucciones** instructions: *instrucciones de uso* instructions for use

instructor/a *nm-nf* instructor

instrumental *nm* instruments [*pl*]

instrumento *nm* instrument

insuficiencia *nf* **1** (*deficiencia*) inadequacy **2** (*Med*) failure: **~ renal** kidney failure

insuficiente *adj* **1** (*escaso*) insufficient **2** (*deficiente*) inadequate

insultar *vt* insult

insulto *nm* insult

insuperable *adj* **1** (*hazaña, belleza*) matchless **2** (*dificultad*) insuperable **3** (*calidad, oferta*) unbeatable

insustituible *adj* irreplaceable

intachable *adj* irreproachable

intacto *adj* **1** (*no tocado*) untouched **2** (*no dañado*) intact

integración *nf* integration (*into sth*)

integral *adj* **1** (*total*) comprehensive **2** (*alimentos*) wholemeal

integrarse *vp* (*adaptarse*) integrate (*into sth*)

integridad *nf* integrity

integrismo *nm* fundamentalism

integrista *adj, nmf* fundamentalist

íntegro *adj* whole

intelectual *adj, nmf* intellectual

inteligencia *nf* intelligence

inteligente *adj* intelligent

intemperie *nf* ▸ **a la ~** out in the open

intención *nf* intention ▸ **con (mala) ~** maliciously **hacer algo con buena ~** mean well **tener ~ de** intend *to do sth*

intencionado *adj* deliberate ▸ **bien/mal ~** well meaning/malicious

intensidad *nf* **1** intensity **2** (*corriente eléctrica, viento, voz*) strength

intensificar(se) *vt, vp* intensify

intensivo *adj* intensive

intenso *adj* **1** intense: *una ola de frío/calor* ~ intense cold/heat **2** (*vigilancia*) close **3** (*negociaciones*) intensive

intentar *vt* try (*sth/to do sth*): *Inténtelo.* Just try.

intento *nm* attempt ▸ **al primer, segundo, etc. ~** at the first, second, etc. attempt

interactivo *adj* interactive

intercambiar *vt* exchange

intercambio *nm* exchange

interceder *vi* intervene (*on sb's behalf*): *Intercedió por mí.* He intervened on my behalf.

interés *nm* **1** interest (*in sth/sb*): *La novela ha suscitado un gran ~.* The novel has aroused a lot of interest. ◇ **tener ~ en algo** be interested in sth ◇ **a un 10% de ~** at 10% interest **2** (*egoísmo*) self-interest: *Lo hice por puro ~.* I did it out of self-interest. ▸ **hacer algo sin ningún ~** show no interest in sth: *Trabajan sin ningún ~.* They show no interest in their work.

interesante *adj* interesting →BE

interesar *vi* be interested in *sth*: *Me interesa el arte/participar.* I'm interested in art/taking part. ● *vt* ▸ **~ a algn (en algo)** interest sb (*in sth*) ● **interesarse** *vp* **1** (*mostrar interés*) show (an) interest *in sth* **2** (*preocuparse*) ask *after sth/sb*: *Se interesó por mi salud.* He asked after my health.

interferencia *nf* interference [*U*]: *Hay muchas ~s.* We're getting a lot of interference.

interferir *vi* interfere (*in sth*)

interfono (*tb* **interfón** *Mx*) *nm* (*portero electrico*) intercom

interior *adj* **1** inner **2** (*bolsillo*) inside **3** (*Com, Pol*) domestic ● *nm* interior

interjección *nf* interjection

intermediario/a *nm-nf* **1** (*mediador*) mediator **2** (*Com*) middleman [*pl* -men] **3** (*mensajero*) go-between

intermedio *adj* intermediate ● *nm* **1** (*Teat*) intermission, interval (*GB*) **2** (*Dep*) half-time

interminable *adj* endless

intermunicipal *adj* intercity

internacional *adj* international

internado *nm* boarding school

internar *vt* admit: *~ a algn en el hospital/en un asilo* admit sb to hospital/into a home

internet *nm o nf* (the) Internet **NOTA** En inglés **Internet** se suele usar con el artículo definido **the**: *buscar algo en ~* search for sth on the Internet, pero cuando va delante de un sustantivo, no se utiliza el artículo: *un proveedor de servicio de ~* an

Internet service provider.
→COMPUTADORA

interno/a *adj* **1** internal **2** (*dentro de un país*) domestic **3** (*cara, parte*) inner: *la parte interna del muslo* the inner thigh ● *nm-nf* **1** (*alumno*) boarder **2** (*cárcel*) inmate **3** (*residente*) resident

interpretación *nf* interpretation

interpretar *vt* **1** (*explicar*) interpret **2** (*Cine, Teat, Mús*) play

intérprete *nmf* **1** interpreter **2** (*Teat, Cine, Mús*) performer

interrogación *nf* question mark

interrogar *vt* question

interrogatorio *nm* interrogation

interrumpir *vt* **1** interrupt **2** (*tráfico, clase*) disrupt

interruptor *nm* switch

intervalo *nm* interval: *a ~s de media hora* at half-hourly intervals

intervenir *vi* **1** intervene (*in sth*) **2** (*hablar*) speak ● *vt* (*Med*) operate (*on sb*)

intestino *nm* intestine

intimidad *nf* **1** (*vida privada*) private life: *el derecho a la ~* the right to privacy **2** (*relación*) intimacy

íntimo *adj* **1** intimate **2** (*amistad, relación*) close

intolerable *adj* intolerable

intriga *nf* **1** (*Cine, novela*) suspense **2** (*curiosidad*): *¡Qué intriga! Cuéntamelo.* Come on! Don't keep me in suspense. ◇ *¿No tienes ~ por saber dónde está?* Aren't you dying to know where it is? **3** (*enredo*) intrigue

intrigar *vt* intrigue

introducción *nf* introduction

introducir *vt* put *sth* in, put *sth* into *sth*, insert (*más fml*)

introvertido/a *adj* introverted ● *nm-nf* introvert

intruso/a *nm-nf* intruder

intuición *nf* intuition: *Contesté por ~.* I answered intuitively.

intuir *vt* sense

inundación *nf* flood

inundar(se) *vt, vp* flood

inútil *adj* useless: *un esfuerzo ~* a waste of time ◇ *Es ~ que grites.* There's no point in shouting. ● *nmf* good-for-nothing

invadir *vt* invade

inválido/a *adj* (*Med*) disabled ● *nm-nf* disabled person

invasión *nf* **1** (*país, etc.*) invasion **2** (*barrio*) shanty town

invasor/a *adj* invading ● *nm-nf* invader

invencible *adj* invincible

inventar *vt* **1** (*descubrir*) invent **2** (*mentir*) make *sth* up

invento *nm* invention

inventor/a *nm-nf* inventor

invernadero *nm* greenhouse
▸ **efecto ~** greenhouse effect

inversión *nf* (*Fin*) investment

inverso *adj* **1** (*proporción*) inverse **2** (*orden*) reverse **3** (*dirección*) opposite ▸ **a la inversa** the other way around

invertebrado *adj, nm* invertebrate

invertir *vt* (*tiempo, dinero*) invest

investigación *nf* **1** investigation (*into sth*) **2** (*científica, académica*) research [*U*] (*into/on sth*): *hacer un trabajo de ~ sobre algo* do research on sth

investigador/a *nm-nf* **1** investigator **2** (*científico, académico*) researcher ▸ **~ privado** private detective

investigar *vt, vi* **1** investigate **2** (*científico, académico*) do research (*into/on sth*)

invierno *nm* **1** winter **2** (*países tropicales*) rainy season

invisible *adj* invisible

invitación *nf* invitation (*to sth*)

invitado/a *adj, nm-nf* guest: *el artista ~* the guest artist

invitar *vt* invite *sb* (*to sth*) ● *vi* (*pagar*): *Invito yo.* I'll get this one. ◇ *Invita la casa.* It's on the house.

inyección *nf* injection: *poner una ~ a algn* give sb an injection

inyectar *vt* give *sb* an injection

ir *vi* **1** go: *ir en carro/avión* go by car/plane ◇ *ir a pie* go on foot ◇ *¿Cómo te va?* How's it going? ◇ *¿Cómo van las cosas?* How are things going? **NOTA** En inglés "ir" se traduce por **come** cuando se acerca a la persona con la que uno habla: *¡Voy!* Coming! ◇ *Mañana voy a ir a York, así que nos vemos allá.* I'm coming to York tomorrow, so I'll see you there. **2** (*estar, haber diferencia*) be: *Íbamos cansados.* We were tired. ◇ *ir bien vestido* be well dressed ◇ *De nueve a doce van tres.* Nine from twelve is three. **3** (*sentar bien*) suit *sb*: *Le va bien el pelo corto.* Short hair suits you. **4** (*funcionar*) work ● *vaux* **1 ir a hacer algo** (a) we're going to do sth: *Vamos a vender la casa.* We're going to sell the house. (b) (*órdenes*) go and do sth: *Ve a hablar con tu papá.* Go and talk to your dad. ◇ (*sugerencias*): *¡Vamos a ver/comer!* Let's see/ Let's go and eat! **2 ir haciendo**

algo start doing sth: *Vayan preparando la mesa.* Start laying the table. ● **irse** *vp* **1** (*marcharse*) leave: *irse de la casa* leave home **2** (*mancha, luz, dolor*) go **3** (*líquido, gas*) leak ▶ **(a mí) ni me va ni me viene** that's nothing to do with me, you, etc. **ir a dar a** (*calle*) lead to sth **ir a lo suyo** mind your own business **ir con** (*combinar*) go with sth **ir de** be dressed as sth/sb/in sth: *Iba de payaso.* I was dressed as a clown. ◇ *ir de azul* be dressed in blue **ir por 1** (*traer*) go and get sth/sb **2** (*llegar*) be up to sth: *Voy por la página 100.* I'm up to page 100. **¡qué te vaya bien!** all the best! **¡qué va!** no way! **¡vamos!** come on! **¡vaya! 1** (*sorpresa*) good heavens! **2** (*compasión*) oh dear! **¡(ya) voy!** coming!
NOTA Para otras expresiones con **ir**, ver el sustantivo, adjetivo, etc., p.ej. **ir al grano** en **GRANO**.

iris *nm* iris

Irlanda *nf* Ireland ▶ **~ del Norte** Northern Ireland

irlandés/esa *adj, nm* Irish ● *nm-nf* Irishman/woman [*pl* -men/-women]: *los irlandeses* the Irish

ironía *nf* irony [*pl* -ies]

irónico *adj* ironic

irracional *adj* irrational

irreal *adj* unreal

irreconocible *adj* unrecognizable

irregular *adj* **1** irregular: *verbos ~es* irregular verbs ◇ *un latido ~* an irregular heartbeat **2** (*anormal*) abnormal

irremediable *adj* irreparable: *Eso ya es ~.* Nothing can be done about it now.

irreparable *adj* irreparable

irrepetible *adj* (*excelente*) unique

irresistible *adj* irresistible: *Tenía unas ganas ~s de irse.* He was dying to leave.

irrespetuoso *adj* disrespectful (*to/towards sth/sb*)

irrespirable *adj* **1** (*aire*) unbreathable **2** (*ambiente*) unbearable

irresponsable *adj, nmf* irresponsible: *¡Eres un ~!* You're so irresponsible!

irreversible *adj* irreversible

irrompible *adj* unbreakable

isla *nf* island ▶ **~ desierta** desert island **las I~s Británicas** the British Isles

islámico *adj* Islamic

isleño/a *nm-nf* islander

istmo *nm* isthmus

Italia *nf* Italy

italiano/a *adj, nm-nf, nm* Italian

itinerario *nm* itinerary [*pl* -ies]

IVA *nm* sales tax, VAT (*GB*)

izquierda *nf* **1** left: *Siga por/ Voltee a la ~.* Keep/turn left. ◇ *la casa de la ~* the house on the left **2 la Izquierda** (*Pol*) the Left **3** (*mano*) left hand: *escribir con la ~* be left-handed **4** (*pie*) left foot ▶ **de ~** (*Pol*) left-wing

izquierdo *adj* left

J j

jabalí/ina *nm-nf* wild boar

jabalina *nf* (*Dep*) javelin

jabonar(se) = ENJABONAR(SE)

jabonera *nf* soap dish

jacal *nm* (*Mx*) shack

jacinto *nm* hyacinth

jadear *vi* pant

jaguar *nm* jaguar

jalado *adj* **1** (*borracho*) drunk **2** (*Mx, inverosímil*) hard to believe

jalador/a *adj* (*Mx*) ready to join in ● *nm-nf* (*And*) car thief [*pl* thieves]

jalar *vt, vi* **1** pull (on/at sth): *Me jaló la manga.* She pulled at my sleeve. ◇ *una silla* pull up a chair **2** (*Mx, atraer*): *Ahora le jalan más sus amigos.* He's more interested in his friends right now. ● *vi* (*Mx, funcionar*) work ▶ **~ la cadena** flush the toilet **~ parejo** (*Mx*) pull your weight

jalea *nf* jelly [*pl* -ies] ▶ **~ real** royal jelly

jaleo *nm* (*pelea*) fight

jamaica *nf* hibiscus

jamás *adv* never →ALWAYS

jamón *nm* ham ▶ **~ cocido/dulce/ de York** cooked ham **~ serrano** cured ham

Japón *nm* Japan

japonés/esa *adj, nm* Japanese ● *nm-nf* Japanese man/woman [*pl* men/women]: *los japoneses* the Japanese

jaque *nm* check ▶ **~ mate** checkmate: *dar ~ mate* checkmate

jaqueca *nf* migraine

jarabe *nm* syrup

jardín nm garden ▸ ~ **infantil/de niños** preschool, nursery school (GB)

jardinera nf (de ventana) window box

jardinería nf gardening

jardinero/a nm-nf gardener

jarra nf pitcher, jug (GB) ▸ ~ **de cerveza** beer mug

jarro nm (large) pitcher, (large) jug (GB)

jarrón nm vase

jartera nf (And) bore: ¡Qué ~ de libro! What a boring book! ◇ Tengo ~ de levantarme. I can't be bothered to get up.

jarto adj (And) 1 fed up (with sth/ sb): Ya me jarté de él. I'm fed up with him. 2 (aburrido) boring 3 (molesto) annoying

jaula nf cage

jefatura nf 1 (oficina central) headquarters (abrev HQ) 2 (cargo) leadership

jefe/a nm-nf 1 (superior) boss 2 (institución) head: ~ de departamento/estado head of department/state 3 (partido, etc.) leader 4 (policía, tribu) chief ▸ ~ **de ventas** sales manager

jengibre nm ginger

jerarquía nf hierarchy [pl -ies]

jerez nm sherry

jerga nf 1 (profesional) jargon 2 (argot) slang 3 (trapo) floor-cloth

jeringa (tb **jeringuilla**) nf (Med) syringe

jeroglífico nm hieroglyph

Jesucristo n Jesus Christ

jesuita adj, nm Jesuit

Jesús n Jesus ● interj (al estornudar) bless you →**ACHÍS**

jeta nmf mouth ▸ **estar (de)** ~ be in a bad mood

jilguero nm goldfinch

jinete nmf 1 rider 2 (jockey) jockey

jirafa nf giraffe

jitomate nm (Mx) tomato [pl -es]

jockey nmf jockey

jolgorio nm celebrations [pl]

jornada nf 1 day: una ~ laboral de ocho horas an eight-hour working day 2 **jornadas** (congreso) conference [sing] ▸ ~ **completa/ media** ~: trabajar la ~ completa/ media ~ work full-time/part-time

jornalero/a nm-nf casual laborer

joroba nf hump

jorobado/a adj hunchbacked ● nm-nf hunchback

jorobar vt get on sb's nerves

jorongo nm (Mx) poncho [pl -s]

jota nf (cartas) jack →**BARAJA** ▸ **no decir ni** ~ not say a word **no saber/entender ni** ~ not know/ understand a thing (about sth): No sé ni ~ de francés. I don't know a word of French.

joto nm (cartas) jack 2 (Mx, homosexual) gay

joven adj young ● nmf 1 boy/girl, young man/woman [pl men/women] (más fml) 2 **jóvenes** young people

joya nf 1 (a) (sing) piece of jewelry: una ~ preciosa a beautiful piece of jewelry (b) **joyas** jewelry [U] **NOTA** Para "joyas valiosas", también se dice **jewels**: priceless jewels. 2 (cosa, persona) treasure: Eres una ~. You're a treasure.

joyería nf jewelry store/shop (GB) →**CARNICERÍA**

joyero/a nm-nf jeweler ● nm jewelry box

juagada nf (And) ▸ **meterse/pegarse una** ~ get soaked

juagado adj (And) ▸ **estar ~ de la risa** kill yourself laughing: Estaba ~ de la risa con él! He had me in stitches.

juagar(se) (And) = **ENJUAGAR**

juanete nm bunion

jubilación nf 1 (retiro) retirement 2 (pensión) pension

jubilado/a adj retired ● nm-nf pensioner

jubilarse vp retire

judaísmo nm Judaism

judío/a adj Jewish ● nm-nf Jew

judo nm judo: hacer ~ do judo

juego nm 1 game: ~ de mesa/salón board game 2 (azar) gambling 3 (conjunto) set: ~ de llaves set of keys ◇ ~ de cama bedding ▸ **a** ~ matching: Lleva falda y chaqueta a ~. She's wearing a skirt and matching jacket. **en** ~ at stake **hacer** ~ **con** match sth ~ **de azar** game of chance ~ **de manos** conjuring trick ~ **de niños** child's play ~ **de palabras** pun ~ **limpio/ sucio** fair/foul play **J~s Olímpicos** Olympic Games **poner en** ~ put sth at risk

juerga nf partying [sing]: montar una gran ~ have a big party ▸ **ir(se) de** ~ go out (partying)

jueves nm Thursday (abrev Thur(s).) →**LUNES** ▸ **J~ Santo** Holy/Maundy (GB) Thursday

juez nmf judge ▸ ~ **de línea** referee's assistant

jugada nf move ▸ **hacer una mala** ~ play a dirty trick on sb

jugador/a *nm-nf* **1** player **2** *(que apuesta)* gambler

jugar *vt, vi* play: ~ *una partida de cartas* play a game of cards ◊ *El trabajo juega un papel importante en mi vida.* Work plays an important part in my life. → DEPORTE **2** *(apostar)* gamble *(on sth)*: ~ *todo a un caballo* put all your money on a horse ● **jugarse** *vp* **1** *(apostar)* gamble sth *(away)* **2** *(arriesgarse)* risk: ~ *la vida* risk your life ▶ **limpio/sucio** play fair/dirty

jugarreta *nf* ▶ **hacer una ~** play a dirty trick *on sb*

jugo *nm* **1** juice **2** *(salsa)* gravy ▶ **sacar ~ a** get the most out of sth

jugoso *adj* juicy

juguete *nm* toy: *carro de* ~ toy car

juguetería *nf* toy store/shop *(GB)*

juguetón *adj* playful

juicio *nm* **1** *(cualidad)* judgement: *Confío en tu* ~. I trust your judgement. **2** *(sensatez)* (common) sense **3** *(opinión)* opinion: *a mi* ~ in my opinion **4** *(Jur)* trial: *llevar a algn a* ~ take sb to court ▶ **perder el** ~ go crazy

juicioso *adj* **1** *(comportamiento)* sensible **2** *(serio)* conscientious

julio *nm* July *(abrev Jul.)* →MAYO

jungla *nf* jungle

junio *nm* June *(abrev Jun.)* →MAYO

juntar *vt* **1** *(poner juntos)* put sth/sb together: ~ *las mesas* put the tables together **2** *(unir)* join sth *(together)* **3** *(reunir)* get sb together

junto *adj* **1** together: *todos ~s* all together ◊ *Estudiamos ~s.* We study together. **2** *(cerca)* close together: *Los árboles están muy* ~s. The trees are very close together. ● *adv* **1** ~ **a** next to **2** ~ **con** with

Júpiter *nm* Jupiter

jurado *nm* jury *[pl* -ies] **NOTA** Palabras como **jury, committee, crew, government, staff** y **team** pueden llevar el verbo en singular o en plural: *El* ~ *está a punto de adjudicar el premio.* The jury is/are about to award the prize. Si van precedidas de **a, each, every, this** y **that**, se usa el singular: *Cada equipo tiene un líder.* Each team has a leader. Si el verbo está en plural, se usan también pronombre y adjetivo en plural (**them** y **their**): *El personal votó para cambiar el uniforme.* The staff voted to change their uniform.

juramento *nm* oath

jurar *vt, vi* swear ▶ ~ **bandera/lealtad a algn** swear allegiance to the flag/to sb

jurgo *nm* *(And)* an awful lot *(of sth)*

justicia *nf* **1** justice: *Espero que se haga* ~. I hope justice is done. **2** *(del estado)* law: *tomar la* ~ *por su cuenta* take the law into your own hands

justificar *vt* justify

justo *adj* **1** *(razonable)* fair: *un trato* ~ a fair deal **2** *(correcto, exacto)* right: *el precio* ~ the right price **3** *(apretado)* tight: *La falda me queda justa.* The skirt is a bit tight. **4** *(suficiente)* just enough: *Tenemos los platos* ~s. We have just enough plates. ● *adv* just: ~ *a tiempo* just in time ▶ ~ **cuando...** just as...: *Llegó* ~ *cuando me iba.* He arrived just as I was leaving.

juvenil *adj* **1** *(carácter)* youthful: *la moda* ~ young people's fashion **2** *(Dep)* junior

juventud *nf* **1** *(edad)* youth **2** *(los jóvenes)* young people *[pl]*

juzgado *nm* court

juzgar *vt* judge ▶ **a ~ por...** judging by... ▶ ~ **mal** misjudge

K k

karate *nm* karate: *hacer* ~ do karate

kilo *(tb* **kilogramo)** *nm* kilogram *(abrev* **kg)** →Ver pág. 222

kilómetro *nm* kilometer *(abrev* **km)** →Ver pág. 222

kilovatio *nm* kilowatt *(abrev* **kw)**

kinder *nm* preschool, nursery school *(GB)*

kiosco = QUIOSCO

kiwi *nm* kiwi fruit *[pl* kiwi fruit]

kleenex® *nm* kleenex®

koala *nm* koala (bear)

L l

la¹ *art def Ver* EL/LA ▶ THE ● *pron pers* **1** *(ella)* her **2** *(cosa)* it **3** *(usted)* you

la² *nm* A: *la menor* A minor

laberinto *nm* **1** maze **2** *(fig)* labyrinth

labial *nm* lipstick

labio nm lip

labor nf **1** (trabajo) work [U]: Llevó a cabo una gran ~. He did some great work. **2** (de coser) needlework [U] **3** (de punto) knitting [U] ▶ **~es domésticas** housework [U]

laborable adj (día) working

laboratorio nm laboratory [pl -ies], lab (coloq)

labrador/a nm-nf **1** (propietario) small farmer **2** (jornalero) farm laborer

laca nf lacquer

lacio adj (pelo) straight

lacra nf (And, persona) degenerate

lacrimógeno adj ▶ **gas ~** tear gas

ladera nf hillside

lado nm **1** side: Un triángulo tiene tres ~s. A triangle has three sides. ◊ ver el ~ **bueno de** las cosas look on the bright side **2** (lugar) place: de un ~ para otro from one place to another ◊ ¿Nos vamos a otro ~? Should we go somewhere else? ◊ **en algún/ningún ~** somewhere/nowhere **3** (dirección) way: Fueron por otro ~. They went a different way. ◊ mirar a todos ~s look in all directions ▶ **al ~ 1** (cerca) really close **2** (contiguo) next door: la casa de al ~ the house next door ◊ **los vecinos de al ~** the next-door neighbors **al ~ de** next to sth/sb: Ponte a mi ~. Stand next to me. **de ~** sideways: ponerse de ~ turn sideways **estar/ponerse del ~ de** be on/take sb's side: ¿De qué ~ estás? Whose side are you on? **por un lado... por otro (~)** on the one hand... on the other (hand)

ladrar vi bark (at sb/sth)

ladrillo nm brick

ladrón/ona nm-nf **1** thief [pl thieves] **2** (en casa) burglar **3** (en banco) robber → THIEF **●** (Elec) adaptor

lagaña = LEGAÑA

lagartija nf **1** (small) lizard **2** (Mx, gimnasia) push-up [pl -ups]

lagarto/a nm-nf **1** (Zool) lizard **2** (And, persona) crawler

lago nm lake →MAR

lágrima nf tear ▶ **~s de cocodrilo** crocodile tears

laguna nf **1** (lago) (small) lake **2** (omisión) gap

lama nf slime

lambisquear (Mx **lambonear** And) vt suck up to sb

lamentable adj **1** (aspecto, condición) pitiful **2** (desafortunado) regrettable

lamentar vt regret sth: Lamento haberle causado tanto trastorno. I regret having caused you so much trouble. ◊ Lamentamos comunicarle que... We regret to inform you that... ◊ Lo lamento mucho. I am terribly sorry. **●** **lamentarse** vp complain (about sth)

lamer (tb **lamber**) vt (con lengua) lick

lámina nf **1** (hoja) sheet **2** (ilustración) plate

laminar vt laminate

lámpara nf **1** (linterna) lamp: ~ **de pie** floor lamp **2** (calle) street light

lana nf **1** wool: ~ **virgen** new wool **2** (dinero) cash ▶ **de ~** woolen

lancha nf launch ▶ **~ de motor** motor boat

langosta nf **1** (de mar) lobster **2** (insecto) locust

langostino nm jumbo shrimp [pl jumbo shrimp], king prawn (GB)

lánguido adj languid

lanza nf spear

lanzamiento nm **1** (misil, satélite, producto) launch **2** (bomba) dropping **3** (Dep) throw

lanzar vt **1** (juego o deporte) throw sth to sb **2** (con intención de hacer daño) throw sth at sb → THROW **3** (misil, producto) launch **4** (bomba) drop **●** **lanzarse** vp **1** (arrojarse) throw yourself **2** ~ **sobre** pounce on sth/sb

lapicero nm **1** (portaminas) mechanical pencil **2** (bolígrafo) (ballpoint) pen

lápida nf gravestone

lápiz nm pencil ▶ **a ~** in pencil **~ labial** lipstick

largarse vp **1** (irse) clear off **2** ~ **a** start doing sth/to do sth

largo adj long: Te queda muy ~. It's too long for you. **●** nm length: ¿Cuánto mide de ~? How long is it? ◊ Tiene 10m de ~. It's ten meters long. **●** interj ~ **(de aquí)** clear off ▶ **a lo ~** lengthwise **a lo ~ de 1** (espacio) along... **2** (tiempo) throughout...: a lo ~ del día throughout the day **hacerse ~** drag: El día se me está haciendo muy ~. Today is really dragging. **pasar de ~** go straight past sth/sb **tener para ~:** Yo acá tengo para ~. I'm going to be a while.

las Ver LOS/LAS

lasaña nf lasagne

láser nm laser

lástima nf pity: ¡Qué ~! What a pity! ▶ **dar ~ 1** (persona) feel sorry for sb: Él me da mucha ~. I feel very sorry for him. **2** (cosa, situación): Me da ~ que se tengan que ir. I'm sorry you have to go.

lastimar vt hurt

lata nf **1** (envase) can **2** (material) tin **3** (de hornear) baking tray **4** (molestia) pain: ¡Qué ~! What a pain! ▶ **a la ~** (And) very fast **dar ~ 1** (molestar) be a pain: ¡Cuánta ~ das! What a pain you are! **2** (pedir con insistencia) pester

lateral adj, nm side: una calle ~ a side street

latido nm (corazón) (heart)beat

latifundio nm large estate

latigazo nm **1** (golpe) lash **2** (chasquido) crack

látigo nm whip

latín nm Latin

latino adj Latin: la gramática latina Latin grammar ◇ el temperamento ~ the Latin temperament

latir vi beat ▶ **me late que...** (Mx) I have a hunch that...

latitud nf latitude

latón nm brass

latonería nf bodywork

latoso adj **1** (molesto) annoying: ¡Que niño más ~! That kid is such a pain! **2** (aburrido) dull ● nm-nf (persona molesta) pain

laurel nm **1** (Cocina) bay leaf [pl leaves] **2** (árbol) bay tree

lava nf lava

lavabo nm (pila) washbasin

lavada nf wash: Hago dos ~s al día. I do two washes a day. ▶ **pegarse una ~** (And) get soaked

lavadero nm **1** (edificio) washhouse **2** (tina) sink

lavado nm ▶ **~ de dinero** money laundering ● **en seco** dry-cleaning

lavadora nf **1** (ropa) washing machine **2** (platos) dishwasher

lavamanos nm washbasin

lavanda nf lavender

lavandería nf **1** dry-cleaner's **2** (autoservicio) Laundromat®, launderette (GB)

lavaplatos nm sink ▶ **~ (eléctrico)** dishwasher

lavar vt wash: ~ la ropa wash your clothes ● **lavarse** vp **1** (bañarse) wash **2** (And, con la lluvia) get soaked ▶ **~** wash sth by hand **~ en seco** dry clean **~ los platos/la loza** do the dishes **~se la cabeza** wash your hair **~se los dientes** brush your teeth

lavavajillas nm dishwasher

laxante adj, nm laxative

lazo nm **1** (vínculo) bond **2** (cuerda) rope **3** (moño) bow **4** (cinta) ribbon **5** (para enlazar) lasso [pl -s/-es] **6** (And, juego) jumping rope skipping rope (GB) ▶ **jugar/saltar ~** (And) jump rope, skip (GB)

le pron pers **1** (él/ella/ello) (a) (complemento): Le compramos la casa. We bought our house from him/her. ◇ Le vamos a comprar un vestido. We're going to buy her a dress. ◇ No le des importancia. Ignore it. (b) (partes del cuerpo, efectos personales): Le quitaron el pasaporte. They took away his passport. ◇ Le arreglaron la falda. She had her skirt repaired. **2** (usted) (a) (complemento): yo: Le hice una pregunta. I asked you a question. (b) (partes del cuerpo, efectos personales): Tenga cuidado, o le robarán el bolso. Be careful or they'll steal your bag.

leal adj **1** (persona) loyal (to sth/sb) **2** (animal) faithful (to sb)

lealtad nf loyalty [pl -ies] (to sth/sb) ▶ **con ~** loyally

lección nf lesson ▶ **preguntar/tomar la ~** test sb (on sth)

leche nf milk ▶ **~ condensada** condensed milk **~ descremada/entera** skim/whole milk **~ en polvo** powdered milk

lechería nf dairy [pl -ies]

lechero/a adj dairy ● nm-nf milkman [pl -men]

lechón nm (tb lechona nf) suckling pig

lechuga nf lettuce

lector/a nm-nf reader

lectura nf reading

leer vt, vi read ▶ **~ los labios** lipread **~ para sí** read to yourself

legajador nm (And) folder

legal adj **1** (Jur) legal **2** (And, estupendo) great

legalizar vt legalize

legaña nf sleep [U]: Tienes los ojos llenos de ~s. You have sleep in your eyes. ▶ **no es cualquier ~ de mico** (And) it's not to be sneezed at

legislación nf legislation

legislar vi legislate

legua nf ▶ **a la ~/a ~s**: A la ~ se ve que está borracho. It's obvious he's drunk. ◇ Es a ~s el más grande. It's by far the biggest.

legumbre nf **1** (tb leguminosa) pulse **2** (hortaliza) vegetable

lejano adj distant: un lugar/pariente ~ a distant place/relative

lejía *nf* bleach

lejos *adv* far (away), a long way (away) *(from sth/sb)* **NOTA** A **long way (away)** se suele usar en afirmaciones: *Queda ~.* It's a long way (away)., y far en interrogaciones y negaciones: *¿Queda ~?* Is it far? ▸ **a lo ~** in the distance **de/desde ~** from a distance **más ~** further

lema *nm* **1** *(Com, Pol)* slogan **2** *(regla de conducta)* motto *[pl -s/-es]*

lencería *nf (ropa interior)* lingerie

lengua *nf* **1** *(Anat)* tongue: *sacar la ~ a algn* stick your tongue out at sb **2** *(idioma)* language **3** *(And, zapato)* tongue ▸ **darle a la/echar ~** talk too much **irse de la ~** let the cat out of the bag: *Se me fue la ~.* It just slipped out. **las malas ~s** gossip [U]: *Dicen las malas ~s que...* Word has it that... ▸ **materna** mother tongue **media ~:** *Está hablando en media ~.* He's babbling. **soltarle/tirarle la ~ a algn** make sb talk **tener ~ víperina** have a sharp tongue

lenguaje *nm* **1** language **2** *(habla-do)* speech

lengüeta *nf* tongue

lente *nmf/f* lens *[pl lenses]*

lenteja *nf* lentil

lentes *nm* **1** glasses: *No tengo los ~s.* I don't have my glasses on. **2** *(de protección)* goggles ▸ **~s de contacto** contact lenses

lento *adj* slow ▸ **~ pero seguro** slowly but surely

leña *nf* firewood

leñador/a *nm-nf* lumberjack

leño *nm* log

Leo *nm, nmf* Leo *[pl -s]*

león/ona *nm-nf* lion *[fem* lioness*]*

leopardo *nm* leopard

leotardo *nm (gimnasia, etc.)* leotard

lepra *nf* leprosy

leproso/a *adj* leprous ● *nm-nf* leper

les *pron pers* **1** *(a ellos/as)* **(a)** *(complemento)* them: *Les compré un pastel.* I bought them a cake. **(b)** *(partes del cuerpo, efectos personales)*: *Se robaron el bolso.* Their bag was stolen. **2** *(a ustedes)* **(a)** *(complemento)* you: *¿Les gustaría un café?* Would you like a cup of coffee? **(b)** *(partes del cuerpo, efectos personales)*: *¿Les quito los abrigos?* Can I take your coats?

lesbiana *nf* lesbian

lesión *nf* **1** injury *[pl -ies]* **2** *(herida)* wound: *una ~ de bala* a bullet wound **3** *(hígado, cerebro, etc.)* damage [U] → HERIDA

lesionado/a *adj* injured ● *nm-nf* injured person: *la lista de los ~s* the list of people injured

lesionarse *vp* hurt yourself: *Me lesioné la pierna.* I hurt my leg. → HERIDA

letargo *nm* **1** *(sopor)* lethargy **2** *(hibernación)* hibernation

letra *nf* **1** *(abecedario, grafía)* letter **2** *(caracteres)* character: *las ~s chinas* Chinese characters **3** *(escritura)* writing **4** *(canción)* lyrics *[pl]*

letrero *nm* **1** *(nota)* notice *(rótu-lo)* sign

leucemia *nf* leukemia

levadura *nf* yeast

levantamiento *nm* uprising ▸ **~ de pesas** weightlifting

levantar *vt* **1** raise: *~ el brazo/la moral/voz* raise your arm/spirits/voice **2** *(peso, tapa)* lift sth up **3** *(recoger)* pick sth/sb up ● **levantarse** *vp* **1** *(ponerse de pie)* stand up **2** *(de la cama, viento)* get up **3** *(conquistar)* pick sb up ▸ **~se con el pie izquierdo** get up on the wrong side of bed

leve *adj* slight

ley *nf* **1** law: *la ~ de la gravedad* the law of gravity ◇ *ir contra la ~* break the law **2** *(parlamento)* act

leyenda *nf* legend

libélula *nf* dragonfly *[pl -ies]*

liberación *nf* **1** *(país)* liberation **2** *(presos)* release

liberado *adj* **1** freed **2** *(mujer)* liberated

liberal *adj, nmf* liberal

liberar *vt* **1** *(país)* liberate **2** *(prisionero)* free

libertad *nf* freedom ▸ **~ bajo fianza/provisional** bail: *salir en ~ bajo fianza* be released on bail **~ condicional** parole **~ de expresión/prensa** freedom of speech/of the press

Libra *nf, nmf* Libra

libra *nf* **1** *(dinero)* pound: *diez ~s* ten pounds (£10) **2** *(peso)* pound *(abrev* lb*)* → Ver pág. 222

librar *vt* save sth/sb from sth ● **librarse** *vp* **1** *(escapar)* get out of sth: *~ del servicio militar* get out of doing military service **2** *(desembarazarse)* get rid of sth/sb

libre *adj* **1** free: *Soy ~ de hacer lo que quiera.* I'm free to do what I want. ◇ *¿Está ~ la silla?* Is the seat free? **2** *(disponible)* vacant:

No quedan asientos ~s. There are no vacant seats. **3** (*And, natación*): *nadar (estilo)* ~ do the crawl

librería *nf* bookstore, bookshop (GB)

librero/a *nm-nf* bookseller ● *nm* (*Mx, mueble*) bookcase

libreta *nf* notebook ▸ ~ **de ahorro(s)** savings book

libro *nm* book ▸ ~ **de bolsillo** paperback ▸ **de cocina/texto** cookbook/textbook

licencia *nf* license: ~ *de manejar/conducción* driver's license

licenciado/a *adj, nm-nf* (person) with a degree (*in sth*): (*un*) ~ *en Derecho* (a person) with a degree in law

licenciarse *vp* graduate (*in sth*): ~ *de la UNAM* graduate from the UNAM

licenciatura *nf* **1** (*título*) degree **2** (*estudios*) program of study

licor *nm* liqueur

licorera *nf* **1** (*mueble*) drinks cabinet **2** (*recipiente*) decanter

licuado *nm* (milk) shake

licuadora *nf* blender

líder *nmf* leader

liebre *nf* hare

liendre *nm* nit

lienzo *nm* canvas

liga *nf* **1** (*deporte*) league **2** (*cinta*) garter **3** (*banda elástica*) rubber band **4** (*pelo*) hairband

ligamento *nm* ligament: *sufrir una fractura/rotura de ~s* tear a ligament

ligar(se) *vi, vp* make out with sb, get off with sb (GB): *Se ligó a la más bonita.* He made out with the best looking girl. ◇ *mucho* have a lot of success with boys/girls

ligeramente *adv* slightly

ligero *adj* **1** light: *comida/ropa ligera* light food/clothing ◇ *tener el sueño* ~ sleep lightly **2** (*que casi no se nota*) slight: *un* ~ *acento norteño* a slight Northern accent **3** (*ágil*) agile ▸ **hacer/tomarse algo a la ligera** do sth hastily/take sth lightly

light *adj* (*refresco*) diet: *Coca-Cola* ~ Diet Coke →LOW-CALORIE

lija *nf* sandpaper

lijar *vt* sand

lila *nf*, *nm* (*flor, color*) lilac

lima *nf* **1** (*herramienta*) file: ~ *de uñas* nail file **2** (*fruta*) lime

limar *vt* file ▸ ~ **asperezas** smooth things over

limbo *nm* limbo ▸ **estar en el** ~ have your head in the clouds

limitación *nf* limitation

limitado *adj* limited

limitar *vt* limit ● *vi* (*Geog*) ~ **con** border on... ● **limitarse** *vp*: *Limítese a responder a la pregunta.* Just answer the question.

límite *nm* **1** limit: *el* ~ *de velocidad* the speed limit **2** (*Geog, Pol*) boundary [*pl* -ies] → BORDER ▸ **sin** ~ unlimited: *kilometraje sin* ~ unlimited mileage

limón *nm* **1** (*fruto*) (a) lemon (b) (*Mx*) lime **2** (*color*): *verde* ~ lime green **3** (*tb limonero*) (*árbol*) (a) lemon (tree) (b) (*Mx*) lime (tree) ▸ ~ **dulce/real** (*Mx*) lemon

limonada *nf* (traditional) lemonade

limonero/a *nm-nf* beggar

limosna *nf*: *Le di una* ~. I gave him some money. ◇ *Una* ~ *por favor.* Could you spare some change, please? ▸ **pedir** ~ beg

limosnero/a *nm-nf* beggar

limpiabotas *nmf* shoeshine

limpiaparabrisas (*tb* limpiabrisas *And*) *nm* windshield wiper, windscreen wiper (GB)

limpiar *vt* **1** clean **2** (*pasar un trapo*) wipe **3** (*sacar brillo*) polish ● **limpiarse** *vp* clean yourself up ▸ **se la nariz** wipe your nose

limpio *adj* **1** clean **2** (*pelado*) broke ● *adv* fair: *jugar* ~ play fair ▸ **pasar/poner en** ~ make a final copy of sth **sacar en** ~ **1** (*entender*) get sth out of sth: *No saqué nada en* ~. I didn't get anything out of it. **2** (*dinero*) clear sth: *sacar en* ~ *$800 al mes* clear 800 dollars a month

limpión *nm* dish towel, tea towel (GB)

lindo *adj* **1** (*bonito*) pretty **2** (*agradable*) nice: *Fue un detalle muy* ~. It was a very nice gesture. ● *adv* beautifully: *Escribe muy* ~. She writes beautifully. ▸ **de lo** ~: *divertirse de lo* ~ have a great time

línea *nf* line ▸ **cuidar/mantener la** ~ watch your weight ~ **de meta** finishing line ~ **divisoria** dividing line **por** ~ **materna/paterna** on my, your, etc. mother's/father's side

lingote *nm* ingot

lingüística *nf* linguistics [*sing*]

lino *nm* **1** (*Bot*) flax **2** (*tela*) linen

linterna *nf* flashlight, torch (GB)

lío *nm*: *¡Qué* ~! What a mess! ◇ *No se meta en* ~s. Don't get into trouble. ▸ **hacerse un** ~ (*confundirse*) get into a muddle **hecho un** ~ really confused

liquidación nf 1 (rebaja) sale: ~ por cierre de negocio clearance sale 2 (Mx, pago) severance pay

liquidar vt 1 (deuda) settle 2 (negocio) liquidate 3 (matar) bump sb off

líquido adj, nm liquid

lirio nm iris

liso adj 1 (llano) flat 2 (suave) smooth 3 (sin adornos, de un solo color) plain 4 (pelo) straight

lista nf list ► ~ de espera/compras waiting/shopping list ~ de éxitos (Mús) charts [pl] pasar ~ take attendance, take the register (GB)

listo adj 1 (preparado) ready: Estoy ~ para salir. I'm ready to leave. 2 (inteligente) smart 3 (And, de acuerdo) OK

listón nm (Mx, cinta) ribbon

litera nf bunk

literatura nf literature

litro nm liter (abrev l): medio ~ half a liter →Ver pág. 222

llaga nf ulcer

llama¹ nf (fuego) flame ► en ~s ablaze

llama² nf (animal) llama

llamada nf call: hacer una ~ (telefónica) make a (phone) call ◊ la ~ del deber the call of duty ► dar/pegar una ~ give sb a call ~ de larga distancia long-distance call: hacer una ~ de larga distancia make a long-distance call ~ por cobrar/cobro revertido collect call, reverse charge call (GB)

llamado adj so-called: el ~ Tercer Mundo the so-called Third World

llamar vt call: ~ a la policía call the police ● vi 1 (teléfono) call: ¿Quién llama? Who's calling? 2 (puerta) knock: ~ a la puerta knock at the door 3 (timbre) ring: ~ al timbre ring the bell ● **llamarse** vp be called: ¿Cómo te llamas? What's your name? ◊ Me llamo Ana. I'm called Ana./My name's Ana. ► ~ por cobrar/cobro revertido call collect, reverse (the) charges (GB) ~ por teléfono telephone sb, give sb a call (más coloq)

llamativo adj 1 (noticia, persona) striking 2 (ostentoso) flashy

llano adj 1 flat 2 (sencillo) simple ● nm (tb **llanura** nf) plain

llanta nf tire

llanto nm crying

llave nf 1 key (to sth) 2 (agua) faucet, tap (GB) ► No tomes agua de la ~. Don't drink the tap water. 3 (Mec) wrench, spanner

(GB) ► bajo ~ under lock and key echar ~ lock up ~ de contacto/encendido ignition key ~ de paso (del agua) stopcock ~ inglesa monkey wrench, adjustable spanner

llavero nm keyring

llegada nf arrival

llegar vi 1 arrive (at/in...): ~ al hospital/a México arrive at the hospital/in Mexico 2 (alcanzar) reach: ¿Llegas? Can you reach? ◊ ~ a una conclusión reach a conclusion 3 (altura) come up to sth: Mi hija ya me llega al hombro. My daughter comes up to my shoulder. 4 ~ hasta (extenderse) go as far as...: La finca llega hasta el río. The estate goes as far as the river. 5 (tiempo) come: Ha llegado el momento de... The time has come to... ► estar por ~ be due to arrive any time ~ a golpes/las manos come to blows ~ a hacer algo (lograr) manage to do sth ~ a la casa get home ~ a ser become ~ a tiempo be on time ~ lejos go far ~ tarde/temprano be late/early si no llega a ser por él if it hadn't been for him, her, etc.

llenar vt 1 fill sth/sb (with sth) 2 (satisfacer) satisfy 3 (formulario, etc., impreso) fill sth out ● **llenarse** vp 1 fill (up) (with sth) 2 (comiendo) stuff yourself (with sth)

lleno adj 1 full (of sth): El autobús estaba ~ hasta el tope. The bus was packed full. ◊ No quiero más, estoy ~. I don't want any more, I'm full. 2 (cubierto) covered in/with sth

llevadero adj bearable

llevar vt 1 take: Lleve la caja a la cocina. Take the box to the kitchen. ◊ Me llevará un día arreglarlo. It'll take me a day to fix it. **NOTA** Para ofrecerse a llevar algo a algn se usa bring: No hace falta que vengas, te lo llevo el lunes. You don't need to come, I'll bring it on Monday. 2 (carga) carry: ~ una maleta carry a suitcase 3 (ropa, sombrero, peinado, etc.) wear 4 (manejar) drive: ¿Quién llevaba el carro? Who was driving? 5 (tener) have: No llevo dinero encima. I don't have any cash on me. 6 (tiempo) have been (doing sth): Lleva una hora esperando. He's been waiting for an hour. ◊ ¿Cuánto tiempo llevas aquí? How long have you been here? ● vi (camino, etc.) lead to sth ● v aux + **participio** have:

Llevo vistas tres películas este mes. I've seen three movies this month. ● **llevarse** *vp* **1** *(robar)* take **2** *(estar de moda)* be in: *Este año se lleva el gris.* Gray is in this year. **3** *(Mat)* carry: *22 y llevo dos.* 22 and carry two. ▶ **llevarle a algn dos años, etc.** be two years, etc. older than sb: *Me lleva un año.* She's a year older than me. **~se bien/mal** get along well/badly (with sb) **para ~** to go, to take away (GB): *una pizza para ~* a pizza to go **NOTA** Para otras expresiones con **llevar**, ver el sustantivo, adjetivo, etc., p. ej. **llevar a cabo** en CABO.

llorar *vi* **1** cry: *~ de rabia* cry with rage ◊ *ponerse a ~* burst into tears **2** *(ojos)* water: *Me lloran los ojos.* My eyes are watering. ▶ **a lágrima viva/a moco tendido** cry your eyes out

llorón/ona *adj, nm-nf* crybaby [pl -ies]: *No seas tan ~.* Don't be such a crybaby.

llover *vi* rain: *¿Llueve?* Is it raining? ▶ **~ a cántaros** pour

llovizna *nf* drizzle

lloviznar *vi* drizzle

lluvia *nf* **1** rain: *bajo la ~* in the rain ◊ *un día de ~* a rainy day ◊ *botas para la ~* boots for wet weather **2** *(estrellas, regalos, polvo)* shower of sth **3** *(balas, piedras, golpes, insultos)* hail of sth ▶ **~ ácida** acid rain ▶ **radiactiva** radioactive fallout

lluvioso *adj* **1** *(zona, temporada)* wet **2** *(día, tiempo)* rainy

lo *art def (para sustantivar)* the... thing: *lo bueno/malo es...* the good/bad thing is... ● *pron pers* **1** *(él)* him **2** *(cosa)* it: *No lo creo.* I don't believe it. **NOTA** Al usarse como complemento directo de algunos verbos como "decir", "saber" y "ser" no se traduce: *Te lo digo mañana.* I'll tell you tomorrow. ◊ *Todavía no eres médico pero lo serás.* You are not a doctor yet, but you will be. **3** *(usted)* you ▶ **lo cual** which **lo de...** **1** *(posesión):* *Todo ese equipaje es lo de Juan.* All that baggage is Juan's. **2** *(asunto): Lo del viaje fue inesperado.* The journey came as a surprise. ◊ *Lo de la fiesta era una broma ¿no?* What you said about the party was a joke, wasn't it? **lo mío** **1** *(posesión)* my, your, etc. things: *Todo lo mío es tuyo.* Everything I have is yours. **2** *(afición)* my, your etc. thing: *Lo suyo es la música.* Music's his thing. **lo que...** what: *No te imaginas lo*

que fue aquello. You can't imagine what it was like. ◊ *Haré lo que diga.* I'll do anything you say.

lobo/a *nm-nf* wolf [pl wolves] ● *adj (And)* **1** *(objeto, estilo)* tacky **2** *(color)* garish

local *adj* local ● *nm* premises [pl]

localidad *nf* **1** *(pueblo)* village **2** *(ciudad pequeña)* town **3** *(Cine, Teat)* seat ▶ **no hay ~es** sold out

localizar *vt* **1** *(encontrar)* locate **2** *(contactar)* get hold of sb

locha *nf (And)* laziness ▶ **tener ~** feel lazy

lochar *vi (And)* laze around

locho *adj (And)* lazy

loción *nf* lotion

locker *nm* locker

loco/a *adj* crazy: *volverse ~* go crazy ◊ *El chocolate me vuelve ~.* I'm crazy about chocolate. ● *nm-nf* madman/woman [pl -men/-women] ▶ **estar como ~** *(encantado)* be crazy about sth/sb **hacerse el ~** pretend not to notice **~ de atar** beside yourself with sth: *Está ~ de alegría.* He's beside himself with joy. **~ de remate** totally nuts

locomotora *nf* engine

locura *nf (disparate)* crazy thing: *Es una ~ ir solo.* It's crazy to go alone.

locutor/a *nm-nf (noticias)* newsreader

lodo *nm* mud

lógico *adj* **1** *(normal)* natural **2** *(conclusión, etc.)* logical

logotipo *nm* logo [pl -s]

lograr *vt* **1** get, achieve *(más fml)* **2** + *inf* manage to do sth: *Logré hacerlo.* I managed to do it. **3** **~ que...** get sb to do sth: *No lograrás que venga.* You'll never get her to come.

logro *nm* achievement

lombriz *nf* worm

lomo *nm* **1** *(Anat)* back **2** *(Cocina)* loin **3** *(libro)* spine **4** *(cuchillo)* back

lonchera *nf* lunch box

longitud *nf* **1** length: *Tiene 1m de ~.* It is a meter long. **2** *(Geog)* longitude

lonja *nf (loncha)* slice ▶ **en ~s** sliced

loquear *vi* clown around

loro *nm (tb* **lora** *fig, And)* **1** *(ave)* parrot **2** *(persona)* windbag

los/las *art def* the ● *pron pers* **1** *(a ellos)* them: *~ vi ayer.* I saw them yesterday. **2** *(a ustedes)* you ▶ **de ~ de...:** *un terremoto de los de verdad* a really violent earthquake ◊ *El carro es de los de antes.* The car is old-fashioned. **~ de...** 1 (*posesión*): *~ de mi mamá* my mother's 2 (*característica*) the ones (with...): *Prefiero ~ de punta fina/de cuadros.* I prefer the ones with a fine point/the plaid ones. 3 (*ropa*) the ones in...: *~ de rojo* the ones in red 4 (*procedencia*) the ones from...: *~ de Cali* the ones from Cali **~ hay:** *~ hay muy grandes.* There are some really big ones. ◊ *Dígame si ~ hay o no.* Tell me if there are any or not. **~ que...** 1 (*personas*): *~ que estaban en la casa* the ones who were in the house ◊ *~ que tenemos que madrugar* those of us who have to get up early ◊ *Hablé con todos los que vinieron.* I spoke to everyone who came. 2 (*cosas*) the ones (which/that)...: *~ que compré ayer* the ones I bought yesterday

losa *nf* flagstone

lote *nm* 1 (Com) batch 2 (*terreno*) plot

lotería *nf* lottery [*pl* -ies]: *jugar (a) la ~* do the lottery

loza *nf* china

lucha *nf* fight (*for/against sth/sb*) ▸ **~ libre** wrestling

luchador/a *adj, nm-nf* fighter: *Es muy ~.* He's a real fighter. ● *nm-nf* (*deportista*) wrestler

luchar *vi* 1 fight (*for/against sth/sb*): *~ por la libertad/contra el racismo* fight for freedom/against racism 2 (Dep) wrestle

lúcido *adj* lucid

lucir *vt* (*ropa*) wear ● *vi* 1 (*resaltar*) look nice: *Esa figura luce mucho ahí.* That figure looks very nice there. 2 (*aparecer*) look: *El panorama lucía esperanzador.* Prospects looked hopeful. ● **lucirse** *vp* show off

luego *adv* 1 (*más tarde*) later 2 (*a continuación*) then: *Se baten los huevos y ~ se añade el azúcar.* Beat the eggs and then stir in the sugar. ◊ *Primero está el hospital y ~ el banco.* First there's the hospital and then the bank. ● *conj* therefore ▸ **desde ~** of course: *¡Desde ~ que no!* Of course not! **hasta ~** bye

lugar *nm* 1 place: *estar fuera de ~* feel out of place 2 (*posición, puesto*) position: *ocupar un ~ importante* have an important position 3 (*pueblo*) town: *los del ~* people from the town ▸ **dar ~ a** cause sth en **el ~ de los hechos** on the spot **en ~ de** instead of sth/sb: *En ~ de salir tanto, más le*

valdría estudiar. Instead of going out so much, you'd be better off studying. **en primer, segundo, etc. ~** 1 (*posición*) first, second, etc.: *quedar clasificado en último ~* come last 2 (*en discurso*) first of all, secondly, etc.: *En último ~...* Last of all... **~ de nacimiento** 1 birthplace 2 (*en impresos*) place of birth **sin ~ a dudas** undoubtedly **tener ~** take place **yo en tu ~** if I were you

lúgubre *adj* gloomy

lujo *nm* luxury [*pl* -ies] ▸ **a todo ~** in style **de ~** luxury: *un apartamento de ~* a luxury apartment

lujoso *adj* luxurious

lujuria *nf* lust

lumbre *nf* 1 fire: *al calor de la ~* by the fire 2 (*estufa*) stove

luminoso *adj* 1 bright: *una habitación/idea luminosa* a bright room/idea 2 (*que despide luz*) luminous: *un reloj ~* a luminous watch

luna *nf* 1 moon 2 (*espejo*) mirror ▸ **estar en la ~** be lost in thought **~ creciente/menguante** waxing/waning moon **~ de miel** honeymoon **~ llena/nueva** full/new moon

lunar *adj* lunar ● *nm* 1 (*piel*) mole 2 (*dibujo*) polka dot: *una falda de ~es* a polka-dot skirt ▸ **~ de nacimiento** birthmark

lunático/a *adj, nm-nf* lunatic

lunes *nm* Monday (*abrev* **Mon.**): *el ~ por la mañana* on Monday morning ◊ *Los ~ no trabajo.* I don't work on Mondays. ◊ *un ~ sí y otro no* every other Monday ◊ *el ~ pasado/que viene* last/next Monday ◊ *el ~ 25 de mayo* on Monday May 25 **NOTA** See *lee* "Monday, May twenty-fifth".

lupa *nf* magnifying glass

luto *nm* mourning ▸ **estar de ~** be in mourning (*for sb*) **ir de/llevar ~** be dressed in mourning

luz *nf* 1 light: *encender/apagar la ~* turn the light on/off 2 (*electricidad*) electricity: *Se fue la ~.* The electricity went off. 3 (*día*) daylight 4 **luces** (*inteligencia*): *tener muchas/pocas luces* be bright/dim 5 **luces** (Aut) headlights: *hacer señas con las luces* flash your lights 6 **luces** (*pelo*) highlights ▸ **a plena ~ del día** in broad daylight **dar a ~** give birth (*to sb*) **luces altas** high beams, headlights (GB) **luces bajas** low beams, dipped headlights (GB): *poner las luces bajas* use your low beams/dim your headlights (GB) **sacar a la ~** bring sth (out) into the open **salir a la ~** (*secreto*) come to light

M m

macabro *adj* macabre

macarrones *nm* macaroni [U]

maceta *nf* flowerpot

machacar *vt* **1** (*aplastar*) (a) crush: *~ ajo/nueces* crush garlic/nuts (b) (*fruta, papa, etc.*) mash **2** (*romper*) smash: *El niño machacó los juguetes.* The boy smashed his toys to pieces. ● *vt, vi* (*repetir*) go over (and over) sth

machete *nm* machete

machetero/a *adj, nm-nf* **1** (*Mx, estudiante*) grind, swot (GB): *Es muy ~.* He's a real grind. **2** (*And, persona*) slapdash: *Ese plomero es un ~.* That plumber is really slapdash.

machismo *nm* machismo

machista *adj, nmf* sexist

macho *adj, nm* **1** male: *¿Es ~ o hembra?* Is it male or female? →FEMALE **2** (*machote*) macho: *Se cree muy ~.* He likes to think he's so macho. ● *nm* (*enchufe*) plug

macizo *adj* (*objeto*) solid

madera *nf* **1** (*material*) wood **2** (*tabla*) piece of wood **3** (*de construcción*) timber, lumber (GB): *las ~s del techo* the roof beams ▶ **~ de** → wooden → **de pino, roble, etc.** pine, oak, etc.: *una mesa de ~ de pino* a pine table **tener ~ de artista, líder, etc.** be a born artist, leader, etc. **¡toca ~!** knock on wood!, touch wood! (GB)

madero *nm* **1** (*tronco*) log **2** (*tablón*) piece of lumber, piece of timber (GB)

madrastra *nf* stepmother

madre *nf* mother: *ser ~ de dos hijos* be the mother of two children ▶ **¡~ mía!** good heavens! **~ soltera** single parent

madriguera *nf* **1** den **2** (*conejo, etc.*) burrow

madrina *nf* **1** (*bautizo*) godmother **2** (*confirmación*) sponsor **3** (*matrimonio*) woman who accompanies the bride and groom →MATRIMONIO

madrugada *nf: a las dos de la ~* at two in the morning ◊ *en la ~* in the early hours

madrugar *vi* get up early

madurar *vi* **1** (*fruta*) ripen **2** (*persona*) mature

maduro *adj* **1** (*fruta*) ripe **2** (*de mediana edad*) middle-aged **3** (*sensato*) mature ● *nm* (*And*) plantain

maestría *nf* (*Educ*) master's: *hacer una ~* do a master's

maestro/a *nm-nf* **1** (*educador*) teacher **2** (*figura destacada*) master: *un ~ del ajedrez* a chess master

mafia *nf* mafia: *la M~* the Mafia

magdalena *nf* cupcake

magia *nf* magic

mágico *adj* magic

magisterio *nm* (*profesión*) teaching: *ejercer el ~* be a teacher ◊ *la huelga del ~* the teachers' strike

magma *nm* magma

magnate *nmf* tycoon

magnético *adj* magnetic

magnetismo *nm* magnetism

magnífico *adj* wonderful

mago/a *nm-nf* (*ilusionista*) magician

maguey *nm* maguey plant

magullado *adj* **1** (*fruta*) bruised **2** (*carro, etc.*) dented

maicena® *nf* cornstarch, cornflour (GB)

maíz *nm* **1** (*planta*) corn, maize (GB) **2** (*grano*) corn, sweetcorn (GB) ▶ **~ pira** (*And*) popcorn [U]

Majestad *nf* Majesty [*pl* -ies]

mal *adj* → MALO ● *adv* badly: *portarse ~* behave badly ◊ *un trabajo ~ pagado* a poorly/badly paid job ◊ *Oigo muy ~.* My hearing is very bad. ◊ *¡Qué ~ la pasé!* What a terrible time I had! **2** (*calidad, aspecto*) bad: *Esa camisa no está ~.* That shirt's not bad. **3** (*equivocadamente, moralmente*) wrong: *escoger ~* make the wrong choice ◊ *contestar ~ a una pregunta* give the wrong answer ● *nm* **1** evil: *el bien y el ~* good and evil **2** (*daño*) harm **3** (*problema*) problem: *La venta de la casa nos salvó de ~es mayores.* The sale of the house saved us any further problems. ▶ **andar/estar ~ de** be short of sth **estar/encontrarse ~** be/feel ill **no hay ~ que por bien no venga** every cloud has a silver lining **¡qué ~!** oh no! **NOTA** Para otras expresiones con **mal**, ver el sustantivo, adjetivo, etc., p. ej. **¡menos mal!** en MENOS.

malcriado *adj* spoiled

malcriar *vt* spoil

maldad nf wickedness [U]: *Ha sido una ~ de su parte.* It was a wicked thing to do.

maldecir vt curse

maldición nf curse: *echarle una ~ a algn* put a curse on sb ◇ *Nos cayó una ~.* There's a curse on us. ◇ *soltar maldiciones* curse and swear

maldito adj damned

maleducado/a adj, nm-nf rude: *Es un ~.* He's so rude!

malentendido nm misunderstanding

malestar nm 1 (*indisposición*): *Siento un ~ general.* I don't feel very well. 2 (*inquietud*) unease

maleta nf 1 (*equipaje*) (suit)case 2 (*Aut*) trunk, boot (GB) ▸ **empacar/desempacar la(s) ~(s)** pack/unpack

maletero nm 1 (*And*) porter

maletín nm 1 (*documentos*) briefcase 2 (*médico*) (doctor's) bag

malgastar vt waste

malgeniado/a adj (*And*) bad-tempered

malhablado/a adj, nm-nf foulmouthed: *ser un ~* be foulmouthed

malherido adj badly injured

maligno adj (*Med*) malignant

malinchista adj, nmf (*Mx*) (person) preferring imported things

malla nf 1 (*ballet, gimnasia*) leotard 2 (*Dep*) net 3 (*alambre*) wire mesh

malo/a adj 1 bad 2 (*inadecuado*) poor: *mala alimentación/visibilidad* poor food/visibility ◇ *el mal estado del terreno* the poor condition of the ground 3 (*travieso*) naughty 4 (*torpe*) bad *at sth*: *Soy malísimo en matemáticas.* I'm hopeless at math. ● nm-nf villain, bad guy (coloq) ▸ **estar de malas** be unlucky **estar ~** be ill **lo ~ es que...** the trouble is (that)...

NOTA Para otras expresiones con **malo**, ver el sustantivo, p.ej. **mala hierba** EN HIERBA.

malpensado/a adj, nm-nf 1 (*que siempre sospecha*) suspicious: *Eres un ~.* You have a really suspicious mind. 2 (*obsceno*) dirty-minded: *¡Cómo eres de ~!* What a dirty mind you have!

malteada nf milkshake

maltratar vt mistreat: *Me maltrataron física y verbalmente.* I was subjected to physical and verbal abuse.

maluco/a adj 1 (tb **maluchо**) (*enfermo*) under the weather 2 (*comida*) bad

malva nf (*flor*) mallow ● adj, nm (*color*) mauve

malvado adj wicked

mama nf breast

mamá nf mom, mum (GB)

NOTA Los niños pequeños suelen decir **mommy** o **mummy** (GB).

mamado adj (*And, cansado*) exhausted

mamar vi feed ● **mamarse** vp 1 (*aguantarse*): *No me mamo esa clase tan aburrida.* I can't stand that boring class. ◇ *Se mamó todo el discurso.* He sat through the whole speech. 2 (*And, cansarse*) get tired *of sth/sb* ▸ **~ gallo** (*And*) joke around

mamera nf (*And*) *¡Qué ~!* What a drag!

mamífero nm mammal

mamila nf (*biberón*) baby bottle

mamón adj (*And*) boring

mampara nf 1 (*en banco*) screen 2 (*pared*) partition

manada nf 1 (a) herd (b) (*lobos, perros*) pack (c) (*leones*) pride 2 (*gente*) crowd

manantial nm spring

manar vi flow (*from sth/sb*)

mancha nf 1 (*suciedad*) stain 2 (*leopardo*) spot

manchado adj 1 (*embadurnado*) stained (*with sth*): *Llevas la camisa manchada de vino.* You have a wine stain on your shirt. ◇ *una carta manchada de sangre/tinta* a bloodstained/ink-stained letter 2 (*animal*) spotted

manchar vt get sth dirty: *Manchaste el suelo de barro.* You've gotten mud on the floor. ● **mancharse** vp get dirty

manco adj 1 (*sin brazo*) onearmed 2 (*sin mano*) one-handed

mancuernilla (*Mx*) (**mancorna** *And*) cufflink

mandado nm errand: *hacer un ~* run an errand ▸ **hacer los ~s a** algn do what sb tells you **ir al ~** (*Mx*) go shopping

mandamiento nm (*Rel*) commandment

mandar vt 1 (*ordenar*) tell sb to do sth: *Mandó a los niños que se callaran.* He told the children to be quiet. 2 (*enviar*) send 3 (*llevar*) have sth done: *Lo voy a ~ limpiar.* I'm going to have it cleaned. ● vi 1 (*gobierno*) be in power 2 (*ser el jefe*) be in charge, be the boss (coloq) ▸ **~ a la goma/porra** tell sb to get lost

mandarina nf mandarin

mandíbula nf jaw

mando nm 1 (liderazgo) leadership: tener don de ~ be a born leader (b) (Mil) command: entregar/tomar ~ hand over/take command 2 (Comp) joystick 3 **mandos** controls: tablero de ~s control panel

mandón/ona adj, nm-nf bossy: Eres un ~. You're so bossy.

manecilla nf (reloj) hand

manejar vt 1 handle 2 (carro) drive 3 (moto) ride 4 (máquina) operate 5 (manipular) manipulate ● vi drive ● **manejarse** vp (And, portarse) behave: Manéjese bien. Behave yourself.

manera nf 1 (modo) way (of doing sth) 2 **maneras** manners: buenas ~s good manners ◊ pedir algo de buenas ~s ask nicely for sth ▶ a mi ~, my, your, etc. way **de todas (las) ~s** anyway ▶ **de ser**: Es mi ~ de ser. It's just the way I am. **no haber ~ de** be impossible to do sth: No hay ~ de abrirlo. It's impossible to open it. **¡qué ~ de...!** what a way to...!

manga nf 1 sleeve: una camisa de ~ larga/corta a long-sleeved/short-sleeved shirt ▶ **por hombro** in a mess **sacarse algo de la ~** make sth up **sin ~s** sleeveless

mango[1] nm (asa) handle

mango[2] nm (fruta) mango [pl -es]

mango[3] nm (Mx, persona atractiva) stunner

mangonear vi boss sb around

manguera nf hose

maní nm peanut

manía nf quirk: ¡Qué ~! You're getting obsessed about it! ▶ **tener la ~ de** have the strange habit of doing sth **tener ~** a hate sth/sb

maniático adj (quisquilloso) fussy

manicomio nm psychiatric hospital

manifestación nf 1 (protesta) demonstration 2 (expresión) expression 3 (declaración) statement

manifestante nmf demonstrator

manifestar vt 1 (opinión) express 2 (mostrar) show ● **manifestarse** vp (Pol) demonstrate

manifiesto nm manifesto [pl -s]

manija nf handle

maniobra nf maneuver

maniobrar vi 1 maneuver 2 (Mil) be on maneuvers

manipular vt 1 (deshonestamente) manipulate 2 (lícitamente) handle: ~ alimentos handle food

maniquí nm mannequin, dummy [pl -ies] (GB)

manirroto/a nm-nf big spender

manivela nf crank

manjar nm delicacy [pl -ies] ▶ ~ **blanco** (And) soft fudge

mano nf 1 hand: Levanta la ~. Put your hand up. ◊ en buenas ~s in good hands ▶**my** 2 (animal) front foot [pl feet] 3 (pintura) coat ▶ **a (la)** ~ at hand: ¿Tienes la lista a la ~? Do you have the list at hand? **a ~** by hand: Hay que lavarlo a ~. It needs to be washed by hand. ◊ **hecho a** ~ handmade **a ~ derecha/izquierda** on the right/left **atraco/robo a ~ armada** 1 armed robbery [pl -ies] 2 (fig) daylight robbery **con las ~s en la masa** red-handed **dar/echar una** ~ give sb a hand **dar la** ~ hold sb's hand **dar(se) la** ~ shake hands (with sb): Se dieron la ~. They shook hands. **de la** ~ hand in hand (with sb): pasear (tomados) de la ~ walk along hand in hand **en** ~ in person: Entréguesela en ~. Give it to her in person. **estar/quedar a** ~ be even **la ~ asesina** the murderer **mano a mano** clash: un ~ a ~ entre los dos líderes a clash between the two leaders **~ de obra** labor **~ dura** firm hand **¡~s arriba!** hands up! **sacar la** ~ (And) have bad it: La tele ya sacó la ~. The TV has had it. **tener buena** ~ be good at sth/with sb

manojo nm bunch

manopla nf 1 mitten 2 (béisbol) glove

manosear vt touch

manotazo nm slap

mansión nf mansion

manso adj 1 (animal) tame 2 (persona) meek

manta nf blanket

manteca nf fat ▶ ~ **(de cerdo)** lard

mantel nm tablecloth

mantener vt 1 (conservar) keep: ~ algo caliente keep sth hot ◊ ~ una promesa keep a promise 2 (económicamente) support 3 (afirmar) maintain 4 (sujetar) hold: Mantén bien sujeta la botella. Hold the bottle tight. ● **mantenerse** vp live on sth: ~ a base de arroz live on rice ▶ **~se en pie** stand (up) **~se firme** stand your ground **~ vivo** keep sth/sb alive

mantenimiento nm maintenance

mantequilla nf butter

manual adj, nm manual: ~ de instrucciones instruction manual

manubrio nm handlebars [pl]

manufacturar vt manufacture

manuscrito nm manuscript

manzana nf 1 (fruta) apple 2 (casas) block ▶ ~ de Adán Adam's apple

manzanilla nf 1 (planta) camomile 2 (infusión) camomile tea

manzano nm apple (tree)

maña nf 1 (habilidad) skill 2 mañas cunning [U] 3 (manía) bad habit ▶ darse ~ (ser bueno en algo) be good at sth

mañana nf morning: a la ~ siguiente the following morning ◊ a las dos de la ~ at two (o'clock) in the morning ◊ el lunes en/por la ~ on Monday morning ◊ en/por la ~ tomorrow morning →MORNING ● nm future: No pienses en el ~. Don't think about the future. ● adv tomorrow: el periódico de ~ tomorrow's paper

mañoso adj fussy

mapa nm map

mapache nm raccoon

maqueta nf model

maquiladora nf (Mx) assembly plant

maquillaje nm make-up [U]: Ana se compra un ~ carísimo. Ana buys very expensive make-up.

maquillar vt make sb up ● **maquillarse** vp put on your make-up

máquina nf machine: ~ de coser sewing machine ▶ **escribir/pasar a ~** type ~ **de afeitar/rasurar** razor ~ **de escribir** typewriter ~ **tragamonedas** slot machine

maquinaria nf machinery

mar nm o nf sea: Este verano me voy al ~. I'm going to the beach this summer. **NOTA** Sea, river, lake, etc., se escriben con mayúscula si van con un nombre: el ~ Negro the Black Sea. ▶ **alta ~** on the high sea(s) **hacerse a la ~** put out to sea ~ **adentro** out to sea **por ~** by sea

maracuyá nm passion fruit

maratón nm o nf marathon

maravilla nf wonder ▶ hacer ~s work wonders ¡qué ~! how wonderful!

maravilloso adj wonderful

marca nf 1 (señal) mark 2 (productos de limpieza, alimentos, ropa) brand 3 (carros, electrodomésticos, etc.) make 4 (récord) record: batir/establecer una ~ beat/set a record ▶ **de ~**: productos de ~ brand name goods ◊ ropa de ~ designer clothes ~ **(registrada)** (registered) trademark

marcado adj (fuerte) strong: con acento ~ with a strong accent

marcador nm 1 (Dep) scoreboard 2 (rotulador) marker 3 (para libros) bookmark

marcar vt 1 mark 2 (ganado) brand 3 (indicar) say: El reloj marcaba la una. The clock said one o'clock. ● vt, vi 1 (Dep) score 2 (teléfono) dial: ~ mal dial the wrong number ▶ ~ **el compás/ritmo** beat time/the rhythm ~ **tarjeta** (en el trabajo) punch in/out

marcha nf 1 (Mil, Mús, manifestación) march 2 (velocidad) speed: reducir la ~ reduce speed ▶ **a toda** ~ at top speed **dar** ~ **atrás** reverse **sobre la** ~ as I, you, etc. go (along)

marchar vi go: Todo marcha a las mil maravillas. Everything's going wonderfully. ● **marcharse** vp leave

marchito adj (flor) withered

marcial adj martial

marciano/a adj, nm-nf Martian

marco nm 1 (cuadro, puerta) frame 2 (entorno) setting

marea nf tide: ~ alta/baja high/low tide ◊ Subió/bajó la ~. The tide has come in/gone out. ▶ ~ **negra** oil slick

mareado/a adj 1 sick: estar ~ feel sick 2 (harto) sick and tired: Me tiene ~ con esa idea. I'm sick and tired of him going on about that.

marear vt 1 make sb feel sick 2 (hartar) get on sb's nerves: ¡No me marees! Don't bug me! ● **marearse** vp 1 get sick 2 (perder el equilibrio) feel dizzy 3 (en el mar) get seasick

maremoto nm tidal wave

mareo nm dizziness: sufrir/tener ~s feel dizzy

marfil nm ivory

margarina nf margarine

margarita nf daisy [pl -ies]

margen nf bank ● nm 1 (en página) margin 2 (espacio) room (for sth): ~ de duda room for doubt ▶ **al** ~: Lo dejan al ~ de todo. They leave him out of everything.

marginado/a adj 1 (persona) left out 2 (zona) deprived ● nm-nf outcast

marginar vt shun

marica nm gay

marido nm husband

marihuana nf marijuana

marina nf navy: la M~ Mercante the Merchant Marine

marinero/a adj, nm sailor

marino adj 1 marine 2 (aves, sal) sea ◆ nm sailor

marioneta nf 1 puppet 2 **marionetas** puppet show [sing]

mariposa nf butterfly [pl -ies]: nadar (de) ~ do (the) butterfly

mariquita nf ladybug, ladybird (GB)

marisco nm shellfish

marisma nf marsh

marítimo adj 1 (pueblo, zona) coastal 2 (puerto, ruta) sea

marketing nm marketing

mármol nm marble

maroma nf 1 (Mx) (tb **marometa**) (voltereta) somersault 2 (And) trick

marqués/esa nm-nf marquis [fem marchioness]

marranada nf 1 dirty trick: hacerle una ~ a algn play a dirty trick on sb 2 (acción grosera): Siempre anda haciendo ~s. He's always doing disgusting things.

marrano/a nm-nf (animal) pig →CERDO ◆ nm (And, carne) pork ◆ adj filthy

marrón adj, nm brown

Marte nm Mars

martes nm Tuesday (abrev Tue(s).) →LUNES ~ de Carnaval Shrove Tuesday ~ **trece** **N O T A** El equivalente en EE.UU. y Gran Bretaña es **Friday the thirteenth.**

martillo nm hammer

mártir nmf martyr

marxismo nm marxism

marzo nm March (abrev Mar.) →MAYO

más adv

● comparativo more (than sth/sb): Es ~ alta/inteligente que yo. She's taller/more intelligent than me. ◇ Tú has viajado ~ que yo. You've traveled more than me/than I have. ◇ ~ de un año more than a year ◇ durar/trabajar ~ last longer/work harder ◇ Son ~ de las dos. It's after two. **N O T A** En comparaciones como "más blanco que la nieve", etc., se usa la construcción as... as: as white as snow, etc.

● superlativo most (in/of...): la casa ~ antigua de la ciudad the oldest house in the town ◇ el ~ bonito de todos the nicest one of all ◇ la tienda que ~ libros ha vendido the store that has sold most books **N O T A** Al referirse al superlativo a dos cosas o personas, se usa la forma more o -er: ¿Cuál es la cama ~ cómoda (de las dos)? Which bed is more

comfortable? ◇ ¿Cuál es la cama ~ cómoda de la casa? Which is the most comfortable bed in the house?

● **+ pron negativo, interrogativo e indefinido** else: Si tienes algo ~ que decir... If you have anything else to say... ◇ ¿Alguien ~? Anyone else? ◇ nada/nadie ~ nothing/nobody else ◇ ¿Qué ~ puedo hacer? What else can I do?

● **otras construcciones 1** (exclamaciones): ¡Qué carro ~ bonito! What a lovely car! ◇ ¡Es ~ aburrido! He's so boring! **2** (negaciones): solo No sabemos ~ que lo que dijo el radio. We only know what it said on the radio. ◇ Esto no lo sabe nadie ~ que tú. Only you know this.

● nm, prep plus: Dos ~ dos, cuatro. Two plus two is four. ▶ **a ~ no poder:** Grité a ~ no poder. I shouted as loud as I could. **de lo ~...:** really: una cara de lo ~ antipática a really nasty face **de ~ 1** (que sobra): Hay dos sillas de ~. There are two chairs too many. ◇ pagar dos dólares de ~ pay two dollars too much **2** (de sobra): No te preocupes, yo llevo un lápiz de ~. Don't worry. I have a spare pencil. ~ **bien** rather: Es ~ bien feo, pero simpático. He's rather ugly, but nice. ~ **o menos** more or less ~ **que nada** particularly **por ~ que** however much: Por ~ que grites... However much you shout... **¿qué ~ da?** what difference does it make? **sin ~ ni ~** just like that **N O T A** Para otras expresiones con **más**, ver el adjetivo, adverbio, etc., p. ej. **más que nunca** en NUNCA.

masa nf 1 mass: ~ atómica atomic mass ◇ una ~ de gente a mass of people 2 (pan) dough 3 (para tartas, etc.) pastry ▶ **de ~s** mass: cultura de ~s mass culture

masaje nm massage: ¿Me das un poco de ~ en la espalda? Can you massage my back for me?

mascada nf (Mx) scarf [pl -s o scarves]

mascar vt, vi chew

máscara nf mask

mascota nf 1 mascot 2 (animal doméstico) pet

masculino adj 1 male 2 (Dep, moda) men's: el equipo ~ the men's team 3 (característico del hombre, Gram) masculine: un corte de pelo muy ~ a very masculine haircut →MALE

masivo adj 1 (de masas) mass: *transporte ~* mass transport 2 (enorme) huge

máster nm master's (degree): *un ~ de economía* a master's in economics

masticar vt, vi chew

mástil nm 1 (barco) mast 2 (bandera) flagpole

masturbarse vp masturbate

mata nf 1 (planta) plant 2 (arbusto) bush

matadero nm slaughterhouse

matado adj, nm-nf (Mx) grind, swot (GB): *Él es muy ~.* He's such a grind.

matanza nf slaughter

matar vt, vi kill: ~ *el tiempo* kill time ▸ ~ **a tiros/de un tiro** shoot *sb* dead ~ **el hambre**: *Compré fruta para ~ el hambre.* I bought some fruit to keep us going. **~se estudiando/trabajando** work like crazy

matasellos nm postmark

mate¹ nm (ajedrez) mate

mate² adj (sin brillo) matt

matemáticas nf mathematics, math (coloq), maths (GB) (coloq)

matemático/a adj mathematical ● nm-nf mathematician

matera nf (And) flowerpot

materia nf 1 matter 2 (asignatura, tema) subject ▸ ~ **prima** raw material

material adj material ● nm 1 (materia, datos) material: *un ~ resistente al fuego* fire-resistant material ◇ *Tengo todo el ~ que necesito.* I have all the material I need. 2 (equipo) equipment [U]: ~ *deportivo* sports equipment ▸ ~ **didáctico/educativo** teaching materials

materialista adj materialistic ● nmf materialist

maternidad nf 1 (condición) motherhood 2 (sala) maternity ward

materno (tb **maternal**) adj maternal

matinal adj morning: *un vuelo ~* a morning flight

matiz nm 1 (color) shade 2 (rasgo) nuance: *un ~ irónico* a touch of irony

matizar vt 1 (palabras, etc.) qualify 2 (colores) blend

matón nm bully [pl -ies]

matorral nm scrub [U]: *entre unos ~es* in the scrub

matrícula nf 1 (inscripción) registration: *Están abiertas las ~s.* Registration has begun. 2 (Aut) (a) (número) license

plate number (b) (placa) license plate, number plate (GB)

matricular(se) vt, vp enroll

matrimonio nm 1 marriage 2 (ceremonia) wedding **NOTA** Wedding es la ceremonia, y **marriage** suele referirse al matrimonio como institución. En EE.UU. y Gran Bretaña los matrimonios se pueden celebrar en una iglesia (a **church wedding**) o en un juzgado (a **civil ceremony**). La novia (**bride**) suele llevar **bridesmaids** (damas de honor). El novio (**groom**) no lleva madrina, sino que va acompañado del **best man** (normalmente su mejor amigo). Tampoco se habla del padrino, aunque la novia suele entrar con su padre. Después se da un banquete (**have a reception**). 3 (pareja) (married) couple

matriz nf 1 (Anat) womb 2 (Mat) matrix [pl -rices]

matutino adj morning: *la sesión matutina* the morning session

maullar vi meow

maullido nm miaow

maxilar nm jawbone

máximo adj, nm maximum: *Hay un plazo ~ de diez días para pagar.* There is a maximum of ten days in which to pay. ◇ *el ~ goleador de la liga* the top scorer in the league ● **máxima** nf maximum temperature ▸ **al ~**: *aprovechar los recursos al ~* make maximum use of resources ◇ *Me esforcé al ~.* I tried my best. **como ~** at most

mayo nm May: *el 12 de ~* (on) May 12 **NOTA** Se dice "May twelfth" o "the twelfth of May".

mayonesa nf mayonnaise

mayor adj
- comparativo 1 bigger (than sth): *Londres es ~ que Madrid.* London is bigger than Madrid. ◇ ~ *de lo que parece* bigger than it looks 2 (edad) older (than sb)
  →ELDER
- superlativo (edad) oldest: *Es el alumno ~ de la clase.* He's the oldest student in the class.
  →ELDER
- otros usos 1 (adulto) grown-up 2 (anciano) old 3 (principal) main: *la calle ~* the main street 4 (Mús) major: *do ~* C major
- nmf 1 oldest (one) (in/of...): *El ~ tiene diez años.* The oldest (one) is ten. 2 mayores (adultos) grown-ups ▸ **al por ~** wholesale **de ~** when I, you, etc.

grow up: *De* ~ *quiero ser médico*. I want to be a doctor when I grow up. *de* ~ *importancia, prestigio*, etc. the most important, prestigious, etc.: *la zona de* ~ *riesgo* the most dangerous area **hacerse** ~ grow up **la** ~ **parte (de)** most (of *sth/sb*): *La* ~ *parte son católicos*. Most of them are Catholics. *Most of us like it.* **ser** ~ **de edad**: *Cuando sea* ~ *de edad podré votar*. I'll be able to vote when I'm eighteen. ◇ *Puede comprar alcohol porque es* ~ *de edad*. He can buy alcohol because he's over eighteen.

mayordomo *nm* butler

mayoreo *nm* wholesale

mayoría *nf* majority [*pl* -ies]: *obtener la* ~ *absoluta* get an absolute majority ▶ **la** ~ **de...** most (of...): *A la* ~ *de nosotros nos gusta*. Most of us like it. → MOST

mayúscula *nf* capital letter: *en* ~s in capitals

mazacote *nm* lump

mazapán *nm* marzipan

mazo *nm* (*martillo*) mallet

me *pron pers* (*complemento*) me: *Dámelo*. Give it to me. ◇ *¡Cómpramelo!* Buy it for me. **2** (*partes del cuerpo, efectos personales*): *Me voy a lavar las manos*. I'm going to wash my hands. **3** (*reflexivo*): *Me vi en el espejo*. I saw myself in the mirror. ◇ *Me vestí enseguida*. I got dressed right away.

mear *vi* pee

mecánica *nf* mechanics [*sing*]

mecánico/a *adj* mechanical ● *nm-nf* mechanic

mecanismo *nm* mechanism

mecanografía *nf* typing

mecanografiar *v* type

mecanógrafo/a *nm-nf* typist

mecate *nm* string

mecato *nm* (*And*) snack

mecedora *nf* rocking chair

mecer(se) *vt, vp* **1** (*columpio*) swing **2** (*cuna, bebé, barca*) rock

mecha *nf* **1** (*vela*) wick **2** (*bomba*) fuse **3** mechas (a) (*rayitos*) highlights (b) (*pelo*) hair: *hacerse cortar las* ~ have your hair cut ▶ **a toda** ~ at full speed

mechón *nm* **1** (*porción de pelo*) lock **2** mechones (*And, rayitos*) highlights: *hacerse mechones* have highlights put in

mechudo/a *adj, nm-nf* long-haired (person)

medalla *nf* medal: ~ *de oro* gold medal

media¹ *nf* **1** (*promedio*) average **2** (*Mat*) mean ▶ **las dos**, etc. **y** ~ half after/past (*GB*) two, etc.

media² *nf* **1** (*corta*) sock **2** medias (~s pantalón *And*) (*largas*) pantyhose [*pl*], tights [*pl*] (*GB*) **3** (*hasta el muslo*) stocking → PANTALÓN ▶ **irse las** ~s: *Se me fueron las* ~s. I have a run in my pantyhose. ~ **tobillera** (*And*) anklet, ankle sock (*GB*) ~s **veladas** (*And*) nylon stockings

mediados ▶ **a/hacia** ~ **de...** in/around the middle of...

mediano *adj* **1** medium: *Uso la talla mediana*. I wear a medium size. **2** (*regular*) average: *de mediana estatura* of average height ▶ **de mediana edad** middle-aged

medianoche *nf* midnight: *a* ~ at midnight

medicamento *nm* medicine

medicina *nf* medicine

médico/a *adj* medical ● *nm-nf* doctor (*abrev* **Dr.**): *ir al* ~ go to the doctor's ▶ ~ **de cabecera** family doctor, GP (*GB*)

medida *nf* **1** (*extensión*) measurement: *¿Qué* ~s *tiene esta sala?* What are the measurements of this room? ◇ *El sastre me tomó las* ~s. The tailor took my measurements. **2** (*unidad, norma*) measure: *pesos y* ~s weights and measures ▶ **Habrá que tomar** ~ **al respecto**. Something must be done about it. ▶ (*hecho*) **a la** ~ (made) to measure

medieval *adj* medieval

medio *adj* **1** (*la mitad de*) half a/an: *media botella* half a bottle ◇ *media hora* half an hour **2** (*promedio, normal*) average: *de tamaño* ~ of average size ● *adv* half: ~ *dormido* half asleep ● *nm* **1** (*centro*) middle **2** (*entorno*) environment **3** (*Mat*) half [*pl* halves] **4** (*procedimiento, recurso*) means [*pl* means]: ~ *de transporte* means of transport ◇ *No tengo* ~s *para hacerlo*. I lack the means to do it. ▶ **a media mañana/tarde** in the middle of the morning/afternoon **NOTA** In the middle of the morning suele referirse a las 10 u 11 de la mañana, y para una hora alrededor de las 12 se dice **midday**. In the middle of the afternoon suele ser a las 3 de la tarde, y para referirse a las 5 o 6, se dice **between 5 and 6** (**in the evening**). **en** ~ **de** in the middle of *sth* **estar/ponerse en** (**el**) ~ be/get in the way **medias tintas** half measures ~ **ambiente** environment ~ **campo** (*Dep*) midfield ~ **(de comunicación)** medium [*pl* media] ● **tiempo 1** (*Dep*) half-time **2** (*trabajo*) part-time: *trabajar* ~ *tiempo* have a part-time job **y** ~ and a half: *Demoré una hora y media.* It took me one and a half hours.

mediodía *nm* **1** (*hora exacta*) noon **2** (*aproximada*) lunchtime

medir *vt* measure ● *vi*: —*¿Cuánto mides?* "How tall are you?" ◊ *La mesa mide 1,50 m de largo.* The table is 1.50m long. ▶ **medírsele a algo/algn** take sth/sb on

meditar *vt*, *vi* think (*about* sth)

mediterráneo *adj, nm* Mediterranean

médula (*tb* medula) *nf* marrow

medusa *nf* jellyfish [*pl* jellyfish]

mejilla *nf* cheek → MY

mejillón *nm* mussel

mejor *adj, adv* (*comparativo*) better (*than* sth/sb): ~ *que nunca* better than ever ◊ *cuanto antes* ~ the sooner the better ◊ *adj, adv, nmf* (*superlativo*) best (*in/of/ that...*): *Es la* ~ *de la clase.* She's the best in the class. ◊ *el que* ~ *canta* the one who sings best ▶ **a lo** ~ maybe **hacer algo lo** ~ **posible** do your best ~ **dicho** I mean: *cinco, ~ dicho, seis* five, I mean six ~ **que nunca** better than ever

mejorar *vt, vi* improve: *Esto te va a* ~. This will make you feel better. ● **mejorarse** *vp* get better: *¡Que te mejores!* Get well soon!

mejoría *nf* improvement (*in* sth/ sb)

melancólico *adj* sad

melena *nf* hair

mellizo/a *adj, nm-nf* twin

melodía *nf* tune ▶ **hecho/vuelto una** ~ (*And*) in a mess: *La novia lo dejó y quedó vuelto una* ~. His girlfriend left him and he's shattered.

melón *nm* melon

membrillo *nm* quince

memorable *adj* memorable

memoria *nf* **1** memory: *tener buena* ~ have a good memory **2** memorias (*texto*) memoirs ▶ **de** ~ by heart **hacer** ~ try to remember

memorizar *vt* memorize

menaje *nm* ▶ ~ **de cocina** kitchenware

mención *nf* mention

mencionar *vt* mention ▶ **sin** ~ not to mention

mendigar *vt, vi* beg (*for* sth): ~ *comida* beg for food

mendigo/a *nm-nf* beggar

mendrugo *nm* crust

menear *vt* **1** (*sacudir*) shake **2** (*cabeza*) (a) (*para decir que sí*) nod (b) (*para decir que no*) shake **3** (*cola*) wag

menguante *adj* (*luna*) waning

menopausia *nf* menopause

menor *adj* **1** (*comparativo*) (a) smaller (b) (*edad*) younger: *Eres* ~ *que ella.* You're younger than her. **2** (*Mús*) minor: *en mi* ~ in E minor ● *adj, nmf* (*superlativo*) youngest (one): *el* (*alumno*) ~ *de la clase* the youngest (student) in the class ▶ **al** par ~ retail ~ **de 18, etc. años:** *Prohibida la entrada a* ~*es de 18 años.* No entry for persons under 18. ~ **(de edad)** minor: *No se sirve alcohol a* ~*es.* Alcohol will not be served to minors.

menos *adv* **1** (*comparativo*) less: *Tardé* ~ *de lo que yo pensaba.* It took me less time than I thought it would. **NOTA** Con sustantivos contables es más correcto **fewer**, aunque también se usa **less**: *Había* ~ *gente que ayer.* There were fewer people than yesterday. → LESS **2** (*superlativo*) least: *la* ~ *habladora de la familia* the least talkative member of the family **NOTA** Con sustantivos contables es más correcto **fewest**, aunque también se usa **least**: *la clase con* ~ *alumnos* the class with fewest pupils. → LESS ● *prep* **1** (*excepto*) except: *Fueron todos* ~ *yo.* Everybody went except me. **2** (*Mat, temperatura*) minus: *Estamos a* ~ *diez grados.* It's minus ten. ● *nm* (*signo matemático*) minus (sign) ▶ **al** ~ at least **a** ~ **que** unless: *a* ~ *que deje de llover* unless it stops raining **de** ~ too little, too few: *mil pesos de* ~ a thousand pesos too little **echar de** ~ miss: *Echaré de* ~ *el ir a cine.* I'll miss going to the movies. **lo** ~ the least: *¡Es lo* ~ *que puedo hacer!* It's the least I can do! ◊ *lo* ~ *posible* as little as possible **¡**~ **mal!** thank goodness! **por lo** ~ at least

mensaje *nm* message ▶ ~ **de texto** text message

mensajero/a *nm-nf* messenger

menso/a *adj* stupid ● *nm-nf* fool

menstruación *nf* menstruation

mensual *adj* monthly

menta *nf* mint

mental *adj* mental

mentalidad *nf* mentality [*pl* ies] ▶ **tener una** ~ **abierta/estrecha** be open-minded/narrow-minded

mentalizar vt make sb aware (of sth)

mente nf mind: *tener algo en ~* have something in mind

mentir vi lie: *¡No me mientas!* Don't lie to me!

mentira nf lie: *decir/meter ~s* tell lies ◊ *¡Eso es ~!* That isn't true! ▸ **de ~(s)**: *una corona de ~* a pretend crown *¡mentiras!* nonsense! *parece ~*: *¡Parece ~!* I can hardly believe it! *una ~ piadosa* a white lie

mentiroso/a adj deceitful: *una persona mentirosa* a deceitful person ● nm-nf liar

mentón nm chin

menú nm menu

menudencias nf giblets

menudeo nm retail trade

menudo adj 1 (*pequeño*) small 2 (*en exclamaciones*): ¡Menuda suerte tienes! You're so lucky! ◊ *¡En ~ lío te metiste!* You've gotten yourself into a real mess! ● nm 1 (*cocina*) tripe 2 (*And*) (tb menuda nf) (*cambio*) small change ▸ **a ~** often

meñique nm 1 (*mano*) little finger 2 (*pie*) little toe

mercadeo nm marketing

mercadillo nm street market

mercado nm market: *en el ~ at the market* ◊ *la lista del ~* the shopping list ▸ **hacer (el) ~** do the shopping ~ **negro** black market

mercancía nf goods [pl]

mercar vi do the shopping

mercería nf (*sección*) sewing notions, haberdashery (GB)

mercurio nm 1 (*Quím*) mercury 2 **Mercurio** (*planeta*) Mercury

merecer(se) vt, vp deserve: *El equipo mereció perder.* The team deserved to lose.

merecido adj well deserved ▸ **lo tienes bien ~** it serves you right

merendar vt have sth as an afternoon snack ● vi 1 have an afternoon snack 2 (*al aire libre*) have a picnic

merengue nm 1 (*Cocina*) meringue 2 (*baile*) merengue

meridiano nm meridian

merienda nf 1 afternoon snack 2 (*al aire libre*) picnic

mérito nm merit ▸ **tener ~** be praiseworthy

merluza nf hake [pl hake]

mermelada nf jam

mero adj 1 mere: *una mera casualidad* mere coincidence 2 (*mismo*) very: *la mera orilla del río* the very edge of the river 3 (*preciso*) exact: *a la mera hora*

when it comes down to it ● adv soon: *Ya ~ acaba.* It's almost finished. ▸ **el mero mero** (*Mx*) the top dog

mes nm month: *el ~ pasado/que viene* last/next month ▸ **al ~** 1 (*cada mes*) a month: *¿Cuánto gastas al ~?* How much do you spend a month? 2 (*transcurrido un mes*) within a month: *al ~ de empezar* within a month of starting *estar de dos, etc. ~es/tener dos, etc. ~es de embarazo* be two, etc. months pregnant *por ~es* monthly *un ~ sí y otro no* every other month

mesa nf table: *¿Nos sentamos a la ~?* Shall we sit at the table? ▸ **levantar/recoger la ~** clear the table ~ **auxiliar** (*occasional*) table ~ **redonda** round table **poner la ~** set the table

mesada nf allowance

mesero/a nm-nf waiter [fem waitress]

meseta nf plateau

mesita (tb **mesilla**) nf ▸ ~ (**de noche**) bedside table ~ (**de ruedas**) trolley

mesón nm inn

mestizo/a adj, nm-nf (person) of mixed race

meta nf (*Dep*) finishing line: *cruzar la ~* cross the finishing line 2 (*objetivo*) goal

metáfora nf metaphor

metal nm metal

metálico adj 1 metal: *una barra metálica* a metal bar 2 (*color, sonido*) metallic ▸ **en ~** cash: *un premio en ~* a cash prize

metedura nf = METIDA

meteorito nm meteor

meteorológico adj weather: *un informe ~* a weather bulletin

meter vt 1 put: *¿Dónde metiste mis llaves?* Where did you put my keys? 2 (*gol, canasta*) score ● **meterse** vp 1 (*introducirse*) get into sth: *~ en la cama* get into bed ◊ *Se me metió una piedra en el zapato.* I have a stone in my shoe. 2 (*involucrarse, interesarse*) get involved: *~ en política* get involved in politics 3 (*en los asuntos de otro*) interfere 4 **~ con** (*criticar*) pick on sb **NOTA** Para expresiones, ver el sustantivo, p.ej. **meter miedo** en MIEDO.

metiche (metete *And*) adj nosy ● nmf busybody [pl -ies]

metida nf ▸ ~ **de pata** blunder

metido/a adj ● nm-nf busybody [pl -ies] ▸ **dejar ~** (*And*) stand sb up

método nm method

metralleta nf sub-machine gun

métrico adj metric

metro nm 1 (medida) meter (abrev **m**): Se vende por ~s. It's sold by the meter. 2 (cinta para medir) tape measure 3 (tren) subway, underground (GB)

mexicano/a adj, nm-nf Mexican

México nm Mexico

mezcla nf 1 mixture 2 (tabaco, alcohol, café, té) blend 3 (racial, social, musical) mix

mezclar vt 1 mix: Hay que ~ bien los ingredientes. Mix the ingredients well. 2 (desordenar) get sth mixed up: No mezcles las fotos. Don't get the pictures mixed up. ● **mezclarse** vp 1 (alternar) mix: No quiere ~ con la gente del pueblo. He doesn't want to mix with people from the town. 2 (meterse) get mixed up: No quiero mezclarme en asuntos de familia. I don't want to get mixed up in family affairs.

mezclilla nf (tela) denim: pantalón de ~ jeans

mezquita nf mosque

mi¹ adj my

mi² nm E: mi mayor E major

mí pron pers me

miau nm meow →GATO

mico/a nm-nf monkey

microbio nm microbe

micrófono nm microphone, mike (más coloq)

microondas nm microwave

microscopio nm microscope

miedo nm fear: el ~ a volar/al fracaso fear of flying/failure ▸ **dar** ~ frighten, scare (más coloq): Sus amenazas no me dan ningún ~. His threats don't frighten me. ◊ **por** ~ a/de algo for fear of sth **meter** ~ frighten, scare (más coloq) **pasar** ~ be frightened, be scared (más coloq) **¡qué** ~! how scary! **tener** ~ be afraid, be scared (más coloq): tener ~ a los perros be scared of dogs ◊ ¿Tenías ~ de caerte? Were you afraid of falling?

miel nf honey

miembro nm 1 member: hacerse ~ become a member 2 (Anat) limb

mientras adv in the meantime ● conj 1 (simultaneidad) while: Canta ~ pinta. He sings while he paints. 2 (tanto tiempo como, siempre que) as long as: Aguanta ~ puedas. Put up with it as long as you can. ▸ ~ más/menos... the

more/less...: ~ más tiene, más quiere. The more he has, the more he wants. ~ **que** while ~ **tanto** in the meantime

miércoles nm Wednesday (abrev **Wed.**) →LUNES ▸ ~ **de Ceniza** Ash Wednesday

miga nf crumb ▸ **hacer buenas ~s** get along well (with sb)

migración nf migration

mijo/a pron dear

mil adj, nm, pron 1 (a) thousand: ~ personas a thousand people ◊ un billete de cinco ~ a five-thousand peso bill **NOTA** Mil se traduce por **one thousand** cuando va seguido de otro número: ~ trescientos one thousand three hundred, o para dar énfasis: Te dije ~, no dos ~. I said one thousand, not two. De 1.100 a 1.900 se usan también las formas **eleven/twelve hundred**, etc. De **años**): en 1600 in sixteen hundred ◊ en 2004 in two thousand and four ▸ ~**es de...** thousands of... ~ **millones** (a) billion: tres ~ millones de dólares three billion dollars **por** ~**es** in their thousands

milagro nm miracle

milésimo/a adj, nm-nf, pron thousandth: una milésima de segundo a thousandth of a second

miligramo nm milligram (abrev **mg**)

milímetro nm millimetre (abrev **mm**)

militar adj military ● nmf soldier

milla nf mile

millar nm thousand [pl thousand]: dos ~es de libros two thousand books ▸ ~**es de...** thousands of...

millón nm million [pl million]: dos millones trescientos quince two million three hundred and fifteen ◊ Tengo un ~ de cosas que hacer. I have a million things to do. ▸ **millones de...** millions of...: millones de partículas millions of particles

millonario/a nm-nf millionaire

mimar vt spoil

mimbre nm wicker

mímica nf (lenguaje) sign language ▸ **hacer** ~ mime

mimo nm 1 (cariño) fuss [U]: Los niños necesitan ~s. Children need to be made a fuss of. 2 (excesiva tolerancia) No le des tantos ~s. Don't spoil him. ● nmf mime artist

mina nf 1 mine: una ~ de carbón a coal mine 2 (lápiz) lead

mineral nm mineral

M

minero/a adj mining: *una empresa minera* a mining company ● *nm-nf* miner

miniatura nf miniature

minifalda nf miniskirt

mínimo adj **1** (*menor*) minimum: *el salario* ~ the minimum wage **2** (*insignificante*) minimal: *una diferencia mínima* a minimal difference ● *nm* minimum: *reducir algo al* ~ cut sth to a minimum ▶ **como** ~ at least

ministerio nm **1** (Pol) department, ministry [pl -ies] (GB): *M~ de Relaciones Exteriores/del Interior* Department of Foreign Affairs/the Interior ◊ *M~ de Hacienda* Treasury Department **2** (Rel) ministry

ministro/a nm-nf secretary [pl -ies]: *M~ de Relaciones Exteriores/del Interior* Secretary of Foreign Affairs/the Interior ◊ *M~ de Hacienda* Treasury Secretary **NOTA** En Gran Bretaña y en algunos otros países se dice también **minister**.

minoría nf minority [pl -ies] ▶ **ser** ~ be in the minority

minúsculo adj **1** (*diminuto*) tiny **2** (*letra*) small: *una "m" minúscula* a small "m" ● **minúscula** nf small letter

minusválido adj disabled: *asientos reservados para los* ~s seats for disabled people

minutero nm minute hand

minuto nm minute

mío/a adj, pron mine: *un amigo* ~ a friend of mine

miope adj near-sighted

miopía nf near-sightedness

mirada nf **1** look: *una* ~ *inexpresiva* a blank look **2** (*vistazo*) glance: *echarle una* ~ *rápida al periódico* take a quick glance at the newspaper

mirador nm viewpoint

mirar vt, vi look (at sth/sb): ~ *el reloj* look at the clock ◊ ~ *hacia arriba/abajo* look up/down ◊ ~ *por una ventana* look out of a window **NOTA** En inglés hay varias formas de decir "mirar". Las más comunes son **look at** y, para "observar", **watch**. Los demás verbos tienen algún matiz que los distingue:
gaze = mirar fijamente durante un tiempo
glance = echar una mirada rápida
glare = mirar con ira
peep = mirar rápida y cautelosamente
peer = mirar de manera prolon-

gada y a veces con esfuerzo **stare at sth/sb** = mirar fijamente durante mucho tiempo con interés o sorpresa.

▶ **mira que...**: *Mira que mi paciencia tiene un límite.* Be careful, there's a limit to my patience. ◊ *¡Mira que eres despistado!* You're so absent-minded! **se mire como/por donde se mire** whichever way you look at it **NOTA** Para otras expresiones, ver el sustantivo, etc., p. ej. **mirar de reojo** en REOJO.

mirilla nf peephole

mirlo nm blackbird

misa nf mass ▶ ~ **de(l) gallo** midnight mass

miserable adj **1** (*sórdido, escaso*) miserable: *un cuarto/sueldo* ~ a miserable room/salary **2** (*persona, vida*) wretched ● nmf **1** (*malvado*) wretch **2** (*tacaño*) miser

miseria nf **1** (*pobreza*) poverty **2** (*cantidad pequeña*) pittance

misil nm missile

misión nf mission

misionero/a nm-nf missionary [pl -ies]

mismo adj **1** (*idéntico*) same: *Vivo en la misma casa que él.* I live in the same house as him. **2** (*énfasis*): *Yo* ~ *lo vi.* I saw it myself. ◊ *la princesa misma* the princess herself ● pron same one: *el* ~ *que vino ayer* the same one who came yesterday ● adv: *delante* ~ *de mi casa* right in front of my house ◊ *Le prometo hacerlo hoy* ~. I promise you I'll get it done today. ▶ **lo** ~ the same: *lo* ~ *de siempre* the same as usual **me da lo** ~ I, you, etc. don't mind **quedarse en las mismas** not understand a thing

misterio nm mystery [pl -ies]

misterioso adj mysterious

mitad nf half [pl halves]: *la primera* ~ *del partido* the first half of the game ◊ *partir algo por la* ~ cut sth in half ▶ **a/en/por (la)** ~: *en la* ~ *del camino* halfway ◊ *La botella estaba a/por la* ~. The bottle was half empty. **a** ~ **de precio** half-price

mitin nm (*reunión política*) meeting: *hacer un* ~ hold a meeting

mito nm **1** (*leyenda*) myth **2** (*persona famosa*) legend

mitología nf mythology

mixto adj (Educ) coeducational

mobiliario nm furniture

mocasín nm moccasin

mochila nf **1** (*de viaje*) backpack **2** (And, bolso) shoulder bag

mocho adj: Tiene una oreja mocha. He only has one ear.

moco (tb **mocos**) nm mucus ► **tener ~s** have a runny nose

moda nf fashion ► **(estar/ponerse) de ~** (be/become) fashionable: un bar de ~ a fashionable bar **pasarse de ~** go out of fashion: pasado de ~ unfashionable

modales nm manners

modelar vt model

modelo nm 1 model: un ~ a escala a scale model 2 (ropa) style: varios ~s de chaqueta several styles of jacket ● nmf (persona) model

módem nm modem

moderado adj moderate

moderador/a nm-nf moderator

moderar vt 1 (velocidad) reduce 2 (lenguaje) watch: Modera tus palabras. Watch your language.

modernizar(se) vt, vp modernize

moderno adj modern

modestia nf modesty

modesto adj modest

modificar vt 1 (cambiar) change 2 (Gram) modify

modisto/a nm-nf (diseñador) designer ● nmf (costurera) dressmaker

modo nm 1 way (of doing sth): un ~ especial de reír a special way of laughing ◊ Lo hace del mismo ~ que yo. He does it the same way as me. 2 (modales) manners ► **a mi ~** my, your, etc. way **de ~ que** (por tanto) so **de todos ~s** anyway ¡ni ~! no way: ¡Ni ~, así soy yo! Tough, that's the way I am.

módulo nm module

moflete nm chubby cheek

mogolla nf (And) bread roll

moho nm mold ► **criar/tener ~** get/be moldy

mojado adj wet

mojar vt 1 get sth/sb wet: No mojes el suelo. Don't get the floor wet. 2 (comida) dip: ~ el pan en la sopa dip your bread in the soup ● **mojarse** vp get wet: ~ los pies get your feet wet

molcajete nm (Mx) mortar

molde nm 1 (Cocina) pan, tin (GB) 2 (de yeso) cast

mole nm 1 (salsa) chocolate chili sauce 2 (fig): Las matemáticas son su mero ~. Math is his best subject.

molécula nf molecule

moler vt (café, trigo, carne) grind ● vi (trabajar) work ► **a palos** give sb a beating

molestar vt 1 (importunar) bother: ¿Te molesta que fume?

Does it bother you if I smoke? 2 (interrumpir) disturb: No quiere que la molesten mientras trabaja. She doesn't want to be disturbed while she's working. 3 (ofender) upset ● vi be a nuisance: No quiero ~. I don't want to be a nuisance. ● **molestarse** vp 1 (disgustarse) get upset (at/about sth): Se molestó por mis comentarios. She got upset at my remarks. 2 (tomarse trabajo) bother (to do sth): Ni se molestó en contestar. He didn't even bother to reply. ► **no ~** do not disturb

molestia nf 1 (dolor) discomfort [U] 2 **molestias** inconvenience [U]: Disculpen las ~s. We apologize for any inconvenience. ► **si no es ~** if it's no bother **tomarse la ~ de** take the trouble to do sth

molesto adj 1 (que fastidia) annoying 2 (disgustado) annoyed: Está ~ conmigo por lo que dije. He's annoyed with me about what I said.

molido adj 1 (cansado) pooped (out), shattered (GB) 2 (And, cuerpo) stiff

molinillo nm (para batir) whisk

molino nm mill ► **de agua/viento** watermill/windmill

momento nm 1 moment: Espera un ~. Wait a moment. 2 (periodo) time: en estos ~s de crisis at this time of crisis ◊ el mejor cantante del ~ the best singer of our time ► **al ~** immediately **de ~** for the moment **de un ~ a otro** from one minute to the next **en el ~ menos pensado** when I, you, etc. least expect it **por/en el ~** for the time being

momia nf mummy [pl -ies]

monaguillo nm altar boy

monarca nmf monarch

monarquía nf monarchy [pl -ies]

monasterio nm monastery [pl -ies]

moneda nf 1 (pieza) coin: ¿Tienes una ~ de 20? Do you have a 20 peso coin? 2 (unidad monetaria) currency [pl -ies]

monedero nm coin purse, purse (GB)

monitor/a nm-nf 1 instructor 2 (And, universidad) student who acts as an assistant teacher ● nm (pantalla) monitor

monje nm-nf monk [fem nun]

mono/a adj 1 (lindo) pretty 2 (And, rubio) fair, blond(e) → **RUBIO** ● nm-nf (animal) monkey ● nm (dibujo): pintar ~s en el cuaderno doodle in your exercise book ◇ los ~s del periódico the cartoons in the newspaper

monolito nm monolith

monólogo nm monologue

monopatín nm 1 (con manillar) scooter 2 (sin manillar) skateboard

monopolio nm monopoly [pl -ies]

monótono adj monotonous

monóxido nm monoxide: ~ de carbono carbon monoxide

monstruo nm monster: un ~ de tres ojos a three-eyed monster 2 (genio) genius: un ~ de las matemáticas a mathematical genius

montado adj: ~ en un caballo/una moto riding a horse/motorcycle

montadura nf (joyas) setting

montaje nm 1 (máquina) assembly: una cadena/línea de ~ an assembly line 2 (truco) set-up 3 (Cine) montage

montaña nf 1 mountain: en lo alto de una ~ at the top of a mountain 2 la montaña (tipo de paisaje) mountains [pl] ► ~ rusa roller coaster

montañismo nm mountaineering

montañoso adj mountainous

montar vt 1 (establecer) set up: ~ un negocio set up a business 2 (piedras preciosas, exposición, campaña) mount 3 (máquina) assemble 4 (Teat, etc.) put sth on ● vi ride: ~ en bicicleta ride a bicycle ◇ botas de ~ riding boots ● montar(se) vi, vp get on (sth): Se montaron dos pasajeros. Two passengers got on. ► ~ a caballo go horseback riding

monte nm 1 mountain 2 (con nombre propio) Mount: el ~ Everest Mount Everest

montón nm 1 (pila) pile: un ~ de arena a pile of sand 2 (muchos) a load of: un ~ de problemas a load of problems ◇ Gastas dinero a montones. You spend a load of money. ► del ~ ordinary: una muchacha del ~ an ordinary girl

montura nf 1 (caballo) saddle 2 (gafas) frames [pl]

monumento nm monument

moño nm 1 (lazo) bow 2 (pelo) bun ► ponerse ~s give yourself airs

moñona nf (bolos, etc.) strike

mora nf 1 (de arbusto) blackberry [pl -ies] 2 (de árbol) mulberry [pl -ies]

morado adj, nm (color) purple ● nm bruise

moral adj moral ● nf 1 (principios) morality 2 (ánimo) morale: La ~ está baja. Morale is low. ► estar bajo de ~/bajársele a algn la ~ be in low spirits

moraleja nf moral

morcilla nf blood sausage, black pudding (GB)

mordaza nf gag: Los asaltantes le pusieron una ~. The robbers gagged him.

mordedura nf bite

morder(se) vt, vi, vp bite: El perro me mordió (en) la pierna. The dog bit my leg. ◇ ~se las uñas bite your nails ► estar que muerde: No le preguntes, que muerde. Don't ask him; he'll bite your head off. ► el anzuelo swallow the bait ~se la lengua (lit y fig) hold your tongue

mordida nf 1 bite 2 (Mx, soborno) bribe

mordisco nm bite ► dar/pegar un ~ bite

mordisquear vt nibble

moreno adj 1 (pelo, piel) dark 2 (bronceado, azúcar, pan) brown: ponerse ~ go brown

moretón nm bruise

morfina nf morphine

morgue nf morgue

moribundo adj dying

morir(se) vi, vp die: ~ de un infarto/en un accidente die of a heart attack/in an accident ► ~se de aburrimiento/aburrición be bored stiff ~se de frío be freezing ~se del susto get the fright of your life ~se de miedo be scared stiff ~se de risa fall about laughing ~se por hacer algo be dying to do sth

moro adj Moorish ● nm-nf Moor

morocho adj black

morral nm backpack

morralla nf small change

morro nm (avión) nose

morsa nf walrus

morse nm Morse Code

mortadela nf bologna, mortadella (GB)

mortal adj 1 mortal: pecado ~ mortal sin 2 (enfermedad, accidente) fatal 3 (veneno, enemigo) deadly 4 (aburrimiento, ruido, trabajo) dreadful ● nmf mortal

mortalidad nf mortality

mortero nm mortar

mosaico nm mosaic

mosca nf fly [pl flies] ► caer/morir como ~s drop like flies ponerse ~ smell a rat ¿qué ~ te ha picado? what's eating you?

mosquito nm mosquito [pl -s/-es]

mostaza *nf* mustard

mostrador *nm* **1** (*tienda*) counter **2** (*bar*) bar **3** (*aeropuerto*) check-in desk

mostrar *vt* show ● **mostrarse** *vp* (*parecer*) seem: *Se mostraba pesimista.* He seemed pessimistic.

mota *nf* speck

mote *nm* nickname

motilado *nm* (*And*) haircut

motilar *vt* cut *sb's* hair ● **motilarse** *vp* have your hair cut

motín *nm* mutiny [*pl* -ies]

motivar *vt* **1** (*causar*) cause **2** (*incentivar*) motivate

motivo *nm* reason: *el ~ del viaje* the reason for the trip ◊ *sin ~ alguno* for no reason ▶ **¡que sea un ~!** (*And*) let's drink to that

moto (*tb* **motocicleta**) *nf* motorcycle: *ir en ~* ride a motorcycle

motociclismo *nm* motorcycling

motociclista *nmf* motorcyclist

motocross *nm* motocross

motor *adj* motor: *potencia motora* motive power ● *nm* engine, motor →ENGINE

mover(se) *vt, vi, vp* move: *~ una pieza del ajedrez* move a chess piece ◊ *Muévete un poco para que me siente.* Move over and let me sit down.

movido *adj* **1** (*ajetreado*) busy **2** (*foto*) blurry

móvil *adj, nm* mobile

movimiento *nm* **1** movement: *un leve ~ de la mano* a slight movement of the hand ◊ *el ~ obrero* the labor movement **2** (*marcha*) motion: *poner algo en ~* set sth in motion **3** (*actividad*) activity

mu *nm* moo ▶ **no decir ni ~** not open your mouth

muchacho/a *nm-nf* **1** boy, guy (*más coloq*) [*fem* girl] **2 muchachos** (*chicos y chicas*) young people, kids (*más coloq*)

muchedumbre *nf* crowd

mucho *adj*
● **frases afirmativas** a lot of *sth*: *Tengo ~ trabajo.* I have a lot of work.
● **frases negativas/interrogativas 1** (+ *sustantivo incontable*) much, a lot of *sth* (*más coloq*): *No tiene mucha suerte.* He doesn't have much luck. ◊ *¿Tomas ~ café?* Do you drink a lot of coffee? **2** (+ *sustantivo contable*) many, a lot of *sth* (*más coloq*): *No había ~s ingleses.* There weren't many English people.
● **otras construcciones**: *¿Tienes mucha hambre?* Are you very hungry? ◊ *hace ~ tiempo* a long

time ago ● *pron* **1** (*afirmativo*) a lot: *~s de mis amigos* a lot of my friends **2** (*negativo/interrogativo*) much [*pl* many] →MANY
● *adv* **1** a lot: *Se parece ~ al papá.* He's a lot like his father. ◊ *trabajar ~* work hard **2** (+ *comparativo*) much: *Eres ~ mayor que ella.* You're much older than her. ◊ *~ más interesante* much more interesting **3** (*mucho tiempo*) a long time: *hace ~* a long time ago **4** (*en respuestas*) very: —*¿Está cansado?* —*No ~.* "Are you tired?" "Not very." ▶ **ni ~ menos** far from it **por ~ que...** however much... *Por ~ que insistas...* However much you insist...

mudanza *nf* (*de casa*) move: *estar de ~* be moving (house)

mudar(se) *vt, vp* **1** (*cambiar*) change: *~se de camisa* change your shirt **2** (*casa*) move

mudo *adj* **1** (*Med*) mute **2** (*Cine*) silent

mueble *nm* **1** (*en singular*) piece of furniture **2 muebles** furniture [U]: *Los ~s estaban cubiertos de polvo.* The furniture was covered in dust.

mueca *nf* ▶ **hacer ~s** make faces

mueco *adj* gap-toothed

muela *nf* molar ▶ **~ del juicio** wisdom tooth **ser buena ~** (*And*) **1** (*buena persona*) be a good sort **2** (*apetito*) enjoy your food

muelle *nm* **1** (*resorte*) spring **2** (*puerto*) wharf [*pl* -s o wharves]

muenda *nf* beating

muerte *nf* death ▶ **dar ~** kill *sb* **de mala ~** horrible: *un pueblo de mala ~* a horrible village

muerto/a *adj, nm-nf* dead: *los ~s en la guerra* the war dead ◊ *Hubo tres ~s en el accidente.* Three people were killed in the accident. ▶ **~ de cansancio** tired as a dog **~ de envidia** green with envy **~ de frío/hambre** freezing/starving **~ de miedo** scared to death **~ de sed** dying of thirst

muestra *nf* **1** (*Med, Estadística, mercancía*) sample: *una ~ de sangre* a blood sample **2** (*prueba*) token: *una ~ de amor* a token of love **3** (*señal*) sign: *dar ~s de cansancio* show signs of fatigue

mugir *vi* **1** (*vaca*) moo **2** (*toro*) bellow

mugre *nf* filth

mujer *nf* **1** woman [*pl* women] **2** (*esposa*) wife [*pl* wives]

mula *nf* mule ● *adj* (*Mx*) mean

muleta *nf* crutch: *andar con ~s* walk on crutches

mullido *adj* soft

multa *nf* fine ▸ **poner una ~** fine

multicultural *adj* multicultural

multimedia *adj* multimedia ● *nm* multimedia system

multinacional *adj* multinational ● *nf* multinational company [*pl* -ies]

múltiple *adj* **1** (*no simple*) multiple **2** (*numerosos*) numerous

multiplicación *nf* multiplication

multiplicar *vt, vi* (*Mat*) multiply: *~ dos por cuatro* multiply two by four

multirracial *adj* multiracial

multitud *nf* **1** (*muchedumbre*) crowd **2 ~ de** (*muchos*) a lot of *sth*: (*una*) *~ de problemas* a lot of problems

mundial *adj* world: *el récord ~* the world record ● *nm* world championship: *los M~es de Atletismo* the World Athletics Championships ◇ *el M~* the World Cup

mundo *nm* **1** world **2 un mundo** (**de**) (*gran número*) lots of ▸ **medio ~** lots of people **todo el ~** everybody

munición *nf* ammunition [U]

municipal *adj* municipal

municipio *nm* **1** (*territorio*) municipality [*pl* -ies] **2** (*ayuntamiento*) city council

muñeca *nf* **1** (*juguete*) doll **2** (*Anat*) wrist

muñeco *nm* **1** (*juguete*) doll: *un ~ de trapo* a rag doll **2** (*de ventrílocuo, maniquí*) dummy [*pl* -ies] ▸ **~ de nieve** snowman [*pl* -men] **~ de peluche/felpa** stuffed toy

muñequera *nf* wristband

mural *nm* mural

muralla *nf* wall(s): *la ~ medieval* the medieval walls

murciélago *nm* bat

murmullo *nm* murmur

murmurar *vt, vi* (*en voz baja*) mutter ▸ *vi* (*chismosear*) gossip

muro *nm* wall

musa *nf* muse

musaraña *nf* ▸ **pensar en las ~s** daydream

muscular *adj* muscle: *una lesión ~* a muscle injury

músculo *nm* muscle

musculoso *adj* muscular

museo *nm* museum

musgo *nm* moss

música *nf* music: *~ en vivo* live music

musical *adj, nm* musical

músico *nmf* musician

muslo *nm* **1** thigh →MY **2** (*ave*) leg

mustio *adj* (*Mx*) hypocritical

musulmán/ana *adj, nm-nf* Muslim

mutante *adj, nmf* mutant

mutilar *vt* mutilate

mutuamente *adv* each other: *Se odian ~.* They hate each other.

mutuo *adj* mutual

muy *adv* **1** very: *~ cansados/despacio* very tired/slowly **2** (+ *sustantivo*): *Es ~ hombre.* He's a real man. ▸ **~ bien** (*de acuerdo*) OK **por muy... que...** however...: *Por ~ simpático que sea...* However nice he is...

N n

nabo *nm* turnip

nácar *nm* mother-of-pearl

nacer *vi* **1** (*persona, animal*) be born: *Nací en 1981.* I was born in 1981. **2** (*río*) rise **3** (*planta, pelo, plumas*) grow ▸ **para actor, cantante, etc.** be a born actor, singer, etc.

naciente *adj* (*sol*) rising

nacimiento *nm* **1** birth: *fecha de ~* date of birth **2** (*río*) source **3** (*pelo, uña*) root **4** (*belén*) crib ▸ **de ~**: *ser chileno de ~* be Chilean by birth ◇ *Es ciega de ~.* She was born blind.

nación *nf* nation

nacional *adj* **1** (*de la nación*) national: *la bandera ~* the national flag **2** (*no internacional*) domestic: *vuelos/salidas ~es* domestic flights/departures

nacionalidad *nf* **1** nationality [*pl* -ies] **2** (*ciudadanía*) citizenship

nacionalista *adj, nmf* nationalist

nacionalizar *vt* nationalize ● **nacionalizarse** *vp* become a British, US, etc. citizen

naco *adj* (*Mx*) tacky

nada *pron* nothing, anything **NOTA** Se usa **nothing** en afirmaciones y **anything** en negaciones: *No queda ~.* There's nothing left. ◇ *No quiero ~.* I don't want anything. ● *adv* at all: *No está ~ claro.* It's not at all clear. ▸ **con ~ más que** *Con ~ más que verlo.* I recognized him as soon as I saw him. **de ~** you're welcome: *—Gracias por la comida. —¡De ~!* "Thanks for the meal." "You're welcome!" **~ más 1** (*eso es todo*) that's all **2** (*sólo*) only: *Tengo un hijo*

~ más. I only have one son.
~ más y ~ menos que...
1 (persona) none other than...
2 (cantidad) no less than...
~ más y ~ menos que 100 personas no less than 100 people
~ que...: —¿Hablaste con Paola? —Nada que me diga. "Did you talk to Paola?" "She hasn't called me yet."

nadador/a nm-nf swimmer

nadar vi swim: **~ cinco largos** swim five lengths ◊ **~ (de) espalda/mariposa** do the back-stroke/butterfly

nadie pron nobody, anybody
NOTA Se usa **nobody** en afirmaciones y **anybody** en negaciones: *Eso no lo sabe ~.* Nobody knows that. ◊ *No quiere hablar con ~.* He won't talk to anybody.

nado ▸ a ~: *Cruzaron el río a ~.* They swam across the river.
~ libre crawl

naipe nm playing card

nalga nf **1** buttock **2** nalgas bottom [sing]

nana nf (niñera) nanny [pl -ies]

naranja adj, nm, nf (fruta, color) orange

naranjada nf orangeade

naranjo nm orange (tree)

narcótico nm drug

narcotraficante (tb narco) nmf drug trafficker

narcotráfico nm drug trafficking

nariz nf nose → MY ▸ **cerrar la puerta en las narices a algn** shut the door in sb's face **en las propias narices de** under sb's nose **hasta las narices (de)** fed up (with sth/sb) **meter las narices** poke/stick your nose into sth

narrador/a nm-nf narrator

narrar vt tell

nata nf (de leche hervida) skin ▸ **la crema/flor y ~** the crème de la crème

natación nf swimming

natal adj native: *país ~* native country

natalidad nf birth rate

nativo/a adj, nm-nf native

nato adj born

natural adj natural: *¡Es ~!* It's only natural! **2** (fruta, flor) fresh **3** (espontáneo) unaffected: *un gesto ~* an unaffected gesture ▸ **ser ~ de...** come from...

naturaleza nf nature ▸ **~ muerta** still life por **~ by nature**

naturalidad nf: *con la mayor ~ del mundo* as if it were the most natural thing in the world ▸ **con ~** naturally

naturalmente adv of course

naufragar vi be wrecked

naufragio nm shipwreck

náufrago/a nm-nf castaway

náusea nf ▸ **dar ~s** make sb feel nauseous, make sb feel sick (GB) **sentir/tener ~s** feel nauseous, feel sick (GB)

náutico adj sailing: *club ~* sailing club

navaja nf **1** (pequeña) penknife [pl -knives] **2** (arma) knife [pl knives]: *Me sacaron una ~.* They pulled a knife on me.

navajazo nm knife wound ▸ **dar un ~** stab

nave nf **1** (Náut) ship **2** (iglesia) nave ▸ **~ espacial** spaceship

navegación nf navigation

navegador nm (Comp) browser

navegar vi **1** (barcos) sail **2** (Comp) surf: **~ en/por internet** surf the Net

navidad nf Christmas: *¡Feliz Navidad!* Merry Christmas!
NOTA En EE.UU. y Gran Bretaña apenas se celebra la Nochebuena o **Christmas Eve**. Es más importante el 25 de diciembre (**Christmas Day**), cuando se abren los regalos que trae **Santa Claus** o **Father Christmas** (GB).

navideño adj Christmas

neblina nf mist

necesario adj necessary
NOTA "Es necesario" suele traducirse por **have to**: *No es ~ que vengas.* You don't have to come.

neceser nm sponge bag

necesidad nf **1** (cosa imprescindible) necessity [pl -ies]: *Comer es una ~.* Food is a necessity. **2 ~ (de)** need (for sth/to do sth): *No veo la ~ de ir en avión.* I don't see the need to fly. ◊ *No hay ~ de...* There's no need to... ▸ **pasar ~** suffer hardship

necesitado/a adj, nm-nf (pobre) poor: *ayudar a los ~s* help the poor

necesitar vt need

necio adj **1** (tonto) dumb, stupid (GB) **2** (travieso) naughty

nectarina nf nectarine

negado adj useless: *Soy ~ para las matemáticas.* I'm useless at math.

negar vt **1** (hecho) deny: *Negó haberlo robado.* He denied stealing it. **2** (permiso, ayuda) refuse: **~ a algn la entrada a un país** refuse sb entry into a country ● **negarse** vp refuse to do sth: *Se negó a pagar.* He refused to pay.

negativa nf refusal

negativo *adj, nm* negative

negociación *nf* negotiation

negociante *nmf* businessman/ woman [pl -men/-women]

negociar *vt, vi* negotiate

negocio *nm* 1 (*comercio, asunto*) business: *hacer* ~s do business ◊ *Estoy aquí de* ~s. I'm here on business. ◊ *un hombre/una mujer de* ~s a businessman/ -woman 2 (*irónicamente*) bargain: *¡Qué* ~ *que hemos hecho!* Some bargain we got there!

negro *adj, nm* black

neón *nm* neon

Neptuno *nm* Neptune

nervio *nm* 1 nerve: *un ataque de* ~s a nervous breakdown 2 (*carne*) gristle ▶ **poner los** ~**s de punta** set sb's nerves on edge

nerviosismo *nm* nervousness

nervioso *adj* 1 (*síntoma, tensión*) nervous (*b*) (*célula, fibra*) nerve: *células nerviosas* nerve cells 2 (*agitado, intranquilo*) nervous, tense 3 (*fácilmente excitable*) high strung, highly strung (GB) ▶ **poner** ~ **a algn** get on sb's nerves **ponerse** ~ get worked up

neto *adj* net: *ingresos* ~s net income

neumático *nm* inner tube

neumonía *nf* pneumonia [U]: *pescar una* ~ catch pneumonia

neurótico/a *adj, nm-nf* neurotic

neutral *adj* neutral

neutro *adj* 1 neutral 2 (*Biol, Gram*) neuter ● *nm* (*Aut*) neutral

neutrón *nm* neutron

nevada *nf* snowfall

nevado *adj* (*cubierto de nieve*) snow-covered ● *nm* (*montaña*) snow-capped mountain

nevar *vi* snow

nevera *nf* refrigerator

ni *conj* 1 (*doble negación*) neither... nor...: *Ni tú ni yo hablamos inglés.* Neither you nor I speak English. ◊ *No dijo ni que sí ni que no.* He didn't say either yes or no. 2 (*ni siquiera*) not even: *Ni él mismo sabe lo que gana.* Not even he knows how much he earns. ▶ **ni aunque** even if: *ni aunque me dieran dinero* not even if they paid me **ni nada** or anything *¡Ni que fuera...!* anyone would think...: *¡Ni que yo fuera millonario!* Anyone would think I was a millionaire! **ni una palabra, un día, etc. más** not another word, day, etc. more **ni uno** not a single (one): *No me queda ni un peso.* I don't have a single peso

left. **ni yo** (*tampoco*) neither am I, do I, have I, etc.: —*Yo no voy a la fiesta.* —*Ni yo tampoco.* "I'm not going to the party." "Neither am I."

Nicaragua *nf* Nicaragua

nicaragüense *adj, nmf* Nicaraguan

nicotina *nf* nicotine

nido *nm* nest: *hacer un* ~ build a nest

niebla *nf* fog: *Hay* ~. It's foggy.

nieto/a *nm-nf* 1 grandson [*fem* granddaughter] 2 **nietos** grandchildren

nieve *nf* snow

ninguno/a *adj* no, any: *No es ningún imbécil.* He's no fool. **NOTA** Se usa **no** en afirmaciones: *Aún no ha llegado ningún alumno.* No students have arrived yet., y **any** en negaciones: *No le dio ninguna importancia.* He didn't pay any attention to it. ● *pron* 1 (*entre dos personas/ cosas*) neither, either **NOTA** Se usa **neither** en afirmaciones: —*¿Cuál de los dos prefieres?* —*Ninguno.* "Which one do you prefer?" "Neither (of them).", y **either** en negaciones: *No hablé con* ~ *de los dos.* I didn't talk to either of them. 2 (*entre más de dos personas/cosas*) none: *Había tres, pero no queda* ~. There were three, but there are none left. ▶ **de ninguna manera/de ningún modo** no way: *No quiso irse de ninguna manera.* He absolutely refused to go. **en ningún lugar/sitio/en ninguna parte** nowhere, anywhere **NOTA** Se usa **nowhere** en afirmaciones: *Al fin no iremos a ningún sitio.* We'll go nowhere in the end., y **anywhere** en negaciones: *No lo encuentro en ninguna parte.* I can't find it anywhere. **en ningún momento** to never: *En ningún momento pensé que lo harían.* I never thought they would do it.

niñez *nf* childhood

niño/a *nm-nf* 1 level: - *del mar* sea level ◊ *a todos los* ~*es* in every respect 2 (*calidad, preparación*) standard: *un excelente* ~ *de juego* an excellent standard of play ▶ ~ **de vida** standard of living

niño/a *nm-nf* 1 (*sin distinción de sexo*) (*a*) child [*pl* children] (*b*) (*recién nacido*) baby [*pl* -ies] 2 (*masc*) boy 3 (*fem*) girl ▶ **la niña de los ojos de algn** the apple of sb's eye ~ **bien/popis** rich kid

nitrógeno *nm* nitrogen

nivel *nm* 1 level: - *del mar* sea level ◊ *a todos los* ~*es* in every respect 2 (*calidad, preparación*) standard: *un excelente* ~ *de juego* an excellent standard of play ▶ ~ **de vida** standard of living

nivelar vt 1 (*superficie, etc.*) level 2 (*desigualdades*) even sth out

no adv 1 (*respuesta*) no: *He dicho que no.* I said no. ◊ *dije que no.* Said no. 2 (*con verbos, adverbios, frases*) not: *No lo sé.* I don't know. ◊ *No lo sé.* I don't know. ◊ *Por supuesto que no.* Of course not. ◊ *Que yo sepa, no.* Not as far as I know. 3 (*doble negación*): *No sale nunca.* He never goes out. ◊ *No sé nada de deporte.* I know nothing about sport. 4 (*palabras compuestas*) non-: *no fumador* non-smoker ◊ *fuentes no oficiales* unofficial sources ● **no** nm [pl noes]: *un no categórico* a categorical no ▶ **¿a que no...?** 1 (*confirmando*): *¿A que no vino?* He didn't come, did he? 2 (*desafío*) I bet...: *un no ganas?* I bet you don't win. **¿no?** *Hoy es lunes ¿no?* Today is Monday, isn't it? ◊ *Lo compraste, ¿no?* You did buy it, didn't you? **NOTA** Para otras expresiones con **no**, ver el verbo, sustantivo, etc., p.ej. **no pegar el ojo** en ojo.

noble adj 1 noble 2 (*madera, material*) fine ● nmf nobleman/woman [pl -men/-women]

nobleza nf nobility

noche nf night, evening: *el lunes en la ~* on Monday evening/night ◊ *las diez de la ~* ten o'clock at night **NOTA** Night tiene un uso más general y suele referirse al período en que la gente está dormida. Evening se refiere al período entre las seis y las diez aproximadamente. ▶ **dar las buenas ~s** (*despedida*) say good night 2 (*saludo*) say good evening **de la ~ a la mañana** overnight **de ~ 1** (*trabajar, estudiar*) at night 2 (*vestido*) evening **esta ~** tonight **hacerse de ~** get dark **¡que pase buena ~!** good night!

Nochebuena nf Christmas Eve → NAVIDAD

Nochevieja nf New Year's Eve

noción nf notion ▶ **tener nociones de** have a basic grasp of sth

nocivo adj harmful (*to sth/sb*)

nocturno adj 1 night 2 (*clases, etc.*) evening: *función nocturna* evening performance

nogal nm walnut (tree)

nómada adj nomadic ● nmf nomad

nombrar vt 1 (*citar*) mention sb's name 2 (*para cargo*) appoint

nombre nm 1 (a) name (b) (*en formularios*) first name → MIDDLE NAME 2 (*Gram*) noun ▶ **en ~ de** on behalf of sb **de pila** given name **~ propio** proper

noun nombre(s) y apellidos full name

nómina nf (*sueldo*) payroll

nominar vt nominate sth/sb

nones nm odd numbers

nono adj odd: *Tengo la media nona.* This is an odd sock.

nopal nm prickly pear

noreste (*tb* nordeste) nm 1 (*punto cardinal, región*) north-east (*abrev* NE) 2 (*viento, dirección*) north-easterly

norma nf rule ▶ **tener por ~** always/never do sth: *Tengo por ~ no comer entre horas.* I never eat between meals.

normal adj 1 (*común*) normal: *Es lo ~.* That's the normal thing. 2 (*corriente*) ordinary: *un empleo ~* an ordinary job 3 (*estándar*) standard: *el procedimiento ~* the standard procedure

normalizar vt (*situación*) restore sth to normal ● **normalizarse** vp return to normal

noroccidental adj north-western: *la zona ~ de la ciudad* the north-west of the city

noroeste (*tb* noroccidente) nm 1 (*punto cardinal, región*) north-west (*abrev* NW) 2 (*dirección, viento*) north-westerly

nororiental adj north-eastern: *la zona ~ de la ciudad* the north-east of the city

nororiente nm north-east (*abrev* NE)

norte nm north: *en la costa ~* on the north coast

Noruega nf Norway

noruego/a adj, nm-nf, nm Norwegian

nos pron pers 1 (*complemento*) us: *~ vieron.* They saw us. ◊ *~ mintió.* He lied to us. 2 (*partes del cuerpo, efectos personales*): *~ quitamos el abrigo.* We took our coats off. 3 (*reflexivo*): *~ divertimos.* We enjoyed ourselves. ◊ *~ acabamos de bañar.* We've just taken a shower. ◊ *¡Vámonos!* Let's go! 4 (*recíproco*) each other, one another: *~ queremos.* We love each other. → EACH OTHER

nosotros/as pron pers 1 (*sujeto*) we 2 (*complemento, en comparaciones*) us: *¿Vienes con ~?* Are you coming with us? ▶ **de ~** ours: *un amigo de ~* a friend of ours **entre ~** (*confidencialmente*) between ourselves **somos ~** it's us

nostalgia nf 1 (*del pasado*) nostalgia 2 (*del hogar, país, etc.*) homesickness: *Cada vez que* *estoy fuera, me entra una* ~ *terrible*. Whenever I'm away I feel really homesick. ▶ *sentir/tener* ~ miss *sth/sb*

nota *nf* **1** note **2** (*Educ*) grade, mark (GB): *sacar buenas* ~*s get good grades* ▶ **las** ~**s** (*Educ*) report (card) [*sing*]: *Hoy me dan las* ~*s. I get my report card today.* **tomar** ~ note (*of sth*)

notable *adj* noteworthy

notar *vt* **1** (*advertir*) notice **2** (*encontrar*) find: *No noto muy triste.* He seems very sad. ● **notarse** *vp* **1** (*sentirse*) feel: *Se nota la tensión.* You can feel the tension. **2** (*verse*) show: *No se le notan los años.* He doesn't look his age. ▶ **se nota...** you can tell...: *Se notaba que estaba nerviosa.* You could tell she was nervous.

notario/a *nm-nf* notary public, solicitor (GB) → ABOGADO/A

noticia *nf* **1** news [*U*]: *una mala* ~ *some bad news* ◊ *Las* ~*s son alarmantes.* The news is alarming. → CONSEJO **2** (*Period, TV*) news item ▶ **las** ~**s** the news [*sing*]: *las* ~*s de las dos* the two o'clock news **tener** ~**s** hear from *sb*: *¿Tienes* ~ *de ella?* Have you heard from her?

noticiero (*tb* **noticiario**) *nm* news [*sing*]: *¿A qué hora es el* ~? What time is the news on?

notificar *vt* notify *sb of sth*

novato/a *adj* inexperienced ● *nm-nf* **1** beginner **2** (*universidad*) freshman **3** (*Mil*) new recruit

novecientos/as *adj, nm, pron* nine hundred

novedad *nf* **1** novelty [*pl* -ies]: *la gran* ~ *de la temporada* the latest thing **2** (*cambio*) change **3** (*noticia*) news [*U*]

novela *nf* novel ▶ ~ **rosa/policiaca** romance/detective novel

novelista *nmf* novelist

noveno/a *adj, nm-nf, pron* ninth

noventa *adj, nm, pron* **1** ninety **2** (*nonagésimo*) ninetieth

noviembre *nm* November (*abrev* Nov.) → MAYO

novillo/a *nm-nf* bullock [*fem* heifer]

novio/a *nm-nf* boyfriend [*fem* girlfriend]: *¿Tienes novia?* Do you have a girlfriend? **2** (*prometido*) fiancé [*fem* fiancée] **3** (*en boda, recién casado*) groom [*fem* bride] → MATRIMONIO ▶ **los** ~**s 1** (*en boda*) the bride and groom **2** (*recién casados*) the newly-weds **ser** ~**s**: *Hace un año que somos* ~*s.* We've been going out together for a year.

nube *nf* cloud ▶ **estar en las** ~**s** have your head in the clouds

nublado *adj* cloudy

nublarse *vp* **1** (*cielo*) cloud over **2** (*vista*) be blurred

nubosidad *nf* ▶ ~ **variable** patchy cloud

nuca *nf* nape (of the neck)

nuclear *adj* nuclear

núcleo *nm* nucleus [*pl* -lei]

nudillo *nm* knuckle

nudo *nm* knot: *hacer/deshacer un* ~ *tie/undo a knot* ▶ **tener un** ~ **en la garganta** have a lump in your throat

nuera *nf* daughter-in-law [*pl* -ers-in-law]

nuestro/a *adj* ● *pron* ours: *Su carro es mejor que el* ~. Your car is better than ours. ◊ *un amigo* ~ a friend of ours

nueve *adj, nm, pron* **1** nine **2** (*fecha*) ninth

nuevo *adj* **1** new **2** (*adicional*) further: *Se han presentado* ~*s problemas.* Further problems have arisen. ▶ **de** ~ again

nuez *nf* **1** pecan **2** *nueces* nuts ▶ ~ **de Castilla** walnut ~ **moscada** nutmeg

nulo *adj* **1** (*inválido*) invalid **2** (*inexistente*) non-existent **3** ~ **en/para** hopeless at *sth*

numeración *nf* numbers [*pl*] ▶ ~ **arábica/romana** Arabic/Roman numerals [*pl*]

numeral *nm* numeral

numerar *vt* number ● **numerarse** *vp* number off

número *nm* **1** number: *el de teléfono* telephone number **2** (*talla*) size: *¿Qué* ~ *de zapatos usas?* What size shoe do you wear? **3** (*publicación*) issue **4** (*Teat*) act: *un* ~ *circense* a circus act ▶ **en** ~**s rojos** in the red ~ **de placa** license (plate) number ~ **par/impar/primo** even/odd/prime number ~**s arábicos/romanos** Arabic/Roman numerals

numeroso *adj* **1** (*grande*) large: *una familia numerosa* a large family **2** (*muchos*) numerous: *en numerosas ocasiones* on numerous occasions

nunca *adv* never, ever **NOTA** Se usa **never** en afirmaciones: ~ *he estado en Roma.* I've never been to Rome. y **ever** en negaciones o con palabras como **nobody**, **nothing**, etc.: ~ *pasa nada.* Nothing ever happens. ▶ **casi** ~ hardly ever: *No nos vemos casi* ~. We hardly ever see each other. **como** ~ better than ever **más que** ~ more than ever: *Hace más* *calor que* ~. It's hotter than ever. **~ jamás** never ever **~ más** never again

nupcial *adj* wedding
nutria *nf* otter
nutrición *nf* nutrition
nutritivo *adj* nutritious

Ñ ñ

ñame *nm* yam
ñapa *nf*: *Me las dio de* ~. He gave them to me for free.
ñato *adj* snub-nosed
ñoño/a *adj*, *nm-nf* **1** (*remilgado*) affected: *Es un* ~. He's so affected. **2** (*puritano*) prim

O o

o *conj* or ▶ **o... o...** (either...) or...: *O es rusa o es polaca.* She's either Russian or Polish. ◇ *O lo comes o no sales.* Eat it or you're not going out.
oasis *nm* oasis [*pl* oases]
obedecer *vt*, *vi* obey: *¡Obedece!* Do as you're told!
obediente *adj* obedient
obispo *nm* bishop
obituario *nm* obituary [*pl* -ies]
objetar *vt* object
objetivo *nm* **1** (*finalidad*) objective **2** (*Mil*) target **3** (*Fot*) lens ● *adj* objective
objeto *nm* **1** (*cosa*, *Gram*) object **2** (*propósito*) purpose ▶ **~s perdidos** lost and found, lost property [*sing*] (*GB*)
objetor/a *nm-nf* ▶ **~ (de conciencia)** conscientious objector
oblicuo *adj* oblique
obligación *nf* obligation ▶ **tener (la) ~ de** be obliged to do sth
obligado *adj* obliged
obligar *vt* force sb to do sth
obligatorio *adj* compulsory
oboe *nm* oboe
obra *nf* **1** work: ~ *de arte* work of art ◇ *la* ~ *completa de Borges* the complete works of Borges **2** (*acción*) deed: *realizar buenas* ~*s* do good deeds **3** (*lugar en construcción*) site **4 obras** (*carretera*) road construction [*sing*], road-

works (*GB*) ▶ **~ maestra** masterpiece **~ (teatral/de teatro)** play
obrero/a *adj* **1** (*familia*, *barrio*) working-class **2** (*sindicato*) labor: *el movimiento* ~ the labor movement ● *nm-nf* worker
obsceno *adj* obscene
observación *nf* observation: *en* ~ under observation
observador/a *adj* observant ● *nm-nf* observer
observar *vt* **1** (*mirar*) watch, observe (*más fml*) **2** (*notar*) notice
observatorio *nm* observatory [*pl* -ies]
obsesión *nf* obsession ▶ **tener ~ por** be obsessed with sth/sb
obsesionar *vt* obsess ● **obsesionarse** *vp* become obsessed (*with* sth/sb)
obstaculizar *vt* block
obstáculo *nm* obstacle
obstante ▶ **no ~** nevertheless
obstruir *vt* **1** (*cañería*, *etc*.) block **2** (*dificultar*) obstruct
obtener *vt* get, obtain (*fml*)
obvio *adj* obvious
ocasión *nf* **1** (*vez*) occasion **2** (*oportunidad*) opportunity [*pl* -ies], chance (*más coloq*) (*to do* sth) ▶ **de ~**: *anuncios/avisos de* ~ classified ads ◇ *precios/libros de* ~ bargain prices/second-hand books
occidental *adj* western ● *nmf* westerner
occidente *nm* west
océano *nm* ocean →MAR
ochenta *adj*, *nm*, *pron* **1** eighty **2** (*octogésimo*) eightieth
ocho *adj*, *nm*, *pron* **1** eight **2** (*fecha*) eighth
ochocientos *adj*, *nm*, *pron* eight hundred
ocio *nm* leisure
ocioso *adj* idle
octavo/a *adj*, *nm-nf*, *pron* eighth ▶ **~s de final** round prior to quarter-finals
octubre *nm* October (*abrev* Oct.) →MAYO
oculista *nmf* eye specialist
ocultar(se) *vt*, *vp* hide (sth/sb) (*from* sth/sb)
ocupado *adj* **1** (*persona*) busy (*with* sth/sb; *doing* sth) **2** (*teléfono*) busy, engaged (*GB*) **3** (*baño*) occupied, engaged (*GB*) **4** (*asiento*, *taxi*) taken **5** (*país*) occupied
ocupar *vt* **1** (*espacio*, *tiempo*) take up sth **2** (*cargo*) hold **3** (*país*) occupy
ocurrencia *nf* idea: *¡Qué* ~! What a bright idea!

ocurrir vi happen ● **ocurrirse** vp occur to sb ▸ *Se me acaba de ~ que...* It has just occurred to me that... ◊ *¿Se te ocurre algo?* Can you think of anything?

odiar vt hate

odio nm hatred (*for/of sth/sb*)

odioso adj horrible

oeste nm west: *en la costa ~* on the west coast

ofender vt offend ● **ofenderse** vp take offense (*at sth*)

ofensa nf offense

ofensiva nf offensive

ofensivo adj offensive

oferta nf 1 (*Econ*) supply: *~ y demanda* supply and demand ▸ **de/en ~** on special offer **~s de empleo** job vacancies

oficial adj official: *no ~* unofficial ● nmf (*policía, Mil*) officer

oficina nf office ▸ **~ de correos/empleo** post/employment office

oficinista nmf office worker

oficio nm trade: *Es carpintero de ~.* He's a carpenter by trade.

ofrecer vt offer ● **ofrecerse** vp volunteer (*to do sth*)

oftalmólogo/a nm-nf ophthalmologist

ofuscar vt annoy ● **ofuscarse** vp get annoyed (*with sb*) (*about sth*)

oída ▸ **de ~s**: *Lo conozco de ~s.* I've heard of him.

oído nm 1 (*Anat*) ear: *Dímelo al ~.* Whisper it in my ear. **2** (*sentido*) hearing ▸ **de ~** by ear: *Toco el piano de ~.* I play the piano by ear. **tener buen ~** have a good ear

oír vt 1 hear →HEAR **2** (*escuchar*) listen (*to sth/sb*): *~ música* listen to music ▸ **¡oiga!** excuse me!

ojal nm buttonhole

ojalá interj 1 (*espero que*) I hope: *¡~ ganen!* I hope they win! *¡~ —Verás como pasas.—¡Ojalá!* "I'm sure it'll pass.""I hope so." **2** (*ya quisiera yo*) if only: *¡~ pudiera ir!* If only I could go!

ojeada nf glance ▸ **echar una ~** have a (quick) look (*at sth*)

ojeras nf bags: *¡Qué ~ tienes!* You have huge bags under your eyes.

ojo nm 1 eye: *mirarse a los ~s* look into each other's eyes →MY **2** (*cerradura*) keyhole ● interj (be) careful ▸ **andar con cien ~s** have eyes in the back of your head **a ~** roughly: *Lo calculé a ~.* I worked it out roughly. **con los ~s vendados** blindfold **echar un ~ a** (*cuidar*) keep an eye on *sth/sb* **no pegar (el) ~** not sleep a wink **no quitar los ~s de (encima)** not take your eyes off *sth/sb*

~ de agua (*Mx*) spring **~ de buey** (*ventana*) porthole **sacarse un ~** (*And*): *Casi me saco un ~ para entenderlo.* I'm going crazy trying to understand it. **tener ~** be careful

ola nf wave

olé interj bravo

oleaje nm swell

óleo nm oil: *pintura al ~* oil painting

oler vt, vi smell (*of sth*): *~ a pintura/quemado* smell of paint/burning →HEAR ▸ **~ fatal/a diablos/que apesta** stink **~ raro** smell fishy **~se algo/olérsela** smell a rat

olfatear vt 1 (*oler*) sniff **2** (*seguir el rastro*) scent

olfato nm (*sentido*) smell ▸ **tener ~** (*fig*) have a nose *for sth*

olimpiada (*tb* **olimpíada**) nf Olympics [*pl*]

olímpico adj Olympic

oliva nf olive

olivo nm olive (tree)

olla nf pot ▸ **~ exprés/a presión** pressure cooker

olmo nm elm

olor nm smell (*of sth*)

oloroso adj sweet-smelling

olvidadizo adj forgetful

olvidado adj forgotten ▸ **dejar ~** leave *sth* (*behind*)

olvidar(se) vt, vp 1 (*no recordar*) forget **2** (*dejar*) leave *sth* (*behind*)

ombligo nm navel

omitir vt leave *sth* out, omit (*fml*)

once adj, nm, pron 1 eleven **2** (*fecha*) eleventh ● nm (*And*) snack: *tomar ~s* have a bite to eat

onceavo adj, nm eleventh

onda nf wave: *~ expansiva* shock wave ▸ **agarrar la ~** get it **buena/mala ~** cool/uncool **en la ~** up to date, hip (*coloq*) *¿qué ~?* how's it going? **tirar la ~** flirt *with sb*

ondear vt wave ● vi (*bandera*) fly

ondulado adj 1 (*pelo*) wavy **2** (*superficie*) undulating **3** (*cartón, etc.*) corrugated

ONG nf NGO [*pl ~s*], charity [*pl -ies*] **NOTA** El término *NGO* se utiliza sobre todo en un contexto político. Para las organizaciones como UNICEF, Greenpeace, etc. se suele usar **charity**.

ONU nf UN

opa interj careful

opaco adj opaque

opción nf option: *No tiene otra ~.* He has no option.

opcional adj optional

ópera nf opera

operación nf **1** operation: *una ~ cardíaca/policial* a heart/police operation **2** (*Fin*) transaction ▸ *~ tortuga* (*And*) slowdown, go-slow (*GB*)

operador/a nm-nf operator

operar vt, vi operate (*on sb*): *Me operaron del corazón.* I had a heart operation. ● **operarse** vp have an operation

opinar vt think

opinión nf opinion ▸ *tener buena/mala ~ de* have a high/low opinion of *sth/sb*

oponente nmf opponent

oponer vt offer ● **oponerse** vp **1** (*oponer ~*) *~ a una idea* oppose an idea **2** (*poner reparos*) object: *Iré si mis padres no se oponen.* I'll go if my parents don't object.

oportunidad nf **1** (*ocasión*) opportunity [*pl* -ies], chance (*más colog*) (*to do sth*) **2** (*ganga*) bargain

oportuno adj **1** (*en buen momento*) timely **2** (*adecuado*) appropriate

oposición nf opposition

opresión nf oppression

opresivo adj oppressive

oprimir vt **1** oppress **2** (*apretar*) be too tight

optar vi **1** opt for *sth/to do sth* **2** (*solicitar*) apply for *sth*: *~ a una plaza en el gobierno* apply for a job with the government

optativo adj optional

óptico adj **1** optical **2** (*nervio*) optic ● nm-nf optometrist, optician (*GB*) ● **óptica** nf (*negocio*) optical establishment, optician's (*GB*)

optimismo nm optimism

optimista adj optimistic ● nmf optimist

optómetra nmf optometrist

opuesto adj **1** (*lado, dirección*) opposite: *Intentó calmarla, pero tuvo el efecto ~.* He tried to calm her down, but it had the opposite effect. ◇ *en sentidos ~s* in opposite directions ◇ *(dispar)* different: *Mis dos hermanos son totalmente ~s.* My two brothers are totally different.

oración nf **1** (*Rel*) prayer: *rezar una ~* say a prayer **2** (*Gram*) (a) sentence (b) (*proposición*) clause: *~ subordinada* subordinate clause

oral adj oral

orar vi pray

órbita nf orbit

orden nm **1** order: *en/por ~ alfabético* in alphabetical order **2** (*tipo*) nature: *problemas de ~ jurídico* problems of a legal nature ● nf **1** order: *por ~ del juez* by order of the court ◇ *la ~ franciscana* the Franciscan Order **2** (*Jur*) warrant: *~ de cateo/registro* search warrant ▸ **a sus órdenes/a la ~** can I help you? ~ **del día** agenda

ordenado adj tidy

ordenar vt **1** (*habitación*) tidy *sth* (up) **2** (*apuntes, etc.*) put *sth* in order **3** (*mandar*) order *sb* to do *sth*: *Me ordenó que me sentara.* He ordered me to sit down. →ORDER

ordeñar vt milk

ordinario adj **1** (*habitual*) ordinary **2** (*vulgar*) common

orégano nm oregano

oreja nf ear →MY

orfanato (*tb* orfanatorio) nm orphanage

orgánico adj organic

organismo nm **1** (*Biol*) organism **2** (*organización*) organization

organización nf organization

organizador/a nm-nf organizer ● adj organizing

organizar vt organize ● **organizarse** vp (*persona*) get yourself organized

órgano nm (*Anat, Mús*) organ

orgullo nm pride

orgulloso adj proud

orientado adj ▸ **estar ~** (*edificio, etc.*) face: *Está ~ hacia el sur.* It faces south.

oriental adj eastern ● nmf person from the Far East

orientar vt **1** (*colocar*) position **2** (*dirigir*) direct ● **orientarse** vp (*encontrar el camino*) find your way around

oriente nm east ▸ **Extremo/Lejano ~** Far East **~ Medio** Middle East

origen nm origin ▸ **dar ~** give rise to *sth*

original adj, nm original

originar vt lead to *sth* ● **originarse** vp start

orilla nf **1** (*borde*) edge **2** (*río*) bank: *a ~s del Nilo* on the banks of the Nile **3** (*lago, mar*) shore

orillarse vp pull over

orina nf urine

orinar vi urinate ● **orinarse** vp wet yourself

oro nm **1** gold **2** **oros** (*cartas*) →BARAJA

orozuz nm licorice

orquesta nf 1 (música clásica) orchestra 2 (música popular) band

ortografía nf spelling

orzuelo nm stye

oscilar vi 1 (moverse) swing 2 (cifras) vary (between sth and sth)

oscurecer vt darken • **oscurecer(se)** vi, vp get dark

oscuridad nf 1 darkness 2 (fig) obscurity

oscuro adj 1 dark: azul ~ dark blue 2 (desconocido) obscure ► a **oscuras** in the dark

oso/a nm-nf bear ► hacer el ~ make a fool of yourself ~ **polar/de peluche** polar/teddy bear ~ **hormiguero** anteater

ostra nf (ostión Mx, nm) oyster

otoño nm fall, autumn (GB)

otorgar vt award

otro adj another, other NOTA Another se usa con sustantivos en singular y other con sustantivos en plural: en otra ocasión on another occasion ◊ ¿Hay ~s colores? Are there any other colors? Other también se usa en expresiones como: la otra noche the other night ◊ mi ~ hermano my other brother. Cuando "otros" va seguido de un número y un sustantivo plural, se traduce por more: Me quedan ~s dos exámenes. I have two more exams to take. • pron another (one) [pl others]: un día u ~ one day or another ◊ ¿Tienen ~? Do you have another (one)? ◊ ¿Tienen ~s? Do you have any others? NOTA "El otro, la otra" se traducen por the other one: ¿Dónde está el ~? Where's the other one? ► en ~ **lugar/sitio/en otra parte** somewhere else **lo ~** 1 (la otra cosa) the other thing 2 (lo demás) the rest: Lo ~ no importa. The rest doesn't matter. **nada del ~ jueves/mundo** nothing special **otra cosa** something else NOTA En una negación, se usa nothing else o anything else (si hay otra partícula negativa en la frase): No hay otra cosa. There's nothing else./There isn't anything else. **~(s) tanto(s)** as much/as many again: Me pagó 100 euros y me debe ~ tanto. He paid me 100 euros and owes me as much again. **por ~ lado/otra parte** on the other hand

oval adj (tb ovalado) adj oval

ovario nm ovary [pl -ies]

oveja nf sheep [pl sheep] →CARNE ► ~ **negra** black sheep

overol (tb overoles) nm 1 (de trabajo) coveralls [pl], overalls [pl] (GB) 2 (de tirantes) overalls [pl], dungarees [pl] (GB) →PANTALÓN

ovillo nm (lana) ball ► hacerse un ~ curl up

ovni nm UFO [pl -s]

oxidado adj rusty

oxidar(se) vt, vp rust

oxígeno nm oxygen

oyente nmf 1 (Radio) listener 2 (Educ) unregistered student

ozono nm ozone

P p

pabellón nm 1 (exposición) pavilion 2 (hospital) block 3 (Dep) sports hall

pacer vi graze

pachanga nf party [pl -ies] ► **irse de** ~ go out partying

paciencia nf patience: Hay que tener ~. You must be patient. • interj be patient

paciente adj, nmf patient

pacificar vt pacify • **pacificarse** vp calm down

pacífico adj 1 peaceful 2 (océano) Pacific • **el Pacífico** nm the Pacific (Ocean)

pacifista nmf pacifist

pactar vt agree on sth • vi make an agreement (with sb) (to do sth)

pacto nm agreement

padecer vi suffer (from sth) ► ~ **del corazón, riñón, etc.** have heart, kidney, etc. trouble

padrastro nm 1 (familiar) stepfather 2 (en dedo) hangnail

padre nm 1 father: Es ~ de dos hijos. He is the father of two children. ◊ el ~ García Father García 2 padres parents ► ¡qué ~! (Mx) that's really cool!

padrenuestro nm Our Father

padrino nm 1 (bautizo) godfather 2 (boda) man who accompanies the bride →MATRIMONIO 3 padrinos godparents

padrón nm: ~ **electoral** electoral register

paga nf (sueldo) pay

pagano/a adj, nmf pagan

pagar vt, vi pay: ~ los impuestos pay your taxes ◊ Mi tío me paga los estudios. My uncle is paying for my education. ◊ ~ con cheque/tarjeta pay by check/credit card ▶ **¡me las vas a ~!** you'll pay for this! ~ **el pato** carry the can ~ **el servicio (militar)** do your military service

página *nf* page: *en la ~ tres* on page three ◊ ~s **amarillas** yellow pages

pago *nm* payment: *hacer un ~* make a payment ▶ ~ **contra/a la entrega** cash on delivery

país *nm* country [*pl* -íes]

paisaje *nm* landscape →SCENERY

paisano/a *nm-nf* 1 (*del mismo país*) fellow countryman/woman [*pl* -men/-women] 2 (*de la misma región, ciudad*): *ser ~ (de algn)* be from the same place (as sb) ▶ **de ~** 1 (*militar*) in civilian dress 2 (*policía*) in plain clothes

paja *nf* 1 straw 2 (*en texto/discurso*) waffle ▶ **hablar/echar ~** 1 (*decir mentiras*) tell lies 2 (*charlar*) chat

pajar *nm* hay loft

pájaro *nm* bird ▶ **más vale ~ en mano...** a bird in the hand is worth two in the bush **matar dos ~s de un tiro** kill two birds with one stone

paje *nm* page

pala *nf* 1 shovel 2 (*playa*) spade

palabra *nf* word: *una ~ de tres letras* a three-letter word ◊ *No dijo ni ~.* He didn't say a word. ◊ *Te doy mi ~.* I give you my word. ▶ **dejar con la ~ en la boca** cut sb short **dirigir la ~** speak to sb **no soltar ~** not say a word **¡~ (de honor)!** honest! **tener la última ~** have the last word

palabrota *nf* swear word: *decir ~s* swear

palacio *nm* palace

paladar *nm* palate

palanca *nf* 1 (*Mec*) lever 2 (*contactos*) connections [*pl*] ▶ ~ **de cambios** gear shift, gear lever (*GB*) **tener ~** be well connected: *Tiene ~ con el alcalde.* He's well in with the mayor.

palangana *nf* bowl

palanquear *vt, vi* pull strings (for sb): *Su amigo lo palanqueó para conseguir ese trabajo.* A friend pulled some strings to get him that job.

palco *nm* box

paleta *nf* 1 (*de albañil*) trowel 2 (*Arte*) palette 3 (*piruli*) lollipop ▶ **~ helada** Popsicle®, ice lolly [*pl* -ies] (*GB*)

paliacate *nm* (*Mx*) bandanna

palidecer *vi* go pale

pálido *adj* pale: *ponerse/quedar ~* go pale

palillo *nm* 1 (*dientes*) toothpick 2 **palillos** (a) (*tambor*) drumsticks (b) (*comida*) chopsticks ▶ **hecho un ~** as thin as a rake

palma *nf* 1 (*mano*) palm 2 (*tb* **palmera**) (*árbol*) palm (tree): *~ de coco* coconut palm ▶ **dar ~s** clap: *acompañar a algn dando ~s* clap in time to the music

palmada *nf* 1 (*gesto amistoso*) pat: *Me dio una ~ en la espalda.* He gave me a pat on the back. 2 (*de castigo*) smack ▶ **dar ~s** clap

palmo *nm*: *Es un ~ más alto que yo.* He's several inches taller than me. ▶ **dejar con un ~ de narices** snub *sb* **~ a ~** inch by inch

palo *nm* 1 stick 2 (*barco*) mast 3 (*cartas*) suit →BARAJA 4 (*golf*) (golf) club ▶ **a ~ seco** on its own **de ~** wooden: *cuchara/pata de ~* wooden spoon/leg **de tal ~, tal astilla** like father like son **ni a ~(s)** for love nor money: *Este niño no come ni a ~.* This child won't eat for love nor money.

paloma *nf* 1 pigeon: *una ~ mensajera* a carrier pigeon 2 (*blanca*) dove: *la ~ de la paz* the dove of peace ▶ **se me fue la ~** (*And*) it went right out of my head

palomar *nm* dovecote

palomita *nf* (*marca*) check, tick (*GB*) ▶ ~**s de maíz**) popcorn [*U*]

palpar(se) *vt, vi, vp* feel: *Se palpó los bolsillos.* He felt his pockets.

palpitar *vi* beat

palta *nf* avocado [*pl* -s]

palurdo *nm-nf* hick

palustre *nm* trowel

pan *nm* 1 (*sustancia*) bread [*U*]: *¿Quieres ~?* Do you want some bread? →BREAD 2 (*pieza grande*) loaf [*pl* loaves] 3 (*pieza pequeña*) roll 4 (*jabón*) bar ▶ (**llamar**) **al pan pan y al vino vino** call a spade a spade **~ dulce** pastry [*pl* -ies] **~ duro** stale bread **~ francés** baguette **~ integral** wholemeal bread **~ molido/rallado** breadcrumbs [*pl*] **~ tostado/de caja** sliced bread **~ tostado** toast [*U*] **ser ~ comido** be a piece of cake

pana *nf* corduroy

panadería *nf* bakery [*pl* -ies]

panadero/a *nm-nf* baker

panal *nm* honeycomb

Panamá *nm* Panama

panameño/a *adj, nm-nf* Panamanian

pancarta nf 1 (cartón) placard 2 (tela) banner

páncreas nm pancreas

panda nm panda

pandereta nf tambourine

pandilla nf gang

pando adj shallow

panel nm panel

panfleto nm pamphlet

pánico nm panic ▶ **dar ~**: Me dio ~. I was scared stiff. ◇ Le da ~ salir sola. She's scared stiff of going out alone. **entrarle a algn el ~** be panic-stricken **tener ~** be scared stiff of sth/sb

panorama nm 1 (vista) view 2 (perspectiva) prospect: un oscuro ~ a bleak prospect

panqué nm (Mx) pound cake, Madeira cake (GB)

pantalla nf 1 (Comp, TV) screen 2 (lámpara) lampshade 3 (fig) front: La empresa es sólo una ~. The company is just a front.

pantalón (tb **pantalones**) nm pants [pl], trousers [pl] (GB) **NOTA** Pants, trousers, pyjamas, shorts etc. son palabras plurales. Para referirnos a "un pantalón" o "un piyama", se usa some/a pair of pants/pajamas: Llevaba un ~ viejo. He was wearing an old pair of pants/trousers. ◇ dos piyamas two pairs of pajamas →PAIR ▶ **~ corto/de deporte** shorts [pl]

pantaloncillos nm underpants →PANTALÓN

pantaloneta nf shorts [pl] ▶ **~ de baño** swimming trunks [pl] →PANTALÓN

pantano nm 1 (embalse) reservoir 2 (terreno) swamp

pantera nf panther

pantimedia nf (Mx) pantyhose, tights [pl] (GB) →PANTALÓN

pants nm sweats [pl], tracksuit bottoms [pl] (GB) →PANTALÓN

pantufla nf slipper

panza nf 1 (estómago) belly [pl -ies] 2 (barriga) paunch: echar ~ get a paunch

pañal nm diaper, nappy [pl -ies] (GB): cambiar el ~ a un niño change a baby's diaper

paño nm 1 (tejido) woolen cloth: un vestido de ~ a woolen suit 2 (bayeta) cloth ▶ **en ~s menores** in your underwear ~ **de cocina** dish towel, tea towel (GB) **~s calientes/paños de agua tibia** half measures

pañuelo nm 1 (para sonarse) handkerchief [pl -s o -chieves] 2 (cuello) scarf [pl -s o scarves]

papa¹ nm pope

papa² nf 1 potato [pl -es] ▶ **ni ~** not a thing: No oigo ni ~. I can't hear a thing. **~s fritas** 1 (de bolsa) chips, crisps (GB) 2 (tb **~s a la francesa**) (French) fries, chips (GB) **ser buena ~** (And) be nice

papá nm 1 (padre) dad **NOTA** Los niños pequeños suelen decir **daddy.** 2 **papás** mom and dad, parents (más fml) ▶ **P~ Noel** Santa Claus

papagayo nm parrot

papalote nm (Mx) kite

papaya nf papaya

papel nm 1 (material) paper [U]: una hoja de ~ a sheet of paper 2 (recorte, cuartilla) piece of paper: anotar algo en un ~ note sth down on a piece of paper 3 (personaje, función) part: hacer el ~ de Otelo play the part of Othello ▶ **~ cuadriculado** graph paper ~ **(de) aluminio** foil ~ **de envolver/regalo** wrapping paper ~ **de seda/china/~ globo** tissue paper ~ **higiénico** toilet paper ~ **principal/secundario** (Cine, Teat) starring/supporting role ~ **tapiz/de colgadura** wallpaper

papeleo nm paperwork

papelera nf wastebasket

papelería nf office supply store, stationer's (GB)

papeleta nf 1 (electoral) ballot paper 2 (sorteo, rifa) raffle ticket

paperas nf mumps: tener ~ have (the) mumps

papilla nf (de bebé) baby food

paprika nf paprika

paquete nm 1 (comida, tabaco) pack, packet (GB): un ~ de cigarrillos a pack of cigarettes 2 (bulto) package, parcel (GB): mandar un ~ por correo mail a package 3 (Comp) package

par adj even: números ~es even numbers ● nm 1 (pareja) pair: un ~ de zapatos a pair of shoes 2 (algunos) couple: hace un ~ de meses a couple of months ago ▶ **a la ~ (a la vez)** at the same time **de ~ en ~** wide open

para prep 1 for: muy útil ~ la lluvia very useful for the rain ◇ demasiado fácil ~ mí too easy for me 2 **+ inf** to do sth: comer ~ vivir eat to live 3 **+ no + inf** so as not to do sth: Lo hice ~ no molestarte. I did it so as not to bother you. 4 (futuro) for: Lo necesito ~ el lunes. I need it for Monday. 5 (dirección): Voy ~ la casa. I'm going home. ◇ Van ~ allá. They're on their way. ▶ **~ eso**: ~ eso, me compro uno *nuevo.* I might as well buy a new one. ◇ *¿- eso me hiciste venir?* You got me here just for that? **~ que...** so (that)... **~ sí:** *hablar ~ sí* talk to yourself

parábola *nf* **1** (*Biblia*) parable **2** (*Geom*) parabola

parabólico *adj*: *antena parabólica* satellite dish

parabrisas *nm* windshield, windscreen (*GB*)

paracaídas *nm* parachute ▸ **lanzarse/tirarse en ~** parachute

paracaidista *nmf* parachutist

parachoques *nm* bumper

parada *nf* **1** stop: *hacer una ~ para almorzar* make a stop for lunch ◇ *~ de camión/autobús* bus stop **2** (*Dep*) save

paradero *nm* **1** (*de persona*) whereabouts **2** (*autobús*) bus stop **3** (*taxi*) taxi stand

parado *adj* **1** (*de pie*) standing up **2** (*paralizado*) at a standstill ▸ **salir bien/mal ~** come off well/badly

paraguas *nm* umbrella

Paraguay *nm* Paraguay

paraguayo/a *adj, nm-nf* Paraguayan

paragüero *nm* umbrella stand

paraíso *nm* paradise ▸ **~ terrenal** heaven on earth

paraje *nm* spot

paralelas *nf* parallel bars

paralelo *adj* parallel (*to sth*)

parálisis *nf* paralysis

paralítico *adj* paralyzed

paralizar *vt* **1** (*Med*) paralyze **2** (*parar*) bring *sth* to a standstill

paramilitar *adj, nmf* paramilitary [*pl* -ies]

páramo *nm* **1** (*tierras altas*) uplands [*pl*] **2** (*lugar desolado*) moor

parapente *nm* paragliding

parar *vt, vi* stop ▸ **pararse** *vp* **1** (*detenerse*) stop **2** (*ponerse de pie*) stand (up): *Me paré en la cola.* I stood in line. ▸ **ir a ~** end up no *me* be always on the go **sin ~** non-stop: *trabajar sin ~* work non-stop

pararrayos *nm* lightning rod, lightning conductor (*GB*)

parásito *nm* parasite

parcela *nf* (*terreno*) plot

parche *nm* patch

parchís *nm* Parcheesi®, ludo (*GB*)

parcial *adj* **1** (*incompleto*) partial: *una solución ~* a partial solution **2** (*partidista*) biased ● *nm* end of semester/year exam

pareado *adj* semi-detached ● *nm* semi-detached house, semi [*pl* -s] (*más coloq*) →CASA

parecer *vi* **1** (*dar la impresión*) seem: *Parece que fue ayer.* It seems like only yesterday. **2** (*tener aspecto*) (a) **+ adj** look: *~ joven* look young (b) **+ sustantivo** look like *sth/sb*: *Parece una actriz.* She looks like an actress. **3** (*opinar*) think: *Me pareció que tenía razón.* I thought he was right. ◇ *¿Qué te pareció mi primo?* What did you think of my cousin? ● **parecerse** *vp* **1** (*físicamente*) look alike, look like *sth/sb*: *Se parecen mucho.* They look very much alike. ◇ *Te pareces a tu mamá.* You look like your mom. **2** (*carácter*) be alike, be like *sb*: *Te pareces a tu papá en eso.* You're like your dad in that. ▸ **al ~/según parecer** apparently **parece mentira**: *¡Parece mentira!* I can hardly believe it! **parece que...** it looks like...: *Parece que va a llover.* It looks like rain.

parecido *adj* similar (*to sth/sb*): *Eres muy ~ a tu papá.* You're very like your father. ● *nm* similarity ▸ **algo ~** something like that

pared *nf* wall ▸ **las ~s oyen** walls have ears

pareja *nf* **1** (*relación amorosa*) couple: *Hacen muy buena ~.* They make a very nice couple. **2** (*animales, equipo*) pair: *la ~ vencedora del torneo* the winning pair **3** (*cónyuge, compañero*) partner: *Pedro y su ~* Pedro and his partner ◇ *No tengo ~ para jugar.* I don't have a partner to play with. ▸ **en ~s** two by two: *Entraron en ~s.* They went in two by two. **sacar ~** ask *sb* to dance

parejo *adj* **1** (*sin desniveles*) even **2** (*justo*) fair ● *nm* (*de baile*) partner ▸ **ir ~:** *Los ciclistas van muy ~s.* The two cyclists are neck and neck.

parentela *nf* relations [*pl*]

parentesco *nm* relationship ▸ **tener ~** be related to *sb*

paréntesis *nm* (*signo*) parenthesis [*pl* -theses], brackets [*pl*] (*GB*) ▸ **entre ~** in parentheses/brackets

pargo *nm* (*red*) snapper

pariente/a *nm-nf* relation

parir *vt, vi* give birth (*to sth/sb*)

parlamentario/a *adj* parliamentary ● *nm-nf* member of parliament

parlamento nm parliament

parlanchín/ina adj talkative ● nm-nf chatterbox

parlante nm speaker

paro nm (huelga) strike: estar en/de ~ be on strike ▸ ~ cívico community protest

parpadear vi 1 (ojos) blink 2 (luz) flicker

párpado nm eyelid

parque nm 1 park 2 (munición) ammunition ▸ ~ de diversiones funfair ~ eólico wind farm ~ infantil playground ~ temático theme park

parqueadero nm (And) 1 parking lot, car park (GB) 2 (espacio) parking space: No encuentro ~. I can't find a parking space.

parquear vt, vi park

parqueo nm parking

párrafo nm paragraph

parranda nf party

parrandear vi go out partying

parrilla nf 1 (Cocina) grill 2 (Aut) roof rack ▸ a la ~ grilled

párroco nm parish priest

parroquia nf 1 (iglesia) parish church 2 (comunidad) parish

parte¹ nf 1 part: tres ~s iguales three equal parts ◊ Vete a otra ~. Go somewhere else. 2 (persona) party [pl -ies]: la ~ contraria the opposing party ▸ de ~ de algn on behalf of sb ¿de ~ de quién? (por teléfono) who's calling? en/por todas ~s everywhere la ~ de abajo/arriba the bottom/top la ~ de atrás/delante the back/front la/una tercera, cuarta, quinta, etc. parte a third, a quarter, a fifth, etc. por mi ~ as far as I am, you are, etc. concerned por su ~ little by little por una ~... por la otra... on the one hand... on the other... tomar ~ en algo take part in sth

parte² nm 1 (informe) report: ~ médico medical report 2 (And, multa) fine: Me pusieron un ~ por exceso de velocidad. I got fined for speeding. ▸ dar ~ inform sb (of/about sth

partero/a nm-nf midwife [pl -wives]

participación nf 1 (intervención) participation: la ~ del público audience participation 2 (Fin) share

participante adj participating ● nmf participant

participar vi take part (in sth), participate (in sth) (más fml)

partícula nf particle

particular adj 1 characteristic 2 (privado) private: clases ~ es private classes

partida nf 1 (juego) game 2 (nacimiento, matrimonio, etc.) certificate

partidario/a adj in favor of sth ● nm-nf supporter

partido nm 1 (Pol) party [pl -ies] 2 (Dep) game, match (GB): un ~ de basquetbol a basketball game ▸ ~ de desempate play-off ~ de ida/vuelta first/second leg sacar ~ a/de algo make the most of sth

partir vt 1 (con cuchillo) cut sth (up): ~ el pastel cut up the cake 2 (con las manos) break sth (off) 3 (quebrar) crack 4 (marcharse) leave ● partirse vp 1 split: ~ la cabeza split your head open 2 (diente, alma) break ▸ a ~ de from... (on): a ~ de mañana starting from tomorrow

partitura nf score

parto nm birth: estar de ~ be in labor

pasa (tb uva ~) nf raisin

pasabordo nm boarding pass

pasada nf wipe ▸ de ~ in passing hacer/jugar una mala ~ play a dirty trick on sb

pasadizo nm passage

pasado/a adj 1 (día, semana, etc.) last: el año ~ last year 2 (Gram, época) past: siglos ~s past centuries 3 (comida) (a) (demasiado cocinada) overdone (b) (estropeada) bad ● nm past ▸ ~ de fecha (producto) past its expiration/expiry (GB) date ~ de moda unfashionable ~ mañana the day after tomorrow

pasador nm 1 (puerta) bolt 2 (pelo) bobby pin, hairgrip (GB)

pasaje nm 1 (boleto/tiquete) ticket 2 (calle) side street

pasajero/a nm-nf passenger

pasamontañas nm ski mask, balaclava (GB)

pasaporte nm passport

pasar vi 1 pass: Pasaron tres horas. Three hours passed. ◊ Ese autobús pasa por el museo. That bus goes past the museum. 2 (entrar) come in: ¿Puedo ~? May I come in? 3 (ir) go: Voy a ~ por el banco. I'll go to the bank. 4 (ocurrir) happen: A mí me pasó lo mismo. The same thing happened to me. ● vt 1 pass: ¿Me pasas ese libro? Can you pass me that book? ◊ ~ el tiempo/un examen pass the time/an exam 2 (período de tiempo) spend: Pasamos el día charlando. We spent the day chatting. **3** (*página*) turn *sth* over **4** (*Cine, TV*): *¿Qué van a ~ en la tele?* What's on TV? **5** (*película*) show **6** (*Teat*) put *sth* on ● **pasarse** *vp* **1** (*ir demasiado lejos*): *No te pases comiendo.* Don't eat too much. ◊ *¡Esta vez te pasaste!* You've gone too far this time! **2** (*comida*) (a) (*demasiado cocinada*) be overcooked (b) (*ponerse mala*) be bad **3** (*olvidarse*) forget (*about sth*) ● **¿Pasa algo?** is anything the matter? **pasarlo/la bien/mal** have a good/hard time **por algo/algn 1** (*aparentar*) pass for *sth/sb*: *~ por italiano* pass for an Italian **2** (*recoger*) pick *sth/sb* up: *Paso por ti a las dos.* I'll pick you up at two. **¿qué pasa?** (*¿hay problemas?*) what's the matter? **NOTA** Para otras expresiones, ver el sustantivo, adjetivo, etc., p.ej. *pasar el rato* en RATO.

pasatiempo *nm* **1** (*afición*) hobby [*pl* -ies] **2** **pasatiempos** (*en periódico*): *la página de ~s* the puzzle page

pascua *nf* **1** (*Semana Santa*) Easter **2** **pascuas** (*Navidad*) Christmas: *¡Felices Pascuas!* Merry Christmas!

pase *nm* **1** (*autorización*) pass: *~ de abordar* boarding pass **2** (*And, de conducción*) driver's license, driving licence (GB)

pasear *vt, vi* walk: *salir a ~* go out for a walk

paseo *nm* **1** (*a pie*) walk **2** (*en bicicleta, caballo*) ride ▶ **dar un ~** go for a walk/ride

pasillo *nm* **1** (*casa*) corridor **2** (*iglesia, avión, teatro*) aisle

pasión *nf* passion ▶ **tener ~ por** be crazy about *sth/sb*

pasito *adv* (*And*) quietly

pasivo/a *adj* passive ● **pasiva** *nf* (*Gram*) passive (voice)

pasmado/a *adj* amazed: *Me quedé ~ ante su insolencia.* I was amazed at their insolence. ● *nm-nf* halfwit

paso *nm* **1** step: *un ~ hacia la paz* a step toward peace ◊ *dar un ~ atrás* step back ◊ *~ a ~* step by step **2** (*acción de pasar*) passage: *el ~ del tiempo* the passage of time **3** (*camino*) way (*through*): *Por aquí no hay ~.* There's no way through. **4** (*de montaña*) pass **5** (*pasos*) footsteps: *Me pareció oír ~s.* I thought I heard footsteps. ▶ **abrir/dar/dejar ~** make way (*for sth/sb*) **a ~ de tortuga** at a snail's pace **de ~ 1** (*en el camino*) on the way: *Me queda de ~.* It's on my way. **2** (*al*

mismo tiempo): *Cuando vayas, de ~ pides una cita.* While you're there, make an appointment. **~ a nivel** railroad crossing, level crossing (GB) **~ de cebra** zebra crossing **~ peatonal/de peatones** crosswalk, pedestrian crossing (GB) **~ subterráneo/a desnivel** underpass **salir del ~** get by

pasta *nf* **1** (*masa, concentrado*) paste **2** (*fideos, macarrones, etc.*) pasta **3** (*de pan*) dough **4** (*de pay*) pastry **5** (*de libro*) cover ▶ **~ de dientes** toothpaste

pastar *vt, vi* graze

pastel *nm* **1** (*dulce*) cake: *~ de chocolate* chocolate cake **2** (*salado, de hojaldre*) pie: *~ de pollo/manzana* chicken/apple pie **3** (*Arte*) pastel

pastelería *nf* cake shop

pastilla *nf* **1** tablet: *~s contra el mareo* travel-sickness tablets (b) **la pastilla** (*anticonceptiva*) the pill **2** (*jabón*) bar ▶ **~ de chocolate 1** (*tableta*) candy bar **2** (*pedazo*) square

pasto *nm* **1** (*hierba*) grass **2** (*para animales*) pasture

pastor/a *nm-nf* shepherd ▶ **~ alemán** German shepherd

pata *nf* **1** leg: *la ~ de la mesa* the table leg **2** (*pie*) (a) (*de cuadrúpedo con uñas*) paw: *El perro se hizo daño en la ~.* The dog hurt its paw. (b) (*pezuña*) hoof [*pl* -s o -hooves]: *las ~s de un caballo* a horse's hooves ▶ **andar/saltar a la ~ coja** hop **en cuatro ~s** on all fours: *ponerse en cuatro ~s* get down on all fours **mala ~** bad luck **meter la ~** put your foot in it **~s arriba** in a mess **~s de gallo** crow's feet

patada *nf* **1** kick: *Le dio una ~ a la mesa.* She kicked the table. **2** (*en el suelo*) stamp ▶ **caer/sentar como una ~ (en el estómago)** be like a kick in the teeth **echar a ~s** kick *sb* out **ir de la ~** (*Mx*): *Me fue de la ~ en el examen.* I did badly in the test.

patalear *vi* **1** (*en el suelo*) stamp **2** (*en el aire*) kick

pataleta *nf* tantrum: *agarrarse/dar una ~* throw a tantrum

patán *adj* loutish ● *nm* lout

patatús *nm* ▶ **darle a algn un ~ 1** (*desmayarse*) faint **2** (*disgustarse*) have a fit

paté *nm* pâté

patear *vt* kick

patente *nf* patent

paternidad *nf* paternity

paterno (*tb* **paternal**) *adj* paternal

patilla nf 1 (pelo) sideburn 2 (And, fruta) watermelon

patín nm 1 (ruedas) roller skate 2 (cuchilla) ice skate ▸ ~ del diablo (Mx) scooter ~ en línea in-line skate

patinador/a nm-nf skater

patinaje nm skating: ~ sobre hielo/artístico ice/figure skating

patinar vi 1 (persona) skate 2 (vehículo) skid

patineta nf 1 (con manillar) scooter 2 (sin manillar) skateboard

patio nm 1 courtyard 2 (colegio) playground

patito/a (tb patico/a) nm-nf duckling

pato/a nm-nf duck **NOTA** Duck es el sustantivo genérico. El macho es drake. ▸ ir de ~ (And) ride pillion

patonearse vp tramp around

patria nf (native) country

patriota nmf patriot

patriotismo nm patriotism

patrocinador/a nm-nf sponsor

patrocinar vt sponsor

patrón/ona nm-nf 1 (jefe) boss 2 (Rel) patron saint ● nm (costura) pattern

patrulla nf patrol

patrullar vt, vi patrol

pausa nf pause ▸ hacer una ~ have a short break

pavimento nm pavement, surface (GB)

pavo/a nm-nf turkey ▸ ~ real peacock [fem peahen]

pay nm pie →PIE

payasada nf ▸ hacer ~s goof around, play the fool (GB)

payaso/a nm-nf clown ▸ hacer(se) el ~ clown around

paz nf peace: en tiempos(s) de ~ in peacetime ▸ dejar en ~ leave sth/sb alone hacer las paces make up (with sb)

pe nf ▸ de pe a pa from beginning to end

peaje nm toll

peatón nm pedestrian

peatonal adj pedestrian

peca nf freckle

pecado nm sin

pecador/a nm-nf sinner

pecar vi 1 sin 2 ~ de be too...: Pecas de confiado. You're too trusting.

pecera nf fish bowl

pecho nm 1 chest: gripa de ~ a chest cold 2 (mujer) (a) (busto) bust (b) (mama) breast 3 (natación) breastroke: nadar (de)

~ do (the) breaststroke ▸ dar ~ breastfeed tomar(se) algo a ~ 1 (en serio) take sth seriously 2 (ofenderse) take sth to heart

pechuga nf breast: ~ de pollo chicken breast

pedagogía nf education

pedagógico adj educational

pedal nm pedal

pedalear vi pedal

pedante adj pedantic ● nmf pedant

pedazo nm piece: un ~ de pastel/ponqué a piece of cake ▸ caerse a ~s fall apart hacerse ~s smash (to pieces)

pedestal nm pedestal

pediatra nmf pediatrician

pedido nm order: hacer un ~ place an order

pedir vt 1 ask (sb) for sth: ~ la cuenta ask for the check ◊ ~ ayuda a los vecinos ask the neighbors for help 2 (permiso, favor, cantidad) ask (sb) sth: Te quiero ~ un favor. I want to ask you a favor. 3 ~ a algn que haga algo ask sb to do sth: Me pidió que esperara. He asked me to wait. 4 (encargar) order: Pedí sopa. I ordered soup. ▸ ~ cita make an appointment ~ disculpas/perdón apologize ~ limosna beg ~ prestado borrow: Me pidió prestado el carro. He borrowed my car. te pido por Dios/por lo que más quieras que... I beg you to...

pedo nm (gases) fart ▸ tirarse/echarse un ~ fart

pedrada nf: Lo recibieron a ~s. They threw stones at him.

pega nf trick ▸ hacer ~s play tricks/jokes (on sb)

pegado adj ~ estar ~ a (muy cerca) be right next to sth ~ del teléfono on the phone

pegajoso adj 1 (tb pegachento) sticky 2 (molesto) clingy 3 (música) catchy

pegamento (tb pegante And) nm glue

pegar vt 1 (golpear) hit 2 (adherir) stick: ~ una etiqueta en un paquete stick a label on a package ◊ ~ una taza rota glue a broken cup together 3 (acercar) put sth against sth: Pegó la cama a la pared. He put his bed against the wall. 4 (contagiar) give: Me pegaste la gripa. You've given me your flu. ● vi 1 (ropa, colores) go (with sth): La chaqueta no pega con la falda. The jacket doesn't go with the skirt. 2 (sol, bebida) be strong ● pegarse vp

1 (*pelearse*) fight **2** (*adherirse, comida*) stick **3** (*enfermedad*) be catching **4** (*golpearse*) knock: *Me pegué con la silla.* I knocked myself on the chair. ◇ ~ *en la cabeza* knock your head **5** (*acento*): *Se me pegó el acento cubano.* I picked up a Cuban accent. ▶ **dale que te pego** like mad **NOTA** Para otras expresiones, ver el sustantivo, p.ej. **no pegar ojo** en OJO.

pegoste *nm* (*Mx*) groupie

pegote *nm* sticky mess

peinado *adj*: *¿Todavía no estás peinada?* Haven't you done your hair yet? ● *nm* hairstyle: *hacerse un* ~ have your hair styled ▶ *ir bien/mal* ~: *Iba muy bien peinada.* Her hair looked really nice. ◇ *Siempre va muy mal* ~. His hair is always a mess.

peinar *vt* **1** comb sb's hair **2** (*peluquero*) do sb's hair: *Voy a que me peinen.* I'm going to have my hair done. **3** (*zona*) comb ● **peinarse** *vp* comb your hair

peine *nm* (*tb* **peinilla** *nf*) comb

pela *nf* (*golpe*) smack ▶ **dar/pegar una** ~ slap sb

pelado *adj* **1** (*cabeza*) shaven **2** (*sin dinero*) broke **3** (*Mx, persona*) rude ● *nm-nf* (*niño*) kid

pelar *vt* **1** peel: ~ *una naranja* peel an orange **2** (*arvejas/chícharos, mariscos*) shell **3** (*dulce*) unwrap ● **pelarse** *vp* peel: *Se te va a* ~ *la nariz.* Your nose will peel.

peldaño *nm* step

pelea *nf* fight: *meterse en una* ~ get into a fight

pelear(se) *vi, vp* **1** (*luchar*) fight: *Los niños (se) peleaban por los juguetes.* The children were fighting over the toys. **2** (*reñir*) quarrel

peleón (**peleonero** *Mx*) *adj* **1** (*que discute*) argumentative **2** (*que pelea*) No *me gustan los niños peleones.* I don't like children who are always fighting.

pelícano (*tb* **pelicano**) *nm* pelican

película *nf* movie, film (*GB*): *pasar/dar una* ~ show a movie ▶ ~ *cómica/de risa* comedy [*pl* -ies] ~ *del oeste* western ~ *de miedo/terror* horror movie/film ~ *muda* silent movie/film ~ *policíaca/de suspenso* thriller

peligrar *vi* be in danger

peligro *nm* danger

peligroso/a *adj* dangerous

pelirrojo/a *adj* red-haired ● *nm-nf* redhead

pellejo *nm* **1** skin **2** (*en una uña*) hangnail ▶ **arriesgar/jugarse el** ~ risk your neck

pellizcar *vt* pinch

pellizco *nm* **1** (*sal, en la piel*) pinch **2** (*pedacito*) little bit: *un* ~ *de pan* a little bit of bread ▶ **dar/pegar un** ~ pinch

pelo *nm* **1** hair: *tener el* ~ *crespo/chino* have curly/straight hair → MY **2** (*animal*) coat ▶ **de** ~**s** (*Mx*) cool **no tener** ~**s en la lengua** not mince your words **ponerse los** ~**s de punta**: *Se me pusieron los* ~*s de punta.* My hair stood on end. **por un** ~**/los** ~**s** by the skin of your teeth **soltarse el** ~ let your hair down **tomar el** ~ pull sb's leg

pelón *adj* **1** (*calvo*) bald **2** (*con mucho pelo*) hairy

pelota *nf* ball: *una* ~ *de tenis* a tennis ball ● *nmf* (*persona*) jerk: *No seas* ~. Don't be such a jerk. ▶ **en** ~ stark naked

pelotera *nf* **1** (*pelea*) rumpus **2** (*ruido*) uproar

pelotón *nm* **1** (*ciclismo*) bunch **2** (*Mil*) platoon

peluca *nf* wig

peluche *nm* plush

peludo *adj* **1** hairy **2** (*animal*) long-haired

peluquería *nf* **1** hairdressing salon **2** (*para hombres*) barber shop, barber's (*GB*)

peluquero/a *nm-nf* **1** hair stylist **2** (*para hombres*) barber

peluquín *nm* toupee

pelusa (*tb* **pelusilla**) *nf* **1** (*fruta*) fuzz **2** (*tela, suciedad*) piece of lint

pena *nf* **1** (*tristeza*) sorrow: *ahogar las* ~*s* drown your sorrows **2** (*lástima*) shame: *¡Qué* ~ *que no puedas venir!* What a shame you can't come! **3** (*vergüenza*) embarrassment: *¡Qué* ~! How embarrassing! **4** (*condena*) sentence **5** **penas** (*problemas*) troubles ▶ **dar** ~ **1** (*lástima*) be/feel sorry: *Me da* ~ *que se tenga que ir.* I'm sorry you have to leave. ◇ *Me da mucha* ~. I feel really sorry for him. **2** (*vergüenza*) be/feel embarrassed: *Le dio* ~ *que lo vieran así.* He was embarrassed to be seen like that. **merecer/valer la** ~ be worth sth: *Vale la* ~ *leerlo.* It's worth reading. ◇ *No merece la* ~. It's not worth it. ~ **de muerte** death penalty

penal *adj* penal

penalty (tb **pénal** And) nm penalty [pl -ies]: *meter un (gol de) ~* score from a penalty

pendiente adj 1 (*factura, etc.*) outstanding 2 (*decisión, veredicto*) pending ● nf slope: *una ~ suave* a gentle slope ▶ **asunto/asignatura ~** unresolved matter **dar ~** (*preocupar*) worry **por estar ~ de 1** (*vigilar*) keep an eye on sth/sb **2** (*estar atento*) be attentive to sth/sb: *Estaba muy atento a sus invitados.* He was very attentive to his guests. **3** (*estar esperando*) be waiting for sth: *Estamos ~s de su decisión.* We're waiting for his decision.

pene nm penis

penetrante adj 1 penetrating: *una mirada ~* a penetrating look 2 (*frío, viento*) bitter

penetrar vt, vi enter sth: *El agua penetró en las casas.* The water entered the houses. ◇ *La bala le penetró la cabeza.* The bullet entered into his head.

penicilina nf penicillin

península nf peninsula

penitencia nf penance: *hacer ~* do penance

penitenciaría nf penitentiary [pl -ies]

pensamiento nm thought ▶ **adivinar el ~** read sb's mind

pensar vt, vi 1 think (*about/of sth/sb*): *Piensa un número.* Think of a number. ◇ *Estamos pensando en casarnos.* We're thinking about/of getting married. **2** (*opinar*) think sth of sth/sb: *¿Qué piensas de él?* What do you think of him? **3** (*tener decidido*) be going to do sth: *Pensaba irme ya.* I was going to leave now. ◇ *¿Piensas venir?* Are you going to come? ▶ **¡ni ~lo!** no way! **pensándolo bien...** on second thoughts... **piénsalo** think it over

pensativo adj thoughtful

pensión nf 1 (*jubilación, subsidio*) pension 2 (*hospedaje*) guest house **3** (And, *mensualidad*) tuition fees [pl] ▶ **~ completa/media** full/half board

pensionista nmf (tb **pensionado/a** nm-nf) senior, pensioner (GB)

pentagrama nm staff

penúltimo adj penultimate

peña nf rock

peñón nm rock

peón nm 1 (*obrero*) laborer 2 (*ajedrez*) pawn

peor adj, adv (*comparativo*) worse: *Fue ~ de lo que me espe-* raba. It was worse than I'd expected. ● adj, adv, nmf (*superlativo*) worst: *el ~ equipo del mundo* the worst team in the world ◇ *la ~ de todas* the worst of all

pepa nf 1 (*limón, uva*) pip 2 (*aceituna, aguacate*) pit, stone (GB)

pepinillo nm pickle, gherkin (GB)

pepino nm cucumber

pepita nf 1 (*semilla*) seed 2 (*oro*) nugget

pequeño adj 1 small → SMALL 2 (*joven*) little: *los niños ~s* little children 3 (*el más joven*) youngest: *mi hijo ~* my youngest son

pera nf pear

peral nm pear (tree)

percha nf 1 (*de pie*) coat stand 2 (*de pared*) coat hook 3 (*de pájaro*) perch

perdedor adj losing ● nm-nf loser: *un buen/mal ~* a good/bad loser

perder vt 1 lose: *~ las llaves* lose your keys ◇ *~ altura/peso* lose height/weight 2 (*medio de transporte, oportunidad*) miss 3 (*desperdiciar*) waste: *~ el tiempo/dinero* waste time/money 4 (*reprobar*) fail: *Perdí francés.* I failed French. **5** (*líquido, gas*) leak ● vi 1 lose: *~ a/en ajedrez* lose at chess 2 (*salir perjudicado*) lose out ● **perderse** vi get lost: *Te vas a perder.* You'll get lost. ◇ *¡Piérdete!* Get lost! 2 (*película, espectáculo*) miss ▶ **echar algo a ~** ruin sth **salir perdiendo** lose out **NOTA** Para otras expresiones, ver el sustantivo, p.ej. **perder la cabeza** en CABEZA.

pérdida nf 1 loss: *~s y ganancias* profit and loss ◇ *sufrir ~s económicas* lose money 2 (*desperdicio*) waste: *una ~ de tiempo* a waste of time **2 pérdidas** (*daños*) damage [U]

perdido adj 1 lost 2 (*perro*) stray

perdigón nm pellet

perdiz nf partridge

perdón nm forgiveness ● interj sorry →EXCUSE

perdonar vt 1 forgive: *Jamás le perdonaré lo que me hizo.* I'll never forgive him for what he did. 2 (*deuda*) write sth off: *Me perdonó los mil dólares que le debía.* He wrote off the thousand dollars I owed him. 3 (*castigo, condena*) let sb off sth ▶ **perdona, perdone, etc.** 1 (*para pedir disculpas*) sorry: *Perdone el ~.* Sorry for/about the mess. 2 (*para llamar la atención*) excuse me 3 (*cuando no se ha oído bien*) sorry, I beg your pardon (*más fml*) →EXCUSE

perecear *vi* (And) laze around

peregrinación *nf* (tb **peregrinaje** *nm*) pilgrimage: *ir en ~* go on a pilgrimage

peregrino/a *nm-nf* pilgrim

perejil *nm* parsley

pereque *nm* (And) nuisance: *No me ponga ~.* Don't be a nuisance.

pereza *nf* laziness ▶ **me da ~** I, you, etc. can't be bothered (*to do sth*) ¡**qué ~!** what a drag! **tener/sentir ~** feel lazy

perezosa *nf* (silla) deckchair

perezoso *adj* lazy: *Mi hermano es un ~.* My brother's very lazy. ● *nm* (animal) sloth

perfeccionar *vt* (mejorar) improve

perfecto *adj* perfect: *Nos salió ~.* It turned out perfectly.

perfil *nm* 1 (persona) profile: *un retrato de ~* a profile portrait 2 (edificio, montaña) outline

perfilar *vt* (dibujo) draw the outline of *sth*

perfumado *adj* scented

perfumar *vt* perfume ● **perfumarse** *vp* put perfume on

perfume *nm* perfume

perfumería *nf* perfumery [*pl* -ies]

perico *nm* 1 (pájaro) parakeet 2 (cocaína) coke 3 (And, café) coffee with milk

perilla *nf* (puerta, cajón) knob

perímetro *nm* perimeter

periódico *adj* periodic ● *nm* newspaper

periodismo *nm* journalism

periodista *nmf* journalist

período *nm* (tb **periodo**) (*nm*) period: *tener el ~* have your period ◊ *hacer algo en ~ de prueba* do *sth* for a trial period

periquito *nm* 1 parakeet 2 (australiano) budgie

perito/a *nm-nf* expert ▶ **~ en agronomía** agronomist

perjudicar *vt* 1 (salud) damage 2 (intereses) prejudice

perjudicial *adj* bad: *El tabaco es ~ para la salud.* Smoking is bad for your health.

perjuicio *nm* harm ▶ **ir en ~ de algn** go against *sb*

perla *nf* pearl ▶ **de ~s**: *Me viene de ~s.* It'll come in very handy.

permanecer *vi* remain

permanente *adj* permanent ● *nm o nf* perm: *hacerse la/un ~* have your hair permed

permiso *nm* 1 (autorización) permission: *pedir/dar ~* ask for/give

permission 2 (documento) permit: *~ de residencia/trabajo* residence/work permit 3 (vacación) leave: *estar de/en ~* be on leave ▶ **con (su) ~**: *Me siento aquí, con su ~.* I'll sit here, if you don't mind.

permitir *vt* 1 (dejar) let: *Permítame ayudarla.* Let me help you. 2 (autorizar) allow: *No permiten entrar sin corbata.* You are not allowed in without a tie. →ALLOW ● **permitirse** *vp* 1 (atreverse, tomarse) take: *Se permite demasiadas confianzas.* He takes too many liberties. 2 (económicamente) afford: *No nos lo podemos ~.* We can't afford it. ▶ ¿**me permite...?** may I...?

permutación *nf* permutation

pero *conj* but ● *nm* (defecto) fault: *Le encuentras ~s a todo.* You find fault with everything.

perpendicular *adj, nf* perpendicular

perpetuo *adj* perpetual

perplejo *adj* puzzled

perra *nf* 1 bitch 2 (And, borrachera): *pegarse una ~* get drunk

perrera *nf* kennel

perrito/a *nm-nf* puppy [*pl* -ies]

perro *nm* dog **NOTA** Cuando se quiere recalcar que es hembra, se dice **bitch**. ▶ **de ~s** lousy: *un día de ~s* a lousy day **llevarse como el ~ y el gato** fight like cat and dog **~/perrito caliente** hot dog **~ faldero** lapdog **~ guardián** guard dog **~ lobo** German shepherd **~ pastor** sheepdog **~ que ladra no muerde** his/her bark is worse than his/her bite

persecución *nf* 1 pursuit: *ir en ~ de algn* go in pursuit of *sb* 2 (Pol, Rel) persecution

perseguir *vt* 1 pursue: *~ a algn/un objetivo* pursue *sb/an* objective 2 (Pol, Rel) persecute

persiana *nf* blind: *subir/bajar las ~s* raise/lower the blinds

persistente *adj* persistent

persistir *vi* persist (*in sth*)

persona *nf* person [*pl* people]: *miles de ~s* thousands of people ▶ **en ~** in person **~ mayor** grown-up **por ~**: *1.000 pesos por ~* 1,000 pesos a head **ser (una) buena ~** be nice

personaje *nm* 1 (libro, película) character 2 (persona importante) personality [*pl* -ies]

personal *adj* personal ● *nm* staff →JURADO

personalidad *nf* personality [*pl* -ies]

perspectiva nf 1 (Arte) perspective 2 (vista) view 3 (en el futuro) prospect: buenas ~s good prospects

perspicacia nf insight

perspicaz adj perceptive

persuadir vt persuade ● **persuadirse** vp become convinced (of sth)

persuasivo adj persuasive

pertenecer vi belong to sth/sb

perteneciente adj belonging to sth/sb

pertenencia nf 1 (partido, club, etc.) membership 2 **pertenencias** belongings

pertinente adj relevant

Perú nm Peru

peruano/a adj, nm-nf Peruvian

pervertir vt pervert

pesa nf 1 weight 2 (balanza) scales [pl] ▶ hacer ~s lift weights

pesadez nf 1 (aburrimiento): ¡Qué ~ de película! What a boring movie! 2 (molestia) nuisance: Las moscas son una ~. These flies are a nuisance.

pesadilla nf nightmare

pesado/a adj 1 (físico) heavy: una maleta/comida pesada a heavy suitcase/meal 2 (aburrido) boring ● adj, nm-nf (persona): ser (un) ~ be a pain

pésame nm condolences [pl] ▶ dar el ~ offer sb your condolences

pesar¹ vt weigh ● vi 1 weigh: ¿Cuánto pesas? How much do you weigh? 2 (tener mucho peso) be heavy: ¡Este paquete sí que pesa! This package is very heavy. ◊ ¡Cómo pesa! It weighs a ton! ◊ ¡No pesa nada! It hardly weighs a thing!

pesar² nm 1 (tristeza) sorrow 2 (lástima) pity: Es un ~... It's a pity... ◊ ¡Qué ~! What a pity! ▶ a ~ de algo in spite of sth: a ~ del calor in spite of the heat a ~ de que... although...: A ~ de que no pude ir... Although I couldn't go...

pesca nf fishing: ir de ~ go fishing

pescadería nf fish market

pescadero/a nm-nf fish seller

pescado nm fish: Voy a comprar ~. I'm going to buy some fish.

pescador/a nm-nf fisherman/woman [pl -men/-women]

pescar vi salir a ~ go out fishing ● vt (pescado, enfermedad) catch

pesebre nm (nacimiento) creche, crib (GB)

pesero nm (Mx) minibus

pesimista adj pessimistic ● nmf pessimist

pésimo adj dreadful

pesista nmf (And) weightlifter

peso nm 1 weight: ganar/perder ~ put on/lose weight 2 (moneda) peso [pl -s] ▶ de ~ (persona) influential 2 (asunto) weighty no tener ni un ~ not have a dime/penny (GB) quitarse un ~ de encima: Me quité un gran ~ de encima. That was a great weight off my mind.

pesquero adj fishing: un puerto ~ a fishing port ● nm fishing boat

pestaña nf (ojo) eyelash ▶ quemarse las ~s study

pestañeada (tb pestañada) nf ▶ echarse una ~ have a nap

pestañear vi blink ▶ sin ~ without batting an eye/eyelid (GB)

pestañina nf mascara

peste nf 1 (epidemia) plague 2 (resfriado) cold 3 (mal olor) smell ▶ decir/echar ~s (de) rag on sth/sb, slag sth/sb off (GB)

pestillo nm catch: echar el ~ put the catch on

petaca nf 1 (para tabaco) tobacco pouch 2 (cesto) basket 3 (maleta) suitcase ▶ echarse por/con las ~s go to pieces

pétalo nm petal

petardo nm firecracker

petatearse vp kick the bucket

petición nf 1 request: hacer una ~ de ayuda make a request for help 2 (instancia) petition

petirrojo nm robin

petróleo nm oil

petrolero nm oil tanker

pez nm fish [pl fish] →FISH ▶ ~ de colores goldfish [pl goldfish] ~ gordo big shot

pezón nm 1 (persona) nipple 2 (animal) teat

pezuña nf hoof [pl -s o hooves]

piadoso adj devout

pianista nmf pianist

piano nm piano [pl -s]: tocar una pieza al/en el ~ play a piece of music on the piano ▶ ~ de cola grand piano

piar vi chirp

pica nf 1 (herramienta) pick 2 picas (cartas) spades →BARAJA

picada nf 1 (comida) (hot) appetizer 2 (dolor) shooting pain ▶ caer en ~ nosedive

picadero nm riding school

picado adj 1 (diente) bad 2 (mar) choppy 3 (enfadado) mad, angry (GB): Creo que está ~ conmigo. I think he's mad at me.

picadura nf 1 (mosquito, serpiente) bite 2 (abeja, avispa) bite

picante adj (Cocina) hot: una salsa ~ a hot sauce

picaporte nm door handle

picar vt 1 (pájaro) peck 2 (mosquito, serpiente) bite 3 (abeja, avispa) sting 4 (comer): ¿Quieres ~ algo? Do you want something to eat? ◊ Nos pusieron unas cosas para ~. They gave us some munchies/nibbles (GB). 5 (cebolla, verdura) chop 6 (hielo) crush ● vi 1 (producir picor) itch: Este suéter pica. This sweater makes me itch. 2 (planta espinosa) be prickly 3 (pez) bite 4 (ser picante) be hot ► **picarse** vp 1 (diente, fruta, crema) go bad 2 (molestarse) get annoyed (with sb) (about sth) 3 (interesarse) get interested in sth ► **el ojo** wink

picardía nf craftiness: tener ~ be crafty

pichón nm young pigeon

picnic nm picnic: ir de ~ go for a picnic

pico nm 1 (pájaro) beak 2 (montaña) peak 3 (herramienta) pick ► **y** ~: dos mil y ~ de personas two thousand odd people ◊ Tiene treinta y ~ de años. He's thirty something. ◊ Es la una y ~. It's just after one.

picor nm 1 (picazón) itch: Tengo ~ en la espalda. My back itches. 2 (escozor) stinging 3 (garganta) tickle

picoso adj hot

picotazo nm 1 (mosquito) bite 2 (abeja, avispa) sting 3 (pájaro) peck

pie¹ nm 1 foot [pl feet] → MY 2 (estatua, columna) pedestal 3 (copa) stem 4 (lámpara) stand ► **al** ~ **(de)** near: al ~ de la casa near the house al ~ de la letra word for word **andar con ~s de plomo** tread carefully **a** ~ on foot **de** ~ **a cabeza** from top to toe **estar de** ~ be standing (up) **hacer** ~: No hago ~. My feet don't touch the bottom. **no tener ni** ~**s ni cabeza** be absurd **ponerse de** ~ stand up

pie² nm (pay) pie →PIE

piedad nf 1 (compasión) mercy 2 (devoción) piety 3 (imagen, escultura) pietà

piedra nf stone: una pared de ~ a stone wall ► **quedarse una** ~ be speechless **sacar la** ~ **a algn** (And) get on sb's nerves

piel nf 1 (Anat) skin: tener la ~ blanca have fair skin (con pelo) fur: un abrigo de ~es a fur coat 3 (cuero) leather 4 (fruta) skin ► **~ de gallina** goose bumps

pierde nm ► **no tiene** ~ you can't miss it

pierna nf leg ► MY ► **con las** ~**s cruzadas** cross-legged

pieza nf 1 (ajedrez, Mús) piece 2 (Mec) part: una ~ de repuesto a spare part 3 (habitación) (bed)room ► **quedarse de una** ~ be speechless

pigmento nm pigment

pijama = PIYAMA

pila nf 1 (montón) pile: una ~ de periódicos a pile of newspapers (gran cantidad) loads of...: una ~ de trabajo loads of work 3 (Elec) battery [pl -ies] 4 (fuente) fountain ► **ponerse las** ~**s** get cracking

pilar nm pillar

píldora nf pill

pillaje nm plunder

pillar vt catch: ~ a algn con las manos en la masa catch sb red-handed ► **¡nos pillamos!** see you later!

pilotear (tb pilotar) vt 1 (avión) fly 2 (Aut) drive

piloto nmf 1 (avión) pilot 2 (Aut) racing driver

pimentón nm 1 (especia) (a) (dulce) paprika (b) (picante) cayenne pepper 2 (And, fruto) = PIMIENTO

pimienta nf pepper

pimiento nm bell pepper, pepper (GB)

pin nm badge

pinar nm pine forest

pincel nm paintbrush

pinchar vt 1 (balón, llanta) puncture 2 (picar) prick ● vi (tener pinchazo) have a flat (tire) ► **pincharse** vp 1 (llanta) puncture: Se me pinchó una rueda. I have a flat (tire). 2 (~ con) prick yourself (on/with sth)

pinchazo nm puncture

pincho nm 1 (varilla para asar) spit 2 (de carne) shish kebab

ping-pong® nm ping-pong®

pingüino nm penguin

pino nm pine (tree)

pinta nf 1 (aspecto) look 2 (medida) pint ► **irse de** ~ (Mx) play hooky **ponerse de** ~ get dressed up **tener** ~ **(de)** look (like): Tienes ~ de payaso. You look like a clown. ◊ tener muy buena ~ look very nice

pintada nf graffiti [U]

pintado adj ▶ ~ **de** painted: _Están ~s de azul._ They are painted blue. **quedar/salir/venir que ni** ~ be perfect

pintar vt, vi paint: ~ _una pared de rojo_ paint a wall red ◇ ~ _al óleo/a la acuarela_ paint in oils/water-colors ● **pintarse** vp 1 paint: ~ _las uñas_ paint your nails 2 (_maquillarse_) put on your make-up: ~ _los ojos_ put on your eye make-up

pintor/a nm-nf painter

pintoresco adj picturesque

pintura nf 1 (_actividad, cuadro_) painting 2 (_producto_) paint

pinza nf 1 (_para tender_) clothes-pin, clothes peg (GB) 2 (_de pelo_) clip 3 (_cangrejo, langosta_) pincer 4 **pinzas** (_crustáceo_) tweezers: _unas ~s para las cejas_ tweezers (b) (_azúcar, hielo, carbón_) tongs (c) (_alicates_) pliers →PAIR

piña nf 1 (_fruta tropical_) pineapple 2 (_pino_) pine cone

piñón nm (Bot) pine nut

pío nm (_sonido_) tweet ▶ **no decir ni** ~ not open your mouth

piocha nf (Mx) goatee

piojo nm louse [pl lice]

pionero/a adj pioneering ● nm-nf pioneer: ~ _de la cirugía estética_ a pioneer in cosmetic surgery

pipa nf pipe

pique nm (_enfado_) quarrel ▶ **irse a** ~ 1 (_negocio_) go broke 2 (_plan_) fall through 3 (_barco_) sink

piquete nm 1 (_soldados_) squad 2 (Mx) (_aguja_) prick 3 (_jeringa_) jab 2 (_insecto_) bite 3 (_And, comida_) picnic

pirado adj crazy

piragua nf large canoe

piragüismo nm canoeing: _hacer_ ~ go canoeing

pirámide nf pyramid

pirata adj, nmf pirate: _una emisora_ ~ a pirate radio station

piratear vt 1 (_disco, video_) pirate 2 (_entrar en sistema informático_) hack into sth

pirómano/a nm-nf arsonist

piropo nm (_cumplido_) compliment 2 (_en la calle_): _echar un_ ~ _a algn_ whistle at sb

pirueta nf pirouette

pirulí nm lollipop

pis nm pee ▶ **hacer** ~ pee

pisada nf 1 (_sonido_) footstep 2 (_huella_) footprint

pisar vt 1 step on/in sth: ~_le el pie a algn_ step on sb's foot ◇ ~ _un charco_ step in a puddle 2 (_tierra_) tread sth down 3 (_acelerador,

freno_) put your foot on sth 4 (_dominar_) walk all over sb ● vi tread ● **pisarse** (_tb pisárselas_) vp (And, irse) clear off

piscina nf swimming pool ▶ ~ **climatizada/cubierta** heated/indoor pool

Piscis nm, nmf Pisces

piso nm floor: _en el sexto_ ~ on the sixth floor **NOTA** En EE.UU. la planta baja se dice **ground floor** o **first floor**. En Gran Bretaña, el primer piso se llama **first floor**. ▶ **de dos, etc. ~s** (_edificio_) two-story, etc.: _un bloque de cinco ~s_ a five-story block

pisotear vt 1 (_pisar_) stamp on sth 2 (_fig_) trample on sth: ~ _los derechos de algn_ trample on sb's rights

pisotón nm ▶ **dar un** ~ step on sb's foot

pista nf 1 (_huella_) track(s): _seguir la ~ de un animal_ follow an animal's tracks ◇ _Le perdí la ~ a Raúl._ I lost track of Raúl. 2 (_dato_) clue: _Dame más ~s._ Give me more clues. 3 (_carreras_) track: _una ~ cubierta_ an indoor track ▶ ~ **de aterrizaje** runway ~ **de baile** dance floor ~ **de esquí** ski slope ~ **de hielo/patinaje** ice/skating rink **sobre la** ~ **de algn** on sb's trail

pistacho nm pistachio [pl -s]

pistola nf gun, pistol ▶ ~ **de aire comprimido** airgun

pita nf (And) twine

pitar vi 1 (_policía, árbitro_) blow your whistle: _El policía nos pitó._ The policeman blew his whistle at us. 2 (Aut) honk, hoot (GB): _El conductor me pitó._ The driver honked at me. ● **irse/salir pitando** dash off ● ~ **un penalty/una falta** award a penalty/free kick

pitido nm 1 (_tren, árbitro, policía_) whistle 2 (Aut) honk, hoot (GB)

pitillo nm (And) straw

pito nm whistle ▶ **entre** ~**s y flautas** what with one thing and another

pitón nm python

piyama nf pajamas [pl], pyjamas [pl] (GB) →PANTALÓN

pizarra nf slate

pizarrón nm blackboard

pizca nf: _una_ ~ _de sal/humor_ a pinch of salt/a touch of humor ▶ **ni** ~ not at all: _No tiene ni_ ~ _de gracia._ It's not funny at all.

pizza nf pizza

placa nf 1 (_lámina, Fot, Geol_) plate: ~_s de acero_ steel plates 2 (Aut) license plate, number plate (GB) 3 (conmemorativa) plaque 4 (policía) badge

placer nm pleasure: un viaje de ~ a pleasure trip

plaga nf plague

plan nm 1 plan: ¿Tienes ~ para el sábado? Do you have anything planned for Saturday? 2 (humor): Si sigues en ese ~, me voy. If you're going to keep this up, I'm leaving.

plancha nf (electrodoméstico) iron ▸ **a la ~** grilled

planchar vt iron • vi do the ironing: Hoy me toca ~. I have to do the ironing today.

planeador nm glider

planear vt plan: ~ la fuga plan your escape • vi (avión, pájaro) glide

planeo nm gliding

planeta nm planet

planificación nf planning

plano adj flat • nm 1 (nivel) level: en el ~ personal on a personal level 2 (diagrama) (a) (ciudad, metro) map (b) (de arquitecto) plan 3 (Cine) shot

planta nf 1 (Bot) plant 2 (piso) floor: en la ~ baja on the first/ ground floor →PISO 3 (personal) staff →JURADO ▸ **del pie** sole

plantación nf plantation

plantado adj ▸ **dejar ~** stand sb up

plantar vt 1 plant 2 (dejar plantado) stand sb up

planteamiento nm approach

plantear vt raise: ~ dudas raise doubts • **plantearse** vp think (about sth): ¡Eso ni me lo planteo! I don't even think about that!

plantel nm 1 (personal) staff →JURADO 2 (Dep) squad 3 (escuela) school

plantilla nf 1 (zapato) insole 2 (para dibujar) template

plantón nm (espera larga) long wait ▸ **dar un ~** 1 (retrasarse) keep sb waiting 2 (no acudir) stand sb up

plástico adj plastic: cirugía plástica plastic surgery • nm plastic: un envase de ~ a plastic container ◇ un ~ a plastic sheet

plastificar vt laminate

plastilina® nf modeling clay, plasticine® (GB)

plata nf 1 (metal) silver: un anillo de ~ a silver ring 2 (dinero) money: ¿Tienes ~? Do you have any money? ▸ **andar/estar mal de ~** be short of money

plataforma nf platform

platal nm fortune

plátano nm 1 (a) (para comer crudo) banana (b) (~ macho (Mx, para cocinar) plantain 2 (árbol frutal) banana (tree)

platea nf orchestra, stalls (GB)

plateado adj 1 (color) silver 2 (con baño de plata) silver-plated

platicar vi chat • vt tell

platillo nm 1 (taza) saucer 2 platillos (Mús) cymbals 3 (guiso) dish ▸ **~ volador** flying saucer

platino nm platinum

plato nm 1 (utensilio) (a) plate (b) (debajo de la taza) saucer 2 (guiso) dish 3 (parte de la comida) course ▸ **~ de postre** dessert plate ~ **extendido/pando** dinner plate ~ **fuerte** main course ~ **hondo/sopero** soup plate **ser un ~** (divertido) be a scream

platón nm 1 (Mx) serving dish 2 (And) washbowl

platudo adj well-heeled

playa nf beach: pasar un mes en la ~ spend a month at the beach

playera nf 1 (zapato) canvas shoe 2 (Mx, camiseta) T-shirt

plaza nf 1 (espacio abierto) square 2 (mercado) market (place) 3 (asiento) seat: un avión de cuatro ~s a four-seater plane 4 (puesto de trabajo) position 5 (en curso) place ▸ **~ de toros** bullring

plazo nm 1 (período): el ~ de inscripción the registration period ◇ Tengo un mes de ~ para pagar. I have a month to pay. ◇ El ~ vence mañana. The deadline is tomorrow. 2 (pago) installment: pagar/comprar algo a ~s pay for/buy sth in installments

plectro nm (Mús) plectrum

plegable adj folding

plegar vt fold

pleito nm 1 (Jur) lawsuit 2 (pelea) fight

pleno adj full ▸ **a plena luz del día** in broad daylight **en pleno...** (right) in the middle of...: en ~ invierno in the middle of winter

pliegue nm 1 fold 2 (falda) pleat

plomero/a nm-nf plumber

plomo nm lead

pluma nf 1 feather: un colchón de ~s a feather mattress 2 (para escribir) pen

plumero nm feather duster

plumón nm felt-tip pen

plural adj, nm plural

Plutón nm Pluto

plutonio nm plutonium

población nf 1 (conjunto de personas) population 2 (localidad) (a) (ciudad grande) city [pl -ies] (b) (ciudad pequeña) town

poblado nm small town

pobre adj poor ● nmf 1 poor man/woman [pl men/women]: los ricos y los ~s the rich and the poor 2 (desgraciado) poor thing

pobreza nf poverty

pocilga nf pigsty [pl -ies]

pocillo nm (taza) cup

poco/a adj 1 (+ sustantivo incontable) little, not much (más coloq): Tienen muy ~ interés. They don't have much interest. 2 (+ sustantivo contable) few, not many (más coloq): Tiene ~s amigos. He doesn't have many friends. → LESS ● pron little [pl few]: Vinieron muy ~s. Very few came. ● adv 1 (+ verbo) ~. Come ~. He doesn't eat much. 2 (poco tiempo) not long: hace ~ not long ago 3 + adj not very: Es ~ inteligente. He's not very intelligent. ▶ ¿a ~? (Mx) really a ~ de shortly after poco a poco gradually → más/menos (de) just over/under: ~ menos de 5.000 personas just under 5,000 people por ~ nearly: Por ~ me atropellan. I was almost run over. un ~ a little: un ~ de sal a little salt ◊ Espera un ~. Wait a moment. unos ~s a few **NOTA** Para otras expresiones, ver el sustantivo, adjetivo, etc., p.ej. **ser poca cosa** en COSA

podar vt prune

poder¹ vt, vi 1 can do sth, be able to do sth: No podía creerlo. I couldn't believe it. → CAN 2 (tener permiso) can, may (más fml): ¿Puedo hablar con Ana? Can I talk to Ana? → MAY 3 (probabilidad) may, could, might **NOTA** El uso de **may, could** y **might** depende del grado de probabilidad de realizarse la acción: **could** y **might** expresan menor probabilidad que **may**: Puede llegar en cualquier momento. He could/might come at any minute. ◊ Podría ser peligroso. It could/might be dangerous. ▶ ¡bien puedal (go right) ahead! no ~ más (estar cansado) be exhausted ~ con cope with sth: No puedo con tanto trabajo. I can't cope with so much work. **puede (que...)** maybe: Puede que sí, puede que no. Maybe, maybe not. **se puede/no se puede** ¿Se puede? May I come in? ◊ No se puede fumar aquí. You can't smoke in here. **NOTA** Para otras expresiones, ver el adjeti-

vo, verbo etc., p. ej. **sálvese quien pueda** en SALVAR.

poder² nm power: tomar el ~ seize power ▶ el ~ ejecutivo/judicial/legislativo the executive/judiciary/legislature

poderoso adj powerful

podrido adj rotten ▶ ~ en dinero/plata stinking rich

poema nm poem

poesía nf 1 poetry: la ~ épica epic poetry 2 (poema) poem

poeta nmf poet

poético adj poetic

polaco adj, nm Polish ● nm-nf Pole

polar adj polar

polea nf pulley

polémica nf controversy [pl -ies]

polémico adj controversial

polen nm pollen

poli nmf cop ● nf cops [pl]

policía nf police officer ● nmf police [pl]

polideportivo nm sports center

polígono nm (Geom) polygon

polilla nf moth

politécnico adj polytechnic ● nm technical college

política nf 1 (Pol) politics: meterse en ~ get involved in politics 2 (postura, programa) policy [pl -ies]: la ~ exterior foreign policy

político/a adj 1 (Pol) political: un partido ~ a political party 2 (diplomático) diplomatic 3 (familia): mi familia política my in-laws ● nm-nf politician

póliza nf policy [pl -ies]: tomar una ~ take out a policy

polizón nmf stowaway

pollito (tb polluelo) nm chick

pollo nm chicken: ~ asado/rostizado roast chicken

polo nm 1 (Geog, Fís) pole: el ~ Norte/Sur the North/South Pole 2 (camisa) polo shirt ▶ ser ~s opuestos (carácter) be like chalk and cheese

Polonia nf Poland

polución nf pollution

polvareda nf cloud of dust

polvo nm 1 (suciedad) dust 2 (Cocina, Quím) powder 3 polvos (tocador) powder [U] ▶ hecho ~ (cansado) shattered **limpiar/quitar el ~** dust

pólvora nf gunpowder

polvoriento adj dusty

pomada nf ointment

pomo nm 1 (puerta) doorknob 2 (cajón) knob

pompa nf 1 (burbuja) bubble: hacer ~s de jabón blow bubbles

2 (solemnidad) pomp ▸ **~s fúnebres 1** (entierro) funeral **2** (funeraria) funeral home

pomposo adj pompous

pómulo nm cheekbone

ponchadura nf (Mx) puncture

ponchar vt (Mx) puncture ● **poncharse** vp (Mx) Se ponchó la llanta. The tire is flat.

poner vt **1** (colocar) put: Pon los libros en una caja. Put the books in a box. **2** (aparato) turn sth on: ~ el radio turn on the radio **3** (disco, CD) play **4** (reloj) set: Pon el despertador a las seis. Set the alarm for six. **5** (vestir) put sth on: Ponle la bufanda a tu hermano. Put your brother's scarf on for him. **6** (servir) give: Ponme más sopa. Give me some more soup. **7** (huevos) lay **8** (tarea) set **9** (sábana, mantel) put sth on: Pon el mantel. Put the tablecloth on the table. **10** (correo) mail: ~ una carta (en el correo) mail a letter ● **ponerse** vp **1** (de pie) stand: Ponte a mi lado. Stand next to me. **2** (sentado) sit **3** (vestirse) put sth on: ¿Qué me pongo? What should I put on? **4** (sol) set **5** + adj get: Se puso enfermo. He got sick. **6** ~ a start doing sth/to do sth: Se puso a llover. It started raining. ▸ ~ **atención** pay attention **NOTA** Para otras expresiones, ver el sustantivo, adjetivo, etc., p.ej. **ponerse la pinta** en PINTA.

ponqué nm (And) cake

pontífice nm pontiff

pony (tb poni) nm pony [pl -ies]

popa nf stern

popis adj (Mx) posh

popote nm (Mx) (drinking) straw

popular adj popular

por prep

● **lugar 1** (con verbos de movimiento): circular ~ la derecha drive on the right ◊ ¿Pasas ~ una farmacia? Are you going past a drugstore? ◊ pasar ~ el centro go through the center ◊ viajar ~ Asia travel around Asia **2** (con verbos como agarrar) by: Lo agarré ~ el brazo. I grabbed him by the arm.

● **tiempo 1** (tiempo determinado): ~ la mañana/tarde in the morning/afternoon ◊ ~ la noche at night ◊ mañana ~ la noche tomorrow night **2** (duración) for: ~ unos días for a few days →FOR

● **causa**: Se suspende ~ el mal tiempo. It's been canceled because of bad weather. ◊ hacer

algo ~ dinero do sth for money ◊ Lo despidieron ~ robar. He was fired for stealing.

● **finalidad**: ~ ti haría cualquier cosa. I'd do anything for you. ◊ ~ no molestar so as not to annoy

● **agente** by: pintado ~ Botero painted by Botero

● **hacia/en favor de** for: sentir cariño ~ algn feel affection for sb ◊ ¡Vote ~ nosotros! Vote for us!

● **expresiones numéricas**: cuatro ~ tres four times three ◊ Mide siete ~ dos. It measures seven by two. ◊ $50 ~ hora 50 dollars an/per hour

● **otras construcciones 1** (medio, instrumento): ~ correo/avión by mail/air **2** (sustitución): Ella irá ~ mí. She'll go instead of me. ◊ Cámbialo ~ una camisa. Exchange it for a shirt. ◊ Lo compré ~ mil euros. I bought it for a thousand euros. **3** (sucesión) by: paso ~ paso step by step **4** + adj/adv however: ~ simple que... However simple... ◊ ~ mucho que trabajas... However much you work... ▸ ~ **mí** as far as I am, you are, etc. concerned ~ **qué** why: No dijo ~ qué no venía. He didn't say why he wasn't coming. ◊ ¿~ qué no? Why not?

porcelana nf porcelain

porcentaje nm percentage

porción nf portion

pornografía nf pornography

pornográfico adj pornographic

poro nm **1** (Anat, Biol) pore **2** (puerro) leek

poroso adj porous

porque conj because

porqué nm reason: el ~ de la huelga the reason for the strike ▸ ¿por qué? ver POR

porquería nf **1** (suciedad): La calle quedó hecha una ~. The street was filthy. **2** (asquerosidad): No hagas ~ con la comida. What you're doing with your food is disgusting. **3** (cosa) junk [U] **4** (golosina) junk food [U]

porra nf nightstick, truncheon (GB)

portada nf **1** (libro, revista) cover **2** (disco) sleeve

portafolios nm briefcase

portal nm **1** (casa) (entrance) hall **2** (internet) portal

portarse vp behave: ~ bien behave well

portátil adj portable: un televisor ~ a portable television ● nmf (Comp) laptop

portavasos *nm* coaster

portaviones *nm* aircraft carrier

portavoz *nmf* spokesman [*fem* spokeswoman] [*pl* -men/ -women] →CHAIRMAN

portazo *nm* bang ▸ **dar un ~** slam the door

portería *nf* 1 (*edificio*) superintendent's room, porter's lodge (GB) 2 (*Dep*) goal

portero/a *nm-nf* 1 (*edificio*) superintendent, caretaker (GB) 2 (*Dep*) goalkeeper

portón *nm* main door

Portugal *nm* Portugal

portugués/esa *adj, nm* Portuguese ● *nm-nf* Portuguese man/ woman [*pl* men/women]

porvenir *nm* future

posar *vi* (*para una foto*) pose ● **posarse** *vp* 1 (*aves, insectos*) land 2 (*polvo, sedimento*) settle

posdata *nf* postscript (*abrev* PS)

poseer *vt* own

posesivo *adj* possessive

posibilidad *nf* possibility [*pl* -ies] ▸ **tener (muchas) ~es de...** have a (good) chance of sth

posible *adj* 1 possible: *Es ~ que ya haya llegado.* It's possible he's here already. 2 (*potencial*) potential: *un ~ accidente* a potential accident ▸ **hacer (todo) lo ~ por/ para** do your best to do sth

posición *nf* position

positivo *adj* positive

poso *nm* (*sedimento*) dregs [*pl*]

postal *adj* postal ● *nf* postcard

poste *nm* post: *El balón dio en el ~.* The ball hit the post. ◇ **~ telegráfico** telegraph pole

póster *nm* poster

posterior *adj* 1 (*tiempo*): *los años ~es a la guerra* the years after the war ◇ *un suceso ~* a subsequent event 2 (*lugar*): *la fila ~ a la de ustedes* the row behind yours ◇ *en la parte ~ del autobús* in the back of the bus

postizo *adj* false: *dentadura postiza* false teeth

postre *nm* dessert: *¿Qué hay de ~?* What's for dessert?

postura *nf* 1 (*del cuerpo*) position 2 (*actitud*) stance

potable *adj* drinkable: *agua ~* drinking water

potencia *nf* power: *~ atómica/ económica* atomic/economic power ◇ **de alta/gran ~** ◇ *~* **(en caballos)** horsepower (*abrev* hp)

potente *adj* powerful

potro/a *nm-nf* foal **NOTA** *Foal* es el sustantivo genérico. El macho

es **colt** y la hembra **filly.** ● *nm* (*gimnasia*) (vaulting) horse

pozo *nm* well: *un ~ de petróleo* an oil well

práctica *nf* 1 practice: *en la ~* in practice ◇ **poner algo en ~** put sth into practice 2 (*Educ, sesión práctica*) practical

prácticamente *adv* practically

practicante *adj* practicing: *un católico ~* a practicing Catholic ● *nmf* 1 (*enfermera*) nurse 2 (*Educ*) student teacher

practicar *vt* 1 practice: *~ la medicina* practice medicine 2 (*deporte*) play: *¿Practicas algún deporte?* Do you do any sports?

práctico *adj* 1 practical 2 (*útil*) handy: *una excusa práctica* a handy excuse

pradera *nf* meadow

prado *nm* meadow

preámbulo *nm* 1 (*prólogo*) introduction 2 (*rodeos*): *Déjate de ~s.* Stop beating about the bush.

precaución *nf* precaution: *tomar precauciones contra incendios* take precautions against fire ▸ **con ~** carefully **por ~** as a precaution

preceder *vt* precede *sth/sb*

precepto *nm* rule

precinto *nm* seal

precio *nm* price: *¿Qué ~ tiene?* How much is it?

preciosidad *nf*: *Ese vestido es una ~.* That dress is lovely.

precioso *adj* 1 (*valioso*) precious: *una piedra preciosa* a precious stone 2 (*persona, cosa*) cute: *¡Qué gemelos tan ~s!* What cute twins!

precipicio *nm* precipice

precipitaciones *nf* (*lluvia*) rainfall [U]

precipitado *adj* hasty

precipitarse *vp* 1 (*sin pensar*) be hasty: *No te precipites, piénsalo bien.* Don't be hasty. Think it over. 2 (*arrojarse*) jump out of sth: *~ al vacío* jump into the void

precisamente *adv* exactly: *Es ~ por eso que no quiero ir.* This is exactly why I don't want to go. ◇ *~ ahora no puedo recibirlo.* I can't see you right now. 2 (*de hecho*) actually: *Fuiste ~ tú el que lo sugirió.* Actually, it was you who suggested it.

precisar *vt* 1 (*necesitar*) need 2 (*especificar*) specify: *~ hasta el más mínimo detalle* specify every last detail

precisión *nf* accuracy: *con ~* accurately

preciso adj: decir algo en el momento ~ say sth at the right moment ▶ **ser** ~ (necesario): Es ~ que vengas. You must come.

precoz adj (niño) precocious

predecir vt foretell

predicar vt, vi preach

predominante adj predominant

predominar adj predominant

preescolar adj pre-school ● nm kindergarten

prefabricado adj prefabricated

prefacio nm preface

preferencia nf preference

preferible adj preferable ▶ **ser** ~: Es ~ que no entres ahora. It's better if you don't go in now.

preferido/a adj, nm-nf favorite

preferir vt prefer: Prefiero el té al café. I prefer tea to coffee. **NOTA** En preguntas se usa **would prefer** si se trata de dos cosas o **would rather** si se trata de dos acciones: ¿Prefieres té o café? Would you prefer tea or coffee? ◇ ¿Prefieres ir al cine o ver un video? Would you rather go to the movies or watch a video? Para contestar a estas preguntas se usa **I would** o **I'd rather** + infinitivo sin to: Prefiero té. I'd rather have tea. ◇ No, prefiero quedarme en casa hoy. No, I'd rather stay home today.

prefijo nm 1 prefix 2 (teléfono) area code

pregunta nf question: contestar a/hacer una ~ answer/ask a question

preguntar vt, vi ask ● vi ~ **por** 1 (buscando algo/a algn) ask for sth/sb 2 (interesándose por algo/algn) ask about sth/sb ● **preguntarse** vp wonder

preguntón adj nosy

prehistórico adj prehistoric

prejuicio nm prejudice

prematuro adj premature

premiar vt award sb a prize: Fue premiado con un Oscar. He was awarded an Oscar.

premio nm 1 prize: ~ de consolación consolation prize 2 (recompensa) reward: como ~ a tu esfuerzo as a reward for your efforts

prenatal adj prenatal, antenatal (GB)

prenda nf 1 (ropa) garment 2 prendas (juego) forfeits ▶ **no soltar** ~ not say a word

prender vt 1 (luz, aparato) turn sth on: ~ la televisión turn on the TV 2 (Aut) start (con alfileres) pin sth (to/on sth) ● vi 1 (fuego) light 2 (Aut) start ● **prenderse** vp

1 (aparato) come on: Se prendió una luz. A light came on. 2 (madera, etc.) catch fire ▶ ~ **fuego** set fire to sth

prensa nf 1 (Mec, imprenta) press 2 (periódicos) papers [pl] 3 **la prensa** (periodistas) the press ▶ **conferencia/rueda de** ~ press conference ~ **amarilla/amarillista** gutter press

prensar vt press

preñada adj pregnant

preocupación nf worry [pl -ies]

preocupar vt worry: Me preocupa la salud de mi papá. I'm worried about my father's health. ● **preocuparse** vp worry: ~ por algn worry about sb

preparación nf 1 preparation 2 (entrenamiento) training: ~ física physical training

preparado adj 1 (listo) ready 2 (persona) qualified ▶ ~**s, listos, ¡ya!** ready, set, go!

preparador/a nm-nf trainer

preparar(se) vt, vp prepare, get (sth/sb) ready (más coloq): ~se para un examen prepare for a test

preparativos nm preparations

preparatoria nf senior high school

preposición nf preposition

presa nf 1 prey: aves de ~ birds of prey 2 (embalse) dam 3 (And, pollo) piece ▶ **ser** ~ **del pánico** be seized by panic

presagio nm omen

prescindir vi ~ **de** 1 (privarse) do without sth 2 (deshacerse) dispense with sb

presencia nf 1 presence 2 (apariencia) appearance: tener buena/mala ~ look pleasant/unattractive

presenciar vt 1 (ser testigo) witness: ~ un accidente witness an accident 2 (estar presente) attend: ~ un partido attend a game

presentación nf 1 presentation 2 **presentaciones** introductions

presentador/a nm-nf host

presentar vt 1 present: Presentó las pruebas ante el juez. He presented the evidence to the judge. ◇ ~ un programa present a program 2 (renuncia) submit 3 (denuncia, demanda, queja): make: ~ una denuncia make an official complaint 4 (persona) introduce: ¿Cuándo nos la presentas? When are you going to introduce her to us? ◇ Les presento a mi esposo. This is my husband. 5 (Cine, TV): ¿Qué van a ~ en la tele? What's on TV? ● **presentarse** vp

1 (*Pol*) run, stand (*GB*): ~ *para diputado* run/stand for Congress **2** (*cargo*) apply: ~ *a un puesto* apply for a job **3** (*examen*) take: ~ *a un examen* take an exam **4** (*aparecer*) turn up

presente *adj, nmf* present: *los ~s* those present ● *nm* (*Gram*) present

presentimiento *nm* feeling

presentir *vt* have a feeling: *Presiento que vas a aprobar.* I have a feeling you're going to pass.

preservativo *nm* **1** (*condón*) condom **2** (*Quím*) preservative

presidencia *nf* **1** presidency [*pl* -ies]: *la ~ de un país* the presidency of a country **2** (*club, comité, partido*) chairmanship

presidencial *adj* presidential

presidente/a *nm-nf* **1** president **2** (*club, comité, partido*) chair

presidiario/a *nm-nf* convict

presidio *nm* prison

presidir *vt* preside at/over sth

presión *nf* pressure: ~ *arterial* blood pressure

presionar *vt* **1** (*apretar*) press **2** (*forzar*) put pressure on sb

preso/a *adj*: *estar* ~ be in prison ◊ *Se lo llevaron* ~. They took him prisoner. ● *nm-nf* prisoner

prestado *adj*: *No es mío, es* ~. It's not mine. I borrowed it. ◊ *¿Por qué no lo pides* ~? Why don't you ask to borrow it? ▸ **dejar** ~ lend

préstamo *nm* loan

prestar *vt* lend: *Le presté mis libros.* I lent her my books. ▸ ~ **atención** pay attention ~ **declaración** testify ~ **juramento** take an oath

prestigio *nm* prestige ▸ **de mucho** ~ very prestigious

presumido *adj* vain

presumir *vi* **1** show off **2** ~ **de** (*a*) (*creerse algo*) like to think you are...: *Presume de inteligente.* He likes to thinks he's so smart. (b) (*fanfarronear*) brag about sth: *Siempre está presumiendo de su carro.* He's always bragging about his car.

presunto *adj* alleged

presupuesto *nm* **1** (*cálculo anticipado*) estimate: *pedir un* ~ ask for an estimate **2** (*fondos*) budget: *pasarse del* ~ exceed your budget

pretender *vt* **1** (*querer*): *¿Qué pretendes de mí?* What do you want from me? **2** *No pretenderás que lo crea, ¿no?* You don't expect me to believe that, do you?

2 (*intentar*) try: *¿Qué pretende decirnos?* What's he trying to tell us?

pretexto *nm* excuse: *encontrar un* ~ *para no hacer algo* find an excuse not to do sth

prevención *nf* prevention

prevenido *adj* **1** (*preparado*) prepared **2** (*prudente*) prudent

prevenir *vt* **1** (*evitar*) prevent **2** (*avisar*) warn: *Te previne de lo que planeaban.* I warned you about what they were planning.

preventiva *nf* (*Mx*) yellow light, amber light (*GB*)

prever *vt* foresee

previo *adj*: *experiencia previa* previous experience ◊ *sin* ~ *aviso* without prior warning

previsor *adj* far-sighted

prieto *adj* (*Mx*) dark-skinned

prima *nf* bonus [*pl* -es]

primario *adj* **1** primary: *color* ~ primary color **2** (*Educ*) elementary, primary (*GB*): *enseñanza primaria* elementary/primary education ● **primaria** *nf* (*escuela*) elementary school, primary school (*GB*)

primavera *nf* spring: *en* ~ in (the) spring

primera *nf* **1** (*Aut*) first (gear): *Puse la* ~. I put it into first. **2** (*clase*) first class: *viajar en* ~ travel first class ▸ **a la** ~ first time

primero/a *adj* first: *el* ~ *de mayo* the first of May ◊ *primera clase* first class **2** (*principal*) main ● *pron, nm-nf* **1** first (one): *los* ~s *en salir* the first (ones) to leave **2** (*mejor*) top: *Eres el* ~ *de la clase.* You're at the top of the class. ● *adv* first ▸ **de primera necesidad** absolutely essential **(de)** ~ first: *Llegó (de)* ~. He came in first. **primer ministro** prime minister ~s **auxilios** first aid **primer plano** close-up

primitivo *adj* primitive

primo/a *nm-nf* (*pariente*) cousin ▸ ~ **hermano/segundo** first/second cousin

princesa *nf* princess

principal *adj* main: *comida/oración* ~ main meal/clause **2** *Eso es lo* ~. That's the main thing.

príncipe *nm* prince **NOTA** Para "los príncipes", refiriéndonos a príncipe y princesa, se dice **the prince and princess**. ▸ ~ **azul** Prince Charming ~ **heredero** crown prince

principiante *nmf* beginner

principio *nm* **1** (*comienzo*) beginning: *al* ~ at the beginning **2** (*concepto, moral*) principle

▶ **al ~** at first **a ~(s) de...** at the beginning of...: *a ~s de mayo* in early May

prioridad *nf* priority [*pl* -ies]

prisa *nf* hurry: *No hay ~*. There's no hurry. ▶ **darse ~** hurry up **tener ~** be in a hurry

prisión *nf* prison

prisionero/a *nm-nf* prisoner ▶ **hacer ~** take sb prisoner

prismáticos *nm* binoculars

privada *nf* (*Mx*) private road

privado *adj* private: *en ~* in private

privarse *vp* **1 ~ de** do without sth **2** (*desmayarse*) pass out

privilegiado *adj* **1** (*excepcional*) exceptional **2** (*favorecido*) privileged: *las clases privilegiadas* the privileged classes ◇ *Soy un ~.* I'm a privileged person.

privilegio *nm* privilege

pro *prep* for: *la organización pro ciegos* the association for the blind ▶ **en ~ de** in favor of sth/sb **los ~s y los contras** the pros and cons

proa *nf* bow(s)

probabilidad *nf* chance: *tener muchas/pocas ~s de hacer algo* have a good chance/no chance of doing sth

probable *adj* likely, probable (*más fml*): *Es ~ que no esté en casa.* He probably won't be in. ◇ *Es muy ~ que llueva.* It's likely to rain. ▶ **poco ~** unlikely

probador *nm* fitting room

probar *vt* **1** (*demostrar*) prove: *Esto prueba que yo tenía razón.* This proves I was right. **2** (*comprobar que funciona*) try sth out: *~ la lavadora* try out the washing machine **3** (*comida, bebida*) try ● *vi* try (*doing sth*): *¿Probaste a abrir la ventana?* Did you try opening the window? ● **probar(se)** *vt, vp* (*ropa*) try sth on

probeta *nf* test tube: *bebé/niño ~* test-tube baby

problema *nm* problem

procedencia *nf* origin

procedente *adj* **~ de** from...: *el avión ~ de Quito* the plane from Quito

proceder *vi* **~ de** come from...

procedimiento *nm* procedure: *según los ~s establecidos* according to established procedure

procesador *nm* processor

procesamiento *nm* processing ▶ **~ de textos** word processing

procesar *vt* **1** (*juzgar*) prosecute: *La procesaron por fraude.* She

was prosecuted for fraud. **2** (*producto, Comp*) process

procesión *nf* procession

proceso *nm* **1** process: *un ~ químico* a chemical process **2** (*Jur*) proceedings [*pl*]

procurar *vt* **1 ~ hacer algo** try to do sth: *Procuremos descansar.* Let's try to rest. **2 ~ que** make sure: *Procuraré que vengan.* I'll make sure they come.

prodigio *nm* (*persona*) prodigy [*pl* -ies]: *niño ~* child prodigy

producción *nf* **1** production: *la ~ del acero* steel production **2** (*agrícola*) harvest **3** (*industrial, artística*) output

producir *vt* produce

producto *nm* **1** product: *~s de belleza/limpieza* beauty/cleaning products **2** (*agrícola*): *~s agrícolas/del campo* agricultural/farm produce →PRODUCE

productor *adj* producing: *un país ~ de petróleo* an oil-producing country ● *nm-nf* producer ● **productora** *nf* (*empresa*) production company [*pl* -ies]

profesión *nf* profession, occupation →WORK

profesional *adj, nmf* professional: *un ~ del ajedrez* a professional chess player

profesor/a *nm-nf* **1** teacher: *un ~ de inglés* an English teacher **2** (*universitario*) professor, lecturer (*GB*)

profesorado *nm* teachers [*pl*]: *El ~ está inquieto.* The teachers are worried. ◇ *la formación del ~* teacher training

profeta/isa *nm-nf* prophet

profundidad *nf* depth

programa *nm* **1** program: *un ~ de televisión/software* a TV/software program **2** (*temario de una asignatura*) syllabus ▶ **~ de estudios** curriculum

programación *nf* programs [*pl*]: *la ~ infantil* children's programs

programador/a *nm-nf* (*Comp*) programmer

programar *vt* **1** (*elaborar*) plan **2** (*aparato*) set: *~ el vídeo* set the VCR ● *vt, vi* (*Comp*) program

progresar *vi* make progress: *~ mucho* make good progress

progreso *nm* progress [*U*]: *hacer ~s* make progress

prohibido *adj* ▶ **~ el paso/prohibida la entrada** no entry **~ fijar avisos/carteles** post no bills **~ fumar** no smoking **~ pisar el pasto/prado** keep off the grass

prohibir vt 1 forbid: ~le a algn los dulces/salir de noche forbid sb to eat sweets/to go out at night 2 (oficialmente) prohibit: Prohibieron la circulación/el tráfico por el centro. Traffic has been prohibited downtown. ▶ se prohibe...: Se prohibe fumar. No smoking.

prójimo nm neighbor

prólogo nm prologue

prolongar vt prolong ● prolongarse vp: La reunión se prolongó demasiado. The meeting went on too long.

promedio nm average: en ~ on average

promesa nf promise: cumplir/ hacer una ~ keep/make a promise

prometer vt promise: Te prometo que volveré. I promise I'll come back.

prometido/a nm-nf fiancé [fem fiancée]

promoción nf 1 promotion: la ~ de una película the promotion of a movie 2 (curso) year: un compañero de mi ~ someone in my year

promover vt (fomentar) promote

pronombre nm pronoun

pronosticar vt forecast

pronóstico nm 1 (predicción) forecast 2 (Med) prognosis [pl -noses]: heridas de ~ grave serious injuries

pronto adv 1 (enseguida) soon: lo más ~ posible as soon as possible 2 (rápidamente) quickly ▶ de ~ 1 (tal vez) maybe: Cuidado, que de ~ te caes. Be careful, you might fall. 2 (de repente) suddenly **hasta ~** see you soon

pronunciación nf pronunciation

pronunciar vt 1 (sonidos) pronounce 2 (discurso) give ● pronunciarse vp speak out against/ in favor of sth

propaganda nf 1 (publicidad) advertising: hacer ~ de un producto advertise a product ◇ una ~ de chicles an ad for chewing gum 2 (Pol) propaganda

propagar(se) vt, vp spread

propenso adj prone to sth

propiedad nf property [pl -ies]

propietario/a nm-nf owner

propina nf tip: Le di dos dólares de ~. I gave him a two-dollar tip.

propio adj 1 (de uno) my, your, etc. own: en beneficio ~ for your own benefit 2 (mismo) himself, herself, etc.: Los ~s médicos no saben qué es. The doctors themselves don't know what it is. 3 (característico) typical: Esto es ~ de ella. This is typical of her.

proponer vt 1 (medida, plan) propose 2 (acción) suggest: Propongo ir al cine hoy. I suggest going to the movies today. ◇ Propuso que nos fuéramos. He suggested we should leave. ● proponerse vp set out to do sth: Me propuse acabarlo. I set out to finish it.

proporción nf proportion

proposición nf 1 proposal ▶ hacer proposiciones indecorosas make improper suggestions ~ de matrimonio proposal (of marriage)

propósito nm 1 (intención) intention: buenos ~s good intentions 2 (objetivo) purpose ▶ a ~ 1 (adrede) on purpose 2 (por cierto) by the way

propuesta nf proposal

prórroga nf 1 (de plazo) extension 2 (Dep) overtime, extra time (GB)

prosa nf prose

prospecto nm leaflet

prosperar vi prosper

prosperidad nf prosperity

próspero adj prosperous

prostituta nf prostitute

protagonista nmf main character

protagonizar vt star in sth: ~ una película star in a movie

protección nf protection

protector adj protective (toward sb)

proteger vt protect

proteína nf protein

protesta nf protest

protestante adj, nmf Protestant

protestantismo nm Protestantism

protestar vi 1 (quejarse) complain (about sth) 2 (reivindicar) protest (against/about sth): ~ contra una ley protest against a law

prototipo nm prototype

provecho nm benefit ▶ ¡buen ~! enjoy your meal! **sacar ~** benefit from sth

proverbio nm proverb

providencia nf providence

provincia nf 1 (región) province 2 (fuera de la capital) the provinces [pl]: un hombre de ~ a man from the provinces

provisional adj provisional

provocar vt 1 (hacer enfadar) provoke 2 (causar) cause: ~ un accidente cause an accident 3 (incendio) start ● vi (And) like sth/to

do sth: *¿Le provoca un trago?* Would you like to go for a drink?

proximidad *nf* nearness

próximo *adj* 1 (*siguiente*) next: *el mes/martes ~* next month/Tuesday 2 (*cerca*): *La Navidad está próxima.* It will soon be Christmas.

proyectar *vt* 1 (*reflejar*) project: *~ una imagen sobre una pantalla* project an image onto a screen 2 (*película*) show

proyectil *nm* projectile

proyecto *nm* 1 project 2 (*plan*) plan: *¿Tienes algún ~ para el futuro?* Do you have any plans for the future? ► **~ de ley** bill

proyector *nm* projector

prudencia *nf* good sense ► **con ~** carefully: *manejar con ~* drive carefully

prudente *adj* 1 (*sensato*) sensible: *una decisión ~* a sensible decision 2 (*cauto*) careful

prueba *nf* 1 test: *una ~ de aptitud* an aptitude test 2 (*Mat, señal*) proof 3 (*Dep*) event 4 (*Jur*) evidence [U]: *No hay ~s contra mí.* There's no evidence against me ► **a ~** on trial **a ~ de balas** bulletproof **poner a ~** test sb

psicología *nf* psychology

psicólogo/a *nm-nf* psychologist

psiquiatra *nmf* psychiatrist

psiquiatría *nf* psychiatry

psiquiátrico *adj* psychiatric

púa *nf* 1 (*punta aguda*) spike 2 (*animal*) spine 3 (*peine*) tooth [*pl* teeth]

pubertad *nf* puberty

pubis *nm* pubic area

publicación *nf* publication ► **de ~ semanal** weekly

publicar *vt* 1 publish: *~ una novela* publish a novel 2 (*divulgar*) publicize

publicidad *nf* 1 publicity 2 (*propaganda*) advertising: *hacer ~ en la televisión* advertise on TV

publicitario *adj* advertising: *una campaña publicitaria* an advertising campaign

público *adj* ● *nm* 1 public: *abierto al ~* open to the public ◊ *hablar en ~* speak in public 2 (*clientela*) clientele 3 (*espectadores*) audience

puchero *nm* 1 (*recipiente*) cooking pot 2 (*cocido*) stew ► **hacer ~s** pout

pucho *nm* cigarette

pudiente *adj* wealthy

pudor *nm* shame

pudrirse *vp* rot

pueblo *nm* 1 (*gente*) people [*pl*]: *el ~ mexicano* the Mexican people 2 (*población*) town

puente *nm* bridge ► **hacer ~** have a long weekend **~ aéreo** shuttle service

puerco/a *adj* filthy ● *nm-nf* pig ► **~ espín** porcupine

puericultor/a *nm-nf* paediatrician

puerro *nm* leek

puerta *nf* 1 door: *Llaman a la ~.* There's somebody at the door. 2 (*ciudad, palacio*) gate ► **~ corrediza/giratoria** sliding/revolving door **~ de abordar/embarque** gate

puerto *nm* 1 port: *un ~ comercial/pesquero* a commercial/fishing port 2 (*de montaña*) pass

pues *conj* well

puesta *nf* ► **~ de sol** sunset

puesto *nm* 1 (*lugar*) place: *Ocupa el primer ~.* He's in first place. 2 (*empleo*) job: *solicitar un ~ de trabajo* apply for a job ➡ WORK 3 (*caseta*) (a) (*en mercado*) stall (b) (*en feria*) stand 4 (*asiento*) seat ► **bien ~** well dressed **~ de periódicos** news-stand **~ de primeros auxilios** first-aid post

puf *nm* footstool ► *interj* you bet

pugilista (*tb* **púgil**) *nmf* boxer

pulcritud *nf* neatness

pulcro *adj* neat

pulga *nf* flea ► **tener malas ~s** have a bad temper

pulgada *nf* inch (*abrev* in.)

pulgar *nm* 1 (*mano*) thumb 2 (*pie*) big toe

pulir *vt* polish ● **pulirse** *vp* (*refinarse*) become more refined

pullman *nm* (*autobús*) bus

pulmón *nm* lung

pulmonar *adj* lung: *una infección ~* a lung infection

pulmonía *nf* pneumonia [*U*]: *agarrar una ~* catch pneumonia

pulpa *nf* pulp

púlpito *nm* pulpit

pulpo *nm* octopus

pulsación *nf* (*Anat*) pulse rate

pulsar *vt* 1 press: *Pulse la tecla.* Press the key. 2 (*Comp*) click (*on sth*) 3 (*timbre*) ring

pulsera *nf* 1 (*brazalete*) bracelet 2 (*de reloj*) strap

pulso *nm* 1 (*Med*) pulse: *El médico me tomó el ~.* The doctor took my pulse. 2 (*mano firme*): *tener buen ~* have a steady hand ◊ *Me tiembla el ~.* My hand is trembling. ► **a ~** with my, your, etc. bare hands **echar un ~** arm wrestle

pulverizador nm spray
pulverizar vt 1 (rociar) spray 2 (destrozar) pulverize
puma nm puma
punk adj, nmf punk
punta nf 1 (cuchillo, arma, lápiz) point 2 (lengua, dedo, isla, iceberg) tip: Lo tengo en la ~ de la lengua. It's on the tip of my tongue. 3 (extremo, pelo) end: en la otra ~ de la mesa at the other end of the table ▸ a ~ de navaja/pistola at knifepoint/gunpoint de ~ a ~: de ~ a ~ de la ciudad from one side of town to the other de ~ en blanco dressed up to the nines sacar ~ (afilar) sharpen
puntada nf 1 (costura) stitch 2 (Mx) witty comment
puntapié nm kick: Le di un ~. I kicked him.
puntagudo adj pointed
puntilla nf ▸ en ~s on tiptoe
punto nm 1 point: Perdimos por dos ~s. We lost by two points. ◇ diez ~ cinco (10,5) ten point five (10·5) 2 (signo de puntuación) period, full stop (GB) 3 (grado) extent: ¿Hasta qué ~ es cierto? To what extent is this true? 4 (costura, Med) stitch ▸ a ~ de nieve stiffly beaten con ~s y comas down to the last detail de ~ knitted: un vestido de ~ a knit dress en ~ precisely: las dos en ~ two o'clock precisely en su ~ (carne) medium rare estar a ~ de hacer algo to be about to do sth: Está a ~ de terminar. It's about to finish. 2 (por poco) almost do sth: Estuvo a ~ de perder la vida. He almost lost his life. hacer ~ knit ~ débil/flaco weak point ~ de vista point of view ~ final period, full stop (GB) ~ muerto deadlock ~s suspensivos ellipsis ~ y aparte new paragraph ~ y coma semicolon
puntuación nf 1 (escritura) punctuation 2 (Dep) score(s)
puntual adj punctual
NOTA Punctual se refiere a la cualidad o virtud de una persona: Es importante ser ~. It's important to be punctual. Al referirnos a la idea de "llegar a tiempo", se usa on time: Procura ser/llegar ~. Try to get there on time.
puntualidad nf punctuality
puntuar vt 1 (escritura) punctuate 2 (calificar) mark

puñado nm handful
puñal nm dagger
puñalada nf stab
puñetazo nm punch: Me dio un ~. He punched me.
puño nm 1 (mano cerrada) fist 2 (manga) cuff 3 (bastón, paraguas) handle 4 (espada) hilt ▸ de su ~ y letra in his/her own handwriting
punzada nf sharp pain
punzante adj sharp
pupila nf pupil
pupitre nm desk
purasangre nm thoroughbred
puré nm purée: ~ de manzana apple purée ▸ estar hecho ~ be dead beat ~ de papa(s) mashed potato
pureza nf purity
purgatorio nm purgatory
purificar vt purify
puritanismo nm puritanism
puritano/a adj 1 (mojigato) puritanical 2 (Rel) Puritan ● nm-nf Puritan
púrpura adj purple
pus nm pus

Q q

que pron
● sujeto 1 (personas) who: el hombre ~ vino ayer the man who came yesterday 2 (cosas) that: la bici ~ está ahí the bike that's over there **NOTA** Cuando que equivale a "el/la cual" se traduce por which: El edificio, ~ antes fue sede del gobierno,... The building, which previously housed the government,...
● complemento **NOTA** El inglés no suele traducir que cuando funciona como complemento, aunque también es correcto usar that/who para personas y that/which para cosas: el muchacho ~ conocí en Roma the boy (that/who) I met in Rome ◇ el libro ~ me prestaste the book (that/which) you lent me ● conj 1 (con oraciones subordinadas) (that): Dijo ~ vendría esta semana. He said (that) he would come this week. ◇ Quiero ~ viajes en primera clase. I want you to travel first class. 2 (en com-

paraciones) than: *Es más alto ~ tú.* He's taller than you. **3** (*en mandatos*): *¡~ te calles!* Shut up! ◊ *¡~ la pasen bien!* Have a good time! **4** (*resultado*) (that): *Estaba tan cansada ~ me quedé dormida.* I was so tired (that) I fell asleep.

qué *adj*
• **interrogación** what: *¿~ hora es?* What time is it? ◊ *¿En ~ piso vive?* What floor do you live on? **NOTA** Cuando hay pocas opciones se usa **which**: *¿~ tarjeta uso? ¿La tuya o la mía?* Which card shall I use? Yours or mine?
• **exclamación 1** (+ *sustantivos contables en plural e incontables*) what: *¡~ casas tan bonitas!* What lovely houses! ◊ *¡~ valor!* What courage!* **2** (+ *sustantivos contables en singular*) what a: *¡~ vida!* What a life! **3** (*cuando se traduce por adjetivo*) how: *¡~ rabia/horror!* How annoying/awful!
• *pron* what: *¿Qué? Habla más alto.* What? Speak up. ◊ *No sé ~ quieres.* I don't know what you want. • *adv* how: *¡~ interesante!* How interesting! ▶ **¡~ de...!** what a lot of...!: *¡~ de turistas!* What a lot of tourists! **¿~ tal?** *Ver* TAL **¡~ va!** no way! *¿y a mí ~?* what's it to me, you, etc.?

quebrado *nm* fraction

quebrar *vt* break: *~ un vaso/ plato* break a glass/plate **2** (*lápiz*) snap **3** (*rajar*) crack **4** (*diente*) chip • *vi* go bankrupt ▶ **quebrarse** *vp* break: *Me quebré el brazo.* I broke my arm.

quedada *nf* (*Mx*) spinster

quedar *vi* **1** (*haber*) be left: *¿Queda café?* Is there any coffee left? **2** (*tener*) have *sth* left: *No me queda dinero.* I don't have any money left. **3** (*estar situado, llegar*) be: *¿Dónde queda el hotel?* Where is the hotel? ◊ *Quedé tercero en el concurso.* I was third in the competition. **4** (*arreglo personal*): *¿Qué tal le queda la chaqueta?* How does the jacket look on her? ◊ *El pelo corto le queda muy bien.* Short hair looks really good on you. **5** (*citarse*) meet: *¿Dónde quedamos?* Where should we meet? ◊ *Quedé con ella a las dos.* I arranged to meet her at two. **6** ~ **de/en** agree to do *sth*: *Quedamos de/en vernos el lunes.* We agreed to meet on Monday. • **quedarse** *vp* **1** (*en un sitio*) stay: *~ en la cama* stay in bed **2** + *adj* go: *~ calvo/ciego* go bald/blind **3** ~ **con** keep: *Quédese con el*

cambio. Keep the change. ▶ **~ bien/mal** make a good/bad impression: *Quedé muy mal con él.* I made a bad impression on him. **~ fácil/difícil** (*convenir*) be good/bad for *sb*: *Mañana me quedaría más ~.* It would be better if we left it till tomorrow. **~se sin algo** run out of sth: *~ sin dinero* run out of money **NOTA** Para otras expresiones, ver el sustantivo, adjetivo, etc., p. ej. **quedarse de piedra** en PIEDRA.

queja *nf* complaint

quejarse *vp* complain (*about sth/ sb*)

quejido *nm* **1** (*dolor*) moan **2** (*lamento, suspiro*) sigh **3** (*animal*) whine

quemado *adj* **1** burned **2** (*bronceado*) tanned ▶ **saber a ~** taste burned

quemador *nm* burner

quemadura *nf* **1** burn: *~s de segundo grado* second-degree burns **2** (*con líquido hirviendo*) scald ▶ **~ de sol** sunburn [U]

quemar *vt* burn: *Vas a ~ la carne.* You're going to burn the meat. **2** (*edificio, bosque*) burn *sth* down • *vi* be hot: *¡Cómo quema!* It's very hot! ▶ **quemarse** *vp* **1** (*persona*) burn *sth/yourself* (*on sth*): *~ la lengua* burn your tongue ◊ *~ con la sartén* burn yourself on the frying pan **2** (*comida*) be burned **3** (*agotarse*) burn yourself out **4** (*con el sol*) get sunburned ▶ **~se las pestañas** cram

querer *vt* **1** (*amar*) love **2** (*algo, hacer algo*) want: *¿Cuál quieres? Which one do you want? ◊ Quiero salir.* I want to go out. ◊ *De entrada, quiero sopa.* I'd like soup to start with. → WANT • *vi* want to: *No quiero.* I don't want to. ▶ **~ decir** mean **queriendo** (*a propósito*) on purpose **quisiera...** I, he, etc. would like to *do sth*: *Quisiera saber por qué...* I'd like to know why... **sin ~**: *Perdona, fue sin ~.* Sorry, it was an accident.

querido *adj* **1** (*apreciado, cartas*) dear **2** (*simpático*) nice: *Es muy ~.* He's really nice.

queso *nm* cheese

quicio *nm* ▶ **sacar de ~** drive *sb* crazy

quiebra *nf* bankruptcy [*pl* -ies]

quien *pron* **1** (*sujeto*) who: *Fue mi tío ~ me lo dijo.* It was my uncle who told me. **2** (*complemento*) **NOTA** El inglés no suele traducir **quien** cuando funciona como complemento, aunque también es correcto usar **who** o **whom**: *el muchacho con ~ la vi ayer* the boy (who) I saw her with yesterday ◊ *la actriz de ~ se ha escrito tanto* the actress about whom so much has been written **3** (*cualquiera*) whoever: *Invite a ~ quiera.* Invite whoever you want. ◊ *~ esté a favor, que levante la mano.* Those in favor, raise your hands.

quién *pron* who: *¿~ es?* Who is it? ◊ *¿A ~ viste?* Who did you see? ◊ *¿De ~ hablas?* Who are you talking about? ▶ **¿de ~?** whose: *¿De ~ es este abrigo?* Whose coat is this?

quienquiera *pron* whoever

quieto *adj* still: *estarse/quedarse ~* keep still

química *nf* chemistry

químico/a *adj* chemical ● *nm-nf* chemist

quince *adj, nm, pron* **1** fifteen **2** (*fecha*) fifteenth ▶ *~ días* two weeks, fortnight (GB)

quinceañero/a *nm-nf* (*adolescente*) teenager

quincena *nf* (*quince días*) two weeks

quinientos/as *adj, nm, pron* five hundred

quinto/a *adj, nm-nf, pron* fifth ● **quinta** *nf* (*Aut*) fifth (gear) ▶ **en el ~ infierno**, **la quinta porra**, etc. in the middle of nowhere

quiosco *nm* stand ▶ *~ de periódicos* news-stand

quirófano *nm* operating room, (operating) theatre (GB)

quirúrgico *adj* surgical: *una intervención quirúrgica* an operation

quisquilloso *adj* **1** (*exigente*) fussy **2** (*susceptible*) touchy

quitaesmalte *nm* nail polish remover

quitamanchas *nm* stain remover

quitar *vt* **1** take *sth* off/down/out: *Quita tus cosas de mi escritorio.* Take your things off my desk. ◊ *Quítale el suéter.* Take his sweater off. **2** (*Mat, sustraer*) take *sth* away: *Si a tres le quitas uno...* Take one (away) from three... ◊ *Me quitaron el pasaporte.* I had my passport taken away. **3** (*mancha*) remove **4** (*dolor*) relieve **5** (*tiempo*): *Los niños me quitan mucho tiempo.* The children take up a lot of my time. ● **quitarse** *vp* **1** take *sth* off: *~ los zapatos* take your shoes off **2** (*mancha*): *Esta mancha no se quita.* This stain won't come out. **3** (*costumbre,*

manía) kick: *~ la costumbre de morderse las uñas* kick the habit of biting your nails **NOTA** Para expresiones, ver al sustantivo, adjetivo, etc., p. ej. **quitarse las ganas** en GANA.

quizá (*tb* **quizás**) *adv* maybe

R r

rábano *nm* radish

rabia *nf* **1** anger **2** (*Med*) rabies ▶ **dar ~** make *sb* mad: *Me da mucha ~.* It makes me really mad.

rabieta *nf* tantrum

rabillo *nm* ▶ **con/por el ~ del ojo** out of the corner of your eye

rabioso 1 (*furioso*) furious **2** (*Med*) rabid

rabo *nm* (*animal*) tail

racha *nf* **1** (*serie*) run: *una ~ de suerte* a run of good luck **2** (*viento*) gust ▶ **pasar una mala ~** be going through a bad spell

racial *adj* racial: *la discriminación ~* racial discrimination ◊ *relaciones ~es* race relations

racimo *nm* bunch

racional *adj* rational

racionamiento *nm* rationing

racismo *nm* racism

racista *adj, nmf* racist

radar *nm* radar

radiactivo *adj* radioactive

radiador *nm* radiator

radial *adj* radio: *una cadena ~* a radio station

radiante *adj* **1** (*brillante*) bright **2** (*persona*) radiant: *~ de alegría* radiant with happiness

radical *adj, nmf* radical

radicar *vi* lie in *sth*

radio *nm* **1** (*Geom*) radius [*pl* radii] **2** (*rueda*) spoke **3** (*Quím*) radium ● *nm* o *nf* radio [*pl* -s]: *oír/escuchar la ~* listen to the radio ◊ *en la ~* on the radio

radioaficionado/a *nm-nf* ham radio operator

radioescucha *nmf* listener

radiograbadora *nf* radio cassette player

radiografía *nf* X-ray: *hacer una ~* take an X-ray

ráfaga *nf* **1** (*viento*) gust **2** (*disparos*) burst

rafting *nm* white-water rafting

raído *adj* threadbare

raíz *nf* root ▶ echar raíces **1** (*planta*) take root **2** (*persona*) put down roots ~ **cuadrada/cúbica** square/cube root

raja *nf* **1** (*fisura*) crack **2** (*herida*) cut **3** (*alimentos*) slice

rajadura *nf* crack

rajar *vt* **1** (*cortar*) cut **2** (*llanta*) slash **3** (*apuñalar*) stab ● **rajarse** *vp* **1** (*romperse*) crack **2** (*echarse atrás*) back out **3** (*And, en examen*) flunk, fail (*GB*)

ralladura *nf* ▶ ~ **de limón/naranja** grated lemon/orange rind

rallar *vt* grate

rama *nf* branch ▶ andar/irse por las ~s beat about the bush

ramo *nm* **1** (*flores*) bunch **2** (*sector*) sector

rampa *nf* ramp

rana *nf* frog

ranchero/a *nm-nf* (*Mx*) rancher

rancho *nm* (*Mx*) ranch

rancio *adj* **1** (*mantequilla*) rancid **2** (*pan*) stale **3** (*olor*) musty

rango *nm* rank

ranking *nm* ranking(s): *primero en el ~ mundial* number one in the world rankings

ranura *nf* slot

rapar *vt* (*pelo*) crop

rapaz *nf* (*ave*) bird of prey

rapidez *nf* speed

rápido *adj* **1** (*breve*) quick: *una llamada rápida* a quick phone call **2** (*veloz*) fast ● *adv* quickly ● **rápidos** *nm* (*río*) rapids

raponazo *nm* mugging

rappel (*tb* **rápel**) *nm* rappel, abseiling (*GB*)

raptar *vt* kidnap

rapto *nm* kidnapping

raptor *nm-nf* kidnapper

raqueta *nf* racket

raro *adj* **1** (*extraño*) strange **2** (*poco común*) rare: *una planta rara* a rare plant

ras *nm* ▶ a ~ **de** level with sth: *a ~ del suelo* along the floor

rasca *nf* (*And*): *pegarse una ~* get drunk

rascacielos *nm* skyscraper

rascar(se) *vt*, *vp* scratch: ~*se la cabeza* scratch your head

rasgar(se) *vt*, *vp* tear

rasgo *nm* **1** feature **2** (*de pluma*) stroke

rasguño *nm* scratch

raso *adj* **1** (*llano*) flat **2** (*cucharada, medida*) level **3** (*balón*) low ● *nm* satin

raspar *vt* **1** (*arañar*) scratch **2** (*quitar*) scrape sth (*off sth*) ● *vi* be rough: *Esta toalla raspa.*

This towel's rough. ● **rasparse** *vp* graze: ~ *la mano* graze your hand

rastra *nf* ▶ a ~s: *Se acercó a ~s.* He crawled over.

rastrear *vt* **1** (*seguir la pista*) follow **2** (*zona*) comb

rastreo *nm* search

rastrillo *nm* **1** rake **2** (*Mx, para rasurar*) razor

rastro *nm* **1** (*pista*) trail **2** (*vestigio, señal*) trace: *Desaparecieron sin dejar ~.* They disappeared without trace. **3** (*Mx, matadero*) slaughterhouse ▶ **perder el ~** lose track of sth/sb

rasurar(se) *vt*, *vp* shave

rata *nf* rat ● *adj* (*tacaño*) stingy ● *nmf* (*persona*) skinflint

ratero/a *nm-nf* pickpocket
→THIEF

ratificar *vt* **1** (*tratado, acuerdo*) ratify **2** (*noticia*) confirm

rato *nm* while: *dentro de un ~* in a while ▶ **al (poco)** ~ shortly afterwards **a ~s** sometimes **para ~**: *Todavía tengo para ~.* I still have a lot to do. **pasar el ~** pass the time

ratón *nm* mouse [*pl* mice] ▶ **el ~/ratoncito Pérez** the tooth fairy **~ de biblioteca** bookworm

ratonera *nf* **1** (*trampa*) mousetrap **2** (*madriguera*) mousehole

raya *nf* **1** line: *marcar una ~* draw a line **2** (*listas*) stripe: *una camisa de ~s* a striped shirt **3** (*pelo*) part, parting (*GB*) **4** (*pantalón*) crease ▶ **pasarse de la ~** overstep the mark **tener a ~** keep a tight rein on sb

rayado *adj* (*loco*) crazy

rayar *vt* scratch ● *vi* border on sth: ~ **en** el fanatismo be bordering on fanaticism

rayo *nm* **1** ray: *un ~ de sol* a ray of sunshine ◊ ~s X X-rays **2** (*tormenta*) (flash of) lightning **3** **rayitos** (*pelo*) highlights ▶ ~ **láser** laser beam

raza *nf* **1** (*humana*) race **2** (*animal*) breed ▶ **de** ~: *un perro de ~* a pedigree dog

razón *nf* **1** (*argumento, motivo*) reason (*for sth*): *la ~ de su renuncia* the reason for his resignation **2** (*mensaje*) message ▶ **tener/no tener** ~ be right/wrong

razonable *adj* reasonable

razonamiento *nm* reasoning

razonar *vi* (*pensar*) think ● *vt* (*explicar*) give reasons for sth: *Razona tu respuesta.* Give reasons for your answer.

re *nm* (*Mús*) D ● **re-** *pref: un libro re-aburrido* an incredibly boring book ◊ *Está rebueno.* He's really gorgeous.

reabastecer(se) *vt, vp* (*combustible*) refuel

reacción *nf* reaction

reaccionar *vi* react

reactor *nm* **1** (*motor*) jet engine **2** (*avión*) jet ▶ **~ atómico/nuclear** nuclear reactor

readmitir *vt* readmit

real *adj* **1** (*caso, historia*) true **2** (*de reyes*) royal

realidad *nf* reality [*pl* -ies] ▶ **en ~** actually **hacerse ~** come true

realismo *nm* realism

realista *adj* realistic ● *nmf* realist

realización *nf* **1** (*proyecto, trabajo*): *Yo me encargaré de la ~ del plan.* I'll take charge of carrying out the plan. **2** (*objetivo, sueño*) fulfillment

realizar *vt* **1** (*llevar a cabo*) carry sth out: *~ un proyecto* carry out a project **2** (*sueño, objetivo*) fulfill ● **realizarse** *vp* **1** (*hacerse realidad*) come true: *Mis sueños se realizaron.* My dreams came true. **2** (*persona*) fulfill yourself

realmente *adve* really

realzar *vt* enhance

reanimar *vt* revive ● **reanimarse** *vp* **1** (*fortalecerse*) get your strength back **2** (*volver en sí*) regain consciousness

reanudar *vt* **1** resume: *~ el trabajo* resume work **2** (*amistad, relación*) renew

rearme *nm* rearmament

rebaja *nf* **1** (*descuento*) discount **2 rebajas** (*saldo*) sales

rebajar *vt* **1** (*reducir*) reduce **2** (*color*) soften **3** (*humillar*) humiliate ● **rebajarse** *vp* **1 ~ (a hacer algo)** lower yourself (by doing sth) **2 ~ ante algn** bow down to sb

rebanada *nf* slice

rebaño *nm* **1** (*ovejas*) flock **2** (*ganado*) herd

rebasar *vi* (*Mx, Aut*) pass

rebelarse *vp* rebel

rebelde *adj* **1** rebel: *el general ~* the rebel general **2** (*espíritu*) rebellious **3** (*niño*) difficult ● *nmf* rebel

rebelión *nf* rebellion

rebobinar *vt* rewind

rebosante *adj* overflowing: *~ de alegría* overflowing with joy

rebosar *vi, vt* be overflowing with sth

rebotar *vi* **1** (*balón*) bounce (*off sth*) **2** (*bala*) ricochet (*off sth*)

rebote *nm* rebound ▶ **de ~** on the rebound

rebuscarse (*tb* **rebuscárselas**) *vp* get by

rebuznar *vi* bray

recado *nm* **1** (*mensaje*) message **2** (*encargo*) errand: *hacer unos ~s* run a few errands

recaer *vi* **1** (*Med*) have a relapse **2** (*vicio*) go back to your old ways **3 ~ en** (a) (*responsabilidad, sospecha*) fall on sb: *Todas las sospechas recayeron sobre mí.* Everyone suspected me. (b) (*premio*) go to sb/sth

recalcar *vt* stress

recalentar *vt* warm sth up ● **recalentarse** *vp* overheat

recámara *nf* (*Mx, dormitorio*) bedroom

recapacitar *vt* think sth over ● *vi* think things over

recargado *adj* **1** over-elaborate **2** (*de peso*) overloaded

recargar *vt* **1** (*cargar de nuevo*) (a) (*pila, batería*) recharge (b) (*arma*) reload (c) (*pluma*) refill **2** (*de peso*) overload **3** (*apoyar*) lean sth against sth ● **recargarse** *vp* (*apoyarse*) lean against sth

recargo *nm* surcharge

recaudar *vt* collect

recepción *nf* reception

recepcionista *nmf* receptionist

recesión *nf* recession

receta *nf* **1** (*Cocina*) recipe: *la ~ de un plato* the recipe for a dish **2** (*Med*) prescription

recetar *vt* prescribe

rechazar *vt* turn sth/sb down

rechupete ▶ **de ~** delicious

recibir *vt* **1** receive, get (*más coloq*): *Recibí tu carta.* I received/got your letter. **2** (*persona*) welcome: *Salí a ~los.* I went out to welcome them.

recibo *nm* **1** (*comprobante*) receipt **2** (*factura*) bill: *el ~ de la luz* the electric bill

reciclaje *nm* (*materiales*) recycling

reciclar *vt* (*materiales*) recycle

recién *adv* **1** recently: *~ creado* recently formed **2** (*hace poco*) (only) just: *~ llegó.* He's just arrived. ▶ **~ pintado** (*cartel*) wet paint **un ~ nacido** a newborn baby [*pl* -ies]

reciente *adj* **1** (*huella*) fresh **2** (*acontecimiento*) recent

recipiente *nm* container

recitar *vt* recite

reclamación *nf* (*tb* **reclamo** *nm*) complaint ▶ **hacer/presentar una ~** make/lodge a complaint

reclamar vt demand ● vi complain

reclinable adj (asiento) reclining

reclinar vt lean sth (on sth/sb): Reclinó la cabeza en mi hombro. He leaned his head on my shoulder. ● **reclinarse** vp (persona) lean back (against sth/sb)

recluso/a nm-nf prisoner

recluta nmf recruit

recobrar vt get sth back: ~ el dinero/la memoria get your money/memory back ● **recobrarse** vp recover: ~ de una enfermedad recover from an illness

recogedor nm dustpan

recoger vt 1 pick sth up: Recoge tu ropa. Pick up your clothes. ◊ ~ el correo pick up your mail 2 (reunir) collect: ~ firmas collect signatures 3 (ordenar) clean sth up 4 (ir a buscar) pick sb/sth up: ~ a los niños del colegio pick the kids up from school ● vi clean up ▶ ~se el pelo tie your hair back

recogida nf ▶ ~ de basura garbage collection

recogido adj 1 (tranquilo) quiet 2 (pelo): con el pelo ~ with your hair up

recomendación nf recommendation: por ~ de mi hermano on my brother's recommendation

recomendado adj 1 recommended: muy ~ highly recommended 2 (correo) certified, registered (GB): mandar una carta recomendada send a letter by certified mail

recomendar vt recommend

recompensa nf reward ▶ en/como ~ as a reward

recompensar vt reward sb (for sth)

reconciliarse vp make up

reconocer vt 1 recognize 2 (admitir) admit: ~ un error admit a mistake 3 (examinar) examine

reconocido adj well known: un ~ sociólogo a well-known sociologist

reconocimiento nm recognition ▶ ~ médico physical (examination): hacerse un ~ médico have a physical

reconquista nf reconquest

reconstruir vt 1 rebuild 2 (hechos, suceso) reconstruct

recopilar vt collect

récord nm record: batir/tener un ~ break/hold a record

recordar vt 1 recordarle algo a algn remind sb (about sth/to do sth): Recuérdame que compre pan. Remind me to buy some bread. 2 (por asociación) remind sb of sth/sb: Me recuerda a mi hermano. He reminds me of my brother. → REMIND 3 (acordarse) remember sth/doing sth: No recuerdo su nombre. I can't remember his name. ▶ que yo recuerde as far as I remember

recorrer vt 1 go around: ~ Ecuador en autobús go around Ecuador by bus 2 (distancia) cover

recorrido nm route

recortar vt 1 (artículo, figura) cut sth out 2 (lo que sobra) trim 3 (gastos) cut

recostado adj lying: Está ~ en el sofá. He's lying on the couch.

recostar vt (apoyar) lean: Lo recosté contra la pared. I leaned it (up) against the wall. ● **recostarse** vp lie down

recrearse vp take pleasure in sth

recreo nm recess, break (GB) ▶ de ~ recreational

recta nf straight line ▶ ~ final 1 (Dep) home stretch 2 (fig) closing stages [pl]: la ~ final de la campaña the closing stages of the campaign

rectangular adj rectangular

rectángulo nm rectangle ● adj (triángulo) right, right-angled (GB)

rectificar vt 1 rectify: ~ el error rectify the mistake 2 (actitud, conducta) improve

recto adj straight ● nm rectum ▶ todo ~ straight ahead

recuadro nm box

recuerdo nm 1 (memoria) memory [pl -ies] 2 (souvenir) souvenir 3 recuerdos regards: Mi mamá te manda ~s. My mother sends her regards.

recuperar vt 1 recover: ~ la vista recover your sight 2 (tiempo, clases) make sth up: Tienes que ~ tus horas de trabajo. You must make up the time. 3 (Educ): Recuperé francés. I passed in French the second time around. ● **recuperarse** vp recover from sth

recurrir vi 1 (utilizar) resort to sth 2 (pedir ayuda) turn to sb

recurso nm 1 (medio) resort: como último ~ as a last resort 2 recursos resources: ~s económicos economic resources

red nf 1 (Dep, caza, pesca) net 2 (sistema) network: la ~ de carreteras the road network 3 (organizaciones) chain 2 (Internet) the Net ▶ caer en la ~ fall into the trap

redacción nf essay

redactar vt, vi write

redactor/a nm-nf (Period) editor

redada nf raid

redoblar vi (tambor) roll

redomado adj out-and-out

redondear vt 1 round sth off: ~ un negocio round off a business deal 2 (precio, cifra) round sth up/down

redondo adj 1 round ▸ **a la redonda**: en 10 km a la redonda within ten kilometers **salir** ~ turn out perfectly

reducción nf reduction

reducido adj (pequeño) small

reducir vt reduce ▸ **todo se reduce a...** it all comes down to...

redundancia nf redundancy

reelegir vt re-elect

reembolsar vt 1 (devolución) refund 2 (gastos) reimburse

reembolso nm refund ▸ **envío/pago contra ~** cash on delivery (abrev COD)

reemplazar vt replace sth/sb (with sth/sb)

reencarnación nf reincarnation

reencarnarse vp be reincarnated (as sth/sb)

refacción nf (Mx) spare part

referencia nf reference: Con ~ a su carta... With reference to your letter... ▸ **hacer ~** a refer to sth/sb

referéndum (tb **referendo**) nm referendum

referente adj ~ a regarding sth/sb ▸ **(en lo) ~ a** with regard to sth

referirse vp refer to sth/sb

refilón ▸ **de ~** out of the corner of your eye

refinería nf refinery [pl -ies]

reflector nm 1 (edificio) spotlight 2 (estadio) floodlight

reflejar vt reflect

reflejo adj reflex: un acto ~ a reflex action ● nm 1 (imagen) reflection 2 (reacción) reflex

reflexionar vi reflect (on sth)

reforestación nf reforestation

reforma nf 1 reform 2 (en un edificio) alteration

reformar vt 1 reform: ~ una ley/a un delincuente reform a law/delinquent 2 (edificio) make alterations to sth ● **reformarse** vp mend your ways

reformatorio nm juvenile detention center

reforzar vt reinforce

refrán nm saying

refrescante adj refreshing

refrescar vt 1 (enfriar) cool 2 (memoria) refresh 3 (conocimientos) brush up on sth: Necesito ~ mi inglés. I have to brush up on my English. ● vi get cooler ● **refrescarse** vp freshen up

refresco nm soda, soft drink (GB)

refrigerador nm (tb **refrigeradora** nf) refrigerator

refrigerar vt refrigerate

refuerzo nm reinforcement

refugiado/a nm-nf refugee

refugiar(se) vt, vp shelter: ~se de la lluvia shelter from the rain

refugio nm refuge

refunfuñar vi grumble (about sth)

regadera nf 1 (jardín) watering can 2 (ducha) shower

regadío nm irrigation: tierra de ~ irrigated land

regalado adj 1 (muy barato) dirt cheap 2 (muy fácil) dead easy

regalar vt 1 (hacer un regalo) give 2 (cuando no se quiere algo) give sth away

regaliz nm licorice

regalo nm gift: La última pregunta fue un ~. The last question was an absolute gift.

regañadientes ▸ **a ~** reluctantly

regañar vt tell sb off (for sth)

regaño nm good talking-to

regar vt 1 (planta, jardín) water 2 (esparcir) scatter

regata nf boat race

regatear vt, vi 1 (precio) haggle (over/about sth) 2 (fútbol) dribble

regazo nm lap

regenerar vt regenerate ● **regenerarse** vp 1 regenerate 2 (persona) mend your ways

regente adj, nmf regent

régimen nm 1 (Pol, normas) regime 2 (dieta) diet: estar a ~ be on a diet

regimiento nm regiment

región nf region

regional adj regional

regir vt 1 (país, sociedad) rule 2 (empresa, proyecto) run ● vi (ley) be in force

registradora nf (And, puerta) turnstile

registrar vt 1 (inspeccionar) search 2 (grabar, hacer constar) record: ~ información record information 3 (correo) register 4 (en aeropuerto) check sth in ● **registrarse** vp register

registro nm 1 (inscripción) registration 2 (inspección) search 3 (lugar, oficina) registry [pl -ies] ▸ **~ civil** registry office

regla *nf* **1** rule: *por ~ general* as a general rule **2** *(instrumento)* ruler **3** *(menstruación)* period ▶ **en ~** in order

reglamentario *adj* regulation: *uniforme ~* regulation uniform

reglamento *nm* regulations *[pl]*

regocijarse *vp* be delighted: *Se regocijaron con la noticia.* They were delighted at the news.

regocijo *nm* joy

regresar *vt* **1** *(cosa)* return **2** *(persona)* send *sb* back ● go/come back: *No quieren ~ a su país.* They don't want to go back home.

regreso *nm* return: *a mi ~ a la ciudad* on my return to the city

reguero *nm* trickle

regular¹ *vt* regulate

regular² *adj* **1** regular: *verbos ~es* regular verbs **2** *(mediocre)* poor **3** *(mediano)* medium: *de altura ~* of medium height ● *adv*: *El negocio va ~.* Business isn't going too well. ◊ *La abuela está ~ (de salud).* Grandma isn't doing too well.

regularidad *nf* regularity ▶ **con ~** regularly

rehabilitación *nf* rehabilitation

rehabilitar *vt* rehabilitate

rehacer *vt* redo ▶ **~ la vida** rebuild your life

rehén *nmf* hostage

rehuir *vt* avoid *(doing sth)*

rehusar *vt* refuse: *Rehusaron venir.* They refused to come.

reina *nf* queen

reinado *nm* reign

reinar *vi* **1** *(gobernar)* reign **2** *(prevalecer)* prevail

reincidir *vi* *(Jur)* reoffend

reiniciar *vt* resume

reino *nm* kingdom: *el ~ animal* the animal kingdom **2** *(ámbito)* realm ▶ **el R~ Unido** the United Kingdom *(abrev* **UK***)*

reintegro *nm* **1** refund **2** *(en sorteo)* return of stake

reír *vi* laugh ● *~ (chiste, etc.)* laugh at *sth* ● **reírse** *vp* **1** *~ con algn* have a laugh with *sb* **2** *~ con algo* laugh at *sth* **3** *~ de* laugh at *sth/sb*: *Siempre se ríen de mí.* They always laugh at me.

reivindicación *nf* **1** *(derecho)* claim **2** *(atentado)*: *No se produjo una ~ de la bomba.* Nobody claimed responsibility for the bomb.

reivindicar *vt* **1** *(reclamar)* claim **2** *(atentado)* claim responsibility for *sth*

reja *nf* **1** *(ventana)* grille **2** *(cerca)* railing(s) **3** **rejas** bars: *entre ~s* behind bars

rejilla *nf* **1** grille **2** *(alcantarilla)* grating

rejuvenecer *vt* make *sb* look younger

relación *nf* **1** relationship: *mantener relaciones con algn* have a relationship with *sb* **2** *(conexión)* connection *(between...)* ▶ **con/en ~ a** in/with relation to *sth/sb* **relaciones públicas** public relations *(abrev* **PR***)*

relacionado *adj* related *(to sth)*

relacionar *vt* relate *sth (to/with sth)* ● **relacionarse** *vp* mix *(with sb)*

relajación *nf* **1** relaxation **2** *(tensión)* easing: *la ~ de las tensiones internacionales* the easing of international tension

relajar *vt* relax ● **relajarse** *vp* **1** relax **2** *(reglas, disciplina)* become lax

relajo *nm* **1** mess: *¡Qué ~ el que tienes en la oficina!* What a mess your office is! **2** *(ruido)* racket

relamer *vt* lick *sth* clean ● **relamerse** *vp* lick your lips

relámpago *nm* lightning *[U]*: *Me asustan los ~s.* Lightning frightens me. *~ un ~* a flash of lightning ◊ *una visita ~* a lightning visit

relatar *vt* relate

relatividad *nf* relativity

relativo/a *adj* **1** *(no absoluto)* relative **2** *~ a* relating to *sth*

relato *nm* **1** *(cuento)* story *[pl -ies]* **2** *(descripción)* account: *hacer un ~ de los hechos* give an account of events

relax *nm* relaxation

relevante *adj* important

relevar *vt* **1** *(sustituir)* take over *(from sb)*: *Me relevó un compañero.* A colleague took over from me. **2** *(de un cargo)* relieve *sb* of *sth*: *Fue relevado del cargo.* He was relieved of his duties. ● **relevarse** *vp* take turns *(at sth)*

relevo *nm* **1** relief **2** *(turno)* shift **3** **relevos** *(Dep)*: *una carrera de ~s* a relay race

relieve *nm* **1** *(Geog)*: *un mapa en ~* a relief map ◊ *una región de ~ accidentado* an area with a rugged landscape **2** *(importancia)* significance

religión *nf* religion

religioso/a *adj* religious ● *nm-nf* monk *[fem* nun*]*

relinchar *vi* neigh

reliquia *nf* relic

rellenar vt **1** fill: ~ *un pastel de/ con fruta* fill a cake with fruit **2** (*volver a llenar*) refill **3** (*formulario*) fill sth out

relleno nm **1** filling: *pasteles con ~ de guayaba* pastries filled with guava **2** (*cojín*) stuffing

reloj nm **1** (*de pared, mesa*) clock **2** (*de pulsera, de bolsillo*) watch ▶ **contra ~** against the clock ◆ **~ (de) cucú** cuckoo clock ◆ **~ de sol** sundial

relojería nf watch repair shop

relojero/a nm-nf watchmaker

relucir vi shine

remangar(se) vt, vp roll sth up: *Se remangó los pantalones.* He rolled up his pants.

remar vi row

rematar vt **1** (*terminar*) finish sth/ sb off **2** (*Dep*): *Ronaldo remató la jugada.* Ronaldo shot at goal.

remate nm **1** (*término*) end **2** (*extremo*) top: *el ~ de una torre* the top of a tower **3** (*borde*) border: *un ~ de encaje* a lace border **4** (*Dep*) shot ▶ **de ~**: *un imbécil de ~* a prize idiot

remediar vt **1** (*solucionar*) remedy **2** (*daño*) repair ▶ **no lo puedo ~** I, you, etc. can't help it

remedio nm **1** (*cura*) remedy [pl -ies] (*for sth*) **2** (*medicamento*) medicine ▶ **no tener más ~ (que...)** have no choice (but to...)

remendar vt mend

remiendo nm (*costura*) patch

remite nm return address

remitente nmf sender

remo nm **1** (*instrumento*) oar **2** (*actividad*) rowing: *un club de ~* a rowing club ▶ **a ~**: *cruzar un río a ~* row across a river

remojar vt soak

remojo nm: *Pon los garbanzos en ~.* Soak the garbanzo beans.

remolacha nf beet, beetroot (GB)

remolcar vt tow

remolino nm **1** eddy [pl -ies] **2** (*río*) whirlpool **3** (*pelo*) cowlick

remolón/ona adj lazy ◆ nm-nf slacker

remolque nm (*vehículo*) trailer

remontar vt **1** (*subir*) go up sth **2** (*dificultad*) overcome **3** (*el partido/marcador*) turn the game around ◆ **remontarse** vp (*hecho, tradición*) date back to sth ▶ **el vuelo** soar

remorder vt ▶ **remorderle a algn la conciencia** have a guilty conscience

remordimiento nm remorse ▶ **tener ~s (de conciencia)** feel guilty

remoto adj remote

remover vt **1** (*líquido*) stir **2** (*ensalada*) toss **3** (*tierra*) turn sth over **4** (*asunto*) bring sth up

renacimiento nm **1** (*resurgimiento*) revival **2 el Renacimiento** the Renaissance

renacuajo nm tadpole

rencor nm resentment ▶ **guardar ~** bear sb a grudge

rencoroso adj resentful

rendición nf surrender

rendido adj (*agotado*) worn out

rendija nf crack

rendimiento nm **1** performance: *un motor de alto ~* a high-performance engine **2** (*producción*) output

rendir vt (*cansar*) tire sb out ◆ vi **1** (*alimento, etc.*): *El arroz rinde mucho.* Rice goes a long way. **2** (*persona*): *Rindo más por la mañana.* I work better in the mornings. ◆ **rendirse** vp **1** give up **2** (*Mil*) surrender ▶ **~ culto** worship

renegar vi **1** renounce: *~ de la religión* renounce your religion **2** (*quejarse*) grumble (*about sth*)

renglón nm line

reno nm reindeer [pl reindeer]

renombre nm renown: *un médico de mucho ~* a renowned doctor

renovación nf **1** renewal **2** (*estructural*) renovation

renovar vt **1** renew: *~ un contrato/ el pasaporte* renew a contract/ your passport **2** (*edificio*) renovate **3** (*modernizar*) modernize

renta nf **1** (*alquiler*) rent **2** (*Fin, ingresos*) income: *el impuesto sobre la ~* income tax

rentable adj profitable

rentar vt (*Mx*) rent ▶ **se renta** for rent, to let (GB) →ALQUILAR

renuncia nf resignation: *entregar la ~* hand in your resignation

renunciar vi **1** renounce: *~ a una herencia/un derecho* renounce an inheritance/a right **2** (*puesto*) resign: *Renunció a su cargo.* She resigned from her position.

reñido adj hard-fought: *El partido estuvo muy ~.* It was a hard-fought game.

reñir vi (*discutir*) argue (*with sb*) (*about/over sth*): *No riñan por eso.* Don't argue over something like that.

reo nmf accused ▶ **~ de muerte** condemned person

reojo ▸ mirar de ~ look at sb out of the corner of your eye

reparación nf repair

reparar vt repair ● vi ~ **en** notice: *Reparé en que estaba cansado.* I noticed he was tired.

reparo nm reservation ▸ **poner ~s** find fault with sth

repartidor/a nm-nf delivery man/woman [pl men/women] ▸ **~ de periódicos** paperboy [fem papergirl]

repartir vt **1** (*dividir*) divide sth up: ~ *el trabajo* divide up the work **2** (a) (*distribuir*) distribute (b) (*correo, mercancías*) deliver (c) (*naipes, golpes*) deal →BARAJA

reparto nm **1** (*distribución*) distribution **2** (*mercancías, correo*) delivery [pl -ies] **3** (*Cine, Teat*) cast

repasar vt **1** (*revisar*) check: ~ *un texto* check a text **2** (*Educ, estudiar*) review, revise (GB)

repaso nm **1** (*Educ*) review, revision (GB): *dar un ~ a algo* review/revise sth **2** (*revisión, inspección*) check

repatriar vt repatriate

repelar vi (*Mx*) complain (about sth)

repelente adj (*persona*) horrible ● nm (*insecto*) repellent

repente nm ▸ **de ~** suddenly

repentino adj sudden

repercusión nf repercussion

repercutir vi have repercussions: ~ *en la economía* have repercussions on the economy

repertorio nm (*Mús*) repertoire

repetición nf repetition

repetir vt **1** (*volver a decir*) repeat, say sth again (*más coloq*) **2** (*volver a hacer*) do sth again **3** (*ajo, cebolla, pimiento*): *Estoy repitiendo el pimiento.* I can still taste the peppers. ● vi (*servirse otro poco*) have another helping ● **repetirse** vp (*acontecimiento*) happen again **2** (*persona*) repeat yourself

repicar vt, vi ring

repisa nf **1** ledge **2** (*chimenea*) mantelpiece **3** (*ventana*) windowsill **4** (*estante*) shelf [pl shelves]

repleto adj full

replicar vt retort ● vi answer back: *¡No me repliques!* Don't answer me back!

repollito nm ▸ **~s de Bruselas** Brussels sprouts

repollo nm cabbage

reponer vt **1** (*combustible, provisiones*) replenish **2** (*película*)

rerun ● **reponerse** vp recover (*from sth*)

reportaje nm documentary [pl -ies]

reportar ▸

reportero/a nm-nf reporter ▸ **~ gráfico** press photographer

reposacabezas nm headrest

reposar vi **1** (*descansar*) rest **2** (*yacer*) lie

reposo nm **1** (*descanso*) rest **2** (*paz*) peace

repostería nf baking

represa nf dam

represalia nf reprisal

representación nf **1** representation **2** (*Teat*) performance

representante nmf **1** representative **2** (*Cine, Teat*) agent

representar vt **1** (*organización, país*) represent **2** (*cuadro, etc.*) depict **3** (*Teat*) (a) (*obra*) perform (b) (*papel*) play **4** (*edad*) look: *Representa unos 30 años.* She looks about 30.

representativo/a adj representative

represión nf repression

represivo adj repressive

reprimido adj repressed

reprobar vt, vi fail: ~ *en dos asignaturas* fail two subjects

reprochar vt reproach sb (*for sth*)

reproducción nf reproduction

reproducir(se) vt, vp reproduce

réptil nm crawl

reptil nm reptile

república nf republic

republicano/a adj, nm-nf republican

repuesto nm spare part ▸ **de ~** spare: *un rollo de ~* a spare roll of film

repugnante adj revolting

reputación nf reputation

requisar vt **1** (*confiscar*) seize **2** (*registrar*) search

requisito nm requirement

res nf **1** (farm) animal **2** (*carne*) beef

resaltar vt **1** (*color, belleza*) bring sth out **2** (*poner énfasis*) highlight ● vi stand out (*from sth*) ▸ **hacer ~** bring sth out

resbaladilla nf (*Mx*) slide

resbaladizo adj slippery

resbalar vi **1** (*Aut*) skid **2** (*superficie*) be slippery **3** ~ **(por)** slide (*along/down sth*): *La lluvia resbalaba por la ventana.* The rain slid down the window. **4** (*ser indiferente*): *Los estudios le resbalan.* He doesn't care about school. ● **resbalarse** vp slip (*on sth*)

resbalón *nm* slip: *dar/pegarse un ~* slip

resbaloso *adj* slippery

rescatar *vt* 1 (*salvar*) rescue 2 (*recuperar*) recover: *Pudo ~ el dinero.* He recovered the money.

rescate *nm* 1 (*salvación*) rescue 2 (*pago*) ransom: *pedir un ~ elevado* demand a high ransom

rescoldo *nm* embers [*pl*]

reseco *adj* very dry

resentirse *vp* 1 (*deteriorarse*) deteriorate 2 (*enfadarse*) be annoyed (*with sb*) (*about sth*) 3 (*dolerse*) hurt: *La pierna aún se resiente de la caída.* My leg still hurts from the fall.

reserva *nf* 1 reserve(s): *~s de petróleo* oil reserves 2 (*gasolina*) reserve tank 3 (*animales, plantas*) reserve ● *nmf* (*persona*) reserve

reservación *nf* reservation: *hacer una ~* make a reservation

reservado *adj* reserved

reservar *vt* 1 (*guardar*) save: *Resérvame un sitio.* Save me a place. 2 (*pedir con antelación*) reserve

resfriado *adj*: *Estoy ~.* I have a cold. ● *nm* cold

resfriarse *vp* catch a cold

resguardar *vt* protect ● **resguardarse** *vp* shelter: *~ de la lluvia* shelter from the rain

resguardo *nm* protection

residencia *nf* residence ▸ **~ de estudiantes** dormitory [*pl* -ies], hall of residence (GB)

residuos *nm* waste [*U*]: *~s tóxicos* toxic waste

resina *nf* resin

resistencia *nf* (*física*) strength

resistir *vt* 1 (*soportar*) withstand 2 (*peso*) take: *El puente no va a ~ el peso de ese camión.* The bridge won't take the weight of that truck. 3 (*tentación*) resist *sth* ● *vi* hold up ● **resistirse** *vp* refuse: *Me resistía a creerlo.* I refused to believe it.

resolver *vt* 1 (*solucionar*) solve 2 *~ hacer algo* (*decidir*) resolve to do *sth*

resonar *vi* 1 (*metal, voz*) ring 2 (*retumbar*) resound

resoplar *vi* huff and puff

resortera *nf* (*Mx*) slingshot, catapult (GB)

respaldar *vt* back *sth/sb* up

respaldo *nm* 1 (*silla*) back 2 (*apoyo*) support

respectivo *adj* respective

respecto *nm* ▸ **con ~** a with regard to *sth/sb*

respetable *adj* respectable

respetar *vt* 1 (*estimar*) respect *sth/sb* (*for sth*) 2 (*código, signo*) obey

respeto *nm* 1 (*consideración, veneración*) respect: *el ~ a los demás* respect for other people 2 (*miedo*) fear of *sth*: *tenerle ~ al agua* be afraid of water

respetuoso *adj* respectful

respiración *nf*: *ejercicios de ~* breathing exercises ◊ *contener la ~* hold your breath ▸ **~ artificial** artificial respiration ● **~ boca a boca** mouth-to-mouth resuscitation

respirar *vt, vi* breathe: *Respira hondo.* Take a deep breath. ▸ **no dejar ni ~** not give *sb* a minute's rest

respiratorio *adj* respiratory

resplandecer *vi* shine

resplandeciente *adj* shining

resplandor *nm* 1 brightness 2 (*fuego*) blaze

responder *vt, vi* answer: *~ a una pregunta* answer a question ● *vi* 1 (*reaccionar*) respond: *~ a un tratamiento* respond to treatment 2 *~ por* answer for *sth/sb*: *¡No respondo por mis acciones!* I won't answer for my actions!

responsabilidad *nf* responsibility [*pl* -ies]

responsabilizarse *vp* assume responsibility (*for sth*)

responsable *adj* responsible (*for sth*) ● *nmf*: *Los ~s se entregaron.* Those responsible gave themselves up. ◊ *el ~ de las obras* the person in charge of the construction work

respuesta *nf* 1 (*contestación*) answer: *una ~ a mi pregunta* an answer to my question 2 (*reacción*) response

resquebrajar(se) *vt, vp* crack

resta *nf* (*Mat*) subtraction

restablecer *vt* 1 restore: *~ el orden* restore order 2 (*diálogo, negociaciones*) resume ● **restablecerse** *vp* recover

restar *vt* take *sth* away: *~ dos de diez* take two away from ten

restauración *nf* restoration

restaurador/a *nm-nf* restorer

restaurante *nm* restaurant

restaurar *vt* restore

resto *nm* 1 rest 2 (*Mat*) remainder 3 **restos** (a) (*comida*) leftovers (b) (*edificio*) remains

restregar *vt* scrub ● **restregarse** *vp* rub: *~ los ojos* rub your eyes

resucitar *vt* 1 (*Rel*) rise from the dead ● *vt* (*Med*) resuscitate

resultado nm result: *como ~ de algo* as a result of sth ▶ **dar/lo dar** = be successful/unsuccessful ~ **final** (*Dep*) final score

resultar vi **1** (*ser*) be: *Resulta difícil de creer.* It's hard to believe. **2** ~ *que...* turn out (that...)

resumen nm summary [*pl* -ies] ▶ **en ~** in short

resumir vt **1** summarize: *~ un libro* summarize a book **2** (*concluir*) sum sth up

resurrección nf resurrection

retablo nm (*altar*) altarpiece

retador/a nm-nf challenger

retar vt challenge

retardado adj delayed: *de acción retardada* delayed-action

retazo nm remnant

retención nf (*tráfico*) hold-up

retener vt **1** (*guardar*) keep **2** (*memorizar*) remember **3** (*detener*) hold: *~ a algn en contra de su voluntad* hold sb against their will

retina nf retina

retirada nf retreat

retirado adj **1** (*remoto*) remote **2** (*jubilado*) retired

retirar vt withdraw: *~le el pasaporte a algn* withdraw sb's passport ◊ *~ una revista de circulación* withdraw a magazine from circulation ● **retirarse** vp **1** (*irse*) withdraw: *~ de una lucha* withdraw from a fight **2** (*jubilarse*) retire: *~ de la política* retire from politics **3** (*Mil*) retreat

retiro nm **1** (*jubilación, de una profesión*) retirement: *Anunció su ~ del fútbol.* He announced his retirement from football. **2** (*pensión*) retirement pension **3** (*lugar*) retreat

reto nm challenge

retocar vt (*pintura, fotos*) retouch

retoque nm finishing touch: *dar los últimos ~s a algo* put the finishing touches to sth

retorcer vt twist: *Me retorció el brazo.* He twisted my arm. ● **retorcerse** vp **1** ~ *de dolor* writhe in pain **2** ~ *de risa* double up with laughter

retorcijón nm cramp

retornable adj returnable

retorno nm return

retransmisión nf broadcast: *una ~ en directo/diferido* a live/recorded broadcast

retransmitir vt broadcast

retrasado adj **1** (*Med*) mentally disabled **2** (*atrasado*) behind: *Voy muy ~ en mi trabajo.* I'm

very behind with my work. **3** (*país, región*) backward

retrasar vt **1** delay: *Retrasaron todos los vuelos.* All the flights were delayed. **2** (*reloj*) put sth back: *~ el reloj una hora* put your watch back an hour ● **retrasarse** vp **1** (*llegar tarde*) be late **2** (*en trabajo*) fall behind: *Empezó a ~ en sus estudios.* He began to fall behind in his studies. **3** (*reloj*) be slow: *Este reloj se retrasa diez minutos.* This watch is ten minutes slow.

retraso nm **1** (*demora*) delay **2** (*subdesarrollo*) backwardness ▶ **con ~** cinco minutos, horas, etc. **de ~** five minutes, hours, etc. late **llevar/tener ~** be late: *El avión lleva cinco horas de ~.* The plane is five hours late.

retratar vt **1** (*pintar*) paint sb's portrait **2** (*Fot*) take a photograph (of sth/sb) **3** (*describir*) portray

retrato nm **1** (*cuadro*) portrait **2** (*foto*) photograph **3** (*descripción*) portrayal ▶ **~ hablado** composite (sketch), identikit® (*GB*)

retroceder vi **1** (*volver atrás*) go back **2** (*echarse atrás*) back down

retroceso nm **1** (*movimiento*) backward movement **2** (*de arma*) recoil

retrovisor nm rear-view mirror

retumbar vi resound

reuma nm o nf (*tb* reumatismo nm) rheumatism

reunión nf **1** meeting **2** (*encuentro informal*) gathering

reunir vt **1** gather sth/sb together **2** (*información*) collect **3** (*dinero*) raise **4** (*cualidades*) have ● **reunirse** vp meet

revancha nf revenge ▶ **tomar (la) ~** get/take your revenge

revelado nm developing

revelar vt **1** reveal: *~ un secreto* reveal a secret **2** (*Fot*) develop

reventar(se) vt, vi, vp burst: *Si comes más, vas a ~.* If you eat any more you'll burst. ▶ **me reventar** I, you, etc. hate sth

reventón nm (*Mex*) party [*pl* -ies]

reverencia nf ▶ **hacer una ~ 1** (*hombre*) bow **2** (*mujer*) curtsy [*pl* -ies]

reversa nf (*velocidad*) reverse (gear)

reversible adj reversible

reverso nm **1** (*papel*) back **2** (*moneda*) reverse

revés nm **1** (*tela*) wrong side **2** (*Dep*) backhand **3** (*bofetada*) slap **4** (*contratiempo*) setback:

sufrir un ~ suffer a setback ▶ **al/ del ~ 1** (con lo de arriba hacia abajo) upside down **2** (con lo de dentro hacia afuera) inside out **3** (con lo de delante hacia atrás) backwards, back to front (GB) **al ~ 1** (mal) wrong: ¡Todo está saliendo al ~! Everything's going wrong for me! **2** (al contrario) the other way around: Lo hice al ~ que tú. I did it the other way around than you did.

revestir vt (cubrir) cover

revisar vt check

revisión nf **1** revision **2** (Med) check-up [pl -ups]

revista nf **1** (publicación) magazine **2** (Teat) revue **3** (Mil) review

revivir vt relive: ~ el pasado relive the past ● vi revive

revolcar vt knock sth/sb over ● **revolcarse** vp **1** roll around: ~ en el pasto roll around on the grass **2** (en agua, lodo) wallow

revolotear vi fly around

revoltoso adj naughty

revolución nf revolution

revolucionar vt **1** (cambiar) revolutionize **2** (alborotar) stir sb up

revolucionario/a adj, nm-nf revolutionary [pl -ies]

revolver vt **1** (remover) (a) stir (b) (ensalada) toss **2** (desordenar) mess sth up: Los ladrones revolvieron todo el apartamento. The burglars turned the apartment upside down. **3** (estómago) turn ● vi (fisgar) rummage

revólver nm revolver

revuelta nf **1** (alzamiento) revolt **2** (desorden) ruckus

revuelto adj **1** (desordenado) messy **2** (agitado) worked up **3** (estómago): Tengo el estómago ~. I have an upset stomach.

rey nm **1** king **NOTA** Para los reyes, refiriéndonos a rey y reina, se dice the **king and queen. 2 Reyes** Epiphany ▶ **los Reyes Magos** the Three Wise Men

rezagado/a adj: Ven, no te quedes ~. Come on, don't get left behind. ● nm-nf straggler

rezar vt say: ~ una plegaria say a prayer ● vi pray (for sth/sb)

riachuelo nm stream

ribera nf **1** (orilla) bank **2** (vega) riverside

rico/a adj **1** rich: ~ en minerales rich in minerals **2** (delicioso) delicious **3** (mono) sweet: ¡Qué bebé más ~! What a sweet little baby! **4** (cómodo) comfortable ●

nm-nf rich man/woman [pl men/women]: los ~s the rich

ridiculez nf: ¡Qué ~! How ridiculous! ◇ Lo que dice es una ~. He's talking nonsense.

ridiculizar vt ridicule

ridículo adj ridiculous ▶ **dejar/ poner en ~** make a fool of sb **hacer el ~** make a fool of yourself

riego nm (Agricultura) irrigation ▶ ~ **sanguíneo** circulation

riel nm rail

rienda nf rein ▶ **dar ~ suelta** give free rein to sth/sb **llevar las ~s** be in charge (of sth)

riesgo nm risk: correr el ~ de hacer algo run the risk of doing sth ▶ **a/contra todo ~** (seguro) comprehensive

rifa nf raffle

rifar vt raffle

rifle nm rifle

rígido adj **1** (tieso) rigid **2** (severo) strict

riguroso adj **1** (estricto) strict **2** (minucioso) thorough **3** (castigo) harsh

rima nf rhyme

rimar vt rhyme

rimbombante adj (lenguaje) pompous

rímel® nm mascara

rincón nm corner

rinoceronte nm rhino [pl -s]

riña nf **1** (pelea) fight **2** (discusión) argument

riñón nm **1** (órgano) kidney **2** riñones (zona lumbar) lower back

riñonera nf fanny pack, bumbag (GB)

río nm river ▶MAR ▶ ~ **abajo/arriba** downstream/upstream

riqueza nf **1** (dinero) wealth [U]: acumular ~s amass wealth **2** (cualidad) richness: la ~ del terreno the richness of the land

risa nf laugh: ¡Qué ~! What a laugh! ▶ **dar ~** make sb laugh **me dio la ~** I, you, etc. got the giggles

risueño adj **1** (cara) smiling **2** (persona) cheerful

ritmo nm **1** (Mús) rhythm: seguir el ~ keep time **2** (velocidad) rate: el ~ de crecimiento the growth rate ▶ ~ **de vida** pace of life **tener ~ 1** (persona) have a good sense of rhythm **2** (melodía) have a good beat

rito nm rite

ritual nm ritual

rival adj, nm-nf rival

rizado adj curly: Tengo el pelo ~. I have curly hair.

rizar vt curl ● **rizarse** vp go curly

rizo *nm* curl

robar *vt* **1** (*banco, tienda, persona*) rob **2** (*dinero, objetos*) steal **3** (*casa, caja fuerte*) break into *sth* **4** (*cartas*) draw ● *vi* **1** steal **2** (*a una persona*) rob **3** (*en una casa*): *Robaron en casa de los vecinos.* Our neighbors' house was broken into. ➔ROB

robo *nm* **1** (*banco, tienda, persona*) robbery [*pl* -ies] **2** (*objetos*) theft **3** (*casa, oficina*) burglary [*pl* -ies] ➔THEFT **4** (*estafa*) rip-off [*pl* -offs]

robot *nm* robot

robusto *adj* robust

roca *nf* rock

roce *nm* **1** (*rozamiento*) rubbing **2** (*discusión*) clash

rociar *vt* spray *sth* (*with sth*)

rocío *nm* dew

rock *nm* rock: *un grupo de ~* a rock band

rocoso *adj* rocky

rodaja *nf* slice

rodaje *nm* (*Cine*) filming

rodar *vi* **1** (*dar vueltas*) roll **2** (*ir de un lado a otro*) lie around ● *vt* (*película*) film

rodear *vt* **1** surround *sth/sb* (*with sth/sb*) **2** (*con los brazos*): *Sus brazos me rodearon.* He put his arms around me. ● *vt, vi* make a detour: *~ (por) el bosque* make a detour through the woods ● **rodearse** *vp* surround yourself *with sth/sb*

rodeo *nm* **1** (*desvío*) detour: *dar un ~ de 5km* make a five-kilometer detour **2** (*espectáculo*) rodeo [*pl* -s] ▶ **andar con ~s** beat about the bush

rodilla *nf* knee ➔MY ▶ **de ~s**: *Todos estaban de ~s.* Everyone was kneeling down. ◇ *Tendrás que pedírmelo de ~s.* You'll have to get down on your knees and beg. **ponerse de ~s** kneel (down)

rodillera *nf* **1** (*Dep*) kneepad **2** (*Med*) knee support **3** (*parche*) knee patch

rodillo *nm* **1** (*Cocina*) rolling pin **2** (*pintura*) roller

roedor *nm* rodent

roer *vt* gnaw (at) *sth*

rogar *vt* **1** (*suplicar*) beg (*sb*) for *sth*; beg (*sth*) *of sb*: *Les rogué que me soltaran.* I begged them to let me go. **2** (*pedir*): *Tranquilízate, te lo ruego.* Calm down, please. ◇ *Me rogaron que me fuera.* They asked me to go. **3** (*rezar*) pray: *Roguemos al Señor.* Let us pray. ▶ **hacerse de ~** play hard to get **se ruega no fumar** no smoking **se ruega silencio** silence please

rojizo *adj* reddish

rojo *adj, nm* red ▶ **al ~ vivo** (*metal*) red-hot **ponerse ~** turn red

rollo *nm* **1** roll: *~s de papel higiénico* rolls of toilet paper ◇ *Se me veló todo el ~.* The whole film is out of focus. **2** (*pesadez*): *¡Qué ~ de libro!* What a boring book! ◇ *Esa clase es un ~.* That class is boring. **3** (*asunto*): *¿Cuál es el ~?* What are you up to? ◇ *Está metido en un ~ muy raro.* He's involved in something very odd. **4** (*sermón*) lecture

románico *adj* Romanesque

romano *adj* Roman

romántico/a *adj, nm-nf* romantic

rombo *nm* rhombus [*pl* -es]

romero *nm* rosemary

rompecabezas *nm* **1** (*para armar*) jigsaw **2** (*acertijo*) puzzle

rompeolas *nm* breakwater

romper *vt* **1** break: *~ una promesa* break a promise **2** (*papel, tela*) tear: *Rompió la carta.* He tore up the letter. **3** (*ropa, zapatos*) wear *sth* out ● *vi* **1** **~ con** fall out with *sb* **2** (*novios*) split up (with *sb*) ● **romperse** *vp* **1** (*quebrarse*) break **2** (*tela, papel*) tear **3** (*cuerda*) snap **4** (*ropa, zapatos*) wear out ▶ **~ el hielo** break the ice

ron *nm* rum

roncar *vi* snore

ronco *adj* (*afónico*) hoarse

ronda *nf* round ▶ **hacer la ~** **1** (*policía*) walk a beat **2** (*soldado, vigilante* [illegible]

rondín *nm* watchman [*pl* -men]

ronronear *vi* purr

ronroneo *nm* purr

roña *nf* (*mugre*) dirt

roñoso *adj* **1** (*mugriento*) grimy **2** (*tacaño*) stingy

ropa *nf* **1** (*de persona*) clothes [*pl*]: *~ infantil* children's clothes **2** (*de uso doméstico*) linen: *~ blanca* household linen ▶ **~ de deporte** sportswear **~ interior** underwear

ropero *nm* wardrobe

rosa *nf* rose ● *adj, nm* (*color*) pink

rosado *adj* **1** pink **2** (*vino*) rosé

rosal *nm* rose bush

rosario *nm* (*Rel*) rosary [*pl* -ies]: *rezar el ~* say the rosary

rosca *nf* **1** (*pan*) (ring-shaped) roll **2** (*tornillo*) thread ▶ **pasarse de ~** go over the top

rostizado *adj* (*Mx*) roast

rostizar *vt* (*Mx*) roast

rostro *nm* face

rotación *nf* rotation: *~ de cultivos* crop rotation

rotar *vt* rotate

rótula *nf* kneecap

rotular *vt* (*poner rótulos*) put the lettering on *sth*

rótulo *nm* **1** (*en cartel, mapa*) lettering [U] **2** (*letrero*) sign

rotundo *adj* **1** (*contundente*) resounding: *un fracaso ~* a resounding flop **2** (*negativa*) emphatic

rozar *vt* **1** brush (*against sth/sb*): *Le rocé el vestido.* I brushed against her dress. **2** (*raspar*) rub: *Las botas me rozan atrás.* My boots rub at the back. **3** (*hacer un rozón*) scratch: *No me roces la pintura.* Don't scratch the paint.

ruana *nf* (*And*) poncho [*pl* -s]

rubéola (*tb* **rubéola**) *nf* German measles [*sing*]

rubí *nm* ruby [*pl* -ies]

rubio *adj* fair, blond(e) **NOTA** Fair se usa sólo si el rubio es natural y **blond(e)** tanto si es natural como si es teñido: *Es ~.* He has fair/blond hair.

rubor *nm* (*maquillaje*) blusher

rueda *nf* **1** wheel: *~ delantera/ trasera* front/back wheel **2** (*neumático*) tire ▸ **ir sobre ~s** go really well ▸ **rueda de la fortuna/Chicago** Ferris wheel, big wheel (*GB*)

ruedo *nm* **1** (*toros*) ring **2** (*dobladillo*) hem

ruego *nm* plea

rugby *nm* rugby

rugido *nm* roar

rugir *vi* roar

ruido *nm* noise: *No hagas ~.* Don't make any noise.

ruidoso *adj* noisy

ruina *nf* ruin: *La ciudad estaba en ~s.* The city was in ruins. **2** (*hundimiento*) collapse ▸ **en la ~** flat broke **ser la/una ~** cost a fortune

ruiseñor *nm* nightingale

ruleta *nf* roulette

rulo *nm* roller

rumba *nf* **1** (*Mús*) rumba **2** (*parranda*) partying ▸ **ir(se) de ~** go out

rumbear *vi* (*And*) party

rumbo *nm* **1** (*camino, dirección*) direction **2** (*avión, barco*) course: *tomar ~ al sur* set course southward ▸ (**con**) **~ a** bound for: *El barco iba con ~ a Vigo.* The ship was bound for Vigo.

rumiante *nm* ruminant

rumiar *vi* (*vaca*) chew the cud

rumor *nm* **1** (*noticia*) rumor **2** (*murmullo*) murmur

rumorear (**rumorar** *And*) *vt* ▸ **se rumora que...** there are rumors (that...): *Se rumora que han hecho un fraude.* There are rumors of a fraud.

rural *adj* rural

Rusia *nf* Russia

ruso/a *adj, nm-nf, nm* Russian

rústico/a *adj* rustic

ruta *nf* route

rutina *nf* routine: *inspecciones de ~* routine inspections ◊ *la ~ diaria* the daily routine

S s

sábado *nm* Saturday (*abrev* Sat.) →LUNES

sábana *nf* sheet

saber *vt* **1** know: *No sé nada de arte.* I don't know anything about art. ◊ *¡Ya lo sé!* I know! **2 ~ hacer algo** can: *¿Sabes nadar?* Can you swim? **3** (*enterarse*) find out: *Lo supe ayer.* I found out yesterday. ● *vi* **1** know: *Le tengo mucho aprecio, ¿sabes?* I'm very fond of her, you know. ◊ *Nunca se sabe.* You never know. **2 ~ de** (*tener noticias*) hear of *sth/sb*: *Nunca más supimos de él.* That was the last we heard of him. **3** (*tener sabor*) taste (*of sth*): *Sabe a menta.* It tastes of mint. ◊ *¡Qué bueno sabe!* It tastes really good! ▸ **no sé qué/cuántos** something or other: *Me habló de no sé qué.* He talked to me about something or other. **¡qué sé yo!/yo qué sé!** how should I know? **que yo sepa** as far as I know ▸ **~ mal** have a nasty taste

sabiduría *nf* wisdom

sabio *adj* wise

sabor *nm* **1** (*gusto*) taste (*of sth*): *Tiene un ~ muy raro.* It tastes very odd. **2** (*gusto que se añade a un producto*) flavor: *Viene en seis ~es distintos.* It comes in six different flavors. ▸ **con ~ a** flavored: *un yogurt con ~ a durazno* a peach-flavored yogurt

saborear *vt* savor

sabotaje *nm* sabotage

sabotear *vt* sabotage

sabroso *adj* **1** (*comida*) delicious **2** (*música, fiesta, etc.*) great **3** (*clima*) beautiful

sacacorchos *nm* corkscrew

sacapuntas nm pencil sharpener

sacar vt 1 take sth/sb out: ~ una carpeta del cajón take a folder out of the drawer ◊ El dentista le sacó una muela. The dentist took his tooth out. 2 (conseguir) get: ¿Cuánto sacaste en matemáticas? What did you get in math? ◊ No sé de dónde saqué el dinero. I don't know where she got the money from. 3 (parte del cuerpo) stick sth out: ~ la cabeza por la ventanilla stick your head out of the window 4 (producir) make sth: ~ el queso de la leche make cheese from milk 5 vt, vi (tenis) serve ● sacarse vp: ¡Sácate las manos de los bolsillos! Take your hands out of your pockets! **NOTA** Para expresiones, ver el sustantivo, adjetivo, etc., p. ej. sacar de quicio en QUICIO.

sacarina nf saccharin

sacerdote nm priest

saciar vt 1 (hambre, ambición, deseo) satisfy 2 (sed) quench

saco nm 1 (prenda) (a) (de punto) sweater (b) (de tela) jacket 2 (costal) sack

sacramento nm sacrament

sacrificar vt sacrifice ● sacrificarse vp make sacrifices

sacrificio nm sacrifice: hacer ~s make sacrifices

sacudida nf (eléctrica) shock

sacudidor nm duster

sacudir vt shake: ~ la arena (de la toalla) shake the sand off (the towel) 2 (pegar) give sb a smack 3 (limpiar el polvo) dust ● sacudirse vp brush off

sádico/a nm-nf sadist

Sagitario nm, nmf Sagittarius

sagrado adj 1 (Rel) holy: la Sagrada Familia the Holy Family 2 (intocable) sacred: Los domingos para mí son ~s. My Sundays are sacred.

sal nf salt ▸ ~es de baño bath salts ~ fina table salt ~ gruesa/de cocina cooking salt

sala nf 1 room: ~ de espera/juntas waiting/meeting room 2 (tb ~ de estar) living room 3 (Cine) screen 4 (hospital) ward

salado adj 1 (gusto) salty: agua salada salt water 2 (desafortunado) jinxed

salario nm salary [pl -ies] ▸ ~ base/mínimo basic/minimum wage

salchicha nf sausage

salchichón nm salami [U]

saldar vt (cuenta, deuda) settle

saldo nm 1 (cuenta bancaria) balance 2 (rebaja) sale

salero nm (para la sal) salt shaker, salt cellar (GB)

salida nf 1 (acción de salir) way out (of sth): a la ~ del teatro on the way out of the theater 2 (puerta) exit: la ~ de emergencia the emergency exit 3 (avión, tren) departure: ~s nacionales/internacionales domestic/international departures ▸ ~ del sol sunrise

salir vi 1 (ir/venir fuera) go/come out: Salí a ver qué pasaba. I went out to see what was going on. ◊ No quería ~ del baño. He wouldn't come out of the bathroom. 2 (partir) leave: Salimos de la casa a las dos. We left home at two. ◊ ~ para Cuzco leave for Cuzco 3 (alternar) go out: ~ a cenar go out for a meal ◊ Sale con un estudiante. She's going out with a student. 4 (producto, flor) come out: El libro sale en abril. The book is coming out in April. 5 (sol) (a) (amanecer) rise (b) (de entre las nubes) come out 6 ~ de (superar): ~ de una operación pull through an operation ◊ ~ de la droga quit drugs 7 ~ a algn (parecerse) take after sb 8 ~ a/por (costar) work out at sth: Sale a 60 pesos el metro. It works out at 60 pesos a meter. 9 (al hacer cuentas): A mí me sale 18. I make it 18. 10 (resultar) turn out: El viaje salió muy bien. The trip turned out really well. ● salirse vp 1 come off: La moto se salió de la carretera. The motorcycle came off the road. 2 (líquido) leak ▸ ~se con la suya get your own way **NOTA** Para otras expresiones, ver el sustantivo, adjetivo, etc., p. ej. salir a flote en FLOTE.

saliva nf saliva

salmo nm psalm

salmón nm salmon [pl salmon]

salón nm 1 (casa) living room 2 (hotel) lounge 3 (escuela) classroom 4 (universidad) lecture room ▸ ~ de actos main hall ~ de belleza beauty salon ~ de fiestas function room

salpicadera nf (Mx) fender, mudguard (GB)

salpicar vt splash

salpicón nm (de frutas) fruit cocktail

salsa nf 1 (Cocina) sauce 2 (Mús) salsa

saltamontes nm grasshopper

saltar vt, vi jump: ~ al agua/por la ventana jump into the water/out of the window ● **saltarse** vp **1** (omitir) skip: ~ una comida skip a meal **2** (cola, semáforo) jump: ~ un semáforo jump the lights ▸ **~ a la vista** be obvious ~ **la cuerda** jump rope, skip (GB)

salto nm **1** jump: dar ~s de alegría jump for joy **2** (pájaro, conejo, etc.) hop **3** (de trampolín) dive **4** (salto vigoroso, progreso) leap ▸ **~ alto/de altitud** high jump ~ **largo/de longitud** long jump

saltón adj (ojos) bulging

salud nf health: estar bien/mal de ~ be in good/poor health ● interj **1** (para brindar) cheers **2** (al estornudar) bless you

saludable adj healthy

saludar vt say hello (to sb) ▸ **lo/la saluda atentamente** sincerely yours, yours sincerely/faithfully (GB) → **ATENTAMENTE** ~ **con la mano** wave

saludo nm **1** greeting **2 saludos** (en carta) best wishes

salvación nf salvation

salvador/a nm-nf savior

salvadoreño/a adj, nm-nf Salvadoran, Salvadorean (GB)

salvajada nf atrocity [pl -ies]

salvaje adj **1** wild: animales ~s wild animals **2** (pueblo, tribu) uncivilized

salvamento nm rescue

salvar vt **1** save: La operación le salvó la vida. The operation saved his life. **2** (obstáculo) cross: ~ un río cross a river ● **salvarse** vp survive ▸ **¡sálvese quien pueda!** every man for himself!

salvavidas nm **1** (llanta) lifesaver, lifebelt (GB) **2** (persona) lifeguard

salvo prep except: todos ~ él. everybody except for him ▸ **estar a ~** be safe ~ **que...** unless...: ~ que sea necesario unless it's necessary

San adj Saint (abrev St.)

sanar vi **1** (herida) heal **2** (enfermo) recover

sanción nf **1** (castigo) sanction **2** (multa) fine

sancionar vt **1** (penalizar) penalize **2** (económicamente) sanction

sandalia nf sandal

sandía nf watermelon

sándwich (**sánduche** And) nm sandwich

sangrar vt, vi bleed

sangre nf blood ▸ **a ~ fría** in cold blood **tener ~ fría** (serenidad) keep your cool

sangría nf sangria

sangriento adj **1** (lucha) bloody **2** (herida) bleeding

sangrón/ona adj (Mx) annoying ● **~** (Mx) nuisance

sanguíneo adj blood: grupo ~ blood group

sanidad nf **1** (pública) public health **2** (higiene) sanitation

sanitario/a adj (de salud) health: riesgos ~s health risks **2** (de higiene) sanitary

sano adj **1** (clima, vida, ambiente, cuerpo, comida) healthy **2** (en forma) fit **3** (madera) sound ▸ **no estar en su ~ juicio** not be in your right mind ~ **y salvo** safe and sound

santiamén nm ▸ **en un ~** in no time at all

santo/a adj **1** (Rel) holy **2** (en títulos) Saint (abrev St.) **3** (énfasis): en todo el ~ día all day ● nm-nf saint ▸ **ser un ~ varón** be a saint **¡y santas pascuas!** and that's that!

santuario nm sanctuary

sapear vt, vi (And) tell: Me sapearon la última pregunta. They told me the answer to the last question. ◊ Me vio copiando y le sapeó al profesor. He saw me copying and told on me to the teacher.

sapo nm toad

saque nm **1** (fútbol) kick-off [pl -offs] **2** (tenis) serve ▸ **~ de banda** throw-in [pl -ins]

saquear vt **1** (ciudad) sack **2** (despensa) raid **3** (robar) loot

sarampión nm measles [sing]

sarcástico adj sarcastic

sardina nf sardine

sardinel nm (And) **1** (andén) sidewalk, pavement (GB) **2** (borde exterior del andén) curb

sardino/a nm-nf (And) kid

sargento nmf sergeant

sarta nf string ▸ **decir una ~ de disparates/tonterías** talk nonsense **una ~ de mentiras** a pack of lies

sartén nm o nf frying pan

sastre/a nm-nf tailor

satélite nm satellite

satín nm satin

satisfacción nf satisfaction

satisfacer vt **1** satisfy: ~ el hambre/la curiosidad satisfy your hunger/curiosity **2** (sed) quench **3** (ambición, etc.) fulfill

satisfactorio adj satisfactory

satisfecho adj satisfied (with sth) ▸ **~ de sí mismo** self-satisfied

Saturno nm Saturn

sauce nm willow ▸ **~ llorón** weeping willow

sauna nf sauna

savia nf (Bot) sap

saxofón nm saxophone (abrev **sax**)

sazonar vt season

se pron
- reflexivo 1 (él, ella, ello) himself, herself, itself: **Se compró un CD.** He bought himself a CD. 2 (usted, ustedes) yourself [pl yourselves] 3 (ellos, ellas) themselves 4 (partes del cuerpo, efectos personales): **Se secó el pelo.** She dried her hair.
- recíproco each other, one another: **Se quieren.** They love each other.
- pasivo: **Se construyó hace años.** It was built a long time ago. ◊ **Se dice que está muerta.** People say she's dead. ◊ **Se prohíbe fumar.** No smoking.
- impersonal: **Se vive bien aquí.** Life here is terrific.
- en lugar de le, les him, her, you, them: **Se lo di.** I gave it to him/her. ◊ **Se lo robamos.** We stole it from them.

secadora nf (tb **secador** nm) 1 (ropa) dryer 2 (pelo) hairdryer

secar vt, vi dry: **~ los platos** dry the dishes ▸ **secarse** vp 1 dry 2 (planta, río, estanque, tierra, herida) dry up

sección nf 1 section: **la ~ deportiva** the sports section 2 (tienda) department: **~ de hombres** mens' clothing department ▸ **~ transversal** cross section

seco adj 1 dry: **un clima ~** a dry climate 2 (persona) unfriendly 3 (sin vida) dead: **hojas secas** dead leaves 4 (frutos, flores) dried 5 (sonido, golpe) sharp ▸ **a secas** just **frenar/parar en ~** stop dead

secretaría nf 1 (oficina para matricularse) admissions office 2 (cargo) secretariat: **la ~ de la ONU** the UN secretariat 3 (oficina del secretario) secretary's office 4 (Mx, Pol) department, ministry [pl -ies] (GB): **S~ de Relaciones Exteriores** Department of Foreign Affairs

secretariado nm (estudios) secretarial course

secretario/a nm-nf secretary [pl -ies]: **S~ de Relaciones Exteriores** Secretary of Foreign Affairs

secreto adj, nm secret ▸ **en ~** secretly

secta nf sect

sector nm 1 (zona, industria) sector 2 (grupo de personas) section: **un pequeño ~ de la población** a small section of the population

secuencia nf sequence

secuestrador/a nm-nf 1 (de persona) kidnapper 2 (de avión) hijacker

secuestrar vt 1 (persona) kidnap 2 (avión) hijack

secuestro nm 1 (persona) kidnapping 2 (avión) hijacking

secundaria nf high school

secundario adj secondary

sed nf thirst ▸ **tener/pasar ~** be thirsty: **Tengo mucha ~.** I'm very thirsty.

seda nf silk

sedante nm sedative

sede nf headquarters

sediento adj thirsty

sedimento nm sediment

seducción nf seduction

seducir vt seduce

seductor/a adj seductive ● nm-nf seducer

segadora nf combine harvester

segar vt cut

segmento nm segment

segregar vt segregate

seguido adj in a row: **cuatro veces seguidas** four times in a row ◊ **Lo hizo tres días ~s.** He did it three days running.

seguir vt follow: **Sígueme.** Follow me. ● vi 1 go on (doing sth): **Siga hasta la avenida sexta.** Go on till you reach Sixth Avenue. ◊ **Siguieron trabajando hasta las dos.** They went on working till two. 2 (en una situación) be still...: **¿Sigue enferma?** Is she still sick?

según prep according to: **~ ella/ los planes** according to her/the plans ● adv 1 (dependiendo de) depending on...: **~ sea el tamaño** depending on the size 2 (a medida que) as: **~ van entrando** as they come in

segundero nm second hand

segundo/a adj, nm-nf, pron second ● nm (tiempo) second ● **segunda** nf (marcha) second (gear) ▸ **de segunda mano** second-hand

seguramente adv probably

seguridad nf 1 (contra accidente) safety: **~ vial** road safety 2 (contra ataque/robo, garantía) security: **controles de ~** security checks 3 (certeza) certainty: **No**

S

lo saben con ~. They don't know for certain. **4** (*en sí mismo*) self-confidence

seguro *adj* **1** (*sin riesgo*) safe: *un lugar ~* a safe place **2** (*convencido*) sure: *Estoy ~ de que vendrá.* I'm sure he'll come. **3** (*firme, bien sujeto*) secure ● *nm* **1** (*póliza*) insurance [U]: *sacarse un ~ de vida* take out life insurance **2** (*mecanismo*) safety catch ▶ *~ que...: ~ que llegan tarde.* They're bound to be late. **~ social** social security

seis *adj, nm, pron* **1** six **2** (*fecha, sexto*) sixth ▶ **a las ~** at six o'clock *cinco, etc. para las seis* five, etc. to six **y cinco, etc.** five, etc. after/past (*GB*) six **de cada diez** six out of ten **son las ~** it's six o'clock

seiscientos/as *adj, nm, pron* six hundred

selección *nf* **1** selection **2** (*equipo*) (national) team: *la ~ peruana de basquetbol* the Peruvian basketball team

seleccionar *vt* select

selecto *adj* select

sellar *vt* **1** seal: *~ un sobre/una amistad* seal an envelope/a friendship **2** (*timbrar*) stamp: *~ un pasaporte* stamp a passport

sello *nm* **1** (*correos, pasaporte*) stamp **2** (*oficial*) seal

selva *nf* jungle

semáforo *nm* traffic light(s): *un ~ en rojo* a red light

semana *nf* week: *la ~ pasada/que viene* last/next week ◇ *dos veces por ~* twice a week **S~ Santa** Easter **una ~ sí y otra no** every other week

semanal *adj* **1** (*de cada semana*) weekly: *una revista ~* a weekly magazine **2** (*a la semana*): *Tenemos una hora ~ de gimnasia.* We have one hour of gymnastics a week.

sembrar *vt* **1** sow: *~ trigo/un campo* sow wheat/a field **2** (*hortalizas*) plant: *~ un campo de papas* plant a field with potatoes

semejante *adj* **1** (*parecido*) similar: *un modelo ~ a este* a model similar to this one **2** (*tal*): *¿Cómo pudiste hacer ~ cosa?* How could you do such a thing?

semejanza *nf* similarity [*pl* -ies]

semen *nm* semen

semicírculo *nm* semicircle

semifinal *nf* semifinal

semifinalista *nmf* semifinalist

semilla *nf* seed

seminario *nm* **1** (*clase*) seminar **2** (*Rel*) seminary [*pl* -ies]

senado *nm* senate

senador/a *nm-nf* senator

sencillez *nf* simplicity

sencillo *adj* **1** simple **2** (*persona*) straightforward ● *nm* **1** (*dinero*) small change **2** (*disco*) single

senda *nf* path

senderismo *nm* hiking: *hacer ~* go hiking

seno *nm* breast

sensación *nf* feeling ▶ **causar/hacer ~** (*hacer furor*) cause a sensation

sensacional *adj* sensational

sensatez *nf* good sense

sensato *adj* sensible

sensibilidad *nf* sensitivity

sensible *adj* **1** sensitive: *Mi piel es muy ~ al sol.* My skin is very sensitive to the sun. **2** (*grande*) noticeable: *una mejora ~* a noticeable improvement

sensual *adj* sensual

sentada *nf* (*protesta*) sit-in ▶ **de/en una ~** in one go

sentado *adj* sitting, seated (*fml*): *Estaban ~s a la mesa.* They were sitting at the table. ◇ *Se quedaron ~s.* They remained seated. ▶ **dar por ~** assume *sth*

sentar *vt* sit: *Sentó al bebé en el sofá.* He sat the baby on the couch. ● *vi* look good: *Te sienta mejor el rojo.* The red one looks better on you. ◇ *¿Qué tal me sienta?* How does it look? ● **sentarse** *vp* sit (down): *Siéntese.* Sit down. ◇ *~ en el suelo* sit (down) on the floor ▶ **~ bien/mal 1** (*ropa*) look good/bad on *sb*: *Este vestido me sienta muy mal.* This dress doesn't look good on me at all. **2** (*alimentos*) agree/not agree with *sth* **3** (*hacer buen efecto*) do *sb* good/no good: *Me sentó bien el descanso.* The rest did me good. **4** (*tomar bien/mal*): *Me sentó mal que no me invitaran.* I was upset that I wasn't invited. **~ cabeza** settle down

sentencia *nf* **1** (*Jur*) sentence **2** (*dicho*) maxim

sentenciar *vt* sentence

sentido *nm* **1** sense: *~ del humor* sense of humor ◇ *No tiene ~.* It doesn't make sense. **2** (*significado*) meaning **3** (*dirección*) direction ▶ **de doble ~** (*chiste, palabra*) with a double meaning **~ común** common sense **sexto ~** sixth sense

sentimental *adj* **1** sentimental: *valor ~* sentimental value **2** love: *vida ~* love life

sentimiento *nm* feeling

sentir vt 1 feel: ~ frío/hambre feel cold/hungry ◊ (oír) hear 3 (lamentar) be sorry about sth/(that...): Siento no poder ayudarle. I'm sorry (that) I can't help you. ◊ Sentimos mucho su desgracia. We're very sorry about your bad luck. ● **sentirse** vp feel: Me siento bien. I feel good. ► **lo siento (mucho)** I'm (very) sorry

seña nf 1 (gesto) sign 2 **señas** (dirección) address ► **hacer ~s** signal: Me hacían ~s para que parara. They were signaling to me to stop.

señal nf 1 sign: ~es de tránsito road signs ◊ en ~ de protesta as a sign of protest 2 (marca) mark 3 (teléfono) tone: la ~ para marcar/de ocupado the dial tone/busy signal ► **dar ~es** show signs of sth **hacer ~es/una ~** signal

señalar vt 1 (marcar) mark 2 (mostrar, afirmar) point sth out: ~ algo en un mapa point sth out on a map ◊ Señaló que... He pointed out that...

señalizar vt signpost

señor/a nm-nf 1 (adulto) man [pl men], [fem lady] [pl ~ies]: ropa para señoras ladies' clothing 2 (delante del apellido) Mr. [fem Mrs.] [pl Mr. and Mrs.]: ¿Está el ~ López? Is Mr. López in? ◊ los ~es de Soler Mr. and Mrs. Soler 3 (delante del nombre o de cargos): La señora Luisa es la costurera. Luisa is the dressmaker. ◊ el ~ alcalde the mayor 4 (para llamar la atención) excuse me!: ¡Señor! Se le cayó el tíquete. Excuse me! You dropped your ticket. 5 (de cortesía) sir [fem madam] [pl ~ies]: Buenos días ~. Good morning, sir. ◊ Señoras y señores... Ladies and gentlemen... ● **Señor** nm Lord ● **señora** nf (esposa) wife ► **¡no ~!** no way! **¡señor!** good Lord! **¡sí ~!** that's right!

señorita nf 1 (fórmula de cortesía) Miss, Ms. **NOTA** Miss y Ms. se usan con el apellido o con nombre y apellido: "Miss/Ms. Jones" o "Miss/Ms. Mary Jones". **Ms.** se usa para no especificar el estado civil. 2 (maestra) teacher 3 (para llamar la atención) excuse me

separación nf 1 separation 2 (distancia) gap: Hay 7m de ~. There's a seven-meter gap.

separado adj 1 (matrimonio) separated 2 (distinto) separate: llevar vidas separadas lead separate lives ► **por ~** separately

separar vt 1 separate sth/sb: Separa las rojas de las verdes. Separate the red ones from the green. 2 (alejar) move sth/sb away: ~ la silla de la mesa move the chair away from the table 3 (guardar) save: Sepárame un pan. Save a loaf of bread for me. ● **separarse** vp 1 separate, split up (más coloq): Se separó de su marido. She separated from her husband. 2 (apartarse) move away: ~ de la familia move away from your family

separo nm (Mx) cell

sepia nf cuttlefish [pl cuttlefish]

septiembre nm September (abrev Sept.) →MAYO

séptimo/a adj, nm-nf, pron seventh ► **en el ~ cielo** in seventh heaven

sepultura nf grave

sequía nf drought

ser¹ vi 1 be: Es alta. She's tall. ◊ Soy de La Paz. I'm from La Paz. ◊ Son las siete. It's seven o'clock. ◊ —¿Quién es? —Soy Ana. "Who's that?" "It's Ana." **NOTA** No se usa el artículo indefinido a/an delante de profesiones con el verbo be: Es médico/ingeniero. He's a doctor/an engineer. 2 ~ de (material) be made of sth: Es de acero. It's made of steel. ● v aux be: Será juzgado el lunes. He will be tried on Monday. ► **a no ~ que...** unless... **es más** what's more **¡eso es!** that's right! **es que...** Es que no me apetece. I just don't feel like it. ◊ ¡Es que es muy caro! It's very expensive! **lo que sea** whatever no sea que/no vaya a ~ que (just) in case o **sea** ◊ ¿O sea que se van mañana? So you're leaving tomorrow, are you? ◊ El 17, o sea el martes pasado. The 17th, that is to say last Tuesday. **por si fuera poco** to top it all **¿qué es/ha sido de...?** ¿Qué es de tu hermana? What's your sister been up to? ◊ ¿Qué ha sido de tu vida? What have you been up to? **sea como sea/sea lo que sea sea quien sea** no matter how/what/who **si no es/fuera por** if it weren't for sth/sb **si yo fuera** if I were **soy yo** it's me, you, etc. **NOTA** Para otras expresiones, ver el sustantivo, adjetivo, etc., p.ej. **ser el colmo** en COLMO.

ser² nm being: un ~ humano a human being

serial nm serial →SERIES

serie nf series [pl ~ies]: una ~ de desgracias a series of disasters ◊

S

una nueva ~ televisiva a new TV series →SERIES

serio *adj* **1** serious: *un libro/asunto ~* a serious book/matter **2** *(cumplidor)* reliable ▶ **en ~** seriously: *tomar algo en ~* take sth seriously ◊ *¿Lo dices en ~?* Are you serious? ▶ **ponerse ~ con algn** get annoyed with sb

sermón *nm (Rel)* sermon ▶ **echar/soltar un ~** give *sb* a lecture

seropositivo *adj* HIV positive

serpentina *nf* streamer

serpiente *nf* snake

serrar *vt* saw sth (up)

servicio *nm* **1** service: *~ de autobuses* bus service **2** *(tenis)* service **3** *(doméstico)* domestic help: *muchacha/señora del ~* maid

servidor *nm (Comp)* server ▶ **~ de internet** Internet service provider *(abrev* ISP)

servilleta *nf* napkin

servilletero *nm* napkin ring

servir *vt* serve: *¿Te sirvo más?* Would you like some more? ● *vi* **1** serve: *~ en la marina* serve in the navy **2** *~ de/como/que* serve as *sth/to do sth*: *Sirvió para aclarar las cosas.* It served to clarify things. **3** *~ para (usarse)* be used for *sth*: *Sirve para cortar.* It is used for cutting. ◊ *¿Para qué sirve?* What do you use it for? **4** *(ropa)* fit: *Ya no me sirve este pantalón.* These pants don't fit me any more. **5** *(tenis)* serve ● **servirse** *vp (comida)* help yourself: *~ ensalada* help yourself to salad ▶ **no ~** be no good: *Este cuchillo no sirve para cortar carne.* This knife is no good for cutting meat. ◊ *No sirvo para enseñar.* I'm no good at teaching. ◊ *Este libro no sirve para nada.* This book's useless.

sesenta *adj, nm, pron* **1** sixty **2** *(sexagésimo)* sixtieth

sesión *nf* **1** session: *~ de entrenamiento* training session **2** *(Cine)* showing **3** *(Teat)* performance

seso *nm* brain ▶ **calentarse/devanarse los ~s** rack your brains

setecientos *adj, nm, pron* seven hundred

setenta *adj, nm, pron* **1** seventy **2** *(septuagésimo)* seventieth

seudónimo *nm* pseudonym

severo *adj* **1** *(intenso)* severe: *un golpe ~* a severe blow **2** *(estricto)* strict: *Mi papá era muy ~ con nosotros.* My father was very strict with us. **3** *(castigo, crítica)* harsh

sexista *adj, nmf* sexist

sexo *nm* sex

sexto/a *adj, nm-nf, pron* sixth: *Fui el ~ en cruzar la meta.* I was the sixth to finish. ◊ *Felipe VI Philip VI* **NOTA** Se lee "Philip the Sixth".

sexual *adj* sexual: *acoso ~* sexual harassment ◊ *(educación, órganos, vida)* sex: *vida ~* sex life

sexualidad *nf* sexuality

short *(tb* shorts) *nm* shorts *[pl]* →PANTALÓN

si¹ *nm* B: *si mayor* B major

si² *conj* **1** if: *Si llueve no iremos.* If it rains, we won't go. **2** *(duda)* whether: *No sé si quedarme o irme.* I don't know whether to stay or go. **3** *(deseo)* if only: *¡Si me lo hubieras dicho antes!* If only you had told me before! **4** *(protesta)* but: *¡Si no me lo habías dicho!* But you didn't tell me! ▶ **si no** otherwise

sí¹ *adv* **1** yes **2** *(énfasis)*: *Ella no irá, pero yo sí.* She's not going but I am. ● *nm*: *Aún no me ha dado el sí.* He still hasn't said yes. ▶ **¡eso sí que no!** definitely not

sí² *pron pers* **1** *(él)* himself **2** *(ella)* herself **3** *(ello)* itself: *El problema se solucionó por sí mismo.* The problem solved itself. **4** *(ellos, ellas)* themselves **5** *(impersonal, usted)* yourself **6** *(ustedes)* yourselves ▶ **dar(se) de sí** *(prendas, zapatos)* stretch ▶ **de por sí/en sí (mismo)** in itself

sida *(tb* SIDA) *nm* AIDS

siderurgia *nf* iron and steel industry

siderúrgico *adj* iron and steel: *el sector ~* the iron and steel sector

siembra *nf* sowing

siempre *adv* always: *~ dices lo mismo.* You always say the same thing. →ALWAYS ▶ **como ~** as usual **de ~** *(acostumbrado)* usual: *el sitio de ~* the usual place **lo de ~** the usual **para ~** *(permanentemente)* for good: *Me voy para ~.* I'm leaving for good. **2** *(eternamente)* forever: *Nuestro amor es para ~.* Our love will last forever. ▶ **que...** whenever...: *~ que vamos de vacaciones* whenever we go on vacation

sien *nf* temple

sierra *nf* **1** *(herramienta)* saw **2** *(región)* mountains **3** *(Geog)* mountain range

siesta *nf* siesta ▶ **dormir/echar la ~** take a siesta

siete *adj, nm, pron* **1** seven **2** *(fecha)* seventh ▸ **tener ~ vidas** have nine lives

sigilosamente *adv* very quietly

siglas *nf* abbreviation: *¿Cuáles son las ~s de...?* What's the abbreviation for...?

siglo *nm* **1** *(centuria)* century [pl -ies]: *en el ~ XXI* in the 21st century **NOTA** Se lee "in the twentieth-first century". **2** *(era)* age: *el ~ de las computadoras* the computer age

significado *nm* meaning

significar *vt, vi* mean: *Él significa mucho para mí.* He means a lot to me.

signo *nm* **1** sign: *los ~s del zodíaco* the signs of the zodiac **2** *(imprenta, fonética)* symbol ▸ **~ de admiración/interrogación** exclamation point/question mark

siguiente *adj* next: *al día ~* the next day ● *nmf* next one: *Que pase la ~.* Next, please!

sílaba *nf* syllable

silbar *vt, vi* **1** whistle: *~ una canción* whistle a tune **2** *(abuchear)* boo

silbato *nm* whistle

silbido *nm* **1** whistle: *el ~ del viento* the whistling of the wind **2** *(protesta, serpiente)* hiss **3** *(oídos)* buzzing

silenciar *vt* **1** *(persona)* silence **2** *(suceso)* hush sth up

silencio *nm* silence ● *interj* be quiet

silencioso *adj* **1** *(en silencio, callado)* silent: *un motor ~* a silent engine **2** *(tranquilo)* quiet: *una calle silenciosa* a quiet street

silla *nf* chair: *en una ~* on a chair ▸ **~ de montar** saddle **~ de ruedas** wheelchair

sillón *nm* armchair: *sentado en un ~* sitting in an armchair

silueta *nf* silhouette

silvestre *adj* wild

simbólico *adj* symbolic

simbolizar *vt* symbolize

símbolo *nm* symbol

simétrico *adj* symmetrical

similar *adj* similar

simio *nm-nf* ape

simpatía *nf* charm ▸ **sentir/tener ~ hacia/por algn** like sb

simpático *adj* nice: *un hombre muy ~* a very nice man **NOTA** Sympathetic no significa "simpático" sino "comprensivo", "compasivo". ▸ **hacerse el ~** try to be nice

simpatizante *nmf* sympathizer

simpatizar *vi* *(llevarse bien)* get along (well) *(with sb)*

simple *adj* **1** *(sencillo, fácil)* simple **2** *(soso)* tasteless: *La sopa está algo ~.* This soup needs salt. **3** *(mero)* *Es un ~ apodo.* It's just a nickname. ▸ **a ~ vista** at first glance

simplemente *adv* simply, just *(más coloq)*

simplificar *vt* simplify

simultáneo *adj* simultaneous

sin *prep* **1** without: *~ pensar* without thinking **NOTA** Cuando "sin" va seguido de una palabra negativa como "nada" o "nadie", estas se traducen por **anything** o **anybody**: *Salió sin decir nada.* She left without saying anything. **2** *(por hacer)*: *Los platos estaban sin lavar.* The dishes hadn't been done. ◊ *Dejé el trabajo sin terminar.* I left the work unfinished.

sinagoga *nf* synagogue

sinceridad *nf* sincerity

sincero *adj* sincere

sincronización *nf* *(motor)* tuning

sincronizar *vt* synchronize

sindicato *nm* *(labor)* union, *(trade)* union *(GB)*: *el ~ de trabajadores* the workers' union

síndrome *nm* syndrome ▸ **~ de abstinencia** withdrawal symptoms [pl] **~ de inmunodeficiencia adquirida** Acquired Immune Deficiency Syndrome *(abrev* AIDS*)*

sinfonía *nf* symphony [pl -ies]

sinfónico *adj* symphonic: *orquesta sinfónica* symphony orchestra

single *nm* *(Mús)* single

singular *adj* *(Gram)* singular

siniestro *adj* sinister

sino *conj* but: *no sólo en Lima, ~ también en otros sitios* not only in Lima but also in other places ◊ *No haces ~ criticar.* You do nothing but criticize.

sinónimo *adj* synonymous *(with sth)* ● *nm* synonym

sintetizador *nm* *(Mús)* synthesizer

síntoma *nm* symptom

sintonizar *vt, vi* tune in: *~ (con) la BBC* tune in to the BBC

sinvergüenza *nmf* scoundrel

siquiera *adv* **1** *(frases negativas)* even: *Ni ~ me llamaste.* You didn't even call me. **2** *(al menos)* at least: *Deme ~ una idea.* At least give me an idea.

sirena *nf* **1** *(señal acústica)* siren: *~ de policía* police siren **2** *(mujer-pez)* mermaid

sirviente/a *nm-nf* servant ● **sirvienta** *nf* maid

sísmico *adj* seismic

sistema *nm* **1** system: *el ~ solar* the solar system **2** (*método*) method: *los ~s pedagógicos modernos* modern teaching methods ▸ **~ montañoso** mountain range

sitio *nm* **1** place: *un ~ para dormir* a place to sleep (*espacio*) room: *¿Hay ~?* Is there any room? ◊ *Creo que no habrá ~ para todos.* I don't think there'll be enough room for everybody. **3** (*asiento*) seat **4** (*Mx, para taxi*) taxi stand ▸ **hacer ~** make room (*for sth/sb*) **ir de un ~ a/para otro** rush around ● **web** website

situación *nf* situation

situar *vt* **1** (*colocar*) put: *Me sitúa en una posición muy comprometida.* This puts me in a very awkward position. **2** (*en un mapa*) find: *Sitúeme León en el mapa.* Find León on the map. ● **situarse** *vp* (*clasificación*) be: *~ entre las cinco primeras* be among the top five ▸ **~se a la cabeza** lead the field

slogan *nm* slogan

smoking *nm* tuxedo [*pl* -s]

snob *adj* snobbish ● *nmf* snob

sobaco *nm* armpit

sobar *vt* **1** (*cosa*) finger **2** (*persona*) paw

soberano/a *adj, nm-nf* sovereign

sobornar *vt* bribe

soborno *nm* **1** (*acción*) bribery **2** (*obsequio*) bribe: *aceptar ~s* take bribes

sobra *nf* **1** (*exceso*) surplus **2** **sobras** (*restos*) leftovers ▸ **de ~** **1** (*suficiente*) plenty of (*sth*): *Tenemos tiempo de ~.* We have plenty of time. **2** (*muy bien*) well: *Sabes de ~ que...* You know very well that...

sobrado *adv* easily

sobrar *vi* **1** (*quedar*): *Sobra queso de anoche.* There's some cheese left (over) from last night. **2** (*haber más de lo necesario*): *Sobra tela para la falda.* There's plenty of material for the skirt. ◊ *Sobran dos sillas.* There are two chairs too many. **3** (*estar de más*) (a) (*cosa*) be unnecessary: *Sobran las palabras.* Words are unnecessary. (b) (*persona*) be in the way ▸ **sobrarle algo a algn 1** (*quedar*) have sth left: *Me sobran unos pesos.* I have a few pesos left. **2** (*tener demasiado*) have too much/many...: *Me sobra trabajo.* I have too much work.

sobre¹ *nm* **1** (*carta*) envelope **2** (*envase*) package, packet (*GB*)

sobre² *prep* **1** (*encima de*) on: *~ la mesa* on the table **2** (*por encima, sin tocar*) over: *Volamos ~ Cancún.* We flew over Cancún. **3** (*temperatura*) above: *diez grados ~ cero* ten degrees above zero **4** (*acerca de, expresando aproximación*) about: *una película ~ Neruda* a movie about Neruda ◊ *Llegaré ~ las ocho.* I'll arrive about eight.

sobrecargado *adj* overloaded

sobrecargo *nmf* flight attendant

sobredosis *nf* overdose

sobremesa *nf* (*conversación*) after-dinner chat

sobrenatural *adj* supernatural

sobrentenderse (*tb* **sobreentenderse**) *vp* be understood

sobrepasar *vt* **1** (*cantidad, límite, medida, esperanzas*) exceed: *Sobrepasó los 170 km por hora.* It exceeded 170 km an hour. **2** (*rival, récord*) beat

sobrepoblado *adj* overpopulated

sobresaliente *adj* outstanding

sobresalir *vi* **1** (*objeto, parte del cuerpo*) protrude **2** (*destacar, resaltar*) stand out: *Sobresale entre sus compañeras.* She stands out from her friends.

sobresaltar *vt* startle

sobreviviente *adj* surviving ● *nmf* survivor

sobrevivir *vi* survive

sobrino/a *nm-nf* nephew [*fem* niece]: *¿Cuántos ~s tienes?* How many nephews and nieces do you have?

sobrio *adj* sober

sociable *adj* sociable

social *adj* social

socialismo *nm* socialism

socialista *adj, nmf* socialist

sociedad *nf* **1** society [*pl* -ies]: *~ de consumo* consumer society **2** (*Com*) company [*pl* -ies] ▸ **~ anónima** public limited company, public limited corporation (*abrev* **plc**) (*GB*) **~ limitada** limited company (*abrev* **Ltd**)

socio/a *nm-nf* **1** (*club*) member: *hacerse ~ de un club* become a member of a club **2** (*Com*) partner

sociología *nf* sociology

sociólogo/a *nm-nf* sociologist

socorrer *vt* help

socorrido *adj* handy

socorrismo *nm* life-saving

socorrista *nmf* lifeguard

socorro *nm* help

sofá nm sofa ► ~ **cama** sofa bed

sofisticado adj sophisticated

sofocante adj stifling

sofocar vt 1 (fuego) smother 2 (rebelión) put sth down ● **sofocarse** vp 1 (de calor) suffocate 2 (quedarse sin aliento) get out of breath 3 (irritarse) get worked up

sofoco nm 1 (vergüenza) embarrassment: ¡Qué ~! How embarrassing! 2 (sudores) hot flash, hot flush (GB)

sofreír vt fry sth lightly

software nm software [U]: crear un nuevo ~ develop a new piece of software

soga nf rope ► **con la** ~ **al cuello** in a bind

sol nm 1 sun: sentarse al ~ sit in the sun ◊ una tarde de ~ a sunny afternoon 2 (Mús) G ► **de** ~ **a** ~ from morning to night **gafas/lentes de** ~ sunglasses **hacer** ~ be sunny **no dejar ni a** ~ **ni a sombra** not leave sb in peace **tomar el** ~ sunbathe

solamente adv only

solapa nf 1 (chaqueta) lapel 2 (libro, sobre) flap

solar adj (del sol) solar ● nm (terreno) plot

soldado nmf soldier

soldar vt solder

soleado adj sunny

solemne adj solemn

soler vi 1 (en presente) usually do sth: No suelo desayunar. I don't usually have breakfast. →ALWAYS 2 (en pasado) used to do sth: Solíamos visitarlo en el verano. We used to visit him in the summer. →USED TO

solfeo nm music theory

solicitante nmf applicant

solicitar vt 1 request: ~ una entrevista request an interview 2 (empleo, beca) apply for sth

solicitud nf 1 (petición) request: una ~ de información a request for information 2 (instancia) application: una ~ de trabajo a job application ◊ llenar una ~ fill out an application (form)

solidez nf solidity

solidificar(se) vt, vp 1 solidify 2 (agua) freeze

sólido adj, nm solid

solista nmf soloist

solitario adj 1 (sin compañía) solitary: Lleva una vida solitaria. She leads a solitary life. 2 (lugar) lonely ● nm (cartas) solitaire, patience (GB): hacer un ~ play a game of solitaire/patience

sollozo nm sob

solo adj 1 (sin compañía) alone: Estaba ~ en la casa. I was alone in the house. 2 (sin ayuda) by myself, yourself, etc.: El niño ya come ~. He can eat by himself now. →ALONE ● (tb **sólo**) adv only: Trabajo ~ los sábados. I only work on Saturdays. ◊ Es ~ un niño. He's only a child. ● nm **solo** [pl -s]: hacer un ~ play/sing a solo ► **a solas** alone **estar/sentirse** ~ feel/be lonely **no sólo... sino también...** not only... but also... **quedarse** ~ be (left) on your own

solomillo (tb **solomito**) nm filet mignon, fillet steak (GB)

soltar vt 1 (desasir) let go of sth/sb: ¡Suéltame! Let go of me! 2 (dejar caer) drop 3 (dejar libre) set sth/sb free 4 (perro) set sth loose 5 (cable, cuerda) let sth out 6 (olor, humo) give sth off 7 (dinero) cough sth up 8 (grito, suspiro) let sth out ● **soltarse** vp 1 (separarse) let go (of sth/sb): No te sueltes de mi mano. Don't let go of my hand. 2 ~ **(en)** get the hang of sth: Ya se está soltando en inglés. She's getting the hang of English now.

soltero adj single

solterón/ona nm-nf bachelor [fem old maid]

soltura nf 1 (desparpajo) self-confidence 2 (facilidad): Habla francés con ~. She speaks fluent French. ◊ manejar con ~ drive well ◊ adquirir ~ en la computadora get the hang of the computer

soluble adj soluble

solución nf solution: encontrar la ~ del problema find the solution to the problem

solucionar vt solve

solvente adj, nm solvent

sombra nf 1 (ausencia de sol) shade: sentarse en la ~ sit in the shade 2 (silueta) shadow: proyectar una ~ cast a shadow ► ~ **de ojos** eyeshadow

sombreado adj shady

sombrero nm hat

sombrilla nf (playa) sunshade

someter vt 1 (dominar) subdue 2 (exponer) subject: ~ a los presos a torturas subject prisoners to torture ◊ Sometieron el metal al calor. The metal was subjected to heat. 3 (buscar aprobación) submit ● **someterse** vp (rendirse) surrender ► ~ **a votación** put sth to the vote

somnífero nm sleeping pill

sonado *adj* (*comentado*) much talked-about

sonajero *nm* (*tb* **sonaja** *Mx, nf*) rattle

sonámbulo/a *nm-nf* sleepwalker

sonar *vi* **1** sound: *El piano suena de maravilla.* The piano sounds great. ◇ *¿Cómo te suena esto?* How does this sound to you? **2** (*alarma, sirena*) go off **3** (*timbre, campanilla, teléfono*) ring **4** (*ser familiar*) ring a bell: *El nombre me suena.* The name rings a bell. **5** (*tripas*) rumble: *Me sonaban las tripas.* My tummy was rumbling. ● **sonarse** *vp* **1** (*nariz*) blow your nose **2** (*Mx, dar una paliza*) beat sb up

sonda *nf* (*Med*) probe

sondear *vt* **1** (*persona*) sound sb out **2** (*opinión, mercado*) test

sondeo *nm* (*opinión, mercado, etc.*) poll: *un ~ de opinión* an opinion poll

sonido *nm* sound

sonoro *adj* **1** sound: *efectos ~s* sound effects **2** (*voz*) loud

sonreír *vi* smile: *Me sonrió.* He smiled at me.

sonriente *adj* smiling

sonrisa *nf* smile

sonrojarse *vp* blush

sonrosado *adj* rosy

soñador/a *nm-nf* dreamer

soñar *vi* **1** (*durmiendo*) dream (*about sth/sb*): *Anoche soñé contigo.* I dreamed about you last night. **2** (*desear*) dream of: *sth*: *~ con ser famoso* dream of being famous ● *vt* dream: *No sé si lo soñé.* I don't know if I dreamed it. ▶ **~ con los angelitos** have sweet dreams ◆ **despierto** daydream

sopa *nf* soup ▶ **hasta en la ~** all over the place

sopera *nf* soup tureen

sopero *adj* soup: *una cuchara sopera* a soup spoon

soplar *vt* **1** (*para apagar algo*) blow sth out: *~ una vela* blow out a candle **2** (*para enfriar algo*) blow on sth: *~ la sopa* blow on your soup **3** (*decir en voz baja*) whisper: *Me soplaba las respuestas.* He whispered the answers to me. **4** (*delatar*) (a) (*entre niños*) tell (*on sb*): *Devuélvemelo o se lo soplo a la maestra.* Give it back or I'll tell the teacher on you. (b) (*a la policía*) squeal ● *vi* **1** (*persona, viento*) blow **2** (*beber*) drink

soplo *nm* (*tb* **soplido**) *nm* **1** blow: *Apagó todas las velas de un ~.* He blew out the candles in one go. **2** (*viento*) gust

soplón/ona *nm-nf* **1** tattletale, telltale (*GB*) **2** (*de la policía*) informant

soportar *vt* put up with sth/sb: *~ el calor* put up with the heat **NOTA** En negaciones se dice **stand**: *No lo soporto.* I can't stand her. *No soporta esperar.* He can't stand waiting.

soporte *nm* **1** support **2** (*estantería*) bracket

soprano *nmf* [*pl* -s]

sorber *vt, vi* **1** (*líquido*) (a) sip (b) (*con pajita*) suck **2** (*por las narices*) sniff

sorbete *nm* sorbet

sorbo *nm* sip

sordera *nf* deafness

sórdido *adj* sordid

sordo *adj* deaf: *quedarse ~* go deaf ◇ *un colegio especial para ~s* a special school for the deaf ▶ **hacerse el ~** turn a deaf ear ◆ **como una tapia** deaf as a post

sordomudo *adj* deaf and dumb

soroche *nm* altitude sickness

sorprendente *adj* surprising

sorprender *vt* **1** surprise: *Me sorprende que no haya llegado todavía.* I'm surprised he's not here yet. **2** (*agarrar desprevenido*) catch sb (*unawares*): *Los sorprendió robando.* He caught them stealing. ● **sorprenderse** *vp* be surprised

sorpresa *nf* surprise ▶ **tomar por ~** take sb by surprise

sortear *vt* **1** (*echar a suertes*) draw straws, draw lots (*GB*) for sth **2** (*rifar*) raffle **3** (*golpe, obstáculo*) dodge **4** (*dificultad, trabas*) overcome

sorteo *nm* **1** (*lotería, adjudicación*) draw **2** (*rifa*) raffle

sortija *nf* ring

SOS *nm* SOS

sosegado *adj* calm

sosegarse *vp* calm down

sosiego *nm* calm

soso *adj* **1** (*comida*) tasteless **2** (*persona*) dull

sospecha *nf* suspicion

sospechar *vt, vi* suspect: *No sospechaban de mí.* They didn't suspect me. ◇ *¡Ya (me) lo sospechaba!* Just as I suspected!

sospechoso/a *adj* suspicious ● *nm-nf* suspect

sostén *nm* (*prenda*) bra

sostener *vt* **1** (*sujetar*) hold **2** (*peso, carga*) support **3** (*afirmar*) maintain ● **sostenerse** *vp* stand up

sostenido *adj* (*Mús*) sharp: *fa ~ F* sharp

sotana nf cassock

sótano nm basement

soya nf soy, soya (GB)

sport adj, nm: zapatos/ropa (de) ~ casual shoes/clothes

spray nm spray, atomizador

squash nm squash

stop nm (señal) stop light

su adj **1** (de él) his **2** (de ella) her **3** (de objeto, animal, concepto) its **4** (de ellos/ellas) their **5** (impersonal) their: Cada cual tiene su opinión. Everyone has their own opinion. **6** (de usted, de ustedes) your

suave adj **1** (color, luz, música, piel, ropa, voz) soft **2** (superficie) smooth **3** (brisa, persona, curva, pendiente, sonido) gentle **4** (castigo, clima, sabor) mild **5** (ejercicios, lluvia, viento) light **6** (café, té) weak

suavizante nm conditioner

suavizar vt **1** (piel) moisturize **2** (pelo) condition

subasta nf auction

subcampeón/ona nm-nf runner-up [pl -ers-up]

subconsciente adj, nm subconscious

subdesarrollado adj underdeveloped

subdesarrollo nm underdevelopment

súbdito/a nm-nf subject

subida nf **1** (acción) ascent **2** (pendiente) hill **3** (aumento) rise: una ~ de precios a rise in prices

subido adj (color) bright

subir vt **1** (llevar) take/bring sth up: Subió las maletas a la habitación. He took the bags up to the room. **2** (poner más arriba) put sth up: Súbelo un poco más. Put it up a little higher. **3** (levantar) lift sth (up): Subí el equipaje al tren. I lifted the baggage onto the train. **4** (ir/venir arriba)/go/come up: ~ (por) una calle go up a street **5** (volumen) turn sth up **6** (precios) raise ● vi **1** (ir/venir arriba)/go/come up: ~ al tejado go up onto the roof **2** (temperatura, río, precio) rise: Subió la gasolina. The price of gasoline rose. **3** (marea) come in **4** (volumen, voz) get louder ● **subir(se)** vi, vp **1** (automóvil): Subí al taxi. I got into the taxi. **2** (transporte público, caballo, bicicleta) get on (sth) ▸ **~se a la cabeza** go to your head **~se a las barbas** walk all over sb **subírsele los humos a algn** become high and

mighty **~se por las paredes** hit the roof

subjetivo adj subjective

subjuntivo adj, nm subjunctive

sublevación nf uprising

sublime adj sublime

submarino adj underwater ● nm submarine

subnormal adj subnormal

subordinado/a adj, nm-nf subordinate

subrayar vt underline

subsidio nm subsidy [pl -ies]

subsistir vi subsist (on sth)

subterráneo adj underground

subtítulo nm subtitle

suburbio nm **1** (alrededores) suburb **2** (barrio pobre) slum

subvencionar vt subsidize

sucedáneo nm substitute (for sth)

suceder vi (ocurrir) happen ● vt (en un cargo, etc.) succeed

sucesión nf succession

sucesivamente adv successively

suceso nm **1** (acontecimiento) event **2** (incidente) incident

sucesor/a nm-nf successor

suciedad nf dirt

sucio adj, adv dirty: jugar ~ play dirty ▸ **en ~**: escribir algo en ~ write a rough draft of sth

suculento/a adj succulent

sucursal nf branch

sudadera nf **1** sweatshirt **2** (And, conjunto) sweats [pl], tracksuit (GB) →**PANTALÓN**

sudado nm (And) stew

sudar vi sweat ▸ **~ la gota gorda/sangre/tinta** sweat blood

sudeste nm Ver SURESTE

sudoeste nm Ver SUROESTE

sudor nm sweat

sudoroso adj sweaty

Suecia nf Sweden

sueco/a adj, nm Swedish ● nm-nf Swede

suegro/a nm-nf father-in-law [fem mother-in-law] **2 suegros** parents-in-law

suela nf sole

sueldo nm **1** pay: un aumento de ~ a pay increase **2** (mensual) salary [pl -ies]

suelo nm **1** (superficie de la tierra) ground: caer al ~ fall to the ground **2** (dentro de un edificio) floor **3** (terreno) land

suelto adj loose: Siempre llevo el pelo ~. I always wear my hair loose. ◇ dinero ~ loose change ● nm small change

sueño nm **1** (descanso) sleep: debido a la falta de ~ due to lack of sleep **2** (*somnolencia*) drowsiness: *Estas pastillas dan/producen ~.* These pills make you drowsy. **3** (*lo soñado, ilusión*) dream: *Fue un ~ hecho realidad.* It was a dream come true. ▶ **caerse de ~** be dead on your feet **tener ~** be sleepy

suerte *nf* **1** (*fortuna*) luck: *¡Buena ~!* Good luck! ◇ *dar/traer mala ~* bring bad luck **2** (*destino*) fate ▶ **de la ~:** *mi número de la ~* my lucky number **echar a ~s** toss for *sth* **por ~** fortunately **tener mala ~** be unlucky **tener ~** be lucky

suéter *nm* sweater →SWEATER

suficiente *adj* enough: *lo ~ para vivir* enough to live on

sufrido *adj* (*persona*) long-suffering

sufrimiento *nm* suffering

sufrir *vt* **1** (*tener*) have: *~ un accidente/un ataque al corazón* have an accident/a heart attack ◇ *La ciudad sufre problemas de tráfico.* The city has traffic problems. **2** (*derrota, lesión*) suffer **3** (*cambio*) undergo ● *vi* suffer: *Sufre del corazón.* He suffers from heart trouble.

sugerencia *nf* suggestion

sugerir *vt* suggest

sugestionar *vt* influence ● **sugestionarse** *vp* convince yourself *that...*

suicidarse *vp* commit suicide

suicidio *nm* suicide

Suiza *nf* Switzerland

suizo/a *adj* Swiss ● *nm-nf* Swiss man/woman [*pl* men/women]: *los ~s* the Swiss

sujetar *vt* **1** (*agarrar*) hold **2** (*asegurar*) fasten ● **sujetarse** *vp* (*agarrarse*) hold on (*to sth*): *Sujétate a mi brazo.* Hold on to my arm.

sujeto *adj* **1** (*atado*) fastened **2** (*agarrado*): *Dos policías lo tenían ~.* Two policemen were holding him down. **3** (*fijo*) secure: *El gancho no estaba bien ~.* The hook wasn't secure. **4** (*sometido*) subject to: *Estamos ~s a las reglas del club.* We are subject to the rules of the club. ● *nm* **1** (*tipo*) character **2** (*Gram*) subject

suma *nf* sum: *hacer una ~* do a sum

sumar *vt, vi* add (*sth*) up

sumergible *adj* water-resistant

sumergir(se) *vt, vp* submerge

suministrar *vt* supply *sb* (with *sth*)

sumiso *adj* submissive

superar *vt* **1** (*dificultad, problema*) overcome, get over *sth* (*más coloq*): *Superé el miedo a volar.* I've gotten over my fear of flying. **2** (*récord*) beat **3** (*prueba*) pass **4** (*ser mejor*) surpass: *~ las expectativas* surpass expectations ● **superarse** *vp* better yourself

superdotado/a *adj* gifted ● *nm-nf*: *un colegio para ~s* a school for gifted children

superficial *adj* superficial

superficie *nf* **1** surface **2** (*Geom*) area

superfluo *adj* unnecessary

superior *adj* **1** higher (*than sth/sb*): *una cifra diez veces ~ a la normal* a figure ten times higher than normal ◇ *estudios ~es* higher education **2** (*en calidad*) superior (*to sth/sb*) **3** (*posición*) top: *el ángulo ~ izquierdo* the top left-hand corner

superiora *nf* (*Rel*) Mother Superior

superioridad *nf* superiority

supermercado *nm* supermarket

superpoblado *adj* overpopulated

superstición *nf* superstition

supersticioso *adj* superstitious

supervisar *vt* supervise

suplemento *nm* supplement

suplente *adj, nmf* **1** relief: *un conductor ~* a relief driver **2** (*tb* **maestro ~**) substitute teacher, supply teacher (*GB*) **3** (*Dep*) substitute

súplica *nf* plea

suplicar *vt* beg (*sb*) (for *sth*): *Le supliqué que no lo hiciera.* I begged him not to do it. ◇ *~ piedad* beg for mercy

suplicio *nm* **1** (*molestia*) torture [*U*]: *Estos tacones son un ~.* These high heels are torture. **2** (*sufrimiento*) ordeal

suponer *vt* **1** (*creer*) suppose: *Supongo que sí/no.* I suppose so/not. ◇ *Supongamos que...* Supposing... **2** (*significar*) mean: *Supone mucho para nosotros.* It means a lot to us.

suposición *nf* supposition

supositorio *nm* suppository [*pl* -ies]

supremo *adj* supreme

suprimir *vt* **1** (*omitir, excluir*) leave *sth* out **2** (*abolir*) abolish

supuesto *adj* **1** (*presunto*) alleged **2** (*nombre*) assumed ▶ **dar por ~** take *sth* for granted **por ~ (que...)** of course

sur *nm* south

surco nm **1** (agricultura, arruga) furrow **2** (en el agua) wake **3** (disco, metal) groove

sureste nm **1** (punto cardinal, región) south-east (abrev **SE**) **2** (viento, dirección) south-easterly

surf nm surfing: hacer/practicar el ~ go surfing

surgir vi arise

suroeste nm **1** (punto cardinal, región) south-west (abrev **SW**) **2** (viento, dirección) south-westerly

surtido adj (variado) assorted ● nm selection: Hay muy poco ~. There's a very poor selection.

surtidor nm **1** (fuente) fountain **2** (gasolina) pump

surtir vt supply ▸ ~ efecto have an effect

susceptible adj (irritable) touchy

suscribirse vp **1** (publicación, opinión) subscribe (to sth) **2** (asociación) become a member (of sth)

suscripción nf subscription

susodicho adj above-mentioned: los ~s the above-mentioned

suspender vt suspend

suspenso nm suspense ▸ **libro/película de ~** thriller

suspensores nm (tirantes) suspenders, braces (GB)

suspirar vi sigh

suspiro nm sigh

sustancia nf substance

sustancial adj substantial

sustancioso adj (comida) nourishing

sustantivo nm noun

sustento nm **1** (alimento) sustenance **2** (soporte, apoyo) support

sustitución nf **1** (permanente) replacement **2** (temporal, Dep) substitution

sustituir (suplir) stand in for sb

sustituto/a nm-nf **1** (permanente) replacement **2** (suplente) stand-in

susto nm **1** (miedo, sobresalto) fright: ¡Qué ~ me diste! What a fright you gave me! **2** (falsa alarma) scare

sustraer vt (Mat) subtract

susurrar vt, vi whisper

susurro nm whisper

sutil adj subtle

sutura nf suture

suyo/a adj, pron **1** (de usted/ustedes) yours: un amigo ~ a friend of yours **2** (de él) his **3** (de ella) hers **4** (de ellas/ellos) theirs

T t

tabaco nm **1** tobacco: ~ de pipa pipe tobacco **2** (And, puro) cigar

taberna nf bar

tabique nm **1** (pared) partition **2** (ladrillo) brick ▸ ~ **nasal** nasal septum

tabla nf **1** (madera sin alisar) plank **2** (madera pulida, plancha) board: ~ de planchar/windsurf ironing board/sailboard **3** (lista, índice, Mat) table: las ~s (de multiplicar) (multiplication) tables ◇ la ~ del tres the three times table

tablero nm **1** board: pasar al ~ go up to the board ◇ ~ de ajedrez chessboard ◇ ~ de anuncios bulletin board/noticeboard (GB) **2** (panel) panel: ~ de control control panel

tableta nf **1** (Med) tablet **2** (tablilla Mx) (chocolate) bar

tablón nm plank

tabú nm taboo: una palabra ~ a taboo word

taburete nm stool

tacaño/a adj stingy ● nm-nf skin-flint

tachar vt cross sth out

tachón nm crossed-out word

tachuela nf tack

taco nm **1** (para tapar) plug **2** (para tornillo) Rawl®, Rawl-plug® (GB) **3** (Dep, calzado) cleat, stud (GB) **4** (billar) pool/billiard cue **5** (tortilla) taco ▸ **a todo ~** (And) **1** (con lujo) in style **2** (muy rápido) at top speed **3** (volumen) (at) full blast

tacón nm heel: llevar tacones wear high heels ◇ sandalias de ~ high-heeled sandals

táctica nf **1** (estrategia) tactics [pl]: un cambio de ~ a change of tactics **2** (maniobra) tactic: una ~ electoral an electoral tactic

tacto nm sense of touch: reconocer algo por el ~ recognize sth by touch

tajada nf slice

tajante adj adamant

tal adj such: en ~es situaciones in such situations ◇ un hecho de ~ gravedad a matter of such importance ◇ actividades ~es como leer y pintar activities such as reading and painting **NOTA** Con sustantivos contables en singular se dice such a: ¿Cómo puedes decir ~ cosa? How can you say such a thing?

▶ **con ~ de** to: *Haría cualquier cosa con ~ de ganar.* I'd do anything to win. **el/la ~** *(supuesto)* the so-called: *la ~ amiga* her so-called friend **¿qué ~?** **1** *(saludo)* how are things? **2** *(¿cómo está(n)?)* how is/are...?: *¿Qué ~ tus papás?* How are your parents? **3** *(¿cómo es/son?)* what is/are *sth* like?: *¿Qué ~ la película?* What was the movie like? **ser ~ para cual** be two of a kind ▶ **como como** the way: *Se escribe ~ como suena.* It's spelled the way it sounds. **un/una ~:** *Lo llamó un ~ Luis Blanco.* A Luis Blanco called you.

taladrar *vt* drill a hole in *sth*

taladro *nm* drill

talar *vt (árbol)* cut *sth* down

talco *nm* talcum powder

talego *nm (And)* bag

talento *nm* talent: *Tiene ~ para la música/pintar.* He has a talent for music/painting.

talla *nf* **1** *(prenda)* size: *¿Qué ~ de camisa usas?* What size shirt do you wear? ◊ *No tienen la ~.* They don't have the right size. **2** *(escultura)* sculpture

tallar *vt* **1** *(madera, piedra)* carve: *~ algo en coral* carve *sth* in coral **2** *(joya, cristal)* cut **3** *(Mx, piso, ropa)* scrub ▶ **~se los ojos** *(Mx)* rub your eyes

taller *nm* **1** workshop: *un ~ de teatro/carpintería* a theater/carpenter's workshop **2** *(Aut)* garage **3** *(Arte)* studio *[pl -s]*

tallo *nm* stem

talón *nm* **1** *(pie, zapato)* heel **2** *(cheque)* stub

talonario *nm* **1** *(cheques)* checkbook **2** *(recibos, etc.)* book

tamal *nm* tamale

tamaño *nm* size: *¿Qué ~ tiene la caja?* What size is the box?

tamarindo *nm* tamarind

también *adv* also, too, as well **NOTA** Too y **as well** van al final de la frase: *Yo ~.* Me too. I want to go too/as well. **Also** es más formal y va delante del verbo principal, o detrás si es un verbo auxiliar: *venden zapatos.* They also sell shoes. ◊ *Conocí a Jane y ~ a sus papás.* I've met Jane and I've also met her parents. ▶ **yo ~** me too: *—Voy a casa. —Yo ~.* "I'm going home." "Me too."

tambor *nm* drum

tampoco *adv* neither, nor, either: *—No he leído ese libro. —Yo ~.* "I haven't read that book." "Neither/Nor have I./Me neither." ◊

—No me gusta. —A mí ~. "I don't like it." "I don't either./Neither/Nor do I." ◊ *Yo ~ fui.* I didn't go either. ▶ **NEITHER**

tampón *nm* tampon

tan *adv* **1** *(delante de adj o adv)* so: *Es ~ difícil que...* It's so hard that... ◊ *No creí que llegarías ~ tarde.* I didn't think you'd be so late. **2** *(detrás de sustantivo)* such: *No me esperaba un regalo ~ caro.* I wasn't expecting such an expensive gift. ◊ *¡Qué casa ~ bonita!* What a lovely house! ▶ **tan... como...** as... as...: *Es ~ alto como su padre.* He's as tall as his father. ◊ *~ pronto como llegues* as soon as you arrive

tangente *nf* tangent

tanque *nm* tank

tantear *vt* **1** *(persona)* sound *sb* out **2** *(situación)* weigh *sth* up

tanto/a *adj, pron* **1** *(referido a sustantivo incontable)* so much: *No me pongas ~ arroz.* Don't give me so much rice. **2** *(referido a sustantivo contable)* so many: *¿Por qué compraste ~s?* Why did you buy so many? ● *adv* **1** so much: *He comido ~ que no me puedo mover.* I've eaten so much I can't move. **2** *(tanto tiempo)* so long: *¡Hace ~ que no te veo!* I haven't seen you for so long! **3** *(tan rápido)* so fast: *No corras ~.* Don't go so fast. **4** *(tan a menudo)* so often ● *nm* **1** *(cantidad)* so much: *Me dan un ~ al mes.* They give me so much a month. **2** *(gol)* goal ▶ **entre ~ = ENTRETANTO no ser para ~:** *No es para ~.* It's not that important. **poner al ~** fill *sb* in: *Me puso al ~ de la situación.* He filled me in on the situation. **por (lo) ~** therefore **tanto... como...** **1** *(en comparaciones)* **(a)** *(+ sustantivo incontable)* as much... as...: *Tomé ~ vino como tú.* I drank as much wine as you. **(b)** *(+ sustantivo contable)* as many... as...: *No tengo ~s amigos como antes.* I don't have as many friends as before. **2** *(los dos)* both...: *Lo sabían ~ él como su hermana.* He and his sister both knew. **un ~** *(bastante)* rather **un ~ por ciento** a percentage **y ~s 1** *(con cantidad)* odd: *treinta y ~s km* thirty-odd kilometers **2** *(con año, edades)*: *mil novecientos sesenta y ~s* nineteen sixty something

tap *nm* tap dancing

tapa *nf* **1** *(olla)* lid **2** *(bolígrafo, botella)* top **3** *(zapatos)* heel **4** *(libro)* cover **5** *(diente)* filling

tapada *nf (And, Dep)* save

tapadera nf 1 (tapa) lid 2 (fig) cover

tapado adj (And, tonto) dumb

tapanco nm (Mx) loft

tapar vt 1 (cubrir) cover 2 (abrigar) wrap sth/sb up: La tapé con una cobija. I wrapped her up in a blanket. 3 (con tapa) put the lid on sth: Tapa la olla. Put the lid on the pan. 4 (con tapón) put the top on sth 5 (agujero, gotera) plug sth (up) 6 (obstruir) block: La basura tapó el desagüe. The garbage blocked the drainpipe. ◊ No me tapes la tele. Don't block my view of the TV. 7 (diente) fill ● **taparse** vp 1 (abrigarse) wrap up (in sth): Tápate bien. Wrap up warm. 2 (obstruirse) get blocked

tapete nm (alfombra) rug ▸ **mover el ~** pull the rug from under sb

tapia nf wall

tapicería nf upholstery

tapiz nm tapestry [pl -ies]

tapizar vt upholster

tapón nm 1 top: ~ de rosca screw top 2 (de corcho) cork 3 (Mec, bañera, para los oídos) plug

taquete nm (Mx) Rawl®, Rawlplug® (GB)

taquigrafía nf shorthand

taquilla nf 1 ticket office 2 (de un teatro/cine) box office

tarántula nf tarantula

tararear vt, vi hum

tardar vi take (time) to do sth: Tardaron bastante en contestar. They took a long time to reply. ◊ En tren se tarda una hora. It takes an hour by train. ▸ **no ~ nada** not be long

tarde nf afternoon, evening: El concierto es por la ~. The concert is in the afternoon/evening. ◊ Llegó el domingo por la ~. He arrived on Sunday afternoon/evening. ◊ a las tres de la ~ at three o'clock in the afternoon ● adv 1 late: Se hace ~. It's getting late. ◊ llegar ~ be late 2 (demasiado tarde) too late: Es ~ para llamarlos. It's too late to call them. ▸ **¡buenas ~s!** good afternoon/evening! **~ o temprano** sooner or later

tarea nf 1 (actividad) task 2 (Educ) homework [U]: poner ~ set homework ◊ la ~ de geografía your geography homework

tarima nf platform

tarjeta nf card: ~ de crédito/identidad credit/identity card

tarro nm 1 (vidrio) jar 2 (metal) can 3 (taza) mug

tartamudear vt stutter

tartamudo/a adj, nm-nf: ser ~ have a stammer ◊ los ~s people with a stammer

tarugada nf (Mx) stupid thing: Eso que dices es una ~. What you're saying is stupid.

tasa nf 1 (índice) rate: ~ de natalidad birth rate 2 (impuesto) tax 3 (cuota) fee: ~s académicas tuition fees

tatarabuelo/a nm-nf 1 great-great-grandfather [fem great-great-grandmother] 2 **tatarabuelos** great-great-grandparents

tatuaje nm tattoo

Tauro nm, nmf Taurus

taxi nm taxi

taxista nmf taxi driver

taza nf 1 cup: una ~ de café a cup of coffee 2 (inodoro) bowl

tazón nm bowl

te pron pers 1 (complemento) you: Te lo compré. I bought it for you. 2 (partes del cuerpo, efectos personales): Quítate el abrigo. Take your coat off. ◊ ¿Te duele la espalda? Does your back hurt? 3 (reflexivo) (yourself): Vístete. Get dressed.

té nm tea

teatro nm 1 theater 2 (cine) (movie) theater, cinema (GB) ▸ **hacer ~** (exagerar) put on an act

techo nm 1 (interior) ceiling 2 (exterior, Aut) roof

tecla nf key

teclado nm keyboard

teclear vt key sth in

técnica nf 1 (método) technique 2 (tecnología) technology [pl -ies]

técnico/a adj technical ● nm-nf technician

tecnología nf technology ▸ **alta ~** high technology

teja nf tile

tejado nm roof

tejer vt 1 (hacer punto) knit 2 (en un telar) weave 3 (araña, gusano) spin

tejido nm 1 (tela) fabric → TELA 2 (Anat) tissue

tela nf cloth, material, fabric **NOTA** Cloth es la traducción más general si se usa para la tela con la que se hacen los trajes, cortinas, etc. y para describir de qué está hecha una cosa: Está hecho de ~. It's made of cloth. ◊ *una bolsa de* ~ a cloth bag. **Material** y **fabric** se usan sólo para la tela utilizada en sastrería y tapicería, aunque **fabric** suele indicar que tiene varios colores. **Material** y **fabric** son sustantivos contables e incontables, pero **cloth** suele ser incontable cuando significa tela.

telaraña *nf* cobweb

tele *nf* TV

telecomunicaciones *nf* telecommunications

teleférico *nm* cable car

telefonazo *nm* call

telefonear *vt, vi* telephone

telefónico *adj* telephone, phone (*coloq*): *una llamada telefónica* a phone call

telefonista *nmf* telephonist

teléfono *nm* **1** (*aparato*) telephone, phone (*coloq*): *hablar por* ~ *con algn* be on the phone with sb **2** (*número*) phone number

telegrama *nm* telegram

telenovela *nf* soap (opera)

teleobjetivo *nm* telephoto lens

telepatía *nf* telepathy

telescopio *nm* telescope

telespectador/a *nm-nf* viewer

teletexto *nm* teletext

televidente *nmf* viewer

televisar *vt* televise

televisión *nf* television, TV (*más coloq*): *salir en la* ~ *la televisión* ◊ *Prende/apaga la* ~. Turn the TV on/off. ◊ *ver (la)* ~ watch television

televisor *nm* television (set)

telón *nm* curtain

tema *nm* **1** subject: *el* ~ *de una charla* the subject of a talk ◊ *No cambies de* ~. Don't change the subject. **2** (*cuestión*) matter: *un* ~ *personal/político* a private/political matter **3** (*canción*) track **4** (*música clásica*) theme

temario *nm* syllabus

temblar *vi* **1** tremble: ~ *de miedo* tremble with fear ◊ *Le temblaba la mano/voz*. His hand/voice was trembling. **2** (*de frío, fiebre*) shiver **3** (*edificio, muebles*) shake

temblor *nm* tremor

temer *vt* be afraid of sth/sb ● **temerse** *vp* be afraid: *Me temo que no van a venir*. I'm afraid they won't come.

temible *adj* fearful

temor *nm* fear: *por* ~ *a asustarlos* for fear of scaring them

temperamento *nm* temperament ▸ **tener** ~ have spirit

temperatura *nf* temperature

tempestad *nf* storm

templado *adj* **1** (*clima*) mild **2** (*comida, líquidos*) lukewarm

templo *nm* temple

temporada *nf* **1** (*período de tiempo*) time **2** (*época*) season: *la* ~ *alta/baja* the high/low season ▸ *de* ~ seasonal

temporal *adj* temporary

temprano *adj, adv* early: *Llegó por la mañana* ~. He arrived early in the morning. ◊ *tarde o* ~ sooner or later

tenaz *adj* tenacious

tenazas *nf* **1** (*Mec*) pliers **2** (*Cocina*) tongs ➔PAIR

tendedero *nm* **1** (*cuerda*) clothes line **2** (*plegable*) (clothes) drying rack **3** (*lugar*) drying room

tendencia *nf* **1** tendency [*pl* -ies]: *Tiene* ~ *a engordar*. He has a tendency to put on weight. **2** (*moda*) trend: *las últimas* ~*s de la moda* the latest trends in fashion

tender *vt* **1** (*ropa*) hang sth out **2** (*cama*) make ● *vi* ~ **a**: *Tiende a complicar las cosas*. He tends to complicate things. ◊ *La economía tiende a recuperarse*. The economy is recovering. ● **tenderse** *vp* lie down

tendero/a *nm-nf* store owner, shopkeeper (*GB*)

tendido *nm* ▸ ~ *eléctrico* cables [*pl*]

tendón *nm* tendon

tenebroso *adj* sinister

tenedor *nm* fork

tenencia *nf* (*Mx, Aut*) road tax

tener *vt*
● **posesión** have **NOTA** Hay dos formas para expresar "tener" en presente: **have** y **have got**. **Have** es más común en EE.UU. y siempre va acompañado de un auxiliar en interrogaciones o negaciones. **Have got** no necesita un auxiliar: *¿Tienes lápiz?* Do you have/Have you got a pencil? ◊ *No tengo dinero*. I don't have/I haven't got any money. En los demás tiempos verbales se usa **have**: *Tuve una bicicleta cuando era chiquito*. I had a bicycle when I was little.
● **estados, actitudes 1** (*edad, tamaño*) be: *Tiene diez años*. She's ten (years old). ◊ *Tiene 3m de largo*. It's three meters long. **2** (*sentir, tener una actitud*) **NOTA** Cuando **tener** significa "sentir", el inglés usa el verbo **be** con adjetivo, mientras que en español se usa un sustantivo:

Tengo mucha hambre. I'm very hungry. ◊ ~ *calor/frío/sed/miedo* be hot/cold/thirsty/frightened ◊ ~ *cuidado/paciencia* be careful/patient.

● **en construcciones con adj:** *Me tiene harta de tanto esperar.* I'm sick of waiting for him. ◊ *Tienes las manos sucias.* Your hands are dirty. ◊ *Tengo a mi mamá enferma.* My mother is sick.

● **v aux 1 ~ que hacer algo** have to do sth: *Tuvieron que irse enseguida.* They had to leave straight away. ◊ *Tienes que decírselo.* You must tell him. → MUST **2 + participio:** *Lo tienen todo planeado.* It's all arranged. ◊ *Su comportamiento nos tiene preocupados.* We're worried about the way he's been behaving. ▶ ~ **que ver** (*asunto*) have to do with *sth/sb: Eso no tiene nada que ver.* That has nothing to do with it. **NOTA** Para otras expresiones, ver el sustantivo, adjetivo, etc., p.ej. **tener afán** en AFÁN.

teniente *nmf* lieutenant

tenis *nm* **1** (*Dep*) tennis **2** (*zapatos*) sneakers, trainers (*GB*) ▶ ~ **de mesa** table tennis

tenista *nmf* tennis player

tenor *nm* tenor

tensar *vt* tighten

tensión *nf* **1** tension: ~ *nerviosa* nervous tension **2** (*eléctrica*) voltage **3** (*arterial*) blood pressure

tenso *adj* tense

tentación *nf* temptation: *resistir la ~ de hacer algo* resist the temptation to do sth ◊ *caer en la ~* fall into temptation

tentáculo *nm* tentacle

tentador *adj* tempting

tentar *vt* **1** (*inducir*) tempt: *Me tienta la idea de...* I'm tempted to... **2** (*palpar*) feel

tentativa *nf* attempt

tenue *adj* (*luz, sonido, línea*) faint

teñir *vt* dye: ~ *una camisa de rojo* dye a shirt red ● **teñirse** *vp* dye your hair: ~ *de castaño* dye your hair brown

teología *nf* theology

teoría *nf* theory [*pl* -ies]

teórico *adj* theoretical

terapia *nf* therapy [*pl* -ies]

tercero/a *adj, nm-nf, pron* third (*abrev* **3rd**) ● *nm* third party: *seguro a/contra ~s* third-party insurance ● **tercera** *nf* (*Aut*) third (gear) ▶ **a la tercera va la vencida, la tercera es la vencida** third time lucky **tercera edad:** *actividades para la tercera edad* activities for senior citizens

tercio *nm* third

terciopelo *nm* velvet

terco *adj* stubborn

térmico *adj* thermal

terminación *nf* ending

terminal *adj, nmf* terminal: *enfermos ~es* terminally ill patients ◊ ~ *de pasajeros* passenger terminal ▶ ~ **de autobuses** bus station

terminar *vt* finish ● *vi* **1** end: ~ *en tragedia* end in tragedy **2** ~ (**de hacer algo**) finish (doing sth) **3** ~ **haciendo/por hacer algo** end up doing sth **4** ~ **como/igual que...** end up like *sth/sb: Vas a ~ igual que tu papá.* You'll end up like your father. ● **terminarse** *vp* **1** be over: *Se terminó la fiesta.* The party's over. **2** (*pan, café, etc.*) run out: *Se nos terminó el pan.* We've run out of bread.

término *nm* **1** term: *en ~s generales* in general terms **2** (*fin*) end

termo *nm* Thermos® bottle, Thermos® (*GB*)

termómetro *nm* thermometer ▶ **poner el ~** take *sb's* temperature

termostato *nm* thermostat

ternero/a *nm-nf* calf [*pl* calves] ● **ternera** *nf* (*carne*) veal

ternura *nf* tenderness

terracería *nf* (*Mx*) ▶ **camino de ~** dirt road

terrateniente *nmf* landowner

terraza *nf* **1** (*balcón*) balcony [*pl* -ies] **2** (*bar*): *sentarse en la ~* sit outside **3** (*Agricultura*) terrace

terregal *nm* dust cloud

terremoto *nm* earthquake

terreno *nm* **1** (*tierra*) land [*U*]: *un ~ muy fértil* very fertile land ◊ *Compré un ~.* I bought some land. **2** (*fig*) field: *el ~ de la biología* the field of biology ▶ **sobre el ~ 1** (*en el lugar*) on the spot **2** (*sobre la marcha*) as I, you, etc. go along ▶ ~ **de juego** pitch

terrestre *adj* land: *un ataque ~* a land attack

terrible *adj* terrible

territorio *nm* territory [*pl* -ies]

terrón *nm* (*azúcar*) cube, lump (*GB*)

terror *nm* terror

terrorífico *adj* terrifying

terrorismo *nm* terrorism

terrorista *adj, nmf* terrorist

tertulia *nf* **1** get-together **2** (*TV*) talk show

tesis *nf* thesis [*pl* theses]

tesón *nm* determination

tesorero/a *nm-nf* treasurer

tesoro nm treasure

testamento nm 1 (Jur) will: hacer ~ make a will 2 **Testamento** (Rel) Testament

testarudo adj stubborn

testículo nm testicle

testigo nmf witness: ser ~ de algo witness sth ● nm (Dep) baton
▶ ~ presencial eyewitness

tetera nf 1 (para té) teapot 2 (para hervir agua) kettle

tetero nm (And) baby's bottle

Tetra Brik® nm carton

tétrico adj gloomy

textil adj textile

texto nm text: libro de ~ textbook
▶ procesamiento/tratamiento de ~ word processing

textura nf texture

tez nf complexion

tezontle nm (Mx) volcanic rock

ti pron pers you

tianguis nm (Mx) street market

tibio adj lukewarm

tiburón nm shark

tiempo nm 1 (cronológico) time: Hace mucho ~ que vivo acá. I've been living here for a long time. 2 (Dep) half [pl halves]: el primer ~ the first half 3 (Gram) tense 4 (meteorológico) weather: Hace buen/mal ~. The weather's good/bad. ▶ al poco ~ soon afterwards al ~ (bebida) at room temperature a ~: Todavía estás a ~ de enviarlo. You've still got time to send it. ◇ llegar a ~ be on time con el ~ in time con ~ (de sobra) in good time hacer ~ while away your time ~ completo full-time ~ muerto (Dep) timeout

tienda nf store, shop (GB) ▶ ir de ~s go shopping ~ de (abarrotes/comestibles) grocery store, grocer's (GB) ~ (de campaña) tent

tierno adj 1 (pan, verdura) fresh

tierra nf 1 (por oposición al mar, campo, fincas) land [U]: cultivar la ~ work the land 2 (para plantas, terreno) soil: una ~ fértil fertile soil 3 (suelo) ground: Cayó a ~. He fell to the ground. 4 (patria) home 5 **Tierra** (planeta) earth ▶ echar por ~ ruin ~ adentro inland ~ caliente/fría lowlands/highlands [pl] ~ firme dry land tomar ~ land

tieso adj stiff: quedarse ~ (de frío) be frozen stiff ▶ dejar ~ (asombrar) leave sb speechless

tiestazo nm (And) 1 (golpe) bump 2 (ruido) racket ▶ darse un ~ (manejando) have a crash

tifón nm typhoon

tifus nm typhus

tigre/esa nm-nf tiger [fem tigress]

tijera nf scissors [pl]: unas ~s some scissors/a pair of scissors → PAIR

tila nf (tb **tilo** nm) (infusión) lime tea

tilde nf 1 (acento) accent 2 (en la eñe) tilde

tiliches nm (Mx) 1 (pertenencias) stuff [U] 2 (trastos) junk [U]

timbrar vt 1 (impreso) print 2 (documento) stamp ● vi ring the bell
● **timbrarse** vp (And, ponerse nervioso) get jumpy

timbre nm 1 (campanilla) bell: tocar el ~ ring the bell 2 (voz) pitch: un ~ de voz muy alto a very high-pitched voice 3 (Mx, correos) stamp

tímido adj shy

timón nm 1 (barco) rudder 2 (Aut) steering wheel

tímpano nm (Anat) eardrum

tina nf bathtub

tinieblas nf darkness [sing]

tinta nf ink ▶ medias ~s half measures **saber algo de buena** ~ have sth on good authority ~ **china** Indian ink

tinte nm dye

tinto adj, nm 1 (vino) red (wine) 2 (And, café) black (coffee)

tintorería nf dry-cleaner's

tinturar vt (And) dye ● **tinturarse** vp (And) dye your hair

tío/a nm-nf uncle [fem aunt]: el ~ Daniel Uncle Daniel ◇ Vivo con mis ~s. I live with my aunt and uncle.

típico adj 1 (característico) typical 2 (tradicional) traditional: un baile ~ a traditional dance

tipo nm 1 kind: todo ~ de gente all kinds of people ◇ No es mi ~. He's not my type. 2 (cuerpo) (a) (mujer) figure: Tiene un ~ bonito. She has a nice figure. (b) (hombre) body 3 (individuo) guy

tiquete nm 1 (entrada, transporte) ticket 2 (recibo) receipt

tira¹ nf 1 (papel, tela) strip 2 (zapato) strap

tira² nmf (policía) cop ● **la tira** nf (Mx) the cops

tirada nf 1 (turno) throw 2 (distancia) way: Hay una buena ~. It's quite a way. ▶ de/en una ~ in one go

tirado adj lying (around): ~ en el suelo lying on the ground

tirador/a nm-nf (persona) shot ● nm (cajón, puerta) knob

tiranizar vt tyrannize

tirante adj 1 tight: *Pon la cuerda bien* ~. Make sure the rope is tight. 2 (*ambiente, situación*) tense ● nm 1 (*vestido*) shoulder strap 2 tirantes suspenders, braces (GB)

tirar vt 1 (*lanzar*) throw: *Tírale la pelota a tu compañero.* Throw the ball to your teammate. **NOTA** Cuando se tira algo a algn con intención de hacerle daño, se usa **throw sth at sb**: *Le tiraban piedras al gato.* They were throwing stones at the cat. 2 (*desechar*) throw away 3 (*residuos*) dump 4 (*derramar*) spill 5 (*tumbar*) knock sth over ● vi 1 pull: ~ *de la cadena* pull the chain 2 ~ *a: rosa tirando a rojo* pinkish red ◊ *Tira un poco a la familia de la mamá.* He looks a little like his mother's side of the family. 3 (*disparar, Dep*) shoot (at *sth/sb*): ~ *a la portería* shoot at goal ● **tirarse** vp 1 jump: ~ *por la ventana* jump out of the window 2 (*And, echar a perderse*) ruin **NOTA** Para otras expresiones, ver el sustantivo, p. ej. **tirar la toalla** en TOALLA.

tiritar vi shiver: ~ *de frío* shiver with cold

tiro nm 1 (*lanzamiento*) throw 2 (*disparo, Dep*) shot: *un* ~ *a gol* a shot at goal 3 (*herida de disparo*) bullet wound 4 (*chimenea*) draft ▶ **a** ~ **de piedra** a stone's throw away **caer/sentar como un** ~: *Me cayó como un* ~ *que me dijera eso.* I was really upset when he said that. ◊ *La comida me sentó como un* ~. The meal didn't agree with me. **de a** ~ (*Mx*) *Nos fue de a* ~ *mal.* We did really badly. **ni a** ~ **s** for love nor money **pegar un** ~ **s** shoot: *Se pegó un tiro.* He shot himself. **salir como un** ~ rush out **salir el** ~ **por la culata** backfire: *Me salió el* ~ *por la culata.* It backfired on me. ~ **al blanco** target shooting ~ **con arco** archery ~ **de esquina** (*Dep*) corner

tirón nm tug: *dar un* ~ *de pelo* give sb's hair a tug

tiroteo nm 1 (*delincuentes*) shootout 2 (*durante una guerra*) fighting 3 (*ruido de disparos*) shots [*pl*]: *Escuchamos un* ~ *desde la calle.* We heard shots in the street.

tirria nf grudge: *tenerle* ~ *a algn* have a grudge against sb

títere nm 1 puppet 2 títeres (*representación*) puppet show

titipuchal nm (*Mx*) loads [*pl*]: *un* ~ *de gente* loads of people

titular¹ vt call

titular² adj: *el equipo* ~ the first team ◊ *un jugador* ~ a first-team player ● nmf (*pasaporte, cuenta bancaria*) holder ● nm headline

título nm 1 title: *el* ~ *de una novela* the title of a novel 2 (*estudios*) degree: *obtener el* ~ *de abogado* get a degree in law

tiza nf chalk: *Dame una* ~. Give me a piece of chalk. ◊ ~s *de colores* colored chalks

tlapalería nf (*Mx*) hardware store/shop (GB)

toalla nf towel ▶ **tirar la** ~ throw in the towel

tobillo nm ankle →MY

tobogán nm (*parque*) slide

tocadiscos nm record player

tocar vt 1 touch: *¡No lo toques!* Don't touch it! 2 (*palpar*) feel: *¿Me dejas* ~ *la tela?* Can I feel the fabric? 3 (*Mús*) play: ~ *la guitarra/un villancico* play the guitar/a carol 4 (*hacer sonar*) (a) (*campana, timbre*) ring (b) (*bocina, sirena*) sound (c) (*silbato*) blow ● vi 1 (*Mús*) play 2 (*turno*) be sb's turn (*to do sth*): *Te toca tirar.* It's your turn to throw. 3 (*corresponder*) (a) (*seguido de acción*) have *to do sth*: *Hoy nos toca ir a comprar.* We have to go shopping today. (b) (*en reparto*) get: *Me tocó el mismo profesor que el año pasado.* I have the same teacher as last year. (c) (*en sorteo*) win: *Me tocó una muñeca.* I won a doll.

tocayo/a nm-nf namesake

tocineta nf (*And*) bacon

tocino nm pork fat

todavía adv 1 (*frases afirmativas e interrogativas*) still: *¿* ~ *vives allá?* Do you still live there? 2 (*frases negativas e interrogativas-negativas*) yet: ~ *no están maduras.* They're not ripe yet. ◊ *—¿* ~ *no te contestan? —No,* ~ *no.* "Haven't they written back yet?" "No, not yet." → STILL 3 (*frases comparativas*) even: ~ *mejor* even better

todo adj 1 all: *Ya hice* ~ *el trabajo.* I've done all the work. ◊ *Lleva* ~ *mes enfermo.* He's been sick all month. ◊ ~s *los edificios del pueblo* all the buildings in town **NOTA** Con un sustantivo contable en singular se suele decir **the whole**: *Van a limpiar* ~ *el edificio.* They're going to clean the whole building. 2 (*cada*) every: ~s *los días me levanto a las seis.* I get up at six every day. →EVERY ● pron 1 (*en singular*) (a) all: *Eso es ~ por hoy.* That's all for today. (b) *(todas las cosas)* everything: *~ lo que te dije era verdad.* I told you everything was true. (c) *(cualquier cosa)* anything: *Mi loro come de ~.* My parrot eats anything. **2** *todos* everybody, we/you/they all: *~s dicen lo mismo.* Everybody says the same thing/They all say the same thing. ◊ *A ~s nos gustó la obra.* We all/All of us liked the play. **NOTA** Everybody lleva el verbo en singular, pero le sigue el pronombre en plural (**their**): *¿~s tienen sus lápices?* Does everybody have their pencils? ● *nm* whole: *considerar como un ~* taken as a whole ▸ **ante/después de ~** above/after all ▸ **por ~ México, el mundo, etc.** throughout Mexico, the world, etc. ▸ **sobre ~** especially **NOTA** Para otras expresiones, ver el sustantivo, adjetivo, etc., p.ej. **todo el mundo** en MUNDO.

todoterreno *nm* **1** *(carro)* four-by-four *(abrev* **4x4)** **2** *(bicicleta)* mountain bike

toldo *nm* awning

tolerar *vt* **1** *(soportar)* put up with *sth/sb* → SOPORTAR **2** *(consentir)* let *sb* get away with *sth*: *Te toleran todo.* You can get away with anything.

toma *nf* **1** *(Mil)* taking: *la ~ de la ciudad* the taking of the city **2** *(medicina)* dose **3** *(Cine, TV)* take ▸ **~ de corriente** outlet, socket *(GB)* ▸ **~ de tierra** ground, earth *(GB)*

tomadura *(tb* **tomada)** *nf* ▸ **~ de pelo** joke

tomar *vt* **1** take: *~ una decisión* take a decision ◊ *¿Por quién me tomas?* What do you take me for? **2** *(consumir)* have: *¿Qué vas a ~?* What are you going to have? ● *vi* take: *Toma, es para ti.* Here, it's for you. **2** *(beber)* drink: *Mi hermano toma mucho.* My brother drinks a lot. ● **tomarse** *vp*: *~ unos días de descanso* take a few days off **NOTA** Para expresiones, ver el sustantivo, adjetivo, etc., p. ej. **tomar el sol** en SOL.

tomate *nm* tomato [*pl* -es] ▸ **ponerse como un ~** get as red as a beet, go as red as a beetroot *(GB)* ▸ **~ de árbol** tree tomato

tombo *nm (And)* cop

tomillo *nm* thyme

tomo *nm* volume

ton *nm* ▸ **sin ~ ni son** for no particular reason

tonalidad *nf* **1** *(Mús)* key **2** *(color)* tone

tonel *nm* barrel

tonelada *nf* ton

tónica *nf (bebida)* tonic

tónico *adj (sílaba)* stressed ● *nm* tonic

tono *nm* **1** tone: *¡No me hables en ese ~!* Don't speak to me in that tone of voice! **2** *(color)* shade **3** *(Mús)* key

tontear *vi* fool around

tontería *nf* stupid (little) thing ▸ **decir ~s** talk nonsense **dejarse de ~s** stop messing around

tonto/a *adj* dumb, stupid ● *nm-nf* idiot

toparse *vp* **~ con** bump into *sth/ sb*

tope *nm* **1** *(límite)* limit: *¿Hay una edad ~?* Is there an age limit? **2** *(punto más alto)* top: *en el ~ del cerro* at the top of the hill **3** *(Mx, calle)* speed bump ▸ **hasta el ~:** *El supermercado estaba hasta el ~.* The supermarket was packed. ◊ *Estoy hasta el ~ de trabajo.* I'm up to my neck in work.

tópico *nm* **1** *(tema)* subject **2** *(cliché)* cliché

topo *nm* mole

toque *nm* **1** *(golpecito)* tap **2** *(matiz)* touch: *dar el ~ final a algo* put the finishing touch to *sth* **3** *(Mx, descarga)* electric shock ▸ **~ de queda** curfew

tórax *nm* thorax

torbellino *nm* whirlwind

torcedura *nf* sprain

torcer *vt* **1** twist: *Le torció el brazo.* She twisted his arm. **2** *(cabeza)* turn ● *vi* turn ● **torcerse** *vp (tobillo, muñeca)* sprain: *Se torció el tobillo.* He sprained his ankle.

torcido *adj* crooked

torear *vt, vi (toro)* fight ● *vt (persona)* tease

torero/a *nm-nf* bullfighter

tormenta *nf* storm

tormento *nm* **1** *(tortura)* torture **2** *(persona, animal)* pest: *Este niño es un ~.* This kid's a pest.

tornado *nm* tornado [*pl* -es]

torneo *nm* **1** tournament **2** *(atletismo)* meeting

tornillo *nm* **1** screw **2** *(para tuerca)* bolt

torniquete *nm (Med)* tourniquet

torno *nm* **1** *(para elevar)* winch **2** *(alfarero)* (potter's) wheel **3** *(carpintero)* lathe

toro *nm (animal)* bull **2** *toros:* *ir a los ~s* go to a bullfight ◊ *Le*

encantan los ~s. He loves bull-fighting.

toronja nf grapefruit

torpe adj 1 (manazas) clumsy 2 (zoquete) slow

torpedo nm torpedo [pl -es]

torpeza nf 1 clumsiness 2 (lentitud) slowness

torrar(se) vt, vp roast

torre nf 1 tower: ~ de vigilancia watch tower 2 (electricidad) pylon 3 (ajedrez) rook, castle

torrencial adj torrential

torrente nm torrent

torrija nf French toast [U]

torso nm torso [pl -s]

torta nf 1 (de verduras) pie 2 (frita) fritter 3 (dulce) cake: ~ helada ice cream cake 4 (Mx, sandwich) large sandwich

tortícolis nm/nf crick in your neck

tortilla nf 1 (de maíz o trigo) tortilla 2 (de huevo) omelette

tortuga nf 1 (de tierra) tortoise 2 (de mar) turtle ▶ a paso de ~/ más lento que una ~ at snail's pace

tortura nf torture

torturar vt torture

tos nf cough: tener ~ have a cough

toser vi cough

tostada nf 1 (pan) slice of toast 2 (Mx) fried tortilla

tostador nm (tb **tostadora** nf) toaster

tostar vt 1 (pan, frutos secos) toast 2 (café) roast 3 (piel) tan

total adj, nm total ▶ en ~ altogether: Somos diez en ~. There are ten of us altogether.

totalmente adv totally

tóxico adj toxic

toxicómano/a nm-nf drug addict

trabajador/a adj hard-working ● nm-nf worker

trabajar vi, vt work: ~ de profesora work as a teacher ◊ ¿En qué trabaja tu hermana? What does your sister do?

trabajo nm 1 work [U]: Tengo mucho ~. I have a lot of work. ◊ Me dieron la noticia en el ~. I heard the news at work. 2 (empleo, tarea) job: un ~ bien pagado a well-paid job ◊ estar sin ~ be out of work/a job →WORK 3 (obra escrita) piece of work: hacer un ~ sobre el medio ambiente do a piece of work on the environment ▶ costar ~ be hard to...: Me cuesta ~... I find it hard to... **dar** ~ be a lot of work ● **de/en equipo** teamwork ~ **de parto** labor ~s

forzados hard labor ~s manuales arts and crafts

trabalenguas nm tongue-twister

trabarse vp (And) get high (on sth) ▶ **trabársele la lengua** get tongue-tied

tractor nm tractor

tradición nf tradition

tradicional adj traditional

traducción nf translation: hacer una ~ del español al ruso do a translation from Spanish into Russian

traducir vt, vi translate: ~ un libro del francés al inglés translate a book from French into English →INTERPRET

traductor/a nm-nf translator

traer vt 1 bring 2 (causar) cause: El nuevo sistema nos va a ~ problemas. The new system is going to cause problems. ● **traerse** vp bring sth/sb (with you): Tráete una almohada. Bring a pillow with you. ▶ ~**se algo (entre manos)** be up to sth

traficante nmf dealer: un ~ de armas an arms dealer

traficar vi deal in sth: Traficaban con drogas. They dealt in drugs.

tráfico nm 1 (vehículos) traffic 2 (armas) arms dealing 3 (drogas) drug trafficking

tragar vt, vp 1 swallow: ~se una aceituna/el orgullo swallow an olive/your pride 2 (soportar) put up with sth/sb

tragedia nf tragedy [pl -ies]

trágico adj tragic

trago nm 1 drink: un ~ de agua a drink of water ◊ ir a tomar unos ~s go for a few drinks 2 (mal) ~ (mal momento) shock ▶ **de un** ~: Se lo bebió de un ~. He drank it down in one gulp.

traición nf 1 betrayal: cometer ~ contra algn betray sb 2 (Pol) treason: Lo juzgaron por alta ~. He was tried for high treason. ▶ **a** ~: Lo hicieron a ~. They went behind his back.

traicionar vt 1 betray: ~ a un compañero/una causa betray a friend/cause 2 (fallar) let sb down: Los nervios me traicionaron. My nerves let me down.

traidor/a nm-nf traitor

trailer nm 1 (casa) trailer, caravan (GB) 2 (Mx, camión) trailer

trailero/a nm-nf (Mx) truck driver

traje nm 1 (dos piezas) suit 2 (nacional, regional) dress [U]: vestido con el ~ típico wearing traditional dress ▶ ~ **de baño**

swimsuit **~ de noche** evening dress **~ espacial** spacesuit

trama *nf* plot

tramar *vt* plot: *Están tramando algo.* They're up to something.

tramitar *vt* process

trámite *nm* procedure [U]: *los ~s habituales* usual procedure ▶ **en ~(s) de** *Estamos en ~s de divorcio.* We are in the process of getting a divorce.

tramo *nm* **1** (*carretera*) stretch **2** (*escalera*) flight

trampa *nf* trap: *caer en una ~* fall into a trap ◊ *tenderle una ~ a algn* set a trap for sb **2** (*en un juego*): *¡Eso es ~!* That's cheating! ◊ *hacer ~* (*s*) cheat

trampilla *nf* trapdoor

trampolín *nm* **1** (*gimnasia*) springboard **2** (*natación*) diving board

tramposo/a *adj, nm-nf* cheater, cheat (*GB*): *No seas tan ~.* Don't be such a cheater.

trancón *nm* (*And*) traffic jam

tranquilidad *nf* peace: *un ambiente de ~* a peaceful atmosphere ◊ *Para tu ~, te diré que es cierto.* For your peace of mind, I can tell you it is true.

tranquilizante *nm* tranquilizer

tranquilizar(se) *vt, vp* calm (*sb*) down: *Tranquilízate, que están por llegar.* Calm down, they'll soon be here.

tranquilo *adj* **1** calm: *un hombre/ mar ~* a calm man/sea **2** (*apacible*) quiet: *una zona tranquila* a quiet area **3** (*conciencia*) clear ▶ **tan ~** not worried: *Perdió el año y se quedó tan tranquila.* She failed but didn't seem worried.

transatlántico *nm* (ocean) liner

transbordador *nm* ferry [*pl* -ies] ▶ **~ espacial** space shuttle

transbordo *nm* ▶ **hacer ~** change: *Tuvimos que hacer dos ~s.* We had to change twice.

transcripción *nf* transcription

transcurrir *vi* **1** (*tiempo*) pass **2** (*ocurrir*) take place

transeúnte *nmf* passer-by [*pl* -ers-by]

transferencia *nf* transfer: *~ bancaria* credit transfer

transferir *vt* transfer

transformador *nm* transformer

transformar *vt* transform *sth/sb* (*into sth*) ● **transformarse** *vp* turn *into sth/sb*: *La rana se transformó en príncipe.* The frog turned into a prince.

transfusión *nf* transfusion

transgénico *adj, nm* genetically modified (foods)

transición *nf* transition

transistor *nm* (*transistor*) radio

transitivo *adj* transitive

tránsito *nm* traffic: *accidente de ~* traffic accident ▶ **agente/policía de ~** traffic police officer

transmisión *nf* (*programa*) broadcast

transmitir *vt* **1** (*comunicar, contagiar*) transmit **2** (*TV, Radio*) broadcast

transparente *adj* **1** transparent **2** (*ropa*) see-through

transportar *vt* carry

transporte *nm* transportation, transport (*GB*): *~ público/escolar* public/school transportation

transportista *nmf* carrier

transversal *adj* **1** transverse: *eje ~* transverse axis **2** (*calle*): *La 47 es ~ a la avenida 50.* 47th Street crosses 50th Avenue. ▶ **corte/ sección ~** cross section

tranvía *nm* streetcar, tram (*GB*)

trapeador *nm* mop

trapear *vt, vi* mop (the floor)

trapecio *nm* **1** (*circo*) trapeze **2** (*Geom*) trapezoid, trapezium (*GB*)

trapecista *nmf* trapeze artist

trapo *nm* **1** (*limpieza*) cloth **2 trapos** (*ropa*) clothes ▶ **sacar** (*a relucir*) **los ~s sucios** wash your dirty linen in public **~ de cocina** dish towel, tea towel (*GB*) **~ del polvo** duster **~ viejo** old rag

tráquea *nf* windpipe

tras *prep* **1** (*después de, en busca de*) after: *día ~ día* day after day ◊ *andar/ir ~ algo* be after sth **2** (*detrás de*) behind **3** (*más allá de*) beyond

trasatlántico, trasbordo, etc. = TRANSATLÁNTICO, TRANSBORDO, ETC.

trasbocar *vt, vi* throw (*sth*) up

trasero *adj* back ● *nm* butt, bum (*GB*) **NOTA** Estas palabras son coloquiales. Es más formal **bottom.**

trasladar(se) *vt, vp* move: *Nos trasladamos al número tres.* We moved to number three.

traslado *nm* move

traslucir *vt* reveal

trasluz *nm* ▶ **al ~** against the light

trasmano *nm* ▶ **a ~** out of the way

trasnochar *vi* stay up late

traspapelarse *vp* be mislaid

traspasar *vt* **1** (*atravesar*) go through *sth*: *~ la barrera del sonido* go through the sound barrier **2** (*líquido*) soak **3** (*negocio*) sell

traspié *nm* ▶ **dar un ~** trip

trasplantar *vt* transplant

trasplante *nm* transplant

traste *nm* dish: *lavar los ~s* do the dishes ▶ **~s de cocina** kitchen utensils

trastearse *vp* (*And*) move house

trasteo *nm* (*And*) move

trasto *nm* (*cosa*) junk [*U*]

trastornar *vt* **1** upset: *La huelga trastornó mis planes.* The strike upset my plans. **2** (*volver loco*) drive *sb* crazy ● **trastornarse** *vp* (*enloquecer*) go crazy

tratado *nm* treaty [*pl* -ies]

tratamiento *nm* treatment

tratar *vt* **1** treat: *~ una enfermedad/ a un paciente* treat an illness/a patient **2** (*discutir*) deal with *sth*: *Trataremos estas cuestiones mañana.* We will deal with these matters tomorrow. ● *vi* **1** **~ de/sobre** deal with *sth/sb*: *El programa trata sobre el arte.* The program's about art. **2** **~ con** deal with *sth/sb*: *No trato con ese tipo de gente.* I don't have any dealings with people like that. **3** (*intentar*) try to *do sth*: *Trata de llegar a tiempo.* Try to be on time. →TRY ● **tratarse** *vp* **~ de** be about *sth/sb*: *Se trata de aprender, no de aprobar.* It's about learning, not just passing. ▶ **~ de tú/usted** be on first-name/formal terms *with sb*

trato *nm* **1** (*relación*): *Debemos meorar nuestro ~ con los vecinos.* We must try to get along better with our neighbors. ◊ *No tengo demasiado ~ con ellos.* I don't see much of them. **2** (*acuerdo*) deal: *hacer/cerrar un ~* make/close a deal ◊ *¡~ hecho!* It's a deal! ▶ **malos ~s** mistreatment [*U*]

trauma *nm* trauma

través ▶ **a ~ de** through

travesti *nmf* transvestite

travesura *nf* prank: *hacer ~s* play pranks

travieso *adj* naughty

trayecto *nm* route

trayectoria *nf* trajectory [*pl* -ies]

trazar *vt* **1** (*línea, plano*) draw **2** (*plan, proyecto*) draw *sth* up

trébol *nm* **1** (*Bot*) clover **2 tréboles** (*cartas*) clubs →BARAJA

trece *adj, nm, pron* **1** thirteen **2** (*fecha*) thirteenth

treceavo *adj, nm* thirteenth

trecho *nm* stretch: *un ~ peligroso* a dangerous stretch of road

tregua *nf* truce

treinta *adj, nm, pron* **1** thirty **2** (*trigésimo*) thirtieth

tremendo *adj* **1** (*horrible*) terrible: *un dolor ~* a terrible pain **2** (*enorme*) tremendous: *Tuvo un éxito ~.* It was a tremendous success.

tren *nm* train: *tomar/perder el ~* catch/miss the train ◊ *Fui en ~.* I went by train. ▶ **a todo ~ 1** (*con lujo*) in style **2** (*muy rápido*) flat out **~ correo/de mercancías** mail/freight train **~ de aterrizaje** undercarriage **~ de vida** lifestyle

trenza *nf* braid, plait (*GB*)

trepar *vi* climb: *~ a un árbol* climb a tree

tres *adj, nm, pron* **1** three **2** (*fecha*) third

trescientos/as *adj, nm, pron* three hundred

triangular *adj* triangular

triángulo *nm* triangle

tribu *nf* tribe

tribuna *nf* bleachers [*pl*], stand (*GB*)

tribunal *nm* court: *llevar a algn a los ~es* take *sb* to court

triciclo *nm* tricycle

trigo *nm* wheat

trillar *vt* thresh

trillizos/as *nm-nf* triplets

trimestral *adj* quarterly

trimestre *nm* **1** quarter **2** (*Educ*) term

trinar *vi* (*pájaro*) sing

trinchera *nf* trench

trineo *nm* **1** sled **2** (*de caballos*) sleigh

trinidad *nf* trinity

trino *nm* trill

trío *nm* trio [*pl* -s]

tripa *nf* (*tb* **tripas**) *nf* **1** (*intestino*) gut **2** (*vientre*) stomach: *dolor de ~* stomach ache ◊ *Me suenan las ~s.* My stomach's rumbling. →MY

triple *adj* triple: *~ salto* triple jump ● *nm* **el ~ (de** (grande, etc.) **que...** three times (as big, etc.) as...: *Gana el ~ que yo.* He earns three times as much as me.

triplicar(se) *vt, vp* treble

tripulación *nf* crew →JURADO

tripular *vt* **1** (*barco*) sail **2** (*avión*) fly

triste *adj* **1** sad: *sentirse ~* feel sad **2** (*deprimente*) gloomy

tristeza *nf* **1** sadness **2** (*melancolía*) gloominess

triturar *vt* **1** (*carne*) mince **2** (*cosas duras*) crush **3** (*papel*) shred

triunfal adj 1 (arco, entrada) triumphal 2 (gesto, regreso) triumphant

triunfar vi 1 (tener éxito) succeed: ~ en la vida succeed in life 2 (ganar) win: ~ a cualquier precio win at any price 3 ~ (sobre) triumph (over sth/sb): ~ sobre los enemigos triumph over your enemies

triunfo nm 1 (Pol, Mil) victory [pl -ies] 2 (logro personal, proeza) triumph: un ~ de la ingeniería a triumph of engineering 3 (Mús, éxito) hit 4 (cartas) trump

trivial adj trivial

trivialidad nf 1 (cosa trivial) triviality [pl -ies] 2 (comentario) trite remark

triza nf ▸ **hacer ~s** tear sth to shreds **hecho ~s** (triste) shattered

trocear vt cut sth into pieces

trofeo nm trophy [pl -ies]

tromba nf ▸ ~ **(de agua)** downpour

trombón nm trombone

trompa nf 1 (elefante) trunk 2 (insecto) proboscis

trompeta nf trumpet

trompo nm spinning top

tronar vi 1 (haber truenos) thunder 2 (Mx, suspender) fail: ~ en matemáticas fail math

tronco nm 1 (árbol, Anat) trunk 2 (leño) log

trono nm throne

tropa nf troop

tropezar(se) vi, vp ~ **(con)** 1 (caerse) trip (over sth) 2 (problemas) come up against sth

tropical adj tropical

trópico nm 1 tropic: el ~ de Cáncer the tropic of Cancer 2 el trópico (región) the tropics [pl]: vivir en el ~ live in the tropics

trotar vi 1 (caballo) trot 2 (correr) go jogging

trote nm 1 trot: ir al ~ go at a trot 2 (actividad intensa): Tanto ~ va a acabar conmigo. All this rushing around will finish me off. ▸ **no estar para muchos/esos ~s**: Ya no estoy para esos ~s. I'm not up to it any more.

trozo nm piece

trucha nf trout [pl trout]

truco nm trick ▸ **agarrar/pillar el ~** get the hang of sth **tener ~** have a catch

trueno nm thunder [U]: rayos y ~s thunder and lightning ◇ un ~ a clap of thunder

tu adj your

tú pron pers you: ¿Eres tú? Is that you?

tuberculosis nf tuberculosis (abrev TB)

tubería nf pipe: ~ de desagüe waste pipe

tubo nm 1 (de conducción) pipe 2 (recipiente) tube: un ~ de dentífrico a tube of toothpaste ▸ ~ **de escape/exhosto** exhaust (pipe)

tuerca nf nut

tuerto adj one-eyed ▸ **ser ~** be blind in one eye

tufo nm stink

tugurio nm 1 (cuchitril) hovel: barrio de ~s shanty town 2 (bar) dive

tulipán nm tulip

tumba nf 1 grave 2 (mausoleo) tomb

tumbar vt knock sth/sb down/over ● **tumbarse** vp lie down

tumbo nm ▸ **dar ~s 1** (tambalearse) stagger 2 (tener dificultades) lurch from one crisis to another

tumbona nf deckchair

tumor nm tumor: ~ benigno/cerebral benign/brain tumor

tumulto nm (multitud) crowd

tuna nf prickly pear

túnel nm tunnel

túnica nf tunic

turbante nm turban

turbio adj 1 (líquido) cloudy 2 (asunto) shady

turismo nm tourism: oficina de ~ tourist office ▸ **hacer ~** tour around: hacer ~ por Cuba tour around Cuba

turista nmf tourist

turistear vi tour around

turnarse vp take turns (with sb) (doing sth): Nos turnamos para hacer la limpieza. We take turns doing the cleaning.

turno nm 1 (orden) turn: Espere su ~ en la cola. Wait your turn in line. 2 (trabajo) shift: ~ de día day shift ▸ **de ~** on duty

turquesa adj, nm, nf turquoise

turrón nm Spanish nougat

tutear vt, vp be on first-name terms (with sb)

tutor/a nm-nf 1 (Jur) guardian 2 (profesor) tutor

tuyo/a adj, pron yours: un amigo ~ a friend of yours

U u

u *conj* or

uchuvas *nf* physalis [*sing*]

UCI = UTI

úlcera *nf* ulcer

últimamente *adv* lately

ultimátum *nm* ultimatum

último/a *adj* **1** *por última vez* for the last time **2** (*más reciente*) latest: *la última moda* the latest fashion **NOTA** Last se dice del último de una serie que ya se terminó: *el ~ álbum de John Lennon* John Lennon's last album. **Latest** se dice del último de una serie que puede continuar: *su última película* his latest movie. →LATE **3** (*más alto*) top: *en el ~ piso* on the top floor **4** (*más bajo*) bottom ● *nm-nf* **1** last (one): *Fuimos los ~s en llegar.* We were the last (ones) to arrive. **2** (*mencionado en último lugar*) latter ▸ **a última hora 1** (*en último momento*) at the last moment **2** (*al final de un día*) late: *a última hora del martes* late last Tuesday **ir/vestir a la última** to be fashionably dressed

ultraderecha *nf* extreme right

umbilical *adj* umbilical

umbral *nm* threshold

un/una *art indef* a, an **NOTA** La forma **an** se emplea delante de sonido vocálico: *un árbol* a tree ◊ *un brazo* an arm ◊ *una hora* an hour ◊ *un árbol* some: *Necesito unos zapatos nuevos.* I need some new shoes. ◊ *Tienes unos ojos preciosos.* You have beautiful eyes.

unanimidad *nf* unanimity ▸ **por ~** unanimously

undécimo/a *adj, nm-nf, pron* eleventh

único/a *adj* **1** (*solo*) only: *la única excepción* the only exception ◊ *ser hijo ~* be an only child **2** (*excepcional*) extraordinary **3** (*sin igual*) unique: *una obra de arte única* a unique work of art ● *nm-nf* only one: *el ~ que sabe hacerlo* the only one who can do it

unidad *nf* **1** unit: *~ de medida* unit of measurement **2** (*unión*) unity: *falta de ~* lack of unity **3** (*Comp*) drive: *~ de disco* disk drive

unido *adj* close: *una familia muy unida* a very close family

unificar *vt* unify

uniforme *adj, nm* uniform: *soldados de ~* soldiers in uniform

unión *nf* **1** union: *~ monetaria* monetary union ◊ *Unión Europea* European Union **2** (*acción*) merger

unir *vt* **1** (*intereses, personas*) unite **2** (*piezas, objetos*) join **3** (*carretera, ferrocarril*) link ● **unirse** *vp* join: *Se unieron al grupo.* They joined the group.

universal *adj* **1** universal: *un problema ~* a universal problem **2** (*historia, literatura*) world

universidad *nf* university [*pl* -ies] **NOTA**: *Mi prima estudia en la ~/va a la ~* se dice "My cousin is at college/goes to college" en EE.UU. y "... is at university/goes to university" en Gran Bretaña.

universo *nm* universe

uno/a *adj* **1** one **2** *unos* (*aproximadamente*) ~: *Tendrá ~s 50 años.* He must be around 50. ◊ *una ~s dos semanas* around two weeks ◊ *Tendrá ~s 50 años.* He must be around 50. ● *pron* **1** one **2** (*uso impersonal*) you, one (*más fml*) **3** *unos* some (people) ● *nm* one ▸ **¡a la una, a las dos, a las tres!** ready, set, go! **de ~ en ~** one by one **es la una** it's one o'clock **(los) ~s a (los) otros** each other: *Se ayudaban (los) ~s a (los) otros.* They helped each other.

untar *vt* spread: *~ el pan con/de mermelada* spread jam on bread ◊ *~ un molde con aceite* grease a tin

uña *nf* **1** (*mano*) (finger)nail: *comerse/morderse las ~s* bite your nails **2** (*pie*) toenail ▸ **ser ~ y carne/mugre** be inseparable

uranio *nm* uranium

Urano *nm* Uranus

urbanización *nf* development

urbano/a *adj* urban

urgencia *nf* **1** emergency [*pl* -ies] **2** *urgencias* (*en hospital*) emergency room, accident and emergency (*GB*)

urgente *adj* **1** urgent **2** (*correo*) express

urna *nf* **1** (*cenizas*) urn **2** (*Pol*) ballot box

urraca *nf* magpie

Uruguay *nm* Uruguay

uruguayo/a *adj, nm-nf* Uruguayan

usado *adj* **1** (*ropa*) second-hand **2** (*vehículo*) used **3** (*gastado*) worn

usar *vt* **1** (*utilizar*) use **2** (*ponerse, talla*) wear: *¿Qué perfume usas?* What perfume do you wear? ◊ *~ pantalones talla 40* wear size forty pants ● **usarse** *vp* (*estar de moda*) be fashionable

uso *nm* use ▶ **de ~ externo/tópico** (*pomada*) for external application

usted, ustedes *pron pers* you

usuario/a *nm-nf* user

utensilio *nm* **1** (*herramienta*) tool **2** (*cocina*) utensil

útero *nm* womb

UTI *nf* intensive care unit (*abrev* ICU)

útil *adj* useful ● **útiles** *nm* equipment [*U*]

utilidad *nf* usefulness

utilizar *vt* use

utopía *nf* Utopia

uva *nf* grape ▶ **~ pasa** raisin

V v

vaca *nf* **1** (*animal*) cow **2** (*carne*) beef ▶ CARNE ● **hacer (una) ~/vaquita** club together: *Hicieron (una) ~ para comprar el regalo.* They clubbed together to buy the gift.

vacación *nf* vacation, holiday (*GB*) ▶ **de/en vacaciones** on vacation, on holiday (*GB*)

vacacionista *nmf* (*Mx*) vacationer, holidaymaker (*GB*)

vaciar *vt* empty

vacilar *vt* (*tomar el pelo*) tease ● *vi* (*dudar*) hesitate

vacío *adj* empty ● *nm* vacuum

vacuna *nf* vaccine: *la ~ contra la gripa* the flu vaccine

vacunar *vt* vaccinate *sth/sb* (*against sth*)

vado *nm* (*de río*) ford

vagabundo/a *adj* **1** (*persona*) wandering **2** (*animal*) stray ● *nm-nf* vagrant

vagar *vi* wander: *~ por las calles* wander the streets

vagina *nf* vagina

vago/a *adj* **1** (*holgazán*) lazy **2** (*impreciso*) vague: *una respuesta vaga* a vague answer ● *nm-nf* slacker

vagón *nm* (*train*) car, carriage (*GB*): *~ de pasajeros* passenger car/carriage ▶ **~ de mercancías** freight car, freight wagon (*GB*) **~ restaurante** dining car

vaho *nm* **1** (*vapor*) steam **2** (*aliento*) breath

vaina *nf* **1** (*legumbres*) pod **2** (*And, problema*) nuisance,

drag (*más coloq*): *Es una ~ que no puedas venir.* It's a drag you can't come. **3** (*And, cosa*) thing: *esa ~ roja de allá* that red thing over there

vainilla *nf* vanilla

vaivén *nm* swinging

vajilla *nf* **1** stoneware, crockery (*GB*) **2** (*juego completo*) dinner service

vale *nm* **1** (*cupón*) voucher **2** (*entrada*) (free) ticket ▶ **~ de despensa** (*Mx*) food coupon

valentía *nf* courage

valer *vt* **1** (*costar*) cost: *¿Cuánto vale el libro?* How much does this book cost? **2** (*tener valor de*) be worth: *Un dólar vale unos 10 pesos.* One dollar is worth around 10 pesos. ● *vi* **1** **~ por** entitle *sb* to *sth*: *Este cupón vale por un descuento.* This coupon entitles you to a discount. **2** **~ (para)** (*persona*) be good (as *sth*): *Yo no valdría para maestra.* I'd be no good as a teacher. **3** (*estar permitido*) be allowed: *No vale hacer trampas.* No cheating. **4** (*documento*) be valid ● **valerse** *vp* **~ de** use: *~ de un pretexto* use a pretext ▶ **más vale...** it's better (if...): *Más vale así.* It's better like that. ◇ *Más te vale decir la verdad.* It's better if you tell the truth. **¡me vale!** (*Mx*) I don't give a damn! **¡no vale!** (*no es justo*) that's not fair **no ~ para nada** be useless **~se (por sí mismo)** manage (on your own)

válido *adj* valid

valiente *adj* brave

valioso *adj* valuable

valla *nf* **1** (*cerca*) fence **2** (*Dep*) hurdle: *los 500m ~s* the 500 meter hurdles ▶ **~ publicitaria** billboard, hoarding (*GB*)

valle *nm* valley

valor *nm* **1** value: *tener un gran ~ sentimental* have great sentimental value **2** (*precio*) price: *Las joyas alcanzaron un ~ muy alto.* The jewels reached a very high price. **3** (*valentía*) courage ▶ **sin ~** worthless

valorar *vt* **1** (*poner precio, apreciar*) value *sth* (*at sth*): *Lo valoraron en $1 000.* It was valued at a thousand dollars. **2** (*evaluar*) evaluate: *~ los resultados* evaluate the results

vals *nm* waltz

válvula *nf* valve: *~ de seguridad* safety valve

vampiro *nm* vampire

vandalismo *nm* vandalism

vándalo/a *nm-nf* vandal

vanguardia nf 1 (Mil) vanguard 2 (Arte) avant-garde

vanidad nf vanity

vanidoso/a adj

vano adj vain ▸ **en ~** in vain

vapor nm steam: barco de ~ steamship ▸ **al ~** steamed

vaquero/a nm-nf (persona) cowhand ● **vaqueros** nm (pantalón) jeans: unos ~s a pair of jeans

vara nf 1 (palo) stick 2 (rama) branch

vararse vp (And, Aut) break down

variable adj (carácter) changeable ● nf variable

variación nf variation

variado/a adj varied

variar vt, vi 1 (dar variedad, ser variado) vary: Los precios varían según el bar. Prices vary depending on the bar. 2 (cambiar) change: No varía en plural. It doesn't change in the plural. ▸ **para ~** for a change

varicela nf chickenpox

variedad nf variety [pl -ies]

varilla nf rod

varios/as adj, pron several

varita nf stick ▸ **~ mágica** magic wand

variz nf varicose vein

varón nm 1 (hombre) man [pl men] 2 (niño) boy

varonil adj manly

vasija nf vessel

vaso nm 1 glass: un ~ de agua a glass of water 2 (Anat, Bot) vessel: ~s sanguíneos blood vessels ▸ **~ de plástico/papel** plastic/paper cup

vatio nm watt

vecindario nm neighborhood

vecino/a adj neighboring ● nm-nf neighbor

vegetación nf 1 (plantas) vegetation 2 **vegetaciones** (Med) adenoids

vegetal adj vegetable: aceites ~es vegetable oils ● nm vegetable

vegetar vi 1 (Bot) grow 2 (persona) vegetate

vegetariano/a adj, nm-nf vegetarian

vehículo nm vehicle

veinte adj, nm, pron 1 twenty 2 (vigésimo) twentieth: el siglo ~ the twentieth century

vejestorio nm old relic

vejez nf old age

vejiga nf bladder

vela nf 1 candle 2 (de barco) sail 3 (deporte) sailing: hacer ~ go sailing ▸ **estar/pasarse la noche**

en ~ 1 (trasnochar) stay up all night 2 (con un enfermo) keep watch (over sb) **no tener ~s en el entierro**: ¿Quién te ha dado ~s en este entierro? What business is it of yours? ◇ No tengo ~s en el entierro. It's none of my business.

velada nf evening

velador/a nm-nf (persona) (night) watchman

veladora nf (Mx, vela) candle

velar vt 1 (cadáver) keep vigil over sb 2 (enfermo) sit up with sb ● vi **~ por** look after sth/sb: Tu padrino velará por ti. Your godfather will look after you. ● **velarse** vp (película) be exposed

velatorio nm wake

velero nm sailboat, sailing boat (GB)

veleta nf weathervane

vello nm hair

velo nm veil ▸ **~ del paladar** soft palate

velocidad nf 1 (rapidez) speed: la ~ del sonido the speed of sound 2 (Mec) gear: cambiar de ~ shift gear

velocímetro nm speedometer

velocista nmf sprinter

velódromo nm velodrome

velorio nm wake

veloz adj fast →FAST

vena nf vein

vencedor/a adj 1 winning: el equipo ~ the winning team 2 (país, ejército) victorious ● nm-nf 1 winner 2 (Mil) victor

vencer vt 1 (Dep) beat 2 (Mil) defeat 3 (rendir) overcome: Me venció el sueño. I was overcome with sleep. ● vi 1 (triunfar) win 2 (plazo) expire: El plazo venció ayer. The deadline expired yesterday. 3 (pago) be due

vencido/a adj: darse por ~ give in ● nm-nf loser: vencedores y ~s winners and losers

venda nf bandage

vendar vt bandage ▸ **~ los ojos** blindfold sb

vendaval nm gale

vendedor/a nm-nf 1 (viajante) salesman/woman [pl -men/-women] 2 (en tienda) sales clerk, shop assistant (GB) ▸ **~ ambulante** hawker

vender vt sell: Se venden en el mercado. They are on sale in the market. ● **venderse** vp (persona) sell out ▸ **se vende** for sale **~se como pan caliente** sell like hot cakes

vendimia nf grape harvest

V

veneno nm poison

venenoso adj poisonous

venezolano/a adj, nm-nf Venezuelan

Venezuela nf Venezuela

venganza nf revenge

vengarse vp take revenge (on sb) (for sth): Me vengaré de él. I'll get my revenge on him.

venida nf ▸ a la ~ on the way back

venir vi 1 come: ¡Ven acá! Come here! 2 (volver) be back: Vengo enseguida. I'll be back in a minute. 3 (estar) be: Viene en todos los periódicos. It's in all the papers. • v aux ~ haciendo algo have been doing sth: Hace años que te vengo diciendo lo mismo. I've been telling you the same thing for years. ▸ que viene next: el lunes que viene next Monday ~ bien/mal (convenir) be good/bad (for sb): Mañana me viene mal. Tomorrow isn't good for me. **NOTA** Para otras expresiones, ver el sustantivo, adjetivo, etc., p.ej. **no venir a cuento** en CUENTO.

venta nf sale: en ~ for sale

ventaja nf advantage: llevar ~ a algn have an advantage over sb

ventana nf window

ventanilla nf window

ventear vi be windy

ventilación nf ventilation

ventilador nm fan

ventilar vt (habitación, ropa) air

ventrílocuo/a nm-nf ventriloquist

ver vt 1 see: Hace mucho que no la veo. I haven't seen her for a long time. ◊ No veo por qué. I don't see why. → HEAR 2 (televisión) watch 3 (examinar) look at sth: Necesito verlo con más calma. I need more time to look at it. • v see • verse vp 1 ~ (con) meet (sb): Me vi con ella en el parque. I met her in the park. 2 (estar) be: Nunca me había visto en una situación igual. I'd never been in a situation like that. 3 (apariencia) look: Mi mamá se ve mucho mejor. My mom is looking much better. ▸ a ~ let's see ▸ a ~ si... (deseo) I hope...: A ~ si paso el examen esta vez. I hope I pass this time. (temor) what if...?: ¡A ~ si les pasó algo! What if something has happened to them? (ruego, mandato) how about...?: A ~ si me escribes. How about writing to me? ~ venir algo see sth coming: Lo estaba viendo venir. I could see it coming. **NOTA** Para otras ex-

presiones, ver el sustantivo, adjetivo, etc., p.ej. **ver estrellas** en ESTRELLA.

veraneante nmf vacationer, holidaymaker (GB)

veranear vi spend the summer

veraneo nm vacation, holiday (GB): estar/ir de ~ be/go on vacation/holiday

verano nm 1 summer 2 (países tropicales) dry season

verbena nf (baile) open-air dance

verbo nm verb

verdad nf truth: Di la ~. Tell the truth. ▸ **ser** ~ be true **¿verdad?**: Este es mejor, ¿verdad? This one's better, isn't it? ◊ No te gusta la leche, ¿verdad? You don't like milk, do you?

verdadero adj true

verde adj 1 (color) green 2 (fruta) unripe 3 (obsceno) dirty: chistes ~s dirty jokes • nm 1 (color) green 2 (hierbas) greenery ▸ ~ botella bottle green

verdugo nm executioner

verdura nf vegetable(s)

vergonzoso adj 1 (tímido) shy 2 (indignante) shameful

vergüenza nf 1 (timidez, sentido del ridículo) embarrassment 2 (sentido de culpabilidad, modestia) shame ▸ **dar/pasar** ~ 1 (sentirse ridículo) be embarrassed: Me da ~ preguntarles. I'm too embarrassed to ask them. 2 (sentirse culpable) be ashamed: Le daba ~ confesarlo. He was ashamed to admit it.

verídico adj true

verificación nf inspection ▸ ~ ambiental emissions control

verificar vt check

verja nf 1 (cerca) railing(s) 2 (puerta) gate

verraco nm (And) (estupendo) fantastic: Es un ~. He's fantastic. 2 (valiente) gutsy

verraquera nf (And, valentía) guts ▸ **ser la** ~ be fantastic **tener** ~ be angry

verruga nf wart

versión nf version ▸ **en** ~ **original** (Cine) with subtitles

verso nm 1 (línea de un poema) line 2 (género literario) poetry 3 (poema) verse

vértebra nf [pl -brae]

vertebrado adj, nm vertebrate

vertedero nm dump

verter vt 1 (en recipiente) pour: ~ leche en una taza pour milk into a cup 2 (residuos) dump

vertical adj 1 vertical: una línea ~ a vertical line 2 (posición) upright: *en posición ~* in an upright position

vértice *nm* vertex [*pl* -tices]

vértigo *nm* vertigo: *tener ~* get vertigo ▸ *dar/producir ~* make sb dizzy

vesícula *nf* ▸ *~ biliar* gall bladder

vespa® *nf* scooter

vestíbulo *nm* **1** (*entrada, recibidor*) hall **2** (*hotel, teatro, etc.*) foyer

vestido *nm* **1** (*de mujer*) dress: *~ de novia* wedding dress **2** (*And, de hombre*) suit ▸ *~ de baño* swimsuit

vestidor *nm* **1** (*en casa*) dressing room **2** (*gimnasio, etc.*) locker room, changing room (GB)

vestier *nm* (*And*) **1** (*tienda*) fitting room **2** (*gimnasio, etc.*) locker room, changing room (GB)

vestir *vt* **1** (*a una persona*) dress **2** (*llevar puesto*) wear: *Vestía un pantalón gris.* He was wearing gray pants. ● **vestir(se)** *vi, vp* dress (*in sth*): *vestirse bien/de blanco* dress well/in white ● **vestirse** *vp* get dressed: *Vístete o vas a llegar tarde.* Get dressed or you'll be late.

vestuario *nm* wardrobe

vetar *vt* **1** (*rechazar*) veto: *~ una propuesta* veto a proposal **2** (*prohibir*) ban

veterano/a *adj* experienced ● *nm-nf* veteran

veterinaria *nf* veterinary science

veterinario/a *nm-nf* veterinarian, vet (GB)

veto *nm* veto [*pl* -es]

vez *nf* time: *tres veces al año* three times a year ◇ *Gano cuatro veces más que él.* I earn four times as much as he does. ▸ *a la ~ (que)* at the same time (as): *a la ~ que yo* at the same time as me *alguna ~* ever: *¿Has estado allá alguna ~?* Have you ever been there? *a veces/algunas veces* sometimes *cada ~ más/menos* more and more/less and less *cada ~ mejor/peor* better and better/worse and worse *cada ~ que...* whenever *demasiadas veces* too often *de una ~!: ¡Contéstalo de una ~!* Hurry up and answer! *de una ~ por todas* once and for all *de ~ en cuando* from time to time *dos veces* twice *en ~ de* instead of *había/érase una vez...* once upon a time there was... *otra ~* again *tal ~* maybe *una ~* once

vía *nf* **1** (*de tren*) track **2** (*calle*) road **3** vías (*Med*) tract: *~s respiratorias* respiratory tract ▸ *de una ~* one-way *en ~s de desarrollo* developing (*por*) *~ aérea* (by) airmail *Vía Láctea* Milky Way *~ satélite* satellite: *una conexión ~ satélite* a satellite link

viajante *nmf* sales rep

viajar *vi* travel: *~ en avión/tren* travel by plane/train

viaje *nm* journey, trip, travel **NOTA** Travel es incontable y se refiere a la actividad de viajar en general: *Sus principales aficiones son los libros y los ~s.* Her main interests are reading and travel. *Journey* y *trip* se refieren a un viaje concreto: *El ~ fue agotador.* The journey was exhausting. *Trip* incluye también la estancia: *¿Qué tal tu ~ a París?* How was your trip to Paris? ◇ *un ~ de negocios* a business trip. *Voyage* es un viaje largo por mar, y también se usa en sentido figurativo: *un ~ de autodescubrimiento* a voyage of self-discovery. *Tour* un viaje organizado con varias paradas: *un ~ por Tierra Santa* a tour of the Holy Land. ▸ *¡buen/feliz ~!* have a good trip! *estar/irse de ~* be/go away *~ organizado* package tour

viajero/a *nm-nf* **1** (*pasajero*) passenger **2** (*turista*) traveler

vial *adj* road: *seguridad ~* road safety

viáticos *nm* traveling expenses

víbora *nf* viper

vibrar *vi* vibrate

vicepresidente/a *nm-nf* vice-president

vicesecretario/a *nm-nf* deputy secretary [*pl* -ies]

viceversa *adv* vice versa

viciarse = ENVICIARSE

vicio *nm* **1** (*adicción*) addiction: *agarrar/tener el ~ de algo* get/be addicted to sth ◇ *darse al ~* turn to drink, drugs, etc. **2** (*defecto*) vice

vicioso/a *adj* depraved ● *nm-nf* (*drogadicto*) drug addict

víctima *nf* victim

victoria *nf* **1** victory [*pl* -ies] **2** (*Dep*) win

victorioso/a *adj* ▸ *salir ~* triumph

vid *nf* vine

vida *nf* **1** life [*pl* lives] **2** (*sustento*) living: *ganarse la ~* make a living ◇ *nivel de ~* standard of living ▸ *con ~* alive: *Siguen con ~.* They're still alive. *darse la gran ~* live the good life *de toda la ~: La conozco de toda la ~.* I've known her all my life. ◇ *amigos de toda la ~* lifelong friends *en la ~* never: *En la ~ he visto una cosa*

V

igual. I've never seen anything like it. **¡esto (sí) es ~!** this is the life! **llevar una ~ de perros** lead a dog's life **para toda la ~** for life

video nm 1 video [pl -s] 2 (aparato) VCR, video [pl -s] (GB)

videocámara nf camcorder

videoclip nm video [pl -s]

vidriera nf glazier's

vidrio nm glass

viejo/a adj old ● nm-nf old man/woman [pl men/women] ▶ ~ **verde** dirty old man

viento nm wind: Hace mucho ~. It's very windy. ▶ **contra ~ y marea** come hell or high water

vientre nm 1 (abdomen) belly [pl -ies] 2 (matriz) womb

viernes nm Friday (abrev **Fri.**) →LUNES ▶ **V~ Santo** Good Friday

viga nf 1 (madera) beam 2 (metal) girder

vigente adj current ▶ **estar ~** be in force

vigía nmf lookout

vigilancia nf surveillance

vigilante nmf guard

vigilar vt 1 (prestar atención, atender) keep an eye on sth/sb 2 (enfermo) look after sb 3 (custodiar) guard: ~ la frontera guard the border 2 (examen) proctor, invigilate (GB)

vigor nm 1 (Jur) force: entrar en ~ come into force 2 (energía) vigor

villa nf 1 (casa) villa ▶ ~ **olímpica** Olympic village

villancico nm (Christmas) carol

vilo ▶ **en ~** (intranquilo) on tenterhooks: tener a algn en ~ keep sb on tenterhooks

vinagre nm vinegar

vinagreta nf vinaigrette

vínculo nm link

vinícola adj wine: industria ~ wine industry ◇ región ~ wine-growing region

vinicultor/a nm-nf wine grower

vinicultura nf wine growing

vino nm wine: ~ tinto/blanco red/white wine

viña nf (tb **viñedo** nm) vineyard

violación nf 1 (agresión sexual) rape 2 (falta de respeto) violation

violador/a nm-nf rapist

violar vt 1 (agresión sexual) rape 2 (incumplir) break 3 (profanar) violate

violencia nf violence

violentar vt force: ~ una cerradura force a lock

violento/a adj 1 violent: una película violenta a violent film 2 (incómodo) embarrassing

violeta adj, nf, nm violet

violín nm violin

violinista nmf violinist

violoncelo nm cello [pl -s]

virar vi swerve: ~ hacia la derecha swerve to the right

virgen adj 1 virgin: bosques vírgenes virgin forests ◇ ser ~ be a virgin 2 (cassette) blank ● nmf virgin

virginidad nf virginity

Virgo nm, nmf Virgo [pl -s]

viril adj manly, virile (más fml)

virilidad nf manliness

virtual adj virtual

virtualmente adv virtually

virtud nf virtue

virtuoso/a adj (honesto) virtuous

viruela nf smallpox

virus nm virus

visa nf visa

viscoso adj viscous

visera nf visor

visibilidad nf visibility: poca ~ poor visibility

visible adj visible

visillo nm net curtain

visión nf 1 (vista) (eye)sight: perder la ~ en un ojo lose the sight of one eye 2 (punto de vista) view 3 (alucinación) vision: ver visiones hallucinate

visita nf 1 visit: horario de ~s visiting hours 2 (visitante) visitor ▶ **hacer una ~** pay sb a visit

visitante adj visiting ● nmf visitor

visitar vt visit

visón nm mink

víspera nf day before: la ~ del examen the day before the test ▶ **en ~s de** just before sth

vista nf 1 (sentido) (eye)sight: La zanahoria es muy buena para la ~. Carrots are very good for your eyesight. ◇ corto de ~ near-sighted 2 (ojos) eyes: Lo operaron de la ~. He had an eye operation. 3 (panorama) view 4 (instinto) vision: un político con mucha ~ a politician of vision ◇ Tiene mucha ~ para los negocios. He has an eye for business. ▶ **dejar/poner algo a la ~** leave sth where it can be seen **de ~** by sight: La conozco de ~. I know her by sight. **en ~ de** in view of: en ~ de lo ocurrido in view of what has happened **hacer (de) la ~ gorda** turn a blind eye (to sth) **¡hasta la ~!** see you later! **no quitar la ~ (de encima)** not take your eyes off sth/sb **perder de ~** lose sight of sth/sb

vistazo nm look: dar/echar un ~ a algo have a look at sth

visto adj ▸ bien ~ well thought of · mal ~ frowned upon · por lo ~ apparently · bueno ~ approval

vistoso adj colorful

visual adj visual

visualizar vt 1 (Comp) display: ~ una página de internet display a Web page 2 (conceptualizar) visualize

vital adj 1 (Biol) life: ciclo ~ life cycle 2 (persona) full of life 3 (decisivo) vital

vitalidad nf vitality

vitamina nf vitamin

viticultura nf wine growing

vitral nm stained-glass window

vitrina nf 1 (armario) glass cabinet 2 (de tienda) store window, shop window (GB)

viudo/a adj widowed ● nm-nf widower [fem widow]

viva nm cheer: ¡Tres ~s al campeón! Three cheers for the champion! ● interj 1 hooray 2 ~ el amor, la reina, etc. long live love, the queen, etc.

víveres nm provisions

vivero nm 1 (plantas) nursery [pl -ies] 2 (peces) fish farm

vividor/a nm-nf freeloader

vivienda nf 1 (casa) house 2 (en un bloque) apartment 3 (casas en general) housing: el problema de la ~ the housing problem

vivir vi 1 (casa) live: ¿Dónde vives? Where do you live? ◊ Vivió casi noventa años. He lived for almost ninety years. 2 (subsistir) live on sth: ~ con $300 al mes live on 300 dollars a month 3 (existir) be alive: Mi abuelo aún vive. My grandfather is still alive. ● vt live through (sth): Vive tu vida. Live your own life. ◊ una mala experiencia live through a bad experience ▸ no dejar ~ (en paz/tranquilo) not leave sb in peace · ~ al día live from hand to mouth

vivo adj 1 (con vida) living. NOTA Se traduce por living cuando va delante del sustantivo en inglés: seres ~s living beings ◊ lenguas vivas living languages, y alive cuando va después del verbo: ¿Está ~? Is he alive? ◊ Su valor lo mantuvo ~. His courage kept him alive. 2 (persona) bright 3 (luz, color, ojos) bright 4 (activo) lively: una ciudad muy viva a lively city ▸ en ~ (en directo) live · ~ o muerto dead or alive

vocabulario nm vocabulary [pl -ies]

vocación nf vocation

vocal adj vocal ● nf (letra) vowel ● nmf (persona) member

vocalizar vi speak clearly

vocear vt, vi shout

vodka nm vodka

volada nf ▸ de ~ (Mx) double speed

volado adj (dientes, etc.) protruding ● nm ▸ echar un ~ (Mx) toss for sth

volador adj flying

volante nm 1 (Aut) steering wheel 2 (propaganda) flier 3 (tela) frill

volar vi 1 fly: Volamos a Lima desde Bogotá. We flew to Lima from Bogotá. 2 (con el viento) blow away: El sombrero voló por los aires. His hat flew away. ● vt 1 (hacer explotar) blow sth up 2 (Mx, robar) swipe ▸ volando in a flash: Fuimos volando a la estación. We rushed off to the station.

volcán nm volcano [pl -es]

volcar vi, vt 1 (derribar) knock over 2 (vaciar) empty sth out ● **volcarse** vp overturn: The car skidded and overturned. El carro se volcó al patinar.

voleibol nm volleyball

voleo nm ▸ a ~ at random

voltaje nm voltage

voltear vt 1 turn: ~ la cabeza turn your head 2 (carne, página) turn sth over ● vi turn: ~ a la derecha turn right ● **voltearse** vp 1 turn 2 (volcarse) overturn

voltereta nf somersault

voltio nm volt

voluble adj changeable

volumen nm volume: bajar/subir el ~ turn the volume down/up

voluntad nf will: contra mi ~ against my will ◊ tener ~ propia have a will of your own ◊ fuerza de ~ willpower ▸ buena ~ goodwill

voluntario/a adj voluntary ● nm-nf volunteer ▸ presentarse como/ofrecerse de ~ volunteer

volver vi 1 go/come back: Volví a mi casa. I went back home. ◊ Vuelve acá. Come back here. ● vi aux ▸ ~ a hacer algo do sth again: No vuelvas a decirlo. Don't say that again. ● vt turn: Me volvió la espalda. He turned his back on me. ● **volverse** vp 1 (girar) turn: Se volvió hacia Ana. He turned towards Ana. 2 (convertirse) become: ~ loco go insane ▸ ~ el estómago throw up · en sí come around

vomitar vt, vi throw (sth) up

vómito nm vomit

votación nf vote: *hacer una ~* vote

votar vi vote: *~ a favor/en contra de algo* vote for/against sth

voto nm **1** (Pol) vote **2** (Rel) vow ▶ *~ nulo* spoiled ballot

voz nf voice ▶ *a ~ en grito* at the top of your voice **correr la ~** spread the word (*that...*) **en ~ alta**: *decir algo en ~ alta* say sth in a loud voice ◊ *leer algo en ~ alta* read sth out loud **en ~ baja** quietly **llevar la ~ cantante** be the boss

vuelo nm **1** flight: *~ nacional/internacional/regular* domestic/international/scheduled flight **2** (prenda): *Esa falda tiene mucho ~.* That skirt's very full.

vuelta nf **1** (regreso) return: *la ~ a la normalidad* the return to normality **2** (Dep) lap: *Dieron tres ~s a la pista.* They did three laps of the track. ▶ **a la ~ de la esquina** (just) around the corner **dar (dos, etc.) ~s a/alrededor de algo** go around sth (twice, etc.) **dar la ~ a la manzana/al mundo** go around the block/world **darle ~s a algo 1** turn sth: *Siempre le doy dos ~s a la llave.* I always turn the key twice. **2** (comida) stir sth: *darle ~s al caldo* stir the broth **2** (pensar) worry about sth: *Deja de darle ~s al asunto.* Stop worrying about it. **dar media ~** turn around **dar ~s** spin (ir/salir a) **dar una ~** go (out) for a walk **~ ciclística** cycle race **~ de campana** somersault: *El carro dio dos ~s de campana.* The car somersaulted twice. **~ de carro/estrella** cartwheel

vuelto nm change: *Quédese con el ~.* Keep the change.

vulgar adj vulgar

W w

walkie-talkie nm walkie-talkie

walkman® nm Walkman®

waterpolo nm water polo

web nf **1** (sitio web) website: *página ~* web page **2 la web** (red) the Web

whisky nm whiskey

windsurf nm windsurfing

X x

xenofobia nf xenophobia

xilófono nm xylophone

Y y

y conj **1** (copulativa) and **2** (en interrogaciones) and what about...?: *¿Y tú?* And what about you? **3** (para expresar las horas) after, past (GB): *Son las dos y diez.* It's ten after/past two. ▶ *¿y qué?* so what?

ya adv **1** (presente/pasado) already: *Ya son las tres.* It's already three o'clock. ◊ *¿Ya lo terminaste?* Have you finished it already? → YET **2** (futuro): *Ya veremos.* We'll see. ◊ *Ya le escribirán.* They'll write to you sometime. **3** (énfasis): *Ya lo sé.* I know. ▶ **ya mismo** right away **ya no...** not... anymore: *Ya no vivo allá.* I don't live there anymore. **¡ya no más!** that's enough! **ya que** as **¡ya voy!** coming!

yacimiento nm **1** (Geol) deposit **2** (Arqueología) site

yanqui adj, nmf Yankee

yate nm yacht

yegua nf mare

yema nf **1** (huevo) (egg) yolk **2** (dedo) (finger)tip **3** (Bot) bud

yerba nf **1** (marihuana) pot **2** = HIERBA

yerbabuena = HIERBABUENA

yerno nm son-in-law

yeso nm plaster

yo pron pers **1** (sujeto) I **2** (en comparaciones, con prep) me: *antes que yo* before me ◊ *excepto yo* except (for) me ▶ **soy yo** it's me *¿yo?: ¿Quién dices? ¿Yo?* Who do you mean? Me? **yo que tú** if I were you

yodo nm iodine

yoga nm yoga: *hacer ~* practice yoga

yogur (tb yogurt) nm yogurt

yuca nf cassava

yudo nm judo

yugular adj, nf jugular

Z z

zacate nm 1 (*pasto*) grass 2 (*estropajo*) scourer

zafiro nm sapphire

zaguán nm 1 hallway 2 (*Mx, puerta*) front door

zamarra nf jacket

zambullirse vp dive

zanahoria nf carrot

zancada nf stride

zancadilla nf ▸ hacer ~ trip *sb* up

zancudo nm mosquito [*pl* -s/-es]

zángano/a nm-nf slacker

zanja nf trench

zanjar vt put an end to *sth*

zapatería nf shoe store/shop (GB)

zapatero/a nm-nf shoemaker

zapatilla nf 1 (*pantufla*) slipper 2 (*de ballet*) (ballet) shoe 3 (*Mx, de mujer*) (woman's) shoe

zapato nm shoe: ~s planos/de tacón flat/high-heeled shoes

zapping nm channel-hopping: hacer ~ channel-hop

zarandear vt shake

zarcillo nm earring

zarpa nf paw

zarpar vi set sail: *El barco zarpó hacia Cuba.* The boat set sail for Cuba.

zarza nf bramble

zigzag nm zigzag

zinc nm zinc

zíper nm zipper, zip (GB)

zócalo nf (*Mx*) (town) square

zodíaco (*tb* zodiaco) nm zodiac

zombi nmf zombie

zona nf 1 (*área*) area: ~ industrial/ residencial industrial/residential area 2 (Geog, Mil, Pol) zone ▸ ~ norte, etc.: *la ~ norte/sur de la ciudad* the north/south of the city ~s verdes parkland

zoológico nm zoo

zopenco/a adj stupid ● nm-nf jerk

zoquete adj dimwitted ● nmf dimwit

zorrillo nm skunk

zorro/a nm-nf (*animal*) fox [*fem* vixen] ● nm (*piel*) fox fur

zueco nm clog

zumbar vt, vi 1 (*insecto, oídos*) buzz: *zumbarle los oídos a algn* have a buzzing in your ears 2 (*máquina*) hum ▸ salir zumbando rush off

zumbido nm 1 (*insecto*) buzzing 2 (*máquina*) humming

zurcir vt darn

zurdo adj left-handed

zurrar vt wallop

zurrón nm bag

Expresiones numéricas

Números

	Cardinales		Ordinales
1	one	1st	first
2	two	2nd	second
3	three	3rd	third
4	four	4th	fourth
5	five	5th	fifth
6	six	6th	sixth
7	seven	7th	seventh
8	eight	8th	eighth
9	nine	9th	ninth
10	ten	10th	tenth
11	eleven	11th	eleventh
12	twelve	12th	twelfth
13	thirteen	13th	thirteenth
14	fourteen	14th	fourteenth
15	fifteen	15th	fifteenth
16	sixteen	16th	sixteenth
17	seventeen	17th	seventeenth
18	eighteen	18th	eighteenth
19	nineteen	19th	nineteenth
20	twenty	20th	twentieth
21	twenty-one	21st	twenty-first
30	thirty	30th	thirtieth
40	forty	40th	fortieth
50	fifty	50th	fiftieth
60	sixty	60th	sixtieth
70	seventy	70th	seventieth
80	eighty	80th	eightieth
90	ninety	90th	ninetieth
100	a/one hundred	100th	hundredth
101	a/one hundred and one	101st	hundred and first
200	two hundred	200th	two hundredth
1,000	a/one thousand	1,000th	thousandth
10,000	ten thousand	10,000th	ten thousandth
1,000,000	a/one million	1,000,000th	millionth

* En inglés se utiliza una coma para marcar el millar, por ejemplo 25,000.

Quebrados y decimales

½	a half	$\frac{1}{10}$	a/one tenth
⅓	a/one third	$\frac{1}{16}$	a/one sixteenth
¼	a quarter	1½	one and a half
⅛	an/one eighth	2⅓	two and a third

0.1	(zero) (nought *GB*) point one
0.25	(zero) (nought *GB*) point two five
1.75	one point seven five

* En inglés se utiliza un punto para marcar los decimales.

Expresiones matemáticas

+	plus	%	per cent
−	minus	3^2	three squared
×	times *o* multiplied by	5^3	five cubed
÷	divided by	6^{10}	six to the power of ten
=	equals		

Pesos y medidas

Peso

	Sistema en EE.UU.	Sistema métrico
	1 ounce (oz.)	= 28.35 grams (g)
16 ounces	= 1 pound (lb.)	= 0.454 kilogram (kg)
2,000 pounds	= 1 ton (t.)	= 0.907 metric ton (m.t.)

Capacidad (líquidos)

	Sistema en EE.UU.	Sistema métrico
1 cup		= 0.2371 liter (l)
2 cups	= 1 pint (pt.)	= 0.4731 liter (l)
2 pints	= 1 quart (qt.)	= 0.9461 liter (l)
8 pints	= 1 gallon (gal.)	= 3.7851 liters

Longitud

	Sistema en EE.UU.	Sistema métrico
	1 inch (in.)	= 25.4 millimeters (mm)
12 inches	= 1 foot (ft.)	= 30.48 centimeters (cm)
3 feet	= 1 yard (yd.)	= 0.914 meter (m)
1,760 yards	= 1 mile	= 1.609 kilometers (km)

Superficie

	Sistema en EE.UU.	Sistema métrico
	1 square inch (sq in.)	= 6.452 square centimeters
144 square inches	= 1 square foot (sq ft.)	= 929.03 square centimeters
9 square feet	= 1 square yard (sq yd.)	= 0.836 square meter
4,840 square yards	= 1 acre	= 0.405 hectare
640 acres	= 1 square mile	= 2.59 square kilometers/ 259 hectares

Expresiones de tiempo

APRIL
15

Las fechas

Cómo escribirlas:
4/15/04 (15/4/04 *GB*)   April 15, 2004 (15 April 2004 *GB*)

Cómo decirlas:
April fifteenth, two thousand and four
The fifteenth of April (April the fifteenth *GB*), two thousand
and four

Cómo decir los años:

1900 nineteen hundred	2004 two thousand and four
1999 nineteen ninety-nine	2050 two thousand and fifty

La hora

10:00   ten o'clock

11:10   ten after eleven,
        ten past eleven (*GB*),
        eleven ten

5:15   (a) quarter after five,
        (a) quarter past five (*GB*),
        five fifteen

11:40   twenty to/of twelve,
        twenty to twelve (*GB*),
        eleven forty

6:30   half after six,
        half past six (*GB*),
        six thirty

14:07   seven minutes after two,
        seven minutes past two
        (*GB*),
        two o seven

3:45   (a) quarter to/of four,
        (a) quarter to four (*GB*),
        three forty-five

12:00   twelve o'clock,
        twelve noon/midnight

---

*La palabra **minutes** se puede omitir después de 5, 10, 20 y 25.
Casi siempre se utiliza después de los demás números:
It's five after/past (*GB*) *two.*
It's eleven minutes after/past (*GB*) *five.*

*El "reloj de veinticuatro horas" (**the 24-hour clock**) no suele ser
usado en el lenguaje hablado, excepto para leer los horarios de
trenes, aviones, etc.
Para especificar que son 04:00 y no 16:00, se puede decir *four
o'clock **in the morning***. En un lenguaje más formal, se dice *4 **a.m.***

La moneda

EE.UU.	Valor de moneda/billete	Nombre de moneda/billete
1¢	a cent	a penny
5¢	five cents	a nickel
10¢	ten cents	a dime
25¢	twenty-five cents	a quarter
$1	a dollar	a dollar (bill/coin)
$5	five dollars (five bucks*)	a five-dollar bill
$10	ten dollars (ten bucks)	a ten-dollar bill
$20	twenty dollars (twenty bucks)	a twenty-dollar bill
$50	fifty dollars (fifty bucks)	a fifty-dollar bill
$100	a hundred dollars (a hundred bucks)	a hundred-dollar bill

* La palabra **buck** es más coloquial.

Reino Unido	Valor de moneda/billete	Nombre de moneda/billete
1p	a penny (one p*)	a penny
2p	two pence (two p)	a two-pence piece
5p	five pence (five p)	a five-pence piece
10p	ten pence (ten p)	a ten-pence piece
20p	twenty pence (twenty p)	a twenty-pence piece
50p	fifty pence (fifty p)	a fifty-pence piece
£1	a pound	a pound (coin)
£2	two pounds	a two-pound coin
£5	five pounds	a five-pound note
£10	ten pounds	a ten-pound note
£20	twenty pounds	a twenty-pound note
£50	fifty pounds	a fifty-pound note

* Note que *1p*, *2p* etc. se pronuncian /wʌn piː/, /tuː piː/, etc.

El teléfono

637-2335	*six three seven, two three three five*
(617) 731-0293	*area code* six one seven, seven three one, zero** two nine three*

* El **area code** es el prefijo.
** En inglés británico, el número 0 también se pronuncia "ou":
01865 o one eight six five

Los mensajes de texto

Para mandar mensajes de texto y en los emails y chats, hay cada vez más gente que utiliza las siguientes formas abreviadas:

> hello! :o) RU OK? Want2 meet 2moro? That would B gr8! ((( ))) xoxoxo

2	to, too, two	**l8r**	later
2day	today	**lol**	laugh out loud
2moro	tomorrow	**luvu**	love you
2nite	tonight	**msg**	message
4	for, four	**myob**	mind your own business
4eva	forever		
4rom	from	**ne1**	anyone
afaik	as far as I know	**neway**	anyway
asap	as soon as possible	**no1**	no one
		otoh	on the other hand
b	be	**pls**	please
b4	before	**ppl**	people
brb	be right back	**rofl**	roll on the floor laughing
btw	by the way		
cu	see you	**ru ok?**	are you OK?
dak	does anyone know	**sn**	soon
		spksn	speak soon
evry1	everyone	**thanx** o **thx**	thanks
ez	easy	**tia**	thanks in advance
fone	phone		
fyi	for your information	**tic**	tongue in cheek
		txt	text
gd	good	**u**	you
gr8	great	**u r**	you are
hth	hope that helps	**v**	very
imo	in my opinion	**w**	with
iyswim	if you see what I mean	**xoxoxo**	hugs and kisses
		yr	your, you're
l8	late		

*Estas formas suelen utilizarse en minúsculas. El uso de mayúsculas normalmente indica que la persona está "gritando", o que quiere enfatizar algo.

Emoticones

:) o ;-) o :o)	happy
;) o ;-) o P-)	wink, wink
:(o :-(	sad
>:-l	angry
%	confused
((( )))	hugs
:D	laughter
:-D	I'm laughing at you
:-X	I'm not saying anything
:-/	hmm, I'm not sure

Falsos amigos

La palabra en inglés...	significa en español...
actual	exacto; verdadero
actually	en realidad, de hecho
advice	consejo
agenda	orden del día
assist	ayudar
attend	asistir
casual	informal; ocasional; superficial; fortuito; sin importancia
casualty	víctima, baja
comprehensive	global, completo
compromise	acuerdo
conductor	director/a (de orquesta); cobrador/a (de autobús)
crude	burdo; grosero
deception	engaño
disgrace	desgracia, deshonra; vergüenza
disgust	asco, repugnancia
diversion	desviación
embarrassed	avergonzado
exit	salida
fabric	tela
genial	simpático
intend	tener la intención
large	grande; amplio
lecture	conferencia; sermón
library	biblioteca
mascara	rímel®
molest	agredir sexualmente
notice	anuncio, cartel; aviso; (carta de) despido
parent	madre, padre
presume	asumir, suponer
realize	darse cuenta; cumplir
receipt	recibo, factura
record	registrar; grabar; marcar
resume	reanudar; recobrar
sensible	sensato; acertado
stranger	desconocido; forastero
sympathetic	comprensivo, compasivo

y no...	que en inglés se dice...
actual	current; present-day
actualmente	at the moment
aviso	notice; warning; advertisement
agenda	datebook, diary (GB); address book
asistir	attend; treat
atender	see; serve; deal with; answer
casual	chance
casualidad	chance
comprensivo	understanding
compromiso	commitment; agreement; engagement; awkward position
conductor	driver
crudo	raw; underdone; harsh; shocking
decepción	disappointment
desgracia	misfortune
disgusto	sorrow; accident
diversión	pastime; fun; entertainment
embarazada	pregnant
éxito	success; hit
fábrica	factory; works
genial	brilliant
intentar	try
largo	long
lectura	reading
librería	bookstore, bookshop (GB)
máscara	mask
molestar	bother; disturb; upset
noticia	news; news item
pariente	relation
presumir	show off, brag
realizar	carry out; fulfill
receta	recipe; prescription
recordar	remind; remember
resumir	summarize; sum up
sensible	sensitive; noticeable
extranjero	foreigner
simpático	nice

Nombres de lugar

País	Nacionalidad
Afghanistan /æfˈgænɪstæn; -stɑːn *GB*/	Afghan /ˈæfgæn/ Afghani /æfˈgæni/
Africa /ˈæfrɪkə/	African /ˈæfrɪkən/
Albania /ælˈbeɪniə/	Albanian /ælˈbeɪniən/
Algeria /ælˈdʒɪəriə/	Algerian /ælˈdʒɪəriən/
America /əˈmerɪkə/	American /əˈmerɪkən/
Antarctica /ænˈtɑːktɪkə/	Antarctic /ænˈtɑːktɪk/
(the) Arctic /ˈɑːktɪk/	Arctic /ˈɑːktɪk/
Argentina /ˌɑːdʒənˈtiːnə/	Argentinian /ˌɑːdʒənˈtɪniən/, Argentine /ˈɑːdʒəntaɪn/
Asia /ˈeɪʒə, ˈeɪʃə/	Asian /ˈeɪʒn, ˈeɪʃn/
(the) Atlantic /ətˈlæntɪk/	Atlantic /ətˈlæntɪk/
Australia /ɒˈstreɪliə; ɒˈs- *GB*/	Australian /ɒˈstreɪliən; ɒˈs- *GB*/
Austria /ˈɔːstriə; ˈɒs- *GB*/	Austrian /ˈɔːstriən; ˈɒs- *GB*/
(the) Bahamas /bəˈhɑːməz/	Bahamian /bəˈheɪmiən/
Bangladesh /ˌbæŋɡləˈdeʃ/	Bangladeshi /ˌbæŋɡləˈdeʃi/
Barbados /bɑːˈbeɪdɒs; -dəs *GB*/	Barbadian /bɑːˈbeɪdiən/
Belgium /ˈbeldʒəm/	Belgian /ˈbeldʒən/
Belize /bəˈliːz/	Belizean /bəˈliːziən/
Bolivia /bəˈlɪviə/	Bolivian /bəˈlɪviən/
Bosnia-Herzegovina /ˌbɒzniə ˌhɜːrtsəɡəˈviːnə/	Bosnian /ˈbɒzniən/
Brazil /brəˈzɪl/	Brazilian /brəˈzɪliən/
Bulgaria /bʌlˈɡeəriə/	Bulgarian /bʌlˈɡeəriən/
Burma (Myanmar) /ˈbɜːrmə/	Burmese /bɜːrˈmiːz/
Cameroon /ˌkæməˈruːn/	Cameroonian /ˌkæməˈruːniən/
Canada /ˈkænədə/	Canadian /kəˈneɪdiən/
(the) Caribbean /ˌkærəˈbiːən, kəˈrɪbiən/	
Chile /ˈtʃɪli/	Chilean /ˈtʃɪliən/
China /ˈtʃaɪnə/	Chinese /tʃaɪˈniːz/
Colombia /kəˈlʌmbiə/	Colombian /kəˈlʌmbiən/
(the Democratic Republic of the) Congo /ˈkɒŋɡoʊ/	Congolese /ˌkɒŋɡəˈliːz/
Costa Rica /ˌkɒstə ˈriːkə/	Costa Rican /ˌkɒstə ˈriːkən/
Croatia /kroʊˈeɪʃə/	Croatian /kroʊˈeɪʃən/
Cuba /ˈkjuːbə/	Cuban /ˈkjuːbən/
Cyprus /ˈsaɪprəs/	Cypriot /ˈsɪpriət/
(the) Czech Republic /ˌtʃek rɪˈpʌblɪk/	Czech /tʃek/
Denmark /ˈdenmɑːrk/	Danish /ˈdeɪnɪʃ/, Dane /deɪn/
(the) Dominican Republic /dəˌmɪnɪkən rɪˈpʌblɪk/	Dominican /dəˈmɪnɪkən/
Ecuador /ˈekwədɔːr/	Ecuadoran, Ecuadorean /ˌekwəˈdɔːriən/
Egypt /ˈiːdʒɪpt/	Egyptian /iˈdʒɪpʃn/
El Salvador /el ˈsælvədɔːr/	Salvadoran /ˌsælvəˈdɔːriən/
England /ˈɪŋɡlənd/	English /ˈɪŋɡlɪʃ/, Englishman, Englishwoman
Estonia /eˈstoʊniə/	Estonian /eˈstoʊniən/
Ethiopia /ˌiːθiˈoʊpiə/	Ethiopian /ˌiːθiˈoʊpiən/
Europe /ˈjʊərəp/	European /ˌjʊərəˈpiːən/
Finland /ˈfɪnlənd/	Finnish /ˈfɪnɪʃ/, Finn /fɪn/
France /fræns; frɑːns *GB*/	French /frentʃ/, Frenchman, Frenchwoman
Germany /ˈdʒɜːrməni/	German /ˈdʒɜːrmən/
Ghana /ˈɡɑːnə/	Ghanaian /ɡɑːˈneɪən/

País	Nacionalidad
Great Britain /ˌɡreɪt ˈbrɪtn/	British /ˈbrɪtɪʃ/, Briton /ˈbrɪtn/
Greece /ɡriːs/	Greek /ɡriːk/
Guatemala /ˌɡwɑːtəˈmɑːlə/	Guatemalan /ˌɡwɑːtəˈmɑːlən/
Guinea /ˈɡɪni/	Guinean /ˈɡɪniən/
Guyana /ɡaɪˈænə/	Guyanese /ˌɡaɪəˈniːz/
Haiti /ˈheɪti/	Haitian /ˈheɪʃn/
Holland /ˈhɒlənd/	→ (the) Netherlands
Honduras /hɒnˈdʊərəs; -ˈdjʊə- GB/	Honduran /hɒnˈdʊərən; -ˈdjʊə- GB/
Hungary /ˈhʌŋɡəri/	Hungarian /hʌŋˈɡeəriən/
Iceland /ˈaɪslənd/	Icelandic /aɪsˈlændɪk/, Icelander /ˈaɪsləndər/
India /ˈɪndiə/	Indian /ˈɪndiən/
Indonesia /ˌɪndəˈniːʒə/	Indonesian /ˌɪndəˈniːʒn/
Iran /ɪˈrɑːn/	Iranian /ɪˈreɪniən/
Iraq /ɪˈrɑːk/	Iraqi /ɪˈrɑːki/
(the Republic of) Ireland /ˈaɪərlənd/	Irish /ˈaɪrɪʃ/, Irishman, Irishwoman
Israel /ˈɪzreɪl/	Israeli /ɪzˈreɪli/
Italy /ˈɪtəli/	Italian /ɪˈtæliən/
Jamaica /dʒəˈmeɪkə/	Jamaican /dʒəˈmeɪkən/
Japan /dʒəˈpæn/	Japanese /ˌdʒæpəˈniːz/
Jordan /ˈdʒɔːrdn/	Jordanian /dʒɔːrˈdeɪniən/
Kenya /ˈkenjə/	Kenyan /ˈkenjən/
Korea /kəˈriə/ **North Korea, South Korea**	North Korean /ˌnɔːrθ kəˈriən/ South Korean /ˌsaʊθ kəˈriən/
Latvia /ˈlætviə/	Latvian /ˈlætviən/
Lebanon /ˈlebənən/	Lebanese /ˌlebəˈniːz/
Libya /ˈlɪbiə/	Libyan /ˈlɪbiən/
Lithuania /ˌlɪθjuˈeɪniə/	Lithuanian /ˌlɪθjuˈeɪniən/
Malaysia /məˈleɪʒə/	Malaysian /məˈleɪʒn/
(the) Mediterranean /ˌmedɪtəˈreɪniən/	
Mexico /ˈmeksɪkoʊ/	Mexican /ˈmeksɪkən/
Montenegro /ˌmɒntəˈneɡroʊ/	Montenegrin /ˌmɒntəˈneɡrɪn/
Morocco /məˈrɑːkoʊ/	Moroccan /məˈrɑːkən/
Nepal /nɪˈpɑːl, nɪˈpɔːl/	Nepalese /ˌnepəˈliːz/
(the) Netherlands /ˈneðərləndz/	Dutch /dʌtʃ/, Dutchman, Dutchwoman
New Zealand /ˌnuː ˈziːlənd; ˌnjuː GB/	New Zealander /ˌnuː ˈziːləndər; ˌnjuː GB/
Nicaragua /ˌnɪkəˈræɡwə/	Nicaraguan /ˌnɪkəˈræɡwən/
Nigeria /naɪˈdʒɪəriə/	Nigerian /naɪˈdʒɪəriən/
Northern Ireland /ˌnɔːrðərn ˈaɪərlənd/	Northern Irish /ˌnɔːrðərn ˈaɪrɪʃ/
Norway /ˈnɔːrweɪ/	Norwegian /nɔːrˈwiːdʒən/
Oceania /ˌoʊsiˈɑːniə/	Oceanian /ˈoʊsiɑːniən/
(the) Pacific /pəˈsɪfɪk/	Pacific /pəˈsɪfɪk/
Pakistan /ˌpækɪˈstæn; ˌpɑːkɪˈstɑːn GB/	Pakistani /ˌpækɪˈstæni; ˌpɑːkɪˈstɑːni GB/
Panama /ˈpænəmɑː/	Panamanian /ˌpænəˈmeɪniən/
Paraguay /ˈpærəɡwaɪ/	Paraguayan /ˌpærəˈɡwaɪən/
Peru /pəˈruː/	Peruvian /pəˈruːviən/
(the) Philippines /ˈfɪlɪpiːnz/	Philippine /ˈfɪlɪpiːn/, Filipino /ˌfɪlɪˈpiːnoʊ/
Poland /ˈpoʊlənd/	Polish /ˈpoʊlɪʃ/, Pole /poʊl/

País	Nacionalidad
Portugal /ˈpɔːrtʃʊgl/	Portuguese /ˌpɔːrtʃʊˈgiːz/
Romania /ruˈmeɪniə/	Romanian /ruˈmeɪniən/
Russia /ˈrʌʃə/	Russian /ˈrʌʃn/
Saudi Arabia /ˌsaʊdi əˈreɪbiə/	Saudi /ˈsaʊdi/, Saudi Arabian /ˌsaʊdi əˈreɪbiən/
Scotland /ˈskɑtlənd/	Scottish /ˈskɑtɪʃ/, Scots /ˈskɑts/, Scot /skɑt/, Scotsman, Scotswoman
Serbia /ˈsɜːrbiə/	Serbian /ˈsɜːrbiən/
Singapore /ˈsɪŋɡəpɔːr; ˌsɪŋəˈpɔːr GB/	Singaporean /ˌsɪŋəˈpɔːriən/
Slovakia /sloʊˈvækiə; slə- GB/	Slovak /ˈsloʊvæk/, Slovakian /sloʊˈvækiən; slə- GB/
Slovenia /sloʊˈviːniə; slə- GB/	Slovene /ˈsloʊviːn/, Slovenian /sloʊˈviːniən; slə- GB/
South Africa /ˌsaʊθ ˈæfrɪkə/	South African /ˌsaʊθ ˈæfrɪkən/
Spain /speɪn/	Spanish /ˈspænɪʃ/, Spaniard /ˈspænjərd/
Sudan /suˈdæn; suːˈdɑːn GB/	Sudanese /ˌsuːdəˈniːz/
Suriname /ˌsʊərɪˈnæm/	Surinamese /ˌsʊərɪmæˈmiːz/
Sweden /ˈswiːdn/	Swedish /ˈswiːdɪʃ/, Swede /swiːd/
Switzerland /ˈswɪtsərlənd/	Swiss /swɪs/
Syria /ˈsɪriə/	Syrian /ˈsɪriən/
Tanzania /ˌtænzəˈniːə/	Tanzanian /ˌtænzəˈniːən/
Thailand /ˈtaɪlænd/	Thai /taɪ/
Trinidad and Tobago /ˌtrɪnɪdæd ən təˈbeɪɡoʊ/	Trinidadian /ˌtrɪnɪˈdædiən/, Tobagonian /ˌtoʊbəˈɡoʊniən/, Tobagan /təˈbeɪɡən/
Tunisia /tuˈniːʒə; tjuˈnɪziə GB/	Tunisian /tuˈniːʒn; tjuˈnɪziən GB/
Turkey /ˈtɜːrki/	Turkish /ˈtɜːrkɪʃ/, Turk /tɜːrk/
Uganda /juːˈɡændə/	Ugandan /juːˈɡændən/
Ukraine /juːˈkreɪn/	Ukrainian /juːˈkreɪniən/
(the) United States of America /juːˌnaɪtɪd ˌsterts əv əˈmerɪkə/	American /əˈmerɪkən/
Uruguay /ˈjʊərəɡwaɪ/	Uruguayan /ˌjʊərəˈɡwaɪən/
Venezuela /ˌvenəˈzweɪlə/	Venezuelan /ˌvenəˈzweɪlən/
Vietnam /vjetˈnæm, ˌviːet-/	Vietnamese /ˌvjetnəˈmiːz, viːet-/
Wales /weɪlz/	Welsh /welʃ/, Welshman, Welshwoman
Yemen Republic /ˌjemən rɪˈpʌblɪk/	Yemeni /ˈjeməni/
Zimbabwe /zɪmˈbɑːbwi/	Zimbabwean /zɪmˈbɑːbwiən/

Cómo construir el plural

Para construir el plural se debe añadir una **-s** al final (p. ej. *a Cuban, two Cubans*), excepto en el caso de **Swiss** y de palabras terminadas en **-ese** (p. ej. *Japanese*), que son invariables.

Ciudades de EE.UU. y Canadá

Ciudades principales de EE.UU.

Atlanta	/æt'lænta; at- *GB*/
Austin	/'ɔːstɪn; 'ɒs- *GB*/
Baltimore	/'bɔːltɪmɔːr/
Boston	/'bɔːstən; 'bɒs- *GB*/
Chicago	/ʃɪ'kɑɡoʊ/
Cincinnati	/ˌsɪnsɪ'næti/
Cleveland	/'kliːvlənd/
Dallas	/'dæləs/
Detroit	/dɪ'trɔɪt/
Honolulu	/ˌhɑnə'luːluː/
Houston	/'hjuːstən/
Indianapolis	/ˌɪndiə'næpəlɪs/
Kansas City	/ˌkænzəs 'sɪti/
Los Angeles	/ˌlɔːs 'ændʒələs; ˌlɒs 'ændʒəliːz *GB*/
Miami	/maɪ'æmi/
Milwaukee	/mɪl'wɔːki/
New Orleans	/nuː 'ɔrliənz; ˌnjuː ɔː'liːənz *GB*/
New York	/ˌnuː 'jɔːrk; ˌnjuː *GB*/
Philadelphia	/ˌfɪlə'delfiə/
Phoenix	/'fiːnɪks/
Pittsburgh	/'pɪtsbɜːrɡ/
San Antonio	/ˌsæn æn'toʊnioʊ/
San Diego	/ˌsæn di'eɪɡoʊ/
San Francisco	/ˌsæn frən'sɪskoʊ/
Seattle	/si'ætl/
St. Louis	/ˌseɪnt 'luːɪs/
Washington D.C.	/ˌwɑʃɪŋtən diː 'siː/

Ciudades principales de Canadá

Calgary	/'kælɡəri/
Edmonton	/'edməntən/
Montréal	/ˌmɑntri'ɔːl/
Ottawa	/'ɑtəwə/
Quebec	/kwɪ'bek/
Toronto	/tə'rɑntoʊ/
Vancouver	/væn'kuːvər/
Winnipeg	/'wɪnɪpeɡ/

A a

A, a /eɪ/ n (pl **A's, a's**) **1** A, a **2** (Mús) la

a /ə, eɪ/ (tb an /ən, æn/) art indef **NOTA A, an** equivale a "un(a)" excepto en **1** (números): *a hundred people* cien personas **2** (profesiones): *My mother is a lawyer.* Mi madre es abogada. **3** por: *80km an hour* 80 km por hora ◇ *ten dollars a week* $10 a la semana ◇ *2 euros a dozen* dos euros la docena **4** (con desconocidos) un(a) tal

aback /ə'bæk/ adv ▶ **be taken aback** (**by sth/sb**) sorprenderse (ante algo/algn)

abandon /ə'bændən/ vt abandonar

abbess /'æbes/ n abadesa

abbey /'æbi/ n abadía

abbot /'æbət/ n abad

abbreviate /ə'bri:vieɪt/ vt abreviar **abbreviation** n **1** abreviación **2** abreviatura

ABC /ˌeɪ bi: 'si:/ n **1** abecedario **2** abecé

abdicate /'æbdɪkeɪt/ vt, vi abdicar: ~ *all responsibility* declinar toda responsabilidad

abdomen /'æbdəmən/ n abdomen **abdominal** /æb'dɒmɪnl/ adj abdominal

abduct /æb'dʌkt/ vt secuestrar **abduction** n secuestro

abide /ə'baɪd/ vt soportar ■ **abide by sth 1** acatar algo **2** (promesa) cumplir con algo

ability /ə'bɪləti/ n (pl **-ies**) **1** (talento) capacidad, aptitud **2** habilidad

ablaze /ə'bleɪz/ adj **1** en llamas: *set sth* ~ prender fuego a algo **2** be ~ **with** resplandecer de algo

able /'eɪbl/ adj **1** be ~ **to do sth** poder, saber hacer algo →CAN¹ **2** (-er/-est) capaz

abnormal /æb'nɔːrml/ adj anormal **abnormality** /ˌæbnɔːr'mæləti/ n (pl **-ies**) anormalidad

aboard /ə'bɔːrd/ adv, prep a bordo (de)

abode /ə'boʊd/ n (fml) morada

abolish /ə'bɒlɪʃ/ vt abolir **abolition** n abolición

abominable /ə'bɒmɪnəbl/ adj abominable

abort /ə'bɔːrt/ vt, vi abortar: ~ *the launch* detener el lanzamiento

abortion /ə'bɔːrʃn/ n aborto (intencionado): *have an* ~ abortar

abortive /ə'bɔːrtɪv/ adj fracasado

abound /ə'baʊnd/ vi ~ (**with sth**) abundar (en algo)

about /ə'baʊt/ adv **1** más o menos **2** hacia: *at* ~ *half past two* hacia las dos y media →AROUND **3** por aquí: *She's somewhere* ~. Está por aquí. ◇ *There are no jobs* ~ *now.* De momento no hay ningún trabajo. **4** casi **5** de un lado a otro **6** aquí y allá: *People were standing* ~ *in the street.* Había gente parada en la calle. ▶ **about to do sth** a punto de hacer algo **NOTA** Para el uso de **about** en PHRASAL VERBS ver el verbo, p.ej. **be about** en LIE². ● prep **1** por: *She's somewhere* ~ *the place.* Anda por aquí. **2** sobre: *What's the book* ~? ¿De qué trata el libro? **3** [+ adj]: *angry/happy* ~ *sth* enojado por/contento con algo **4** (característica): *There's something* ~ *her I like.* Tiene algo que me atrae. ▶ **how/what about?**: *What* ~ *his car?* ¿Y su carro? ◇ *How* ~ *a drink?* ¿Qué tal si tomamos algo?

above /ə'bʌv/ adv arriba: *children aged ten* ~ niños de diez años o más ● prep **1** por encima de, más arriba de **2** más de: ~ *50%* más del 50% ▶ **above all** sobre todo

abrasive /ə'breɪsɪv/ adj **1** áspero **2** (persona) brusco y desagradable

abreast /ə'brest/ adv: *cycle two* ~ andar en bici al lado de algn ▶ **keep abreast of sth** mantenerse al corriente de algo

abroad /ə'brɔːd/ adv en el extranjero: *go* ~ ir al extranjero

abrupt /ə'brʌpt/ adj (cambio, persona) brusco

abscess /'æbses/ n absceso

abseil /'æbseɪl/ vi (GB) hacer rappel **abseiling** n rappel

absence /'æbsəns/ n ausencia, falta: ~s *due to illness* ausentismo por enfermedad ◇ *in the* ~ *of new evidence* a falta de nuevas pruebas

absent /'æbsənt/ adj **1** ausente **2** distraído

absentee /ˌæbsən'tiː/ n ausente

absent-minded /ˌæbsənt 'maɪndɪd/ adj distraído

absolute /'æbsəluːt/ adj absoluto

absolutely /'æbsəluːtli/ adv **1** absolutamente: *You are* ~ *right.* Tienes toda la razón. ◇ *It's* ~ *essential that...* Es imprescindible que... **2** [en negativa]: ~ *nothing* nada en absoluto

3 /ˌæbsəˈluːtli/ (*mostrando acuerdo*) claro que sí

absolve /əbˈzɒlv/ vt absolver

absorb /əbˈzɔːrb/ vt 1 absorber, asimilar 2 (*golpe*) amortiguar **absorbed** *adj* absorto **absorbing** *adj* absorbente (*libro, etc.*)

absorption /əbˈzɔːrpʃn/ n 1 absorción 2 asimilación

abstain /əbˈsteɪn/ vi abstenerse

abstract /ˈæbstrækt/ *adj* abstracto ● n obra de arte abstracto ▸ **in the abstract** en abstracto

absurd /əbˈsɜːrd/ *adj* absurdo, ridículo **absurdity** n (pl **-ies**) lo absurdo

abundant /əˈbʌndənt/ *adj* abundante **abundance** n abundancia

abuse /əˈbjuːz/ vt 1 abusar de 2 insultar 3 maltratar ● /əˈbjuːs/ n 1 abuso 2 [U] insultos: *They shouted ~ at him.* Lo insultaron. 3 [U] malos tratos **abusive** /əˈbjuːsɪv/ *adj* insultante, grosero

abyss /əˈbɪs/ n abismo

academy /əˈkædəmi/ n (pl **-ies**) academia **academic** /ˌækəˈdemɪk/ *adj* 1 académico 2 teórico

accelerate /əkˈseləreɪt/ vt, vi acelerar **acceleration** n 1 aceleración 2 (*vehículo*) arranque **accelerator** n (GB) acelerador

accent /ˈæksent/ n 1 acento 2 énfasis 3 tilde

accentuate /əkˈsentʃueɪt/ vt 1 acentuar 2 resaltar 3 agravar

accept /əkˈsept/ vt 1 vt, vi aceptar: *The machines only ~ coins.* Las máquinas sólo funcionan con monedas. 2 vt admitir **acceptable** *adj* ~ (**to sb**) aceptable (para algn) **acceptance** n 1 aceptación 2 aprobación

access /ˈækses/ n ~ (**to sth/sb**) acceso (a algo/algn) ● vt (*Comp*) acceder a

accessible /əkˈsesəbl/ *adj* accesible

accessory /əkˈsesəri/ n (pl **-ies**) 1 accesorio 2 ~ (**to sth**) cómplice (de algo)

accident /ˈæksɪdənt/ n 1 accidente 2 casualidad ▸ **by accident** 1 accidentalmente 2 por casualidad 3 por descuido **accidental** /ˌæksɪˈdentl/ *adj* 1 accidental 2 casual

accident and emergency (*abrev* A & E) n (GB) urgencias

acclaim /əˈkleɪm/ vt aclamar ● n [U] elogios

accommodate /əˈkɒmədeɪt/ vt 1 alojar 2 tener capacidad para

accommodations /əˌkɒmə-ˈdeɪʃnz/ n [pl] (**accommodation** GB) alojamiento

accompany /əˈkʌmpəni/ vt (pt/pp **-ied**) acompañar **accompaniment** n acompañamiento

accomplice /əˈkʌmplɪs; əˈkʌm-GB/ n cómplice

accomplish /əˈkʌmplɪʃ; əˈkʌm-GB/ vt llevar a cabo **accomplished** *adj* consumado **accomplishment** n 1 logro 2 talento

accord /əˈkɔːrd/ n acuerdo ▸ **in accord (with sth/sb)** (*fml*) en concordancia (con algo/algn) **of your own accord** por decisión propia ● vt concordar 2 vt otorgar, conceder

accordance /əˈkɔːrdns/ n ▸ **in accordance with sth** de acuerdo con algo

accordingly /əˈkɔːrdɪŋli/ *adv* 1 por lo tanto 2 en consecuencia

according to *prep* según

accordion /əˈkɔːrdiən/ n acordeón

account /əˈkaʊnt/ n 1 (*Fin*) cuenta: *checking/current* (GB) ~ cuenta corriente 2 factura 3 **accounts** [pl] contabilidad 4 relato, relación ▸ **by/from all accounts** por lo que dicen **of no account** (*fml*) sin ninguna importancia **on account of sth** a causa de algo **on no account; not on any account** de ninguna manera **on this/that account** (*fml*) según esto/eso **take account of sth; take sth into account** tener algo en cuenta ● vi ~ (**to sb**) **for sth** rendir cuentas (a algn) de algo **accountable** *adj* ~ (**to sb**) (**for sth**) responsable (ante algn) (de algo)

accountant /əˈkaʊntənt/ n contador/a **accounting** (**accountancy** GB) n contabilidad

accumulate /əˈkjuːmjəleɪt/ vt, vi acumular(se) **accumulation** n acumulación

accurate /ˈækjərət/ *adj* 1 exacto 2 (*disparo, etc.*) certero **accuracy** n precisión

accuse /əˈkjuːz/ vt acusar **the accused** n (pl **the accused**) el/la acusado/a **accusation** n acusación **accusingly** *adv*: *look ~ at sb* lanzar una mirada acusadora a algn

accustomed /əˈkʌstəmd/ *adj* acostumbrado: *become/grow ~ to sth* acostumbrarse a algo

ace /eɪs/ n as

ache /eɪk/ n dolor ● vi doler **aching** *adj* dolorido

achieve /əˈtʃiːv/ vt 1 alcanzar 2 conseguir **achievement** n logro

A

acid /'æsɪd/ *adj, n* ácido: ~ *rain* lluvia ácida **acidic** /ə'sɪdɪk/ *adj* ácido **acidity** *n* acidez

acknowledge /ək'nɒlɪdʒ/ *vt* 1 reconocer 2 acusar recibo de 3 darse por enterado **acknowledge(e)ment** *n* 1 reconocimiento 2 confirmación de recibo 3 agradecimiento (*en un libro, etc.*)

acne /'ækni/ *n* acné

acorn /'eɪkɔ:n/ *n* bellota

acoustic /ə'ku:stɪk/ *adj* acústico **acoustics** *n* [*pl*] acústica

acquaintance /ə'kweɪntəns/ *n* 1 amistad ◊ conocido/a ▶ **make sb's acquaintance/make the acquaintance of sb** (*fml*) conocer a algn (*por primera vez*) **acquainted** *adj* familiarizado: *become/get ~ with sb* (llegar a) conocer a algn

acquiesce /ˌækwi'es/ *vi* (*fml*) ~ **(in sth)** consentir (en algo) **acquiescence** *n* consentimiento

acquire /ə'kwaɪər/ *vt* (*fml*) 1 adquirir 2 obtener **acquisition** /ˌækwɪ'zɪʃn/ *n* adquisición

acquit /ə'kwɪt/ *vt* (**-tt-**) absolver **acquittal** *n* absolución

acre /'eɪkər/ *n* acre (4,047 m²)

acrobat /'ækrəbæt/ *n* acróbata

across /ə'krɔs; ə'krɒs *GB*/ *adv, prep* 1 de un lado a otro: *the path ~ the fields* el camino que atraviesa los campos **NOTA** Muchas veces se traduce por un verbo: *swim ~* cruzar nadando ◊ *walk ~ the border* cruzar la frontera a pie. 2 al otro lado (de): *I was ~ in no time.* Llegué al otro lado en un instante. ◊ *from ~ the room* desde el otro lado de la sala 3 sobre, a lo largo de: *A branch lay ~ the path.* Había una rama atravesada en el camino. 4 de ancho: *The river is a mile ~.* El río tiene una milla de ancho. 5 ~ **from** **NOTA** Para el uso de **across** en PHRASAL VERBS ver el verbo, p.ej. **come across** en COME.

acrylic /ə'krɪlɪk/ *adj, n* acrílico

act /ækt/ *n* 1 (*tb Teat*) acto 2 número: *a circus ~* un número de circo 3 (*Jur*) decreto ▶ **get your act together** (*coloq*) organizarse **in the act of doing sth** en el momento de hacer algo **put on an act** (*coloq*) fingir ● *vi* 1 actuar 2 ~ comportarse 3 *vt* (*Teat*) hacer el papel de

acting /'æktɪŋ/ *n* teatro: *his ~ career* su carrera como actor ● *adj* [*antes de sustantivo*] en funciones, interino: *He was ~ chair-*

man at the meeting. Actuó como presidente en la reunión.

action /'ækʃn/ *n* 1 acción: *in ~* en acción ◊ *This machine is out of ~.* Esta máquina no funciona. ◊ *put sth into ~* poner algo en práctica 2 [*U*] medidas: *take ~* tomar medidas 3 acto

activate /'æktɪveɪt/ *vt* activar

active /'æktɪv/ *adj* activo: *take an ~ part in sth* participar activamente en algo ● *n* (*tb* ~ **voice**) (voz) activa

activity /æk'tɪvəti/ *n* (*pl* **-ies**) 1 actividad 2 bullicio

actor /'æktər/ *n* actor, actriz

actress /'æktrəs/ *n* actriz **NOTA** También se usa **actor** para el femenino.

actual /'æktʃuəl/ *adj* 1 exacto: *What were his ~ words?* ¿Qué es lo que dijo exactamente? 2 verdadero: *based on ~ events* basado en hechos reales ◊ *in ~ fact* en realidad 3 *the ~ city center* el centro propiamente dicho

actually /'æktʃuəli/ *adv* 1 en realidad, de hecho: *He's ~ very rich.* La verdad es que es muy rico. 2 exactamente: *What did she ~ say?* ¿Qué dijo exactamente? 3 *Actually, my name's Sue, not Ann.* A propósito, me llamo Sue, no Ann. (*énfasis*): *You ~ met her?* ¿De verdad la conociste? ◊ *He ~ expected me to leave.* Hasta esperaba que me fuera.

acupuncture /'ækjupʌŋktʃər/ *n* acupuntura

acute /ə'kju:t/ *adj* 1 extremo 2 agudo: *~ angle/pain* ángulo/dolor agudo ◊ *become more ~* agudizarse 3 (*remordimiento*) profundo

ad /æd/ *n* (*coloq*) anuncio: *small ads* anuncios por palabras

A.D. /ˌeɪ 'di:/ *abrev* después de Cristo

adamant /'ædəmənt/ *adj* firme, categórico: *He was ~ about staying.* Se empeñó en quedarse.

Adam's apple /ˌædəmz 'æpl/ *n* (*Anat*) manzana (de Adán)

adapt /ə'dæpt/ *vt, vi* adaptar(se) **adaptable** *adj* adaptable **adaptation** *n* adaptación

adaptor /ə'dæptər/ *n* (*Elec*) adaptador

add /æd/ *vt* 1 ~ **sth (on) (to sth)** añadir algo (a algo) 2 ~ **sth (together/up)** sumar algo ■ **add to sth** aumentar, ampliar algo **add up** (*coloq*) encajar: *His story doesn't ~ up.* Hay cosas en su relato que no encaja. **add up to sth** ascender a algo

adder /'ædər/ n víbora

addict /'ædɪkt/ n adicto/a: *drug ~* drogadicto/toxicómano

addiction /ə'dɪkʃn/ n adicción **addicted** adj adicto **addictive** adj adictivo

addition /ə'dɪʃn/ n 1 incorporación 2 adquisición 3 (*Mat*) suma, adición ▶ **in addition (to sth)** además (de algo) **additional** adj adicional

additive /'ædətɪv/ n aditivo

address /ə'dres; adrés *GB*/ n 1 dirección: *~ book* libreta de direcciones 2 discurso ● *vt* /ə'dres/ 1 (*carta, etc.*) dirigir 2 *~ sb* dirigirse a algn 3 *~ (yourself to) sth* hacer frente a algo

adept /ə'dept/ adj hábil

adequate /'ædɪkwət/ adj 1 adecuado 2 aceptable

adhere /əd'hɪər/ vi (*fml*) 1 adherirse 2 *~ to sth* (*creencia, etc.*) observar algo **adherence** n 1 adherencia 2 observación **adherent** n adepto/a

adhesive /əd'hi:sɪv/ adj, n adhesivo

adjacent /ə'dʒeɪsnt/ adj adyacente

adjective /'ædʒɪktɪv/ n adjetivo

adjoining /ə'dʒɔɪnɪŋ/ adj contiguo, colindante

adjourn /ə'dʒɜ:rn/ 1 *vt* aplazar 2 *vt, vi* (*reunión*) suspender(se)

adjust /ə'dʒʌst/ 1 *vt* ajustar, arreglar 2 *vt, vi* adaptar(se) **adjustment** n 1 ajuste, modificación 2 adaptación

administer /əd'mɪnɪstər/ *vt* 1 administrar 2 (*organización*) dirigir 3 (*castigo*) aplicar **administration** n administración, dirección **administrative** adj administrativo **administrator** n administrador/a

admirable /'ædmərəbl/ adj admirable

admiral /'ædmərəl/ n almirante

admiration /ˌædmə'reɪʃn/ n admiración

admire /əd'maɪər/ *vt* admirar, elogiar **admirer** n admirador/a **admiring** adj lleno de admiración

admission /əd'mɪʃn/ n 1 entrada, admisión 2 ingreso 3 reconocimiento

admit /əd'mɪt/ (*-tt-*) 1 *vt, vi* admitir, reconocer: *~ to a crime* confesar un crimen 2 *vt* dejar entrar, admitir: *be admitted to hospital* ser ingresado al hospital **admittedly** adv hay que admitir que...

adolescence /ˌædə'lesns/ n adolescencia **adolescent** adj, n adolescente

adopt /ə'dɑpt/ *vt* adoptar **adopted** adj adoptivo **adoption** n adopción

adore /ə'dɔ:r/ *vt* adorar

adorn /ə'dɔ:rn/ *vt* adornar

adrenalin /ə'drenəlɪn/ n adrenalina

adrift /ə'drɪft/ adj a la deriva

adult /ə'dʌlt, 'ædʌlt/ adj adulto, mayor de edad ● n adulto/a **adulthood** /'ædʌlthʊd/ n edad adulta

adultery /ə'dʌltəri/ n adulterio

advance /əd'væns, əd'vɑ:ns/ n 1 avance 2 adelanto ▶ **in advance** 1 de antemano 2 con antelación 3 por adelantado ● adj anticipado: *~ warning* previo aviso ● *vt, vi* (hacer) avanzar **advanced** adj avanzado **advancement** n 1 desarrollo 2 (*trabajo*) ascenso

advantage /əd'væntɪdʒ; -'vɑ:n- *GB*/ n 1 ventaja 2 provecho ▶ **take advantage of sth** 1 aprovecharse de algo 2 sacar provecho de algo **take advantage of sth/sb** abusar de algo/algn **advantageous** /ˌædvən'teɪdʒəs/ adj ventajoso

advent /'ædvent/ n 1 (*fml*) advenimiento 2 Advent adviento

adventure /əd'ventʃər/ n aventura **adventurer** n aventurero/a **adventurous** adj 1 aventurero 2 aventurado 3 audaz

adverb /'ædvɜ:rb/ n adverbio

adversary /'ædvərseri; -səri *GB*/ n (pl -ies) adversario/a

adverse /'ædvɜ:rs/ adj adverso: *~ criticism* críticas negativas **adversely** adv negativamente

adversity /əd'vɜ:rsəti/ n (pl -ies) adversidad

advertise /'ædvərtaɪz/ 1 *vt* anunciar 2 *vi* hacer publicidad 3 *vi ~ for sth/sb* poner un anuncio solicitando algo/a algn **advertising** n 1 publicidad: *~ campaign* campaña publicitaria 2 anuncios

advertisement /ˌædvər'taɪzmənt; əd'vɜ:rtɪsmənt *GB*/ (*tb* **advert** /'ædvɜ:rt/ *GB*, coloq) n ~ (**for sth/sb**) anuncio (de algo/algn)

advice /əd'vaɪs/ n [U] consejo(s): *a piece of ~* un consejo ◊ *seek/take legal ~* consultar a un abogado →CONSEJO

advise /əd'vaɪz/ *vt, vi* 1 aconsejar: *You would be well advised to...* Sería prudente... 2 asesorar **advisable** adj aconsejable **adviser**

(tb advisor) n consejero/a, asesor/a **advisory** adj consultivo

advocacy /'ædvəkəsi/ n (fml) ~ of sth apoyo a algo

advocate /'ædvəkeɪt/ vt abogar por

aerial /'eəriəl/ n (GB, TV) antena ● adj aéreo

aerobics /ə'rəʊbɪks/ n [sing] aeróbic, aeróbicos

aerodynamic /,eəroʊdaɪ'næmɪk; ,eərəʊ- GB/ adj aerodinámico

aeroplane /'eərəpleɪn/ n (GB) avión

aesthetic /es'θetɪk/ adj estético

affair /ə'feər/ n 1 asunto: the Lewinsky ~ el caso Lewinsky 2 acontecimiento 3 aventura (amorosa)

affect /ə'fekt/ vt afectar, influir en 2 conmover, emocionar

affection /ə'fekʃn/ n cariño **affectionate** adj cariñoso

affinity /ə'fɪnəti/ n (pl -ies) (fml) 1 afinidad 2 simpatía

affirm /ə'fɜːrm/ vt afirmar

afflict /ə'flɪkt/ vt afligir: be afflicted with sth sufrir de algo

affluent /'æfluənt/ adj rico **affluence** n riqueza

afford /ə'fɔːrd/ vt 1 permitirse (el lujo de) 2 proporcionar **affordable** adj asequible

afield /ə'fiːld/ adv ▸ far/further afield muy lejos/más allá: from as far ~ as... desde lugares tan lejanos como...

afloat /ə'fləʊt/ adj y adv a flote

afraid /ə'freɪd/ adj 1 be ~ (of sth/ sb) tener miedo (a algo/algn) 2 be ~ to do sth no atreverse a hacer algo 3 be ~ for sb temer por algn ▸ I'm afraid so lo siento, pero...: I'm ~ so/not. Me temo que sí/no.

afresh /ə'freʃ/ adv de nuevo

after /'æftər; 'ɑːf- GB/ prep 1 después de: the day ~ tomorrow pasado mañana 2 detrás de, tras: time ~ time una y otra vez 3 (búsqueda): What are you ~? ¿Qué buscas? 4 I named him ~ you. Le puse tu nombre. ▸ after all al fin y al cabo ● conj después de que ● adv después: the day ~ el día siguiente

aftermath /'æftərmæθ; 'ɑːf- GB/ n [sing] secuelas: in the ~ of sth en el período subsiguiente a algo

afternoon /,æftər'nuːn; ,ɑːf- GB/ n tarde ▸ good afternoon buenas tardes →MORNING, MEDIO, TARDE

aftershave /'æftərʃeɪv; 'ɑːf- GB/ n loción para después del afeitado

afterthought /'æftərθɔːt; 'ɑːf- GB/ n ocurrencia tardía

afterwards /'æftərwərdz; 'ɑːf- GB/ (tb afterward USA) adv después: shortly/soon ~ poco después

again /ə'gen, ə'geɪn/ adv otra vez, de nuevo: once/over ~ una vez más/nunca más ◇ Don't do it ~. No vuelvas a hacerlo. ◇ ~ and ~ una y otra vez ▸ then/there again por otra parte

against /ə'genst, ə'geɪnst/ prep 1 contra 2 (oposición) en contra de 3 (contraste) sobre: His red clothes stood out ~ the snow. Su ropa roja se recortaba sobre la nieve. **NOTA** Para el uso de against en PHRASAL VERBS ver el verbo, p.ej. come up against en COME.

age /eɪdʒ/ n 1 edad: be six years of ~ tener seis años ◇ It improves with ~. Mejora con el tiempo. 3 época, era 4 ages (tb an age) (coloq) eternidad: It's ~s since I saw her. Hace siglos que no la veo. ● come of age alcanzar la mayoría de edad **look your age** aparentar una tu edad que tiene **under age** menor de edad ● vt, vi (pt pres aging pt/pp aged /eɪdʒd/) (hacer) envejecer

aged adj 1 /eɪdʒd/ de... años de edad: He died ~ 81. Murió a la edad de 81 años. 2 /'eɪdʒɪd/ anciano ● the aged /'eɪdʒɪd/ n [pl] los ancianos **NOTA** Es más común usar **old people** o the **elderly** para referirnos a las personas mayores. "Tercera edad" se dice **senior citizens**: activities for senior citizens.

ageing = AGING

agency /'eɪdʒənsi/ n (pl -ies) agencia, organismo

agenda /ə'dʒendə/ n orden del día

agent /'eɪdʒənt/ n agente, representante

aggravate /'ægrəveɪt/ vt 1 agravar 2 fastidiar **aggravating** adj irritante **aggravation** n 1 fastidio 2 agravamiento

aggressive /ə'gresɪv/ adj agresivo **aggression** n [U] agresión, agresividad

agile /'ædʒl; 'ædʒaɪl GB/ adj ágil **agility** /ə'dʒɪləti/ n agilidad

aging /'eɪdʒɪŋ/ adj 1 avejentado 2 no tan joven ● n envejecimiento

agitated /'ædʒɪteɪtɪd/ adj agitado: get ~ ponerse nervioso **agitation** n 1 perturbación 2 (Pol) agitación

ago /əˈgoʊ/ adv hace: How long ~ did she die? ¿Cuánto hace que murió? ◊ as long ~ as 1950 ya en 1950 **NOTA** **Ago** se usa con el simple past y el past continuous, pero nunca con el present perfect: She arrived a few minutes ~. Con el past perfect se usa before o earlier: She had arrived two days before.

agonize /ˈægənaɪz/ vi atormentarse: ~ over a decision angustiarse tratando de decidir algo **agonized** adj angustiado **1** angustioso **2** (dolor) horroroso

agony /ˈægəni/ n (pl -ies) sufrimiento: be in ~ tener unos dolores horrorosos ◊ It was ~! ¡Fue una pesadilla!

agree /əˈgriː/ (pt, pp **agreed**) **1** vi ~ (with sb) (on/about sth) estar de acuerdo (con algn) (en/sobre algo) **2** vi ~ (to sth) consentir (en algo), acceder (a algo) **3** vt acordar **4** vi llegar a un acuerdo **5** vi concordar **6** vt (informe, etc.) aprobar ■ **agree with sb** sentarle bien a algn (comida, clima) **agreeable** adj **1** agradable **2** ~ (to sth) conforme (con algo)

agreement /əˈgriːmənt/ n **1** conformidad, acuerdo: in ~ with de acuerdo con **2** convenio **3** (Com) contrato

agriculture /ˈægrɪkʌltʃər/ n agricultura **agricultural** /ˌægrɪˈkʌltʃərəl/ adj agrícola

ah /ɑː/ interj ah

aha /ɑːˈhɑː/ interj ajá

ahead /əˈhed/ adv **1** hacia/por adelante **2** próximo: during the days ~ durante los próximos días **NOTA** Para el uso de **ahead** en PHRASAL VERBS ver el verbo, p.ej. **press ahead** en PRESS. ● **ahead of** prep **1** (por) delante de: be/get ~ of sb llevar ventaja/adelantarse a algn ◊ ~ of time adelantado **2** antes de

aid /eɪd/ n **1** ayuda **2** auxilio: come/go to sb's ~ acudir en auxilio de algn **3** apoyo ▶ **in aid of sth/sb** a beneficio de algo/algn ● vt ayudar, facilitar

AIDS /eɪdz/ n (abrev de **Acquired Immune Deficiency Syndrome**) sida

ailment /ˈeɪlmənt/ n achaque

aim /eɪm/ **1** vt, vi ~ (sth) (at sth/sb) (arma) apuntar (a algo/algn) (con algo) **2** vt ~ sth at sth/sb dirigir algo contra algo/algn: be aimed at sth tener algo como objetivo **3** vi ~ at/for sth aspirar a algo **4** vi ~ to do sth tener la intención de hacer algo ● n

1 objetivo **2** puntería ▶ **take aim** apuntar

aimless /ˈeɪmləs/ adj sin objeto **aimlessly** adv sin rumbo

ain't /eɪnt/ (coloq) **1** = AM/IS/ARE NOT **2** = HAS/HAVE NOT

air /eər/ n aire: ~ fares tarifas aéreas ◊ ~ pollution contaminación atmosférica ◊ by ~ en avión/por vía aérea ▶ **give yourself/put on airs** darse aires in the air: There's something in the ~. Se está tramando algo. **on the air** (TV, Radio) al aire **up in the air**: The plan is still up in the ~. El proyecto sigue en el aire. ● vt **1** airear **2** (ropa) orear **3** (queja) ventilar

air conditioning n aire acondicionado **air-conditioned** adj climatizado

aircraft /ˈeərkræft; -krɑːft GB/ n (pl aircraft) avión

airfield /ˈeərfiːld/ n aeródromo

air force n fuerza(s) aérea(s)

air hostess n azafata

airline /ˈeərlaɪn/ n línea aérea

airmail /ˈeərmeɪl/ n correo aéreo: by ~ por vía aérea

airplane /ˈeərpleɪn/ n (USA) avión

airport /ˈeərpɔːrt/ n aeropuerto

airtight /ˈeərtaɪt/ adj hermético

aisle /aɪl/ n pasillo (avión, iglesia, teatro)

akin /əˈkɪn/ adj semejante

alarm /əˈlɑːrm/ n **1** alarma: raise/ sound the ~ dar la alarma **2** (tb ~ clock) despertador **3** (tb ~ bell) timbre de alarma ▶ **a false alarm** una falsa alarma ● vt alarmar **alarming** adj alarmante

alas /əˈlæs/ interj por desgracia

albeit /ˌɔːlˈbiːɪt/ conj (fml) aunque

album /ˈælbəm/ n álbum

alcohol /ˈælkəhɔːl; -hɒl GB/ n alcohol: alcohol-free sin alcohol **alcoholic** /ˌælkəˈhɔːlɪk/ adj, n alcohólico/a **alcoholism** /ˈælkəhɔːlɪzəm; -hɒl- GB/ n alcoholismo

ale /eɪl/ n cerveza

alert /əˈlɜːrt/ adj despierto ● n **1** alerta: be on the ~ estar alerta **2** aviso: bomb ~ aviso de bomba ● vt alertar

algae /ˈældʒiː; ˈælgiː/ n algas

algebra /ˈældʒɪbrə/ n álgebra

alibi /ˈæləbaɪ/ n coartada

alien /ˈeɪliən/ adj **1** extraño **2** extranjero **3** ajeno ● n **1** (fml) extranjero/a: illegal ~ inmigrante ilegal **2** extraterrestre **alienate** vt enajenar

alight /əˈlaɪt/ adj: be ~ estar ardiendo ◊ set sth ~ prender fuego a algo

align /əˈlaɪn/ vt 1 alinear 2 ~ yourself with sb (Pol) aliarse con algn

alike /əˈlaɪk/ adj 1 parecido: be/look ~ parecerse 2 igual: No two are ~. No hay dos iguales. ● adv igual, del mismo modo: It appeals to young and old ~. Atrae a viejos y jóvenes por igual.

alive /əˈlaɪv/ adj [después del verbo] vivo, con vida: stay ~ sobrevivir → VIVO ▸ alive and kicking vivito y coleando keep sth alive 1 (tradición) conservar algo 2 (recuerdo) mantener fresco algo

all /ɔːl/ adj, pron todo: All three of us liked it. Nos gustó a los tres. ◊ I ate ~ of it. Me lo comí todo. ◊ All I want is... Lo único que quiero es... ▸ all in all en conjunto **all the more** tanto más/aún más **at all:** if it's at ~ possible si hay la más mínima posibilidad **in all** en total **on all fours** a gatas ● adv 1 todo, completamente: ~ in white todo de blanco ◊ ~ alone completamente solo 2 muy: ~ excited muy emocionado **solo 2** muy: ~ excited muy emocionado (Dep): The score is two ~. Están empatados a dos. ▸ **all along** todo el tiempo **all but** casi: It was ~ but impossible. Era casi imposible. **all for sth** totalmente a favor de algo **all over 1** por todas partes **2** That's her ~ over. Eso es muy típico de ella. **all the better** tanto mejor **all too** demasiado

all-around adj **1** general **2** (persona) completo

allegation /ˌæləˈɡeɪʃn/ n acusación

allege /əˈledʒ/ vt (fml) alegar **alleged** /əˈledʒɪd/ adj (fml) presunto **allegedly** adv supuestamente

allegiance /əˈliːdʒəns/ n lealtad

allergy /ˈælədʒi/ n (pl -ies) alergia **allergic** /əˈlɜːrdʒɪk/ adj: be ~ to tener alergia a algo

alleviate /əˈliːvieɪt/ vt aliviar **alleviation** n alivio

alley /ˈæli/ n (tb **alleyway** /ˈæliweɪ/) callejón ▸ **(right) up your alley** (USA, coloq) ideal para ti

alliance /əˈlaɪəns/ n alianza

allied /ˈælaɪd, əˈlaɪd/ adj **1** relacionado **2** (Pol) aliado

alligator /ˈælɪɡeɪtər/ n caimán

allocate /ˈæləkeɪt/ vt asignar **allocation** n asignación

allot /əˈlɒt/ vt (-tt-) asignar **allotment** n **1** asignación **2** (GB) parcela

all-out adj total **all out** adv: go ~ no reparar en nada

allow /əˈlaʊ/ vt **1** ~ sth/sb to do sth permitir a algo/algn que haga algo: Dogs are not allowed. No se admiten perros. **NOTA** Allow se usa en inglés formal y coloquial. La forma pasiva **be allowed to** es muy común. Se usa **permit** (más fml) en lenguaje escrito, y **let** (coloq) en inglés hablado. **2** conceder **3** calcular **4** admitir ■ **allow for sth** tener algo en cuenta **allowable** adj permisible

allowance /əˈlaʊəns/ n **1** límite permitido **2** subvención ▸ **make allowances for sth/sb** tener algo en cuenta/ser indulgente con algn

alloy /ˈælɔɪ/ n aleación

all right adj, adv **1** bien: Are you getting on ~? Te está yendo bien? **2** (adecuado): The food was ~. La comida no estaba mal. **3** de acuerdo **4** That's him ~. Seguro que es él.

all-round (GB) = ALL-AROUND

all-time adj de todos los tiempos

ally /əˈlaɪ/ vt, vi (pt/pp **-ied**) ~ (yourself) with/to sth/sb aliarse con algn/algo ● /ˈælaɪ/ n (pl **-ies**) aliado/a

almond /ˈɑːmənd/ n **1** almendra **2** (tb ~ **tree**) almendro

almost /ˈɔːlmoʊst/ adv casi → NEARLY

alone /əˈloʊn/ adj solo: Are you ~? ¿Estás solita? **NOTA** Alone, palabra neutra, nunca va delante de un sustantivo; **lonely** sí puede ir delante de un sustantivo y tiene siempre connotaciones negativas: I want to be ~. Quiero estar solo. ◊ feel lonely sentirse solo ◊ a lonely house una casa solitaria. ▸ **leave/let sb/sth alone** dejar algo o a algn en paz **let alone** mucho menos: I can't afford new clothes, let ~ a vacation. No me puedo permitir ropa nueva, y mucho menos unas vacaciones. ● adv solo, sólo: You ~ can help me. Sólo tú me puedes ayudar.

along /əˈlɒŋ/ prep por, a lo largo de ● adv: I was driving ~. Iba manejando. ◊ Bring a friend ~. Tráete a un amigo. **NOTA** Es común usar **along** con verbos de movimiento en tiempos continuos cuando no se menciona ningún destino. Generalmente no se traduce en español. ▸ **along with** junto con

come along! ¡vamos!
NOTA Para el uso de *along* en PHRASAL VERBS ver el verbo, p.ej. **get along** en GET.

alongside /əˌlɒŋˈsaɪd; əˌlɒŋ- *GB*/ *prep, adv* al lado (de)

aloud /əˈlaʊd/ *adv* 1 en voz alta 2 a voces

alphabet /ˈælfəbet/ *n* alfabeto **alphabetical** /ˌælfəˈbetɪkl/ *adj* alfabético

already /ɔːlˈredi/ *adv* ya: *Why are you not going ~?* ¿Ya te vas? →YET

alright /ɔːlˈraɪt/ Ver ALL RIGHT

also /ˈɔːlsəʊ/ *adv* también, además →TAMBIÉN

altar /ˈɔːltər/ *n* altar

alter /ˈɔːltər/ 1 *vt, vi* cambiar 2 *vt* (*ropa*) arreglar **alteration** *n* 1 cambio 2 (*ropa*) arreglo

alternate /ˈɔːltɜːnət; ɔːlˈtɜːnət *GB*/ *adj* alterno ♦ /ˈɔːltɜːneɪt/ *vt, vi* alternar(se)

alternative /ɔːlˈtɜːnətɪv/ *n* alternativa: *She had no ~ but to...* No tuvo más remedio que... ● *adj* alternativo

although (*tb* altho *USA, coloq*) /ɔːlˈðəʊ/ *conj* aunque →AUNQUE

altitude /ˈæltɪtuːd; -tjuːd *GB*/ *n* altitud

altogether /ˌɔːltəˈɡeðər/ *adv* 1 completamente 2 en total 3 en general

aluminum /əˈluːmɪnəm/ (aluminium /ˌæljəˈmɪniəm/ *GB*) *n* aluminio

always /ˈɔːlweɪz/ *adv* siempre
NOTA La posición de los adverbios de frecuencia **always**, **never**, **usually**, etc. depende del verbo que acompañan. Van detrás de los verbos auxiliares y modales y delante de los demás verbos: *I'm ~ tired.* ◊ *I've never visited her.* ◊ *I usually go shopping on Mondays.*

am /əm, æm/ Ver BE

a.m. /ˌeɪ ˈem/ *abrev* de la mañana →P.M.

amalgam /əˈmælɡəm/ *n* amalgama **amalgamate** *vt, vi* fusionar(se)

amateur /ˈæmətər/ *adj, n* 1 aficionado/a 2 (*pey*) chapucero/a

amaze /əˈmeɪz/ *vt* asombrar **amazement** *n* asombro **amazing** *adj* asombroso

ambassador /æmˈbæsədər/ *n* embajador/a

amber /ˈæmbər/ *n, adj* ámbar

ambiguous /æmˈbɪɡjuəs/ *adj* ambiguo **ambiguity** /ˌæmbɪˈɡjuːəti/ *n* (*pl* -ies) ambigüedad

ambitious /æmˈbɪʃəs/ *adj* ambicioso **ambition** *n* ambición

ambulance /ˈæmbjələns/ *n* ambulancia

ambush /ˈæmbʊʃ/ *n* emboscada

amen /ɑːˈmen, eɪˈmen/ *interj, n* amén

amend /əˈmend/ *vt* enmendar **amendment** *n* enmienda

amends /əˈmendz/ *n* [*pl*] ▶ **make amends** (**for sth**) compensar (por algo)

amenities /əˈmenətiz; əˈmiːn- *GB*/ *n* [*pl*] 1 comodidades 2 instalaciones (*públicas*)

amiable /ˈeɪmiəbl/ *adj* amable

amicable /ˈæmɪkəbl/ *adj* amistoso

amid /əˈmɪd/ (*tb* amidst /əˈmɪdst/) *prep* (*fml*) entre, en medio de

ammunition /ˌæmjuˈnɪʃn/ *n* [*U*] 1 municiones: *live* ~ fuego real 2 argumentos (*para discutir*)

amnesty /ˈæmnəsti/ *n* (*pl* -ies) amnistía

among /əˈmʌŋ/ (*tb* amongst /əˈmʌŋst/) *prep* entre (*más de dos personas o cosas*): *I was ~ the last to leave.* Fui de los últimos en irse.

amount /əˈmaʊnt/ *n* 1 cantidad: *any ~ of money* todo el dinero que quiera 2 (*factura*) importe 3 (*dinero*) suma ■ **amount to sth** 1 ascender a algo: *The information doesn't ~ to much.* No hay muchos datos. ◊ *He'll never ~ to much.* Nunca llegará a nada. 2 equivaler a algo

amphibian /æmˈfɪbiən/ *n* anfibio

amphitheater (-theatre *GB*) /ˈæmfɪθiətər/ *n* anfiteatro

ample /ˈæmpl/ *adj* 1 abundante 2 bastante 3 (*extenso*) amplio **amply** *adv* ampliamente

amplify /ˈæmplɪfaɪ/ *vt* (*pt/pp* -ied) 1 amplificar 2 ampliar **amplifier** *n* amplificador

amuse /əˈmjuːz/ *vt* 1 hacer gracia 2 distraer, divertir **amusement** *n* 1 diversión 2 atracción: ~ *arcade/park* salón de juegos/parque de atracciones **amusing** *adj* divertido, gracioso

an Ver A

anaemia (*GB*) = ANEMIA

anaesthetic (*GB*) = ANESTHETIC

analogy /əˈnælədʒi/ *n* (*pl* -ies) analogía

analysis /əˈnæləsɪs/ *n* (*pl* -lyses /-ləsiːz/) 1 análisis 2 psicoanálisis ▶ **in the last/final analysis** a fin de cuentas **analytical** /ˌænəˈlɪtɪkl/ *adj* analítico **analyst**

/'ænəlɪst/ n 1 analista 2 psicoanalista

analyze (**analyse** GB) /'ænəlaɪz/ vt analizar

anarchism /'ænərkɪzəm/ n anarquismo **anarchist** adj, n anarquista

anarchy /'ænərki/ n anarquía **anarchic** /ə'nɑːrkɪk/ adj anárquico

anatomy /ə'nætəmi/ n (pl -ies) anatomía

ancestor /'ænsestər/ n antepasado/a **ancestral** /æn'sestrəl/ adj ancestral **ancestry** /'ænsestri/ n (pl -ies) ascendencia

anchor /'æŋkər/ n 1 ancla: at ~ anclado 2 (fig) soporte ● vt, vi anclar

anchovy /'æntʃoʊvi; -tʃəvi GB/ n (pl -ies) anchoa

ancient /'eɪnʃənt/ adj 1 antiguo 2 (coloq) viejísimo

and /ænd, ənd/ conj 1 y: bread ~ butter pan con mantequilla ◊ one hundred ~ two ciento dos 2 come, go, stay, etc. and: Come ~ help me. Ven a ayudarme. ◊ Try ~ finish soon. Intenta acabar pronto. 3 (repetición): They shouted ~ shouted. Gritaron sin parar. ◊ I've tried ~ tried. Lo he intentado muchísimas veces.

anecdote /'ænɪkdoʊt/ n anécdota

anemia /ə'niːmiə/ n anemia **anemic** adj anémico

anesthetic /ˌænəs'θetɪk/ n anestesia: give sb an ~ anestesiar a algn

angel /'eɪndʒl/ n ángel

anger /'æŋgər/ n ira ● vt enojar

angle /'æŋgl/ n ángulo ▶ at an angle inclinado

angling /'æŋglɪŋ/ n pesca (con caña)

angry /'æŋgri/ adj (-ier/-iest) 1 ~ (at/about sth) enojado (por algo): make sb/get ~ enojar a algn/enojarse 2 (cielo) tormentoso **angrily** adv con ira

anguish /'æŋgwɪʃ/ n angustia **anguished** adj angustiado

angular /'æŋgjələr/ adj 1 angular 2 (complexión) huesudo

animal /'ænɪml/ n animal

animate /'ænɪmət/ adj animado (vivo) ● /'ænɪmeɪt/ vt animar

ankle /'æŋkl/ n tobillo

anniversary /ˌænɪ'vɜːrsəri/ n (pl -ies) aniversario

announce /ə'naʊns/ vt anunciar (hacer público) **announcement** n anuncio, comunicado: make an ~ comunicar algo **announcer** n

1 locutor/a (TV, etc.) 2 (USA) presentador/a

annoy /ə'nɔɪ/ vt molestar **annoyance** n fastidio **annoyed** adj enojado: get ~ enojarse **annoying** adj molesto

annual /'ænjuəl/ adj anual

anonymous /ə'nɑnɪməs/ adj anónimo **anonymity** /ˌænə'nɪməti/ n anonimato

anorak /'ænəræk/ n (GB) abrigo

anorexia /ˌænə'reksiə/ n anorexia **anorexic** adj, n anoréxico/a

another /ə'nʌðər/ adj, pron otro/a: ~ five cinco más ~ otro **NOTA** El plural del pron another es others.

answer /'ænsər/ /'ɑːn- GB/ n 1 respuesta: in ~ to sth en respuesta a algo ◊ There was no ~. No contestaban. 2 solución 3 (Mat) resultado ▶ have/know all the answers saberlo todo ● 1 vt, vi contestar: ~ the door abrir la puerta 2 vt responder a 3 vt (ruegos) oír ■ **answer back** contestar (con insolencia) **answer for sth/sb** responder de algo/por algn **answer to sb (for sth)** responder ante algn (de algo) **answer to sth** responder a algo (descripción)

answering machine (tb answerphone GB /'ænsərfoʊn; 'ɑːn- GB/) n contestador (automático)

ant /ænt/ n hormiga

antagonism /æn'tægənɪzəm/ n antagonismo **antagonistic** /ænˌtægə'nɪstɪk/ adj hostil

anteater /'æntiːtər/ n oso hormiguero

antenna /æn'tenə/ n 1 (pl -nae /-niː/) (insecto) antena 2 (pl -s) (USA, TV, etc.) antena

anthem /'ænθəm/ n himno

anthology /æn'θɑlədʒi/ n (pl -ies) antología

anthropology /ˌænθrə'pɑlədʒi/ n antropología **anthropological** /ˌænθrəpə'lɑdʒɪkl/ adj antropológico **anthropologist** /ˌænθrə'pɑlədʒɪst/ n antropólogo/a

antibiotic /ˌæntibaɪ'ɑtɪk/ adj, n antibiótico

antibody /'æntibɑdi/ n (pl -ies) anticuerpo

anticipate /æn'tɪsɪpeɪt/ vt 1 prever: as anticipated de acuerdo con lo previsto 2 anticiparse a **anticipation** n 1 previsión 2 expectación

antics /'æntɪks/ n [pl] payasadas

antidote /'æntidoʊt/ n ~ (for/to sth) antídoto (contra algo)

antiquated /'æntɪkweɪtɪd/ adj anticuado

antique /ænˈtiːk/ n antigüedad (objeto) ● adj antiguo (y valioso)
antiquity /ænˈtɪkwəti/ n (pl -ies) antigüedad
antithesis /ænˈtɪθəsɪs/ n (pl -theses /-θəsiːz/) antítesis
antlers /ˈæntlərz/ n [pl] cornamenta
anus /ˈeɪnəs/ n ano
anxiety /æŋˈzaɪəti/ n (pl -ies) 1 preocupación 2 ansiedad 3 ~ for sth/to do sth ansia de algo
anxious /ˈæŋkʃəs/ adj 1 preocupado (por algo): an ~ moment un momento de inquietud 2 ~ to do sth ansioso por hacer algo **anxiously** adv con ansia
any /ˈeni/ adv [+ comparativo] más: She doesn't work here ~ longer. Ya no trabaja acá. ● adj, pron →SOME
● frases interrogativas 1 Do you have ~ cash? ¿Tienes dinero? 2 algo (de): Do you know ~ Greek? ¿Sabes algo de griego? 3 algún: Are there ~ problems? ¿Hay algún problema? **NOTA** En este sentido el sustantivo suele ir en plural en inglés.
● frases negativas: He doesn't have ~ friends. No tiene amigos. ◊ There isn't ~ left. No queda nada. ◊ We won't do you ~ harm. No le vamos a hacer ningún daño. →NINGUNO
● frases condicionales 1 If I had ~ relatives... Si tuviera parientes... 2 algo (de): If he has ~ sense, he won't go. Si tiene un mínimo de sentido común, no irá. 3 algún **NOTA** En este sentido el sustantivo suele ir en plural en inglés. En muchos casos se puede usar some en vez de any: If you need some/any help, tell me.
● frases afirmativas 1 cualquier (a): Take ~ one you like. Toma el que quieras. 2 todo: Give her ~ help she needs. Préstale toda la ayuda que necesite.
anybody /ˈenibɑdi/ pron 1 (frases interrogativas) alguien: Is ~ there? ¿Hay alguien? 2 (frases negativas/comparativas) nadie: I can't see ~. No veo a nadie. ◊ He spoke more than ~. Habló más que nadie. →NOBODY **3** (frases afirmativas) cualquier(a): Anybody else would have refused. Cualquier otro se habría negado. ◊ Invite ~ you like. Invita a quien quieras. →EVERYBODY, SOMEBODY
anyhow /ˈenihaʊ/ adv 1 (tb any old how GB, coloq) de cualquier manera 2 de todas formas

anymore /eniˈmɔːr/ (any more GB) adv: She doesn't live here ~. Ya no vive acá.
anyone /ˈeniwʌn/ Ver ANYBODY
anyplace /ˈenipleɪs/ (USA) Ver ANYWHERE
anything /ˈeniθɪŋ/ pron 1 algo: Is ~ wrong? ¿Pasa algo? 2 (frases afirmativas) cualquier cosa, todo: We'll do ~ you say. Haremos lo que nos digas. 3 (frases negativas y comparativas) nada: He never says ~. Nunca dice nada. →NOBODY, SOMETHING ▸ anything but: It was ~ but pleasant. Fue de todo menos agradable. ◊ "Are you tired?" "Anything but." —¿Estás cansado? —Para nada! **as... as anything** (coloq) muy: I was as ~ frightened as ~. Estaba muerto de miedo. **if anything** más bien, en todo caso
anyway /ˈeniweɪ/ adv de todas formas
anywhere /ˈeniweər/ adv, pron 1 en/a alguna parte 2 (frases afirmativas): I'd live ~. Viviría en cualquier lugar. ◊ ~ you like donde quieras 3 (frases negativas/comparativas) en/a por ninguna parte: more beautiful than ~ más bonito que ningún otro lugar ◊ I don't have ~ to stay. No tengo donde alojarme. →NOBODY, SOMEWHERE
apart /əˈpɑːrt/ adv 1 They're ten meters ~. Están a diez metros uno del otro. 2 They are a long way ~. Están muy lejos el uno del otro. 2 aislado 3 separado: They live ~. Viven separados. ◊ I can't pull them ~. No puedo separarlos. ▸ **take sth apart** 1 desmontar algo 2 hacer pedazos algo
apart from prep aparte de
apartment /əˈpɑːrtmənt/ n apartamento, departamento
apathy /ˈæpəθi/ n apatía **apathetic** /ˌæpəˈθetɪk/ adj apático
ape /eɪp/ n simio ● vt remedar
apologetic /əˌpɑləˈdʒetɪk/ adj de disculpa: an ~ look una mirada de disculpa ◊ be ~ about sth disculparse por algo
apologize /əˈpɑlədʒaɪz/ vi disculparse
apology /əˈpɑlədʒi/ n (pl -ies) disculpa: make an ~ disculparse
apostle /əˈpɑsl/ n apóstol
apostrophe /əˈpɑstrəfi/ n apóstrofo
appall (appal GB) /əˈpɔːl/ vt (-ll-) horrorizar **appalling** adj espantoso, horrible

apparatus /ˌæpəˈrætəs; -ˈreɪtəs *GB*/ *n* [U] aparato (*de gimnasio, laboratorio*)

apparent /əˈpærənt/ *adj* 1 evidente 2 aparente **apparently** *adv* al parecer: *Apparently not.* Parece que no.

appeal /əˈpiːl/ *vi* 1 ~ (**to sb**) **for sth** pedir algo (a algn) 2 ~ **to sb to do sth** hacer un llamado a algn para que haga algo 3 apelar 4 ~ (**to sb**) atraer (a algn) 5 ~ (**against sth**) (*Jur*) recurrir (algo) ● *n* 1 llamado: *an ~ for help* un llamado pidiendo ayuda 2 súplica 3 atractivo 4 (*Jur*) recurso: *~s court* tribunal de apelación **appealing** *adj* 1 atractivo 2 suplicante

appear /əˈpɪər/ *vi* 1 aparecer: ~ *on TV* salir en televisión 2 parecer: *You've made a mistake.* Parece que cometiste un error. 3 (*Jur*) comparecer **appearance** *n* 1 apariencia: *keep up ~s* mantener las apariencias 2 aparición

appendicitis /əˌpendəˈsaɪtɪs/ *n* apendicitis

appendix /əˈpendɪks/ *n* (*pl* **-dices** /-dɪsiːz/) apéndice (*Anat, libro*)

appetite /ˈæpɪtaɪt/ *n* 1 apetito: *give sb an ~* abrir el apetito a algn 2 apetencia **appetizer** *n* antojito (*Mx*), pasabocas (*And*)

applaud /əˈplɔːd/ *vt, vi* aplaudir **applause** *n* [U] aplausos: *a big round of ~* un fuerte aplauso

apple /ˈæpl/ *n* 1 manzana 2 (*tb ~ tree*) manzano

appliance /əˈplaɪəns/ *n* aparato: *electrical/kitchen ~s* electrodomésticos

applicable /ˈæplɪkəbl, əˈplɪkəbl/ *adj* aplicable

applicant /ˈæplɪkənt/ *n* solicitante, aspirante

application /ˌæplɪˈkeɪʃn/ *n* 1 solicitud 2 (*Comp*) aplicación

apply /əˈplaɪ/ (*pt/pp* **-ied**) 1 *vt* aplicar 2 *vt* (*fuerza, etc.*) ejercer: ~ *the brakes* frenar 3 *vi* ~ (**to sb**) (**for sth**) hacer una solicitud, solicitar algo (a algn) 4 *vi* ~ **to sth/sb**) ser aplicable (a algo/algn): *This applies to men too.* Esto se aplica a los hombres también. 5 *vt* ~ **yourself** (**to sth**) aplicarse (a algo) **applied** *adj* aplicado

appoint /əˈpɔɪnt/ *vt* nombrar **appointment** *n* 1 (*acto*) nombramiento 2 puesto 3 cita (*profesional*)

appraisal /əˈpreɪzl/ *n* evaluación

appreciate /əˈpriːʃieɪt/ 1 *vt* apreciar 2 *vt* agradecer 3 *vt* comprender 4 *vi* revalorizarse **appreciation** *n* 1 apreciación

2 agradecimiento 3 valoración **appreciative** *adj* 1 ~ (**of sth**) agradecido (por algo) 2 (*mirada, etc.*) de admiración

apprehend /ˌæprɪˈhend/ *vt* detener **apprehension** *n* aprensión **apprehensive** *adj* aprensivo

apprentice /əˈprentɪs/ *n* 1 aprendiz/a 2 principiante **apprenticeship** *n* aprendizaje (*oficio*)

approach /əˈprəʊtʃ/ 1 *vt, vi* acercarse (a) 2 *vt* (*para ayuda*) acudir a 3 *vt* abordar ● *n* 1 llegada 2 aproximación 3 acceso 4 enfoque

appropriate /əˈprəʊpriət/ *adj* 1 apropiado, adecuado 2 oportuno ● /əˈprəʊprieɪt/ *vt* apropiarse de

approve /əˈpruːv/ 1 *vt* aprobar 2 *vi* ~ (**of sth**) estar de acuerdo (con algo) 3 *vi* ~ (**of sb**): *I don't ~ of him.* No tengo un buen concepto de él. **approval** *n* aprobación, visto bueno ▸ **on approval** a prueba **approving** *adj* de aprobación

approximate /əˈprɒksɪmət/ *adj* aproximado ● /əˈprɒksɪmeɪt/ *vt, vi* aproximarse (a) **approximately** *adv* aproximadamente

apricot /ˈeɪprɪkɒt/ *n* 1 albaricoque, chabacano (*Mx*) 2 (*tb ~ tree*) albaricoquero, chabacano (*Mx*)

April /ˈeɪprəl/ *n* (*abrev* Apr.) abril →JUNE

April Fool's Day *n* 1 de abril (*equivale al día de los inocentes*)

apron /ˈeɪprən/ *n* delantal

apt /æpt/ *adj* 1 acertado 2 **be ~ to do sth** tener tendencia a hacer algo

aptitude /ˈæptɪtuːd; -tjuːd *GB*/ *n* aptitud

aquarium /əˈkweəriəm/ *n* acuario

Aquarius /əˈkweəriəs/ *n* Acuario

aquatic /əˈkwætɪk/ *adj* acuático

arable /ˈærəbl/ *adj* cultivable: ~ *land* tierra de cultivo

arbitrary /ˈɑːbɪtreri; -trəri *GB*/ *adj* 1 arbitrario 2 indiscriminado

arbitrate /ˈɑːbɪtreɪt/ *vt, vi* arbitrar **arbitration** *n* arbitraje

arc /ɑːk/ *n* (*Geom*) arco

arcade /ɑːˈkeɪd/ *n* 1 galería: *amusement ~* sala de juegos 2 [*sing*] portales

arch /ɑːtʃ/ *n* arco (*arquitectónico*) ● *vt, vi* arquear(se)

archaic /ɑːˈkeɪɪk/ *adj* arcaico

archbishop /ˌɑːtʃˈbɪʃəp/ *n* arzobispo

A

archeology (archae- *GB*) /ˌɑːkɪ-'ɒlədʒɪ/ n arqueología **archeological** /ˌɑːkɪə'lɒdʒɪkl/ adj arqueológico **archeologist** /ˌɑːkɪ'ɒlədʒɪst/ n arqueólogo/a

archery /'ɑːtʃərɪ/ n tiro con arco **archer** n arquero/a

architect /'ɑːkɪtekt/ n arquitecto/a

architecture /'ɑːkɪtektʃər/ n arquitectura **architectural** /ˌɑːkɪ-'tektʃərəl/ adj arquitectónico

archive /'ɑːkaɪv/ n archivo

archway /'ɑːtʃweɪ/ n arco (*arquitectónico*)

ardent /'ɑːdnt/ adj ferviente, entusiasta

ardor (-our *GB*) /'ɑːdər/ n fervor

arduous /'ɑːdʒʊəs/ adj arduo

are /ər, ɑːr/ *Ver* BE

area /'eərɪə/ n 1 superficie 2 área 3 (*Geog*) zona, región: ~ manager director regional 4 (*de uso específico*) recinto

area code n (*teléfono*) prefijo

arena /ə'riːnə/ n 1 estadio 2 (*circo*) pista 3 (*plaza de toros*) ruedo 4 (*fig*) ámbito

aren't /ɑːnt/ = ARE NOT

arguable /'ɑːgjuəbl/ adj 1 *It is ~ that...* Podría decirse que... 2 discutible **arguably** adv probablemente

argue /'ɑːgjuː/ 1 vi discutir 2 vt, ~ (for/against sth) argumentar (a favor de/en contra de algo)

argument /'ɑːgjumənt/ n 1 discusión: *have an ~* discutir 2 ~ (for/against sth) argumento (a favor de/en contra de algo)

arid /'ærɪd/ adj árido

Aries /'eəriːz/ n Aries

arise /ə'raɪz/ vi (pt **arose** /ə'rəʊz/ pp **arisen** /ə'rɪzn/) 1 (*problema, etc.*) surgir: *should the need* ~ si fuera preciso 2 (*oportunidad*) presentarse 3 (*tormenta*) levantarse 4 (*cuestión, etc.*) plantearse

aristocrat /ə'rɪstəkræt; 'ærɪst-*GB*/ n aristócrata **aristocracy** /ˌærɪ'stɒkrəsɪ/ n (pl -ies) aristocracia **aristocratic** /ˌærɪstə-'krætɪk; ər-*GB*/ adj aristocrático

arithmetic /ə'rɪθmətɪk/ n aritmética: *mental* ~ cálculo mental

ark /ɑːk/ n arca

arm /ɑːm/ n 1 brazo: ~ *in* ~ *with sb* del brazo de algn 2 manga ● vt, vi armar(se)

armament /'ɑːməmənt/ n armamento

armchair /ˌɑːm'tʃeər/ n sillón

armed /ɑːmd/ adj armado: ~ *forces* fuerzas armadas ◊ ~ *robbery* asalto a mano armada

armistice /'ɑːmɪstɪs/ n armisticio

armor (-our *GB*) /'ɑːmər/ n [U] 1 armadura: *a suit of* ~ una armadura 2 blindaje **armored** adj 1 blindado 2 acorazado

armpit /'ɑːmpɪt/ n axila

arms /ɑːmz/ n [pl] 1 armas: ~ *race* carrera armamentista 2 escudo (*de armas*) ▶ **be up in arms (about/over sth)** poner el grito en el cielo (por algo)

army /'ɑːmɪ/ n (pl -ies) ejército

aroma /ə'rəʊmə/ n aroma **aromatic** /ˌærə'mætɪk/ adj aromático

aromatherapy /əˌrəʊmə-'θerəpɪ/ n aromaterapia

arose /ə'rəʊz/ pt de ARISE

around /ə'raʊnd/ adv 1 más o menos 2 hacia: ~ *1850* hacia 1850 **NOTA** En expresiones temporales, **about** suele ir precedido por las preposiciones *at, on, in*, etc., pero **around** no requiere preposición: *around/at about one o'clock* ◊ *around/on about 9 May.* 3 por aquí 4 de aquí para allá: *I've been dashing ~ all day.* Llevo todo el día de aquí para allá. 5 a su alrededor **NOTA** Para el uso de **around** en PHRASAL VERBS *ver* el verbo, p.ej. **lie around** en LIE. ● prep 1 por: *travel ~ the world* viajar por todo el mundo ◊ *show sb ~ the house* enseñarle a algn la casa 2 alrededor de 3 a la vuelta de: *just ~ the corner* a la vuelta de la esquina

arouse /ə'raʊz/ vt 1 suscitar 2 excitar (*sexualmente*) 3 despertar

arrange /ə'reɪndʒ/ 1 vt disponer 2 vt ordenar 3 vt organizar 4 vi ~ *for sb to do sth* asegurarse de que algn haga algo 5 vi ~ **to do sth/that...** quedar en hacer algo/en que... 6 vt (*Mús*) arreglar **arrangement** n 1 disposición 2 arreglo 3 acuerdo 4 **arrangements** preparativos

arrest /ə'rest/ vt 1 detener 2 (*fml*) (*inflación, etc.*) contener 3 (*fml*) (*atención*) atraer ● n 1 detención: *be under* ~ estar detenido 2 *cardiac* ~ paro cardíaco

arrive /ə'raɪv/ vi 1 llegar **NOTA** Se usa **arrive in** cuando se llega a un país o a una ciudad: *When did you ~ in Oxford?* **Arrive at** se usa con lugares específicos como un edificio, una estación, etc.: *I'll call as soon as I ~ at the airport.* "Llegar a la casa" se dice *arrive home.* 2

(coloq) (éxito) llegar a la cima

arrival /ə'raɪvl/ n **1** llegada **2** new/recent ~s recién llegados

arrogant /'ærəgənt/ adj arrogante **arrogance** n arrogancia

arrow /'ærəʊ/ n flecha

arson /'ɑːsn/ n [U] incendio provocado

art /ɑːt/ n **1** arte: a work of ~ una obra de arte **2** the arts cultura, las Bellas Artes: ~s centre centro cultural **3** arts (asignatura) letras **4** maña

artery /'ɑːtəri/ n (pl -ies) arteria

arthritis /ɑː'θraɪtɪs/ n artritis **arthritic** /ɑː'θrɪtɪk/ adj, n artrítico/a

artichoke /'ɑːtɪtʃəʊk/ n alcachofa

article /'ɑːtɪkl/ n **1** artículo **2** ~s of clothing prendas de vestir

articulate /ɑː'tɪkjələt/ adj capaz de expresarse con claridad ● /ɑː'tɪkjuleɪt/ vt, vi articular

artificial /ˌɑːtɪ'fɪʃl/ adj artificial

artillery /ɑː'tɪləri/ n artillería

artisan /ˈɑːtɪzæn/ n artesano/a

artist /'ɑːtɪst/ n artista **artistic** /ɑː'tɪstɪk/ adj artístico/a

artwork /'ɑːtwɜːk/ n **1** material gráfico (en libro, etc.) **2** obra de arte

as /əz, æz/ prep **1** como: Treat me as a friend. Trátame como a un amigo. **2** (en función de) de: work as a doctor trabajar de médico ◊ as a child de pequeño **NOTA** En comparaciones y ejemplos se usa like: a car like yours ◊ Romantic poets like Byron. ● adv as... as tan... como: as soon as possible lo antes posible ◊ I earn as much as her/as she does. Gano tanto como ella. ● conj **1** mientras **2** como: as you weren't there... como no estabas... **3** tal como **as well** así en cuanto a algo/algn **as from/of**: as of 1 May a partir del 1 de mayo **as if/though** como si **as it is** tal como está la situación **as many 1** tantos: I didn't win as many as him. No gané tantos como él. ◊ You ate three times as many as I did. Comiste tres veces más que yo. **2** six jobs in as many months seis trabajos en otros tantos meses **as many as** hasta: as many as ten people hasta diez personas **as much 1** tanto: I don't have as much as you. No tengo tanto como tú. **2** I thought as much. Eso pensé. **as much/many again** otro(s) tanto(s) **as to sth/as regards sth** en cuanto a algo **as yet** hasta ahora

asbestos /æs'bestəs/ n asbesto

ascend /ə'send/ n **1** vi ascender **2** vt subir ▶

ascendancy /ə'sendənsi/ n ascendiente

ascent /ə'sent/ n ascenso

ascertain /ˌæsər'teɪn/ vt (fml) averiguar

ascribe /ə'skraɪb/ vt atribuir

ash /æʃ/ n **1** ceniza (tb ~ tree) fresno

ashamed /ə'ʃeɪmd/ adj avergonzado: be ~ to do sth darle vergüenza a uno hacer algo

ashore /ə'ʃɔːr/ adv en/a tierra: go ~ desembarcar

ashtray /'æʃtreɪ/ n cenicero

Ash Wednesday n miércoles de Ceniza

aside /ə'saɪd/ adv **1** a un lado **2** en reserva ● n aparte (Teat)

aside from prep aparte de

ask /æsk, ɑːsk GB/ vt **1** vi ~ (sb) (sth) preguntar (algo) (a algn): ~ a question hacer una pregunta **2** vt, vi ~ (sb) for sth; ~ sb to do sth pedir algo (a algn): pedir a algn que haga algo **3** vt ~ sb (to sth) invitar a algn (a algo): ~ sb around invitar a algn (a tu casa) ▶ **be asking for trouble/it** (coloq) buscársela **don't ask me!** (coloq) ¡yo qué sé! **for the asking** con sólo pedirlo ■ **ask after sb** preguntar cómo está algn **ask for sb** preguntar por algn (para verlo) **ask sb out** pedirle a algn que salga con uno (como pareja)

asleep /ə'sliːp/ adj dormido: fall ~ dormirse **~ fast/sound** profundamente dormido **NOTA** Asleep no se usa antes de un sustantivo. "Un niño dormido" se dice a sleeping baby.

asparagus /ə'spærəgəs/ n [U] espárrago(s)

aspect /'æspekt/ n **1** aspecto **2** (edificio, etc.) orientación

asphalt /'æsfɔːlt; -fælt GB/ n asfalto, chapapote (Mx)

asphyxiate /əs'fɪksieɪt/ vt asfixiar

aspire /ə'spaɪər/ vi aspirar: aspiring musicians aspirantes a músicos **aspiration** /ˌæspə'reɪʃn/ n aspiración

aspirin /'æsprɪn/ n aspirina

ass /æs/ n **1** asno **2** (idiota) burro

assailant /ə'seɪlənt/ n (fml) agresor/a

assassin /ə'sæsn/ -sɪn GB/ n asesino/a **assassinate** vt asesinar **assassination** n asesinato
→ ASESINATO

assault /əˈsɔːlt/ vt agredir ● n
1 agresión 2 ~ (on sth/sb) ataque
(contra algo/algn)

assemble /əˈsembl/ 1 vt, vi reu-
nir(se) 2 vt (Mec) montar

assembly /əˈsembli/ n (pl -ies)
1 asamblea 2 (colegio) reunión
matinal 3 montaje: ~ line línea de
montaje

assert /əˈsɜːt/ vt 1 afirmar (derechos, etc.) hacer valer 3 ~ yourself imponerse **assertion** n
afirmación **assertive** adj firme,
que se hace valer

assess /əˈses/ vt 1 valorar 2 calcular **assessment** n 1 valoración
2 análisis **assessor** n tasador/a

asset /ˈæset/ n 1 ventaja, baza: to
be an ~ to sth/sb ser muy valioso
para algo/algn 2 **assets** (Com)
bienes

assign /əˈsaɪn/ vt asignar

assignment /əˈsaɪnmənt/ n 1 (colegio) trabajo 2 misión

assimilate /əˈsɪməleɪt/ 1 vt, vi
asimilar(se)

assist /əˈsɪst/ vt, vi ayudar **assistance** n (fml) 1 ayuda 2 auxilio

assistant /əˈsɪstənt/ n 1 ayudante
2 (GB) (tb shop ~) dependiente/a
3 ~ manager subdirector/a

associate /əˈsəʊʃieɪt/ vt 1 relacionar 2 vi ~ with sb tratar con
algn ● adj /əˈsəʊʃiət/ n socio/a

association /əˌsəʊsiˈeɪʃn/ n
1 asociación 2 implicación

assorted /əˈsɔːtɪd/ adj 1 variado
2 (galletas, etc.) surtido

assortment /əˈsɔːtmənt/ n variedad, surtido

assume /əˈsjuːm; əˈsuːm GB/ vt
1 suponer 2 dar por hecho 3 (expresión, etc.) adoptar 4 (significado) adquirir 5 (control) asumir

assumption /əˈsʌmpʃn/ n
1 supuesto 2 (poder) toma

assurance /əˈʃʊərəns/ n 1 garantía 2 confianza

assure /əˈʃʊər/ vt 1 ~ sb (of sth)
asegurar (algo) a algn 2 ~ sb of
sth convencer a algn de algo
3 ~ yourself that... cerciorarse
de que... **assured** adj seguro: to
be ~ of sth tener asegurado algo

asterisk /ˈæstərɪsk/ n asterisco

asthma /ˈæsmə; ˈæsmə GB/ n
asma **asthmatic** /æzˈmætɪk; æs-
ˈm- GB/ adj, n asmático/a

astonish /əˈstɒnɪʃ/ vt asombrar
astonishing adj asombroso **as-
tonishment** n asombro

astound /əˈstaʊnd/ vt dejar atónito: We were astounded to see
him. Nos quedamos atónitos al
verlo. **astounding** adj increíble

astray /əˈstreɪ/ adv ▶ **lead sb/go
astray** descarriar a algn/descar-
riarse

astride /əˈstraɪd/ adv, prep a hor-
cajadas (en)

astrology /əˈstrɒlədʒi/ n astrología

astronaut /ˈæstrənɔːt/ n astronauta

astronomy /əˈstrɒnəmi/ n astronomía **astronomer** n astróno-
mo/a **astronomical** /ˌæstrə-
ˈnɒmɪkl/ adj astronómico

astute /əˈstjuːt; əˈstuːt GB/ adj
astuto

asylum /əˈsaɪləm/ n 1 asilo:
~ seekers personas que buscan
asilo político 2 manicomio

at /æt, ət/ prep 1 (posición) en: at
home en la casa ◇ at the top en lo
alto →EN 2 (tiempo): at 3.35 a las
3.35 ◇ at times a veces ◇ at night
por la noche ◇ at Christmas en
(la) Navidad ◇ at the moment of
momento 3 (precio, frecuencia,
velocidad): a: at full volume a todo
volumen ◇ two at a time de dos
en dos 4 (hacia): stare at sb mirar
fijamente a algn 5 (reacción):
surprised at sth sorprendido
por algo ◇ At this, she fainted.
Y entonces, se desmayó. 6 (actividad) en: She's at work. Está en
el trabajo. ◇ children at play
niños jugando

ate /eɪt; et GB/ pt de EAT

atheism /ˈeɪθiɪzəm/ n ateísmo
atheist n ateo/a

athlete /ˈæθliːt/ n atleta

athletic /æθˈletɪk/ adj atlético
athletics n [sing] atletismo

atlas /ˈætləs/ n 1 atlas 2 mapa de
carreteras

ATM /ˌeɪ tiː ˈem/ n cajero automático

atmosphere /ˈætməsfɪər/ n 1 atmósfera 2 ambiente

atom /ˈætəm/ n 1 átomo 2 (fig)
ápice

atomic /əˈtɒmɪk/ adj atómico

atrocious /əˈtrəʊʃəs/ adj 1 atroz
2 pésimo **atrocity** /əˈtrɒsəti/ n (pl
-ies) atrocidad

attach /əˈtætʃ/ vt 1 atar 2 unir
3 (documentos) adjuntar 4 ~ importance to sth dar importancia a
algo **attached** adj: be ~ to sb
tenerle cariño a algn **attachment**
n 1 accesorio 2 apego 3 (Comp)
(archivo) adjunto

attack /əˈtæk/ n ~ (on sth/sb)
ataque (contra algo/algn) ● vt,
vi atacar **attacker** n agresor/a

attain /əˈteɪn/ vt alcanzar **attain-
ment** n logro

attempt /əˈtempt/ vt intentar ● n **1** ~ (at doing/to do sth) intento (de hacer algo) **2** atentado **attempted** adj: ~ robbery/murder intento de robo/asesinato frustrado

attend /əˈtend/ vt **1** vt, vi asistir (a) **2** vi ~ **to sth/sb** ocuparse de algo/algn **attendance** n asistencia: in ~ presente

attendant /əˈtendənt/ n encargado/a

attention /əˈtenʃn/ n atención: pay ~ prestar atención ● interj (Mil) firmes **attentive** adj atento

attic /ˈætɪk/ n desván

attitude /ˈætɪtuːd; -tjuːd GB/ n actitud

attorney /əˈtɜːrni/ n **1** (USA) abogado/a → ABOGADO **2** apoderado/a

Attorney-General n **1** asesor legal del gobierno **2** procurador/a general (en EE.UU.)

attract /əˈtrækt/ vt **1** atraer **2** (atención) llamar **attraction** n **1** atracción **2** atractivo **attractive** adj atractivo

attribute /ˈætrɪbjuːt/ n atributo ● /əˈtrɪbjuːt/ vt atribuir

aubergine /ˈoʊbərʒiːn/ n (GB) berenjena ● adj (color) morado

auction /ˈɔːkʃn/ n subasta ● vt subastar **auctioneer** /ˌɔːkʃəˈnɪər/ n subastador/a

audible /ˈɔːdəbl/ adj audible

audience /ˈɔːdiəns/ n **1** (espectáculo) público **2** audiencia

audit /ˈɔːdɪt/ n auditoría ● vt auditar

audition /ɔːˈdɪʃn/ n audición ● vi presentarse a una audición

auditor /ˈɔːdɪtər/ n auditor/a

auditorium /ˌɔːdɪˈtɔːriəm/ n auditorio

August /ˈɔːɡəst/ n (abrev Aug.) agosto →JUNE

aunt /ænt; ɑːnt GB/ (coloq **auntie, aunty**) n tía: my ~ and uncle mis tíos

au pair /ˌoʊ ˈpeər/ n (GB) estudiante extranjero que ayuda en las tareas domésticas y/o hace de niñero a cambio de hospedaje y pequeño sueldo

austere /ɔːˈstɪr/ adj austero **austerity** /ɔːˈsterəti/ n austeridad

authentic /ɔːˈθentɪk/ adj auténtico **authenticity** /ˌɔːθenˈtɪsəti/ n autenticidad

author /ˈɔːθər/ n autor/a

authoritarian /ɔːˌθɒrɪˈteəriən/ adj, n autoritario/a

authoritative /ɔːˈθɒrətətɪv; -tətɪv GB/ adj **1** de gran autoridad **2** autoritario

authority /əˈθɒrəti/ n (pl -ies) autoridad: local ~ (GB) gobierno local/regional ► **have sth on good authority** saber algo de buena fuente

authorize /ˈɔːθəraɪz/ vt autorizar **authorization** n autorización

autobiography /ˌɔːtəbaɪˈɒɡrəfi/ n (pl -ies) autobiografía **autobiographical** /ˌɔːtəˌbaɪəˈɡræfɪkl/ adj autobiográfico

autograph /ˈɔːtəɡræf; -ɡrɑːf GB/ n autógrafo ● vt autografiar

automate /ˈɔːtəmeɪt/ vt automatizar **automation** n automatización

automatic /ˌɔːtəˈmætɪk/ adj automático ● n **1** arma automática **2** carro automático

automobile /ˈɔːtəməbiːl/ n (USA) automóvil

autonomous /ɔːˈtɒnəməs/ adj autónomo **autonomy** n autonomía

autopsy /ˈɔːtɒpsi/ n (pl -ies) autopsia

autumn /ˈɔːtəm/ n (GB) otoño

auxiliary /ɔːɡˈzɪliəri/ adj, n (pl -ies) auxiliar

avail /əˈveɪl/ n ► **to no avail** en vano

available /əˈveɪləbl/ adj disponible **availability** /əˌveɪləˈbɪləti/ n disponibilidad

avalanche /ˈævəlænʃ; -lɑːnʃ GB/ n avalancha

avant-garde /ˌævɒ̃ ˈɡɑːrd/ adj vanguardista ● n vanguardia

avenue /ˈævənjuː; -njuː GB/ n **1** (abrev **Ave**) avenida → STREET **2** (fig) camino

average /ˈævərɪdʒ/ n promedio: on ~ en promedio ● adj **1** medio: ~ earnings el sueldo medio **2** mediocre ■ **average out (at sth)**: It ~s out at 5%. Sale a un promedio del 5%.

aversion /əˈvɜːrʒn/ n aversión

avert /əˈvɜːrt/ vt **1** (mirada) apartar **2** (crisis, etc.) evitar

aviation /ˌeɪviˈeɪʃn/ n aviación

avid /ˈævɪd/ adj ávido

avocado /ˌævəˈkɑːdoʊ/ n (pl -s) aguacate, palta

avoid /əˈvɔɪd/ vt **1** evitar **2** eludir

await /əˈweɪt/ vt (fml) **1** estar a la espera de **2** aguardar

awake /əˈweɪk/ adj **1** despierto **2** ~ **to sth** consciente de algo ● vt, vi (pret **awoke** pp **awoken**) (fml) despertar(se) **NOTA** Es más común **wake (sb) up**.

awaken /əˈweɪkən/ (fml) **1** vt, vi despertar(se) **2** vt ~ **sb to sth** advertir a algn de algo

award /əˈwɔːd/ vt conceder ● n premio, galardón

award-winning adj galardonado

aware /əˈweər/ adj consciente: as far as I am ~ que yo sepa ◊ become ~ of sth darse cuenta de algo ◊ make sb ~ of sth informar; concientizar a algn de algo

awareness n conciencia

away /əˈweɪ/ adv **1** (distancia): The hotel is two kilometres ~. El hotel está a 2km. ◊ It's a long way ~. Queda muy lejos. ◊ She moved ~ from him. Se alejó de él. ◊ He limped ~. Se fue cojeando. **2** (énfasis): I was working ~ all night. Pasé toda la noche trabajando. ◊ The snow had melted ~. La nieve se había derretido del todo. **3** (Dep) fuera (de casa): an ~ win una victoria fuera de casa **NOTA** Para el uso de away en PHRASAL VERBS ver el verbo, p.ej. **get away** en GET.

awe /ɔː/ n admiración: be in ~ of sb sentirse intimidado por algn

awesome /ˈɔːsəm/ adj **1** impresionante **2** (coloq) genial

awful /ˈɔːfl/ adj **1** horroroso **2** an ~ lot of money muchísimo dinero

awfully adv terriblemente: I'm ~ sorry. Lo siento muchísimo.

awkward /ˈɔːkwəd/ adj **1** inoportuno **2** incómodo **3** torpe **4** (persona) difícil

awoke /əˈwoʊk/ pt de AWAKE

awoken /əˈwoʊkən/ pp de AWAKE

ax (**axe** GB) /æks/ n hacha ▸ **have an ax to grind** tener un interés particular en algo ● vt **1** (servicio, etc.) cortar **2** despedir

axis /ˈæksɪs/ n (pl **axes** /ˈæksiːz/) (Geog, Pol) eje

axle /ˈæksl/ n eje (de ruedas)

aye (tb **ay**) /aɪ/ interj, n (Esc, N de Inglaterra) sí: The ~s have it. Ganaron los síes.

B b

B, b /biː/ n (pl **B's, b's**) **1** B, b **2** (Mús) si

babble /ˈbæbl/ n **1** (voces) murmullo **2** (bebé) balbuceo ● vt, vi farfullar, balbucear

babe /beɪb/ n (coloq) nena

baby /ˈbeɪbi/ n (pl **-ies**) **1** bebé: a newborn ~ un recién nacido ◊ a ~ girl una niña **2** (animal) cría **3** (coloq) cariño

baby carriage n (USA) coche (de niño) (estilo moisés)

babysit /ˈbeɪbisɪt/ vi (-**tt**-) (pt/pp -**sat**) ~ (**for sb**) cuidar a un niño (de algn) **babysitter** n babysitter

bachelor /ˈbætʃələr/ n soltero

back /bæk/ n **1** parte de atrás; detrás **2** dorso **3** revés **4** espalda: lie on your ~ acostarse boca arriba → MY **5** (silla) respaldo ▸ **back to back** espalda con espalda **back to front** (GB) al revés **be glad, pleased, etc. to see the back of sth/sb** (coloq) alegrarse de librarse de algo/algn **behind sb's back** a espaldas de algn **be on sb's back** (coloq) estar encima de algn **get/put sb's back up** (coloq) sacar de quicio a algn **have sth at the back of your mind** tener muy presente (en la mente) **have your back to the wall** estar entre la espada y la pared **turn your back on sth/algn** volverle la espalda a algo/algn ● adj **1** trasero: ~ door/seat puerta trasera/asiento trasero **2** (número) atrasado ▸ **by/through the back door** (fig) por la puerta de atrás **take a back seat** pasar a segundo plano ● adv **1** (movimiento, posición) hacia atrás: Stand well ~. Manténganse alejados. ◊ a mile ~ una milla más atrás **2** (regreso, repetición) de vuelta: on the way ~ de regreso ◊ ~ in power en el poder otra vez ◊ go there and ~ ir y volver ◊ He smiled ~ (at her). Le devolvió la sonrisa. **3** (tiempo) atrás: a few years ~ hace algunos años ▸ **back and forth** de aquí para allá **get/have your own back (on sb)** (coloq) vengarse (de algn) **NOTA** Para el uso de back en PHRASAL VERBS ver el verbo, p.ej. **go back** en GO. ● n **1** vt ~ **sth/sb** (**up**) respaldar algo/a algn **2** vt financiar **3** vt apostar por **4** vi ~ (**up**) dar marcha atrás ■ **back away (from sth/sb)** retroceder (ante algo/algn) **back down/off** (USA) retractarse **back onto sth** (GB) dar a algo (casa) **back out (of sth)** echarse atrás (de algo)

backache /ˈbækeɪk/ n dolor de espalda

backbone /ˈbækboʊn/ n **1** columna vertebral **2** fortaleza, agallas

back door n puerta de atrás

backdrop (tb **backcloth** GB) /ˈbækdrɒp-klɔːθ/ n telón de fondo

backfire /ˌbækˈfaɪər/ vi 1 (Aut) petardear 2 ~ (on sb) salirle (a algn) el tiro por la culata

background /ˈbækɡraʊnd/ n 1 fondo 2 contexto 3 clase social, educación, formación

backing /ˈbækɪŋ/ n 1 apoyo 2 (Mús) acompañamiento

backlash /ˈbæklæʃ/ n reacción violenta

backlog /ˈbæklɒɡ/ n atraso: a huge ~ of work un montón de trabajo atrasado

backpack /ˈbækpæk/ n mochila ● vi viajar con mochila

backside /ˈbæksaɪd/ n (coloq) trasero

backslash /ˈbækslæʃ/ n barra oblicua

backstage /ˌbækˈsteɪdʒ/ adv entre bastidores

backstroke /ˈbækstrəʊk/ n (natación) (estilo) espalda

back-up n 1 [sing] refuerzos, asistencia 2 (pl **-ups**) (Comp) copia (de seguridad)

backward /ˈbækwəd/ adj 1 hacia atrás 2 atrasado ● adv (tb **backwards**) 1 hacia atrás 2 de espaldas 3 al revés ▶ **backward(s) and forward(s)** de un lado a otro

backyard /ˌbækˈjɑːd/ n 1 (USA) jardín de atrás 2 (GB) patio de atrás

bacon /ˈbeɪkən/ n tocino, tocineta (And)

bacteria /bækˈtɪəriə/ n [pl] bacterias

bad /bæd/ adj (comp **worse** superl **worst**) 1 malo: be ~ at Latin ser malo en latín 2 grave 3 (dolor, etc.) fuerte ▶ **too bad** (coloq) 1 una pena: It's too ~ you can't come. Es una pena que no puedas venir. 2 ¡peor para ti! **badly** adv (comp **worse** superl **worst**) 1 mal: behave ~ portarse mal 2 muy: The house was ~ damaged. La casa sufrió muchos daños. 3 mucho: I miss her ~. La extraño muchísimo. ◇ He ~ needs a vacation. Necesita unas vacaciones desesperadamente. ▶ **badly off** mal de dinero

badge /bædʒ/ n 1 insignia, chapa 2 símbolo

badger /ˈbædʒər/ n tejón

badminton /ˈbædmɪntən/ n bádminton

bad-tempered adj de mal genio

baffle /ˈbæfl/ vt desconcertar **baffling** adj desconcertante

bag /bæɡ/ n bolsa, bolso ▶ **bags of sth** (coloq) un montón de algo **be**

in the bag (coloq) estar asegurado

bagel /ˈbeɪɡl/ n bollo de pan en forma de rosca bagel

baggage /ˈbæɡɪdʒ/ n equipaje

baggy /ˈbæɡi/ adj ancho, flojo (ropa)

bag lunch n (USA) comida de mediodía que se lleva de casa

bagpipes /ˈbæɡpaɪps/ n [pl] gaita (escocesa, gallega)

baguette /bæˈɡet/ n barra de pan, baguette

bail /beɪl/ n [U] (libertad bajo) fianza: go/stand ~ for sb pagar la fianza de algn

bailiff /ˈbeɪlɪf/ n (GB) alguacil

bait /beɪt/ n cebo

bake /beɪk/ vt, vi hacer(se): a baking tin un molde de hornear ◇ baked potatoes papas asadas **baker** n panadero/a **bakery** (pl **-ies**) (tb **baker's** GB) n panadería

baked beans n frijoles en salsa de tomate

balance /ˈbæləns/ n 1 equilibrio 2 (Fin) saldo, balance 3 balanza ▶ **catch sb off balance** agarrar desprevenido a algn **on balance** bien mirado ● 1 vi mantener el equilibrio 2 vt mantener en equilibrio 3 vt equilibrar 4 vt compensar, contrarrestar 5 vt, vi (cuentas) (hacer) cuadrar

balcony /ˈbælkəni/ n (pl **-ies**) balcón

bald /bɔːld/ adj calvo

ball /bɔːl/ n 1 balón, pelota, bola 2 esfera, ovillo 3 baile (de etiqueta) ▶ **have a ball** (coloq) pasarla buenísimo **on the ball** al tanto **start/set the ball rolling** empezar

ballad /ˈbæləd/ n balada

ballet /ˈbæleɪ; bæˈleɪ GB/ n ballet: ~ dancer bailarín/ina

balloon /bəˈluːn/ n globo

ballot /ˈbælət/ n votación: ~ box urna electoral

ballpark /ˈbɔːlpɑːk/ n (USA) campo de beisbol ▶ **a ballpark figure** una cifra aproximada

ballpoint /ˈbɔːlpɔɪnt/ (tb ~ **pen**) n bolígrafo, esfero (And)

ballroom /ˈbɔːlruːm/ n salón de baile: ~ dancing baile de salón

bamboo /ˌbæmˈbuː/ n bambú

ban /bæn/ vt (-nn-) prohibir ● n ~ (on sth) prohibición (de algo)

banana /bəˈnænə; bəˈnɑːnə GB/ n plátano, banano (And)

band /bænd/ n 1 (Mús) banda, grupo 2 cinta, franja 3 banda (de valores), escala 4 (Radio) banda 5 (ladrones, etc.) banda

bandage /'bændɪdʒ/ n vendaje ● vt vendar

Band-Aid® n (USA) curita

bandwagon /'bændwægən/ n
▸ **climb/jump on the bandwagon** (coloq) subirse al mismo carro/tren

bang /bæŋ/ 1 vt dar un golpe en: *I banged the box down on the floor.* Tiré la caja al suelo de un golpe. 2 vt ~ **your head, etc. (against/on sth)** darse en la cabeza, etc. (con algo) 3 vi ~ **into sth/sb** darse contra algo/algn 4 vi (*petardo, etc.*) estallar 5 vi (*puerta, etc.*) dar golpes ● n 1 golpe 2 estallido ● adv (coloq) justo, completamente: ~ **on time** justo a tiempo
▸ **go bang** (coloq) estallar ● interj pum

banger /'bæŋər/ n (GB, coloq) 1 salchicha 2 petardo 3 carracha

bangs /bæŋz/ n (USA) flequillo

banish /'bænɪʃ/ vt desterrar

banister /'bænɪstər/ n barandilla, pasamanos

bank /bæŋk/ n 1 banco: ~ **account** cuenta bancaria ◇ ~ **statement/balance** extracto/saldo bancario 2 (*río, lago*) orilla **banker** n banquero/a ● 1 vt (*dinero*) depositar 2 vi tener cuenta (*en un banco*) ▸ **bank on sth/sb** contar con algo/algn

bank holiday n (GB) día festivo: ~ **Monday** el lunes del puente **NOTA** En Gran Bretaña los días festivos suelen ser los lunes, y el puente se llama **bank holiday weekend**.

banknote /'bæŋknoʊt/ n billete

bankrupt /'bæŋkrʌpt/ adj en bancarrota: *go* ~ ir a la bancarrota **bankruptcy** n bancarrota, quiebra

banner /'bænər/ n pancarta, estandarte

banning /'bænɪŋ/ n prohibición

banquet /'bæŋkwɪt/ n banquete

bap /bæp/ n (GB) bollo (*de pan*)

baptize /'bæptaɪz/ bæp'taɪz GB/ vt bautizar **baptism** /'bæptɪzəm/ n bautismo, bautizo **Baptist** n Bautista

bar /bɑr/ n 1 barra 2 bar 3 (*chocolate*) tableta 4 (*jabón*) pastilla 5 (*Mús*) compás 6 prohibición ▸ **behind bars** (coloq) entre rejas ● vt (**-rr-**) 1 ~ **sb from (doing) sth** prohibir (hacer) algo a algn 2 ~ **the way** cerrar el paso ● prep excepto

barbarian /bɑr'beəriən/ n bárbaro/a **barbaric** /bɑr'bærɪk/ adj bárbaro

barbecue /'bɑrbɪkju:/ n barbacoa, parrillada (*Mx*)

barbed wire /,bɑrbd 'waɪər/ n alambre de espino/púas

barber /'bɑrbər/ n peluquero **barbershop** /'bɑrbərʃɑp/ (**barber's** GB) n peluquería (*de caballeros*)

bar chart n gráfico de barras

bar code n código de barras

bare /beər/ adj (**-er/-est**) 1 desnudo → NAKED 2 descubierto 3 ~ **(of sth):** *a room ~ of furniture* una habitación sin muebles 4 mínimo **barely** adv apenas

barefoot /'beərfʊt/ adv descalzo

bargain /'bɑrgən/ n 1 trato 2 ganga ● vi 1 negociar 2 regatear ■ **bargain for sth** esperar algo **bargaining** n 1 negociación 2 regateo

barge /bɑrdʒ/ n barcaza

baritone /'bærɪtoʊn/ n barítono

bark /bɑrk/ n 1 corteza (*árbol*) 2 ladrido ● 1 vi ladrar 2 vt, vi (*persona*) gritar **barking** n ladridos

barley /'bɑrli/ n cebada

barmaid /'bɑrmeɪd/ n (GB) mesera de barra

barman /'bɑrmən/ n (GB) (*pl* **-men**) mesero de barra

barn /bɑrn/ n granero

barometer /bə'rɑmɪtər/ n barómetro

baron, baroness /'bærən, bærə'nəs; 'bærən GB/ n barón, baronesa

barracks /'bærəks/ n [pl] cuartel

barrage /bə'rɑʒ; 'bærɑʒ GB/ n 1 (*Mil*) descarga de fuego 2 (*preguntas, etc.*) bombardeo

barrel /'bærəl/ n 1 barril 2 cañón

barren /'bærən/ adj árido, improductivo (*tierra, etc.*)

barricade /,bærɪ'keɪd/ n barricada ● vt bloquear (con barricada): ~ **yourself in** encerrarse con barricadas

barrier /'bæriər/ n barrera

barrister /'bærɪstər/ n abogado/a →ABOGADO

barrow /'bæroʊ/ n carretilla (*de mano*)

bartender /'bɑrtendər/ n (USA) mesero/a de barra

base /beɪs/ n base ● vt 1 basar 2 **be based in/at...** tener base en...

baseball /'beɪsbɔ:l/ n béisbol, beisbol (*Mx*)

baseboard /'beɪsbɔrd/ n rodapié, zócalo

basement /'beɪsmənt/ n sótano

bash /bæʃ/ *vt, vi* (*coloq*) golpear fuertemente: ~ *your head against/on/into sth* darse un golpe en la cabeza con algo ● *n* golpe fuerte ▸ **have a bash (at sth)** (*coloq*) intentar (algo)

basic /ˈbeɪsɪk/ *adj* **1** fundamental **2** básico **3** elemental ● **the basics** *n* [*pl*] lo esencial, la base **basically** *adv* básicamente

basil /ˈbæzl/ *n* albahaca

basin /ˈbeɪsn/ *n* **1** lavabo **2** cuenco **3** (*Geog*) cuenca

basis /ˈbeɪsɪs/ *n* (*pl* **bases** /ˈbeɪsiːz/) base: *on the ~ of sth* basándose en algo

basket /ˈbæskɪt; ˈbɑːs- *GB*/ *n* cesto/a, canasta

basketball /ˈbæskɪtbɔːl; ˈbɑːs- *GB*/ *n* basquetbol, basket

bass /beɪs/ *n* **1** (*cantante*) bajo **2** [*U*] graves **3** (*tb* ~ **guitar**) bajo **4** (*tb* **double ~**) contrabajo ● *adj* bajo

bat /bæt/ *n* **1** bate **2** murciélago ● *vt, vi* (**-tt-**) batear ▸ **not bat an eyelid** (*coloq*) no inmutarse

batch /bætʃ/ *n* **1** tanda **2** hornada

bath /bæθ; bɑːθ *GB*/ *n* (*pl* **-s** /bæðz; bɑːðz *GB*/) **1** baño **2** bañera, tina ● *vt* (*GB*) bañar

bathe /beɪð/ *vt* **1** lavar **2** (*USA*) bañar

bathrobe /ˈbæθroʊb; ˈbɑːθ- *GB*/ *n* (*USA*) bata (*de baño*)

bathroom /ˈbæθruːm; ˈbɑːθ- *GB*/ *n* (cuarto de) baño →TOILET

baton /bəˈtɑn; ˈbætɒn *GB*/ *n* **1** (*policía*) porra, macana (*Mx*) **2** (*Mús*) batuta **3** (*Dep*) testigo

battalion /bəˈtæliən/ *n* batallón

batter /ˈbætər/ **1** *vt* apalear: ~ *sb to death* matar a algn a palos **2** *vt, vi* ~ **(at/on) sth** aporrear algo ■ **batter sth down** derribar algo a golpes **battered** *adj* deformado

battery /ˈbætəri/ *n* (*pl* **-ies**) **1** (*Elec*) batería, pila **2** *a ~ hen* una gallina ponedora

battle /ˈbætl/ *n* batalla, lucha ● *vi* luchar

battlefield (*tb* **battleground**) /ˈbætlfiːld/-graʊnd/ *n* campo de batalla

battlements /ˈbætlmənts/ *n* [*pl*] almenas

battleship /ˈbætlʃɪp/ *n* acorazado

bauble /ˈbɔːbl/ *n* chuchería (*baratija*)

bawl /bɔːl/ **1** *vi* berrear **2** *vt* gritar

bay /beɪ/ *n* **1** bahía **2** (*zona*): *loading ~* zona de carga **3** (*tb* **~ tree**) laurel **4** caballo pardo ▸ **hold/keep sth/sb at bay** mantener algo/a algn a raya ● *vi* aullar

bayonet /ˈbeɪənət/ *n* bayoneta

bay window *n* ventana (*saliente*)

bazaar /bəˈzɑr/ *n* **1** bazar **2** mercadillo benéfico

BBQ *Ver* BARBECUE

B.C. /ˌbiː ˈsiː/ *abrev* antes de Cristo

be /bi, biː/ (*pt* **was/were** *pp* **been**) →Para el uso de **be** con **there**, ver THERE.

● **v intransitivo** **1** ser: *It's me.* Soy yo. ◇ *She's from here.* Es de acá. ◇ *Be quick!* ¡Date prisa! ◇ *I was late.* Llegué tarde. **2** (*estado, lugar*) estar **NOTA** Compara las dos oraciones: *He's bored.* Está aburrido. ◇ *He's boring.* Es aburrido. Con adjetivos terminados en **-ed**, como **interested**, **tired**, etc., el verbo **be** expresa un estado y se traduce por "estar". Con adjetivos terminados en **-ing**, como **interesting**, **tiring**, etc., expresa una cualidad y se traduce por "ser". **3** [*sólo en tiempo perfecto*] visitar: *I've never been to Chile.* Nunca he estado en Chile. ◇ *I've been into town.* Fui al centro. **NOTA** A veces **been** se usa como participio de **go**. →GO[1] **4** tener: *I'm hot/afraid.* Tengo calor/miedo. ◇ *He is ten (years old).* Tiene diez años. → OLD **NOTA** En español se usa **tener** con sustantivos como "frío", "sed", etc., mientras que en inglés se usa **be** con el adjetivo. **5** (*tiempo*): *It's cold/foggy.* Hace frío/Hay niebla. **6** (*medida*) medir: *He is six feet tall.* Mide 1,80 m. **7** (*hora, Mat*) ser: *It's two o'clock.* Son las dos. ◇ *Two and two is/are four.* Dos y dos son cuatro. **8** (*precio*) costar

● **v auxiliar** **1** [*voz pasiva*]: *He was killed in the war.* Lo mataron en la guerra. ◇ *It is said that he is rich/He is said to ~ rich.* Dicen que es rico. **2** [*tiempos continuos*]: *What are you doing?* ¿Qué haces/estás haciendo? ◇ *I'm just coming!* ¡Ya voy! **3** [+ *infinitivo*]: *I am to inform you that...* Debo informarle que... ◇ *They were to be married.* Se iban a casar. **NOTA** Para expresiones, ver el sustantivo, adjetivo, etc., p.ej. **be all ears** en EAR. ■ **be through (to sth/sb)** tener línea (con algo/algn) **be through (with sth/sb)** haber terminado (con algo/algn)

beach /biːtʃ/ *n* playa ● *vt* varar

beacon /ˈbiːkən/ *n* **1** faro **2** (*hoguera*) almenara **3** radiobaliza

bead /biːd/ n 1 cuenta 2 beads [pl] collar de cuentas 3 (sudor, etc.) gota

beak /biːk/ n pico

beaker /ˈbiːkər/ n vaso (plástico)

beam /biːm/ n 1 viga, travesaño 2 (luz) rayo 3 (linterna, etc.) haz de luz 4 sonrisa radiante ● 1 vi sonreír con alegría 2 vt transmitir (programa)

bean /biːn/ n 1 frijol: green ~s ejotes (Mx)/habichuelas (And) ◇ broad ~s habas 2 (café, cacao) grano

bear /beər/ n oso ● (pt bore pp borne) 1 vt aguantar 2 vt (firma, etc.) llevar 3 vt (peso) soportar 4 vt (gastos) hacerse cargo de 5 vt (responsabilidad) asumir 6 vt resistir: It won't ~ close examination. No resistirá un examen a fondo. 7 vt (fml) dar a luz 8 vt (cosecha, resultado) producir 9 vi (carretera, etc.) torcer ▶ bear a grudge guardar rencor bear a resemblance to sth/sb tener un parecido a algo/algn bear no relation to sth no tener relación con algo bear sth/sb in mind tener algo/a algn en cuenta ■ bear sth/sb out confirmar algo/lo que algn ha dicho bear up (under sth) aguantar (algo): He's bearing up under the strain. Lo está llevando bien. bear with sb tener paciencia con algn bearable adj tolerable

beard /bɪrd/ n barba bearded adj barbudo, con barba

bearer /ˈbeərər/ n 1 (noticias, cheque) portador/a 2 (documento) titular

bearing /ˈbeərɪŋ/ n (Náut) marcación ▶ get/lose your bearings orientarse/desorientarse have a bearing on sth tener que ver con algo

beast /biːst/ n animal, bestia: wild ~ fiera

beat /biːt/ (pt beat pp beaten /ˈbiːtn/) 1 vt, vi golpear, dar golpes (en) 2 vt (metal, huevos, alas, récord) batir 3 vt (tambor) tocar 4 vi (corazón) latir 5 vt ~ sb (at sth) ganar a algn (a algo) 6 vt: Nothing ~s home cooking. No hay nada como la cocina casera. ▶beat around/about (GB) the bush andarse con rodeos off the beaten track no ir lugar apartado ■ beat sb up dar una paliza a algn ● 1 n ritmo 2 (tambor) redoble 3 (policía) ronda beating n 1 paliza 2 batir 3 (corazón) latido ▶take some beating (GB) ser difícil de superar

beautiful /ˈbjuːtɪfl/ adj 1 hermoso 2 magnífico

beauty /ˈbjuːti/ n (pl -ies) 1 belleza 2 (persona o cosa) preciosidad

beaver /ˈbiːvər/ n castor

became /brˈkeɪm/ pt de BECOME

because /brˈkɔːz; -ˈkɒz GB/ conj porque because of prep a causa de a: ~ of you por ti

beckon /ˈbekən/ 1 vi hacer señas 2 vt llamar con señas

become /brˈkʌm/ vi (pt became pp become) 1 [+ sustantivo] llegar a ser, convertirse en, hacerse 2 [+ adj] ponerse, volverse ■ become of sth/sb pasar con algo/algn: What will ~ of me? ¿Qué será de mí?

bed /bed/ n 1 cama NOTA No se usa el artículo en las expresiones: go to ~ ◇ It's time for ~. 2 (tb river ~) lecho (del río) 3 (tb sea ~) fondo (del mar) 4 (flores) arriate

bed and breakfast abrev (tb B & B) n hotel (desayuno incluido)

bedding (tb bedclothes) /ˈbedɪŋ/ -kloʊðz/ n [pl] ropa de cama

bedroom /ˈbedruːm/ n dormitorio, recámara (Mx)

bedside /ˈbedsaɪd/ n cabecera: ~ lamp lámpara de noche

bedsit /ˈbedsɪt/ n (GB) habitación con cama y cocina

bedspread /ˈbedspred/ n colcha

bedtime /ˈbedtaɪm/ n hora de acostarse

bee /biː/ n abeja

beech /biːtʃ/ (tb ~ tree) n haya

beef /biːf/ n carne de res: roast ~ rosbif →CARNE

beehive /ˈbiːhaɪv/ n colmena

been /bɪn, tb biːn GB/ pp de BE

beer /bɪər/ n cerveza

beet /biːt/ (beetroot /ˈbiːtruːt/ GB) n remolacha, betabel (Mx)

beetle /ˈbiːtl/ n escarabajo

before /brˈfɔːr/ adv antes: the week ~ la semana anterior ● prep 1 antes de/que 2 ante 3 delante de ● conj antes de que

beforehand /brˈfɔːrhænd/ adv de antemano

beg /beg/ (-gg-) 1 vt, vi ~ (sth/for sth) (from sb) mendigar (algo) (de/a algn) 2 vt ~ sb to do sth suplicar a algn que haga algo ▶ beg sb's pardon 1 pedir perdón a algn 2 I ~ your pardon? ¿Cómo dijo? beggar n mendigo/a

begin /brˈgɪn/ vt, vi (-nn-) (pt began /brˈgæn/ pp begun /brˈgʌn/) empezar NOTA Begin y start pueden ir seguidos de un infinitivo o de una forma en

-ing, pero en tiempo continuo sólo se usa el ritmo: *It is starting to rain.* ► **to begin with 1** para empezar **2** al principio **beginner** *n* principiante **beginning** *n* **1** comienzo, principio **2** origen

begrudge /bɪˈgrʌdʒ/ *vt* **1** ~ (**sb**) **sth** envidiar algo (a algn) **2** escatimar

behalf /bɪˈhæf; -ˈhɑːf *GB*/ *n* ► **on behalf of sb/in sb's behalf (on ~ of sb/on sb's ~** *GB*) en nombre de algn

behave /bɪˈheɪv/ *vi* ~ **well, badly, etc. (towards sb)** comportarse bien, mal, etc. (con algn): *Behave yourself!* ¡Pórtate bien! ◊ **well behaved** bien educado

behavior (-our *GB*) /bɪˈheɪvjər/ *n* comportamiento

behind /bɪˈhaɪnd/ *prep* **1** detrás de, tras **2** *be ~ schedule* ir retrasado (con respecto a los planes) **3** a favor de ● *adv* **1** atrás: *He was shot from ~.* Le dispararon por la espalda. ◊ *stay ~* quedarse **2** ~ **(in/with sth)** atrasado (en/con algo) ● *n* trasero

being /ˈbiːɪŋ/ *n* **1** ser **2** existencia ► **come into being** crearse

belated /bɪˈleɪtɪd/ *adj* tardío

belch /beltʃ/ *vi* eructar ● *n* eructo

belief /bɪˈliːf/ *n* **1** creencia **2** confianza, fe ► **beyond belief** increíble **in the belief that...** confiando en que...

believe /bɪˈliːv/ *vt, vi* creer: ~ *it or not* aunque no te lo creas ■ **believe in sth/sb creer**, confiar en algo/algn **believable** *adj* creíble **believer** *n* creyente: *be a great/firm ~ in sth* ser gran partidario de algo

bell /bel/ *n* **1** campana, campanilla **2** timbre

bellow /ˈbeloʊ/ **1** *vi* bramar **2** *vt, vi* gritar ● *n* **1** bramido **2** grito

belly /ˈbeli/ *n* (*pl* **-ies**) barriga, panza

belly button *n* (*coloq*) ombligo

belong /bɪˈlɔːŋ; -ˈlɒŋ *GB*/ *vi* **1** pertenecer: *Who does this ~ to?* ¿De quién es esto? **2** deber estar: *Where does this ~?* ¿Dónde va esto? **belongings** *n* pertenencias

below /bɪˈloʊ/ *prep* (por) debajo de, bajo ● *adv* (más) abajo

belt /belt/ *n* **1** cinturón **2** (*Mec*) correa: *conveyor ~* banda transportadora **3** (*Geog*) zona ► **below the belt**: *That was below the ~.* Eso fue un golpe bajo. **have sth under your belt** tener algo ya hecho

bemused /bɪˈmjuːzd/ *adj* perplejo

bench /bentʃ/ *n* **1** (*asiento*) banco **2** (*GB, Pol*) escaño **3 the bench** (*Jur*) el tribunal

benchmark /ˈbentʃmɑːrk/ *n* punto de referencia

bend /bend/ (*pt/pp* **bent**) **1** *vt, vi* doblar(se) **2** *vi* ~ (**down**) agacharse, inclinarse ● *n* **1** curva **2** (*tubería*) codo ► **round the bend** (*GB*) chiflado

beneath /bɪˈniːθ/ *prep* (*fml*) **1** bajo, debajo de **2** indigno de ● *adv* abajo

benefactor /ˈbenɪfæktər/ *n* benefactor/a

beneficial /ˌbenɪˈfɪʃl/ *adj* beneficioso, provechoso

benefit /ˈbenɪfɪt/ *n* **1** beneficio: *be of ~ to sb* ser beneficioso para algn **2** subsidio: *unemployment ~* subsidio de desempleo **3** función benéfica ► **give sb the benefit of the doubt** darle a algn el beneficio de la duda ● *vt, vi* beneficiar(se)

benevolent /bəˈnevələnt/ *adj* **1** benévolo **2** benéfico

benign /bɪˈnaɪn/ *adj* benigno

bent /bent/ *pt, pp de* BEND ► **bent on sth** empeñado en algo

bequeath /bɪˈkwiːð/ *vt* (*fml*) legar

bequest /bɪˈkwest/ *n* (*fml*) legado

bereaved /bɪˈriːvd/ *adj* afligido por la muerte de un ser querido **bereavement** *n* pérdida (de un ser querido)

beret /bəˈreɪ; ˈbereɪ *GB*/ *n* boina

berry /ˈberi/ *n* (*pl* **-ies**) baya

berserk /bəˈsɜːrk/ *adj* loco: *go ~* volverse loco

berth /bɜːrθ/ *n* **1** (*barco*) camarote **2** (*tren*) litera **3** (*Náut*) atracadero

beside /bɪˈsaɪd/ *prep* junto a, al lado de ► **beside yourself (with sth)** fuera de sí (por algo)

besides /bɪˈsaɪdz/ *prep* **1** además de **2** excepto: *No one writes to me ~ you.* Nadie me escribe excepto tú. ● *adv* además

besiege /bɪˈsiːdʒ/ *vt* **1** asediar **2** acosar

besotted /bɪˈsɒtɪd/ *adj* ~ (**by/with sth/sb)** loco (con algo/por algn)

best /best/ *adj* mejor: *the ~ in the world* el mejor del mundo ► **best before**: ~ *before 2006* consumir antes de 2006 **best wishes**: *Best wishes, Ann.* Un fuerte abrazo, Ann. ◊ *Give her my ~ wishes.* Dale muchos recuerdos. ● *adv* **1** mejor **2** más: *best-known* más conocido ► **as best you can** lo

mejor que puedas ● n 1 el/la
mejor: *He's the ~ by far.* Él es mil
veces mejor. 2 lo mejor 3 (the)
~ of sth: *We're (the) ~ of friends.*
Somos excelentes amigos. ▶ **all
the best** (cartas, etc.) un abrazo
at best en el mejor de los casos
at its/your best en su mejor momento **do/try your (level/very)
best** hacer todo lo posible **make
the best of sth** sacar el máximo
partido de algo **to the best of
your belief/knowledge** que tú
sepas

best man *n* padrino (de boda)
→MATRIMONIO

best-seller *n* éxito de ventas

bet /bet/ *vt, vi* (-tt-) (*pt/pp* bet)
~ (**on**) **sth** apostar ((en) algo): *I
~ you he doesn't come.* ¡A que no
viene! ▶ **you bet!** (coloq) ¡claro!
● *n* apuesta: *place/put a ~ on sth*
apostar por algo ▶ **the/your best
bet** (coloq) la mejor opción

betray /bɪ'treɪ/ *vt* 1 traicionar
2 (*secreto*) revelar **betrayal** *n*
traición

better /'betər/ *adj* mejor: *get ~*
mejorar ▶ **be little/no better
than...** no valer más que... **have
seen/known better days** no ser lo
que era ● *adv* 1 mejor 2 más ▶ **be
better off (without sth/sb)** estar
mejor (sin algo/algn): *He'd be
~ off leaving now.* Más le valdría
irse ahora. **better late than never**
más vale tarde que nunca **better
safe than sorry** más vale prevenir que curar/lamentar **I'd,
you'd, etc. better/best** (que haga,
hagas, etc. algo): *You'd ~ go.* Es mejor
que vayas. ● *n* (algo) mejor: *I
expected ~ of him.* Esperaba más
de él. ▶ **get the better of sb**
vencer a algn

betting shop *n* agencia de
apuestas

between /bɪ'twiːn/ *prep* entre
(*dos cosas/personas*) ● *adv* (*tb*
in ~) en medio

beverage /'bevərɪdʒ/ *n* (*fml*) bebida

beware /bɪ'weər/ *vi* ~ (**of sth/sb**)
tener cuidado (con algo/algn)

bewilder /bɪ'wɪldər/ *vt* dejar perplejo **bewildered** *adj* perplejo
bewildering *adj* desconcertante
bewilderment *n* perplejidad

bewitch /bɪ'wɪtʃ/ *vt* hechizar

beyond /bɪ'jɒnd/ *prep, adv* más
allá (de) ▶ **be beyond sb** (coloq):
It's ~ me. No lo puedo entender.

bias /'baɪəs/ *n* 1 ~ **towards sth/sb**
predisposición a favor de algo/
algn 2 ~ **against sth/sb** prejuicios

contra algo/algn 3 parcialidad
biased (*tb* -ss-) *adj* parcial

bib /bɪb/ *n* 1 babero o peto (*de
delantal*)

bible /'baɪbl/ *n* biblia **biblical** *adj*
bíblico

bibliography /ˌbɪbli'ɒɡrəfi/ *n* (*pl*
-ies) bibliografía

biceps /'baɪseps/ *n* (*pl* biceps)
biceps

bicker /'bɪkər/ *vi* discutir (*por
asuntos triviales*)

bicycle /'baɪsɪkl/ *n* bicicleta

bid /bɪd/ *vt, vi* (-dd-) (*pt/pp* bid)
1 (*subasta*) pujar 2 (Com) hacer
ofertas ● *n* 1 (subasta) puja
2 (Com) oferta 3 intento: *make
a ~ for sth* intentar conseguir
algo **bidder** *n* postor/a

bide /baɪd/ *vt* ▶ **bide your time**
esperar el momento oportuno

biennial /baɪ'eniəl/ *adj* bienal

big /bɪɡ/ (**bigger**, **-est**) *adj* 1 grande
2 mayor: *my ~ sister* mi hermana
mayor 3 (*decisión*) importante
4 (*error*) grave ▶ **a big cheese/
fish/shot** (coloq) un pez gordo
big business: *This is ~ business.*
Esto es una mina. **the big time**
(coloq) el estrellato ● *adv* (coloq):
think ~ planearlo a lo grande

bigamy /'bɪɡəmi/ *n* bigamia

big-head *n* (coloq) engreído/a
big-headed *adj* (coloq) engreído

bigoted /'bɪɡətɪd/ *adj* intolerante

bike /baɪk/ *n* (coloq) 1 bici 2 moto

bikini /bɪ'kiːni/ *n* bikini

bilingual /ˌbaɪ'lɪŋɡwəl/ *adj, n* bilingüe

bill /bɪl/ *n* 1 factura, cuenta: *gas ~*
recibo del gas 2 programa (*cine,
etc.*) 3 proyecto de ley 4 (USA)
billete 5 pico (*ave*) ▶ **fill/fit the bill**
satisfacer los requisitos ● *vt*
1 ~ **sb for sth** pasar la factura
de algo a algn 2 anunciar (*en un
programa*)

billboard /'bɪlbɔːrd/ *n* (USA) valla
publicitaria

billiards /'bɪliərdz/ *n* [*sing*] billar:
billiard ball bola de billar

billing /'bɪlɪŋ/ *n*: *get top/star ~*
encabezar el cartel/reparto

billion /'bɪljən/ *adj, n* mil millones
NOTA En Gran Bretaña, a **billion** antes equivalía a un billón,
pero hoy son mil millones. A
trillion equivale a un millón de
millones, es decir, un billón.

bin /bɪn/ *n* (GB) bote (*Mx*), caneca
(*And*) (*de basura*)

binary /'baɪnəri/ *adj* binario

bind /baɪnd/ *vt* (*pt/pp* bound)
1 atar 2 unir, ligar 3 ~ **sb/yourself
(to sth)** obligar(se) (a algn) (a

algo) ● **n** (coloq) **1** lata: It's a terrible ~. Es una lata. **2** apuro

binder /'baɪndər/ n carpeta

binding /'baɪmdɪŋ/ n **1** encuadernación **2** ribete ● adj ~ (on/upon sb) vinculante (para algn)

binge /bɪndʒ/ n (coloq) juerga, comilona ● vi atracarse de comida, emborracharse

bingo /'bɪŋgoʊ/ n bingo (juego)

binoculars /bɪ'nɑkjələrz/ n [pl] binoculares

biochemistry /ˌbaɪoʊ'kemɪstri/ n bioquímica **biochemical** adj bioquímico **biochemist** n bioquímico/a

biodegradable /ˌbaɪoʊdɪ-'greɪdəbl/ adj biodegradable

biodiversity /ˌbaɪoʊdaɪvɜ:rsəti/ n biodiversidad

biography /baɪ'ɑgrəfi/ n (pl -ies) biografía **biographer** n biógrafo/a **biographical** /ˌbaɪə'græfɪkl/ adj biográfico

biological /ˌbaɪə'lɑdʒɪkl/ adj biológico

biology /baɪ'ɑlədʒi/ n biología **biologist** n biólogo/a

bird /bɜ:rd/ n ave, pájaro: ~ of prey ave de rapiña

Biro® /'baɪroʊ/ n (GB) (pl -s) bolígrafo, esfero (And)

birth /bɜ:rθ/ n **1** nacimiento **2** natalidad: ~ control control de natalidad **3** parto **4** cuna, origen ▸ **give birth (to sth/sb)** dar a luz (a algo/algn)

birthday /'bɜ:rθdeɪ/ n cumpleaños

birthmark /'bɜ:rθmɑrk/ n mancha de nacimiento

birthplace /'bɜ:rθpleɪs/ n lugar de nacimiento

biscuit /'bɪskɪt/ (GB) n galleta

bisexual adj, n bisexual

bishop /'bɪʃəp/ n **1** (Rel) obispo **2** (ajedrez) alfil

bit /bɪt/ pt de BITE ● n **1** trocito, pedacito: I have a ~ of shopping to do. Tengo que hacer algunas compras. **2** (caballo) bocado ▸ **a bit 1** un poco **2** un rato: Wait a ~! ¡Espera un poco! **3** It rained quite a ~. Llovió bastante. **a bit much** (coloq) demasiado **bit by bit** a poco a poco **bits and pieces** (coloq) cosillas **do your bit** (coloq) hacer tu parte **not a bit; not one (little) ~**. No me gusta nada. **to bits**: pull/tear sth to ~s hacer algo pedazos ◇ fall to ~s hacerse pedazos ◇ take sth to ~s desarmar algo

bitch /bɪtʃ/ n perra →PERRO

bite /baɪt/ (pt bit pp bitten /'bɪtn/) **1** vt, vi ~ (into sth) morder (algo) **2** vt (insecto) picar ● n **1** mordisco **2** bocado **3** picadura, piquete (Mx)

bitter /'bɪtər/ adj **1** amargo **2** resentido **3** (frío) glacial ● n (GB) cerveza (amarga) ▸ **bitterly** adv amargamente: It's ~ cold. Hace un frío glacial. **bitterness** n amargura

bizarre /bɪ'zɑr/ adj **1** extraño, raro **2** (aspecto) estrafalario

black /blæk/ adj (-er/-est) **1** negro: ~ market mercado negro ◇ ~ eye ojo morado **2** oscuro **3** (café, té) negro, sin leche ◇ ~ and white **1** negro **2** (persona) negro/a ■ **black out** perder el conocimiento

blackberry n (pl -ies) **1** mora **2** zarza

blackbird /'blækbɜ:rd/ n mirlo

blackboard /'blækbɔrd/ n pizarrón, tablero (And)

blackcurrant /ˌblæk'kʌrənt/ n grosella negra

blacken /'blækən/ vt **1** (reputación, etc.) manchar **2** ennegrecer

blacklist /'blæklɪst/ n lista negra ● vt poner en la lista negra

blackmail /'blækmeɪl/ n chantaje ● vt chantajear **blackmailer** n chantajista

blacksmith /'blæksmɪθ/ n herrero/a

bladder /'blædər/ n vejiga

blade /bleɪd/ n **1** (cuchillo, etc.) hoja **2** (patín, de afeitar) cuchilla **3** (ventilador) aspa **4** (remo) pala **5** (pasto) brizna

blame /bleɪm/ vt **1** ~ **sb (for sth)**; ~ **sth on sb** culpar algn (por algo): He ~s it on her. Le echa la culpa a ella. **2** [frases negativas]: You can't ~ him for being annoyed. No es de extrañar que esté enojado. ▸ **be to blame (for sth)** tener la culpa (de algo) ● n culpa: lay/put the ~ for sth on sb echar la culpa de algo a algn

bland /blænd/ adj (-er/-est) soso, insípido

blank /blæŋk/ adj **1** (papel, cheque, etc.) en blanco **2** (pared, etc.) desnudo **3** (casete) virgen **4** (municiones) de fogueo **5** (expresión) vacío ● n **1** espacio en blanco **2** bala de fogueo

blanket /'blæŋkɪt/ n manta, cobija ● adj general ● vt cubrir (por completo)

blare /bleər/ vi ~ **(out)** sonar a todo volumen

blasphemy /'blæsfəmi/ n blasfemia **blasphemous** adj blasfemo

B

blast /blæst; blɑːst GB/ n 1 explosión 2 onda expansiva 3 ráfaga ▸ **(at) full blast** a tope ● vt volar (con explosivos) ■ **blast off** despegar ● interj maldición **blasted** adj (coloq) maldito

blatant /'bleɪtnt/ adj descarado

blaze /bleɪz/ n 1 incendio 2 hoguera 3 [sing]: a ~ of colour una explosión de color ◇ in a ~ of publicity con mucha publicidad ● vi 1 arder 2 brillar 3 (ojos) echar chispas

blazer /'bleɪzər/ n saco, blazer

bleach /bliːtʃ/ vt 1 blanquear 2 (pelo) aclarar ● n blanqueador

bleak /bliːk/ adj (-er/-est) 1 (paisaje) inhóspito 2 (tiempo) frío, gris y deprimente 3 poco prometedor **bleakness** n 1 desolación 2 crudeza

bleed /bliːd/ vi (pt/pp bled /bled/) sangrar **bleeding** n [U] hemorragia

blemish /'blemɪʃ/ n mancha ● vt manchar

blend /blend/ 1 vt, vi mezclar(se) 2 vi difuminarse ■ **blend in** armonizar ● n mezcla

blender /'blendər/ n licuadora

bless /bles/ vt bendecir ▸ **be blessed with sth** gozar de algo **bless you!** 1 ¡que Dios te bendiga! 2 ¡salud!, ¡Jesús! (al estornudar) →ACHÍS

blessed /'blesɪd/ adj 1 santo 2 bendito 3 (coloq): the whole ~ day todo el santo día

blessing /'blesɪŋ/ n 1 bendición 2 visto bueno ▸ **it's a blessing in disguise** no hay mal que por bien no venga

blew /bluː/ pt de BLOW

blind /blaɪnd/ adj ciego ▸ **turn a blind eye (to sth)** hacer la vista gorda (ante algo) ● vt 1 deslumbrar 2 cegar ● n 1 persiana 2 **the blind** [pl] los ciegos **blindness** n ceguera

blindfold /'blaɪndfoʊld/ n venda (ojos) ● vt vendar los ojos a ● adv con los ojos vendados

blink /blɪŋk/ vi parpadear ● n parpadeo

bliss /blɪs/ n dicha **blissful** adj dichoso

blister /'blɪstər/ n ampolla

blistering /'blɪstərɪŋ/ adj abrasador (calor)

blitz /blɪts/ n 1 (Mil) ataque relámpago 2 ~ (on sth) campaña (contra algo)

blizzard /'blɪzərd/ n ventisca (de nieve)

bloated /'bloʊtɪd/ adj hinchado

blob /blɑb/ n gota (líquido espeso)

bloc /blɑk/ n bloque (Pol)

block /blɑk/ n 1 bloque 2 (edificios) cuadra 3 (entradas, acciones, etc.) paquete: a ~ booking una reserva en grupo 4 obstáculo: a mental ~ un bloqueo mental ● vt 1 atascar, bloquear 2 tapar impedir

blockade /blɑ'keɪd/ n (Mil) bloqueo ● vt bloquear (puerto, etc.)

blockage /'blɑkɪdʒ/ n 1 obstrucción 2 bloqueo 3 atasco

blockbuster /'blɑkbʌstər/ (coloq) n éxito rotundo (Cine, etc.)

block capitals (tb **block letters**) n [pl] mayúsculas

bloke /bloʊk/ n (GB, coloq) tipo

blonde (tb **blond**) /blɑnd/ adj rubio ● **blonde** n rubia →RUBIO

blood /blʌd/ n sangre: ~ group/pressure grupo sanguíneo/presión arterial

bloodshed /'blʌdʃed/ n derramamiento de sangre

bloodshot /'blʌdʃɑt/ adj inyectado de sangre

blood sports n [pl] caza

bloodstained /'blʌdsteɪnd/ adj manchado de sangre

bloodstream /'blʌdstriːm/ n flujo sanguíneo

bloody /'blʌdi/ adj (-ier/-iest) 1 ensangrentado 2 sangriento ● adj, adv (GB, coloq): That ~ noise! ¡Ese maldito ruido! ◇ He's ~ useless! ¡Es un maldito inútil!

bloom /bluːm/ n flor ● vi florecer

blossom /'blɑsəm/ n [U] flor (de árbol) ● vi florecer

blot /blɑt/ n mancha ● vt (-tt-) 1 emborronar 2 secar ■ **blot sth out** (memoria, etc.) borrar algo ● 2 (vista, luz, etc.) tapar algo

blotch /blɑtʃ/ n mancha (en la piel) **blotchy** adj lleno de manchas

blouse /blaʊs; blaʊz GB/ n blusa

blow /bloʊ/ (pt **blew** /bluː/ pp **blown** /bloʊn/) 1 vi soplar 2 vt, vi (acción del viento): The wind blew us ashore. El viento nos llevó a tierra. ◇ ~ shut/open cerrarse/abrirse de golpe 3 vt, vi (silbato) tocar, sonar 4 vt (nariz) sonarse ▸ **blow it!** (GB) ¡maldita sea! ■ **blow away** irse volando (con el viento) **blow sth away** llevarse algo (el viento) **blow down/over** ser derribado por el viento **blow sth/sb down/over** derribar algo/algn (el viento) **blow sth out** apagar algo **blow over** pasar sin más (tormenta, escándalo) **blow up 1** (bomba, etc.) explotar 2 (tormenta, escándalo) estallar 3

(coloq) enojarse **blow sth up**
1 (reventar) volar algo 2 (globo,
etc.) inflar algo 3 (Fot) ampliar
algo 4 (asunto) exagerar algo ● n
golpe: at one/a single ~ de un
(solo) golpe ▶ **blow-by-blow
account** un relato con pelos y
señales **come to blows (over sth)**
llegar a las manos (por algo)

blue /bluː/ adj 1 azul 2 (coloq)
triste (película) porno ● n 1 (coloq)
azul 2 **blues** (Mús) blues 3 **the blues**
la depre ▶ **out of the blue** de
repente **bluish** adj azulado

blueberry /ˈbluːberi/ -bəri GB/ n
(pl -ies) arándano

blue-collar adj: ~ workers obre-
ros

blueprint /ˈbluːprɪnt/ n ~ (for sth)
anteproyecto de algo

bluff /blʌf/ vi fanfarronear, faro-
lear(se) ● n fanfarronada

blunder /ˈblʌndər/ n metedura de
pata ● vi meter la pata

blunt /blʌnt/ vt embotar ● adj
(-er/-est) 1 despuntado, desafilado 2 romo: a ~ instrument un
instrumento contundente
3 brusco: To be ~... Para serte
franco... ◇ be ~ with sb hablar a
algn sin rodeos

blur /blɜːr/ n imagen borrosa ● vt,
vi (-rr-) 1 hacer(se) borroso 2 ate-
nuar(se) **blurred** adj borroso

blurt /blɜːrt/ v ■ **blurt sth out**
soltar algo

blush /blʌʃ/ vi sonrojarse ● n
sonrojo **blusher** n (maquillaje)
rubor

boar /bɔːr/ n 1 jabalí 2 verraco
→CERDO

board /bɔːrd/ n 1 tabla 2 tablero
3 pizarrón 4 tablero de anuncios,
cartelera (And) 5 cartoné, pasta
dura 6 (tb ~ of directors) junta/
mesa directiva 7 pensión: full/
half ~ pensión completa/media
pensión ▶ **above board** correcto
across the board en todos los
niveles **on board** a bordo (de) ●
1 vt ~ sth (up/over) cubrir algo
con tablas 2 vt, vi embarcar (en),
abordar

boarder /ˈbɔːrdər/ n 1 (colegio)
interno/a 2 (pensión) huésped

boarding card (tb **boarding
pass**) n tarjeta de embarque

boarding house n casa de hués-
pedes

boarding school n internado

boast /boʊst/ vi 1 alardear 2 vt
(fml) gozar de: The town ~s a
museum. La ciudad tiene un
museo. ● n alarde **boastful** adj
1 presuntuoso 2 pretencioso

boat /boʊt/ n 1 barco 2 barca:
~ race regata 3 buque **NOTA** A
diferencia de **ship**, **boat** se suele
usar para embarcaciones peque-
ñas.

bob /bɑb/ vi (-bb-) ~ (up and
down) (en agua) balancearse

bobby /ˈbɑbi/ n (pl -ies) (GB,
coloq) policía

bode /boʊd/ vt (fml) presagiar,
augurar: ~ ill/well for sb ser de
mal agüero/buena señal para
algn

bodice /ˈbɑdɪs/ n corpiño

bodily /ˈbɑdɪli/ adj del cuerpo,
corporal ● adv a la fuerza

body /ˈbɑdi/ n (pl -ies) 1 cuerpo:
~ odor olor corporal 2 cadáver
3 grupo: a government ~ un
organismo gubernamental 4 conjunto 5 (GB, ropa) body ▶ **body
and soul** en cuerpo y alma

bodybuilding /ˈbɑdibɪldɪŋ/ n fisiculturismo

bodyguard /ˈbɑdigɑrd/ n 1 guardaespaldas 2 (grupo) guardia
personal

bodysuit /ˈbɑdisuːt/ n (USA) body

bodywork /ˈbɑdiwɜːrk/ n [U] carrocería

bog /bɔːg/ n 1 ciénaga 2 (GB,
coloq) retrete, baño ● v (-gg-) ■
get bogged down 1 estancarse
2 atascarse **boggy** adj pantanoso

bogeyman /ˈboʊɡimæn/ Ver
BOOGEYMAN

bogus /ˈboʊɡəs/ adj falso, fraudulento

boil /bɔɪl/ n 1 forúnculo 2 **be on
the** ~ estar hirviendo ● 1 vt, vi
hervir 2 vt cocer ■ **boil down to
sth** reducirse a algo **boil over**
rebosar **boiling** adj hirviendo:
~ point punto de ebullición ◇
~ hot hirviendo

boiler /ˈbɔɪlər/ n caldera, boiler

boiler suit n (GB) overol

boisterous /ˈbɔɪstərəs/ adj bullicioso, alborotado

bold /boʊld/ adj (-er/-est) 1 valiente, atrevido 2 bien definido,
marcado 3 (color) llamativo 4 (tipografía) negrilla **boldness** n
1 valentía 2 audacia, atrevimiento

bolt /boʊlt/ n 1 cerrojo 2 tornillo,
perno 3 a ~ of lightning un rayo
▶ **make a bolt for it** intentar
escapar ● 1 vt cerrar con cerrojo
2 vt atornillar 3 vt ~ sth (down)
engullir algo 4 vi (caballo)
desbocarse 5 vi salir disparado

bomb /bɑm/ n 1 bomba: plant a ~
poner una bomba 2 (GB) costar a
~ costar un dineral ▶ **go like a
bomb** (GB, coloq) ir como un

rayo ● **1** *vt* bombardear **2** *vt* poner una bomba en **3** *vi* ~ **along, down, up, etc.** (GB, coloq) ir zumbando **bombing** *n* **1** bombardeo **2** atentado con explosivos

bombard /bɑm'bɑrd/ *vt* **1** bombardear **2** (*a preguntas, etc.*) acosar **bombardment** *n* bombardeo

bomber /'bɑmər/ *n* **1** (*avión*) bombardero **2** persona que pone bombas

bombshell /'bɑmʃel/ *n* bomba: *The news came as a ~.* La noticia cayó como una bomba

bond /bɑnd/ *vt* unir ● *n* **1** pacto **2** lazos **3** bono: *Government ~s* bonos del Tesoro **4** bonds cadenas

bone /boʊn/ *n* **1** hueso **2** (*pez*) espina ▸ **a bone of contention** la manzana de la discordia **bone dry** completamente seco **have a bone to pick with sb** tener que ajustar las cuentas con algn **make no bones about sth** no andarse con rodeos en cuanto a algo ● *vt* deshuesar

bone marrow *n* médula

bonfire /'bɑnfaɪər/ *n* hoguera

Bonfire Night *n* NOTA El 5 de noviembre, en Gran Bretaña, se celebra el **Bonfire Night**, y hay hogueras y fuegos artificiales para recordar el intento de quemar el Parlamento en 1605.

bonnet /'bɑnɪt/ *n* **1** (*bebé*) gorrito **2** (*señora*) sombrero **3** (GB, Aut) capó, cofre (Mx)

bonus /'boʊnəs/ *n* **1** plus, bonificación (*fig*) ventaja añadida

bony /'boʊni/ *adj* **1** óseo **2** lleno de espinas/huesos **3** huesudo

boo /buː/ *vt, vi* abuchear ● *n* abucheo ● *interj* bu

booby trap /'buːbi træp/ *n* trampa (explosiva)

boogeyman /'buːgimæn/ *n* (*pl* -men) coco (*espíritu maligno*)

book /bʊk/ *n* **1** libro **2** libreta **3** cuaderno **4** the books las cuentas ▸ **be in sb's good/bad books** gozar del favor/estar en la lista negra de algn **by the book** según las normas ● *vt, vi* **1** reservar, hacer una reservación **2** *vt* contratar **3** (GB) (*policía*) fichar **4** *vt* (Dep) sancionar ▸ **be booked up 1** agotarse las localidades **2** *I'm booked up.* Tengo la agenda llena. ■ **book in** registrarse

bookcase /'bʊkkeɪs/ *n* estantería, librero

booking /'bʊkɪŋ/ *n* reservación: *~ office* taquilla

booklet /'bʊklət/ *n* folleto

bookmaker /'bʊkmeɪkər/ (*tb* **bookie**) *n* corredor/a de apuestas

bookmark /'bʊkmɑrk/ *n* **1** separador (libros) **2** (Comp) bookmark ● *vt* (Comp) agregar como bookmark

bookseller /'bʊkselər/ *n* librero/a

bookshelf /'bʊkʃelf/ *n* (*pl* -shelves /-ʃelvz/) estante, repisa (*para libros*)

bookstore (**bookshop** GB) /'bʊkstɔːr/-ʃɑːp/ *n* librería

boom /buːm/ *vi* **1** resonar, retumbar ● *n* **1** estruendo **2** boom

boost /buːst/ *vt* **1** aumentar **2** (*moral*) levantar ● *n* **1** aumento **2** estímulo grato

boot /buːt/ *n* **1** bota **2** (GB, Aut) baúl (Mx), cajuela (And) ▸ **get the boot** (coloq) ser despedido ● **1** *vt* dar una patada a **2** *vt, vi* (Comp) ~ (**sth**) (**up**) arrancar (algo) ■ **boot sb out** (coloq) echar a algn

booth /buːθ; buːð GB/ *n* **1** caseta **2** cabina

booty /'buːti/ *n* botín

booze /buːz/ *n* (coloq) bebida (alcohólica) ● *vi* (coloq): *go out boozing* salir de juerga/parranda

border /'bɔːrdər/ *n* **1** frontera NOTA La división entre países o estados puede ser **border** o **frontier**, pero una frontera natural siempre se llama **border**: *The river forms the ~ between the countries.* **Boundary** se usa para las divisiones entre áreas más pequeñas, como los condados. **2** (*jardín*) arriate **3** borde, ribete ● *vt* limitar con, lindar con ■ **border on sth** rayar en algo

borderline /'bɔːrdərlaɪn/ *n* límite ● *adj* dudoso

bore /bɔːr/ *pt de* BEAR ● *vt* **1** aburrir **2** (*agujero*) hacer (con taladro) ● *n* **1** (*persona*) aburrido/a **2** rollo, lata **3** (*escopeta*) calibre **bored** *adj* aburrido →BE **boredom** *n* aburrimiento **boring** *adj* aburrido →BE

born /bɔːrn/ *pp* nacido ▸ **be born** nacer: *He was ~ blind.* Es ciego de nacimiento. ● *adj* [*antes de sustantivo*] nato

borne /bɔːrn/ *pp de* BEAR

borough /'bʌroʊ; 'bʌrə GB/ *n* municipio

borrow /'bɑroʊ/ *vt* ~ **sth** (**from sth/sb**) pedir (prestado) algo (a algo/algn) NOTA En español se suele usar el verbo "prestar": *Could I ~ a dollar?* ¿Me presta un dólar? **borrower** n prestatario/a **borrowing** n crédito

bosom /'bʊzəm/ n seno

boss /bɒs/ n jefe/a ● vt ~ **sb about/around** (pey) dar órdenes, mangonear a algn **bossy** adj (-ier/-iest) mandón

botanical /bə'tænɪkl/ adj botánico

botany /'bɒtəni/ n botánica **botanist** n botánico/a

both /bəʊθ/ adj, pron ambos/as, los/las dos: ~ of you ustedes dos ◊ Both of us went./We ~ went. Los dos fuimos. ● adv **both... and...** a la vez..., y...: ~ you and me tanto tú como yo

bother /'bɒðər/ 1 vt molestar 2 vt preocupar 3 vi ~ (**to do sth**) molestarse (en algo) 4 vi ~ **about sth/sb** preocuparse por algo/algn ▶ **I can't be bothered (to do sth)** me da pereza (hacer algo) **I'm not bothered** me da igual ● n molestia ● (GB) interj caray (Mx), qué vaina (And)

bottle /'bɒtl/ n 1 botella 2 frasco 3 mamila (Mx), tetero (And) ● vt 1 embotellar 2 envasar

bottle bank n (GB) contenedor de botellas

bottle opener n abrebotellas

bottom /'bɒtəm/ n 1 fondo 2 (colina, página, escaleras) pie 3 (Anat) trasero 4 (calle) final 5 último: He's ~ of the class. Es el último de la clase. 6 (ropa) pantalón ▶ **at the bottom of sth** (fig) detrás de algo **get to the bottom of sth** llegar al fondo de algo

bough /baʊ/ n rama

bought /bɔːt/ pt, pp de BUY

boulder /'bəʊldər/ n roca (grande)

bounce /baʊns/ 1 vt, vi botar, rebotar 2 vi (coloq) (cheque) ser devuelto ■ **bounce back** recuperarse ● n bote, rebote **bouncy** adj 1 (pelota) que bota/rebota mucho 2 (persona) animado

bouncer /'baʊnsər/ n portero (discotecas, etc.), cadrulas (Mx)

bound /baʊnd/ pt, pp de BIND ● adj ~ **to do sth**: You're ~ to pass. Seguro que apruebas. 2 obligado (por ley o deber) 3 ~ **for...** con destino a... ▶ **bound up with sth** ligado a algo ● vi saltar ● n salto

boundary /'baʊndri/ n (pl -ies) límite, frontera →BORDER

boundless /'baʊndləs/ adj ilimitado

bounds /baʊndz/ n [pl] límites ▶ **out of bounds** prohibido

bouquet /bu'keɪ/ n 1 (flores) ramo 2 buqué

bourgeois /,bʊr'ʒwɑ/ adj, n burgués/esa

bout /baʊt/ n 1 racha 2 (enfermedad) ataque 3 (boxeo) combate

bow¹ /bəʊ/ n 1 lazo 2 (Dep, violín) arco

bow² /baʊ/ 1 vi inclinarse, hacer una reverencia 2 vt (cabeza) inclinar, bajar ● n 1 reverencia 2 (tb bows [pl]) (Náut) proa

bowel /'baʊəl/ n 1 intestino(s) 2 **bowels** (fig) entrañas

bowl /bəʊl/ n 1 cuenco, tazón: a fruit/sugar/salad ~ un frutero/azucarero/una ensaladera 2 plato hondo 3 (retrete) taza 4 **bowls** [sing] bochas ● vt, vi lanzar (pelota)

bowler /'bəʊlər/ n 1 (Dep) lanzador/a 2 (tb ~ **hat**) bombín

bowling /'bəʊlɪŋ/ n [U] bolos: ~ alley boliche/cancha de bolos

bow tie /,bəʊ 'taɪ/ n corbata de moño (Mx), corbatín (And)

box /bɒks/ n 1 caja 2 estuche 3 (correo) buzón 4 (Teat) palco 5 **the box** (coloq) la tele ● 1 vt embalar **box** 2 vt, vi boxear (contra) **boxing** n boxeo

boxer /'bɒksər/ n 1 boxeador 2 (perro) bóxer 3 **boxers** (tb ~ **shorts**) boxers (calzoncillos) →PAIR

Boxing Day n 26 de diciembre →NAVIDAD

box number n apartado postal/de correos

box office n taquilla

boy /bɔɪ/ n 1 niño 2 hijo 3 chico, muchacho

boycott /'bɔɪkɑt/ vt boicotear ● n boicot

boyfriend /'bɔɪfrend/ n novio

boyhood /'bɔɪhʊd/ n niñez

boyish /'bɔɪʃ/ adj juvenil: She has a ~ figure. Tiene tipo de muchacho.

bra /brɑ/ n sostén, brasier

brace /breɪs/ vt ~ **yourself** prepararse **bracing** adj estimulante

bracelet /'breɪslət/ n pulsera

braces /'breɪsɪz/ n [pl] 1 (**brace** GB) aparato (dental), frenos (Mx) 2 (GB) tirantes

bracket /'brækɪt/ n 1 paréntesis: in ~s entre paréntesis 2 soporte 3 categoría: the 20-30 age ~ el grupo de edad de 20 a 30 años ● vt 1 poner entre paréntesis 2 agrupar

brag /bræg/ vi (-gg-) fanfarronear, jactarse

braid /breɪd/ n trenza

brain /breɪn/ n 1 cerebro: the ~s of the family el cerebro de la familia **2 brains** sesos **3** mente ▸ **have sth on the brain** (coloq) tener algo metido en la cabeza **brainless** adj estúpido **brainy** adj (coloq) inteligente

brainstorming /'breɪnstɔːrmɪŋ/ n lluvia de ideas: *have a ~ session* reunirse para intercambiar ideas

brainwash /'breɪnwɒʃ/ vt ~ **sb (into sth)** lavarle el cerebro a algn (para que haga algo) **brainwashing** n lavado de cerebro

brainwave /'breɪnweɪv/ n idea brillante

brake /breɪk/ n freno ● vt, vi frenar

bramble /'bræmbl/ n zarza

bran /bræn/ n salvado

branch /brɑːntʃ; brɑːntʃ GB/ n **1** rama **2** sucursal ■ **branch of** desviarse, ramificarse **branch out (into sth)** extenderse (a algo), comenzar (con algo)

brand /brænd/ n **1** (Com) marca (tabaco, ropa, etc.) **2** forma: *a strange ~ of humour* un sentido del humor muy peculiar ● vt **1** (ganado) marcar **2** ~ **sb (as sth)** etiquetar a algn (de algo)

brandish /'brændɪʃ/ vt blandir

brand new adj completamente nuevo

brandy /'brændi/ n coñac

brash /bræʃ/ adj descarado **brashness** n desparpajo

brass /brɑːs; brɑːs GB/ n **1** latón **2** (Mús) metales

bravado /brə'vɑːdoʊ/ n bravuconería

brave /breɪv/ adj (-er/-est) valiente ▸ **put a brave face on sth** poner al mal tiempo buena cara ● vt **1** desafiar **2** (dificultades) soportar

brawl /brɔːl/ n bronca, pelea

breach /briːtʃ/ n **1** (contrato, etc.) incumplimiento: ~ *of confidence* abuso de confianza **2** (ley) violación **3** (relaciones) ruptura **4** (seguridad) falla ● vt **1** (contrato, etc.) incumplir **2** (ley) violar **3** (muro, etc.) abrir una brecha en

breadcrumbs /'bredkrʌmz/ n [pl] pan rallado/molido: *fish in ~* pescado empanizado/apanado

breadth /bredθ/ n **1** amplitud **2** anchura

break /breɪk/ n **1** rotura, abertura **2** descanso, vacaciones cortas, recreo **3** ruptura, cambio **4** (coloq) golpe de suerte ▸ **give sb a break** dejar en paz a algn **make a break (for it)** intentar escapar ●

(pt **broke** pp **broken**) **1** vt, vi romper **NOTA Break** no se usa con materiales flexibles, como la tela o el papel. **2** vi romperse, hacerse pedazos **3** vt (ley) violar **4** vt (promesa, etc.) no cumplir **5** vt (récord) batir **6** vt (caída) amortiguar **7** vt (viaje) interrumpir **8** vi hacer un descanso: ~ *for coffee* parar para tomar un café **9** vt (voluntad) quebrantar **10** vt (mala costumbre) dejar **11** vt (código) descifrar **12** vt (caja fuerte) forzar **13** vi (tiempo) cambiar **14** vi (tormenta, escándalo) estallar **15** vi (noticia, etc.) hacerse público **16** vi (voz) quebrarse, cambiar ▸ **break it up!** ¡basta ya! **break the bank** (coloq): *A meal out won't ~ the bank.* Comer fuera no nos va a arruinar. **break the news** dar la (mala) noticia **break your back (to do sth)** sudar sangre (para hacer algo) ■ **break away (from sth)** separarse (de algo), romper (con algo) **break down 1** (Aut) averiarse **2** (máquina) estropearse **3** (persona) venirse abajo: ~ *down and cry* romper a llorar **4** (negociaciones) fracasar **break sth down 1** echar abajo algo **2** vencer algo **3** descomponer algo **break in** forzar la entrada **break into sth 1** (ladrón) entrar en algo **2** (mercado) introducirse en algo **3** empezar a hacer algo: ~ *into a run* echar a correr ◊ *He broke into a cold sweat.* Le dio un sudor frío. **break off** dejar de hablar **break sth off 1** partir algo **2** (compromiso) romper algo **break out 1** (epidemia) declararse **2** (guerra, etc.) estallar **3** (incendio) producirse **4** llenarse: ~ *out in spots* llenarse de granos **break through sth** abrirse camino a través de algo **break up 1** (reunión) disolverse **2** (relación) terminarse **3** *School ~s up soon.* Las clases terminan pronto. **break (up) with sb** romper con algn **break sth up** disolver, hacer fracasar algo

breakdown /'breɪkdaʊn/ n **1** avería **2** (salud) crisis **3** (estadística) análisis

breakdown lane n (USA) acotamiento (Mx), berma (And)

breakfast /'brekfəst/ n desayuno: *have* ~ desayunar

break-in n (pl **-ins**) robo (de una casa)

breakthrough /'breɪkθruː/ n avance (importante)

breast /brest/ n seno, pecho (mujer): ~ *cancer* cáncer de mama

breaststroke /'breststrouk/ n (natación) (estilo) pecho, braza

breath /breθ/ n aliento: *out of/ short of* ~ sin aliento ◊ *hold your* ~/*get your* ~ *back* contener/recuperar el aliento ◊ *take a deep* ~ respirar hondo ▸ **a breath of fresh air** un soplo de aire fresco **catch your breath 1** recuperar el aliento **2** contener la respiración **don't hold your breath!** (coloq) ¡espérate sentado! **say sth under your breath** decir algo en voz baja **take sb's breath away** dejar a algn boquiabierto **waste your breath** perder el tiempo

breathe /briːð/ vt, vi **1** respirar **2** ~ (sth) in/out aspirar, espirar (algo) ▸ **breathe down sb's neck** (coloq) estar encima de algn **breathe life into sth/sb** infundir vida a algo/algn **not breathe a word** (of/about sth) no soltar ni una palabra (de algo) **breathing** n respiración: *heavy* ~ jadeo

breathless /'breθləs/ adj jadeante, sin aliento

breathtaking /'breθteɪkɪŋ/ adj impresionante, vertiginoso

breed /briːd/ (pt/pp **bred** /bred/) **1** vi reproducirse **2** vt criar **3** vt (fig) producir ● n raza, casta

breeze /briːz/ n brisa

brew /bruː/ **1** vt (cerveza) elaborar **2** vt, vi (té) hacer(se) **3** vi prepararse: *Trouble is brewing.* Se está armando un lío. **brewery** /'bruːəri/ n (pl **-ies**) fábrica de cerveza

bribe /braɪb/ n soborno (dinero) ● vt ~ **sb** (into doing sth) sobornar a algn (para que haga algo) **bribery** /'braɪbəri/ n soborno (acto)

brick /brɪk/ n ladrillo ■ **brick sth in/up** enladrillar algo

bride /braɪd/ n novia (durante la boda) →MATRIMONIO

bridegroom /'braɪdɡruːm/ n novio (durante la boda) →MATRIMONIO

bridesmaid /'braɪdzmeɪd/ n dama de honor →MATRIMONIO

bridge /brɪdʒ/ n **1** puente **2** vínculo ● vt ▸ **bridge the gap between...** acortar la distancia entre...

bridle /'braɪdl/ n brida

brief /briːf/ adj (**-er/-est**) breve ▸ **in brief** en pocas palabras ● vt dar instrucciones a algn **briefly** adv **1** brevemente **2** en pocas palabras

briefcase /'briːfkeɪs/ n portafolio(s)

briefs /briːfs/ n [pl] **1** calzoncillos **2** calzones →PAIR

bright /braɪt/ (**-er/-est**) adj **1** brillante, luminoso: ~ *eyes* ojos vivos **2** (color) vivo **3** (sonrisa, carácter) radiante, alegre **4** inteligente ▸ **look on the bright side** mirar el lado bueno de las cosas ● adv brillantemente

brighten /'braɪtn/ **1** vt, vi ~ (up) animar(se) (algo) **2** vi ~ (up) (tiempo) despejar

brightness /'braɪtnəs/ n **1** brillo, claridad **2** alegría **3** inteligencia

brilliant /'brɪliənt/ adj **1** brillante **2** (coloq) genial **brilliance** n **1** brillo, resplandor **2** inteligencia

brim /brɪm/ n **1** borde **2** ala (sombrero)

bring /brɪŋ/ vt (pt/pp **brought**) →LLEVAR **1** traer, llevar: ~ *sb to justice* llevar a algn ante los tribunales **2** (acciones judiciales) entablar **3** ~ *yourself to do sth: I couldn't* ~ *myself to tell her.* No tuve valor para decírselo. ■ **bring sth about** provocar algo **bring sb around** lograr que algn vuelva en sí **bring sb around (to sth)** convencer a algn (de algo) **bring sth back 1** reintroducir algo **2** hacer pensar en algo **bring sth down 1** derribar, derrocar algo **2** (inflación, etc.) reducir algo **bring sth forward** adelantar algo **bring sth in** introducir algo (ley) **bring sth off** lograr algo **bring sth on** provocar algo **bring sth on yourself** buscarse algo **bring sth out 1** producir algo **2** publicar algo **3** realzar algo **bring sb over (to sth)** convencer a algn (de algo) **bring sb to** hacer que algn vuelva en sí **bring sth/sb together** reconciliar, unir algo/a algn **bring sb up** criar a algn **bring sth up 1** vomitar algo **2** sacar algo a colación

brink /brɪŋk/ n borde

brisk /brɪsk/ adj (**-er/-est**) **1** enérgico **2** (negocio) activo

brittle /'brɪtl/ adj **1** quebradizo **2** (fig) frágil

broach /broʊtʃ/ vt abordar

broad /brɔːd/ adj (**-er/-est**) **1** ancho **2** amplio **3** (esquema, etc.) general **NOTA** Para la distancia entre dos extremos, es más común **wide**: *The gate is two meters wide.* Broad se usa para características geográficas: *a* ~ *expanse of desert*, y en frases como: ~ *shoulders*. ▸ **in broad daylight** en pleno día **broadly** adv **1** *smiling* ~ con una amplia sonrisa **2** en general: ~ *speaking* hablando en términos generales

broadcast /'brɔːdkɑːst; -kæst GB/ (pt/pp **broadcast**) **1** vt transmitir

2 vt (opinión, etc.) propagar 3 vi emitir ● n transmisión: party political ~ espacio electoral

broaden /'brɔːdn/ vt, vi ~ (sth) (out) ensanchar(se) (algo)

broccoli /'brɒkəli/ n brócoli

brochure /'brəʊʃər; 'brəʊʃə(r) GB/ n folleto (esp de viajes o publicidad)

broil /brɔɪl/ vt asar a la parrilla

broke /brəʊk/ pt de BREAK ● adj (coloq) sin dinero ▶ go broke quebrar (negocio)

broken /'brəʊkən/ pp de BREAK

broker /'brəʊkər/ n corredor/a de bolsa

brolly /'brɒli/ n (pl -ies) (GB, coloq) paraguas

bronchitis /brɒŋ'kaɪtɪs/ n bronquitis

brooch /brəʊtʃ/ n broche

brood /bruːd/ vi ~ (on/over sth) dar vueltas a algo

brook /brʊk/ n arroyo

broom /bruːm/ n escoba **broomstick** /'bruːmstɪk/ n (palo de) escoba

broth /brɒθ; brɔːθ GB/ n caldo

brothel /'brɒθl/ n burdel

brother /'brʌðər/ n 1 hermano 2 cofrade **brotherhood** n 1 hermandad 2 cofradía **brother-in-law** n (pl -ers-in-law) cuñado **brotherly** adj fraternal

brought /brɔːt/ pt, pp de BRING

brow /braʊ/ n 1 (Anat) frente 2 (gen pl) ceja 3 (colina) cima

brown /braʊn/ adj (-er/-est) 1 (color) café 2 (pelo) castaño 3 (piel, azúcar) moreno 4 (oso) pardo 5 ~ bread/rice pan/arroz integral ◇ ~ paper papel de embalar o empacar ● n café ● vt, vi dorar(se) **brownish** adj pardusco

brownie /'braʊni/ n 1 bizcocho/pastelillo de chocolate 2 Brownie niña scout, hadita (Mx)

browse /braʊz/ vi 1 ~ (through sth) echar un vistazo (a algo), hojear (algo) 2 pacer **browser** /'braʊzər/ n (Comp) navegador

bruise /bruːz/ n 1 moretón 2 (fruta) golpe ● vt 1 ~ (yourself) (persona) magullar(se) 2 vt (fruta) golpear **bruising** n [U] magulladuras

brush /brʌʃ/ n 1 cepillo 2 escoba 3 pincel 4 brocha 5 cepillado 6 ~ with sth roce con algo ● vt 1 cepillar 2 vt barrer 3 vt, vi ~ (past/against) sth rozarse contra/con algo/con algn ▶ brush sth aside hacer caso omiso de algo brush sth up/brush up on sth pulir algo (idioma, etc.)

brusque /brʌsk; bruːsk GB/ adj brusco (comportamiento, voz)

brutal /'bruːtl/ adj brutal **brutality** /bruː'tæləti/ n (pl -ies) brutalidad

brute /bruːt/ n 1 bestia 2 bruto ● adj bruto **brutish** adj brutal

bubble /'bʌbl/ n 1 burbuja: ~ bath espuma para baño 2 pompa: blow ~s hacer pompas ● vi 1 borbotear 2 burbujear **bubbly** adj (-ier/-iest) 1 efervescente 2 (persona) animado

bubblegum /'bʌblgʌm/ n [U] chicle (que hace bombas)

buck /bʌk/ n 1 (USA, coloq) dólar: big ~s mucha plata/lana 2 (animal) macho → CONEJO, CONEJA ▶ make a fast/quick buck hacer dinero fácil **the buck stops here** yo soy el último responsable ● vi dar brincos ▶ buck the trend ir contra la corriente ■ buck (sb) up (coloq) animarse, animar a algn

bucket /'bʌkɪt/ n balde, cubeta

buckle /'bʌkl/ n 1 hebilla ● 1 vt abrochar 2 vi (piernas) doblarse 3 vt, vi (metal) deformar(se)

bud /bʌd/ n (Bot) capullo

Buddhism /'bʊdɪzəm/ n budismo **Buddhist** adj, n budista

budding /'bʌdɪŋ/ adj en ciernes

buddy /'bʌdi/ n (pl -ies) (USA, coloq) compa, mano (Aml)

budge /bʌdʒ/ 1 vt, vi mover(se) 2 vi (opinión) ceder

budgerigar /'bʌdʒərɪgɑːr/ (coloq **budgie**) n (GB) periquito

budget /'bʌdʒɪt/ n presupuesto: a ~ deficit un déficit presupuestario ● 1 vt, vi presupuestar(se) 2 vi ~ for sth contar con algo **budgetary** adj presupuestario

buff /bʌf/ n 1 entusiasta ● adj, n beige

buffalo /'bʌfələʊ/ n (pl buffalo o -es) 1 búfalo 2 (USA) bisonte

buffer /'bʌfər/ n 1 amortiguador 2 (GB, vía) tope

buffet¹ /'bəˈfeɪ; 'bʊfeɪ GB/ n 1 cafetería: ~ car coche bar/restaurante 2 bufé

buffet² /'bʌfɪt/ vt zarandear

bug /bʌg/ n 1 insecto, bicho 2 (coloq) infección 3 (Comp) error de programación 4 (coloq) micrófono oculto ● vt (-gg-) 1 poner un micrófono oculto en 2 escuchar mediante un micrófono oculto 3 (coloq) sacar de quicio

buggy /'bʌgi/ n (pl -ies) (GB) 1 carrito 2 cochecito de niño

build /bɪld/ vt (pt/pp built) 1 construir 2 crear, producir ■ build sth in 1 empotrar algo 2 incorporar algo **build on sth** partir de la base de algo **build up** 1 intensificarse 2 acumularse **build sth/sb up** poner algo/a algn muy bien **build sth up** 1 acumular algo 2 (*negocio*) crear algo

builder /'bɪldər/ n constructor/a

building /'bɪldɪŋ/ n 1 edificio 2 construcción

building site n 1 solar 2 (*construcción*) obra

building society n (GB) banco hipotecario, corporación de ahorro y vivienda

build-up n 1 aumento gradual 2 acumulación 3 ~ (**to sth**) preparación (para algo) 4 propaganda

built /bɪlt/ pt, pp de BUILD

built-in adj 1 empotrado 2 incorporado

built-up adj urbanizado

bulb /bʌlb/ n 1 (*Bot*) bulbo 2 foco (*Mx*), bombillo (*And*)

bulge /bʌldʒ/ n 1 bulto 2 aumento (transitorio) ● vi 1 ~ (**with sth**) rebosar (de algo) 2 abombarse

bulimia n bulimia **bulimic** adj, n bulímico/a

bulk /bʌlk/ n 1 volumen: ~ *buying* compra al por mayor 2 mole 3 **the bulk** la mayor parte ▸ **in bulk** 1 al por mayor 2 a granel **bulky** adj (**-ier/-iest**) voluminoso

bull /bʊl/ n 1 toro 2 Ver BULLSEYE

bulldozer /'bʊldoʊzər/ n buldózer **bulldoze** vt 1 aplanar 2 derribar

bullet /'bʊlɪt/ n bala

bulletin /'bʊlətɪn/ n 1 (*declaración*) parte 2 boletín: ~ *board* tablero/cartelera (de avisos)

bulletproof /'bʊlɪtpruːf/ adj a prueba de balas

bullfight /'bʊlfaɪt/ n corrida de toros **bullfighter** n torero/a **bullfighting** n toreo

bullion /'bʊliən/ n oro/plata (en lingotes)

bullring /'bʊlrɪŋ/ n plaza de toros

bullseye /'bʊlzaɪ/ n (centro de la) diana

bully /'bʊli/ n (pl **-ies**) abusón/ona (*esp en la escuela*) ● vt (pt/pp **-ied**) intimidar, meterse con algn

bum /bʌm/ n 1 (*coloq*) (GB) trasero 2 (USA) vagabundo/a ● v (**-mm-**) ■ **bum around** (*coloq*) vagar, vagabundear

bumbag n (GB) riñonera

bumblebee /'bʌmblbiː/ n abejorro

bump /bʌmp/ vt, vi ~ **sth** (**against/on sth**); ~ **into sth** dar(se) con algo/algn (contra/en algo) ■ **bump into sb** (*coloq*) toparse con algn **bump sb off** (*coloq*) matar a algn **bump sth up** (*coloq*) (hacer) subir algo ● n 1 golpe 2 sacudida 3 (*Anat*) chichón 4 bache 5 abolladura

bumper /'bʌmpər/ n 1 parachoques, defensa (*Mx*): ~ *car* carro chocón ● adj abundante

bumpy /'bʌmpi/ adj (**-ier/-iest**) 1 (*superficie*) desigual 2 lleno de baches 3 (*viaje*) agitado

bun /bʌn/ n 1 panecillo (*redondo*) 2 (GB) bollo (dulce) 3 moña (*And*), chongo (*Mx*)

bunch /bʌntʃ/ n 1 manojo 2 (*frutas*) racimo 3 (*flores*) ramo 4 (*coloq*) grupo ● vt, vi agrupar(se), apiñar(se)

bundle /'bʌndl/ n 1 (*papeles, ropa*) fardo 2 haz 3 (*billetes*) fajo ● vt ~ **sth** (**together/up**) empaquetar algo

bung /bʌŋ/ n tapón ● vt 1 taponar 2 (GB, *coloq*) poner

bungalow /'bʌŋgəloʊ/ n casa de un solo piso

bungee jumping /'bʌndʒi dʒʌmpɪŋ/ n bungee

bungle /'bʌŋgl/ vt echar a perder

bunk /bʌŋk/ n 1 litera ▸ **do a bunk** (GB, *coloq*) largarse ■ **bunk off** (**sth**) (GB, *coloq*) irse de pinta (*Mx*), capar clase/trabajo (*And*)

bunny /'bʌni/ n (pl **-ies**) (tb ~ *rabbit*) conejito →CONEJO

bunting /'bʌntɪŋ/ n [U] banderolas

buoy /bɔɪ/ n boya ● vt 1 ~ **sb** (**up**) animar a algn 2 ~ **sth** (**up**) mantener algo a flote

buoyant /'buːjənt; 'bɔɪənt GB/ adj boyante

burble /'bɜːrbl/ vi 1 (*arroyo*) susurrar 2 ~ (**on**) (**about sth**) (GB) farfullar (algo)

burden /'bɜːrdn/ n 1 carga 2 peso ● vt 1 cargar 2 agobiar

bureau /'bjʊroʊ/ n 1 (USA) cómoda 2 (GB) escritorio 3 (USA, *Pol*) departamento (*gobierno*) 4 agencia

bureaucracy /bjʊə'rɑkrəsi/ n (pl **-ies**) burocracia **bureaucrat** /'bjʊərəkræt/ n burócrata **bureaucratic** /ˌbjʊərə'krætɪk/ adj burocrático

burger /'bɜːrgər/ n hamburguesa

burglar /'bɜːrglər/ n ladrón/ona: ~ *alarm* alarma antirrobo **burglary** n (pl **-ies**) robo (de una casa) **burglarize** (**burgle** GB) vt robar en →ROB, THIEF

burial /'beriəl/ n entierro

burly /'bɜːrli/ adj fornido

burn /bɜːrn/ (pt/pp burned/burnt)
→DREAM 1 vi, vt quemar: *to be badly
burnt* sufrir graves quemaduras
2 vi arder: *a burning building* un
edificio en llamas 3 vi escocer
4 vi (luz, etc.) arder 5 ~ *the lamp
burning* dejar una lámpara encendida 6 vt: *The boiler ~s oil.* La
caldera funciona con petróleo. ●
n quemadura **burning** adj 1 ardiente 2 intenso 3 (*tema*) candente

burner /'bɜːrnər/ n quemador
(*cocina*)

burp /bɜːrp/ 1 vi eructar 2 vt
(*bebé*) hacer eructar ● n eructo

burrow /'bɜːroʊ/ n madriguera ●
vt excavar

burst /bɜːrst/ n 1 (*ira, etc.*) arranque 2 (*disparos*) ráfaga 3 (*aplausos*) salva ● (pt/pp burst) 1 vt,
vi reventar(se) 2 vi explotar 3 vt:
The river ~ its banks. El río se
desbordó. ▶ **be bursting to** do sth
reventar de ganas de hacer algo
burst into tears romper a llorar
burst open abrirse de golpe
burst out laughing echar(se) a
reír ■ **burst into/out of sth** irrumpir en/salir de algo

bury /'beri/ vt (pt/pp -ied) 1 enterrar 2 sepultar: *~ your face in
your hands* ocultar la cara en las
manos 3 (*cuchillo, etc.*) clavar

bus /bʌs/ n (pl -es) autobús,
camión (de pasajeros) (*Mx*)

bush /bʊʃ/ n 1 arbusto: *a rose ~*
un rosal 2 **the bush** el monte
bushy adj 1 (*barba*) poblado
2 (*cola*) peludo 3 (*planta*) frondoso

busily /'bɪzɪli/ adv atareadamente

business /'bɪznəs/ n 1 [U] negocios: *I'm here on ~.* Estoy acá por
cuestión de negocios. ◇ *~ card*
tarjeta de visita ◇ *~ studies* ciencias empresariales 2 negocio,
empresa 3 asunto: *It's none of
your ~!* ¡No es asunto suyo!
4 (*reunión*): *any other ~* ruegos
y preguntas ▶ **business before
pleasure** primero es la obligación que la devoción **get down to
business** ir al grano **go out of
business** quebrar **have no business doing sth** no tener derecho
a hacer algo **mean business** ir en
serio

businesslike /'bɪznəslaɪk/ adj
1 formal 2 sistemático

businessman, **businesswoman** /'bɪznəsmæn/-wʊmən/

n (pl -men/-women) hombre/mujer de negocios

busk /bʌsk/ vi tocar música (*en la
calle, etc.*) **busker** n músico callejero

bust /bʌst/ vt, vi (pt/pp busted/
bust) (*coloq*) romper(se)
→ DREAM ● adj (*coloq*) roto ▶ **go
bust** ir a la quiebra ● n 1 busto
2 (*Anat*) pecho

bustle /'bʌsl/ vi ~ (about) trajinar
● n (*tb* hustle and ~) bullicio,
ajetreo **bustling** adj bullicioso

busy /'bɪzi/ adj (-ier/-iest) 1 ocupado 2 concurrido 3 (*temporada*)
de mucha actividad 4 (*programa*)
apretado 5 (*USA, teléfono*) ocupado ● vt ~ **yourself** ocuparse

busybody /'bɪzibɒdi/ n (pl -ies)
entrometido/a, metiche

but /bət, bʌt/ conj 1 pero 2 sino:
What could I do ~ cry? ¿Qué
podía hacer sino llorar? ● prep
excepto: *nobody ~ you* solo tú
▶ **but for sth/sb** de no haber sido
por algo/algn

butcher /'bʊtʃər/ n carnicero/a
butcher's n carnicería ● vt 1 (*animal*) matar 2 (*persona*) matar
brutalmente

butler /'bʌtlər/ n mayordomo

butt /bʌt/ n 1 tonel 2 aljibe 3 culata 4 (*cigarrillo*) colilla 5 (*USA,
coloq*) trasero ▶ **be the butt of sth**
ser el blanco de algo ● vt dar un
cabezazo a ■ **butt in** interrumpir

butter /'bʌtər/ n mantequilla ● vt
untar con mantequilla

buttercup /'bʌtərkʌp/ n ranúnculo

butterfly /'bʌtərflaɪ/ n (pl -ies)
mariposa ▶ **have butterflies (in
your stomach)** tener los nervios
en el estómago

buttock /'bʌtək/ n nalga

button /'bʌtn/ n botón ● vt, vi
~ (sth) (up) abrochar(se) (algo)

buttonhole /'bʌtnhoʊl/ n ojal

buy /baɪ/ vt (pt/pp bought) comprar: *~ a bike for sb/~ sb a bike*
comprar una bici para algn ◇ *I
bought this bike from Marta.* Le
compré la bici a Marta. ● n
compra **buyer** n comprador/a

buzz /bʌz/ n 1 zumbido 2 (*voces*)
murmullo 3 *I get a real ~ out of
flying.* En avión me entusiasma. 4 (*coloq*): *give sb a ~* llamar a
algn (por teléfono) ● vi zumbar ■
buzz off! (*coloq*) ¡lárgate!

buzzard /'bʌzərd/ n (USA) zopilote (*Mx*), gallinazo (*And*)

buzzer /'bʌzər/ n timbre eléctrico

by /baɪ/ prep 1 por 2 al lado de,
junto a 3 antes de, para: *be home
by ten o'clock* estar en casa para

las diez **4** de: *by day/night* de día/
noche ◇ *by birth/profession* de
nacimiento/profesión ◇ *a novel
by Joyce* una novela de Joyce
5 en: *by boat/train* en barco/tren
6 según: *by my watch* según mi
reloj **7** con: *pay by check* pagar
con un cheque **8** a: *little by little*
poco a poco **9** *by doing sth: Let
me begin by saying...* Permítan-
me que empiece diciendo... ◇ *by
working hard* a base de trabajar
duro ▸ **have/keep sth by** tener
tener algo a mano ● *adv* ▸ **by
and by** dentro de poco **by the by**
a propósito **go, drive, etc. by**
pasar (por delante) (en carro,
etc.) **keep/put sth by** guardar
algo para más tarde

bye /baɪ/ (*tb* **bye-bye**) *interj*
(*coloq*) chao, adiós

by-election *n* elecciones extraor-
dinarias

bygone /ˈbaɪɡɒn/ *adj* pasado

by-law (*tb* **bye-law**) *n* (*GB*) orde-
nanza municipal

bypass /ˈbaɪpæs; -pɑːs *GB*/ *n*
1 (carretera de) circunvalación
2 (*Med*) bypass ● *vt* circunvalar
2 evitar

by-product *n* **1** subproducto
2 (*fig*) consecuencia

bystander /ˈbaɪstændər/ *n* presente

byte /baɪt/ *n* (*Comp*) byte

C c

C, c /siː/ *n* (*pl* **C's, c's**) **1** C, c
2 (*Mús*) do

cab /kæb/ *n* **1** taxi: *~ driver* taxista
2 cabina (*de camión*)

cabbage /ˈkæbɪdʒ/ *n* repollo, col

cabin /ˈkæbɪn/ *n* **1** (*Náut*) camarote **2** (*avión*) cabina (*de pasajeros*) **3** cabaña

cabinet /ˈkæbɪnət/ *n* **1** armario:
drinks ~ (mueble) bar **2 the Cabinet** el gabinete

cable /ˈkeɪbl/ *n* **1** cable **2** amarra

cable car *n* **1** teleférico **2** (*USA*)
funicular

cackle /ˈkækl/ *n* **1** cacareo **2** carcajada desagradable ● *vi* **1** cacarear **2** reírse a carcajadas

cactus /ˈkæktəs/ *n* (*pl* **-es** o **cacti**
/ˈkæktaɪ/) cactus

cadet /kəˈdet/ *n* cadete

Caesarean (*tb* **Caesarian**) /si-
ˈzeəriən/ (*tb* **~ section**) *n* cesárea

cafe /ˈkæfeɪ, ˈkæfeɪ/ *n* café

cafeteria /ˌkæfəˈtɪəriə/ *n* restaurante de autoservicio

caffeine /ˈkæfiːn/ *n* cafeína

cage /keɪdʒ/ *n* jaula ● *vt* enjaular

cagey /ˈkeɪdʒi/ *adj* (**-ier/-iest**)
(*coloq*) reservado: *He's very
~ about his family.* No suelta
nada sobre su familia.

cake /keɪk/ *n* pastel, ponqué
(*And*) ▸ **have your cake and eat
it** (*coloq*) repicar y andar en la
procesión

caked /keɪkt/ *adj* *~ with sth*
cubierto de algo

calamity /kəˈlæməti/ *n* (*pl* **-ies**)
calamidad

calculate /ˈkælkjuleɪt/ *vt* calcular ▸ **be calculated to do sth** estar
pensado para hacer algo **calcu-
lating** *adj* calculador **calculation**
n cálculo

calculator /ˈkælkjuleɪtər/ *n*
calculadora

caldron (*USA*) = CAULDRON

calendar /ˈkælɪndər/ *n* calendario

calf /kæf, kɑːf/ *n* (*pl* **calves**)
1 becerro, ternero →CARNE **2** cría
(*foca, etc.*) **3** pantorrilla

caliber (**calibre** *GB*) /ˈkælɪbər/ *n*
calibre, valía

call /kɔːl/ *n* **1** grito, llamada
2 canto (*de pájaro*) **3** visita (*tb*
(**tele)phone ~**) llamada (telefónica): *a ~ for* llamada en demanda para algo ▸ **on call** de guardia
● **1** *vi* *~ (out) (for sth)* llamar a
voces (pidiendo algo): *She called
for help.* Pidió ayuda a gritos. **2** *vt*
~ sth (out) gritar, llamar algo (a
voces) **3** *vt, vi* llamar (por teléfono): *~ a taxi* llamar un taxi ◇
~ collect llamar por cobrar/cobro
revertido **4** *vt* llamar: *What's
your dog called?* ¿Cómo se llama
tu perro? **5** *vi* pasar por (la) casa
de algn: *Let's ~ on John/at John's
house.* Vamos a visitar a John.
6 *vi* (*GB, tren*) parar **7** *vt* (*reunión, elección*) convocar ▸ **call it
a day** (*coloq*) dejarlo por hoy **call
sb names** insultar a algn ■ **call
at...** (*GB, tren*) parar en... **call for
sb** ir a buscar a algn **call for sth**
requerir algo **call sth off** cancelar, abandonar algo **call sb out**
llamar a algn **call sb up 1** (*USA,
teléfono*) llamar a algn **2** llamar a
algn a filas

call box (*GB*) *Ver* PHONE BOX

caller /ˈkɔːlər/ *n* **1** el/la que llama
(por teléfono) **2** visita

call-in *n* (*pl* **-ins**) (*USA*) programa
de radio o televisión abierto a las
llamadas del público

callous /'kæləs/ *adj* cruel

calm /kɑːm/ *adj* (**-er/-est**) tranquilo ● *n* calma ● *vt, vi* ~ (**sth/sb**) (**down**) calmar(se) (algo/a algn)

calorie /'kæləri/ *n* caloría

calves /kɑːvz, kævz/ *pl de* CALF

camcorder /'kæmkɔːrdər/ *n* videocámara

came /keɪm/ *pt de* COME

camel /'kæml/ *n* camello

camera /'kæmərə/ *n* cámara (fotográfica)

camouflage /'kæməflɑːʒ/ *n* camuflaje ● *vt* camuflar

camp /kæmp/ *n* campamento: *concentration ~ campo* de concentración ● *vi* acampar **camping** *n* camping (*actividad*) **NOTA** Camping en inglés no es un lugar para acampar. Un camping se llama **campground** o **campsite** (*GB*).

campaign /kæm'peɪn/ *n* campaña ● *vi* hacer campaña **campaigner** *n* defensor/a

campground (**campsite** *GB*) /'kæmpgraʊnd/-saɪt/ *n* camping (*lugar*) →CAMP

campus /'kæmpəs/ *n* campus

can¹ /kən, kæn/ *v* (*neg* **cannot** /'kænɒt/ *o* **can't** /kænt, kɑːnt *GB*/ *pt* **could** *neg* **could not/ couldn't**) **NOTA** Can es un verbo modal al que sigue un infinitivo sin **to**, y que no usa el auxiliar **do** en interrogativas y negaciones. Sólo tiene presente: *I can't swim.* No sé nadar., y pasado, que también tiene un valor condicional: *He couldn't do it.* No pudo hacerlo. ◊ *Could you come?* ¿Podrías venir? Para otras formas se usa **be able to**: *Will you be able to come?* ¿Podrás venir? ◊ *I'd like to be able to go.* Me gustaría poder ir.
● **posibilidad** poder: *We ~ go by train.* Podemos ir en tren. ◊ *It ~ be very cold here.* A veces hace mucho frío acá.
● **conocimientos, habilidades** saber: *They can't read.* No saben leer.
● **permiso** poder: *You can't go swimming.* No puedes ir a nadar. →MAY
● **sugerencias, peticiones, etc.** poder: *Can I help?* ¿Puedo ayudar? ◊ *Could you help me with this?* ¿Me puede ayudar con esto? →MUST
● **con verbos de percepción:** *I can't see/hear you.* No te veo/ oigo.
● **incredulidad:** *I can't believe it.* No lo puedo creer. ◊ *Where*

~ she have put it? ¿Dónde lo habrá puesto?

can² /kæn/ *n* lata: *a petrol ~* un bote/tarro de gasolina ▸ **carry the can** (**for sth**) (*GB, coloq*) cargar con la culpa (de algo) ● *vt* (**-nn-**) enlatar

canal /kə'næl/ *n* **1** canal **2** tubo, conducto

canary /kə'neəri/ *n* (*pl* **-ies**) canario

cancel /'kænsl/ *vt, vi* (**-l-, -ll-** *GB*) **1** cancelar **2** anular ■ **cancel (sth) out** eliminar(se) (algo) **cancellation** *n* cancelación

Cancer /'kænsər/ *n* Cáncer

cancer /'kænsər/ *n* cáncer (*Med*)

candid /'kændɪd/ *adj* franco

candidate /'kændɪdət, -deɪt/ *n* **1** candidato/a **2** (*GB*) persona que se presenta a un examen **candidacy** /'kændɪdəsi/ *n* candidatura

candle /'kændl/ *n* vela

candlelight /'kændllaɪt/ *n* luz de una vela

candlestick /'kændlstɪk/ *n* **1** candelero **2** candelabro

candy /'kændi/ *n* (*pl* **-ies**) (*USA*) golosinas, dulces **NOTA** Candy se usa mucho como sustantivo incontable: *She loves ~.* A ella le gustan mucho las golosinas.

cane /keɪn/ *n* **1** (*Bot*) caña **2** mimbre **3** bastón **4 the cane** la vara (*para castigar*)

canister /'kænɪstər/ *n* **1** lata, tarro (*té, galletas, etc.*) **2** bomba (*de gas*)

cannabis /'kænəbɪs/ *n* marihuana

canned /kænd/ *adj* enlatado

cannibal /'kænɪbl/ *n* caníbal

cannon /'kænən/ *n* cañón

canoe /kə'nuː/ *n* canoa, piragua **canoeing** *n* canotaje

can-opener *n* (*USA*) abrelatas

canopy /'kænəpi/ *n* (*pl* **-ies**) **1** toldo **2** dosel **3** (*fig*) techo

canteen /kæn'tiːn/ *n* **1** comedor (*colegio, fábrica, etc.*)

canter /'kæntər/ *n* medio galope

canvas /'kænvəs/ *n* **1** lona **2** (*Arte*) lienzo

canvass /'kænvəs/ **1** *vt, vi* pedir apoyo **2** *vt, vi* (*Pol*): ~ *for/on behalf of sb* hacer campaña por algn ◊ *go out canvassing (for votes)* salir a buscar votos **3** *vt* (*opinión*) sondear

canyon /'kænjən/ *n* cañón (*Geol*)

cap /kæp/ *n* **1** gorra **2** cofia **3** gorro **4** tapa, tapón ● *vt* (**-pp-**) superar ▸ **to cap it all** para colmo

C

capable /'keɪpəbl/ *adj* capaz **capability** *n* (*pl* -ies) **1** capacidad, aptitud **2** potencial

capacity /kə'pæsəti/ *n* (*pl* -ies) **1** capacidad: *filled to* ~ completo **2** nivel máximo: *at full* ~ a pleno rendimiento **3** *in your* ~ *as* sth en su calidad de algo

cape /keɪp/ *n* **1** capa (*ropa*) **2** (*Geog*) cabo

caper /'keɪpər/ *vi* ~ (*about*) brincar ● *n* **1** alcaparra **2** (*coloq*) travesura

capillary /'kæpəleri; kə'pɪləri *GB*/ *n* (*pl* -ies) capilar

capital /'kæpɪtl/ *n* **1** (*tb* ~ **city**) capital **2** (*tb* ~ **letter**) mayúscula **3** (*Fin*) capital: ~ *gains* plusvalía ▸ **make capital (out) of** sth sacar partido de algo ● *adj* **1** capital: ~ *punishment* pena de muerte **2** mayúsculo **capitalism** *n* capitalismo **capitalist** *adj*, *n* capitalista **capitalize** *vt* (*Fin*) capitalizar ■ **capitalize on** sth aprovecharse, sacar partido de algo

capitulate /kə'pɪtʃuleɪt/ *vi* ~ (*to* sth/sb) capitular (ante algo/algn)

capricious /kə'prɪʃəs/ *adj* caprichoso

Capricorn /'kæprɪkɔːrn/ *n* Capricornio

capsize /kæp'saɪz; kæp'saɪz *GB*/ *vt*, *vi* volcar(se)

capsule /'kæpsl, -sjuːl/ *n* cápsula

captain /'kæptɪn/ *n* (*Dep*, *Náut*) capitán/ana **2** (*avión*) comandante ● *vt* ser el capitán de **captaincy** *n* capitanía

caption /'kæpʃn/ *n* **1** encabezamiento, título **2** pie (*de foto*) **3** (*Cine*, *TV*) rótulo, letrero

captivate /'kæptɪveɪt/ *vt* cautivar **captivating** *adj* encantador

captive /'kæptɪv/ *adj* cautivo: *hold/take* sb ~ tener preso/apresar a algn ● *n* preso/a, cautivo/a **captivity** /kæp'tɪvəti/ *n* cautividad

captor /'kæptər/ *n* captor/a

capture /'kæptʃər/ *vt* **1** capturar **2** (*interés*, *etc.*) atraer **3** (*Mil*) tomar **4** *She captured his heart.* Le conquistó el corazón. **5** (*Arte*) captar ● *n* **1** captura **2** (*ciudad*) toma

car /kɑr/ *n* **1** carro, coche, auto: *by* ~ en carro **2** (*USA*, *tren*) vagón

caramel /'kærəmel/ *n* caramelo (*azúcar quemado*)

carat (*GB*) = KARAT

caravan /'kærəvæn/ *n* **1** (*GB*) trailer, casa rodante **2** caravana (*de camellos*)

carbohydrate /,kɑrboʊ'haɪdreɪt/ *n* hidrato de carbono

carbon /'kɑrbən/ *n* carbono

carbon copy *n* (*pl* -ies) **1** copia al carbón **2** réplica: *She's a* ~ *of her Mom.* Es idéntica a su mamá.

carburetor /'kɑrbəreɪtər/ (**carburettor** /ˌkɑrbə'retər/ *GB*) *n* carburador

carcass /'kɑrkəs/ *n* **1** restos (*de pollo*, *etc.*) **2** res muerta lista para trocear

card /kɑrd/ *n* **1** tarjeta • ficha: ~ *index* fichero **3** (*de socio*, *etc.*) carné **4** (*naipes*) carta **5** [*U*] cartulina ▸ **get your cards/give sb their cards** (*GB*, *coloq*) ser despedido/despedir a algn **lay your cards on the table** poner las cartas sobre la mesa **play your cards right** jugar bien sus cartas

cardboard /'kɑrdbɔːrd/ *n* cartón

cardholder /'kɑrdhoʊldər/ *n* titular de tarjeta (*de crédito*)

cardiac /'kɑrdiæk/ *adj* cardíaco

cardigan /'kɑrdɪgən/ *n* suéter, saco (*de botones*)

cardinal /'kɑrdml/ *adj* **1** cardinal **2** fundamental ● *n* (*Rel*) cardenal

care /keər/ *n* **1** ~ (*over* sth/*in doing* sth) cuidado (con algo/al hacer algo): *take* ~ tener cuidado **2** atención ▸ **preocupación** ▸ **care of** sb (*correos*) a la atención de algn **in care** (*GB*, *niños*) al cuidado de una institución **take care of** sth/sb cuidarse/cuidar algo/a algn **take care of yourself/sth/sb** cuidarse/cuidar algo/a algn **that takes care of that** así se da por terminado ● *vi* **1** ~ (*about* sth) importarle a algn (algo): *See if I* ~. ¿Y a mí qué me importa? **2** ~ **to do** sth querer hacer algo ▸ **for all I, you, etc. care** para lo que a mí me, a ti te, etc. importa **I, you, etc. couldn't care less** me, te, etc. importa un comino ■ **care for** sb **1** querer a algn **2** cuidar a algn **care for** sth **1** gustarle algo a algn **2** apetecerle algo a algn

career /kə'rɪər/ *n* (*actividad profesional*) carrera: ~ *prospects* perspectivas profesionales ● *vi* correr a toda velocidad

carefree /'keərfriː/ *adj* libre de preocupaciones

careful /'keərfl/ *adj* **1** *be* ~ (*about/of/with* sth) tener cuidado (con algo) **2** (*trabajo*, *etc.*) cuidadoso **carefully** *adv* con cuidado, cuidadosamente: *listen/think* ~ escuchar con atención/pensar bien

caregiver /'keərgɪvər/ (**carer** /'keərər/ GB) n cuidador/a (de persona anciana o enferma)

careless /'keərləs/ adj 1 ~ (**about** sth) descuidado (con algo) 2 imprudente

caress /kə'res/ n caricia ● vt acariciar

caretaker /'keərteɪkər/ n (GB) portero/a, vigilante ● adj interino

cargo /'kɑːgoʊ/ n (pl **-s/-es**) 1 carga 2 cargamento

caricature /'kærɪkətʃər/ n caricatura ● vt caricaturizar

caring /'keərɪŋ/ adj caritativo

carnation /kɑːr'neɪʃn/ n clavel

carnival /'kɑːrnɪvl/ n carnaval

carnivore /'kɑːrnɪvɔːr/ n carnívoro **carnivorous** /kɑːr'nɪvərəs/ adj carnívoro

carol /'kærəl/ n villancico

carousel /ˌkærə'sel/ n (USA) carrusel

car park n (GB) estacionamiento, parqueadero (And)

carpenter /'kɑːrpəntər/ n carpintero/a **carpentry** n carpintería

carpet /'kɑːrpɪt/ n alfombra, tapete ● vt alfombrar

carriage /'kærɪdʒ/ n 1 carruaje 2 (GB, tren) vagón 3 (USA) baby ~ coche (de niño) **carriageway** /'kærɪdʒweɪ/ n (GB) carril

carrier /'kæriər/ n 1 portador/a: mail/letter ~ cartero/a 2 empresa de transportes

carrier bag n (GB) bolsa (de plástico/papel)

carrot /'kærət/ n 1 zanahoria 2 (fig) incentivo

carry /'kæri/ (pt/pp **-ied**) vt 1 llevar: ~ a gun estar armado → WEAR 2 vt soportar 3 vt (votación) aprobar 4 vi oírse: Her voice carries well. Tiene una voz muy potente. ▶ **carry the day** triunfar **carry weight** tener gran peso **get carried away** 1 entusiasmarse 2 perder los estribos ■ **carry sth off** 1 salir airoso de algo 2 realizar algo **carry sth/sb on** llevar(se) algo a algn **carry on** (**with sth**) seguir con algo **carry sth on** continuar (con algo) **carry sth out** 1 cumplir algo 2 llevar algo a cabo **carry sth through** llevar a término algo

carry-on n (GB, coloq) lío

cart /kɑːrt/ n 1 carro ● vt (coloq) 1 ~ sth/sb **off/away** llevarse algo/a algn 2 ~ sth **about/around** cargar con algo

carton /'kɑːrtn/ n caja, cartón

cartoon /kɑːr'tuːn/ n 1 caricatura 2 tira cómica 3 dibujos animados 4 (Arte) boceto **cartoonist** n caricaturista

cartridge /'kɑːrtrɪdʒ/ n 1 cartucho 2 (Fot, etc.) carrete, rollo

carve /kɑːrv/ 1 vt, vi esculpir 2 vt, vi tallar 3 vt grabar 4 vt, vi (carne) trinchar ■ **carve sth out** (**for yourself**) ganarse algo **carve sth up** repartir algo **carving** n escultura, talla

cascade /kæ'skeɪd/ n cascada

case /keɪs/ n 1 (Med, Gram, etc.) caso: It's a ~ of... Se trata de... 2 argumento(s): There is a ~ for... Hay razones para... 3 (Jur) causa: the ~ for the defence/prosecution la defensa/la acusación 4 estuche 5 cajón (de embalaje) 6 caja (de vino) 7 maleta ▶ **in any case** en cualquier caso **in case...** por si...: ~ in ~ it rains por si llueve (**just**) **in case** por si acaso **make** (**out**) **a case** (**for sth**) presentar argumentos (para algo)

cash /kæʃ/ n [U] dinero (en efectivo): be short of ~ andar mal de dinero ◊ pay ~ pagar en efectivo ◊ ~ price precio al contado ◊ ~ flow movimiento de fondos ◊ ~ desk caja ▶ **cash on delivery** (abrev COD) pago contra reembolso **cash up front**; **cash down** (GB) pago de contado ● vt hacer efectivo ■ **cash in on sth** aprovecharse (de algo) **cash sth in** canjear algo

cashier /kæ'ʃɪər/ n cajero/a

cash machine (tb **cashpoint®** /'kæʃpɔɪnt/ GB) n cajero automático

cashmere /ˌkæʃ'mɪər/ n cachemir

casino /kə'siːnoʊ/ n (pl **-s**) casino

cask /kæsk; kɑːsk GB/ n barril

casket /'kæskɪt, 'kɑːskɪt/ n 1 cofre (joyas, etc.) 2 (USA) ataúd

casserole /'kæsəroʊl/ n 1 (tb ~ **dish**) cazuela 2 estofado

cassette /kə'set/ n cassette: ~ player/recorder grabadora

cast /kæst; kɑːst GB/ n (Teat) reparto ● vt (pt/pp **cast**) 1 (Teat): ~ sb as Othello dar a algn el papel de Otelo 2 lanzar 3 (mirada): ~ an eye over sth echar un vistazo a algo 4 (sombra) proyectar 5 ~ your vote votar ▶ **cast a spell on sth/sb** hechizar algo/a algn **cast doubt** (**on sth**) hacer dudar (de algo) ■ **cast sth/sb aside** (fml) dejar de lado algo/a algn **cast sth off** (fml) deshacerse de algo

castaway /'kæstəweɪ; 'kɑːst- GB/ n náufrago/a

caste /kæst; kɑːst GB/ n casta

cast iron n hierro fundido **cast-iron** adj 1 de hierro fundido 2 (constitución) de hierro 3 (coartada) sólido

castle /ˈkæsl; ˈkɑːsl GB/ n 1 castillo 2 (ajedrez) torre

castrate /kæˈstreɪt; ˈkæˌstreɪt GB/ vt castrar **castration** n castración

casual /ˈkæʒuəl/ adj 1 (ropa) informal 2 (GB, trabajo) ocasional: ~ worker trabajador eventual 3 superficial: a ~ acquaintance un conocido ◇ a ~ glance un vistazo 4 (encuentro) fortuito 5 (comentario) sin importancia 6 (actitud) despreocupado, informal: ~ sex sexo sin compromiso

casualty /ˈkæʒuəlti/ n (pl -ies) víctima, baja

cat /kæt/ n 1 gato →GATO 2 felino: big ~ felino salvaje ▶ **let the cat out of the bag** irse de la lengua

catalog (tb **catalogue**) /ˈkætəlɔːg; -lɒg GB/ n 1 catálogo 2 a ~ of disasters una serie de desastres ● vt catalogar

catalyst /ˈkætəlɪst/ n catalizador

catapult /ˈkætəpʌlt/ n catapulta ● vt catapultar

cataract /ˈkætərækt/ n catarata

catarrh /kəˈtɑːr/ n catarro, flujo catarral

catastrophe /kəˈtæstrəfi/ n catástrofe **catastrophic** /ˌkætəˈstrɒfɪk/ adj catastrófico

catch /kætʃ/ (pt/pp caught) 1 vt agarrar, atrapar 2 vt sorprender 3 vt (coloq) pillar 4 vt ir a ver: I'll ~ you later. Te veré luego. 5 vt ~ sth (in/on sth) enganchar algo (en/con algo): ~ your thumb in the door agarrarse el dedo con la puerta 6 vt (Med) contagiarse de 7 vt oír, entender 8 vi (fuego) prenderse ▶ **catch fire** incendiarse **catch it** (GB, coloq): You'll ~ it! ¡Te la vas a ganar! **catch sb's attention/eye** captar la atención de algn **catch sight/a glimpse of sth/sb** vislumbrar algo/a algn ▶ **catch at sth** agarrarse a/de algo **catch on** hacerse popular **catch on (to sth)** (coloq) entender (algo) **catch sb out** 1 agarrar en falta a algn 2 (Dep) eliminar a algn al agarrar la pelota **be caught up in sth** estar metido en algo **catch up (on sth)** ponerse al día (con algo) **catch up (with sb)** alcanzar a algn ● n 1 atrapada (pelota, etc.) 2 captura 3 (peces) pesca 4 partido: He's a good ~. Es un buen partido. 5 cierre, cerradura 6 trampa: It's catch-22. Es una situación

sin salida. **catching** adj contagioso **catchy** adj (-ier/-iest) pegajoso

catchment area n (GB) área (que cubre un colegio, hospital, etc.)

catchphrase /ˈkætʃfreɪz/ n dicho (de persona famosa)

catechism /ˈkætəkɪzəm/ n catecismo

categorical /ˌkætəˈgɒrɪkl; -ˈgɔːr- GB/ adj 1 (respuesta) categórico 2 (rechazo) rotundo 3 (regla) terminante

category /ˈkætəgɔːri; -gəri GB/ n (pl -ies) categoría **categorize** vt clasificar

cater /ˈkeɪtər/ vi abastecer: ~ for all tastes atender a todos los gustos **catering** n comida: the ~ industry la preparación y distribución de alimentos

caterpillar /ˈkætərpɪlər/ n oruga

cathedral /kəˈθiːdrəl/ n catedral

Catholic /ˈkæθlɪk/ adj, n católico/a **Catholicism** /kəˈθɒləsɪzəm/ n catolicismo

cattle /ˈkætl/ n [pl] ganado

caught /kɔːt/ pt, pp de CATCH

cauldron /ˈkɔːldrən/ n caldera

cauliflower /ˈkɔːlɪflaʊər; ˈkɒlɪ- GB/ n coliflor

cause /kɔːz/ vt causar ● n 1 causa 2 motivo, razón: ~ for complaint motivo de queja

causeway /ˈkɔːzweɪ/ n camino/carretera más elevado/a que el terreno a los lados

caustic /ˈkɔːstɪk/ adj 1 cáustico 2 mordaz

caution /ˈkɔːʃn/ 1 vt, vi advertir 2 vt amonestar ● n 1 precaución, cautela: exercise extreme ~ extremar las precauciones 2 amonestación ▶ **throw/fling caution to the winds** abandonar la prudencia **cautionary** adj de advertencia: a ~ tale un relato ejemplar

cautious /ˈkɔːʃəs/ adj ~ (about/of sth) cauteloso (con algo): a ~ driver un conductor prudente **cautiously** adv con cautela

cavalry /ˈkævlri/ n caballería

cave /keɪv/ n cueva: ~ painting pintura rupestre ■ **cave in** 1 derrumbarse 2 ceder

cavern /ˈkævərn/ n caverna **cavernous** adj cavernoso

cavity /ˈkævəti/ n (pl -ies) 1 cavidad 2 caries

CD /ˌsiː ˈdiː/ n CD

CD-ROM /ˌsiː diː ˈrɒm/ n CD-ROM

cease /si:s/ *vt, vi* (*fml*) cesar, terminar: ~ *to do sth* dejar de hacer algo

ceasefire /'si:sfaɪər/ *n* cese del fuego

ceaseless /'si:sləs/ *adj* incesante

cede /si:d/ *vt* (*fml*) ceder

ceiling /'si:lɪŋ/ *n* 1 techo 2 tope, límite

celebrate /'selɪbreɪt/ 1 *vt* celebrar 2 *vi* festejar **celebrated** *adj* célebre **celebration** *n* celebración: *in ~ of sth* en conmemoración de algo **celebratory** /'seləbrə,tɔːri, ,selə'breɪtəri/ *adj* conmemorativo, festivo

celebrity /sə'lebrəti/ *n* (*pl* **-ies**) celebridad

celery /'seləri/ *n* apio

cell /sel/ *n* 1 celda 2 (*Anat, Pol*) célula 3 (*Elec*) pila

cellar /'selər/ *n* sótano

cello /'tʃeloʊ/ *n* (*pl* **-s**) violonchelo **cellist** *n* violonchelista

cellphone /'selfoʊn/ (*tb* **cellular phone**) *n* (*USA*) (teléfono) celular

cellular /'seljələr/ *adj* celular

Celsius /'selsiəs/ *adj* (*abrev* **C**) centígrado

cement /sɪ'ment/ *n* cemento ● *vt* 1 revestir de/pegar con cemento 2 cimentar

cemetery /'semətəri, -tri/ *n* (*pl* **-ies**) cementerio

censor /'sensər/ *n* censor/a ● *vt* censurar **censorship** *n* [U] censura

censure /'senʃər/ *vt* censurar ● *n* censura

census /'sensəs/ *n* (*pl* **-es**) censo

cent /sent/ *n* 1 (*dólar*) centavo ➤ Ver pág. 224 2 (*euro*) céntimo

centennial /sen'teniəl/ *n* (*tb* **centenary** /sen'tenəri, -'ti:n-/ (*GB* *pl* **-ies**)) centenario

center /'sentər/ *n* 1 centro: *the ~ of the town* = el centro de la ciudad 2 núcleo 3 (*USA, Dep*) delantero centro ● *vi, vt* centrar(se) ■ **center (sth) on/upon/around sth/sb** centrar(se) (algo) en/alrededor de algo/algn

center back (**centre back** *GB*) *n* defensor central

centimeter (**-metre** *GB*) /'sentiˌmi:tər/ *n* (*abrev* **cm**) centímetro

centipede /'sentɪpi:d/ *n* ciempiés

central /'sentrəl/ *adj* 1 (*en ciudad*) céntrico: ~ *London* el centro de Londres 2 central: ~ *air conditioning* aire acondicionado central 3 principal **centralize** *vt* centralizar **centralization** *n* centralización

---

centre (*GB*) = CENTER

century /'sentʃəri/ *n* (*pl* **-ies**) siglo

cereal /'stəriəl/ *n* cereal(es)

cerebral /sə'ri:brəl, 'serəb-/ *adj* cerebral

ceremonial /,serɪ'moʊniəl/ *adj, n* ceremonial

ceremony /'serəmoʊni, -məni/ *n* (*pl* **-ies**) ceremonia

certain /'sɜːrtn/ *adj* 1 seguro 2 cierto: *to a ~ extent* hasta cierto punto 3 tal: *a ~ Mr Lee* un tal Sr. Lee ▶ **for certain** con seguridad **make certain (of sth/that...)** asegurarse (de algo/de que...) **certainly** *adv* 1 con toda certeza 2 (*como respuesta*) cómo no: *Certainly not!* ¡Desde luego que no! **certainty** *n* (*pl* **-ies**) certeza

certificate /sər'tɪfɪkət/ *n* 1 certificado 2 (*nacimiento, etc.*) partida, acta

certify /'sɜːrtɪfaɪ/ *vt* (*pt/pp* **-ied**) 1 certificar 2 *He was certified* (*insane*). Lo declararon demente. **certification** *n* certificación

cesarean (*tb* **cesarian**) (*USA*) = CAESAREAN

chain /tʃeɪn/ *n* 1 cadena: ~ *reaction* reacción en cadena ◇ *in ~s* encadenado 2 (*Geog*) cordillera ● *vt* ~ **sth/sb (up)** encadenar algo/a algn

chainsaw /'tʃeɪnsɔː/ *n* sierra mecánica

chain-smoke *vi* fumar uno tras otro

chair /tʃeər/ *n* 1 silla: *easy* ~ sillón 2 **the chair** (*reunión*) la presidencia, el/la presidente/a 3 **the (electric)** ~ la silla eléctrica 4 cátedra ● *vt* presidir (*reunión*)

chairman, chairwoman /'tʃeərmən-wʊmən/ *n* (*pl* **-men/-women**) presidente/a **NOTA** Algunas personas prefieren usar **chairperson, spokesperson**, etc. tanto para un hombre como para una mujer.

chalet /ʃæ'leɪ, 'ʃæleɪ/ *n* chalé (*esp de estilo suizo*)

chalk /tʃɔːk/ *n* [*gen* U] 1 (*Geol*) creta 2 tiza, gis (*Mx*): *a piece/stick of* ~ una tiza/un gis ■ **chalk sth up** apuntarse algo

chalkboard /'tʃɔːkbɔːrd/ *n* (*USA*) pizarrón, tablero (*And*)

challenge /'tʃælɪndʒ/ *n* 1 desafío: *issue a* ~ *to sb* desafiar a algn 2 reto ● *vt* 1 desafiar 2 dar el alto a 3 poner en duda 4 (*trabajo, etc.*) estimular **challenger** *n* 1 (*Dep*) aspirante 2 desafiador/a **challenging** *adj* estimulante, exigente

chamber /'tʃeɪmbər/ n cámara: ~ *music* música de cámara ◇ *of commerce* cámara de comercio

champagne /ʃæm'peɪn/ n champán

champion /'tʃæmpɪən/ n 1 campeón/ona: *the defending/reigning* ~ el actual campeón 2 (*causa*) defensor/a ■ vt defender **championship** n campeonato

chance /tʃæns; tʃɑːns GB/ n 1 azar o casualidad: by (any) ~ por casualidad ◇ a ~ *meeting* un encuentro casual 2 posibilidad 4 oportunidad 5 riesgo: *take a* ~ *on sth* correr el riesgo de algo ◇ *take* ~ arriesgarse ▶ **on the (off) chance** por si acaso **the chances are (that)...** (*coloq*) lo más probable es que... ■ vt ~ *doing sth* correr el riesgo de hacer algo ▶ **chance your arm** (*GB, coloq*) arriesgarse ■ **chance on/upon sth/sb** encontrarse con algo/a algn por casualidad

chancellor /'tʃænsələr; 'tʃɑːns-GB/ n 1 canciller: *Chancellor of the Exchequer* (*GB*) Ministro/Secretario de Hacienda (*GB*) 2 (*GB, universidad*) rector/a o honorario/a

chandelier /ˌʃændə'lɪər/ n lámpara de araña

change /tʃeɪndʒ/ 1 vt, vi cambiar(se) (de): ~ (*your*) *clothes* cambiarse (de ropa) ◇ ~ *a tire* cambiar una llanta 2 vt ~ **sth/sb (into)** convertir a algn (en algo) 3 vi ~ **from sth to/into sth** pasar de algo a algo ▶ **change hands** cambiar de manos **change places (with sb)** cambiar de lugar (con algn) **change your mind/tune** cambiar de opinión/actitud ■ **change back into sth** 1 (*ropa*) ponerse algo otra vez 2 volver a convertirse en algo **change into sth** 1 (*ropa*) ponerse algo 2 transformarse en algo **change over (from sth to sth)** cambiar (de algo a algo) ● n 1 cambio: *a* ~ *of shoes* otro par de zapatos 2 transbordo 3 [*U*] monedas: *loose* ~ *dinero suelto* 4 (*dinero*) vuelto ▶ **a change for the better/worse** un cambio para mejor/peor **a change of heart** un cambio de actitud **for a change** para variar **make a change**: *It makes a* ~ *to get good news*. Una vez son buenas noticias. ◇ *It makes a* ~ *from pasta*. Por lo menos no es pasta otra vez. **the change of life** la menopausia **changeable** adj variable

changeover /'tʃeɪndʒoʊvər/ n cambio (*sistema político, etc.*)

change room (**changing room** *GB*) n probador, vestier (*And*)

channel /'tʃænl/ n 1 (*TV, Radio*) cadena, canal 2 canal 3 canal (*de navegación*) 4 (*fig*) vía ● vt (-l-, -ll-*GB*) 1 encauzar 2 acanalar

chant /tʃænt, tʃɑːnt/ n 1 (*Rel*) canto (litúrgico) 2 (*multitud*) consigna, canción ● vt, vi 1 (*Rel*) cantar 2 (*multitud*) gritar, corear

chaos /'keɪɑs/ n caos **chaotic** /keɪ'ɑtɪk/ adj caótico

chap /tʃæp/ n (*GB, coloq*) tipo

chapel /'tʃæpl/ n capilla

chaplain /'tʃæplɪn/ n capellán

chapped /tʃæpt/ adj agrietado

chapter /'tʃæptər/ n 1 capítulo 2 época ▶ **chapter and verse** con pelos y señales

char /tʃɑr/ vt, vi (-rr-) carbonizar(se), chamuscar(se)

character /'kærəktər/ n 1 carácter: ~ *references* referencias personales ◇ ~ *assassination* difamación 2 (*Cine, libro*) personaje: *the main* ~ el protagonista 3 reputación 4 (*coloq*) tipo ▶ **in/out of character** típico/poco típico (de algn)

characteristic /ˌkærəktə'rɪstɪk/ adj característico ● n rasgo, característica **characteristically** adv: *His answer was* ~ *frank*. Respondió con la franqueza que lo caracteriza.

characterize /'kærəktəraɪz/ vt 1 ~ **sth/sb as sth** calificar algo/a algn de algo 2 caracterizar **characterization** n descripción, caracterización

charade /ʃə'reɪd, ʃə'rɑːd/ n farsa

charcoal /'tʃɑrkoʊl/ n 1 carbón vegetal 2 (*Arte*) carboncillo 3 (*tb* ~ *grey*) (*color*) gris oscuro

charge /tʃɑrdʒ/ n 1 acusación: *bring/press* ~ *s against sb* presentar cargos contra algn 2 (*Mil*) carga 3 (*Dep*) ataque 4 (*animales*) embestida 5 cargo, cobro: *free of* ~ gratis 6 cargo: *have/take* ~ *of sth* estar a cargo de/hacerse cargo de algo ◇ *leave sb in* ~ *of sth* dejar a algn a cargo de algo ◇ *Who's in* ~? ¿Quién es el encargado? ◇ *under sb's* ~ bajo el cuidado de algn 7 carga (*eléctrica o de un arma*) ● vt ~ **sb (with sth)** acusar a algn (de algo) 2 vt, vi ~ **(at) (sth/sb)** atacar: *Charge!* ¡Al ataque! 3 vt, vi ~ **(at) (sth/sb)** (*animal*) embestir (algo/a algn) 4 vi ~ **down, in, up, etc.** lanzarse: ~ *down/up the stairs* lanzarse escaleras abajo/arriba 5 vt, vi cobrar 6 vt cargar: *Charge*

C

it to my account. Cárgalo a mi cuenta. **7** *vt* (*pistola, pila*) cargar **8** *vt* (*fml*) encomendar **chargeable** *adj* **1** imponible, sujeto a pago **2** ~ **to sb** a cargo de algn

chariot /ˈtʃæriət/ *n* carroza (*de tipo romana*)

charisma /kəˈrɪzmə/ *n* carisma **charismatic** /ˌkærɪzˈmætɪk/ *adj* carismático

charity /ˈtʃærəti/ *n* (*pl* **-ies**) **1** caridad **2** comprensión **3** organización benéfica, ONG: *for* ~ con fines benéficos ◇ **ONG charitable** *adj* **1** caritativo **2** bondadoso **3** (*organismo*) benéfico

charm /tʃɑːm/ *n* **1** encanto **2** amuleto, dije **3** hechizo ▸ **work like a charm** tener un efecto mágico ● *vt* encantar: *a charmed life* una vida afortunada ■ **charm sth out of sb** conseguir algo de algn por medio del encanto **charming** *adj* encantador

chart /tʃɑːt/ *n* **1** carta de navegación **2** gráfica: *flow* ~ diagrama de flujo **3** **the charts** los discos más vendidos ● *vt*: ~ *the course of sth* hacer una gráfica de la trayectoria de algo

charter /ˈtʃɑːtə(r)/ *n* **1** flete: *a ~ flight* un vuelo chárter **2** estatutos: *royal* ~ autorización real ● *vt* **1** (*avión, etc.*) fletar **2** otorgar autorización a **chartered** *adj* diplomado: ~ *accountant* (*GB*) auditor

chase /tʃeɪs/ **1** *vt, vi* perseguir: *He's always chasing (after) women.* Siempre anda persiguiendo mujeres. **2** *vt* andar detrás de **3** *vi* ~ **around, about, etc.** correr de un lado para otro ■ **chase sb/sb away, off, etc.** echar, ahuyentar algo/a algn **chase sth up** (*GB*) averiguar qué pasó con algo **chase sb up** recordar a algn (*que haga lo que olvidó hacer*) ● *n* **1** persecución **2** (*animales*) caza

chasm /ˈkæzəm/ *n* abismo

chassis /ˈʃæsi/ *n* (*pl* **chassis** /ˈʃæsiz/) chasis

chaste /tʃeɪst/ *adj* casto

chastened /ˈtʃeɪsnd/ *adj* **1** escarmentado **2** (*tono*) sumiso **chastening** *adj* que sirve de escarmiento

chastity /ˈtʃæstəti/ *n* castidad

chat /tʃæt/ *n* charla, plática: ~ *show* programa de entrevistas ◇ ~ *room* chat ● *vi* (**-tt-**) charlar, platicar ■ **chat sb up** (*GB, coloq*) tratar de ligar con algn, encartalar a algn (*And*)

chatty *adj* (**-ier/-iest**) **1** parlanchín **2** (*carta*) informal

chatter /ˈtʃætə(r)/ *vi* **1** ~ (*away/on*) parlotear **2** (*pájaro, animal*) chillar **3** (*dientes*) castañear ● *n* parloteo

chauffeur /ˈʃəʊfə; ˈʃəʊfə(r) *GB*/ *n* chofer ● *vt* ~ **sb around** hacer de chofer para, llevar a algn

chauvinism /ˈʃəʊvɪnɪzəm/ *n* chovinismo **chauvinist** *n* chovinista **chauvinistic** /ˌʃəʊvɪˈnɪstɪk/ *adj* chovinista

cheap /tʃiːp/ *adj* (**-er/-est**) **1** barato **2** económico **3** de mala calidad **4** (*comentario, chiste, etc.*) ordinario **5** (*USA, coloq*) tacaño ▸ **cheap at (twice) the price** regalado **on the cheap** barato ● *adv* (*coloq*) barato ▸ **be going cheap** estar en oferta **not come cheap**: *Success doesn't come* ~. El éxito no lo regalan. **cheapen** *vt* abaratar: ~ *yourself* rebajarse

cheat /tʃiːt/ **1** *vi* hacer trampas **2** *vt* engañar ■ **cheat on sb** ser infiel a algn **cheat sb (out) of sth** quitar algo a algn (*por medio de engaños*) ● *n* **1** tramposo/a **2** engaño, trampa

check /tʃek/ *vt* **1** comprobar, checar (*Mx*): ~ (*sth*) *for sth* comprobar que no haya algo (*en algo*) **2** *vt, vi* asegurar(se) **3** *vt* contener **4** *vt* detenerse **5** *vt* (*USA*) marcar (*con señal*) ■ **check in (at...)**; **check into...** registrarse (*en un hotel*) **check sth in** registrar algo **check sth/sb off** tachar algo/a algn (*de una lista*) **check out (of...)** saldar la cuenta e irse de un hotel **check sth/sb out 1** (*coloq*) mirar algo/a algn: *Check out these prices!* ¡No te pierdas esos precios! **2** (*tb* **check (up) on sth/sb**) hacer averiguaciones sobre algo/algn ● *n* **1** comprobación, revisión **2** investigación **3** jaque **4** (*USA*) cheque: *by* ~ con cheque **5** (*USA*) cuenta ▸ **hold/keep sth in check** contener/controlar algo **checked** (*tb* **check**) *adj* a cuadros

checkbook /ˈtʃekbʊk/ *n* chequera

checkers /ˈtʃekərz/ *n* (*USA*) damas

check-in *n* facturación, registro (*en aeropuerto*)

checklist /ˈtʃeklɪst/ *n* lista

checkmate /ˌtʃekˈmeɪt/ *n* jaque mate

checkout /ˈtʃekaʊt/ *n* **1** caja (*en tienda*) **2** acto de pagar e irse de un hotel

checkpoint /'tʃekpɔɪnt/ n puesto de control

check-up n (pl **-ups**) (Med) chequeo

cheek /tʃi:k/ n 1 mejilla 2 (GB) descaro **cheeky** adj (-ier/-iest) descarado

cheer /tʃɪər/ 1 vt, vi aclamar, vitorear 2 vt se cheered by sth animarse con algo ■ **cheer sb on** alentar a algn **cheer up** animarse, alegrar (algo/a algn) ● n ovación, vítor: *Three ~s for Joe!* ¡Tres hurras por Joe! **cheerful** adj alegre **cheery** adj (-ier/-iest) alegre

cheering /'tʃɪərɪŋ/ n [U] vítores ● adj alentador, reconfortante

cheerio /,tʃɪəri'oʊ/ interj (GB, coloq) hasta luego

cheerleader /'tʃɪərli:dər/ n porrista

cheers /tʃɪərz/ interj 1 salud 2 (GB, coloq) adiós 3 (GB, coloq) gracias

cheese /tʃi:z/ n queso

cheesecake /'tʃi:zkeɪk/ n pastel de queso, cheesecake

cheetah /'tʃi:tə/ n guepardo

chef /ʃef/ n chef

chemical /'kemɪkl/ adj químico ● n sustancia química

chemist /'kemɪst/ n 1 (GB) farmacéutico/a 2 químico/a **chemist's** n (GB) farmacia

chemistry /'kemɪstri/ n química

cheque /tʃek/ n cheque

chequebook n (GB) chequera

cherish /'tʃerɪʃ/ vt 1 valorar 2 (persona) querer, cuidar 3 (esperanza) abrigar 4 (recuerdo) guardar con cariño

cherry /'tʃeri/ n (pl -ies) 1 cereza 2 (tb ~ tree) cerezo ● adj, n (tb ~ red) rojo cereza

cherub /'tʃerəb/ n querubín

chess /tʃes/ n ajedrez

chessboard /'tʃesbɔ:rd/ n tablero de ajedrez

chest /tʃest/ n 1 baúl: *~ of drawers* cómoda 2 pecho (tórax) ▸ **get sth/something off your chest** desahogarse

chestnut /'tʃesnʌt/ n 1 castaña 2 castaño 3 (coloq) chiste viejo ● adj (color) caoba

chew /tʃu:/ vt masticar ■ **chew sth over** rumiar algo **chewy** adj 1 (caramelo) masticable 2 (alimento) cauchudo

chewing gum n [U] chicle

chick /tʃɪk/ n polluelo

chicken /'tʃɪkɪn/ n 1 (carne) pollo 2 (ave) gallina ● adj, n (coloq)

cobarde ■ **chicken out** (coloq) acobardarse

chickenpox /'tʃɪkɪmpɑks/ n varicela

chickpea /'tʃɪkpi:/ n (esp GB) garbanzo

chicory /'tʃɪkəri/ n [U] 1 endibia 2 achicoria

chief /tʃi:f/ n jefe/a ● adj principal **chiefly** adv 1 sobre todo 2 principalmente

chieftain /'tʃi:ftən/ n cacique (de tribu o clan)

child /tʃaɪld/ n (pl **children** /'tʃɪldrən/) 1 niño/a: *children's TV* programación infantil ◊ *~ benefit* subsidio familiar 2 hijo/a: *an only ~* un hijo único 3 (fig) producto ▸ **child's play** (coloq) juego de niños **childhood** n infancia, niñez **childish** adj infantil: *be ~* portarse como un niño **childless** adj sin hijos **child-like** adj de (un) niño

childbirth /'tʃaɪldbɜ:rθ/ n parto

childcare /'tʃaɪldkeər/ n servicio de cuidado de los niños

childminder /'tʃaɪldmaɪndər/ n (GB) persona que cuida niños en su casa

chili (chili GB) /'tʃɪli/ n (pl -ies) (tb ~ pepper) chile, ají

chill /tʃɪl/ n 1 frío 2 resfriado: *catch a ~* resfriarse 3 escalofrío ● 1 vt helar 2 vt, vi (comestibles) enfriar(se), refrigerar(se) ■ **chill out** (coloq) relajarse **chilling** adj escalofriante **chilly** adj (-ier/-iest) frío

chime /tʃaɪm/ n 1 repique 2 campanada ● vi repicar ■ **chime in (with sth)** interrumpir (diciendo algo)

chimney /'tʃɪmni/ n chimenea (conducto): *~ piece* (GB) repisa de la chimenea

chimpanzee /,tʃɪmpæn'zi:/ (coloq **chimp**) n chimpancé

chin /tʃɪn/ n barbilla ▸ **keep your chin up** (coloq) poner al mal tiempo buena cara

china /'tʃaɪnə/ n 1 porcelana 2 vajilla (de porcelana)

chink /tʃɪŋk/ n grieta, abertura ▸ **a chink in sb's armor** el punto débil de algn

chip /tʃɪp/ n 1 trocito 2 (madera) astilla 3 desportilladura 4 (US) papa frita (de bolsa) 5 (GB) papa frita (larga) 6 (casino) ficha 7 (Comp) chip ▸ **a chip off the old block** (coloq) de tal palo tal astilla **have a chip on your shoulder** (coloq) estar resentido ● vt, vi (-pp-) desportillarse ■ **chip away at sth** minar algo (destruir *poco a poco* **chip in (with sth)** (coloq) **1** (*comentario*) interrumpir (diciendo algo) **2** (*dinero*) contribuir (con algo) **chippings** n [pl] **1** grava, cascajo **2** (tb **wood** ~) virutas de madera

chipmunk /'tʃɪpmʌŋk/ n ardilla listada

chirp /tʃɜːrp/ n **1** pío **2** (*grillo*) canto ● vi **1** piar **2** (*grillo*) cantar **chirpy** adj alegre

chisel /'tʃɪzl/ n cincel ● vt tallar: *chiseled features* rasgos elegantes

chivalry /'ʃɪvəlri/ n **1** caballería **2** caballerosidad

chives /tʃaɪvz/ n [pl] cebollín

chloride /'klɔːraɪd/ n cloruro

chlorine /'klɔːriːn/ n cloro

chock-a-block adj ~ **(with sth)** atestado (de algo)

chock-full adj lleno a rebosar

chocolate /'tʃɒklət/ n **1** chocolate: *plain/milk* ~ chocolate negro/con leche **2** bombón, chocolate

choice /tʃɔɪs/ n **1** elección: *make a* ~ escoger **2** selección **3** posibilidad: *If I had the* ~... Si de mí dependiera... ► **by choice** por decisión propia **have no choice** no tener más remedio ● adj **(-er/-est)** de calidad, escogido

choir /'kwaɪər/ n coro

choke /tʃəʊk/ **1** vi ~ **(on sth)** atragantarse con algo: ~ *to death* asfixiarse **2** vt estrangular **3** vt ~ **(up)** atascar algo ■ **choke sth back** contener algo ● n (*Aut*) ahogador, choke

cholera /'kɒlərə/ n cólera

cholesterol /kə'lestərɒl/ n colesterol

choose /tʃuːz/ (*pt chose pp chosen*) **1** vt, vi elegir, escoger **2** vt (*Dep*) seleccionar **3** vt, vi ~ **(to do sth)** decidir (hacer algo) **4** vi preferir: *whenever I* ~ cuando quiera **choosy** adj (coloq) quisquilloso

chop /tʃɒp/ vt, vi **(-pp-) 1** ~ **sth (up) (into sth)** cortar, picar algo (en algo): ~ *sth in two* partir algo por la mitad ◇ *chopping board* tabla de cortar **2** (coloq) reducir ► **chop and change** (GB, coloq) cambiar de opinión varias veces ■ **chop sth down** talar algo **chop sth off** cortar algo (de golpe) ● n **1** hachazo **2** golpe **3** (*carne*) chuleta **chopper** n **1** hacha **2** (*carne*) tajadera **3** (coloq) helicóptero **choppy** adj picado (*mar*)

chopsticks /'tʃɒpstɪks/ n [pl] palillos (chinos)

choral /'kɔːrəl/ adj coral

chord /kɔːd/ n acorde

chore /tʃɔːr/ n tarea (*rutinaria*): *household* ~s quehaceres domésticos

choreography /ˌkɔːriˈɒɡrəfi; ˌkɒri- GB/ n coreografía **choreographer** n coreógrafo/a

chorus /'kɔːrəs/ n **1** (*Mús, Teat*) coro: *in* ~ a coro ◇ ~ *girl* corista **2** estribillo ● vt corear

chose /tʃəʊz/ pt de CHOOSE

chosen /'tʃəʊzn/ pp de CHOOSE

Christ /kraɪst/ n Cristo

christen /'krɪsn/ vt bautizar (con el nombre de) **christening** /ˈkrɪsnɪŋ/ n bautismo

Christian /'krɪstʃən/ adj, n cristiano/a **Christianity** /ˌkrɪstiˈænəti/ n cristianismo

Christian name n nombre de pila

Christmas /'krɪsməs/ n Navidad: ~ *Eve* Nochebuena →NAVIDAD

Christmas pudding n pastel de frutos secos que se come el día de Navidad

chrome /krəʊm/ n cromo

chromium /'krəʊmiəm/ n cromo: *chromium-plated* cromado

chromosome /'krəʊməsəʊm/ n cromosoma

chronic /'krɒnɪk/ adj **1** crónico **2** (*alcohólico, etc.*) empedernido

chronicle /'krɒnɪkl/ n crónica ● vt registrar

chrysalis /'krɪsəlɪs/ n (pl **-es**) crisálida

chubby /'tʃʌbi/ adj regordete

chuck /tʃʌk/ vt (coloq) **1** tirar: ~ *sth away/out* tirar algo a la basura **2** ~ **sth (in/up)** dejar algo ■ **chuck sth out** echar a algn

chuckle /'tʃʌkl/ vi reírse entre dientes ● n risita

chum /tʃʌm/ n (coloq) compa, (her)mano (*And*)

chunk /tʃʌŋk/ n trozo **chunky** adj fornido

church /tʃɜːrtʃ/ n iglesia: *go to* ~ ir a misa ◇ ~ *hall* salón parroquial →SCHOOL

churchyard /'tʃɜːrtʃjɑːrd/ n cementerio (*alrededor de iglesia*)

churn /tʃɜːrn/ n, vi ~ **(sth) (up)** (*agua, barro*) agitarse, remover algo **2** vi (*estómago*) revolverse ■ **churn sth out** (coloq) fabricar algo en serie (*libros, etc.*)

chute /ʃuːt/ n tobogán

cider /'saɪdər/ n sidra

cigar /sɪ'ɡɑːr/ n puro (*tabaco*)

cigarette /ˌsɪɡə'ret; 'sɪɡəret GB/ n cigarrillo: ~ *butt* colilla

cinder /'sɪndər/ n ceniza

cinema /'sɪnəmə/ n (GB) cine

C

cinnamon /'sɪnəmən/ n canela

circle /'sɜːkl/ n 1 círculo, circunferencia: *stand in a ~* formar un círculo 2 *(Teat)* anfiteatro *(primer piso)* ▶ **go around in circles** no hacer progresos ● vt 1 dar vueltas a 2 rodear 3 encerrar en un círculo

circuit /'sɜːkɪt/ n 1 gira 2 vuelta 3 pista 4 *(Elec)* circuito

circular /'sɜːkjələr/ adj redondo, circular ● n circular

circulate /'sɜːkjəleɪt/ vt, vi (hacer) circular

circulation /ˌsɜːrkjə'leɪʃn/ n 1 circulación 2 *(Period)* tirada

circumcise /'sɜːrkəmsaɪz/ vt circuncidar **circumcision** /ˌsɜːrkəm'sɪʒn/ n circuncisión

circumference /sər'kʌmfərəns/ n circunferencia: *the ~ of a circle* el perímetro de una circunferencia

circumstance /'sɜːrkəmstæns/ n 1 circunstancia 2 **circumstances** *[pl]* situación económica ▶ **in/under no circumstances** en ningún caso **in/under the circumstances** dadas las circunstancias

circus /'sɜːrkəs/ n circo

cistern /'sɪstərn/ n 1 cisterna 2 depósito, tinaco *(Mx)*

cite /saɪt/ vt citar

citizen /'sɪtɪzn/ n ciudadano/a **citizenship** n ciudadanía

citrus /'sɪtrəs/ adj cítrico: *~ fruit* cítricos

city /'sɪti/ n *(pl* -ies**)** 1 ciudad →CIUDAD 2 **the City** *(GB)* el centro financiero de Londres

city hall n *(USA)* ayuntamiento, alcaldía

civic /'sɪvɪk/ adj 1 municipal: *~ centre* centro municipal 2 cívico

civil /'sɪvl/ adj 1 civil: *~ strife* disensión social ◇ *~ rights/liberties* derechos civiles ◇ *~ servant* funcionario *(del Estado)*/burócrata ◇ *the Civil Service* la Administración Pública 2 educado, atento

civilian /sə'vɪliən/ n civil

civilization /ˌsɪvəlaɪ'zeɪʃn; -lar'z- GB/ n civilización **civilized** adj civilizado

clad /klæd/ adj ~ **(in sth)** *(fml)* vestido *(de algo)*

claim /kleɪm/ vt 1 reclamar 2 afirmar, pretender 3 *(atención)* merecer 4 *(vidas)* cobrarse ● n 1 ~ **(for sth)** solicitud *(de algo)*; demanda 2 ~ **(against sth/sb)** *(against algo/algn)*: *insurance* ~ reclamación al seguro ▶ **lay** ~ **to sth** reclamar algo 2 ~ **(to sth)**;

~ **(on sth/sb)** derecho *(a algo)*; *(sobre algo/algn)* 3 afirmación, pretensión **claimant** n demandante

clam /klæm/ n almeja ● v *(-mm-)* ▶ **clam up** *(coloq)* cerrar el pico

clamber /'klæmbər/ vi trepar *(con dificultad)*

clammy /'klæmi/ adj sudoroso, pegajoso

clamor *(-our GB)* /'klæmər/ n clamor, griterío ● vi 1 clamar 2 ~ **for sth** pedir algo a voces

clamp /klæmp/ n 1 grapa 2 abrazadera 3 *(GB)* cepo ● vt 1 sujetar 2 poner el cepo a ■ **clamp down (on sth/sb)** apretar los tornillos (a algo/algn)

clampdown /'klæmpdaʊn/ n ~ **(on sth)** restricción *(de algo)*, medidas drásticas *(contra algo)*

clan /klæn/ n clan

clandestine /klæn'destɪn/ adj *(fml)* clandestino

clang /klæŋ/ n tañido *(metálico)* ● vt, vi (hacer) sonar

clank /klæŋk/ vi hacer un ruido metálico *(cadenas, maquinaria)*

clap /klæp/ *(-pp-)* 1 vt, vi aplaudir 2 vt: ~ *your hands (together)* batir palmas ◇ ~ *sb on the back* dar una palmada en la espalda a algn ● n 1 aplauso 2 *a ~ of thunder* un trueno **clapping** n *[U]* aplausos

clarify /'klærəfaɪ/ vt *(pt/pp* -ied**)** aclarar **clarification** n aclaración

clarinet /ˌklærə'net/ n clarinete

clarity /'klærəti/ n lucidez, claridad

clash /klæʃ/ 1 vt, vi (hacer) chocar *(con ruido)* 2 vi tener un enfrentamiento 3 vi ~ **(on/over sth)** discrepar *(en algo)* 4 vi *(fechas)* coincidir 5 vi *(colores)* desentonar ● n 1 estruendo 2 enfrentamiento 3 ~ **(on/over sth)** discrepancia *(por algo)*: *a ~ of interests* un conflicto de intereses

clasp /klæsp; klɑːsp GB/ n cierre ● vt apretar

class /klæs, klɑːs/ n 1 clase: *He's in ~.* Está en clase. ◇ *~ system* sistema de clases 2 categoría: *They're not in the same ~.* No tienen comparación. ◇ *in a ~ of its own* sin par ● vt clasificar

classic /'klæsɪk/ adj, clásico, típico

classical /'klæsɪkl/ adj clásico

classify /'klæsɪfaɪ/ vt *(pt/pp* -ied**)** clasificar **classification** n 1 clasificación 2 categoría **classified** adj 1 clasificado 2 confidencial

classmate /ˈklæsmeɪt; ˈklɑːs- GB/ n compañero/a de clase

classroom /ˈklæsruːm, ˈklɑːs-/ n aula, salón de clase

classy /ˈklæsi; ˈklɑːsi GB/ adj (-ier/-iest) con mucho estilo

clatter /ˈklætər/ n (tb **clattering**) 1 estrépito 2 (tren) traqueteo ● 1 vt, vi hacer ruido (con platos, etc.) 2 vi (tren) traquetear

clause /klɔːz/ n 1 (Gram) proposición 2 (Jur) cláusula

claw /klɔː/ n 1 garra 2 (gato) uña 3 (cangrejo) pinza 4 (máquina) garfio ● vt arañar

clay /kleɪ/ n arcilla, barro

clean /kliːn/ adj (-er/-est) 1 limpio: *wipe sth ~* limpiar algo 2 (papel, etc.) en blanco ▸ **make a clean break (with sth)** romper (con algo) ● vt, vi ~ (**sth**) (**up**) limpiar(se) (algo): *~ mud off your shoes* limpiar el barro de los zapatos ◇ *~ up your image* mejorar su imagen ■ **clean sb out** (coloq) dejar a algn sin un peso **clean sth out** limpiar algo a fondo **cleaning** n limpieza (*trabajo*) **cleanliness** /ˈklenlinəs/ n limpieza (*cualidad*)

clean-cut adj 1 pulcro 2 (*rasgos*) muy bien perfilado

cleaner /ˈkliːnər/ n limpiador/a **cleaner's** n lavandería

cleanse /klenz/ vt 1 limpiar en profundidad 2 purificar **cleanser** n 1 producto de limpieza 2 (*para cara*) crema limpiadora

clean-shaven adj afeitado

clean-up n limpieza (*de un lugar*)

clear /klɪər/ adj (-er/-est) 1 claro: *make sth ~* dejar algo claro 2 (*cielo, carretera*) despejado 3 (*vidrio*) transparente 4 (*recepción, recuerdo*) nítido 5 (*conciencia*) tranquilo 6 libre: *~ of debt* libre de deudas ◇ *keep next week ~* dejar libre la semana que viene ▸ **(as) clear as day/mud** más claro que el agua/nada claro **in the clear** (coloq) fuera de sospecha/peligro ● adv 1 claramente 2 completamente ▸ **keep/stay/steer clear** mantenerse alejado ● 1 vt, vi despejar(se) 2 vt (*tubería*) destapar 3 vt (*de agua*) desalojar 4 vi (*agua*) aclararse 5 vt ~ **sb** (**of sth**) absolver a algn (*de algo*): *~ your name* limpiar su nombre 6 vt (*obstáculo*) salvar 7 vt, vi ~ (**sth**) (**away/up**) recoger (*algo*): *~ the table* recoger la mesa ▸ **clear the air** aclarar las cosas ■ **clear off** (coloq) largarse **clear sth out** ordenar algo **clear up** (*tiempo*) despejarse **clear sth up** dejar algo claro

clearance /ˈklɪərəns/ n 1 despeje: *a ~ sale* una liquidación 2 espacio libre 3 autorización

clear-cut adj definido

clear-headed adj de mente despejada

clearing /ˈklɪərɪŋ/ n claro (*de bosque*)

clearly /ˈklɪərli/ adv claramente

clear-sighted adj lúcido

cleavage /ˈkliːvɪdʒ/ n escote

clef /klef/ n (Mús) clave

clench /klentʃ/ vt apretar (*puños, dientes*)

clergy /ˈklɜːrdʒi/ n [pl] clero

clergyman /ˈklɜːrdʒimən/ n (pl -men) 1 clérigo 2 sacerdote anglicano

clerical /ˈklerɪkl/ adj 1 de oficina: *~ staff* personal administrativo 2 (Rel) eclesiástico

clerk /klɜːrk; klɑːk GB/ n 1 oficinista, empleado/a 2 (*juzgado, etc.*) actuario/a 3 (USA) (tb **desk ~**) recepcionista 4 (USA) (tb **sales/store ~**) (*en tienda*) dependiente/a, vendedor/a

clever /ˈklevər/ adj (-er/-est) 1 inteligente: *be too ~* pasarse de listo 2 hábil: *be ~ at sth* tener aptitud para algo 3 ingenioso 4 astuto **cleverness** n inteligencia, habilidad, astucia

cliché /kliːˈʃeɪ; ˈkliːʃeɪ GB/ n cliché

click /klɪk/ n 1 clic 2 chasquido 3 taconazo ● 1 vt, vi: *~ your heels/fingers* chasquear los dedos ◇ *~ open/shut* abrirse/cerrarse con un clic 2 vi ~ (**on sth**) (Comp) hacer clic (en algo) 3 vi (*hacerse amigos*) conectar 4 vi caer en la cuenta

client /ˈklaɪənt/ n cliente

clientele /ˌklaɪənˈtel; ˌkliː- GB/ n clientela

cliff /klɪf/ n acantilado, precipicio

climate /ˈklaɪmət/ n clima: *social ~* las condiciones sociales

climax /ˈklaɪmæks/ n clímax

climb /klaɪm/ vt, vi 1 escalar 2 subir: *The path ~s steeply.* El camino es muy empinado. 3 ~ (**up**) (**sth**) trepar (por algo): *~ up (on to) sth* subirse a algo 4 ~ **out of sth** bajarse de algo: *~ out of bed* levantarse de la cama 5 (*sociedad*) ascender ■ **climb down** dar marcha atrás ● n 1 escalada, subida 2 pendiente **climber** n alpinista **climbing** n escalada: *go climbing* hacer alpinismo

c

clinch /klɪntʃ/ vt 1 (trato, etc.) cerrar 2 (victoria, etc.) ganar: *That clinched it.* Eso fue decisivo.

cling /klɪŋ/ vi (pt/pp **clung**) **~ (on) to sth/sb** agarrarse, aferrarse a algo/algn: *~ to each other* abrazarse estrechamente **clinging** (tb **clingy**) adj 1 (ropa) ceñido 2 (persona) pegajoso

clinic /ˈklɪnɪk/ n clínica

clinical /ˈklɪnɪkl/ adj 1 clínico 2 (fig) imparcial

clink /klɪŋk/ 1 vi tintinear 2 vt: *~ glasses* brindar

clip /klɪp/ n 1 clip 2 (joya) broche, prendedor ● vt (-pp-) 1 cortar, recortar 2 **~ sth (on) to sth** prender algo a algo (con clip) 3 **~ sth together** unir algo (con clip)

clique /kliːk/ n camarilla

cloak /kləʊk/ n capa ● vt envolver: *cloaked in secrecy* rodeado de un gran secreto

cloakroom /ˈkləʊkruːm/ n 1 guardarropa 2 (GB) baño →TOILET

clock /klɒk/ n 1 reloj (de pared o de mesa) 2 (coloq) cuentakilómetros 3 (coloq) taxímetro ► **around the clock** las veinticuatro horas **turn back the clock** volver al pasado ● vt cronometrar ■ **clock in/on** marcar/checar tarjeta **clock off/out** marcar/marcar tarjeta **clock up sth** registrar, acumular algo **clockwise** adv, adj en el sentido del reloj

clockwork /ˈklɒkwɜːk/ adj con mecanismo de relojería ► **like clockwork** como un reloj

clog /klɒɡ/ n zueco ● vt, vi (-gg-) **~ (sth) (up)** atascar(se) (algo)

cloister /ˈklɔɪstər/ n claustro

clone /kləʊn/ n 1 (Biol) clon 2 (Comp) clónico ● vt clonar

close¹ /kləʊs/ (-er/-est) adj 1 (pariente) cercano 2 (amigo) íntimo: *~ to sb* unido a algn 3 (vínculos, etc.) estrecho 4 (vigilancia) estricto 5 (examen) detallado 6 (partido) muy reñido 7 (tiempo) bochornoso 8 **~ to sth** cerca de, al lado de algo: *~ to tears* casi llorando ► **it/that was a close call/shave** (coloq) por un pelo me, te... **keep a close eye/watch on sth/sb** mantener algo/a algn bajo vigilancia ● adv (tb **~ by**) cerca ► **close on** casi **close together** juntos **closeness** n 1 proximidad 2 intimidad

close² /kləʊz/ vt, vi 1 cerrar(se) 2 (reunión, etc.) concluir(se) ► **close your mind to sth** no querer saber nada de algo ■

close (sth) down cerrar (algo) (definitivamente) **close in** (día) acortarse **close in (on sth/sb)** (noche, enemigo, etc.) venirse encima (de algo/algn) ● n final: *towards the ~ of* a finales de ◊ *come/draw to a ~* llegar a su fin ► **bring sth to a close** concluir algo **closed** adj cerrado

close-knit adj muy unido

closet /ˈklɒzət/ n (USA) clóset

close-up n (pl **-ups**) primer plano

closing /ˈkləʊzɪŋ/ adj último: *~ time/date* hora de cierre/fecha límite

closure /ˈkləʊʒər/ n cierre

clot /klɒt/ n coágulo

cloth /klɒθ; klɒθ GB/ n (pl **-s** /klɔːðz; klɒðz GB/) 1 tela, paño →TELA 2 trapo

clothe /kləʊð/ vt **~ sb/yourself (in sth)** vestir a algn; vestirse (de algo)

clothes /kləʊðz; kləʊðz GB/ n [pl] ropa: *~ line* cuerda de la ropa

clothespin /ˈkləʊðzpɪn/ n pinza, gancho (And)

clothing /ˈkləʊðɪŋ/ n ropa: *the ~ industry* la industria textil

cloud /klaʊd/ n nube ● 1 vt ofuscar 2 vt complicar 3 vi **~ over** nublarse 4 vi (expresión) ensombrecerse **cloudless** adj despejado **cloudy** adj (-ier/-iest) nublado

clout /klaʊt/ n 1 (coloq) golpe 2 influencia ● vt (coloq) darle un golpe a

clove /kləʊv/ n 1 (especia) clavo 2 (ajo) diente

clover /ˈkləʊvər/ n trébol

clown /klaʊn/ n payaso/a

club /klʌb/ n 1 club 2 discoteca 3 garrote 4 (palo de golf) 5 **clubs** (cartas) tréboles →BARAJA ● (-bb-) 1 vt aporrear: *~ sb to death* matar a algn a garrotazos 2 vi: *go clubbing* ir de parranda/rumba ■ **club together** (GB) hacer un fondo (dinero)

clue /kluː/ n 1 **~ (to sth)** pista (de algo) 2 indicio 3 (crucigrama) definición ► **not have a clue** (coloq) 1 no tener ni idea 2 ser un inútil

clump /klʌmp/ n grupo (plantas, etc.)

clumsy /ˈklʌmzi/ adj (-ier/-iest) 1 torpe 2 tosco

clung /klʌŋ/ pt, pp de CLING

cluster /ˈklʌstər/ n grupo ● vi **~ (together)** apiñarse

clutch /klʌtʃ/ 1 vt apretar, estrechar 2 vt, vi **~ (at) sth** agarrar, agarrarse a/de algo ● n

1 embrague, clutch 2 **clutches** (*coloq*) garras

clutter /ˈklʌtər/ n desorden, confusión ● vt (*pey*) ~ **sth** (**up**) atestar algo

coach /koʊtʃ/ n 1 (*GB*) autobús, camión (de pasajeros) (*Mx*) 2 (*GB*, *tren*) vagón 3 carroza 4 entrenador/a 5 (*USA*, *avión*) de tarifa reducida ● 1 vt (*Dep*) entrenar 2 vt, vi ~ (**sb**) (**for/in sth**) dar clases particulares (de algo) (a algn) **coaching** n entrenamiento, preparación

coal /koʊl/ n 1 carbón 2 trozo de carbón: *hot/live ~s* brasas

coalfield /ˈkoʊlfiːld/ n yacimiento de carbón

coalition /ˌkoʊəˈlɪʃn/ n coalición

coarse /kɔːrs/ adj (-**er/-est**) 1 (*arena*, etc.) grueso 2 áspero 3 vulgar 4 grosero

coast /koʊst/ n costa ● vi 1 (*Aut*) ir en neutro 2 (*bicicleta*) ir sin pedalear **coastal** adj costero

coastguard /ˈkoʊstɡɑːrd/ n (servicio de) guardacostas

coastline /ˈkoʊstlaɪn/ n litoral

coat /koʊt/ n 1 abrigo: *white ~* bata (blanca) 2 (*animal*) pelo, lana 3 (*pintura*) capa ● vt ~ **sth** (**in/with sth**) cubrir algo (de algo) **coating** n capa, baño

coax /koʊks/ vt 1 ~ **sb** **into/out of sth**; ~ **sb** **to do sth** engatusar, persuadir a algn (para que haga/deje de hacer algo) 2 ~ **sth** **out of/from sb** sonsacar algo a algn

cobblestones /ˈkɒblstoʊnz/ (*tb* **cobbles**) n adoquines

cobweb /ˈkɒbweb/ n telaraña

cocaine /koʊˈkeɪn/ n cocaína

cock /kɒk/ n 1 (*GB*) gallo 2 (*pájaro*) macho ● vt levantar (*pata*, *orejas*, etc.)

cockney /ˈkɒkni/ adj, n (persona/dialecto) del este de Londres

cockpit /ˈkɒkpɪt/ n (*avión*) cabina

cockroach /ˈkɒkroʊtʃ/ n cucaracha

cocktail /ˈkɒkteɪl/ n coctel

cocoa /ˈkoʊkoʊ/ n 1 cacao 2 (*bebida*) chocolate

coconut /ˈkoʊkənʌt/ n coco

cocoon /kəˈkuːn/ n 1 (*gusano*) capullo 2 (*fig*) caparazón

cod /kɒd/ n (*pl* **cod**) bacalao

code /koʊd/ n 1 código 2 (*mensaje*) clave

coercion /koʊˈɜːrʃn/ n coacción

coffee /ˈkɔːfi; ˈkɒfi *GB*/ n café: *~ bar/shop* cafetería

coffin /ˈkɔːfɪn; ˈkɒf- *GB*/ n ataúd

cog /kɒɡ/ n 1 rueda dentada 2 (de piñón) diente

cogent /ˈkoʊdʒənt/ adj (*fml*) convincente

coherent /koʊˈhɪərənt/ adj 1 coherente 2 (*habla*) inteligible

coil /kɔɪl/ n 1 rollo 2 (*serpiente*) anillo 3 (*anticonceptivo*) diu ● 1 vt ~ **sth** (**up**) enrollar algo 2 vt, vi ~ (**yourself**) (**around sth**) enroscarse (en algo)

coin /kɔɪn/ n 1 moneda ● vt acuñar

coincide /ˌkoʊɪnˈsaɪd/ vi coincidir

coincidence /koʊˈɪnsɪdəns/ n casualidad

coke /koʊk/ n 1 **Coke®** Coca Cola® 2 (*coloq*) (*cocaína*) coca 3 coque

cold /koʊld/ adj (-**er/-est**) frío: *I'm ~*. Tengo frío. ◇ *It's ~ today*. Hace frío hoy. ◇ *get ~* enfriarse →FRÍO ▸ **get/have cold feet** (*coloq*) sentir/dar mieditis ◇ *catch a ~* resfriarse ● adv de improviso

cold-blooded adj 1 (*Biol*) de sangre fría 2 desalmado

collaboration /kəˌlæbəˈreɪʃn/ n 1 colaboración 2 colaboracionismo

collapse /kəˈlæps/ vi 1 derrumbarse, desplomarse 2 caer desmayado 3 (*negocio*, etc.) hundirse 4 (*valor*) caer en picada 5 (*mueble*, etc.) plegarse ● n 1 derrumbamiento 2 caída en picada 3 (*Med*) colapso

collar /ˈkɒlər/ n 1 (*camisa*, etc.) cuello 2 (*perro*) collar

collateral /kəˈlætərəl/ n garantía

colleague /ˈkɒliːɡ/ n colega, compañero/a (*de profesión*)

collect /kəˈlekt/ 1 vt recoger: *collected works* obras completas 2 vt juntar, reunir 3 vt (*datos*) recopilar 4 vt (*fondos*) recaudar 5 vt coleccionar 6 vi (*muchedumbre*) reunirse 7 vi (*polvo*, *agua*) acumularse ● adj, adv (*USA*, *teléfono*) a cobro revertido, por cobrar **collection** n 1 colección 2 recogida 3 (*en iglesia*) colecta 4 conjunto, grupo **collector** n coleccionista

collective /kəˈlektɪv/ adj, n colectivo

college /ˈkɒlɪdʒ/ n 1 centro de educación superior (*USA*) o universidad 2 (*GB*) colegio universitario (*Oxford*, *Cambridge*, etc.)

collide /kəˈlaɪd/ vi chocar

colliery /ˈkɒliəri/ n (*pl* -**ies**) (*GB*) mina de carbón

collision /kəˈlɪʒn/ n choque

colloquial /kəˈloʊkwiəl/ adj coloquial

colon /'koʊlən/ n 1 colon 2 dos puntos

colonel /'kɜːnl/ n coronel

colonial /kə'loʊniəl/ adj colonial

colony /'kɑləni/ n (pl -ies) colonia

color (-our GB) /'kʌlər/ n 1 color 2 **colors** [pl] (GB) bandera ► **be/ feel off color** (GB, coloq) no estar muy bien ● vt ~ **sth (in)** colorear, pintar algo 2 vt (afectar) marcar 3 vt (juicio) ofuscar 4 vi ~ **(at sth)** (fml) ruborizarse (ante algo) **colored** adj 1 cream-colored de color crema 2 (pey) (persona) de color **colorful** adj 1 lleno de color, llamativo 2 (vida, etc.) interesante **coloring** n 1 colorido 2 tez 3 colorante **colorless** adj 1 incoloro, sin color 2 (personaje, estilo) gris

color-blind (-our- GB) adj daltónico

colossal /kə'lɑsl/ adj colosal

colt /koʊlt/ n potro →POTRO

column /'kɑləm/ n columna

coma /'koʊmə/ n (Med) coma

comb /koʊm/ n 1 peine, peinilla 2 (adorno) peineta ● 1 vt peinar 2 vt, vi ~ **(through) (sth for sth/sb)** rastrear algo (en busca de algo/algn)

combat /'kɑmbæt/ n [U] combate ● vt combatir

combination /ˌkɑmbɪ'neɪʃn/ n combinación

combine /kəm'baɪn/ 1 vt, vi combinar(se) 2 vt (cualidades) reunir

come /kʌm/ vi (pt came pp come) 1 venir 2 llegar 3 recorrer 4 (posición) ser: ~ *first* ser él/ella primero/a ◊ *It came as a surprise.* Fue una sorpresa. 5 ~ **undone** desatarse 6 ~ **to/into + sustantivo:** ~ *to a halt* pararse ◊ ~ *into a fortune* heredar una fortuna ► **come to nothing/ come to anything** quedar en nada **come what may** pase lo que pase **when it comes to sth** cuando se trata de algo **NOTA** Para otras expresiones, ver el sustantivo, adjetivo, etc., p.ej. **come of age** en AGE. ■ **come about** ocurrir **come across/with sb** encontrar algo/encontrar con algn **come along 1** aparecer, presentarse 2 venir también 3 progresar **come apart** deshacerse **come around** volver en sí **come around (to...)** venir (a...) **come away (from sth)** desprenderse (de algo) **come away with sth** irse con algo **come back**

volver **come by sth 1** conseguir algo 2 adquirir algo **come down 1** bajar 2 desplomarse **come forward** ofrecerse **come from...** ser de... **come in 1** entrar: *Come in!* ¡Adelante! 2 llegar **come in for sth** (crítica, etc.) recibir algo **come off 1** (mancha, pieza) quitarse 2 (coloq) (plan) tener éxito **come off (sth)** caerse, desprenderse (de algo) **come on 1** (actor) salir a la escena 2 hacer progresos **come out 1** salir 2 ponerse de manifiesto 3 declararse homosexual **come out with sth** soltar, salir con algo **come over (to...)** venir (a...) **come over sb** invadir a algn: *I can't think what came over me.* No sé qué me pasó. **come through (sth)** sobrevivir (a algo) **come to** volver en sí **come to sth 1** ascender a algo 2 llegar a algo **come up 1** (planta, sol) salir 2 (tema) surgir **come up against sth** tropezar con algo **come up to sb** acercarse a algn

comeback /'kʌmbæk/ n retorno: *make a ~* reaparecer en escena

comedian /kə'miːdiən/ n humorista, cómico/a

comedy /'kɑmədi/ n (pl -ies) 1 comedia 2 comicidad

comet /'kɑmɪt/ n cometa

comfort /'kʌmfərt/ n 1 bienestar, comodidad 2 consuelo 3 **comforts** comodidades ● vt consolar

comfortable /'kʌmftəbl/ adj 1 cómodo 2 (victoria) fácil 3 (mayoría) amplio ► **be comfortably off** vivir con holgura

comforter /'kʌmfərtər/ n (USA) edredón

comic /'kɑmɪk/ adj cómico ● n 1 (~ book USA) cómic 2 humorista, cómico/a

coming /'kʌmɪŋ/ n 1 llegada 2 (Rel) advenimiento ● adj próximo

comma /'kɑmə/ n coma (ortografía)

command /kə'mænd; -'mɑːnd GB/ 1 vt ordenar →ORDER 2 vt, vi tener el mando de 3 vt (recursos) disponer de 4 vt (vista) tener 5 vt (respeto) infundir 6 vt (atención) llamar ● n 1 orden 2 (Mil) mando 3 (idioma) dominio **commander** n 1 (Mil) comandante 2 jefe/a

commemorate /kə'meməreɪt/ vt conmemorar

commence /kə'mens/ vt, vi (fml) dar comienzo a

commend /kə'mend/ vt 1 elogiar 2 (fml) recomendar **commendable** adj meritorio

comment /'kɒment/ n comentario ● vi **1** comentar **1** hacer comentarios

commentary /'kɒmənteri; -tri GB/ n (pl -ies) **1** (Dep) comentarios **2** (texto) comentario

commentator /'kɒmənteɪtər/ n comentarista

commerce /'kɒmɜːrs/ n comercio NOTA Es más común **trade**.

commercial /kə'mɜːrʃl/ adj **1** comercial **2** (Jur) mercantil **3** (TV, etc.) financiado por medio de la publicidad ● n anuncio, comercial

commission /kə'mɪʃn/ n **1** comisión **2** encargo ● vt encargar

commissioner n **1** comisario/a, comisionado/a **2** jefe/a de policía

commit /kə'mɪt/ vt (-tt-) vt **1** cometer **2** entregar: ~ sth to memory aprenderse algo de memoria **3** ~ yourself (to sth) comprometerse (a algo) **4** ~ yourself (on sth) definirse (en algo) **commitment** n **1** ~ (to sth) compromiso (con algo/de hacer algo) **2** entrega

committee /kə'mɪti/ n comité →JURADO

commodity /kə'mɒdəti/ n (pl -ies) **1** producto **2** (Fin) mercancía

common /'kɒmən/ adj **1** corriente **2** común: ~ sense sentido común **3** ordinario, vulgar ▸ in common en común ● n **1** (tb ~ land) tierra comunal **2** the Commons (GB) la Cámara de los Comunes **commonly** adv generalmente

commonplace /'kɒmənpleɪs/ adj normal

commotion /kə'moʊʃn/ n revuelo

commune /'kɒmjuːn/ n comuna **communal** adj comunal

communicate /kə'mjuːnɪkeɪt/ vt, vi comunicar(se) **communication** n **1** comunicación **2** mensaje

communion /kə'mjuːniən/ (tb **Holy Communion**) n comunión

communiqué /kə'mjuːnə-ˈkeɪ; kəˌmjuːnɪˈkeɪ GB/ n comunicado

communism /'kɒmjunɪzəm/ n comunismo **communist** adj, n comunista

community /kə'mjuːnəti/ n (pl -ies) **1** comunidad: ~ center centro social **2** (expatriados, etc.) colonia

commute /kə'mjuːt/ vi viajar para ir al trabajo **commuter** n persona que tiene que viajar para ir al trabajo

compact /kəm'pækt/ adj compacto ● /'kɒmpækt/ n polvera

compact disc n CD

companion /kəm'pæniən/ n compañero/a **companionship** n compañerismo

company /'kʌmpəni/ n (pl -ies) **1** compañía: keep sb ~ hacer compañía a algn **2** (Com) empresa

comparable /'kɒmpərəbl/ adj comparable

comparative /kəm'pærətɪv/ adj **1** comparativo **2** relativo

compare /kəm'peər/ vt, vi comparar(se)

comparison /kəm'pærɪsn/ n comparación

compartment /kəm'pɑːrtmənt/ n compartimento

compass /'kʌmpəs/ n **1** brújula **2** (tb **compasses** [pl]) compás

compassion /kəm'pæʃn/ n compasión **compassionate** adj compasivo

compatible /kəm'pætəbl/ adj compatible

compel /kəm'pel/ vt (-ll-) (fml) **1** obligar **2** forzar **compelling** adj **1** irresistible **2** apremiante **3** (argumento) convincente

compensate /'kɒmpenseɪt/ **1** vt, vi ~ (sb)(for sth) compensar (algo)(a algn) **2** vt indemnizar **compensation** n **1** compensación **2** indemnización

compete /kəm'piːt/ vi competir

competent /'kɒmpɪtənt/ adj competente **competence** n aptitud, eficiencia

competition /ˌkɒmpə'tɪʃn/ n **1** concurso **2** competencia **3** the competition la competencia **competitive** /kəm'petətɪv/ adj competitivo

competitor /kəm'petɪtər/ n competidor/a, concursante

compile /kəm'paɪl/ vt compilar

complacency /kəm'pleɪsnsi/ n ~ (about sth/sb) autosatisfacción (con algo/algn) **complacent** adj satisfecho de sí mismo

complain /kəm'pleɪn/ vi quejarse **complaint** n **1** queja, reclamación **2** (Med) afección

complement /'kɒmplɪmənt/ n **1** ~ (to sth) complemento (para algo) **2** dotación ● vt complementar **complementary** /ˌkɒmplɪ'mentri/ adj complementario

complete /kəm'pliːt/ vt **1** completar **2** terminar **3** (impreso) llenar ● adj **1** completo **2** total **3** (éxito) rotundo **4** terminado

completely adv completamente
completion n conclusión
complex /kəm'pleks; 'kɒmpleks GB/ adj, n complejo
complexion /kəm'plekʃn/ n 1 tez, cutis 2 (fig) pinta
compliance /kəm'plaɪəns/ n obediencia: in ~ with sth conforme a algo
complicate /'kɒmplɪkeɪt/ vt complicar **complicated** adj complicado **complication** n complicación
compliment /'kɒmplɪmənt/ n 1 cumplido: pay sb a ~ hacer un cumplido a algn 2 **compliments** (fml) saludos ● vt ~ **sb** (on sth) felicitar, hacerle un cumplido a algn (por algo) **complimentary** /,kɒmplɪ'mentri/ adj 1 elogioso, favorable 2 (entrada, etc.) gratuito
comply /kəm'plaɪ/ vi (pt/pp -ied) ~ (with sth) obedecer (algo)
component /kəm'pəʊnənt/ n 1 componente 2 (Mec) pieza ● adj: ~ parts piezas integrantes
compose /kəm'pəʊz/ vt 1 (Mús) componer 2 (escrito) redactar 3 (pensamientos) poner en orden 4 ~ **yourself** serenarse **composed** adj sereno **composer** n compositor/a
composition /,kɒmpə'zɪʃn/ n composición
compost /'kɒmpɒst/ n abono
composure /kəm'pəʊʒər/ n calma
compound /'kɒmpaʊnd/ adj, n compuesto ● n recinto ● /kəm-'paʊnd/ vt agravar
comprehend /,kɒmprɪ'hend/ vt comprender (en su totalidad) **comprehensible** adj ~ (to sb) comprensible (para algn) **comprehension** n comprensión
comprehensive /,kɒmprɪ-'hensɪv/ adj global, completo ● n (tb ~ school) (GB) colegio de enseñanza secundaria
compress /kəm'pres/ vt 1 comprimir 2 condensar **compression** n compresión
comprise /kəm'praɪz/ vt 1 constar de 2 formar
compromise /'kɒmprəmaɪz/ n acuerdo ● vi 1 llegar a un acuerdo 2 vt comprometer **compromising** adj comprometedor
compulsive /kəm'pʌlsɪv/ adj 1 compulsivo 2 (novela) absorbente 3 (jugador) empedernido **compulsion** n ~ (to do sth) obligación, deseo irresistible (de hacer algo)

compulsory /kəm'pʌlsəri/ adj 1 obligatorio 2 (despido) forzoso
computer /kəm'pju:tər/ n computadora, computador: computer-literate con experiencia en el uso de computadoras ◇ ~ studies informática → COMPUTADORA **computerize** vt informatizar **computing** n informática
comrade /'kɒmreɪd/ n 1 (Pol) camarada 2 compañero/a
con /kɒn/ n 1 (coloq) estafa: ~ artist/man estafador 2 the pros and ~s los pros y los contras ● vt (-nn-) (coloq) ~ **sb** (out of sth) estafar (algo) a algn
conceal /kən'si:l/ vt 1 ocultar 2 (alegría) disimular
concede /kən'si:d/ vt 1 conceder 2 admitir
conceit /kən'si:t/ n vanidad **conceited** adj vanidoso
conceivable /kən'si:vəbl/ adj concebible **conceivably** adv posiblemente
conceive /kən'si:v/ vt, vi concebir 1 ~ (of) sth imaginar algo
concentrate /'kɒnsntreɪt/ vt, vi concentrar(se) **concentration** n concentración
concept /'kɒnsept/ n concepto
conception /kən'sepʃn/ n 1 concepción 2 idea
concern /kən'sɜ:rn/ vt 1 tener que ver con: as far as I am concerned en cuanto a mí 2 referirse a 3 preocupar 4 ~ **yourself with sth** interesarse por algo ● n 1 preocupación 2 interés 3 (empresa) negocio **concerned** adj preocupado ▸ **be concerned with sth** tratar de algo **concerning** prep 1 acerca de 2 en lo que se refiere a
concert /'kɒnsərt/ n concierto
concerted /kən'sɜ:rtɪd/ adj 1 (ataque) coordinado 2 (intento, esfuerzo) conjunto
concerto /kən'tʃɜ:rtoʊ/ n (pl -s) concierto
concession /kən'seʃn/ n 1 concesión 2 (Fin) exención
conciliation /kən,sɪli'eɪʃn/ n conciliación **conciliatory** /kən-'sɪliətɔ:ri; -təri GB/ adj conciliador
concise /kən'saɪs/ adj conciso
conclude /kən'klu:d/ 1 vt, vi concluir 2 vt ~ that... llegar a la conclusión de que... 3 vt (acuerdo) concertar **conclusion** n conclusión **conclusive** adj definitivo, decisivo
concoct /kən'kɒkt/ vt 1 elaborar 2 (pretexto) inventar 3 (plan)

tramar **concoction** n 1 mezcolanza 2 mejunje

concord /'kɒŋkɔ:rd/ n (fml) concordia, armonía

concourse /'kɒŋkɔ:rs/ n vestíbulo (de edificio)

concrete /'kɒŋkri:t/ adj, n concreto

concur /kən'kɜ:r/ vi (-rr-) (fml) estar de acuerdo, coincidir **concurrence** /kən'kɜ:rəns/ n acuerdo **concurrent** adj simultáneo

concussion /kən'kʌʃn/ n [U] conmoción cerebral

condemn /kən'dem/ vt 1 condenar 2 (edificio) declarar ruinoso **condemnation** n condena

condense /kən'dens/ vt, vi (-rr-) (fml) 1 condensar(se), resumir(se) (algo) (en algo) (into/to sth) condensar(se) **condensation** n 1 condensación 2 vaho

condescend /ˌkɒndɪ'send/ vi ~ to do sth dignarse a hacer algo **condescending** adj condescendiente

condition /kən'dɪʃn/ n 1 condición: on ~ that... a condición de que... ◇ on one ~ con una condición 2 be out of ~ no estar en forma 3 **conditions** circunstancias, condiciones ▸ on no condition (fml) bajo ningún concepto ● vt 1 condicionar, determinar 2 acondicionar **conditional** adj condicional: be ~ upon sth depender de algo **conditioner** n suavizante

condolence /kən'doʊləns/ n: give/send your ~s dar el pésame

condom /'kɒndəm; 'kɒndɒm GB/ n preservativo, condón

condominium /ˌkɒndə'mɪniəm/ n (USA) condominio

condone /kən'doʊn/ vt aprobar

conducive /kən'du:sɪv; -'dju:- GB/ adj ~ to sth propicio para algo

conduct /'kɒndʌkt/ n 1 conducta 2 ~ of sth gestión de algo ● /kən'dʌkt/ vt 1 guiar 2 dirigir 3 (investigación) llevar a cabo 4 ~ yourself (fml) comportarse 5 (Elec) conducir **conductor** n 1 (Mús) director/a 2 (GB, autobús) cobrador/a **NOTA** El conductor del autobús se llama **driver**. 3 jefe/a de tren 4 (Elec) conductor

cone /koʊn/ n 1 cono 2 (helado) barquillo, cono 3 (Bot) piña (de pino, etc.)

confectionery /kən'fekʃəneri/ n [U] dulces

confederation /kənˌfedə'reɪʃn/ n confederación

confer /kən'fɜ:r/ (-rr-) 1 vi deliberar 2 vi consultar 3 vt ~ sth (on sb) conceder algo (a algn)

conference /'kɒnfərəns/ n 1 congreso: ~ hall sala de conferencias 2 (discusión) reunión: press ~ rueda de prensa

confess /kən'fes/ vt, vi confesar(se): ~ to sth confesar algo **confession** n confesión

confide /kən'faɪd/ 1 vt, vi confiar 2 vi ~ in sb hacer confidencias a algn

confidence /'kɒnfɪdəns/ n 1 confianza: ~ trick estafa 2 confidencia: take sb into your ~ hacer confidencias a algn **confident** adj 1 seguro (de sí mismo) 2 be ~ of sth/that... confiar en algo/que... **confidently** adv con toda confianza

confidential /ˌkɒnfɪ'denʃl/ adj 1 confidencial 2 (tono, etc.) de confianza

confine /kən'faɪn/ vt 1 confinar 2 limitar **confined** adj limitado (espacio) **confinement** n confinamiento: solitary ~ incomunicación

confines /'kɒnfaɪnz/ n (fml) límites

confirm /kən'fɜ:rm/ vt confirmar **confirmation** n confirmación **confirmed** adj empedernido

confiscate /'kɒnfɪskeɪt/ vt confiscar

conflict /'kɒnflɪkt/ n conflicto ● /kən'flɪkt/ vi ~ (with sth) discrepar (de algo) **conflicting** adj contradictorio

conform /kən'fɔ:rm/ vi 1 atenerse 2 seguir las reglas **conformist** n conformista **conformity** n (fml) conformidad: in ~ with sth de conformidad con algo

confront /kən'frʌnt/ vt 1 hacer frente a, afrontar 2 ~ sb with sth hacer (a algn) afrontar algo **confrontation** /ˌkɒnfrən'teɪʃn/ n enfrentamiento

confuse /kən'fju:z/ vt 1 confundir 2 (asunto) complicar **confused** adj confuso: get ~ desorientarse/ofuscarse **confusing** adj confuso **confusion** n confusión

congeal /kən'dʒi:l/ vi coagularse

congenial /kən'dʒi:niəl/ adj 1 ~ (to sb) agradable (para algn) 2 ~ (to sth) propicio (para algo)

congenital /kən'dʒenɪtl/ adj congénito

congested /kən'dʒestɪd/ adj ~ (with sth) congestionado (de algo) **congestion** n congestión

conglomerate /kən'glɒmərət/ n grupo (de empresas)

c

congratulate /kənˈgrætʃuleɪt/ vt ~ sb (on sth) felicitar a algn (por algo) **congratulations** n felicitaciones

congregate /ˈkɑŋgrɪgeɪt/ vi congregarse **congregation** n [sing] feligreses

congress /ˈkɑŋgrəs/ n congreso **congressional** /kənˈgreʃənl/ adj del congreso

congressman, congresswoman /ˈkɑŋgrəsmən-ˌwʊmən/ n (pl -men/-women) congresista

conical /ˈkɑnɪkl/ adj cónico

conifer /ˈkɑnɪfər/ n conifera

conjecture /kənˈdʒektʃər/ n conjetura

conjunction /kənˈdʒʌŋkʃn/ n (Gram) conjunción ▸ in conjunction with conjuntamente con

conjure /ˈkɑndʒər/ vi hacer magia con las manos ▪ conjure sth up 1 evocar algo 2 hacer aparecer algo como por arte de magia 3 invocar algo **conjurer** n mago/a

connect /kəˈnekt/ 1 vt, vi conectar(se) 2 vt (habitaciones) comunicar 3 vt relacionar: connected by marriage emparentados políticamente 4 vt ~ sb (with sb) (teléfono) comunicar a algn (con algn) **connection** n 1 conexión 2 relación 3 (transporte) enlace 4 **connections** palancas ▸ in connection with en relación con

connoisseur /ˌkɑnəˈsɜːr/ n conocedor/a, experto/a

conquer /ˈkɑŋkər/ vt 1 conquistar 2 vencer **conqueror** n 1 conquistador/a 2 vencedor/a

conquest /ˈkɑŋkwest/ n conquista

conscience /ˈkɑnʃəns/ n conciencia (moral): have sth on your ~ pesar algo sobre la conciencia de algn

conscientious /ˌkɑnʃiˈenʃəs/ adj concienzudo: ~ objector objetor de conciencia

conscious /ˈkɑnʃəs/ adj 1 consciente 2 deliberado **consciousness** n 1 conocimiento 2 conciencia

conscript /ˈkɑnskrɪpt/ n recluta **conscription** n reclutamiento (obligatorio)

consecrate /ˈkɑnsɪkreɪt/ vt consagrar

consecutive /kənˈsekjətɪv/ adj consecutivo

consent /kənˈsent/ vi acceder ● n consentimiento ▸ age of consent edad legal para mantener relaciones sexuales

consequence /ˈkɑnsəkwens/ n 1 consecuencia 2 (fml) importancia

consequent /ˈkɑnsɪkwənt/ adj (fml) 1 consiguiente 2 ~ on/upon sth que resulta de algo **consequently** adv por consiguiente

conservation /ˌkɑnsərˈveɪʃn/ n 1 conservación: ~ area zona protegida 2 (recursos) ahorro

conservative /kənˈsɜːrvətɪv/ adj, n conservador/a

conservatory /kənˈsɜːrvətɔːri; -tri GB/ n (pl -ies) 1 (GB) galería acristalada contigua a una casa 2 (Mús) conservatorio

conserve /kənˈsɜːrv/ vt 1 conservar 2 (energía) ahorrar 3 (naturaleza) proteger

consider /kənˈsɪdər/ vt 1 considerar: ~ doing sth pensar hacer algo 2 tener en cuenta

considerable /kənˈsɪdərəbl/ adj considerable **considerably** adv bastante

considerate /kənˈsɪdərət/ adj considerado

consideration /kənˌsɪdəˈreɪʃn/ n 1 consideración: It is under ~. Lo están considerando. ◇ take sth into ~ tener algo en cuenta 2 factor

considering /kənˈsɪdərɪŋ/ conj teniendo en cuenta

consign /kənˈsaɪn/ vt abandonar: consigned to oblivion relegado al olvido **consignment** n 1 envío 2 pedido

consist /kənˈsɪst/ 1 ~ of sth constar de, estar formado por algo 2 ~ in sth consistir en algo

consistent /kənˈsɪstənt/ adj 1 (persona) consecuente 2 en concordancia **consistency** n (pl -ies) 1 consistencia 2 coherencia **consistently** adv 1 constantemente 2 (actuar) consecuentemente

consolation /ˌkɑnsəˈleɪʃn/ n consuelo

console /kənˈsoʊl/ vt consolar

consolidate /kənˈsɑlɪdeɪt/ vt, vi consolidar(se)

consonant /ˈkɑnsənənt/ n consonante

consortium /kənˈsɔːrtiəm/ n (pl -tia /-tiə/) consorcio

conspicuous /kənˈspɪkjuəs/ adj 1 llamativo: make yourself ~ llamar la atención 2 visible ▸ be conspicuous by your/its absence brillar algn/algo por su ausencia **conspicuously** adv notablemente

conspiracy /kənˈspɪrəsi/ n (pl -ies) 1 conspiración 2 conjura

conspiratorial /kənˌspɪrəˈtɔːriəl/ adj conspirador

conspire /kənˈspaɪər/ vi conspirar

constable /ˈkʌnstəbl/ n (agente de) policía

constant /ˈkɒnstənt/ adj 1 constante, continuo 2 (amigo, etc.) fiel ● n constante

constipation /ˌkɒnstɪˈpeɪʃn/ n estreñimiento **constipated** adj estreñido

constituency /kənˈstɪtjuənsi/ n (pl -ies) 1 distrito electoral 2 votantes

constituent /kənˈstɪtjuənt/ n 1 (Pol) elector/a 2 componente

constitute /ˈkɒnstɪtjuːt; -tjuːt/ vt constituir

constitution /ˌkɒnstɪˈtjuːʃn; -ˈtjuːʃn GB/ n constitución **constitutional** adj constitucional

constraint /kənˈstreɪnt/ n 1 coacción 2 limitación

constrict /kənˈstrɪkt/ vt 1 apretar 2 limitar

construct /kənˈstrʌkt/ vt construir **NOTA** Es más común build. **construction** n construcción

construe /kənˈstruː/ vt interpretar

consul /ˈkɒnsl/ n cónsul

consulate /ˈkɒnsələt; -sjəl- GB/ n consulado

consult /kənˈsʌlt/ vt, vi consultar: consulting room consultorio **consultant** n 1 asesor/a 2 (Med) especialista **consultancy** n asesoría **consultation** n consulta

consume /kənˈsuːm; -ˈsjuːm GB/ vt consumir **consumer** n consumidor/a

consummate /ˈkɒnsəmət/ (fml) adj 1 consumado 2 (habilidad, etc.) extraordinario ● /ˈkɒnsəmeɪt/ vt 1 culminar 2 (matrimonio) consumar

consumption /kənˈsʌmpʃn/ n consumo

contact /ˈkɒntækt/ n contacto: make ~ ponerse en contacto ● vt ponerse en contacto con

contact lens n (pl contact lenses) lente de contacto

contagious /kənˈteɪdʒəs/ adj contagioso

contain /kənˈteɪn/ vt contener: ~ yourself contenerse **container** n 1 recipiente 2 contenedor: ~ ship buque contenedor

contaminate /kənˈtæmɪneɪt/ vt contaminar

contemplate /ˈkɒntəmpleɪt/ 1 contemplar 2 considerar

contemporary /kənˈtemprəri; -prəri GB/ adj 1 contemporáneo 2 de la época ● n (pl -ies) contemporáneo/a

contempt /kənˈtempt/ n 1 desprecio: beneath ~ despreciable 2 (tb ~ of court) desacato (al tribunal) ▸ hold sth/sb in contempt despreciar algo/a algn **contemptible** adj despreciable **contemptuous** adj desdeñoso, despectivo

contend /kənˈtend/ 1 vi ~ with sth enfrentarse a algo 2 vi ~ (for sth) luchar (por algo) 3 vt afirmar **contender** n contendiente

content¹ /ˈkɒntent/ (tb contents [pl]) n contenido

content² /kənˈtent/ adj contento, satisfecho ● vt ~ yourself with sth contentarse con algo **contented** adj satisfecho **contentment** n contento, satisfacción

contention /kənˈtenʃn/ n 1 contienda 2 controversia **contentious** adj 1 polémico 2 pendenciero

contest /kənˈtest/ vt 1 rebatir 2 impugnar 3 (premio, etc.) disputar ● /ˈkɒntest/ n 1 concurso, competencia 2 lucha **contestant** /kənˈtestənt/ n concursante

context /ˈkɒntekst/ n contexto

continent /ˈkɒntɪnənt/ n 1 continente 2 the Continent (GB) el continente europeo **continental** /ˌkɒntɪˈnentl/ adj continental

contingency /kənˈtɪndʒənsi/ n (pl -ies) 1 eventualidad 2 contingencia: ~ plan plan de emergencia

contingent /kənˈtɪndʒənt/ n 1 (Mil) contingente 2 representación

continual /kənˈtɪnjuəl/ adj continuo **continually** adv continuamente **NOTA** Continual suele describir acciones que se repiten. A menudo tiene un matiz negativo: His continual phone calls started to annoy her. **Continuous** se usa para describir acciones ininterrumpidas: There has been a continuous improvement in his work. ◇ It rained continuously all day.

continue /kənˈtɪnjuː/ 1 vi continuar, seguir 2 vt continuar: To be continued... Continuará... **continuation** n continuación **continued** adj continuo **continuing** adj continuado

continuity /ˌkɒntɪˈnjuːəti; -ˈnjuː- GB/ n continuidad

continuous /kənˈtɪnjuəs/ *adj* constante, continuo **continuously** *adv* continuamente, sin parar →CONTINUAL

contort /kənˈtɔːrt/ *vt, vi* retorcer(se), contorsionar(se)

contour /ˈkɑntʊər/ *n* contorno

contraband /ˈkɑntrəbænd/ *n* contrabando

contraception /ˌkɑntrəˈsepʃn/ *n* anticoncepción **contraceptive** *adj, n* anticonceptivo

contract /ˈkɑntrækt/ *n* contrato: *under ~ to sb* bajo contrato con algn ● /kənˈtrækt/ **1** *vt* contratar **2** *vt, vi* contraer(se) **contraction** *n* contracción **contractor** *n* contratista

contradict /ˌkɑntrəˈdɪkt/ *vt* contradecir **contradiction** *n* contradicción **contradictory** *adj* contradictorio

contrary /ˈkɑntreri; -trəri *GB*/ *adj* contrario ♦ *adv* ~ **to sth** en contra de algo, contrario a algo ● **the contrary** *n* lo contrario ▶ **on the contrary** por el contrario

contrast /kənˈtræst; -ˈtrɑːst *GB*/ *vt, vi* contrastar ● /ˈkɑntræst; -trɑːst *GB*/ *n* contraste

contribute /kənˈtrɪbjuːt/ **1** *vt, vi* contribuir **2** *vt, vi* ~ **(sth) to sth** (*artículo*) escribir (algo) para algo **3** *vi* ~ **to sth** (*debate*) participar en algo **contributor** *n* **1** contribuyente **2** (*publicación*) colaborador/a **contribution** *n* **1** contribución, aporte **2** (*Period*) artículo **contributory** *adj* **1** que contribuye **2** (*plan de jubilación*) contributivo

control /kənˈtrəʊl/ *n* **1** control, mando, dominio: *be in ~ of sth* tener el control de algo ◇ *The taxi went out of ~.* Perdió el control del taxi. **2 controls** mandos ▶ **be out of control 1** estar fuera de control **2** (*persona*) desmandarse ● (-**ll**-) **1** *vt* controlar, tener el mando de **2** *vt* (*Aut*) manejar **3** *vt* ~ **yourself** dominarse **4** *vt* (*ley*) regular **5** *vt* (*gastos, etc.*) controlar

controversial /ˌkɑntrəˈvɜːrʃl/ *adj* controvertido, polémico

controversy /ˈkɑntrəvɜːrsi/ *n* (*pl* -**ies**) ~ **(about/over sth)** polémica, controversia (sobre algo)

convene /kənˈviːn/ **1** *vt* convocar **2** *vi* reunirse

convenience /kənˈviːniəns/ *n* **1** comodidad: *~ food* comida rápida ◇ *public ~s* (*GB*) baños públicos **2** conveniencia

convenient /kənˈviːniənt/ *adj* **1** *if it's ~ (for you)* si le viene bien **2** oportuno **3** práctico **4** a mano **5** ~ **for sth** bien situado en relación con algo **conveniently** *adv* oportunamente

convent /ˈkɑnvent/ *n* convento

convention /kənˈvenʃn/ *n* **1** congreso **2** convención **3** convencionalismo **conventional** *adj* convencional: *~ wisdom* sabiduría popular

converge /kənˈvɜːrdʒ/ *vi* **1** converger **2** ~ **(on...)** (*personas*) juntarse (en...) **convergence** *n* convergencia

conversant /kənˈvɜːrsnt/ *adj* ~ **with sth** (*fml*) versado en algo: *become ~ with sth* familiarizarse con algo

conversation /ˌkɑnvərˈseɪʃn/ *n* conversación

converse /kənˈvɜːrs/ *vi* (*fml*) conversar

the converse /ˈkɑnvɜːrs/ *n* lo contrario **conversely** *adv* a la inversa

conversion /kənˈvɜːrʒn/ *n* conversión

convert /kənˈvɜːrt/ *vt, vi* convertir(se) ● /ˈkɑnvɜːrt/ *n* converso/a

convertible /kənˈvɜːrtəbl/ *adj, n* convertible

convey /kənˈveɪ/ *vt* **1** expresar **2** (*saludos*) enviar **3** (*fml*) llevar, transportar **conveyor** *n* banda transportadora

convict /kənˈvɪkt/ *vt* declarar culpable ● /ˈkɑnvɪkt/ *n* preso/a **conviction** *n* **1** (*Jur*) condena **2** convicción: *lack ~* no ser convincente

convince /kənˈvɪns/ *vt* convencer **convinced** *adj* convencido **convincing** *adj* convincente

convulse /kənˈvʌls/ *vt, vi* convulsionar: *convulsed with laughter* muerto de risa **convulsion** *n* convulsión

cook /kʊk/ **1** *vt, vi* cocinar **2** *vi* (*comida*) cocer: *The potatoes aren't cooked.* Las papas no están cocidas. ▶ **cook the books** (*coloq*) falsificar los libros de contabilidad ■ **cook sth up** (*coloq*) inventar (*excusa, etc.*) ● *n* cocinero/a

cooker /ˈkʊkər/ *n* (*GB*) estufa

cookery /ˈkʊkəri/ *n* [U] cocina: *Oriental ~* la cocina oriental

cookie /ˈkʊki/ *n* (*USA*) galleta

cooking /ˈkʊkɪŋ/ *n* [U] cocina: *French ~* la cocina francesa ◇ *do the ~* cocinar

cool /kuːl/ *adj* (-**er/-est**) **1** fresco →FRÍO **2** (*coloq*) chévere, padre

(Mx): "I'll meet you at three." "Cool." —Quedamos a las tres. —Vale. **3** (coloq) impasible **4 ~ (about sth/towards sb)** indiferente (a algo/algn) **5** (acogida) frío ▸ **keep/stay cool** no perder la calma: Keep ~! ¡Tranquilo! ● vt, vi **1 ~ (sth) (down/off)** enfriar(se) (algo) **2 ~ (sb) (down/off)** refrescar(se) (a algn) ■ **cool (sb) down/off** calmar(se) (a algn) ● **the cool** el fresco ▸ **keep/lose your cool** (coloq) mantener/perder la calma

cooperate /koʊˈɑpəreɪt/ vi cooperar **2** colaborar **cooperation** n **1** cooperación **2** colaboración

cooperative /koʊˈɑpərətɪv/ adj **1** cooperativo **2** dispuesto a colaborar ● n cooperativa

coordinate /koʊˈɔːrdɪneɪt/ vt coordinar

cop /kɑp/ n (coloq) poli

cope /koʊp/ vi ~ **(with sth)** arreglárselas (con algo), hacer frente a algo: I can't ~. No doy abasto.

copious /ˈkoʊpiəs/ adj abundante

copper /ˈkɑpər/ n **1** cobre **2** (GB, coloq) policía

copy /ˈkɑpi/ n (pl -ies) **1** copia **2** ejemplar **3** (Period) número **4** texto (para imprimir) ● vt (pt/pp -ied) **1 ~ sth (down/out)** copiar algo **2** fotocopiar **3** imitar

copyright /ˈkɑpiraɪt/ n copyright ● adj registrado, protegido por copyright

coral /ˈkɔːrəl; ˈkɒrəl GB/ n coral ● adj de coral, coralino

cord /kɔːrd/ n **1** cordón **2** (USA) cable eléctrico **3** pana **4** cords [pl] pantalón de pana →PAIR

cordless /ˈkɔːrdləs/ adj inalámbrico

cordon /ˈkɔːrdn/ n cordón ● ~ **sth off** acordonar algo

corduroy /ˈkɔːrdərɔɪ/ n pana

core /kɔːr/ n **1** (fruta), corazón **2** centro, núcleo ▸ **to the core** hasta la médula

cork /kɔːrk/ n corcho

corkscrew /ˈkɔːrkskruː/ n sacacorchos, descorchador

corn /kɔːrn/ n **1** (USA) maíz **2** (GB) cereal **3** callo

corner /ˈkɔːrnər/ n **1** (desde dentro) rincón **2** (desde fuera) esquina **3** (tb ~ **kick**) córner, tiro/saque de esquina ▸ **(just) around the corner** a la vuelta de la esquina ● **1** vt acorralar **2** vi tomar una curva **3** vt (mercado) monopolizar

cornerstone /ˈkɔːrnərstoʊn/ n piedra angular

cornstarch (**cornflour** GB) /ˈkɔːrnstɑːrtʃ/-flaʊər/ n maicena®

corollary /ˈkɔːrəleri; kəˈrɒləri GB/ n (pl -ies) (fml) consecuencia lógica

coronation /ˌkɔːrəˈneɪʃn; ˌkɒr-GB/ n coronación

coroner /ˈkɔːrənər; ˈkɒr- GB/ n juez de instrucción (en casos de muerte violenta o accidentes)

corporal /ˈkɔːrpərəl/ n (Mil) cabo ● adj: ~ **punishment** castigo corporal

corporate /ˈkɔːrpərət/ adj **1** colectivo **2** corporativo

corporation /ˌkɔːrpəˈreɪʃn/ n corporación

corps /kɔːr/ n (pl corps /kɔːrz/) cuerpo

corpse /kɔːrps/ n cadáver

correct /kəˈrekt/ adj correcto: Am I ~ in saying...? ¿Me equivoco si digo...? ● vt corregir

correlation /ˌkɔːrəˈleɪʃn; ˌkɒr-GB/ n correlación

correspond /ˌkɔːrəˈspɒnd; ˌkɒr-GB/ vi **1** coincidir **2** equivaler **3** (fml) mantener correspondencia **correspondence** n correspondencia **correspondent** n corresponsal **corresponding** adj correspondiente

corridor /ˈkɔːrɪdɔːr; ˈkɒr- GB/ n pasillo

corrosion /kəˈroʊʒn/ n corrosión

corrugated /ˈkɔːrəgeɪtɪd/ adj corrugado

corrupt /kəˈrʌpt/ adj **1** corrupto, deshonesto **2** depravado ● vt corromper **corruption** n corrupción

cosmetic /kɑzˈmetɪk/ adj cosmético: ~ **surgery** cirugía estética **cosmetics** n cosméticos

cosmopolitan /ˌkɑzməˈpɑlɪtən/ adj, n cosmopolita

cost /kɔːst; kɒst GB/ vt **1** (pt/pp cost) costar, valer **2** (pt/pp costed) (Com) presupuestar ● n **1** costo: whatever the ~ cueste lo que cueste ◇ **cost-effective** rentable **2** costs gastos, costos ▸ **at all costs** a toda costa **costly** adj (-ier/-iest) costoso

co-star n coprotagonista

costume /ˈkɑstuːm; -tjuːm GB/ n **1** traje, disfraz **2** costumes [pl] (Teat) vestuario

cosy (GB) = COZY

cot /kɑt/ n **1** (USA) camastro, catre **2** (GB) cuna

cottage /ˈkɑtɪdʒ/ n casita (de campo)

cotton /'kɒtn/ n 1 algodón: ~ *wool* (GB) algodón (de farmacia) 2 hilo (de algodón)

couch /kaʊtʃ/ n diván ● vt ~ **sth** (**in sth**) (fml) expresar algo (en algo)

cough /kɒf; kɔːf GB/ n tos ● 1 vi toser 2 vt ~ **sth up** escupir algo ▶ **cough** (**sth**) **up** (coloq) soltar (algo)

could /kəd, kʊd/ pt de CAN¹

council /'kaʊnsl/ n 1 ayuntamiento, concejo 2 consejo **councillor** (tb -l- USA) n concejal/a

counsel /'kaʊnsl/ n 1 (fml) consejo **NOTA** Es más común *advice*. 2 (pl **counsel**) abogado →ABOGADO ● vt (-l-, -ll- GB) (fml) aconsejar **counseling** (-ll- GB) n asesoramiento, orientación **counselor** (-ll- GB) n 1 asesor/a, consejero/a 2 (USA, Irl) abogado/a

count /kaʊnt/ n 1 conde 2 recuento ● 1 vt, vi ~ (**sth**) (**up**) contar (algo) 2 vt, vi ~ (**as sth**) contar (como algo): ~ *yourself lucky* considerarse afortunado 3 vi ~ (**for sth**) importar (para algo) 4 vi valer ▶ **count the cost** pagar las consecuencias ■ **count down** hacer la cuenta regresiva **count sth/sb in/out** contar/no contar con algo/algn **count on sth/sb** contar con algo/algn **count towards sth** contribuir a algo

countdown /'kaʊntdaʊn/ n ~ (**to sth**) cuenta regresiva

countenance /'kaʊntənəns/ n (fml) aprobar, tolerar ● n rostro

counter /'kaʊntər/ 1 vi rebatir, contraatacar 2 vt responder a ● n 1 (juego) ficha 2 contador 3 mostrador ● adv ~ **to sth** en contra de algo

counteract /ˌkaʊntərˈækt/ vt contrarrestar

counter-attack n contraataque

counterpart /'kaʊntərpɑːrt/ n 1 homólogo/a 2 equivalente

counter-productive adj contraproducente

countess /'kaʊntəs/ n condesa

countless /'kaʊntləs/ adj innumerable

country /'kʌntri/ n (pl -**ies**) 1 país 2 [sing] patria 3 [U] (tb the ~) campo: ~ *life* la vida rural 4 zona, tierra

countryman, countrywoman /'kʌntrimən, -wʊmən/ n (pl -**men**/-**women**) 1 compatriota 2 campesino/a

countryside /'kʌntrisaɪd/ n [U] 1 campo, campiña 2 paisaje

county /'kaʊnti/ n (pl -**ies**) condado

coup /kuː/ n (pl -**s** /kuːz/) 1 (tb ~ **d'état** /kuː deɪˈtɑː/) (pl -**s d'état**) golpe (de estado) 2 éxito

couple /'kʌpl/ n 1 pareja (relación amorosa): *a married* ~ un matrimonio 2 **a couple** un par, unos cuantos ● vt 1 asociar, acompañar: *coupled with sth* junto con algo 2 acoplar, enganchar

coupon /'kuːpɒn/ n cupón, vale

courage /'kʌrɪdʒ/ n valor **courageous** /kəˈreɪdʒəs/ adj valiente

courgette /kʊərˈʒet/ n (GB) calabacín, calabacita (Mx)

courier /'kʊəriər/ n 1 mensajero/a 2 (GB) guía turístico/a (persona)

course /kɔːrs/ n 1 curso: *in the* ~ *of sth* en el transcurso de algo 2 (avión, etc.) rumbo: *be on/off* ~ seguir el rumbo/un rumbo equivocado 3 ~ (**in/on sth**) (Educ) curso (de algo) 4 (Med) tratamiento 5 (golf) campo 6 (comida) plato ▶ **a course of action** una línea de acción **of course** por supuesto: *of* ~ *not* claro que no

court /kɔːrt/ n 1 (tb ~ **of law**) juzgado, tribunal: *go to* ~ (over *sth*) ir a juicio (por algo) ◊ *take sb to* ~ demandar a algn ◊ *a* ~ *case/order* un pleito/una orden judicial 2 (Dep) cancha 3 corte ● vt 1 cortejar (peligro, etc.) exponerse a

courteous /'kɜːrtiəs/ adj cortés

courtesy /'kɜːrtəsi/ n (pl -**ies**) cortesía ▶ (**by**) **courtesy of sb** (por) gentileza de algn

court martial n (pl **courts martial**) consejo de guerra

courtship /'kɔːrtʃɪp/ n noviazgo

courtyard /'kɔːrtjɑːrd/ n patio

cousin /'kʌzn/ n primo/a

cove /kəʊv/ n bahía, rada

covenant /'kʌvənənt/ n pacto

cover /'kʌvər/ 1 vt ~ **sth/sb** (**in/ with sth**) cubrir algo/a algn (de algo) 2 vt tapar 3 vt (timidez, etc.) disimular 4 vt abarcar 5 vt tratar, encargarse de ■ **cover for sb** sustituir a algn (tb ~ **up for sb**) cubrir las espaldas a algn **cover** (**sth**) **up** (pey) ocultar (algo) ● n 1 cubierta 2 funda 3 tapa (libro, etc.) portada 5 **the covers** las cobijas 6 (fig) tapadera, identidad falsa 7 protección: *take* ~ *from* algo resguardarse de algo 8 ~ (**for sb**) sustitución (de algn) 9 ~ (**against sth**) seguro (contra algo) ▶ **from cover to**

cover de principio a fin **under cover of sth** al amparo de algo **coverage** n cobertura **covering** n 1 envoltura 2 capa

coveralls /'kʌvərɔːlz/ n [pl] (USA) overol →PAIR

covert /'kʌvəːrt; 'kʌvət GB/ adj 1 secreto, encubierto 2 (mirada) furtivo

cover-up n (pl -ups) (pey) encubrimiento

covet /'kʌvət/ vt codiciar

cow /kaʊ/ n vaca →CARNE

coward /'kaʊərd/ n cobarde **cowardice** n [U] cobardía **cowardly** adj cobarde

cowboy /'kaʊbɔɪ/ n 1 vaquero 2 (GB, coloq) pirata (albañil, etc.)

co-worker n compañero/a de trabajo

coy /kɔɪ/ adj 1 tímido (por coquetería) 2 reservado

cozy /'kəʊzi/ adj (-ier/-iest) acogedor

crab /kræb/ n cangrejo

crack /kræk/ n 1 grieta 2 (fig) defecto 3 rendija, abertura 4 chasquido, estallido ▶ **at the crack of dawn** (coloq) al amanecer ● 1 vt, vi resquebrajar(se): a cracked cup una taza agrietada 2 vt, vi ~ (sth) (open) abrir(se) (algo) 3 vt (nuez) cascar 4 vt ~ sth (on/against sth) golpear algo (contra algo) 5 vt, vi chascar, chasquear 6 vt (látigo) restallar 7 vi desmoronarse 8 vt (resistencia) quebrantar 9 vt ~ (sth) (coloq) resolver 10 vt (voz) quebrarse 11 vt (coloq) contar ▶ **to get cracking** (coloq) poner manos a la obra ■ **crack down (on sth/sb)** tomar medidas enérgicas (contra algo/algn) **crack up** (coloq) 1 agotarse (física o mentalmente) 2 echarse a reír

crackdown /'krækdaʊn/ n ~ on sth) medidas enérgicas (contra algo)

cracker /'krækər/ n 1 galleta salada 2 (GB) (tb Christmas ~) petardo sorpresa

crackle /'krækl/ vi crepitar ● n (tb crackling) crujido, chisporroteo

cradle /'kreɪdl/ n cuna ● vt acunar

craft /kræft; krɑːft GB/ n 1 artesanía 2 oficio 3 embarcación ● vt fabricar artesanalmente

craftsman, craftswoman /'kræftsmən/-wʊmən; 'krɑːfts-GB/ n (pl -men/-women) 1 artesano/a 2 artista **craftsmanship** n 1 artesanía 2 arte

crafty /'kræfti; 'krɑːfti GB/ adj (-ier/-iest) astuto, ladino

crag /kræg/ n peñasco, risco **craggy** adj escarpado

cram /kræm/ (-mm-) 1 vt ~ A into B atiborrar, llenar B de A; meter A en B (a presión) 2 vi ~ into meterse con dificultad en, abarrotar algo

cramp /kræmp/ n 1 (muscular) calambre, jalón (And) 2 (stomach) cramps retortijones ● vt (movimiento, etc.) obstaculizar **cramped** adj (espacio) estrecho

crane /kreɪn/ n 1 (Mec) grúa 2 (ave) grulla

crank /kræŋk/ n 1 (Mec) manivela 2 bicho raro 3 (USA) cascarrabias

crash /kræʃ/ n 1 estrépito 2 accidente, choque: ~ helmet casco protector 3 (Com) quiebra 4 (Fin) caída 5 (Comp) falla ● 1 vt, vi ~ (sth) (into sth) (Aut) estrellar(se) (algo) (contra algo): He crashed his car yesterday. Chocó ayer. 2 vi (Comp) dejar de funcionar 3 vi ~ (out) (coloq) dormirse ● adj (curso, dieta) intensivo

crash landing n aterrizaje de emergencia

crass /kræs/ adj (pey) 1 sumo 2 majadero

crate /kreɪt/ n 1 cajón 2 caja (para botellas)

crater /'kreɪtər/ n cráter

crave /kreɪv/ vt, vi ~ (for) sth anhelar algo **craving** n ~ (for sth) ansia, antojo (de algo)

crawl /krɔːl/ vi 1 gatear, arrastrarse 2 ~ (along) (tráfico) avanzar a paso de tortuga 3 (coloq) lamber ▶ **crawling with sth** (coloq) lleno/cubierto de algo ● n 1 paso de tortuga 2 (natación) estilo libre, crol

crayon /'kreɪən/ n 1 cera (de colores), crayola® 2 (Arte) pastel

craze /kreɪz/ n moda, fiebre

crazy /'kreɪzi/ adj (-ier/-iest) (coloq) loco ▶ **like crazy** (coloq) como loco

creak /kriːk/ vi crujir, chirriar

cream /kriːm/ n 1 crema 2 pomada 3 **the ~ of sth** la crema y nata de algo ● adj, n (color) crema **creamy** adj (-ier/-iest) cremoso ● vt batir ■ **cream sth off** quedarse con lo mejor de algo

crease /kriːs/ n 1 arruga, pliegue 2 (pantalón) raya ● vt, vi arrugar(se)

create /kriˈeɪt/ vt crear, producir: ~ a fuss hacer un escándalo

creation n creación **creative** adj creativo **creator** n creador/a

creature /'kri:tʃər/ n criatura: *living ~* ser vivo ◊ *a ~ of habit* un animal de costumbres ◊ *~ comforts* comodidades de la vida

crèche /kreʃ/ n (GB) guardería infantil

credentials /krə'denʃlz/ n [pl] 1 documentos 2 (*para un trabajo*) calificaciones

credible /'kredəbl/ adj creíble **credibility** /ˌkredə'bɪləti/ n credibilidad

credit /'kredɪt/ n 1 crédito: *on ~* a crédito ◊ *a ~* tener saldo positivo 3 (*contabilidad*) haber 4 mérito: *be a ~ to sth/sb* hacer honor a algo/algn ◊ *do sb ~* honrar a algn ◊ *to sb's ~* a algn 5 **credits** (*Cine*) créditos ● vt 1 ~ **sth/sb with sth** atribuir el mérito de algo a algn/algn 2 (*Fin*) consignar 3 creer **creditable** adj encomiable **creditor** n acreedor/a

credit card n tarjeta de crédito

creed /kri:d/ n credo

creek /kri:k/ n 1 (*USA*) riachuelo 2 (*GB*) estero ▶ **be up the creek (without a paddle)** (*coloq*) en un apuro

creep /kri:p/ vi (*pt/pp* crept) 1 deslizarse (*sigilosamente*): *~ up on sb* aproximarse sigilosamente a algn 2 (*fig*): *A feeling of drowsiness crept over him.* Lo invadió una sensación de sopor. 3 (*planta*) trepar ● n (*coloq*) lambiscón/ona (*Mx*), lambón/ona (*And*) ▶ **give sb the creeps** (*coloq*) ponerle los pelos de punta a algn **creepy** adj (*-ier/-iest*) (*coloq*) espeluznante

cremation /krə'meɪʃn/ n cremación

crematorium /ˌkremə'tɔːriəm/ n (*tb* **crematory** /'kri:mətɔːri/ *USA*) crematorio

crescendo /krə'ʃendəʊ/ n (*pl* -s) 1 (*Mús*) crescendo 2 (*fig*) cúspide

crescent /'kresnt/ n 1 media luna: *a ~ moon* la media luna 2 calle en forma de media luna

crest /krest/ n 1 cresta 2 (*colina*) cima 3 (*Heráldica*) emblema **crestfallen** /'krestfɔːlən/ adj cabizbajo

crevice /'krevɪs/ n grieta (*en roca*)

crew /kru:/ n 1 tripulación 2 (*remo, Cine*) equipo →JURADO

crew cut n corte de pelo a cepillo

crib /krɪb/ n 1 pesebre 2 (*USA*) cuna 3 (*plagio*) copia ● vt, vi (*-bb-*) copiar

cricket /'krɪkɪt/ n 1 (*Zool*) grillo 2 (*Dep*) críquet **cricketer** n jugador/a de críquet

crime /kraɪm/ n 1 delito, crimen 2 delincuencia

criminal /'krɪmɪnl/ adj 1 *~ damage* delito de daños ◊ *a ~ record* antecedentes penales 2 (*derecho*) penal 3 inmoral ● n delincuente, criminal

crimson /'krɪmzn/ adj carmesí

cringe /krɪndʒ/ vi 1 (*miedo*) encogerse 2 morirse de vergüenza

cripple /'krɪpl/ n inválido/a ● vt 1 dejar inválido 2 perjudicar seriamente **crippling** adj 1 (*enfermedad*) que deja inválido 2 (*deuda*) agobiante

crisis /'kraɪsɪs/ n (*pl* **crises** /-siːz/) crisis

crisp /krɪsp/ adj (*-er/-est*) 1 crujiente 2 (*verduras*) fresco 3 (*billete*) nuevo 4 (*ropa*) liso 5 (*tiempo*) frío y frío 6 (*manera*) tajante ● n (*GB*) papa frita (*de bolsa*) **crispy** adj (*-ier/-iest*) crujiente

criterion /kraɪ'tɪəriən/ n (*pl* **-ria** /-riə/) criterio

critic /'krɪtɪk/ n 1 detractor/a 2 crítico/a **critical** adj 1 crítico: *be ~ of sth/sb* criticar algo/a algn ◊ *~ acclaim* el aplauso de la crítica ◊ *a ~ moment* un momento crucial 2 (*persona*) criticón **critically** adv 1 críticamente 2 *~ ill* gravemente enfermo

criticism /'krɪtɪsɪzəm/ n [*gen U*] crítica(s): *He can't take ~.* No soporta que le critiquen.

criticize /'krɪtɪsaɪz/ vt criticar

critique /krɪ'tiːk/ n análisis crítico

croak /krəʊk/ vi 1 croar 2 gruñir ● n croar

crochet /'krəʊʃeɪ; krəʊ'ʃeɪ GB/ n (*labor de*) ganchillo, crochet

crockery /'krɒkəri/ n [*U*] loza, vajilla

crocodile /'krɒkədaɪl/ n cocodrilo

crocus /'krəʊkəs/ n azafrán (*de primavera*)

croissant /'krwʌsɒɴ/ n croissant

crony /'krəʊni/ n (*pl* -ies) (*pey*) compinche

crook /krʊk/ n (*coloq*) criminal

crooked /'krʊkɪd/ adj 1 torcido 2 (*camino*) tortuoso 3 deshonesto

crop /krɒp/ n 1 cosecha 2 cultivo ● vt (*-pp-*) 1 (*pelo*) cortar muy corto 2 (*animales*) pacer ■ **crop up** surgir

croquet /krou'keɪ; 'krəʊkeɪ *GB*/ *n* croquet

cross /krɔːs; krɒs *GB*/ *n* **1** cruz **2** ~ (between...) cruce, mezcla (de...) ● **1** *vt, vi* cruzar: *Shall we ~ over?* ¿Pasamos al otro lado? **2** *vt* ~ **yourself** santiguarse **3** *vt* llevar la contraria a **4** *vt* (*Zool, Bot*) cruzar ▸ **cross your fingers (for me)** deséame suerte **cross your mind** ocurrírsele a uno ■ **cross sth off/through** tachar algo ● *adj* (**-er/-est**) **1** enojado: *get ~ enojarse* **2** (*viento*) de costado

crossbar /'krɔːsbɑr; 'krɒs- *GB*/ *n* **1** (*bicicleta*) barra **2** (*Dep*) larguero, travesaño

crossbow /'krɔːsbou; 'krɒs- *GB*/ *n* ballesta

cross-country *adj, adv* a campo traviesa

cross-examine *vt* interrogar

cross-eyed *adj* bizco

crossfire /'krɔːsfaɪər; 'krɒs- *GB*/ *n* tiroteo: *get caught in the ~* encontrarse entre dos fuegos

crossing /'krɔːsɪŋ; 'krɒsɪŋ *GB*/ *n* **1** travesía **2** (*carretera*) cruce **3** paso a nivel **4** (*GB*) paso/cruce peatonal **5** *border* ~ frontera

cross-legged *adj, adv* con las piernas cruzadas

crossly /'krɔːsli; 'krɒs- *GB*/ *adv* con enojo

crossover /'krɔːsouvər; 'krɒs- *GB*/ *n* mezcla (*música, etc.*)

cross purposes *n*: *We're at* ~. Aquí hay un malentendido.

cross-reference *n* remisión

crossroads /'krɔːsroudz; 'krɒs- *GB*/ *n* cruce, crucero (*Mx*)

cross section *n* **1** corte **2** muestra representativa

crosswalk /'krɔːswɔːk; 'krɒs- *GB*/ *n* paso de peatones

crossword /'krɔːswɜːrd; 'krɒs- *GB*/ (*tb* ~ **puzzle**) *n* crucigrama

crotch /krɑtʃ/ *n* entrepierna

crouch /krautʃ/ *vi* agacharse, agazaparse

crow /krou/ *n* cuervo ▸ **as the crow flies** en línea recta ● *vi* **1** cantar **2** ~ (**about/over sth**) jactarse (de algo)

crowbar /'kroubɑr/ *n* palanca

crowd /kraud/ *n* **1** multitud: *~s of people* un montón de gente **2** (*en show*) concurrencia **3** the crowd (*pey*) las masas **4** (*coloq*) gente, grupo (*de amigos*) ● *vt* (*espacio*) llenar ■ **crowd around (sth/sb)** apiñarse (alrededor de algo/algn) **crowd in** entrar en tropel **crowd sth/sb in** apiñar algo/a

algn crowded *adj* **1** lleno (de gente) **2** repleto

crown /kraun/ *n* **1** corona: *~ prince* príncipe heredero **2** the Crown (*GB*) el estado **3** (*cabeza*) coronilla **4** (*sombrero*) copa **5** (*colina*) cumbre **6** (*diente*) corona ● *vt* coronar

crucial /'kruːʃl/ *adj* crucial

crucifix /'kruːsəfɪks/ *n* crucifijo

crucify /'kruːsɪfaɪ/ *vt* (*pt/pp* **-ied**) crucificar

crude /kruːd/ *adj* (**-er/-est**) **1** burdo **2** grosero ● *n* (*tb* ~ **oil**) crudo (*petróleo*)

cruel /'kruːəl/ *adj* (**crueller, -est** ~ (**to sth/sb**) cruel (con algo/algn) **cruelty** *n* (*pl* **-ies**) crueldad

cruise /kruːz/ *vi* **1** hacer un crucero **2** (*Aut, avión*) ir a velocidad constante ● *n* crucero (*viaje*) **cruiser** *n* **1** (*Mil*) crucero **2** (*tb* **cabin** ~) lancha de motor con camarotes

crumb /krʌm/ *n* migaja

crumble /'krʌmbl/ **1** *vi* ~ (**away**) desmoronarse, deshacerse **2** *vt* deshacer **3** *vt, vi* (*Cocina*) desmenuzar(se) **crumbly** *adj* (**-ier/-iest**) que se desmorona

crumple /'krʌmpl/ *vt, vi* ~ (**sth**) (**up**) arrugar(se) (algo)

crunch /krʌntʃ/ *vt* **1** morder (*haciendo ruido*) **2** *vt, vi* (*hacer*) crujir ● *n* crujido **crunchy** *adj* (**-ier/-iest**) crujiente

crusade /kruː'seɪd/ *n* cruzada **crusader** *n* **1** (*Hist*) cruzado **2** luchador/a

crush /krʌʃ/ *vt* **1** aplastar: *be crushed to death* morir aplastado **2** ~ **sth** (**up**) triturar algo: *crushed ice* hielo picado **3** (*ajo, etc.*) machacar **4** (*fruta*) exprimir **5** moler **6** (*ropa*) arrugar **7** (*ánimo*) abatir ● *n* **1** aglomeración **2** ~ (**on sb**) enamoramiento (breve) (*de algn*): *have a ~ on sb* clavarse (*Mx*)/tragarse (*And*) de algn **3** (*fruta*) jugo **crushing** *adj* aplastante

crust /krʌst/ *n* corteza

crutch /krʌtʃ/ *n* **1** muleta **2** apoyo

crux /krʌks/ *n* quid

cry /kraɪ/ (*pt/pp* **cried**) **1** *vi* ~ (**over sth/sb**) llorar (por algo/algn): *~ for joy* llorar de alegría **2** *vt, vi* ~ (**sth**) (**out**) gritar ▸ **a crying shame** una verdadera lástima **cry your eyes out** llorar a lágrima viva **it's no use crying over spilled/spilt** (*GB*) **milk** a lo hecho, pecho ■ **cry off** (*GB*) echarse atrás **cry out for sth** (*fig*) pedir algo a gritos ● *n* (*pl* **cries**) **1** grito **2** llorera, lloradera

C

(*And*): **have a** (*good*) ~ desahogarse llorando

crybaby /'kraɪbeɪbi/ *n* (*pl* **-ies**) (*coloq*) llorón/ona

crypt /krɪpt/ *n* cripta

cryptic /'krɪptɪk/ *adj* críptico

crystal /'krɪstl/ *n* cristal ▸ **crystal clear** 1 cristalino 2 (*significado*) claro como el agua

cub /kʌb/ *n* 1 (*león, etc.*) cachorro 2 osezno 3 lobezno 4 **the Cubs** los lobatos

cube /kju:b/ *n* 1 cubo 2 cubito: *sugar* ~ terrón/cubo de azúcar **cubic** *adj* cúbico

cubicle /'kju:bɪkl/ *n* 1 cubículo 2 (*GB*) probador, vestier (*And*)

cuckoo /'kʊku:/ *n* cuco

cucumber /'kju:kʌmbər/ *n* pepino, cocombro (*And*)

cuddle /'kʌdl/ 1 *vt* tener en brazos 2 *vt, vi* abrazar(se) 3 ~ **up to sb**) acurrucarse (junto a algn) ● *n* abrazo **cuddly** *adj* (**-ier/-iest**) (*coloq*) adorable: ~ *toy* muñeco de peluche

cue /kju:/ *n* 1 señal 2 (*Teat*) entrada 3 ejemplo: *take your* ~ *from sb* seguir el ejemplo de algn 4 taco (*billar, etc.*) ▸ **(right) on cue** en el momento preciso ● *vt* 1 dar la señal a 2 (*Teat*) dar la entrada a

cuff /kʌf/ *n* 1 (*ropa*) puño 2 manotazo ▸ **off the cuff** de improviso ● *vt* dar un manotazo a

cufflink /'kʌflɪŋk/ *n* mancuernilla (*Mx*), mancorna (*And*)

cuisine /kwɪ'zi:n/ *n* cocina: *Italian* ~ cocina italiana

cul-de-sac /'kʌl də sæk/ *n* (*pl* **-s**) (*calle*) cerrada

cull /kʌl/ *vt* 1 (*animales*) matar (*para controlar el número*) 2 seleccionar

culminate /'kʌlmɪneɪt/ *vi* (*fml*) culminar **culmination** *n* culminación

culottes /ku:'lɒts; kju:- *GB*/ *n* [*pl*] falda pantalón

culprit /'kʌlprɪt/ *n* culpable

cult /kʌlt/ *n* 1 culto: *a* ~ *movie* una película de culto 2 secta

cultivate /'kʌltɪveɪt/ *vt* 1 cultivar 2 fomentar **cultivated** *adj* 1 culto 2 cultivado **cultivation** *n* cultivo

culture /'kʌltʃər/ *n* 1 cultura: ~ *shock* choque cultural 2 (*Biol, Bot*) cultivo **cultural** *adj* cultural **cultured** *adj* 1 culto 2 ~ *pearl* perla cultivada

cum /kʌm/ *prep*: *a kitchen-cum-dining room* una cocina-comedor

cumbersome /'kʌmbərsəm/ *adj* 1 engorroso 2 voluminoso

cumulative /'kju:mjələtɪv; -lətɪv *GB*/ *adj* 1 acumulado 2 acumulativo

cunning /'kʌnɪŋ/ *adj* 1 astuto 2 (*aparato*) ingenioso ● *n* [*U*] astucia

cup /kʌp/ *n* 1 taza: *paper* ~ vaso de papel 2 (*premio*) copa ▸ **sb's cup of tea** (*coloq*) del gusto de algn ● *vt* (**-pp-**) (*manos*) hacer bocina con: ~ *a hand over sth* tapar algo con la mano ◇ ~ *your face in your hands* apoyar la cara en las manos

cupboard /'kʌbərd/ *n* armario ▸ **cupboard love** (*GB*) amor interesado

cupful /'kʌpfʊl/ *n* taza (*cantidad*)

curate /'kjʊərət/ *n* (*iglesia anglicana*) coadjutor/a (*del párroco*)

curative /'kjʊərətɪv/ *adj* curativo

curator /kjʊə'reɪtər/ *n* conservador/a (*museo*)

curb /kɜ:rb/ *n* 1 (*fig*) freno 2 borde (*de la acera*) ● *vt* frenar

curd /kɜ:rd/ *n* cuajada: ~ *cheese* requesón

curdle /'kɜ:rdl/ *vt, vi* cortar(se) (*leche, etc.*)

cure /kjʊər/ *vt* 1 curar 2 sanear ● *n* 1 cura, curación 2 remedio

curfew /'kɜ:rfju:/ *n* toque de queda

curious /'kjʊəriəs/ *adj* curioso: *I'm* ~ *to know...* Tengo curiosidad por saber... **curiosity** /ˌkjʊəri'ɒsəti/ *n* (*pl* **-ies**) 1 curiosidad 2 cosa rara

curl /kɜ:rl/ *n* 1 rizo 2 (*humo*) espiral ● *vt, vi* rizar(se) 2 *vi*: *The smoke curled upwards.* El humo subía en espiral. ■ **curl up** 1 rizarse 2 acurrucarse **curly** *adj* (**-ier/-iest**) rizado, chino (*Mx*)

currant /'kʌrənt/ *n* 1 pasa 2 grosella (*negra o roja*)

currency /'kʌrənsi/ *n* (*pl* **-ies**) 1 moneda: *hard* ~ divisa fuerte 2 aceptación: *gain* ~ generalizarse

current /'kʌrənt/ *n* corriente ● *adj* actual: ~ *affairs* temas de actualidad 2 generalizado **currently** *adv* actualmente

curriculum /kə'rɪkjələm/ *n* plan de estudios, currículo

curriculum vitae /kə,rɪkjələm 'vi:taɪ/ (*GB*) *Ver* cv

curry /'kʌri/ *n* (*pl* **-ies**) (*plato al*) curry ● *vt* (*pt/pp* **-ied**) ▸ **curry favor** congraciarse

curse /kɜ:rs/ *n* 1 maldición 2 maleficio 3 desgracia ● *vt, vi*

maldecir ▸ **be cursed with sth** padecer de algo

cursory /ˈkɜːrsəri/ adj rápido, superficial

curt /kɜːrt/ adj (tono) cortante

curtail /kɜːrˈteɪl/ vt acortar **curtailment** n limitación

curtain /ˈkɜːrtn/ n 1 cortina: *lace/net* ~s visillos 2 (*Teat*) telón 3 **curtains** [*pl*] (*coloq*) el fin

curtsy (*tb* **curtsey**) /ˈkɜːrtsi/ n (*pt/pp* **-ied/curtseyed**) (*solo mujeres*) hacer una reverencia ● n (*pl* **-ies** *o* **-eys**) reverencia

curve /kɜːrv/ n curva ● vi describir/hacer una curva **curved** adj 1 curvo 2 arqueado

cushion /ˈkʊʃn/ n 1 cojín 2 (*fig*) colchón ● vt 1 amortiguar 2 proteger

cushy adj (**-ier/-iest**) (*coloq*) fácil

custard /ˈkʌstərd/ n [U] crema inglesa

custodian /kʌˈstoʊdiən/ n 1 guardián/ana 2 (*museo, etc.*) conservador/a

custody /ˈkʌstədi/ n 1 custodia: *in* ~ bajo custodia 2 **remand sb in** ~ ordenar la detención de algn

custom /ˈkʌstəm/ n 1 costumbre 2 clientela **customary** adj acostumbrado: *It is* ~ *to...* Es costumbre...

customer /ˈkʌstəmər/ n cliente/a

customs /ˈkʌstəmz/ n [*pl*] 1 (*tb* ~ **duty**) derechos de aduana 2 aduana

cut /kʌt/ n 1 corte, incisión 2 reducción, recorte 3 (*carne*) pieza 4 (*ropa*) corte 5 (*ganancias*) parte ▸ **a cut above sth/sb** mejor que algo/algn ● (**-tt-**) (*pt/pp* **cut**) 1 *vt, vi* cortar(se): ~ *sth in half* partir algo por la mitad 2 *vt* reducir 3 *vt* tallar: ~ *glass* cristal tallado 4 *vt* herir ▸ **cut it/that out!** (*coloq*) ¡ya no más! **cut it/things fine** (*coloq*) dejar algo hasta el último momento **cut sth short** truncar algo ■ **cut across sth** 1 rebasar algo 2 cortar camino por algo **cut back (on sth)** recortar algo **cut sth back** podar algo **cut down (on sth):** ~ *down on smoking* fumar menos **cut sth down** 1 talar algo 2 reducir algo **cut in (USA)** colarse **cut in (on sth/sb)** 1 interrumpir (algo/a algn) 2 (*Aut*) meterse (delante de algo/algn) **cut sb off** 1 (*teléfono*): *I was* ~ *off*. Se cortó la comunicación. 2 desheredar a algn **cut sth off** 1 cortar algo: ~ *a second off the record* mejorar el récord en un segundo 2 (*pueblo*) aislar algo: *be* ~ *off* quedar incomuni-

cado **be cut out for sth/to be sth** (*coloq*) estar hecho para algo **cut sth out** 1 recortar algo 2 (*información*) suprimir algo 3 dejar de hacer algo **cut sth up** picar algo

cutback /ˈkʌtbæk/ n recorte

cute /kjuːt/ adj (**-er/-est**) mono, cuco (*And*)

cutlery /ˈkʌtləri/ n [U] cubiertos

cutlet /ˈkʌtlət/ n chuleta

cut-off (*tb* ~ **point**) n límite

cut-rate (**cut-price** GB) adj, adv a precio rebajado

cut-throat adj despiadado

cutting /ˈkʌtɪŋ/ n 1 recorte 2 (*Bot*) esqueje ● adj mordaz

CV /ˌsiː ˈviː/ n (GB) hoja de vida, currículum vitae

cyanide /ˈsaɪənaɪd/ n cianuro

cybercafe /ˈsaɪbərkæfeɪ/ n café internet

cyberspace /ˈsaɪbərspeɪs/ n ciberespacio

cycle /ˈsaɪkl/ n 1 ciclo 2 (*obras*) serie 3 bicicleta ● vi ir en bicicleta **cyclic** adj cíclico **cycling** n ciclismo **cyclist** n ciclista

cyclone /ˈsaɪkloʊn/ n ciclón

cylinder /ˈsɪlɪndər/ n cilindro **cylindrical** /səˈlɪndrɪkl/ adj cilíndrico

cymbal /ˈsɪmbl/ n (*Mús*) platillo

cynic /ˈsɪnɪk/ n cínico/a **cynical** adj 1 que desconfía de todo 2 sin escrúpulos **cynicism** n 1 desconfianza 2 falta de escrúpulos

cypress /ˈsaɪprəs/ n ciprés

cyst /sɪst/ n quiste

D d

D, d /diː/ n (*pl* **D's, d's**) 1 D, d 2 (*Mús*) re

dab /dæb/ n (**-bb-**) 1 *vt, vi* ~ (**at**) **sth** tocar algo ligeramente 2 *vt* ~ **sth on (sth)** poner un poco de algo (en algo) ● n poquito

dad /dæd/ (*tb* **daddy** /ˈdædi/) n (*coloq*) papá →PAPÁ

daffodil /ˈdæfədɪl/ n narciso

daft /dæft; dɑːft GB/ adj (**-er/-est**) (GB, *coloq*) bobo, ridículo

dagger /ˈdægər/ n puñal

daily /ˈdeɪli/ adj cotidiano, diario ● adv a diario, diariamente ● n (*pl* **-ies**) periódico

dairy /ˈdeəri/ n (*pl* **-ies**) lechería ● adj [*antes de sustantivo*] lechero: ~ *farming* la industria lechera ◊ ~ *products/produce* productos lácteos

D

daisy /'deɪzi/ n (pl **-ies**) margarita

dale /deɪl/ n (GB) valle

dam /dæm/ n presa (de un río) ● vt (**-mm-**) represar

damage /'dæmɪdʒ/ vt 1 dañar 2 perjudicar ● n 1 [U] daño 2 **damages** daños y perjuicios **damaging** adj perjudicial

Dame /deɪm/ n (GB) título aristocrático concedido a mujeres

damn /dæm/ vt condenar ● adj (tb **damned**) (coloq) maldito ● interj ¡maldita sea! ● n ▶ **not give a damn (about sth/sb)** (coloq) importarle a algn un comino (algo/algn) **damnation** /dæm'neɪʃn/ n condenación **damning** /'dæmɪŋ/ adj contundente

damp /dæmp/ adj (**-er/-est**) húmedo →HÚMEDO ● n humedad ● vt ■ **damp sth down** 1 apaciguar algo 2 reducir la intensidad de algo **dampen** /'dæmpən/ vt 1 mojar 2 amortiguar, sofocar

dance /dɑːns; dɑːns GB/ vt, vi bailar ● n baile **dancer** n bailarín/ina **dancing** n baile

dandelion /'dændɪlaɪən/ n diente de león (flor)

dandruff /'dændrʌf/ n caspa

danger /'deɪndʒər/ n peligro: be in ~ of sth estar en peligro de algo **dangerous** adj 1 peligroso 2 nocivo

dangle /'dæŋgl/ vi colgar

dank /dæŋk/ adj húmedo y frío

dare /deər/ 1 v modal, vi (neg **dare not/daren't** o **don't/doesn't dare** pt **dared not/didn't dare**) (frases negativas/interrogativas) atreverse a 2 vt ~ **sb (to do sth)** desafiar a algn (a hacer algo) ▶ **don't you dare** ni se te ocurra **how dare you!** ¡cómo te atreves! **I dare say** diría yo **NOTA** Normalmente **dare** se usa como un verbo normal: I didn't ~ to ask. Puede funcionar también como verbo modal M (esp en negaciones en inglés británico), y entonces se le sigue un infinitivo sin **to**: I daren't ask for a day off.

daring /'deərɪŋ/ n atrevimiento, osadía ● adj atrevido, osado

dark /dɑːrk/ adj (**-er/-est**) 1 oscuro: get ~ anochecer 2 (persona) moreno 3 secreto 4 triste: These are ~ days. Son tiempos difíciles. ▶ **a dark horse** una persona de talentos ocultos **in the** ~ a oscuras ▶ **before/after dark** antes/después del anochecer **darken** vt, vi oscurecer(se) **darkly** adv

1 misteriosamente 2 con pesimismo **darkness** n oscuridad, tinieblas: in ~ a oscuras

dark glasses n gafas oscuras, lentes oscuros →PAIR

darkroom /'dɑːrkruːm/ n cuarto oscuro

darling /'dɑːrlɪŋ/ n cariño (persona)

dart /dɑːrt/ n 1 dardo ● vi 1 precipitarse 2 ~ **away/off** salir disparado

dash /dæʃ/ n 1 pizca 2 raya 3 guión ▶ **make a dash for sth** precipitarse hacia algo ● 1 vi apurarse 2 vi ir muy rápido: ~ **upstairs** subir las escaleras corriendo 3 vt (esperanzas) desbaratar ■ **dash sth off** escribir algo rápidamente

dashboard /'dæʃbɔːrd/ n tablero de instrumentos (vehículo)

data /'deɪtə/ n [U] 1 (Comp) datos 2 información

database (tb **databank**) /'deɪtəbeɪs/-bæŋk/ n base de datos

date /deɪt/ n 1 fecha 2 cita 3 dátil ▶ **out of date** 1 pasado de moda 2 desfasado 3 caducado **to date** hasta la fecha **up to date** 1 al día 2 actualizado ● vt 1 fechar (fósiles, etc.) 2 datar **dated** adj pasado de moda

daughter /'dɔːtər/ n hija **daughter-in-law** n (pl **-ers-in-law**) nuera

daunting /'dɔːntɪŋ/ adj sobrecogedor

dawn /dɔːn/ n amanecer: from ~ till dusk de sol a sol ● vi amanecer

day /deɪ/ n 1 día: the ~ after tomorrow pasado mañana ◇ the ~ before yesterday anteayer 2 jornada 3 days [pl] época: these ~s hoy en día ▶ **day by/after day** día a/tras día **day in, day out** todos los días **from day to day; from one day to the next** de un día para otro **one/some day** algún día, un día de estos **to this day** aun ahora

daydream /'deɪdriːm/ n ensueño ● vi soñar despierto

daylight /'deɪlaɪt/ n luz del día

day off n (pl **days off**) día libre

day return n (GB) boleto/tiquete de ida y vuelta para un mismo día

daytime /'deɪtaɪm/ n día: in the ~ de día

day-to-day adj 1 día a día 2 diario

day trip n excursión de un día

daze /deɪz/ n ▶ **in a daze** aturdido **dazed** adj aturdido

dazzle /'dæzl/ vt deslumbrar

D

dead /ded/ *adj* **1** muerto **2** (*hojas*) seco **3** (*parte del cuerpo*) dormido **4** (*pila, batería*) gastado **5** (*teléfono*): *The line's gone* ~. Se cortó la comunicación. ● *adv* (*coloq*) completamente: *You're* ~ *right.* Tienes toda la razón. ● *n* ▶ **in the dead of night** en plena noche **deaden** *vt* **1** (*sonido*) amortiguar **2** (*dolor*) aliviar

dead end *n* callejón sin salida

dead heat *n* empate

deadline /'dedlaɪn/ *n* fecha/hora límite

deadlock /'dedlɒk/ *n* punto muerto

deadly /'dedli/ *adj* (**-ier/-iest**) mortal

deaf /def/ *adj* (**-er/-est**) sordo: ~ *and dumb* sordomudo **deafen** *vt* ensordecer **deafening** *adj* ensordecedor **deafness** *n* sordera

deal /di:l/ *vt, vi* (*pt/pp* **dealt** /delt/) (*golpe, naipes*) dar ■ **deal in sth** comerciar en algo: ~ *in drugs* traficar con drogas **deal with sb 1** tratar a/con algn **2** castigar a algn **3** ocuparse de algn **deal with sth 1** resolver algo **2** manejar algo **3** (*tema*) tratar de algo ● *n* **1** trato **2** contrato ▶ **a good/great deal** mucho: *It's a good* ~ *colder today.* Hace mucho más frío hoy. **big deal!** (*coloq*) ¡vaya cosa! ¡vaya gracia!

dealer /'di:lər/ *n* **1** vendedor/a, comerciante **2** (*drogas, armas*) traficante **3** (*cartas*) tallador/a

dealing /'di:lɪŋ/ *n* (*drogas, armas*) tráfico ▶ **have dealings with sth/sb** tratar con algo/algn

dean /di:n/ *n* **1** deán **2** decano/a

dear /dɪər/ *adj* (**-er/-est**) **1** querido **2** (*carta*): *Dear Sir* Muy señor mío ◊ *Dear Tom* Querido Tom **3** (*GB*) caro ▶ **oh dear!** ¡caramba! ● *n* cariño (*persona*) **dearly** *adv* mucho

death /deθ/ *n* muerte: ~ *certificate* acta/certificado de defunción ◊ *put/beat sb to* ~ dar muerte a algn/matar a algn a golpes **deathly** *adj* sepulcral: ~ *pale* pálido como un muerto

debase /dɪ'beɪs/ *vt* degradar

debatable /dɪ'beɪtəbl/ *adj* discutible

debate /dɪ'beɪt/ *n* debate ● *vt, vi* debatir

debit /'debɪt/ *n* débito ● *vt* cobrar

debris /də'briː; 'debriː *GB*/ *n* [U] escombros

debt /det/ *n* deuda: *be in* ~ tener deudas **debtor** *n* deudor/a

decade /'dekeɪd, dɪ'keɪd/ *n* década

decadent /'dekədənt/ *adj* decadente **decadence** *n* decadencia

decaffeinated /ˌdiː'kæfɪneɪtɪd/ (*coloq* **decaf** /'diːkæf/) *adj* descafeinado

decay /dɪ'keɪ/ *vi* **1** (*dientes*) picarse **2** descomponerse **3** decaer ● *n* [U] **1** (*tb tooth* ~) caries **2** descomposición

deceased /dɪ'siːst/ *adj* (*fml*) difunto ● **the deceased** *n* el/la difunto/a

deceit /dɪ'siːt/ *n* **1** falsedad **2** engaño **deceitful** *adj* **1** mentiroso **2** engañoso

deceive /dɪ'siːv/ *vt* engañar

December /dɪ'sembər/ *n* (*abrev* **Dec.**) diciembre →JUNE

decency /'diːsnsi/ *n* decencia, decoro

decent /'diːsnt/ *adj* **1** decente **2** adecuado **3** amable

deception /dɪ'sepʃn/ *n* engaño **deceptive** *adj* engañoso

decide /dɪ'saɪd/ **1** *vt, vi* decidir(se) **2** *vi* ~ *on sth/sb* optar por algo/algn **decided** *adj* **1** marcado **2** ~ (*about sth*) decidido (en algo)

decimal /'desɪml/ *adj, n* decimal

decipher /dɪ'saɪfər/ *vt* descifrar

decision /dɪ'sɪʒn/ *n* decisión: *decision-making* toma de decisiones

decisive /dɪ'saɪsɪv/ *adj* **1** decisivo **2** decidido

deck /dek/ *n* **1** (*Náut*) cubierta **2** (*USA, cartas*) baraja **3** (*autobús*) piso **4** (*tb cassette/tape* ~) grabadora **5** terraza (*de madera*)

deckchair /'dektʃeər/ *n* tumbona, silla de playa

declare /dɪ'kleər/ *vt* declarar **declaration** *n* declaración

decline /dɪ'klaɪn/ **1** *vt, vi* disminuir **2** *vt* (*fml*) declinar **3** *vt* (*fml*) ~ **to do sth** negarse a hacer algo ● *n* **1** disminución **2** decadencia

decoder /ˌdiː'kəʊdər/ *n* decodificador

decompose /ˌdiːkəm'pəʊz/ *vi* descomponerse, pudrirse

decor /'deɪkɔːr, deɪkɔː(r)/ *n* [U] decoración

decorate /'dekəreɪt/ *vt* **1** adornar **2** empapelar, pintar **3** condecorar **decoration** *n* **1** decoración **2** adorno **3** condecoración **decorative** /'dekərətɪv; -rətɪv *GB*/ *adj* decorativo

decoy /'diːkɔɪ/ *n* señuelo

decrease /dɪ'kriːs/ **1** *vi* disminuir **2** *vt* reducir ● /'diːkriːs/ *n* disminución, reducción

decree /dɪ'kriː/ n decreto ● vt (pt/ pp **decreed**) decretar

decrepit /dɪ'krepɪt/ adj decrépito

dedicate /'dedɪkeɪt/ vt dedicar, consagrar **dedication** n 1 dedicación 2 dedicatoria

deduce /dɪ'djuːs; dɪ'duːs GB/ vt deducir, concluir

deduct /dɪ'dʌkt/ vt deducir (impuestos, gastos, etc.) **deduction** n deducción

deed /diːd/ n 1 (fml) acción, obra 2 (fml) hazaña (Jur) escritura

deem /diːm/ vt (fml) considerar

deep /diːp/ (-er/-est) adj 1 profundo: The water is one meter ~. El agua tiene un metro de profundidad. 2 (respiración) hondo 3 (voz, etc.) grave 4 (color) intenso 5 ~ in absorto en algo ● adv muy profundo, con profundidad ▶ **deep down** en el fondo **go/run deep** estar muy arraigado **deeply** adv profundamente

deepen /'diːpən/ vt, vi hacer(se) más profundo, aumentar

deep freeze n congelador

deer /dɪər/ n (pl deer) ciervo →CIERVO

default /dɪ'fɔːlt/ n 1 incumplimiento 2 incomparecencia: by ~ por incomparecencia 3 (Comp): the ~ option la opción predeterminada ● vi 1 no comparecer 2 ~ (on sth) dejar incumplido (algo)

defeat /dɪ'fiːt/ vt 1 derrotar 2 frustrar ● n derrota: admit/accept ~ darse por vencido

defect¹ /dɪ'fekt/ vi 1 desertar 2 ~ to pasarse a algo **defection** n deserción **defector** n desertor/a

defect² /'diːfekt, dɪ'fekt/ n defecto → MISTAKE **defective** /dɪ-'fektɪv/ adj defectuoso

defend /dɪ'fend/ vt defender **defendant** n acusado/a **defender** n 1 (Dep) defensa 2 defensor/a

defense (**defence** GB) /dɪ-'fens/ n 1 defensa 2 **the defense** (Jur) la defensa **defenseless** adj indefenso

defensive /dɪ'fensɪv/ adj a la defensiva ▶ **on the defensive** a la defensiva

defer /dɪ'fɜːr/ vt (-rr-) ~ sth (to sth) posponer algo (para algo)

deference /'defərəns/ n reverencia: in ~ to sth por deferencia a algo

defiance /dɪ'faɪəns/ n desafío, desobediencia **defiant** adj desafiante

deficiency /dɪ'fɪʃnsi/ n (pl -ies) deficiencia **deficient** adj deficiente

define /dɪ'faɪn/ vt definir

definite /'defɪnət/ adj 1 definitivo, concreto 2 seguro 3 (Gram) definido **definitely** adv 1 definitivamente 2 sin duda alguna **definition** n definición

definitive /dɪ'fɪnətɪv/ adj definitivo, determinante

deflate /dɪ'fleɪt/ vt, vi desinflar(se)

deflect /dɪ'flekt/ vt desviar

deforestation /ˌdiːˌfɔːrɪ'steɪʃn/ n deforestación

deform /dɪ'fɔːrm/ vt deformar **deformed** adj deforme **deformity** n (pl -ies) deformidad

defrost /ˌdiːˈfrɔːst; -ˈfrɒst GB/ vt descongelar

deft /deft/ adj hábil

defunct /dɪ'fʌŋkt/ adj (fml) muerto, extinto

defuse /ˌdiːˈfjuːz/ vt 1 (bomba) desactivar 2 (crisis) atenuar

defy /dɪ'faɪ/ vt (pt/pp -ied) 1 desafiar 2 ~ sb to do sth retar a algn a que haga algo

degenerate /dɪ'dʒenəreɪt/ vi degenerar **degeneration** n degeneración

degrade /dɪ'greɪd/ vt degradar **degradation** /ˌdegrə'deɪʃn/ n degradación

degree /dɪ'griː/ n 1 grado 2 título (universitario): a ~ course una carrera/licenciatura (universitaria) ▶ **by degrees** poco a poco

deity /'deɪəti/ n (pl -ies) deidad

dejected /dɪ'dʒektɪd/ adj desanimado

delay /dɪ'leɪ/ 1 vt retrasar 2 vi esperar, tardar 3 vt aplazar: delayed action de acción retardada ● n retraso: without ~ sin demora **delaying** adj dilatorio

delegate /'delɪgət/ n delegado/a ● /'delɪgeɪt/ vt encomendar **delegation** n delegación

delete /dɪ'liːt/ vt borrar, tachar **deletion** n borrado, eliminación

deliberate /dɪ'lɪbərət/ adj deliberado ● /dɪ'lɪbəreɪt/ vi deliberar **deliberation** n deliberación

delicacy /'delɪkəsi/ n (pl -ies) 1 delicadeza 2 manjar

delicate /'delɪkət/ adj 1 delicado 2 (color, olor, etc.) suave: a ~ flavour un sabor exquisito

delicatessen /ˌdelɪkə'tesn/ (tb **deli** /'deli/) n delicatessen

delicious /dɪ'lɪʃəs/ adj delicioso

delight /dɪ'laɪt/ n deleite: take ~ in sth deleitarse en algo ◇ the

~s of traveling el placer de viajar ● **1** *vt* encantar **2** *vi* ~ **in sth** regodearse en algo **delighted** /dɪ'laɪtɪd/ *adj* ~ **(at/with sth)** encantado (de algo) **delightful** *adj* encantador

delinquent /dɪ'lɪŋkwənt/ *adj, n* delincuente **delinquency** *n* delincuencia

delirious /dɪ'lɪrɪəs/ *adj* delirante: ~ *with joy* loco de alegría **delirium** /dɪ'lɪrɪəm/ *n* delirio

deliver /dɪ'lɪvər/ *vt* **1** (*carta, etc.*) entregar **2** (*recado*) dar **3** (*discurso*) pronunciar **4** (*Med*): ~ *a baby* asistir a algn en un parto **5** (*golpe*) dar **delivery** *n* (*pl* **-ies**) **1** reparto **2** entrega **3** parto

delta /'deltə/ *n* delta

delude /dɪ'lu:d/ *vt* engañar

deluge /'delju:dʒ/ *n* **1** diluvio **2** (*fig*) lluvia ● *vt* ~ **sth/sb (with sth)** inundar algo/a algn (de algo)

delusion /dɪ'lu:ʒn/ *n* engaño, espejismo

de luxe /də 'lʌks/ *adj* de lujo

demand /dɪ'mænd; dɪ'mɑːnd *GB*/ *n* **1** ~ **(for sb to do sth)** exigencia (de que algn haga algo) **2** ~ **(for sth/sb)** demanda (de algo/algn) ▸ **in demand** solicitado on demand a petición ● *vt* **1** exigir **2** requerir **demanding** *adj* exigente

demise /dɪ'maɪz/ *n* **1** fracaso **2** (*fml*) fallecimiento

demo /'deməʊ/ *n* (*pl* **-s**) (*coloq*) **1** manifestación **2** (*Mús*) demo

democracy /dɪ'mɒkrəsi/ *n* (*pl* **-ies**) democracia **democrat** /'deməkræt/ *n* demócrata **democratic** /ˌdeməˈkrætɪk/ *adj* democrático

demographic /ˌdeməˈɡræfɪk/ *adj* demográfico

demolish /dɪ'mɒlɪʃ/ *vt* derribar **demolition** *n* demolición

demon /'diːmən/ *n* demonio **demonic** /dɪ'mɒnɪk/ *adj* diabólico

demonstrate /'demənstreɪt/ **1** *vt* demostrar **2** *vi* manifestarse **demonstration** *n* **1** demostración **2** manifestación **demonstrator** *n* manifestante

demonstrative /dɪ'mɒnstrətɪv/ *adj* **1** cariñoso **2** (*Gram*) demostrativo

demoralize /dɪ'mɒrəlaɪz; -'mɒr- *GB*/ *vt* desmoralizar

demure /dɪ'mjʊər/ *adj* recatado

den /den/ *n* guarida

denial /dɪ'naɪəl/ *n* **1** negación **2** denegación, rechazo

denim /'denɪm/ *n* tela de mezclilla, tela de bluyín (*And*)

denomination /dɪˌnɒmɪ'neɪʃn/ *n* confesión

denounce /dɪ'naʊns/ *vt* denunciar

dense /dens/ *adj* (**-er/-est**) denso **density** *n* (*pl* **-ies**) densidad

dent /dent/ *n* abolladura ● *vt, vi* abollar(se)

dental /'dentl/ *adj* dental

dentist /'dentɪst/ *n* dentista

denunciation /dɪˌnʌnsi'eɪʃn/ *n* denuncia

deny /dɪ'naɪ/ *vt* (*pt/pp* **-ied**) **1** negar **2** (*rumor, etc.*) desmentir

deodorant /di'əʊdərənt/ *n* desodorante

depart /dɪ'pɑːt/ *vi* (*fml*) salir

department /dɪ'pɑːtmənt/ *n* (*abrev* **Dept**) **1** departamento, sección **2** ministerio **departmental** /ˌdiːpɑːt'mentl/ *adj* de departamento

department store *n* [*sing*] (grandes) almacenes

departure /dɪ'pɑːtʃər/ *n* **1** partida **2** (*avión, etc.*) salida

depend /dɪ'pend/ *vi* ~ **on/upon sth/sb** depender de algo/algn **2** confiar en algo/algn ▸ **that/it depends** depende **dependable** *adj* fiable

dependent (*tb* **-ant** *GB*) /dɪ'pendənt/ *n* persona bajo el cargo de otra ● *adj* **1** be ~ **on/upon sth/sb** depender de algo/algn **2** (*persona*) poco independiente **dependence** *n* ~ **(on/upon sth/sb)** dependencia (de algo/algn)

depict /dɪ'pɪkt/ *vt* representar

depleted /dɪ'pliːtɪd/ *adj* reducido

deplore /dɪ'plɔːr/ *vt* **1** condenar **2** lamentar

deploy /dɪ'plɔɪ/ *vt* desplegar(se)

deport /dɪ'pɔːt/ *vt* deportar **deportation** *n* deportación

depose /dɪ'pəʊz/ *vt* destituir

deposit /dɪ'pɒzɪt/ *vt* **1** (*dinero*) depositar **2** ~ **sth (with sb)** (*bienes*) dejar algo (a cargo de algn) ● *n* **1** (*Fin*) depósito: *safety ~ box* caja de seguridad **2** ~ **(on sth)** cuota inicial (para algo) **3** sedimento

depot /'diːpəʊ; 'depəʊ *GB*/ *n* **1** depósito **2** (*GB, para vehículos*) garaje **3** (*USA*) terminal (*tren, buses*)

depress /dɪ'pres/ *vt* deprimir **depression** *n* depresión

deprivation /ˌdeprɪ'veɪʃn/ *n* pobreza, privación

deprive /dɪ'praɪv/ *vt* privar **deprived** *adj* necesitado

depth /depθ/ *n* profundidad ▸ **in depth** a fondo, en profundidad

deputation /ˌdepjuˈteɪʃn/ n delegación

deputy /ˈdepjuti/ n (pl -ies) 1 sustituto/a, suplente: ~ chairman vicepresidente 2 (Pol) diputado/a **deputize** vi ~ (for sb) sustituir a algn

deranged /dɪˈreɪndʒd/ adj trastornado, loco

deregulation /ˌdiːregjuˈleɪʃn/ n liberalización (servicios, etc.)

derelict /ˈderəlɪkt/ adj abandonado (edificio)

deride /dɪˈraɪd/ vt ridiculizar, burlarse de

derision /dɪˈrɪʒn/ n burla(s) **derisive** /dɪˈraɪsɪv/ adj burlón **derisory** /dɪˈraɪsəri/ adj irrisorio

derivative /dɪˈrɪvətɪv/ n derivado

derive /dɪˈraɪv/ 1 vt (fml) obtener: ~ comfort from sth hallar consuelo en algo 2 vi ~ from sth derivar de algo **derivation** n derivación

derogatory /dɪˈrɒɡətɔːri; -tri GB/ adj despectivo

descend /dɪˈsend/ vt, vi (fml) descender **descendant** n descendiente

descent /dɪˈsent/ n 1 descenso 2 ascendencia

describe /dɪˈskraɪb/ vt describir **description** n descripción

desert[1] /ˈdezət/ n desierto

desert[2] /dɪˈzɜːt/ 1 vt abandonar 2 vi (Mil) desertar **deserted** adj desierto **deserter** n desertor/a **desertification** /dɪˌzɜːtɪfɪˈkeɪʃn/ n desertificación

deserve /dɪˈzɜːv/ vt merecer **deserving** adj digno

design /dɪˈzaɪn/ n 1 diseño 2 plan 3 dibujo ● vt diseñar, concebir

designate /ˈdezɪɡneɪt/ vt 1 designar 2 nombrar

designer /dɪˈzaɪnər/ n diseñador/a ● adj [antes de sustantivo] de marca

desire /dɪˈzaɪər/ n 1 deseo 2 ~ (for sth/to do sth) ansias (de algo): He had no ~ to see her. No sentía ninguna gana de verla. ● vt desear **desirable** adj deseable

desk /desk/ n escritorio

desktop /ˈdesktɒp/ adj: ~ computer computador(a) personal ◇ ~ publishing autoedición

desolate /ˈdesələt/ adj 1 desolado 2 (futuro) desolador **desolation** n 1 desolación 2 desconsuelo

despair /dɪˈspeər/ vi ~ perder las esperanzas ● n desesperación **despairing** adj desesperado

despatch (GB) = DISPATCH

desperate /ˈdespərət/ adj desesperado

despicable /dɪˈspɪkəbl/ adj despreciable

despise /dɪˈspaɪz/ vt despreciar

despite /dɪˈspaɪt/ prep a pesar de

despondent /dɪˈspɒndənt/ adj abatido, desalentado

despot /ˈdespɒt/ n déspota

dessert /dɪˈzɜːt/ n postre

dessertspoon /dɪˈzɜːtspuːn/ n 1 cuchara de postre 2 (tb dessertspoonful) cucharada (de postre)

destination /ˌdestɪˈneɪʃn/ n destino (avión, barco, etc.)

destined /ˈdestɪnd/ adj (fml) destinado: It was ~ to fail. Estaba condenado a fracasar.

destiny /ˈdestəni/ n (pl -ies) destino (sino)

destitute /ˈdestɪtuːt; -tjuːt GB/ adj indigente

destroy /dɪˈstrɔɪ/ vt destruir **destroyer** n destructor

destruction /dɪˈstrʌkʃn/ n destrucción **destructive** adj destructivo

detach /dɪˈtætʃ/ vt separar **detachable** adj que se puede separar **detachment** n 1 imparcialidad 2 (Mil) destacamento

detached /dɪˈtætʃt/ adj 1 imparcial 2 (casa) independiente (no pareado)

detail /ˈdiːteɪl; dɪˈteɪl GB/ n detalle, pormenor: go into ~s entrar en detalles ◇ in ~ detalladamente ● vt detallar **detailed** adj detallado

detain /dɪˈteɪn/ vt retener **detainee** /ˌdiːteɪˈniː/ n detenido/a

detect /dɪˈtekt/ vt 1 detectar 2 descubrir **detectable** adj detectable **detection** n descubrimiento: escape ~ pasar inadvertido

detective /dɪˈtektɪv/ n detective: ~ story novela policíaca

detention /dɪˈtenʃn/ n detención

deter /dɪˈtɜːr/ vt (-rr-) disuadir

detergent /dɪˈtɜːdʒənt/ adj, n detergente

deteriorate /dɪˈtɪəriəreɪt/ vi deteriorarse, empeorar **deterioration** n deterioro

determine /dɪˈtɜːmɪn/ vt determinar, decidir: determining factor factor determinante **determination** n determinación **determined** adj resuelto

determiner /dɪˈtɜːmɪnər/ n (Gram) determinante

deterrent /dɪˈterənt; -ˈtɜːr- GB/ n 1 escarmiento 2 elemento disuasorio 3 (*Mil*): *nuclear* ~ fuerza disuasoria nuclear

detest /dɪ'test/ vt detestar

detonate /'detəneɪt/ vt, vi detonar

detour /'diː'tʊər/ n desvío

detract /dɪ'trækt/ vi ~ **from sth** restar mérito a algo: ~ *from sb's enjoyment of sth* restar placer a algo

detriment /'detrɪmənt/ n ▸ **to the detriment of sth/sb** (*fml*) en detrimento de algo/algn **detrimental** /ˌdetrɪ'mentl/ adj perjudicial

devalue /ˌdiː'væljuː/ vt, vi devaluar(se) **devaluation** n devaluación

devastate /'devəsteɪt/ vt 1 devastar, asolar 2 (*persona*) destrozar **devastating** adj 1 devastador 2 desastroso **devastation** n devastación

develop /dɪ'veləp/ 1 vt, vi desarrollar(se) 2 vt (*plan*) elaborar 3 vt (*Fot*) revelar 4 vt urbanizar **developed** adj desarrollado **developer** n promotor/a **developing** adj en (vías de) desarrollo **development** n 1 desarrollo, evolución: *There has been a new* ~. Ha cambiado la situación. 2 urbanización 3 complejo habitacional, fraccionamiento (*Mx*)

deviant /'diːviənt/ adj, n 1 desviado/a 2 (*sexual*) pervertido/a

deviate /'diːvieɪt/ vi desviarse **deviation** n desviación

device /dɪ'vaɪs/ n 1 aparato, dispositivo: *explosive* ~ artefacto explosivo 2 (*plan*) estrategema

devil /'devl/ n demonio, diablo: *You lucky* ~! ¡Qué suerte tienes!

devious /'diːviəs/ adj 1 enrevesado 2 poco escrupuloso

devise /dɪ'vaɪz/ vt idear, elaborar

devoid /dɪ'vɔɪd/ adj ~ **of sth** desprovisto, exento de algo

devolution /ˌdiːvə'luːʃn, ˌdiːv-/ n 1 descentralización 2 (*de poderes*) delegación

devote /dɪ'vəʊt/ vt 1 ~ **sth/yourself to sth/sb** dedicar(se) (algo) a algo/algn 2 (*recursos*) destinar **devoted** adj fiel, leal: *They're* ~ *to each other*. Están entregados el uno al otro. **devotion** n devoción

devotee /ˌdevə'tiː/ n devoto/a

devour /dɪ'vaʊər/ vt devorar

devout /dɪ'vaʊt/ adj 1 devoto, piadoso 2 sincero

dew /duː; dju: GB/ n rocío

dexterity /dek'sterəti/ n destreza

diabetes /ˌdaɪə'biːtiːz/ n diabetes **diabetic** /ˌdaɪə'betɪk/ adj, n diabético/a

diabolical /ˌdaɪə'bɒlɪkl/ adj diabólico

diagnose /ˌdaɪəg'nəʊs; 'daɪəgnəʊz GB/ vt diagnosticar: *She was diagnosed with cancer.* Le diagnosticaron cáncer. **diagnosis** n (*pl* -noses /-'nəʊsiːz/) diagnóstico **diagnostic** /ˌdaɪəg'nɒstɪk/ adj diagnóstico

diagonal /daɪ'ægənl/ adj, n diagonal

diagram /'daɪəgræm/ n diagrama

dial /'daɪəl/ n 1 indicador 2 (*reloj*) cara, carátula 3 (*Radio*) dial ● vt (-l-, -ll- GB) marcar

dialect /'daɪəlekt/ n dialecto

dialling code n (GB, *teléfono*) prefijo, indicativo

dialogue (*tb* dialog USA) /'daɪəlɔːg; -lɑːg GB/ n diálogo

dial tone (**dialling tone** GB) n tono de marcar

diameter /daɪ'æmɪtər/ n diámetro: *It is 15cm in* ~. Tiene 15cm de diámetro.

diamond /'daɪəmənd/ n 1 diamante 2 rombo 3 ~ *jubilee* sexagésimo aniversario 4 **diamonds** (*cartas*) diamantes →BARAJA

diaper /'daɪpər/ n (USA) pañal

diaphragm /'daɪəfræm/ n diafragma

diarrhea (**diarrhoea** GB) /ˌdaɪə'riːə/ n diarrea

diary /'daɪəri/ n (*pl* -ies) 1 diario 2 (GB) agenda

dice /daɪs/ n (*pl* dice) dado ● vt cortar en cubitos

dictate /dɪk'teɪt; 'dɪk'teɪt GB/ 1 vt, vi dictar 2 vi ~ **to sb** dar órdenes a algn **dictation** n dictado

dictator /dɪk'teɪtər; dɪk'teɪtə(r) GB/ n dictador **dictatorship** n dictadura

dictionary /'dɪkʃənəri; -nri GB/ n (*pl* -ies) diccionario

did *pt de* DO²

didactic /daɪ'dæktɪk/ adj (*fml*) didáctico

didn't /'dɪdnt/ = DID NOT

die /daɪ/ vi (*pt/pp* died *pt pres* dying) morir ▸ **be dying for sth/to do sth** morirse por (hacer) algo ■ **die away** disminuir poco a poco **die down** 1 apagarse gradualmente 2 amainar **die off** morir uno tras otro **die out** 1 (*Zool*) extinguirse 2 desaparecer

diesel /'diːzl/ n diesel: ~ *fuel/oil* diesel/ACPM (*And*)

diet /'daɪət/ n dieta: *go on a* ~ ponerse a dieta ● vi estar a/hacer dieta **dietary** adj dietético

differ /'dɪfər/ vi 1 ser diferente 2 no estar de acuerdo

difference /'dɪfrəns/ n diferencia: *a ~ of opinion* una desavenencia ▸ **it makes all the difference** lo cambia todo **it makes no difference** da lo mismo **what difference does it make?** ¿qué más da?

different /'dɪfrənt/ adj ~ (**than/ from sth/sb**) diferente, distinto (a/de algo/algn) **differently** adv de otra manera

differentiate /,dɪfə'renʃieɪt/ vt, vi distinguir, diferenciar **differentiation** n diferenciación

difficult /'dɪfɪkəlt/ adj difícil **difficulty** n (pl **-ies**) 1 dificultad 2 apuro, aprieto: *make difficulties for sb* poner obstáculos a algn

diffident /'dɪfɪdənt/ adj poco seguro de sí mismo **diffidence** n falta de confianza en sí mismo

dig /dɪg/ vt, vi (**-gg-**) (pt/pp **dug**) 1 cavar: *~ for sth* cavar en busca de algo ◇ *~ sth out* sacar algo (cavando) 2 *~* (sth) **into sth** clavar(se) (algo) en algo ▸ **dig your heels in** cerrarse en banda ■ **dig in** (coloq) (comida) atacar **dig sth up** 1 sacar algo de la tierra 2 desenterrar algo 3 (calle) levantar algo ● n excavación **digger** n excavadora

digest /'daɪdʒest/ n 1 resumen 2 compendio ● /dar'dʒest/ vt, vi digerir(se) **digestion** n digestión

digit /'dɪdʒɪt/ n dígito **digital** adj digital

dignified /'dɪgnɪfaɪd/ adj digno

dignitary /'dɪgnɪteri; -təri GB/ n dignatario/a

dignity /'dɪgnəti/ n dignidad

digression /dar'greʃn/ n digresión

dike = DYKE

dilapidated /dɪ'læpɪdeɪtɪd/ adj 1 ruinoso 2 destartalado

dilemma /dɪ'lemə, daɪ-/ n dilema

dilute /daɪ'luːt/ vt 1 diluir 2 suavizar, debilitar

dim /dɪm/ adj (**dimmer, -est**) 1 (luz) débil, tenue 2 (recuerdo, etc.) vago 3 (porvenir) poco prometedor 4 (GB, coloq) tonto 5 (vista) turbio ● (**-mm-**) 1 vt (luz) bajar 2 vi (luz) apagarse poco a poco 3 vt, vi empañar(se), apagar(se)

dime /daɪm/ n (Can, USA) moneda de 10 centavos

dimension /dɪ'menʃn, daɪ-/ n dimensión

diminish /dɪ'mɪnɪʃ/ vt, vi disminuir

diminutive /dɪ'mɪnjətɪv/ adj, n diminuto ● adj, n diminutivo

dimly /'dɪmli/ adv 1 débilmente 2 vagamente 3 (ver) apenas

dimple /'dɪmpl/ n hoyuelo

din /dɪn/ n [sing] 1 alboroto 2 estruendo

dine /daɪn/ vi ~ (**on sth**) (fml) cenar, comer (algo): *~ out* cenar/comer fuera **diner** n 1 comensal 2 (USA) pequeño restaurante

dinghy /'dɪŋgi/ n (pl **-ies**) 1 bote, barca 2 lancha (de goma)

dingy /'dɪndʒi/ adj (**-ier/-iest**) 1 sombrío 2 sucio

dining room n comedor

dinner /'dɪnər/ n 1 comida de mediodía o al final de la tarde: *have ~* cenar/comer (And): *~ party* cena entre amigos **NOTA** El uso de los términos **dinner, lunch, supper** y **tea** varía mucho en los países anglohablantes. **Lunch** es la comida del mediodía, que suele ser ligera. Hay gente en Gran Bretaña que llama **dinner** a esta comida. **Dinner** y **supper** (y **tea** en Gran Bretaña) pueden referirse a la comida principal del día, que se toma al final de la tarde. **Supper** puede ser también algo ligero que se toma antes de acostarse, y **tea** puede consistir en té con galletas o pasteles en la tarde. 2 cena (de gala)

dinner jacket n (GB) smoking

dinosaur /'daɪnəsɔːr/ n dinosaurio

diocese /'daɪəsɪs/ n diócesis

dioxide /daɪ'ɑksaɪd/ n dióxido

dip /dɪp/ (**-pp-**) 1 vt meter, mojar 2 vt, vi bajar ● n 1 (coloq) chapuzón 2 (precios, etc.) baja 3 declive 4 (Cocina) dip (salsa fría en la que se mojan papas fritas, etc.) 5 (Geog) depresión

diploma /dɪ'pləʊmə/ n diploma

diplomacy /dɪ'pləʊməsi/ n diplomacia **diplomat** /'dɪpləmæt/ n diplomático/a **diplomatic** /,dɪplə'mætɪk/ adj diplomático

dire /'daɪər/ adj (**direr, -est**) 1 (fml) horrible, extremo 2 (GB, coloq) fatal

direct /dɪ'rekt, daɪ-/ vt dirigir: *Could you ~ me to...?* ¿Podría indicarme el camino a...? ● adj 1 directo 2 franco 3 total ● adv 1 directamente: *The train goes ~ to London.* El tren va directo a Londres. 2 en persona **directly** adv 1 directamente: *~ opposite* justo enfrente 2 enseguida **directness** n franqueza

direct debit n (GB) débito bancario/automático

direction /dɪˈrekʃn, daɪ-/ n 1 dirección, sentido 2 **directions** instrucciones: ask for ~s preguntar el camino a algún sitio

directive /dɪˈrektɪv, daɪ-/ n directiva

director /dɪˈrektər, daɪ-/ n director/a

directorate /dɪˈrektərət, daɪ-/ n 1 junta directiva 2 Dirección General

directory /dəˈrektəri, daɪ-/ n (pl -ies) guía (telefónica), directorio

dirt /dɜːrt/ n 1 suciedad, mugre 2 tierra 3 (coloq) grosería, porquería

dirty /ˈdɜːrti/ adj (-ier/-iest) 1 sucio: ~ trick mala pasada 2 (chiste, etc.) verde, colorado (Mx): ~ word grosería ● vt, vi (pt/pp -ied) ensuciar(se)

disability /ˌdɪsəˈbɪləti/ n (pl -ies) 1 discapacidad 2 incapacidad

disabled /dɪsˈeɪbld/ adj minusválido ● **the disabled** n [pl] los minusválidos

disadvantage /ˌdɪsədˈvæntɪdʒ; -ˈvɑːn- GB/ n desventaja **disadvantaged** adj perjudicado **disadvantageous** /ˌdɪsædvænˈteɪdʒəs/ adj desventajoso

disagree /ˌdɪsəˈɡriː/ vi no estar de acuerdo ● **disagree with** sb sentarle mal a algn (comida, clima) **disagreeable** adj desagradable **disagreement** n 1 desacuerdo 2 discrepancia

disappear /ˌdɪsəˈpɪər/ vi desaparecer **disappearance** n desaparición

disappoint /ˌdɪsəˈpɔɪnt/ vt decepcionar, defraudar **disappointed** adj decepcionado: I'm ~ in you. Me decepcionaste. **disappointing** adj decepcionante **disappointment** n decepción

disapprove /ˌdɪsəˈpruːv/ vi 1 ~ (of sth) desaprobar (algo) 2 ~ (of sb) tener mala opinión (de algn) **disapproval** n desaprobación **disapproving** adj desaprobación

disarm /dɪsˈɑːrm/ vt, vi desarmar(se) **disarmament** n desarme

disassociate /ˌdɪsəˈsoʊʃieɪt/ Ver DISSOCIATE

disaster /dɪˈzæstər; -ˈzɑːs- GB/ n desastre **disastrous** adj desastroso, catastrófico

disband /dɪsˈbænd/ vt, vi disolver(se)

disbelief /ˌdɪsbɪˈliːf/ n incredulidad

disc /dɪsk/ n disco

discard /dɪsˈkɑːrd/ vt desechar, deshacerse de

discern /dɪˈsɜːrn/ vt 1 percibir 2 discernir **discernible** adj perceptible

discharge /dɪsˈtʃɑːrdʒ/ vt 1 (residuos) verter 2 (Mil) licenciar 3 (Med) dar de alta 4 (deber) desempeñar ● /dɪsˈtʃɑːrdʒ/ n 1 descarga 2 (residuo) vertido 3 (Mil) licenciamiento 4 (Jur): conditional ~ libertad condicional 5 (Med) supuración

disciple /dɪˈsaɪpl/ n discípulo/a

discipline /ˈdɪsəplɪn/ n disciplina ● vt disciplinar **disciplinary** adj disciplinario

disc jockey n DJ

disclose /dɪsˈkloʊz/ vt revelar **disclosure** /dɪsˈkloʊʒər/ n revelación

disco /ˈdɪskoʊ/ n (pl -s) discoteca

discolour (-or GB) /dɪsˈkʌlər/ vt, vi decolorar(se)

discomfort /dɪsˈkʌmfərt/ n [U] incomodidad

disconcerted /ˌdɪskənˈsɜːrtɪd/ adj desconcertado **disconcerting** adj desconcertante

disconnect /ˌdɪskəˈnekt/ vt 1 desconectar 2 (luz) cortar **disconnected** adj inconexo, incoherente

discontent /ˌdɪskənˈtent/ (tb **discontentment**) n descontento **discontented** adj descontento

discontinue /ˌdɪskənˈtɪnjuː/ vt suspender, descontinuar

discord /ˈdɪskɔːrd/ n 1 (fml) discordia 2 (Mús) disonancia **discordant** /dɪsˈkɔːrdənt/ adj 1 discorde 2 (Mús) disonante

discount /dɪsˈkaʊnt/ vt 1 descartar, ignorar 2 (Com) descontar ● /ˈdɪskaʊnt/ n descuento: at a ~ a precio rebajado

discourage /dɪsˈkʌrɪdʒ/ vt 1 desanimar 2 ~ sth oponerse a algo, aconsejar que no se haga algo 3 ~ sb from doing sth disuadir a algn de hacer algo **discouraging** adj desalentador

discover /dɪsˈkʌvər/ vt descubrir **discovery** n (pl -ies) descubrimiento

discredit /dɪsˈkredɪt/ vt desacreditar

discreet /dɪsˈkriːt/ adj discreto

discrepancy /dɪsˈkrepənsi/ n (pl -ies) discrepancia

discretion /dɪsˈkreʃn/ n 1 discreción 2 albedrío ▶ **at sb's discretion** a juicio de algn

discriminate /dɪˈskrɪmɪneɪt/ vi 1 distinguir 2 ~ against/in favor of sb discriminar, favorecer a algn **discriminating** adj perspicaz **discrimination** n 1 discriminación 2 discernimiento

discuss /dɪˈskʌs/ vt ~ sth hablar, tratar de algo **discussion** n debate, deliberación

disdain /dɪsˈdeɪn/ n desdén

disease /dɪˈziːz/ n enfermedad, afección **NOTA** En general, **disease** se usa para enfermedades específicas: heart ~ ◇ Parkinson's ~. **Illness** se refiere a la enfermedad como estado o al período en que uno está enfermo: mental illness. **diseased** adj enfermo

disembark /ˌdɪsɪmˈbɑːk/ vi desembarcar

disenchanted /ˌdɪsɪnˈtʃæntɪd; -ˈtʃɑːnt GB/ adj desengañado, desilusionado

disentangle /ˌdɪsɪnˈtæŋgl/ vt 1 desenredar 2 liberar

disfigure /dɪsˈfɪgjər; -gə(r) GB/ vt desfigurar

disgrace /dɪsˈgreɪs/ vt deshonrar ● n 1 desgracia, deshonra: in ~ with sb desacreditado ante algn 2 a ~ (to sth/sb) una vergüenza (para algo/algn) **disgraceful** adj vergonzoso

disgruntled /dɪsˈgrʌntld/ adj disgustado

disguise /dɪsˈgaɪz/ vt ~ sth/sb (as sth/sb) disfrazar, disimular algo/a algn (de algo/algn) ● n disfraz: in ~ disfrazado

disgust /dɪsˈgʌst/ n asco, repugnancia **disgusting** adj asqueroso

dish /dɪʃ/ n plato: the national ~ el plato nacional ◇ wash/do the dishes lavar los platos ■ **dish sth out 1** (tb ~ sth up) (comida) servir algo **2** (coloq) (dinero) repartir a manos llenas

disheartened /dɪsˈhɑːtnd/ adj desalentado, desanimado **disheartening** adj desalentador

disheveled (-ll- GB) /dɪˈʃevld/ adj 1 (pelo) despeinado 2 (ropa, etc.) desaliñado

dishonest /dɪsˈɑnɪst/ adj 1 deshonesto 2 fraudulento **dishonesty** n deshonestidad

dishonor (-our GB) /dɪsˈɑnər/ n deshonor, deshonra ● vt deshonrar **dishonorable** adj deshonroso

dishwasher /ˈdɪʃwɑʃər/ n lavavajillas, lavaplatos

disillusion /ˌdɪsɪˈluːʒn/ n (tb disillusionment) desengaño, desencanto ● vt desengañar, desencantar

disinfect /ˌdɪsɪnˈfekt/ vt desinfectar **disinfectant** n desinfectante

disintegrate /dɪsˈɪntɪgreɪt/ vt, vi desintegrar(se) **disintegration** n desintegración

disinterested /dɪsˈɪntrəstɪd/ adj desinteresado

disjointed /dɪsˈdʒɔɪntɪd/ adj inconexo

disk /dɪsk/ n disco

disk drive n unidad de disco

diskette /dɪsˈket/ n disquete

dislike /dɪsˈlaɪk/ vt no gustar, tener aversión ● n ~ (of sth/sb) aversión (por/a algo/algn), antipatía (a/hacia algn)

dislocate /ˈdɪsloʊkeɪt; -lək- GB/ vt dislocar **dislocation** n dislocación

dislodge /dɪsˈlɑdʒ/ vt desalojar

disloyal /dɪsˈlɔɪəl/ adj ~ (to sb) desleal (a algo/con algn) **disloyalty** n deslealtad

dismal /ˈdɪzməl/ adj 1 triste 2 (coloq) pésimo

dismantle /dɪsˈmæntl/ vt 1 desarmar 2 desmantelar

dismay /dɪsˈmeɪ/ n ~ (at sth) consternación (ante algo) ● vt llenar de consternación

dismember /dɪsˈmembər/ vt desmembrar

dismiss /dɪsˈmɪs/ vt 1 despedir 2 ~ sth/sb (as sth) descartar, desechar algo/a algn (por ser algo) **dismissal** n 1 despido 2 rechazo **dismissive** adj desdeñoso

dismount /dɪsˈmaʊnt/ vi desmontar, apearse

disobedient /ˌdɪsəˈbiːdiənt/ adj desobediente **disobedience** n desobediencia

disobey /ˌdɪsəˈbeɪ/ vt, vi desobedecer

disorder /dɪsˈɔːrdər/ n desorden: in ~ desordenado **disorderly** adj 1 desordenado 2 indisciplinado: be charged with being drunk and ~ ser acusado de borrachera y alboroto

disorganized /dɪsˈɔːrgənaɪzd/ adj desorganizado

disorient /dɪsˈɔːriənt/ (disorientate /dɪsˈɔːriənteɪt/ GB) vt desorientar

disown /dɪsˈoʊn/ vt renegar de

dispatch /dɪsˈpætʃ/ vt (fml) enviar ● n 1 envío 2 (Period) despacho

dispel /dɪˈspel/ vt (-ll-) disipar

dispense /dɪˈspens/ vt repartir ■ **dispense with sth/sb** prescindir de algo/algn

disperse /dɪˈspɜːrs/ *vt*, *vi* dispersar(se) **dispersal** *n* dispersión (*tb* **dispersion**) *n* dispersión

displace /dɪsˈpleɪs/ *vt* **1** desplazar **2** reemplazar

display /dɪsˈpleɪ/ *vt* **1** exhibir **2** (*emoción, etc.*) mostrar **3** (*Comp*) mostrar en pantalla ● *n* **1** exhibición **2** demostración **3** (*Comp*) pantalla (*de información*) ▸ **on display** expuesto

disposable /dɪsˈpoʊzəbl/ *adj* **1** desechable **2** (*Fin*) disponible

disposal /dɪsˈpoʊzl/ *n* desecho ▸ **at your/sb's disposal** a su disposición/a la disposición de algn

disposed /dɪsˈpoʊzd/ *adj* dispuesto: *be ill/well ~ towards sb* estar mal/bien dispuesto hacia algn

disposition /ˌdɪspəˈzɪʃn/ *n* manera de ser

disproportionate /ˌdɪsprəˈpɔːrʃənət/ *adj* desproporcionado

disprove /ˌdɪsˈpruːv/ *vt* refutar

dispute /dɪsˈpjuːt/ *n* **1** discusión **2** conflicto, disputa ▸ **in dispute 1** en discusión **2** (*Jur*) en litigio ● *vt*, *vi* discutir, poner en duda

disqualify /dɪsˈkwɑːlɪfaɪ/ *vt* (*pt/pp* **-ied**) descalificar: *~ sb from doing sth* inhabilitar a algn para hacer algo

disregard /ˌdɪsrɪˈɡɑːrd/ *vt* hacer caso omiso de ● *n* ~ (**for/of sth/sb**) indiferencia (hacia algo/algn)

disrepute /ˌdɪsrɪˈpjuːt/ *n* desprestigio **disreputable** /dɪsˈrepjətəbl/ *adj* **1** de mala reputación **2** vergonzoso

disrespect /ˌdɪsrɪˈspekt/ *n* falta de respeto

disrupt /dɪsˈrʌpt/ *vt* interrumpir **disruption** *n* trastorno, molestia(s) **disruptive** *adj* molesto, que causa molestias

dissatisfaction /ˌdɪsˌsætɪsˈfækʃn/ *n* descontento **dissatisfied** /dɪsˈsætɪsfaɪd/ *adj* insatisfecho

dissent /dɪˈsent/ *n* desacuerdo **dissenting** *adj* en desacuerdo, contrario

dissertation /ˌdɪsərˈteɪʃn/ *n* tesis

dissident /ˈdɪsɪdənt/ *adj*, *n* disidente

dissimilar /dɪˈsɪmɪlər/ *adj* distinto

dissociate /dɪˈsoʊʃieɪt/ *vt* **1** ~ **yourself from sth/sb** desligarse de algo/algn **2** disociar

dissolve /dɪˈzɑːlv/ **1** *vt*, *vi* disolver(se) **2** *vi* desvanecerse

dissuade /dɪˈsweɪd/ *vt* disuadir

distance /ˈdɪstəns/ *n* distancia: *from/at a ~* a la distancia ◇ *in the ~* a lo lejos ● *vt* distanciar **distant** *adj* **1** distante **2** lejano

distaste /dɪsˈteɪst/ *n* ~ (**for sth/sb**) aversión (a algo/algn) **distasteful** *adj* desagradable

distill (**distil** *GB*) /dɪsˈtɪl/ *vt* (**-ll-**) destilar **distillery** *n* (*pl* **-ies**) destilería

distinct /dɪsˈtɪŋkt/ *adj* **1** claro **2** distinto: *as ~ from sth* en contraposición a algo **distinction** *n* **1** distinción **2** honor **distinctive** *adj* particular

distinguish /dɪsˈtɪŋɡwɪʃ/ **1** *vt*, *vi* distinguir **2** *vt* ~ **yourself** distinguirse

distort /dɪsˈtɔːrt/ *vt* **1** distorsionar **2** tergiversar **distortion** *n* **1** distorsión **2** tergiversación

distract /dɪsˈtrækt/ *vt* distraer **distracted** *adj* distraído **distraction** *n* distracción: *drive sb to ~* sacar a algn de quicio

distraught /dɪsˈtrɔːt/ *adj* consternado

distress /dɪsˈtres/ *n* **1** angustia **2** dolor **3** peligro **distressed** *adj* afligido **distressing** *adj* angustioso

distribute /dɪsˈtrɪbjuːt/ *vt* repartir, distribuir **distribution** *n* distribución **distributor** *n* distribuidor/a

district /ˈdɪstrɪkt/ *n* **1** distrito, región **2** zona

distrust /dɪsˈtrʌst/ *n* desconfianza ● *vt* desconfiar de **distrustful** *adj* desconfiado

disturb /dɪsˈtɜːrb/ *vt* **1** molestar, interrumpir: *I'm sorry to ~ you.* Siento molestarle. ◇ *Do not ~.* No molestar. **2** perturbar **disturbance** *n* **1** molestia **2** [*sing*] disturbios: *cause a ~* armar un alboroto **disturbed** *adj* trastornado **disturbing** *adj* inquietante

disuse /dɪsˈjuːs/ *n* desuso **disused** /dɪsˈjuːzd/ *adj* abandonado

ditch /dɪtʃ/ *n* zanja ● *vt* (*coloq*) abandonar

dither /ˈdɪðər/ *vi* (*GB, coloq*) vacilar

ditto /ˈdɪtoʊ/ *n* ídem **NOTA** Se refiere al símbolo (") que se usa para evitar las repeticiones en una lista.

dive /daɪv/ *vi* (*pt* **dove** *pp* **dived**, *pt/pp* **dived** *GB*) **1** tirarse de cabeza **2** (*submarino*) sumergirse **3** ~ (**down**) (**for sth**) bucear (en busca de algo) **4** (*avión*) bajar en picada **5** ~ (**into/under sth**) meterse (en/debajo de algo):

~ *for cover* meterse en/debajo de algo para protegerse ∎ salto, clavado **diver** n buzo

diverge /daɪˈvɜːdʒ/ vi 1 divergir 2 (fml) (opiniones) diferir **divergence** n divergencia **divergent** adj divergente

diverse /daɪˈvɜːs/ adj diverso **diversification** n diversificación **diversify** vt, vi (pt/pp -ied) diversificar(se) **diversity** n diversidad

diversion /daɪˈvɜːʒn; -ˈvɜːʃn GB/ n desviación (por obras, etc.)

divert /daɪˈvɜːt/ vt desviar

divide /dɪˈvaɪd/ 1 vt, vi ~ (sth) (up) (into sth) dividir(se) (algo) (en algo) 2 vt ~ sth (out/up) (between/among sb) repartir algo (entre algn) 3 vt separar 4 vt ~ sth by sth (Mat) dividir algo por algo **divided** adj dividido

divided highway n (USA) autopista, carretera de doble pista

dividend /ˈdɪvɪdend/ n dividendo

divine /dɪˈvaɪn/ adj divino

diving /ˈdaɪvɪŋ/ n buceo

diving board n trampolín

division /dɪˈvɪʒn/ n 1 división 2 (Com) sección, departamento **divisional** adj divisionario

divorce /dɪˈvɔːs/ n divorcio ∎ vt divorciarse de: get divorced divorciarse **divorcé** n /dɪˈvɔːˈseɪ/ (USA) divorciado **divorcee** /dɪˌvɔːˈseɪ; -ˈsiː GB/ n divorciado/a **NOTA** Divorcee se usa en Gran Bretaña para hombres y mujeres, y en EE.UU. sólo para mujeres.

divulge /daɪˈvʌldʒ/ vt revelar

DIY /ˌdiː aɪ ˈwaɪ/ n (GB) bricolaje

dizzy /ˈdɪzi/ adj mareado **dizziness** n mareo, vértigo

DJ /ˈdiː dʒeɪ/ n DJ

DNA /ˌdiː en ˈeɪ/ n AND

do¹ /duː/ n [pl **dos/do's** /duːz/]
▶ **do's and don'ts** reglas

do² /duː/ (3ᵃ pers sing pres **does** pt **did** pp **done**)
∎ vt, vi hacer **NOTA** Se usa do al hablar de una actividad sin decir exactamente de qué se trata, como cuando va acompañado de palabras como something, nothing, etc.: Are you doing anything tomorrow? ¿Vas a hacer algo mañana? ◇ I have nothing to do. No tengo nada que hacer. ◇ What can I do for you? ¿En qué puedo servirlo? ◇ Do as you please. Haz lo que quieras.

● **do + the, my, etc. + -ing** vt (obligaciones, hobbies) hacer:

do the ironing/shopping planchar/hacer las compras

● **do + (the, my, etc.) + sustantivo** vt: do your homework hacer las tareas ◇ do business hacer negocios ◇ do your best hacer lo que se pueda ◇ do your duty cumplir con tu deber ◇ do your hair/have your hair done arreglarse el pelo/ir a la peluquería →DEPORTE

● **otros usos** vi 1 ser suficiente, servir: Will ten dollars do? ¿Será suficiente con $10? 2 quedar bien: Will next Monday do? ¿Te queda bien el lunes? 3 ir: How's the business doing? ¿Qué tal va el negocio? ◇ He did badly in the exam. Le fue mal en el examen. ▶ **be/have to do with sth/sb** tener que ver con algo/algn: What does it have to do with you? ¿Y a ti qué te importa! **it/that won't do**: It (simply) won't do. No puede ser. ◇ It would never do to... No estaría bien que... **that does it!** (coloq) ¡se acabó! **that's done it!** (coloq) ¡la regamos! (Mx), ¡la embarramos! (And) **that will do!** ¡ya está bien! **NOTA** Para otras expresiones, ver el sustantivo, adjetivo, etc., p. ej. **do your bit** en BIT. ∎ **do away with sth** abolir algo, deshacerse de algo **do sth up** 1 abrochar(se) algo 2 amarrar(se) algo 3 envolver algo 4 (GB) renovar algo **do with sth**: I could do with a vacation. Me sentaría bien unas vacaciones. **do without (sth/sb)** arreglárselas sin (algo/algn)

∎ v aux **NOTA** No se traduce el auxiliar do. Lleva el tiempo y la persona del verbo principal de la oración.

● **frases interrogativas y negativas**: Do you speak English? ¿Hablas inglés? ◇ She didn't go to Paris. No fue a París.

● **question tags** 1 [oración afirmativa]: do + n't + sujeto (pron pers)?: John lives here, doesn't he? John vive acá, ¿verdad? 2 [oración negativa]: do + sujeto (pron pers)?: You don't know, do you? No lo sabes, ¿verdad? 3 [oración afirmativa]: do + sujeto (pron pers)?: So you told him, did you? O sea que le contaste, ¿no?

● **en afirmativo** (énfasis): He does look tired. De verdad se ve cansado. ◇ Oh, do be quiet! ¡Cállate ya!

● **para evitar repeticiones**: She knows more than he does. Ella sabe más que él. ◇ "Who won?"

"I did." —¿Quién ganó? —Yo. ◇ "He smokes." "So do I." —Él fuma. —Yo también. ◇ **Anna didn't go and neither did I.** Anna no fue y yo tampoco.

docile /'dəsl; 'dəʊsaɪl GB/ *adj* dócil

dock /dɑk/ *n* **1** muelle **2 docks** [*pl*] puerto **3** (*Jur*) banquillo (de los acusados) ● *vt, vi* (*Náut*) (hacer) entrar en dique, atracar (en un muelle) **2** *vi* llegar en barco **3** *vt* reducir (*sueldo*)

doctor /'dɑktər/ *n* **1** médico/a (*abrev* Dr.) **2** doctor/a (en algo) ● *vt* **1** amañar **2** (*comestibles*) adulterar

doctorate /'dɑktərət/ *n* doctorado

doctrine /'dɑktrɪn/ *n* doctrina

document /'dɑkjumənt/ *n* documento ● *vt* documentar

documentary /,dɑkju'mentri/ *adj, n* (*pl* **-ies**) documental

dodge /dɑdʒ/ **1** *vi* hacerse a un lado: ~ *around the corner* esconderse a la vuelta de la esquina **2** *vt* eludir **3** *vt* (*golpe*) esquivar

dodgy /'dɑdʒi/ *adj* (GB, *coloq*) problemático: *Sounds a bit* ~ *to me.* Me suena un poco sospechoso. ◇ *a* ~ *wheel* una rueda defectuosa

doe /doʊ/ *n* cierva, coneja, liebre hembra →CIERVO, CONEJO

does /dʌz/ Ver DO²

doesn't /'dʌznt/ = DOES NOT

dog /dɔːɡ; dɑɡ GB/ *n* perro ● *vt* (**-gg-**) perseguir

dogged /'dɔːɡɪd; 'dɑɡɪd GB/ *adj* tenaz

doggy (*tb* **doggie**) /'dɔːɡi; 'dɑɡi GB/ *n* (*coloq*) perrito

dogsbody /'dɔːɡzbɑdi; 'dɑɡ-GB/ *n* (*pl* **-ies**) (GB) chico/a para todo

do it yourself *n* bricolaje

the dole /doʊl/ *n* (GB, *coloq*) subsidio de desempleo: *on the* ~ desempleado

doll /dɑl/ *n* muñeca

dollar /'dɑlər/ *n* dólar →Ver pág. 224

dolly /'dɑli/ *n* (*pl* **-ies**) muñequita

dolphin /'dɑlfɪn/ *n* delfín

domain /doʊ'meɪn; də'm-GB/ *n* **1** campo: *outside my* ~ fuera de mi competencia **2** propiedad

dome /doʊm/ *n* cúpula **domed** *adj* abovedado

domestic /də'mestɪk/ *adj* **1** doméstico **2** nacional **domesticated** *adj* **1** doméstico **2** casero

dominant /'dɑmɪnənt/ *adj* dominante **dominance** *n* dominación

dominate /'dɑmɪneɪt/ *vt, vi* dominar **domination** *n* dominio

domineering /,dɑmɪ'nɪərɪŋ/ *adj* (*pey*) dominante

dominion /də'mɪniən/ *n* dominio

domino /'dɑmɪnoʊ/ *n* (*pl* **-es**) ficha de dominó: *play* ~s jugar dominó

donate /'doʊneɪt; doʊ'neɪt GB/ *vt* donar **donation** *n* **1** donativo **2** donación

done /dʌn/ *pp* de DO² ● *adj* hecho, terminado

donkey /'dɑŋki/ *n* burro

donor /'doʊnər/ *n* donante

don't /doʊnt/ = DO NOT

donut /'doʊnʌt/ *n* dona

doom /duːm/ *n* **1** perdición: *send sb to his* ~ mandar a algn a la muerte **2** pesimismo **doomed** *adj* condenado: ~ *to failure* destinado al fracaso

door /dɔːr/ *n* **1** puerta **2** entrada ▶ **(from) door to door** de puerta en puerta: *a door-to-door sales-man* un vendedor ambulante **out of doors** al aire libre

doorbell /'dɔːrbel/ *n* timbre

doormat /'dɔːrmæt/ *n* tapete (en la entrada)

doorstep /'dɔːrstep/ *n* peldaño (de la puerta) ▶ **on your doorstep** a un paso

doorway /'dɔːrweɪ/ *n* entrada

dope /doʊp/ *n* (*coloq*) **1** [*U*] droga (*esp* marihuana) **2** imbécil ● *vt* dopar

dope test *n* prueba antidoping

dormant /'dɔːrmənt/ *adj* inactivo

dormitory /'dɔːrmətɔːri; -tri GB/ *n* (*pl* **-ies**) **1** dormitorio **2** (USA) residencia universitaria

dosage /'doʊsɪdʒ/ *n* dosificación

dose /doʊs/ *n* dosis

dot /dɑt/ *n* punto ▶ **on the dot** (*coloq*) a la hora en punto ● *vt* (**-tt-**) poner un punto sobre ▶ **dot your i's and cross your t's** dar los últimos retoques

dote /doʊt/ *vi* ~ **on sth/sb** adorar algo/a algn **doting** *adj* devoto

double /'dʌbl/ *adj* doble: ~ *figures* número de dos cifras ● *adv*: *see* ~ ver doble ◇ *encima* ◇ ~ *fold sth* ~ doblar algo en dos ● *n* **1** doble: *She earns* ~ *what he does.* Gana el doble que él. **2 doubles** (*Dep*) dobles ● **1** *vt, vi* duplicar(se) **2** *vt* ~ **sth (up/over/across/back)** doblar algo (en dos) **3** *vi* ~ **on sth** hacer de algo ■ **double back** volver sobre sus pasos **double (sb) up:** *be doubled up with laughter/pain* doblarse de risa/de dolor

double-barreled (**-ll-** *GB*) *adj* **1** (*arma*) de dos cañones **2** (*GB*, *apellido*) compuesto

double bass *n* contrabajo

double bed *n* cama matrimonial

double-breasted *adj* cruzado

double-check *vt* volver a comprobar

double-click *vi* (*Comp*) hacer doble clic

double-cross *vt* engañar

double-decker *n* (*GB*) autobús de dos pisos

double-edged *adj* de doble filo

double glazing *n* doble vidrio **double-glazed** *adj* con cristal/vidrio doble

doubly /'dʌbli/ *adv* doblemente: *make ~ sure of sth* asegurarse bien de algo

doubt /daʊt/ *n* duda: *beyond ~* fuera de toda duda ▸ *in doubt* dudoso **no doubt** sin duda ● *vt*, *vi* dudar (de) **doubter** *n* escéptico/a **doubtless** *adv* sin duda

doubtful /'daʊtfl/ *adj* dudoso: *be ~ about sth* tener dudas sobre algo **doubtfully** *adv* sin convicción

dough /doʊ/ *n* masa

doughnut (*GB*) = DONUT®

dour /dʊər/ *adj* austero

douse /daʊs/ *vt* empapar

dove¹ /dʌv/ *n* paloma

dove² /doʊv/ (*USA*) *pt* de DIVE

dowdy /'daʊdi/ *adj* sin gracia

down /daʊn/ *n* **1** [*U*] plumones **2** **pelusa** ● *adj* **1** (*coloq*) (*persona*) deprimido **2** (*Comp*): *The server's ~*. El servidor no funciona. ● *prep* abajo: *~ the hill* colina abajo ◇ *~ the corridor on the right* por el pasillo a la derecha ◇ *He ran his eyes ~ the list*. Recorrió la lista de arriba abajo. ● *adv* **1** abajo: *face ~* boca abajo **2** bajo: *Inflation is ~ this month.* La inflación bajó este mes. ◇ *be 50 dollars ~* faltarle a algn \$50 **3** *Ten ~, five to go.* Van diez, quedan cinco. ▸ **Down with sth/sb!** ¡abajo algo/algn! **NOTA** Para el uso de **down** en PHRASAL VERBS ver el verbo, p.ej. **go down** en GO¹.

down and out *n* vagabundo/a

downcast /'daʊnkæst; -kɑːst *GB*/ *adj* abatido

downfall /'daʊnfɔːl/ *n* [*sing*] ruina

downgrade /daʊn'greɪd/ *vt* bajar de categoría

downhearted /,daʊn'hɑːrtɪd/ *adj* desanimado

downhill /,daʊn'hɪl/ *adv*, *adj* cuesta abajo ▸ **be downhill (from**

here/there) ser fácil (a partir de ahora/entonces) **go downhill** ir cuesta abajo

download /,daʊn'loʊd/ *vt* (*Comp*) bajar

downmarket /,daʊn'mɑːrkɪt/ *adj* de/para la gran masa, vulgar

downpour /'daʊnpɔːr/ *n* aguacero

downright /'daʊnraɪt/ *adj* total ● *adv* completamente

downside /'daʊnsaɪd/ *n* inconveniente

Down's syndrome *n* síndrome de Down

downstairs /,daʊn'steərz/ *adv* (en el piso de abajo): *fall ~* caerse escaleras abajo ● *adj* en el/del piso de abajo ● *n* [*sing*] planta baja, piso de abajo

downstream /,daʊn'striːm/ *adv* río abajo

down-to-earth *adj* práctico, con los pies en la tierra

downtown /,daʊn'taʊn/ *adv* (*USA*) a/en el centro (*de la ciudad*)

downtrodden /'daʊntrɒdn/ *adj* oprimido

downturn /'daʊntɜːrn/ *n* **1** bajada **2** (*ventas, etc.*) descenso

down under *adv* (*coloq*) a/en Australia/Nueva Zelanda

downward /'daʊnwərd/ *adj* hacia abajo: *a ~ trend* una tendencia a la baja ● *adv* (*tb* **downwards**) hacia abajo

downy /'daʊni/ *adj* con pelusa

dowry /'daʊri/ *n* (*pl* **-ies**) dote

dowse /daʊz/ = DOUSE

doze /doʊz/ *vi* dormitar ■ **doze off** quedarse dormido ● *n* cabezada, pestañ(ead)a **dozy** *adj* amodorrado

dozen /'dʌzn/ *n* (*abrev* **doz.**) docena

drab /dræb/ *adj* monótono, gris

draft /dræft; drɑːft *GB*/ *vt* **1** hacer un borrador de **2** (*USA, Mil*) reclutar **3** *~ sth/sb* (*in*) destacar algo/a algn ▸ **on draft** de barril ● *n* **1** corriente (*de aire*) **2** borrador: *a ~ bill* un anteproyecto de ley **3** (*Fin*) orden de pago **4** (*USA*) **the draft** la llamada al servicio militar **drafty** *adj* (**-ier/-iest**) con muchas corrientes (*de aire*)

draftsman, **draftswoman** /'dræftsmən-wʊmən; 'drɑːfts- *GB*/ *n* (*pl* **-men/-women**) delineante, proyectista →CHAIRMAN

drag /dræg/ (**-gg-**) **1** *vt, vi* arrastrar(se) **2** *vi* (*tiempo*) pasar lentamente, hacerse eterno **3** *vt* (*Náut*) rastrear ● *n* (*coloq*) **1**

a drag un rollo **2** *a man in* ~ un hombre vestido de mujer

dragon /ˈdrægən/ *n* dragón

dragonfly /ˈdrægənflaɪ/ *n* (*pl* -ies) libélula

drain /dreɪn/ *n* **1** desagüe **2** alcantarilla **3** ~ *on sth* un continuo desangramiento de algo ● *vt* **1** (*platos, etc.*) escurrir **2** drenar ■ **drain away** irse (*por un desagüe*) **2** consumirse **drainage** *n* drenaje **drained** *adj* agotado

draining board *n* (*GB*) escurridero

drainpipe /ˈdreɪnpaɪp/ *n* tubería de desagüe

drama /ˈdrɑːmə/ *n* **1** obra de teatro **2** drama: ~ *student* estudiante de arte dramático **dramatic** /drəˈmætɪk/ *adj* dramático

dramatist /ˈdræmətɪst/ *n* dramaturgo **dramatization** *n* dramatización **dramatize** *vt*, *vi* dramatizar

drank /dræŋk/ *pt de* DRINK

drape /dreɪp/ *vt* **1** ~ *sth across/around/over sth* (*tejido*) colgar algo sobre algo **2** ~ *sth/sb* (*in/with sth*) cubrir, envolver algo/a algn (*en/con algo*) **drapes** (*tb* **draperies**) *n* (*USA*) cortinas (*gruesas*)

drastic /ˈdræstɪk/ *adj* **1** drástico **2** grave

draught (*GB*) = DRAFT

draughts /drɑːfts; ˈdrɑːfts *GB*/ *n* (*GB*) damas (*juego*)

draughtsman, **draughtswoman** (*GB*) = DRAFTSMAN, DRAFTSWOMAN

draw /drɔː/ *n* **1** sorteo **2** empate ● (*pt* **drew** *pp* **drawn**) **1** *vt*, *vi* dibujar, trazar **2** *vi*: ~ *level with sb* alcanzar a algn ◇ ~ *near* acercarse **3** *vt* (*cortinas*) correr, descorrer **4** *vt*: ~ *a conclusion* sacar una conclusión ◇ ~ *comfort from sth/sb* hallar consuelo en algo/algn ◇ ~ *inspiration from sth* inspirarse en algo ◇ ~ *a distinction/an analogy* hacer una distinción/establecer una analogía **5** *vt* (*sueldo*) cobrar **6** *vt* provocar, causar **7** *vt* ~ *sb to sth/sb* atraer a algn (*hacia algo/algn*) **8** *vt* (*Dep*) empatar ■ **draw back** retroceder, retirarse **draw sth back** retirar, descorrer algo **draw in** (*día*) acortarse **draw on/upon sth** hacer uso de algo **draw out** (*día*) alargarse **draw up** pararse **draw sth up 1** redactar algo **2** (*silla*) acercar algo

drawback /ˈdrɔːbæk/ *n* inconveniente, desventaja

drawer /drɔːr/ *n* cajón

drawing /ˈdrɔːɪŋ/ *n* dibujo

drawing pin *n* (*GB*) chinche

drawing room *n* (*fml*) salón

drawl /drɔːl/ *n* voz lenta y pesada

drawn /drɔːn/ *pp de* DRAW ● *adj* demacrado

dread /dred/ *n* terror ● *vt* tener terror a: *I* ~ *to think what will happen.* Sólo pensar qué pasará me horroriza. **dreadful** *adj* **1** terrible **2** horrible, pésimo: *I feel* ~. Me siento fatal. ◇ *I feel* ~ *about what happened.* Me siento muy mal por lo que pasó. ◇ *How* ~! ¡Qué horror! **dreadfully** *adv* **1** terriblemente **2** muy mal **3** muy: *I'm* ~ *sorry.* Lo siento muchísimo.

dreadlocks /ˈdredlɒks/ (*coloq* **dreads**) *n* [*pl*] rizos al estilo de los rastafaris

dream /driːm/ *n* sueño: *have a* ~ *about sth* soñar con algo ◇ *live in a* ~ *world* vivir de ensueños ● (*pt/pp* **dreamed/dreamt** /dremt/) **1** *vt*, *vi* ~ (*of/about sth/sb*) soñar (*con algo/algn*) **2** *vt* imaginar **NOTA** Algunos verbos tienen formas regulares e irregulares para el *past simple* y el *past participle*: **dream: dreamed/dreamt**, **spoil: spoiled/spoilt**, etc. En inglés británico se prefieren las formas irregulares, y en inglés americano las regulares. Cuando el *participle* funciona como adjetivo siempre se usa la forma irregular: *a spoilt child.* **dreamer** *n* soñador/a **dreamy** *adj* (-ier/-iest) soñador, distraído

dreary /ˈdrɪəri/ *adj* (-ier/-iest) **1** deprimente **2** aburrido

dredge /dredʒ/ *vt*, *vi* dragar **dredger** *n* draga

drench /drentʃ/ *vt* empapar

dress /dres/ *n* **1** vestido **2** [*U*] ropa: *have no* ~ *sense* no saber vestirse ● **1** *vt*, *vi* vestir(se): *dressed in/as sth* vestido de algo **NOTA** Para la acción de vestirse se dice **get dressed**. **2** *vt* (*herida*) curar **3** *vt* (*ensalada*) aliñar ■ **dress up (as sth/sb)/(in sth)** disfrazarse (*de algo/algn*)/(*con algo*) **dress sb up (as sth/sb)/(in sth)** disfrazar(se) (*a algn* (*de algo/algn*)/(*con algo*)) **dress sth up** disfrazar algo **dress up** engalanarse

dress circle *n* (*GB, Teat*) principal, platea alta

dresser /ˈdresər/ *n* **1** (*USA*) cómoda **2** (*GB*) aparador

dressing /ˈdresɪŋ/ *n* **1** vendaje **2** aliño

dressing gown n (GB) bata

dressing room n vestidor, camerino

dressing table n tocador

dressmaker /'dresmeɪkər/ n modista **dressmaking** n corte y confección

drew /dru:/ pt de DRAW

dribble /'drɪbl/ 1 vi babear 2 vt, vi (Dep) driblar

dried /draɪd/ pt, pp de DRY ● adj seco

drier = DRYER

drift /drɪft/ vi 1 flotar 2 (arena, nieve) amontonarse 3 ir a la deriva ~ into sth hacer algo a la deriva ▶ n [sing] idea general **drifter** n vagabundo/a

drill /drɪl/ n 1 taladro 2 (dentista) torno, fresa 3 instrucción 4 ejercicio ● vt 1 taladrar, perforar 2 instruir

drily /'draɪli/ en tono seco

drink /drɪŋk/ n bebida: a ~ of water un trago de agua ◇ go for a ~ ir a tomar algo ◇ a soft ~ un refresco ● vt, vi (pt **drank** pp **drunk**) beber: ~ sth down/up tomarse algo de un trago ▶ drink sb's health (GB) tomar a la salud de algn ■ drink sth in embeberse en algo drink (a toast) to sth/sb brindar por algo/algn **drinker** n bebedor/a **drinking** n el tomar

drinking water n agua potable

drip /drɪp/ vi (-pp-) gotear ▶ dripping with sth: dripping with sweat/jewels empapado en sudor/cargado de joyas ● n 1 gota 2 (Med) gotero: be on a ~ estar con suero

drive /draɪv/ (pt **drove** pp **driven** /'drɪvn/) 1 vt, vi manejar 2 vi viajar en carro 3 vt llevar (en carro) 4 vt (ganado) arrear 5 vt impulsar: ~ sb to drink llevar a algn a la bebida ▶ be driving at sth: What are you driving at? ¿Qué insinúas? drive a hard bargain ser un negociador duro ■ drive away/off alejarse en carro drive sth/sb back/off ahuyentar algo/a algn drive sb on empujar a algn ● n 1 vuelta, viaje: go for a ~ dar una vuelta en carro 2 (tb **driveway** /'draɪvweɪ/) camino de entrada (en una casa) 3 (Dep) golpe directo, drive 4 empuje 5 campaña 6 (Mec) mecanismo de transmisión: four-wheel ~ tracción en las cuatro llantas 7 (Comp) unidad: disk ~ unidad de disco

drive-in n (pl -ins) (USA) cine o restaurante donde se sirve a los clientes en sus vehículos

driver /'draɪvər/ n conductor/a, chófer: train ~ maquinista ▶ be in the driver's seat tener la sartén por el mango

driver's license (**driving licence** GB) n licencia de manejo, pase

driving school n escuela de manejo/conducción

driving test n examen de manejo/conducción

drizzle /'drɪzl/ n llovizna ● vi lloviznar

drone /droʊn/ n zumbido ● vi zumbar ■ drone on (about sth) hablar (largo) sobre algo) en tono monótono

drool /dru:l/ vi babear: ~ over sb caérsele la baba a uno por algn

droop /dru:p/ vi 1 caer 2 (flor) marchitarse 2 (ánimo) decaer

drop /drɒp/ n 1 gota: Would you like a ~ of wine? ¿Te gustaría un vinito? 2 caída: a ~ in prices/temperature una caída de los precios/un descenso de la temperatura ◇ a sheer ~ un precipicio ▶ a drop in the bucket/ocean (GB) un grano de arena en la desierto at the drop of a hat sin pensarlo dos veces ■ (-pp-) 1 vi caer: ~ to your knees caer de rodillas 2 vt (sin querer): She dropped her book. Se le cayó el libro. NOTA Si se trata de un objeto, se usa drop: Be careful you don't ~ that plate! y para un líquido, spill: She spilt coffee on her skirt. 3 vt (a propósito) dejar caer: ~ a bomb lanzar una bomba ◇ ~ anchor echar el ancla 4 vi desplomarse: I'm ready to ~. Estoy que me caigo. ◇ work till you ~ matarse trabajando 5 vt, vi disminuir, reducir(se) 6 vt ~ sth/sb (off) dejar algo/a algn 7 vt omitir 8 vt ~ sb romper con algn 9 vt (hábito, etc.) dejar: Can we ~ the subject? ¿Podemos olvidar el tema? ▶ drop a brick (GB, coloq) meter la pata drop dead (coloq) quedarse en el sitio: Drop dead! ¡Vete al carajo! drop (sb) a hint soltar una indirecta (a algn) drop sb a line (coloq) mandarle unas líneas a algn ■ drop back/behind quedarse atrás drop by/in/over/round: Why don't you ~ by? ¿Por qué no pasas por la casa? ◇ Drop round/over. Ven a vernos. drop in on sb hacer una visita informal a algn drop off (GB, coloq) quedarse dormido drop out (of sth) retirarse (de algo): ~ out (of university/society) dejar los estudios/automarginarse

drop-dead adv (coloq) (persona): He's ~ gorgeous! ¡Está buenísimo!

dropout /'drɒpaʊt/ n marginado/a

droppings /'drɒpɪŋz/ n [pl] excrementos (animales o pájaros)

drought /draʊt/ n sequía

drove /droʊv/ pt de DRIVE

drown /draʊn/ vt, vi ahogar(se) ∎ **drown sth/sb out** (ruido, etc.) ahogar algo/a algn

drowsy /'draʊzi/ adj (-ier/-iest) adormilado: This drug can make you ~. Este medicamento puede producir somnolencia.

drudgery /'drʌdʒəri/ n trabajo pesado

drug /drʌɡ/ n 1 (Med) medicamento: ~ company empresa farmacéutica ◊ 2 droga: be on ~s consumir drogas habitualmente ◇ ~ abuse abuso de drogas ● vt (-gg-) drogar

drug addict n drogadicto/a

druggist /'drʌɡɪst/ n (USA) farmacéutico/a

drugstore /'drʌɡstɔːr/ n (USA) farmacia (que también vende comestibles, periódicos, etc.)

drum /drʌm/ n 1 (Mús) tambor, batería 2 bidón ● (-mm-) 1 vi tocar al tambor 2 vi, vt ~ (sth) on sth tamborilear (con algo) en algo ∎ **drum sth into sb('s head)** machacarle algo a algn **drum sb out (of sth)** echar a algn de algún sitio **drum sth up** esforzarse por conseguir algo (apoyo, clientes, etc.): ~ up interest in sth fomentar el interés en algo **drummer** n batería

drumstick /'drʌmstɪk/ n 1 (Mús) baqueta 2 (Cocina) pata (de pollo, etc.)

drunk /drʌŋk/ pp de DRINK ● adj borracho: get ~ emborracharse ◇ ~ with joy ebrio de alegría

drunkard /'drʌŋkərd/ n borracho/a

drunken /'drʌŋkən/ adj borracho: be charged with ~ driving ser acusado de manejar en estado de embriaguez **drunkenness** n embriaguez

dry /draɪ/ adj (drier, driest) 1 seco: Today will be ~. Hoy no va a llover. 2 árido 3 (humor) irónico ▶ **run dry** secarse ● vt, vi (pt/pp dried) ~ (sth) (up/out) secar(se) (algo) ● n ▶ **in the dry** a cubierto **dryness** n 1 sequedad 2 aridez 3 (humor) ironía

dry-clean vt limpiar en seco **dry-cleaner's** n tintorería **dry-cleaning** n lavado en seco

dryer /'draɪər/ n secador(a)

dry land n tierra firme

dryly = DRILY

dual /'duːəl; 'djuːəl GB/ adj doble

dual carriageway n (GB) autopista, carretera de doble pista

dub /dʌb/ vt (-bb-) doblar **dubbing** n doblaje

dubious /'duːbiəs; 'djuː- GB/ adj 1 be ~ about sth tener dudas acerca de algo 2 (conducta) sospechoso 3 (honor) discutible

duchess /'dʌtʃəs/ n duquesa

duck /dʌk/ n pato/a →PATO ● 1 vi agachar la cabeza: ~ behind a rock esconderse detrás de una roca 2 vt (responsabilidad) eludir 3 vt, vi ~ (out of) sth sacarle el cuerpo a algo

duct /dʌkt/ n conducto

dud /dʌd/ adj 1 defectuoso 2 inútil 3 (cheque) sin fondos ● n (coloq): This battery is a ~. Esta pila no es defectuosa.

due /duː; djuː GB/ adj 1 the money ~ to him el dinero que se le debe ◇ Our thanks are ~ to... Quedamos agradecidos a... ◇ The payment is ~ on the sixth. El pago vence el seis. 2 The train is ~ (in) at five. El tren debe llegar a las cinco. ◇ She's ~ back on Thursday. Vuelve el jueves. 3 ~ (for) sth: I'm ~ (for) a rest. Me merezco un descanso. 4 debido: It's ~ to her efforts. Se lo debemos al esfuerzo de ella. ▶ **in due course** a su debido tiempo ◆ **dues** n [pl] cuota ▶ **give sb their due** para ser justo ● adv: ~ south directamente al sur

duel /'duːəl; 'djuːəl GB/ n duelo

duet /du'et; dju'et GB/ n dúo (pieza musical)

duffel coat /'dʌfl kout/ n abrigo tres cuartos (con capucha)

dug /dʌɡ/ pt, pp de DIG

duke /duːk; djuːk GB/ n duque

dull /dʌl/ adj (-er/-est) 1 (tiempo) gris 2 (color) apagado 3 (superficie) deslustrado 4 (luz) sombrío: a ~ glow un brillo pálido 5 (dolor, ruido) sordo 6 aburrido, soso 7 sin filo **dully** adv con desgano

duly /'duːli; 'djuːli GB/ adv 1 debidamente 2 a su debido tiempo

dumb /dʌm/ adj (-er/-est) 1 mudo: deaf and ~ sordomudo 2 (coloq) tonto **dumbly** adv sin hablar

dumbfounded /dʌm'faʊndɪd/ (tb **dumbstruck** /'dʌmstrʌk/) adj mudo de asombro

dummy /'dʌmi/ n (pl -ies) 1 maniquí, muñeco 2 imitación 3 (GB) chupón, chupo 4 (USA, coloq) imbécil ● adj falso, de mentiras: ~ run (GB) ensayo

dump /dʌmp/ 1 vt, vi verter, tirar: dumping ground basurero/tiradero 2 vt (coloq) abandonar 3 vt deshacerse de ● n 1 vertedero 2 (Mil) depósito 3 (coloq) antro

dumpling /'dʌmplɪŋ/ n bola de masa que se come en los guisos

dumps /dʌmps/ n [pl] ▸ (down) in the dumps (coloq) deprimido

Dumpster® /'dʌmpstər/ n (USA) contenedor (para escombros)

dune /duːn; djuːn GB/ n duna

dung /dʌŋ/ n boñiga(s)

dungarees /ˌdʌŋɡə'riːz/ n (GB) [pl] pantalones de peto, overol

dungeon /'dʌndʒən/ n mazmorra

duo /'duːoʊ; 'djuːəʊ GB/ n (pl -s) dúo (personas)

dupe /duːp; djuːp GB/ vt engañar

duplicate /'duːplɪkeɪt; 'djuː- GB/ vt duplicar ● /'duːplɪkət; 'djuː- GB/ adj, n duplicado: a ~ (letter) letter) una copia

durable /'dʊərəbl; 'djʊə- GB/ adj duradero ● **(consumer) durables** n electrodomésticos **durability** /ˌdʊərə'bɪləti; ˌdjʊə- GB/ n durabilidad

duration /du'reɪʃn; dju- GB/ n duración ▸ for the duration (coloq) durante el tiempo que dure

duress /du'res; dju- GB/ n ▸ under duress bajo coacción

during /'dʊərɪŋ; 'djʊər- GB/ prep durante →DURANTE

dusk /dʌsk/ n atardecer

dusky /'dʌski/ adj moreno

dust /dʌst/ n polvo: gold ~ oro en polvo ● vt, vi limpiar el polvo ■ **dust sth/sb down/off** quitarle el polvo a algo/algn **dust sth with sth** espolvorear algo de algo

dustbin /'dʌstbɪn/ n (GB) bote (Mx), caneca (And) (de basura)

duster /'dʌstər/ n trapo (del polvo): feather ~ plumero

dustman /'dʌstmən/ n (pl -men) (GB) basurero

dustpan /'dʌstpæn/ n recogedor

dusty /'dʌsti/ adj (-ier/-iest) polvoriento

Dutch /dʌtʃ/ adj ▸ **Dutch courage** (GB, coloq) valor infundido por el alcohol **go Dutch (with sb)** pagar cada uno su parte

duty /'duːti; 'djuːti GB/ n (pl -ies) 1 deber, obligación: do your ~ cumplir uno con su deber 2 función: ~ officer oficial de guardia

3 ~ **(on sth)** aranceles (sobre algo) ▸ **be on/off duty** estar/no estar de servicio **dutiful** /'duːtɪfl; 'djuː- GB/ adj (fml) obediente, concienzudo

duty-free adj libre de impuestos

duvet /'duːveɪ/ n (GB) edredón (cobija)

DVD /ˌdiː viː 'diː/ n DVD

dwarf /dwɔːrf/ n (pl -s o dwarves /dwɔːrvz/) enano/a ● vt empequeñecer

dwell /dwel/ vi (pt/pp dwelled/dwelt) (fml) morar ■ **dwell on/upon sth** 1 insistir en algo 2 dejarse obsesionar por algo **dwelling** n (fml) vivienda

dwindle /'dwɪndl/ vi disminuir, reducirse

dye /daɪ/ vt, vi (3ª pers sing pres **dyes** pt/pp **dyed** pt pres **dyeing**) teñir(se) ● n tintura (pelo, ropa, etc.)

dying /'daɪŋ/ Ver DIE ● adj 1 (persona) moribundo, agonizante 2 (palabras, etc.) último: a ~ breed una raza en vías de extinción

dyke /daɪk/ n 1 dique 2 (pey) lesbiana

dynamics /daɪ'næmɪks/ n [pl] dinámica

dynamism /'daɪnəmɪzəm/ n dinamismo **dynamic** /daɪ'næmɪk/ adj dinámico

dynamite /'daɪnəmaɪt/ n dinamita ● vt dinamitar

dynamo /'daɪnəmoʊ/ n (pl -s) dínamo, dinamo

dynasty /'daɪnəsti; 'dɪ- GB/ n (pl -ies) dinastía

dysentery /'dɪsənteri; -tri GB/ n disentería

dyslexia /dɪs'leksiə/ n dislexia **dyslexic** adj, n disléxico/a

dystrophy /'dɪstrəfi/ n distrofia

E e

E, e /iː/ n (pl **E's**, **e's**) 1 E, e 2 (Mús) mi

each /iːtʃ/ adj cada **NOTA** Each se suele traducir por "cada (uno)" y **every** por "todo(s)", excepto cuando se expresa la repetición de algo en intervalos fijos de tiempo: The Olympics are held every four years. →EVERY ● adv, pron cada uno: We have two ~. Tenemos dos cada uno. ◇ ~ for himself cada cual por su cuenta

each other *pron* el uno al otro (*mutuamente*)

eager /'iːɡər/ *adj* ~ (**for sth/to do sth**) ávido (de algo), ansioso (por hacer algo) **eagerly** *adv* con impaciencia/ilusión **eagerness** *n* ansia

eagle /'iːɡl/ *n* águila

ear /ɪər/ *n* 1 oreja → MY 2 oído: *have an ~ for sth* tener buen oído para algo 3 (*trigo, etc.*) espiga ► **be all ears** (*coloq*) ser todo oídos **up to your ears in sth** hasta el cuello de algo

earache /'ɪəreɪk/ *n* dolor de oídos

eardrum /'ɪərdrʌm/ *n* tímpano

earl /ɜːrl/ *n* conde

early /'ɜːrli/ (**-ier/-iest**) *adj* 1 temprano: *at an ~ age* a una edad temprana 2 (*muerte*) prematuro 3 (*jubilación*) anticipado 4 primero: *my earliest memories* mis primeros recuerdos ● *adv* 1 temprano: *as ~ as 1988* ya en 1988 2 con anticipación 3 prematuramente 4 a principios de: ~ *last year* a principios del año pasado ► **at the earliest** lo más pronto **early bird** madrugador **early on** al poco tiempo de empezar: *earlier on* anteriormente **it's early days (yet)** (*GB*) es demasiado pronto **the early hours** la madrugada

earmark /'ɪərmɑːrk/ *vt* destinar

earn /ɜːrn/ *vt* 1 (*dinero*) ganar: ~ *a living* ganarse la vida 2 merecer(se)

earnest /'ɜːrnɪst/ *adj* 1 serio 2 (*deseo, etc.*) ferviente ► **in earnest** 1 de veras 2 en serio: *in deadly ~* con la mayor seriedad **earnestly** *adv* con seriedad **earnestness** *n* fervor

earnings /'ɜːrnɪŋz/ *n* [*pl*] ingresos

earphones /'ɪərfoʊnz/ *n* [*pl*] audífonos

earring /'ɪərɪŋ/ *n* pendiente, arete

earshot /'ɪərʃɑːt/ *n* ► **out of/within earshot** fuera del/al alcance del oído

earth /ɜːrθ/ *n* 1 (*tb* **the Earth**) la Tierra 2 (*Geol, Elec*) tierra ► **charge/cost/pay the earth** (*GB, coloq*) cobrar/costar/pagar un dineral **come back/down to earth** (**with a bang/bump**) (*coloq*) bajar de las nubes **how, what, etc. on earth** (*coloq*) ¿cómo, qué, etc. demonios? ● *vt* (*GB, Elec*) conectar a tierra

earthenware /'ɜːrθənweər/ *n* barro (*cocido*)

earthly /'ɜːrθli/ *adj* 1 terrenal 2 (*coloq*) concebible: *You haven't*

an ~ chance of winning. No tienes la más remota posibilidad de ganar.

earthquake /'ɜːrθkweɪk/ *n* terremoto

earthworm /'ɜːrθwɜːrm/ *n* lombriz

ease /iːz/ *n* 1 facilidad 2 desahogo 3 alivio ► **at (your) ease** a gusto ● *vt* 1 (*dolor, etc.*) aliviar: ~ *sb's mind/conscience* tranquilizar a algn 2 (*tensión, tráfico*) reducir 3 (*situación*) suavizar 4 (*restricción*) aflojar ■ **ease (sth/sb) across, along, etc. sth** mover (algo/a algn) cuidadosamente a través de, a lo largo de, etc. algo **ease off/up** aligerarse **ease up on sth/sb** moderarse con algo/algn

easel /'iːzl/ *n* (*Arte*) caballete

easily /'iːzəli/ *adv* 1 fácilmente 2 seguramente 3 muy probablemente

east /iːst/ *n* 1 (*abrev* **E.**) este 2 **the East** (el) Oriente ● *adj* (del) este, oriental ● *adv* al este

eastbound *adj* en/con dirección este

Easter /'iːstər/ *n* Pascua

eastern /'iːstərn/ *adj* (del) este, oriental

eastwards /'iːstwərdz/ (*tb* **eastward**) *adv* hacia el este

easy /'iːzi/ (**-ier/-iest**) *adj* 1 fácil 2 tranquilo ► **I'm easy** (*GB, coloq*) me da igual ● *adv* 1 **easier said than done** más fácil decirlo que hacerlo **go easy on/with sth/sb** (*coloq*) tomárselo con tranquilidad con algo/algn **take it easy** tomarse las cosas con calma: *Take it ~!* ¡Cálmate!

easy-going *adj* tolerante: *She's very ~.* Es de trato muy fácil.

eat /iːt/ *vt, vi* (*pt* **ate** *pp* **eaten** /'iːtn/) comer: ~ *out* comer fuera ► **be eaten up with sth** estar consumido por algo **be eating sb** (*coloq*) estar inquietando a algn **eat out of sb's hand** estar sometido a algn **eat your words** tragarse las palabras ■ **eat away at sth/eat sth away** 1 roer/corroer algo 2 consumir algo **eat into sth** 1 corroer, desgastar algo 2 mermar algo (*reservas*) **eat sth up** 1 comérselo todo 2 devorar algo: *The van ~s up gas!* La camioneta traga un montón de gasolina. **eater** *n*: *a big ~* un comelón

eavesdrop /'iːvzdrɑːp/ *vi* (**-pp-**) ~ (**on sth/sb**) escuchar (algo/a algn) a escondidas

ebb /eb/ *vi* 1 (*marea*) bajar 2 ~ (**away**) disminuir ● **the ebb** *n* el reflujo ► **on the ebb** en decadencia **the ebb and flow** los altibajos

ebony /'ebəni/ n ébano

eccentric /ɪk'sentrɪk/ adj, n excéntrico/a **eccentricity** /ˌeksen'trɪsəti/ n (pl -ies) excentricidad

echo /'ekoʊ/ n (pl -es) 1 eco, resonancia 2 imitación ● 1 vt ~ **sth (back)** repetir, reflejar algo 2 vi resonar

eclipse /ɪ'klɪps/ n eclipse ● vt eclipsar

ecology /i:'kɒlədʒi/ n ecología **ecologist** n ecologista **ecological** /ˌi:kə'lɒdʒɪkl/ adj ecológico

e-commerce /'i: kɒmɜːrs/ n comercio electrónico

economic /ˌi:kə'nɒmɪk, ˌekə-/ adj 1 (Pol, etc.) económico 2 rentable

economical /ˌi:kə'nɒmɪkl, ˌekə-/ adj (combustible, aparato, estilo) económico **NOTA** A diferencia de **economic**, **economical** puede ser calificado por palabras como **more**, **very**, etc.: *a more ~ car.* ▸ **be economical with the truth** decir las verdades a medias

economics /ˌi:kə'nɒmɪks, ˌekə-/ n [sing] economía **economist** n economista

economize /ɪ'kɒnəmaɪz/ vi ~ **(on sth)** economizar algo

economy /ɪ'kɒnəmi/ n (pl -ies) economía: *make economies* economizar ◇ ~ *size* de tamaño familiar

ecosystem /'i:koʊsɪstəm/ n ecosistema

ecstasy /'ekstəsi/ n (pl -ies) éxtasis: *be in/go into ~ over sth* extasiarse con algo **ecstatic** /ɪk'stætɪk/ adj extasiado

edge /edʒ/ n 1 filo (cuchillo, etc.) 2 borde 3 ~ **(on/over sth/sb)** ventaja (sobre algo/algn) ▸ **on edge** con los nervios de punta **take the edge off sth** suavizar algo ● vt, vi 1 ~ **(sth) (with sth)** bordear (algo) (de algo) 2 ~ **(your) way)** along, away, etc. avanzar, alejarse, etc. poco a poco: ~ *towards the door* ir acercándose hacia la puerta

edgy /'edʒi/ adj (coloq) nervioso

edible /'edəbl/ adj comestible

edit /'edɪt/ vt 1 (libro) preparar una edición de 2 (texto) editar **edition** n edición

editor /'edɪtər/ n 1 (Period) director/a 2 (libros) editor/a

educate /'edʒukeɪt/ vt educar (académicamente) **educated** adj culto ▸ **an educated guess** una conjetura con fundamento

education /ˌedʒu'keɪʃn/ n 1 educación, enseñanza 2 pedagogía **educational** adj educativo, educacional

eel /i:l/ n anguila

eerie /'ɪəri/ adj misterioso, horripilante

effect /ɪ'fekt/ n efecto: *special ~s* efectos especiales ▸ **for effect** para impresionar **in effect** en realidad **take effect** 1 surtir efecto 2 (tb **come into ~**) entrar en vigor **to no effect** inútilmente **to this effect** con este propósito ● vt (fml) efectuar (cura, cambio)

effective /ɪ'fektɪv/ adj 1 ~ **(in sth)** eficaz (para algo) 2 de mucho efecto **effectively** adv 1 eficazmente 2 en efecto **effectiveness** n eficacia

effeminate /ɪ'femɪnət/ adj afeminado

efficient /ɪ'fɪʃnt/ adj 1 (persona) eficiente 2 (máquina, etc.) eficaz **efficiency** n eficiencia

effort /'efərt/ n 1 esfuerzo: *make an ~* esforzarse 2 intento

e.g. /ˌi: 'dʒi:/ abrev por ejemplo

egg /eg/ n huevo ▸ **put all your eggs in one basket** jugárselo todo a una carta ■ **egg sb on (to do sth)** animar mucho a algn (que haga algo)

eggplant /'egplænt; -plɑ:nt GB/ n (USA) berenjena

eggshell /'egʃel/ n cáscara de huevo

ego /'i:goʊ/ n (pl -s) ego: *boost sb's ~* alimentar el ego a algn

eight /eɪt/ adj, n, pron ocho **eighth** adj, adv, n, pron octavo

eighteen /ˌeɪ'ti:n/ adj, n, pron dieciocho **eighteenth** 1 adj, pron decimoctavo 2 n dieciochava parte, dieciochavo

eighty /'eɪti/ adj, n, pron ochenta **eightieth** 1 adj, pron octogésimo 2 n ochentava parte, ochentavo

either /'aɪðər, 'i:ðər GB/ adj 1 cualquiera de los dos: ~ *way...* de cualquiera de las dos maneras... 2 ambos: *on ~ side of the road* en ambos lados de la calle 3 [frases negativas] ninguno de los dos ● pron 1 cualquiera, uno u otro 2 [frases negativas] ninguno →NINGUNO ● adv 1 [frases negativas] tampoco: *"I'm not going." "I'm not ~."* —No voy a ir. —Yo tampoco. 2 **either... or...** o..., o..., ni...ni... →NEITHER

eject /i'dʒekt/ 1 vt (fml) expulsar 2 vt arrojar 3 vi eyectar(se)

elaborate /ɪ'læbərət/ adj intrincado ● /ɪ'læbəreɪt/ vi dar detalles

E

elapse /ɪ'læps/ vi (fml) pasar (tiempo)

elastic /ɪ'læstɪk/ adj, n elástico

elastic band n (GB) banda (elástica), caucho (And)

elated /i'leɪtɪd/ adj jubiloso

elbow /'elbəʊ/ n codo

elder, eldest /'eldər/-ɪst/ adj, pron mayor **NOTA** El comparativo de **elder** es **elder** y el superlativo **eldest**, pero **older** y **oldest** son más comunes: *He is older than me.* ◊ *The oldest building in the city.* Al comparar las edades de las personas, esp en una familia, se suele usar **elder** y **eldest**: *my eldest brother* ◊ *the elder of the two brothers.* **Elder** y **eldest** no se usan con **than** y sólo pueden ir delante del sustantivo.

elderly /'eldərli/ adj anciano: *the ~ los ancianos*

elect /ɪ'lekt/ vt elegir **election** n elección **electoral** adj electoral **electorate** n electorado

electric /ɪ'lektrɪk/ adj eléctrico **electrical** adj eléctrico → ELÉCTRICO **electrification** n electrificación **electrify** vt (pt/pp -ied) **1** electrificar **2** (fig) electrizar

electricity /ɪ,lek'trɪsəti/ n electricidad: *switch off the ~* cortar la luz **electrician** n electricista

electrocute /ɪ'lektrəkju:t/ vt electrocutar

electrode /ɪ'lektrəʊd/ n electrodo

electron /ɪ'lektrɒn/ n electrón

electronic /ɪ,lek'trɒnɪk/ adj electrónico **electronics** n [sing] electrónica

elegant /'elɪgənt/ adj elegante **elegance** n elegancia

element /'elɪmənt/ n elemento

elementary /,elɪ'mentri/ adj elemental: *~ school* escuela primaria

elephant /'elɪfənt/ n elefante

elevator /'elɪveɪtər/ n (USA) ascensor, elevador (Mx)

eleven /ɪ'levn/ adj, n, pron once **eleventh** adj, n undécimo **2** n onceavo

elicit /ɪ'lɪsɪt/ vt (fml) obtener

eligible /'elɪdʒəbl/ adj: *be ~ for sth* tener derecho a algo ◊ *be ~ to do sth* llenar los requisitos para hacer algo ◊ *an ~ bachelor* un soltero disponible

eliminate /ɪ'lɪmɪneɪt/ vt **1** eliminar **2** (pobreza, etc.) erradicar

elk /elk/ n (GB) alce

elm /elm/ n (tb ~ tree) n olmo

elope /ɪ'ləʊp/ vi fugarse (con su amante)

eloquent /'eləkwənt/ adj elocuente

else /els/ adv: *Did you see anybody ~?* ¿Viste a alguien más? ◊ *anyone ~* cualquier otra persona ◊ *everyone/everything ~* todos los/todo lo demás ◊ *It must have been somebody ~.* Debe haber sido otro. ◊ *nobody ~* nadie más ◊ *Anything ~?* ¿Algo más? ◊ *somewhere ~* a/en otra parte ◊ *What ~?* ¿Qué más? ▶ **or else 1** o, o si no: *Run or ~ you'll be late.* Corre o llegarás tarde. **2** (coloq) (como amenaza): *Stop that, or ~!* ¡Deja de hacer eso, o verás!

elsewhere /,els'weər/ adv a/en otra parte

elude /i'lu:d/ vt escaparse de **elusive** /i'lu:sɪv/ adj escurridizo: *an ~ word* una palabra difícil de recordar

email /'i:meɪl/ n **1** correo electrónico: *My ~ address is jones@oup. com.* Mi email es jones@oup. com. **NOTA** Se lee "jones at oup dot com" (/ dʒəʊnz æt əʊp ju: pi: dɒt kɒm/). **2** (mensaje) email ● vt mandar un email a: *~ sth to sb* enviar algo a algn por email

emanate /'eməneɪt/ vi *~ from sth/ sb* emanar, provenir de algo/ algn

emancipation /ɪ,mænsɪ'peɪʃn/ n emancipación

embankment /ɪm'bæŋkmənt/ n terraplén

embargo /ɪm'bɑːgəʊ/ n (pl -es) prohibición, embargo

embark /ɪm'bɑːk/ vi **1** embarcar **2** *~ on sth* emprender algo

embarrass /ɪm'bærəs/ vt avergonzar: *I'm embarrassed.* Me da pena. **embarrassing** adj embarazoso **embarrassment** n vergüenza: *be an ~ to sb* ser la vergüenza de algn

embassy /'embəsi/ n (pl -ies) embajada

embedded /ɪm'bedɪd/ adj **1** empotrado **2** (dientes, espada) clavado

ember /'embər/ n ascua, brasa

embezzlement /ɪm'bezlmənt/ n desfalco

embittered /ɪm'bɪtərd/ adj amargado

embody /ɪm'bɒdi/ vt (pt/pp -ied) encarnar **embodiment** n personificación

embrace /ɪm'breɪs/ vt, vi abrazar(se) ● n abrazo

embroider /ɪmˈbrɔɪdər/ vt, vi bordar **embroidery** n [U] bordado

embryo /ˈembriəʊ/ n (pl -s) embrión

emerald /ˈemərəld/ n esmeralda

emerge /iˈmɜːrdʒ/ vi emerger, surgir: *It emerged that...* Salió a relucir que... **emergence** n aparición, surgimiento

emergency /iˈmɜːrdʒənsi/ n (pl -ies) emergencia

emergency room (abrev **ER**) n (USA) urgencias

emigrate /ˈemɪɡreɪt/ vi emigrar **emigrant** n emigrante **emigration** n emigración

eminent /ˈemɪnənt/ adj eminente

emit /iˈmɪt/ vt (-tt-) 1 emitir 2 (olor, vapor) despedir **emission** n emisión

emotion /iˈməʊʃn/ n emoción **emotional** adj 1 emocional 2 emotivo **emotive** adj emotivo

empathy /ˈempəθi/ n empatía

emperor /ˈempərər/ n emperador

emphasis /ˈemfəsɪs/ n (pl emphases /ˈemfəsiːz/) énfasis **emphasize** vt enfatizar, recalcar **emphatic** /ɪmˈfætɪk/ adj categórico, enfático

empire /ˈempaɪər/ n imperio

employ /ɪmˈplɔɪ/ vt emplear, contratar **employee** n empleado/a **employer** n patrón/ona **employment** n empleo, trabajo →WORK

empress /ˈemprəs/ n emperatriz

empty /ˈempti/ adj 1 vacío 2 vano, inútil ● (pt/pp -ied) 1 vt ~ sth (out) vaciar algo 2 vt (habitación, etc.) desalojar 3 vi quedar vacío **emptiness** n 1 vacío 2 futilidad

empty-handed adj con las manos vacías

enable /ɪˈneɪbl/ vt permitir

enact /ɪˈnækt/ vt 1 (fml) (Teat) representar 2 llevar a cabo

enamel /ɪˈnæml/ n esmalte

enchanting /ɪnˈtʃɑːntɪŋ; -ˈtʃænt- GB/ adj encantador

encircle /ɪnˈsɜːrkl/ vt rodear

enclose /ɪnˈkləʊz/ vt 1 ~ sth (with sth) encerrar algo (con algo) 2 adjuntar **enclosure** n 1 recinto 2 (documento) anexo

encore /ˈɑːŋkɔːr/ n repetición, bis

encounter /ɪnˈkaʊntər/ vt (fml) encontrarse con ● n encuentro

encourage /ɪnˈkɜːrɪdʒ/ vt 1 animar 2 fomentar **encouragement** n aliento, estímulo **encouraging** adj alentador

encyclopedia (tb -paedia GB) /ɪnˌsaɪkləˈpiːdiə/ n enciclopedia

end /end/ n 1 final, extremo: *from ~ to ~* de punta a punta 2 (palo, etc.) punta 3 (hilo, etc.) cabo 4 *the east ~ of town* la parte/zona oriental de la ciudad 5 (tiempo) fin, final: *at the ~ of* al final/a finales de algo ◊ *from beginning to ~* de principio a fin → FINAL 6 propósito 7 (Dep) campo, lado ▸ **be at an end** tocar a su fin, haber terminado (ya) **in the end** al final **on end 1** de punta 2 *for days on ~* durante muchos días ● vt, vi terminar ▸ **end in sth** 1 terminar en algo (resultado) 2 acabar en algo **end up (as sth)** terminar (siendo algo) **end up (in...)** ir a parar (a...) (lugar)

endanger /ɪnˈdeɪndʒər/ vt poner en peligro: *an endangered species* una especie amenazada

endear /ɪnˈdɪər/ vt ~ sb/yourself **to sb** granjear(se) la simpatía de algn **endearing** adj atractivo

endeavour (-our **US**) /ɪnˈdevər/ n (fml) esfuerzo ● vi (fml) ~ **to do sth** esforzarse por hacer algo

ending /ˈendɪŋ/ n final

endless /ˈendləs/ adj interminable, infinito

endorse /ɪnˈdɔːrs/ vt 1 aprobar 2 (cheque) endosar **endorsement** n 1 aprobación 2 endoso 3 (carné de conducir) nota de sanción

endow /ɪnˈdaʊ/ vt dotar **endowment** n dotación (dinero)

endure /ɪnˈdʊər; -ˈdjʊə(r) GB/ 1 vt aguantar **NOTA** En negaciones es más común can't bear/stand. 2 vi perdurar **endurance** n resistencia **enduring** adj duradero

enemy /ˈenəmi/ n (pl -ies) enemigo/a

energy /ˈenərdʒi/ n (pl -ies) energía **energetic** /ˌenərˈdʒetɪk/ adj enérgico

enforce /ɪnˈfɔːrs/ vt hacer cumplir **enforcement** n aplicación

engage /ɪnˈɡeɪdʒ/ 1 vt (fml) contratar 2 vt (fml) (persona, tiempo, etc.) ocupar 3 vt (fml) (atención) llamar 4 vi (Mec) encajar ▸ **engage in sth** dedicarse a algo **engaged** adj 1 (com)prometido: *get ~* comprometerse 2 (baño) ocupado 3 (GB, teléfono) ocupado **engaging** adj atractivo

engagement /ɪnˈɡeɪdʒmənt/ n 1 compromiso matrimonial 2 noviazgo 3 (cita) compromiso

engine /ˈendʒɪn/ n 1 motor **NOTA** Se usa engine para vehículos y motor para electrodomésticos. 2 locomotora

engineer /ˌendʒɪˈnɪər/ n 1 ingeniero/a 2 (mantenimiento,

E 314

etc.) técnico/a **3** (*USA*) maquinista ● *vt* **1** (*colog*) maquinar **2** construir **erfgineering** *n* ingeniería

engrave /ɪnˈɡreɪv/ *vt* grabar **engraving** *n* grabado

engrossed /ɪnˈɡrəʊst/ *adj* absorto

enhance /ɪnˈhæns; -ˈhɑːns *GB*/ *vt* **1** aumentar, mejorar **2** realzar

enjoy /ɪnˈdʒɔɪ/ *vt* **1** disfrutar de: *Enjoy your meal!* ¡Buen provecho! **2** ~ **doing sth** gustarle a algn hacer algo **3** ~ **yourself** pasarla bien **enjoyable** *adj* agradable, divertido **enjoyment** *n* disfrute: *get a lot of ~ from sth* disfrutar algo mucho

enlarge /ɪnˈlɑːdʒ/ *vt* ampliar **enlargement** *n* ampliación

enlighten /ɪnˈlaɪtn/ *vt* (*fml*) ~ **sb** (**about/as to/on sth**) aclarar (algo) a algn **enlightened** *adj* **1** (*persona*) culto **2** (*política*) inteligente **enlightenment** *n* **1** aclaración **2** **the Enlightenment** (*Hist*) la Ilustración

enlist /ɪnˈlɪst/ **1** *vi* (*Mil*) alistarse **2** *vt* reclutar

enmity /ˈenmɪti/ *n* enemistad

enormous /ɪˈnɔːrməs/ *adj* enorme **enormously** *adv* muy, muchísimo

enough /ɪˈnʌf/ *adj, pron* suficiente, bastante: *Is that ~ food for ten?* ¿Será suficiente comida para diez? ◇ *That's ~!* ¡Ya basta! ▸ **have had enough** estar harto/jarto (*And*) ● *adv* (*lo*) bastante: *Is it near ~ to go on foot?* ¿Está lo bastante cerca como para ir a pie? **NOTA** Enough siempre va después del adjetivo y **too** delante: *You're not old ~./You're too young.* Eres demasiado joven. ▸ **funnily, strangely, etc. enough** lo curioso, extraño, etc. es que...

enquire = INQUIRE

enrage /ɪnˈreɪdʒ/ *vt* enfurecer

enrich /ɪnˈrɪtʃ/ *vt* enriquecer

enroll (**enrol** *GB*) /ɪnˈrəʊl/ *vt, vi* (-ll-) inscribir(se), matricular(se) **enrollment** (-l- *GB*) *n* inscripción, matrícula

ensure /ɪnˈʃʊər/ *vt* asegurar, garantizar

entail /ɪnˈteɪl/ *vt* suponer, conllevar

entangle /ɪnˈtæŋɡl/ *vt* enredar **entanglement** *n* enredo

enter /ˈentər/ **1** *vt, vi* entrar (*en*): *It never entered my head.* Ni se me pasó por la cabeza. **2** *vt, vi* ~ (**for**) **sth** inscribirse, matricularse en algo **3** *vt* ingresar a/en algo **4** *vt* ~ **sth** (**in sth**) anotar

algo (*en algo*) ■ **enter into sth 1** (*negociaciones*) iniciar algo **2** (*acuerdo*) llegar a algo **3** tener que ver con algo

enterprise /ˈentərpraɪz/ *n* **1** empresa **2** espíritu emprendedor **enterprising** *adj* emprendedor

entertain /ˌentərˈteɪn/ **1** *vt* entretener **2** *vt, vi* recibir (*en casa*) **3** *vt* (*idea*) albergar **entertainer** *n* artista del mundo del espectáculo **entertaining** *adj* entretenido **entertainment** *n* entretenimiento

enthralling /ɪnˈθrɔːlɪŋ/ *adj* cautivador

enthusiasm /ɪnˈθuːziæzəm; -ˈθjuː- *GB*/ *n* ~ (**for/about sth**) entusiasmo (por algo) **enthusiast** *n* entusiasta **enthusiastic** /ɪnˌθuːziˈæstɪk; -ˌθjuː- *GB*/ *adj* entusiasta

entice /ɪnˈtaɪs/ *vt* tentar

entire /ɪnˈtaɪər/ *adj* entero, todo **entirely** *adv* totalmente **entirety** /ɪnˈtaɪərəti/ *n* totalidad

entitle /ɪnˈtaɪtl/ *vt* **1** dar derecho a **2** (*libro*) titular **entitlement** *n* derecho

entity /ˈentəti/ *n* (*pl* -ies) entidad, ente

entrance /ˈentrəns/ *n* ~ (**to sth**) entrada (a/de algo)

entrant /ˈentrənt/ *n* ~ (**for sth**) participante (en algo)

entrepreneur /ˌɑːntrəprəˈnɜːr/ *n* empresario/a

entrust /ɪnˈtrʌst/ *vt* ~ **sb with sth/sth to sb** confiar algo a algn

entry /ˈentri/ *n* (*pl* -ies) **1** entrada, ingreso: *No ~.* Prohibido el paso. **2** (*diario*) anotación **3** (*diccionario*) entrada

enunciate /ɪˈnʌnsieɪt/ *vt, vi* pronunciar, articular

envelop /ɪnˈveləp/ *vt* envolver

envelope /ˈenvələʊp, ˈɑːn-/ *n* sobre (*para carta*)

enviable /ˈenviəbl/ *adj* envidiable

envious /ˈenviəs/ *adj* envidioso: *be ~ of sth* tener envidia de algn

environment /ɪnˈvaɪrənmənt/ *n* medio ambiente **environmental** /ɪnˌvaɪrənˈmentl/ *adj* ambiental **environmentalist** *n* ecologista **environmentally** *adv*: ~ *friendly products* productos ecológicos

envisage /ɪnˈvɪzɪdʒ/ *vt* imaginar(se)

envoy /ˈenvɔɪ/ *n* enviado/a

envy /ˈenvi/ *n* envidia ● *vt* (*pt/pp* -ied) envidiar

enzyme /ˈenzaɪm/ *n* enzima

ephemeral /ɪˈfemərəl/ *adj* efímero

epic /'epɪk/ n épica, epopeya ● adj épico

epidemic /ˌepɪ'demɪk/ n epidemia

epilepsy /'epɪlepsi/ n epilepsia **epileptic** /ˌepɪ'leptɪk/ adj, n epiléptico/a

episode /'epɪsoʊd/ n episodio

epitaph /'epɪtæf; -tɑːf GB/ n epitafio

epitome /ɪ'pɪtəmi/ n **the ~ of sth** la más pura expresión de algo

epoch /'epɒk; 'iːpɒk GB/ n (fml) época

equal /'iːkwəl/ adj, n igual: ~ opportunities igualdad de oportunidades ▸ **be on equal terms (with sb)** tener una relación de igual a igual (con algn) ● vt (-l-, -ll- GB) igualar (Mat): 7 plus 9 ~s 16. 7 más 9 son 16. **equality** /ɪ'kwɒləti/ n igualdad **equalize**, **-ise** /'iːkwəlaɪz/ vi (Dep) lograr el empate, empatar **equally** adv **1** igualmente **2** equitativamente

equate /i'kweɪt/ vt equiparar

equation /ɪ'kweɪʒn/ n ecuación

equator /ɪ'kweɪtər/ n ecuador

equilibrium /ˌiːkwɪ'lɪbriəm, ˌek-/ n equilibrio

equinox /'iːkwɪnɒks, 'ek-/ n equinoccio

equip /ɪ'kwɪp/ vt (-pp-) equipar, proveer **equipment** n [U] equipo, material

equitable /'ekwɪtəbl/ adj (fml) equitativo, justo

equivalent /ɪ'kwɪvələnt/ adj, n equivalente

era /'ɪərə/ n era

eradicate /ɪ'rædɪkeɪt/ vt erradicar

erase /ɪ'reɪs; ɪ'reɪz GB/ vt borrar **eraser** (USA) n goma, borrador

erect /ɪ'rekt/ vt erigir ● adj **1** erguido **2** erecto **erection** n erección

erode /ɪ'roʊd/ vt erosionar

erotic /ɪ'rɒtɪk/ adj erótico

errand /'erənd/ n mandado: run ~s hacer mandados

erratic /ɪ'rætɪk/ adj irregular

error /'erər/ n error: make an ~ cometer un error **NOTA** Mistake es más común que **error**, pero en algunos casos sólo se puede usar **error**: human ~ error humano ◇ an ~ of judgement una equivocación. →MISTAKE

erupt /ɪ'rʌpt/ vi **1** hacer/entrar en erupción **2** (violencia) estallar

escalate /'eskəleɪt/ vt, vi **1** aumentar **2** intensificar(se) **escal-**

-ation n **1** aumento **2** intensificación

escalator /'eskəleɪtər/ n escalera mecánica/eléctrica

escapade /'eskəpeɪd, ˌeskə'peɪd/ n aventura

escape /ɪ'skeɪp/ **1** vi escapar(se) **2** vt, vi salvarse (de): ~ unharmed salir ileso ● n **1** fuga: make your ~ darse a la fuga **2** (gas, etc.) escape

escort /'eskɔːrt/ n **1** escolta **2** (fml) acompañante ● /ɪ'skɔːrt/ vt acompañar

especially /ɪ'speʃəli/ adv especialmente, sobre todo →SPECIALLY

espionage /'espiənɑːʒ/ n espionaje

essay /'eseɪ/ n **1** ensayo **2** (colegio) redacción, trabajo

essence /'esns/ n esencia **essential** /ɪ'senʃl/ adj **1** imprescindible **2** fundamental **essentially** adv básicamente

establish /ɪ'stæblɪʃ/ vt establecer **established** adj **1** (negocio) sólido **2** (religión) oficial **establishment** n **1** establecimiento **2** institución **3** the Establishment el sistema

estate /ɪ'steɪt/ n **1** hacienda, finca **2** (bienes) herencia **3** (GB) Ver HOUSING DEVELOPMENT **4** (GB) industrial ~ zona industrial

estate agent (GB) corredor/a de bienes raíces

estate car (tb estate) n (GB) camioneta

esteem /ɪ'stiːm/ n ▸ **hold sth/sb in high/low esteem** tener una buena/mala opinión de algo/algn

esthetic (USA) = AESTHETIC

estimate /'estɪmət/ n **1** cálculo **2** valoración **3** presupuesto ● /'estɪmeɪt/ vt calcular

estimation /ˌestɪ'meɪʃn/ n juicio

estranged /ɪ'streɪndʒd/ adj ▸ **be estranged from sb 1** vivir separado de algn **2** estar enemistado con algn

estuary /'estʃueri; -əri GB/ n (pl -ies) estuario

etching /'etʃɪŋ/ n grabado (al aguafuerte)

eternal /ɪ'tɜːrnl/ adj eterno **eternity** n eternidad

ether /'iːθər/ n éter **ethereal** /ɪ'θɪəriəl/ adj etéreo

ethics /'eθɪks/ n [pl] ética **ethical** adj ético

ethnic /'eθnɪk/ adj étnico

ethos /'iːθɒs/ n (fml) carácter, espíritu

etiquette /'etɪket/ n etiqueta (modales)

EU /ˌiː ˈjuː/ *abrev de* **European Union** Unión Europea

euro /ˈjʊərəʊ/ *n* (*pl* -**s**) euro

euthanasia /ˌjuːθəˈneɪʒə; -ˈneɪziə *GB*/ *n* eutanasia

evacuate /ɪˈvækjueɪt/ *vt* evacuar (*a personas*) **evacuee** /ɪˌvækjuˈiː/ *n* evacuado/a

evade /ɪˈveɪd/ *vt* evadir, eludir

evaluate /ɪˈvæljueɪt/ *vt* evaluar

evaporate /ɪˈvæpəreɪt/ *vt, vi* evaporar(se) **evaporation** *n* evaporación

evasion /ɪˈveɪʒn/ *n* evasión **evasive** /ɪˈveɪsɪv/ *adj* evasivo

eve /iːv/ *n* ◇ **on the eve of sth** la víspera de algo **en vísperas de algo**

even /ˈiːvn/ *adv* 1 [*énfasis*] aun, hasta: *He didn't ~ open the letter.* Ni siquiera abrió la carta. 2 [+ *comparativo*] aún ► **even if/though** aunque, aun cuando **even so** aun así, no obstante ● *adj* 1 (*superficie*) parejo 2 (*color*) uniforme 3 (*temperatura*) constante 4 empatado 5 (*número*) par ■ **even out** nivelarse **even sth up** nivelar algo **evenly** *adv* 1 de modo uniforme 2 equitativamente

evening /ˈiːvnɪŋ/ *n* 1 tarde, noche: *an ~ class/dress* una clase nocturna/un traje de noche → MORNING, TARDE 2 atardecer ► **good evening** buenas tardes/noches →NOCHE

event /ɪˈvent/ *n* suceso, acontecimiento ► **at all events/in any event** en todo caso **in the event** al final **in the event of sth** en caso de (que) **eventful** *adj* lleno de incidentes

eventual /ɪˈventʃuəl/ *adj* final **eventually** *adv* finalmente

ever /ˈevər/ *adv* nunca, jamás: *for ~ (and ~)* para siempre ◇ *Did it ~ happen before?* ¿Ha pasado alguna vez antes? ► **ever since** desde entonces →ALWAYS, NUNCA

every /ˈevri/ *adj* cada, todos los: *~ (single) time* cada vez **NOTA** Se usa **every** para referirnos a todos los elementos de un grupo en conjunto: *Every player was on top form.* **Each** se usa para referirnos individualmente a cada uno de ellos: *The Queen shook hands with each player after the game.* → EACH ► **every last...** hasta el último... **every now and again/then** de vez en cuando **every other** uno sí y otro no: *~ other week* una semana sí y otra no **every so often** alguna que otra vez

everybody /ˈevribɒdi/ (*tb* **everyone** /ˈevriwʌn/) *pron* todos, todo el mundo **NOTA** Everybody, **anybody** y **somebody** llevan el verbo en singular, pero van seguidos de **they, their** o **them**: *Everybody does what they want.*

everyday /ˈevrideɪ/ *adj* cotidiano, de todos los días: *for/in - use* para uso diario/de uso corriente **NOTA** Everyday sólo se usa antes de un sustantivo. No se debe confundir con **every day**, que significa "todos los días"

everything /ˈevriθɪŋ/ *pron* todo

everywhere /ˈevriweər/ *adv* en/a/por todas partes

evict /ɪˈvɪkt/ *vt* desalojar

evidence /ˈevɪdəns/ *n* [U] 1 pruebas: *insufficient ~* falta de pruebas 2 (*Jur*) testimonio **evident** *adj* evidente **evidently** *adv* obviamente

evil /ˈiːvl/ *adj* malvado, muy malo ● *n* (*fml*) mal

evocative /ɪˈvɒkətɪv/ *adj* evocador

evoke /ɪˈvəʊk/ *vt* evocar

evolution /ˌiːvəˈluːʃn, ˌiːv-/ *n* evolución

evolve /ɪˈvɒlv/ *vi* evolucionar

ewe /juː/ *n* oveja hembra

exact /ɪgˈzækt/ *adj* exacto

exacting /ɪgˈzæktɪŋ/ *adj* exigente

exactly /ɪgˈzæktli/ *adv* exactamente ● *interj* exacto

exaggerate /ɪgˈzædʒəreɪt/ *vt* exagerar **exaggerated** *adj* exagerado

exam /ɪgˈzæm/ *n* (*Educ*) examen

examination /ɪgˌzæmɪˈneɪʃn/ *n* 1 (*fml*) examen 2 reconocimiento, revisión **examine** *vt* examinar, revisar

example /ɪgˈzɑːmpl; -ˈzæmpl *GB*/ *n* ejemplo: *set a good/bad ~* dar buen/mal ejemplo ► **for example** (*abrev* **e.g.**) por ejemplo

exasperate /ɪgˈzæspəreɪt; -ˈzɑːs *GB*/ *vt* exasperar **exasperation** *n* exasperación

excavate /ˈekskəveɪt/ *vt, vi* excavar

exceed /ɪkˈsiːd/ *vt* exceder(se en), superar **exceedingly** *adv* sumamente

excel /ɪkˈsel/ *vi* (**-ll-**) ~ **in/at sth** sobresalir, destacar en algo

excellent /ˈeksələnt/ *adj* excelente **excellence** *n* excelencia

except /ɪkˈsept/ *prep* ~ (**for**) **sth/sb** excepto algo/algn **exception** *n* excepción **exceptional** *adj* excepcional

excerpt /ˈeksɜːpt/ *n* extracto

excess /ɪk'ses/ n exceso **excessive** adj excesivo

exchange /ɪks'tʃeɪndʒ/ n cambio, intercambio ● vt cambiar

the Exchequer /ɪks'tʃekər/ n Ministerio de Hacienda y Crédito Público (en GB)

excite /ɪk'saɪt/ vt excitar **excitable** adj excitable **excited** adj 1 emocionado 2 excitado **excitement** n emoción **exciting** adj emocionante

exclaim /ɪk'skleɪm/ vi exclamar **exclamation** n exclamación

exclamation point (exclamation mark GB**)** n signo de exclamación

exclude /ɪk'skluːd/ vt excluir **exclusion** n exclusión

exclusive /ɪk'skluːsɪv/ adj 1 exclusivo 2 ~ of sth/sb sin incluir algo/a algn

excursion /ɪk'skɜːrʃn; -3:ʃn GB/ n excursión

excuse /ɪk'skjuːs/ n excusa ● /ɪk'skjuːz/ vt 1 disculpar 2 ~ sb (from sth) dispensar a algn (de algo) **NOTA** Se usa **excuse me** para interrumpir o abordar a algn: *Excuse me, sir!* ¡Disculpe, señor! o para pedir paso: *Excuse me, please.* ¿Me deja, por favor?/¿Con permiso, por favor? En Gran Bretaña se usa **sorry** en lugar de **excuse me** para pedir perdón por algo: *I'm sorry I'm late.* ◇ *Did I hit you? Sorry!* →ACHÍS

execute /'eksɪkjuːt/ vt ejecutar **execution** n ejecución **executioner** n verdugo

executive /ɪg'zekjətɪv/ n ejecutivo/a

exempt /ɪg'zempt/ adj exento ● vt eximir **exemption** n exención

exercise /'eksərsaɪz/ n ejercicio ● 1 vi hacer ejercicio 2 vt (derecho, poder) ejercer

exert /ɪg'zɜːrt/ vt 1 ejercer 2 ~ yourself esforzarse **exertion** n esfuerzo

exhaust /ɪg'zɔːst/ n 1 (tb ~ pipe) escape, exhosto (And) 2 [U] (tb ~ fumes [pl]) gases del escape/exhosto ● vt agotar **exhausted** adj exhausto **exhausting** adj agotador **exhaustion** n agotamiento **exhaustive** adj exhaustivo

exhibit /ɪg'zɪbɪt/ n objeto expuesto ● 1 vt, vi exponer 2 vt manifestar

exhibition /ˌeksɪ'bɪʃn/ n exposición

exhilarating /ɪg'zɪləreɪtɪŋ/ adj estimulante, emocionante **exhilaration** n euforia

exile /'egzaɪl, 'eksaɪl/ n 1 exilio 2 (persona) exiliado/a ● vt exiliar

exist /ɪg'zɪst/ vi 1 existir 2 ~ (on sth) subsistir (a base de algo) **existence** n existencia **existing** adj existente

exit /'eksɪt/ n salida

exotic /ɪg'zɑːtɪk/ adj exótico

expand /ɪk'spænd/ vt, vi 1 dilatar(se) 2 ampliar(se) ■ **expand on sth** ampliar algo **expansion** n 1 expansión 2 desarrollo **expansive** adj expansivo, comunicativo

expanse /ɪk'spæns/ n extensión

expatriate /ˌeks'peɪtriət; -'pæt- GB/ n expatriado/a

expect /ɪk'spekt/ vt 1 esperar → ESPERAR 2 (coloq) suponer **expectant** adj 1 expectante 2 (madre) embarazada **expectancy** n expectación **expectation** n expectativa: *against/contrary to ~s* contra todas las previsiones

expedition /ˌekspə'dɪʃn/ n expedición

expel /ɪk'spel/ vt (-ll-) expulsar

expend /ɪk'spend/ vt (fml) emplear

expendable /ɪk'spendəbl/ adj (fml) 1 (cosas) desechable 2 (personas) prescindible

expenditure /ɪk'spendɪtʃər/ n gasto(s)

expense /ɪk'spens/ n gasto(s), costo **expensive** adj caro, costoso

experience /ɪk'spɪəriəns/ n experiencia ● vt experimentar **experienced** adj experimentado

experiment /ɪk'sperɪmənt/ n experimento ● vi hacer experimentos, experimentar

expert /'ekspɜːrt/ adj, n experto/a, perito/a **expertise** /ˌekspɜːr-'tiːz/ n conocimientos (técnicos), pericia

expire /ɪk'spaɪər/ vi vencer, caducar: *My passport's expired.* Mi pasaporte está vencido. **expiry** (**expiry** GB) n vencimiento

explain /ɪk'spleɪn/ vt explicar **explanation** n explicación **explanatory** /ɪk'splænətɔːri; -tri GB/ adj explicativo

explicit /ɪk'splɪsɪt/ adj explícito

explode /ɪk'sploʊd/ vt, vi (hacer) estallar, (hacer) explotar

exploit /'eksplɔɪt/ n proeza, hazaña ● /ɪk'splɔɪt/ vt explotar (personas, recursos) **exploitation** n explotación

explore /ɪk'splɔːr/ vt, vi explorar **exploration** n exploración, investigación **explorer** n explorador/a

explosion /ɪkˈsploʊʒn/ n explosión **explosive** adj, n explosivo

export /ɪkˈspɔːrt/ vt, vi exportar ● /ˈekspɔːrt/ n (artículo de) exportación

expose /ɪkˈspoʊz/ vt **1** exponer **2** (persona culpable) desenmascarar **exposed** adj descubierto **exposure** n **1** exposición: die of ~ morir de frío (a la intemperie) **2** (de falta) revelación

express /ɪkˈspres/ adj **1** (tren) rápido **2** (entrega) inmediato **3** (deseo, etc.) expreso ● adv **1** (por envío) urgente **2** en tren rápido ● vt expresar ● n **1** (tb ~ train) rápido **2** (GB) servicio/envío urgente **expressly** adv expresamente

expression /ɪkˈspreʃn/ n **1** expresión **2** muestra **3** expresividad **expressive** /ɪkˈspresɪv/ adj expresivo

expressway /ɪkˈspresweɪ/ n (USA) carretera, autopista

expulsion /ɪkˈspʌlʃn/ n expulsión

exquisite /ɪkˈskwɪzɪt, ˈekskwɪzɪt/ adj exquisito

extend /ɪkˈstend/ **1** vt extender, ampliar **2** vi extenderse **3** vt prolongar **4** vt (plazo) prorrogar **5** vt (mano) tender **6** vt (bienvenida) dar

extension /ɪkˈstenʃn/ n **1** extensión **2** ~ (to sth) ampliación, anexo (de algo) **3** prolongación **4** (plazo) prórroga **5** (teléfono) extensión

extensive /ɪkˈstensɪv/ adj **1** extenso **2** amplio **3** (daños) cuantioso **4** (uso) frecuente **extensively** adv **1** extensamente **2** comúnmente

extent /ɪkˈstent/ n alcance, grado: the full ~ of the losses el valor real de las pérdidas ▸ **to a large/great extent** en gran parte ▸ **to a lesser extent** en menor grado ▸ **to some/what extent** hasta cierto/qué punto

exterior /ɪkˈstɪəriər/ adj exterior ● n **1** exterior **2** (persona) aspecto

exterminate /ɪkˈstɜːrmɪneɪt/ vt exterminar

external /ɪkˈstɜːrnl/ adj externo, exterior

extinct /ɪkˈstɪŋkt/ adj **1** (animal) extinto, desaparecido: become ~ extinguirse **2** (volcán) inactivo **extinction** n extinción

extinguish /ɪkˈstɪŋgwɪʃ/ vt extinguir, apagar **NOTA** Es más común **put out**. **extinguisher** n extinguidor

extort /ɪkˈstɔːrt/ vt **1** obtener (mediante extorsión) **2** (confesión) sacar a la fuerza **extortion** n extorsión

extortionate /ɪkˈstɔːrʃənət/ adj excesivo

extra /ˈekstrə/ adj **1** adicional, de más, extra: ~ charge recargo ◊ Wine is ~. El vino no está incluido. **2** de sobra (Dep): ~ time prórroga/tiempo suplementario ● adv súper, extra: pay ~ pagar un suplemento ● n **1** extra **2** (precio) suplemento

extract /ɪkˈstrækt/ vt **1** extraer **2** conseguir ● /ˈekstrækt/ n **1** extracto **2** pasaje

extraordinary /ɪkˈstrɔːrdəneri, -dnri GB/ adj extraordinario

extravagant /ɪkˈstrævəgənt/ adj **1** extravagante **2** exagerado **extravagance** n extravagancia

extreme /ɪkˈstriːm/ adj, n extremo: with ~ care con sumo cuidado **extremely** adv extremadamente **extremist** n extremista **extremity** /ɪkˈstremɪti/ n (pl -ies) extremidad

extricate /ˈekstrɪkeɪt/ vt (fml) sacar

extrovert /ˈekstrəvɜːrt/ n extrovertido/a

exuberant /ɪgˈzuːbərənt; -ˈzjuː- GB/ adj desbordante de vida y entusiasmo

exude /ɪgˈzuːd; ɪgˈzjuːd GB/ **1** vt, vi exudar **2** vt rebosar

eye /aɪ/ n ojo: have sharp ~s tener muy buena vista ◊ private ~ detective privado → MY ▸ **before your (very) eyes** delante de tus propias narices **in the eyes of sb/in sb's eyes** en opinión de algn **in the eyes of the law** a los ojos de la ley **keep an eye on sth/sb** echarle un ojo a algo/algn **see eye to eye with sb** estar plenamente de acuerdo con algn **up to your eyes in sth** hasta el cuello de algo ● vt (pt pres eyeing) mirar

eyeball /ˈaɪbɔːl/ n globo ocular

eyebrow /ˈaɪbraʊ/ n ceja

eye-catching adj vistoso

eyelash /ˈaɪlæʃ/ n pestaña

eye-level adj a la altura de los ojos

eyelid /ˈaɪlɪd/ n párpado

eyeshadow /ˈaɪʃædoʊ/ n sombra de ojos

eyesight /ˈaɪsaɪt/ n vista

eyesore /ˈaɪsɔːr/ n monstruosidad

eyewitness /ˈaɪwɪtnəs/ n testigo ocular

F f

F, f /ef/ n (pl **F's, f's**) **1** F, f **2** (Mús) fa

fable /'feɪbl/ n fábula

fabric /'fæbrɪk/ n **1** tejido, tela →TELA **2** (fml): the ~ of society los cimientos de la sociedad

fabulous /'fæbjələs/ adj **1** fabuloso **2** de leyenda

façade /fə'sɑːd/ n fachada

face /feɪs/ n **1** cara, rostro: ~ down/up boca abajo/arriba **2** cara: the south ~ la cara sur ◊ a rock ~ una pared de roca **3** (reloj) cara, carátula **4** superficie ▶ **face to face** cara a cara: come ~ to ~ with sth enfrentarse con algo **in the face of sth 1** a pesar de algo **2** frente a algo **make/pull faces/a face** hacer muecas **on the face of it** (coloq) a primera vista **to sb's face** a la cara ● vt **1** estar de cara a: They sat facing each other. Se sentaron uno frente al otro. **2** dar a: The house ~s the river. La casa da al río. **3** enfrentarse con **4** afrontar **5** (sentencia, etc.) correr el riesgo de recibir **6** revestir ▶ **let's face it** reconozcámoslo ■ **face up to sth/ sb** enfrentarse a algo/algn

faceless /'feɪsləs/ adj anónimo

facelift /'feɪslɪft/ n **1** estiramiento (facial) **2** (fig) remodelación superficial

facet /'fæsɪt/ n faceta

facetious /fə'siːʃəs/ adj (pey) gracioso

face value n valor nominal ▶ **accept/take sth at (its) face value** tomar algo literalmente

facial /'feɪʃl/ adj facial ● n (tratamiento) facial

facile /'fæsl/ -saɪl GB/ adj simplista

facilitate /fə'sɪlɪteɪt/ vt (fml) facilitar

facility /fə'sɪləti/ n **1** [sing] facilidad **2** **facilities**: sports/banking facilities instalaciones deportivas/servicios bancarios

fact /fækt/ n hecho: in ~ de hecho ▶ **facts and figures** detalles precisos **the facts of life** de dónde vienen los niños, la sexualidad

factor /'fæktər/ n factor

factory /'fæktəri/ n (pl -ies) fábrica

factual /'fæktʃuəl/ adj basado en los hechos

faculty /'fæklti/ n (pl -ies) **1** facultad **2** (USA) profesorado

fad /fæd/ n **1** manía **2** moda

fade /feɪd/ vt, vi **1** decolorar(se) **2** desteñir(se) ■ **fade away** ir desapareciendo poco a poco

fag /fæg/ n **1** (USA, pey) maricón **2** (GB, coloq) cigarrillo **3** [sing] (GB, coloq): What a ~! ¡Qué cruz!

fail /feɪl/ vt **1** (examen, etc.) reprobar **2** vi fracasar: ~ in your duty faltar al deber **3** vi ~ **to do sth**: He never ~s to write. Nunca deja de escribir. ◊ The letter failed to arrive. La carta no llegó. **4** vi fallar **5** vi (salud) deteriorarse **6** vi (cosecha) arruinarse **7** vt (negocio) quebrar ● n reprobado ▶ **without fail** sin falta

failing /'feɪlɪŋ/ n **1** debilidad **2** defecto ● prep a falta de: ~ this si esto no es posible

failure /'feɪljər/ n **1** fracaso **2** falla: heart ~ paro cardíaco ◊ engine ~ daño en el motor **3** ~ **to do sth**: His ~ to answer puzzled her. Le extrañó que no contestara.

faint /feɪnt/ adj (-er/-est) **1** (sonido) débil **2** (rastro) leve **3** (parecido) ligero **4** (esperanza) pequeño **5** ~ (from/with sth) mareado (de/por algo) ● vi desmayarse ● n [sing] desmayo

fair /feər/ n **1** parque de diversiones **2** feria: a trade ~ una feria de muestras ● adj (-er/-est) **1** ~ (to/ on sb) justo, imparcial (con algn): It's not ~! ¡No hay derecho! **2** (tiempo) bueno **3** (pelo) rubio, güero (Mx) →RUBIO **4** (idea) bastante bueno: a ~ size bastante grande ▶ **fair and square 1** merecidamente **2** (GB) claramente **fair game** objeto legítimo de persecución/burla **fair play** juego limpio **have, etc. (more than) your fair share of sth**: We had more than our ~ share of rain. Nos llovió más de lo que podíamos esperarse.

fair-haired adj rubio, güero (Mx)

fairly /'feərli/ adv **1** justamente, equitativamente **2** [+ adj/adv] bastante: It's ~ good. No está mal. **NOTA** Los adverbios **fairly** y **pretty** (y **rather** y **quite** en Gran Bretaña) modifican los adjetivos o adverbios que acompañan, y pueden significar "bastante", "hasta cierto punto" o "no muy". **Fairly** es el de grado más bajo.

fairy /'feəri/ n (pl -ies) hada

faith /feɪθ/ n fe ▶ **in bad/good faith** de mala/buena fe **put your faith in sth/sb** confiar en algo/algn

faithful /'feɪθfl/ adj fiel, leal **faithfully** adv fielmente

fake /feɪk/ n imitación ● adj falso
● 1 vt falsificar 2 vt, vi fingir

falcon /ˈfælkən; ˈfɔːl- GB/ n halcón

fall /fɔːl/ n 1 caída 2 baja, descenso 3 a ~ of snow una nevada 4 (USA) otoño 5 falls [pl] catarata ● vi (pt fell pp fallen /ˈfɔːlən/) 1 caer(se) 2 bajar **NOTA** A veces el verbo **fall** puede tener el sentido de "volverse", "quedarse", "ponerse", p. ej.: ~ asleep/ill quedarse dormido/caer enfermo. ■ **fall apart** deshacerse **fall back** retroceder **fall back on sth/sb** recurrir a algo/algn **fall behind (sth/sb)** quedar(se) atrás/detrás de algo/algn **fall behind with sth** retrasarse con algo/en hacer algo **fall down 1** caerse 2 (plan) fracasar **fall for sb** (coloq) enamorarse de algn **fall for sth** (coloq) tragarse algo (trampa) **fall in 1** (techo) hundirse 2 (Mil) formar **fall off** caer(se) **fall on/upon sb** recaer en algn **fall out (with sb)** pelearse (con algn) **fall over** caerse **fall over sth/sb** tropezar con algo/algn **fall through** fracasar, irse a pique

false /fɔːls/ adj falso 2 (dientes, etc.) postizo 3 fraudulento

falsify /ˈfɔːlsɪfaɪ/ vt (pt/pp -ied) falsificar

falter /ˈfɔːltər/ vi 1 (persona) vacilar 2 (voz) titubear

fame /feɪm/ n fama

familiar /fəˈmɪliər/ adj 1 familiar (conocido) 2 familiarizado **familiarity** /fəˌmɪliˈærəti/ n 1 ~ with sth conocimientos de algo 2 familiaridad

family /ˈfæməli/ n (pl -ies) familia: ~ name apellido ◇ ~ tree árbol genealógico ◇ → FAMILIA ▸ **run in the family** ser de familia

famine /ˈfæmɪn/ n hambre →HAMBRE

famous /ˈfeɪməs/ adj famoso

fan /fæn/ n 1 abanico 2 ventilador 3 fan, hincha ● vt (-nn-) 1 abanicar 2 (disputa, fuego) atizar ■ **fan out** desplegarse en abanico

fanatic /fəˈnætɪk/ n fanático/a **fanatical** adj fanático

fanciful /ˈfænsɪfl/ adj 1 extravagante 2 (persona) fantasioso

fancy /ˈfænsi/ n 1 capricho 2 fantasía ▸ **catch/take sb's fancy** cautivar a algn: whatever takes your ~ lo que más se te antoje **take a fancy to sth/sb** encapricharse con algo/algn ● adj fuera de lo corriente: nothing ~ nada extravagante ● vt (pt/pp -ied) 1 imaginarse 2 (GB, coloq) que-

rer 3 (GB, coloq) gustar: I don't ~ him. Él no me gusta. 4 (GB, coloq) ~ **yourself (as sth)** dárselas de algo ◇ **fancy (that)!** ¡quién lo iba a creer!

fancy dress n [U] (GB) disfraz

fantastic /fænˈtæstɪk/ adj fantástico

fantasy /ˈfæntəsi/ n (pl -ies) fantasía

FAQ /ˌef eɪ ˈkjuː/ abrev de frequently asked questions preguntas más frecuentes

far /fɑːr/ (comp further/farther superl furthest/farthest) adj 1 extremo: the ~ end el otro extremo 2 opuesto: on the ~ bank en la margen opuesta ● adv 1 lejos: How ~ is it? ¿A qué distancia está? **NOTA** En este sentido se usa en negaciones o interrogaciones. En afirmaciones es más común **a long way**. 2 [+ prep y comp] muy, mucho: ~ above/beyond sth muy por encima/mucho más allá de algo ◇ It's ~ better. Es mucho mejor. ▸ **as far as** hasta **as/so far as** por lo que: as ~ as I know que yo sepa **as/so far as sth/sb is concerned** por lo que se refiere a algo/algn **be far from sth** distar mucho de algo **by far** con mucho **far and wide** por todas partes **far away** muy lejos **far from it** (coloq) ni mucho menos **go too far** pasarse **in so far as** en la medida en que **so far 1** hasta ahora 2 hasta cierto punto

faraway /ˈfɑːrəweɪ/ adj 1 remoto 2 (expresión) distraído

fare /feər/ n tarifa, precio del boleto/tiquete ● vi: ~ well/badly irle bien/mal a uno

farewell /ˌfeərˈwel/ interj (fml) adiós ● n despedida: bid/say ~ to sb despedirse de algn

farm /fɑːm/ n granja, hacienda ● 1 vt, vi labrar, cultivar 2 vt criar

farmer /ˈfɑːrmər/ n granjero/a, agricultor/a

farmhouse /ˈfɑːrmhaʊs/ n casa (de granja, hacienda, etc.)

farming /ˈfɑːrmɪŋ/ n agricultura, ganadería

farmland /ˈfɑːrmlænd/ n [U] tierras de cultivo

farmyard /ˈfɑːrmjɑːrd/ n corral

far-sighted adj 1 con visión de futuro 2 (USA) hipermétrope

fart /fɑːrt/ n (coloq) pedo ● vi (coloq) echarse un pedo

farther /ˈfɑːrðər/ adj, adv más lejos →FURTHER

farthest /ˈfɑːrðɪst/ Ver FURTHEST

fascinate /'fæsɪneɪt/ vt fascinar **fascinating** adj fascinante

fascism /'fæʃɪzəm/ n fascismo **fascist** adj, n fascista

fashion /'fæʃn/ n moda: in/out of ~ de moda/pasado de moda ◊ come into/go out of ~ ponerse/ pasar de moda ● vt moldear, hacer **fashionable** adj de moda

fast /fæst; fɑːst GB/ (-er/-est) adj **1** rápido **NOTA** Fast suele usarse para describir a una persona o cosa que se mueve a mucha velocidad: a ~ car/runner, mientras **quick** se refiere a algo que se realiza en un breve espacio de tiempo: a quick decision/ visit. **2** (reloj) adelantado **3** (color) que no destiñe ● adv **1** rápido, rápidamente **2** ~ asleep profundamente dormido ▸ **stand fast** mantenerse firme ● vi ayunar ● n ayuno

fasten /'fæsn; 'fɑːsn GB/ vt **1** ~ **sth** (down) asegurar algo **2** vt, vi ~ (sth) (up) abrochar(se) (algo) **3** vt sujetar, fijar: ~ sth together unir algo

fast food n comida rápida

fastidious /fæ'stɪdiəs/ adj meticuloso, quisquilloso

fat /fæt/ adj (fatter, -est) gordo: get ~ engordar **NOTA** Hay palabras menos directas que **fat**, p. ej. **chubby, stout, plump** y **overweight**. ● n **1** grasa **2** manteca

fatal /'feɪtl/ adj **1** ~ (to sth/sb) mortal (para algo/algn) **2** fatídico **fatality** /fə'tæləti/ n (pl -ies) víctima mortal

fate /feɪt/ n destino **fated** adj predestinado **fateful** adj fatídico

father /'fɑːðər/ n padre: Father Christmas (GB) Papá Noel → NAVIDAD ▸ **like father, like son** de tal palo, tal astilla ● vt engendrar **fatherhood** n paternidad **father-in-law** n (pl -ers-in-law) suegro **fatherly** adj paternal

Father's Day n día del padre

fatigue /fə'tiːɡ/ n fatiga, cansancio ● vt fatigar

fatten /'fætn/ vt (animal) cebar **fattening** adj: Butter is very ~. La mantequilla engorda mucho.

fatty /'fæti/ adj (-ier/-iest) **1** (Med) adiposo **2** (-ier/-iest) (alimento) grasoso

faucet /'fɔːsət/ n (USA) llave (de agua)

fault /fɔːlt/ n **1** defecto, falla → MISTAKE **2** culpa: be at ~ tener la culpa **3** (Dep) falta **4** (Geol) falla ● vt criticar: He can't be faulted. Es irreprochable. **faultless** adj sin tacha, impecable **faulty** adj defectuoso

fauna /'fɔːnə/ n fauna

favor (-our GB) n favor ▸ **in favor of sth** a favor de algo ● vt **1** favorecer **2** preferir, ser partidario de (idea) **favorable** adj **1** favorable **2** ~ (to/toward sth/ sb) a favor de (algo/algn)

favorite (-our- GB) n favorito/a ● adj preferido

fawn /fɔːn/ n venado menor de un año → CIERVO ● adj, n beige

fax /fæks/ n fax ● vt **1** mandar un fax a **2** mandar algo por fax

fear /fɪər/ n miedo, temor: in ~ of sth/sb con miedo de algo/algn ▸ **for fear of sth** por temor a algo ● vt temer a **fearful** adj (fml) temeroso **fearless** adj intrépido **fearsome** adj (fml) terrible

feasible /'fiːzəbl/ adj factible **feasibility** /ˌfiːzə'bɪləti/ n viabilidad

feast /fiːst/ n **1** festín **2** (Rel) fiesta ● vi darse un festín

feat /fiːt/ n proeza, hazaña

feather /'feðər/ n pluma

feature /'fiːtʃər/ n **1** característica **2 features** facciones ● vt: featuring Brad Pitt protagonizada por Brad Pitt **featureless** adj sin rasgos característicos

February /'februeri; -uari GB/ n (abrev Feb.) febrero → JUNE

fed /fed/ pt, pp de FEED

federal /'fedərəl/ adj federal

federation /ˌfedə'reɪʃn/ n federación

fed up adj ~ (about/with sth/sb) harto, jarto (And) (de algo/algn)

fee /fiː/ n **1** honorarios **2** cuota (club) **3** school ~s colegiatura (Mx)/pensión y matrícula (And)

feeble /'fiːbl/ adj (-er/-est) débil

feed /fiːd/ (pt/pp fed) **1** vi ~ (on sth) alimentarse (de algo) **2** vt dar de comer a, alimentar **3** vt (datos, etc.) suministrar ● n **1** comida (de animales) **2** alimento

feedback /'fiːdbæk/ n reacción

feel /fiːl/ (pt/pp felt) **1** vt sentir, tocar: ~ the cold ser friolento ◊ She felt the water. Probó la temperatura del agua. **2** vi sentirse: ~ good/sad sentirse bien/triste ◊ ~ cold/hungry tener frío/hambre **3** vt, vi opinar: How do you ~ about it? ¿Qué opinas? **4** vi parecer: It ~s like silk. Parece seda. ▸ **feel like/as if/though...:** I ~ as if I'm going to be sick. Creo que voy a vomitar. **feel like sth:** I felt like hitting him. Me dieron ganas de agarrarlo a golpes. **feel yourself** sentirse bien ■ feel **about/around for sth** buscar algo a tientas **feel for sb** sentir lástima por algn **feel up to sth** sentirse capaz de algo ● *n*: *Let me have a ~*. Déjame tocarlo. ▶ **get the feel of sth** familiarizarse con algo

feeling /'fi:lɪŋ/ *n* **1** sensación **2** [*sing*] (*opinión*) sentir **3 feelings** sentimientos **4** sensibilidad ▶ **bad/ill feelings** resentimiento

feet /fi:t/ *pl de* FOOT

fell /fel/ *pt de* FALL ● **1** *vt* (*árbol*) talar **2** *vt* derribar

fellow /'feloʊ/ *n* **1** compañero: *~ countryman* compatriota ◊ *~ passenger* compañero de viaje **2** (*coloq*) tipo

fellowship /'feloʊʃɪp/ *n* compañerismo

felt /felt/ *pt, pp de* FEEL ● *n* fieltro

felt-tip pen (*tb* **felt tip**) *n* marcador, plumón

female /'fi:meɪl/ *adj* **1** femenino → FEMENINO **2** hembra **NOTA Female** y **male** especifican el sexo de personas o animales: *a female/male friend, rabbit*, etc. **3** de la mujer: *equality* la igualdad de la mujer ● *n* hembra

feminine /'femənɪn/ *adj, n* femenino (*propio de la mujer*) → FEMALE

feminism /'femənɪzəm/ *n* feminismo **feminist** *n* feminista

fence /fens/ *n* **1** cerca o alambrada, malla (*And*) ● **1** *vt* cercar **2** *vi* practicar la esgrima **fencing** *n* esgrima

fend /fend/ *v* ■ **fend for yourself** valerse por sí mismo **fend sth/sb off** rechazar algo/a algn

fender /'fendər/ *n* (*USA*) **1** guardabarros, salpicadera **2** aleta

ferment /fər'ment/ *vt, vi* fermentar ● /'fɜːment/ *n* (*fml*) ebullición

fern /fɜːrn/ *n* helecho

ferocious /fə'roʊʃəs/ *adj* feroz

ferocity /fə'rɒsəti/ *n* ferocidad

ferry /'feri/ *n* (*pl* **-ies**) ferry, transbordador **2** balsa (*para cruzar ríos*) ● *vt* (*pt/pp* **-ied**) transportar

fertile /'fɜːrtl; -taɪl *GB*/ *adj* fértil, fecundo **fertility** /fər'tɪləti/ *n* fertilidad

fertilize /'fɜːrtəlaɪz/ *vt* **1** fertilizar **2** abonar **3** fecundar **fertilizer** *n* **1** fertilizante **2** abono **fertilization** *n* **1** fertilización **2** fecundación

fervent /'fɜːrvənt/ *adj* ferviente

fester /'festər/ *vi* infectarse

festival /'festɪvl/ *n* **1** (*Cine, Mús*, etc.) festival **2** (*Rel*) fiesta

fetch /fetʃ/ *vt* **1** traer **2** buscar, ir a recoger **3** alcanzar (*precio*)

fête /feɪt/ *n* fiesta

fetus /'fi:təs/ *n* feto

feud /fju:d/ *n* rencilla ● *vi* tener un pleito

feudal /'fju:dl/ *adj* feudal **feudalism** *n* feudalismo

fever /'fi:vər/ *n* fiebre **feverish** *adj* febril

few /fju:/ *adj, pron* **1** (*-er/-est*) pocos: *every ~ minutes* cada pocos minutos ◊ *fewer than six* menos de seis → LESS **2 a few** unos cuantos, algunos **NOTA Few** tiene un sentido negativo y significa "poco". A **few** tiene un sentido más positivo y equivale a "unos cuantos", "algunos": *Few people turned up*. Vino poca gente. ◊ *I have a ~ friends coming*. Vienen unos cuantos amigos. ▶ **few and far between** contadísimos **quite a few; a good few** (*GB*) un buen número (de), bastante(s)

fiancé (*fem* **fiancée**) /ˌfiːɑːnˈseɪ; friˈɒnseɪ *GB*/ *n* prometido/a

fiasco /fiˈæskoʊ/ *n* (*pl* **-s/-es**) desastre

fib /fɪb/ *n* (*coloq*) cuento (*mentira*) ● *vi* (*coloq*) (**-bb-**) decir mentiras

fiber (**fibre** *GB*) /'faɪbər/ *n* fibra **fibrous** *adj* fibroso

fickle /'fɪkl/ *adj* voluble

fiction /'fɪkʃn/ *n* ficción

fiddle /'fɪdl/ *n* (*coloq*) **1** violín **2** (*GB*) estafa ● **1** *vi* ~ (*about/around*) juguetear **2** *vt* (*coloq*) (*gastos*, etc.) falsificar **3** *vi* tocar el violín ■ **fiddle about/around** perder el tiempo **fiddler** *n* violinista

fiddly /'fɪdli/ *adj* (*coloq*) complicado

fidelity /fɪ'deləti/ *n* fidelidad **NOTA** Es más común **faithfulness**.

field /fi:ld/ *n* campo

fiend /fi:nd/ *n* **1** desalmado/a **2** (*coloq*) fanático/a **fiendish** *adj* (*coloq*) endiablado

fierce /fɪərs/ *adj* (*-er/-est*) **1** (*animal*) feroz **2** (*oposición*) fuerte

fifteen /ˌfɪf'ti:n/ *adj, n, pron* quince **fifteenth** **1** *adj, pron* decimoquinto **2** *n* quinceavo

fifth (*abrev* **5th**) /fɪfθ/ *adj, adv, pron* quinto ● *n* **1** quinto **2 the fifth** el (día) cinco **3** (*tb* ~ **gear**) quinta: *change into ~* meter la quinta

fifty /'fɪfti/ *adj, n, pron* cincuenta ▶ **go fifty-fifty** pagar por partes iguales **fiftieth** 1 *adj, pron* quincuagésimo 2 *n* cincuentavo

fig /fɪg/ *n* 1 higo 2 (*tb* ~ tree) higuera

fight /faɪt/ *n* 1 lucha, pelea 2 combate **NOTA** Para un conflicto continuado, se usa más **fighting**: *There has been heavy fighting in the capital.* ▸ **give up without a fight** rendirse sin luchar **put up a good fight** oponer resistencia ● (*pt/pp* fought) 1 *vi, vt* luchar (contra): *a battle against algo* 2 *vi, vt* pelearse (con) 3 *vt* combatir ▸ **fight it out**: *They must ~ it out between them.* Deben arreglarlo entre ellos. **fight your way across, into, etc.** abrirse paso a la fuerza hacia, en, etc. algo ■ **fight back** contraatacar **fight sth/sb off** repeler a algn

fighter /ˈfaɪtər/ *n* 1 luchador/a, combatiente 2 caza (*avión*)

figure /ˈfɪɡjər; ˈfɪɡə(r) *GB*/ *n* 1 cifra, número 2 cantidad, suma 3 figura: *a key* ~ un personaje clave 4 cuerpo 5 silueta ▸ **put a figure on sth** poner precio a, dar una cifra sobre algo ● 1 *vi* figurar 2 *vi* (*coloq*): *It/That ~s.* Se comprende. 3 *vt* figurarse ■ **figure sth/sb out** entender algo/a algn

file /faɪl/ *n* 1 carpeta **expediente**: *be on* ~ estar archivado 2 (*Comp*) archivo 3 lima ▸ **in single file** en fila india ● 1 *vt* archivar 2 *vt* (*demanda*) presentar 3 *vt* limar 4 *vi* ~ (*past sth*) desfilar (ante algo) 5 *vi* ~ **in, out, etc.** entrar, salir, etc. en fila

filet (**fillet** *GB*) /ˈfɪlɪt/ *n* filete

fill /fɪl/ 1 *vt, vi* ~ (**sth**) (**with sth**) llenar(se) (algo) (de algo) 2 *vt* (*grieta*) rellenar 3 *vt* (*diente*) tapar (*Mx*), calzar (*And*) 4 *vt* (*cargo*) ocupar ■ **fill in (for sb)** sustituir (a algn) **fill sb in (on sth)** poner a algn al tanto (de algo) **fill sth in/out** llenar algo (*formulario*, *etc.*)

filling /ˈfɪlɪŋ/ *n* 1 tapadura (*Mx*), calza (*And*) 2 relleno

film /fɪlm/ *n* 1 (*GB*) película: ~ *star* estrella de cine 2 película (*capa fina*) ● *vt, vi* **film** rodar **filming** *n* rodaje

film-maker *n* cineasta **film-making** *n* cinematografía

filter /ˈfɪltər/ *n* filtro ● *vt, vi* filtrar(se)

filth /fɪlθ/ *n* 1 porquería, mugre 2 groserías 3 inmundicias, porquerías (*revistas, etc.*)

filthy /ˈfɪlθi/ *adj* (**-ier/-iest**) 1 asqueroso 2 sucio 3 obsceno 4 (*carácter, etc.*) desagradable

fin /fɪn/ *n* aleta

final /ˈfaɪnl/ *adj* último, final ● *n* 1 final 2 finals (*exámenes*) finales **finalist** *n* finalista

finally /ˈfaɪnəli/ *adv* 1 por último 2 finalmente 3 por fin

finance /ˈfaɪnæns, fəˈnæns/ *n* finanzas: ~ *company* (compañía) financiera ◇ *the ~ minister* el ministro de Hacienda ● *vt* financiar **financial** /faɪˈnænʃl, fəˈnæ-/ *adj* financiero: ~ *year* año fiscal

find /faɪnd/ *vt* (*pt/pp* found) 1 encontrar: ~ *your way* encontrar el camino 2 buscar 3 (*Jur*): ~ *sb guilty* declarar a algn culpable ▸ **find fault (with sth/sb)** criticar (a algo/algn) **find your feet** adaptarse ■ **find sth out** enterarse (de algo) **find sb out** descubrirle el juego a algn **finding** *n* 1 **findings** conclusiones 2 (*Jur*) fallo

fine /faɪn/ *adj* (**-er/-est**) 1 excelente: *I'm* ~. Estoy bien. ◇ *You're a* ~ *one to talk!* ¡Mira quién habla! 2 fino 3 (*tiempo*) bueno 4 (*distinción*) sutil ▸ **one fine day** un buen día ● *adv* (*coloq*) bien: *That suits me* ~. Eso me cae/queda muy bien. ● *n* multa ● *vt* multar

fine arts *n* (*tb* **fine art**) bellas artes

finger /ˈfɪŋɡər/ *n* dedo (*de la mano*) →**MY** ▸ **be all fingers and thumbs** ser torpe **put your finger on sth** identificar algo (*con precisión*) **work your fingers to the bone** matarse trabajando

fingernail /ˈfɪŋɡərneɪl/ *n* uña (*de la mano*)

fingerprint /ˈfɪŋɡərprɪnt/ *n* huella digital

fingertip /ˈfɪŋɡərtɪp/ *n* yema del dedo ▸ **have sth at your fingertips** saber(se) algo al dedillo

finish /ˈfɪnɪʃ/ 1 *vt, vi* terminar 2 *vt* ~ **sth (off/up)** (*comida*) acabar algo ■ **finish up** acabar ● *n* 1 final 2 (*tb* ~ **line** *USA*, **finishing line** *GB*) (línea de) meta 3 acabado

finishing line *n* línea de meta

fir /fɜːr/ *n* (*tb* ~ tree) abeto

fire /ˈfaɪər/ *n* 1 fuego 2 incendio 3 calentador 4 [*U*] disparos ▸ **be/come under fire** 1 encontrarse bajo fuego enemigo 2 ser objeto de severas críticas **on fire** en llamas: *be on* ~ estar ardiendo **set fire to sth/set sth on fire** prender fuego a algo ● 1 *vt, vi* disparar 2 *vt* (*insultos*) soltar 3 *vt* despedir (*del trabajo*) 4 *vt* (*imaginación*) estimular

firearm /ˈfaɪərɑːrm/ *n* [*gen pl*] (*fml*) arma de fuego

fire department (**fire brigade** /ˈfaɪər brɪˌɡeɪd/ GB) n cuerpo de bomberos

fire engine n carro de bomberos

fire escape n escalera de incendios

fire extinguisher n extinguidor

firefighter /ˈfaɪərfaɪtər/ (tb **fireman** /ˈfaɪərmən/) (pl **-men**) n bombero →BOMBERO

fireplace /ˈfaɪərpleɪs/ n chimenea (hogar)

fire station n estación de bomberos

firewood /ˈfaɪərwʊd/ n leña

firework /ˈfaɪərwɜːk/ n 1 cohete 2 **fireworks** fuegos artificiales

firing /ˈfaɪərɪŋ/ n tiroteo: ~ line línea de fuego ◇ ~ squad pelotón de fusilamiento

firm /fɜːrm/ n firma, empresa ● adj (**-er/-est**) firme ▶ **a firm hand** mano dura **be on firm ground** pisar terreno firme ● adv ▶ **stand firm** mantenerse firme

first /fɜːrst/ (abrev **1st**) adj primero: a ~ night un estreno ◇ ~ name nombre de pila ▶ **at first hand** de primera mano **first thing** a primera hora **first things first** lo primero es lo primero ● adv 1 primero: come ~ in the race ganar la carrera 2 por primera vez 3 en primer lugar ▶ **at first** al principio **first come, first served** por orden de llegada **first of all** 1 al principio 2 en primer lugar **put sth/sb first** poner algo/a algn por encima de todo ● pron el/la primero/a, los/las primeros/as ● n 1 **the first** el (día) primero 2 (tb ~ **gear**) primera ▶ **from first to last** de principio a fin **from the (very) first** desde el primer momento

first aid n primeros auxilios: ~ kit botiquín

first class n 1 primera (clase) 2 servicio de correo rápido ● adv en primera (clase): send sth ~ mandar algo urgente **first-class** adj de primera (clase/categoría): a ~ stamp una estampilla/un timbre urgente

first-hand adj, adv de primera mano

firstly /ˈfɜːrstli/ adv en primer lugar

first-rate adj excelente, de primera (categoría)

fish /fɪʃ/ n 1 pez 2 [U] pescado: ~ and chips pescado con papas fritas **NOTA** Fish como sustantivo contable tiene dos formas para el plural: **fish** y **fishes**. Fish es más común. ▶ **like a fish**

out of water como gallina en corral ajeno ● vi pescar

fisherman /ˈfɪʃərmən/ n (pl **-men**) pescador

fishing /ˈfɪʃɪŋ/ n pesca

fishmonger /ˈfɪʃmʌŋɡər/ n pescadero/a **fishmonger's** n pescadería

fishy /ˈfɪʃi/ adj (**-ier/-iest**) 1 a pescado (oler, etc.) 2 (coloq) sospechoso: There's something ~ going on. Aquí hay gato encerrado.

fist /fɪst/ n puño **fistful** n puñado

fit /fɪt/ adj (**fitter, -est**) 1 en forma 2 ~ **for sth/sb**; ~ **to do sth** apto para algo/algn; en condiciones de hacer algo 3 ~ **to do sth** (GB, coloq) a punto de hacer algo ▶ (**as**) **fit as a fiddle** en muy buena forma (física) **fit for a king** digno de un rey **keep fit** mantenerse en forma ● (**-tt-**) (pt/pp **fit** GB **fitted**) 1 vi caber 2 vt, vi entrar (en): These shoes don't ~ (me). Estos zapatos no me quedan bien. 3 vt equipar 4 vt ~ **sth (on)to) sth** poner algo a/en algo 5 vt cuadrar con ▶ **fit (sb) like a glove** quedar (a algn) como anillo al dedo ■ **fit in (with sth/sb)** encajar (con algo/algn) ● n 1 ataque (risa, tos, etc.) 2 (ropa): be a good/tight ~ quedar a algn bien/ajustado ▶ **have/throw a fit:** She'll have a ~! ¡Le va a dar un ataque!

fitness /ˈfɪtnəs/ n forma (física)

fitted /ˈfɪtɪd/ adj 1 instalado: ~ cupboards armarios empotrados 2 (habitación) amueblado

fitting /ˈfɪtɪŋ/ adj apropiado ● n 1 repuesto, pieza 2 (vestido) prueba: ~ room probador/vestier (And)

five /faɪv/ adj, pron, n cinco **fiver** n (GB, coloq) (billete de) cinco libras

fix /fɪks/ vt 1 fijar 2 arreglar 3 establecer 4 (comida) preparar 5 (coloq) falsificar 6 (coloq) ajustar las cuentas a ■ **fix on sth/sb** decidirse por algo/algn **fix sb up (with sth)** (coloq) conseguirle algo a algn **fix sth up** 1 arreglar algo 2 reparar, retocar algo ● n [sing] lío: be in/get yourself into a ~ estar/meterse en un lío

fixed /fɪkst/ adj fijo ▶ (**of**) **no fixed abode/address** sin domicilio fijo

fixture /ˈfɪkstʃər/ n 1 accesorio fijo de una casa 2 (GB) cita deportiva

fizz /fɪz/ vi 1 burbujear 2 silbar **fizzy** adj con gas, gaseoso

flabby /ˈflæbi/ adj (coloq) fofo

F

flag /flæg/ n 1 bandera 2 banderín ● vi (-gg-) flaquear

flagrant /'fleɪgrənt/ adj flagrante

flair /fleər/ n 1 [sing] aptitud 2 estilo, elegancia

flake /fleɪk/ n copo ● vi ~ (off/ away) desprenderse (en escamas)

flamboyant /flæm'bɔɪənt/ adj 1 extravagante 2 llamativo

flame /fleɪm/ n llama

flamingo /flə'mɪŋgoʊ/ n (pl -s/ -es) flamenco

flammable /'flæməbl/ adj inflamable →INFLAMMABLE

flan /flæn/ n pay (dulce) → PIE
NOTA La palabra española "flan" se traduce por **crème caramel**.

flank /flæŋk/ n 1 (persona) costado 2 (animal) ijar 3 (Mil) flanco ● vt flanquear

flannel /'flænl/ n 1 franela 2 (GB) toalla de cara

flap /flæp/ n 1 (sobre) solapa 2 (bolso) tapa 3 (mesa) hoja plegable 4 (avión) alerón ● (-pp-) 1 vt, vi agitar(se) 2 vt (alas) batir

flare /fleər/ n 1 bengala 2 destello 3 **flares** pantalón acampanado ● vi 1 llamear 2 estallar: Tempers flared. Se encendieron los ánimos. ■ **flare up 1** (re)avivarse 2 (conflicto) estallar

flash /flæʃ/ n 1 destello: a ~ of lightning un relámpago 2 golpe: a ~ of genius un golpe de genio 3 (Fot) flash 4 noticia de última hora ▸ **a flash in the pan**: It was no ~ in the pan. No fue flor de un día. **in a/like a flash** en un abrir y cerrar de ojos ● vi 1 centellear, brillar: It flashed on and off. Se encendía y apagaba. 2 vt dirigir (luz): ~ your headlights hacer señales con los faros 3 vt mostrar rápidamente (imagen) ■ **flash by, past, etc.** pasar, cruzar, etc. como un rayo

flashlight /'flæʃlaɪt/ n (USA) linterna

flashy /'flæʃi/ adj (-ier/-iest) ostentoso, llamativo

flask /flæsk; flɑːsk GB/ n 1 (GB) termo 2 licorera (de bolsillo)

flat /flæt/ n 1 (GB) apartamento, departamento 2 (de la mano) palma 3 [gen pl] (Geog): mud ~s marismas 4 (Mús) bemol 5 (USA) pinchazo, ponchadura (Mx) ● adj (flatter, -est) 1 plano 2 (llanta) desinflado, ponchado (Mx) 3 (GB, batería) descargado 4 (bebida) sin gas 5 (Mús) desafinado ● adv: lie down ~ acostarse completamente ▸ **flat out** (coloq) a tope (trabajar, correr, etc.). **in five seconds, etc. flat** (coloq) en sólo cinco segundos, etc. **flatly** rotundamente

flatten /'flætn/ 1 vt ~ sth (out) aplanar, alisar algo 2 vt aplastar 3 vi ~ (out) (paisaje) allanarse

flatter /'flætər/ vt 1 adular, halagar 2 (ropa, etc.) favorecer 3 ~ yourself hacerse ilusiones **flattering** adj favorecedor, halagador

flaunt /flɔːnt/ vt (pey) alardear de

flavor (-our GB) /'fleɪvər/ n sabor, gusto ● vt dar sabor a, condimentar

flaw /flɔː/ n 1 imperfección 2 falla, defecto **flawed** adj defectuoso **flawless** adj impecable

flea /fliː/ n pulga: ~ market mercado de pulgas/cháchara

fleck /flek/ n mota (polvo, color)

flee /fliː/ (pt/pp fled /fled/) 1 vi huir, escapar 2 vt abandonar

fleece n 1 lana 2 saco (de felpa)

fleet /fliːt/ n flota

flesh /fleʃ/ n 1 carne 2 (fruta) pulpa ▸ **flesh and blood** carne y hueso **in the flesh** en persona **your own flesh and blood** (pariente) de tu propia sangre

flew /fluː/ pt de FLY

flex /fleks/ n cable eléctrico ● vt flexionar

flexible /'fleksəbl/ adj flexible

flick /flɪk/ n 1 movimiento rápido: a ~ of the wrist un giro de la muñeca 2 capirotazo ● vt 1 pegar 2 ~ sth (off, on, etc.) mover algo rápidamente ■ **flick through sth** hojear algo rápidamente

flicker /'flɪkər/ vi parpadear: a flickering light una luz titilante ● n 1 (luz) parpadeo 2 atisbo

flies n (GB) [pl] bragueta

flight /flaɪt/ n 1 vuelo 2 huida 3 (aves) bandada 4 (escalera) tramo ▸ **take flight** darse a la fuga

flight attendant n auxiliar de vuelo, sobrecargo

flimsy /'flɪmzi/ adj (-ier/-iest) 1 enebre, débil 2 (tela) fino

flinch /flɪntʃ/ vi 1 retroceder 2 ~ from sth echarse atrás ante algo/a la hora de hacer algo

fling /flɪŋ/ vt (pt/pp flung) 1 ~ sth (at sth) arrojar, lanzar algo (contra algo): She flung her arms around him. Le echó los brazos al cuello. 2 dar un empujón a: ~ open the door abrir la puerta de un golpe ● n (coloq) 1 juerga 2 aventura (amorosa)

flint /flɪnt/ n **1** pedernal **2** piedra (de encendedor)

flip /flɪp/ (**-pp-**) **1** vt echar a cara **2** vt, vi ~ (**sth**) (**over**) dar(se) (a algo) la vuelta **3** vi (coloq) enloquecer

flip-flop n chancla (de plástico)

flippant /ˈflɪpənt/ adj frívolo

flirt /flɜːrt/ vi coquetear ● n coqueto/a: He's a great ~. Siempre está coqueteando.

flit /flɪt/ vi (**-tt-**) revolotear

float /floʊt/ vi **1** flotar **2** vt (barco) poner a flote **3** vt (idea) proponer ● n **1** (carnaval) carroza, carro alegórico **2** boya **3** flotador

flock /flɑːk/ n **1** rebaño (ovejas) **2** bandada **3** multitud ● vi **1** agruparse **2** acudir en tropel

flog /flɑːɡ/ vt (**-gg-**) **1** azotar **2** ~ **sth** (**off**) (GB, coloq) vender algo ▸ **flog a dead horse** (GB, coloq) malgastar saliva

flood /flʌd/ n **1** inundación **2 the Flood** el Diluvio **3** (fig) avalancha ● vt, vi inundar(se) **2** vi ~ **in** llegar en avalancha

flooding /ˈflʌdɪŋ/ n [U] inundaciones

floodlight /ˈflʌdlaɪt/ n foco, reflector ● vt (pt/pp **-lit** /-lɪt/) iluminar con focos/reflectores

floor /flɔːr/ n **1** suelo **2** planta, piso ⇒PISO **3** (mar, valle) fondo ● vt **1** dejar a algn sin saber qué decir **2** (contrincante) tumbar

floorboard /ˈflɔːrbɔːrd/ n tabla (del suelo)

flop /flɑːp/ n **1** fracaso ● vi (**-pp-**) **1** desplomarse **2** (coloq) fracasar

floppy /ˈflɑːpi/ adj (**-ier/-iest**) **1** flojo, flexible **2** (orejas) caído ● n (tb ~ **disk**) disquete

flora /ˈflɔːrə/ n flora **floral** adj de flores

florist /ˈflɔːrɪst; ˈflɑːr- GB/ n florista, vendedor/a de flores **florist's** n floristería

flounder /ˈflaʊndər/ vi **1** tambalearse **2** balbucear **3** caminar con dificultad

flour /ˈflaʊər/ n harina

flourish /ˈflɜːrɪʃ; ˈflʌr- GB/ vi **1** prosperar **2** vt (arma) blandir ● n floreo

flow /floʊ/ n **1** flujo **2** caudal **3** circulación **4** suministro ● vi **1** fluir: ~ into the sea desembocar en el mar **2** circular **3** flotar **4** ~ **in/out** (marea) subir/bajar

flower /ˈflaʊər/ n flor ● vi florecer

flowering /ˈflaʊərɪŋ/ n floreciomiento ● adj (planta) que da flores

flowerpot /ˈflaʊərpɑːt/ n maceta, matera (And)

flown /floʊn/ /floʊn/ pp de FLY

flu /fluː/ n [U] gripa

fluctuate /ˈflʌktʃueɪt/ vi variar

fluent /ˈfluːənt/ adj **1** She's ~ in Russian. Habla ruso con fluidez. ◇ **speak ~ English** dominar el inglés **2** (orador) elocuente **3** (estilo) fluido

fluff /flʌf/ n **1** pelusa: a piece of ~ una pelusa **2** (aves) plumón **fluffy** adj (**-ier/-iest**) **1** de pelusa **2** mullido, esponjoso

fluid /ˈfluːɪd/ adj **1** fluido, líquido **2** (fml) (situación) variable, inestable **3** (fml) (estilo, etc.) fluido, suelto ● n **1** líquido **2** fluido

fluke /fluːk/ n (coloq) chiripa

flung /flʌŋ/ pt, pp de FLING

flurry /ˈflɜːri; ˈflʌri GB/ n (pl **-ies**) **1** (actividad, etc.) frenesí **2** ráfaga

flush /flʌʃ/ n rubor: hot flushes sofocos/calores ● vi **1** ponerse colorado **2** vt (sanitario) vaciar

fluster /ˈflʌstər/ vt aturdir: get flustered ponerse nervioso

flute /fluːt/ n flauta (traversa)

flutter /ˈflʌtər/ vi (pájaro) revolotear **2** vt, vi (alas) agitar(se), batir(se) **3** vi ondear ● n **1** (alas) aleteo **2** pestañeo

fly /flaɪ/ n (pl **flies**) **1** mosca **2** bragueta ● (pt **flew** pp **flown**) **1** vi volar: ~ away/off irse volando **2** vi (persona) ir/viajar en avión: ~ in/out/back llegar/partir/regresar (en avión) **3** vt pilotear **4** vt transportar (en avión) **5** vi de prisa: I must ~. Me voy corriendo. **6** vi (repentinamente): The wheel flew off. La rueda salió disparada. ◇ The door flew open. La puerta se abrió de golpe. **7** vi ondear **8** vt (bandera) enarbolar **9** vt (cometa) volar ▸ **fly high** ser ambicioso **let fly at sth/sb** atacar algo/a algn **let fly with sth** disparar con algo ▸ **fly at sb** lanzarse sobre algn

flying /ˈflaɪɪŋ/ n volar: ~ lessons clases de vuelo ● adj volador

flying saucer n platillo volador

flying start ▸ **get off to a flying start** empezar con el pie derecho

flyover /ˈflaɪoʊvər/ n (GB) paso elevado

foal /foʊl/ n potro ⇒POTRO

foam /foʊm/ n **1** espuma **2** (tb ~ **rubber**) hule/caucho espuma ● vi echar espuma

focus /ˈfoʊkəs/ n foco ▸ **in focus/out of focus** enfocado/desenfocado ● **1** vt, vi enfocar **2** vt concentrar: ~ your attention on sth concentrarse en algo

fodder /ˈfɑːdər/ n forraje

foetus /GB/ = FETUS

fog /fɔːg; fɒg GB/ n niebla ● vi (-gg-) ~ (up) empañarse **foggy** adj (-ier/-iest): a ~ day un día de niebla

foil /fɔɪl/ n lámina: aluminum ~ papel de aluminio ● vt frustrar

fold /fəʊld/ 1 vt, vi doblar(se), plegar(se): ~ your arms cruzar los brazos 2 vi (empresa) irse abajo 3 vi (obra de teatro) cerrar ■ **fold (sth) back/down/up** doblar(se) (algo) ● n 1 pliegue 2 redil **folding** adj [antes de sustantivo] plegable

folder /ˈfəʊldər/ n carpeta

folk /fəʊk/ n (coloq) 1 [tb folks [pl]] gente: country ~ gente de pueblo **folks** [pl] familia ● adj folklórico, popular

follow /ˈfɒləʊ/ 1 vt, vi seguir 2 vt, vi entender 3 vi ~ (on) (from sth) resultar, ser la consecuencia de (algo) ■ **as follows** como sigue **follow the crowd** hacer lo que hacen los demás ■ **follow on** seguir **follow sth through** seguir con algo hasta el final **follow sth up** 1 Follow up your call with a letter. Confirma por carta lo hablado por teléfono. 2 (investigar) seguir algo **follower** n seguidor/a

following /ˈfɒləʊɪŋ/ adj siguiente ● n **the following** lo siguiente/lo que sigue ● prep tras, después de

follow-up n (pl -ups) continuación

fond /fɒnd/ adj (-er/-est) 1 [antes de sustantivo] cariñoso: ~ memories recuerdos gratos **2 be ~ of sb** tenerle cariño a algn **3 be ~ of sth** ser aficionado a algo

fondle /ˈfɒndl/ vt acariciar

font /fɒnt/ n 1 (Comp) tipo de letra 2 pila (bautismal)

food /fuːd/ n [gen U] comida, alimento: Italian ~ la comida italiana ◊ frozen ~ comida congelada ■ **food for thought** algo en que pensar

food processor n procesador de alimentos

foodstuffs /ˈfuːdstʌfs/ n [pl] alimentos

fool /fuːl/ n tonto, bobo ▶ **act/play the fool** hacer(se) el tonto **be no/nobody's fool** no tener un pelo de tonto, no dejarse engañar por nadie **make a fool of yourself/sb** ponerse/poner a algn en ridículo ● vi 1 bromear 2 vt engañar ■ **fool around/about** perder el tiempo: Stop fooling around! ¡Deja de jugar! **foolish** adj 1 tonto 2 ridículo

foolproof /ˈfuːlpruːf/ adj infalible

foot /fʊt/ n 1 (pl feet) pie: at the ~ of the stairs al pie de las escaleras → MY 2 (pl feet o foot) (abrev ft.) (medida) pie (30,48 cm) → Ver pág. 222 ▶ **fall/land on your feet** salirle las cosas bien a algn **on foot** a pie **put your feet up** descansar **put your foot down** oponerse (enérgicamente) **put your foot in your mouth/in it** (GB) meter la pata ● vt ▶ **foot the bill (for sth)** (coloq) pagar los gastos (de algo)

football /ˈfʊtbɔːl/ n 1 (USA) fútbol americano 2 (GB) fútbol 3 balón (de fútbol) **footballer** n futbolista

footing /ˈfʊtɪŋ/ n [sing] 1 equilibrio 2 situación: on an equal ~ en igualdad de condiciones

footnote /ˈfʊtnəʊt/ n nota (a pie de página)

footpath /ˈfʊtpɑːθ; -pæθ GB/ n sendero: public ~ camino público

footprint /ˈfʊtprɪnt/ n huella

footstep /ˈfʊtstep/ n pisada, paso

footwear /ˈfʊtweər/ n [U] calzado

for /fər, fɔːr/ prep 1 para: What's it ~? ¿Para qué sirve? ◊ the train ~ London el tren que va a Londres ◊ It's time ~ bed. Es hora de acostarse. 2 por: ~ her own good por su propio bien 3 (expresiones de tiempo) durante, desde hace: I'm going ~ a month. Me voy por un mes. ◊ How long are you here ~? ¿Cuánto tiempo vas a estar acá? ◊ I haven't seen him ~ two days. No lo veo desde hace dos días. **NOTA** Cuando for se traduce por "desde hace" se puede confundir con since. Ambas palabras se usan para expresar el tiempo que ha durado la acción del verbo, pero for especifica la duración de la acción y since el comienzo: I've been here ~ three months. ◊ I've been here since May. En ambos casos se usa el present perfect o el past perfect, nunca el presente. 4 (apoyo) a favor de 5 [+ infinitivo]: There's no need ~ you to go. No hace falta que vayas. ◊ It's impossible ~ me to do it. Me es imposible hacerlo. 6 (otros usos): I ~ Irene I de Irene ◊ ~ miles and miles millas tras milla ◊ What does he do ~ a job? ¿Qué trabajo tiene? ▶ **be (in) for it** (coloq): He's ~ it now! ¡Se va a meter en la grande! **for all 1** a pesar de **2 For all I know...** Que yo sepa... **NOTA** Para el uso de for en PHRASAL VERBS ver el verbo, p. ej. **look for** en LOOK. ● conj (fml) ya que

F

forbid /fərˈbɪd/ vt (pt **forbade** /fərˈbæd, -ˈbeɪd/ pp **forbidden** /fərˈbɪdn/) prohibir: They forbade them from entering. Se prohibieron entrar. **forbidding** adj imponente, amenazadora

force /fɔːrs/ n fuerza: by ~ a la fuerza ▸ **be in/come into force** estar/entrar en vigor ● vt forzar, obligar ■ **force sth on/upon sb** imponer algo a algn **forceful** adj 1 fuerte, con carácter 2 (argumento) convincente 3 (ataque) con fuerza

forcible /ˈfɔːrsəbl/ adj 1 a/por la fuerza 2 convincente **forcibly** adv 1 por la fuerza 2 enérgicamente

ford /fɔːrd/ n vado ● vt vadear

fore /fɔːr/ adj delantero, anterior ● n ▸ **be at the fore** destacarse ▸ **come to the fore** hacerse importante

forearm /ˈfɔːrɑːrm/ n antebrazo

forecast /ˈfɔːrkæst; -kɑːst GB/ vt (pt/pp **forecast/forecasted**) pronosticar ● n pronóstico

forefinger /ˈfɔːrfɪŋɡər/ n dedo índice

forefront /ˈfɔːrfrʌnt/ n ▸ **at/in the forefront of sth** en la vanguardia de algo

foreground /ˈfɔːrɡraʊnd/ n primer plano

forehead /ˈfɔːrhed, ˈfɔːrəd; ˈfɒrɪd GB/ n (Anat) frente

foreign /ˈfɔːrən; ˈfɒr- GB/ adj 1 extranjero 2 exterior: ~ exchange divisas ◊ Foreign Office/ Secretary Secretaría/Secretario de Asuntos Exteriores 3 ~ to sth/sb (fml) ajeno a algo/algn **foreigner** n extranjero/a

foremost /ˈfɔːrmoʊst/ adj más destacado ● adv principalmente

forerunner /ˈfɔːrʌnər/ n precursor/a

foresee /fɔːrˈsiː/ vt (pt **foresaw** /fɔːrˈsɔː/ pp **foreseen** /fɔːrˈsiːn/) prever **foreseeable** adj previsible: for the ~ future en un futuro previsible

foresight /ˈfɔːrsaɪt/ n previsión

forest /ˈfɔːrɪst; ˈfɒr- GB/ n bosque **NOTA** Un wood suele ser más pequeño que un **forest**.

foretell /fɔːrˈtel/ vt (pt/pp **foretold** /fɔːrˈtoʊld/) (fml) predecir

forever /fəˈrevər/ adv 1 (tb **for ever** GB) para siempre 2 siempre

foreword /ˈfɔːrwɜːrd/ n prefacio

forge /fɔːrdʒ/ n fragua ● vt 1 forjar 2 (dinero, etc.) falsificar ■ **forge ahead** progresar con rapidez **forgery** n (pl -ies) falsificación

forget /fərˈɡet/ (pt **forgot** /fərˈɡɑːt/ pp **forgotten** /fərˈɡɑːtn/) vt, vi ~ ((about) sth/sb) olvidar algo/a algn: olvidarse (de algo/algn) ▸ **not forgetting...** (GB) sin olvidarse de... **forgetful** adj olvidadizo

forgive /fərˈɡɪv/ vt (pt **forgave** /fərˈɡeɪv/ pp **forgiven** /fərˈɡɪvn/) perdonar **forgiveness** n perdón **forgiving** adj indulgente

fork /fɔːrk/ n 1 tenedor 2 (para cultivar) horqueta 3 bifurcación ● vi 1 bifurcarse 2 ~ left torcer a la izquierda ■ **fork out** (for/on sth) (coloq) desembolsar dinero (para algo)

form /fɔːrm/ n 1 forma 2 formulario, forma (Mx): application ~ hoja de solicitud 3 formas: as a matter of ~ porque así se acostumbra 4 (GB, Educ) año: in the first ~ en primero 5 (GB) in/off ~ en forma/en baja forma ● 1 vt formar, constituir 2 vi formarse

formal /ˈfɔːrml/ adj 1 (ademán, etc.) ceremonioso 2 (comida, ropa) formal 3 (declaración, etc.) oficial **formally** adv 1 oficialmente 2 de etiqueta

formality /fɔːrˈmæləti/ n (pl -ies) 1 formalidad, ceremonia 2 trámite: legal formalities requisitos legales

format /ˈfɔːrmæt/ n formato ● vt (-tt-) (Comp) formatear

formation /fɔːrˈmeɪʃn/ n formación

former /ˈfɔːrmər/ adj 1 antiguo: the ~ president el ex-presidente 2 anterior: in ~ times en otros tiempos 3 primero ● the **former** pron aquel/la, aquello, aquellos/as ▸ **formerly** adv 1 anteriormente 2 antiguamente

formidable /ˈfɔːrmɪdəbl/ adj 1 extraordinario, formidable 2 (tarea) tremendo

formula /ˈfɔːrmjələ/ n (pl -s) fórmula **NOTA** En lenguaje científico, el plural es **formulae** /ˈfɔːrmjuliː/.

forsake /fərˈseɪk/ vt (pt **forsook** /fərˈsʊk/ pp **forsaken** /fərˈseɪkən/) (fml) 1 renunciar a 2 abandonar

fort /fɔːrt/ n fortificación, fuerte

forth /fɔːrθ/ adv (fml) en adelante: from that day ~ desde aquel día ▸ **and** (so on and) so forth etcétera

forthcoming /ˌfɔːrθˈkʌmɪŋ/ adj 1 próximo 2 de próxima aparición 3 disponible: No offer was ~. No hubo ninguna oferta. 4 (persona) comunicativo

F

forthright /ˈfɔːrθraɪt/ *adj* **1** directo **2** (*opinión*) franco

fortieth /ˈfɔːrtiəθ/ *adj, pron* cuadragésimo **2** *n* cuarentavo

fortify /ˈfɔːrtɪfaɪ/ *vt* (*pt/pp* -**ied**) **1** fortificar **2** (*persona*) fortalecer **fortification** *n* fortalecimiento

fortnight /ˈfɔːrtnaɪt/ *n* (GB) quincena: *a ~ today* de hoy en quince días

fortnightly /ˈfɔːrtnaɪtli/ (GB) *adj* quincenal ● *adv* cada quince días, quincenalmente

fortress /ˈfɔːrtrəs/ *n* fortaleza

fortunate /ˈfɔːrtʃənət/ *adj* afortunado: *be ~* tener suerte **fortunately** *adv* afortunadamente

fortune /ˈfɔːrtʃuːn/ *n* **1** fortuna **2** suerte

forty /ˈfɔːrti/ *adj, n, pron* cuarenta

forward /ˈfɔːrwərd/ *adj* **1** hacia adelante **2** delantero: *a ~ position* una posición avanzada **3** *~ planning* planificación para el futuro **4** atrevido ● *adv* **1** (*tb* **forwards**) (hacia) adelante **2** en adelante: *from that day ~* a partir de entonces ● *vt* remitir: *Please ~... Remítase a...* ◊ *forwarding address* nueva dirección (a la que han de remitirse las cartas) ● *n* delantero/a

fossil /ˈfɒsl/ *n* fósil

foster /ˈfɒstər/ *vt* **1** (*fml*) fomentar **2** acoger en una familia

fought /fɔːt/ *pt, pp* de FIGHT

foul /faʊl/ *adj* **1** sucio **2** asqueroso **3** (*carácter, humor, tiempo*) horrible ● *n* (*Dep*) falta ● *vt* (*Dep*) cometer una falta contra ● **foul sth up** (*coloq*) dañar algo

foul play *n* [U] acto delictivo

found /faʊnd/ *pt, pp* de FIND ● *vt* **1** fundar **2** fundamentar: *founded on fact* basado en la realidad

foundation /faʊnˈdeɪʃn/ *n* **1** fundación **2** **the foundations** los cimientos **3** fundamento **4** (*tb ~ cream*) (*maquillaje*) base

fountain /ˈfaʊntn/ *n* fuente

fountain pen *n* pluma fuente

four /fɔːr/ *adj, n, pron* cuatro

fourteen /ˌfɔːrˈtiːn/ *adj, n, pron* catorce **fourteenth** **1** *adj, pron* decimocuarto **2** *n* catorceavo

fourth (*abrev* **4th**) /fɔːrθ/ *adj, adv, pron* cuarto ● *n* **1** **the fourth** el (día) cuatro **2** (*tb ~ gear*) cuarta NOTA Para hablar de proporciones, "un cuarto" se dice a **quarter**: *We ate a quarter of the cake each.*

fowl /faʊl/ *n* ave (de corral)

fox /fɒks/ *n* zorro

foyer /ˈfɔɪər; ˈfɔɪeɪ GB/ *n* vestíbulo, foyer

fraction /ˈfrækʃn/ *n* fracción

fracture /ˈfræktʃər/ *n* fractura ● *vt, vi* fracturar(se)

fragile /ˈfrædʒl; -dʒaɪl GB/ *adj* frágil, delicado

fragment /ˈfrægmənt/ *n* fragmento, parte ● /frægˈment/ *vt, vi* fragmentar(se)

fragrance /ˈfreɪɡrəns/ *n* fragancia, aroma, perfume **fragrant** *adj* aromático

frail /freɪl/ *adj* frágil, delicado (*esp personas ancianas*)

frame /freɪm/ *n* **1** marco **2** armazón, estructura **3** montura ▸ **frame of mind** estado de ánimo ● *vt* **1** enmarcar **2** (*pregunta, etc.*) formular **3** (*coloq*) ~ **sb** declarar en falso para incriminar a algn

framework /ˈfreɪmwɜːrk/ *n* **1** armazón, estructura **2** marco

frank /fræŋk/ *adj* franco

frantic /ˈfræntɪk/ *adj* frenético, desesperado

fraternal /frəˈtɜːrnl/ *adj* fraternal

fraternity /frəˈtɜːrnəti/ *n* (*pl* -**ies**) **1** hermandad, cofradía, sociedad **2** (*fml*) fraternidad **fraternal** *adj* fraternal

fraud /frɔːd/ *n* **1** (*delito*) fraude **2** (*persona*) impostor/a

fraught /frɔːt/ *adj* **1** ~ **with sth** lleno, cargado de algo **2** preocupante, tenso

fray /freɪ/ *vt, vi* desgastar(se), raer(se), deshilachar(se)

freak /friːk/ *n* **1** (*coloq*) fanático/a **2** (*pey*) bicho raro ● *adj* [*antes de sustantivo*] insólito, inesperado

freckle /ˈfrekl/ *n* peca **freckled** *adj* pecoso

free /friː/ *adj* (**freer** /ˈfriːər/ **freest** /ˈfriːɪst/) **1** libre: ~ *speech* libertad de expresión ◊ ~ *kick* tiro libre ◊ *set sb ~* poner a algn en libertad **2** (*sin atar*) suelto **3** gratuito: ~ *of charge* gratis ◊ ~ *admission* entrada libre **4** ~ **with sth** generoso con algo ▸ **free and easy** relajado, informal **get, have, etc. a free hand** tener las manos libres ● *vt* (*pt/pp* **freed**) **1** liberar **2** librar, eximir **3** soltar ● *adv* gratis **freely** *adv* **1** libremente, copiosamente **2** generosamente

freedom /ˈfriːdəm/ *n* **1** libertad **2** ~ **from sth** inmunidad contra algo

free-range *adj* de granja

freeway /ˈfriːweɪ/ *n* (*USA*) carretera, autopista

free will *n* libre albedrío ▸ **of your own free will** por voluntad propia

freeze /friːz/ (pt **froze** pp **frozen**)
1 vt, vi congelar(se): *I'm freezing!*
¡Estoy muerto de frío! ◇ *freezing
point* punto de congelación 2 vt
(*comida, precios, etc.*) congelar
3 vi quedarse inmóvil: *Freeze!*
¡No te muevas! ● n 1 helada
2 (*precios, etc.*) congelación

freezer /ˈfriːzər/ n congelador

freight /freɪt/ n 1 carga: ~ *car*
vagón de carga 2 transporte

French door (**French window**
GB) n puerta (*que da al jardín*)

French fry (*esp USA*) Ver **FRY**

frenzy /ˈfrenzi/ n **frenesí** **frenzied**
adj frenético, enloquecido

frequency /ˈfriːkwənsi/ n (pl
-ies) frecuencia

frequent /ˈfriːkwənt/ adj frecuente ● /frɪˈkwent/ vt frecuentar

frequently /ˈfriːkwəntli/ adv con
frecuencia →ALWAYS

fresh /freʃ/ adj (-er/-est) 1 fresco
2 nuevo, otro 3 reciente 4 (*agua*)
dulce **freshly** adv recién: ~ *baked*
recién sacado del horno **fresh-
ness** n 1 frescura 2 novedad

freshen /ˈfreʃn/ 1 vt ~ **sth (up)** dar
nueva vida a algo 2 vi (*viento*)
refrescar ■ **freshen (yourself) up**
arreglarse

freshman /ˈfreʃmən/ n (pl **-men**)
estudiante de primer año

freshwater /ˈfreʃwɔːtər/ adj de
agua dulce

fret /fret/ vi (**-tt-**) ~ (**about/at/over**
sth) preocuparse (por algo)

friar /ˈfraɪər/ n fraile

friction /ˈfrɪkʃn/ n 1 fricción, rozamiento 2 desavenencia

Friday /ˈfraɪdeɪ, -di/ n (*abrev* **Fri.**)
viernes ▸ **Good Friday** Viernes
Santo

fridge /frɪdʒ/ n (*GB, coloq*) nevera, refrigerador

fried /fraɪd/ pt, pp de FRY ● adj
frito

friend /frend/ n 1 amigo/a 2 ~ **of/
to sth** partidario/a de algo ▸ **be/
make friends with sb** ser/hacerse
amigo de algn **have friends in
high places** tener palancas **make
friends** hacer amigos

friendly /ˈfrendli/ adj (-ier/-iest)
1 simpático **NOTA** Sympathetic
significa "compasivo". 2 (*relación,
partido*) amistoso 3 (*gesto, etc.*)
amable 4 (*ambiente*) acogedor
friendliness n simpatía, cordiali-
dad

friendship /ˈfrendʃɪp/ n amistad

fright /fraɪt/ n susto

frighten /ˈfraɪtn/ vt asustar, dar
miedo a **frightened** adj asustado

be ~ **of sth** tener miedo de algo
frightening adj alarmante

frigid /ˈfrɪdʒɪd/ adj frígido

frill /frɪl/ n 1 (*GB, costura*) volante, olán 2 **frills** adornos

fringe /frɪndʒ/ n 1 (*GB*) flequillo,
fleco (*Mx*) 2 flecos 3 margen ● vt
▸ **fringed by/with sth** bordeado
por/con algo

frisk /frɪsk/ 1 vt cachear 2 vi
juguetear **frisky** adj juguetón

frivolity /frɪˈvɒləti/ n frivolidad

frivolous /ˈfrɪvələs/ adj frívolo

fro /frəʊ/ adv ▸ **to and fro** de un
lado a otro

frock /frɒk/ n vestido

frog /frɒg/ n 1 rana
2 (*coloq, pey*) franchute/a

from /frʌm, frəm/ prep 1 (*procedencia*) de: *I'm ~ Texas.*
Soy de Texas. ◇ ~ *bad to worse*
de mal en peor 2 (*tiem-
po, situación*) desde: ~ *above/be-
low* desde arriba/abajo ◇ ~ *time
to time* de vez en cuando →SINCE
3 por: ~ *what I can gather* por lo
que yo entiendo 4 entre: *choose
~... elegir entre...* 5 con: *Wine is
made ~ grapes.* El vino se hace
con uvas. 6 (*Mat*): *13 – 34 leaves
21.* 34 menos 13 son 21. ▸ **from...
on**: ~ *now/then on* de ahora en
adelante/desde entonces
NOTA Para los usos de **from**
en PHRASAL VERBS ver el verbo,
p.ej. **hear from** en **HEAR**.

front /frʌnt/ n 1 **the front** el
frente, la (parte) delantera: *Sit
at the ~.* Siéntate adelante. 2 **the
front** (*Mil*) el frente 3 fachada
4 terreno: *on the economic ~* en el
terreno económico ● adj delantero, de delante: ~ *cover/page*
portada/primera plana ◇ ~ *row*
primera fila ● adv ▸ **in front**
adelante: *the row in ~* la fila de
adelante **up front** (*coloq*) por
adelantado ● prep ▸ **in front of**
1 delante de 2 ante
NOTA Enfrente de se traduce
por **opposite**.

front door n puerta de entrada

frontier /frʌnˈtɪər; ˈfrʌntɪə(r) *GB*/
n frontera →BORDER

frost /frɒst; frɔːst *GB*/ n 1 helada
2 escarcha ● vt, vi ~ (**sth**) (**over/
up**) cubrirse, cubrir algo de escarcha **frosty** adj (-ier/-iest) 1 helado 2 cubierto de escarcha

froth /frɒθ; frɔːθ *GB*/ n espuma ●
vi hacer espuma

frown /fraʊn/ n ceño ● vi fruncir
el ceño ■ **frown on/upon sth**
desaprobar algo

froze /frəʊz/ pt de FREEZE

frozen /'frəʊzn/ *pp de* FREEZE

fruit /fru:t/ *n* **1** [*gen* U] fruta: *~ and vegetables* frutas y verduras **2** fruto

fruitful /'fru:tfl/ *adj* fructífero

fruition /fru'ɪʃn/ *n* realización: *come to ~* verse realizado

fruitless /'fru:tləs/ *adj* infructuoso

frustrate /frʌ'streɪt; frə'streɪt *GB*/ *vt* frustrar, desbaratar **frustrating** *adj* frustrante

fry /fraɪ/ *vt, vi* (*pt/pp* fried) freír(se) ● *n* (*pl* fries) papa frita

frying pan *n* sartén ▶ *out of the frying pan into the fire* de Guatemala a guatepeor

fudge /fʌdʒ/ *n* (caramelo de) dulce de leche

fuel /'fju:əl/ *n* **1** combustible **2** carburante

fugitive /'fju:dʒətɪv/ *adj, n* fugitivo/a

fulfill (fulfil *GB*) /fʊl'fɪl/ *vt* (-ll-) **1** (*promesa*) cumplir (con) **2** (*tarea, función*) realizar **3** (*deseo*) satisfacer

full /fʊl/ *adj* (-er/-est) **1** lleno **2** *~ of sth* obsesionado por algo **3** *(fit ~ up GB)* repleto: *I'm ~ (up)*. Estoy lleno. **4** completo **5** (*discusiones*) extenso **6** (*sentido*) amplio **7** (*investigación*) detallado ▶ *full of yourself*: *be ~ of yourself* ser un creído **in full** detalladamente, íntegramente **to the full** al máximo ● *adv* **1** *~ in the face* en plena cara **2** muy: *You know ~ well that...* Sabes muy bien que... **fully** *adv* completamente, del todo

full-length *adj* **1** (*espejo*) de cuerpo entero **2** (*ropa*) largo

full stop *n* (*GB*) punto (y seguido)

full-time *adj, adv* (a/de) tiempo completo

fumble /'fʌmbl/ *vi* **1** *~ (with sth)* manipular algo (*torpemente*) **2** *~ for sth* buscar algo a tientas

fume /fju:m/ *vi* echar humo (*de rabia*) ● **fumes** *n* [*pl*] humo: *poisonous ~s* gases tóxicos

fun /fʌn/ *n* diversión: *be great/good ~* ser muy divertido ◊ *have ~* pasarla bien ◊ *take the ~ out of sth* quitar toda la gracia a algo **NOTA Fun** se usa con el verbo **be** para decir que alguien/algo es entretenido o divertido. Es más coloquial que **enjoyable**: *The party was good ~.* ◊ *Aerobics is more ~ than jogging.* **Funny** se usa para hablar de algo que se hace reír: *a funny joke* ◊ *The clowns were very funny.* Puede

significar también "extraño, raro": *The car's making a funny noise.* ▶ **make fun of sth/sb** reírse de algo/algn

function /'fʌŋkʃn/ *n* **1** función **2** ceremonia ● *vi* **1** funcionar **2** *~ as sth* servir, hacer de algo

fund /fʌnd/ *n* **1** fondo (*dinero*) **2** **funds** fondos ● *vt* financiar

fundamental /,fʌndə'mentl/ *adj* fundamental ● *n* **fundamentals** fundamentos

funeral /'fju:nərəl/ *n* **1** funeral, entierro: *~ parlor* funeraria **2** cortejo fúnebre

funfair /'fʌnfeər/ *n* (*GB*) parque de diversiones

fungus /'fʌŋgəs/ *n* (*pl* -gi /-gaɪ, -dʒaɪ/) hongo (*no comestible*)

funnel /'fʌnl/ *n* **1** embudo **2** (*barco*) chimenea ● *vt* (-l-, -ll-*GB*) canalizar

funny /'fʌni/ *adj* (-ier/-iest) **1** gracioso, divertido **2** extraño, raro →FUN

fur /fɜ:r/ *n* **1** pelo (*de animal*) **2** piel: *a ~ coat* un abrigo de piel

furious /'fjʊəriəs/ *adj* **1** *~ (at sth/with sb)* furioso (con algo/algn) **2** (*esfuerzo, lucha, tormenta*) violento **3** (*debate*) acalorado

furnace /'fɜ:rnɪs/ *n* caldera

furnish /'fɜ:rnɪʃ/ *vt* **1** amueblar **2** *~ sth/sb with sth* suministrar algo a algo/algn **furnishings** *n* [*pl*] mobiliario

furniture /'fɜ:rnɪtʃər/ *n* [U] mobiliario, muebles: *a piece of ~* un mueble

furrow /'fʌrəʊ/ *n* surco ● *vt* hacer surcos en: *a furrowed brow* una frente arrugada

furry /'fɜ:ri/ *adj* **1** peludo **2** de peluche

further /'fɜ:rðər/ *adj* **1** más lejos **2** más: *for ~ details...* para mayor información... ▶ *until ~ notice* hasta nuevo aviso ● *adv* **1** más lejos: *How much ~ is it to Oxford?* ¿Cuánto falta para Oxford? **2** además: *Further to my letter...* En relación a mi carta... **3** más: *hear nothing ~* no tener más noticias **NOTA Farther** y **further** son ambos comparativos de **far**, pero sólo se usan **further** al referirse a distancias: *Which is ~/farther?* ¿Cuál está más lejos?

furthermore /ˌfɜ:rðə'mɔ:r/ *adv* además

furthest /'fɜ:rðɪst/ *adj, adv* (*superl de* far) más lejano/alejado

fury /'fjʊəri/ *n* furia, rabia

fuse /fjuːz/ n **1** fusible **2** mecha **3** detonador ● **1** vi fundirse **2** vt ~ **sth (together)** soldar algo

fusion /ˈfjuːʒn/ n fusión

fuss /fʌs/ n [U] alboroto, lío ▸ **make a fuss of/over sb** hacer fiestas a algn **make/kick up a fuss (about/over sth)** armar un escándalo (por algo) ● vi **1** ~ **(about)** preocuparse (por menudencia) **2** ~ **over sb** mimar a algn

fussy /ˈfʌsi/ adj **(-ier/-iest) 1** quisquilloso **2** ~ **(about sth)** exigente (con algo)

futile /ˈfjuːtl; -taɪl GB/ adj inútil

future /ˈfjuːtʃər/ n **1** futuro: in (the) ~ en el futuro/de ahora en adelante **2** porvenir ● adj futuro

fuze /fjuːz/ n (USA) detonador

fuzzy /ˈfʌzi/ adj **1** velludo, peludo **2** borroso **3** (mente) confuso

G g

G, g /dʒiː/ n (pl **G's, g's**) **1** G, g **2** (Mús) sol

gab /gæb/ n ▸ **have the gift of (the) gab** tener mucha labia

gable /ˈgeɪbl/ n hastial (triángulo de fachada que soporta el tejado)

gadget /ˈgædʒɪt/ n aparato

gag /gæg/ n **1** mordaza **2** gag ● vt (-gg-) amordazar

gage (USA) = GAUGE

gaiety /ˈgeɪəti/ n alegría

gain /geɪn/ n **1** ganancia **2** aumento ● **1** vt adquirir, ganar **2** vt aumentar: ~ two kilos engordar dos kilos **3** vi ~ **by/from sth** beneficiarse de algo **4** vi (reloj) adelantarse ▸ **gain on sth/sb** ir alcanzando algo/a algn

gait /geɪt/ n [sing] paso, andar

galaxy /ˈgæləksi/ n (pl **-ies**) galaxia

gale /geɪl/ n vendaval

gallant /ˈgælənt/ adj (fml) valiente **gallantry** n valentía

gallery /ˈgæləri/ n (pl **-ies**) **1** (tb art ~) museo →MUSEUM **2** (tienda, Teat) galería

galley /ˈgæli/ n **1** cocina (de avión o barco) **2** (Náut) galera

gallon /ˈgælən/ n (abrev **gal.**) galón →Ver pág. 222

gallop /ˈgæləp/ vt, vi (hacer) galopar ● n galope

the gallows /ˈgæləʊz/ n la horca

gamble /ˈgæmbl/ vt, vi (dinero) jugar, apostar ■ **gamble on sth** confiar en algo, arriesgarse a algo ● n **1** jugada **2** be a ~ ser arriesgado **gambler** n jugador/a **gambling** n juego

game /geɪm/ n **1** juego **2** partido **3** (cartas, ajedrez) partido **4** [U] caza ● adj: Are you ~? ¿Te animas?

gammon /ˈgæmən/ n (GB) [U] jamón (fresco salado)

gander /ˈgændər/ n ganso (macho)

gang /gæŋ/ n **1** banda, grupo (de amigos) **2** cuadrilla, brigada (trabajadores) ■ **gang up on sb** juntarse contra algn

gangster /ˈgæŋstər/ n gángster

gangway /ˈgæŋweɪ/ n **1** pasarela **2** (GB) pasillo (entre sillas, etc.)

gaol /dʒeɪl/ (GB) Ver JAIL

gap /gæp/ n **1** hueco, abertura **2** espacio (tiempo) intervalo **3** espacio **4** separación **5** (deficiencia) laguna

gape /geɪp/ vi **1** ~ **(at sth/sb)** mirar boquiabierto (algo/a algn) **2** abrirse, quedar abierto **gaping** adj enorme

garage /ˈgærɑːʒ; gəˈrɑːʒ, -rɪdʒ GB/ n **1** garaje, cochera **2** taller **3** estación de servicio

garbage /ˈgɑːrbɪdʒ/ n (esp USA) basura: ~ can bote/caneca de basura **NOTA** En inglés británico **garbage** sólo se usa en sentido figurado.

garbled /ˈgɑːrbld/ adj confuso

garden /ˈgɑːrdn/ n jardín ● vi trabajar en el jardín **gardener** n jardinero/a **gardening** n jardinería

gargle /ˈgɑːrgl/ vi hacer gárgaras

garish /ˈgeərɪʃ/ adj chillón (color)

garland /ˈgɑːrlənd/ n guirnalda

garlic /ˈgɑːrlɪk/ n [U] ajo

garment /ˈgɑːrmənt/ n (fml) prenda (de vestir)

garnish /ˈgɑːrnɪʃ/ vt adornar, aderezar ● n adorno

garrison /ˈgærɪsn/ n guarnición (militar)

garter /ˈgɑːrtər/ n (USA) liga (para medias)

gas /gæs/ n **1** gas: ~ mask máscara antigás **2** (USA) (tb **gasoline** /ˈgæsəliːn/) gasolina: ~ station gasolinera **3** (USA) [U] gases ● vt (-ss-) asfixiar con gas

gash /gæʃ/ n herida profunda

gasp /gæsp; gɑːsp GB/ **1** vi dar un grito ahogado /o/ jadear: ~ for air hacer esfuerzos para respirar **3** vt ~ **sth (out)** decir algo con voz entrecortada ● n jadeo, grito ahogado

gas pedal n (Aut) acelerador

gate /geɪt/ n puerta, reja

gatecrash /'geɪtkræʃ/ vt, vi colarse (en)

gateway /'geɪtweɪ/ n **1** entrada, puerta **2** ~ to sth pasaporte hacia algo

gather /'gæðər/ **1** vi juntarse, reunirse: ~ around acercarse ◊ ~ around sth agruparse en torno a algo **2** vi (muchedumbre) formarse **3** vt ~ sth/sb (together) reunir algo/a algn **4** vt ~ sth (in) (costura) recoger **5** vt deducir, tener entendido **6** vt ~ sth (up) recoger algo **7** vt (velocidad) ganar **gathering** n reunión

gaudy /'gɔːdi/ adj (-ier/-iest) chillón, llamativo

gauge /geɪdʒ/ n **1** medida **2** (tren) ancho de vía **3** indicador ● vt **1** calibrar, calcular **2** juzgar

gaunt /gɔːnt/ adj demacrado

gauze /gɔːz/ n gasa

gave /geɪv/ pt de GIVE

gay /geɪ/ adj, n gay, homosexual

gaze /geɪz/ vi ~ (at sth/sb) mirar fijamente (algo/a algn) →MIRAR ■ n mirada fija y larga

gear /gɪər/ n **1** equipo: camping ~ equipo de acampar **2** (Aut) marcha, cambio: out of ~ en neutral/neutro ◊ ~ shift → cambiar de velocidad **3** (Mec) engranaje ■ **gear sth to/towards sth** adaptar, enfocar algo a algo **gear (sth/sb) up** prepararse, preparar algo/a algn

gearbox /'gɪərbɒks/ n caja de cambios

geese /giːs/ pl de GOOSE

gem /dʒem/ n **1** piedra preciosa **2** (fig) joya

Gemini /'dʒemɪnaɪ/ n Géminis

gender /'dʒendər/ n **1** (Gram) género **2** sexo

gene /dʒiːn/ n gen

general /'dʒenrəl/ adj general: the ~ public el público (en general) ▸ **in general** en general ● n general **generally** adv generalmente, por lo general: ~ speaking... en términos generales...

general election n elecciones generales

generalize /'dʒenrəlaɪz/ vi generalizar **generalization** n generalización

general practice n (GB) medicina general

general practitioner Ver GP

general purpose adj de uso general

generate /'dʒenəreɪt/ vt generar

generation /ˌdʒenə'reɪʃn/ n generación: the older/younger ~ los mayores/jóvenes ◊ the ~ gap la brecha generacional

generator /'dʒenəreɪtər/ n generador

generosity /ˌdʒenə'rɒsəti/ n generosidad

generous /'dʒenərəs/ adj **1** generoso **2** (porción) abundante

genetic /dʒə'netɪk/ adj genético **genetics** n [sing] genética

genetically modified Ver GM

genial /'dʒiːniəl/ adj simpático

genital /'dʒenɪtl/ adj genital **genitals** (tb **genitalia** /ˌdʒenɪ'teɪliə/) n [pl] genitales

genius /'dʒiːniəs/ n genio

genocide /'dʒenəsaɪd/ n genocidio

gent /dʒent/ n (GB) **1** caballero **2 the Gents** [sing] (coloq) el baño (de caballeros) →TOILET

genteel /dʒen'tiːl/ adj fino, elegante **gentility** /dʒen'tɪləti/ n (fml) finura

gentle /'dʒentl/ adj (-er/-est) **1** amable, benévolo **2** suave **3** (animal) manso **gentleness** n **1** amabilidad **2** suavidad **3** mansedumbre **gently** adv **1** suavemente **2** (freír) a fuego lento

gentleman /'dʒentlmən/ n (pl -men) caballero

genuine /'dʒenjuɪn/ adj **1** auténtico **2** (persona) sincero

geography /dʒi'ɒɡrəfi/ n geografía **geographer** n geógrafo/a **geographical** /ˌdʒiːə'ɡræfɪkl/ adj geográfico

geology /dʒi'ɒlədʒi/ n geología **geological** /ˌdʒiːə'lɒdʒɪkl/ adj geológico **geologist** /dʒi'ɒlədʒɪst/ n geólogo/a

geometry /dʒi'ɒmətri/ n geometría **geometric** /ˌdʒiːə'metrɪk/ adj geométrico

geriatric /ˌdʒeri'ætrɪk/ adj, n geriátrico/a

germ /dʒɜːrm/ n germen, microbio

gesture /'dʒestʃər/ n gesto ● vi hacer señas: ~ at/to/towards sth señalar algo con la mano

get /get/ (-tt-) (pt got pp gotten, got GB)
● **get + n/pron** vt recibir, conseguir: ~ a shock llevarse un susto ◊ ~ headaches sufrir de dolores de cabeza ◊ ~ a joke entender un chiste
● **get + objeto + -ing/infinitivo** vt ~ sth/sb doing sth/to do sth hacer, conseguir que algo/algn haga algo: ~ him talking hacerle hablar

● **get + objeto + participio** *vt* (*cuando queremos que otra persona realice algo para nosotros*): ~ *your hair cut* cortarse el pelo ◊ ~ *your watch repaired* llevar el reloj a arreglar

● **get + objeto + adj** *vt* (*conseguir que algo se vuelva/haga...*): ~ *sth right* acertar algo ◊ ~ (*sb*) *ready* arreglarse/arreglar a algn

● **get + adj** *vi* volverse, hacerse: ~ *wet* mojarse ◊ ~ *better* mejorar/recuperarse

● **get + participio** *vi*: ~ *fed up with sth* cansarse de algo ◊ ~ *used to sth* acostumbrarse a algo ◊ ~ *lost* perderse **NOTA** Algunas combinaciones comunes de **get + participio** se traducen por verbos pronominales: ~ *bored* aburrirse ◊ ~ *dressed* vestirse ◊ ~ *drunk* emborracharse ◊ ~ *married* casarse. Para conjugarlos, añadimos la forma correspondiente de **get**: *She soon got used to it.* Se acostumbró enseguida. ◊ *I'm getting dressed.* Me estoy vistiendo. **Get + participio** también expresa acciones que ocurren o se realizan de forma accidental, inesperada o repentina: *I got caught in a heavy rainstorm.* Me agarró una tormenta muy fuerte. ◊ *He got hit by a ball.* Le dieron un pelotazo.

● **otros usos** ▶ **vi ~ to...** (*movimiento*) llegar a...: *Where have they got to?* ¿Dónde se metieron? **2 have get** *Ver* HAVE (1, 2) ▶ **get away from it all** (*coloq*) huir de todo y de todos **get (sb) nowhere; not get (sb) anywhere** no llevar a (algn) a ninguna parte **get there** lograrlo **NOTA** Para otras expresiones, ver el sustantivo, adjetivo, etc, p. ej. **get the hang of sth** en HANG. ■ **get about** (*GB*) *Ver* GET AROUND **get sth across** comunicar algo **get ahead (of sb)** adelantarse (a algn) **get along 1** *How did you ~ along?* ¿Cómo te fue? **2** arreglárselas **get along (together/with sb)** llevarse bien (con algn) **get around 1** moverse **2** (*rumor, etc.*) circular **get around sb** convencer a algn **get around to sth** encontrar tiempo para algo **get at sth** insinuar algo: *What are you getting at?* ¿Qué quieres decir? **get away (from...)** irse, salir (de...) **get away with sth** salvarse de un castigo por algo **get back** regresar **get back at sb** (*coloq*) vengarse de algn **get sth back** recuperar algo **get behind (with**

sth) retrasarse (con/en algo) **get by** arreglárselas **get down** bajar **get down to sth** ponerse a hacer algo **get sb down** (*coloq*) deprimir a algn **get into sth; get in 1** llegar (a un sitio) **2** (*persona*) volver a (casa) **3** subirse a (algo) (*vehículo*) bajar de algo, recoger algo **get off (sth) 1** salir (del trabajo) **2** (*vehículo*) bajar (de algo) **get off with sb** (*GB, coloq*) ligar, encariñarse con algn **get sth off (sth)** quitar algo (de algo) **get on 1** *Ver* GET ALONG **2** tener éxito en algo; *Ver* GET ONTO; **get onto sth** subirse a (algo) **get on to sth** pasar a considerar, ponerse a hablar de algo **get on (together/with sb)** llevarse bien (con algn) **get on with sth** seguir con algo **get on** poner(se) algo **get out (of sth) 1** salir (de algo): *Get out (of here)!* ¡Fuera de aquí! **2** (*vehículo*) bajar (de algo) **get out of sth** librarse de algo **get sth out of sth/sb** sacar algo de algo/algn **get over sth 1** superar algo **2** olvidar algo **3** recuperarse de algo **get through sth 1** consumir algo **2** (*tarea*) terminar algo **get through (to sb)** (*por teléfono*) ponerse en contacto (con algn) **get through to sb** entenderse con algn **get (sb/sth) together** reunir(se) (algo/a algn con algo) **get (sb) up** levantar(se) (a algn) **get sb up** levantar a algn **get up to sth 1** llegar a algo **2** meterse en algo

getaway /'getɔweɪ/ *n* fuga

ghastly /'gæstli; 'gɑː- *GB*/ *adj* (**-ier/-iest**) espantoso

ghetto /'getɔʊ/ *n* (*pl* **-s/-es**) gueto

ghost /gɔʊst/ *n* fantasma: ~ *story* historia de terror ▶ **give up the ghost** estirar la pata **ghostly** *adj* fantasmal

giant /'dʒaɪənt/ *n* gigante

gibberish /'dʒɪbərɪʃ/ *n* [U] tonterías

giddy /'gɪdi/ *adj* (**-ier/-iest**) mareado: *The wine made her* ~. El vino la mareó.

gift /gɪft/ *n* **1** regalo **2** don **3** (*coloq*) ganga ▶ **don't look a gift horse in the mouth** a caballo regalado no se le mira el diente **gifted** *adj* dotado

gift certificate (gift token/ voucher *GB*) *n* vale de regalo

gift-wrap *vt* envolver en papel de regalo

gig /gɪg/ *n* actuación (*musical*)

gigantic /dʒaɪ'gæntɪk/ *adj* gigantesco

giggle /'gɪgl/ *vi* ~ (**at sb/sth**) reírse tontamente (de algo/algn) ● *n*

1 risita **2** (GB, coloq) broma **3** the giggles [pl] (coloq): *a fit of the ~s* un ataque de risa

gilded /ˈgɪldɪd/ (tb gilt) adj dorado

gimmick /ˈgɪmɪk/ n truco publicitario o de promoción

gin /dʒɪn/ n ginebra: *a ~ and tonic* un gin-tonic

ginger /ˈdʒɪndʒər/ n jengibre ● adj (GB) pelirrojo

gingerly /ˈdʒɪndʒərli/ adv cautelosamente, sigilosamente

gipsy = GYPSY

giraffe /dʒəˈræf; -ˈrɑːf GB/ n jirafa

girl /gɜːrl/ n niña, chica

girlfriend /ˈgɜːrlfrend/ n **1** novia **2** (esp USA) amiga

gist /dʒɪst/ n ▸ **get the gist of sth** captar lo esencial de algo

give /gɪv/ n ▸ **give and take** toma y daca ● (pt gave pp given) **1** vt ~ sth ~ (to sb) dar algo (a algn): *~ a lecture* dar una conferencia **2** vt ~ (to sth) dar dinero (para algo) **3** vt ceder **4** vt (tiempo, etc.) dedicar **5** vt contagiar: *You've given me your cold.* Me pegaste tu resfriado. **6** vt conceder: *I'll ~ you that.* Te reconozco eso. ▸ **don't give me that!** (coloq) ¡no me salgas con eso! **give or take sth:** *an hour, ~ or take a few minutes* una hora, más o menos **NOTA** Para otras expresiones, ver la entrada del sustantivo, adjetivo, etc., p. ej. **give rise to sth** en RISE. ■ **give sth away** regalar algo **give sth/sb away** delatar algo/a algn **give (sb) back sth; give sth back (to sb)** devolver algo (a algn) **give in** ceder **give sth in** entregar algo **give sth out** repartir algo **give up** abandonar, rendirse **give up sth** dejar algo: *~ up hope* perder las esperanzas

given /ˈgɪvn/ pp de GIVE ● adj, prep dado: *~ name* nombre de pila

glacier /ˈgleɪʃər/ n glaciar

glad /glæd/ adj **1** be ~ (about sth/ to do sth) alegrarse (de algo): *I'm ~ (that) you could come.* Me alegro de que pudieras venir. **2** be ~ to do sth tener mucho gusto en hacer algo: *"Can I help?" "I'd be ~ to."* —¿Puede ayudar? —Con mucho gusto. **3** be ~ of sth agradecer algo **NOTA Glad** y **pleased** se refieren a circunstancias o hechos concretos: *Are you ~/pleased about getting the job?* **Happy** describe un estado mental y puede preceder al sustantivo: *Are you happy in your new job?*

◇ *a happy occasion/memory*

gladly adv con gusto

glamor (-our GB) /ˈglæmər/ n glamour **glamorous** adj glamoroso

glance /glæns; glɑːns GB/ vi ~ at/ down/over/through sth echar un vistazo a algo →MIRAR ● n vistazo: *take a ~ at sth* echar un vistazo a algo ▸ **at a glance** a simple vista

gland /glænd/ n glándula

glare /gleər/ n **1** luz deslumbrante **2** mirada desafiante ● vi ~ at sth/sb mirar de una manera desafiante algo/a algn → MIRAR

glaring adj **1** (error) evidente **2** desafiante **3** deslumbrante **glaringly** adv: *~ obvious* muy evidente

glass /glæs; glɑːs GB/ n **1** [U] vidrio: *a pane of ~* un vidrio **2** copa, vaso

glasses /ˈglæsɪz, ˈglɑːsɪz/ n gafas, lentes →PAIR

glaze /gleɪz/ n **1** barniz **2** (Cocina) glaseado ● **1** vi (ojos) ~ (over) ponerse vidrioso **2** vt barnizar **3** vt (Cocina) glasear **glazed** adj **1** (ojos) inexpresivo **2** barnizado

gleam /gliːm/ n **1** destello **2** brillo ● vi **1** destellar **2** brillar **gleaming** adj reluciente

glean /gliːn/ vt sacar (información)

glee /gliː/ n regocijo **gleeful** adj eufórico

glen /glen/ n valle estrecho

glide /glaɪd/ n deslizamiento ● vi **1** deslizarse **2** (en el aire) planear **glider** n planeador

glimmer /ˈglɪmər/ n **1** luz tenue **2** ~ (of sth) chispa (de algo): *a ~ of hope* un rayo de esperanza

glimpse /glɪmps/ n visión momentánea ● vt vislumbrar

glint /glɪnt/ vi **1** destellar **2** brillar ● n **1** destello **2** (ojos) chispa

glisten /ˈglɪsn/ vi brillar (esp superficie mojada)

glitter /ˈglɪtər/ vi relucir ● n **1** brillo **2** esplendor

gloat /gloʊt/ vi ~ (about/over sth) regodearse (de algo)

global /ˈgloʊbl/ adj **1** mundial **2** global **globalization** n globalización

globe /gloʊb/ n **1** globo **2** globo terráqueo

gloom /gluːm/ n **1** penumbra **2** tristeza **3** pesimismo **gloomy** adj (-ier/-iest) **1** oscuro **2** (día, voz, etc.) triste **3** poco prometedor **4** melancólico

glory /ˈglɔːri/ n **1** gloria **2** esplendor ● vi (pt/pp -ied) ~ in sth (fml) vanagloriarse, enorgullecerse de algo **glorious** adj 1 glorioso 2 espléndido

gloss /glɔːs; glɒs GB/ n 1 brillo 2 (tb ~ paint) (pintura de) esmalte 3 (fig) lustre 4 ~ (on sth) glosa (de algo) ■ **gloss over sth** pasar algo por alto **glossy** adj (-ier/-iest) reluciente, lustroso

glossary /ˈglɒsəri; ˈglɔːs- GB/ n (pl -ies) glosario

glove /glʌv/ n guante

glow /gloʊ/ vi 1 estar al rojo vivo 2 brillar (suavemente) 3 (cara) enrojecerse 4 ~ (with sth) rebosar (de algo) ● n 1 luz suave 2 arrebol 3 satisfacción

glucose /ˈgluːkəʊs/ n glucosa

glue /gluː/ n pegamento, pegante (And) ● vt (pt pres gluing) pegar

glutton /ˈglʌtn/ n 1 tragón/ona 2 a ~ for sth (coloq) amante de algo: be a ~ for punishment ser masoquista

GM /ˌdʒiː ˈem/ adj (abrev de genetically modified) transgénico

gnarled /nɑːld/ adj 1 (árbol, mano) retorcido 2 (tronco) nudoso

gnaw /nɔː/ vt, vi 1 ~ (at) sth roer algo 2 ~ (at) sb atormentar a algn

gnome /nəʊm/ n gnomo

go¹ /gəʊ/ vi (3ª pers sing pres goes /gəʊz/ pt went pp gone) 1 ir **NOTA** Been se usa para expresar que alguien ha ido a un lugar y ha vuelto: Have you ever been to London? **Gone** implica que esa persona no ha regresado todavía: John's gone to Paris. He'll be back in May. → **IR** 2 irse, marcharse 3 (tren, etc.) salir 4 **go + -ing** ir: go swimming/camping ir a nadar/de camping →**DEPORTE** 5 **go for a + sustantivo** ir: go for a walk ir a dar un paseo 6 (progreso) ir, salir: How's it going? ¿Cómo te va? ◊ All went well. Todo salió bien. 7 (máquina) funcionar 8 volverse, quedarse: go mad/blind volverse loco/quedarse ciego 9 hacer (sonido): Cats go "miaow". Los gatos hacen "miau". 10 desaparecer: My cough's gone. Se me quitó la tos. ◊ Is it all gone? ¿Se acabó? 11 gastarse, romperse 12 (tiempo) pasar ▶ **be going to do sth** ir a hacer algo: I'm going to buy a house. Voy a comprar una casa. **NOTA** Para otras expresiones, ver el sustantivo, adjetivo, etc., p. ej. **go astray** en ASTRAY. ■ **go about** (GB) Ver **go AROUND** (3, 4) **go about sth**: How should I go about telling him? ¿Cómo debería decírselo? **go ahead** seguir adelante **go along with sth/sb** estar conforme con algo/con lo que dice algn **go around 1** girar, dar vueltas 2 (cantidad) alcanzar 3 [con adj o -ing] andar: go around naked andar desnudo 4 (rumor) circular **go away 1** irse (de viaje) 2 (mancha) desaparecer **go back** volver (a algún sitio) **go back on sth** faltar a algo (promesa, etc.) **go by** pasar: as time goes by con el tiempo **go down 1** bajar 2 (barco) hundirse 3 (sol) ponerse **go down (with sb)** (obra, etc.) ser recibido (por algn) **go for sb** atacar a algn **go for sth/sb** ir por algo/algn: That goes for you too. Eso va para ti también. **go in** entrar **go in (sth)** caber (en algo) **go in for sth** interesarse por algo (hobby, etc.) **go into sth 1** decidir dedicarse a algo (profesión) 2 examinar algo: go into details entrar en detalles **go off 1** irse, marcharse 2 (arma) dispararse 3 (bomba) explotar 4 (alarma) sonar 5 (luz) apagarse 6 (alimentos) pasarse 7 salir: It went off well. Salió muy bien. **go off sth/sb** perder interés en algo/algn **go off with sth/sb** llevarse algo o algn **go on 1** seguir adelante 2 (luz) encenderse 3 suceder: What's going on? ¿Qué pasa? 4 continuar, seguir **go on (about sth/sb)** no parar de hablar (de algo/algn) **go out 1** salir 2 (luz) apagarse **go over sth 1** examinar algo 2 repasar algo **go over to sth** pasarse a algo (partido, etc.) **go through** ser aprobado (ley, etc.) **go through sth 1** revisar, registrar algo 2 repasar algo 3 sufrir, pasar (por) algo **go through with sth** llevar algo a cabo, seguir adelante con algo **go together; go with sth** ir bien, hacer juego (con algo) **go up 1** subir 2 (edificio) levantarse 3 estallar, explotar **go without** pasar privaciones **go without sth** arreglárselas sin algo

go² /gəʊ/ n (pl goes /gəʊz/) (GB) 1 turno: Whose go is it? ¿A quién le toca? 2 (coloq) empuje ▶ **be on the go** (coloq) no parar **have a go (at sth)** probar suerte (con algo), intentar (hacer algo)

goad /gəʊd/ vt ~ sb (into sth) incitar a algn (a hacer algo)

go-ahead the go-ahead n luz verde ● adj emprendedor

goal /gəʊl/ n 1 portería 2 gol 3 meta **goalkeeper** /ˈgəʊlkiːpər/ (coloq **goalie**) n arquero/a **goalpost** /ˈgəʊlpəʊst/ n poste de la portería

goat /gəʊt/ n cabra

gobble /'gɒbl/ vt ~ sth (up/down) engullir algo

go-between n intermediario/a

god /gɒd/ n 1 dios 2 **God** Dios

godchild /'gɒdtʃaɪld/ n (pl **-children**) ahijado/a

god-daughter n ahijada

goddess /'gɒdes/ n diosa

godfather /'gɒdfɑːðər/ n padrino

godmother /'gɒdmʌðər/ n madrina

godparent /'gɒdpeərənt/ n 1 padrino, madrina 2 **godparents** padrinos

godsend /'gɒdsend/ n regalo del cielo

godson /'gɒdsʌn/ n ahijado

goggles /'gɒglz/ n gafas, anteojos (de protección)

going /'gəʊɪŋ/ n 1 [sing] (marcha) ida: I was sad as I left the ~. Sentí que me marchaba. 2 Good ~! ¡Bien hecho! ◊ That was good ~. Fue muy rápido. ◊ The journey was hard ~. El viaje fue muy duro. ▶ **get out, etc. while the going is good** (GB) irse, etc. mientras se puede ● adj ▶ **a going concern** un negocio próspero **the going rate** la tarifa existente

gold /gəʊld/ n oro: gold-plated chapado en oro ▶ **(as) good as gold** más bueno que el pan

golden /'gəʊldən/ adj 1 de oro 2 dorado

goldfish /'gəʊldfɪʃ/ n (pl **goldfish**) pez de colores

golf /gɒlf/ n golf **golfer** n golfista

golf club n 1 club de golf 2 palo de golf

gone /gɒn; gɒn GB/ pp de GO¹ ● prep (GB, coloq): It was ~ midnight. Eran las doce pasadas.

gonna /'gɒːnə; 'gənə GB/ (coloq) Ver GOING TO

good /gʊd/ adj (ccmp **better** superl **best**) 1 bueno: Fruit is ~ for you. La fruta es buena para la salud. ◊ ~ nature bondad 2 be ~ at sth tener aptitud para algo 3 ~ to sb amable con algn ▶ **as good as** prácticamente **(as) good as new** como nuevo **good for you, her, etc.!** (coloq) ¡bien hecho! **NOTA** Para otras expresiones, ver el sustantivo, adjetivo, etc., p.ej. **a good many** en MANY. ● n 1 bien 2 **the good** [pl] los buenos ▶ **be no good (doing sth)** no servir de nada (hacer algo) **do sb good** hacerle bien a algn **for good** para siempre

goodbye /ˌgʊd'baɪ/ interj, n adiós: say ~ despedirse **NOTA** Es más

informal **bye** o **cheerio/cheers** (GB).

good-humored (-oured GB) adj 1 afable 2 de buen humor

good-looking adj atractivo

good-natured adj 1 amable 2 de buen corazón

goodness /'gʊdnəs/ n 1 bondad 2 valor nutritivo ● interj Dios mío

goods /gʊdz/ n [pl] 1 bienes 2 artículos, mercancías

goodwill /ˌgʊd'wɪl/ n buena voluntad

goose /guːs/ n (pl **geese**) ganso/a

gooseberry /'gʊzbəri; 'gʊzberi GB/ n (pl **-ies**) grosella verde espinosa que se usa en dulces

goose bumps (**goose pimples** GB) n [pl] (tb **gooseflesh** /'guːsfleʃ/) carne/piel de gallina

gorge /gɔːrdʒ/ n (Geog) cañón

gorgeous /'gɔːrdʒəs/ adj 1 (coloq) buenísimo 2 precioso

gorilla /gə'rɪlə/ n gorila

gory /'gɔːri/ adj 1 sangriento 2 morboso

gosh /gɒʃ/ interj Dios mío

go-slow n (GB) huelga pasiva, operación tortuga (And)

gospel /'gɒspl/ n evangelio

gossip /'gɒsɪp/ n 1 [U] (pey) chismes 2 (pey) chismoso/a ● vi chismear

got /gɒt/ pt, pp de GET

Gothic /'gɒθɪk/ adj gótico

gotten /'gɒtn/ (USA) pp de GET

gouge /gaʊdʒ/ vt: ~ a hole in sth hacer un agujero en algo ■ **gouge sth out** sacar algo

gout /gaʊt/ n gota (enfermedad)

govern /'gʌvərn/ vt, vi 1 gobernar 2 (acto, negocio) regir **governing** adj rector

governess /'gʌvərnəs/ n institutriz

government /'gʌvərnmənt/ n gobierno →JURADO **governmental** /ˌgʌvərn'mentl/ adj gubernamental

governor /'gʌvərnər/ n 1 gobernador/a 2 director/a

gown /gaʊn/ n 1 vestido largo 2 (Educ, Jur) toga 3 (Med) bata

GP /ˌdʒiː 'piː/ n (abrev de **general practitioner**) (GB) médico/a de medicina general

grab /græb/ (**-bb-**) 1 vt ~ sth (**hold of**) sth/sb agarrar algo/a algn 2 vt (atención) captar 3 vi ~ **at sth/sb** tratar de agarrar algo/a algn 4 vt ~ sth (from sth/sb) quitar algo (a algo/algn) ● n ▶ **make a grab for/at sth** intentar agarrar algo

grace /greɪs/ n 1 gracia, elegancia 2 plazo: five days' ~ cinco días de gracia 3 *say* ~ bendecir la mesa ● *vt* **1** adornar **2** honrar **graceful** *adj* **1** grácil, elegante **2** delicado (*cortés*)

gracious /'greɪʃəs/ *adj* **1** afable **2** elegante, lujoso

grade /greɪd/ *n* **1** clase, categoría **2** (*Educ*) nota **3** (*USA, Educ*) año **4** (*USA, Geog*) pendiente ▶ **make the grade** (*coloq*) tener éxito ● *vt* **1** clasificar **2** (*USA, Educ*) calificar (*examen*) **grading** *n* clasificación

gradient /'greɪdiənt/ *n* pendiente

gradual /'grædʒuəl/ *adj* **1** gradual, paulatino **2** (*pendiente*) suave **gradually** *adv* paulatinamente, poco a poco

graduate /'grædʒuət/ *n* **1** licenciado/a **2** (*USA*) graduado/a ● /'grædʒueɪt/ **1** *vi* licenciarse **2** (*USA*) graduarse **3** *vt* graduar **graduation** *n* graduación

graffiti /grə'fi:ti/ *n* [U] graffiti

graft /grɑːft/ /græft/ GB/ *n* (*Bot, Med*) injerto ● *vt* injertar

grain /greɪn/ *n* **1** [U] cereales **2** grano **3** veta (*madera*) ▶ **against the grain** contra la naturaleza

gram (*tb* **gramme** GB) /græm/ *n* (*abrev* **g**) gramo → Ver pág. 222

grammar /'græmər/ *n* gramática **grammatical** /grə'mætɪkl/ *adj* **1** gramatical **2** (*gramaticalmente*) correcto

grammar school *n* (GB) colegio de enseñanza secundaria

grand /grænd/ *adj* (**-er/-est**) **1** espléndido, grandioso **2** (*coloq*) estupendo **3** (*títulos*) gran ● *n* **1** (*pl* **grand**) (*coloq*) mil dólares/libras **2** (*tb* ~ **piano**) piano de cola

grandad /'grændæd/ *n* (*coloq*) abuelito

grandchild /'græntʃaɪld/ *n* (*pl* **grandchildren**) nieto/a

granddaughter /'grændɔːtər/ *n* nieta

grandeur /'grændʒər/ *n* grandiosidad, grandeza

grandfather /'grænfɑːðər/ *n* abuelo

grandma /'grænmɑ/ *n* (*coloq*) abuelita

grandmother /'grænmʌðər/ *n* abuela

grandpa /'grænpɑ/ *n* (*coloq*) abuelito

grandparent /'grænpeərənt/ *n* abuelo/a

grandson /'grænsʌn/ *n* nieto

grandstand /'grænstænd/ *n* (*Dep*) tribuna

granite /'grænɪt/ *n* granito

granny /'græni/ *n* (*pl* **-ies**) (*coloq*) abuelita

grant /grænt/ /grɑːnt GB/ *vt* conceder ▶ **take sth/sb for granted** dar algo por sentado, no darse cuenta de lo que vale algn ● *n* **1** subvención **2** (*Educ*) beca

grape /greɪp/ *n* uva

grapefruit /'greɪpfruːt/ *n* toronja

grapevine /'greɪpvaɪn/ *n* viña ▶ **on/through the grapevine**: *hear sth on the* ~ oír algo por ahí

graph /græf/ /grɑːf GB/ *n* gráfico

graphic /'græfɪk/ *adj* gráfico **graphics** *n* gráficas

grapple /'græpl/ *vi* luchar

grasp /græsp/ /grɑːsp GB/ *vt* **1** agarrar **2** (*oportunidad*) aprovechar **3** comprender ● *n* **1** alcance: *within/beyond the* ~ *of* al alcance/fuera del alcance de **2** conocimiento **grasping** *adj* codicioso

grass /græs/ /grɑːs GB/ *n* pasto **grassy** *adj* cubierto de pasto

grasshopper /'græshɑpər/ /'grɑːs- GB/ *n* saltamontes, chapulín

grassland /'græslænd/ /'grɑːs- GB/ *n* praderas

grass roots *n* (GB) base popular

grate /greɪt/ **1** *vt* rallar **2** *vi* chirriar **3** *vi* ~ **(on sth/sb)** irritar (*algo/a algn*) ● *n* parrilla (*de chimenea*) **grater** *n* rallador

grateful /'greɪtfl/ *adj* agradecido

gratitude /'grætɪtuːd/ /-tjuːd GB/ *n* gratitud

grave /greɪv/ *adj* (**-er/-est**) (*fml*) grave, serio **NOTA** Es más común **serious**. ● *n* tumba

gravel /'grævl/ *n* gravilla, grava

graveyard /'greɪvjɑrd/ *n* cementerio (*alrededor de una iglesia*)

gravity /'grævəti/ *n* **1** (*Fís*) gravedad **2** (*fml*) seriedad **NOTA** Es más común **seriousness**.

gravy /'greɪvi/ *n* salsa (*hecha con el jugo de la carne*)

gray /greɪ/ *adj* **1** gris **2** (*pelo*) blanco: *go/turn* ~ encanecer ◇ *gray-haired* canoso ◇ *n* gris **grayish** *adj* grisáceo

graze /greɪz/ **1** *vi* pacer **2** *vt* (*piel*) raspar(se) **3** *vt* rozar ● *n* (*Med*) raspadura

grease /griːs/ *n* **1** grasa **2** lubricante **3** gel, gomina ● *vt* engrasar **greasy** *adj* (**-ier/-iest**) grasiento

great /greɪt/ *adj* (**-er/-est**) **1** grande, gran: *the world's greatest tennis player* la mejor tenista del mundo ◇ *We're* ~ *friends.*

Somos muy amigos. ◊ *I'm not a ~ reader.* No soy muy aficionado a la lectura. **5** (*distancia*) largo **3** (*edad*) avanzado **4** (*cuidado*) mucho **5** (*coloq*) estupendo: *We had a ~ time.* La pasamos genial. ◊ *It's ~ to see you!* ¡Qué alegría verte! **6 ~ at** muy bueno en algo **7** (*coloq*) muy: *a ~ big dog* un perro enorme ● *n* (*coloq*): *one of the jazz ~s* una de las grandes figuras del jazz **greatly** *adv* muy, mucho **greatness** *n*

great-grandfather *n* bisabuelo

great-grandmother *n* bisabuela

greed /griːd/ *n* **1 ~ (for sth)** codicia (de algo) **2** (*distancia*)

greedy /ˈgriːdi/ *adj* (**-ier/-iest**) **1 ~ (for sth)** codicioso (de algo) **2** glotón **greedily** *adv* **1** codiciosamente **2** vorazmente

green /griːn/ *adj* (**-er/-est**) verde ● *n* **1** verde **2 greens** verduras **3** (*GB*) prado **greenery** *n* verde, follaje **greenish** *adj* verdoso

greengrocer /ˈgriːnɡrəʊsər/ *n* (*GB*) verdulero/a **o greengrocer's** *n* (*GB*) verdulería

greenhouse /ˈgriːnhaʊs/ *n* invernadero: *~ effect* efecto invernadero

greet /griːt/ *vt* saludar: *~ sb with a smile* recibir a algn con una sonrisa **2** acoger **greeting** *n* **1** saludo **2** recibimiento

grenade /grəˈneɪd/ *n* granada (de mano)

grew /gruː/ *pt de* GROW

grey (*GB*) = GRAY

greyhound /ˈgreɪhaʊnd/ *n* galgo

grid /grɪd/ *n* **1** rejilla **2** (*GB*) (*gas, luz*) red **3** (*mapa*) cuadrícula

grief /griːf/ *n ~* **(over/at sth)** dolor, pesar (por algo) ▶ **come to grief** (*coloq*) **1** fracasar **2** sufrir un accidente

grievance /ˈgriːvns/ *n* **1** (*motivo de*) queja **2** reivindicación

grieve /griːv/ *vt* **1** (*fml*) afligir, apenar **2** *vi ~* **(for/over sth/sb)** llorar la pérdida (de algo/algn) **3** *vi ~* **at/about/over sth** afligirse por algo

grill /grɪl/ *n* **1** parrilla **2** parrillada ● **1** *vt, vi* asar(se) a la parrilla **2** *vt* freír a preguntas

grille (*tb* **grill**) /grɪl/ *n* rejilla, reja

grim /grɪm/ *adj* (**grimmer, -est**) **1** (*persona*) severo, ceñudo **2** (*lugar*) triste, lúgubre **3** deprimente **4** macabro

grimace /ˈɡrɪməs, grɪˈmeɪs/ *n* mueca ● *vi ~* **(at sth/sb)** hacer muecas (a algo/algn)

grime /graɪm/ *n* mugre **grimy** *adj* (**-ier/-iest**) mugriento

grin /grɪn/ *vi* (**-nn-**) **~ (at sth/sb)** sonreír de oreja a oreja (a algo/algn) ▶ **grin and bear it** aguantarse ● *n* sonrisa

grind /graɪnd/ (*pt/pp* **ground**) **1** *vt, vi* moler(se) **2** *vt* (*dientes*) rechinar **4** *vt* (*USA*, *carne*) moler ▶ **grind to a halt/standstill 1** detenerse con un chirrido **2** (*proceso*) detenerse gradualmente ● *n* (*coloq*): *the daily ~* la rutina cotidiana

grip /grɪp/ *n* (**-pp-**) **1** *vt, vi* agarrar(se) **2** *vt* (*mano*) coger **3** *vt* (*atención*) absorber ● *n* **1** agarre, adherencia: *release your ~ on sth* soltar algo **2** (*fig*) dominio, control **3** agarradera ▶ **come/get to grips with sth** enfrentarse a algo **gripping** *adj* fascinante

grit /grɪt/ *n* **1** arena, arenilla **2** valor, determinación ● *vt* (**-tt-**) cubrir con arena ▶ **grit your teeth 1** apretar los dientes **2** armarse de valor

groan /grəʊn/ *vi* **1 ~ (with sth)** gemir (de algo) **2** (*muebles, etc.*) crujir **3 ~ (on (about/over sth); ~ at (sth/sb)** quejarse (de algo; (a algo/algn) ● *n* **1** gemido **2** quejido **3** crujido

grocer /ˈgrəʊsər/ *n* tendero/a, abarrotero/a **groceries** *n* comestibles **grocery store** (**grocer's** *GB*) *n* tienda de abarrotes

groggy /ˈgrɒgi/ *adj* mareado

groin /grɔɪn/ *n* ingle

groom /gruːm/ *n* **1** mozo/a de cuadra **2** *Ver* BRIDEGROOM ● *vt* **1** (*caballo*) cepillar **2** (*pelo*) arreglar **3 ~ sb (for sth/to do sth)** preparar a algn (para algo)

groove /gruːv/ *n* ranura

grope /grəʊp/ *vi* **1** andar a tientas **2 ~ (around) for sth** buscar algo a tientas

gross /grəʊs/ *n* gruesa (*doce docenas*) ● *adj* (**-er/-est**) **1** repulsivamente gordo **2** grosero **3** (*exageración*) flagrante **4** (*error*) craso **5** (*injusticia, etc.*) grave **6** (*total*) bruto ● *vt* recaudar, ganar (en bruto) **grossly** *adv* extremadamente

grotesque /grəʊˈtesk/ *adj* grotesco

ground /graʊnd/ *pt, pp de* GRIND ● *adj* **1** molido **2** (*USA*, *carne*) molido ● *vt* **1** (*avión*) impedir el despegue **2** (*niño*) castigar sin salir **3** (*USA*, *Elec*) conectar a tierra ● *n* **1** suelo, tierra **2** terreno **3** zona, campo (*de juego*) **4 grounds** [*pl*] jardines **5** [*gen pl*] motivo, razón **6 grounds** [*pl*] sedimento ▶ **get off the ground 1** ponerse en marcha, resultar factible **2** (*avión*) despegar **give/lose ground (to sth/sb)** ceder/perder terreno (frente a algo/algn) **on the ground** en el suelo, sobre el terreno **to the ground** (*destruir*) completamente **grounding** *n* [*sing*] **~ (in sth)** base, conceptos fundamentales (de algo) **groundless** *adj* infundado

ground floor *n* (*GB*) planta baja

group /gru:p/ *n* grupo ● *vt, vi* **~ (sth/sb) (together)** agrupar(se) (algo/a algn) **grouping** *n* agrupación

grouse /graʊs/ *n* (*pl* **grouse**) urogallo (*de Escocia*)

grove /grəʊv/ *n* arboleda

grovel /ˈɡrɒvl/ *vi* (**-l-, -ll-** *GB*) (*pey*) **~ (to sb)** humillarse (ante algn) **grovelling** *adj* servil

grow /grəʊ/ (*pt* **grew** *pp* **grown**) **1** *vi* crecer **2** *vi* (*pelo, barba*) dejar crecer **3** *vt* cultivar **4** *vi* [+ *adj*] hacerse: **~ old/rich** envejecer/enriquecerse **5** *vi* **~ to do sth** llegar a hacer algo ■ **grow into sth** convertirse en algo **grow on sb** empezar a gustarle a algn cada vez más **grow up 1** desarrollarse **2** crecer: *when I ~ up* cuando sea mayor ◊ *Grow up!* ¡Madure! **growing** *adj* creciente

growl /graʊl/ *vi* gruñir ● *n* gruñido

grown /grəʊn/ *pp de* GROW ● *adj* adulto

grown-up /ˌgrəʊn ˈʌp/ *adj* mayor ● /ˈgrəʊn ʌp/ *n* (*pl* **-ups**) adulto/a

growth /grəʊθ/ *n* **1** crecimiento **2** aumento **3** [*sing*] brotes **4** tumor

grub /grʌb/ *n* **1** larva **2** (*coloq*) comida

grubby /ˈgrʌbi/ *adj* (**-ier/-iest**) sucio

grudge /grʌdʒ/ *vt* **1** resentirse por **2** escatimar ● *n* rencor: *bear sb a ~/have a ~ against sb* guardarle rencor a algn **grudgingly** *adv* de mala gana

grueling (**gruelling** *GB*) /ˈgru:əlɪŋ/ *adj* muy duro, penoso

gruesome /ˈgru:səm/ *adj* espantoso, horrible

gruff /grʌf/ *adj* tosco, áspero

grumble /ˈgrʌmbl/ *vi* refunfuñar: **~ about/at sth** quejarse de algo ● *n* queja

grumpy /ˈgrʌmpi/ *adj* (**-ier/-iest**) (*coloq*) gruñón

grunt /grʌnt/ *vi* gruñir ● *n* gruñido

guarantee /ˌgærənˈtiː/ *n* garantía ● *vt* **1** garantizar **2** avalar

guard /gɑːd/ *vt* **1** proteger, guardar **2** vigilar ■ **guard against sth** protegerse contra algo ● *n* **1** guardia, vigilancia: *on ~* de guardia ◊ **~ dog** perro guardián **2** dispositivo de seguridad **3** (*GB, tren*) jefe/a de tren ▸ **off/on your guard** desprevenido/alerta **guarded** *adj* cauteloso

guardian /ˈgɑːdiən/ *n* **1** guardián/ana: **~ angel** ángel de la guarda **2** tutor/a

guerrilla (**tb guerilla**) /gəˈrɪlə/ *n* guerrillero/a: **~ warfare** guerra de guerrillas

guess /ges/ **1** *vt, vi* adivinar **2** *vi* **~ at sth** imaginar algo **3** *vi* (*esp USA, coloq*) creer: *I ~ so/not.* Supongo que sí/no. ● *n* conjetura, cálculo: *have/make a ~ (at sth)* intentar adivinar algo ▸ **it's anybody's guess** (*coloq*) nadie lo sabe

guesswork /ˈgeswɜːk/ *n* [*U*] conjeturas

guest /gest/ *n* **1** invitado/a **2** huésped/a: *house ~* pensión

guide /gaɪd/ *n* **1** (*persona*) guía **2** (*tb* **guidebook** /ˈgaɪdbʊk/) guía (*turística*) **3** (*GB*) (*tb* **Girl Guide**) guía (*scouts*) ● *vt* **1** guiar, orientar: **~ sb to sth** llevar a algn hasta algo **2** influenciar **guidance** *n* orientación, supervisión **guided** *adj* con guía

guideline /ˈgaɪdlaɪn/ *n* directriz, pauta

guilt /gɪlt/ *n* culpa, culpabilidad **guilty** *adj* (**-ier/-iest**) culpable

guinea pig *n* **1** conejillo de Indias (*lit y fig*)

guise /gaɪz/ *n* apariencia

guitar /gɪˈtɑː(r)/ *n* guitarra **guitarist** *n* guitarrista

gulf /gʌlf/ *n* **1** (*Geog*) golfo **2** abismo

gull /gʌl/ *n* gaviota

gullible /ˈgʌləbl/ *adj* crédulo

gulp /gʌlp/ **1** *vt* **~ (down)** tragarse algo **2** *vi* tragar saliva ● *n* trago

gum /gʌm/ *n* **1** (*Anat*) encía **2** pegamento, pegante (*And*) **3** [*U*] chicle

gun /gʌn/ *n* **1** arma (*de fuego*) **2** escopeta ● *v* (**-nn-**) ■ **gun sb down** matar/herir gravemente a algn a tiros

gunfire /ˈgʌnfaɪə(r)/ *n* disparos

gunman /ˈgʌnmən/ *n* (*pl* **-men**) pistolero

gunpoint /ˈgʌnpɔɪnt/ *n* ▸ **at gunpoint** a punta de pistola

gunpowder /ˈgʌnpaʊdə(r)/ *n* pólvora

gunshot /'gʌnʃɑt/ n disparo

gurgle /'gɜːrgl/ vi 1 gorgotear 2 (bebé) gorjear

gush /gʌʃ/ vi 1 ~ (out) salir a borbotones, manar 2 ~ (over sth/sb) hablar con demasiado entusiasmo (de algo/algn)

gust /gʌst/ n ráfaga

gusto /'gʌstoʊ/ n entusiasmo

gut /gʌt/ n 1 **guts** (coloq) tripas 2 **guts** (coloq) agallas 3 intestino: a ~ reaction/feeling una reacción visceral/un presentimiento ● vt 1 destripar 2 destruir por dentro

gutter /'gʌtər/ n 1 alcantarilla: the ~ press la prensa amarilla 2 canal de desagüe (en tejado)

guy /gaɪ/ n (coloq) tipo

guzzle /'gʌzl/ vt ~ sth (down/up) (coloq) tragarse algo

gym /dʒɪm/ n 1 (tb **gymnasium** /dʒɪm'neɪziəm/ fml) gimnasio 2 (tb **gymnastics** /dʒɪm'næstɪks/ [sing]) gimnasia

gymnast /'dʒɪmnæst/ n gimnasta

gynecologist (**gynae-** GB) /ˌgaɪnə'kɑlədʒɪst/ n ginecólogo/a

gypsy /'dʒɪpsi/ n (pl **-ies**) gitano/a

H h

H, h /eɪtʃ/ n (pl **H's, h's**) H, h

habit /'hæbɪt/ n 1 costumbre: get into the ~ of sth acostumbrarse a algo 2 (Rel) hábito

habitat /'hæbɪtæt/ n hábitat

habitual /hə'bɪtʃuəl/ adj habitual

hack /hæk/ vt, vi 1 ~ (at) (sth) dar golpes a (algo) (con algo cortante) 2 ~ (into) (sth) (Comp) entrar sin autorización (en algo) **hacker** n pirata informático/a **hacking** n acceso ilegal

had /həd, hæd/ pt, pp de HAVE

hadn't /'hædnt/ = HAD NOT

haemo- (GB) = **HEMO-**

haggard /'hægərd/ adj demacrado

haggle /'hægl/ vi ~ (over/about sth) regatear (por algo)

hail /heɪl/ n [U] granizo ● 1 vt ~ sth/sb as sth aclamar algo/algn como algo 2 vt llamar (para atraer la atención) 3 vi granizar

hailstone /'heɪlstoʊn/ n piedra (de granizo)

hailstorm /'heɪlstɔːrm/ n granizada

hair /heər/ n 1 pelo, cabello 2 vello

hairbrush /'heərbrʌʃ/ n cepillo (para el pelo)

haircut /'heərkʌt/ n corte de pelo: have a ~ cortarse el pelo

hairdo /'heərduː/ n (pl **-s**) (coloq) peinado

hairdresser /'heərdresər/ n peluquero/a **hairdresser's** n peluquería (negocio) **hairdressing** n peluquería (arte)

hairdryer (tb **hairdrier**) /'heərdraɪər/ n secador(a) (pelo)

hairpin /'heərpɪn/ n pasador, gancho (pelo): ~ turn/bend (GB) curva muy cerrada

hairspray /'heərspreɪ/ n laca

hairstyle /'heərstaɪl/ n peinado

hairy /'heəri/ adj (**-ier/-iest**) peludo

half /hæf; hɑːf GB/ adj, n, pron (pl **halves**) 1 medio, mitad: ~ an hour media hora ◊ break sth in ~ partir algo por la mitad ◊ cut sth by ~ reducir algo a la mitad 2 (Dep): the first ~ el primer tiempo ▶ go halves (on sth) pagar algo por mitades half after/past (GB) one, two, etc. la una, las dos, etc. y media **NOTA** En inglés británico es muy común la forma coloquial half one, half two, etc. ● adv a medio, a medias: ~ built a medio construir

half-brother n hermano por parte de padre/madre

half-hearted adj poco entusiasta

half-heartedly adv sin entusiasmo

half-sister n hermana por parte de padre/madre

half-term n (GB) vacaciones cortas a mediados de trimestre

half-time n (Dep) descanso, intermedio (And)

halfway /ˌhæf'weɪ; ˌhɑːf- GB/ adj, adv a medio camino, a la mitad

hall /hɔːl/ n 1 (tb **hallway** /'hɔːlweɪ/) vestíbulo, entrada 2 (conciertos, etc.) sala 3 (tb **residence** ~) (~ of residence GB) residencia universitaria

hallmark /'hɔːlmɑrk/ n 1 (metales preciosos) contraste 2 (fig) sello

Halloween (tb **Hallowe'en**) /ˌhæloʊ'iːn/ n halloween **NOTA** Halloween (31 de octubre) es la víspera de Todos los Santos, la noche de fantasmas y brujas. La gente vacía una calabaza, le da forma de cara y pone una vela dentro. Los niños se disfrazan y piden caramelos o dinero en las casas. Al abrir la puerta dicen trick or treat ("nos das algo o te gastamos una broma").

hallucination /həˌluːsɪˈneɪʃn/ n alucinación

halo /ˈheɪləʊ/ n (pl **-s/-es**) halo, aureola

halt /hɔːlt/ n parada, interrupción ● vt, vi parar(se): *Halt!* ¡Alto!

halting /ˈhɔːltɪŋ/ adj vacilante

halve /hæv; hɑːv GB/ vt 1 partir por la mitad 2 reducir a la mitad

halves /hævz; hɑːvz GB/ pl de HALF

ham /hæm/ n jamón (cocido)

hamburger /ˈhæmbɜːrgər/ hamburguesa

hamlet /ˈhæmlət/ n caserío

hammer /ˈhæmər/ n martillo ● 1 vt martillear: ~ *sth in* clavar algo (a martillazos) 2 vi ~ *(at/on sth)* dar golpes (en algo) 3 vt (coloq) dar una paliza a

hammock /ˈhæmək/ n hamaca

hamper /ˈhæmpər/ n cesta (alimentos) ● vt obstaculizar

hamster /ˈhæmstər/ n hámster

hand /hænd/ n 1 mano → MY 2 (reloj) manecilla 3 peón, jornalero 4 (Náut) tripulante ▶ *by hand* a mano: *delivered by ~* entregado en mano *(close/near)* *at hand* a mano, cerca *give/lend sb a hand* darle una mano a algn *hand in hand* 1 de la mano 2 muy unido, a la par *hands up* manos arriba: *Hands up if you know the answer.* El que sepa la respuesta que levante la mano. *in hand* 1 *(tb in ~)* disponible 2 entre manos *on the one hand... on the other (hand)...* por una lado... por otro... *out of hand* 1 descontrolado 2 sin pensarlo a mano ● vt pasar ■ *hand sth back* devolver algo *hand sth in* entregar algo *hand sth out* repartir algo

handbag /ˈhændbæg/ n bolso, bolsa *(Mx)*

handbook /ˈhændbʊk/ n manual, guía

handbrake /ˈhændbreɪk/ n freno de mano

handcuff /ˈhændkʌf/ vt esposar **handcuffs** n esposas

handful /ˈhændfʊl/ n puñado: *a ~ of girls* un puñado de chicas ▶ *be a (real) handful (coloq)* ser muy travieso

handgun /ˈhændɡʌn/ n pistola

handicap /ˈhændikæp/ n 1 *(Med)* minusvalía 2 *(Dep)* desventaja ● vt *(-pp-)* 1 perjudicar 2 *(Dep)* compensar **handicapped** adj minusválido

handicrafts /ˈhændikræfts; -krɑːfts GB/ n [pl] artesanía(s)

handkerchief /ˈhæŋkərtʃɪf/ n (pl **-s/-chieves** /-tʃiːvz/) pañuelo (de bolsillo)

handle /ˈhændl/ n 1 mango 2 manija 3 asa ● vt 1 manejar 2 *(máquina)* operar 3 *(gente)* tratar 4 soportar

handlebars /ˈhændlbɑːrz/ n [pl] manubrio

handmade /ˌhændˈmeɪd/ adj hecho a mano, artesanal **NOTA** Hay adjetivos compuestos para muchas destrezas manuales: p. ej. **hand-built**, **hand-painted** (construido/pintado a mano), etc.

handout /ˈhændaʊt/ n 1 donativo 2 folleto 3 fotocopia

handshake /ˈhændʃeɪk/ n apretón de manos

handsome /ˈhænsəm/ adj 1 guapo, atractivo **NOTA** Se aplica sobre todo a los hombres. 2 *(regalo)* generoso

handwriting /ˈhændraɪtɪŋ/ n 1 escritura 2 letra **handwritten** /ˌhændˈrɪtn/ adj escrito a mano

handy /ˈhændi/ adj (-ier/-iest) 1 práctico 2 a mano

hang /hæŋ/ (pt/pp hung) 1 vt colgar 2 vi estar colgado 3 vi *(ropa, pelo)* caer 4 vi ~ *(above/over sth/sb)* pender (sobre algo/algn) 5 *(pt/pp hanged)* vt, vi ahorcar(se) ■ *hang about/around (coloq)* 1 holgazanear 2 esperar *(sin hacer nada)* *hang on* 1 agarrarse 2 *(coloq)* esperar *hang out (with sb) (coloq)* andar (con algn) *hang sth out* tender algo *hang up* colgar *hang up (on sb) (coloq)* colgar(le) (a algn) *(teléfono)* ● n ▶ *get the hang of sth (coloq)* agarrar la onda/el tiro a algo

hangar /ˈhæŋər/ n hangar

hanger /ˈhæŋər/ n *(tb clothes/coat ~)* n gancho

hang-glider n ala delta **hanggliding** n (vuelo con) ala delta

hangman /ˈhæŋmən/ n (pl **-men**) 1 verdugo *(de horca)* 2 *(juego)* el ahorcado

hangover /ˈhæŋəʊvər/ n resaca

hang-up n (pl **-ups**) *(coloq)* trauma, complejo

haphazard /hæpˈhæzərd/ adj al azar, de cualquier manera

happen /ˈhæpən/ vi 1 ocurrir, pasar: *whatever ~s/no matter what ~s* pase lo que pase ◇ *if you ~ to see her* si por casualidad la ves **happening** n suceso, acontecimiento

happy /ˈhæpi/ adj (-ier/-iest) 1 feliz 2 contento → GLAD **happily** adv

1 felizmente **2** afortunadamente **happiness** n felicidad

harass /'hærəs, hə'ræs/ vt hostigar, acosar **harassment** n hostigamiento, acoso

harbor (-our GB) /'hɑrbər/ n puerto ● vt **1** proteger, dar cobijo a **2** (dudas, etc.) albergar

hard /hɑrd/ (-er/-est) adj **1** duro: a ~ worker una persona trabajadora **2** difícil: ~ to please exigente **3** (persona, trato) severo, cruel **4** (bebida) alcohólico ▸ **hard cash** (GB) dinero contante **hard luck** mala suerte **have/give sb a hard time** (hacer) pasar a (algn) un mal rato **take a hard line** adoptar una postura tajante **the hard way** por la vía difícil ● adv **1** mucho, duro: She hit her head ~. Se dio un fuerte golpe en la cabeza. ~ try ~ esforzarse **2** (pensar) detenidamente **3** (mirar) fijamente ▸ **be hard put to do sth** tener dificultad en hacer algo **hard up** (coloq) mal de dinero

hardback /'hɑrdbæk/ n libro de tapa dura

hard disk (tb hard drive) n (Comp) disco duro

harden /'hɑrdn/ vt, vi endurecer(se): a hardened criminal un criminal habitual **hardening** n endurecimiento

hardly /'hɑrdli/ adv **1** apenas **2** difícilmente: It's ~ surprising. No es ninguna sorpresa. **3** casi: ~ anybody/ever casi nadie/nunca

hardship /'hɑrdʃɪp/ n privación

hard shoulder (GB) acotamiento (Mx), berma (And)

hardware /'hɑrdweər/ n **1** ferretería: ~ store ferretería/tlapalería (Mx) **2** (Mil) armamentos **3** (Comp) hardware

hard-working adj trabajador

hardy /'hɑrdi/ adj (-ier/-iest) robusto

hare /heər/ n liebre

harm /hɑrm/ n daño, mal: mean no ~ no tener malas intenciones ◇ There's no ~ done. No pasó nada. ◇ You'll come to no ~. No te va a pasar nada. ▸ **do more harm than good** ser peor el remedio que la enfermedad **out of harm's way** a salvo ● vt **1** (persona) hacer daño a **2** (cosa) dañar **harmful** adj dañino, perjudicial **harmless** adj **1** inocuo **2** inocente, inofensivo

harmony /'hɑrməni/ n (pl -ies) armonía

harness /'hɑrnɪs/ n [sing] arreos ● vt **1** (caballo) ponerle los arreos a **2** (recursos) aprovechar

harp /hɑrp/ n arpa ■ **harp on (about) sth** hablar repetidamente de algo

harsh /hɑrʃ/ adj (-er/-est) **1** áspero **2** duro **3** (color, luz) chillón, fuerte **4** (ruido) estridente **5** (clima, etc.) riguroso **6** (castigo, etc.) severo

harvest /'hɑrvɪst/ n cosecha ● vt cosechar

has /həz, hæz/ Ver HAVE

hashish /'hæʃiːʃ/ (coloq hash /'hæʃ/) n hachís

hasn't /'hæznt/ = HAS NOT

hassle /'hæsl/ n (coloq) **1** lío: It's a lot of ~. Es mucho lío. **2** molestias: Don't give me any ~! ¡Déjame en paz! ● vt (coloq) molestar

haste /heɪst/ n prisa: in ~ de prisa **hasten** /'heɪsn/ **1** vi darse prisa, apurarse **2** vt acelerar **hasty** adj (-ier/-iest) precipitado

hat /hæt/ n sombrero

hatch /hætʃ/ **1** vi ~ (out) salir del huevo **2** vi (huevo) abrirse al incubar **3** vt ~ sth (up) tramar algo ● n **1** escotilla **2** ventanilla (para comida)

hatchback /'hætʃbæk/ n carro con puerta trasera

hate /heɪt/ vt **1** odiar **2** lamentar: I ~ to bother you, but... Siento molestarle, pero... ● n **1** odio **2** my pet ~ la cosa que más odio **hateful** adj odioso **hatred** /'heɪtrəd/ n odio

haul /hɔːl/ vt arrastrar ● n **1** camino, recorrido: long-haul flight vuelo de larga distancia **2** redada (peces) **3** botín

haunt /hɔːnt/ vt **1** (fantasma) aparecerse en **2** frecuentar **3** (pensamiento) atormentar ● n lugar predilecto **haunted** adj embrujado (edificio)

have /həv, hæv/ v aux haber: "I've finished." "So ~ I." —Terminé. —Yo también. ◇ He's gone home, hasn't he? Se ha ido/Se fue a casa, ¿no? ◇ "Have you seen it?" "Yes, I ~./No, I haven't." —¿Lo has visto/viste? —Sí./No. ● vt **1** (tb have → got) tener: ~ a headache tener dolor de cabeza → TENER **2** ~ (got) sth to do; ~ (got) to do sth tener algo que hacer; tener que hacer algo **3** tomar: ~ a coffee tomar un café **NOTA** La estructura **have + sustantivo** a menudo se expresa en español con un verbo: ~ breakfast/a wash desayunar/lavarse **4** ~ sth done hacer/mandar hacer algo: ~ your hair cut cortarse el pelo ◇ She had her bag stolen. Le robaron el bolso. **5** I won't ~ it! ¡No lo consentiré! ▶ **have had it** (*coloq*): *The TV's had it.* La tele ya no funciona. **have it (that)**: *Rumour has it that...* Se dice que... ◊ *As luck would ~ it...* Como quiso la suerte... **have to do with sth/sb** tener que ver con algo/algn **NOTA** Para otras expresiones, ver el sustantivo, adjetivo, etc., p. ej. **have a sweet tooth** en SWEET. ■ **have sth back**: *Let me ~ it back soon.* Devuélvemelo pronto. **have sb on** (*coloq*) tomar el pelo a algn **have sth on** 1 (*ropa*) llevar algo (puesto) 2 estar ocupado con algo: *Do you have anything on today?* ¿Tienes algún plan para hoy?

haven /ˈheɪvn/ *n* refugio

haven't /ˈhævnt/ = HAVE NOT

havoc /ˈhævək/ *n* [U] estragos: *wreak/cause/play ~ with sth* hacer estragos en algo

hawk /hɔːk/ *n* halcón

hay /heɪ/ *n* heno: *~ fever* alergia al polen

hazard /ˈhæzərd/ *n* peligro: *a health ~* un peligro para la salud ● *vt*: *~ a guess* aventurar una opinión **hazardous** *adj* peligroso

haze /heɪz/ *n* bruma

hazel /ˈheɪzl/ *n* avellano ● *adj*, *n* (*color*) avellana

hazelnut /ˈheɪzlnʌt/ *n* avellana

hazy /ˈheɪzi/ *adj* (**-ier/-iest**) 1 brumoso 2 vago, confuso

he /hiː/ *pron* ● *vt* **NOTA** El *pron pers* no puede omitirse en inglés. ● *n*: *Is it a he or a she?* ¿Es macho o hembra?

head /hed/ *n* 1 cabeza 2 (*Dep*) cabecear ■ **head for sth** dirigirse a algn ● *n* 1 cabeza: *It never entered my ~.* Jamás se me ocurrió. ◊ *have a good ~ for business* tener talento para los negocios 2 (*mesa, cama*) cabecera 3 jefe/a 4 (*GB*) director/a (*colegio*) ▶ **heads or tails?** ¿águila o sol? (*Mx*) ¿cara o sello? (*And*) **a/per head** por cabeza: *ten euros a ~* diez euros por cabeza **go up above/over your head** pasarle por encima de **go to sb's head** subírsele a la cabeza a algn **head first** de cabeza **not make head or tail of sth** no conseguir entender algo

headache /ˈhedeɪk/ *n* 1 dolor de cabeza 2 quebradero de cabeza

heading /ˈhedɪŋ/ *n* encabezamiento, título

headlight (*tb* **headlamp**) /ˈhedlaɪt/ -læmp/ *n* (*Aut*) faro, farola (*And*)

headline /ˈhedlaɪn/ *n* 1 titular, encabezado (*Mx*) 2 **headlines** [*pl*] resumen de noticias

headmaster, headmistress /ˌhedˈmɑːstər, ˌhedˈmɪstrəs/ *n* director/a (*colegio*)

head office *n* sede central

head-on *adj*, *adv* de frente: *a ~ collision* una colisión de frente

headphones /ˈhedfəʊnz/ *n* [*pl*] auriculares, audífonos

headquarters /ˌhedˈkwɔːtərz/ *n* (*abrev* **HQ**) 1 (sede) central 2 (*Mil*) cuartel general

head teacher *n* director/a (*de colegio*)

headway /ˈhedweɪ/ *n* ▶ **make headway** avanzar, progresar

heal /hiːl/ 1 *vi* cicatrizar, sanar 2 *vt* sanar, curar

health /helθ/ *n* salud: *~ centre* centro médico **healthy** *adj* (**-ier/-iest**) 1 sano 2 saludable

heap /hiːp/ *n* montón ● *vt* **~ sth (up)** amontonar algo

hear /hɪər/ (*pt/pp* **heard** /hɜːrd/) 1 *vt*, *vi* oír, escuchar: *I heard someone laughing.* Oí a alguien que se reía. **NOTA** Hear, see, smell y taste no suelen usarse en tiempos continuos, sino con **can** y **could**: *No se oía nada.* You couldn't hear a thing. ◊ *¿Ves la casa de allá?* Can you see the house over there? 2 *vt* (*Jur*) ver ■ **hear about sth** enterarse de algo **hear from sb** tener noticias de algn **hear of sth/sb** oír hablar de algo/algn

hearing /ˈhɪərɪŋ/ *n* 1 (*tb* **sense of ~**) oído 2 (*Jur*) vista, audiencia

heart /hɑːrt/ *n* 1 corazón: *~ attack/failure* infarto/paro cardíaco 2 (*clave*): *the ~ of the matter* el meollo del asunto 3 (*lechuga, etc.*) cogollo 4 **hearts** (*cartas*) corazones →BARAJA ▶ **at heart** en el fondo **by heart** de memoria **lose heart** descorazonarse **set your heart on sth** poner el corazón en algo **take heart** alentarse **take sth to heart** tomar algo a pecho

heartbeat /ˈhɑːrtbiːt/ *n* latido (*del corazón*)

heartbreak /ˈhɑːrtbreɪk/ *n* angustia **heartbreaking** *adj* que parte el corazón **heartbroken** *adj* desconsolado

hearten /ˈhɑːrtn/ *vt* animar **heartening** *adj* alentador

heartfelt /ˈhɑːrtfelt/ *adj* sincero

hearth /hɑːrθ/ *n* chimenea (*hogar*)

heartless /ˈhɑːtləs/ adj cruel

hearty /ˈhɑːti/ adj (-ier/-iest) 1 (enhorabuena) cordial 2 (persona) jovial (a veces en exceso) 3 (comida) abundante

heat /hiːt/ n 1 calor 2 (Dep) prueba clasificatoria ▸ **in/on** (GB) **heat on** celo ● vt, vi ~ (sth) (up) calentar(se) (algo) **heated** adj 1 centrally ~ con calefacción central 2 (discusión, etc.) acalorado **heater** n calentador

heath /hiːθ/ n monte

heathen /ˈhiːðn/ n no creyente

heather /ˈheðər/ n brezo

heating /ˈhiːtɪŋ/ n calefacción

heatwave /ˈhiːtweɪv/ n ola de calor

heave /hiːv/ vt, vi ~ (at/on) (sth) arrastrar(se) (algo), tirar con esfuerzo (de algo) ● n tirón, empujón

heaven /ˈhevn/ n (Rel) cielo **NOTA** Heaven y hell pueden escribirse con mayúscula, pero no llevan el artículo: She has gone to Heaven. **heavenly** adj 1 (Rel) celestial 2 (astro) celeste 3 (coloq) divino

heavy /ˈhevi/ adj (-ier/-iest) 1 pesado: How ~ is it? ¿Cuánto pesa? 2 más de lo normal: be a ~ drinker beber mucho ◇ The traffic was very ~. Había mucho tráfico. 3 (facciones, movimiento) torpe ▸ **with a heavy hand** con mano dura **heavily** adv 1 muy, mucho: ~ loaded muy cargado ◇ ~ rain llover muchísimo 2 pesadamente

heavyweight /ˈheviweɪt/ n 1 (boxeo) peso pesado 2 figura (importante)

heckle /ˈhekl/ vt, vi interrumpir (con comentarios molestos)

hectare /ˈhekteər/ n hectárea

hectic /ˈhektɪk/ adj frenético

he'd /hiːd/ 1 = HE HAD 2 = HE WOULD

hedge /hedʒ/ n 1 seto 2 protección ● vi salirse por la tangente

hedgehog /ˈhedʒhɒg; -hɔːg GB/ n erizo (mamífero)

heed /hiːd/ vt (fml) prestar atención a ● n ▸ **take heed (of sth)** hacer caso (de algo)

heel /hiːl/ n 1 talón 2 tacón

hefty /ˈhefti/ adj (-ier/-iest) 1 (persona) fornido 2 (objeto) pesado 3 (golpe) fuerte

height /haɪt/ n 1 estatura 2 altura 3 (Geog) altitud 4 (fig) cumbre, colmo: at/in the ~ of summer en pleno verano ◇ the ~ of fashion la última moda →ALTO **heighten**

vt, vi intensificar(se), aumentar(se)

heir, heiress /eər/ˈeəres/ n ~ (to sth) heredero/a (de algo)

held /held/ pt, pp de HOLD

helicopter /ˈhelɪkɒptər/ n helicóptero

he'll /hiːl/ = HE WILL

hell /hel/ n infierno → HEAVEN ▸ **a/one hell of a...** (coloq): a ~ of a shock un susto terrible **hellish** adj infernal

hello /həˈləʊ/ interj, n 1 hola: say ~ to sb saludar a algn → HOLA 2 (teléfono) aló, bueno (Mx)

helm /helm/ n timón

helmet /ˈhelmɪt/ n casco

help /help/ 1 vt, vi ayudar: Help! ¡Socorro! ◇ How can I ~ you? ¿En qué puedo servirlo? 2 vt ~ **yourself (to sth)** servirse (algo) ▸ **can't help sth** no poder evitar algo: It can't be helped. No hay remedio. ◇ I couldn't ~ laughing. No pude contener la risa. **give/ lend a helping hand** dar una mano ■ **help (sb) out** dar una mano (a algn) ● n [U] ayuda: It wasn't much ~. No sirvió de mucho. 2 asistencia **helper** n ayudante **helpful** adj 1 servicial 2 amable (consejo, etc.) **helpless** adj indefenso, desamparado

helping /ˈhelpɪŋ/ n porción

helpline /ˈhelplaɪn/ n línea telefónica de ayuda

helter-skelter n tobogán (en espiral), resbaladilla (Mx) ● adj precipitado

hem /hem/ n dobladillo ● v (-mm-) ■ **hem sth/sb in** 1 cercar algo/a algn 2 cohibir a algn

hemisphere /ˈhemɪsfɪər/ n hemisferio

hemoglobin /ˌhiːməˈgləʊbɪn/ n hemoglobina

hemophilia /ˌhiːməˈfɪliə/ n hemofilia **haemophiliac** n hemofílico/a

hemorrhage /ˈhemərɪdʒ/ n hemorragia

hemorrhoids /ˈhemərɔɪdz/ n hemorroides

hen /hen/ n gallina

hence /hens/ adv (fml) 1 desde ahora: two years ~ de aquí a dos años 2 (por eso) de ahí

henceforth /ˌhensˈfɔːrθ/ adv (fml) de ahora en adelante

hen night (tb hen party) n (GB) despedida de soltera

hepatitis /ˌhepəˈtaɪtɪs/ n hepatitis

her /hɜːr, ər/ pron 1 [objeto directo] la 2 [objeto indirecto] le, a ella

3 [después de prep o verbo be] ella: *She took it with* ~. Se lo llevó consigo. ● *adj* suy (*de ella*) → MY NOTA Her se usa también para referirse a vehículos, barcos o naciones.

herald /'herəld/ *n* heraldo ● *vt* anunciar (*llegada, comienzo*)

heraldry /'herəldri/ *n* heráldica

herb /3:rb; hɜ:b *GB*/ *n* hierba (fina) **herbal** *adj* (a base de hierbas: ~ *tea* infusión

herd /hɜ:rd/ *n* manada (*vacas, cabras, cerdos*) ● *vt* llevar en manada

here /hɪər/ *adv* aquí: *He'll be* ~ *soon.* Llegará pronto. ◇ *Here they are, at last!* ◇ *Here it is, on the table!* o bien **here** + *verbo* + *sustantivo*: *Here comes the bus.* ▶ **here and there** aquí y allá **here you are** aquí tiene ● *interj* **1** oye **2** (*para ofrecer*) toma **3** presente

NOTA Cuando una frase empieza con here, la estructura es here + pronombre + verbo: *Here they are, at last!* ◇ *Here it is, on the table!*, o bien here + verbo + sustantivo: *Here comes the bus.*

hereditary /həˈredɪteri; -tri *GB*/ *adj* hereditario

heresy /'herəsi/ *n* (*pl* -ies) herejía

heritage /'herɪtɪdʒ/ *n* patrimonio

hermit /'hɜ:rmɪt/ *n* ermitaño/a

hero /'hɪəroʊ/ *n* (*pl* -es) **1** protagonista **2** héroe, heroína **heroic** /həˈroʊɪk/ *adj* heroico **heroism** /'heroʊɪzəm/ *n* heroísmo

heroin /'heroʊɪn/ *n* heroína (*droga*)

heroine /'heroʊɪn/ *n* heroína (*persona*)

herring /'herɪŋ/ *n* arenque ▶ a red herring una pista falsa

hers /hɜ:rz/ *pron* suyo (*de ella*): *a friend of* ~ un amigo suyo ◇ *Where are* ~? ¿Dónde están los suyos?

herself /hɜ:rˈself/ *pron* **1** [uso reflexivo] se (*a ella misma*) **2** [después de prep] sí (*misma*) **3** [énfasis] ella misma ▶ (all) by herself sola

he's /hi:z/ **1** = HE IS **2** = HE HAS

hesitate /'hezɪteɪt/ *vi* **1** dudar: *Don't* ~ *to call.* No dudes en llamar. **2** vacilar **hesitant** *adj* vacilante, indeciso **hesitation** *n* vacilación, duda

heterogeneous /ˌhetərəˈdʒi:niəs/ *adj* heterogéneo

heterosexual /ˌhetərəˈsekʃuəl/ *adj*, *n* heterosexual

hexagon /'heksəgən/ *n* hexágono

hey /heɪ/ *interj* oye, eh

heyday /'heɪdeɪ/ *n* apogeo

hi /haɪ/ *interj* (*coloq*) hola →HOLA

hibernate /'haɪbərneɪt/ *vi* hibernar **hibernation** *n* hibernación

hiccup (*tb* hiccough) /'hɪkʌp/ *n* **1 the hiccups** [*pl*] hipo **2** (*coloq*) problema

hide /haɪd/ (*pt* hid /hɪd/ *pp* hidden /'hɪdn/) **1** esconderse **2** ~ **sth** (from sb) ocultar algo (a algn) ● *n* piel (*de animal*)

hide-and-seek *n* escondidillas

hideous /'hɪdiəs/ *adj* espantoso

hiding /'haɪdɪŋ/ *n* (*coloq*) paliza ▶ be in/go into hiding estar escondido/esconderse

hierarchy /'haɪərɑːrki/ *n* (*pl* -ies) jerarquía

hieroglyphics /ˌhaɪərəˈɡlɪfɪks/ *n* [*pl*] jeroglíficos

hi-fi *adj* de alta fidelidad ● *n* equipo de música

high /haɪ/ *adj*, *adv* (-er/-est) **1** (*precio, techo, velocidad*) alto: *The wall is six feet* ~. La pared mide seis pies de altura. ◇ *How* ~ *is it?* ¿Cuánto mide de altura? ◇ *high-risk/level* de alto riesgo/nivel →ALTO **2** elevado: *have a* ~ *opinion of sb* tener buena opinión de algn ◇ ~ *hopes* grandes esperanzas ◇ *I have it on the highest authority.* Lo sé de muy buena fuente. ◇ *friends in* ~ *places* amigos muy influyentes **3** (*viento*) fuerte **4** *the* ~ *life* la vida de lujo ◇ *the* ~ *point of the day* el mejor momento del día **5** (*season*) agudo **6** ~ *summer* pleno verano ◇ ~ *season* temporada alta **7** ~ (on sth) (*coloq*) atizado (*Mx*), trabado (*And*) (de/con algo) (*drogas*) ▶ high and dry plantado ● *adv* alto ▶ n punto alto

highbrow /'haɪbraʊ/ *adj* (*frec pey*) intelectual

high-class *adj* de categoría

High Court *n* Tribunal Supremo

higher education *n* educación superior

high jump *n* salto alto

highland /'haɪlənd/ *n* tierra alta ● *adj* de las tierras altas

highlight /'haɪlaɪt/ *n* **1** punto culminante/notable **2** [*gen pl*] (*pelo*) luces (*Mx*), mechones (*And*) ● *vt* (hacer) resaltar

highly /'haɪli/ *adv* **1** muy, sumamente **2** *think* ~ *of sb* tener muy buena opinión de algn

highly strung *adj* nervioso

Highness /'haɪnəs/ *n* alteza

high-pitched *adj* (*sonido*) agudo

high-powered *adj* **1** de gran potencia **2** (*persona*) dinámico **3** (*trabajo, etc.*) de mucha responsabilidad

H

high pressure n alta presión ● **high-pressure** adj estresante

high-rise n torre (de muchos pisos) ● adj de muchos pisos: a ~ apartment un apartamento en un edificio alto

high school n colegio de enseñanza secundaria

high street n (GB) calle principal

high-tech adj de alta tecnología

highway /ˈhaɪweɪ/ n 1 (USA) carretera, autopista 2 vía pública: Highway Code código de circulación

hijack /ˈhaɪdʒæk/ vt 1 secuestrar (avión) 2 acaparar ● n secuestro **hijacker** n secuestrador/a

hike /haɪk/ n caminata ● vi ir a caminar **hiker** n caminante

hilarious /hɪˈleəriəs/ adj divertidísimo, muy cómico

hill /hɪl/ n 1 colina, cerro 2 cuesta **hilly** adj (-ier/-iest) montañoso

hillside /ˈhɪlsaɪd/ n ladera

hilt /hɪlt/ n empuñadura ▶ (up) to the hilt 1 hasta el cuello 2 (apoyar) incondicionalmente

him /hɪm/ pron 1 [objeto directo] lo, le 2 [objeto indirecto] le, se 3 [después de prep o verbo be] él: He always has it with ~. Siempre lo tiene consigo.

himself /hɪmˈself/ pron 1 [uso reflexivo] se (a él mismo) 2 [después de prep] sí (mismo) 3 [énfasis] él mismo ▶ (all) by himself solo

hinder /ˈhɪndər/ vt dificultar

hindrance /ˈhɪndrəns/ n estorbo, obstáculo

hindsight /ˈhaɪndsaɪt/ n: with/in ~ viéndolo a posteriori

Hindu /ˈhɪndu/ adj, n hindú **Hinduism** n hinduismo

hinge /hɪndʒ/ n bisagra ■ **hinge on sth** depender de algo

hint /hɪnt/ n 1 insinuación, indirecta 2 indicio 3 consejo ● 1 vi ~ at sth referirse indirectamente a algo 2 vt, vi insinuar

hip /hɪp/ n cadera ● adj (hipper, -est) (coloq) de moda, en la onda

hippo /ˈhɪpoʊ/ n (pl -s) (tb hippopotamus /ˌhɪpəˈpɒtəməs/) hipopótamo

hire /ˈhaɪər/ vt 1 alquilar, rentar (Mx) →ALQUILAR 2 contratar ● n alquiler, renta (Mx): ~ purchase (GB) compra a plazos ▶ for hire se alquila(n), se renta(n) (Mx)

his /hɪz/ adj su (de él) →MY ● pron suyo (de él): a friend of ~ un amigo suyo

hiss /hɪs/ vt, vi silbar, sisear ● n silbido, siseo

historian /hɪˈstɔːriən/ n historiador/a

historic /hɪˈstɒrɪk; -ˈstɔːr- GB/ adj histórico (importante) **historical** adj histórico

history /ˈhɪstri/ n (pl -ies) 1 historia 2 (Med) historial

hit /hɪt/ n 1 golpe 2 éxitazo ● vt (-tt-) (pt/pp hit) 1 golpear: I ~ my knee on/against the table. Me golpeé la rodilla contra la mesa. ◇ ~ a nail darle a un clavo ◇ ~ the ball pegar a la pelota 2 dar: He was ~ by a bullet. Fue alcanzado por una bala. 3 chocar contra 4 afectar: the areas ~ by the drought las zonas afectadas por la sequía ▶ hit it off (with sb) (coloq): They ~ it off immediately. Se cayeron bien desde el principio. ■ **hit back (at sb/sth)** contestar (a algo/algn) ■ **hit out (at sth/sb)** lanzarse (contra algo/algn)

hit-and-run adj: a ~ driver conductor que atropella a alguien y se da a la fuga

hitch /hɪtʃ/ vt, vi ~ (a ride/lift) pedir aventón, echar dedo ■ **hitch sth up** (ropa) subirse algo ● n problema

hitch-hike vi pedir aventón, echar dedo **hitch-hiker** n autostopista

hi-tech = HIGH-TECH

hive /haɪv/ n colmena

hiya /ˈhaɪjə/ interj (coloq) hola

hoard /hɔːrd/ n 1 tesoro 2 provisión ● vt acaparar

hoarding /ˈhɔːrdɪŋ/ n (GB) valla publicitaria

hoarse /hɔːrs/ adj ronco

hoax /hoʊks/ n broma de mal gusto: a bomb ~ un aviso de bomba falso

hob /hɒb/ n quemador, hornilla (de la estufa)

hobby /ˈhɒbi/ n (pl -ies) hobby

hockey /ˈhɒki/ n 1 (USA) (ice GB) hockey sobre hielo 2 (GB) (field ~ USA) hockey sobre hierba

hoe /hoʊ/ n azada, azadón

hog /hɒɡ; hɔːɡ GB/ n cerdo ● vt (-gg-) acaparar

hoist /hɔɪst/ vt izar, levantar

hold /hoʊld/ (pt/pp held) 1 vt sostener, tener en la mano: ~ sth out/up tender/levantar algo 2 ~ sth ~ on to sth/sb) vt, vi agarrar algo, agarrarse (a algo/algn) 3 vt, vi (peso) aguantar 4 vt (criminal, etc.) tener detenido 5 vt (opinión) sostener 6 vt tener espacio para: It won't ~ everyone. No van a caber todos. 7 vt (cargo) ocupar **8** vt (conversación) mantener **9** vt (reunión, elecciones) tener **10** vt (poseer) tener **11** vt (fml) considerar **12** vi (oferta, etc.) ser válido **13** vt (título) ostentar **14** vi (al teléfono) esperar ▸ **hold fast/firm to sth** aferrarse a/mantenerse firme en algo **hold hands** ir de la mano **hold it** (coloq) espera ∎ **hold sth against sb** tener algo en contra de algn **hold sth back** ocultar algo **hold sth/sb back** refrenar algo/a algn **hold sth down** no sujetar algo **hold forth** echar un discurso **hold on 1** (coloq) esperar **2** aguantar **hold out 1** durar **2** aguantar **hold sth/sb up** retrasar algo/a algn **hold sb up** atracar algo (banco, etc.) **hold with sth** estar de acuerdo con algo ∘ **n 1** keep a firm ~/take~ of sth tener algo bien agarrado/agarrar algo **2** (judo) llave **3** ~ **(on/over sth/sb)** influencia, control (sobre algo/ algn) **4** (barco, avión) bodega ▸ **get hold of sb** ponerse en contacto con algn **get hold of sth** hacerse con algo

holdall /'hoʊldɔːl/ n (GB) bolso de viaje

holder /'hoʊldər/ n **1** titular **2** poseedor/a **3** recipiente

hold-up n (pl **-ups**) **1** (tráfico) atasco, trancón (And) **2** (retraso) **3** asalto

hole /hoʊl/ n **1** agujero **2** perforación **3** (carretera) bache **4** boquete **5** madriguera **6** (coloq) aprieto **7** (Dep) hoyo

holiday /'hɒlədeɪ/ n **1** (GB) vacaciones **2** fiesta ∘ vi (GB) estar de vacaciones

holidaymaker /'hɒlədeɪmeɪkər/ n (GB) vacacionista

hollow /'hɒloʊ/ adj **1** hueco **2** (cara, ojos) hundido **3** (sonido) sordo **4** poco sincero, falso ∘ n **1** hoyo **2** hondonada **3** hueco ∘ vt ~ **sth out** ahuecar algo

holly /'hɒli/ n (pl **-ies**) acebo

holocaust /'hɒləkɔːst/ n holocausto

holy /'hoʊli/ adj (**-ier/-iest**) **1** santo **2** sagrado **3** bendito **holiness** n santidad

homage /'hɒmɪdʒ/ n [U] (fml) homenaje

home /hoʊm/ n **1** casa, hogar **2** (ancianos, etc.) residencia **3** (fig) (Zool) hábitat **4** (carrera) meta ▸ **at home 1** en la casa **2** a sus anchas **3** en su país **bring sth home to sb** hacer que algn comprenda algo ∘ adj **1** casero **2** ~ **comforts** las comodidades del hogar **3** nacional: the

Home Office el Ministerio del Interior **4** (Dep) de/en casa **5** natal ∘ adv **1** go ~ irse a la casa **2** (fijar, clavar, etc.) a fondo ▸ **home free/home and dry** (GB) a salvo **hit/strike home** dar en el blanco

homeland /'hoʊmlænd/ n tierra natal, patria

homeless /'hoʊmləs/ adj sin hogar ∘ **the homeless** n [pl] las personas sin hogar

homely /'hoʊmli/ adj (**-ier/-iest**) **1** (lugar) familiar, acogedor **2** (GB) sencillo **3** (USA) feo

home-made adj casero, hecho en casa

home page n página principal

homesick /'hoʊmsɪk/ adj nostálgico: be/feel ~ tener nostalgia (de casa, de su país)

homework /'hoʊmwɜːrk/ n [U] (colegio) tarea

homicide /'hɒmɪsaɪd/ n homicidio **homicidal** /ˌhɒmɪ'saɪdl/ adj homicida

homogeneous /ˌhoʊmə'dʒiːniəs/ adj homogéneo

homosexual /ˌhoʊmə'sekʃuəl/ adj, n homosexual **homosexuality** /ˌhoʊməsekʃu'æləti/ n homosexualidad

honest /'ɒnɪst/ adj **1** honrado **2** sincero **3** (sueldo) justo **honestly** adv **1** honradamente **2** de verdad, francamente

honesty /'ɒnəsti/ n **1** honradez, honestidad **2** franqueza

honey /'hʌni/ n **1** miel **2** (coloq) (tratamiento) mi amor, cariño

honeymoon /'hʌnimuːn/ n luna de miel

honk /hɒŋk/ vt, vi tocar el claxon/ pito (And)

honor (**-our** GB) /'ɒnər/ n **1** honor **2** condecoración **3** honors [pl] distinción: (first class) ~s degree licenciatura (con la nota más alta) **4** your/his/her Honor su Señoría ▸ **in honor of sth/sb; in sth's/sb's honor** en honor de/a algo/algn ∘ vt **1** honrar **2** condecorar **3** (opinión, etc.) respetar **4** (compromiso, deuda) cumplir (con) **honorable** adj **1** honorable **2** honroso

honorary /'ɒnəreri, -rəri/ adj **1** honorífico **2** honorario

hood /hʊd/ n **1** capucha **2** (USA, Aut) capó, cofre (Mx) **3** (GB, Aut) capota

hoof /huːf/ n (pl **-s** o **hooves**) casco, pezuña

hook /hʊk/ n **1** gancho, garfio **2** (pesca) anzuelo ▸ **let sb/get sb off the hook** dejar que algn se salve/sacar a algn del apuro **off the hook** descolgado (*teléfono*) ● *vt, vi* enganchar **hooked 1** ~ (on sth) enganchado (a algo) **2** ~ (on sb) chiflado (por algn)

hooligan /'huːlɪgən/ *n* vándalo/a **hooliganism** *n* vandalismo

hoop /huːp/ *n* aro

hooray /huˈreɪ/ *interj* ~ (for sth/sb) viva (algo/algn)

hoot /huːt/ *n* **1** ululato **2** pitazo ● **1** *vi* ulular **2** *vi* pitar **3** *vt* (*claxon*) tocar

Hoover® /'huːvər/ (*GB*) *n* aspiradora ● **hoover** *vt, vi* pasar la aspiradora (a/por)

hooves /huːvz/ *pl* de HOOF

hop /hɒp/ *vi* (**-pp-**) **1** saltar con un solo pie (*animal*) dar saltitos ● *n* **1** salto **2** (*Bot*) lúpulo

hope /hoʊp/ *n* esperanza ● **1** *vi* ~ (for sth) esperar (algo) **2** *vt* ~ (to do sth) esperar (hacer algo): *I* ~ *not/so.* Espero que no/sí. ▸ **I should hope not!** ¡faltaría más! →ESPERAR

hopeful /'hoʊpfl/ *adj* confiado: *be* ~ *that...* tener la esperanza de que... **2** (*situación*) prometedor **hopefully** *adv* con esperanzas **2** con suerte

hopeless /'hoʊpləs/ *adj* **1** inútil **2** (*tarea*) imposible **hopelessly** *adv* totalmente

horde /hɔːrd/ *n* multitud: *~s of people* un mar de gente

horizon /hə'raɪzn/ *n* **1** horizonte **2** horizons [*pl*] perspectiva

horizontal /ˌhɔːrɪ'zɒntl, ˌhɒrɪ'zɒntl *GB*/ *adj, n* horizontal

hormone /'hɔːrmoʊn/ *n* hormona

horn /hɔːrn/ *n* **1** cuerno, asta **2** (*Mús*) cuerno **3** (*Aut*) claxon

horoscope /'hɔːrəskoʊp, 'hɒr- *GB*/ *n* horóscopo

horrendous /hɔː'rendəs, hɒ'r- *GB*/ *adj* horrendo

horrible /'hɔːrəbl, 'hɒr- *GB*/ *adj* horrible

horrid /'hɔːrɪd, 'hɒrɪd *GB*/ *adj* horrible, horroroso

horrific /hə'rɪfɪk/ *adj* espantoso

horror /'hɔːrər, 'hɒr- *GB*/ *n* horror: ~ *movie* película de terror **horrify** (*pt/pp* **-ied**) horrorizar **horrifying** *adj* horroroso

horse /hɔːrs/ *n* caballo

horseback riding /'hɔːrsbæk raɪdɪŋ/ *n* (*USA*) equitación

horseman, horsewoman /'hɔːrsmən/-wʊmən/ *n* (*pl* **-men/-women**) jinete, amazona

horsepower /'hɔːrspaʊər/ *n* (*abrev* **hp**) caballo de vapor

horseshoe /'hɔːrsʃuː/ *n* herradura

horticulture /'hɔːrtɪkʌltʃər/ *n* horticultura **horticultural** /ˌhɔːrtɪ'kʌltʃərəl/ *adj* hortícola

hose /hoʊz/ (*tb* **hosepipe** /'hoʊzpaɪp/) *n* manguera

hospice /'hɒspɪs/ *n* hospital (*para incurables*)

hospitable /hɒ'spɪtəbl, 'hɒs-/ *adj* hospitalario

hospital /'hɒspɪtl/ *n* hospital →SCHOOL

hospitality /ˌhɒspɪ'tæləti/ *n* hospitalidad

host /hoʊst/ *n* **1** anfitrión/ona **2** (*TV*) presentador/a **3** montón: *a ~ of fans* una multitud de admiradores **4 the Host** la hostia ● *vt* (*evento*) ser la sede de

hostage /'hɒstɪdʒ/ *n* rehén

hostel /'hɒstl/ *n* hostal: *youth* ~ albergue juvenil

hostess /'hoʊstəs/ *n* **1** anfitriona **2** (*TV*) presentadora **3** azafata

hostile /'hɒstl, -taɪl *GB*/ *adj* hostil **2** (*territorio*) enemigo **hostility** /hɒ'stɪləti/ *n* hostilidad

hot /hɒt/ *adj* (**-tt-**) **1** caliente: *I'm* ~. Tengo calor. ◆ FRÍO **2** (*tiempo*) caluroso: *It's* ~. Hace calor. **3** picante, picoso (*Mx*) **hotly** *adv* enérgicamente

hot dog *n* perrito caliente

hotel /hoʊ'tel/ *n* hotel

hound /haʊnd/ *n* perro de caza ● *vt* acosar

hour /'aʊər/ *n* **1** hora: *on the* ~ a la hora en punto **2 hours** [*pl*] horario: *after* ~s después del horario de trabajo/apertura **3** momento **hourly** *adj, adv* cada hora

house /haʊs/ *n* **1** casa **2** (*Teat*) sala de espectáculos: *There was a full* ~. Se llenó al completo. ▸ **on the house** cortesía de la casa ● /haʊz/ *vt* alojar, albergar

household /'haʊshoʊld/ *n*: *a large* ~ una casa de mucha gente ◇ ~ *chores* quehaceres domésticos **householder** *n* dueño/a de la casa

housekeeper /'haʊskiːpər/ *n* ama de llaves **housekeeping** *n* gobierno/gastos de la casa

the House of Commons (*tb* **the Commons**) *n* la Cámara de los Comunes

the House of Lords (*tb* **the Lords**) *n* la Cámara de los Lores

the Houses of Parliament *n* [*pl*] el Parlamento (*británico*)

housewife /'haʊswaɪf/ *n* (*pl* **-wives** /-waɪvz/) ama de casa

housework /'haʊswɜːrk/ n [U] quehaceres domésticos

housing /'haʊzɪŋ/ n [U] vivienda, alojamiento

housing development (tb **housing estate** GB) n complejo habitacional, fraccionamiento (Mx)

hover /'hʌvər; 'hɒvə(r) GB/ vi 1 planear o quedarse suspendido (en el aire) 3 (persona) rondar

how /haʊ/ adv cómo: How are you? ¿Cómo estás? ◊ I dress ~ I like. Me visto como quiero. ◊ How old are you? ¿Cuántos años tienes? ◊ How fast were you going? ¿A qué velocidad ibas? ◊ How cold it is! ¡Qué frío hace! ▸ **how come...?** ¿cómo es que...? **how do you do?** mucho gusto NOTA **How do you do?** se usa en presentaciones formales, y se contesta con **how do you do?** En cambio, **how are you?** se usa en situaciones informales, y se responde según se encuentre uno: fine, very well, not too well, etc. **how ever** cómo **how many** cuántos **how much** cuánto **how's that?** (coloq) ¿y eso?

however /haʊ'evər/ adv 1 sin embargo 2 por muy/mucho que: ~ strong you are por muy fuerte que seas 3 ~ you like como quieras ◊ ~ you look at it no mires por donde lo mires

howl /haʊl/ n 1 aullido 2 grito ● vi 1 aullar 2 dar alaridos

hub /hʌb/ n 1 (rueda) cubo 2 eje

hubbub /'hʌbʌb/ n algarabía, barullo

huddle /'hʌdl/ vi 1 acurrucarse 2 apiñarse ● n grupo (cerrado)

hue /hjuː/ n (fml) 1 matiz 2 color ▸ **hue and cry** griterío

huff /hʌf/ n: be in a ~ estar enfadado/tener una rabieta

hug /hʌg/ n abrazo ● vt (-gg-) abrazar

huge /hjuːdʒ/ adj enorme

hull /hʌl/ n casco (de barco)

hullo = HELLO

hum /hʌm/ n 1 zumbido 2 murmullo ● (-mm-) 1 vi zumbar 2 vt, vi tararear 3 vi (coloq): ~ with activity bullir de actividad

human /'hjuːmən/ adj, n humano

humane /hjuː'meɪn/ adj humanitario, humano

humanity /hjuː'mænəti/ n 1 humanidad 2 **humanities** humanidades **humanitarian** /hjuːˌmænɪˈteəriən/ adj humanitario

humble /'hʌmbl/ adj (-er/-est) humilde ● vt: ~ yourself adoptar una actitud humilde

humid /'hjuːmɪd/ adj húmedo **humidity** /hjuː'mɪdəti/ n humedad →HÚMEDO

humiliate /hjuː'mɪlieɪt/ vt humillar **humiliating** adj humillante **humiliation** n humillación

humility /hjuː'mɪləti/ n humildad

hummingbird /'hʌmɪŋbɜːrd/ n colibrí

humor (-our GB) /'hjuːmər/ n 1 humor 2 gracia ● vt seguir la corriente a, complacer **humorous** adj humorístico, divertido

hump /hʌmp/ n joroba, giba

hunch /hʌntʃ/ vt, vi ~ (sth) (up) encorvar(se) (algo) ● n corazonada

hundred /'hʌndrəd/ adj, pron cien, ciento →CIEN ● n ciento, centenar **hundredth** 1 adj, pron centésimo 2 n centésima parte

hung /hʌŋ/ pt, pp de HANG

hunger /'hʌŋgər/ n hambre →HAMBRE ▸ **hunger for/after sth** anhelar, tener sed de algo

hungry /'hʌŋgri/ adj (-ier/-iest) hambriento: I'm ~. Tengo hambre.

hunk /hʌŋk/ n (buen) trozo

hunt /hʌnt/ vt, vi 1 cazar, ir de cacería 2 ~ (for sth/sb) buscar (algo/a algn) ● n 1 caza, cacería 2 búsqueda **hunter** n cazador/a **hunting** n caza

hurdle /'hɜːrdl/ n obstáculo

hurl /hɜːrl/ vt 1 lanzar, arrojar 2 (insultos, etc.) soltar

hurrah /hə'rɑː/ = HOORAY

hurricane /'hɜːrəkən; 'hʌrɪ GB/ n huracán

hurry /'hɜːri; 'hʌri GB/ n [U] prisa, afán (And): be in a ~ tener prisa/afán ● vt, vi (pt/pp -ied) apurar(se) ■ **hurry up** darse prisa **hurried** adj apresurado

hurt /hɜːrt/ (pt/pp hurt) 1 vt hacer daño a, lastimar: get ~ hacerse daño 2 vi doler 3 vt herir, ofender 4 vt (reputación, etc.) perjudicar **hurtful** adj hiriente, cruel

hurtle /'hɜːrtl/ vi precipitarse

husband /'hʌzbənd/ n marido

hush /hʌʃ/ n [sing] silencio ● 1 vt, vi callar: Hush! ¡Calla! 2 vt ~ sth up ocultar algo

husky /'hʌski/ adj (-ier/-iest) ronco ● n (pl -ies) husky

hustle /'hʌsl/ vt 1 empujar 2 meterle prisa, apurar ● n ▸ **hustle and bustle** ajetreo

hut /hʌt/ n choza, cabaña

hybrid /'haɪbrɪd/ adj, n híbrido

hydrant /'haɪdrənt/ n toma de agua: fire ~ boca de incendio

hydraulic /haɪˈdrɔːlɪk/ adj hidráulico

hydroelectric /ˌhaɪdrəʊɪˈlektrɪk/ adj hidroeléctrico

hydrogen /ˈhaɪdrədʒən/ n hidrógeno

hyena /haɪˈiːnə/ n hiena

hygiene /ˈhaɪdʒiːn/ n higiene **hygienic** /haɪˈdʒiːnɪk/ adj higiénico

hymn /hɪm/ n himno

hype /haɪp/ n propaganda (exagerada) ● vt ~ sth (up) anunciar algo exageradamente

hyperlink /ˈhaɪpəlɪŋk/ n enlace

hyphen /ˈhaɪfn/ n guión

hypnosis /hɪpˈnəʊsɪs/ n hipnosis

hypnotic /hɪpˈnɒtɪk/ adj hipnótico

hypnotism /ˈhɪpnətɪzəm/ n hipnotismo **hypnotist** n hipnotizador/a **hypnotize** vt hipnotizar

hypochondriac /ˌhaɪpəˈkɒndriæk/ n hipocondríaco/a

hypocrite /ˈhɪpəkrɪt/ n hipócrita **hypocrisy** /hɪˈpɒkrəsi/ n hipocresía **hypocritical** /ˌhɪpəˈkrɪtɪkl/ adj hipócrita

hypothesis /haɪˈpɒθəsɪs/ n (pl **-theses** /-θəsiːz/) hipótesis **hypothetical** /ˌhaɪpəˈθetɪkl/ adj hipotético

hysteria /hɪˈstɪəriə/ n histeria **hysterics** /hɪˈsterɪks/ n [pl] 1 crisis de histeria 2 (coloq) ataque de risa **hysterical** adj 1 histérico 2 (coloq) chistosísimo

I i

I, i /aɪ/ n (pl **I's, i's**) I, i

I /aɪ/ pron yo →YOU

ice /aɪs/ n [U] hielo ● vt glasear

iceberg /ˈaɪsbɜːɡ/ n iceberg

icebox /ˈaɪsbɒks/ n (USA) refrigerador, nevera

ice cream n helado

ice skate n patín de hielo ● **ice-skate** vi patinar sobre hielo **ice skating** n patinaje sobre hielo

icicle /ˈaɪsɪkl/ n carámbano

icing /ˈaɪsɪŋ/ n glaseado: ~ *sugar* (GB) azúcar glas/en polvo

icon /ˈaɪkɒn/ n (Comp, Rel) icono

icy /ˈaɪsi/ adj 1 helado 2 gélido

I'd /aɪd/ 1 = I HAD 2 = I WOULD

ID /aɪ ˈdiː/ n identificación, documento de identidad

idea /aɪˈdɪə/ n 1 idea: *get the* ~ sacar la idea 2 ocurrencia ▸ **give sb ideas** meterle a algn ideas en

la cabeza **have no idea** no tener ni idea

ideal /aɪˈdiːəl/ adj, n ideal **ideally** adv en el mejor de los casos: *be* ~ *suited* complementarse perfectamente ◊ *Ideally, they should all help.* Lo ideal sería que todos ayudaran.

idealism /aɪˈdiːəlɪzəm/ n idealismo **idealist** n idealista **idealize** vt idealizar **idealistic** /ˌaɪdiəˈlɪstɪk/ adj idealista

identical /aɪˈdentɪkl/ adj idéntico

identify /aɪˈdentɪfaɪ/ vt, vi identificar(se) **identification** n identificación

identity /aɪˈdentəti/ n (pl **-ies**) identidad: *a case of mistaken ~* una confusión de identidades

ideology /ˌaɪdiˈɒlədʒi/ n (pl **-ies**) ideología

idiom /ˈɪdiəm/ n modismo, locución

idiosyncrasy /ˌɪdiəˈsɪŋkrəsi/ n (pl **-ies**) idiosincrasia

idiot /ˈɪdiət/ n (coloq) idiota **idiotic** /ˌɪdiˈɒtɪk/ adj estúpido

idle /ˈaɪdl/ adj (**-er/-est**) 1 holgazán 2 desocupado 3 (*maquinaria*) parado 4 vano, inútil ▸ **idle sth away** desperdiciar algo **idleness** n holgazanería

idol /ˈaɪdl/ n ídolo **idolize** vt idolatrar

idyllic /aɪˈdɪlɪk; rˈd- GB/ adj idílico

i.e. /ˌaɪ ˈiː/ abrev es decir

if /ɪf/ conj 1 si 2 cuando, siempre que: *if in doubt* en caso de duda 3 (*tb* **even if**) aunque, incluso si ▸ **if I were you** yo que tú/usted **if only** ojalá: *If only I had known!* ¡De haberlo sabido! **if so** de ser así

igloo /ˈɪɡluː/ n iglú

ignite /ɪɡˈnaɪt/ vt, vi prender (fuego a), encender(se) **ignition** n 1 ignición 2 (Mec) encendido

ignominious /ˌɪɡnəˈmɪniəs/ adj vergonzoso

ignorant /ˈɪɡnərənt/ adj ignorante: *be ~ of sth* desconocer algo **ignorance** n ignorancia

ignore /ɪɡˈnɔːr/ vt 1 no hacer caso de 2 ignorar **NOTA** "Ignorar" en el sentido de "desconocer" se traduce por **not know**: *They don't know why it happened.* Ignoran las causas de lo sucedido. 3 pasar por alto

I'll /aɪl/ 1 = I SHALL 2 = I WILL

ill /ɪl/ adj 1 (*esp GB*) enfermo: *fall/ be taken ~* enfermarse ◊ *feel ~* sentirse mal →ENFERMO 2 malo ● adv mal **NOTA** Se usa mucho en compuestos, p. ej. **ill-fated** (infortunado), **ill-equipped** (mal equipado), **ill-advised** (imprudente). ► **ill at ease** incómodo, molesto **speak/think ill of sb** hablar/pensar mal de algn ● *n* (*fml*) mal, daño

illegal /ɪˈliːgl/ *adj* ilegal

illegible /ɪˈledʒəbl/ *adj* ilegible

illegitimate /ˌɪləˈdʒɪtəmət/ *adj* ilegítimo

ill feeling *n* rencor

ill health *n* mala salud

illicit /ɪˈlɪsɪt/ *adj* ilícito

illiterate /ɪˈlɪtərət/ *adj* 1 analfabeto 2 ignorante

illness /ˈɪlnəs/ *n* enfermedad
→DISEASE

illogical /ɪˈlɒdʒɪkl/ *adj* ilógico

ill-treatment *n* [U] maltrato **ill-treat** *vt* maltratar

illuminate /ɪˈluːmɪneɪt/ *vt* iluminar **illuminating** *adj* revelador **illumination** *n* 1 iluminación 2 **illuminations** (*GB*) luces

illusion /ɪˈluːʒn/ *n* ilusión (*idea equivocada*): *be under the ~ that...* hacerse ilusiones de que...

illusory /ɪˈluːsəri/ *adj* ilusorio

illustrate /ˈɪləstreɪt/ *vt* ilustrar **illustration** *n* 1 ilustración 2 ejemplo

illustrious /ɪˈlʌstriəs/ *adj* ilustre

I'm /aɪm/ = I AM

image /ˈɪmɪdʒ/ *n* imagen **imagery** *n* [U] imágenes

imaginary /ɪˈmædʒɪnəri; -neri *GB*/ *adj* imaginario

imagine /ɪˈmædʒɪn/ *vt* imaginar(se) **imagination** *n* imaginación **imaginative** /ɪˈmædʒɪnətɪv/ *adj* imaginativo

imbalance /ɪmˈbæləns/ *n* desequilibrio

imbecile /ˈɪmbəsl; -siːl *GB*/ *n* imbécil

imitate /ˈɪmɪteɪt/ *vt* imitar **imitation** *n* 1 imitación 2 copia, reproducción

immaculate /ɪˈmækjələt/ *adj* 1 inmaculado 2 impecable

immaterial /ˌɪməˈtɪəriəl/ *adj* irrelevante

immature /ˌɪməˈtʃʊər; -tjʊə(r) *GB*/ *adj* inmaduro

immeasurable /ɪˈmeʒərəbl/ *adj* inconmensurable

immediate /ɪˈmiːdiət/ *adj* 1 inmediato 2 (*familia, etc.*) más cercano 3 (*necesidad, etc.*) urgente

immediately /ɪˈmiːdiətli/ *adv* 1 inmediatamente 2 directamente ● *conj* (*GB*) en cuanto: ~ *I saw her* en cuanto/apenas la vi

immense /ɪˈmens/ *adj* inmenso

immerse /ɪˈmɜːrs/ *vt* sumergir (se) **immersion** *n* inmersión

immigrant /ˈɪmɪgrənt/ *adj, n* inmigrante

immigration /ˌɪmɪˈgreɪʃn/ *n* inmigración

imminent /ˈɪmɪnənt/ *adj* inminente

immobile /ɪˈməʊbl; -baɪl *GB*/ *adj* inmóvil **immobilize** *vt* inmovilizar

immoral /ɪˈmɔːrəl; ɪˈmɒrəl *GB*/ *adj* inmoral

immortal /ɪˈmɔːrtl/ *adj* 1 inmortal 2 (*fama*) imperecedero **immortality** /ˌɪmɔːrˈtæləti/ *n* inmortalidad

immovable /ɪˈmuːvəbl/ *adj* 1 (*objeto*) inmóvil 2 (*persona*) inflexible

immune /ɪˈmjuːn/ *adj* inmune **immunity** *n* inmunidad

immunize /ˈɪmjunaɪz/ *vt* inmunizar **immunization** *n* inmunización

imp /ɪmp/ *n* 1 diablillo 2 (*niño*) pillo, diablito

impact /ˈɪmpækt/ *n* 1 impacto 2 (*Aut*) choque

impair /ɪmˈpeər/ *vt* deteriorar: *impaired vision* visión debilitada **impairment** *n* deficiencia

impart /ɪmˈpɑːrt/ *vt* 1 conferir 2 impartir

impartial /ɪmˈpɑːrʃl/ *adj* imparcial

impasse /ˈɪmpæs; ˈæmpɑːs *GB*/ *n* impase, callejón sin salida

impassioned /ɪmˈpæʃnd/ *adj* apasionado

impassive /ɪmˈpæsɪv/ *adj* impasible

impatient /ɪmˈpeɪʃnt/ *adj* impaciente **impatience** *n* impaciencia

impeccable /ɪmˈpekəbl/ *adj* impecable

impede /ɪmˈpiːd/ *vt* obstaculizar

impediment /ɪmˈpedɪmənt/ *n* 1 ~ (**to sth/sb**) obstáculo (para algo/algn) 2 (*habla*) defecto

impel /ɪmˈpel/ *vt* (-ll-) impulsar

impending /ɪmˈpendɪŋ/ *adj* inminente

impenetrable /ɪmˈpenɪtrəbl/ *adj* impenetrable

imperative /ɪmˈperətɪv/ *adj* 1 urgente, imprescindible 2 (*voz*) imperativo ● *n* imperativo

imperceptible /ˌɪmpərˈseptəbl/ *adj* imperceptible

imperfect /ɪmˈpɜːrfɪkt/ *adj, n* imperfecto

imperial /ɪmˈpɪəriəl/ *adj* imperial **imperialism** *n* imperialismo

impersonal /ɪmˈpɜːrsənl/ *adj* impersonal

impersonate /ɪmˈpɜːrsəneɪt/ *vt* **1** imitar **2** hacerse pasar por

impertinent /ɪmˈpɜːrtɪmənt/ *adj* impertinente

impetus /ˈɪmpɪtəs/ *n* impulso

implant /ˈɪmplænt; -plɑːnt GB/ *n* implante ● /ɪmˈplænt; -ˈplɑːnt GB/ *vt* **1** (*Med*) implantar **2** inculcar

implausible /ɪmˈplɔːzəbl/ *adj* inverosímil

implement /ˈɪmplɪmənt/ *n* utensilio ● *vt* **1** llevar a cabo, realizar **2** poner en práctica **3** (*ley*) aplicar **implementation** *n* **1** realización, puesta en práctica **2** (*ley*) aplicación

implicate /ˈɪmplɪkeɪt/ *vt* involucrar **implication** *n* **1** consecuencia **2** implicación (*delito*)

implicit /ɪmˈplɪsɪt/ *adj* **1** implícito **2** absoluto

implore /ɪmˈplɔːr/ *vt* suplicar

imply /ɪmˈplaɪ/ *vt* (*pt/pp* **-ied**) **1** insinuar, dar a entender **2** implicar, suponer

impolite /ˌɪmpəˈlaɪt/ *adj* mal educado

import /ɪmˈpɔːrt/ *vt* importar ● /ˈɪmpɔːt/ *n* importación

important /ɪmˈpɔːrtnt/ *adj* importante: *vitally ~* de suma importancia **importance** *n* importancia

impose /ɪmˈpoʊz/ **1** *vt* imponer **2** *vi* ~ **on/upon sth/sb** abusar (de la hospitalidad) de algo/algn **imposing** *adj* imponente **imposition** *n* **1** imposición (*restricción, etc.*) **2** molestia

impossible /ɪmˈpɑsəbl/ *adj* **1** imposible **2** intolerable ● **the impossible** *n* lo imposible **impossibility** *n* /ɪm,pɑsəˈbɪləti/ imposibilidad

impotent /ˈɪmpətənt/ *n* impotente **impotence** *adj* impotencia

impoverished /ɪmˈpɑvərɪʃt/ *adj* empobrecido

impractical /ɪmˈpræktɪkl/ *adj* poco práctico

impress /ɪmˈpres/ **1** *vt* impresionar **a 2** *vt* ~ **sth on/upon sb** recalcar algo a algn **3** *vi* causar buena impresión

impression /ɪmˈpreʃn/ *n* **1** impresión: *be under the ~ that...* tener la impresión de que... **2** imitación

impressive /ɪmˈpresɪv/ *adj* impresionante

imprison /ɪmˈprɪzn/ *vt* encarcelar **imprisonment** *n* encarcelamiento

improbable /ɪmˈprɑbəbl/ *adj* improbable, poco probable

impromptu /ɪmˈprɑmptuː; -tjuː GB/ *adj* improvisado

improper /ɪmˈprɑpər/ *adj* **1** incorrecto, indebido **2** impropio **3** (*transacción*) irregular

improve /ɪmˈpruːv/ *vt, vi* mejorar **■ improve on/upon sth** superar algo **improvement** *n* **1** ~ **(on/in sth)** mejora (de algo) **2** reforma

improvise /ˈɪmprəvaɪz/ *vt, vi* improvisar

impulse /ˈɪmpʌls/ *n* impulso ▸ **on impulse** sin pensar **impulsive** *adj* impulsivo

in /ɪn/ *prep* **1** en: *in here/there* aquí/ahí dentro **2** [después de superl] de: *the best store in town* el mejor almacén de la ciudad **3** (*tiempo*) de: *in the morning/daytime* en la mañana/de día **4** dentro de: *I'll see you in two days (time).* Te veo dentro de dos días. ◇ *He did it in a day.* Lo hizo en un día. **5** por: *5p in the pound* (*GB*) cinco peniques por libra ◇ *one in ten people* una de cada diez personas **6** (*descripción, método*): *the girl in blue* la chica de azul ◇ *covered in mud* cubierto de barro ◇ *Speak in English.* Habla en inglés. **7** + **-ing**: *In saying that, you're contradicting yourself.* Al decir eso te contradices a ti mismo. ▸ **in that** en tanto que ● *adv* **1** en la casa: *Is anyone in?* ¿Hay alguien? **2** (*tren, etc.*): *get in* llegar **3** *Applications must be in by...* Las solicitudes deberán llegar antes del... ▸ **be/get in on sth** (*colog*) participar en algo, enterarse de algo **be in for sth** (*colog*) esperarle a uno algo: *He's in for a surprise!* ¡Qué sorpresa se va a llevar! **have (got) it in for sb** (*colog*): *He has it in for me.* Me tiene rabia/bronca. **NOTA** Para el uso de **in** en PHRASAL VERBS ver el verbo, p.ej. **go in** en *go*¹. ● *adj* (*colog*) de moda ● *n* ▸ **the ins and outs (of sth)** los pormenores (de algo)

inability /ˌɪnəˈbɪləti/ *n* incapacidad

inaccessible /ˌɪnækˈsesəbl/ *adj* **1** inaccesible **2** incomprensible

inaccurate /ɪnˈækjərət/ *adj* inexacto, impreciso

inaction /ɪnˈækʃn/ *n* pasividad

inadequate /ɪnˈædɪkwət/ *adj* **1** insuficiente **2** incapaz

inadvertently /ˌɪnəd'vɜːrtəntli/ *adv* sin querer, sin darse cuenta

inappropriate /ˌɪnə'proupriət/ *adj* poco apropiado, impropio

inaugural /ɪ'nɔːɡjərəl/ *adj* 1 inaugural 2 (*discurso*) de apertura

inaugurate /ɪ'nɔːɡjəreɪt/ *vt* 1 investir 2 inaugurar

incapable /ɪn'keɪpəbl/ *adj* 1 incapaz 2 incompetente

incapacity /ˌɪnkə'pæsəti/ *n* incapacidad

incense /'ɪnsens/ *n* incienso

incensed /ɪn'senst/ *adj* furioso

incentive /ɪn'sentɪv/ *n* incentivo, aliciente

incessant /ɪn'sesnt/ *adj* incesante **incessantly** *adv* sin parar

incest /'ɪnsest/ *n* incesto

inch /ɪntʃ/ *n* (*abrev* **in.**) pulgada (25,4 *mm*) → Ver pág. 222 ▸ **not give an inch** no ceder ni un palmo

incidence /'ɪnsɪdəns/ *n* ~ **of** frecuencia, tasa, casos de algo

incident /'ɪnsɪdənt/ *n* incidente: *without* ~ sin novedad

incidental /ˌɪnsɪ'dentl/ *adj* 1 ocasional, fortuito 2 secundario, marginal **incidentally** *adv* 1 a propósito 2 de paso

incisive /ɪn'saɪsɪv/ *adj* 1 (*comentario*) incisivo 2 (*tono*) mordaz 3 (*mente*) penetrante

incite /ɪn'saɪt/ *vt* incitar

inclination /ˌɪnklɪ'neɪʃn/ *n* inclinación, tendencia: *not have the time nor* ~ *to do sth* no tener ni tiempo ni ganas de hacer algo

incline /ɪn'klaɪn/ *n* pendiente ● /ɪn'klaɪn/ *vt, vi* inclinar(se) **inclined** *adj* **be** ~ **to do sth** 1 (*voluntad*) inclinarse, estar dispuesto a hacer algo 2 (*tendencia*) ser propenso a (hacer) algo

include /ɪn'kluːd/ *vt* incluir **including** *prep* incluir, inclusive **inclusion** *n* inclusión **inclusive** *adj* 1 incluido: **be** ~ **of** sth incluir algo 2 inclusive

incoherent /ˌɪnkou'hɪərənt/ *adj* incoherente

income /'ɪnkʌm/ *n* ingresos: ~ *tax* impuesto sobre la renta

incoming /'ɪnkʌmɪŋ/ *adj* entrante

incompetent /ɪn'kɒmpɪtənt/ *adj, n* incompetente

incomplete /ˌɪnkəm'pliːt/ *adj* incompleto

incomprehensible /ɪnˌkɒmprɪ'hensəbl/ *adj* incomprensible

inconceivable /ˌɪnkən'siːvəbl/ *adj* inconcebible

inconclusive /ˌɪnkən'kluːsɪv/ *adj* no concluyente: *The meeting was* ~. La reunión no llegó a ninguna conclusión.

incongruous /ɪn'kɒŋɡruəs/ *adj* incongruente

inconsiderate /ˌɪnkən'sɪdərət/ *adj* desconsiderado

inconsistent /ˌɪnkən'sɪstənt/ *adj* inconsecuente

inconspicuous /ˌɪnkən'spɪkjuəs/ *adj* 1 apenas visible 2 poco llamativo: *make yourself* ~ procurar pasar inadvertido

inconvenience /ˌɪnkən'viːniəns/ *n* [U] 1 inconveniente 2 molestia ● *vt* incomodar **inconvenient** *adj* 1 molesto 2 inoportuno

incorporate /ɪn'kɔːrpəreɪt/ *vt* 1 incorporar 2 incluir 3 *incorporated company* sociedad anónima

incorrect /ˌɪnkə'rekt/ *adj* incorrecto

increase /'ɪnkriːs/ *n* ~ **(in sth)** aumento (de algo): *on the* ~ en aumento ● /ɪn'kriːs/ *vt, vi* 1 aumentar 2 incrementar(se) **increasing** *adj* creciente **increasingly** *adv* cada vez más

incredible /ɪn'kredəbl/ *adj* increíble

indecisive /ˌɪndɪ'saɪsɪv/ *adj* 1 indeciso 2 no concluyente

indeed /ɪn'diːd/ *adv* 1 (*énfasis*) de verdad: *Thank you very much* ~! ¡Muchísimas gracias! 2 de veras: *Did you* ~? ¿De veras? 3 (*fml*) de hecho

indefensible /ˌɪndɪ'fensəbl/ *adj* intolerable (*comportamiento*)

indefinite /ɪn'defɪnət/ *adj* 1 vago 2 (*tb Gram*) indefinido **indefinitely** *adv* 1 indefinidamente 2 por tiempo indefinido

indelible /ɪn'deləbl/ *adj* imborrable, indeleble

indemnity /ɪn'demnəti/ *n* (*pl* -ies) 1 indemnización 2 indemnidad

independence /ˌɪndɪ'pendəns/ *n* independencia

Independence Day *n* día de la Independencia **NOTA** Se celebra en EE.UU. el 4 de julio, con fuegos artificiales y desfiles. También se le llama **Fourth of July**.

independent /ˌɪndɪ'pendənt/ *adj* 1 independiente 2 (*colegio*) privado

in-depth *adj* a fondo, exhaustivo

indescribable /ˌɪndɪ'skraɪbəbl/ *adj* indescriptible

index /'ɪndeks/ *n* 1 (*libro*) índice: ~ *finger* dedo índice ◊ *index-linked* actualizado según el costo de la vida **2** (GB) (tb **card ~**) (archivo) ficha **3** (pl **indices** /'ındisiːz/) (Mat) exponente

indicate /'ındıkeıt/ **1** vt indicar **2** vi poner las direcciones **indication** n **1** indicación **2** indicio, señal

indicative /ın'dıkǝtıv/ adj, n indicativo

indicator /'ındıkeıtǝr/ n **1** indicador **2** (GB, Aut) direccional

indictment /ın'daıtmǝnt/ n **1** acusación **2** procesamiento **indict** vt

indifferent /ın'dıfrǝnt/ adj **1** indiferente **2** mediocre **indifference** n indiferencia

indigenous /ın'dıdʒǝnǝs/ adj (fml) indígena

indigestion /,ındı'dʒestʃǝn/ n indigestión

indignant /ın'dıgnǝnt/ adj indignado **indignation** n indignación

indignity /ın'dıgnǝti/ n (pl -ies) humillación

indirect /,ındǝ'rekt, ,ındaı-/ adj indirecto **indirectly** adv indirectamente

indiscreet /,ındı'skriːt/ adj indiscreto **indiscretion** /,ındı'skreʃn/ n indiscreción

indiscriminate /,ındı'skrımınǝt/ adj indiscriminado

indispensable /,ındı'spensǝbl/ adj imprescindible

indisputable /,ındı'spjuːtǝbl/ adj irrefutable

indistinct /,ındı'stıŋkt/ adj poco claro

individual /,ındı'vıdʒuǝl/ adj **1** individual **2** suelto **3** personal **4** particular, original ● n individuo **individualism** n individualismo **individually** adv **1** por separado **2** individualmente

indoctrination /ın,dɒktrı'neıʃn/ n adoctrinamiento

indoor /'ındɔːr/ adj (de) interior: **~ pool** piscina/alberca cubierta ◇ **~ activities** juegos de salón **indoors** adv en casa

induce /ın'duːs; ın'djuːs GB/ vt **1 ~ sb to do sth** inducir a algn a que haga algo **2** causar **3** (Med) inducir el parto de

induction /ın'dʌkʃn/ n iniciación: **an ~ course** un curso de introducción

indulge /ın'dʌldʒ/ **1** vt: **~ yourself** darse el placer **2** vt complacer, satisfacer **3** vi **~ (in sth)** darse el gusto (de algo)

indulgence /ın'dʌldʒǝns/ n **1** indulgencia, tolerancia **2** vicio, placer **indulgent** adj indulgente

industrial /ın'dʌstrıǝl/ adj **1** industrial **2** laboral **industrialist** n empresario/a, industrial

industrialize /ın'dʌstrıǝlaız/ vt industrializar **industrialization** n industrialización

industrious /ın'dʌstrıǝs/ adj trabajador

industry /'ındǝstri/ n (pl -ies) **1** industria **2** (fml) aplicación

inedible /ın'edǝbl/ adj no comestible, incomible

ineffective /,ını'fektıv/ adj **1** ineficaz **2** (persona) incapaz

inefficiency /,ını'fıʃnsi/ n **1** incompetencia **2** ineficacia **inefficient** adj **1** ineficaz **2** incompetente

ineligible /ın'elıdʒǝbl/ adj **be ~ (for sth/to do sth)** no tener derecho (a algo)

inept /ı'nept/ adj inepto

inequality /,ını'kwɒlǝti/ n (pl -ies) desigualdad

inert /ı'nɜːrt/ adj inerte

inertia /ı'nɜːrʃǝ/ n inercia

inescapable /,ını'skeıpǝbl/ adj ineludible

inevitable /ın'evıtǝbl/ adj inevitable **inevitably** adv inevitablemente

inexcusable /,ınık'skjuːzǝbl/ adj imperdonable

inexhaustible /,ınıg'zɔːstǝbl/ adj inagotable

inexpensive /,ınık'spensıv/ adj económico

inexperience /,ınık'spıǝrıǝns/ n inexperiencia **inexperienced** adj sin experiencia, inexperto

inexplicable /,ınık'splıkǝbl/ adj inexplicable

infallible /ın'fælǝbl/ adj infalible **infallibility** /ın,fælǝ'bılǝti/ n infalibilidad

infamous /'ınfǝmǝs/ adj infame

infancy /'ınfǝnsi/ n **1** infancia: **in ~ de niño 2** It's still in its **~**. Todavía está en desarrollo.

infant /'ınfǝnt/ n niño pequeño: **~ school** escuela primaria (hasta los 7 años) ◇ **~ mortality rate** tasa de mortalidad infantil **NOTA** Baby, toddler y child son más comunes. ● adj naciente

infantile /'ınfǝntaıl/ adj (pey) infantil

infantry /'ınfǝntri/ n infantería

infatuated /ın'fætʃueıtıd/ adj encaprichado **infatuation** n encaprichamiento

infect /ın'fekt/ vt **1** infectar **2** contagiar **infection** n infección **infectious** adj infeccioso

I

infer /ɪnˈfɜːr/ vt (-rr-) **1** deducir **2** insinuar **inference** /ˈɪnfərəns/ n conclusión: by ~ por deducción

inferior /ɪnˈfɪəriər/ adj, n inferior **inferiority** /ɪnˌfɪəriˈɒrəti/ n inferioridad

infertile /ɪnˈfɜːtl; -tail GB/ adj estéril **infertility** /ˌɪnfɜːˈtɪləti/ n esterilidad

infest /ɪnˈfest/ vt infestar **infestation** n plaga

infidelity /ˌɪnfɪˈdeləti/ n infidelidad

infiltrate /ˈɪnfɪltreɪt/ vt, vi infiltrar(se)

infinite /ˈɪnfɪnət/ adj infinito **infinitely** adv muchísimo

infinitive /ɪnˈfɪnətɪv/ n infinitivo

infinity /ɪnˈfɪnəti/ n **1** infinidad **2** infinito

infirm /ɪnˈfɜːm/ adj débil, achacoso **infirmity** n (pl -ies) **1** debilidad **2** achaque

infirmary /ɪnˈfɜːrməri/ n (pl -ies) hospital

inflamed /ɪnˈfleɪmd/ adj **1** (Med) inflamado **2** acalorado

inflammable /ɪnˈflæməbl/ adj inflamable **NOTA** Flammable es sinónimo de inflammable.

inflammation /ˌɪnfləˈmeɪʃn/ n inflamación

inflate /ɪnˈfleɪt/ vt, vi inflar(se)

inflation /ɪnˈfleɪʃn/ n inflación

inflexible /ɪnˈfleksəbl/ adj inflexible

inflict /ɪnˈflɪkt/ vt **1** infligir **2** (daño) causar **3** imponer

influence /ˈɪnfluəns/ n **1** influencia **2** palancas ● vt **1** ~ sth en/sobre algo **2** ~ sb influenciar a algn **influential** /ˌɪnfluˈenʃl/ adj influyente

influenza /ˌɪnfluˈenzə/ n [U] (fml) gripa

influx /ˈɪnflʌks/ n afluencia

inform /ɪnˈfɔːrm/ vt **1** informar **2** vi ~ against/on sb delatar a algn **informant** n informante

informal /ɪnˈfɔːrml/ adj **1** informal, no oficial **2** (persona, tono) familiar, sencillo

information /ˌɪnfərˈmeɪʃn/ n [U] información: a piece of ~ un dato →CONSEJO

information technology Ver IT

informative /ɪnˈfɔːrmətɪv/ adj informativo

informer /ɪnˈfɔːrmər/ n soplón, -ona

infrastructure /ˈɪnfrəstrʌktʃər/ n infraestructura

infrequent /ɪnˈfriːkwənt/ adj poco frecuente

infringe /ɪnˈfrɪndʒ/ vt infringir

infuriate /ɪnˈfjʊərieɪt/ vt enfurecer **infuriating** adj desesperante

ingenious /ɪnˈdʒiːniəs/ adj ingenioso

ingenuity /ˌɪndʒəˈnuːəti; -ˈnjuː- GB/ n ingenio

ingrained /ɪnˈɡreɪnd/ adj arraigado

ingredient /ɪnˈɡriːdiənt/ n ingrediente

inhabit /ɪnˈhæbɪt/ vt habitar

inhabitant /ɪnˈhæbɪtənt/ n habitante

inhale /ɪnˈheɪl/ vt, vi inhalar (el humo)

inherent /ɪnˈhɪərənt/ adj inherente **inherently** adv intrínsecamente

inherit /ɪnˈherɪt/ vt heredar **inheritance** n herencia

inhibit /ɪnˈhɪbɪt/ vt **1** ~ sb (from doing sth) impedir a algn (hacer algo) **2** dificultar **inhibited** adj cohibido **inhibition** n inhibición

inhospitable /ˌɪnhɒˈspɪtəbl/ adj **1** inhospitalario **2** inhóspito

inhuman /ɪnˈhjuːmən/ adj inhumano, despiadado

initial /ɪˈnɪʃl/ adj, n inicial ● vt (-l-, -ll- GB) poner las iniciales (en, **initially** adj en un principio, inicialmente

initiate /ɪˈnɪʃieɪt/ vt **1** (fml) iniciar **2** (juicio) entablar **initiation** n iniciación

initiative /ɪˈnɪʃətɪv/ n iniciativa

inject /ɪnˈdʒekt/ vt inyectar **injection** n inyección

injure /ˈɪndʒər/ vt herir, lesionar: Six people were injured. Seis personas resultaron heridas. → HERIDA **injured** adj **1** herido, lesionado **2** (tono) ofendido

injury /ˈɪndʒəri/ n (pl -ies) **1** herida, lesión: ~ time (GB) tiempo de descuento → HERIDA **2** perjuicio

injustice /ɪnˈdʒʌstɪs/ n injusticia

ink /ɪŋk/ n tinta

inkling /ˈɪŋklɪŋ/ n indicio, idea

inland /ˈɪnlænd/ adj (del) interior ● /ˌɪnˈlænd/ adv hacia el interior

Inland Revenue n (GB) Hacienda, Dirección de Impuestos

in-laws /ˈɪn lɔːz/ n [pl] (coloq) **1** familia política **2** suegros

inlet /ˈɪnlet/ n **1** ensenada **2** entrada

in-line skate n patín en línea

inmate /ˈɪnmeɪt/ n interno/a (en un recinto vigilado)

inn /ɪn/ n **1** (USA) posada **2** (GB) taberna

innate /ɪˈneɪt/ adj innato

inner /'mər/ *adj* **1** interior, interno **2** íntimo

innermost /'məmoʊst/ *adj* **1** más íntimo **2** más recóndito

innocent /'məsnt/ *adj* inocente **innocence** *n* inocencia

innocuous /r'nɑkjuəs/ *adj* inofensivo **2** inocuo

innovate /'məveɪt/ *vi* introducir novedades **innovation** *n* innovación **innovative** /'məveɪtɪv; -vət- *GB/ adj* innovador

innuendo /ˌmju'endoʊ/ *n* (*pey*) insinuación

innumerable /r'nuːmərəbl; r'njuː-GB/ *adj* innumerable

inoculate /r'nɑkjuleɪt/ *vt* vacunar **inoculation** *n* vacuna

input /'mpʊt/ *n* **1** contribución, aporte **2** (*Comp*) entrada

inquest /'mkwest/ *n* ~ (**on sb/into sth**) investigación (judicial) (acerca de algn/algo)

inquire /m'kwaɪər/ (*fml*) **1** *vt* preguntar **2** *vi* pedir información **inquiring** *adj* (*mente*) curioso **2** inquisitivo **inquiry** (*pl* **-ies**) **1** ~ (**into sth**) investigación (sobre algo) **2** pregunta **3** inquiries (*GB*) [*pl*] oficina de información

inquisition /ˌmkwr'zɪʃn/ *n* (*fml*) interrogatorio

inquisitive /m'kwɪzətɪv/ *adj* inquisitivo

insane /m'seɪn/ *adj* loco

insanity /m'sænəti/ *n* demencia, locura

insatiable /m'seɪʃəbl/ *adj* insaciable

inscribe /m'skraɪb/ *vt* grabar **inscription** /m'skrɪpʃn/ *n* **1** inscripción **2** dedicatoria

insect /'msekt/ *n* insecto **insecticide** /m'sektɪsaɪd/ *n* insecticida

insecure /ˌmsr'kjʊər/ *adj* inseguro **insecurity** *n* inseguridad

insensitive /m'sensətɪv/ *adj* **1** insensible **2** (*acto*) falto de sensibilidad **insensitivity** /m,sensə-'tɪvəti/ *n* insensibilidad

inseparable /m'seprəbl/ *adj* inseparable

insert /m'sɜːrt/ *vt* insertar, meter

inside /m'saɪd/ *n* **1** interior: *on/from the ~* por/desde dentro **2 insides** [*pl*] (*coloq*) tripas ▸ **inside out 1** al revés: *You have your sweater on ~ out.* Llevas el suéter al revés. **2** de arriba abajo: *know sth ~ out* conocer algo como la palma de la mano (*tb ~ of USA*) dentro de ● *adv* (a)dentro ● /'msaɪd/ *adj* [*antes de sustantivo*] interior, interno

insider /m'saɪdər/ *n* alguien de adentro (*empresa, grupo*)

insight /'msaɪt/ *n* **1** perspicacia **2** ~ (**into sth**) idea (de algo)

insignificant /ˌmsɪg'nɪfɪkənt/ *adj* insignificante **insignificance** *n* insignificancia

insincere /ˌmsɪn'sɪər/ *adj* falso, hipócrita **insincerity** /ˌmsɪn-'serəti/ *n* insinceridad

insinuate /m'smjueɪt/ *vt* insinuar **insinuation** *n* insinuación

insist /m'sɪst/ *vi* **1** insistir **2** empeñarse **insistence** *n* insistencia **insistent** *n* insistente

insolent /'msələnt/ *adj* insolente **insolence** *n* insolencia

insomnia /m'sɑmniə/ *n* insomnio

inspect /m'spekt/ *vt* **1** inspeccionar **2** (*equipaje*) registrar **inspection** *n* inspección **inspector** *n* **1** inspector/a **2** (*tren, etc.*) revisor/a

inspiration /ˌmspə'reɪʃn/ *n* inspiración

inspire /m'spaɪər/ *vt* **1** inspirar **2** ~ **sth** (**in sb**); ~ **sb** **with sth** infundir algo (en algn)

instability /ˌmstə'bɪləti/ *n* inestabilidad

install /m'stɔːl/ *vt* instalar **installation** /ˌmstə'leɪʃn/ *n* instalación

installment (**instalment** *GB*) /m'stɔːlmənt/ *n* **1** entrega, fascículo **2** (*TV*) episodio **3** ~ (**on sth**) (*pago*) plazo (de algo)

instance /'mstəns/ *n* caso ▸ **for instance** por ejemplo

instant /'mstənt/ *n* instante ● *adj* **1** inmediato **2** (*café*) instantáneo **instantly** *adv* inmediatamente

instantaneous /ˌmstən'temiəs/ *adj* instantáneo

instead /m'sted/ *adv* en vez de eso ● *prep* ~ **of** en vez de

instigate /'mstɪgeɪt/ *vt* instigar **instigation** *n* instigación

instinct /'mstɪŋkt/ *n* instinto **instinctive** /m'stɪŋktɪv/ *adj* instintivo

institute /'mstɪtuːt; -tjuːt *GB/ n* instituto, centro ● *vt* (*fml*) iniciar, introducir

institution /ˌmstɪ'tuːʃn; -'tjuːʃn *GB/ n* institución **institutional** *adj* institucional

instruct /m'strʌkt/ *vt* (*fml*) **1** ~ **sb** (**in sth**) enseñar (algo) a algn **2** dar instrucciones a **instructive** *adj* instructivo

instruction /m'strʌkʃn/ *n* **1** instructions instrucciones **2** ~ (**in sth**) formación (en algo)

instructor /m'strʌktər/ *n* profesor/a, instructor/a

instrument /'mstrəmənt/ n instrumento

instrumental /ˌmstrə'mentl/ adj 1 be ~ in sth contribuir materialmente a algo 2 (Mús) instrumental

insufferable /m'sʌfrəbl/ adj insufrible

insufficient /ˌmsə'fɪʃnt/ adj insuficiente

insular /'msələr; -sjələ(r) GB/ adj estrecho de miras

insulate /'msəleɪt; -sjul- GB/ vt aislar **insulation** n material aislante

insult /'msʌlt/ n insulto ● /m-'sʌlt/ vt insultar **insulting** adj insultante

insurance /m'ʃʊərəns/ n [U] seguro (Fin)

insure /m'ʃʊər/ vt 1 ~ sth/sb (for/against sth) asegurar algo/a algn (contra algo) 2 (USA) garantizar

intact /m'tækt/ adj intacto

intake /'mteɪk/ n 1 (comida, etc.) consumo 2 número admitido: We have an annual ~ of 20. Admitimos a 20 cada año.

integral /'mtɪgrəl/ adj esencial

integrate /'mtɪgreɪt/ vt, vi integrar(se) **integration** n integración

integrity /m'tegrəti/ n integridad

intellectual /ˌmtə'lektʃuəl/ adj, n intelectual

intelligence /m'telɪdʒəns/ n inteligencia **intelligent** adj inteligente

intend /m'tend/ vt 1 ~ to do sth pensar hacer algo, tener la intención de hacer algo 2 ~ sth for sth/sb destinar algo a algo/algn: They're not intended for eating. No son para comer. 3 ~ sb to do sth: I ~ you to take over. Mi intención es que te hagas cargo. ◊ You weren't intended to hear that. Tú no tenías que haber oído eso. 4 ~ sth as sth: It was intended as a joke. Se suponía que era una broma.

intense /m'tens/ adj 1 intenso 2 fuerte 3 (persona) serio **intensely** adv intensamente, sumamente **intensify** vt, vi (pt/pp -ied) intensificar(se) **intensity** n intensidad, fuerza

intensive /m'tensɪv/ adj intensivo: ~ care cuidados intensivos

intent /m'tent/ adj 1 (concentrado) atento 2 ~ on/upon sth (fml) resuelto a algo 3 ~ on/upon sth absorto en algo ● n ▸ to/for/to (GB) all intents (and purposes) para los efectos prácticos **intently** adv atentamente

intention /m'tenʃn/ n intención **intentional** adj intencionado

interact /ˌmtər'ækt/ vi 1 (personas) relacionarse entre sí 2 (cosas) influirse mutuamente **interaction** n 1 (personas) relación 2 interacción **interactive** adj interactivo

intercept /ˌmtər'sept/ vt interceptar

interchange /'mtərtʃeɪndʒ/ n intercambio ● /ˌmtər'tʃeɪndʒ/ vt intercambiar **interchangeable** adj intercambiable

interconnect /ˌmtərkə'nekt/ vi 1 conectarse entre sí 2 comunicarse entre sí **interconnected** adj: be ~ tener conexión entre sí **interconnection** n conexión

intercourse /'mtərkɔːrs/ n (fml) relaciones sexuales, coito

interest /'mtrəst/ n 1 ~ (in sth) interés (por algo): It is of no ~ to me. No me interesa. 2 afición: her main ~ lo que más le interesa 3 (Fin) interés ▸ in sb's interest(s) en interés de algn in the interest(s) of sth en aras de/con el fin de algo: in the ~s of safety por razones de seguridad ● vt 1 interesar 2 ~ sb in sth hacer que algn se interese por algo **interested** /'mtrəstɪd/ adj interesado: be ~ in sth interesarse por algo →BE

interesting /'mtrəstɪŋ/ adj interesante **NOTA** Una frase como "Me interesa mucho la informática" se traduce por: I'm very interested in computers. Interesting describe la cualidad y equivale a "interesante": an ~ book. → BE **interestingly** adv curiosamente

interface /'mtərfeɪs/ n (Comp) interface

interfere /ˌmtər'fɪər/ vi 1 entrometerse 2 ~ with sth toquetear algo 3 ~ with sth dificultar, interponerse en algo **interference** n [U] 1 intromisión 2 (Radio) interferencias **interfering** adj entrometido

interim /'mtərɪm/ adj provisional ● n ▸ in the interim mientras tanto

interior /m'tɪəriər/ adj, n interior

interlude /'mtərluːd/ n intermedio

intermediate /ˌmtər'miːdiət/ adj intermedio

intermission /ˌmtər'mɪʃn/ n intermedio

intern /m'tɜːrn/ vt internar

internal /ɪnˈtɜːrnl/ adj interno, interior

international /ˌɪntərˈnæʃnəl/ adj internacional ● n (Dep) 1 partido internacional 2 jugador/a internacional

Internet /ˈɪntərnet/ n internet: on the ~ en internet →INTERNET

interpret /ɪnˈtɜːrprɪt/ vt interpretar **NOTA** Interpret se refiere a la traducción oral, y **translate** a la escrita. **interpretation** n interpretación **interpreter** n intérprete

interrelated /ˌɪntərɪˈleɪtɪd/ adj interrelacionado

interrogate /ɪnˈterəgeɪt/ vt interrogar **interrogation** n interrogación **interrogator** n interrogador/a

interrogative /ˌɪntəˈrɒgətɪv/ adj interrogativo

interrupt /ˌɪntəˈrʌpt/ vt, vi interrumpir **interruption** n interrupción

intersect /ˌɪntərˈsekt/ vi cruzarse **intersection** n intersección, cruce

interspersed /ˌɪntərˈspɜːrst/ adj ~ with sth intercalado con algo

interstate /ˈɪntərsteɪt/ n carretera, autopista

intertwine /ˌɪntərˈtwaɪn/ vt, vi entrelazar(se)

interval /ˈɪntərvl/ n 1 intervalo 2 (GB, Teat, etc.) intermedio

intervene /ˌɪntərˈviːn/ vi 1 intervenir 2 (fml) (tiempo) transcurrir 3 interponerse **intervening** adj intermedio **intervention** n intervención

interview /ˈɪntərvjuː/ n entrevista ● vt entrevistar **interviewee** n entrevistado/a **interviewer** n entrevistador/a

interweave /ˌɪntərˈwiːv/ vt, vi (pt -wove /-ˈwoʊv/ pp -woven /-ˈwoʊvn/) entretejer(se)

intestine /ɪnˈtestɪn/ n intestino

intimacy /ˈɪntɪməsi/ n intimidad

intimate /ˈɪntɪmət/ adj 1 íntimo 2 (amistad) estrecho 3 (conocimiento) profundo ● /ˈɪntɪmeɪt/ vt (fml) dar a entender **intimation** n (fml) indicación, indicio

intimidate /ɪnˈtɪmɪdeɪt/ vt intimidar **intimidation** n intimidación

into /ˈɪntə/ **NOTA** Antes de vocal y al final de la frase se pronuncia /ˈɪntuː/ . prep 1 en, dentro de: come ~ the house entrar en la casa ◇ go ~ town al centro ◇ translate ~ Spanish traducir al español 2 (tiempo, distancia): long ~ the night bien entrada la noche ◇ far ~ the distance a lo lejos 4 (Mat): 12 ~ 144 goes 12 times. 144 dividido por 12 son 12. ▸ **be into sth** (coloq) ser aficionado a algo **NOTA** Para el uso de **into** en PHRASAL VERBS ver el verbo, p.ej. **look into** en LOOK.

intolerable /ɪnˈtɒlərəbl/ adj intolerable, insufrible

intolerant /ɪnˈtɒlərənt/ adj intolerante **intolerance** n intolerancia, intransigencia

intonation /ˌɪntəˈneɪʃn/ n entonación

intoxication /ɪnˌtɒksɪˈkeɪʃn/ n 1 embriaguez 2 (Med) intoxicación **intoxicated** adj (fml) ebrio

Intranet /ˈɪntrənet/ n intranet

intrepid /ɪnˈtrepɪd/ adj intrépido

intricate /ˈɪntrɪkət/ adj intrincado, complejo

intrigue /ˈɪntriːg/ n intriga ● /ɪnˈtriːg/ 1 vi intrigar 2 vt fascinar **intriguing** adj fascinante

intrinsic /ɪnˈtrɪnsɪk/ adj intrínseco

introduce /ˌɪntrəˈduːs; -ˈdjuːs GB/ vt 1 presentar 2 ~ sb to sth iniciar a algn en algo 3 (producto, ley, etc.) introducir

introduction /ˌɪntrəˈdʌkʃn/ n 1 presentación 2 prólogo 3 ~ to sth iniciación a/en algo 4 [U] introducción (producto, ley, etc.) **introductory** 1 preliminar 2 (oferta) introductorio

introvert /ˈɪntrəvɜːrt/ n introvertido/a

intrude /ɪnˈtruːd/ vi 1 molestar 2 ~ (on/upon sth) entrometerse (en algo) **intruder** n intruso/a **intrusion** n 1 [U] invasión 2 intromisión **intrusive** adj intruso

intuition /ˌɪntuˈɪʃn; -tjuː- GB/ n intuición **intuitive** /ɪnˈtuːɪtɪv; -tjuː- GB/ adj intuitivo

inundate /ˈɪnʌndeɪt/ vt ~ sth/sb (with sth) inundar algo/a algn (de algo)

invade /ɪnˈveɪd/ vt, vi invadir **invader** n invasor/a

invalid /ˈɪnvəlɪd/ n inválido/a ● /ɪnˈvælɪd/ adj no válido, nulo

invalidate /ɪnˈvælɪdeɪt/ vt invalidar, anular

invaluable /ɪnˈvæljuəbl/ adj inestimable

invariably /ɪnˈveəriəbli/ adv invariablemente

invasion /ɪnˈveɪʒn/ n invasión

invent /ɪnˈvent/ vt inventar **invention** n 1 invención 2 invento **inventive** adj 1 (poderes) de invención 2 ingenioso **inventiveness** n inventiva **inventor** n inventor/a

inventory /'ɪnvəntəːri; -tri GB/ n (pl -ies) inventario

invert /ɪn'vɜːt/ vt invertir

invertebrate /ɪn'vɜːtɪbrət/ adj, n invertebrado

inverted commas n (GB) comillas

invest /ɪn'vest/ vt, vi (Fin) invertir

investment n inversión **investor** n inversor/a

investigate /ɪn'vestɪgeɪt/ vt, vi investigar **investigation** ~ (into sth) investigación (de algo) **investigative** /ɪn'vestɪgeɪtɪv; -gətɪv GB/ adj: ~ journalism periodismo investigativo **investigator** /ɪn'vestɪgeɪtər/ n investigador/a

invigorating /ɪn'vɪgəreɪtɪŋ/ adj vigorizante, estimulante

invincible /ɪn'vɪnsəbl/ adj invencible

invisible /ɪn'vɪzəbl/ adj invisible

invitation /ˌɪnvɪ'teɪʃn/ n invitación

invite /ɪn'vaɪt/ vt 1 invitar: ~ trouble buscarse problemas 2 (sugerencias, aportes) pedir, solicitar ■ invite sb back 1 devolverle la invitación a algn 2 invitar a algn a volver con uno a su casa **invite sb in/out** invitar a algn a entrar/salir **invite sb over/around** invitar a algn a casa ● /ˈɪnvaɪt/ n (coloq) invitación **inviting** /ɪn'vaɪtɪŋ/ adj 1 atractivo, tentador 2 (comida) apetitoso

invoice /'ɪnvɔɪs/ n factura ● vt pasar factura a

involuntary /ɪn'vɒləntəri; -tri GB/ adj involuntario

involve /ɪn'vɒlv/ vt 1 suponer, implicar: The job ~s me traveling. El trabajo requiere que viaje. 2 hacer participar a: be involved in sth participar en algo 3 meter, enredar: Don't ~ me in your problems. No me mezcles en tus problemas. 4 involucrar: get involved in sth involucrarse en algo 5 be/get involved with sb estar enredado, enredarse con algn **involved** adj complicado **involvement** n 1 ~ (in sth) implicación, compromiso, participación (en algo) 2 ~ (with sb) relación (con algn)

inward /'ɪnwərd/ adj 1 interior, íntimo: give an ~ sigh suspirar para sí 2 (dirección) hacia dentro ● adv (tb **inwards** GB) hacia dentro **inwardly** adv 1 por dentro 2 (suspirar, sonreír, etc.) para sí

IQ /ˌaɪ 'kjuː/ n (abrev de intelligence quotient) coeficiente de inteligencia

iris /'aɪrɪs/ n 1 (Anat) iris 2 (Bot) lirio

iron /'aɪərn; 'aɪən GB/ n 1 hierro 2 (para ropa) plancha ● vt planchar ■ **iron sth out** 1 planchar algo 2 (problema) resolver algo **ironing** n 1 planchado: do the ~ planchar 2 ropa planchada/por planchar

ironic /aɪ'rɒnɪk/ adj irónico: give an ~ smile. sonreír irónicamente.

irony /'aɪrəni/ n (pl -ies) ironía

irrational /ɪ'ræʃənl/ adj irracional **irrationality** /ɪˌræʃə'næləti/ n irracionalidad

irrelevant /ɪ'reləvənt/ adj que no viene al caso **irrelevance** n algo que no viene al caso: the ~ of the curriculum to their lives lo poco que el currículo tiene que ver con sus vidas

irresistible /ˌɪrɪ'zɪstəbl/ adj irresistible

irrespective of /ˌɪrɪ'spektɪv əv/ prep sin consideración a

irresponsible /ˌɪrɪ'spɒnsəbl/ adj irresponsable: It's ~ of you. Es una irresponsabilidad de tu parte. **irresponsibility** /ˌɪrɪˌspɒnsə'bɪləti/ n irresponsabilidad

irrigation /ˌɪrɪ'geɪʃn/ n riego

irritable /'ɪrɪtəbl/ adj irritable **irritability** /ˌɪrɪtə'bɪləti/ n irritabilidad **irritably** adv con irritación

irritate /'ɪrɪteɪt/ vt irritar **irritating** adj irritante: How ~! ¡Qué fastidio! **irritation** n irritación

is /ɪz/ Ver BE

Islam /'ɪzlɑːm/ n Islam **Islamic** /ɪz'læmɪk/ adj islámico

island /'aɪlənd/ n (abrev I, Is.) isla **islander** n isleño/a

isle /aɪl/ n (abrev I, Is.) isla **NOTA** Se usa esp en nombres de lugares, p.ej.: the Isle of Man.

isn't /'ɪznt/ = IS NOT

isolate /'aɪsəleɪt/ vt aislar **isolated** adj aislado **isolation** n aislamiento ▸ **in isolation** aislado: Looked at in isolation... Considerado fuera del contexto...

issue /'ɪʃuː/ n 1 asunto 2 emisión, provisión 3 (Period) número ▸ **make an issue (out) of sth** convertir algo en un problema ● vt 1 distribuir 2 ~ sb with sth proveer a algn de algo 3 (visa, etc.) expedir 4 (libro, revista, etc) publicar 5 (llamada) poner en circulación 6 emitir 7 vi ~ from sth (fml) salir de algo

IT /ˌaɪ 'tiː/ n (abrev de information technology) informática

it /ɪt/ pron ● como sujeto y objeto: It se refiere a un animal o una cosa, o también a un bebé. 1 [como

sujeto] él, ella, ello: *Who is it?* ¿Quién es? ◊ *It's me.* Soy yo. →YOU 2 [*como objeto directo*] lo, la: *Give it to me.* Dámelo. 3 [*como objeto indirecto*] le: *Give it some milk.* Dale un poco de leche. 4 [*después de prep*]: *That box is heavy. What's inside it?* Esa caja pesa mucho, ¿qué hay adentro?
● **frases impersonales**: A menudo **it** carece de significado, y se usa como sujeto gramatical en oraciones que en español suelen ser impersonales. Normalmente no se traduce. 1 (*tiempo, distancia y clima*): *It's ten past two.* Son las dos y diez. ◊ *It's a kilometer to the beach.* Hay un kilómetro hasta la playa. ◊ *It's a long time since he left.* Hace mucho tiempo que se fue. ◊ *It's hot.* Hace calor. 2 (*en otras construcciones*): *Does it really matter?* ¿De verdad importa? ◊ *I'll come at one if it's convenient.* Vendré a la una, si te parece bien. ▸ **that's it** 1 ya está 2 eso es todo 3 ya está bien 4 eso es **that's just it** ahí está el problema **this is it** ya llegó la hora

italics /'ɪtælɪks/ *n* [*pl*] cursiva

itch /ɪtʃ/ *n* picor ● *vi* 1 picar 2 (*coloq*) ~ **for sth/to do sth** tener muchas ganas de algo **itchy** *adj*: *My skin is* ~. Me pica la piel.

it'd /'ɪtəd/ 1 = IT HAD 2 = IT WOULD

item /'aɪtəm/ *n* 1 artículo 2 (*tb* **news** ~) noticia 3 **an item** (*coloq*) pareja (*de novios*)

itinerary /aɪ'tɪnərери; -rəri *GB*/ *n* (*pl* **-ies**) itinerario

it'll /'ɪtl/ = IT WILL

its /ɪts/ *adj* su(s) (*de una cosa, un animal o un bebé*) →

it's /ɪts/ 1 = IT IS 2 = IT HAS

itself /ɪt'self/ *pron* 1 [*reflexivo*] se: *The cat's washing* ~. El gato se está bañando. 2 [*énfasis*] (él) (ella/ello) mismo/a 3 *She is kindness* ~. Es la bondad personificada. ▸ **by itself** 1 por sí mismo 2 solo **in itself** de por sí

I've /aɪv/ = I HAVE

ivory /'aɪvəri/ *n* marfil

ivy /'aɪvi/ *n* hiedra

J j

J, j /dʒeɪ/ *n* (*pl* **J's, j's**) J, j
jab /dʒæb/ *vt, vi* (**-bb-**) 1 *vt, vi* ~ (**at**) **sth** pinchar algo 2 ~ **sth into sth/sb** clavar algo en algo/a algn ● *n* 1 (*GB, coloq*) inyección 2 golpe

jack /dʒæk/ *n* 1 (*Mec*) gato 2 jota (*baraja francesa*) →BARAJA
jackal /'dʒækl/ *n* chacal
jackdaw /'dʒækdɔː/ *n* grajilla
jacket /'dʒækɪt/ *n* 1 chaqueta, saco 2 (*libro*) sobrecubierta
jackpot /'dʒækpɒt/ *n* premio gordo
jade /dʒeɪd/ *adj, n* jade
jaded /'dʒeɪdɪd/ *adj* agotado, con falta de entusiasmo
jagged /'dʒægɪd/ *adj* dentado
jaguar /'dʒægjuər/ *n* jaguar
jail /dʒeɪl/ *n* cárcel ● *vt* encarcelar
jam /dʒæm/ *n* 1 mermelada 2 atasco: *traffic* ~ embotellamiento 3 (*coloq*) aprieto ● (**-mm-**) 1 *vt* ~ **sth into, under, etc. sth** meter algo a la fuerza en, debajo de, etc. algo 2 *vt, vi* apretujar(se) 3 *vt, vi* atascar(se), obstruir(se) 4 *vt* (*Radio*) interferir
jangle /'dʒæŋgl/ *vt, vi* (hacer) sonar de manera discordante
janitor /'dʒænɪtər/ *n* (*USA*) portero/a
January /'dʒænjueri; -əri *GB*/ *n* (*abrev* **Jan.**) enero →JUNE
jar /dʒɑːr/ *n* 1 tarro, frasco 2 jarra ● (**-rr-**) 1 *vi* ~ (**on sth/sb**) irritar (algo/a algn) 2 *vi* ~ (**with sth**) desentonar (con algo) 3 *vt* golpear
jargon /'dʒɑːrgən/ *n* jerga
jasmine /'dʒæzmɪn/ *n* jazmín
jaundice /'dʒɔːndɪs/ *n* icterica **jaundiced** *adj* amargado
javelin /'dʒævlɪn/ *n* jabalina
jaw /dʒɔː/ *n* 1 mandíbula 2 quijada
jazz /dʒæz/ *n* jazz ■ **jazz sth up** animar algo **jazzy** *adj* (*coloq*) vistoso
jealous /'dʒeləs/ *adj* 1 celoso 2 envidioso: *I'm very* ~ *of your new job.* Tu trabajo nuevo me da mucha envidia. **jealousy** *n* (*pl* **-ies**) celos, envidia
jeans /dʒiːnz/ *n* [*pl*] jeans, bluyín (*And*) →PAIR
Jeep® /dʒiːp/ *n* jeep®
jeer /dʒɪər/ *vt, vi* ~ (**at sb**) mofarse (de algn), abuchear (a algn) ● *n* burla, abucheo
Jell-O® /'dʒeləʊ/ gelatina (*de sabores*)
jelly /'dʒeli/ *n* (*pl* **-ies**) 1 (*GB*) Ver JELL-O® 2 jalea
jellyfish /'dʒelifɪʃ/ *n* (*pl* **jellyfish**) medusa
jeopardy /'dʒepərdi/ *n* ▸ **in jeopardy** en peligro **jeopardize** *vt* poner en peligro

jerk /dʒɜːrk/ n 1 sacudida, tirón 2 (coloq) idiota ● vt, vi sacudir(se), mover(se) a sacudidas

jet /dʒet/ n 1 (avión) jet, reactor 2 (agua, gas) chorro 3 azabache

jet lag n desfase horario, jet lag: have ~ estar desfasado

jetty /ˈdʒeti/ n (pl -ies) embarcadero, malecón

Jew /dʒuː/ n judío/a **Jewish** adj judío

jewel /ˈdʒuːəl/ n 1 joya 2 piedra preciosa **jeweler** (-ll- GB) n joyero/a **jewelry** (**jewellery** GB) /ˈdʒuːəlri/ n [U] joyas

jigsaw /ˈdʒɪɡsɔː/ n (tb ~ puzzle) n rompecabezas

jingle /ˈdʒɪŋɡl/ n 1 [sing] tintineo 2 canción publicitaria, jingle ● vt, vi (hacer) tintinear

jinx /dʒɪŋks/ n: There's a ~ on this thing. Esta cosa trae mala suerte.

job /dʒɑb/ n 1 (puesto de) trabajo, empleo: out of a ~ desempleado →WORK 2 tarea 3 deber, responsabilidad ▸ **a good job** (coloq): It's a good ~ you came. Menos mal que viniste. **jobless** adj desempleado

jobcentre /ˈdʒɑbsentər/ n (GB) oficina de empleo

jockey /ˈdʒɑki/ n jockey

jog /dʒɑɡ/ n [sing] 1 go for a ~ ir a trotar 2 empujoncito ● (-gg-) 1 vi ir a trotar 2 vt empujar (ligeramente) ▸ **jog sb's memory** refrescar la memoria a algn **jogging** n trotar

join /dʒɔɪn/ n 1 unión 2 costura ● 1 vt unir, juntar 2 vi ~ up (with sth/sb) juntarse (con algo/algn), unirse (a algo/algn) 3 vt ~ sb reunirse con algn 4 vt, vi hacerse socio (de), afiliarse a 5 vt, vi (empresa, organización) ingresar (en) ■ **join in (sth)** participar (en algo)

joiner /ˈdʒɔɪnər/ n (GB) carpintero/a

joint /dʒɔɪnt/ adj conjunto, colectivo ● n 1 (Anat) articulación 2 junta, ensambladura 3 cuarto/trozo de carne 4 (coloq) antro 5 (coloq) (de marihuana) toque (Mx), bareto (And) **jointed** adj articulado, plegable

joke /dʒoʊk/ n 1 chiste 2 broma: play a ~ on sb hacer una broma a algn 3 [sing] farsa ● vi bromear ▸ **joking apart** bromas aparte **you're joking/you must be joking** (coloq) ¡ni hablar! ¿en serio?

joker /ˈdʒoʊkər/ n 1 bromista 2 (coloq) payaso 3 (cartas) comodín

jolly /ˈdʒɑli/ adj (-ier/-iest) alegre, jovial ● adv (GB, coloq) muy

jolt /dʒoʊlt/ 1 vi traquetear 2 vt sacudir ● n 1 sacudida 2 susto

jostle /ˈdʒɑsl/ vt, vi empujar(se), codear(se)

jot /dʒɑt/ v (-tt-) ■ **jot sth down** apuntar algo

journal /ˈdʒɜːrnl/ n 1 revista (especializada) 2 (viajes, etc.) diario **journalism** n periodismo **journalist** n periodista

journey /ˈdʒɜːrni/ n viaje, recorrido →VIAJE

joy /dʒɔɪ/ n 1 alegría 2 encanto **joyful** adj alegre

joyriding /ˈdʒɔɪraɪdɪŋ/ n pasearse en un carro robado **joyrider** la persona que se pasea en un carro robado

jubilant /ˈdʒuːbɪlənt/ adj jubiloso **jubilation** n júbilo

jubilee /ˈdʒuːbɪliː/ n aniversario

Judaism /ˈdʒuːdeɪɪzəm; -deɪ-ɪzəm GB/ n judaísmo

judge /dʒʌdʒ/ n 1 (Jur, de competencia) juez 2 ~ (of sth) conocedor/a (de algo) ● vt, vi juzgar, considerar, calcular: judging by/from... a juzgar por...

judgement (tb **judgment**) /ˈdʒʌdʒmənt/ n juicio: use your own ~ usar su propio criterio

judicious /dʒuːˈdɪʃəs/ adj juicioso

judo /ˈdʒuːdoʊ/ n judo

jug /dʒʌɡ/ n 1 cántaro 2 (GB) jarra

juggle /ˈdʒʌɡl/ vt, vi 1 hacer malabarismos 2 ~ (with) sth: She ~s home, career and children. Al mismo tiempo maneja casa, trabajo e hijos.

juice /dʒuːs/ n jugo, zumo **juicy** adj (-ier/-iest) jugoso

jukebox /ˈdʒuːkbɑks/ n máquina de discos, rocola

July /dʒuˈlaɪ/ n (abrev **Jul.**) julio →JUNE

jumble /ˈdʒʌmbl/ vt ~ sth (up) revolver algo ● n revoltijo

jumble sale n (GB) venta benéfica de objetos usados

jumbo /ˈdʒʌmboʊ/ adj (coloq) (de) tamaño súper

jump /dʒʌmp/ n 1 salto 2 aumento ● 1 vi, vt saltar: ~ up levantarse de un salto ◇ ~ up and down dar saltos 2 vi sobresaltarse: It made me ~. Me sobresaltó. 3 vi aumentar ▸ **jump the line; jump the queue** (GB) colarse **jump to conclusions** sacar conclusiones precipitadas ■ **jump at sth** aceptar algo sin dudar

jumper /ˈdʒʌmpər/ n 1 (GB) suéter →SWEATER 2 saltador/a

jumpy /'dʒʌmpi/ *adj* (coloq) nervioso

junction /'dʒʌŋkʃn/ *n* cruce, crucero (Mx)

June /dʒuːn/ *n* (abrev **Jun.**) junio: *on ~ 1st* el primero de junio ◊ *every/next ~* cada junio/en junio del año que viene **NOTA** Los nombres de los meses se escriben con mayúscula.

jungle /'dʒʌŋɡl/ *n* jungla, selva

junior /'dʒuːniər/ *adj* **1** subalterno **2** (abrev **Jr**) júnior **3** (GB) *~ school* escuela primaria ● *n* **1** subalterno/a **2** *He's two years her ~.* Es dos años más joven que ella. **3** (GB) alumno/a de escuela primaria

junk /dʒʌŋk/ *n* [U] basura, trastos

junk food (coloq) [U] comida chatarra

junkie /'dʒʌŋki/ *n* (coloq) drogadicto/a

junk mail *n* propaganda (distribuida por correo)

Jupiter /'dʒuːpɪtər/ *n* Júpiter

jury /'dʒʊəri/ *n* (pl **-ies**) jurado → JURADO **juror** *n* (miembro del) jurado

just /dʒʌst/ *adv* **1** justo, exactamente: *That's ~ it!* ¡Exacto! ◊ *~ here* aquí mismo **2** *~ as I thought* justo como/como lo que pensaba: *It's ~ as I thought.* Es justo lo que pensaba. **3** *~ as... as... as... que...: He's ~ as tall as me.* Es igual de alto que yo. **4** *have ~ done sth* acabar de hacer algo: *"Just married"* "Recién casados" **5** (only) *~* por muy poco: *I can only ~ reach the shelf.* Llego al estante a duras penas. **6** *~ over/under* un poco más/menos que... **7** *~* ahora: *I'm ~ going.* Ahora mismo me voy. **8** *be ~ about/going to do sth* estar a punto de hacer algo **9** sencillamente: *It's ~ one of those things.* Es sencillamente una de esas cosas. **10** sólo: *Just let me say something!* ¡Déjame hablar un momento! ◊ *~ for fun* para reírnos un poco ▶ **it is just as well (that...)** menos mal (que)... **just about** (coloq) casi **just in case** por si acaso **just like 1** igual que: *It was ~ like old times.* Fue como en los viejos tiempos. **2** típico de: *It's ~ like her to be late.* Es típico de ella llegar tarde. **just like that** sin más **just now 1** en estos momentos **2** hace un momento ● *adj* **1** justo **2** merecido **justly** *adv* justamente, con razón

justice /'dʒʌstɪs/ *n* **1** justicia **2** juez: *~ of the peace* juez de paz ▶ **do justice to sth/sb 1** ha-

cerle justicia a algo/algn **2** *We couldn't do ~ to her cooking.* No pudimos hacer los honores a su comida. **do yourself justice:** *He didn't do himself ~ in the exam.* Podía haber hecho el examen mucho mejor.

justifiable /ˌdʒʌstɪˈfaɪəbl, 'dʒʌstɪfaɪəbl/ *adj* justificable **justifiably** *adv* justificadamente: *She was ~ angry.* Estaba furiosa, y con razón.

justify /'dʒʌstɪfaɪ/ *vt* (pt/pp **-ied**) justificar

jut /dʒʌt/ (**-tt-**) ▪ **jut out** sobresalir

juvenile /'dʒuːvənl; -naɪl GB/ *n* menor ● *adj* **1** juvenil **2** (pey) pueril

juxtapose /ˌdʒʌkstəˈpoʊz/ *vt* (fml) contraponer **juxtaposition** *n* contraposición

K k

K, k /keɪ/ *n* (pl **K's**, **k's**) K, k

kaleidoscope /kəˈlaɪdəskoʊp/ *n* caleidoscopio

kangaroo /ˌkæŋɡəˈruː/ *n* canguro

karat /'kærət/ *n* quilate

karate /kəˈrɑːti/ *n* karate

kebab /kɪˈbæb/ (tb **shish ~** /'ʃɪʃ kɪbæb/) *n* brocheta

keel /kiːl/ *n* quilla ▪ **keel over** desplomarse

keen /kiːn/ *adj* (**-er/-est**) **1** entusiasta **2** *be ~ (to do sth)* estar ansioso, tener ganas (de hacer algo) **3** *be ~ on sth/sb* (GB, coloq) gustarle a uno algo/algn **4** (interés) grande **5** (olfato) fino **6** (oído, vista) agudo **keenly** *adv* **1** con entusiasmo **2** profundamente

keep /kiːp/ *n* manutención ● (pt/pp **kept** /kept/) **1** *vi* quedarse, permanecer: *Keep still!* ¡Estáte quieto! ◊ *Keep quiet!* ¡Cállate! **2** *vi ~ (on) doing sth* seguir haciendo algo, no parar de hacer algo **3** *vt* [con adj, adv o -ing] mantener, tener: *~ sb happy* tener a algn contento ◊ *~ sb waiting* hacer esperar a algn **4** *vt* entretener, retener: *What kept you?* ¿Por qué tardaste tanto? **5** *vt* guardar: *~ a secret* guardar un secreto **6** *vt* quedarse con **7** *vt* (negocio) ser propietario de **8** *vt* (animales) criar, tener **9** *vi* (alimentos) conservarse (fresco), durar **10** *vi* (diario) escribir **11** *vt* (cuentas, etc.) llevar **12** *vt* (familia) mantener **13** vt (cita) acudir a **14** vt (promesa) cumplir **NOTA** Para expresiones, ver el sustantivo, adjetivo, etc., p. ej. **keep your word** en WORD. ■ **keep (sth/sb) away (from sth/sb)** mantenerse alejado, mantener alejado algo/a algn (de algo/algn) **keep sth (back) from sth** ocultar algo a algn **keep sth down** mantener algo (a)bajo **keep sb from (doing)** impedir, no dejar a algn hacer algo **keep (yourself) from doing sth** evitar hacer algo **keep off** (sth) no acercarse a (algo), no tocar (algo): *Keep off the grass.* Prohibido pisar el pasto. **keep sth/sb off (sth/sb)** no dejar a algn/algo acercarse a (algo/algn): *Keep your hands off me!* ¡No me toques! **keep on (at sb) (about sth/sb)** no dejar de dar lata (a algn) (sobre algo/algn) **keep (sth/sb) out** (of sth) no entrar, no dejar a algo/algn entrar (en algo): *Keep Out!* ¡Prohibida la entrada! **keep (yourself) to yourself** guardar las distancias **keep sth to yourself** guardarse algo (para sí) **keep up (with sth/sb)** seguir el ritmo (de algo/algn) **keep sth up** mantener, seguir haciendo algo: *Keep it up!* ¡Dale!

keeper /ˈkiːpər/ n **1** guarda **2** conservador/a **3** (GB, coloq) (fútbol) portero/a

keeping /ˈkiːpɪŋ/ n ▶ **in/out of keeping (with sth)** de acuerdo/en desacuerdo (con algo) **in sb's keeping** al cuidado de algn

kennel /ˈkenl/ n residencia canina

kerb n (GB) borde de la acera)

kerosene /ˈkerəsiːn/ n queroseno

ketchup /ˈketʃəp/ n catsup

kettle /ˈketl/ n hervidora de agua (eléctrica)

key /kiː/ n **1** llave **2** (Mús) tono **3** tecla **4** ~ (to sth) clave (de algo) ● adj clave ■ vt ~ sth (in) teclear algo →COMPUTADORA

keyboard /ˈkiːbɔːrd/ n teclado

keyhole /ˈkiːhoʊl/ n ojo de la cerradura

key ring n llavero

khaki /ˈkɑːki/ adj, n caqui

kick /kɪk/ **1** vt dar una patada a **2** vt (pelota) darle un puntapié a: ~ *the ball into the river* tirar la pelota al río de una patada **3** vi patear ▶ **kick the bucket** (coloq) estirar la pata ■ **kick off** hacer el saque inicial **kick sb out** (coloq) echar a algn ● n **1** patada **2** pun-

tapié **3** (coloq): *for ~* para divertirse

kick-off n (pl **-offs**) saque inicial

kid /kɪd/ n **1** (coloq) niño/a **2** (esp USA, coloq): *his ~ sister* su hermana menor **3** (Zool) cabrito **4** (piel) cabritilla ● (**-dd-**) **1** vt, vi bromear **2** vt ~ **yourself** engañarse a sí mismo

kidnap /ˈkɪdnæp/ vt (**-pp-**) secuestrar **kidnapper** n secuestrador/a **kidnapping** n secuestro

kidney /ˈkɪdni/ n riñón

kill /kɪl/ vt, vi matar ▶ **kill time** matar el tiempo ■ **kill sth/sb off** exterminar algo, rematar a algn ● n **1** *go/move in for the* ~ entrar a matar **2** (animal matado) presa **killer** n asesino/a

killing /ˈkɪlɪŋ/ n matanza ■ **make a killing** hacer el agosto

kiln /kɪln/ n horno para cerámica

kilo /ˈkiːloʊ/ (pl **-s**) (tb **kilogram** USA, **kilogramme** GB /ˈkɪləɡræm/) n (abrev **kg**) kilo(gramo) →Ver pág. 222

kilometer (**-metre** GB) /kɪˈlɑːmɪtər/ n (abrev **km**) kilómetro →Ver pág. 222

kilt /kɪlt/ n falda escocesa

kin /kɪn/ n [pl] (fml) familia

kind /kaɪnd/ adj (**-er/-est**) amable ● n tipo, clase: *the best of its* ~ el mejor de su categoría ▶ **in kind 1** en especie **2** (fml) con la misma moneda **kind of** (coloq) en cierto modo: ~ *of scared* como asustado **kindness** n **1** amabilidad, bondad **2** favor

kindly /ˈkaɪndli/ adj amable ● adv **1** amablemente **2** *Kindly leave me alone!* ¡Haga el favor de dejarme en paz! ▶ **not take kindly to sth/sb** no gustarle algo/algn a uno

king /kɪŋ/ n rey →REY

kingdom /ˈkɪŋdəm/ n reino

kingfisher /ˈkɪŋfɪʃər/ n martín pescador

kinship /ˈkɪnʃɪp/ n (fml) parentesco

kiosk /ˈkiːɒsk/ n quiosco

kipper /ˈkɪpər/ n arenque ahumado

kiss /kɪs/ vt, vi besar(se) ● n beso ▶ **the kiss of life** (GB) el boca a boca

kit /kɪt/ n **1** equipo **2** conjunto para armar

kitchen /ˈkɪtʃɪn/ n cocina

kite /kaɪt/ n cometa, papalote

kitten /ˈkɪtn/ n gatito →GATO

kitty /ˈkɪti/ n (pl **-ies**) (coloq) fondo (de dinero)

knack /næk/ n maña, tiro: *get the* ~ *of sth* agarrarle el modo/la onda a algo

knead /ni:d/ vt amasar

knee /ni:/ n rodilla ▸ **be/go (down) on your knees** estar/ponerse de rodillas

kneecap /'ni:kæp/ n rótula

kneel /ni:l/ vi (pt/pp **knelt** /nelt/ tb **kneeled** USA) → DREAM ~ **(down)** arrodillarse, hincarse

knew /nu:; nju: GB/ pt de KNOW

knickers /'nɪkərz/ n [pl] (GB) calzones, pantaletas

knife /naɪf/ n (pl **knives** /naɪvz/) cuchillo ● vt acuchillar

knight /naɪt/ n 1 caballero 2 (ajedrez) caballo ● vt nombrar caballero/Sir **knighthood** n título de caballero/Sir

knit /nɪt/ vt, vi tejer **knitting** n [U] tejido: ~ **needle** aguja (de tejer)

knitwear /'nɪtweər/ n [U] (prendas) tejidas

knob /nɑb/ n 1 (puerta, cajón) tirador, perilla 2 (Radio, TV) botón, control (que gira)

knock /nɑk/ n 1 There was a ~ at the door. Llamaron a la puerta. 2 golpe ● 1 vt, vi golpear: ~ your head pegarse en la cabeza 2 vi: ~ at/on the door tocar la puerta 3 vt (coloq) criticar ▸ **knock on wood** tocar madera ■ **knock sb down** atropellar a algn **knock sth down** derribar algo **knock off (sth)** (coloq): ~ off (work) terminar de trabajar **knock sth off** hacer un descuento de algo **knock sb out 1** (boxeo) noquear a algn 2 dejar inconsciente a algn 3 (coloq) dejar boquiabierto a algn **knock sth/sb over** tirar algo/a algn

knockout /'nɑkaʊt/ n 1 nocaut 2 ~ tournament eliminatoria

knot /nɑt/ n 1 nudo 2 grupo (de gente) ● vt (-tt-) hacer un nudo a, anudar

know /noʊ/ n ▸ **in the know** (coloq) enterado ● (pt **knew** /nu:/ pp **known** /noʊn/) 1 vt, vi ~ **(how to do sth)** saber (hacer algo): Not that I ~ of. Que yo sepa, no. ◇ Let me ~ if... Avísame si... 2 vt conocer: get to ~ llegar a conocer a algn 3 vt: I've never known anyone to... Nunca se ha visto que algn... ▸ **for all you know** por lo (poco) que uno sabe **God/goodness/Heaven knows** (bien) sabe Dios **know best** saber uno lo que hace **know better (than that/than to do sth)** You ought to ~ better! ¡Parece mentira que tú hayas hecho eso! ◇ I should have known better. Debí habérmelo

imaginado. **you never know** (coloq) nunca se sabe

knowing /'noʊɪŋ/ adj (mirada, etc.) de complicidad **knowingly** adv intencionadamente

know-it-all (**know-all** GB) n (coloq) sabelotodo

knowledge /'nɑlɪdʒ/ n [U] 1 conocimiento(s): not to my ~ que yo sepa, no 2 saber: in the ~ that... a sabiendas de que... **knowledgeable** adj entendido

knuckle /'nʌkl/ n nudillo ■ **knuckle down (to sth)** (coloq) poner manos a la obra **knuckle under** (coloq) doblegarse

Koran /kə'rɑːn/ n Corán

L l

L, l /el/ n (pl **L's**, **l's**) L, l

label /'leɪbl/ n etiqueta ● vt (-l-, -ll- GB) 1 poner etiqueta a 2 ~ **sth/sb as sth** calificar algo/a algn de algo

labor (-our GB) /'leɪbər/ n 1 [U] trabajo 2 [U] mano de obra: ~ relations relaciones laborales ◇ ~ union sindicato (laboral) 3 [U] parto: go into ~ entrar en trabajo de parto 4 (GB, Pol) laborista ● vi esforzarse **labored** adj 1 difícil 2 pesado **laborer** n trabajador/a

laboratory /'læbrətɔːri; lə-'bɒrətri GB/ n (pl -ies) laboratorio

laborious /lə'bɔːriəs/ adj 1 laborioso 2 penoso

labyrinth /'læbərɪnθ/ n laberinto

lace /leɪs/ n 1 encaje 2 cordón (de zapato), agujeta (Mx) ● vt, vi atar(se) (con lazo) **lacy** adj de encaje

lack /læk/ vt carecer de ▸ **be lacking** faltar **be lacking in sth** carecer de algo ● n [U] falta, carencia

lacquer /'lækər/ n laca

lad /læd/ n (coloq) muchacho

ladder /'lædər/ n 1 escalera de mano 2 I have a ladder in my stocking. Se me fue la media. 3 escala (social, profesional)

laden /'leɪdn/ adj ~ **(with sth)** cargado (de algo)

lady /'leɪdi/ n (pl -ies) 1 señora 2 dama 3 **Lady** Lady (título nobiliario) 4 **the Ladies** [sing] (GB) (ladies' room USA) baño de mujeres →TOILET

ladybug (ladybird GB) /ˈleɪdɪbʌg/-bɜːrd/ n mariquita, catarina (Mx)

lag /læg/ vi (-gg-) ▶ **lag behind** (sth/sb) quedarse atrás (con respecto a algo/algn) ● n (tb time ~) retraso

lager /ˈlɑːgər/ n cerveza (rubia)

lagoon /ləˈguːn/ n laguna

laid /leɪd/ pt, pp de LAY¹

laid-back adj (coloq) tranquilo

lain /leɪn/ pp de LIE²

lake /leɪk/ n lago →MAR

lamb /læm/ n cordero →CARNE

lame /leɪm/ adj 1 cojo 2 (excusa, etc.) poco convincente

lament /ləˈment/ vt, vi ~ (for/over sth/sb) lamentar(se) (de algo/algn)

lamp /læmp/ n lámpara

lamp post n farol/poste de la luz

lampshade /ˈlæmpʃeɪd/ n pantalla (de lámpara)

land /lænd/ n 1 tierra(s): on dry ~ en tierra firme ◇ arable ~ tierra de cultivo ◇ a plot of ~ una parcela 2 **the land** la tierra 3 país ● 1 vt, vi desembarcar 2 vt, vi (avión) (hacer) aterrizar 3 vi caer 4 vi posarse 5 vt (coloq) conseguir ■ **land sb with sth/sb** (coloq) cargar a algn con algo/algn: I got landed with the washing up. A mí me tocó lavar los platos.

landing /ˈlændɪŋ/ n 1 aterrizaje 2 desembarco 3 (escalera) descanso

landlady /ˈlændleɪdi/ n (pl -ies) dueña

landlord /ˈlændlɔːrd/ n dueño

landmark /ˈlændmɑːrk/ n 1 punto destacado 2 hito

landowner /ˈlændoʊnər/ n terrateniente

landscape /ˈlændskeɪp/ n paisaje →SCENERY

landslide /ˈlændslaɪd/ n 1 derrumbe (tierras) 2 (tb ~ victory) victoria aplastante

lane /leɪn/ n 1 camino 2 callejón 3 carril

language /ˈlæŋgwɪdʒ/ n 1 lenguaje: use bad ~ decir groserías 2 idioma, lengua

lantern /ˈlæntərn/ n farol

lap /læp/ n 1 regazo 2 (Dep) vuelta ● vt (-pp-) 1 (agua) chapotear ■ **lap sth up** (coloq) tragarse algo 2 lamer algo

lapel /ləˈpel/ n solapa

lapse /læps/ n 1 error, lapso 2 caída 3 (tiempo) período ● vi 1 caer: ~ into silence quedarse callado 2 caducar

laptop /ˈlæptɒp/ n computador(a) portátil

larder /ˈlɑːrdər/ n despensa

large /lɑːrdʒ/ adj (-er/-est) 1 grande 2 amplio ▶ **by and large** en términos generales ● n ■ **at large** 1 en general: the world at ~ todo el mundo 2 suelto **largely** adv en gran parte

large-scale adj a gran escala

lark /lɑːrk/ n alondra

laser /ˈleɪzər/ n láser

lash /læʃ/ n 1 azote 2 pestaña ● vt 1 azotar 2 (cola) sacudir ■ **lash out at sth/sb** 1 agarrar algo/algn a golpes 2 arremeter contra algo/algn

lass /læs/ n (Esc, N de Inglaterra) muchacha

last /læst; lɑːst GB/ adj 1 último: ~ name apellido →LATE 2 pasado: the night before ~ ante(a)noche ● n **the last** 1 el/la último/a: the ~ but one el penúltimo 2 el/la anterior ▶ **at (long) last** por fin ● adv 1 último: come ~ llegar en último lugar 2 por última vez ▶ **last but not least** y por último, pero no menos importante ● vi 1 durar 2 perdurar **lasting** adj duradero, permanente **lastly** adv por último

latch /lætʃ/ n 1 cerrojo 2 picaporte ■ **latch on (to sth)** (coloq) captar algo

late /leɪt/ (-er/-est) adj 1 tarde, tardío: be ~ llegar tarde ◇ My flight was ~. Mi vuelo se retrasó. 2 in the ~ 20th century a finales del siglo XX ◇ in her ~ twenties llegando a los treinta 3 latest último, más reciente **NOTA** Latest significa el más reciente/nuevo: the latest technology, y last se usa para el último de una serie: The last bus is at twelve. 4 [antes de sustantivo] difunto ▶ **at the latest** a más tardar ● adv tarde: arrive ~ llegar retrasado ▶ **later on** más tarde **lately** adv últimamente

lather /ˈlæðər; ˈlɑːð- GB/ n espuma

latitude /ˈlætɪtuːd; -tjuːd GB/ n latitud

the latter /ˈlætər/ pron el segundo

laugh /læf; lɑːf GB/ vi reír(se) ■ **laugh at sth/sb** 1 reírse de algo/algn 2 burlarse de algo/algn ● n 1 risa, carcajada 2 (coloq): What a ~! ¡Qué risa! ▶ **have the last laugh** reírse el último **laughable** adj risible **laughter** n [U] risa(s): roar with ~ reírse a carcajadas

launch /lɔːntʃ/ *vt* **1** lanzar **2** (*buque*) botar ∎ **launch into sth** comenzar algo • *n* **1** lanzamiento **2** lancha

Laundromat® /'lɔːndrəmæt/ (**launderette** /lɔːn'dret/ *GB*) *n* lavandería (*automática*)

laundry /'lɔːndri/ *n* (*pl* **-ies**) **1** ropa sucia: *do the* ~ lavar la ropa **NOTA** Para "ropa sucia", es más común decir **washing**. **2** lavandería: ~ *service* servicio de lavandería

lava /'lɑːvə/ *n* lava

lavatory /'lævətɔːri; -tri *GB*/ *n* (*pl* **-ies**) (*GB, fml*) **1** inodoro, excusado **2** baño →TOILET

lavender /'lævəndər/ *n* lavanda

lavish /'lævɪʃ/ *adj* **1** pródigo, generoso **2** abundante

law /lɔː/ *n* **1** ley **2** derecho ∎ **law and order** orden público **lawful** *adj* legal, legítimo

lawn /lɔːn/ *n* pasto, césped

lawnmower /'lɔːnməʊər/ *n* cortadora/podadora de pasto

lawsuit /'lɔːsuːt/ *n* pleito, litigio

lawyer /'lɔːjər/ *n* abogado/a →ABOGADO

lay¹ /leɪ/ *vt, pt de* LIE² • *vt* (*pt/pp* **laid**) **1** colocar: ~ *sth aside* poner algo a un lado **2** (*cimientos*) echar **3** tender **4** extender **5** (*huevos*) poner →LIE² ∎ **lay sth down 1** (*armas*) deponer algo **2** (*regla, etc.*) estipular algo ∎ **lay sb off** despedir a algn ∎ **lay sth on** (*GB, coloq*) proveer algo ∎ **lay sth out 1** exhibir algo **2** (*argumento*) exponer algo **3** (*jardín, ciudad*) hacer el plano de algo: *well laid out* bien distribuido

lay² /leɪ/ *adj* **1** laico **2** (*no experto*) lego

lay-by *n* (*GB*) área de descanso (*carretera*)

layer /'leɪər/ *n* **1** capa **2** (*Geol*) estrato **layered** *adj* en capas

lazy /'leɪzi/ *adj* (**-ier/-iest**) **1** vago, flojo **2** perezoso

lead¹ /liːd/ *n* **1** iniciativa **2** (*competición*) ventaja: *be in the* ~ llevar la delantera **3** (*Teat, etc.*) papel principal: *the* ~ *singer* el cantante (*indicio*) pista **5** (*GB, perro*) correa **6** (*GB, Elec*) cable • (*pt/pp* **led**) **1** conducir, guiar **2** vi ~ *to/into sth* (*puerta, etc.*) dar, llevar (a algo): *This road* ~*s back to town.* Por este camino se vuelve a la ciudad. **3** *vt* ~ *to sth* dar lugar a algo **4** *vi* llevar la delantera **5** *vt* encabezar **6** *vt, vi* (*cartas*) salir ▸ **lead the way** mostrar el camino

∎ **lead up to sth** preparar el terreno para algo **leader** *n* líder, dirigente **leadership** *n* **1** liderazgo **2** (*cargo*) jefatura **leading** *adj* principal

lead² /led/ *n* plomo **leaded** *adj* con plomo

leaf /liːf/ *n* (*pl* **leaves**) hoja ▸ **take a leaf out of sb's book** seguir el ejemplo de algn **turn over a new leaf** empezar una nueva vida **leafy** *adj* frondoso

leaflet /'liːflət/ *n* folleto

league /liːg/ *n* **1** liga **2** (*coloq*) clase ▸ **in league (with sb)** confabulado (con algn)

leak /liːk/ *n* **1** agujero, gotera **2** escape **3** filtración • *vi* **1** estar agujereado, tener fuga **2** *vi* (*gas, líquido*) salirse, escaparse **3** *vt* dejar escapar

lean /liːn/ *adj* **1** delgado **2** (*carne*) magro • (*pt/pp* **leaned** *o* **leant** /lent/ *GB*) →DREAM **1** *vi* inclinar(se), ladear(se): ~ *out of the window* asomarse por la ventana **2** *vt, vi* apoyar(se) **leaning** *n* inclinación

leap /liːp/ *vi* (*pt/pp* **leaped** *o* **leapt** /lept/) →DREAM **1** saltar **2** (*corazón*) dar un salto • *n* **1** salto

leap year *n* año bisiesto

learn /lɜːrn/ *vt, vi* (*pt/pp* **learned** *o* **learnt** /lɜːnt/) →DREAM **1** aprender **2** enterarse ▸ **learn your lesson** escarmentar **learner** *n* aprendiz/a, principiante **learning** *n* **1** aprendizaje **2** erudición

lease /liːs/ *n* contrato de arrendamiento ▸ **a new lease on/of life** (*GB*) una nueva vida • *vt* ~ *sth* (*to/from sb*) arrendar algo (a algn)

leash /liːʃ/ *n* correa (*de perro*)

least /liːst/ *adv, pron* menos ▸ **at least** al/por lo menos **not in the least** en absoluto **not least** especialmente • *adj* menor

leather /'leðər/ *n* cuero

leave /liːv/ *vt* (*pt/pp* **left**) *vt* dejar: *Leave it to me.* Yo me encargo. **2** *vt, vi* irse, salir (de) ∎ **leave sth/sb behind** dejar algo/a algn (atrás), olvidar algo/a algn **leave sth/sb out** omitir, excluir algo/a algn **be left over** sobrar • *n* **1** permiso (*de vacaciones*): *on* ~ de permiso ◇ *sick* ~ licencia por enfermedad

leaves /liːvz/ *pl de* LEAF

lecture /'lektʃər/ *n* **1** conferencia: ~ *theater* aula magna **2** (*reprimenda*) sermón • **1** *vi* dar una conferencia **2** *vt* sermonear **lecturer** *n* **1** ~ (**in sth**) (*universidad*) profesor/a (de algo) **2** conferenciante

led /led/ *pt, pp de* LEAD ¹

ledge /ledʒ/ *n* **1** repisa: *the window* ~ el alféizar **2** (*Geog*) plataforma, saliente

leek /liːk/ *n* puerro, poro (*Mx*)

left /left/ *pt, pp de* LEAVE ● *n* **1** izquierda **2** the Left (*Pol*) la Izquierda ● *adj* izquierdo ● *adv* a la izquierda

left-hand *adj* a/de la izquierda: *on the* ~ *side* a mano izquierda **left-handed** *adj* zurdo

left luggage office *n* (*GB*) consigna

leftover /ˈleftəʊvər/ *adj* sobrante **leftovers** *n* sobras

left wing *n* izquierda ● **left-wing** *adj* izquierdista

leg /leg/ *n* **1** pierna → MY **2** pata **3** (*carne*) pierna, muslo **4** (*pantalón*) pernera **5** (*Dep*) vuelta, manga **6** (*viaje*) etapa ▸ **not have a leg to stand on** (*coloq*) no tener nada que lo respalde **pull sb's leg** (*coloq*) tomarle el pelo a algn

legacy /ˈlegəsi/ *n* (*pl* -ies) **1** legado **2** patrimonio

legal /ˈliːgl/ *adj* jurídico, legal: *take* ~ *action* entablar un proceso legal **legality** /liːˈgæləti/ *n* legalidad **legalization** *n* legalización **legalize** *vt* legalizar

legend /ˈledʒənd/ *n* leyenda **legendary** *adj* legendario

leggings /ˈlegɪŋz/ *n* [*pl*] mallones (*Mx*), chicles (*And*)

legible /ˈledʒəbl/ *adj* legible

legion /ˈliːdʒən/ *n* legión

legislate /ˈledʒɪsleɪt/ *vi* legislar **legislation** *n* legislación **legislative** *adj* legislativo **legislature** *n* (*fml*) asamblea legislativa

legitimate /lɪˈdʒɪtɪmət/ *adj* **1** legítimo, legal **2** válido **legitimacy** *n* legitimidad

leisure /ˈliːʒər; ˈleʒə(r) *GB*/ *n* ocio: ~ *time* tiempo libre ◇ ~ *center* (*GB*) centro recreativo ▸ **at your leisure** cuando te quede bien

leisurely /ˈliːʒərli; ˈleʒəli *GB*/ *adj* pausado, relajado

lemon /ˈlemən/ *n* limón (*real/amarillo*)

lemonade /ˌleməˈneɪd/ *n* **1** limonada, agua de limón **2** (*GB*) gaseosa, refresco (*al limón*)

lend /lend/ *vt* (*pt/pp* lent /lent/) prestar

length /leŋθ/ *n* **1** largo, longitud: *20 meters in* ~ 20m de largo **2** duración: *for some* ~ *of time* durante un buen rato/una temporada ▸ **go to any, great, etc. lengths (to do sth)** hacer todo lo posible (por hacer algo) **lengthen** *vt, vi* alargar(se), prolongar(se) **lengthy** *adj* (-ier/-iest) largo

lenient /ˈliːniənt/ *adj* **1** indulgente **2** (*tratamiento*) clemente

lens /lenz/ *n* (*pl* lenses) **1** (*Fot*) objetivo **2** lente

lentil /ˈlentl/ *n* lenteja

Leo /ˈliːəʊ/ *n* (*pl* -s) Leo

leopard /ˈlepərd/ *n* leopardo

lesbian /ˈlezbiən/ *n* lesbiana

less /les/ *adj, adv, pron* menos ▸ **less and less** cada vez menos **NOTA** Como comparativo de *little*, *less* se suele usar con sustantivos incontables: "*I have very little money.*" "*I have even* ~ *money (than you).*" *Fewer* es el comparativo de *few* y se usa con sustantivos en plural: *fewer accidents, people, etc.* En el inglés hablado es más común *less*. **lessen 1** *vi* disminuir **2** *vt* reducir **lesser** *adj* menor: *to a* ~ *extent* en menor grado

lesson /ˈlesn/ *n* **1** clase **2** lección

let ¹ /let/ *vt* (-tt-) (*pt/pp* let) ~ **sb do sth** dejar, permitir a algn hacer algo → ALLOW **NOTA** Let us + infinitivo sin *to* se usa para hacer sugerencias, y es más común la contracción *let's*: *Let's go!* ¡Vamos! En negativa, se usa *let's not*: *Let's not argue.* No discutamos. ▸ **let sb know sth** informar a algn de algo **let's say** digamos **let sth/sb go**; **let go of sth/sb** soltar algo/a algn **let yourself go** dejarse llevar ■ **let sb down** fallar a algn **let sb in/out** dejar entrar/salir a algn **let sb off (sth)** perdonar (algo) a algn **let sth off 1** disparar algo **2** hacer estallar algo

let ² /let/ *vt* (-tt-) (*pt/pp* let) (*GB*) alquilar, rentar (*Mx*) → ALQUILAR ▸ **to let** se alquila(n), se renta(n)

lethal /ˈliːθl/ *adj* letal

lethargy /ˈleθərdʒi/ *n* aletargamiento **lethargic** /ləˈθɑːrdʒɪk/ *adj* aletargado

letter /ˈletər/ *n* **1** carta **2** letra ▸ **to the letter** al pie de la letra

letter box *n* (*GB*) buzón

lettuce /ˈletɪs/ *n* lechuga

leukemia (leukaemia *GB*) /luːˈkiːmiə/ *n* leucemia

level /ˈlevl/ *n* **1** nivel **2** raso **2** ~ (**with sth/sb**) al nivel de (algo/algn) ● *n* nivel ● *vt* (-l-, -ll- *GB*) nivelar ■ **level sth against/at sth/sb** dirigir algo a algo/algn (*críticas, etc.*) **level off/out** estabilizarse

level crossing n (GB) paso a nivel

lever /'levər; 'li:və(r) GB/ n palanca **leverage** n **1** influencia **2** fuerza de la palanca

levy /'levi/ vt (pt/pp **-ied**) imponer (impuestos, etc.) ● n (pl **-ies**) impuesto

liable /'laɪəbl/ adj **1** ~ **(for sth)** responsable de algo **2** ~ **to sth** sujeto a algo **3** ~ **to sth** propenso a algo **liability** /ˌlaɪə'bɪləti/ n (pl **-ies**) **1** responsabilidad **2** (coloq) problema

liaison /li'eɪzɒn; -zn GB/ n **1** vinculación **2** relación sexual

liar /'laɪər/ n mentiroso/a

libel /'laɪbl/ n **1** difamación

liberal /'lɪbərəl/ adj **1** liberal **2** Liberal ● n liberal

liberate /'lɪbəreɪt/ vt liberar **liberated** adj liberado **liberation** n liberación

liberty /'lɪbərti/ n (pl **-ies**) libertad ▸ **take liberties** tomarse libertades

Libra /'li:brə/ n Libra

library /'laɪbreri; -brəri GB/ n (pl **-ies**) biblioteca **librarian** /laɪ'breəriən/ n bibliotecario/a

lice /laɪs/ pl de LOUSE

license (licence GB) /'laɪsns/ n **1** licencia; ~ **plate** placa **2** (fml) permiso

lick /lɪk/ vt lamer ● n lametón

licorice /'lɪkərɪʃ, -rɪs/ n regaliz, orozuz

lid /lɪd/ n **1** tapa **2** párpado

lie¹ /laɪ/ vi (pt/pp **lied** pt pres **lying**) mentir ● n mentira

lie² /laɪ/ vi (pt **lay** pp **lain** pt pres **lying**) **1** echarse, yacer **2** estar: the life that's ahead of us la vida que nos espera **3** extenderse ■ **lie about/around** n pasar el tiempo sin hacer nada **2** estar esparcido: leave your clothes lying around tira la ropa por ahí tirada **lie back** recostarse **lie down** echarse en la cama **lie in** (GB) quedarse en la cama **NOTA lie (lay, lain, lying)** es intransitivo y significa "estar acostado": I lie down on the bed for a while. En cambio, **lie (lied, lied, lying)** también es intransitivo y significa "mentir". **Lay** (laid, laid, laying) es transitivo y tiene el significado de "poner sobre": She laid her dress on the bed.

lieutenant /lu:'tenənt; lef't- GB/ n teniente

life /laɪf/ n (pl **lives**) **1** vida: late in ~ a una avanzada edad **2** (tb ▸ **sentence/imprisonment)** cadena perpetua ▸ **bring sth/sb to life** animar algo/a algn **come to life**

animarse **get a life!** (coloq) ¡vive la vida! **take your (own) life** suicidarse

lifebelt (tb **lifebuoy)** /'laɪf-belt/-bɔɪ/ n salvavidas

lifeboat /'laɪfbəʊt/ n bote salvavidas

life expectancy n esperanza de vida

lifeguard /'laɪfɡɑːrd/ n socorrista

life jacket n chaleco salvavidas

lifelong /'laɪflɔ:ŋ; -lɒŋ GB/ adj de toda la vida

life preserver n (USA) (chaleco) salvavidas

lifestyle /'laɪfstaɪl/ n estilo de vida

lifetime /'laɪftaɪm/ n toda una vida ▸ **the chance, etc. of a lifetime** la oportunidad, etc. de tu vida

lift /lɪft/ vt ~ **sth/sb (up)** levantar algo/a algn vi (neblina, nubes) disiparse ■ **lift off** despegar ● n **1** impulso **2** (GB) ascensor, elevador **3** give sb a ~ llevar a algn en carro

light /laɪt/ n **1** luz **2** (traffic) lights [pl] semáforo **3** a light: Do you have a ~? ¿Tienes fuego/candela? ▸ **come to light** salir a la luz **in the light of sth** considerando algo **set light to sth** prender fuego a algo ● adj **(-er/-est)** **1** (habitación) luminoso **2** (color) claro **3** ligero: two kilos lighter dos kilos menos **4** (golpe, viento) suave ● adv: travel ~ viajar ligero (de equipaje) ■ **light up** encender(se) **1** vt, vi encender(se) **2** vt iluminar **NOTA** Se suele usar **lighted** como adjetivo antes del sustantivo: a lighted candle, y **lit** como verbo: He lit the candle. ■ **light up (with sth)** iluminarse (de algo) (cara, ojos)

light bulb n foco, bombillo

lighten /'laɪtn/ vt, vi **1** iluminar(se) **2** aligerar(se) **3** alegrar(se)

lighter /'laɪtər/ n encendedor

light-headed adj mareado

light-hearted adj **1** despreocupado **2** desenfadado

lighthouse /'laɪthaʊs/ n faro

lighting /'laɪtɪŋ/ n **1** iluminación **2** street ~ alumbrado público

lightly /'laɪtli/ adv **1** ligeramente, suavemente **2** ágilmente **3** a la ligera ▸ **get off/be let off lightly** (coloq) salir bien parado

lightness /'laɪtnəs/ n **1** claridad **2** ligereza **3** suavidad **4** agilidad

lightning /'laɪtnɪŋ/ n [U] relámpago, rayo: a flash of ~ un relámpago

lightweight /ˈlaɪtweɪt/ n (boxeo) peso ligero ● adj 1 ligero 2 (boxeador) de peso ligero

like /laɪk/ prep 1 (comparación) como, igual que: He acted ~ our leader. Se comportó como si fuera nuestro líder. ◊ It's ~ cooking. Es como cocinar. ◊ look/be ~ sb parecerse a algn 2 (ejemplo) (tal) como ▶ **like crazy/mad** (coloq) como loco ● conj (coloq) 1 como 2 como si ● vt gustar: I ~ swimming. Me gusta nadar. ◊ Would you ~ a cup of tea? ¿Quieres un té? →GUSTAR ▶ **if you like** si quieres **likeable** adj agradable

likely /ˈlaɪkli/ adj (-ier/-iest) 1 probable: It isn't ~ to rain. No es probable que llueva. 2 apropiado ● adv ▶ **not likely!** (coloq) ¡ni hablar! **likelihood** n [sing] probabilidad

liken /ˈlaɪkən/ vt (fml) comparar

likeness /ˈlaɪknəs/ n parecido: a family ~ un aire de familia

likewise /ˈlaɪkwaɪz/ adv (fml) 1 de la misma forma: do ~ hacer lo mismo 2 asimismo

liking /ˈlaɪkɪŋ/ n ▶ **take a liking to sb** encariñarse con algn **to sb's liking** del agrado de algn

lilac /ˈlaɪlək/ adj, n lila

lily /ˈlɪli/ n (pl -ies) 1 lirio 2 azucena

limb /lɪm/ n (Anat) miembro, extremidad (de persona)

lime /laɪm/ n 1 cal 2 lima, limón (Mx) ● (tb ~ **green**) adj, n verde limón

limelight /ˈlaɪmlaɪt/ n: be in the ~ ser el foco de atención

limestone /ˈlaɪmstəʊn/ n piedra caliza

limit /ˈlɪmɪt/ n límite: within ~s dentro de ciertos límites ● vt limitar **limitation** n limitación **limited** adj limitado **limiting** adj restrictivo **limitless** adj ilimitado

limousine /ˈlɪməziːn/ n limusina

limp /lɪmp/ adj 1 flácido 2 débil ● vi cojear ● n cojera: have a ~ ser/estar cojo

line /laɪn/ n 1 línea, raya 2 fila, cola 3 lines (Teat): learn your ~s aprender tu papel 4 líneas líneas (castigo) 5 cuerda: a fishing ~ un sedal (de pesca) 6 línea telefónica: The ~ is busy. Está ocupada. ◊ Hold the line. No cuelgue el teléfono. 7 vía 8 [sing]: the official ~ la postura oficial ▶ **along/on the same, etc. lines** del mismo, etc. estilo **in line with sth** conforme a algo ● vt alinear(se) ■ **line up** hacer fila **lined** adj 1 rayado 2 (rostro) arrugado

3 forrado, revestido **lining** n 1 forro 2 revestimiento

line drawing n dibujo a lápiz o pluma

linen /ˈlɪnɪn/ n 1 lino 2 ropa blanca

liner /ˈlaɪnər/ n transatlántico

linger /ˈlɪŋɡər/ vi 1 quedarse mucho tiempo 2 perdurar, persistir

linguist /ˈlɪŋɡwɪst/ n 1 políglota 2 lingüista **linguistic** /lɪŋˈgwɪstɪk/ adj lingüístico **linguistics** n [sing] lingüística

link /lɪŋk/ n 1 eslabón 2 lazo 3 vínculo 4 conexión 5 (Comp) enlace ● vt 1 unir: ~ arms cogerse del brazo 2 vincular ■ **link up (with sth/sb)** unirse (con algo/algn)

lion /ˈlaɪən/ n león

lip /lɪp/ n labio

lip-read /ˈlɪp riːd/ vi (pt/pp lip-read /-red/) leer los labios

lipstick /ˈlɪpstɪk/ n lápiz de labios

liqueur /lɪˈkɜːr; -ˈkjʊə(r) GB/ n licor

liquid /ˈlɪkwɪd/ adj, n líquido **liquidize** vt licuar **liquidizer** n (GB) licuadora

liquor /ˈlɪkər/ n bebida fuerte: ~ store tienda/almacén de licores

liquorice (GB) = LICORICE

lisp /lɪsp/ n ceceo ● vt, vi cecear

list /lɪst/ n lista ● vt 1 enumerar, hacer una lista de 2 (catalogar

listen /ˈlɪsn/ vi 1 ~ (**to sth/sb**) escuchar (algo/a algn) 2 ~ **to sth/sb** hacer caso a algo/algn ■ **listen (out) for sth** estar atento a algo **listener** n 1 (Radio) oyente 2 a good ~ uno que sabe escuchar

lit /lɪt/ pt, pp de LIGHT

liter (litre GB) /ˈliːtər/ n (abrev l) litro →Ver pág. 222

literacy /ˈlɪtərəsi/ n alfabetismo

literate adj que sabe leer y escribir

literal /ˈlɪtərəl/ adj literal

literary /ˈlɪtəreri; -rəri GB/ adj literario

literature /ˈlɪtrətʃər/ n 1 literatura 2 información **literary** adj literario

litter /ˈlɪtər/ n 1 (en la calle) basura 2 (Zool) camada ● vt estar esparcido por: Papers littered the floor. Había papeles tirados por el suelo.

litter bin n (GB) basurero, caneca (And)

little /ˈlɪtl/ adj **NOTA** Para el comparativo y superlativo se suelen usar **smaller** y **smallest**.

1 pequeño: ~ *finger* meñique ◇ *Poor* ~ *thing!* ¡Pobrecito! →**SMALL 2** poco: *a* ~ *while* un poco **NOTA** Little tiene un sentido negativo y significa "poco". **A** little tiene un sentido más positivo y equivale a "algo de": *I have* ~ *hope.* Tengo pocas esperanzas. ◇ *Always carry a* ~ *money.* Lleva siempre algo de dinero. ● *adv. n, pron* poco: *There was* ~ *anyone could do.* No se pudo hacer nada. ▶ **little by little** poco a poco **little or nothing** casi nada

live¹ /lɪv/ *vi* **1** vivir **2** permanecer vivo ■ **live for sth** vivir para algo **live on sth** seguir viviendo **live on sth** vivir de algo **live through sth** sobrevivir a algo **live up to sth** estar a la altura de algo **live with sth** aceptar algo

live² /laɪv/ *adj* **1** vivo **2** (*bomba, etc.*) activado **3** (*Elec*) conectado **4** (*TV, actuación*) en vivo/directo ● *adv* en vivo/directo

livelihood /'laɪvlihʊd/ *n* medio de subsistencia

lively /'laɪvli/ *adj* (**-ier/-iest**) **1** vivo **2** animado

liver /'lɪvər/ *n* hígado

lives /laɪvz/ *pl de* LIFE

livestock /'laɪvstɑk/ *n* ganado

living /'lɪvɪŋ/ *n* vida: *make a* ~ ganarse la vida ◇ *What do you do for a* ~? ¿A qué se dedica? ◇ *standard of* ~ nivel de vida ● *adj* [*antes de sustantivo*] vivo →**VIVO** ▶ **in/within living memory** que se recuerda

living room *n* sala

lizard /'lɪzərd/ *n* lagarto, lagartija

load /loʊd/ *n* **1** carga **2** (*coloq*) montón: *What a* ~ *of rubbish!* ¡Qué cantidad de tonterías! ● **1** *vt, vi* ~ (**up**) (**with sth**) cargar (algo) (con algo) **2** *vt* ~ *sth/sb* (**down**) cargar (con mucho peso) algo/a algn **loaded** *adj* cargado ▶ **a loaded question** una pregunta con segundas

loaf /loʊf/ *n* (*pl* **loaves** /loʊvz/) pan (*de molde, redondo, etc.*): *a* ~ *of bread* un pan

loan /loʊn/ *n* préstamo

loathe /loʊð/ *vt* aborrecer **loathing** *n* aborrecimiento

lobby /'lɑbi/ *n* (*pl* **-ies**) **1** vestíbulo, lobby **2** (*Pol*) grupo (*de presión*) ● *vt, vi* (*pt/pp* **-ied**) presionar, cabildear (*Mx*)

lobster /'lɑbstər/ *n* langosta

local /'loʊkl/ *adj* **1** local, de la zona **2** (*Med*) localizado: ~ *anesthetic* anestesia local

location /loʊ'keɪʃn/ *n* **1** lugar **2** localización **3** (*persona*) paradero ▶ **on location** en exteriores (*Cine*) **locate** *vt* **1** localizar **2** situar

loch /lɑk/ *n* (*Esc*) lago

lock /lɑk/ *n* **1** cerradura **2** esclusa ● *vt, vi* **1** cerrar con llave **2** (*volante/timón*) bloquear(se) ■ **lock sth away/up** guardar algo bajo llave **lock sb up** encerrar a algn

locker /'lɑkər/ *n* casillero (*armario*)

locomotive /,loʊkə'moʊtɪv/ *n* locomotora

lodge /lɑdʒ/ *n* **1** casa del guarda **2** (*caza, pesca, etc.*) pabellón **3** portería ● *vt, vi* hospedar(se) **lodger** *n* inquilino/a **lodging** *n* alojamiento

loft /lɔːft; lɒft GB/ *n* desván

log /lɔːɡ; lɒɡ GB/ *n* **1** tronco **2** leño **3** diario de vuelo/navegación ● *vt* (**-gg-**) anotar ■ **log in/on** (*Comp*) entrar en el sistema **log off/out** (*Comp*) salir del sistema →**COMPUTADORA**

logic /'lɑdʒɪk/ *n* lógica **logical** *adj* lógico

logo /'loʊɡoʊ/ *n* (*pl* **-s**) logotipo

lollipop /'lɑlipɑp/ *n* pirulí (*Mx*), colombina® (*And*)

lolly /'lɑli/ *n* (*pl* **-ies**) (*GB, coloq*) **1** Ver LOLLIPOP **2** paleta (*helada*)

lonely /'loʊnli/ *adj* **1** solo →ALONE **2** solitario **loneliness** *n* soledad **loner** *n* solitario/a

long¹ /lɔːŋ; lɒŋ GB/ (**-er** /'lɔːŋɡər/ **-est** /'lɔːŋɡɪst/) *adj* **1** largo: *It's two meters* ~. Mide 2m de largo. **2** (*tiempo*): *a* ~ *time* mucho tiempo ◇ *How* ~ *is the vacation?* ¿Cuánto duran las vacaciones? ▶ **at the longest** como máximo **in the long run** a la larga ● *adv* **1** mucho (*tiempo*): *Stay as* ~ *as you like.* Quédate cuanto quieras. **2** todo: *all day* ~ todo el día ▶ **as/so long as** con tal de que **for long** mucho tiempo **no/any longer**: *I can't stay any longer.* No me puedo quedar más.

long² /lɔːŋ; lɒŋ GB/ *vi* **1** ~ **for sth/ to do sth** ansiar (hacer) algo **2** ~ **for sb to do sth** desear que algn haga algo **longing** *n* anhelo

long-distance *adj, adv* de larga distancia

longitude /'lɑŋɡɪtuːd; -tjuːd GB/ *n* longitud (*Geog*)

long jump *n* salto largo

long-life *adj* de larga duración

long-range *adj* **1** a largo plazo **2** de largo alcance

long-sighted *adj* hipermétrope

long-standing *adj* de hace mucho tiempo

long-suffering adj sufrido

long-term adj a largo plazo

loo /luː/ n (GB, coloq) baño →TOILET

look /lʊk/ n 1 mirada, vistazo: have/take a ~ at sth echar un vistazo a algo 2 have a ~ for sth buscar algo 3 aspecto 4 moda 5 looks [pl] físico: good ~ s belleza ● vi 1 ~ (at (sth/sb)) mirar (algo/a algn) →MIRAR 2 parecer ▸ look sb up and down mirar a algn de arriba abajo (not) look yourself (no) parecer uno mismo ■ look after yourself/sb cuidar(se) (a algn) look around 1 volver la cabeza para mirar 2 mirar por ahí look around sth visitar algo look at sth 1 examinar algo 2 considerar algo look back (on sth) mirar hacia atrás (recordando algo) look down on sth/sb despreciar algo/a algn look for sth/sb buscar algo/a algn look forward to sth tener ganas de algo look into sth investigar algo look on mirar (sin tomar parte) look out! ¡Cuidado! look out (for sth/sb) fijarse (por si se ve algo/algn) look over examinar algo look through sth repasar, echar un vistazo a algo look up 1 alzar la vista 2 (coloq) mejorar look up to sb admirar a algn ■ look sth up buscar algo (diccionario, etc.)

lookout /ˈlʊkaʊt/ n vigía ▸ be on the lookout/keep a lookout for sth/sb fijarse (por si se ve algo/algn)

loom /luːm/ n 1 telar ● vi 1 ~ (up) surgir, asomar(se) 2 amenazar

loony /ˈluːni/ n (pl -ies) (coloq, pey) loco/a

loop /luːp/ n 1 curva 2 (con nudo) lazo ● 1 vi dar vueltas 2 vt: ~ sth around/over sth pasar algo alrededor de/por algo

loophole /ˈluːphəʊl/ n escapatoria, vacío legal

loose /luːs/ adj (-er/-est) 1 suelto: ~ change dinero suelto 2 flojo 3 (vestido) holgado, ancho 4 (moral) relajado ▸ be at a loose end no tener nada que hacer let sth/sb loose soltar algo/a algn ● n ▸ be on the loose andar suelto loosely adv 1 sin apretar 2 aproximadamente

loosen /ˈluːsn/ 1 vt, vi aflojar(se), soltar(se) 2 vt (control) relajar ■ loosen up 1 relajarse 2 entrar en calor

loot /luːt/ n botín ● vt, vi saquear looting n saqueo

lop /lɒp/ vt (-pp-) 1 podar 2 ~ sth off cortar algo

lopsided /ˌlɒpˈsaɪdɪd/ adj 1 torcido 2 desequilibrado

lord /lɔːd/ n 1 señor 2 the Lord el Señor: the Lord's Prayer el padrenuestro 3 Lord (GB) Lord 4 the Lords la Cámara de los Lores lordship n ▸ your/his Lordship su Señoría

lorry /ˈlɒri; ˈlɔːri (GB)/ n (pl -ies) camión

lose /luːz/ (pt/pp lost) 1 vt, vi perder: ~ your way perderse 2 vt ~ sb sth hacer perder algo a algn: It lost us the game. Nos costó el partido. 3 vi (reloj) atrasarse ■ lose out (on sth)/(to sth/sb) (coloq) salir perdiendo (en algo)/(con respecto a algo/algn) loser n 1 perdedor/a 2 fracasado/a

loss /lɒs; lɒs GB/ n pérdida ▸ at a loss desorientado

lost /lɒst; lɒst/ pt, pp de LOSE ● adj perdido: get ~ perderse ▸ get lost! (coloq) ¡lárgate!

lost and found (lost property GB) n objetos perdidos

lot /lɒt/ adj, adv, pron a lot (of), lots (of) (coloq) mucho(s): Thanks a ~. Muchas gracias. ◊ He spends a ~. Gasta mucho. ◊ ~s of people un montón de gente ◊ What a ~ of CDs! ¡Qué cantidad de CDs! →MANY ● n 1 the (whole) lot (coloq) todo(s) 2 (coloq) grupo: What do you ~ want? ¿Qué quieren ustedes? ◊ I don't go out with that ~. Yo no salgo con esos. 3 terreno 4 suerte (destino)

lotion /ˈləʊʃn/ n loción

lottery /ˈlɒtəri/ n (pl -ies) lotería

loud /laʊd/ (-er/-est) adj 1 alto, fuerte 2 (color) chillón ● adv ▸ out loud en voz alta

loudspeaker /ˌlaʊdˈspiːkər/ n altavoz, parlante

lounge /laʊndʒ/ vi ~ (about/ around) holgazanear ● n sala

louse /laʊs/ n (pl lice) piojo

lousy /ˈlaʊzi/ adj (coloq) terrible

lout /laʊt/ n (GB) patán

lovable /ˈlʌvəbl/ adj encantador

love /lʌv/ n 1 amor be/fall in ~ with sb estar enamorado/enamorarse de algn NOTA Con personas se dice love for somebody y con cosas love of something. 2 (Dep) cero ▸ give/send sb your love dar/mandar saludos a algn make love (to sb) hacer el amor (con algn) ● vt 1 amar, querer 2 adorar: I'd ~ to come. Me encantaría ir.

lovely /ˈlʌvli/ adj (-ier/-iest) 1 precioso 2 encantador 3 muy agradable: *have a ~ time* pasarla muy bien

lovemaking /'lʌvmeɪkɪŋ/ *n* [U] relaciones sexuales

lover /'lʌvər/ *n* amante

loving /'lʌvɪŋ/ *adj* cariñoso **lovingly** *adv* amorosamente

low /loʊ/ (**-er/-est**) *adj* **1** bajo: *lower lip* labio inferior **2** (*sonido*) grave **3** abatido ● *adv* bajo ● *n* mínimo

low-alcohol *adj* bajo en alcohol

low-calorie *adj* bajo en calorías **NOTA** Low-calorie se usa para los productos bajos en calorías o "light". Para bebidas se usa diet: *diet drinks.*

low-cost *adj* barato

lower /'loʊər/ *adj, adv* Ver LOW ● *vt, vi* bajar(se)

low-fat *adj* de bajo contenido graso: *~ milk* leche descremada

low-key *adj* discreto

lowland /'loʊlənd/ *n* tierra baja ● *adj* de las tierras bajas

loyal /'lɔɪəl/ *adj* fiel **loyalist** *n* partidario/a del régimen **loyalty** *n* (*pl* **-ies**) lealtad

luck /lʌk/ *n* suerte ▸ **be in/out of luck** (no) estar de suerte ◊ **no such luck** ¡ojalá!

lucky /'lʌki/ *adj* (**-ier/-iest**) afortunado: *be ~* tener suerte ◊ *It's ~ she's still here.* Suerte que todavía está acá. ◊ *a ~ number* un número de la suerte **luckily** *adv* por suerte

ludicrous /'luːdɪkrəs/ *adj* ridículo

luggage /'lʌgɪdʒ/ *n* [U] equipaje

luggage rack *n* (parrilla) portaequipaje

lukewarm /ˌluːk'wɔːrm/ *adj* tibio

lull /lʌl/ *vt* **1** calmar **2** arrullar ● *n* período de calma

lumber /'lʌmbər/ **1** *vt* ~ **sb with sth/sb** hacer a algn cargar con algo/algn **2** *vi* moverse pesadamente **lumbering** *adj* torpe, pesado

lump /lʌmp/ *n* **1** trozo: *sugar ~* terrón de azúcar **2** grumo **3** (*Med*) bulto ● *vt* ~ **sth/sb together** juntar algo/a algn **lumpy** *adj* lleno de grumos/bolas

lump sum *n* pago único

lunacy /'luːnəsi/ *n* [U] locura

lunatic /'luːnətɪk/ *n* loco/a

lunch /lʌntʃ/ *n* almuerzo, comida (*al mediodía*): *have ~* almorzar, comer ● *vi* almorzar, comer →DINNER

lunchtime /'lʌntʃtaɪm/ *n* la hora de almorzar/comer →DINNER

lung /lʌŋ/ *n* pulmón

lurch /lɜːrtʃ/ *n* sacudida ● *vi* **1** tambalearse **2** dar un bandazo

lure /lʊər/ *n* atractivo ● *vt* atraer

lurid /'lʊərɪd/ *adj* **1** (*color*) chillón **2** horripilante

lurk /lɜːrk/ *vi* acechar

luscious /'lʌʃəs/ *adj* exquisito

lush /lʌʃ/ *adj* exuberante

lust /lʌst/ *n* **1** lujuria **2** ~ **for sth** sed de algo ● *vi* ~ **after/for sth/sb** codiciar algo, desear a algn

luxury /'lʌkʃəri/ *n* (*pl* **-ies**) lujo: *a ~ hotel* un hotel de lujo **luxurious** /lʌg'ʒʊəriəs/ *adj* lujoso

lying Ver LIE

lyrical /'lɪrɪkl/ *adj* lírico

lyrics /'lɪrɪks/ *n* [*pl*] (*Mús*) letra

M m

M, m /em/ *n* (*pl* **M's, m's**) M, m

mac (*tb* **mack**) /mæk/ *n* (*GB, coloq*) impermeable

macabre /məˈkɑːbrə/ *adj* macabro

macaroni /ˌmækəˈroʊni/ *n* [U] macarrones

machine /məˈʃiːn/ *n* máquina

machine-gun *n* ametralladora

machinery /məˈʃiːnəri/ *n* maquinaria

mad /mæd/ *adj* (**madder, -est**) **1** ~ (**about sth/sb**) loco (por algo/algn): *go ~* volverse loco **2** (*coloq*) ~ (**at/with sb**) furioso (con algn) **madly** *adv* locamente: *~ in love with sb* perdidamente enamorado de algn **madness** *n* locura

madam /'mædəm/ *n* [*sing*] (*fml*) señora

maddening /'mædnɪŋ/ *adj* exasperante

made /meɪd/ *pt, pp de* MAKE

magazine /ˈmægəziːn, ˌmægəˈziːn/ *n* (*coloq* **mag**) revista

maggot /'mægət/ *n* gusano

magic /'mædʒɪk/ *n* magia: *like ~* como por arte de magia ● *adj* **1** mágico **2** (*GB, coloq*) genial **magical** *adj* mágico **magician** *n* mago/a

magistrate /'mædʒɪstreɪt/ *n* magistrado/a: *the magistrates' court* el Juzgado de Paz

magnet /'mægnət/ *n* imán **magnetism** *n* magnetismo **magnetize** *vt* imantar

magnetic /mæg'netɪk/ *adj* magnético

magnificent /mæg'nɪfɪsnt/ *adj* magnífico **magnificence** *n* magnificencia

magnify /'mægnɪfaɪ/ *vt, vi* (*pt/pp* -ied) aumentar **magnification** *n* (capacidad de) aumento

magnifying glass *n* lupa

magnitude /'mægnɪtuːd; -tjuːd *GB*/ *n* magnitud

mahogany /mə'hɒgəni/ *adj, n* caoba

maid /meɪd/ *n* 1 criada 2 (*tb* **maiden** /'meɪdn/) doncella

maiden name *n* apellido de soltera **NOTA** En los países de habla inglesa, muchas mujeres toman el apellido del marido al casarse.

mail /meɪl/ *n* [U] correo **NOTA** En Gran Bretaña es más común **post**, aunque **mail** se usa mucho en expresiones como **email, junk mail** y **airmail**. ● *vt* 1 enviar por correo 2 ~ **sb** (*Comp*) mandar un mensaje por email a algn

mailbox /'meɪlbɒks/ (*USA*) *n* buzón (*en la calle*)

mailing list *n* lista de direcciones

mailman /'meɪlmæn/ *n* (*USA*) (*pl* -men) cartero

mail order *n* venta por correo

maim /meɪm/ *vt* mutilar

main /meɪn/ *adj* principal: ~ *street/line* calle/línea principal ◇ *the* ~ *course* segundo plato ◇ *the* ~ *thing* lo principal ● *n* 1 cañería: *a gas* ~ una tubería de gas 2 **the mains** (*GB*) [*pl*] la red de suministros ▸ **in the main** en general **mainly** *adv* principalmente

mainland /'meɪnlænd/ *n* tierra firme, continente

mainstream /'meɪnstriːm/ *n* corriente principal

maintain /meɪn'teɪn/ *vt* 1 mantener 2 conservar: *well maintained* bien cuidado 3 sostener

maintenance /'meɪntənəns/ *n* 1 mantenimiento 2 (*GB, Jur*) pensión de manutención

maize /meɪz/ *n* (*GB*) maíz **NOTA** El maíz cocinado se llama **sweetcorn**.

majesty /'mædʒəsti/ *n* (*pl* -ies) 1 majestuosidad 2 **Majesty** Majestad **majestic** /mə'dʒestɪk/ *adj* majestuoso

major /'meɪdʒər/ *adj* 1 de importancia, principal 2 (*Mús*) mayor ● *n* 1 comandante, mayor 2 (*USA, Educ*) materia principal

majority /mə'dʒɒrəti; -'dʒɔːr- *GB*/ *n* (*pl* -ies) mayoría ▸ *rule* gobierno mayoritario **NOTA** Para "la mayoría de la gente/de mis ami-

gos" se dice *most people/most of my friends*, con el verbo en plural: *Most of my friends live nearby.*

make /meɪk/ *n* marca (*electrodomésticos, etc.*) ● *vt* (*pt/pp* **made**) 1 hacer: ~ *a noise/hole/list* hacer un ruido/un agujero/una lista ◇ ~ *a phone call/visit* hacer una llamada de teléfono/una visita ◇ ~ *an improvement/effort* hacer una mejora/un esfuerzo ◇ ~ *an offer/a promise/plans* hacer una oferta/una promesa/planes ◇ ~ *a movie/cup of tea* hacer una película/taza de té ◇ ~ *money* ganar dinero ◇ ~ *an impression* impresionar ◇ ~ *a note of sth* anotar algo ◇ ~ *a mistake/an excuse* cometer un error/sacar una excusa 2 ~ **sth** (**from/out**) (**of sth**) hacer algo (con/de algo): *What's it made (out) of?* ¿De qué está hecho? ◇ ~ *made in Japan* fabricado en Japón 3 ~ **sth into sth** convertir algo en algo, hacer algo con algo 4 ~ **sth/sb** + *adj/sustantivo*: ~ *sb angry* enojar a algn ◇ ~ *things worse* empeorar las cosas ◇ *He made my life hell.* Me hizo la vida imposible. 5 ~ **sth/sb do sth** hacer que algo/algn haga algo **NOTA** El verbo en infinitivo que viene después de **make** se pone sin **to**, salvo en pasiva: *I can't* ~ *him do it.* ◇ *You made her feel guilty.* ◇ *He was made to wait.* 6 ~ **sb sth** hacer a algo/algn: ~ *sb a rey* hacer a algn rey 7 llegar a ser: *He'll* ~ *a good teacher.* Tiene madera de profesor. 8 (*conseguir, llegar a*): *Can you* ~ *it?* ¿Podrás venir? ▸ **make do (with sth)** arreglárselas (con algo) **make it** triunfar **NOTA** Para otras expresiones, ver el sustantivo, adjetivo, etc., p. ej. **make love** en LOVE. ▸ **be made for sb/each other** estar hecho para algn/estar hechos el uno para el otro **make for sth/sb** dirigirse hacia algo/algn **make for sth** contribuir a (conseguir) algo **make sth of sth/sb** opinar algo de algo/algn **make off (with sth)** largarse (con algo) **make sth out** escribir algo (*cheque, documento*) **make sth/sb out** 1 entender algo/a algn ◇ ~ *out sb's writing* descifrar la escritura de algn 2 distinguir algo/a algn **make up** maquillarse/maquillarse **make sth up** 1 constituir algo 2 inventar algo **make up for sth** compensar algo

maker /'meɪkər/ *n* fabricante

makeshift /ˈmeɪkʃɪft/ *adj* provisional, improvisado

make-up *n* [U] **1** maquillaje **2** constitución **3** carácter

making /ˈmeɪkɪŋ/ *n* fabricación ▶ **be the making of sb** ser la clave del éxito de algn **have the makings of sth 1** tener madera de algo **2** tener los ingredientes para ser algo

male /meɪl/ *adj* **1** masculino **NOTA** Se aplica a las características físicas del hombre: *The ~ voice is deeper than the female.* **2** macho → FEMALE ● *n* macho, varón

malice /ˈmælɪs/ *n* malevolencia, mala intención **malicious** /məˈlɪʃəs/ *adj* mal intencionado

malignant /məˈlɪɡnənt/ *adj* maligno

mall /mɔːl/ *n* centro comercial

malnutrition /ˌmælnuːˈtrɪʃn; -njuː-/ *n* desnutrición

malt /mɔːlt/ *n* malta

mammal /ˈmæml/ *n* mamífero

mammoth /ˈmæməθ/ *n* mamut ● *adj* colosal

man /mæn/ *vt* (**-nn-**) **1** dotar de personal **2** tripular ● *n* (*pl* **men**) hombre: *a young ~* un joven ◊ *a man's shirt* una camisa de caballero ▶ **the man in the street** el ciudadano promedio **NOTA** **Man** y **mankind** se usan con el significado genérico de "todos los hombres y mujeres". Mucha gente prefiere usar palabras como **humanity, the human race** (*sing*) o **humans, human beings, people** (*pl*).

manage /ˈmænɪdʒ/ **1** *vt* dirigir **2** *vt* (*propiedades*) administrar **3** *vi* arreglárselas: *I can't ~ on 80 dollars a week.* No me alcanza con $80 a la semana. **4** *vt, vi*: *~ to do sth* conseguir hacer algo ◊ *Can you ~ all of it?* ¿Puedes con todo eso? ◊ *Can you ~ six o'clock?* ¿Puedes venir a las seis? ◊ *I couldn't ~ another mouthful.* Ya no podría comer ni un bocado más. **manageable** *adj* **1** manejable **2** tratable, dócil

management /ˈmænɪdʒmənt/ *n* dirección, gestión: *a committee/consultant* comité/consejo directivo/asesor de dirección de empresas

manager /ˈmænɪdʒər/ *n* **1** director/a, gerente **2** administrador/a **3** (*Dep*) mánager **managerial** /ˌmænəˈdʒɪəriəl/ *adj* directivo, de gerencia

managing director *n* director/a general

mandate /ˈmændeɪt/ *n* mandato **mandatory** /ˈmændətɔːri; -təri *GB*/ *adj* obligatorio

mane /meɪn/ *n* **1** crin **2** melena

maneuver /məˈnuːvər/ *n* maniobra ● *vt, vi* maniobrar

manfully /ˈmænfəli/ *adv* valientemente

mangle /ˈmæŋɡl/ *vt* destrozar

manhood /ˈmænhʊd/ *n* edad viril, virilidad

mania /ˈmeɪniə/ *n* manía **maniac** *adj, n* maniaco/a

manic /ˈmænɪk/ *adj* **1** (*coloq*) frenético **2** maniaco

manicure /ˈmænɪkjʊər/ *n* manicure

manifest /ˈmænɪfest/ (*fml*) *vt* manifestar ● *adj* visible **manifestation** *n* (*fml*) manifestación

manifesto /ˌmænɪˈfestoʊ/ *n* (*pl* **-s**) manifiesto

manifold /ˈmænɪfoʊld/ *adj* (*fml*) múltiple

manipulate /məˈnɪpjuleɪt/ *vt* manipular, manejar **manipulation** *n* manipulación **manipulative** *adj* manipulador

mankind /mænˈkaɪnd/ *n* género humano → MAN

manly /ˈmænli/ *adj* varonil

man-made *adj* artificial

manned /mænd/ *adj* tripulado

manner /ˈmænər/ *n* **1** manera **2** actitud, modo de comportarse **3 manners** modales: *good/bad ~s* buena/mala educación ◊ *He has no ~s.* Es un mal educado.

mannerism /ˈmænərɪzəm/ *n* gesto, peculiaridad (*forma de hablar, etc.*)

manoeuvre (*GB*) = MANEUVER

manor /ˈmænər/ *n* **1** (*tb ~ house*) casa señorial **2** (*territorio*) señorío

manpower /ˈmænpaʊər/ *n* mano de obra

mansion /ˈmænʃn/ *n* mansión

manslaughter /ˈmænslɔːtər/ *n* homicidio involuntario

mantelpiece /ˈmæntlpiːs/ *n* repisa de la chimenea

manual /ˈmænjuəl/ *adj, n* manual

manufacture /ˌmænjuˈfæktʃər/ *vt* **1** fabricar **2** (*pruebas*) inventar **manufacturer** *n* fabricante

manure /məˈnʊər/ *n* estiércol

manuscript /ˈmænjuskrɪpt/ *n* manuscrito

many /ˈmeni/ *adj, pron* mucho/a, -os/as: *I don't have ~.* No me quedan muchos. ◊ *~ a time* muchas veces ◊ *In ~ ways, I regret it.* En cierta manera, lo lamento. **NOTA** "Mucho" se traduce según el sustantivo al que acompaña o sustituye. En afirmaciones se usa **a lot (of)**: *She has a lot of money*. En negaciones e interrogaciones se usa **many** o **a lot of** cuando el sustantivo es contable: *There aren't ~ women bus drivers.*, y **much** o **a lot of** cuando es incontable: *I haven't eaten much (food)*. ▸ **a good/great many** muchísimos

map /mæp/ n 1 mapa 2 (ciudad) plano ▸ **put sth/sb on the map** dar a conocer algo/a algn ◆ (**-pp-**) trazar el mapa de ■ **map sth out** 1 planear algo 2 (idea) exponer algo

maple /ˈmeɪpl/ n arce, maple

marathon /ˈmærəθən; -θɑn GB/ n maratón: *The meeting was a real ~*. Fue una reunión interminable.

marble /ˈmɑːbl/ n 1 mármol 2 canica

March /mɑːtʃ/ n (abrev **Mar.**) marzo →JUNE

march /mɑːtʃ/ vi 1 vi marchar: ~ *past* desfilar ◇ ~ *in* entrar resueltamente ◇ ~ *up to sb* abordar a algn con resolución 2 vt ~ **sb away/off** llevarse a algn 3 vi manifestarse ▸ **get your marching orders** (GB, coloq) ser despedido ● en marcha: *on the* ~ en marcha **marcher** n manifestante

mare /meər/ n yegua

margarine /ˌmɑːdʒəˈriːn; ˈmɑːdʒəˈriːn GB/ (tb **marge** /mɑːdʒ/ GB, coloq) n margarina

margin /ˈmɑːdʒɪn/ n margen **marginal** adj 1 marginal 2 (notas) al margen **marginally** adv ligeramente

marijuana (tb **marihuana**) /ˌmærəˈwɑːnə/ n marihuana

marina /məˈriːnə/ n puerto de recreo, marina

marine /məˈriːn/ adj 1 marino 2 marítimo ● n infante de marina

marital /ˈmærɪtl/ adj conyugal: ~ *status* estado civil

maritime /ˈmærɪtaɪm/ adj marítimo

mark /mɑːk/ n 1 marca 2 señal: *punctuation* ~ signo de puntuación 3 (Educ) nota ▸ **be up to the mark** (GB) dar la talla **make your mark** alcanzar el éxito **on your marks, (get), set, go!** en sus marcas, listos, ¡fuera! ◆ vt 1 marcar 2 señalar 3 (Educ) corregir ▸ **mark time** 1 hacer tiempo 2 (Mil) marcar el paso ■ **mark sth up/down** aumentar/rebajar el precio de algo **marked** adj notable **markedly** /ˈmɑːkɪdli/ adv de forma notable

marker /ˈmɑːkər/ n 1 marca 2 ~ *buoy* una boya de señalización

market /ˈmɑːkɪt/ n mercado: ~ *research* estudio(s) de mercado ▸ **in the market for sth** interesado en comprar algo **on the market** en el mercado: *put sth on the* ~ poner algo en venta ◆ vt 1 vender 2 ofertar **marketable** adj vendible

marketing /ˈmɑːkɪtɪŋ/ n marketing

marketplace /ˈmɑːkɪtpleɪs/ n 1 (Econ) mercado 2 (tb **market square**) plaza del mercado

marmalade /ˈmɑːməleɪd/ n mermelada (de cítricos)

maroon /məˈruːn/ adj, n granate

marooned /məˈruːnd/ adj abandonado (en isla desierta, etc.)

marquee /mɑːˈkiː/ n carpa

marriage /ˈmærɪdʒ/ n 1 matrimonio 2 boda →MATRIMONIO

marrow /ˈmæroʊ/ n 1 médula 2 (GB) calabaza grande

marry /ˈmæri/ vt, vi (pt/pp **-ied**) casar(se) **married** adj ~ (**to sb**) casado (con algn): *get* ~ casarse ◇ *a* ~ *couple* un matrimonio

Mars /mɑːz/ n Marte

marsh /mɑːʃ/ n ciénaga **marshy** adj pantanoso

marshal /ˈmɑːʃl/ n 1 mariscal 2 jefe de seguridad ● vt (**-l-, -ll-** GB) 1 (tropas) formar 2 (ideas, datos) ordenar

martial /ˈmɑːʃl/ adj marcial

Martian /ˈmɑːʃn/ adj, n marciano

martyr /ˈmɑːtər/ n mártir **martyrdom** /ˈmɑːtərdəm/ n martirio

marvel /ˈmɑːvl/ n maravilla ● vi (**-l-, -ll-** GB) ~ **at sth** maravillarse ante algo **marvelous** (**-ll-** GB) adj maravilloso: *have a* ~ *time* pasarla de maravilla ◇ *That's* ~! ¡Estupendo!

Marxism /ˈmɑːksɪzəm/ n marxismo **Marxist** adj, n marxista

marzipan /ˈmɑːzɪpæn/ n mazapán

mascara /mæˈskærə; -ˈskɑːrə GB/ n rímel®, pestañina (And)

mascot /ˈmæskət/ n mascota

masculine /ˈmæskjəlɪn/ adj, n masculino **NOTA** Se aplica a las cualidades consideradas típicas del hombre. **masculinity** /ˌmæskjuˈlɪnəti/ n masculinidad

mash /mæʃ/ n (GB) puré (de papas) 1 ~ (**up**) machacar algo 2 hacer puré de: *mashed potatoes* puré de papas

mask /mæsk; mɑːsk GB/ n 1 máscara 2 antifaz 3 tapabocas ● vt 1 enmascarar 2 tapar 3 encubrir
masked adj 1 enmascarado 2 encapuchado

mason /'meɪsn/ n 1 albañil 2 (tb **Mason**) masón **masonic** (tb **Masonic**) /mə'sɒnɪk/ adj masónico

masonry /'meɪsənri/ n mampostería

masquerade /ˌmæskə'reɪd; ˌmɑːsk- GB/ n (fml) farsa ● vi ~ **as sth** hacerse pasar por algo

mass /mæs/ n 1 masa 2 **masses** [pl] (coloq) montón, gran cantidad 3 [antes de sustantivo] masivo, de masas: ~ media medios masivos de comunicación ◇ a ~ grave una fosa común ◇ ~ hysteria histeria colectiva 4 the **masses** las masas 5 (tb **Mass**) (Rel, Mús) misa 6 the ~ of... la mayoría de... ▸ **be a mass of sth** estar cubierto/lleno de algo ● vt, vi 1 juntar(se) (en masa) 2 (Mil) concentrar(se)

massacre /'mæsəkər/ n masacre ● vt masacrar

massage /mə'sɑːʒ; 'mæsɑːʒ GB/ vt dar masaje a ● n masaje

massive /'mæsɪv/ adj 1 enorme, monumental 2 macizo

mass production n fabricación en serie **mass-produce** vt fabricar en serie

mast /mæst; mɑːst GB/ n 1 (barco) mástil 2 (TV) torre

master /'mæstər; 'mɑːs- GB/ n 1 amo, dueño 2 maestro 3 (Náut) capitán 4 (cassette, etc.) original 5 ~ bedroom dormitorio principal ◇ a ~ plan un plan infalible ● vt 1 dominar 2 controlar **masterful** adj 1 con autoridad 2 (tb **masterly**) dominante **mastery** n 1 dominio 2 supremacía

mastermind /'mæstərmaɪnd; 'mɑːs- GB/ n cerebro ● vt planear, dirigir

masterpiece /'mæstərpiːs; 'mɑːs- GB/ n obra maestra

master's (tb ~ **degree**) n máster

masturbate /'mæstərbeɪt/ vi masturbarse **masturbation** n masturbación

mat /mæt/ n 1 tapete 2 colchoneta 3 salvamanteles 4 maraña ● adj mate

match /mætʃ/ n 1 fósforo, cerillo 2 (Dep) partido 3 igual 4 complemento ▸ **find/meet your match** encontrar la horma de tu zapato ● 1 vt, vi combinar, hacer juego (con): matching shoes and purse zapatos y bolso que hacen juego 2 vt igualar ■ **match up** coincidir

match up to sth/sb igualar algo/a algn **match sth up (with sth)** acoplar algo (a algo)

matchbox /'mætʃbɒks/ n caja de fósforos/cerillos

mate /meɪt/ n 1 (GB, coloq) amigo, cuate (Mx) 2 ayudante 3 (Náut) segundo de a bordo 4 (Zool) pareja 5 (ajedrez) jaque mate ● vt, vi aparear(se)

material /mə'tɪəriəl/ n 1 material 2 tela → TELA ● adj material **materially** adv sensiblemente

materialism /mə'tɪəriəlɪzəm/ n materialismo **materialist** n materialista **materialistic** /məˌtɪəriə'lɪstɪk/ adj materialista

materialize /mə'tɪəriəlaɪz/ vi convertirse en realidad

maternal /mə'tɜːrnl/ adj 1 maternal 2 materno

maternity /mə'tɜːrnəti/ n maternidad

mathematics /ˌmæθə'mætɪks/ (tb coloq **math** USA, **maths** GB) n [sing] matemáticas **mathematical** adj matemáticos **mathematician** /ˌmæθəmə'tɪʃn/ n matemático/a

matinee /ˌmætɪ'neɪ, 'mætɪneɪ/ n (Cine, Teat) matiné

mating /'meɪtɪŋ/ n apareamiento ▸ **mating season** época de celo

matrimony /'mætrɪmouni; -məni GB/ n (fml) matrimonio **matrimonial** /ˌmætrɪ'mouniəl/ adj matrimonial

matron /'meɪtrən/ n (GB) enfermera jefe

matt /mæt/ adj (GB) mate

matted /'mætɪd/ adj enmarañado

matter /'mætər/ vi importar: It doesn't ~. No importa. ● n 1 asunto: take ~s into your own hands tomar cartas por cuenta propia ◇ I have nothing to say on the ~. No tengo nada que decir al respecto. 2 (Fís) materia 3 material: printed ~ impresos ▸ **a matter of hours, days, etc.** cosa de horas, días, etc. **a matter of opinion/life and death** cuestión de opinión/vida o muerte **as a matter of course** por costumbre **as a matter of fact** en realidad **be the matter (with sth/sb)** (coloq) pasarle a algo/algn: What's the ~? ¿Qué es esto? ◇ Is anything the ~? ¿Pasa algo? **for that matter** si vamos a eso **no matter who, what, etc.** no importa quién, qué, etc.: no ~ what he says diga lo que diga ◇ no ~ how rich he is por muy rico que sea ◇ no ~ what pase lo que pase

matter-of-fact adj 1 prosaico 2 (persona) impasible 3 realista

mattress /'mætrəs/ n colchón

mature /mə'tʊə(r); -'tʃʊə(r) GB/ adj 1 maduro 2 (Com) vencido ● 1 vt, vi (hacer) madurar 2 vi (Com) vencer **maturity** n madurez

maul /mɔːl/ vt 1 maltratar 2 (fiera) herir seriamente

mausoleum /ˌmɔːsə'liːəm/ n mausoleo

mauve /moʊv/ adj, n (color) malva

maverick /'mævərɪk/ n ▸ **be a maverick** ser inconformista

maxim /'mæksɪm/ n máxima

maximum /'mæksɪməm/ adj, n (pl **maxima** /'mæksɪmə/) (abrev **max.**) máximo **maximize** vt potenciar, llevar al máximo

May /meɪ/ n mayo →JUNE

may /meɪ/ v (pt **might** neg **might not**/**mightn't**) NOTA May es un verbo modal al que sigue un infinitivo sin **to**, que no usa el auxiliar **do** en interrogaciones y negaciones. Sólo tiene presente, **may**, y pasado, **might**. 1 (permiso) poder: You – as well go home. Más vale que te vayas a casa. NOTA Para pedir permiso, **may** es más cortés que **can**, aunque **can** es más común: Can I come in? ◊ May I get down from the table? ◊ I'll take a seat, if I –. En el pasado se usa **could** mucho más que **might**: She asked if she could come in. 2 (posibilidad) poder (que): He – not come. Puede que no venga. →PODER ▸ **be that as it may** sea como fuere

maybe /'meɪbi/ adv quizá(s)

mayhem /'meɪhem/ n [U] caos

mayonnaise /ˌmeɪə'neɪz; 'meɪə'neɪz GB/ n mayonesa

mayor /meə(r); 'meɪər GB/ n alcalde/esa **mayoress** /'meərəs; meə'res GB/ n 1 alcaldesa 2 esposa del alcalde

maze /meɪz/ n laberinto

me /miː/ pron 1 [como objeto] me: Don't hit me. No me pegues. ◊ Tell me all about it. Cuéntamelo todo. 2 [después de prep] mí 3 [cuando va sólo o después del verbo be] yo: Hi, it's me. Hola, soy yo.

meadow /'medoʊ/ n prado

meager (**meagre** GB) /'miːgər/ adj escaso, pobre

meal /miːl/ n comida ▸ **make a meal of sth** (coloq) hacer algo con una atención o un esfuerzo exagerado

mean /miːn/ n (Mat) media ● adj (-er/-iest) 1 tacaño 2 – (to sb)

mezquino (con algn) ● vt (pt/pp meant /ment/) 1 querer decir 2 significar: That name meant – anything to me. Ese nombre no me dice nada. 3 suponer 4 pretender: I didn't – to. Fue sin querer. ◊ I meant to finish today. Pensaba terminar hoy. 5 decir en serio: I'm not coming back — I – it! ¡No voy a volver, lo digo en serio! ▸ **be meant for each other** estar hechos el uno para el otro **be meant to do sth**: Is this meant to happen? ¿Es esto lo que se supone que debe pasar? **I mean** (coloq) quiero decir **mean well** tener buenas intenciones

meander /mi'ændər/ vi 1 serpentear 2 (persona) deambular 3 (conversación) divagar

meaning /'miːnɪŋ/ n significado **meaningful** adj trascendente **meaningless** adj sin sentido

means /miːnz/ n 1 (pl **means**) medio: a – to an end un medio para conseguir un fin 2 [pl] medios (económicos) ▸ **by all means** (fml) desde luego

meantime /'miːntaɪm/ n ▸ **in the meantime** mientras tanto

meanwhile /'miːnwaɪl/ adv mientras tanto

measles /'miːzlz/ n sarampión

measure /'meʒər/ vt, vi ~ sth/sb (up) medir algo/a algn: ~ sb up for a suit tomar medidas a algn para un traje ◊ make sth to – hacer algo a medida ■ **measure up (to sth)** estar a la altura (de algo) ● n 1 medida 2 a ~ of sth signo de algo ▸ **for good measure** para no quedarse cortos **half measures** medias tintas **measurable** adj 1 medible 2 sensible **measured** adj 1 (lenguaje) comedido 2 pausado **measurement** n 1 medición 2 medida

meat /miːt/ n carne **meaty** adj (-ier/-iest) 1 carnoso 2 jugoso

meatball /'miːtbɔːl/ n albóndiga

mechanic /mə'kænɪk/ n mecánico/a **mechanical** adj mecánico **mechanically** adv mecánicamente: I'm not ~ minded. Soy malo con las máquinas.

mechanics /mə'kænɪks/ n 1 [sing] mecánica 2 the **mechanics** [pl] (fig) la mecánica

mechanism /'mekənɪzəm/ n mecanismo

medal /medl/ n medalla **medalist** (**-ll-** GB) n medallista

medallion /mə'dæliən/ n medallón

meddle /'medl/ vi (pey) **1** ~ (in sth) entrometerse (en algo) **2** ~ with sth jugar con algo

media /'miːdiə/ n **1** the media [pl] los medios de comunicación: ~ studies estudios de comunicación social **2** pl de MEDIUM (1)

mediaeval = MEDIEVAL

mediate /'miːdieɪt/ vi mediar **mediation** n mediación **mediator** n mediador/a

medic /'medik/ n (coloq) **1** médico/a **2** (GB) estudiante de medicina

medical /'medɪkl/ adj **1** médico: ~ student estudiante de medicina **2** clínico ● n (coloq) reconocimiento médico

medication /,medɪ'keɪʃn/ n medicación

medicine /'medsn; 'medsn GB/ n medicina **medicinal** /mə-'dɪsɪnl/ adj medicinal

medieval /,medi'iːvl/ adj medieval

mediocre /,miːdi'oʊkər/ adj mediocre **mediocrity** /,miːdi-'ɑːkrəti/ n **1** mediocridad **2** (persona) mediocre

meditate /'medɪteɪt/ vi meditar **meditation** n meditación

medium /'miːdiəm/ n **1** (pl media) medio **2** (pl -s) médium ● adj medio: I'm ~. Uso la talla mediana.

medley /'medli/ n popurrí

meek /miːk/ adj (-er/-est) manso, dócil

meet /miːt/ v (pt/pp met) **1** vt, vi ~ (up) encontrar(se) ● (pt/pp met) **1** vt, vi ~ (up) encontrar ● What time shall we ~? ¿A qué hora nos encontramos? ◇ Our eyes met. Nuestras miradas se cruzaron. ◇ ~ sb at the station esperar a algn a la estación **2** vi reunirse **3** vt, vi conocer(se): I'd like you to meet... Quiero presentarte a... **4** vt, vi enfrentar(se) **5** vt (demanda) satisfacer: They failed to ~ payments on their loan. No pudieron pagar las cuotas del préstamo. ▶ meet sb's eye mirar a algn a los ojos

meeting /'miːtɪŋ/ n **1** reunión: Annual General Meeting junta general anual **2** encuentro

megaphone /'megəfoʊn/ n megáfono

melancholy /'melənkɑli/ n melancolía ● adj **1** (persona) melancólico **2** (cosa) triste

melee /'meɪleɪ; 'meleɪ GB/ n pelea, tumulto

mellow /'meloʊ/ adj (-er/-est) **1** (color) suave **2** (sonido) dulce **3** (actitud) comprensivo **4** (coloq) alegre (de beber) ● **1** vt, vi (carácter) ablandar(se) **2** vi (vino) envejecer

melodrama /'melədrɑmə/ n melodrama **melodramatic** /,melədrə'mætɪk/ adj melodramático

melody /'melədi/ n (pl -ies) melodía **melodic** /mə'lɑdɪk/ adj melódico **melodious** /mə'loʊdiəs/ adj melodioso

melon /'melən/ n melón

melt /melt/ **1** vt, vi derretir(se): melting point punto de fusión **2** vi deshacerse **3** vt, vi disolver(se) **4** vt, vi (fig) ablandar(se) ■ **melt away** disolverse **melt sth down** fundir algo **melting** n **1** derretimiento **2** fundición

melting pot n amalgama (razas, culturas, etc.) ▶ in the melting pot en proceso de cambio

member /'membər/ n **1** miembro: Member of Parliament (GB) diputado ◇ ~ of the audience uno de los asistentes **2** (club) socio/a **3** (Anat) miembro **membership** n **1** afiliación: ~ card tarjeta de socio **2** (número de) miembros/socios

membrane /'membreɪn/ n membrana

memento /mə'mentoʊ/ n (pl -s/-es) recuerdo (objeto)

memo /'memoʊ/ n (pl -s) (coloq) circular

memoir /'memwɑːr/ n memoria (escrita)

memorabilia /,memərə'bɪliə/ n [pl] recuerdos (objetos)

memorandum /,memə'rændəm/ n **1** memorándum **2** (Jur) minuta

memorial /mə'mɔːriəl/ n monumento conmemorativo

memory /'meməri/ n (pl -ies) **1** memoria: in ~ of sb/to the ~ of sb en memoria de algn **2** recuerdo **memorable** adj memorable **memorize** vt memorizar

men /men/ pl de MAN

menace /'menəs/ n **1** ~ (to sth/sb) amenaza (para algo/algn) **2** a menace (coloq) un peligro ● vt amenazar **menacing** adj amenazador

menagerie /mə'nædʒəri/ n colección de animales salvajes

mend /mend/ **1** vt arreglar **2** vi curarse ▶ mend your ways reformarse ● n remiendo ▶ on the mend (coloq) mejorando **mending** n **1** arreglo (ropa) **2** ropa para arreglar

meningitis /,menɪn'dʒaɪtɪs/ n meningitis

menopause /'menəpɔːz/ n menopausia

menstruation /ˌmenstru'eɪʃn/ n menstruación **menstrual** adj menstrual

menswear /'menzweər/ n ropa de caballero

mental /'mentl/ adj 1 mental: ~ hospital hospital para enfermos mentales 2 (GB, coloq) mal de la cabeza **mentally** adv mentalmente: ~ ill/disturbed enfermo/trastornado mental

mentality /men'tæləti/ n (pl -ies) mentalidad

mention /'menʃn/ vt mencionar, decir: worth mentioning digno de mención ▶ **don't mention it** no hay de qué **not to mention...** sin contar... ● n mención

mentor /'mentɔːr/ n mentor

menu /'menjuː/ n 1 menú, carta 2 (Comp) menú

meow /mi'aʊ/ interj miau ● n maullido ● vi maullar

mercantile /'mɜːkəntaɪl/ adj mercantil

mercenary /'mɜːsəneri; -nəri GB/ adj 1 mercenario 2 (actitud) interesado ● n (pl -ies) mercenario/a

merchandise /'mɜːtʃəndaɪs/ n [U] mercancía(s) **merchandising** n comercialización

merchant /'mɜːtʃənt/ n 1 comerciante, mayorista (que comercia con el extranjero) 2 (Hist) mercader 3 [antes de sustantivo] mercante: ~ bank banco mercantil

Mercury /'mɜːkjəri/ n Mercurio

mercury /'mɜːkjəri/ n mercurio

mercy /'mɜːsi/ n (pl -ies) 1 compasión: have ~ on sth tener compasión de algn ◇ ~ killing eutanasia 2 It's a ~ that... Es una suerte que... ▶ **at the mercy of sth/sb** a merced de algo/algn **merciful** adj 1 ~ (to/towards sb) compasivo (con algn) 2 (suceso) feliz **merciless** adj ~ (to/towards sb) despiadado (con algn)

mere /mɪər/ adj mero, simple: The merest glimpse was enough. Un simple vistazo fue suficiente. ◇ He's a ~ child. No es más que un niño. ◇ the ~ thought of him con sólo pensar en él **merely** adv sólo, meramente

merge /mɜːdʒ/ vt, vi 1 (Com) fusionar(se) 2 entremezclar(se), unir(se) **merger** n fusión

meringue /mə'ræŋ/ n merengue

merit /'merɪt/ n (fml) mérito ● vt merecer, ser digno de

mermaid /'mɜːrmeɪd/ n sirena

merry /'meri/ adj (-ier/-iest) alegre: Merry Christmas! ¡Feliz Navidad! **merriment** n (fml) alegría, regocijo

merry-go-round n carrusel

mesh /meʃ/ n 1 malla: wire ~ tela metálica 2 (Mec) engranaje ● vi 1 engranar 2 encajar

mesmerize /'mezməraɪz/ vt hipnotizar

mess /mes/ n 1 desastre: The kitchen's a ~! ¡La cocina está hecha una porquería! 2 (coloq) caca 3 enredo, lío 4 desarreglado/a 5 (tb ~ hall USA) (Mil) comedor ● vt (USA, coloq) desordenar ■ **mess about/around** 1 hacer(se) el tonto 2 pasar el rato **mess about/around; mess sth about/around** 1 (GB) tratar con desconsideración a algn **mess sth about/around; mess sth about/around with sth** enredar con algo **mess sb up** (coloq) traumatizar a algn **mess sth up** 1 ensuciar algo 2 estropear algo 3 (pelo) despeinar algo **mess with sth/sb** entrometerse en algo/en los asuntos de algn **messy** adj (-ier/-iest) 1 sucio 2 desordenado 3 enredado

message /'mesɪdʒ/ n 1 recado 2 mensaje ▶ **get the message** (coloq) enterarse

messenger /'mesɪndʒər/ n mensajero/a

Messiah /mə'saɪə/ n Mesías

met /met/ pt, pp de MEET

metabolism /mə'tæbəlɪzəm/ n metabolismo

metal /'metl/ n metal **metallic** /mə'tælɪk/ adj metálico

metalwork /'metlwɜːrk/ n trabajo del metal

metamorphose /ˌmetə'mɔːrfoʊz/ vt, vi (fml) convertir(se) **metamorphosis** /ˌmetə'mɔːrfəsɪs/ n (pl -phoses -fəsiːz/) (fml) metamorfosis

metaphor /'metəfər/ n metáfora **metaphorical** /ˌmetə'fɔːrɪkl; -'fɒr- GB/ adj metafórico

metaphysics /ˌmetə'fɪzɪks/ n [sing] metafísica **metaphysical** adj metafísico

meteor /'miːtiər/ n meteorito **meteoric** /ˌmiːti'ɔːrɪk; -'ɒr- GB/ adj meteórico

meteorite /'miːtiəraɪt/ n meteorito

meter /'miːtər/ n 1 (abrev m) metro →Ver pág. 222 2 medidor ● vt medir

methane /'miːθeɪn/ n metano

method /'meθəd/ n método **methodical** /mə'θɒdɪkl/ adj metódico

methodology /ˌmeθəˈdɒlədʒi/ n (pl **-ies**) metodología

Methodist /ˈmeθədɪst/ adj, n metodista

methylated spirits /ˌmeθəleɪtɪd ˈspɪrɪts/ (coloq **meths**) n alcohol azul/industrial

meticulous /məˈtɪkjələs/ adj meticuloso

metre (GB) = METER (1)

metric /ˈmetrɪk/ adj métrico

metropolis /məˈtrɒpəlɪs/ n metrópoli **metropolitan** /ˌmetrəˈpɒlɪtən/ adj metropolitano

miaow (GB) = MEOW

mice /maɪs/ pl de MOUSE

mickey /ˈmɪki/ n (GB) ▸ take the mickey (out of sb) (coloq) burlarse (de algn)

microbe /ˈmaɪkroʊb/ n microbio

microchip /ˈmaɪkroʊtʃɪp/ n chip

microcosm /ˈmaɪkrəkɒzəm/ n microcosmos

micro-organism n microorganismo

microphone /ˈmaɪkrəfoʊn/ n micrófono

microprocessor /ˌmaɪkroʊˈprɒsesər/ n microprocesador

microscope /ˈmaɪkrəskoʊp/ n microscopio **microscopic** /ˌmaɪkrəˈskɒpɪk/ adj microscópico

microwave /ˈmaɪkrəweɪv/ n (tb ~ **oven**) n microondas

mid /mɪd/ adj: in mid-May a mediados de mayo ◇ mid-morning media mañana ◇ mid-life crisis crisis de los cuarenta

mid-air n en el aire: leave sth in ~ dejar algo sin resolver

midday /ˌmɪdˈdeɪ/ n 1 mediodía →MEDIO

middle /ˈmɪdl/ n 1 the middle [sing] el medio, el centro: in the ~ of the night a mitad de la noche 2 (coloq) cintura ▸ in the middle of nowhere en medio de la nada ● adj central, medio: take a ~ course tomar una línea media ◇ ~ finger dedo corazón ◇ ~ management ejecutivos de nivel intermedio ▸ the middle ground terreno neutral

middle age n madurez **middle-aged** adj de mediana edad

middle class n clase media **middle-class** adj de clase media

middleman /ˈmɪdlmæn/ n (pl **-men**) intermediario

middle name n segundo nombre **NOTA** En los países de habla inglesa, se suele tener dos nombres y un apellido.

middle-of-the-road adj (frec pey) moderado

middleweight /ˈmɪdlweɪt/ n (boxeo) peso medio

midfield /ˌmɪdˈfiːld/ n centro del campo **midfielder** n centrocampista

midge /mɪdʒ/ n mosquito

midget /ˈmɪdʒɪt/ n enano/a

midnight /ˈmɪdnaɪt/ n medianoche

midriff /ˈmɪdrɪf/ n abdomen

midst /mɪdst/ n medio ▸ in our midst entre nosotros

midsummer /ˌmɪdˈsʌmər/ n época del solsticio de verano (21 de junio)

midway /ˌmɪdˈweɪ/ adv a medio camino

midweek /ˌmɪdˈwiːk/ n entre semana: in ~ a mediados de semana

midwife /ˈmɪdwaɪf/ n (pl **-wives** /-waɪvz/) partero/a **midwifery** /mɪdˈwɪfəri/ n obstetricia

midwinter /ˌmɪdˈwɪntər/ n época del solsticio de invierno (21 de diciembre)

miffed /mɪft/ adj ofendido

might¹ /maɪt/ v (neg **might not**/**mightn't** /ˈmaɪtnt/) **NOTA** Might es un verbo modal al que sigue un infinitivo sin to, y que no usa el auxiliar do en interrogaciones y negaciones. **1** pt de MAY **2** (posibilidad) poder (que): They ~ not come. Puede que no vengan. ◇ I ~ be able to. Es posible que pueda. **3** (fml): Might I make a suggestion? ¿Podría hacer una sugerencia? ◇ And why ~ she be? ¿Y esa quién será? ◇ You ~ have told me! ¡Me lo podías haber dicho! → MAY, PODER¹

might² /maɪt/ n [U] fuerza: military ~ poderío militar **mighty** adj (**-ier/-iest**) **1** poderoso, potente **2** enorme

migraine /ˈmaɪɡreɪn; ˈmiː- GB/ n migraña

migrant /ˈmaɪɡrənt/ adj **1** (persona) emigrante **2** (animal, ave) migratorio ● n emigrante

migrate /ˈmaɪɡreɪt; maɪˈɡreɪt GB/ vi migrar **migratory** /ˈmaɪɡrətɔːri; maɪˈɡreɪtəri GB/ adj migratorio

mike /maɪk/ n (coloq) micrófono

mild /maɪld/ adj (**-er/-est**) **1** (clima) templado **2** (sabor, etc.) suave **3** (enfermedad, castigo) leve **4** (carácter) apacible **mildly** adv ligeramente, un tanto ▸ to put it mildly por no decir otra cosa

mildew /ˈmɪlduː; -djuː GB/ n moho

mild-mannered adj apacible

mile /maɪl/ n 1 milla 2 **miles** (coloq): He's ~s better. Él es mucho mejor. ● **miles away** (coloq) en las nubes **miles from anywhere/nowhere** (coloq) en el fin del mundo **see, tell, etc. sth a mile off** (coloq) notar algo a la legua **mileage** /'maɪlɪdʒ/ n 1 recorrido en millas, kilometraje 2 (coloq) ventaja

milestone /'maɪlstəʊn/ n 1 mojón (en carretera) 2 (fig) hito

milieu /mi:'ljɜ:/ n entorno social

militant /'mɪlɪtənt/ adj, n militante

military /'mɪləteri; -tri GB/ adj militar ● **the military** n los militares, el ejército

militia /mə'lɪʃə/ n milicia **militiaman** n (pl -men) miliciano

milk /mɪlk/ n leche: ~ products productos lácteos ● vt 1 ordeñar 2 (explotar) explotar **milky** adj (-ier/-iest) 1 (café, etc.) con leche 2 lechoso

milkman /'mɪlkmən/ n (pl -men) lechero

milkshake /'mɪlkʃeɪk/ n licuado (Mx), malteada (And)

mill /mɪl/ n 1 molino 2 molinillo 3 fábrica: steel ~ acería ● vt moler ■ **mill about/around** arremolinarse **miller** n molinero/a

millennium /mɪ'leniəm/ n milenio

millet /'mɪlɪt/ n mijo

milligram /'mɪlɪgræm/ n (abrev mg) miligramo

millimeter (-metre GB) /'mɪlimi:tər/ n (abrev mm) milímetro

million /'mɪljən/ adj, n 1 millón 2 sinfín ● **one, etc. in a million** excepcional **millionth** 1 adj millonésimo 2 n millonésima parte

millionaire /ˌmɪljə'neər/ n millonario/a

millstone /'mɪlstəʊn/ n piedra de molino ▸ **a millstone around your/sb's neck** una carga enorme (para algn)

mime /maɪm/ n mimo: a ~ artist un(a) mimo ● vt, vi hacer mimo, imitar

mimic /'mɪmɪk/ vt (pt/pp mimicked pt pres mimicking) imitar ● n imitador/a **mimicry** n imitación

mince /mɪns/ vt moler (carne) ▸ **not mince (your) words** no andarse con rodeos ● n (GB) carne molida

mincemeat /'mɪnsmi:t/ n relleno de frutas secas ▸ **make mince-**

meat of sb (coloq) hacer picadillo a algn

mince pie n (GB) pastelito navideño relleno de frutas secas

mind /maɪnd/ n 1 mente, cerebro 2 ánimo 3 pensamiento(s): My ~ was on other things. Estaba pensando en otra cosa. 4 juicio: sound in ~ and body sano en cuerpo y alma ● **be of/in two minds** estar indeciso **come/spring to mind** ocurrírsele a algn **have a good mind/half a mind to do sth** tener ganas de hacer algo **have a mind of your own** ser una persona de mente independiente **have sth/sb in mind (for sth)** tener algo/a algn pensado (para algo) **in your mind's eye** en la imaginación **keep your mind on sth** concentrarse en algo **lose your mind** volverse loco **make up your mind** decidir(se) **my mind:** What's on your ~? ¿Qué te preocupa? **out of your mind** (coloq) loco **put/set/turn your mind to sth** centrarse en algo, proponerse algo **put/set your/sb's mind at ease/rest** tranquilizar(se) (a algn) **take your/sb's mind off sth** distraer(se) (a algn) de algo **to my mind** a mi parecer ● vt 1 cuidar de 2 vt, vi importar: I wouldn't ~ a drink. No me vendría mal tomar algo. ◇ I don't ~. Me da igual. 3 vt preocuparse de: Don't ~ him. No le hagas caso. 4 vt, vi (GB) tener cuidado (con) ▸ **do you mind?** ¿Te importa? **mind (you)** (coloq) a decir verdad **mind your own business** no meterse en lo que no le importa a uno **never mind** no importa **never you mind** (coloq) no te preguntes ■ **mind out (for sth/sb)** (GB) tener cuidado (con algo/algn) **minder** n cuidador/a **mindful** adj (fml) consciente **mindless** adj tonto

mind-boggling adj (coloq) increíble

mine /maɪn/ pron mío: a friend of ~ una amiga mía ● n mina ● vt 1 extraer (minerales) 2 minar 3 sembrar minas en **miner** n minero/a

minefield /'maɪnfi:ld/ n 1 campo de minas 2 (fig) terreno delicado

mineral /'mɪnərəl/ n mineral

mingle /'mɪŋgl/ 1 vi charlar con gente (en fiesta, etc.) 2 vt, vi mezclar(se)

miniature /'mɪnətʃər/ n miniatura

minibus /'mɪnibʌs/ n microbús

minicab /'mɪnikæb/ n (GB) radiotaxi

minidisc /'mɪnɪdɪsk/ n minidisc

minimum /'mɪnɪməm/ adj, n (pl **minima** /'mɪnɪmə/) (abrev **min.**) mínimo: with a ~ of effort con un esfuerzo mínimo ◊ There is a ~ charge of... Se cobra un mínimo de... **minimal** adj mínimo **minimize** vt minimizar

mining /'maɪnɪŋ/ n minería: the ~ industry la industria minera

miniskirt /'mɪniskɜːt/ n minifalda

minister /'mɪnɪstər/ n 1 (GB, Pol) secretario/a 2 ministro/a (protestante) →PRIEST ● vi (fml) atender **ministerial** /ˌmɪnɪ'stɪəriəl/ adj ministerial

ministry /'mɪnɪstri/ n (pl -ies) 1 (GB, Pol) ministerio 2 the ministry el clero (protestante): go into/take up the ~ hacerse sacerdote

mink /mɪŋk/ n visón

minor /'maɪnər/ adj 1 secundario: ~ repairs/injuries pequeñas reparaciones/heridas leves 2 (Mús) menor ● n menor de edad

minority /maɪ'nɒrəti, -'nɔːr- GB/ n (pl -ies) minoría: be in a/the ~ ser minoría ◊ a ~ vote un voto minoritario

mint /mɪnt/ n 1 menta 2 (caramelo de) menta 3 Casa de la Moneda 4 **a mint** (coloq) un dineral ▸ **in mint condition** en perfectas condiciones ● vt acuñar

minus /'maɪnəs/ prep, n menos 2 (temperatura) bajo cero: ~ five cinco bajo cero 3 (coloq) sin: I'm ~ my bike. Estoy sin bici. ● adj 1 (Mat) negativo 2 (Educ) bajo ● n 1 (coloq) desventaja 2 (tb ~ sign) signo menos

minute¹ /'mɪnɪt/ n 1 minuto 2 momento 3 instante 4 nota (oficial) 5 **minutes** actas (de reunión) ▸ **not for a/one minute** no por un segundo **the minute/moment (that)...** en cuanto...

minute² /maɪ'njuːt, -'njuːt GB/ adj 1 diminuto 2 minucioso

miracle /'mɪrəkl/ n milagro: a ~ cure una cura milagrosa ▸ **work miracles** hacer milagros **miraculous** /mɪ'rækjələs/ adj milagroso: have a ~ escape salir ileso de milagro

mirage /mə'rɑːʒ/ n espejismo

mirror /'mɪrər/ n 1 espejo: ~ image réplica exacta/imagen invertida 2 (Aut) retrovisor 3 (fig) reflejo ● vt reflejar

mirth /mɜːθ/ n (fml) 1 risa 2 alegría

misadventure /ˌmɪsəd'ventʃər/ n 1 (fml) desgracia 2 (GB, Jur): death by ~ muerte accidental

misbehave /ˌmɪsbɪ'heɪv/ vi portarse mal **misbehavior** (-**our** GB) n mal comportamiento

miscalculation /ˌmɪskælkjuː-'leɪʃn/ n error de cálculo **miscalculate** vt calcular mal

miscarriage /'mɪskærɪdʒ/ n 1 (Med) aborto (espontáneo) 2 ~ **of justice** (Jur) error judicial

miscellaneous /ˌmɪsə'leɪniəs/ adj variado: ~ expenditure gastos varios

mischief /'mɪstʃɪf/ n [U] 1 travesura: keep out of ~ no hacer travesuras 2 daño **mischievous** adj travieso, pícaro

misconceive /ˌmɪskən'siːv/ vt (fml) 1 interpretar mal 2 plantear mal **misconception** n idea equivocada

misconduct /ˌmɪs'kɒndʌkt/ n (fml) 1 mala conducta 2 (Com) mala administración

miser /'maɪzər/ n avaro/a **miserly** adj 1 avaro 2 mísero

miserable /'mɪzrəbl/ adj 1 triste, infeliz 2 miserable 3 malo, miserable: have a ~ time pasarla mal **miserably** adv 1 tristemente 2 miserablemente: fail ~ ser un fracaso total

misery /'mɪzəri/ n (pl -ies) 1 tristeza, sufrimiento 2 miseria 3 (GB, coloq) aguafiestas ▸ **put sb out of their misery** acabar con el sufrimiento de algn

misfortune /ˌmɪs'fɔːtʃuːn/ n desgracia

misgiving /ˌmɪs'ɡɪvɪŋ/ n duda

misguided /ˌmɪs'ɡaɪdɪd/ adj equivocado

mishap /'mɪshæp/ n 1 contratiempo 2 percance

misinform /ˌmɪsɪn'fɔːm/ vt (fml) informar mal

misinterpret /ˌmɪsɪn'tɜːprɪt/ vt interpretar mal **misinterpretation** n interpretación errónea

misjudge /ˌmɪs'dʒʌdʒ/ vt 1 juzgar mal 2 calcular mal

mislay /ˌmɪs'leɪ/ vt (pt/pp mislaid) extraviar

mislead /ˌmɪs'liːd/ vt (pt/pp misled /-'led/) ~ **sb (about/as to sth)** llevar a conclusiones erróneas a algn (respecto a algo): Don't be misled by... No te dejes engañar por... **misleading** adj engañoso

mismanagement /ˌmɪs'mænɪdʒmənt/ n mala administración

misogynist /mɪ'sɒdʒɪnɪst/ n misógino

misplaced /ˌmɪsˈpleɪst/ adj 1 mal colocado 2 (confianza, etc.) inmerecido 3 fuera de lugar

misprint /ˈmɪsprɪnt/ n errata

misread /ˌmɪsˈriːd/ vt (pt/pp misread /-ˈred/) 1 leer mal 2 interpretar mal

misrepresent /ˌmɪsˌreprɪ-ˈzent/ vt tergiversar (las palabras de)

Miss /mɪs/ n señorita → SEÑORITA

miss /mɪs/ 1 vt, vi no acertar, fallar: ~ your footing no dar un traspié 2 vt no ver: You can't ~ it. Lo va a ver enseguida. ◇ I missed what he said. Se me escapó lo que dijo. 3 vt (ocasión, etc.) perder 4 vt sentir la falta de 5 vt extrañar 6 vt: narrowly ~ (hitting) estar a punto de dar un pelo ▶ not miss much/a trick (coloq) no perderse ni una ▪ miss out (on sth) perder la oportunidad (de algo) miss sth/sb out (GB) olvidarse de algo/algn ● n tiro errado ▶ give sth a miss (coloq) pasar de algo

missile /ˈmɪsl; ˈmɪsaɪl GB/ n 1 (Mil) misil 2 proyectil

missing /ˈmɪsɪŋ/ adj 1 extraviado 2 que falta 3 desaparecido

mission /ˈmɪʃn/ n misión

missionary /ˈmɪʃəneri; -nri GB/ n (pl -ies) misionero/a

mist /mɪst/ n 1 neblina 2 bruma ● vt, vi ~ (sth) over/up empañar(se) (algo)

mistake /mɪˈsteɪk/ n error: by ~ por equivocación ◇ make a ~ equivocarse **NOTA** Mistake y error significan lo mismo, pero error es más formal. **Fault** indica la culpabilidad de una persona: It's all my fault., y también puede indicar una imperfección: an electrical fault ◇ He has many faults. **Defect** es una imperfección más grave: a speech defect. ● vt (pt mistook /mɪˈstʊk/ pp mistaken /mɪˈsteɪkən/) 1 equivocarse de: I mistook your meaning. Entendí mal lo que dijiste. 2 ~ sth/sb for sth/sb confundir algo/algn con algo/algn mistaken adj equivocado: if I'm not ~ si no me equivoco mistakenly adv por equivocación

mister /ˈmɪstər/ n señor

mistletoe /ˈmɪsltoʊ/ n muérdago

mistreat /ˌmɪsˈtriːt/ vt maltratar

mistress /ˈmɪstrəs/ n 1 querida, amante 2 señora 3 (de situación, animal) dueña

mistrust /ˌmɪsˈtrʌst/ vt desconfiar de ● n ~ (of sth/sb) desconfianza (hacia algo/algn)

misty /ˈmɪsti/ adj (-ier/-iest) 1 con neblina 2 borroso

misunderstand /ˌmɪsʌndər-ˈstænd/ vt, vi (pt/pp misunderstood /-ˈstʊd/) entender mal misunderstanding n 1 malentendido 2 desavenencia

misuse /ˌmɪsˈjuːs/ n 1 mal uso 2 (fondos) malversación y abuso

mitigate /ˈmɪtɪɡeɪt/ vt (fml) mitigar, atenuar

mix /mɪks/ 1 vt, vi mezclar(se) 2 ~ with sb vi relacionarse con algn ▶ be/get mixed up in sth estar metido/meterse en algo ▪ mix sth in(to sth) añadir algo (a algo) mix sth/sb up (with sth/sb) confundir algo/algn (con algo/algn) ● n mezcla mixed adj 1 mixto ~ feelings sentimientos encontrados 2 surtido 3 (tiempo) variable mixer n 1 mezclador 2 be a good ~ ser sociable mixture /ˈmɪkstʃər/ n 1 mezcla 2 combinación

mix-up n (pl -ups) (coloq) confusión

moan /moʊn/ 1 vt, vi gemir, decir gimiendo 2 vi (GB, coloq) quejarse ● n 1 gemido 2 (GB, coloq) queja

moat /moʊt/ n foso (castillo)

mob /mɑb/ n 1 chusma 2 (coloq) banda (delincuentes) 3 the Mob la mafia ● vt (-bb-) acosar

mobile /ˈmoʊbl; -baɪl GB/ adj 1 móvil: ~ library biblioteca ambulante ◇ ~ home trailer/casa rodante 2 (cara) cambiante ● n 1 (GB) móvil (tb ~ phone) (teléfono) celular 2 móvil **mobility** /moʊ-ˈbɪləti/ n movilidad

mobilize /ˈmoʊbəlaɪz/ 1 vt, vi movilizar(se) 2 vt organizar

mock /mɑk/ vt, vi ~ (sth/sb) burlarse (de algo/algn): a mocking smile una sonrisa burlona ● adj 1 ficticio: ~ battle simulacro de combate 2 falso, de imitación mockery n 1 burla 2 parodia ▶ make a mockery of sth poner algo en ridículo

mode /moʊd/ n (fml) 1 modo 2 (transporte) medio

model /ˈmɑdl/ n 1 modelo 2 maqueta: airplane avión en miniatura ● vt, vi (-l-, -ll- GB) 1 modelar, ser modelo de ▪ model yourself/sth on sth/sb basarse/basar algo en algo/algn **modeling** (-ll- GB) n 1 modelado 2 trabajo de modelo

modem /ˈmoʊdem/ n módem

moderate /ˈmɑdərət/ adj 1 moderado 2 regular ● n moderado ● /ˈmɑdəreɪt/ vt, vi moderar(se): a *moderating influence* una influencia moderadora **moderation** n moderación

modern /'mɒdərn/ adj moderno **modernity** /mə'dɜ:rnəti/ n modernidad **modernize** /'mɒdərnaɪz/ vt, vi modernizar(se)

modest /'mɒdɪst/ adj **1** ~ (about sth) modesto (con algo) **2** pequeño, moderado **3** (precio, etc.) módico **4** recatado **modesty** n modestia

modify /'mɒdɪfaɪ/ vt (pt/pp -ied) modificar **NOTA** Es más común change.

module /'mɒdʒuːl; 'mɒdjuːl GB/ n módulo **modular** adj modular

mogul /'mɒʊgl/ n magnate

moist /mɔɪst/ adj húmedo: a rich ~ cake un pastel/bizcocho sabroso y esponjoso → HÚMEDO **moisten** /'mɔɪsn/ vt, vi humedecer(se) **moisture** /'mɔɪstʃər/ n humedad **moisturizer** n crema hidratante

molar /'mɒʊlər/ n muela

mold /mɒʊld/ n **1** molde **2** moho ● vt moldear **moldy** adj mohoso

mole /mɒʊl/ n **1** lunar **2** topo

molecule /'mɒlɪkjuːl/ n molécula **molecular** /mə'lekjələr/ adj molecular

molest /mə'lest/ vt agredir sexualmente

mollify /'mɒlɪfaɪ/ vt (pt/pp -ied) calmar, apaciguar

molten /'mɒʊltən/ adj fundido

mom /mɒm/ (tb **mommy** /'mɒmi/) n (coloq) mamá →MAMÁ

moment /'mɒʊmənt/ n momento, instante: I won't be a ~. Enseguida termino. ▸ **at the moment** de momento, por ahora **not for a/one moment** ni por un segundo **the moment of truth** la hora de la verdad **momentary** adj momentáneo

momentous /mɒʊ'mentəs; mə'm- GB/ adj trascendental

momentum /mɒʊ'mentəm, mə'm-/ n ímpetu **2** (Fís) momento: gather ~ cobrar velocidad

monarch /'mɒnərk/ n monarca **monarchy** n (pl -ies) monarquía

monastery /'mɒnəsteri; -tri GB/ n (pl -ies) monasterio **monastic** /mə'næstɪk/ adj monástico

Monday /'mʌndeɪ, -di/ n (abrev **Mon.**) lunes: last/next ~ el lunes pasado/que viene ◇ ~ before last/after next hace dos lunes/ dentro de dos lunes ◇ ~ evening el lunes en la tarde ◇ ~ week/a week on ~ el lunes que viene no,

el siguiente ◇ See you (on) ~. Nos vemos el lunes.

monetary /'mʌnɪteri; -tri GB/ adj monetario

money /'mʌni/ n [U] dinero: ~ problems problemas económicos

monitor /'mɒnɪtər/ n **1** monitor **2** (elecciones) observador/a ● vt monitorear, controlar **monitoring** n monitoreo

monk /mʌŋk/ n monje

monkey /'mʌŋki/ n **1** mono, mico **2** (coloq) (niño) diablillo

monogamy /mə'nɒgəmi/ n monogamia **monogamous** adj monógamo

monolithic /,mɒnə'lɪθɪk/ adj monolítico

monologue (tb **monolog** USA) /'mɒnəlɔːg; -lɒg GB/ n monólogo

monopoly /mə'nɒpəli/ n (pl -ies) monopolio **monopolize** vt monopolizar

monoxide /mə'nɒksaɪd/ n monóxido

monsoon /,mɒn'suːn/ n monzón

monster /'mɒnstər/ n monstruo **monstrous** adj monstruoso **monstrosity** /mɒn'strɒsəti/ n (pl -ies) monstruosidad

month /mʌnθ/ n mes

monthly /'mʌnθli/ adj mensual ● adv mensualmente ● n (pl -ies) publicación mensual

monument /'mɒnjumənt/ n monumento **monumental** /,mɒnju'mentl/ adj **1** monumental **2** excepcional **3** (error, etc.) garrafal

moo /muː/ vi mugir

mood /muːd/ n **1** humor: in a good/bad ~ de buen/mal humor ◇ be in the ~/in no ~ for sth (no) estar de humor para algo **2** mal humor **3** ambiente **4** (Gram) modo **moody** adj (-ier/-iest) **1** de humor caprichoso **2** malhumorado

moon /muːn/ n luna ▸ **over the moon** (coloq) loco de contento ■ **moon about/around** (GB, coloq) ir de aquí para allá distraídamente

moonlight /'muːnlaɪt/ n luz de la luna ● vi (pt/pp -ed) (coloq) tener más de un trabajo **moonlit** adj iluminado por la luna

Moor /mʊər, mɔː(r) GB/ n moro/a **Moorish** adj moro

moor /mʊər, mɔː(r) GB/ (tb **moorland** /'mʊərlənd; 'mɔː- GB/) n páramo ● vt, vi amarrar **mooring** n **1** moorings amarras **2** amarradero

moose /muːs/ n (pl moose) alce

mop /mɒp/ n 1 trapeador 2 (pelo) greña, mata ● vt (-pp-) ~ sth (up) trapear algo

mope /moʊp/ vi abatirse ■ **mope about/around** andar deprimido

moped /ˈmoʊped/ n bicimoto

moral /ˈmɒrəl; ˈmɔːrəl GB/ n 1 moraleja 2 **morals** [pl] moralidad ● adj moral **moralistic** /ˌmɒrəˈlɪstɪk/ adj moralista **morality** /məˈræləti/ n moral, moralidad: standards of ~ valores morales **moralize** /ˈmɒrəlaɪz/ vi moralizar **morally** adv moralmente, honradamente

morale /məˈræl; məˈrɑːl GB/ n moral (ánimo)

morbid /ˈmɔːrbɪd/ adj 1 morboso 2 (Med) patológico **morbidity** /mɔːrˈbɪdəti/ n 1 morbosidad 2 (Med) patología

more /mɔːr/ adj, adv, pron más: ~ than 50 más de 50 ◊ I hope we'll see ~ of you. Espero que te veremos más a menudo. ◊ That's ~ like it! ¡Eso es! **NOTA** Se usa para formar los comparativos de adjetivos y adverbios de dos o más sílabas: ~ expensive. ▸ **be more than happy, willing, etc. to do sth** hacer algo con mucho gusto **more and more** cada vez más **more or less** más o menos: ~ or less finished casi terminado **what is more** es más, además

moreover /mɔːrˈoʊvər/ adv además, por otra parte

morgue /mɔːrg/ n morgue

morning /ˈmɔːrnɪŋ/ n 1 mañana: the ~ paper el periódico de la mañana 2 madrugada: in the early hours of the ~ en la madrugada ▸ **good morning** buenos días **NOTA** También se dice morning!, afternoon!, etc., que es más informal. **in the morning** 1 en la mañana: ten o'clock in the ~ las diez de la mañana 2 (día siguiente): I'll call her in the ~. La llamo mañana en la mañana. **NOTA** Con morning, afternoon y evening, se usa la preposición in para referirnos a un periodo del día: at three o'clock in the ~, y on para hacer referencia a un punto en el calendario: on a May ~ ◊ on Monday ~ ◊ on the ~ of the 4th of July. Sin embargo, con this, that, tomorrow y yesterday no se usa preposición: yesterday ~ ◊ They'll leave this evening. →MEDIO

moron /ˈmɔːrɑːn/ n imbécil

morose /məˈroʊs/ adj huraño

morphine /ˈmɔːrfiːn/ n morfina

morsel /ˈmɔːrsl/ n bocado

mortal /ˈmɔːrtl/ adj, n mortal **mortality** /mɔːrˈtæləti/ n 1 mortalidad 2 mortandad

mortar /ˈmɔːrtər/ n mortero

mortgage /ˈmɔːrgɪdʒ/ n hipoteca: ~ payment pago hipotecario ● vt hipotecar

mortify /ˈmɔːrtɪfaɪ/ vt (pt/pp -ied) humillar, mortificar

mortuary /ˈmɔːrtʃueri; -tʃəri GB/ n (pl -ies) morgue

mosaic /moʊˈzeɪk/ n mosaico

Moslem /ˈmɑːzləm/ = MUSLIM

mosque /mɑːsk/ n mezquita

mosquito /məsˈkiːtoʊ/ n (pl -s/ -es) mosquito, zancudo: ~ net mosquitero

moss /mɔːs; mɒs GB/ n musgo

most /moʊst/ adj, pron 1 más, la mayor parte (de): I ate the ~. Yo fui el que más comió. ◊ the ~ I could give you lo máximo que le podría dar 2 la mayoría (de), casi todo **NOTA** Most es el superlativo de **much/many** y se usa con sustantivos incontables o en plural: Who has ~ time? ◊ ~ children. Delante de pronombres o cuando el sustantivo que precede lleva the o un adjetivo posesivo o demostrativo, se usa **most of**: ~ of us ◊ ~ of the time/ my friends. ▸ **make the most of sth** sacar el mayor provecho de algo ● adv 1 más: What upset me ~ was that... Lo que más me dolió fue que... ◊ ~ of all sobre todo **NOTA** Se usa para formar el superlativo de locuciones adverbiales, adjetivos y adverbios de dos o más sílabas: the ~ exciting film I've seen. 2 muy: ~ likely muy probablemente ▸ **at (the) most** como mucho/máximo **mostly** adv principalmente, por lo general

moth /mɔːθ; mɒθ GB/ n 1 mariposa nocturna, palomilla (Mx) 2 polilla

mother /ˈmʌðər/ n madre: mother-to-be futura madre ◊ ~ tongue lengua materna ● vt 1 criar 2 mimar **motherhood** n maternidad **mother-in-law** n (pl -ers-in-law) suegra **motherly** adj maternal

Mother's Day n día de la madre

motif /moʊˈtiːf/ n 1 motivo, adorno 2 tema

motion /ˈmoʊʃn/ n 1 movimiento: ~ picture película (de cine) ◊ put/set sth in ~ poner algo en marcha 2 (en reunión) moción ▸ **go through the motions (of doing sth)** fingir (hacer algo) ● vt, vi ~ (to/for) sb to do sth hacer señas a algn para que haga algo: ~ **sb in** indicar a algn que entre **motionless** *adj* inmóvil

motivate /ˈmoʊtɪveɪt/ *vt* motivar

motive /ˈmoʊtɪv/ *n* ~ **(for sth)** motivo (de algo): *an ulterior* ~ un motivo oculto **NOTA** Es más común **reason**.

motor /ˈmoʊtər/ *n* motor: ~ *boat* lancha de motor →ENGINE **motoring** *n* automovilismo **motorist** *n* conductor/a de carro **motorize** *vt* motorizar

motorcycle (motorbike GB) /ˈmoʊtərsaɪkl/-baɪk/ *n* moto **motorcycling** *n* motociclismo

motor racing *n* automovilismo

motorway /ˈmoʊtərweɪ/ *n* (GB) autopista

mottled /ˈmɒtld/ *adj* moteado

motto /ˈmɒtoʊ/ *n* (*pl* -**s**/-**es**) lema

mould, mouldy (GB) = MOLD

mound /maʊnd/ *n* 1 montículo 2 montón

mount /maʊnt/ *n* 1 monte 2 soporte 3 montura 4 paspartú ● 1 *vt* (*caballo, etc.*) subirse a (*cuadro*) enmarcar 3 *vt* montar 4 *vi* instalar 5 *vi* crecer **mounting** *adj* creciente

mountain /ˈmaʊntn/ *n* 1 montaña: ~ *range* cordillera 2 ~ **of sth** montón de algo **mountaineer** /ˌmaʊntnˈɪər/ *n* alpinista **mountaineering** *n* alpinismo **mountainous** /ˈmaʊntənəs/ *adj* montañoso

mountain bike *n* bicicleta todo-terreno

mountainside /ˈmaʊntənsaɪd/ *n* ladera de montaña

mourn /mɔːrn/ 1 *vi* lamentarse 2 *vi* estar de luto 3 *vt* llorar la muerte de **mourner** *n* doliente **mournful** *adj* triste, lúgubre **mourning** *n* luto

mouse /maʊs/ *n* (*pl* **mice**) ratón

mousse /muːs/ *n* 1 mousse 2 espuma (*para el pelo*)

moustache (GB) = MUSTACHE

mouth /maʊθ/ *n* (*pl* -**s** /maʊðz/) 1 boca 2 (*río*) desembocadura **mouthful** *n* 1 bocado 2 (*líquido*) trago

mouthpiece /ˈmaʊθpiːs/ *n* 1 boquilla (*teléfono*) micrófono 3 portavoz

move /muːv/ *n* 1 movimiento 2 mudanza 3 (*trabajo*) cambio 4 (*juego*) jugada, turno 5 paso: *a false* ~ un paso en falso ▸ **get a move on** (*coloq*) darse prisa **make a move 1** actuar 2 ponerse en marcha ● 1 *vi* mover(se) 2 *vt, vi* trasladar(se), cambiar(se) (de sitio) 3 *vi* (*tb* ~ **house** GB)

mudarse 4 *vt* conmover a 5 *vt* (*fml*) ~ **sb** (**to do sth**) inducir a algn (a hacer algo) ■ **move about/around** moverse de acá para allá | **move** (**sth**) **away** alejar(se) (algo) | **move forward** avanzar | **move in** instalarse | **move on** seguir (viajando) | **move out** mudarse **movable** *adj* movible

movement /ˈmuːvmənt/ *n* 1 movimiento 2 ~ (**towards/away from sth**) tendencia (hacia/a distanciarse de algo)

movie /ˈmuːvi/ *n* película: *go to the* ~*s* ir al cine ◊ ~ *theater* cine

moving /ˈmuːvɪŋ/ *adj* 1 móvil 2 conmovedor

mow /moʊ/ *vt* (*pt* **mowed** *pp* **mowed/mown** /moʊn/) cortar (*pasto*) ■ **mow sb down** aniquilar a algn **mower** *n* Ver LAWNMOWER

MP /ˌem ˈpiː/ *n* (*abrev de* **Member of Parliament**) GB) diputado/a

Mr. /ˈmɪstər/ *abrev* señor

Mrs. /ˈmɪsɪz/ *abrev* señora

Ms. /mɪz, məz/ *abrev* señora →SEÑORITA

much /mʌtʃ/ *adj, adv, pron* mucho: *so* ~ *traffic* tanto tráfico ◊ *much-needed* muy necesario ◊ ~ *too cold* demasiado frío ◊ *the same* prácticamente igual ◊ *Much to her surprise...* Para gran sorpresa suya... ◊ *How* ~ *is it?* ¿Cuánto es? ◊ *as* ~ *as you can* todo lo que puedas ◊ *for* ~ *of the day* la mayor parte del día ▸ **much** as por más que | **not much of a...**: *He's not* ~ *of an actor.* No es gran cosa como actor. →MANY

muck /mʌk/ *n* 1 estiércol 2 (*coloq*) porquería ■ **muck about/around** (GB, *coloq*) perder el tiempo | **muck sth up** (GB, *coloq*) echar algo a perder **mucky** *adj* (-**ier/-iest**) sucio

mucus /ˈmjuːkəs/ *n* [U] mucosidad

mud /mʌd/ *n* barro **muddy** *adj* (-**ier/-iest**) 1 embarrado: ~ *footprints* pisadas lodosas 2 turbio

muddle /ˈmʌdl/ *vt* 1 ~ **sth** (**up**) revolver algo 2 ~ **sth/sb** (**up**) armar un lío con algo/algn 3 ~ **A and B** (**up**); ~ **A** (**up**) **with B**; ~ **A and B** (**up**) confundir A con B ● *n* 1 desorden, lío (con algo): *get into a* ~ armarse un lío con algo **muddled** *adj* enrevesado

mudguard /ˈmʌdɡɑːrd/ *n* (GB) guardabarros, salpicadera

muffin /ˈmʌfɪn/ *n* 1 mollete, muffin 2 (GB) panecillo que se come caliente con mantequilla

muffled /'mʌfld/ adj 1 (grito) ahogado 2 (voz) apagado

mug /mʌg/ n 1 taza (alta), tarro (Mx) 2 (coloq) jeta 3 (coloq) bobo/a ▸ **a mug's game** (GB) una pérdida de tiempo ● vt (-gg-) asaltar **mugger** n atracador/a **mugging** n asalto

muggy /'mʌgi/ adj bochornoso (tiempo)

mulberry /'mʌlberi; -bəri GB/ n 1 (tb ~ **tree**) morera 2 mora 3 (color) morado

mule /mju:l/ n 1 mulo/a 2 chancla

mull /mʌl/ v ■ **mull sth over** meditar algo

multicolored (-our- GB) /,mʌlti-'kʌlərd/ adj multicolor

multilingual /,mʌlti'lɪŋgwəl/ adj políglota

multimedia /,mʌlti'mi:diə/ adj multimedia

multinational /,mʌlti'næʃnəl/ adj, n multinacional

multiple /'mʌltɪpl/ adj múltiple ● n múltiplo

multiple sclerosis /,mʌltɪpl sklə'rəʊsɪs/ n esclerosis múltiple

multiplex /'mʌltɪpleks/ (tb ~ **cinema** GB) n cine múltiple

multiplicity /,mʌltɪ'plɪsəti/ n multiplicidad

multiply /'mʌltɪplaɪ/ vt, vi (pt/pp -ied) multiplicar(se) **multiplication** n multiplicación

multi-purpose adj multiuso

multi-story (-storey GB) adj de varios pisos: ~ car park (GB) estacionamiento/parqueadero de varios pisos

multitude /'mʌltɪtu:d; -tju:d GB/ n (fml) multitud

mum /mʌm/ (GB) = MOM

mumble /'mʌmbl/ vt, vi hablar entre dientes: Don't ~. Habla alto y claro.

mummy /'mʌmi/ n (pl -ies) 1 momia 2 (GB) mamá

mumps /mʌmps/ n [sing] paperas

munch /mʌntʃ/ vt, vi ~ (on) sth masticar, mascar algo

mundane /mʌn'deɪn/ adj corriente, mundano

municipal /mju:'nɪsɪpl/ adj municipal

munitions /mju:'nɪʃnz/ n [pl] municiones

mural /'mjʊərəl/ n mural

murder /'mɜːrdər/ n 1 asesinato, homicidio 2 (coloq) una pesadilla ▸ **get away with murder** (coloq) hacer lo que le dé la gana a uno ● vt asesinar, matar →ASESINATO **murderer** n asesino/a **murderous**

adj homicida: a ~ look una mirada asesina

murky /'mɜːrki/ adj (-ier/-iest) 1 lóbrego, sombrío 2 turbio

murmur /'mɜːrmər/ n murmullo ▸ **without a murmur** sin rechistar ● vt, vi susurrar

muscle /'mʌsl/ n 1 músculo■: Don't move a ~! ¡No muevas ni un pelo! 2 poder ■ **muscle in** (on **sth/sb**) (coloq) participar sin derecho (en algo) **muscular** /'mʌskjələr/ adj 1 muscular 2 musculoso

muse /mju:z/ n 1 musa ● v 1 vi reflexionar 2 vt: "How strange!" he mused. —¡Qué raro!, dijo pensativo.

museum /mju:'zi:əm/ n museo **NOTA** Museum es un museo en el que se exponen piezas históricas, científicas, etc., y **(art) gallery** un museo para cuadros y esculturas.

mushroom /'mʌʃruːm/ n hongo, champiñón ● vi multiplicarse rápidamente

mushy /'mʌʃi/ adj 1 blando 2 (coloq) sensiblero

music /'mju:zɪk/ n 1 música: a piece of ~ una pieza musical 2 partitura **musician** /mju:-'zɪʃn/ n músico

musical /'mju:zɪkl/ adj musical, de música: be ~ tener talento para la música ● n comedia musical

musk /mʌsk/ n almizcle

musket /'mʌskɪt/ n mosquete **musketeer** /,mʌskə'tɪər/ n mosquetero

Muslim /'mʊzləm/ adj, n musulmán/ana

muslin /'mʌzlɪn/ n muselina

mussel /'mʌsl/ n mejillón

must /mʌst/ n (coloq): It's a ~. Es imprescindible. ◊ His new book is a ~. Su último libro hay que leerlo. ◊ /məst, mʌst/ v (neg **must not/mustn't** /'mʌsnt/) **NOTA** Must es un verbo modal al que sigue un infinitivo sin to, y que usa el auxiliar do en interrogaciones y negaciones: Must you go? ◊ We mustn't tell her. Must sólo tiene presente: I - leave early. Para otras formas se usa **have to**: He'll have to come tomorrow. ◊ We had to eat quickly.

● **obligación y prohibición** deber, tener que **NOTA** Must se usa para dar órdenes o para hacer que alguien o uno mismo siga un determinado comportamiento: You ~ be back by ten. ◊ I

~ quit smoking. Cuando la orden es impuesta por un agente externo, p. ej. por una ley, una regla, etc., se usa **have to**: *The doctor says I have to quit smoking.* ◊ *You have to send it today.* En negativa, **must not/mustn't** expresa una prohibición: *You mustn't open the door.*, y **don't have to** y **haven't got to** expresan que algo no es necesario: *You don't have to do it if you don't want to.* ► **if I, you, etc. must** si no hay más remedio

● **sugerencia** tener que: *You ~ come around.* Tienes que venir a vernos. **NOTA** Para hacer sugerencias y dar consejos se suele usar **ought to** o **should**.

● **probabilidad** deber de: *You ~ be hungry.* Debes de tener hambre.

mustache /'mʌstæʃ/ *n* bigote(s)

mustard /'mʌstəd/ *n* mostaza

muster /'mʌstər/ *vt, vi* reunir(se), juntar(se): ~ **(up) enthusiasm** cobrar entusiasmo ◊ ~ *a smile* conseguir sonreír

musty /'mʌsti/ *adj* rancio

mutant /'mju:tənt/ *adj, n* mutante

mutate /mju:'teɪt; *USA* mju:'teɪt *GB*/ **1** *vt, vi* mutar **2** *vi* transformarse **mutation** *n* mutación

mute /mju:t/ *adj* (*fml*) mudo ● *n* **1** (*Mús*) sordina **2** (*persona*) mudo/a ● *vt* **1** amortiguar **2** (*Mús*) poner sordina a **muted** *adj* **1** (*sonido, color*) apagado **2** (*crítica, etc.*) velado **3** (*Mús*) sordo

mutilate /'mju:tɪleɪt/ *vt* mutilar

mutiny /'mju:tɪni/ *n* (*pl* -ies) motín **mutinous** *adj* rebelde

mutter /'mʌtər/ **1** *vt, vi* hablar entre dientes, murmurar **2** *vi* refunfuñar

mutton /'mʌtn/ *n* (carne de) carnero →CARNE

mutual /'mju:tʃuəl/ *adj* **1** mutuo **2** común **mutually** *adv* mutuamente: ~ *beneficial* beneficioso para ambas partes

muzzle /'mʌzl/ *n* **1** hocico **2** bozal **3** (*arma de fuego*) boca ● *vt* **1** poner bozal **2** amordazar

my /maɪ/ *adj* mi, mío: *My feet are cold.* Tengo los pies fríos. **NOTA** En inglés se usa el posesivo delante de partes del cuerpo y prendas de vestir: *He broke his arm/lost his glasses.*

myopia /maɪ'oʊpiə/ *n* miopía **myopic** /maɪ'ɑpɪk/ *adj* miope

myriad /'mɪriəd/ *n* miríada ● *adj* innumerable

myself /maɪ'self/ *pron* **1** [*reflexivo*] me: *I said to myself...* Dije

para mí... **2** [*énfasis*] yo mismo/a ► **(all) by myself** solo

mystery /'mɪstri/ *n* (*pl* -ies) **1** misterio: *It's a ~ to me.* No logro entenderlo. **2** ~ *tour* viaje sorpresa ◊ *the ~ assailant* el agresor misterioso **3** obra de teatro, novela, etc. de misterio **mysterious** /mɪ'stɪəriəs/ *adj* misterioso

mystic /'mɪstɪk/ *n* místico/a ● *adj* (*tb* **mystical**) místico **mysticism** *n* misticismo, mística

mystify /'mɪstɪfaɪ/ *vt* (*pt/pp* -ied) dejar perplejo **mystification** *n* **1** misterio, perplejidad **2** confusión (*deliberada*) **mystifying** *adj* desconcertante

mystique /mɪ'sti:k/ *n* [*sing*] misterio

myth /mɪθ/ *n* mito **mythical** *adj* mítico

mythology /mɪ'θɒlədʒi/ *n* mitología **mythological** /ˌmɪθə-'lɒdʒɪkl/ *adj* mitológico

N n

N, n /en/ *n* (*pl* **N's, n's**) N, n

naff /næf/ *adj* (GB, *coloq*) de mal gusto

nag /næg/ *vt, vi* (-gg-) **1** dar la lata, moler (*Mx*) **2** regañar **3** (*dolor, sospecha*) corroer **nagging** *adj* **1** (*dolor, sospecha*) persistente **2** (*persona*) crítico

nail /neɪl/ *n* **1** uña **2** clavo ► **hit the nail on the head** dar en el clavo ● *vt* clavar ■ **nail sb down (to sth)** conseguir que algn se comprometa /dé una respuesta concreta (a algo)

naive /naɪ'i:v/ *adj* ingenuo

naked /'neɪkɪd/ *adj* desnudo **NOTA** Naked se refiere generalmente al cuerpo entero: *a ~ body*, **bare** a partes del cuerpo: *bare arms*, y **nude** se usa para desnudos artísticos y eróticos: *a nude figure*. **2** (*fig*): *a ~ light* un foco/un bombillo sin pantalla ◊ ~ *aggression* agresión manifiesta ► **with/to the naked eye** a simple vista

name /neɪm/ *n* **1** nombre: *What's her ~?* ¿Cómo se llama? ◊ *first/ family* ~ nombre (de pila)/apellido **2** fama **3** personaje ► **by name** de nombre **by the name of** (*fml*) llamado ● *vt* **1** llamar **2** poner nombre: *We named him/ after his dad.* Le pusimos el nombre del papá. **3** nombrar

4 (*fecha, precio*) fijar **nameless** *adj* sin nombre, anónimo

namely /ˈneɪmli/ *adv* a saber

namesake /ˈneɪmseɪk/ *n* tocayo/a

nanny /ˈnæni/ *n* (*pl* -**ies**) niñera, nana (*And*)

nap /næp/ *n* sueñecito, siesta

nape /neɪp/ *n* nuca

napkin /ˈnæpkɪn/ *n* servilleta

nappy /ˈnæpi/ *n* (*pl* -**ies**) (*GB*) pañal

narcotic /nɑrˈkɑtɪk/ *adj, n* narcótico

narrate /nəˈreɪt/ *vt* contar **narrator** *n* narrador/a

narrative /ˈnærətɪv/ *n* **1** relato **2** narrativa ● *adj* narrativo

narrow /ˈnærəʊ/ *adj* (-**er/-est**) **1** angosto, estrecho **2** limitado **3** (*ventaja, etc.*) escaso ▶ **have a narrow escape** escaparse por un pelo ● *vi, vt* angostar(se), reducir(se) ■ **narrow sth down** (**to sth**) reducir algo (a algo) **narrowly** *adv* por poco

narrow-minded *adj* de mente cerrada

nasal /ˈneɪzl/ *adj* nasal

nasty /ˈnæsti; ˈnɑːsti *GB*/ *adj* (-**ier/-iest**) **1** desagradable **2** antipático: *be ~ to sb* tratar muy mal a algn **3** (*situación, etc.*) feo, grave: *What a ~ cough!* ¡Qué tos más fea!

nation /ˈneɪʃn/ *n* nación

national /ˈnæʃnəl/ *adj* nacional ● *n* ciudadano/a **nationally** *adv* a escala nacional

National Health Service *n* (*abrev* **NHS**) Servicio Nacional de Salud (*servicio público de asistencia sanitaria en GB*)

National Insurance *n* (*abrev* **NI**) Seguro Social (*en GB*)

nationalism /ˈnæʃnəlɪzəm/ *n* nacionalismo **nationalist** *adj, n* nacionalista

nationality /ˌnæʃəˈnæləti/ *n* (*pl* -**ies**) nacionalidad

nationalize /ˈnæʃnəlaɪz/ *vt* nacionalizar

nationwide /ˌneɪʃnˈwaɪd/ *adj, adv* a escala nacional

native /ˈneɪtɪv/ *n* **1** nativo/a, natural **2** indígena **3** *The koala is a ~ of Australia.* El koala es originario de Australia. ● *adj* **1** natal: *~ land* patria ◇ *~ language* lengua materna **2** indígena, nativo **3** innato **4 ~ to...** originario de...

natural /ˈnætʃrəl/ *adj* **1** natural **2** nato, innato **naturally** *adv* **1** de manera natural **2** por supuesto

naturalist /ˈnætʃrəlɪst/ *n* naturalista

nature /ˈneɪtʃər/ *n* **1** (*tb* **Nature**) naturaleza **2** carácter: *It's not in my ~...* No soy capaz de... **3** índole ▶ **in the nature of sth** algo así como

naughty /ˈnɔːti/ *adj* (-**ier/-iest**) **1** (*coloq*) travieso: *be ~* portarse mal **2** atrevido

nausea /ˈnɔːziə/ *n* náusea **nauseating** /ˈnɔːzieɪtɪŋ/ *adj* nauseabundo

nautical /ˈnɔːtɪkl/ *adj* náutico

naval /ˈneɪvl/ *adj* naval

nave /neɪv/ *n* nave (*iglesia*)

navel /ˈneɪvl/ *n* ombligo

navigate /ˈnævɪɡeɪt/ **1** *vi, vt* navegar (por) **2** *vi* (*Aut*) hacer de copiloto **3** *vt* (*barco*) gobernar **navigation** *n* navegación **2** náutica **navigator** *n* navegante

navy /ˈneɪvi/ *n* (*pl* -**ies**) armada: *the US Navy* la Marina norteamericana ● *adj* (*tb* **~ blue**) *n* azul marino

Nazi /ˈnɑːtsi/ *adj, n* nazi

near /nɪər/ *adj* (-**er/-est**) *adj* **1** cercano **2** próximo **NOTA** Antes de sustantivo se usa **nearby**: *a nearby village.* Sin embargo, con el superlativo se usa **near**: *the nearest bank.* ● *adv* cerca: *get nearer* acercarse ◇ *It's getting ~ to Christmas.* Ya falta poco para la Navidad. **NOTA** *I live nearby* es más común que *I live near*, pero con adverbios como *quite*, *very*, etc. se usa **near**: *I live quite ~.* ▶ **not anywhere near**; **nowhere near** para nada: *The salary isn't anywhere ~ enough.* El sueldo es totalmente insuficiente. ● *prep* cerca de: *~ the beginning* hacia el principio ● *vt* acercarse a

nearby /ˈnɪərbaɪ/ *adj* cercano ● *adv* cerca →NEAR

nearly /ˈnɪərli/ *adv* casi **NOTA** *almost* **1** y **nearly** son intercambiables. Sin embargo, sólo **almost** se usa para calificar otro adverbio en *-ly*: *almost completely*, y sólo **nearly** puede ser calificado por otros adverbios: *I very ~ left.* ▶ **not nearly** para nada

near-sighted *adj* (*USA*) miope

neat /niːt/ *adj* (-**er/-est**) **1** ordenado, bien cuidado **2** pulcro **3** (*USA, coloq*) estupendo **4** (*bebida, GB*) solo **neatly** *adv* **1** ordenadamente **2** hábilmente

necessary /ˈnesəseri; -səri *GB*/ *adj* **1** necesario **2** inevitable **necessarily** /ˌnesəˈserəli/ *adv* necesariamente

necessitate /nə'sesɪteɪt/ *vt* (*fml*) requerir

necessity /nə'sesəti/ *n* (*pl* -**ies**) **1** necesidad **2** artículo de primera necesidad

neck /nek/ *n* **1** cuello ► **neck and neck** a la par **up to your neck in sth** metido hasta el cuello en algo

necklace /'nekləs/ *n* collar

neckline /'neklaɪn/ *n* escote

necktie /'nektaɪ/ *n* (*USA*) corbata

need /ni:d/ *vt* **1** necesitar: *It ~s painting.* Hace falta pintarlo. **2** ~ **to do sth** tener que hacer algo: *Do we ~ to leave so early?* ¿Es necesario que salgamos tan temprano? **NOTA** En este sentido se puede usar el verbo modal en Gran Bretaña, pero es más formal: *Need we leave so early?* ● *v modal* (*neg* **need not/ needn't** /'ni:dnt/ (*GB*) tener que: *You needn't have come.* No hacía falta que vinieras. **NOTA** Cuando **need** es un verbo modal, lo sigue un infinitivo sin **to**, y en interrogaciones y negaciones no se usa el auxiliar **do**. ● *n* ~ (**for sth**) necesidad (de algo): *be in ~ of sth* necesitar algo ► **if need be** si fuera necesario

needle /'ni:dl/ *n* aguja

needless /'ni:dləs/ *adj* innecesario ► **needless to say** no hace falta decir

needlework /'ni:dlwз:rk/ *n* [*U*] costura, bordado

needy /'ni:di/ *adj* (-**ier**/-**iest**) necesitado

negative /'negətɪv/ *adj*, *n* negativo

neglect /nɪ'glekt/ *vt* **1** descuidar **2** ~ **to do sth** olvidar hacer algo ● *n* abandono

negligent /'neglɪdʒənt/ *adj* negligente **negligence** *n* negligencia

negligible /'neglɪdʒəbl/ *adj* insignificante

negotiate /nɪ'gəʊʃieɪt/ **1** *vt, vi* negociar **2** *vt* (*obstáculo*) salvar **negotiation** *n* negociación

neigh /neɪ/ *vi* relinchar ● *n* relincho

neighbor (-**our** *GB*) /'neɪbər/ *n* **1** vecino/a **2** prójimo/a **neighborhood** *n* **1** barrio **2** (*personas*) vecindario **neighboring** *adj* vecino, contiguo

neither /'naɪðər, 'ni:ðər/ *adj*, *pron* ninguno →NINGUNO ● *adv* **1** tampoco **NOTA** Cuando **neither** significa "tampoco" se puede sustituir por **nor**. Con ambos se utiliza la estructura: **neither/ nor + v aux/modal + sujeto:** "*I

didn't go.*" "*Neither/nor did I.*" ◊ *I can't swim and neither/nor can my brother.* **Either** puede significar "tampoco", pero requiere un verbo en negativo y su posición en la frase es distinta: *My sister didn't go either.* ◊ "*I didn't see that movie.*" "*I didn't either.*" **2 neither...nor** ni...ni

neon /'ni:ɑn/ *n* neón

nephew /'nefju:/ *n* sobrino

Neptune /'neptu:n; -tju:n *GB*/ *n* Neptuno

nerd /nз:rd/ *n* (*coloq, pey*) **1** idiota **2** nerd: *He's a computer ~.* Lo único que le interesa es la informática.

nerve /nз:rv/ *n* **1** nervio **2** valor **3** (*coloq*) descaro ► **get on sb's nerves** (*coloq*) ponerle a algn los nervios de punta **lose your nerve** acobardarse

nerve-racking *adj* desesperante

nervous /'nз:rvəs/ *adj* nervioso (*ante algo/la idea de hacer algo*): ~ *breakdown* crisis nerviosa ◊ *I felt ~ about/of going.* Me daba miedo ir. **nervousness** *n* nerviosismo

nest /nest/ *n* nido

nestle /'nesl/ **1** *vi* acurrucarse, arrellanarse **2** *vi* (*pueblo*) estar enclavado **3** *vt, vi* ~ (**sth**) **against/ on, etc. sth/sb** recostar(se) (algo) sobre algn/algn

net /net/ *n* **1** red **2** [*U*] malla, tul: ~ *curtains* visillos **3 the Net** (*coloq*) la red, internet → COMPUTADORA ● *adj* (*tb* **nett** *GB*) **1** (*peso, sueldo*) neto **2** (*resultado*) final **netting** *n* [*U*] red: *wire ~* tela metálica

netball /'netbɔ:l/ *n* tipo de basquetbol

nettle /'netl/ *n* ortiga

network /'netwз:rk/ *n* red (*sistema*) ● *vt* retransmitir

neurotic /nʊ'rɑtɪk; njʊə'r- *GB*/ *adj*, *n* neurótico/a

neutral /'nu:trəl; 'nju:- *GB*/ *adj* **1** neutral **2** (*color*) neutro ● *n* (*Aut*) punto muerto, neutro

never /'nevər/ *adv* **1** nunca **2** *That will ~ do.* Eso es totalmente inaceptable. ► **well, I never (did)!** ¡no me digas! → ALWAYS, NUNCA

nevertheless /ˌnevərðə'les/ *adv* sin embargo

new /nu:; 'nju: *GB*/ *adj* (-**er**/-**est**) nuevo: *What's ~?* ¿Qué hay de nuevo? **newly** *adv* recién **newness** *n* novedad

newcomer /'nu:kʌmər; 'nju:- *GB*/ *n* recién llegado/a

news /nu:z; 'nju:z *GB*/ *n* [*U*] **1** noticia(s): *a piece of ~* una noticia ◊

It's ~ to me. Ahora me entero. →CONSEJO **2 the news** las noticias, el noticiero

newsdealer (newsagent GB) /'nu:zdi:lər/-eidʒənt; 'nju:z- GB/ n vendedor/a de periódicos

newsletter /'nu:zletər; 'nju:z- GB/ n boletín

newspaper /'nu:zpeipər; 'nju:z- GB/ n periódico

newsreader /'nu:zri:dər; 'nju:z- GB/ n presentador/a (noticias)

news-stand n puesto de periódicos

new year n año nuevo: New Year's Eve (noche de) Fin de Año

next /nekst/ adj próximo, siguiente: ~ month el mes que viene ● **next to** prep 1 al lado de, junto a 2 después de 3 casi: ~ to nothing casi nada ◇ ~ to last penúltimo ● adv 1 después, ahora 2 when we ~ meet la próxima vez que nos veamos 3 the ~ oldest el siguiente en antigüedad ● **the next** n [sing] el/la siguiente, el/la próximo/a

next door adv al lado **next-door** adj de al lado

next of kin /,nekst əv 'km/ n pariente(s) más cercano(s)

nibble /'nɪbl/ vt, vi ~ (at) (sth) mordisquear, picar (algo)

nice /naɪs/ adj (-er/-est) 1 agradable, bien: have a ~ time pasarla bien ◇ ~ weather buen tiempo 2 bonito 3 simpático, amable: be ~ to sb tratar bien a algn **NOTA** Sympathetic se traduce por "compasivo": ~ **nice and ...** (coloq) bien: ~ and warm calentito **nicely** adv 1 bien 2 amablemente

niche /nɪtʃ, niːʃ/ n 1 nicho 2 rincón, lugar

nick /nɪk/ n 1 corte pequeño 2 **the nick** (GB, coloq) la pac (Mx), la cana (And) ▶ **in the nick of time** justo a tiempo ● vt 1 hacer(se) un corte en 2 (coloq) robar

nickel /'nɪkl/ n 1 níquel 2 (Can, USA) moneda de 5 centavos

nickname /'nɪkneɪm/ n apodo, mote ● vt apodar

nicotine /'nɪkəti:n/ n nicotina

niece /niːs/ n sobrina

night /naɪt/ n noche: by ~ de noche ◇ ~ school escuela nocturna ◇ the ~ before last anteanoche ▶ **first/opening night** estreno **good night** buenas noches (despedida) →NOCHE, MORNING

nightclub /'naɪtklʌb/ n discoteca

nightfall /'naɪtfɔ:l/ n anochecer

nightgown (**nightdress** GB) /'naɪtgaʊn/-dres/ (coloq **nightie**) n camisón

nightingale /'naɪtɪŋgeɪl/ n ruiseñor

nightlife /'naɪtlaɪf/ n vida nocturna

nightly /'naɪtli/ adj 1 nocturno 2 de todas las noches ● adv cada noche

nightmare /'naɪtmeər/ n pesadilla **nightmarish** adj de pesadilla

night-time n noche

nil /nɪl/ n 1 (esp GB, Dep) cero 2 nulo

nimble /'nɪmbl/ adj (-er/-est) 1 ágil 2 (mente) despierto

nine /naɪn/ adj, n, pron nueve **ninth** (abrev 9th) /naɪnθ/ adj, adv, n, pron noveno

nineteen /,naɪn'ti:n/ adj, n, pron diecinueve **nineteenth** 1 adj, pron decimonoveno 2 n diecinueveava parte

ninety /'naɪnti/ adj, n, pron noventa **ninetieth** 1 adj, pron nonagésimo 2 n noventava parte

nip /nɪp/ (-pp-) 1 vt pellizcar vi (GB, coloq) ~ **down, out, etc.** bajar, salir, etc. un momento

nipple /'nɪpl/ n pezón, tetilla

nitrogen /'naɪtrədʒən/ n nitrógeno

no /nəʊ/ adj 1 ninguno: No two people think alike. No hay dos personas que piensen igual. →NINGUNO 2 No smoking. Prohibido fumar. 3 (énfasis): No ~ fool. No es ninguna tonta. ◇ It's no joke. No es broma. ◇ adv [+ comparativo] no: His house is no bigger than mine. Su casa no es más grande que la mía. ● interj no

nobility /nəʊ'bɪləti/ n nobleza

noble /'nəʊbl/ adj, n (-er/-est) noble

nobody /'nəʊbədi/ pron nadie **NOTA** No se puede usar dos negaciones en la misma frase. Como **nobody**, **nothing** y **nowhere** son negativas, el verbo siempre va en la forma afirmativa: Nobody saw him. ◇ She said nothing. Con un verbo en negativo se usa **anybody**, **anything** y **anywhere**: She didn't say anything. Nobody lleva el verbo en singular, pero va seguido de **they**, **them** y **their**: Nobody else came, did they? ● n (pl **-ies**) don nadie

nocturnal /nɒk'tɜ:rnl/ adj nocturno

nod /nɒd/ (-dd-) 1 vt, vi ~ (your head) asentir con la cabeza 2 vi saludar con la cabeza **3** *vt*, *vi* indicar (algo) con la cabeza **4** *vi* dar cabezadas ■ **nod off** (*coloq*) dormirse ● *n* inclinación de la cabeza ▶ **give sb/sth the nod** (*coloq*) dar permiso a algn/para algo

noise /nɔɪz/ *n* ruido ▶ **make a noise (about sth)** (*coloq*) armar un escándalo (por algo) **noisy** *adj* (**-ier/-iest**) ruidoso

nomad /ˈnoʊmæd/ *n* nómada **nomadic** /noʊˈmædɪk/ *adj* nómada

nominal /ˈnɑmɪnl/ *adj* nominal **nominally** *adv* en principio

nominate /ˈnɑmɪneɪt/ *vt* **1** nombrar **2** designar **nomination** *n* nombramiento

nominee /ˌnɑmɪˈniː/ *n* candidato/a

non- *pref* no

none /nʌn/ *pron* **1** ninguno [+ *sustantivo o pron incontable*] nada ▶ **none but** sólo **none other than** ni más ni menos que ● *adv* **1** **the + comp**: *I'm ~ the wiser.* Sigo sin entender nada. ◇ *He's ~ the worse for it.* No le pasó nada. **2 too + adj/adv**: *~ too clean* nada limpio

nonetheless /ˌnʌnðəˈles/ *adv* sin embargo

non-existent *adj* inexistente

non-fiction *n* obras que no pertenecen al género de ficción

nonsense /ˈnɑnsens/ *n* [*U*] **1** disparates **2** tonterías **nonsensical** /nɑnˈsensɪkl/ *adj* absurdo

non-stop *adj* (*vuelo, etc.*) directo **2** ininterrumpido ● *adv* **1** directamente **2** sin parar

noodle /ˈnuːdl/ *n* fideo

noon /nuːn/ *n* mediodía

no one *Ver* NOBODY

noose /nuːs/ *n* soga, lazo

nor /nɔːr/ *conj*, *adv* ni **1** ni **2** (*ni...*) tampoco: *Nor do I.* Yo tampoco. →NEITHER

norm /nɔːrm/ *n* norma

normal /ˈnɔːrml/ *adj* normal ● *n* lo normal **normally** *adv* normalmente →ALWAYS

north /nɔːrθ/ *n* (*abrev* **N**) norte ● *adj* (del) norte ● *adv* al norte

northbound /ˈnɔːrθbaʊnd/ *adj* en/con dirección norte

north-east *n* (*abrev* **NE**) noreste ● *n* (**north-eastern**) *adj* (del) noreste ● *adv* al noreste

northern /ˈnɔːrðərn/ (*tb* **Northern**) *adj* (del) norte **northerner** *n* norteño/a

northwards /ˈnɔːrθwərdz/ (*tb* **northward**) *adv* hacia el norte

north-west *n* (*abrev* **NW**) noroeste ● (*tb* **north-western**) *adj* noroeste ● *adv* al noroeste

nose /noʊz/ *n* **1** nariz → MY **2** (*avión*) morro **3** olfato ● **nose about/around** husmear

nosebleed /ˈnoʊzbliːd/ *n* hemorragia nasal

nostalgia /nɑˈstældʒə/ *n* nostalgia

nostril /ˈnɑstrəl/ *n* fosa nasal

nosy (*tb* **nosey**) /ˈnoʊzi/ *adj* (*coloq*) entrometido, metiche

not /nɑt/ *adv* no: *I hope ~.* Espero que no. ◇ *Certainly ~!* ¡Ni hablar! ◇ *~ even...* ni siquiera...
NOTA Not suele formar la negación con verbos auxiliares y modales (**be, do, can**, etc.) y se puede usar en su forma contraída **-n't**: *She is not/isn't going.* ◇ *We did not/didn't go.* ◇ *I must not/mustn't go.* La forma no contraída es más formal o enfática y se usa con los verbos subordinados: *He told me ~ to be late.* ◇ *I suppose ~.* **▶ not all that...** no muy... **not as...as all that:** *They're ~ as rich as all that.* No son tan ricos. **not at all 1** en absoluto **2** (*respuesta*) de nada

notable /ˈnoʊtəbl/ *adj* notable **notably** *adv* notablemente

notch /nɑtʃ/ *n* **1** muesca **2** grado ■ **notch sth up** (*coloq*) apuntarse

note /noʊt/ *n* **1** nota: *take ~s* tomar apuntes **2** billete ● *vt* **1** advertir, fijarse en **2** **~ sth (down)** anotar algo **noted** *adj* célebre

notebook /ˈnoʊtbʊk/ *n* **1** cuaderno, libreta **2** (*tb* **~ computer**) computador(a) portátil

notepaper /ˈnoʊtpeɪpər/ *n* papel de cartas

noteworthy /ˈnoʊtwɜːrði/ *adj* digno de mención

nothing /ˈnʌθɪŋ/ *pron* **1** nada: *It's ~ to do with me.* No tiene nada que ver conmigo. →NOBODY **2** cero **▶ for nothing 1** gratis **2** en vano **nothing much** poca cosa

notice /ˈnoʊtɪs/ *n* **1** anuncio, cartel **2** aviso: *give one month's ~* avisar con un mes de antelación **3** (*carta*) de despido: *hand in your ~* presentar la renuncia **▶ at short/a moment's notice** inmediatamente, casi sin aviso **escape sb's notice** pasar inadvertido **take no notice** no hacer caso ● *vt* **1** darse cuenta de **2** prestar atención a, fijarse en **noticeable** *adj* perceptible: *His* *absence was ~*. Se notaba su ausencia.

noticeboard /'nəʊtɪsbɔːrd/ *n* (GB) tablero, cartelera (*de avisos*)

notify /'nəʊtɪfaɪ/ *vt* (*pt/pp* **-ied**) notificar

notion /'nəʊʃn/ *n* noción, idea

notorious /nəʊ'tɔːriəs/ *adj* (pey) conocido, famoso

notwithstanding /ˌnɒtwɪθ-'stændɪŋ/ *prep, adv* (fml) a pesar de, no obstante

nought /nɔːt/ *n* (GB) cero

noughts and crosses *n* (GB) tres en línea/gato (*Mx*)

noun /naʊn/ *n* sustantivo

nourish /'nɜːrɪʃ; 'nʌrɪʃ GB/ *vt* alimentar **nourishing** *adj* nutritivo

novel /'nɒvl/ *adj* original ● *n* novela **novelist** *n* novelista

novelty /'nɒvlti/ *n* (*pl* **-ies**) novedad

November /nəʊ'vembər/ *n* (*abrev* **Nov.**) noviembre →JUNE

novice /'nɒvɪs/ *n* novato/a, principiante

now /naʊ/ *adv* 1 ahora, ya: *right ahorita* 2 ahora bien ▶ (**every**) **now and again/then** de vez en cuando ● *conj* ~ (**that...**) ahora/ya que...

nowadays /'naʊədeɪz/ *adv* hoy (en) día

nowhere /'nəʊweər/ *adv* a/en/ por ninguna parte: *There's ~ to sit*. No hay donde sentarse. →NOBODY ▶ **be nowhere to be found/seen** no aparecer por ninguna parte

nozzle /'nɒzl/ *n* boquilla

nuance /'nuːɑːns; 'njuː- GB/ *n* matiz

nuclear /'nuːkliər; 'njuː- GB/ *adj* nuclear

nucleus /'nuːkliəs; 'njuː- GB/ *n* (*pl* **-lei** /-liaɪ/) núcleo

nude /nuːd; 'njuːd GB/ *adj, n* desnudo (*artístico, erótico*) →NAKED ▶ **in the nude** desnudo **nudity** *n* desnudez

nudge /nʌdʒ/ *vt* 1 dar un codazo a 2 empujar suavemente

nuisance /'nuːsns; 'njuː- GB/ *n* 1 molestia 2 (*persona*) pesado/a

null /nʌl/ *adj* ▶ **null and void** nulo

numb /nʌm/ *adj* entumecido: *~ with shock* paralizado del susto ● *vt* 1 entumecer 2 paralizar

number /'nʌmbər/ *n* 1 (*abrev* **No.**) número 2 *a ~ of...* varios/ ciertos... ● *vt* 1 numerar 2 ascender a

number plate *n* (GB, Aut) placa

numerical /nuː'merɪkl; njuː- GB/ *adj* numérico

numerous /'nuːmərəs; 'njuː- GB/ *adj* (fml) numeroso

nun /nʌn/ *n* monja

nurse /nɜːrs/ *n* enfermero/a ● 1 *vt* cuidar 2 *vi, vt* amamantar(-se) 3 *vt* acunar 4 *vt* (*sentimientos*) alimentar **nursing** *n* 1 enfermería: *~ home* residencia privada de la tercera edad 2 cuidado (*enfermos*)

nursery /'nɜːrsəri/ *n* (*pl* **-ies**) 1 (GB) (*tb* ~ **school**) guardería infantil: *~ education/rhyme* educación/canción infantil 2 vivero

nurture /'nɜːrtʃər/ *vt* 1 (*niño*) criar 2 alimentar

nut /nʌt/ *n* 1 fruto seco 2 tuerca 3 (*coloq*) (*tb* **nutcase** /'nʌtkeɪs/) chiflado/a

nutcrackers /'nʌtkrækərz/ *n* [*pl*] cascanueces

nutmeg /'nʌtmeg/ *n* nuez moscada

nutrient /'nuːtriənt; 'njuː- GB/ *n* (fml) nutriente, sustancia nutritiva

nutrition /nuː'trɪʃn; 'njuː- GB/ *n* nutrición **nutritional** *adj* nutritivo **nutritious** *adj* nutritivo

nuts /nʌts/ *adj* (*coloq*) ~ (**about/on sth/sb**) loco (*por algo/algn*)

nutshell /'nʌtʃel/ *n* cáscara (*fruto seco*) ▶ **in a nutshell** en pocas palabras

nutter /'nʌtə(r)/ /'nʌtər/ (GB) chiflado/a

nutty /'nʌti/ 1 *a ~ flavor* un sabor a fruto seco 2 (*coloq*) chiflado

nylon /'naɪlɒn/ *n* nailon

nymph /nɪmf/ *n* ninfa

O o

O, o /əʊ/ *n* (*pl* **O's, o's**) 1 O, o 2 cero **NOTA** Al nombrar el cero en una serie de números, p. ej. 021, se pronuncia como la letra O: /ˌəʊ tuː 'wʌn/.

oak /əʊk/ *n* (*tb* ~ **tree**) *n* roble

oar /ɔːr/ *n* remo

oasis /əʊ'eɪsɪs/ *n* (*pl* **oases** /əʊ'eɪsiːz/) oasis

oath /əʊθ/ *n* 1 juramento: *on ~* bajo juramento 2 maldición

oats /əʊts/ *n* [*pl*] (copos de) avena

obedient /ə'biːdiənt/ *adj* obediente **obedience** *n* obediencia

obese /əʊ'biːs/ *adj* (fml) obeso

obey /əˈbeɪ/ vt, vi obedecer

obituary /əˈbɪtʃuəri; əˈbɪtʃuəri GB/ n (pl **-ies**) obituario

object /ˈɒbdʒɪkt/ n **1** objeto **2** objetivo **3** (Gram) complemento ● /əbˈdʒekt/ vi oponerse: If he doesn't ~. Si no tiene inconveniente.

objection /əbˈdʒekʃn/ n ~ **(to sth)** objeción (a algo), inconveniente (en algo)

objective /əbˈdʒektɪv/ adj, n objetivo: remain ~ mantener la objetividad

obligation /ˌɒblɪˈɡeɪʃn/ n **1** obligación: be under an/no ~ to do sth (no) tener obligación de hacer algo **2** (Com) compromiso

obligatory /əˈblɪɡətri; -tɔːri GB/ adj (fml) obligatorio, de rigor

oblige /əˈblaɪdʒ/ vt **1** obligar **2** ~ **sb (with/by doing sth)** complacer a algn (haciendo algo) **obliged** adj agradecido ▸ **much obliged** se agradece **obliging** adj atento

obliterate /əˈblɪtəreɪt/ vt eliminar

oblivion /əˈblɪviən/ n olvido **oblivious** adj no consciente

oblong /ˈɒblɒŋ; -lɔːŋ GB/ n rectángulo ● adj rectangular

oboe /ˈoʊboʊ/ n oboe

obscene /əbˈsiːn/ adj obsceno

obscure /əbˈskjʊər/ adj **1** poco claro **2** desconocido ● vt oscurecer, esconder

observatory /əbˈzɜːrvətɔːri; -tri GB/ n (pl **-ies**) observatorio

observe /əbˈzɜːrv/ vt **1** observar **2** (fml) (fiesta) guardar **observant** adj perspicaz **observation** n observación **observer** n observador/a

obsess /əbˈses/ vt obsesionar: become obsessed by/with sth obsesionarse con algo/algn **obsession** n obsesión **obsessive** adj obsesivo

obsolete /ˈɒbsəliːt/ adj obsoleto

obstacle /ˈɒbstəkl/ n obstáculo

obstetrician /ˌɒbstəˈtrɪʃn/ n gineco-obstetra

obstinate /ˈɒbstɪnət/ adj obstinado

obstruct /əbˈstrʌkt/ vt obstruir **obstruction** n obstrucción

obtain /əbˈteɪn/ vt (fml) obtener **obtainable** adj que se puede conseguir

obvious /ˈɒbviəs/ adj obvio **obviously** adv obviamente

occasion /əˈkeɪʒn/ n **1** ocasión, vez **2** acontecimiento ▸ **on the occasion of sth** (fml) con motivo de algo

occasional /əˈkeɪʒənl/ adj algún/uno que otro **occasionally** adv de vez en cuando →ALWAYS

occupant /ˈɒkjəpənt/ n ocupante

occupation /ˌɒkjuˈpeɪʃn/ n **1** ocupación **2** profesión →WORK **occupational** adj **1** laboral: ~ hazards gajes del oficio **2** (terapia) ocupacional

occupy /ˈɒkjupaɪ/ (pt/pp **-ied**) vt **1** ocupar **2** ~ **sb/yourself (in doing sth/with sth)** entretener(se) (a algn) (haciendo algo/con algo) **occupier** (tb **occupant**) n ocupante

occur /əˈkɜːr/ vi (-rr-) **1** (fml) ocurrir(se) **2** encontrarse **3** ~ **to sb** ocurrírsele a algn

occurrence /əˈkɜːrəns/ n **1** caso, hecho **2** existencia, aparición **3** frecuencia

ocean /ˈoʊʃn/ n océano →MAR

o'clock /əˈklɒk/ adv: one ~ la una (en punto) **NOTA** O'clock puede omitirse cuando se entiende que uno habla de las horas en punto: between one and two, pero no cuando va con otro sustantivo: the ten ~ news.

October /ɒkˈtoʊbər/ n (abrev **Oct.**) octubre →JUNE

octopus /ˈɒktəpəs/ n pulpo

odd /ɒd/ adj **1** (-er/-est) raro **2** (número) impar **3** (fascículo) suelto **4** (zapato) sin compañero **5** sobrante **6** ~ y pico: thirty ~ treinta y pico **7** He has the ~ beer. Toma una cerveza de vez en cuando. ▸ **be the odd man/one out** ser la excepción **oddly** adv de forma extraña: Oddly enough... Lo extraño es que...

oddity /ˈɒdəti/ n (pl **-ies**) **1** rareza **2** cosa rara **3** (persona) bicho raro

odds /ɒdz/ n [pl] **1** probabilidades: The ~ are that... Lo más probable es que... **2** apuestas ▸ **be at odds (over/on sth)** estar en desacuerdo (con algo) **it makes no odds** (coloq) da lo mismo **odds and ends** (coloq) cosas sueltas

odor (**odour** GB) /ˈoʊdər/ n (fml) (gen desagradable)

of /əv, ʌv/ prep **1** de: a girl of six una niña de seis años ◇ the first of May el uno de mayo ◇ What did she die of? ¿De qué murió? ◇ It was kind of him. Fue amable de su parte. **2** (con posesivos) de: a friend of Jo's un amigo de Jo ◇ a cousin of mine un primo mío **3** (con cantidades) de: There were six of us. Éramos seis. ◇ most of all más que nada

off /ɔːf; ʊf GB/ adj 1 (comida)
pasado 2 (leche) cortado ● adv
1 (distancia): some way/a mile ~
a cierta/una milla de distancia ◇
not far ~ no (muy) lejos 2 (qui-
tado): You left the lid ~. Lo
dejaste destapado. ◇ with her
shoes ~ descalza 3 I must be ~.
Tengo que irme. 4 The meeting is
~. Se canceló la reunión. 5 (gas,
luz) apagado 6 (máquina) apagado 7 (llave) cerrado 8 a day ~ un
día libre 9 ten percent ~ un diez
por ciento de descuento ▸ **be off
(for sth)** (coloq): How are you
~ for cash? ¿Cómo estás de
dinero? **off and on/on and off**
de cuando en cuando ● prep
1 de: fall ~ sth caerse de algo
2 a street ~ the main road una
calle que sale de la carretera
principal 3 ~ the coast a cierta
distancia de la costa 4 sin ganas
de: ~ your food desganado
▸ **come off it!** ¡anda ya!
NOTA Para el uso de off en
PHRASAL VERBS ver el verbo,
p.ej. **go off** en **GO**¹.

off-duty adj fuera de servicio

offend /əˈfend/ vt ofender: be
offended ofenderse **offender** n
1 infractor/a 2 delincuente

offence (offence GB) /əˈfens/ n
1 delito 2 ofensa: take ~ at sth
ofenderse por algo

offensive /əˈfensɪv/ adj 1 ofensivo
2 repugnante ● n ofensiva

offer /ˈɔːfər; ˈɒf-/ vt, vi ofrecer ● n
oferta **offering** n 1 ofrecimiento
2 ofrenda

offhand /ˌɔːfˈhænd; ˌɒf- GB/ adv
improvisadamente, así de pronto ● adj brusco

office /ˈɔːfɪs; ˈɒfɪs GB/ n 1 oficina
2 despacho 3 cargo: in ~ en el
poder ◇ take ~ asumir funciones

officer /ˈɔːfɪsər; ˈɒf- GB/ n 1 (Mil)
oficial 2 funcionario/a 3 (**police ~**) policía

official /əˈfɪʃl/ adj oficial ● n
funcionario/a

off-licence n (GB) tienda de
vinos y licores

off-peak adj 1 de temporada baja
2 (período) de menor consumo

off-putting adj (coloq) 1 molesto
2 (persona) desagradable

offset /ˈɔːfset; ˈɒf- GB/ vt (-tt-) (pt
pp offset) contrarrestar

offshore /ˌɔːfˈʃɔːr; ˌɒf- GB/ adj
1 cercano a la costa 2 (brisa)
terral 3 (pesca) de bajura

offside /ˌɔːfˈsaɪd; ˌɒf- GB/ adj, adv
(Dep) fuera de juego/lugar

offspring /ˈɔːfsprɪŋ; ˈɒf- GB/ n (pl
offspring) (fml) 1 hijo(s), descendencia 2 cría(s)

often /ˈɔːfn; ˈɒfn/ʹɒftən GB/ adv a
menudo, muchas veces: How
~ do you go? ¿Cada cuánto vas?
→**ALWAYS**

oh interj 1 oh, ah 2 Oh yes I will.
¡Claro que lo haré! ◇ Oh no you
won't! ¡De eso nada!

oil /ɔɪl/ n 1 petróleo: ~ well pozo
petrolífero ◇ ~ rig plataforma/
torre de perforación 2 aceite
3 (Arte) óleo ● vt lubricar **oily**
adj (-ier/-iest) 1 oleoso 2 aceitoso

ointment /ˈɔɪntmənt/ n pomada

OK (tb **okay**) /ˌoʊˈkeɪ/ adj, adv
(coloq) bien ● interj de acuerdo,
listo (And) ● vt dar el visto bueno
a ● n consentimiento

old /oʊld/ adj (-er/-est) → **ELDER**
1 viejo: ~ age vejez ◇ ~ people
(los) ancianos 2 How ~ are you?
¿Cuántos años tienes?
NOTA "Tengo diez años" se dice
I am ten o I am ten years old, y
"un niño de diez años" es a boy of
ten o a ten-year-old boy. 3 antiguo
● **the old** n [pl] los ancianos

old-fashioned adj 1 pasado de
moda 2 tradicional

olive /ˈɒlɪv/ n 1 aceituna: ~ oil
aceite de oliva 2 (~ **tree**) olivo
● adj 1 (tb ~ **green**) verde oliva
2 (piel) aceitunado

the Olympics /ɔɪ əˈlɪmpɪks/ (tb
the Olympic Games) n los Juegos
Olímpicos

omelette (tb **omelet**) /ˈɒmlət/ n
omelet, tortilla (de huevo)

omen /ˈoʊmən/ n presagio

ominous /ˈɒmɪnəs/ adj ominoso

omit /əˈmɪt/ vt (fml) (-tt-) omitir
omission n omisión, olvido

omnipotent /ɒmˈnɪpətənt/ adj
omnipotente

on /ɒn/ adv 1 (continuidad): play
on seguir tocando ◇ further on
más lejos/allá ◇ from that day on
a partir de aquel día 2 (ropa, etc.)
puesto 3 (máquina) conectado,
encendido 4 (llave) abierto 5 pro-
gramado: When is the movie on?
¿A qué hora empieza la película? ▸ **on and on** sin parar ● prep
1 en, sobre 2 (transporte): go on
foot/on the train ir a pie/en el
tren 3 (fechas): on Sunday/on
May 2 el domingo/el dos de
mayo 4 [+ -ing]: on arriving home
al llegar a casa 5 (acerca de)
sobre 6 (consumo): be on drugs
drogarse ◇ live on fruit/on 50
dollars a week vivir de fruta/
mantenerse con $50 a la semana
7 speak on the phone hablar por

teléfono **8** (*actividad, etc.*) de: *on vacation/duty* de vacaciones/servicio **NOTA** Para el uso de **on** en PHRASAL VERBS ver el verbo, p.ej. *get on* en GET.

once /wʌns/ *adv, conj* una vez (que): ~ *a week* una vez a la semana ▶ **at once 1** enseguida **2** a la vez **once again/more** una vez más **once and for all** de una vez por todas **once or twice** un par de veces **once upon a time** érase una vez

oncoming /ˈɒnkʌmɪŋ/ *adj* en dirección contraria

one /wʌn/ *adj* **1** un(o), una **NOTA One** nunca funciona como artículo indefinido (**a/an**). Cuando precede a un sustantivo, indica número o cantidad: *I'm going with just* ~ *friend.* Voy con un amigo solamente. ◊ *I'm going with a friend, not with my family.* No voy con mi familia, sino con un amigo. **2** único: *the* ~ *way to succeed* la única forma de triunfar **3** mismo: *of* ~ *mind* de la misma opinión ● *pron* **1** [*después de adj*]: *the little* ~ los pequeños ◊ *I prefer this.* ~ Prefiero éste. ◊ *Which* ~? ¿Cuál? ◊ *another* ~ otro **2** el/la, los/las que: *the* ~ *at the end* el que está al final **3** uno/a: *I need a pen. Do you have* ~? Necesito un bolígrafo. ¿Tienes uno? ◊ ~ *of her friends* uno de sus amigos **4** [*como sujeto*] (*fml*) uno/a: *One must be sure.* Uno debe estar seguro. ▶ YOU ▶ **(all) in one** a la vez **one by one** uno a uno **one or two** unos cuantos

one another *pron* Ver EACH OTHER

one-off *adj, n* (algo) excepcional/único

oneself /wʌnˈself/ *pron* **1** [*reflexivo*]: *cut* ~ cortarse **2** [*énfasis*] uno mismo: *do it* ~ hacerlo uno mismo

one-sided *adj* **1** parcial **2** desigual

one-way *adj* **1** de sentido único **2** (*boleto/tiquete*) de ida

ongoing /ˈɒngoʊɪŋ/ *adj* **1** en curso **2** actual

onion /ˈʌnjən/ *n* cebolla

online /ˈɒnlaɪn/ *adj, adv* en línea

onlooker /ˈɒnlʊkər/ *n* espectador/a

only /ˈoʊnli/ *adv* solamente, sólo ▶ **not only... but also** no sólo... sino (también) **only just 1** *I've* ~ *just arrived.* Acabo de llegar. **2** *I can* ~ *just see.* Apenas si puedo ver. ● *adj* [*antes de sustantivo*] único: *an* ~ *child* hijo

único ● *conj* (*coloq*) solo que, pero

onset /ˈɒnset/ *n* llegada, inicio

onslaught /ˈɒnslɔːt/ *n* ~ (**on sth/sb**) ataque (contra algo/algn)

onto (*tb* **on to**) /ˈɒntə, ˈɒntu/ *prep* en, sobre, a ▶ **be onto sb** (*coloq*) seguirle la pista a algn **be onto sth** haber dado con algo

onward /ˈɒnwərd/ *adj* (*fml*) hacia delante: *your* ~ *journey* la continuación de tu viaje ● *adv* (*tb* **onwards**) **1** hacia adelante **2** en adelante: *from then* ~s a partir de entonces

oops /ʊps/ *interj* ay

ooze /uːz/ **1** *vi* ~ **from/out of sth** salir de algo **2** *vi* ~ (**with**) **sth** rezumar algo **3** *vt, vi* ~ (**with**) **sth** irradiar algo

opaque /oʊˈpeɪk/ *adj* opaco

open /ˈoʊpən/ *adj* **1** abierto **2** (*vista*) despejado **3** público **4** *leave sth* ~ dejar algo pendiente ▶ **in the open air** al aire libre ● **1** *vt, vi* abrir(se) **2** *vt* empezar **3** *vt, vi* inaugurar(se) ■ **open into/onto sth** dar a algo **open sth out** desplegar algo **open** (**sth**) **up** abrir(se) (algo) ● **the open** (**sth**) **up** el aire libre ▶ **bring/come** (**out**) **into the open** salir/sacar algo a la luz **opener** *n* abridor, destapador **openness** *n* franqueza

open-air *adj* al aire libre

opening /ˈoʊpnɪŋ/ *n* **1** abertura **2** apertura **3** comienzo **4** (*tb* ~ **night**) (*Teat*) estreno **5** inauguración **6** (*trabajo*) vacante **7** oportunidad ● *adj* primero

open-minded *adj* (*mente*) abierto

opera /ˈɒprə/ *n* ópera

operate /ˈɒpəreɪt/ **1** *vi* funcionar **2** *vt* manejar **3** *vi* (*empresa*) operar **4** *vt* (*servicio*) ofrecer **5** *vi* ~ (**on sb**) (**for sth**) (*Med*) operar (a algn) (de algo): *operating room* quirófano

operation /ˌɒpəˈreɪʃn/ *n* **1** operación: *I had an* ~ *on my leg.* Me operaron de la pierna. **2** funcionamiento ▶ **be in/into operation 1** estar/entrar en funcionamiento **2** (*Jur*) estar/entrar en vigor **operational** *adj* del/en funcionamiento

operative /ˈɒpərətɪv, ˈɒprə-/ *adj* **1** en funcionamiento **2** (*Jur*) en vigor **3** (*Med*) operatorio ● *n* operario/a

operator /ˈɒpəreɪtər/ *n* operario/a: (*switchboard*) ~ operador

opinion /əˈpɪniən/ *n* opinión: ~ *poll* sondeo de opinión ▶ **in my opinion** en mi opinión

opponent /əˈpəʊnənt/ n
1 adversario/a 2 **be an ~** of sth
ser contrario a algo

opportunity /ˌɒpəˈtjuːnəti;
-ˈtjuːn- GB/ n (pl -**ies**) oportunidad: *take the ~ of doing sth* aprovechar la ocasión para hacer algo

oppose /əˈpəʊz/ vt 1 oponerse a 2 enfrentarse a **opposed** adj contrario ▸ **as opposed to** (fml): *quality ~ to quantity* calidad más que cantidad **opposing** adj contrario

opposite /ˈɒpəzɪt/ adj 1 de enfrente 2 opuesto ● adv enfrente ● prep enfrente de, frente a: ~ *each other* frente a frente ● n **the ~** lo contrario

opposition /ˌɒpəˈzɪʃn/ n oposición

oppress /əˈpres/ vt 1 oprimir 2 agobiar **oppressed** adj oprimido **oppression** n opresión **oppressive** adj 1 opresivo 2 agobiante, sofocante

opt /ɒpt/ vi 1 ~ **for** sth/**to do** sth optar por algo 2 ~ **out (of** sth) no participar (en algo)

optical /ˈɒptɪkl/ adj óptico

optician /ɒpˈtɪʃn/ n (GB) óptico/a **optician's** n (GB) óptica

optimism /ˈɒptɪmɪzəm/ n optimismo **optimist** n optimista **optimistic** /ˌɒptɪˈmɪstɪk/ adj optimista

optimum /ˈɒptɪməm/ (tb **optimal**) adj óptimo

option /ˈɒpʃn/ n opción **optional** adj opcional, optativo

optometrist /ɒpˈtɒmətrɪst/ n óptico/a

or /ɔːr/ conj 1 o, u 2 si no 3 [después de negativa] ni ▸ **or so**: *an hour or so* una hora más o menos

oral /ˈɔːrəl/ adj 1 oral 2 (Anat) bucal ● n (examen) oral

orange /ˈɒrɪndʒ; ˈɒr- GB/ n naranja ● adj (tb ~ **tree**) naranjo

orbit /ˈɔːbɪt/ n órbita ● vt, vi ~ **((around)** sth) describir una órbita (alrededor de algo)

orchard /ˈɔːtʃəd/ n huerto

orchestra /ˈɔːkɪstrə/ n 1 orquesta 2 (USA, Teat) platea

orchid /ˈɔːkɪd/ n orquídea

ordeal /ɔːˈdiːl/ n experiencia terrible, suplicio

order /ˈɔːdər/ n 1 orden 2 pedido ▸ **be in running/working order** funcionar **in order** en regla **in order to/that…** para/para que… **out of order** estropeado: *It's out of ~.* No funciona. ● vt 1 ~ **sb to do** sth mandar a algn hacer algo/ que haga algo **NOTA** Para decir a algn que haga algo se pueden usar los verbos **tell**, **order** y **command**. **Tell** es el más común y se usa en situaciones cotidianas: *She told him to clean up.* **Order** es más fuerte, y lo usan personas con autoridad: *I'm not asking you, I'm ordering you.* **Command** es un uso principalmente militar: *He commanded his troops to retreat.* 2 vt, vi pedir 3 vt (fml) poner en orden, organizar ■ **order sb about/around** mandar a algn de acá para allá, ser mandón con algn

orderly /ˈɔːdəli/ adj 1 metódico 2 disciplinado, pacífico

ordinary /ˈɔːdnri; -nri GB/ adj corriente, normal ▸ **out of the ordinary** fuera de lo común

ore /ɔːr/ n mineral (metalífero)

oregano /ˌɒrɪˈɡɑːnəʊ; əˈreɡənəʊ GB/ n orégano

organ /ˈɔːɡən/ n órgano

organic /ɔːˈɡænɪk/ adj 1 orgánico 2 ecológico

organism /ˈɔːɡənɪzəm/ n organismo

organize, -ise /ˈɔːɡənaɪz/ vt 1 organizar 2 poner en orden **organizer** n organizador/a **organization** n organización **organizational** adj organizativo

orgy /ˈɔːdʒi/ n (pl -**ies**) orgía

orient /ˈɔːriənt/ vt (tb **orientate** /ˈɔːriəntett/ GB) orientar **orientation** n orientación ● **the Orient** n el Oriente **oriental** /ˌɔːriˈentl/ adj oriental

origin /ˈɒrɪdʒɪn/ n origen

original /əˈrɪdʒənl/ adj 1 original 2 primero, primitivo ● n original ▸ **in the original** en versión original **originality** /əˌrɪdʒəˈnæləti/ n originalidad **originally** adv en un/al principio

originate /əˈrɪdʒɪneɪt/ vi 1 originarse, provenir 2 empezar

ornament /ˈɔːnəmənt/ n (objeto de) adorno **ornamental** /ˌɔːnəˈmentl/ adj decorativo

ornate /ɔːˈneɪt/ adj ornamentado, recargado

orphan /ˈɔːfn/ n huérfano/a ● vt: *be orphaned* quedarse huérfano **orphanage** n orfanato

orthodox /ˈɔːθədɒks/ adj ortodoxo

ostrich /ˈɒstrɪtʃ/ n avestruz

other /ˈʌðər/ adj otro: *some ~ time* otro día → OTRO ▸ **other than** 1 excepto, aparte de 2 (fml) de otra manera ■ **somebody or other/something/somewhere or other** (coloq) alguien/algo/en alguna parte **the other day, week, etc.** el otro día, la otra semana, etc. ● *pron* **the other** *otro/as: Do you have any ~s?* ¿Tienes más? **2 the other** el otro/a la otra **3 the others** los/las demás

otherwise /ˈʌðərwaɪz/ *adv* **1** de otra manera **2** por lo demás ● *conj* si no, de no ser así

otter /ˈɑtər/ *n* nutria

ouch *interj* ay

ought to /ˈɔːt tə, ˈɔːt tuː/ *v* (*neg* **ought not/oughtn't** /ˈɔːtnt/) NOTA Ought to se usa como modal, y no se usa el auxiliar do en interrogaciones y negaciones. **1** (*sugerencias, consejos*): *You ~ do it.* Deberías hacerlo. ◇ *I ~ have gone.* Debería haber ido. **2** (*probabilidad*): *Two ~ be enough.* Con dos debería ser suficiente.

ounce /aʊns/ *n* (*abrev* oz) onza (28,35 gramos) →*Ver pág.* 222

our /ɑr, ˈaʊər/ *adj* nuestro →MY

ours /ɑrz, ˈaʊərz/ *pron* nuestro: *a friend of ~* una amiga nuestra

ourselves /ɑrˈselvz, aʊərˈs-/ *pron* **1** [*reflexivo*] nos **2** [*énfasis*] nosotros mismos ▸ **(all) by ourselves** solos/as

out /aʊt/ *adv* **1** fuera de: *be ~* no estar (en casa)/haber salido *The sun is ~.* Salió el sol. **2** pasado de moda **3** (*posibilidad, etc.*) descartado **3** (*luz, etc.*) apagado **6** call ~ llamar en voz alta **7** (*cálculo*) equivocado **8** (*pelota*) fuera (*de la línea*) eliminado **9** (*pelota*) fuera (*de la línea*) ▸ **out to do sth** decidido a hacer algo NOTA Para el uso de out en PHRASAL VERBS ver el verbo, p.ej. **pick out** en PICK.

outage /ˈaʊtɪdʒ/ *n* (USA) corte eléctrico

outbreak /ˈaʊtbreɪk/ *n* **1** brote **2** (*guerra*) estallido

outburst /ˈaʊtbɜːrst/ *n* **1** explosión **2** (*emoción*) estallido

outcast /ˈaʊtkæst; -kɑːst GB/ *n* marginado/a, paria

outcome /ˈaʊtkʌm/ *n* resultado

outcry /ˈaʊtkraɪ/ *n* (*pl* -ies) protestas

outdated /ˌaʊtˈdeɪtɪd/ *adj* anticuado, pasado de moda

outdo /ˌaʊtˈduː/ *vt* (*3ª pers sing pres* outdoes /-ˈdʌz/ *pt* outdid /-ˈdɪd/ *pp* outdone /-ˈdʌn/) superar

outdoor /ˈaʊtdɔːr/ *adj* al aire libre: *~ swimming pool* piscina/ alberca descubierta

outer /ˈaʊtər/ *adj* **1** exterior, externo **2 ~ space** el espacio sideral

outfit /ˈaʊtfɪt/ *n* (*ropa*) conjunto

outgoing /ˈaʊtɡoʊɪŋ/ *adj* **1** que sale, de salida **2** (*Pol*) saliente **3** extrovertido

outgrow /ˌaʊtˈɡroʊ/ *vt* (*pt* outgrew /-ˈɡruː/ *pp* outgrown /-ˈɡroʊn/) **1** *He's outgrown his shoes.* Ya le quedan pequeños los zapatos. **2** cansarse de, abandonar

outing /ˈaʊtɪŋ/ *n* excursión

outlandish /aʊtˈlændɪʃ/ *adj* estrafalario, extravagante

outlaw /ˈaʊtlɔː/ *vt* declarar ilegal ● *n* bandido/a

outlet /ˈaʊtlet/ *n* **1** desagüe, salida **2** (*fig*) desahogo **3** (*Com*) punto de venta **4** (USA) enchufe (*en pared*)

outline /ˈaʊtlaɪn/ *n* **1** contorno **2** líneas generales, esbozo ● *vt* **1** perfilar, esbozar **2** exponer en líneas generales

outlive /ˌaʊtˈlɪv/ *vt* sobrevivir a

outlook /ˈaʊtlʊk/ *n* **1** punto de vista **2** pronóstico **3** perspectiva

outnumber /ˌaʊtˈnʌmbər/ *vt* superar en número a

out of /ˈaʊt əv/ *prep* **1** fuera de: *jump ~ bed* saltar de la cama **2** *~ interest* por interés **3** de: *eight ~ ten* ocho de cada diez ◇ *copy sth ~ a book* copiar algo de un libro **4** (*material*) de, con: *made ~ wood* de madera **5** *~ work* sin trabajo

outpost /ˈaʊtpoʊst/ *n* (puesto de) avanzada

output /ˈaʊtpʊt/ *n* **1** producción **2** (*Fís*) potencia

outrage /ˈaʊtreɪdʒ/ *n* **1** atrocidad **2** escándalo **3** ira ● *vt* ultrajar **outrageous** /aʊtˈreɪdʒəs/ *adj* **1** escandaloso

outright /ˈaʊtraɪt/ *adj* **1** abierto **2** total **3** (*ganador*) indiscutible **4** (*negativa*) rotundo ● *adv* **1** abiertamente **2** en su totalidad **3** instantáneamente, de golpe **4** (*ganar, etc.*) rotundamente

outset /ˈaʊtset/ *n* principio

outside /ˌaʊtˈsaɪd/ *n* exterior: *on/ from the ~* por/desde (a)fuera ● *prep* (*tb ~ of* USA) fuera de: *Wait ~ the door.* Espera en la puerta. ● *adv* (a)fuera ● /ˈaʊtsaɪd/ *adj* [*antes de sustantivo*] exterior, externo

outsider /ˌaʊtˈsaɪdər/ *n* **1** forastero/a **2** intruso/a **3** (*competidor*) desconocido/a

outskirts /ˈaʊtskɜːrts/ *n* [*pl*] afueras

outspoken /aʊtˈspoʊkən/ *adj* franco

outstanding /aʊtˈstændɪŋ/ adj
1 destacado 2 sobresaliente
3 (pago, trabajo) pendiente

outstretched /aʊtˈstretʃt/ adj
extendido, abierto

outward /ˈaʊtwəd/ adj 1 exterior,
externo 2 (viaje) de ida ● (tb
outwards GB) adv hacia fuera
outwardly adv por fuera, aparentemente

outweigh /ˌaʊtˈweɪ/ vt pesar más
que, importar más que

oval /ˈoʊvl/ adj oval, ovalado

ovary /ˈoʊvəri/ n (pl -ies) ovario

oven /ˈʌvn/ n horno

over /ˈoʊvər/ adv 1 knock sth ~
volcar algo ◊ fall ~ caer(se) 2 turn
sth ~ dar la vuelta a algo 3 (lugar): ~ here/there por acá/allá ◊
She came ~ to see me. Vino a
verme. 4 left ~ de sobra: Is there
any food left ~? ¿Queda algo de
comida? 5 (más): children of five
and ~ niños de cinco años o más
6 terminado: ~ and done with
terminado para siempre ▸ **(all)
over again** de nuevo **over and
over (again)** una y otra vez ●
prep 1 sobre, por encima de 2 al
otro lado de 3 más de 4 durante,
mientras: We'll discuss it over
dinner. Lo discutiremos durante
la cena. 5 a causa de: an argument ~ money una discusión por
cuestiones de dinero ▸ **over and
above** además de NOTA Para el
uso de over en PHRASAL VERBS
ver el verbo, p.ej. **think over** en
THINK.

over- pref 1 excesivamente: over-
ambitious excesivamente ambicioso 2 (edad) mayor de: the
over-60s los mayores de 60 años

overall /ˌoʊvərˈɔːl/ adj 1 total
2 global 3 (ganador) absoluto
● adv 1 en total 2 en general
● /ˈoʊvərɔːl/ n 1 (GB) delantal,
bata 2 **overalls** [pl] (GB) overol
→PAIR

overbearing /ˌoʊvərˈbeərɪŋ/ adj
dominante

overboard /ˈoʊvərbɔːrd/ adv por
la borda

overcast /ˌoʊvərˈkæst; -ˈkɑːst GB/
adj nublado, cubierto

overcharge /ˌoʊvərˈtʃɑːrdʒ/ vt, vi
cobrar de más

overcoat /ˈoʊvərkoʊt/ n abrigo

overcome /ˌoʊvərˈkʌm/ vt (pt
overcame /-ˈkeɪm/ pp **overcome**)
1 superar 2 apoderarse de, invadir: ~ by smoke/emotion vencido
por el humo/embargado por la
emoción

overcrowded /ˌoʊvərˈkraʊdɪd/
adj atestado (de gente) over-
crowding n congestión, hacina-
miento

overdo /ˌoʊvərˈduː/ vt (3ª pers
sing pres -**does** pt -**did** /-ˈdɪd/ pp
-**done** /-ˈdʌn/) 1 exagerar, pasarse con 2 cocer demasiado
▸ **overdo it/things** pasarse (de la
raya)

overdose /ˈoʊvərdoʊs/ n sobredosis

overdraft /ˈoʊvərdræft; -drɑːft
GB/ n sobregiro (banco)

overdue /ˌoʊvərˈduː; -ˈdjuː GB/ adj
1 retrasado 2 (Fin) vencido

overestimate /ˌoʊvərˈestɪmeɪt/
vt sobreestimar

overflow /ˌoʊvərˈfloʊ/ 1 vt, vi
desbordar(se) 2 vi rebosar ●
/ˈoʊvərfloʊ/ n 1 desbordamiento
2 derrame 3 (tb ~ **pipe**) cañería
de desagüe

overgrown /ˌoʊvərˈɡroʊn/ adj
1 crecido, grande 2 ~ (**with sth**)
(jardín) cubierto (de algo)

overhang /ˌoʊvərˈhæŋ/ vt, vi (pt
pp **-hung** /-ˈhʌŋ/) sobresalir, colgar (por encima) **overhanging**
sobresaliente

overhaul /ˌoʊvərˈhɔːl/ vt revisar,
poner a punto ● /ˈoʊvərhɔːl/ n
revisión, puesta a punto

overhead /ˈoʊvərhed/ adj 1 elevado 2 (cable) aéreo 3 (luz) de
techo ● /ˌoʊvərˈhed/ adv por
encima de la cabeza, en lo alto

overhear /ˌoʊvərˈhɪər/ vt (pt/pp
-heard /-ˈhɜːrd/) oír (por casualidad)

overjoyed /ˌoʊvərˈdʒɔɪd/ adj ~ (**at
sth**) contentísimo (con algo)

overland /ˈoʊvərlænd/ adj terrestre ● adv por tierra

overlap /ˌoʊvərˈlæp/ (-**pp-**) 1 vt, vi
superponer(se) 2 vi coincidir en
parte ● /ˈoʊvərlæp/ n 1 superpo-
sición 2 coincidencia

overleaf /ˌoʊvərˈliːf/ adv al dorso

overload /ˌoʊvərˈloʊd/ vt sobre-
cargar ● /ˈoʊvərloʊd/ n sobre-
carga

overlook /ˌoʊvərˈlʊk/ vt 1 tener
vista a 2 pasar por alto 3 no notar
4 (perdonar) dejar pasar

overnight /ˌoʊvərˈnaɪt/ adv 1 durante la noche: travel ~ viajar de
noche 2 de la noche a la mañana
● /ˈoʊvərnaɪt/ adj [antes de sus-
tantivo] 1 de la/para una noche
2 (éxito) repentino

overpass /ˈoʊvərpæs; -pɑːs GB/ n
(USA) paso elevado

overpower /ˌoʊvərˈpaʊər/ vt dominar **overpowering** adj agobiante, arrollador

overran /ˌoʊvəˈræn/ pt de OVER-
RUN

overrate /ˌouvəˈreɪt/ vt sobreestimar, sobrevalorar

overreact /ˌouvəriˈækt/ vi reaccionar de forma exagerada

override /ˌouvəˈraɪd/ vt (pt **overrode** /-ˈroud/ pp **overridden** /-ˈrɪdn/) 1 hacer caso omiso de 2 tener preferencia sobre **overriding** adj [antes de sustantivo] primordial

overrule /ˌouvəˈruːl/ vt anular

overrun /ˌouvəˈrʌn/ (pt **overran** /-ˈræn/ pp **overrun**) 1 vt invadir 2 vt, vi rebasar (su tiempo)

overseas /ˌouvəˈsiːz/ adj exterior, extranjero ● adv en el/al extranjero

oversee /ˌouvəˈsiː/ vt (pt **-saw** /-ˈsɔː/ pp **-seen** /-ˈsiːn/) supervisar

overshadow /ˌouvəˈʃædou/ vt 1 eclipsar 2 (entristecer) ensombrecer

oversight /ˈouvəsaɪt/ n omisión, olvido

oversleep /ˌouvəˈsliːp/ vi (pt/pp **-slept** /-ˈslept/) no despertarse a tiempo

overspend /ˌouvəˈspend/ (pt/pp **-spent** /-ˈspent/) 1 vi gastar en exceso 2 vt (presupuesto) pasarse de

overstate /ˌouvəˈsteɪt/ vt exagerar

overstep /ˌouvəˈstep/ vt (-pp-) pasarse ▶ **overstep the mark** pasarse de la raya

overt /ouˈvɜːt/ adj (fml) abierto

overtake /ˌouvəˈteɪk/ (pt **took** /-ˈtuk/ pp **-taken** /-ˈteɪkən/) 1 vt, vi (GB, Aut) rebasar 2 vt sobrecoger, sobrepasar

overthrow /ˌouvəˈθrou/ vt (pt **-threw** /-ˈθruː/ pp **-thrown** /-ˈθroun/) derrocar ● /ˈouvəθrou/ n derrocamiento

overtime /ˈouvətaɪm/ adv, n horas extras

overtone /ˈouvətoun/ n connotación

overture /ˈouvətʃər/ n 1 (Mús) obertura 2 (entristecer) ensombrecer

overturn /ˌouvəˈtɜːrn/ 1 vt, vi volcar(se) 2 vt (decisión) anular

overview /ˈouvəvjuː/ n perspectiva (general)

overweight /ˌouvəˈweɪt/ adj con exceso de peso →FAT

overwhelm /ˌouvəˈwelm/ vt 1 abrumar 2 abatir, derribar **overwhelming** adj abrumador

overwork /ˌouvəˈwɜːrk/ vt, vi (hacer) trabajar en exceso

ow interj ay

owe /ou/ vt deber, estar en deuda con

owing to /ˈouɪŋ tuː/ prep debido a

owl /aul/ n búho, lechuza

own /oun/ adj, pron propio, mío, tuyo, suyo, nuestro, vuestro: a house of your ~ una casa propia ◊ It was my ~ Fue idea mía. ▶ **(all) on your own 1** (completamente) solo **2** por sí solo, sin ayuda ● vt poseer, ser dueño de ■ **own up (to sth)** confesarse culpable (de algo)

owner /ˈounər/ n dueño/a **ownership** n [U] propiedad

ox /ɑks/ n (pl **oxen** /ˈɑksn/) buey

oxygen /ˈɑksɪdʒən/ n oxígeno

oyster /ˈɔɪstər/ n ostra, ostión (Mx)

ozone /ˈouzoun/ n ozono

P p

P, p /piː/ n (pl **P's**, **p's**) P, p

pace /peɪs/ n 1 paso 2 ritmo ▶ **keep pace (with sth/sb) 1** ir al mismo paso (que algo/algn) **2** mantenerse al corriente (de algo/algn) ● vt, vi pasearse (por): ~ **up and down** pasearse con inquietud

pacemaker /ˈpeɪsmeɪkər/ n (Med) marcapasos

pacifier /ˈpæsɪfaɪər/ n (USA) chupón (Mx), chupo (And)

pacify /ˈpæsɪfaɪ/ vt (pt/pp **-ied**) 1 (ira, etc.) apaciguar 2 pacificar

pack /pæk/ n 1 envase →PACKAGE 2 (cigarrillos) cajetilla 3 mochila 4 (GB, cartas) baraja 5 (animal) carga 6 (perros) jauría 7 (lobos) manada ● 1 vt empacar 2 vi hacer la maleta 3 vt embalar 4 vt ~ **sth into sth** poner algo en algo 5 vt ~ **sth in sth** envolver algo con algo 6 vt (caja) llenar 7 vt (comida) empacar, envasar 8 vt (USA, pistola, etc.) llevar 9 vt (habitación) atestar ▶ **pack your bags** (coloq) irse ■ **pack sth in** (coloq) dejar algo **pack (sth/sb) into sth** apiñarse, apiñar (algo/a algn en algo) **pack up** (coloq) descomponerse **packed** adj 1 al tope 2 ~ **with sth** lleno de algo

package /ˈpækɪdʒ/ n 1 (**packet** /ˈpækɪt/ GB) paquete **NOTA Package** se refiere a los paquetes que se envían por correo o que se entregan en mano. En Gran Bretaña se usa **parcel** para los que se envían por correo.

Pack (packet GB) es un paquete o una bolsa que contiene algún producto que se vende en una tienda: *a pack of cigarettes/chips.* Pack es también un conjunto de cosas diferentes que se venden juntas: *The pack contains needles and thread.* **2** bulto ● vt envasar **packaging** n empaque

package tour *n* (*tb* **package holiday** GB) *n* viaje organizado

packed lunch *n* (GB) comida de mediodía que se lleva de casa

packing /'pækɪŋ/ *n* **1** envase **2** relleno

pact /pækt/ *n* pacto

pad /pæd/ *n* **1** almohadilla **2** (*de papel*) bloc ● vt (**-dd-**) acolchar ■ **pad about, along,** etc. andar (con pasos suaves) **pad sth out** meterle paja/relleno a algo (*libro, discurso*) **padding** n **1** acolchado **2** (*fig*) paja

paddle /'pædl/ *n* **1** pala (*remo*) **2** (GB) **have a ~** mojarse los pies ● vt (*barca*) dirigir (*remando*) **2** vi remar **3** vi (GB) mojarse los pies

paddock /'pædək/ *n* prado (*donde pastan los caballos*)

padlock /'pædlɒk/ *n* candado

paediatrician (GB) = PEDIATRICIAN

pagan /'peɪɡən/ *adj, n* pagano/a

page /peɪdʒ/ *n* (*abrev* **p**) página ● vt llamar por el altavoz/beeper

pager /'peɪdʒər/ *n* beeper, bíper

paid /peɪd/ *pt, pp de* PAY ● *adj* **1** (*empleado*) a sueldo **2** (*trabajo*) remunerado ▸ **put paid to sth** acabar con algo

pain /peɪn/ *n* dolor: *Is she in ~? ¿Le duele mucho?* ◊ *I have a ~ in my arm.* Me duele el brazo. ▸ **a pain (in the neck)** (*coloq*) **1** (*persona*) un/a pesado/a **2** (*cosa*) una lata **be at pains to do sth** esforzarse por hacer algo **take (great) pains with/over sth** esmerarse mucho en algo **pained** *adj* **1** afligido **2** ofendido **painful** *adj* **1** dolorido: *be ~* doler **2** doloroso **3** desagradable **painfully** *adv* terriblemente **painless** *adj* **1** que no duele **2** sin dificultades

painkiller /'peɪnkɪlər/ *n* analgésico

painstaking /'peɪnzteɪkɪŋ/ *adj* **1** laborioso **2** concienzudo

paint /peɪnt/ *n* pintura ● vt, vi pintar **painter** *n* pintor/a **painting** *n* **1** pintura **2** cuadro

paintbrush /'peɪntbrʌʃ/ *n* pincel, brocha

paintwork /'peɪntwɜːrk/ *n* pintura (*superficie*)

pair /peər/ *n* **1** par: *a ~ of pants* unos pantalones/un pantalón **NOTA** Las palabras que designan objetos compuestos por dos elementos (p. ej. pantalones, tijeras, etc.), llevan el verbo en plural: *My pants are very tight.* Al referirse a más de uno, se usa **pair**: *I have two ~s of pants.* **2** pareja (*animales, equipo*) ■ **pair (sb) off/up (with sb)** emparejar(se) (a algn) (*con algn*)

pajamas /pə'dʒæməz; -'dʒɑːm-GB/ *n* [*pl*] piyama →PAIR **pajama** *adj*: **~ bottoms** el pantalón de la piyama

pal /pæl/ *n* (*coloq*) compañero/a

palace /'pæləs/ *n* palacio

palate /'pælət/ *n* paladar

pale /peɪl/ *adj* (**-er/-est**) **1** pálido: *go/turn ~* palidecer **2** (*color*) claro **3** (*luz*) tenue ● *n* ▸ **beyond the pale** inaceptable

pall /pɔːl/ *vi* **~ (on sb)** cansar (a algn) (*de aburrimiento*)

pallid /'pælɪd/ *adj* pálido **pallor** *n* palidez

palm /pɑːm/ *n* **1** (*mano*) palma **2** (*tb* **~ tree**) palmera, palma ▸ **have sb in the palm of your hand** tener a algn en la palma de la mano ■ **palm sth/sb off (on sb)** (*coloq*) meterle algo/algn (a algn)

paltry /'pɔːltri/ *adj* insignificante

pamper /'pæmpər/ *vt* mimar

pamphlet /'pæmflət/ *n* **1** folleto **2** panfleto (*propaganda*)

pan /pæn/ *n* olla, sartén

pancake /'pænkeɪk/ *n* crepe/a

panda /'pændə/ *n* panda

pander /'pændər/ *v* ■ **pander to sth/sb** (*pey*) complacer a algo/algn

pane /peɪn/ *n* cristal: *~ of glass* hoja/lámina de vidrio

panel /'pænl/ *n* **1** panel **2** (*mandos*) tablero **3** (*TV, Radio*) panel **4** jurado **paneled** (**-ll-** GB) *adj* (*revestido*) con paneles **paneling** (**-ll-** GB) *n* revestimiento, páneles

pang /pæŋ/ *n* punzada

panic /'pænɪk/ *n* pánico ● vt, vi (**-ck-**) dejarse llevar por el pánico **panic-stricken** *adj* preso del pánico

pant /pænt/ *vi* jadear

panther /'pænθər/ *n* **1** pantera **2** (*USA*) puma

panties /'pæntiz/ *n* [*pl*] calzones →PAIR

pantomime /'pæntəmaɪm/ *n* (GB) representación teatral navideña

pantry /'pæntri/ n (pl **-ies**) despensa

pants /pænts/ n [pl] **1** (USA) pantalones **2** (GB) calzoncillos, calzones →PAIR

pantyhose /'pæntihəʊz/ n (USA) medias (pantalón), pantimedia

paper /'peɪpər/ n **1** [U] papel: a piece of ~ un papel **2** periódico **3** papel tapiz/de colgadura **4** ~ **papers** [pl] documentación **5 papers** [pl] papeles, papeleo **6** examen (académico) artículo, ponencia ▸ **on paper 1** por escrito **2** en teoría ● **wt** empapelar

paperback /'peɪpəbæk/ n libro de pasta blanda

paper clip n clip (sujetapapeles)

paperwork /'peɪpəwɜːrk/ n [U] **1** papeleo **2** tareas administrativas

par /pɑːr/ n ▸ **below par** en baja forma **on a par with sth/sb** al mismo nivel de algo/algn

parable /'pærəbl/ n parábola (cuento)

parachute /'pærəʃuːt/ n paracaídas

parade /pə'reɪd/ n desfile ● **vi 1** desfilar **2** (Mil) pasar revista **3** **vt** exhibir **4** **vt** (conocimientos) hacer alarde de

paradise /'pærədaɪs/ n paraíso

paradox /'pærədɒks/ n paradoja

paraffin /'pærəfɪn/ n queroseno

paragraph /'pærəgræf, -grɑːf GB/ n párrafo

parallel /'pærəlel/ adj (en) paralelo ● n **1** paralelo **2** paralela

paralyze (**-lyse** GB) /'pærəlaɪz/ vt paralizar **paralysis** /pə'rælɪsɪs/ n **1** parálisis **2** paralización

paramedic /,pærə'medɪk/ n paramédico/a

paramount /'pærəmaʊnt/ adj primordial: of ~ importance de suma importancia

paranoid /'pærənɔɪd/ adj, n **1** paranoico/a **2** maniático/a

paraphrase /'pærəfreɪz/ vt parafrasear

parasite /'pærəsaɪt/ n parásito

parcel /'pɑːrsl/ n paquete →PACKAGE

parched /pɑːrtʃt/ adj **1** reseco **2** (persona) muerto de sed

parchment /'pɑːrtʃmənt/ n pergamino

pardon /'pɑːrdn/ n **1** perdón **2** (Jur) indulto ● **vt** perdonar ▸ **pardon (me)?** ¿cómo dice? **pardon me!** ¡perdón!

parent /'peərənt/ n **1** madre, padre: my ~s mis padres **2** ~ company empresa matriz **parentage**

n **1** ascendencia **2** padres **parenthood** n maternidad, paternidad

parental /pə'rentl/ adj de los padres

parents-in-law n [pl] suegros

parish /'pærɪʃ/ n parroquia: ~ priest párroco

park /pɑːrk/ n **1** parque **2** (USA, Dep) cancha ● **vt**, **vi** estacionar, parquear (And)

parking /'pɑːrkɪŋ/ n [U] estacionamiento: ~ ticket multa por estacionamiento indebido ◇ ~ meter parquímetro ◇ ~ garage estacionamiento/parqueadero de varios pisos

parking lot n (USA) estacionamiento, parqueadero (And)

parkland /'pɑːrklænd/ n zona verde

parliament /'pɑːrləmənt/ n parlamento: Member of Parliament diputado **parliamentary** /,pɑːrlə'mentəri/ adj parlamentario

parlor (**-our** GB) /'pɑːrlər/ n sala (de recibir)

parody /'pærədi/ n (pl **-ies**) parodia

parole /pə'rəʊl/ n libertad condicional

parrot /'pærət/ n loro, papagayo

parsley /'pɑːrsli/ n perejil

parsnip /'pɑːrsnɪp/ n chirivía

part /pɑːrt/ n **1** parte **2** pieza **3** (TV) episodio **4** (Cine, Teat) papel **5 parts** [pl] región **6** (USA, pelo) raya ▸ **for my part** por mi parte **for the most part** por lo general **on the part of sb/on sb's part**: It was an error on my ~. Fue un error de mi parte. **take part (in sth)** tomar parte (en algo) **take sb's part** ponerse de parte de algn **the best/better part of sth** la mayor parte de algo: for the best ~ of a year casi un año ● **vt**, **vi** separar(se) **2** **vt**, **vi** apartar(se) **3** **vt** partir **4** ~ your hair hacerse la raya ▸ **part company (with sb)** separarse, despedirse (de algn) ■ **part with sth** renunciar a algo **2** (dinero) gastar algo

partial /'pɑːrʃl/ adj **1** parcial **2** ~ **to sth** aficionado a algo **partially** adv parcialmente

participate /pɑːr'tɪsɪpeɪt/ vi participar **participant** n participante **participation** n participación

particle /'pɑːrtɪkl/ n partícula

particular /pər'tɪkjələr/ adj **1** (concreto) en particular **2** especial **3** ~ (about sth) exigente (con algo) ● **particulars** n datos **particularly** adv **1** especialmente **2** en particular

parting /'pɑːtɪŋ/ n 1 despedida 2 (GB, pelo) raya

partisan /ˌpɑːtɪ'zæn/ (ˌpɑːtɪ'zæn GB/ adj parcial ● n 1 partidario/a 2 (Mil) partisano/a

partition /pɑː'tɪʃn/ n división

partly /'pɑːtli/ adv en parte

partner /'pɑːtnər/ n 1 pareja 2 (Com) socio/a **partnership** n 1 asociación 2 (Com) sociedad

partridge /'pɑːtrɪdʒ/ n perdiz

part-time adj, adv 1 por horas 2 (curso) de medio tiempo

party /'pɑːti/ n (pl -ies) 1 fiesta 2 (Pol) partido 3 grupo 4 (Jur) parte ▶ **be (a) party to sth** participar en algo

pass /pæs; pɑːs GB/ n 1 (examen) aprobado 2 (permiso, Dep) pase 3 (autobús, etc.) bono 4 (montaña) paso ▶ **make a pass at sb** (coloq) insinuársele a algn ● 1 vt, vi pasar 2 rebasar 3 vt (barrera) cruzar 4 vt (límite) superar 5 vt (examen, ley) aprobar 6 vi suceder ■ **pass around** circular algo **pass as/for sth/sb** ser tomado por algo/algn **pass away** morir **pass by (sth/sb)** pasar al lado (de algo/algn) **pass sth/sb by** dejar algo/a algn de lado **pass sth/sb off as sth/sb** hacer pasar algo/a algn por algo/algn ● **pass out** desmayarse **pass sth up** (coloq) rechazar algo (oportunidad)

passable /'pæsəbl; 'pɑːs- GB/ adj 1 aceptable 2 transitable

passage /'pæsɪdʒ/ n 1 (tb passageway /'pæsɪdʒweɪ/) pasillo 2 (extracto) pasaje 3 paso

passenger /'pæsɪndʒər/ n pasajero/a

passer-by /ˌpæsər 'baɪ/ n (pl passers-by) transeúnte

passing /'pæsɪŋ; 'pɑːs- GB/ adj 1 pasajero 2 (referencia) de pasada 3 (tráfico) que pasa ● n 1 paso 2 (fml) desaparición ▶ **in passing** de pasada

passion /'pæʃn/ n pasión **passionate** /'pæʃənət/ adj apasionado

passive /'pæsɪv/ adj pasivo ● n (tb ~ voice) (voz) pasiva

passport /'pæspɔːt; 'pɑːs- GB/ n pasaporte

password /'pæswɜːrd; 'pɑːs- GB/ n contraseña →COMPUTADORA

past /pæst; pɑːst GB/ adj 1 pasado 2 antiguo 3 último: the ~ few days los últimos días 4 (tiempo) acabado ● n 1 pasado 2 pretérito ● prep 1 half ~ one la una y media ◊ ~ midnight pasada la medianoche ◊ It's ~ two. Son las dos

pasadas. 2 (con verbos de movimiento): walk ~ sth/sb pasar por delante de algo/algn 3 más allá de, después de: It's ~ your bedtime. Ya debías estar acostada. ▶ **not put it past sb (to do sth)** creer a algn capaz (de hacer algo) ● adv al lado, por delante

pasta /'pɑːstə/ n [U] pasta

paste /peɪst/ n 1 pasta, masa 2 engrudo 3 paté ● vt pegar

pastime /'pæstaɪm; 'pɑːs- GB/ n pasatiempo

pastor /'pæstər; 'pɑːs- GB/ n pastor, sacerdote

pastoral /'pæstərəl; 'pɑːs- GB/ adj 1 bucólico 2 ~ care/duties atención/orientación personal

pastry /'peɪstri/ n (pl -ies) 1 masa (pay, etc.) 2 (pl -ies) pastel

pasture /'pæstʃər; 'pɑːs- GB/ n pasto

pat /pæt/ vt (-tt-) 1 dar golpecitos/una palmadita a 2 acariciar ● n 1 palmadita 2 caricia ▶ **give sb a pat on the back** felicitar a algn

patch /pætʃ/ n 1 parche 2 zona 3 (color) mancha 4 pedazo de tierra (para verduras, etc.) ▶ **go through/hit a bad patch** (coloq) pasar una mala racha **not be a patch on sth/sb** (coloq) no tener ni comparación con algo/algn ● vt remendar ■ **patch sth up** 1 parchar algo 2 resolver algo **patchy** adj (-ier/-iest) 1 irregular: ~ rain/fog chubascos/bancos de niebla 2 desigual 3 (conocimientos) con lagunas

patchwork /'pætʃwɜːrk/ n 1 labor manual a base de retazos cosidos en tela 2 (fig) tapiz

patent /'pætnt; 'peɪtnt GB/ n patente ● adj 1 patente 2 (Com) patentado ● vt patentar **patently** adv claramente

paternal /pə'tɜːrnl/ adj 1 paternal 2 paterno

paternity /pə'tɜːrnəti/ n paternidad

path /pæθ; pɑːθ GB/ n 1 sendero 2 paso 3 trayectoria 4 camino

pathetic /pə'θetɪk/ adj 1 patético 2 (coloq) lamentable

pathology /pə'θɑːlədʒi/ n patología **pathological** /ˌpæθə'lɑːdʒɪkl/ adj patológico

pathos /'peɪθɑːs/ n patetismo

patient /'peɪʃnt/ n paciente ● adj paciente **patience** [U] n 1 paciencia 2 (GB, cartas) solitario

patio /'pætioʊ/ n (pl -s) 1 terraza 2 patio

patriarch /'peɪtriɑːrk/ n patriarca

patriot /'peɪtriət/ n patriota **patriotic** /ˌpeɪtri'ɑːtɪk/ adj patriótico

patrol /pə'trəʊl/ vt, vi (-ll-) **1** patrullar **2** (guardia) hacer la ronda (por) ● n patrulla

patron /'peɪtrən/ n **1** patrocinador/a **2** mecenas **3** cliente **patronage** /'pætrənɪdʒ/ n **1** patrocinio **2** (cliente) apoyo **3** patronazgo

patronize /'peɪtrənaɪz; 'pæt- GB/ vt tratar condescendientemente a **patronizing** adj condescendiente

pattern /'pætərn/ n **1** estampado, dibujo **2** (costura) patrón **3** tendencia **patterned** adj estampado

pause /pɔːz/ n pausa ● vi hacer una pausa, pararse

pave /peɪv/ vt pavimentar ▶ **pave the way** (for) preparar el camino (para algo/algn) **paving** n pavimento: ~ stone losa

pavement /'peɪvmənt/ n **1** (USA) pavimento **2** (GB) acera, banqueta (Mx)

pavilion /pə'vɪliən/ n **1** pabellón **2** quiosco

paw /pɔː/ n **1** pata **2** (coloq) mano ● vt manosear

pawn /pɔːn/ n (ajedrez) peón ● vt empeñar

pawnbroker /'pɔːnbrəʊkər/ n prestamista

pay /peɪ/ n [U] sueldo: ~ claim/day reclamación salarial/día de paga ● (pt/pp paid) **1** vt, vi ~ (sb) (for sth) pagar (algo) (a algn) **2** vi ser rentable **3** vt, vi valer la pena **4** vt, vi compensar **5** ~ attention to sth prestar atención a algo ◇ ~ sb a compliment/visit hacer un cumplido/visitar a algn ■ **pay sb back** (sth); **pay sb back sth** devolver algo (a algn) **pay sth in** depositar, consignar algo **pay off** (coloq) dar fruto, valer la pena **pay sb off** pagar y despedir a algn **pay sth off** terminar de pagar algo **pay up** pagar del todo **payable** adj pagadero

payment /'peɪmənt/ n pago: in/as ~ for sth como recompensa/en pago por algo

pay-off n (pl -offs) (coloq) **1** pago, soborno **2** recompensa

payroll /'peɪrəʊl/ n nómina

PC /ˌpiː 'siː/ abrev, n (pl PCs) **1** personal computer computador(a) personal **2** police constable (GB) policía ● adj políticamente correcto **NOTA** Describe la práctica cada vez más común de evitar usar expresiones peyorativas al referirse a ciertos grupos sociales.

P.E. /ˌpiː 'iː/ n (abrev de physical education) educación física

pea /piː/ n arveja, chícharo (Mx)

peace /piːs/ n **1** paz **2** tranquilidad: ~ of mind tranquilidad ◇ at ~ with sth en armonía con algo ▶ **make (your) peace** hacer las paces **peaceful** adj **1** pacífico **2** tranquilo

peach /piːtʃ/ n **1** durazno **2** (tb ~ tree) duraznero

peacock /'piːkɒk/ (fem peahen /'piːhen/) n pavo real

peak /piːk/ n **1** (montaña) pico **2** punta **3** visera **4** punto máximo ● adj máximo: ~ hours horas pico ◇ in ~ condition en condiciones óptimas ● vi alcanzar el punto máximo **peaked** adj **1** en punta **2** con visera

peal /piːl/ n **1** (campanas) repique **2** (risa) carcajada

peanut /'piːnʌt/ n **1** cacahuate, maní **2** peanuts (coloq) una miseria

pear /peər/ n **1** pera **2** (tb ~ tree) peral

pearl /pɜːrl/ n **1** perla **2** (fig) joya

peasant /'pezənt/ n **1** campesino/a → CAMPESINO/A **2** (coloq) palurdo/a, ordinario/a

peat /piːt/ n turba (carbón)

pebble /'pebl/ n guijarro, piedrita

peck /pek/ **1** vt, vi picotear **2** vt (coloq) dar un besito a ▶ **pecking order** (coloq) orden jerárquico ● n **1** picotazo **2** (coloq) besito

peckish /'pekɪʃ/ adj (GB, coloq): feel ~ tener un poco de hambre

peculiar /pɪ'kjuːliər/ adj **1** extraño **2** ~ (to sth/sb) peculiar (de algo/algn) **peculiarity** /pɪˌkjuːli'ærəti/ n (pl -ies) peculiaridad **2** [U] rarezas **peculiarly** adv **1** especialmente **2** característicamente **3** de una manera extraña

pedal /'pedl/ n pedal ● vi (-l-, -ll- GB) pedalear

pedantic /pɪ'dæntɪk/ adj **1** maniático **2** pedante **3** cursi

pedestrian /pə'destriən/ n peatón ● adj **1** peatonal **2** pedestre

pediatrician (paedi- GB) /ˌpiːdiə'trɪʃn/ n pediatra

pedigree /'pedɪɡriː/ n **1** pedigrí **2** genealogía **3** casta ● adj con pedigrí, de raza

pee /piː/ vi (coloq) hacer pis/pipí ● n (coloq) pis, pipí

peek /piːk/ vi ~ at sth/sb echar una mirada furtiva a algo/algn

peel /piːl/ **1** vt, vi pelar(se) **2** vt, vi ~ (sth)(away/back/off) despegar(se) (algo) **3** vi ~ (away/off) (pintura) desprenderse ● n [U] **1** piel **2** corteza

3 cáscara **NOTA** Para cáscaras duras (p.ej. nuez, huevo), se usa **shell**. La corteza del limón es **rind** o **peel**, pero para la naranja sólo se dice **peel**. **Skin** se usa para el plátano y para otras frutas con piel más fina.

peeler /'pi:lər/ n mondador: *potato ~* pelapapas

peep /pi:p/ vi 1 ~ **at sth/sb** echar una mirada (cautelosa) a algo/ algn → MIRAR 2 ~ **over, through, etc. (sth)** atisbar, asomarse por encima de, por, etc. algo ● n 1 vistazo 2 pío

peer /pɪər/ vi 1 ~ **at sth/sb** mirar algo/a algn (*esp con esfuerzo*) → MIRAR 2 ~ **out (of sth)** sacar la cabeza (por algo) ● n 1 igual 2 contemporáneo/a 3 (*GB*) noble **the peerage** n la nobleza

peeved /pi:vd/ adj molesto

peg /peg/ n 1 (*en pared*) percha 2 (*GB*) (*tb clothes ~*) gancho ♦ **bring/take sb down a peg (or two)** bajarle a algn los humos ● vt (**-gg-**) 1 (*precios, etc.*) fijar (*el nivel de*) 2 ~ **sth (out)** tender algo

pejorative /pɪ'dʒɒrətɪv; -'dʒɔr-GB/ adj (*fml*) peyorativo

pelican /'pelɪkən/ n pelícano

pellet /'pelɪt/ n 1 bolita 2 perdigón 3 gránulo

pelt /pelt/ n 1 pellejo 2 piel ● 1 vt ~ **sb with sth** tirar cosas a algn 2 vi ~ **(down)** llover a cántaros 3 (*coloq*) a toda velocidad *por algún sitio*

pelvis /'pelvɪs/ n pelvis **pelvic** adj pélvico

pen /pen/ n 1 bolígrafo, esfero (*And*) 2 corral 3 (*ovejas*) redil

penalize /'pi:nəlaɪz/ vt 1 penalizar, sancionar 2 perjudicar

penalty /'penəlti/ n (pl **-ies**) 1 (*castigo*) pena 2 multa 3 desventaja 4 (*Dep*) penalización 5 (*fútbol*) penalty, penal (*And*)

pence /pens/ n [pl] (*abrev* **p**) peniques

pencil /'pensl/ n lápiz

pencil case n estuche (*lápices*)

pencil sharpener /'pensl ʃɑːrpənər/ n sacapuntas

pendant /'pendənt/ n colgante

pending /'pendɪŋ/ (*fml*) adj pendiente ● *prep* en espera de

pendulum /'pendʒələm; -djə- GB/ n péndulo

penetrate /'penɪtreɪt/ 1 vt, vi penetrar: ~ *into/through sth* introducirse en/atravesar algo 2 vt infiltrar **penetrating** adj 1 penetrante 2 perspicaz

penfriend /'penfrend/ n (*GB*) amigo/a por correspondencia

penguin /'peŋgwɪn/ n pingüino

penicillin /,penɪ'sɪlɪn/ n penicilina

peninsula /pə'nɪnsələ; -sjələ GB/ n península

penis /'pi:nɪs/ n pene

penknife /'pennaɪf/ n (pl **-knives** /-naɪvz/) navaja

penny /'peni/ n 1 (pl **pence** (*abrev* **p**) (*GB*) penique → *Ver* pág. 224 2 (pl **-ies**) (*Can, USA*) centavo **penniless** adj sin dinero

pen pal n amigo/a por correspondencia

pension /'penʃn/ n pensión ■ **pension sb off** jubilar a algn **pensioner** n jubilado/a

pent-up adj 1 (*ira, etc.*) contenido 2 (*deseo*) reprimido

penultimate /pen'ʌltɪmət/ adj penúltimo

people /'pi:pl/ n 1 [pl] gente 2 [pl] personas → PERSON 3 **the people** [pl] el pueblo 4 (*nación*) pueblo ● vt poblar

pepper /'pepər/ n 1 pimienta 2 (*GB*) (*bell ~ USA*) (*legumbre*) pimiento, pimentón (*And*)

peppercorn /'pepərkɔːrn/ n grano de pimienta

peppermint /'pepərmɪnt/ n 1 menta 2 (*dulce de*) menta

per /pər/ prep por: *sixty dollars ~ day* $60 al día ◊ ~ *annum* al año

perceive /pər'siːv/ vt (*fml*) 1 percibir, observar 2 interpretar

percent /pər'sent/ (*tb* **per cent** GB) adj, adv, n por ciento **percentage** /pər'sentɪdʒ/ n porcentaje: ~ *increase* aumento porcentual

perception /pər'sepʃn/ n (*fml*) 1 percepción 2 perspicacia 3 punto de vista **perceptible** adj 1 perceptible 2 (*cambio*) sensible **perceptive** adj perspicaz

perch /pɜːrtʃ/ n 1 (*para pájaros*) percha 2 posición (*elevada*) 3 (*pez*) perca ● vi 1 posarse 2 encaramarse **perched** adj 1 posado 2 encaramado

percussion /pər'kʌʃn/ n percusión

perennial /pə'reniəl/ adj perenne

perfect /pər'fekt/ vt perfeccionar ● /'pɜːrfɪkt/ adj 1 perfecto 2 ideal 3 [*antes de sustantivo*] completo **perfectly** adv 1 completamente 2 perfectamente

perfection /pər'fekʃn/ n perfección **perfectionist** n perfeccionista

perforate /ˈpɜːrfəreɪt/ vt perforar **perforation** n 1 perforación 2 perforado

perform /pərˈfɔːrm/ 1 vt (función) desempeñar 2 vt (operación) realizar 3 vt (compromiso) cumplir 4 vt (Teat, etc.) representar 5 vt (Mús) interpretar 6 vi actuar **performer** n 1 (Mús) intérprete 2 (Teat) actor, actriz 3 (variedades) artista

performance /pərˈfɔːrməns/ n 1 rendimiento 2 (tareas) cumplimiento 3 (Econ) resultados 4 (Cine, Teat) función, representación 5 (Mús) actuación, interpretación

perfume /ˈpɜːfjuːm; pɜːˈfjuːm GB/ n perfume

perhaps /pərˈhæps/ adv quizá(s), tal vez, a lo mejor

peril /ˈperəl/ n peligro, riesgo **perimeter** /pəˈrɪmɪtər/ n perímetro

period /ˈpɪəriəd/ n 1 período: over a ~ of a year a lo largo de un año 2 época 3 (Educ) clase 4 (Med) período 5 (USA, Gram) punto (y seguido) **periodic** /ˌpɪəriˈɑdɪk/ adj periódico

periodical /ˌpɪəriˈɑdɪkl/ n revista ● adj periódico

perish /ˈperɪʃ/ vi (fml) fallecer, perecer **perishable** adj perecedero

perjury /ˈpɜːrdʒəri/ n perjurio

perk /pɜːrk/ n beneficio (adicional) (de un trabajo) ● **perk up** (coloq) 1 animarse 2 mejorar

perm /pɜːrm/ n permanente ● vt: have your hair permed hacerse un/la permanente

permanent /ˈpɜːrmənənt/ adj 1 permanente, fijo 2 (daño) irreparable

permission /pərˈmɪʃn/ n permiso, autorización **permissible** adj permisible, admisible **permissive** adj permisivo

permit /pərˈmɪt/ vt, vi (-tt-) (fml) permitir: If time permits... Si da tiempo... → ALLOW ● /ˈpɜːrmɪt/ n 1 permiso, autorización 2 pase

perpendicular /ˌpɜːrpənˈdɪkjələr/ adj perpendicular

perpetrate /ˈpɜːrpətreɪt/ vt (fml) perpetrar

perpetual /pərˈpetʃuəl/ adj 1 perpetuo 2 constante

perpetuate /pərˈpetʃueɪt/ vt perpetuar

perplexed /pərˈplekst/ adj perplejo

persecute /ˈpɜːrsɪkjuːt/ vt perseguir (por raza, religión, etc.) **persecution** n persecución

persevere /ˌpɜːrsɪˈvɪər/ vi 1 perseverar 2 seguir insistiendo **perseverance** n perseverancia

persist /pərˈsɪst/ vi 1 empeñarse, insistir 2 continuar 3 persistir **persistence** n 1 perseverancia 2 persistencia **persistent** adj 1 porfiado 2 persistente

person /ˈpɜːrsn/ n persona **NOTA** El plural de **person** suele ser **people**: ten people. **Persons** es más formal: a list of missing ~s. ▸ **in person** en persona

personal /ˈpɜːrsənl/ adj personal: get ~ llevar las cosas a lo personal **personalized** adj 1 personalizado 2 marcado con las iniciales de uno 3 con membrete **personally** adv personalmente ▸ **take sth personally** ofenderse por algo

personality /ˌpɜːrsəˈnæləti/ n (pl -ies) personalidad

personify /pərˈsɑnɪfaɪ/ vt (pt/pp -ied) personificar

personnel /ˌpɜːrsəˈnel/ n (departamento de) personal

perspective /pərˈspektɪv/ n perspectiva: get/put sth into ~ poner algo en perspectiva

perspire /pərˈspaɪər/ vi (fml) transpirar **perspiration** n 1 sudor 2 transpiración **NOTA** Es más común **sweat**.

persuade /pərˈsweɪd/ vt 1 ~ sb to do sth persuadir a algn de que haga algo 2 convencer **persuasion** n 1 persuasión 2 creencia **persuasive** adj 1 convincente 2 persuasivo

pertinent /ˈpɜːrtnənt; -tɪnənt GB/ adj (fml) pertinente

perturb /pərˈtɜːrb/ vt perturbar

pervade /pərˈveɪd/ vt 1 (olor) extenderse por 2 (luz) difundirse por 3 (obra) impregnar **pervasive** adj generalizado

perverse /pərˈvɜːrs/ adj 1 (persona) mal intencionado 2 (decisión, etc.) malo 3 perverso **perversion** n 1 corrupción 2 perversión 3 tergiversación

pervert /pərˈvɜːrt/ vt 1 tergiversar 2 corromper ● /ˈpɜːrvɜːrt/ n pervertido/a

pessimism /ˈpesɪmɪzəm/ n pesimismo **pessimist** n pesimista **pessimistic** /ˌpesɪˈmɪstɪk/ adj pesimista

pest /pest/ n 1 insecto/animal dañino: ~ control control de plagas 2 (coloq) molestia

pester /ˈpestər/ vt molestar

pesticide /ˈpestɪsaɪd/ n pesticida

pet /pet/ n 1 animal doméstico 2 (pey) favorito/a ● adj 1 predilecto **2** domesticado ● *vt* acariciar

petal /'petl/ *n* pétalo

peter /'pi:tər/ *v* ■ **peter out** agotarse poco a poco

petition /pə'tɪʃn/ *n* petición

petrol /'petrəl/ *n* (GB) gasolina: ~ *station* gasolinera

petroleum /pə'trəʊliəm/ *n* petróleo

petticoat /'petɪkəʊt/ *n* enaguas

petty /'peti/ *adj* (*pey*) **1** insignificante **2** (*delito, gasto*) menor: ~ *cash* dinero para gastos menores **3** (*conducta*) mezquino

pew /pju:/ *n* banco de iglesia

phantom /'fæntəm/ *n* fantasma ● *adj* ilusorio

pharmaceutical /ˌfɑːmə-'suːtɪkl; -'sjuː- *GB*/ *adj* farmacéutico

pharmacy /'fɑːməsi/ *n* (*pl* -ies) farmacia **pharmacist** *n* farmacéutico/a

phase /feɪz/ *n* fase ● *vt* escalonar: ~ *sth in/out* introducir/retirar algo paulatinamente

Ph. D. /ˌpiː eɪtʃ 'diː/ *n* doctorado

pheasant /'feznt/ *n* faisán

phenomenon /fə'nɒmɪnən/ *n* (*pl* -mena /-mɪnə/) fenómeno **phenomenal** *adj* fenomenal

phew *interj* uf

philanthropist /fɪ'lænθrəpɪst/ *n* filántropo/a

philosophy /fə'lɒsəfi/ *n* (*pl* -ies) filosofía **philosopher** *n* filósofo/a **philosophical** /ˌfɪlə'sɒfɪkl/ *adj* filosófico

phlegm /flem/ *n* flema **phlegmatic** /fleg'mætɪk/ *adj* flemático

phobia /'fəʊbiə/ *n* fobia

phone /fəʊn/ *Ver* TELEPHONE

phone box *n* (GB) cabina/caseta (telefónica)

phonecard /'fəʊnkɑːd/ *n* (GB) tarjeta telefónica

phone-in *n* (*pl* -ins) (GB) programa de radio o televisión abierto a las llamadas del público

phonetic /fə'netɪk/ *adj* fonético ● **phonetics** *n* [U] fonética

phony (**phoney** GB) /'fəʊni/ *adj* (-ier/-iest) (*coloq*) falso

photocopy /'fəʊtəʊkɒpi/ *vt* (*pt/ pp* -ied) fotocopiar ● *n* (*pl* -ies) fotocopia **photocopier** *n* fotocopiadora

photograph /'fəʊtəgrɑːf; -grɑːf *GB*/ *n* (tb **photo** /'fəʊtəʊ/ (*pl* -s)) fotografía: *take a* ~ sacar una foto ● **1** *vt* fotografiar **2** *vi* salir en una foto **photographer** /fə'tɒgrəfər/ *n* fotógrafo/a **photographic** /ˌfəʊtə'græfɪk/ *adj* foto-

gráfico **photography** /fə'tɒgrəfi/ *n* fotografía

phrasal verb /ˌfreɪzl 'vɜːrb/ *n* verbo con preposición o partícula adverbial

phrase /freɪz/ *n* **1** (*Gram*) locución **2** expresión, frase: ~ *book* guía de conversación (para viajeros) ● *vt* **1** expresar **2** (*Mús*) frasear

physical /'fɪzɪkl/ *adj* físico ● *n* revisión médica **physically** *adv* físicamente: ~ *fit/handicapped* en buena forma/minusválido

physician /fɪ'zɪʃn/ *n* (*fml*) médico/a **NOTA** Es más común **doctor**.

physics /'fɪzɪks/ *n* [*sing*] física **physicist** /'fɪzɪsɪst/ *n* físico/a

physiology /ˌfɪzi'ɒlədʒi/ *n* fisiología

physiotherapy /ˌfɪziəʊ'θerəpi/ *n* fisioterapia **physiotherapist** *n* fisioterapeuta

physique /fɪ'ziːk/ *n* físico

piano /pi'ænəʊ/ *n* (*pl* -s) piano **pianist** /'pɪənɪst/ *n* pianista

pick /pɪk/ *n* **1** (derecho de) elección: *Take your* ~. Escoge el/la que quieras. **2** the ~ of sth lo mejor de algo **3** pico (*herramienta*) ● **1** *vt* elegir **2** *vt* (*flor*) cortar **3** *vt* (*fruta*) recoger **4** *vt* escarbar: ~ *your teeth* escarbarse los dientes ◊ ~ *your nose* meterse el dedo a la nariz ◊ ~ *a hole in sth* hacer un agujero en algo **5** *vt* ~ **sth from/off sth** quitar, recoger algo de algo **6** *vt* (*cerradura*) forzar **7** *vi* ~ **at sth** comer algo con poca gana ▸ **pick a fight/ quarrel** buscar pelea **pick and choose** ser muy exigente **pick holes in sth** encontrar defectos en algo **pick sb's brains** (*coloq*) explotar los conocimientos de algn **pick sb's pocket** robarle la cartera a algn **pick up speed** cobrar velocidad ■ **pick on sb** **1** abusar de algn **2** elegir a algn (*para algo desagradable*) **pick sth out** **1** identificar algo **2** destacar algo **pick sth up** **1** escoger algo/a algn **2** (*en un grupo, etc.*) distinguir algo/a algn **pick up 1** mejorar algo **2** (*viento*) soplar más fuerte **pick sb up 1** (*ir a*) recoger a algn **2** (*coloq*) ligar con algn **3** (*coloq*) detener a algn **pick sth up 1** aprender algo **2** (*enfermedad, costumbre*) agarrar algo **pick sth/sb up** (re)coger algo/a algn **pick yourself up** levantarse

pickle /'pɪkl/ *n* **1** encurtidos **2** vinagre ▸ **in a pickle** (*coloq*) en un lío

pickpocket /'pɪkpɒkɪt/ n carterista

picnic /'pɪknɪk/ n picnic

pictorial /pɪk'tɔːriəl/ adj 1 gráfico 2 (Arte) pictórico

picture /'pɪktʃər/ n 1 cuadro 2 ilustración 3 foto 4 retrato 5 imagen 6 película ▸ **be/look a picture** ser una preciosidad **put sb in the picture** poner a algn al corriente ● vt 1 ~ **yourself** imaginarse 2 retratar

picturesque /ˌpɪktʃə'resk/ adj pintoresco

pie /paɪ/ n pay, pie **NOTA** Un pie tiene tapa de masa y relleno dulce o salado. **Tart** y **flan** son pays dulces sin tapa.

piece /piːs/ n 1 pedazo, trozo 2 pieza: take sth to ~s desarmar algo 3 ~ **of paper** papel 4 a ~ **of advice/news** un consejo/una noticia → CONSEJO 5 (Mús) obra 6 (Period) artículo 7 moneda ▸ a **piece of cake** (coloq) pan comido **in one piece** (coloq) sano y salvo ■ **piece sth together** 1 (pruebas, etc.) juntar algo 2 (pasado) reconstruir algo

piecemeal /'piːsmiːl/ adv poco a poco ● adj gradual

pier /pɪər/ n embarcadero, malecón

pierce /pɪərs/ vt 1 (cuchillo, bala) atravesar 2 perforar: have your ears pierced hacerse agujeros en las orejas 3 (sonido, etc.) penetrar en **piercing** adj 1 agudo 2 penetrante

piety /'paɪəti/ n (Rel) piedad

pig /pɪg/ n 1 cerdo → CARNE, CERDO 2 (coloq) tragón/ona

pigeon /'pɪdʒɪn/ n 1 paloma 2 pichón

pigeon-hole n casillero

piglet /'pɪglət/ n cerdito → CERDO

pigment /'pɪgmənt/ n pigmento

pigsty /'pɪgstaɪ/ n (pl -ies) pocilga, chiquero

pigtail /'pɪgteɪl/ n coleta, colita

pile /paɪl/ n montón ● vt, vi ~ **(sth) (up)** amontonar(se) (algo) 2 vi ~ **in/out/on** entrar/salir en tropel

piles /paɪlz/ n hemorroides

pile-up n (pl -ups) (Aut) choque múltiple

pilgrim /'pɪlgrɪm/ n peregrino/a **pilgrimage** /'pɪlgrɪmɪdʒ/ n peregrinación

pill /pɪl/ n 1 píldora 2 **the pill** la píldora (anticonceptiva)

pillar /'pɪlər/ n pilar

pillow /'pɪloʊ/ n almohada

pillowcase /'pɪloʊkeɪs/ n funda de almohada

pilot /'paɪlət/ n 1 piloto 2 (TV) programa piloto ● adj piloto

pimple /'pɪmpl/ n grano (piel)

PIN /pɪn/ (tb ~ number) n (abrev de personal identification number) clave secreta (tarjeta)

pin /pɪn/ n 1 alfiler 2 broche 3 clavija, borne ▸ **pins and needles** hormigueo ● vt (-nn-) 1 (con alfileres) prender 2 sujetar ■ **pin sb down** 1 (en el suelo) inmovilizar a algn 2 hacer que algn concrete

pincer /'pɪnsər/ n pinza → PAIR

pinch /pɪntʃ/ n 1 vt pellizcar 2 vt, vi (zapatos) apretar 3 vt ratear ● n 1 pellizco 2 pizca ▸ **in/at** (GB) **a pinch** en caso de necesidad

pine /paɪn/ n (tb ~ tree) pino ● vi 1 ~ **(away)** languidecer 2 ~ **for sth/sb** añorar algo/a algn

pineapple /'paɪnæpl/ n piña

ping /pɪŋ/ n 1 sonido (metálico) 2 (bala) silbido

ping-pong® /'pɪŋ pɒŋ/ n (coloq) ping-pong®

pink /pɪŋk/ adj 1 rosa, rosado 2 (de vergüenza) colorado ● n 1 rosa 2 (Bot) clavellina **pinkish** adj rosáceo

pinnacle /'pɪnəkl/ n 1 cúspide 2 pináculo 3 (montaña) pico

pinpoint /'pɪnpɔɪnt/ vt 1 localizar exactamente 2 precisar

pint /paɪnt/ n 1 (abrev pt) pinta (0,473 litros, 0,568 litros GB) → Ver pág. 222 3 (GB) have a ~ tomar una cerveza

pin-up n (pl -ups) foto (de persona atractiva, clavada en la pared)

pioneer /ˌpaɪə'nɪər/ n pionero/a ● vt ser pionero en **pioneering** adj pionero

pious /'paɪəs/ adj 1 piadoso, devoto 2 (pey) beato

pip /pɪp/ n pepa, pepita

pipe /paɪp/ n 1 tubería, conducto 2 pipes [pl] cañería(s) 3 pipa 4 (Mús) flauta 5 pipes [pl] Ver BAGPIPES ● vt trasportar (por tubería) ▸ **piping hot** hirviendo ■ **pipe down** (coloq) callarse

pipeline /'paɪplaɪn/ n 1 tubería, gasoducto, oleoducto ▸ **be in the pipeline** 1 estar tramitándose 2 estar preparándose

pirate /'paɪrət/ n pirata ● vt piratear **piracy** n piratería

Pisces /'paɪsiːz/ n Piscis

pistol /'pɪstl/ n pistola

piston /'pɪstən/ n pistón

pit /pɪt/ n 1 foso 2 (*carbón*) pozo 3 (*fruta*) hueso 4 **the pit(s)** (*Aut*) los pits 5 **the pit** (*Teat*) platea ▸ **be the pits** (*coloq*) ser pésimo ● v (-tt-) ■ **pit sth/sb against sth/sb** enfrentar algo/a algn con algo/algn

pitch /pɪtʃ/ n 1 (*GB, Dep*) cancha 2 (*Mús*) tono 3 (*tejado*) inclinación 4 (*GB*) puesto (*mercado, etc.*) 5 brea ● v 1 montar (*tienda, carpa*) 2 vt lanzar, arrojar 3 vt tirarse 4 vi (*barco*) cabecear ■ **pitch in (with sth)** (*coloq*) colaborar (con algo) **pitched** *adj* (*batalla*) campal

pitcher /ˈpɪtʃər/ n 1 jarra 2 (*GB*) cántaro 3 (*USA, Dep*) pitcher

pitfall /ˈpɪtfɔːl/ n escollo

pith /pɪθ/ n médula, meollo

pity /ˈpɪti/ n 1 compasión, pesar: *take ~ on sb* apiadarse de algn 2 lástima ● vt (*pt/pp* -ied) compadecerse de: *I ~ you.* Me das lástima. **pitiful** *adj* 1 conmovedor 2 penoso **pitiless** *adj* 1 despiadado 2 implacable

pivot /ˈpɪvət/ n 1 pivote 2 (*fig*) eje

pizza /ˈpiːtsə/ n pizza

placard /ˈplækɑːd/ n pancarta

placate /pləˈkeɪt; ˈpleɪkeɪt *GB*/ vt apaciguar a

place /pleɪs/ n 1 sitio, lugar 2 (*en superficie*) parte 3 (*asiento, posición*) puesto, sitio 4 *It's not my ~ to...* No me compete... 5 casa ▸ **all over the place** (*coloq*) 1 en todas partes 2 en desorden **in place** en su sitio **in the first, second, etc. place** en primer, segundo, etc. lugar **out of place** 1 desplazado 2 fuera de lugar **take place** ocurrir ● vt 1 poner, colocar 2 identificar a 3 ~ **sth (with sth/sb)** (*pedido, apuesta*) hacer algo (en algo/a algn) 4 situar

plague /pleɪɡ/ n 1 peste 2 plaga ● vt 1 atormentar 2 acosar

plaice /pleɪs/ n (*pl* **plaice**) platija

plain /pleɪn/ *adj* (-er/-est) 1 claro: *make sth ~* dejar algo claro 2 franco, directo 3 sencillo: ~ *flour/chocolate* harina (sin levadura)/chocolate negro 4 liso, en blanco, sin dibujo 5 (*físico*) sin atractivo, simple ● *adv* simplemente **plainly** *adv* 1 claramente 2 evidentemente **plain clothes** *adj* de civil

plaintiff /ˈpleɪntɪf/ n (*Jur*) demandante

plait /plæt/ n (*GB*) trenza

plan /plæn/ n 1 plan, programa 2 plano 3 esquema ● (-nn-) 1 vt planear: *What do you ~ to do?*

¿Qué piensas hacer? 2 vi hacer planes ■ **plan sth out** planificar algo

plane /pleɪn/ n 1 avión 2 plano 3 cepillo (de carpintero)

planet /ˈplænɪt/ n planeta

plank /plæŋk/ n 1 tabla, tablón 2 (*Pol*) elemento fundamental

planning /ˈplænɪŋ/ n 1 planificación: ~ *permission* licencia de construcción 2 (*tb* **town ~**) urbanismo **planner** n 1 planificador/a 2 urbanista

plant /plænt; plɑːnt *GB*/ n 1 planta: ~ *pot* maceta/matera (*And*) 2 (*Mec*) maquinaria 3 fábrica: *power ~* central eléctrica ● vt 1 plantar 2 sembrar 3 colocar (*objeto incriminatorio*)

plantation /plænˈteɪʃn; plɑːnˈ *GB*/ n 1 plantación 2 área forestal (*para uso comercial*)

plaque /plæk; plɑːk *GB*/ n placa

plaster /ˈplæstər; ˈplɑːs- *GB*/ n 1 yeso: *put sth in* ~ enyesar algo 2 (*GB*) curita ● vt 1 enyesar 2 embadurnar 3 cubrir

plastic /ˈplæstɪk/ *adj, n* plástico

Plasticine® /ˈplæstəsiːn/ n (*GB*) plastilina®

plate /pleɪt/ n 1 plato 2 (*metal, etc.*) placa, plancha: ~ *glass* vidrio templado 3 hoja, baño (*oro, plata*) 4 (*imprenta*) lámina

plateau /ˈplætəʊ; plæˈtəʊ *GB*/ n meseta

platform /ˈplætfɔːm/ n 1 tribuna, plataforma 2 andén 3 (*Pol*) programa

platinum /ˈplætɪnəm/ n platino

platoon /pləˈtuːn/ n (*Mil*) pelotón

plausible /ˈplɔːzəbl/ *adj* 1 creíble 2 (*persona*) convincente

play /pleɪ/ n 1 (*Teat*) obra 2 (*movimiento, interacción*) juego: *a ~ on words* un juego de palabras ▸ **in play** en broma ● 1 vt, vi ~ **(sb)** jugar (con/contra algn) →DEPORTE 2 vt, vi (*instrumento*) tocar: ~ *sth by ear* tocar algo de oído 3 vt (*CD, etc.*) poner 4 vi (*música*) sonar 5 vt (*pelota*) pegar 6 vt (*broma*) hacer 7 vt (*papel*) interpretar 8 vt, vi (*obra, etc.*) representar(se) 9 vt hacer(se): ~ *the fool* hacer el tonto ▸ **play it by ear** (*coloq*) improvisar según va la marcha ■ **play along (with sb)** seguirle la corriente a (algn) **play sth down** restar importancia a algo **play A off (against B)** A enfrentar a A y B **play (sb) up** (*coloq*) dar guerra (a algn) **player** n 1 jugador/a 2 (*Mús*) músico **playful** *adj* 1

P

juguetón **2** alegre **3** (*comentario*) en broma

playground /'pleɪgraʊnd/ *n* patio (de recreo), parque infantil

playgroup /'pleɪgruːp/ *n* (*GB*) preescolar, kínder

playing card *n* carta, naipe

playing field *n* campo deportivo

play-off *n* (*pl* -offs) partido de desempate

playpen /'pleɪpen/ *n* corral (*bebé*)

playtime /'pleɪtaɪm/ *n* recreo

playwright /'pleɪraɪt/ *n* dramaturgo/a

plea /pliː/ *n* **1** ~ (**for sth**) petición (de algo): *make a* ~ *for sth* pedir algo **2** súplica **3** pretexto **4** (*Jur*) declaración, alegación

plead /pliːd/ (*pt/pp* pleaded *o tb* pled /pled/ (*USA*)) **1** *vi* ~ suplicar (a algn) **2** *vi* ~ **for sb** pedir algo **3** *vi* ~ **for sb** hablar en favor de algn **4** *vt* (*defensa*) alegar ▸ **plead guilty/not guilty** declararse culpable/inocente

pleasant /'pleznt/ *adj* (**-er/-est**) agradable **pleasantly** *adv* **1** agradablemente **2** con amabilidad

please /pliːz/ **1** *vt, vi* complacer **2** *vi* querer: *for as long as you* ~ todo el tiempo que quieras ◇ *whatever I* ~ lo que me dé la gana ▸ **please yourself!** (*coloq*) ¡Haz lo que te dé la gana! ● *interj* por favor: *Please come in.* Por favor, siga. ◇ *Please do not smoke.* Se ruega no fumar. ▸ **please do!** ¡por supuesto! **pleased** *adj* **1** contento → GLAD **2** satisfecho ▸ **be pleased to do sth** tener el placer de hacer algo: *I'd be* ~ *to come.* Me encantaría ir. **pleased to meet you** encantado de conocerlo **pleasing** *adj* agradable

pleasure /'pleʒər/ *n* placer: *take* ~ *in sth* disfrutar con algo ▸ **with pleasure** (*fml*) con mucho gusto **pleasurable** *adj* placentero

pledge /pledʒ/ *n* **1** promesa, compromiso **2** fianza ● *vt* prometer, comprometerse

plentiful /'plentɪfl/ *adj* abundante: *be in* ~ *supply* abundar

plenty /'plenti/ *pron* **1** mucho, de sobra **2** bastante: *That's* ~. Es suficiente. ● *adv* **1** (*coloq*) bastante: ~ *high enough* lo bastante alto **2** (*USA*) mucho ▸ **plenty more** **1** de sobra **2** (*personas*) otros muchos

pliable /'plaɪəbl/ (*tb* **pliant** /'plaɪənt/) *adj* **1** flexible **2** influenciable

plied /plaɪd/ *pp* de PLY

pliers /'plaɪərz/ *n* [*pl*] alicates, pinzas →PAIR

plight /plaɪt/ *n* **1** mala situación **2** crisis

plod /plɒd/ *vi* (**-dd-**) caminar pesadamente ▸ **plod along/away/on** trabajar con empeño

plonk /plɒŋk/ *vt* ~ **sth** (**down**) dejar caer algo pesadamente

plot /plɒt/ *n* **1** (*libro, etc.*) argumento **2** complot **3** parcela, terreno ● (**-tt-**) **1** *vt* (*ruta*) trazar **2** *vt* (*intriga*) urdir **3** *vi* intrigar

plough (**plow** *GB*) /plaʊ/ *n* arado ● *vt, vi* arar ▸ **plow** (**your way**) **through sth** abrirse camino por/entre algo ▸ **plow sth back** reinvertir algo **plow into sth/sb** estrellarse contra algo/algn

ploy /plɔɪ/ *n* ardid, táctica

pluck /plʌk/ *vt* **1** arrancar **2** desplumar **3** (*cejas*) depilarse **4** (*cuerda*) pulsar ▸ **pluck up courage** armarse de valor

plug /plʌg/ *n* **1** tapón **2** (*Elec*) enchufe (*macho*) **3** (*tb* **spark ~**) bujía **4** (*coloq*) propaganda ● *vt* (**-gg-**) **1** tapar **2** ~ **sth in**(**to sth**) enchufar algo (en algo) **3** (*hueco*) rellenar **4** (*coloq*) hacer propaganda de

plum /plʌm/ *n* **1** ciruela **2** (*tb* ~ **tree**) ciruelo

plumage /'pluːmɪdʒ/ *n* plumaje

plumber /'plʌmər/ *n* plomero/a **plumbing** *n* plomería

plummet /'plʌmɪt/ *vi* **1** caer en picada **2** bajar drásticamente

plump /plʌmp/ *adj* **1** rollizo →FAT **2** mullido ● **plump for sth/sb** (*coloq*) decidirse por algo/algn

plunder /'plʌndər/ *vt* saquear

plunge /plʌndʒ/ **1** *vi* caer (en picada), precipitarse **2** *vt* sumir **3** *vi* zambullirse **4** *vt* sumergir **5** *vt* (*cuchillo, etc.*) hundir ● *n* **1** caída **2** zambullida **3** (*precios*) caída ▸ **take the plunge** (*coloq*) dar el gran paso

plural /'plʊərəl/ *adj, n* plural

plus /plʌs/ *prep* **1** (*Mat*) más **2** además de ● *conj* además ● *adj* **1** como mínimo: *fifty* ~ 50 como mínimo ◇ *He's forty* ~. Tiene cuarenta y pico (de) años. **2** (*Elec, Mat*) positivo ● *n* **1** (*coloq*) punto a favor: *the* ~*es and* ~*inuses* los pros y los contras (*tb* ~ *sign*) signo más

plush /plʌʃ/ *adj* (*coloq*) lujoso

Pluto /'pluːtoʊ/ *n* Plutón

plutonium /pluː'toʊniəm/ *n* plutonio

ply /plaɪ/ *n* **1** (*papel*) capa **2** (*lana*) hebra ● (*pt/pp* plied) *vt* ▸ **ply your trade** (*fml*) desempeñar su trabajo ■ **ply sb with sth 1** dar de beber/comer a algn (constantemente) **2** (*preguntas*) acosar a algn

plywood /'plaɪwʊd/ *n* triplay (*Mx*), triplex (*And*)

p.m. /ˌpiː 'em/ *abrev* de la tarde **NOTA** Cuando se dice **a.m.** o **p.m.**, no se usa **o'clock**: *at 2p.m.*/ *two o'clock*

pneumatic /nuːˈmætɪk; nju:- *GB*/ *adj* neumático

pneumonia /nuːˈmoʊniə; nju:- *GB*/ *n* neumonía

PO /ˌpiː 'oʊ/ *abrev* de **post office**

poach /poʊtʃ/ **1** *vt* cocer **2** *vt* (*huevo*) escalfar, pochar (*Mx*) **3** *vt, vi* cazar/pescar furtivamente **4** *vt* (*idea*) robar **poacher** *n* cazador/a, pescador/a furtivo/a

pocket /'pɑkɪt/ *n* **1** bolsillo: ~ *knife* navaja ◇ *pocket-sized* tamaño (de) bolsillo **2** foco ▸ **be out of pocket** terminar perdiendo dinero ● *vt* **1** meterse en el bolsillo **2** (*robar*) embolsarse

pod /pɑd/ *n* vaina (*legumbres*)

podium /'poʊdiəm/ *n* podio

poem /'poʊəm/ *n* poema

poet /'poʊət/ *n* poeta **poetry** *n* poesía

poetic /poʊˈetɪk/ *adj* poético: ~ *justice* justo castigo

poignant /'pɔɪnjənt/ *adj* conmovedor

point /pɔɪnt/ *n* **1** punto **2** punta **3** (*Mat*) coma **4** cuestión: *miss the* ~ no ver la intención ◇ *prove your* ~ demostrar que se está en lo cierto **5** sentido: *What's the ~?* ¿Para qué? **6** momento **7** (*GB*) (*tb power* ~) enchufe ▸ **be beside the point** no tener nada que ver **make a point of doing sth** asegurarse de hacer algo **make your point** decir algo en claro **point of view** punto de vista **take sb's point** entender lo que algn dice **to the point** al grano ● *vi* ~ **(at/to sth/sb)** señalar (con el dedo) (algo/a algn), apuntar (hacia algo/algn) **2** *vt* ~ **sth at sb** apuntar a algn con algo: ~ *your finger at sth* indicar algo con el dedo ■ **point sth out** señalar algo

point-blank *adj* **1** *at* ~ *range* a quemarropa **2** (*negativa*) rotundo ● *adv* **1** a quemarropa **2** de forma tajante

pointed /'pɔɪntɪd/ *adj* **1** afilado, puntiagudo **2** intencionado

pointer /'pɔɪntər/ *n* **1** indicador **2** puntero **3** (*coloq*) sugerencia **4** pista

pointless /'pɔɪntləs/ *adj* **1** sin sentido **2** inútil

poise /pɔɪz/ *n* **1** elegancia **2** aplomo **poised** *adj* **1** suspendido **2** con aplomo

poison /'pɔɪzn/ *n* veneno ● *vt* envenenar **poisoning** *n* envenenamiento **poisonous** *adj* venenoso

poke /poʊk/ *vt* dar (con el dedo, *etc.*): ~ *your finger into sth* meter el dedo en algo ▸ **poke fun at sth/ sb** burlarse de algo/algn ■ **poke about/around** (*coloq*) **1** fisgonear **2** curiosear **poke out (of sth/ through (sth)** asomar (por algo)

poker /'poʊkər/ *n* **1** atizador, chuzo (*And*) **2** póquer

poker-faced *adj* de rostro impasible

poky /'poʊki/ *adj* diminuto

polar /'poʊlər/ *adj* polar

pole /poʊl/ *n* **1** (*Geog, Fís*) polo **2** palo **3** (*telegráfico*) poste ▸ **poles apart** en extremos opuestos

pole vault *n* salto con garrocha

police /pəˈliːs/ *n* [*pl*] policía: ~ *officer* (agente de) policía ◇ ~ *force* la policía ◇ ~ *state* estado policial ▸ *vt* vigilar policíamente (*fem* **policewoman**) (*pl* **-men/-women**) *n* policía

policy /'pɑləsi/ *n* (*pl* **-ies**) **1** política **2** (*seguros*) póliza

polio /'poʊlioʊ/ *n* polio(mielitis)

polish /'pɑlɪʃ/ *vt* **1** sacar brillo a, encerar, pulir (*zapatos, etc.*) **2** limpiar, bolear (*Mx*) ■ **polish sb off** (*coloq*) matar a algn **polish sth off** (*coloq*) **1** zamparse algo **2** (*trabajo*) despachar algo (rápido) ● *n* **1** lustre **2** brillo **3** (*muebles*) cera **4** (*zapatos*) betún **5** (*uñas*) esmalte **6** finura **polished** *adj* **1** brillante **2** pulido

polite /pəˈlaɪt/ *adj* **1** cortés **2** (*persona*) educado

political /pəˈlɪtɪkl/ *adj* político

politically correct *adj* Ver **PC**

politician /ˌpɑləˈtɪʃn/ *n* político/a

politics /'pɑlətɪks/ *n* **1** política **2** [*pl*] opiniones políticas **3** [*sing*] (*Educ*) ciencias políticas

poll /poʊl/ *n* **1** elección **2** votación **3** **the polls** las urnas **4** (*tb opinion* ~) encuesta

pollen /'pɑlən/ *n* polen

pollute /pəˈluːt/ *vt* **1** contaminar **2** corromper **pollution** *n* **1** contaminación **2** corrupción

polo /'poʊloʊ/ *n* (*Dep*) polo

polo neck *n* (*GB*) (suéter de) cuello alto

polyester /ˌpɑliˈestər/ *n* poliéster

polyethylene (**polythene** *GB*) /ˌpɑliˈeθiliːn/-/θiːn/ *n* polietileno

polystyrene /ˌpɒlɪˈstaɪriːn/ n poliestireno

pomp /pɒmp/ n 1 pompa 2 ostentación **pompous** adj 1 pomposo 2 presumido

pond /pɒnd/ n estanque

ponder /ˈpɒndər/ vt, vi reflexionar

pony /ˈpəʊni/ n (pl -ies) poni

ponytail /ˈpəʊniteɪl/ n cola de caballo

poodle /ˈpuːdl/ n poodle

pool /puːl/ n 1 charco 2 (tb swimming ~) piscina, alberca (Mx) 3 (luz) haz 4 (río) pozo 5 estanque 6 (dinero) fondo (común) 7 billar (pool) 8 the (football) **pools** (GB) apuestas (en fútbol) ● vt (ideas, etc.) juntar

poor /pɔːr/ adj (-er/-est) 1 pobre 2 malo 3 (nivel) bajo ● the poor [pl] los pobres

poorly /ˈpʊərli/ adv mal ● adj (GB) mal, enfermo

pop /pɒp/ n 1 pequeño estallido 2 (USA) papá 3 (tb ~ music) (música) pop ● adv (GB) go ~ hacer ¡pum!, reventar ● (-pp-) 1 vi dar un taponazo 2 vi hacer ¡pum! 3 vt, vi estallar 4 vt (corcho) hacer saltar ► **pop back, down, out, etc.** (GB) volver, bajar, salir, etc. **pop sth back, in, etc.** (GB) devolver, meter, etc. algo **pop in** (GB) visitar **pop up** aparecer **NOTA** Estos phrasal verbs son informales, y denotan una acción rápida o repentina.

popcorn /ˈpɒpkɔːrn/ n [U] palomitas de maíz, maíz pira (And)

pope /pəʊp/ n papa

poplar /ˈpɒplər/ n álamo, chopo

poppy /ˈpɒpi/ n (pl -ies) amapola

Popsicle® /ˈpɒpsɪkl/ n paleta (helada)

popular /ˈpɒpjələr/ adj 1 popular: be ~ with sb caer bien a algn 2 de moda 3 de (las) masas: the ~ press la prensa sensacionalista 4 (creencia) generalizado **popularize** vt 1 popularizar 2 vulgarizar

popularity /ˌpɒpjuˈlærəti/ n popularidad

population /ˌpɒpjuˈleɪʃn/ n población: ~ explosion explosión demográfica

porcelain /ˈpɔːrsəlɪn/ n [U] porcelana

porch /pɔːrtʃ/ n 1 porche 2 (USA) portal

pore /pɔːr/ n poro ■ **pore over sth** estudiar algo detenidamente **porous** adj poroso

pork /pɔːrk/ n (carne de) cerdo/puerco →CARNE

pornography /pɔːrˈnɒɡrəfi/ (coloq **porn**) n porno(grafía)

porpoise /ˈpɔːrpəs/ n marsopa

porridge /ˈpɒrɪdʒ; ˈpɔːr- GB/ n [U] avena (preparada)

port /pɔːrt/ n 1 puerto 2 (barco) babor 3 (vino) oporto

portable /ˈpɔːrtəbl/ adj portátil

porter /ˈpɔːrtər/ n 1 (hotel) mozo, maletero 2 portero/a

porthole /ˈpɔːrthəʊl/ n ventanilla (barco, avión)

portion /ˈpɔːrʃn/ n porción

portrait /ˈpɔːrtreɪt/ n retrato

portray /pɔːrˈtreɪ/ vt 1 retratar 2 representar **portrayal** n representación

pose /pəʊz/ v 1 (para retrato) posar 2 vi comportarse de forma afectada 3 vi ~ as sth/sb hacerse pasar por algo/algn 4 vt (fml) (pregunta) plantear ● n 1 postura 2 pose

posh /pɒʃ/ adj (-er/-est) (coloq) 1 de lujo 2 elegante 3 (acento) afectado

position /pəˈzɪʃn/ n 1 posición 2 situación: in a ~ to do sth en condiciones de hacer algo 3 ~ (on sth) posición (respecto a algo) 4 (fml) (trabajo) puesto ● vt colocar

positive /ˈpɒzətɪv/ adj 1 positivo 2 categórico 3 seguro 4 total, auténtico **positively** adv 1 positivamente 2 con optimismo 3 categóricamente 4 verdaderamente

possess /pəˈzes/ vt 1 (fml) poseer 2 (fml) dominar 3 What possessed you to do that? ¿Cómo se te ocurrió hacer eso? **possession** n 1 posesión: be in ~ of sth tener algo 2 **possessions** pertenencias

possibility /ˌpɒsəˈbɪləti/ n (pl -ies) posibilidad: within/beyond the bounds of ~ dentro/más allá de lo posible

possible /ˈpɒsəbl/ adj posible: as quickly as ~ lo más pronto posible ◊ make sth ~ posibilitar algo **possibly** adv posiblemente: You can't ~ go. No puedes ir de ninguna manera.

post /pəʊst/ n 1 poste, estaca 2 (trabajo) puesto 3 (GB) correo →MAIL ● vt 1 (GB) echar al buzón, mandar 2 (destinar) enviar 3 (Mil) apostar ► **keep sb posted (about/on sth)** mantener a algn al corriente (de algo) **postal** adj postal, de correos

postage /ˈpəʊstɪdʒ/ n valor de envío: ~ stamp estampilla

postbox /'poustbɒks/ n (GB) buzón (para echar cartas)

postcard /'poustkɑːd/ n postal

postcode /'poustkoud/ n (GB) código postal

poster /'poustər/ n 1 (anuncio) cartel 2 póster, afiche

posterity /pɒ'sterəti/ n posteridad

postgraduate /ˌpoust'grædʒuət/ adj, n (estudiante) de posgrado

posthumous /'pɒstʃəməs; 'pɒstʃuməs GB/ adj póstumo

postman /'poustmən/ n (GB) (pl -men) cartero

post-mortem n autopsia

post office n correo

postpone /pous'poun/ vt aplazar

postscript /'poustskrɪpt/ n 1 posdata 2 nota final

posture /'pɒstʃər/ n 1 postura 2 actitud

post-war adj de (la) posguerra

postwoman /'poustwumən/ n (GB) (pl -women) cartero (mujer)

pot /pɒt/ n 1 olla: ~s and pans batería de cocina (And) 3 tarro 3 pieza decorativa (cerámica) 4 (planta) maceta, matera (And) 5 (coloq) marihuana ▶ **go to pot** (coloq) dañarse

potassium /pə'tæsiəm/ n potasio

potato /pə'teɪtou/ n (pl -es) papa

potent /'poutnt/ adj potente, poderoso **potency** n fuerza

potential /pə'tenʃl/ adj, n potencial

pothole /'pɒthoul/ n 1 (en calle) bache, hueco 2 cueva

potted /'pɒtɪd/ adj (GB) 1 en conserva 2 (relato) resumido

potter /'pɒtər/ (GB) = PUTTER

pottery /'pɒtəri/ n 1 cerámica 2 (lugar, arte) alfarería **potter** n alfarero/a

potty /'pɒti/ adj (GB, coloq) ~ (about sth/sb) loco (por algo/algn) ● n (pl -ies) (coloq) bacinica, bacinilla

pouch /pautʃ/ n 1 bolsa pequeña 2 tabaquera 3 (Zool) bolsa

poultry /'poultri/ n [U] aves (de corral)

pounce /pauns/ vi 1 abalanzarse 2 ~ on sth (fig) saltar sobre algo

pound /paund/ n 1 (abrev lb.) libra (0,454 kg) → Ver pág. 222 2 (dinero) libra (£) → Ver pág. 224 ● vt 1 golpear 2 vt corer pesadamente 3 vi (corazón) latir fuertemente 4 vt machacar **pounding** n 1 paliza 2 (olas) embate

pour /pɔːr/ vi 1 fluir, correr 2 vi ~ (with rain) llover a cántaros 3 vt

~ sth (out) (bebida) servir algo 4 vt ~ sth in echar algo ■ **pour in** 1 entrar a raudales 2 inundar **pour out** 1 fluir 2 (personas) salir en tropel **pour sth out** (expresar) sacar algo

pout /paut/ vi hacer un puchero

poverty /'pɒvərti/ n 1 pobreza: poverty-stricken necesitado 2 miseria 3 (ideas) falta

powder /'paudər/ n polvo ● vt empolvar **powdered** adj en polvo

power /'pauər/ n 1 poder 2 poderes [pl] capacidad, facultades 3 fuerza 4 potencia 5 energía 6 electricidad: ~ plant/station (GB) central eléctrica ◇ ~ point (GB) enchufe ▶ **the powers that be** los que mandan ● vt impulsar, propulsar **powerful** adj 1 poderoso 2 potente 3 fuerte 4 (obra, etc.) intenso **powerless** adj impotente

practicable /'præktɪkəbl/ adj factible

practical /'præktɪkl/ adj 1 práctico: ~ joke broma 2 (persona) pragmático **practically** adv prácticamente, de forma práctica

practice /'præktɪs/ n 1 práctica 2 (Dep) entrenamiento 3 (Mús) ejercicios 4 (Med) consultorio 5 (profesión) ejercicio ▶ **out of practice** fuera de práctica ● (**practise** GB) 1 vt, vi practicar 2 vi (Dep) entrenarse 3 vt, vi ~ (**as sth**) (profesión) ejercer (algo) 4 vt (cualidad) ejercitar **practiced** (**practised** GB) adj experto

practitioner /præk'tɪʃənər/ n (fml) experto/a 2 médico/a

pragmatic /præg'mætɪk/ adj pragmático

praise /preɪz/ vt 1 elogiar 2 (Rel) alabar ● n [U] 1 elogio(s) 2 halago 3 (Rel) alabanza **praiseworthy** /'preɪzwɜːrði/ adj loable

pram /præm/ n (GB) coche de niño (estilo moisés)

prank /præŋk/ n travesura

prawn /prɔːn/ n (GB) camarón

pray /preɪ/ vi rezar, orar

prayer /preər/ n oración

preach /priːtʃ/ 1 vt, vi (Rel) predicar 2 vt sermonear 3 vi aconsejar **preacher** n predicador/a

precarious /prɪ'keəriəs/ adj precario

precaution /prɪ'kɔːʃn/ n precaución **precautionary** adj preventivo

precede /prɪ'siːd/ vt 1 preceder a 2 (discurso) introducir **preceding** adj 1 precedente 2 anterior

precedence /'presɪdəns/ n precedencia

precedent /'presɪdənt/ n precedente

precinct /'pri:sɪŋkt/ n 1 (USA) distrito 2 recinto 3 (GB) zona: *pedestrian* ~ zona peatonal

precious /'preʃəs/ adj precioso, valioso ● adv ▶ **precious few/little** (coloq) muy poco/a, -os/as

precipice /'presəpɪs/ n precipicio

precise /prɪ'saɪs/ adj 1 exacto 2 claro 3 (persona) meticuloso **precisely** adv 1 exactamente 2 (hora) en punto 3 con precisión **precision** /prɪ'sɪʒn/ n precisión

preclude /prɪ'klu:d/ vt (fml) excluir

precocious /prɪ'kəʊʃəs/ adj precoz

preconceived /ˌpri:kən'si:vd/ adj preconcebido **preconception** /ˌpri:kən'sepʃn/ n idea preconcebida

precondition /ˌpri:kən'dɪʃn/ n condición previa

predator /'predətər/ n depredador **predatory** /'predətɔ:ri/, -tri GB/ adj 1 depredador 2 (fml) (persona) buitre, rapaz

predecessor /'predəsesər; 'pri:dɪd-GB/ n predecesor/a

predicament /prɪ'dɪkəmənt/ n situación difícil, apuro

predict /prɪ'dɪkt/ vt predecir, prever **predictable** adj previsible, predecible **prediction** n predicción, pronóstico

predominant /prɪ'dɒmɪnənt/ adj predominante

pre-empt vt adelantarse a

preface /'prefəs/ n 1 prólogo 2 (discurso) introducción

prefer /prɪ'fɜ:r/ vt (-rr-) preferir → PREFERIR **preferable** /'prefrəbl/ adj preferible **preference** /'prefrəns/ n preferencia: *in* ~ *to* sth/sb en lugar de algo/algn **preferential** /ˌprefə'renʃl/ adj preferente

prefix /'pri:fɪks/ n prefijo

pregnant /'pregnənt/ adj 1 embarazada 2 preñada **pregnancy** n (pl -ies) embarazo

prejudice /'predʒudɪs/ n 1 [U] prejuicios 2 prejuicio 3 parcialidad 4 (Jur) perjuicio ● vt 1 predisponer 2 (decisión, etc.) influir en 3 (fml) perjudicar **prejudiced** adj 1 parcial 2 intolerante: ~ *against* sth/sb predispuesto contra algo/algn

preliminary /prɪ'lɪmɪnəri; -nəri GB/ adj, n 1 preliminar 2 (Dep) eliminatorio

prelude /'prelju:d/ n 1 (Mús) preludio 2 prólogo

premature /ˌpri:mə'tʃʊər; 'premətʃə(r) GB/ adj prematuro

premier /prɪ'mɪər; 'premiə(r) GB/ n primer(a) ministro/a ● adj principal

premiere /prɪ'mɪər; 'premieə(r) GB/ n estreno

premises /'premɪsɪz/ n [pl] 1 (tienda, bar, etc.) local 2 (empresa) oficinas 3 edificio

premium /'pri:miəm/ n (pago) prima ▶ **be at a premium** escasear

preoccupation /priˌɒkju'peɪʃn/ n ~ (with) (algo) preocupación (por algo) **preoccupied** adj absorto

preparation /ˌprepə'reɪʃn/ n 1 preparación 2 preparativo

preparatory /prɪ'pærətɔ:ri; -tri GB/ adj preparatorio

prepare /prɪ'peər/ vi 1 prepararse, hacer preparativos 2 vt preparar 3 vt **be prepared to do sth** estar dispuesto a hacer algo

preposition /ˌprepə'zɪʃn/ n (Gram) preposición

preposterous /prɪ'pɒstərəs/ adj absurdo

prerequisite /ˌpri:'rekwəzɪt/ n requisito, condición previa

prerogative /prɪ'rɒgətɪv/ n prerrogativa

preschool /'pri:sku:l/ n guardería infantil

prescribe /prɪ'skraɪb/ vt 1 (Med) recetar 2 recomendar

prescription /prɪ'skrɪpʃn/ n 1 (Med) receta 2 (acción) prescripción

presence /'prezns/ n 1 presencia 2 asistencia 3 existencia

present¹ /'preznt/ adj 1 (th Gram) presente: *to the* ~ *day* hasta hoy 2 (tiempo) actual ● n presente: *at* ~ actualmente

present² /'preznt/ n regalo: *give sb a* ~ regalar algo a algn ● /prɪ'zent/ vt 1 presentar **NOTA** Para presentar una persona a otra se usa **introduce**: *Let me introduce you to Jo.* 2 ~ *sb with* sth; ~ sth (*to* sb) hacer entrega de algo (a algn): ~ *sb with a problem* plantearle a algn un problema 3 (argumento) exponer 4 ~ *itself* (ocasión) presentarse 5 (Teat) representar **presentable** /prɪ'zentəbl/ adj presentable

presentation /ˌpri:zen'teɪʃn, ˌprezn-/ n 1 presentación 2 (argumento) exposición 3 (Teat) representación 4 (premio) entrega

present-day adj actual

presenter /prɪˈzentər/ n (GB) presentador/a

presently /ˈprezntli/ adv 1 (USA) actualmente 2 (fml) [pasado] al poco tiempo 3 (fml) [futuro] en un momento, dentro de poco

preservative /prɪˈzɜːrvətɪv/ adj, n conservante

preserve /prɪˈzɜːrv/ vt 1 conservar 2 preservar 3 proteger ● n 1 reserva (de caza): *the exclusive ~ of members* la reserva privada de los socios 2 conserva **preservation** n preservación

preside /prɪˈzaɪd/ vi ~ (over/at sth) presidir (algo)

president /ˈprezɪdənt/ n presidente/a **presidency** n (pl -ies) presidencia **presidential** /ˌprezɪˈdenʃl/ adj presidencial

press /pres/ n 1 (tb the Press) la prensa 2 planchado 3 (tb printing ~) imprenta ● 1 vt, vi apretar 2 vt pulsar, presionar 3 vi ~ (up) against sb arrimarse a algn 4 vt (uvas) pisar 5 vt prensar 6 vt planchar 7 vt, vi ~ (sb) (for sth/to do sth) presionar (a algn) (para que haga algo) ▸ **be pressed for time** andar muy escaso de tiempo ■ **press ahead/on** seguir adelante

pressing /ˈpresɪŋ/ adj urgente

press-up n (GB) Ver PUSH-UP

pressure /ˈpreʃər/ n presión: ~ cooker/gauge olla a presión/ manómetro ◇ ~ group grupo de presión ◇ put ~ on sb to do sth presionar a algn para que haga algo

pressurize /ˈpreʃəraɪz/ vt (GB) (**pressure** USA) ~ sb into sth presionar a algn para que haga algo 2 (Fís) presurizar

prestige /preˈstiːʒ/ n prestigio **prestigious** /preˈstɪdʒəs/ adj prestigioso

presume /prɪˈzuːm; GB -ˈzjuːm/ vt asumir, suponer: I ~ so. Eso creo. **presumably** adv es de suponer que, según parece

presumption /prɪˈzʌmpʃn/ n 1 presunción 2 atrevimiento **presumptuous** adj impertinente

presuppose /ˌpriːsəˈpəʊz/ vt presuponer

pretend /prɪˈtend/ vt, vi 1 fingir 2 pretender 3 ~ to be sth jugar a algo ● adj (coloq) 1 de juguete 2 fingido

pretense (**pretence** GB) /prɪˈtens/ n 1 [U] engaño(s): *abandon all ~ of sth* dejar de fingir algo 2 (fml) ostentación

pretentious /prɪˈtenʃəs/ adj pretencioso

pretext /ˈpriːtekst/ n pretexto

pretty /ˈprɪti/ adj (-ier/-iest) bonito, lindo ▸ **not a pretty sight** nada agradable ● adv bastante → FAIRLY ▸ **pretty much/well** más o menos

prevail /prɪˈveɪl/ vi (fml) 1 imperar 2 predominar 3 prevalecer ■ **prevail (up)on sb to do sth** convencer a algn para que haga algo **prevailing** adj 1 (fml) reinante 2 (viento) predominante

prevalent /ˈprevələnt/ adj (fml) 1 difundido 2 predominante **prevalence** n 1 difusión 2 predominancia

prevent /prɪˈvent/ vt 1 ~ sb from doing sth impedir que algn haga algo 2 evitar, prevenir **prevention** n prevención **preventive** adj preventivo

preview /ˈpriːvjuː/ n preestreno

previous /ˈpriːviəs/ adj anterior ● adv ~ to sth antes de algo

pre-war adj de (la) preguerra

prey /preɪ/ n [U] presa ● vi ~ on sth/sb 1 cazar algo/a algn 2 vivir a costa de algo/algn ▸ **prey on sb's mind** preocupar a algn

price /praɪs/ n precio ▸ **at any price** a toda costa **not at any price** por nada del mundo ● vt 1 fijar el precio de 2 avaluar 3 poner el precio a **priceless** adj que no tiene precio

prick /prɪk/ n 1 punzada 2 pinchazo, piquete (Mx) ● vt 1 pinchar(se) 2 (conciencia) remorder ▸ **prick up your ears** 1 parar las orejas 2 aguzar el oído

prickly /ˈprɪkli/ adj 1 espinoso 2 que pica 3 malhumorado

pride /praɪd/ n 1 ~ (in sth) orgullo (por algo): *take ~ in sth* hacer algo con orgullo 2 soberbia ▸ **sb's pride and joy** la niña de los ojos de algn ■ **pride yourself on sth** preciarse de algo

priest /priːst/ n cura **priesthood** /ˈpriːsthʊd/ n 1 sacerdocio 2 clero **NOTA** Priest suele referirse a los sacerdotes católicos. Para la mayor parte de las religiones protestantes se usa **minister**.

prig /prɪg/ n mojigato/a **priggish** adj mojigato

prim /prɪm/ adj 1 remilgado 2 (aspecto) recatado

primary /ˈpraɪmeri; -məri GB/ adj 1 primario: ~ school (escuela de) primaria 2 primordial 3 principal ● n (pl -ies) (USA) (tb ~ election) elección primaria **primarily** /praɪˈmerəli/ adv principalmente

prime /praɪm/ *adj* **1** principal **2** excelente ● *n*: *in your ~/in the ~ of life* en la flor de la vida ● *vt* **1** preparar **2** ~ **sb (with sth)** poner al tanto a algn (de algo)

prime minister *n* primer/a ministro/a

primeval (*tb* **primaeval**) /praɪ'miːvl/ *adj* primigenio

primitive /'prɪmɪtɪv/ *adj* primitivo

primrose /'prɪmrəʊz/ *n* prímula ● *adj, n* amarillo pálido

prince /prɪns/ (*fem* **princess** /ˌprɪn'ses/) *n* príncipe →PRÍNCIPE

principal /'prɪnsəpl/ *adj* principal ● *n* (*Educ*) director/a, rector/a

principle /'prɪnsəpl/ *n* principio ▶ **in principle** en principio **on principle** por principio

print /prɪnt/ *vt* **1** ~ **sth (out)** imprimir algo **2** (*Period*) publicar **3** escribir en letra de imprenta **4** (*tela*) estampar ● *n* **1** (*tipografía*) letra **2** huella **3** (*Arte*) grabado **4** (*Fot*) copia **5** tela estampada ▶ **in print 1** en venta **2** publicado **out of print** agotado **printer** *n* **1** impresora **2** (*persona*) impresor/a **3** printer's imprenta (*taller*) **printing** *n* **1** imprenta (*proceso*): *a ~ error* una errata **2** (*libros*) impresión **printout** /'prɪntaʊt/ *n* copia impresa

prior /'praɪər/ (*fml*) *adj* previo: ~ *to* **prep 1** ~ *to doing sth* antes de hacer algo **2** ~ *to sth* anterior a algo

priority /praɪ'ɒrəti/ *n* (*pl* **-ies**) prioridad: *get your priorities right* saber cuáles son las prioridades de uno

prise (*GB*) *Ver* PRY (2)

prison /'prɪzn/ *n* cárcel: ~ *camp* campo de concentración **prisoner** *n* **1** preso/a **2** prisionero/a **3** detenido/a

privacy /'praɪvəsi; 'prɪv- *GB*/ *n* intimidad, privacidad

private /'praɪvət/ *adj* **1** privado: ~ *eye* detective privado **2** particular **3** (*persona*) reservado **4** (*lugar*) íntimo ● *n* **1** (*GB, Mil*) soldado raso **2** **privates** (*coloq*) partes (pudendas) ▶ **in private** en privado **privately** *adv* en privado **privatize** *vt* privatizar

privilege /'prɪvəlɪdʒ/ *n* **1** privilegio **2** (*Jur*) inmunidad **privileged** *adj* **1** privilegiado **2** (*información*) confidencial

privy /'prɪvi/ *adj* ▶ **be privy to sth** (*fml*) tener conocimiento de algo

prize /praɪz/ *n* premio ● *adj* **1** premiado **2** de primera **3** de remate **prize** *vt* **1** estimar **2** *Ver* PRY (2)

pro /prəʊ/ *adj, n* (*pl* **-s**) (*coloq*) profesional ● *n*: *the ~s and cons* los pros y los contras

probable /'prɒbəbl/ *adj* probable **probability** /ˌprɒbə'bɪləti/ *n* (*pl* **-ies**) probabilidad **probably** *adv* probablemente **NOTA** Se suele usar el adverbio cuando en español se diría "es probable que": *They will* ~ *go.* Es probable que vayan.

probation /prəʊ'beɪʃn; prə- *GB*/ *n* **1** libertad condicional **2** (*empleado*) prueba

probe /prəʊb/ *n* sonda ● *vt* **1** (*Med*) sondar **2** *vt* examinar **3** *vi* ~ **(into sth)** investigar (algo) **probing** *adj* penetrante

problem /'prɒbləm/ *n* problema **problematic** /ˌprɒblə'mætɪk/ *adj* problemático

procedure /prə'siːdʒər/ *n* **1** procedimiento **2** trámite(s)

proceed /prə'siːd/ *vi* **1** proceder **2** ~ **(to sth)** pasar (a algo) **3** (*fml*) avanzar, ir **4** continuar, seguir adelante **proceedings** *n* [*pl*] (*fml*) **1** acto **2** (*Jur*) proceso **3** (*reunión*) actas

proceeds /'prəʊsiːdz/ *n* [*pl*] ganancias

process /'prəʊses; 'prɒses *GB*/ *n* **1** procedimiento **2** (*Jur*) proceso ▶ **in the process** al hacerlo **in the process of (doing) sth** haciendo algo ● *vt* **1** procesar **2** (*solicitud*) tramitar **3** (*Fot*) revelar **4** (*Comp*) procesar **processing** *n* **1** tratamiento **2** (*Fot*) revelado **3** (*Comp*) procesamiento **processor** *n* procesador

procession /prə'seʃn/ *n* desfile, procesión

proclaim /prə'kleɪm/ *vt* proclamar **proclamation** /ˌprɒklə'meɪʃn/ *n* proclama **2** proclamación

prod /prɒd/ *vt, vi* (**-dd-**) ~ **(at) sth/sb** empujar, picar algo/a algn ● *n* empujón

prodigy /'prɒdədʒi/ *n* (*pl* **-ies**) prodigio **prodigious** /prə-'dɪdʒəs/ *adj* prodigioso

produce /'prɒdjuːs; -duːs *GB*/ *n* [U] productos → PRODUCT ● /prə'djuːs; -'duːs *GB*/ *vt* **1** producir **2** (*cultivo*) dar **3** (*cría*) tener **4** ~ **sth (from/out of sth)** sacar algo (de algo) **5** (*Teat*) poner en escena **producer** *n* **1** productor/a **2** (*Teat*) director/a de escena

product /'prɒdʌkt/ *n* producto **NOTA** Se usa **product** para referirse a productos industriales, y **produce** para los del campo.

production /prəˈdʌkʃn/ n producción: ~ *line* línea de ensamblaje **productive** adj productivo **productivity** /ˌprɒdʌkˈtɪvəti/ n productividad

profess /prəˈfes/ vt (fml) 1 pretender 2 ~ (**yourself**) sth declarar(se) algo 3 (Rel) profesar **professed** adj 1 supuesto 2 declarado

profession /prəˈfeʃn/ n profesión → WORK **professional** adj profesional

professor /prəˈfesər/ n (abrev **Prof.**) 1 (USA) profesor/a de universidad 2 (GB) catedrático/a de universidad

proficiency /prəˈfɪʃnsi/ n [U] ~ (**in** sth) competencia (en algo/para hacer algo) **proficient** adj competente

profile /ˈprəʊfaɪl/ n perfil ▶ a **high/low profile**: a *high-profile campaign* una campaña destacada ◇ *keep a low* ~ procurar pasar desapercibido

profit /ˈprɒfɪt/ n 1 ganancia(s), beneficio(s): *make a* ~ sacar una ganancia ◇ *do sth for* ~ hacer algo con fines de lucro ◇ *profit-making* lucrativo 2 provecho ● vi beneficiarse **profitable** adj 1 rentable 2 provechoso

profound /prəˈfaʊnd/ adj profundo

profuse /prəˈfjuːs/ adj profuso **profusion** n abundancia

program (**programme** GB) /ˈprəʊɡræm/ n 1 programa ● vt, vi programar **programmer** (tb computer ~) n programador/a **programming** n programación

progress /ˈprəʊɡres, ˈprɒ- GB/ n [U] 1 progreso(s) 2 avance: *make* ~ avanzar ▶ **in progress** (fml) en marcha ● /prəˈɡres/ vi avanzar **progressive** 1 progresivo 2 progresista

prohibit /prəˈhɪbɪt/ vt (fml) 1 prohibir 2 impedir **prohibition** /ˌprəʊɪˈbɪʃn/ n prohibición

project /ˈprɒdʒekt/ n proyecto ● /prəˈdʒekt/ 1 vt proyectar 2 vi sobresalir **projection** n proyección **projector** n proyector: *overhead* ~ retroproyector

prolific /prəˈlɪfɪk/ adj prolífico

prologue (tb **prolog** USA) /ˈprəʊlɒɡ; -lɔːɡ GB/ n prólogo

prolong /prəˈlɒŋ; -lɔːŋ GB/ vt prolongar, alargar

prom /prɒm/ n 1 (USA) baile de fin de año 2 (GB, coloq) (tb

promenade /ˌprɒməˈneɪd; -ˈnɑːd GB/) paseo marítimo

prominent /ˈprɒmɪnənt/ adj 1 prominente 2 importante

promiscuous /prəˈmɪskjuəs/ adj promiscuo

promise /ˈprɒmɪs/ n 1 promesa: *show* ~ ser prometedor ● vt, vi prometer **promising** adj prometedor

promote /prəˈməʊt/ vt 1 promover 2 (*en el trabajo*) ascender 3 (Com) promocionar **promoter** n promotor/a **promotion** n 1 ascenso 2 promoción

prompt /prɒmpt/ adj 1 sin dilación 2 rápido 3 (*persona*) puntual ● adv en punto ● 1 vt incitar 2 vt (*reacción*) provocar 3 vt, vi (Teat) apuntar **promptly** adv 1 con prontitud 2 puntualmente 3 al punto

prone /prəʊn/ adj propenso

pronoun /ˈprəʊnaʊn/ n pronombre

pronounce /prəˈnaʊns/ vt 1 pronunciar 2 declarar **pronounced** adj 1 marcado 2 pronunciado

pronunciation /prəˌnʌnsiˈeɪʃn/ n pronunciación

proof /pruːf/ n 1 [U] prueba(s) 2 comprobación

prop /prɒp/ n 1 apoyo 2 soporte ● vt (-pp-) 1 ~ sth (**up**) **against** sth apoyar algo contra algo 2 ~ sth **up** respaldar algo

propaganda /ˌprɒpəˈɡændə/ n propaganda

propel /prəˈpel/ vt (-ll-) 1 impulsar 2 (Mec) propulsar **propellant** n propulsor

propeller /prəˈpelər/ n hélice

propensity /prəˈpensəti/ n (fml) propensión

proper /ˈprɒpər/ adj 1 debido 2 adecuado 3 de verdad 4 correcto 5 decente 6 *the house* ~ la casa propiamente dicha **properly** adv 1 bien 2 (*comportarse*) con propiedad 3 adecuadamente

property /ˈprɒpəti/ n (pl -ies) 1 propiedad 2 [U] bienes

prophecy /ˈprɒfəsi/ n (pl -ies) profecía

prophesy /ˈprɒfəsaɪ/ (pt/pp -ied) 1 vt predecir 2 vi profetizar

prophet /ˈprɒfɪt/ n profeta

proportion /prəˈpɔːʃn/ n porción ▶ **get/keep things in proportion** ver el asunto en su justa medida **out of (all) proportion** 1 desmesuradamente 2 desproporcionado **proportional** adj proporcional

proposal /prəˈpəʊzl/ n propuesta

propose /prə'pəʊz/ **1** vt proponer(se) **2** vi pedir la mano

proposition /ˌprɑpə'zɪʃn/ n proposición **2** propuesta

proprietor /prə'praɪətər/ n propietario/a

prose /prəʊz/ n prosa

prosecute /'prɑsɪkju:t/ vt procesar: *prosecuting lawyer* (abogado/a) fiscal **prosecution** n **1** enjuiciamiento, procesamiento **2 the prosecution** (Jur) la acusación **prosecutor** n fiscal

prospect /'prɑspekt/ n **1** perspectiva **2** probabilidad(es) **prospective** /prə'spektɪv/ adj **1** futuro **2** probable

prospectus /prə'spektəs/ n prospecto (folleto promocional)

prosper /'prɑspər/ vi prosperar **prosperous** adj próspero **prosperity** /prɑ'sperəti/ n prosperidad

prostitute /'prɑstətu:t; -tju:t GB/ n **1** prostituta **2 male ~** prostituto **prostitution** n prostitución

prostrate /'prɑstreɪt/ adj (fml) **1** postrado **2** abatido

protagonist /prə'tægənɪst/ n **1** protagonista **2** defensor/a

protect /prə'tekt/ vt proteger **protection** n protección **protective** adj protector

protein /'prəʊti:n/ n proteína

protest /'prəʊtest/ n protesta ● /prə'test/ **1** vi protestar **2** vt declarar **protester** n manifestante

Protestant /'prɑtɪstənt/ adj, n protestante

prototype /'prəʊtətaɪp/ n prototipo

protrude /prəʊ'tru:d; prə- GB/ vi sobresalir: *protruding teeth* dientes salidos

proud /praʊd/ adj (-er/-est) **1** orgulloso **2** soberbio

prove /pru:v/ (pp proven, proved GB) **1** vt probar, demostrar **2** vi ~ (**to be**) sth resultar (ser) algo **proven** /'pru:vn/ adj comprobado

proverb /'prɑvɜ:rb/ n proverbio **proverbial** /prə'vɜ:rbiəl/ adj **1** proverbial **2** consabido

provide /prə'vaɪd/ **1** vt ~ **sb** (**with sth**); ~ **sth** (**for sb**) proporcionar, suministrar algo a algn ■ **provide for sb** mantener a algn **provide for sth** (fml) **1** prever algo **2** estipular algo

provided /prə'vaɪdɪd/ (tb **providing**) conj ~ (**that...**) con tal (de) que

province /'prɑvɪns/ n **1** provincia **2** (fml) competencia **provincial**

/prə'vɪnʃl/ adj **1** provincial **2** provinciano

provision /prə'vɪʒn/ n **1** suministro **2 make ~ for sth/sb** prever algo/asegurar el porvenir de algn **3 provisions** víveres **4** (Jur) estipulación

provisional /prə'vɪʒənl/ adj provisional

proviso /prə'vaɪzəʊ/ n (pl ~s) condición

provoke /prə'vəʊk/ vt **1** provocar **2** ~ **sb into doing sth** incitar a algn a hacer algo **3** causar **provocation** /ˌprɑvə'keɪʃn/ n provocación **provocative** /prə'vɑkətɪv/ adj provocador

prow /praʊ/ n proa

prowess /'praʊəs/ n **1** proeza **2** habilidad

prowl /praʊl/ vt, vi ~ (**about/around**) (**sth**) rondar, merodear (por algo)

proximity /prɑk'sɪməti/ n proximidad

proxy /'prɑksi/ n (pl -**ies**) **1** apoderado/a **2** poder: by ~ por poder(es)

prude /pru:d/ n mojigato/a

prudent /'pru:dnt/ adj prudente

prune /pru:n/ n ciruela pasa ● vt **1** podar **2** recortar **pruning** n poda

pry /praɪ/ (pt/pp **pried** /praɪd/) **1** vi ~ (**into sth**) entrometerse (en algo), fisgonear **2** vt (USA) ~ **sth apart, off, open, etc. sth** separar, quitar, abrir, etc. algo (**with sth**) hacer palanca con algo)

PS /ˌpi: 'es/ n (abrev de **postscript**) posdata

psalm /sɑm/ n salmo

pseudonym /'su:dənɪm/ n seudónimo

psyche /'saɪki/ n psique

psychiatry /saɪ'kaɪətri/ n psiquiatría **psychiatric** /ˌsaɪki'ætrɪk/ adj psiquiátrico **psychiatrist** /saɪ'kaɪətrɪst/ n psiquiatra

psychic /'saɪkɪk/ adj (tb **psychical**) psíquico **2** be ~ tener poderes parapsicológicos

psychoanalysis /ˌsaɪkəʊə'næləsɪs/ n psicoanálisis

psychological /ˌsaɪkə'lɑdʒɪkl/ adj psicológico

psychology /saɪ'kɑlədʒi/ n psicología **psychologist** n psicólogo/a

pub /pʌb/ n (GB) bar

puberty /'pju:bərti/ n pubertad

pubic /'pju:bɪk/ adj púbico

public /'pʌblɪk/ adj, n público: ~ *house* (GB) bar ▸ **in public** en público

publication /ˌpʌblɪ'keɪʃn/ n publicación

publicity /pʌb'lɪsəti/ n publicidad: ~ campaign campaña publicitaria

publicize /'pʌblɪsaɪz/ vt 1 hacer público 2 promocionar

public school n 1 (USA) colegio público 2 (GB) colegio privado →ESCUELA

publish /'pʌblɪʃ/ vt 1 publicar 2 hacer público **publisher** n 1 editor/a 2 (casa) editorial **publishing** n mundo editorial

pudding /'pʊdɪŋ/ n 1 (GB) postre 2 pudín 3 black ~ (GB) morcilla/ moronga (Mx)

puddle /'pʌdl/ n charco

puff /pʌf/ n 1 soplo, resoplido 2 (humo) bocanada 3 (cigarrillo) fumada 4 (coloq) aliento ● vi resoplar 2 vt, vi ~ (at/on) sth fumar algo 3 vt (humo) echar a bocanadas 4 vt (cigarro, etc.) chupar ■ puff sth out inflar algo **puff up** hincharse **puffed** (tb ~ out) adj (GB, coloq) sin aliento **puffy** adj hinchado (esp cara)

puke /pjuːk/ (coloq) vt, vi vomitar (algo) ● n vómito

pull /pʊl/ n 1 tirón 2 the ~ of sth la atracción de algo ● vt 1 tirar de, jalar 2 vt, vi ~ ((at/on) sth) tirar, jalar (de algo) 3 vt (músculo) desgarrarse 4 vt (gatillo) apretar 5 vt (corcho, muela, pistola) sacar ■ pull sth apart hacer pedazos algo **pull sth down** 1 bajar algo 2 derribar algo **pull in(to) sth** detenerse **pull sth off** (coloq) conseguir algo **pull out** 1 retirarse 2 salir **pull sth out** sacar algo **pull sth/sb out** retirar algo/a algn **pull over** hacerse a un lado (vehículo) **pull yourself together** controlarse **pull up** detenerse **pull sth up** 1 levantar algo 2 (planta) arrancar algo

pull date n (USA) fecha límite de venta

pulley /'pʊli/ n polea

pullover /'pʊləʊvər/ n suéter, saco →SWEATER

pulp /pʌlp/ n 1 pulpa 2 (de madera) pasta

pulpit /'pʊlpɪt/ n púlpito

pulsate /'pʌlseɪt; pʌl'seɪt GB/ (tb pulse) vi palpitar, latir

pulse /pʌls/ n 1 (Med) pulso 2 ritmo 3 pulsación 4 legumbre (seca)

pumice /'pʌmɪs/ (tb ~ stone) n piedra pómez

pummel /'pʌml/ vt (-l-, -ll- GB) aporrear, golpear

pump /pʌmp/ n bomba: gas ~ surtidor de gasolina ● 1 vt, vi bombear 2 vt ~ sth up inflar algo 3 vi (corazón) latir 4 vt ~ sb for sth (coloq) sonsacarle algo a algn

pumpkin /'pʌmpkɪn/ n calabaza, auyama (And)

pun /pʌn/ n juego de palabras

punch /pʌntʃ/ n 1 punzón 2 (tb hole ~) perforadora 3 ponche 4 puñetazo ● vt 1 perforar, picar 2 dar un puñetazo a

punch-up n (pl -ups) pelea a puños

punctual /'pʌŋktʃuəl/ adj puntual → PUNTUAL **punctuality** /ˌpʌŋktʃu'æləti/ n puntualidad

punctuate /'pʌŋktʃueɪt/ vt 1 (Gram) puntuar 2 interrumpir

punctuation /ˌpʌŋktʃu'eɪʃn/ n puntuación

puncture /'pʌŋktʃər/ n (GB) pinchazo, ponchadura (Mx) ● 1 vt, vi pinchar(se), ponchar(se) (Mx) 2 vt (Med) perforar

pundit /'pʌndɪt/ n entendido/a

pungent /'pʌndʒənt/ adj 1 acre 2 punzante 3 mordaz

punish /'pʌnɪʃ/ vt castigar **punishment** n 1 castigo 2 paliza

punitive /'pjuːnətɪv/ adj (fml) 1 punitivo 2 desorbitado

punk /pʌŋk/ n 1 (música) punk 2 (persona) punk 3 (USA, coloq) patán

punt /pʌnt/ n 1 bote plano que se impulsa con pértiga **punter** /'pʌntər/ n (GB, coloq) 1 apostador/a 2 cliente

pup /pʌp/ n 1 cachorro/a 2 cría

pupil /'pjuːpl/ n 1 alumno/a →ALUMNO 2 discípulo/a 3 pupila (del ojo)

puppet /'pʌpɪt/ n 1 marioneta 2 títere

puppy /'pʌpi/ (pl -ies) n cachorro/a

purchase /'pɜːrtʃəs/ (fml) n compra, adquisición ● vt comprar **purchaser** n (fml) comprador/a

pure /pjʊər/ adj (-er/-est) puro **purely** adv puramente **purify** vt (pt/pp -ied) purificar **purity** n pureza

purée /'pjʊəreɪ; 'pjʊəreɪ GB/ n puré

purge /pɜːrdʒ/ vt purgar ● n 1 purga 2 purgante

puritan /'pjʊərɪtən/ adj, n puritano/a **puritanical** /ˌpjʊərɪ'tænɪkl/ adj puritano

purple /'pɜːrpl/ adj, n morado

purport /pər'pɔːrt/ vt (fml): It ~s to be... Pretende ser...

purpose /'pɜːrpəs/ n 1 propósito, fin: **purpose-built** construido con un fin específico 2 determinación: *have no sense of* ~ no tener una meta en la vida ▶ **for the purpose of** para efectos de un propósito **on purpose** a propósito **purposeful** *adj* decidido **purposely** *adv* intencionadamente

purr /pɜːr/ *vi* ronronear

purse /pɜːrs/ *n* 1 (USA) bolso 2 (GB) (coin ~ USA) monedero ● *vt:* ~ *your lips* fruncir los labios

pursue /pər'suː; -'sjuː GB/ *vt* (fml) 1 perseguir **NOTA** Es más común **chase**. 2 (actividad) dedicarse a 3 (conversación) continuar (con)

pursuit /pər'suːt; -'sjuːt GB/ *n* 1 búsqueda: *in ~ of sth* en busca de algo 2 actividad ▶ **in pursuit (of sth/sb)** persiguiendo (a algo/algn)

push /pʊʃ/ *n* empujón ▶ **get the push/give sb the push** (GB, coloq) ser despedido/dar la patada a algn ● 1 *vt, vi* empujar: ~ *past sb* pasar a algn empujando 2 *vt* (botón) apretar 3 *vt* (coloq) promover ▶ **be pushed for sth** (coloq) andar corto de algo ■ **push sb about/around** mangonear a algn **push ahead/forward/on** seguir adelante **push in** (GB, coloq) colarse **push off** (GB, coloq) largarse

pushchair /'pʊʃtʃeər/ *n* coche (de niño), carreola (Mx)

pusher /'pʊʃər/ *n* (tb drug ~) (coloq) dealer, jíbaro (And)

push-up /'pʊʃ ʌps/ (*pl* -ups) flexión (de brazos), lagartija (Mx)

pushy /'pʊʃi/ *adj* (coloq) insistente

pussy /'pʊsi/ *n* (*pl* -ies) (tb ~ cat, puss) gatito/a

put /pʊt/ *vt* (-tt-) (*pt/pp* put) 1 poner, meter: ~ *sb out of work* dejar a algn sin trabajo ◊ *Put them together.* Júntalos. 2 decir 3 (pregunta, etc.) hacer 4 (tiempo, etc.) dedicar **NOTA** Para expresiones con *put*, ver el sustantivo, adjetivo, etc., p.ej. **put sth right** en RIGHT. ■ **put sth/yourself across/over** comunicar algo, expresarse **put sth aside** 1 dejar algo a un lado 2 (tb ~ sth by GB) (dinero) ahorrar, reservar algo **put sth away** guardar algo **put sth back** 1 devolver algo a su lugar, guardar algo 2 (reloj) retrasar algo 3 aplazar algo **put sb down** (coloq) humillar, despreciar a algn **put sth down** 1 poner algo (en el suelo, etc.) 2 dejar, soltar algo 3 anotar algo 4 (rebelión)

sofocar algo 5 (animal) sacrificar algo **put sth down to sth** atribuir algo a algo **put sth forward** 1 (propuesta) presentar algo 2 (sugerencia) hacer algo 3 (reloj) adelantar algo **put sth into sth** 1 dedicar algo a algo 2 invertir algo en algo **put sb off** 1 decir a algn que no venga 2 distraer a algn **put sb off sth** quitarle a algn las ganas (de algo) **put sth on** 1 (ropa) ponerse algo 2 (luz, etc.) encender, prender algo 3 (peso): ~ *on weight/a kilo* engordar (un kilo) 4 (Teat) hacer, montar algo 5 fingir algo **be put out** estar molesto **put sth out** 1 sacar algo 2 apagar algo 3 (mano) tender algo **put yourself out** (coloq) molestarse **put sth through** llevar a cabo algo (plan, etc.) **put sb through sth** someter a algn a algo **put sb through (to sb)** comunicar a algn (con algn) (teléfono) **put sth to sb** sugerir algo a algn **put sth together** montar, hacer algo **put sb up** alojar a algn **put sth up** 1 levantar algo 2 (letrero, etc.) poner algo 3 (precio) subir algo **put up with sth/sb** aguantar algo/a algn

putrid /'pjuːtrɪd/ *adj* 1 podrido 2 (color, etc.) asqueroso

putter /'pʌtər/ *vi* ~ **about/around (sth)** hacer trabajitos (en algo)

putty /'pʌti/ *n* masilla, pasta (para ventanas)

puzzle /'pʌzl/ *n* 1 acertijo 2 misterio 3 rompecabezas ● *vt* desconcertar ■ **puzzle sth out** resolver algo **puzzle over sth** devanarse los sesos sobre algo

pygmy /'pɪgmi/ *n* (*pl* -ies) pigmeo/a ● *adj* enano

pyjamas (GB) = PAJAMAS

pylon /'paɪlən; -lɑn GB/ *n* torre de conducción eléctrica

pyramid /'pɪrəmɪd/ *n* pirámide

python /'paɪθən; -θən GB/ *n* pitón

Q q

Q, q /kjuː/ *n* (*pl* Qs, q's) Q, q

quack /kwæk/ *n* 1 graznido 2 (coloq) (Med) charlatán/ana ● *vi* graznar

quadruple /'kwɑ'druːpl/ *adj* cuádruple ● *vt, vi* cuadruplicar(se)

quagmire /'kwægmaɪər/ *n* atolladero

quail /kweɪl/ *n* codorniz

quaint /kweɪnt/ adj 1 curioso 2 (lugar) pintoresco

quake /kweɪk/ vi temblar ● n (coloq) temblor, terremoto

qualification /ˌkwɒlɪfɪˈkeɪʃn/ n 1 (diploma, etc.) título 2 requisito 3 modificación: without ~ sin reserva 4 calificación

qualify /ˈkwɒlɪfaɪ/ (pt/pp -ied) 1 vt ~ sb (for sth/to do sth) capacitar a algn (para algo), dar derecho a algn a algo 2 vi ~ for sth/to do sth tener derecho a sth/to do sth tener derecho a algo 3 vt (declaración) matizar 4 vi ~ (as sth) obtener el título (de algo) 5 vi ~ (as sth) contar (como algo) 6 vi cumplir los requisitos 7 vi (Dep) clasificar(se) **qualified** adj 1 titulado 2 capacitado 3 (éxito, etc.) limitado **qualifying** adj eliminatorio

quality /ˈkwɒlɪti/ n (pl -ies) 1 calidad 2 clase 3 cualidad 4 característica **qualitative** /ˈkwɒlɪtətɪv; -tət- GB/ adj cualitativo

qualm /kwɑːm/ n escrúpulo, duda

quandary /ˈkwɒndəri/ n dilema

quantify /ˈkwɒntɪfaɪ/ vt (pt/pp -ied) cuantificar

quantity /ˈkwɒntəti/ n (pl -ies) cantidad **quantitative** /ˈkwɒntɪtətɪv; -tət- GB/ adj cuantitativo

quarantine /ˈkwɒrəntiːn; ˈkwɔːr- GB/ n cuarentena

quarrel /ˈkwɒrəl; ˈkwɔː- GB/ n 1 riña, pelea 2 queja ● vi (-l-, -ll- GB) (about/over sth) reñir, pelear (por algo) **quarrelsome** adj pendenciero

quarry /ˈkwɒri; ˈkwɔːri GB/ n (pl -ies) 1 cantera 2 (caza) presa

quart /kwɔːt/ n (abrev qt) cuarto de galón (= 0,95 litros) →Ver pág. 222

quarter /ˈkwɔːrtər/ n 1 cuarto 2 cuarta parte 3 (recibos, etc.) trimestre 4 barrio 5 (Can, USA) 25 centavos 6 quarters [pl] (esp Mil) alojamiento ▸ in/from all quarters en/de todas partes

quarter-back n mariscal de campo, corebac (Mx) (fútbol americano)

quarter-final n cuartos de final

quarterly /ˈkwɔːrtərli/ adj trimestral ● adv trimestralmente ● n (pl -ies) revista trimestral

quartet /kwɔːrˈtet/ n cuarteto

quartz /kwɔːrts/ n cuarzo

quash /kwɒʃ/ vt 1 (sentencia) anular 2 (rebelión) sofocar (rumor, etc.) poner fin a

quay /kiː/ n (tb **quayside** /ˈkiːsaɪd/) n muelle

queasy /ˈkwiːzi/ adj mareado

queen /kwiːn/ n reina

queer /kwɪər/ adj raro ● n (coloq, pey) maricón

quell /kwel/ vt 1 (revuelta, etc.) aplastar 2 (duda, etc.) disipar

quench /kwentʃ/ vt apagar

query /ˈkwɪəri/ n (pl -ies) (pregunta) duda ● vt (pt/pp -ied) cuestionar

quest /kwest/ n (fml) búsqueda

question /ˈkwestʃən/ n 1 pregunta 2 cuestión ▸ bring/call sth into question poner algo en duda out of the question impensable ● vt 1 interrogar, hacer preguntas a 2 dudar de **questionable** adj dudoso

questioning /ˈkwestʃənɪŋ/ n interrogatorio ● adj inquisitivo

question mark n signo de interrogación

questionnaire /ˌkwestʃəˈneər/ n cuestionario

queue /kjuː/ n (GB) fila, cola ● vi ~ (up) hacer fila/cola

quick /kwɪk/ (-er/-est) adj 1 rápido: Be ~! ¡Apúrate! ◊ be ~ to do sth no demorar(se) en hacer algo →FAST 2 (mente, etc.) agudo 3 a ~ temper mal genio ● adv rápido →FAST **quicken** vt, vi (fml) 1 acelerar(se) 2 (interés) avivar(se) **quickly** adv rápidamente

quid /kwɪd/ n (pl quid) (GB, coloq) libra (£)

quiet /ˈkwaɪət/ adj (-er/-est) 1 tranquilo 2 callado: Be ~! ¡Cállate! 3 silencioso ● n 1 silencio 2 tranquilidad ▸ on the quiet a escondidas ● vt, vi (quieten GB) ~ (sth/sb) (down) calmar(se) (algo/a algn) **quietly** adv 1 en silencio 2 tranquilamente 3 en voz baja **quietness** n tranquilidad

quilt /kwɪlt/ n edredón

quintet /kwɪnˈtet/ n quinteto

quirk /kwɜːrk/ n rareza **quirky** adj extraño

quit /kwɪt/ (-tt-) (pt/pp quit o tb quitted GB) (coloq) 1 vt, vi dejar 2 vi irse, marcharse

quite /kwaɪt/ adv 1 muy 2 bastante 3 absolutamente: She played ~ brilliantly. Tocó de maravilla. →FAIRLY ▸ quite a few un número considerable **quite a/ some** todo un: It gave us ~ a shock. Me dio un buen susto.

quiver /ˈkwɪvər/ vi temblar, estremecerse ● n temblor

quiz /kwɪz/ n (pl quizzes) concurso, prueba (de conocimientos) ● vt (-zz-) interrogar

quizzical /ˈkwɪzɪkl/ adj inquisitivo

quorum /ˈkwɔːrəm/ n quórum

quota /ˈkwəʊtə/ n 1 cupo 2 cuota, parte

quotation /kwəʊˈteɪʃn/ n 1 (libro, etc.) cita 2 (Fin) cotización 3 presupuesto

quote /kwəʊt/ 1 vt, vi citar 2 vt dar un presupuesto 3 vt cotizar ● n (coloq) 1 (libro, etc.) cita 2 presupuesto 3 quotes (tb quotation marks) comillas

R r

R, r /ɑːr/ n (pl R's, r's) R, r

rabbit /ˈræbɪt/ n conejo →CONEJO

rabid /ˈræbɪd/ adj rabioso

rabies /ˈreɪbiːz/ n (Med) rabia

race /reɪs/ n 1 carrera 2 raza: ~ relations relaciones raciales ● 1 vi (en carrera) correr 2 vi correr a toda velocidad 3 vi competir 4 vi (pulso) latir muy rápido 5 vt ~ sb echar una carrera con algn 6 vt (caballo) hacer correr

racial /ˈreɪʃl/ adj racial **racing** n carreras: ~ bike bicicleta de carreras

racehorse /ˈreɪshɔːrs/ n caballo de carreras

racetrack /ˈreɪstræk/ n 1 (Aut) circuito 2 (USA) (**racecourse** /ˈreɪskɔːrs/ GB) hipódromo

racism /ˈreɪsɪzəm/ n racismo **racist** adj, n racista

rack /ræk/ n 1 soporte 2 (parrilla) portaequipaje 3 **the rack** el potro ● vt ▸ **rack your brain(s)** devanarse los sesos

racket /ˈrækɪt/ n 1 (tb **racquet**) raqueta 2 (coloq) alboroto, mitote (Mx) 3 (coloq) estafa

racy /ˈreɪsi/ adj (-ier/-iest) 1 (estilo) vivo 2 (chiste) picante, colorado (Mx)

radar /ˈreɪdɑːr/ n [U] radar

radiant /ˈreɪdiənt/ adj radiante **radiance** n resplandor

radiate /ˈreɪdieɪt/ 1 vt, vi irradiar 2 vi (de un punto central) salir **radiation** n radiación

radiator /ˈreɪdieɪtər/ n radiador

radical /ˈrædɪkl/ adj, n radical

radio /ˈreɪdiəʊ/ n (pl -s) radio

radioactive /ˌreɪdiəʊˈæktɪv/ adj radiactivo **radioactivity** /ˌreɪdiəʊæk'tɪvəti/ n radiactividad

radish /ˈrædɪʃ/ n rábano

radius /ˈreɪdiəs/ n (pl radii /-diaɪ/) radio

raffle /ˈræfl/ n rifa

raft /ræft; rɑːft GB/ n balsa: life ~ balsa salvavidas

rafter /ˈræftər; ˈrɑːf- GB/ n viga (del techo)

rag /ræg/ n 1 trapo 2 **rags** andrajos 3 (coloq) periodicucho

rage /reɪdʒ/ n 1 cólera ▸ **be all the rage** (coloq) hacer furor ● vi 1 ponerse furioso 2 (tormenta) rugir 3 (batalla) continuar con furia

ragged /ˈrægɪd/ adj 1 (ropa) roto 2 (persona) andrajoso

raging /ˈreɪdʒɪŋ/ adj 1 (dolor, sed) atroz 2 (mar) enfurecido 3 (tormenta) violento

raid /reɪd/ n 1 ~ (on sth) ataque (contra algo) 2 ~ (on sth) (robo) asalto (a algo) 3 (policial) redada ● vt 1 (policía) allanar 2 saquear **raider** n asaltante

rail /reɪl/ n 1 barandal 2 (cortinas) riel 3 (tren) vía: by ~ por ferrocarril

railing /ˈreɪlɪŋ/ n reja (para cercar)

railroad (**railway** GB) /ˈreɪlrəʊd; -weɪ/ n ferrocarril

rain /reɪn/ n lluvia ● vi llover: ~ hard llover mucho

rainbow /ˈreɪnbəʊ/ n arco iris

raincoat /ˈreɪnkəʊt/ n impermeable

rainfall /ˈreɪnfɔːl/ n [U] precipitaciones

rainforest /ˈreɪnfɔːrɪst; -fɒr- GB/ n selva tropical

rainy /ˈreɪni/ adj (-ier/-iest) lluvioso

raise /reɪz/ n (USA) aumento (salarial) ● vt 1 levantar 2 (precio, etc.) subir 3 aumentar 4 (alarma) dar 5 (tema) plantear 6 (dinero) conseguir 7 (niños, animales) criar 8 (Mil) reclutar ▸ **raise your eyebrows** (at sth) 1 arquear las cejas (por algo) 2 sorprenderse (ante algo) **raise your glass (to sb)** alzar la copa (por algn)

raisin /ˈreɪzn/ n pasa

rake /reɪk/ n rastrillo ● vt, vi rastrillar ▸ **rake it in** forrarse, estar haciendo dinero ■ **rake sth up** sacar a relucir algo (pasado, etc.)

rally /ˈræli/ (pt/pp -ied) 1 vi ~ (around) cerrar filas 2 vt reunir 3 vi recuperarse ● n (pl -ies) 1 mitin 2 (tenis) peloteo 3 (Aut) rally

RAM /ræm/ n (abrev de **random access memory**) (Comp) RAM, memoria de acceso directo

ram /ræm/ n carnero ● (-mm-) 1 vi ~ **into sth** chocar (con algo) 2 vt (puerta, etc.) empujar con fuerza

3 *vt* ~ sth in, into, etc. sth meter algo en algo a la fuerza

ramble /ˈræmbl/ *vi* (GB) ~ (on) divagar ● *n* excursión a pie **rambler** *n* excursionista **rambling** *adj* **1** laberíntico **2** (*Bot*) trepador **3** (*discurso*) que se va por las ramas

ramp /ræmp/ *n* rampa

rampage /ræmˈpeɪdʒ/ *vi* desmandarse ● /ˈræmpeɪdʒ/ *n* desmán: *be/go on the ~* desmandarse

rampant /ˈræmpənt/ *adj* **1** desenfrenado **2** (*Bot*) desarrollado

ramshackle /ˈræmʃækl/ *adj* destartalado

ran /ræn/ *pt de* RUN

ranch /rɑːntʃ; ræntʃ GB/ *n* rancho, granja

rancid /ˈrænsɪd/ *adj* rancio

random /ˈrændəm/ *adj* al azar ● *n* ► **at random** al azar

rang /ræŋ/ *pt de* RING²

range /reɪndʒ/ *n* **1** (*montañas*) cadena **2** gama **3** (*productos*) línea **4** escala **5** (*visión, sonido*) campo (de alcance) **6** (*armas*) alcance ● *vi* **1** ~ from sth to sth extenderse, ir desde algo hasta algo **2** ~ from sth to sth; ~ between sth and sth oscilar entre algo y algo **3** *vt* (*fml*) alinear **4** *vi* ~ (over/through sth) recorrer (algo)

rank /ræŋk/ *n* **1** categoría **2** (*Mil*) grado, rango ► **the rank and file** la(s) base(s) ● *vt* **1** ~ sth/sb (as sth) clasificar, considerar algo/a algn ((como) algo) **2** *vi* situarse: *high-ranking* de alto rango

ransack /ˈrænsæk/ *vt* **1** ~ sth (for sth) registrar algo (en busca de algo) **2** desvalijar

ransom /ˈrænsəm/ *n* rescate ► **hold sb to ransom** chantajear a algn

rap /ræp/ *n* **1** golpe seco **2** (*Mús*) rap ● *vt*, *vi* (-pp-) golpear **rapper** *n* cantante de rap, rapero/a

rape /reɪp/ *vt* violar →VIOLATE ● *n* **1** violación **2** (*Bot*) colza **rapist** *n* violador

rapid /ˈræpɪd/ *adj* rápido **rapidity** /rəˈpɪdəti/ *n* rapidez **rapidly** *adv* rápidamente, (muy) deprisa **rapids** *n* [*pl*] rápidos

rapport /ræˈpɔːr/ *n* compenetración

rapt /ræpt/ *adj* absorto

rapture /ˈræptʃər/ *n* éxtasis **rapturous** *adj* delirante

rare /reər/ *adj* (-er/-est) **1** poco común/frecuente **2** (*carne*) poco hecho →HECHO **rarely** *adv* pocas

veces →ALWAYS **rarity** *n* (*pl* -ies) rareza

rash /ræʃ/ *n* salpullido ● *adj* imprudente, precipitado: *in a ~ moment* en un arrebato

raspberry /ˈræzberi; ˈrɑːzbəri GB/ *n* (*pl* -ies) frambuesa

rat /ræt/ *n* rata ► **the rat race** (*coloq, pey*) las carreras de la vida moderna

rate /reɪt/ *n* **1** *vt* estimar, valorar: *highly rated* tenido en gran estima **2** *vt* considerar como ● *n* **1** ritmo: *at a ~ of ten a day* a razón de diez por día **2** tarifa **3** (*Fin*) tipo: *the exchange ~* el tipo de cambio ◊ **at any rate** (*coloq*) de todos modos ◊ **at this/ that rate** (*coloq*) a este/ese paso

rather /ˈræðər; ˈrɑːðə GB/ *adv* algo, bastante: *I ~ suspect...* Me da la impresión de que... **NOTA** Rather con una palabra de sentido positivo implica sorpresa por parte del hablante: *It was a ~ nice present.* También se usa para criticar algo: *This room looks ~ untidy.* → **FAIRLY** ► **I'd, you'd, etc. rather... (than):** *I'd ~ walk than wait for a taxi.* Prefiero ir a pie que esperar un taxi. →**PREFERIR** or rather o mejor dicho **rather than** *prep* mejor que

rating /ˈreɪtɪŋ/ *n* **1** clasificación: *a low popularity ~* un nivel bajo de popularidad **2** **the ratings** (*TV*) los índices de popularidad

ratio /ˈreɪʃiəʊ/ *n* (*pl* -s) proporción

ration /ˈræʃn/ *n* ración ● *vt* racionar **rationing** *n* racionamiento

rational /ˈræʃnəl/ *adj* racional, razonable **rationalization** *n* racionalización **rationalize** *vt* racionalizar

rationality /ˌræʃəˈnæləti/ *n* racionalidad

rattle /ˈrætl/ **1** *vt* hacer sonar **2** *vi* hacer ruido, tintinear **3** *vi* ~ along, past, etc. traquetear ■ **rattle sth off** farfullar algo ● *n* **1** traqueteo **2** sonajero, sonaja (*Mx*)

ravage /ˈrævɪdʒ/ *vt* devastar

rave /reɪv/ *vi* **1** ~ (at sb) despotricar (contra algn) **2** ~ (on) about sth/sb poner por las nubes algo/a algn

raven /ˈreɪvn/ *n* cuervo

raw /rɔː/ *adj* **1** crudo **2** sin refinar: *~ silk* seda cruda ◊ *~ material* materia prima **3** (*herida*) en carne viva

ray /reɪ/ *n* rayo

razor /ˈreɪzər/ *n* máquina/rastrillo de afeitar/rasurar

razor blade n cuchilla de afeitar/rasurar

reach /riːtʃ/ 1 vi ~ (out) (to sb/for sth) alargar la mano (a algn/para agarrar algo) 2 vt alcanzar 3 vt localizar 4 vt llegar a ● n alcance: within/beyond ~ al/fuera del alcance ▸ within (easy) reach a corta distancia

react /riˈækt/ vi reaccionar **reaction** n reacción **reactionary** adj reaccionario

reactor /riˈæktər/ n reactor

read /riːd/ (pt/pp read /red/) 1 vt, vi leer 2 vt ~ sth (as sth) interpretar algo (como algo) 3 vi (artículo, etc.) decir 4 vt (contador, etc.) marcar ■ **read sth into sth** atribuir algo a algo **read on** seguir leyendo **read sth out** leer algo en voz alta **readable** adj legible **reading** n lectura: ~ glasses gafas/lentes para leer

reader /riːdər/ n lector/a **readership** n [sing] (número de) lectores

ready /redi/ adj (-ier/-iest) listo, preparado: get ~ prepararse 2 dispuesto 3 ~ to do sth a punto de hacer algo 4 a (la) mano **readily** adv 1 de buena gana 2 fácilmente **readiness** n disposición: do sth in ~ hacer algo en preparación

ready-made adj (ropa, etc.) de confección 2 (ya) hecho

real /rɪəl/ adj 1 real 2 auténtico

real estate n (USA) bienes raíces: ~ agent corredor/a de bienes raíces

realism /ˈriːəlɪzəm/ n realismo **realist** n realista **realistic** /ˌriːəˈlɪstɪk/ adj realista

reality /riˈæləti/ n (pl -ies) realidad ▸ **in reality** en realidad

realize /ˈriːəlaɪz/ vt 1 darse cuenta de 2 (plan, etc.) cumplir **realization** n comprensión

really /ˈriːəli/ adv 1 [+ verbo] de verdad 2 [+ adj] muy, realmente 3 (sorpresa, duda, etc.): Really? ¿En serio?

realm /relm/ n terreno: the ~s of possibility el ámbito de lo posible

reap /riːp/ vt segar, cosechar

reappear /ˌriːəˈpɪər/ vi reaparecer **reappearance** n reaparición

rear /rɪər/ 1 vt criar 2 vi ~ (up) (caballo) encabritarse 3 vt erguir ● n the rear [sing] la parte trasera ▸ **bring up the rear** ir a la cola ● adj de atrás, trasero

rearrange /ˌriːəˈreɪndʒ/ vt 1 arreglar, cambiar 2 (planes) volver a organizar

reason /ˈriːzn/ n 1 ~ (why...) razón, motivo (por la/el que...) 2 sentido común: make sb see ~ hacer entrar en razón a algn ◇ within ~ dentro de lo razonable ▸ **it stands to reason** es lógico ● vi razonar **reasonable** adj 1 razonable 2 tolerable, regular **reasonably** adv 1 bastante 2 con sensatez **reasoning** n razonamiento

reassure /ˌriːəˈʃʊər/ vt tranquilizar **reassurance** n 1 consuelo 2 palabras tranquilizadoras **reassuring** adj tranquilizador

rebate /ˈriːbeɪt/ n reembolso

rebel /ˈrebl/ n rebelde ● /rɪˈbel/ vi (-ll-) rebelarse **rebellion** /rɪˈbeljən/ n rebelión **rebellious** /rɪˈbeljəs/ adj rebelde

rebirth /ˌriːˈbɜːθ/ n 1 renacimiento 2 resurgimiento

reboot /ˌriːˈbuːt/ vt, vi (Comp) reiniciar

rebound /rɪˈbaʊnd/ vi 1 ~ (from/off sth) rebotar (en algo) 2 ~ (on sb) repercutir (en algn) ● /ˈriːbaʊnd/ n rebote: on the ~ de rebote

rebuff /rɪˈbʌf/ n 1 desaire 2 rechazo ● vt 1 desairar 2 rechazar

rebuild /ˌriːˈbɪld/ vt (pt/pp rebuilt /ˌriːˈbɪlt/) reconstruir

rebuke /rɪˈbjuːk/ vt reprender, regañar ● n reprimenda

recall /rɪˈkɔːl/ vt 1 (fml) recordar 2 llamar 3 (embajador, etc.) retirar 4 (producto) reclamar 5 (parlamento) convocar

recapture /ˌriːˈkæptʃər/ vt 1 recobrar, reconquistar 2 (fig) revivir

recede /rɪˈsiːd/ vi retroceder: receding hairline entradas

receipt /rɪˈsiːt/ n 1 ~ (for sth) recibo, factura (de algo) 2 **receipts** ingresos

receive /rɪˈsiːv/ vt 1 recibir, acoger 2 (herida) sufrir

receiver /rɪˈsiːvər/ n 1 (Radio, TV) receptor 2 (teléfono) auricular 3 destinatario/a

recent /ˈriːsnt/ adj reciente: in ~ years en los últimos años **recently** adv 1 recientemente: until ~ hasta hace poco 2 recién: a recently-built hotel un hotel recién construido

reception /rɪˈsepʃn/ n 1 recepción 2 acogida **receptionist** n recepcionista

receptive /rɪˈseptɪv/ adj receptivo

recess /rɪˈses, ˈriːses/ n 1 (parlamento) receso 2 descanso

3 (*USA, en escuela*) recreo **4** (*nicho*) hueco **5** lugar recóndito

recession /rɪ'seʃn/ *n* recesión

recharge /ˌriː'tʃɑːrdʒ/ *vt* recargar

recipe /'resəpi/ *n* receta

recipient /rɪ'sɪpiənt/ *n* **1** destinatario/a **2** beneficiario/a

reciprocate /rɪ'sɪprəkeɪt/ *vt, vi* corresponder **reciprocal** *adj* recíproco

recite /rɪ'saɪt/ *vt* **1** recitar **2** enumerar **recital** *n* recital

reckless /'rekləs/ *adj* **1** temerario **2** imprudente

reckon /'rekən/ *vt* **1** considerar **2** (*coloq*) creer **3** calcular ■ **reckon on sth/sb** contar con algo/algn **reckon with sth/sb** contar con algn, tomar algo en consideración: *There's your father to ~ with.* Hay que vérselas con tu padre. **reckoning** *n* [*sing*] **1** cálculos **2** cuentas

reclaim /rɪ'kleɪm/ *vt* **1** recuperar **2** reciclar **reclamation** /ˌreklə'meɪʃn/ *n* recuperación

recline /rɪ'klaɪn/ *vt, vi* reclinar(se) **reclining** *adj* reclinable

recognition /ˌrekəg'nɪʃn/ *n* reconocimiento: *have changed beyond ~* estar irreconocible

recognize /'rekəgnaɪz/ *vt* reconocer **recognizable** *adj* reconocible

recoil /rɪ'kɔɪl/ *vi* **1** sentir repugnancia **2** retroceder

recollect /ˌrekə'lekt/ *vt* recordar **recollection** *n* (*fml*) recuerdo

recommend /ˌrekə'mend/ *vt* recomendar **recommendation** *n* recomendación

recompense /'rekəmpens/ (*fml*) *vt* recompensar ● *n* recompensa

reconcile /'rekənsaɪl/ *vt* **1** conciliar **2** conciliar **3 ~ yourself (to sth)** resignarse (a algo) **reconciliation** [*sing*] **1** conciliación **2** reconciliación

reconnaissance /rɪ'kɒnɪsns/ *n* (*Mil, etc.*) reconocimiento

reconsider /ˌriːkən'sɪdər/ *vt* **1** considerar **2** *vi* recapacitar

reconstruct /ˌriːkən'strʌkt/ *vt* reconstruir

record /rɪ'kɔːrd/ *vt* **1** registrar, anotar **2** *vt, vi* grabar **3** *vt* (*termómetro, etc.*) marcar ● /'rekɔːrd; 'rekɔːd *GB*/ *n* **1** registro **2** historial: *track ~* trayectoria ◇ *a criminal ~* antecedentes penales **3** disco ▪ *company* casa discográfica ◇ *~ player* tocadiscos **4** récord ▶ **put/set the record straight** dejar/poner las cosas claras **recording** /rɪ'kɔːrdɪŋ/ *n* grabación

record-breaking *adj* sin precedentes

recorder /rɪ'kɔːrdər/ *n* **1** flauta (*dulce*) **2** *tape/video ~* grabadora/(aparato de) video

recount /rɪ'kaʊnt/ *vt* referir

recourse /rɪ'kɔːrs/ *n* (*fml*) recurso: *have ~ to sth/sb* recurrir a algo/algn

recover /rɪ'kʌvər/ **1** *vt* recuperar **2** *vi* recuperarse **recovery** *n* (*pl* **-ies**) recuperación, rescate **2** [*sing*] restablecimiento

recreation /ˌrekri'eɪʃn/ *n* pasatiempo, recreación

recruit /rɪ'kruːt/ *n* recluta ● *vt* reclutar **recruitment** *n* reclutamiento

rectangle /'rektæŋgl/ *n* rectángulo

rector /'rektər/ *n* párroco **rectory** *n* (*pl* **-ies**) casa del párroco

recuperate /rɪ'kuːpəreɪt/ *vt, vi* (*fml*) recuperar(se)

recur /rɪ'kɜːr/ *vi* (**-rr-**) repetirse

recycle /ˌriː'saɪkl/ *vt* reciclar **recyclable** *adj* reciclable **recycling** *n* reciclaje

red /red/ *adj* (**redder, -est**) **1** rojo **2** (*rostro*) colorado **3** (*vino*) tinto ● *n* rojo **reddish** *adj* rojizo

redeem /rɪ'diːm/ *vt* **1** redimir: *~ yourself* salvarse **2** recompensar **3** desempeñar **redemption** /rɪ'dempʃn/ *n* (*fml*) redención

redevelopment /ˌriːdɪ'veləpmənt/ *n* reurbanización

redo /ˌriː'duː/ *vt* (*3ª pers sing pres* **redoes** *pt* **redid** /-'dɪd/ *pp* **redone** /-'dʌn/) rehacer

red tape *n* papeleo

reduce /rɪ'djuːs; rɪ'djuːs *GB*/ **1** *vt* **~ sth (by sth)** disminuir algo (en algo) **2** *vt, vi* reducir(se): *The house was reduced to ashes.* La casa quedó reducida a cenizas. ◇ *~ sb to tears* hacer llorar a algn **reduced** *adj* rebajado

reduction /rɪ'dʌkʃn/ *n* **1 ~ (in sth)** reducción (de algo) **2 ~ (in sth)** rebaja, descuento (de algo)

redundant /rɪ'dʌndənt/ *adj* **1** (*GB*) *be made ~* ser despedido (por cierre/reducción de personal) **2** superfluo **redundancy** *n* (*GB*) (*pl* **-ies**) despido (*por cierre/reducción de personal*)

reed /riːd/ *n* junco, carrizo

reef /riːf/ *n* arrecife

reek /riːk/ *vi* **~ (of sth)** apestar (a algo)

reel /riːl/ *n* **1** bobina, carrete **2** (*Fot*) rollo ● *vi* **1** tambalearse **2** (*cabeza*) dar vueltas ■ **reel sth off** recitar algo (de un tirón)

re-enter *vt* volver a entrar a **re-entry** *n* reentrada

refer /rɪ'fɜːr/ (**-rr-**) **1** *vi* referirse **2** *vt*, *vi* remitir(se)

referee /ˌrefə'riː/ *n* **1** árbitro/a **2** juez árbitro **3** (*GB, para empleo*) persona que da una referencia ● *vt, vi* arbitrar

reference /'refərəns/ *n* referencia ▸ **in/with reference to sth/sb** en/con referencia a algo/algn

referendum /ˌrefə'rendəm/ *n* referéndum

refill /ˌriː'fɪl/ *vt* rellenar ● /'riːfɪl/ *n* relleno, repuesto, carga

refine /rɪ'faɪn/ *vt* **1** refinar **2** (*técnica, etc.*) pulir **refined** *adj* **1** refinamiento **2** (*Mec*) refinación **3** sutileza **refinery** *n* (*pl* **-ies**) refinería

reflect /rɪ'flekt/ **1** *vt, vi* reflejar(se) **2** *vi* reflexionar ▸ **reflect well/badly on sth/sb** decir mucho/poco en favor de algo/algn **reflection** *n* **1** reflejo: *be a ~ on sb* decir mucho de algn **2** (*pensamiento*) reflexión: *on ~* pensándolo bien

reflex /'riːfleks/ *n* reflejo

reform /rɪ'fɔːrm/ *vt, vi* reformar(se) ● *n* reforma **reformation** *n* **1** reforma **2** **the Reformation** la Reforma

refrain /rɪ'freɪn/ *vi* (*fml*) abstenerse ● *n* estribillo

refresh /rɪ'freʃ/ *vt* refrescar ▸ **refresh sb's memory** refrescarle la memoria a algn **refreshing** *adj* **1** refrescante **2** alentador

refreshments /rɪ'freʃmənts/ *n* [*pl*] refrescos y botanas (*Mx*), pasabocas (*And*) **NOTA** Se usa en singular cuando precede a un sustantivo: *a refreshment stop* una parada para tomar algo.

refrigerator /rɪ'frɪdʒəreɪtər/ *n* nevera, refrigerador **refrigerate** *vt* refrigerar **refrigeration** *n* refrigeración

refuel /ˌriː'fjuːəl/ *vi* (**-l-, -ll-** *GB*) repostar

refuge /'refjuːdʒ/ *n* **1** refugio: *take ~* refugiarse **2** (*Pol*) asilo

refugee /ˌrefju'dʒiː/ *n* refugiado/a

refund /rɪ'fʌnd/ *vt* reembolsar ● /'riːfʌnd/ *n* reembolso

refuse¹ /rɪ'fjuːz/ *vt* rechazar: *~ sb entry* negar la entrada a algn **2** *vi* negarse a algo **refusal** *n* **1** rechazo **2** negativa

refuse² /'refjuːs/ *n* [*U*] desperdicios

regain /rɪ'geɪn/ *vt* recuperar

regal /'riːgl/ *adj* regio

regard /rɪ'gɑːrd/ *vt* **1** ~ *sth/sb as* **sth** considerar algo/a algn algo **2** (*fml*) mirar ▸ **as regards sth/sb** en/por lo que se refiere a algo/algn ● *n* **1** respeto **2** *regards* (*en cartas*) saludos ▸ **in this/that regard** (*fml*) en este/ese aspecto **in/with regard to sth/sb** (*fml*) con respecto a algo/algn **regarding** *prep* referente a **regardless** *adv* pase lo que pase, a pesar de todo **regardless of** *prep* sin tener en cuenta

regime /reɪ'ʒiːm/ *n* régimen (*gobierno, reglas, etc.*)

regiment /'redʒɪmənt/ *n* regimiento **regimented** *adj* reglamentado

region /'riːdʒən/ *n* región ▸ **in the region of sth** alrededor de algo

register /'redʒɪstər/ *n* **1** registro **2** (*colegio*) lista ● **1** *vt* registrar **2** *vi* inscribirse **3** (*sorpresa, etc.*) mostrar **4** (*correo*) mandar certificado/recomendado

registered mail (**registered post** *GB*) *n* correo certificado/recomendado

registrar /'redʒɪstrɑːr/ *n* **1** funcionario/a (*registro civil, etc.*) **2** (*Educ*) subdirector/a (*admisiones, exámenes, etc.*)

registration /ˌredʒɪ'streɪʃn/ *n* **1** registro **2** inscripción **3** (*GB*) (*tb ~ number*) número de la placa

registry office /'redʒɪstri ɒfɪs/ (*tb* **register office**) *n* (oficina del) registro civil, notaría (*And*)

regret /rɪ'gret/ *n* **1** ~ (*at/about sth*) pesar (por algo) **2** remordimiento ● *vt* (**-tt-**) **1** lamentar **2** arrepentirse de **regretfully** *adv* con pesar/pena **regrettable** *adj* lamentable

regular /'regjələr/ *adj* **1** regular: *on a ~ basis* con regularidad **2** habitual ● *n* cliente habitual **regularity** /ˌregju'lærəti/ *n* regularidad

regulate /'regjuleɪt/ *vt* regular, reglamentar **regulation** *n* **1** regulación **2** norma

rehabilitate /ˌriːə'bɪlɪteɪt/ *vt* rehabilitar **rehabilitation** *n* rehabilitación

rehearse /rɪ'hɜːrs/ *vt, vi* ~ (*sb*) (*for sth*) ensayar (algo) (con algn) **rehearsal** *n* ensayo: *dress ~* ensayo general

reign /reɪn/ *n* reinado ● *vi* reinar

reimburse /ˌriːɪm'bɜːrs/ *vt* reembolsar

rein /reɪn/ *n* rienda

reincarnation /ˌriːɪnkɑːr'neɪʃn/ *n* reencarnación

reindeer /ˈreɪndɪər/ n (pl reindeer) reno

reinforce /ˌriːɪnˈfɔːrs/ vt reforzar **reinforcement** n refuerzo

reinstate /ˌriːɪnˈsteɪt/ vt restituir

reject /rɪˈdʒekt/ vt rechazar ● /ˈriːdʒekt/ n 1 marginado/a 2 cosa defectuosa **rejection** /rɪˈdʒekʃn/ n rechazo

rejoice /rɪˈdʒɔɪs/ vi ~ (at/in/over sth) (fml) alegrarse, regocijarse (por/de algo)

rejoin /ˌriːˈdʒɔɪn/ vt 1 reincorporarse a 2 volver a juntarse con

relapse /rɪˈlæps/ vi recaer ● n recaída

relate /rɪˈleɪt/ vt 1 (fml) relatar 2 relacionar ■ **relate to sth/sb 1** estar relacionado con algo/algn **2** identificarse con algo/algn **related** adj **1** relacionado **2** ~ (to sb) emparentado (con algn): be ~ by marriage ser pariente(s) político(s)

relation /rɪˈleɪʃn/ n **1** ~ (to sth) relación (con algo) **2** pariente **3** parentesco: Is he any ~? ¿Es familiar tuyo? ▸ **in relation to** con relación a **relationship** n **1** relación **2** (relación de) parentesco

relative /ˈrelətɪv/ n pariente ● adj relativo

relax /rɪˈlæks/ **1** vt, vi relajar(se) **2** vt aflojar **relaxation** n **1** descanso **2** pasatiempo **3** relajación **relaxing** adj relajante

relay /ˈriːleɪ/ n **1** (tb ~ race) carrera de relevos **2** (tb /ˈriːleɪ, rɪˈleɪ/ vt) transmitir **2** (GB, TV, Radio) retransmitir

release /rɪˈliːs/ vt **1** poner en libertad **2** soltar **4** (noticia) dar a conocer **5** (CD, etc.) poner a la venta **6** (Cine) estrenar ● n **1** liberación **2** puesta en libertad **3** aparición (CD, etc.), publicación, estreno: The movie is on general ~. Dan la película en todos los cines. **4** press ~ comunicado de prensa

relegate /ˈrelɪɡeɪt/ vt **1** relegar **2** (Dep) bajar **relegation** n (Dep) descenso

relent /rɪˈlent/ vi ceder **relentless** adj **1** implacable **2** tenaz

relevant /ˈreləvənt/ adj relevante **relevance** n relevancia

reliable /rɪˈlaɪəbl/ adj **1** (persona) de confianza **2** confiable **3** (fuente) fidedigno **4** (aparato, etc.) fiable **reliability** /rɪˌlaɪəˈbɪləti/ n confiabilidad

reliance /rɪˈlaɪəns/ n on sth/sb dependencia de algo/algn

relic /ˈrelɪk/ n reliquia

relief /rɪˈliːf/ n **1** alivio: much to my ~ por suerte para mí **2** ayuda **3** (persona) relevo **4** (Arte, Geog) relieve

relieve /rɪˈliːv/ vt **1** aliviar **2** ~ yourself hacer uno sus necesidades **3** relevar ■ **relieve sb of sth** quitar algo a algn

religion /rɪˈlɪdʒən/ n religión **religious** adj religioso

relinquish /rɪˈlɪŋkwɪʃ/ vt (fml) renunciar a **NOTA** Es más común **give sth up**.

relish /ˈrelɪʃ/ n gusto ● vt disfrutar

reluctant /rɪˈlʌktənt/ adj reacio **reluctance** n renuencia **reluctantly** adv de mala gana

rely /rɪˈlaɪ/ vi (pt/pp -ied) ~ on/upon sth/sb depender de, contar con algo/algn

remain /rɪˈmeɪn/ vi (fml) **1** quedar(se) **NOTA** Es más común **stay**. **2** permanecer, seguir siendo **remainder** n [sing] resto (tb Mat) **remains** n [pl] **1** restos **2** ruinas

remand /rɪˈmænd/ /rɪˈmɑːnd/ GB/ vt: ~ sb in custody/on bail poner a algn en prisión preventiva/en libertad bajo fianza ● n custodia: on ~ detenido

remark /rɪˈmɑːrk/ vt, vi comentar, hacer un comentario ● n comentario **remarkable** adj **1** extraordinario **2** notable

remedial /rɪˈmiːdiəl/ adj **1** reparador, de recuperación **2** (clases) para niños con dificultades de aprendizaje

remedy /ˈremədi/ n (pl -ies) remedio ● vt (pt/pp -ied) remediar

remember /rɪˈmembər/ vt, vi acordarse (de): as far as I ~ que yo recuerde **NOTA** Cuando **remember** va seguido de un infinitivo, este hace referencia a una acción que todavía no se ha realizado: Remember to mail the letter. Acuérdate de mandar la carta. Seguido por una forma en -ing, este se refiere a una acción que ya ha tenido lugar: I ~ mailing the letter. Recuerdo haber mandado esa carta. **2** vt ~ sb to sb dar saludos de algn a algn **remembrance** n **1** conmemoración **2** (fml) recuerdo

remind /rɪˈmaɪnd/ vt **1** ~ sb (to do sth) recordarle a algn (que haga algo) **2** ~ sb of sth/sb recordar algo/a algn a algn: He ~s me of John. Me recuerda a John. **reminder** n **1** recuerdo, recordatorio **2** aviso

reminisce /ˌremɪ'nɪs/ vi ~ (about sth) rememorar (algo) **reminiscence** n recuerdo **reminiscent** adj ~ of sth/sb con reminiscencias de algo/algn

remnant /'remnənt/ n 1 resto 2 vestigio 3 retazo (tela)

remorse /rɪ'mɔːrs/ n [U] remordimiento **remorseless** adj 1 despiadado 2 implacable

remote /rɪ'moʊt/ adj (-er/-est) 1 remoto, lejano 2 (persona) distante

remote control n control remoto

remove /rɪ'muːv/ vt 1 ~ quitar(se) **NOTA** Es más común take off, take out, take off. 2 eliminar 3 sacar, destituir **removable** adj que se puede quitar **removal** n 1 eliminación 2 (GB) mudanza, trasteo

the Renaissance /'renəsəns, rɪ-'neɪsns GB/ n el Renacimiento

render /'rendər/ vt (fml) 1 (servicio, etc.) prestar 2 hacer: be rendered speechless quedar mudo 3 (Mús, Arte) interpretar

rendezvous /'rɒndɪvuː/ n (pl rendezvous /-vuːz/) 1 cita 2 lugar de reunión

renegade /'renɪɡeɪd/ n (fml) renegado/a, rebelde

renew /rɪ'nuː; rɪ'njuː GB/ vt 1 renovar 2 reanudar 3 reafirmar **renewable** adj renovable **renewal** n renovación

renounce /rɪ'naʊns/ vt (fml) renunciar a

renovate /'renəveɪt/ vt restaurar

renowned /rɪ'naʊnd/ adj famoso

rent /rent/ n alquiler, renta ▸ for rent se alquila(n), se renta(n) (Mx) →ALQUILAR ● vt 1 ~ sth (from sb) alquilar, rentar (Mx) algo de algn 2 ~ sth (out) (to sb) alquilar, rentar (Mx) algo a (algn) **rental** n alquiler, renta (Mx) (carros, etc.)

reorganize /rɪ'ɔːrɡənaɪz/ vt, vi reorganizar(se)

rep /rep/ n (coloq) representante

repair /rɪ'peər/ vt 1 reparar, arreglar 2 remediar ● n reparación: It's beyond ~. No tiene arreglo. ▸ in (a) good (state of) repair en buen estado

repay /rɪ'peɪ/ vt (pt/pp repaid) 1 devolver 2 (persona) reembolsar 3 (deuda, etc.) pagar 4 (amabilidad) corresponder a **repayment** n 1 reembolso, devolución 2 pago

repeat /rɪ'piːt/ vt, vi repetir(se) 2 vt (confidencia) contar ● n repetición **repeated** adj 1 repetido 2 reiterado

repel /rɪ'pel/ vt (-ll-) 1 repeler 2 rechazar 3 repugnar

repellent /rɪ'pelənt/ adj, n repelente

repent /rɪ'pent/ vt, vi arrepentirse (de) **repentance** n arrepentimiento

repercussion /ˌriːpər'kʌʃn/ n repercusión

repertoire /'repərtwɑːr/ n repertorio (de un músico, actor, etc.)

repertory /'repərtɔːri, -tri GB/ n compañía de repertorio

repetition /ˌrepə'tɪʃn/ n repetición **repetitive** /rɪ'petətɪv/ adj repetitivo

replace /rɪ'pleɪs/ vt 1 colocar de nuevo en su sitio 2 reponer 3 reemplazar 4 (algo roto o desgastado) cambiar 5 destituir **replacement** n 1 sustitución 2 suplente 3 (pieza) repuesto

replay /'riːpleɪ/ n 1 partido de desempate 2 (TV) repetición

reply /rɪ'plaɪ/ vi (pt/pp -ied) responder ● n (pl -ies) respuesta

report /rɪ'pɔːrt/ 1 vt informar de, comunicar 2 vt (crimen, etc.) denunciar 3 vt ~ on sth informar (sobre algo) 4 vi ~ to/for sth presentarse en/a algo: ~ sick informar sobre incapacidad 5 vi ~ to sb rendir cuentas a algn ● n 1 informe 2 noticia 3 (Period) reportaje 4 informe escolar **reportedly** adv según nuestras fuentes **reporter** n reportero/a

represent /ˌreprɪ'zent/ vt 1 representar 2 describir **representation** n representación

representative /ˌreprɪ'zentətɪv/ adj representativo ● n 1 representante: sales ~ representante de ventas 2 (USA, Pol) diputado/a

repress /rɪ'pres/ vt 1 reprimir 2 contener **repression** n represión

reprieve /rɪ'priːv/ n 1 indulto 2 (fig) respiro

reprimand /'reprɪmænd; -mɑːnd GB/ vt reprender ● n reprimenda

reprisal /rɪ'praɪzl/ n represalia

reproach /rɪ'proʊtʃ/ vt ~ sb (for/with sth) reprochar (algo) a algn ● n reproche: above/beyond ~ por encima de toda crítica

reproduce /ˌriːprə'duːs; -'djuːs GB/ vt, vi reproducir(se) **reproduction** n reproducción **reproductive** adj reproductor

reptile /'reptaɪl/ n reptil

republic /rɪ'pʌblɪk/ n república **republican** adj republicano

repugnant /rɪ'pʌɡnənt/ adj repugnante

repulsive /rɪ'pʌlsɪv/ *adj* repulsivo

reputable /'repjətəbl/ *adj* 1 de buena reputación, de confianza 2 (*empresa*) acreditado

reputation /,repju'teɪʃn/ *n* reputación, fama

repute /rɪ'pjuːt/ *n* (*fml*) reputación, fama **reputed** *adj* supuesto: *He is ~ to be...* Tiene fama de ser... **reputedly** *adv* según se dice

request /rɪ'kwest/ *n* ~ (**for sth**) petición, solicitud (de algo): *make a ~ for sth* pedir algo ● *vt* (*fml*) ~ **sth (from/of sb)** pedir algo (a algn): *You are requested not to smoke.* Se ruega no fumar. **NOTA** Es más común **ask for**.

require /rɪ'kwaɪər/ *vt* (*fml*) 1 requerir 2 necesitar **NOTA** Es más común **need**. 3 ~ **sb to do sth** (*fml*) exigir a algn que haga algo **requirement** *n* 1 necesidad 2 requisito

rescue /'reskjuː/ *vt* rescatar, salvar ● *n* rescate **rescuer** *n* salvador/a

research /rɪ'sɜːtʃ, 'riːsɜːtʃ/ *n* [U] investigación (*no policial*) /rɪ'sɜːtʃ/ *vt, vi* investigar **researcher** *n* investigador/a

resemble /rɪ'zembl/ *vt* parecerse a **resemblance** *n* parecido

resent /rɪ'zent/ *vt* resentirse de/por **resentful** *adj* de resentimiento **resentment** *n* resentimiento

reservation /,rezər'veɪʃn/ *n* reserva, reservación

reserve /rɪ'zɜːrv/ *vt* reservar(se) ● *n* 1 reserva(s) 2 **reserves** (*Mil*) reservistas ▸ **in reserve** de reserva **reserved** *adj* reservado

reservoir /'rezərvwɑːr/ *n* 1 embalse, represa 2 (*fig*) reserva

reshuffle /,riː'ʃʌfl/ *n* reorganización

reside /rɪ'zaɪd/ *vi* (*fml*) residir

resident /'rezɪdənt/ *n* 1 residente 2 (*hotel*) huésped ● *adj* residente: *be ~* residir **residence** *n* (*fml*) 1 residencia 2 (*fml*) casa **residential** /,rezɪ'denʃl/ *adj* 1 de viviendas 2 (*curso*) con alojamiento incluido

residue /'rezɪdjuː; -'djuː *GB*/ *n* residuo

resign /rɪ'zaɪn/ 1 *vt, vi* renunciar 2 *vt* ~ **yourself to sth** resignarse a algo **resignation** *n* 1 renuncia, dimisión 2 resignación

resilient /rɪ'zɪliənt/ *adj* resistente **resilience** *n* 1 elasticidad 2 capacidad de recuperación

resist /rɪ'zɪst/ 1 *vt, vi* resistir(se) (a) 2 *vt* oponerse a **resistance** *n* resistencia: *put up ~* oponer resistencia

resolute /'rezəluːt/ *adj* resuelto **NOTA** Es más común **determined**. **resolutely** *adv* 1 con firmeza 2 resueltamente **resolution** *n* 1 resolución 2 propósito: *New Year' ~s* propósitos para el Año Nuevo

resolve /rɪ'zɒlv/ (*fml*) 1 *vt, vi* resolver(se) 2 *vt* acordar 3 *vt* (*disputa, crisis*) resolver

resort /rɪ'zɔːrt/ *n* 1 *a coastal/seaside ~* un centro turístico costero ◇ *a ski ~* una estación de esquí 2 *as a last ~* como último recurso ● *vi* recurrir

resounding /rɪ'zaʊndɪŋ/ *adj* rotundo

resource /'riːsɔːrs/ *n* recurso **resourceful** *adj* de recursos, recursivo (*And*): ~ *tener ingenio para salir de apuros*

respect /rɪ'spekt/ *n* 1 respeto, consideración 2 concepto: *in this ~ en este sentido* ▸ **with respect to sth** (*fml*) por lo que respecta a algo ● *vt* respetar **respectable** *adj* 1 respetable 2 considerable **respectful** *adj* respetuoso **respective** /rɪ'spektɪv/ *adj* respectivo

respite /'respɪt; -paɪt *GB*/ *n* 1 respiro 2 alivio

respond /rɪ'spɒnd/ *vi* 1 responder 2 contestar **NOTA** Es más común **answer** o **reply**. **response** *n* 1 respuesta 2 reacción **responsive** *adj* 1 receptivo 2 sensible

responsible /rɪ'spɒnsəbl/ *adj* ~ (**for sth**); ~ (**to sth/sb**) responsable (de algo); (*ante algn/algn*): *She's ~ for five patients.* Tiene cinco pacientes a su cargo. **responsibility** /rɪ,spɒnsə'bɪləti/ *n* (*pl* -**ies**) ~ (**for sth/sb**); ~ (**to sb**) responsabilidad (por algo/algn; (*ante algn*)

rest /rest/ 1 *vt, vi* descansar 2 *vt, vi* apoyar(se) 3 *vi*: *let the matter ~* dejar el asunto ● *n* 1 [U] el resto 2 [*pl*] los/las demás, los/las otros/as 3 *get some ~* descansar ▸ **at rest** en reposo/paz **come to rest** pararse **restful** *adj* descansado **restless** *adj* 1 agitado 2 inquieto: *become/grow ~* impacientarse 3 *have a ~ night* pasar una mala noche

restaurant /'restrɒnt; -trɒnt *GB*/ *n* restaurante

restore /rɪ'stɔːr/ *vt* 1 devolver 2 restablecer 3 restaurar 4 (*fml*) (*bienes*) restituir **restoration**

R

/ˌrestəˈreɪʃn/ n 1 devolución 2 restauración 3 restablecimiento

restrain /rɪˈstreɪn/ vt contener **restrained** adj medido, comedido **restraint** n 1 compostura 2 restricción 3 moderación

restrict /rɪˈstrɪkt/ vt limitar **restricted** adj limitado, restringido **restriction** n restricción **restrictive** adj restrictivo

restroom /ˈrestruːm/ n (USA) (cuarto de) baño →TOILET

result /rɪˈzʌlt/ n resultado: As a ~ of... Como consecuencia de... ● vi 1 ~ (from sth) ser el resultado (de algo), originarse (por algo) 2 ~ in sth resultar en algo

resume /rɪˈzuːm/ (fml) 1 vt, vi reanudar(se) 2 vt recobrar **resumption** /rɪˈzʌmpʃn/ n (fml) reanudación

resumé /ˈrezəmeɪ; ˈrezjuː GB/ n (USA) currículum vitae

resurgence /rɪˈsɜːrdʒəns/ n resurgimiento

resurrect /ˌrezəˈrekt/ vt resucitar: ~ old traditions hacer revivir viejas tradiciones **resurrection** n resurrección

resuscitate /rɪˈsʌsɪteɪt/ vt reanimar, resucitar **resuscitation** n reanimación

retail /ˈriːteɪl/ n venta al por menor: ~ price precio de venta al público ● vt, vi vender(se) al público **retailer** n (comerciante) minorista

retain /rɪˈteɪn/ vt (fml) 1 quedarse con 2 conservar 3 retener

retaliate /rɪˈtælieɪt/ vi ~ (against sth/sb) vengarse (de algo/algn) **retaliation** n [U] represalia

retarded /rɪˈtɑːrdɪd/ adj retrasado

retch /retʃ/ vi dar arcadas

retention /rɪˈtenʃn/ n (fml) retención, conservación

rethink /ˌriːˈθɪŋk/ vt (pt/pp rethought /-ˈθɔːt/) reconsiderar

reticent /ˈretɪsnt/ adj reservado **reticence** n reserva

retire /rɪˈtaɪər/ 1 vi, vi jubilar(se) 2 vi (fml) retirarse (a sus aposentos) **retired** adj jubilado **retirement** n jubilación, retiro **retiring** adj 1 retraído 2 que se jubila

retort /rɪˈtɔːrt/ n réplica, contestación ● vt replicar

retrace /rɪˈtreɪs/ vt: ~ your steps volver sobre tus pasos

retract /rɪˈtrækt/ (fml) 1 vt retractarse de 2 vt, vi retraer(se), replegar(se)

retreat /rɪˈtriːt/ vi batirse en retirada ● n 1 retirada 2 (Mil) retreta 3 retiro 4 refugio

retrial /ˌriːˈtraɪəl/ n nuevo juicio

retribution /ˌretrɪˈbjuːʃn/ n (fml) 1 justo castigo 2 venganza

retrieve /rɪˈtriːv/ vt 1 (fml) recobrar 2 (Comp) recuperar **retrieval** n recuperación **retriever** n perro de caza

retrograde /ˈretrəgreɪd/ adj (fml) retrógrado

retrospect /ˈretrəspekt/ n ▶ in retrospect mirando hacia atrás

retrospective /ˌretrəˈspektɪv/ adj 1 retrospectivo 2 retroactivo ● n (exposición) retrospectiva

return /rɪˈtɜːrn/ 1 vi regresar, volver 2 vt devolver 3 vt (Jur) declarar 4 vt (Pol, GB) elegir 5 vi (síntoma) reaparecer ● n 1 vuelta, regreso: ~ journey viaje de regreso 2 retorno 3 reaparición 4 devolución, regreso (Mx) 5 declaración: tax ~ declaración de (la) renta 6 ~ (on sth) rendimiento (de algo) 7 (GB) (tb ~ ticket) boleto/tiquete de ida y vuelta ▶ in return (for sth) en recompensa/a cambio (de algo) **returnable** adj 1 (fml) reembolsable 2 (envase) retornable

reunion /riːˈjuːniən/ n reunión

reunite /ˌriːjuːˈnaɪt/ vt, vi 1 reunir(se) 2 reconciliar(se)

rev /rev/ n [gen pl] (coloq) revolución (motor) ● vt, vi (-vv-) ~ (sth) (up) acelerar (algo)

revalue /ˌriːˈvæljuː/ vt revaluar, revalor(iz)ar **revaluation** n revalorización

revamp /ˌriːˈvæmp/ vt modernizar

reveal /rɪˈviːl/ vt 1 revelar 2 mostrar **revealing** adj 1 revelador 2 (vestido) atrevido

revelation /ˌrevəˈleɪʃn/ n revelación

revenge /rɪˈvendʒ/ n venganza: take ~ on sb vengarse de algn ● vt ~ yourself/be revenged on sb (fml) vengarse de algn

revenue /ˈrevənuː; -njuː GB/ n [U] ingresos

reverberate /rɪˈvɜːrbəreɪt/ vi 1 resonar 2 (fml) tener repercusiones **reverberation** n 1 resonancia 2 **reverberations** repercusiones

revere /rɪˈvɪər/ vt (fml) venerar **reverence** /ˈrevərəns/ n (fml) reverencia (veneración) **reverent** adj (fml) reverente

revel /ˈrevl/ vi (-l-, -ll- GB) ~ in sth deleitarse en algo

reverend /'revərənd/ adj (abrev **Rev.**) reverendo

reversal /rɪ'vɜːsl/ n 1 cambio 2 (suerte) revés 3 (Jur) revocación 4 (de papeles) inversión

reverse /rɪ'vɜːs/ n 1 the ~ (of sth) lo contrario (de algo) 2 reverso 3 (papel) dorso 4 (tb ~ gear) reversa ● 1 vt invertir 2 vt, vi poner/ir en reversa 3 vt (decisión) revocar 4 ~ (the) charges (GB) llamar por cobrar/cobro revertido

revert /rɪ'vɜːt/ vi 1 (fml) volver (a un estado o tema anterior) 2 (Jur) revertir

review /rɪ'vjuː/ n 1 examen, revisión 2 (Period) reseña 3 informe 4 (Mil) revista ● 1 vt reconsiderar 2 vt examinar 3 vt hacer una reseña de, vi (USA) repasar 5 vt (Mil) pasar revista a **reviewer** n crítico/a

revise /rɪ'vaɪz/ 1 vt revisar 2 vt modificar 3 vt, vi (GB) repasar **revision** /rɪ'vɪʒn/ n 1 revisión 2 modificación 3 (GB) repaso: do some ~ repasar

revive /rɪ'vaɪv/ 1 vt, vi reanimar(se) 2 vt reavivar 3 vt, vi (Econ) reactivar(se) 4 vt (Teat) reponer **revival** n 1 restablecimiento 2 (moda) resurgimiento 3 (Teat) reposición

revoke /rɪ'vəʊk/ vt (fml) revocar

revolt /rɪ'vəʊlt/ 1 vi sublevarse, rebelarse 2 vt dar asco a ● n sublevación, rebelión

revolting /rɪ'vəʊltɪŋ/ adj repugnante

revolution /ˌrevə'luːʃn/ n revolución **revolutionary** adj, n (pl -ies) revolucionario/a

revolve /rɪ'vɒlv/ vt, vi (hacer) girar ▪ **revolve around** sth/algn girar alrededor de algo/algn

revolver /rɪ'vɒlvə(r)/ n revólver

revulsion /rɪ'vʌlʃn/ n (fml) repugnancia

reward /rɪ'wɔːd/ n recompensa, premio ● vt recompensar **rewarding** adj gratificante

rewind /ˌriː'waɪnd/ vt (pt/pp rewound /-'waʊnd/) rebobinar, devolver

rewrite /ˌriː'raɪt/ vt (pt rewrote /-'rəʊt/ pp rewritten /-'rɪtn/) volver a escribir

rhetoric /'retərɪk/ n retórica

rheumatism /'ruːmətɪzəm/ n reuma, reumatismo

rhino /'raɪnəʊ/ n (pl -s) (tb **rhinoceros** /raɪ'nɒsərəs/) rinoceronte

rhubarb /'ruːbɑːb/ n ruibarbo

rhyme /raɪm/ n 1 rima 2 (poema) verso ● vt, vi rimar

rhythm /'rɪðəm/ n ritmo

rib /rɪb/ n costilla

ribbon /'rɪbən/ n cinta, listón

ribcage /'rɪbkeɪdʒ/ n caja torácica

rice /raɪs/ n arroz: ~ field arrozal

rich /rɪtʃ/ adj (-er/-est) 1 rico: become/get ~ enriquecerse ◊ be ~ in abundar en algo 2 suntuoso 3 (tierra) fértil 4 (comida) pesado, empalagoso ● the rich n [pl] los ricos **riches** n [pl] riqueza(s) **richly** adv: ~ deserve sth tener algo bien merecido

rickety /'rɪkəti/ adj 1 desvencijado 2 (mueble) cojo

rid /rɪd/ vt (-dd-) (pt/pp rid) ~ sth/sb of sth/sb librar algo/a algn de algo/algn, eliminar algo de algo/algn ▶ **be/get rid of sth/sb** deshacerse de algo/algn

ridden /'rɪdn/ pp de RIDE ● adj ~ with sth agobiado por algo

riddle /'rɪdl/ n 1 adivinanza 2 enigma ● vt 1 (a balazos) acribillar 2 riddled with sth plagado de algo

ride /raɪd/ (pt rode pp ridden) 1 vt (caballo) montar a 2 vt (bicicleta, moto) andar en 3 vi montar a caballo 4 vi (en vehículo) viajar, ir ● n 1 (a caballo) paseo 2 (en vehículo) viaje: go for a ~ ir a dar una vuelta ▶ **take sb for a ride** (coloq) dar gato por liebre a algn **rider** n 1 jinete 2 ciclista 3 motociclista

ridge /rɪdʒ/ n 1 (montaña) cresta 2 (tejado) caballete

ridicule /'rɪdɪkjuːl/ n ridículo ● vt ridiculizar **ridiculous** /rɪ'dɪkjələs/ adj ridículo

riding /'raɪdɪŋ/ n equitación: I like ~. Me gusta montar a caballo.

rife /raɪf/ adj ~ with sth plagado de algo

rifle /'raɪfl/ n fusil, rifle

rift /rɪft/ n 1 (Geog) grieta 2 división

rig /rɪg/ vt (-gg-) falsificar ▪ **rig sth up** armar, improvisar algo ● n 1 (Náut) (tb rigging) aparejo 2 aparato

right /raɪt/ adj 1 correcto, cierto: You're quite ~. Tienes toda la razón. 2 adecuado, apropiado: be on the ~ road ir por buen camino 3 (momento) oportuno 4 (pie, mano, etc.) derecho 5 justo 6 (GB, coloq) de remate: a ~ fool un tonto de remate ▶ **get sth right** 1 acertar, hacer algo bien 2 dejar algo claro **put/set sth/sb right** corregir algo/a algn, arreglar algo ● *adv* **1** bien, correctamente **2** exactamente: *~ beside me* justo a mi lado **3** completamente: *~ to the end* hasta el final **4** a la derecha **5** inmediatamente: *I'll be ~ back.* Vuelvo ahora mismo. ▸ **right away/off** enseguida ▸ **right now** ahora mismo, ahorita ● *interj* (GB, colog) **1** **right!** ¡bien!, ¡bueno! **2** **right?** ¿verdad? ● *n* **1** bien: *~ and wrong* el bien y el mal **2** derecho: *human ~s* los derechos humanos **3** **the Right** (Pol) la Derecha ▸ **be in the right** tener razón **by rights** en buena ley **2** en teoría **in your own right** por derecho propio ● *vt* **1** enderezar **2** corregir **rightly** *adv* correctamente, justificadamente: *~ or wrongly* mal que bien

right angle *n* ángulo recto

righteous /'raɪtʃəs/ *adj* (fml) **1** recto, honrado **2** (indignación) justificado **3** (pey) virtuoso

rightful /'raɪtfl/ *adj* legítimo

right-hand *adj* a/de la derecha: *on the ~ side* a mano derecha ▸ **right-hand man** brazo derecho **right-handed** *adj* diestro

right wing *n* derecha ● **right-wing** *adj* derechista

rigid /'rɪdʒɪd/ *adj* **1** rígido **2** (actitud) inflexible

rigor (**-our** GB) /'rɪgər/ *n* rigor **rigorous** *adj* riguroso

rim /rɪm/ *n* **1** borde **2** (gafas, lentes) montura **3** PEEL

rind /raɪnd/ *n* corteza, cáscara (queso, limón, etc.) →PEEL

ring¹ /rɪŋ/ *n* **1** anillo **2** aro **3** círculo **4** (circo) pista **5** (tb **boxing ~**) ring **6** (toros) ruedo ● *vt* (pt/pp **-ed**) **1** ~ **sth/sb** (**with sth**) rodear algo/a algn (de algo) **2** (pájaro) anillar

ring² /rɪŋ/ *(pt* **rang** *pp* **rung**) **1** *vi* sonar **2** *vt* (timbre) tocar **3** *vi* ~ (**for sth/sb**) llamar (a algo/algn) **4** *vi* (oídos) zumbar **5** *vt, vi* (GB) ~ (**sth/sb**) (**up**) llamar (a algo/algn) (por teléfono) ■ **ring sb back** (GB) volver a llamar, devolver la llamada a algn **ring off** (GB) colgar ● *n* **1** timbrazo **2** (campanas) toque **3** [sing] sonido **4** (colog): *give sb a ~* dar un telefonazo a algn

ringleader /'rɪŋliːdər/ *n* cabecilla

ring road *n* (GB, Aut) periférico, circunvalar

rink /rɪŋk/ *n* (*tb* **ice ~**) *n* pista de hielo

rinse /rɪns/ *vt* enjuagar ● *n* **1** enjuagado **2** tintura

riot /'raɪət/ *n* disturbio, motín: *~ police* policía antimotines ▸ **run riot** desmandarse ● *vi*

causar disturbios **rioter** *n* alborotador/a, revoltoso/a **rioting** *n* disturbios **riotous** *adj* **1** (fml) (Jur) alborotador **2** (fiesta, etc.) desenfrenado

rip /rɪp/ (**-pp-**) **1** *vt, vi* rasgar(se): *~ sth open* abrir algo de un rasgón **2** *vt* ~ **sth off/out** arrancar algo **3** *vt* ~ **sth up** desgarrar algo ■ **rip sb off** (colog) estafar a algn ● *n* desgarrón, rasgón

ripe /raɪp/ *adj* (**-er/-est**) **1** maduro **2** listo: *The time is ~ for his return.* Llegó la hora de que regrese. **ripen** *vt, vi* madurar

rip-off *n* (*pl* **-offs**) (colog) estafa, robo

ripple /'rɪpl/ *n* **1** onda, rizo **2** murmullo (*risas, interés, etc.*) ● *vt, vi* ondular(se)

rise /raɪz/ *vi* (*pt* **rose** *pp* **risen** /'rɪzn/) **1** subir **2** (voz) alzarse **3** (fml) (persona, viento) levantarse **NOTA** Para este uso es más común **get up**. **4** ~ (**up**) (fml) sublevarse **5** (rango) ascender **6** (sol, luna) salir **7** (río) nacer ● *n* **1** subida, ascenso **2** (cantidad) aumento **3** cuesta **4** (GB) aumento (salarial) ▸ **give rise to sth** (fml) dar lugar a algo

rising /'raɪzɪŋ/ *n* **1** (Pol) levantamiento **2** (sol, luna) salida ● *adj* **1** creciente **2** (sol) naciente

risk /rɪsk/ *n* riesgo: *take ~s* arriesgarse ▸ **at risk** en peligro **run the risk of sth** correr el riesgo (de algo) ▸ *vt, vi* arriesgar ▸ **risk your neck** arriesgar el pellejo **risky** *adj* (**-ier/-iest**) arriesgado

rite /raɪt/ *n* rito

ritual /'rɪtʃuəl/ *n* ritual, rito ● *adj* ritual

rival /'raɪvl/ *adj, n* rival ● *vt* (**-l-, -ll-** GB) ~ **sth/sb** (**for/in sth**) rivalizar con algo/algn (en algo) **rivalry** *n* (*pl* **-ries**) rivalidad

river /'rɪvər/ *n* río →MAR

riverside /'rɪvərsaɪd/ *n* orilla (río)

rivet /'rɪvɪt/ *vt* **1** fascinar **2** clavar **3** remachar **riveting** *adj* fascinante

road /rəʊd/ *n* **1** carretera: *~ accident/sign* accidente/señal de tránsito ◇ *~ safety* seguridad vial **2** (*abrev* Rd) calle →STREET ▸ **on the road to sth** en camino hacia algo **roadside** /'rəʊdsaɪd/ *n* borde de la carretera **roadway** /'rəʊdweɪ/ *n* calzada

roadblock /'rəʊdblɒk/ *n* control (policial)

road rage *n* violencia al volante

roadworks /'rəʊdwɜːrks/ *n* [*pl*] (GB) obras (*en carretera*)

roam /roʊm/ *vt, vi* vagar (por)

roar /rɔːr/ *n* 1 rugido 2 estruendo ● 1 *vi* rugir 2 *vi* gritar: ~ *with laughter* reírse a carcajadas 3 *vt* decir a gritos **roaring** *adj* ▸ a **roaring trade** (*coloq*) un negocio tremendo

roast /roʊst/ *vt, vi* (*carne*) asar(se) 2 *vt, vi* (*café, etc.*) tostar(se) 3 *vi* (*coloq*) (*persona*) asarse ● *adj, n* asado: ~ *beef* rosbif

rob /rɑb/ *vt* (-bb-) ~ **sth/sb** (**of sth**) robarle (algo) a algo/algn **NOTA** Rob se usa con complementos de persona o lugar: *He robbed me.*, y **steal** al mencionar el objeto robado (de un lugar o a una persona): *He stole all my money* (*from me*). **Burglarize** (**burgle** *GB*) se refiere a robos en casas particulares o tiendas, normalmente cuando los dueños están fuera: *The house has been burgled.* → THIEF **robber** *n* 1 ladrón/ona 2 asaltante **robbery** *n* (*pl* -**ies**) 1 robo 2 asalto → THIEF

robe /roʊb/ *n* 1 (*USA*) bata 2 (*ceremonial*) manto

robin /ˈrɑbɪn/ *n* petirrojo

robot /ˈroʊbɑt/ *n* robot

robust /roʊˈbʌst/ *adj* vigoroso, fuerte

rock /rɑk/ *n* 1 roca 2 (*USA*) piedra 3 (*tb* ~ **music**) rock ▸ **on the rocks** 1 en crisis 2 (*bebida*) en las rocas ● 1 *vt, vi* mecer(se) 2 *vt, vi* arrullar 3 *vt, vi* sacudir(se)

rock-bottom *n* punto más bajo ● *adj* bajísimo: ~ *prices* precios por los suelos

rocket /ˈrɑkɪt/ *n* cohete ● *vi* aumentar muy rápidamente

rocking chair *n* mecedora

rocky /ˈrɑki/ *adj* (-**ier**/-**iest**) 1 rocoso 2 (*fig*) inestable

rod /rɑd/ *n* 1 barra 2 vara 3 (*tb fishing* ~) caña de pescar

rode /roʊd/ *pt de* RIDE

rodent /ˈroʊdnt/ *n* roedor

rogue /roʊg/ *n* 1 sinvergüenza 2 pícaro/a

role /roʊl/ *n* papel: ~ *model* modelo a imitar

roll /roʊl/ *n* 1 rollo 2 pan pequeño, bolillo (*Mx*) 3 (*con relleno*) torta (*Mx*), sánduche (*And*) 4 balanceo 5 registro, lista ● 1 *vt, vi* (hacer) rodar 2 *vt, vi* ~ (**over**) dar(se) vueltas (a algo) 3 *vt, vi* ~ (**up**) enrollar(se) 4 *vt, vi* ~ (**up**) envolver(se) 5 ~ **sth out** extender algo 6 *vt* (*cigarrillo*) hacer 7 *vt* allanar con un rodillo 8 *vt, vi* balancear(se) ▸ **be rolling in it** (*coloq*) nadar en oro ■ **roll in** (*coloq*) llegar en grandes cantidades **roll on** (*GB, coloq*) (*tiempo*) pasar **roll up** (*coloq*) presentarse **rolling** *adj* ondulante

roller /ˈroʊlər/ *n* 1 rodillo 2 (*pelo*) rulo, tubo (*Mx*)

Roller Blade® /ˈroʊlər bleɪd/ *n* patín (*en línea*) ● **rollerblade** *vi* patinar (*con patines en línea*)

roller coaster *n* montaña rusa

roller skate *n* patín (*de ruedas*) ● *vi* patinar (*sobre ruedas*)

rolling pin *n* rodillo (*de cocina*)

ROM /rɑm/ *n* (*abrev de* **read only memory**) (*Comp*) (*memoria*) ROM

romance /roʊˈmæns; roʊˈmæns *GB*/ *n* 1 amorío, aventura 2 romanticismo 3 novela de amor

romantic /roʊˈmæntɪk/ *adj* romántico

romp /rɑmp/ *vi* ~ (**about/around**) retozar, corretear ● *n* (*coloq*) 1 retozo 2 (*Teat, etc.*) obra divertida y sin pretensiones

roof /ruːf/ *n* 1 techo, tejado 2 (*Aut*) techo **roofing** *n* techado

roof rack *n* (*Aut*) portaequipaje

rooftop /ˈruːftɑp/ *n* 1 azotea 2 techo, tejado

rook /rʊk/ *n* 1 grajo 2 (*ajedrez*) torre

room /ruːm/ *n* 1 habitación, cuarto, sala: ~ *temperature* temperatura ambiente 2 sitio: ~ *to breathe* espacio para respirar 3 *There's no* ~ *for doubt.* No cabe duda. ◇ *There's* ~ *for improvement.* Podría mejorarse. **roomy** *adj* (-**ier**/-**iest**) espacioso

roommate /ˈruːmmeɪt/ *n* 1 (*USA*) compañero/a de apartamento 2 (*GB*) compañero/a de habitación

room service *n* servicio de habitaciones

room temperature *n* temperatura ambiente

roost /ruːst/ *n* percha (*para aves*) ● *vi* posarse para dormir

rooster /ˈruːstər/ *n* (*USA*) gallo

root /ruːt/ *n* raíz: *the* ~ *cause* la causa fundamental ▸ **put down roots** echar raíces ■ **root about/around** (**for sth**) revolver (en busca de algo) **root for sth/sb** (*coloq*) apoyar, animar algo/a algn **root sth out** 1 erradicar algo 2 encontrar algo

rope /roʊp/ *n* cuerda ▸ **show sb/know/learn the ropes** (*coloq*) enseñarle a algn/conocer/aprender el oficio ■ **rope sb in** (**to do sth**) (*coloq*) agarrar a algn (para hacer algo) **rope sth off** acordonar un lugar

rope ladder n escala de cuerda

rosary /'rouzəri/ n (pl -**ies**) rosario (*oración y cuentas*)

rose /rouz/ pt de RISE ● n rosa

rosé /'rouzeɪ; 'rəʊzeɪ GB/ n (vino) rosado

rosette /rou'zet/ n escarapela

rosy /'rouzi/ adj (-**ier**/-**iest**) 1 sonrosado 2 prometedor

rot /rɑt/ vt, vi (-tt-) pudrir(se)

rota /'routə/ n (GB) lista (*turnos*)

rotary /'routəri/ n (pl -**ies**) (USA, Aut) glorieta

rotate /'routeɪt; rəʊ'teɪt GB/ vt, vi 1 (hacer) girar 2 alternar(se) **rotation** n 1 rotación 2 alternancia: in ~ por turno

rotten /'rɑtn/ adj 1 podrido 2 asqueroso

rough /rʌf/ (-**er**/-**est**) adj 1 áspero 2 (*mar*) picado 3 (*comportamiento*) violento, brusco 4 ~ (on sb) duro, desconsiderado (con algn) 5 aproximado 6 malo: I feel a bit ~. No me encuentro bien. ● adv duro ● n ▸ in rough en borrador ● vt ▸ rough it (coloq) pasar apuros **roughly** adv 1 aproximadamente 2 bruscamente

roulette /ru:'let/ n ruleta

round /raund/ adj redondo: ~ trip viaje de ida y vuelta ● adv (GB) 1 Ver AROUND 2 all year ~ durante todo el año ◇ a shorter way ~ un camino más corto ◇ ~ the clock las 24 horas ◇ ~ at Tim's en la casa de Tim ▸ **round about 1** de alrededor **2** aproximadamente ● prep (GB) Ver AROUND ● n 1 ronda: It's my ~. Esta ronda la pago yo. **2** recorrido (*cartero*), visitas (*médico*) **3** (Dep) asalto, vuelta **4** ~ of applause aplauso **5** disparo ● vt (*esquina*) doblar ■ **round sth off** terminar algo ■ **round sth/sb up** juntar algo/a algn ■ **round sth up/down** redondear algo por lo alto/bajo (*cifra, etc.*)

roundabout /'raundəbaut/ adj indirecto ● n (GB) 1 carrusel 2 glorieta

rouse /rauz/ vt 1 (*fml*) despertar 2 provocar **rousing** adj 1 (*discurso*) enardecedor 2 (*aplauso*) caluroso

rout /raut/ n derrota ● vt derrotar

route /ru:t/ n ruta

routine /ru:'ti:n/ n rutina ● adj de rutina, rutinario

row¹ /rou/ vt, vi remar: Will you ~ me across the river? ¿Me lleva al otro lado del río? ◇ ~ across the lake cruzar el lago a remo ● n

1 fila, hilera: ~ house casa adosada 2 go for a ~ salir a remar ▸ in a row uno tras otro: six days in a ~ seis días seguidos

row² /rau/ n (coloq) 1 pelea: have a ~ pelearse **NOTA** También se dice **argument**. 2 alboroto 3 ruido ● vi pelear

rowboat /'roubout/ n (USA) (**rowing boat** GB) bote de remos

rowdy /'raudi/ adj (-**ier**/-**iest**) 1 ruidoso, peleón 2 (*reunión*) agitado

royal /'rɔɪəl/ adj real **royalty** n 1 [sing] realeza 2 (pl -**ies**) derechos de autor

rub /rʌb/ (-**bb**-) 1 vt restregar, frotar 2 vi friccionar 3 vi rozar ■ **rub off (on/onto sb)** pegarse (a algn) **rub sth out** (GB) borrar algo ● n frote: give sth a ~ frotar algo

rubber /'rʌbər/ n 1 goma, caucho, hule 2 goma, borrador 3 (USA, coloq) condón

rubber band n banda (elástica), caucho (Amd)

rubbish /'rʌbɪʃ/ n [U] 1 basura: ~ dump/tip basurero/tiradero (Mx) 2 (GB, coloq) tonterías

rubble /'rʌbl/ n [U] escombros

ruby /'ru:bi/ n (pl -**ies**) rubí

rucksack /'rʌksæk/ n (GB) mochila

rudder /'rʌdər/ n timón

rude /ru:d/ adj (-**er**/-**est**) 1 grosero, maleducado: be ~ to do sth ser de mala educación hacer algo 2 indecente (*chiste, etc.*) verde, colorado (Mx) 3 (*fml*) tosco

rudimentary /,ru:dɪ'mentəri/ adj rudimentario

ruffle /'rʌfl/ vt 1 agitar 2 (*pelo*) alborotar 3 (*plumas*) erizar 4 (*tela*) arrugar 5 desconcertar

rug /rʌg/ n 1 alfombra, tapete 2 manta de viaje

rugby /'rʌgbi/ n rugby

rugged /'rʌgɪd/ adj 1 (*terreno*) accidentado 2 (*facciones*) duro

ruin /'ru:ɪn/ n ruina ● vt 1 arruinar, destrozar 2 echar a perder

rule /ru:l/ n 1 regla, norma 2 costumbre 3 dominio, gobierno 4 (*Pol*) mandato 5 reinado ▸ **as a (general) rule** en general 1 vt, vi ~ (over sth/sb) (Pol) gobernar (algo/a algn) 2 vt dominar, regir 3 vt, vi (Jur) fallar, decidir 4 vt (*línea*) trazar ■ **rule sth/sb out** (por algo/algn) descartar algo/a algn **ruler** n 1 gobernante 2 (*instrumento*) regla

ruling /'ru:lɪŋ/ adj 1 imperante 2 (Pol) dirigente ● n (Jur) fallo

rum /rʌm/ n ron

rumble /ˈrʌmbl/ vi 1 retumbar 2 (*estómago*) sonar ● n estruendo

rummage /ˈrʌmɪdʒ/ vi 1 ~ about/around rebuscar 2 ~ among/in/through sth (for sth) escular (en) algo (en busca de algo)

rumor (*-our GB*) /ˈruːmər/ n rumor: *Rumour has it that...* Hay rumores de que...

rump /rʌmp/ n 1 grupa, ancas 2 (*tb ~ steak*) (filete de) cadera

run /rʌn/ n 1 carrera: *go for a ~* salir a correr ◊ *break into a ~* echar a correr 2 (*Aut*) paseo 3 período (*de buena/mal suerte*) 4 (*Teat*) temporada ▶ be on the run haberse fugado de la justicia ● (*-nn-*) (*pt ran pp run*) 1 vt, vi correr 2 vt, vi recorrer: *~ your fingers through sb's hair* pasar los dedos por el pelo de algn ◊ *~ your eyes over sth* echar un vistazo a algo 3 vt, vi (*hacer*) funcionar: *Everything is running smoothly.* Todo marcha sobre ruedas. ◊ *Run the engine before you start.* Tenga el motor en marcha antes de arrancar. 4 vi extenderse: *A fence ~s round the field.* Una valla circunda el prado. 5 vi (*transportes*): *There is a train ~ every hour.* Hay un tren cada hora. ◊ *It's running an hour late.* Lleva una hora de retraso. 6 vt (*coloq*) llevar (*en carro*) 7 vt (*baño*) preparar 8 vi: *leave the faucet running* dejar la llave abierta 9 vi (*nariz*) gotear 10 vt (*tinte*) desteñir 11 vt (*negocio*) administrar, dirigir 12 vt (*servicio, curso*) organizar, ofrecer 13 vt (*Comp*) ejecutar 14 vi ~ (for...) (*Teat*) representar (*durante...*) 15 vt (*nariz*) mantener 16 vi ~ (for sth) (*Pol*) presentarse como candidato (a algo) 17 vt (*Period*) publicar ▶ run for it echar a correr NOTA Para otras expresiones, ver el sustantivo, adjetivo, etc., p.ej. run dry en DRY. ■ run about/around corretear run across sth/sb toparse con algo/algn run after sb perseguir a algn run at sth: *Inflation is running at 25%.* La inflación alcanza el 25%. run away huir run sth/sb down 1 (*tb ~ sth/sb over*) atropellar algo/a algn 2 menospreciar algo/a algn run into sth/sb tropezar con algo/algn 2 chocarse con/contra algo/algn run sth into sth: *He ran the car into a tree.* Se chocó contra un árbol. run off (with sth) huir, escaparse (con algo)

run out 1 caducar **2** acabarse, agotarse **run out of sth** quedarse sin algo **runner** n corredor/a

runaway /ˈrʌnəweɪ/ n 1 fugitivo 2 fuera de control 3 ~ inflation inflación galopante ◊ *a ~ success* un éxito arrollador ● n fugitivo/a

run-down adj 1 en un estado de abandono 2 (*persona*) desmejorado, fatigado

rung /rʌŋ/ pp de RING² ● n peldaño

runner-up n (pl **-ers-up**) subcampeón/ona

running /ˈrʌnɪŋ/ n 1 go (out) ~ salir a correr 2 funcionamiento 3 organización ▶ be in/out of the running (for sth) (*coloq*) tener/no tener posibilidades (de conseguir algo) ● adj 1 continuo 2 consecutivo: *four days* ~ cuatro días seguidos 3 (*agua*) corriente

runny /ˈrʌni/ adj (**-ier/-iest**) 1 líquido 2 (*nariz*) mocoso

run-up n período previo

runway /ˈrʌnweɪ/ n pista (*de aterrizaje*)

rupture /ˈrʌptʃər/ n ruptura ● vt, vi desgarrarse

rural /ˈrʊərəl/ adj rural

rush /rʌʃ/ 1 vi apresurarse, ir con prisa/de afán (*And*): *I rushed out.* Salí corriendo. 2 vi actuar precipitadamente 3 vt apresurar a 4 vt llevar de prisa/afán (*And*): *He was rushed to hospital.* Lo llevaron al hospital con la mayor urgencia. ● n 1 [*sing*] precipitación: *There was a ~ to the exit.* La gente se precipitó hacia la salida. 2 prisa, afán (*And*): *be in a ~* tener prisa/afán ◊ *the ~ hour* la hora pico

rust /rʌst/ n óxido ● vt, vi oxidar(se) **rusty** adj 1 oxidado 2 falto de práctica

rustic /ˈrʌstɪk/ adj rústico

rustle /ˈrʌsl/ vt, vi (*hacer*) crujir ■ rustle sth up (*coloq*) preparar algo ● n crujido, susurro

rut /rʌt/ n bache ▶ be (stuck) in a rut estar estancado

ruthless /ˈruːθləs/ adj despiadado, implacable **ruthlessness** n crueldad, implacabilidad

rye /raɪ/ n centeno

S s

S, s /es/ n (pl S's, s's) S, s

the Sabbath /ˈsæbəθ/ n **1** (cristiano) domingo **2** (judío) sábado

sabotage /ˈsæbətɑːʒ/ n sabotaje ● vt sabotear

saccharin /ˈsækərɪn/ n sacarina

sachet /ˈsæʃeɪ; ˈsæʃeɪ GB/ n bolsita, sobrecito

sack /sæk/ n **1** costal, saco **2 the sack** (coloq): give sb/get the ~ despedir a algn/ser despedido ● vt (coloq) despedir

sacred /ˈseɪkrɪd/ adj sagrado

sacrifice /ˈsækrɪfaɪs/ n sacrificio ● vt sacrificar

sacrilege /ˈsækrəlɪdʒ/ n sacrilegio

sad /sæd/ adj (sadder, -est) **1** triste **2** (situación) lamentable **3** (coloq, pey) aburrido: "She spends all day playing computer games." "That's so ~!" —Se pasa todo el día con los videojuegos. —¡Da pesar! **sadden** vt entristecer **sadness** n tristeza

saddle /ˈsædl/ n **1** (caballo) silla **2** (bicicleta, moto) asiento ● vt **1** ensillar **2 ~ sb with sth** hacer cargar a algn con algo

sadism /ˈseɪdɪzəm/ n sadismo

safari /səˈfɑːri/ n (pl -s) safari

safe /seɪf/ n caja fuerte ● adj (-er/-est) **1 ~ (from sth/sb)** (a salvo (de algo/algn) **2** seguro **3** ileso **4** (conductor) prudente ▶ **be on the safe side** no correr riesgos **safe and sound** sano y salvo **safely** adv **1** sin novedad, sin ningún percance **2** tranquilamente, sin peligro: ~ locked away guardado bajo llave en un lugar seguro

safeguard /ˈseɪfɡɑːd/ n salvaguarda, protección ● vt proteger

safety /ˈseɪfti/ n seguridad: ~ belt/valve cinturón/válvula de seguridad

safety net n **1** red de seguridad **2** red de protección

safety pin n seguro (Mx), gancho (de nodriza) (And)

sag /sæɡ/ vi (-gg-) **1** (cama, sofá) hundirse **2** (madera) pandearse

Sagittarius /ˌsædʒɪˈteəriəs/ n Sagitario

said /sed/ pt, pp de SAY

sail /seɪl/ n vela ▶ **set sail** (to/for) zarpar (rumbo a) ● vi **1** navegar: ~ around the world dar la vuelta al mundo en barco ◇ go sailing navegar a vela **2** (un barco) pilotar **3** vi salir: The ship ~s at noon. El barco zarpa al mediodía. **4** vi (objeto) volar ■ **sail through (sth)** hacer algo sin dificultad: ~ through the exam aprobar el examen sin problemas **sailing** n

1 (Dep) vela **2** There are two ~s a day. Hay dos salidas diarias. **sailor** n marinero/a, marino/a

sailboat /ˈseɪlbəʊt/ n (USA) (sailing boat GB) velero

saint /seɪnt tb snt (GB/ n (abrev St) san, santo/a

sake /seɪk/ n ▶ **for God's, goodness', Heaven's, etc. sake** por (amor de) Dios **for sth's/sb's sake; for the sake of sth/sb** por (el bien de) algo/algn

salad /ˈsæləd/ n ensalada

salary /ˈsæləri/ n (pl -ies) salario, sueldo (mensual)

sale /seɪl/ n **1** venta: ~s department servicio de ventas **2** rebajas **3** subasta **for sale** en venta: For ~. Se vende. **on sale** **1** a la venta **2** (USA) rebajado

salesman, saleswoman /ˈseɪlzmən/-wʊmən/ n (pl -men/-women) vendedor/a, dependiente/a →CHAIRMAN

saliva /səˈlaɪvə/ n saliva

salmon /ˈsæmən/ n (pl salmon) salmón

salon /səˈlɒn; ˈsælɒn GB/ n salón (de belleza)

saloon /səˈluːn/ n **1** salón (barco, etc.) **2** (GB) (tb ~ car) automóvil de cuatro/cinco puertas

salt /sɔːlt/ n sal: ~ shaker/cellar (GB) salero **salted** adj salado **salty** adj (-ier/-iest) salado

saltwater /ˈsɔːltwɔːtər/ adj de agua salada

salutary /ˈsæljətəri; -tri GB/ adj saludable

salute /səˈluːt/ vt, vi saludar (a un militar) ● n **1** saludo **2** salva

salvage /ˈsælvɪdʒ/ n salvamento ● vt recuperar

salvation /sælˈveɪʃn/ n salvación

same /seɪm/ ● adj mismo, igual: the ~ thing lo mismo **NOTA** A veces se usa para dar énfasis: the very ~ man el mismísimo hombre. ▶ **at the same time 1** a la vez **2** sin embargo **in the same boat** en el mismo barco ● **the same** adv de la misma manera, igual ● pron **the same** (as sth/sb) el/la mismo/a, etc. (que algo/algn): I think the ~ as you. Pienso igual que tú. ▶ **all/just the same 1** de todos modos **2** It's all the ~ to me. Me da igual. **same here** (coloq) lo mismo digo **(the) same to you** (coloq) igualmente

sample /ˈsæmpl; ˈsɑːmpl GB/ n muestra ● vt probar

sanatorium /ˌsænəˈtɔːriəm/ n sanatorio

sanction /'sæŋkʃn/ n 1 aprobación 2 sanción ● vt dar el permiso para

sanctuary /'sæŋktʃueri; -uəri GB/ n (pl -ies) 1 refugio: take ~ refugiarse 2 santuario

sand /sænd/ n 1 arena: ~ dune duna 2 [gen pl] playa

sandal /'sændl/ n sandalia

sandcastle /'sændkɑːsl; -kɑːsl GB/ n castillo de arena

sandpaper /'sændpeɪpər/ n papel de lija

sandwich /'sænwɪtʃ/ n sándwich, torta (Mx), sánduche (And) ● vt apretujar (entre dos personas o cosas)

sandy /'sændi/ adj arenoso

sane /seɪn/ adj (-er/-est) 1 cuerdo 2 (idea, etc.) sensato

sang /sæŋ/ pt de SING

sanitarium /ˌsænə'teəriəm/ (USA) n sanatorio

sanitary /'sænəteri; -tri GB/ adj higiénico

sanitary napkin (sanitary towel GB) n toalla sanitaria/feminina

sanitation /ˌsænɪ'teɪʃn/ n saneamiento, sanidad

sanity /'sænəti/ n 1 cordura 2 sensatez

sank /sæŋk/ pt de SINK

Santa Claus /'sæntə klɔːz/ (coloq Santa) n Papá Noel →NAVIDAD

sap /sæp/ n savia ● vt (-pp-) (energía, confianza) minar

sapphire /'sæfaɪər/ n, adj zafiro

sappy /'sæpi/ adj (USA, coloq) sensiblero

sarcasm /'sɑːrkæzəm/ n sarcasmo **sarcastic** /sɑːr'kæstɪk/ adj sarcástico

sardine /ˌsɑːr'diːn/ n sardina

sash /sæʃ/ n faja

sat /sæt/ pt, pp de SIT

satchel /'sætʃəl/ n cartera (de colegio)

satellite /'sætəlaɪt/ n satélite: ~ dish antena parabólica

satin /'sætn; 'sætɪn GB/ n raso, satín

satire /'sætaɪər/ n sátira **satirical** /sə'tɪrɪkl/ adj satírico

satisfaction /ˌsætɪs'fækʃn/ n satisfacción **satisfactory** adj satisfactorio

satisfy /'sætɪsfaɪ/ vt (pt/pp -ied) 1 satisfacer 2 (condiciones, etc.) cumplir con 3 ~ sb (as to sth) convencer a algn (de algo) **satisfied** adj satisfecho **satisfying** adj que satisface, gratificante: a ~ meal una comida que deja satisfecho

satsuma /sæt'suːmə/ n mandarina

saturate /'sætʃəreɪt/ vt 1 empapar 2 (mercado) saturar **saturation** n saturación

Saturday /'sætərdeɪ, -di/ n (abrev Sat.) sábado

Saturn /'sætərn/ n Saturno

sauce /sɔːs/ n salsa

saucepan /'sɔːspæn; -pən GB/ n olla, cacerola

saucer /'sɔːsər/ n plato para taza

sauna /'sɔːnə, 'saʊnə/ n sauna

saunter /'sɔːntər/ vi pasearse: ~ over to the bar irse hacia la barra con mucha tranquilidad

sausage /'sɔːsɪdʒ; 'sɒs- GB/ n salchicha, embutido

sausage roll n (GB) hojaldre relleno de salchicha

savage /'sævɪdʒ/ adj 1 salvaje 2 enfurecido 3 brutal: ~ budget cuts cortes terribles en el presupuesto ● vt atacar con ferocidad **savagery** n salvajismo

save /seɪv/ 1 vt salvar 2 vt, vi ~ (sth) (up) ahorrar (algo) 3 vt (Comp) guardar 4 vt ~ (sb) sth evitar(le) algo a (algn) 5 vt (Dep) parar ▶ **save face** guardar las apariencias ● n (Dep) parada, tapada **saving** n ahorro: make a ~ of five dollars ahorrar $5

savior (-our GB) /'seɪvjər/ n salvador/a

savory (-oury GB) /'seɪvəri/ adj 1 salado 2 sabroso

saw /sɔː/ pt de SEE ● vt, vi (pt sawed o sawn /sɔːn/ o tb sawed USA) serrar ■ **saw sth down** talar algo (con una sierra) **saw sth off (sth)** cortar algo (de algo) (con una sierra): a sawed-off shotgun una escopeta de cañones recortados **saw sth up** serrar algo ● n sierra

sawdust /'sɔːdʌst/ n aserrín

saxophone /'sæksəfoʊn/ n saxofón

say /seɪ/ vt (3ª pers sing says /sez/ pt/pp said) 1 decir NOTA Say suele acompañar las palabras textuales e introduce una oración en estilo indirecto precedida por that: "I'll leave at ten", he said. ◊ He said that he would leave at ten. **Tell** introduce una oración en estilo indirecto y debe ir seguido de un sustantivo, pronombre o nombre propio: He told me that he would leave at ten. Con órdenes o consejos se suele usar tell: I told him to hurry. ◊ She's always telling me what to do. 2 digamos, pongamos (que): Take any writer, ~ Dickens...

Tememos cualquier escritor, digamos Dickens... **3** *What time does it ~ on that clock?* ¿Qué hora tiene ese reloj? ◇ *The map ~s the hotel is here.* El plano dice que el hotel está aquí. ▶ **it is to say** es decir ● *n* ▶ **have a/ some say** tener voz y voto **have your say** expresar su opinión

saying /'seɪŋ/ *n* dicho, refrán

scab /skæb/ *n* costra

scaffold /'skæfəʊld/ *n* cadalso

scaffolding /'skæfəldɪŋ/ *n* [U] andamiaje, andamio

scald /skɔːld/ *vt* escaldar ● *n* escaldadura **scalding** *adj* hirviendo

scale /skeɪl/ *vt* escalar, trepar ● *n* **1** escala: *to ~ a escala* ◇ *a large-scale map* un mapa a gran escala ◇ *a ~ model* una maqueta **2** alcance, magnitud **3** (*tb* **scales** [*pl*]) balanza, báscula **4** escama

scalp /skælp/ *n* cuero cabelludo

scalpel /'skælpl/ *n* bisturí

scamper /'skæmpər/ *vi* corretear

scampi /'skæmpi/ *n* [*pl*] (*GB*) camarones fritas rebozadas

scan /skæn/ *vt* (-**nn**-) **1** escudriñar, examinar con escáner **2** explorar con escáner **3** echar un vistazo a ● *n* escáner, ecografía

scandal /'skændl/ *n* **1** escándalo **2** chisme **3 a scandal** una vergüenza **scandalize** *vt* escandalizar **scandalous** *adj* escandaloso

scanner /'skænər/ *n* escáner (*aparato*)

scanty /'skænti/ (*tb* **scant**) *adj* escaso **scantily** *adv* escasamente: *~ dressed* ligero de ropa

scapegoat /'skeɪpgəʊt/ *n* chivo expiatorio: *She has been made a ~ for what happened.* Cargó con las culpas por lo que pasó.

scar /skɑːr/ *n* cicatriz ● *vt* (-**rr**-) dejar una cicatriz en

scarce /skeərs/ *adj* (-**er/-est**) escaso: *Food was ~.* Los alimentos escaseaban. **scarcity** *n* (*pl* -**ies**) escasez

scarcely /'skeərsli/ *adv* **1** apenas **2** *You can ~ expect me to believe you.* ¿Y espera que le crea?

scare /skeər/ *vt* asustar ▶ **scare sb away/off** ahuyentar a algn ● *n* susto: *bomb ~* amenaza de bomba **scared** *adj* asustado: *be ~* tener miedo ◇ *~ stiff* muerto de miedo **scary** *adj* (-**ier/-iest**) (*coloq*) espeluznante

scarecrow /'skeərkrəʊ/ *n* espantapájaros

scarf /skɑːrf/ *n* (*pl* -**s** *o* **scarves** /skɑːrvz/) **1** bufanda **2** pañuelo

scarlet /'skɑːrlət/ *adj*, *n* escarlata

scathing /'skeɪðɪŋ/ *adj* **1** mordaz **2** feroz

scatter /'skætər/ **1** *vt*, *vi* dispersar(se) **2** *vt* esparcir **scattered** *adj* esparcido: *~ showers* chubascos/ aguaceros aislados

scavenge /'skævɪndʒ/ *vi* **1** buscar carroña **2** (*persona*) buscar (*en la basura*) **scavenger** *n* **1** animal, ave de carroña **2** persona que busca en las basuras, pepenador (*Mx*)

scenario /sə'nærioʊ; -'nɑːr- *GB*/ *n* (*pl* -**s**) **1** marco hipotético **2** (*Teat*) argumento

scene /siːn/ *n* **1** escena: *a change of ~* un cambio de aires **2** escenario: *the ~ of the crime* el lugar del crimen **3** escándalo ● **the scene** (*coloq*) el mundo: *the music ~* el mundo de la música ▶ **set the scene 1** describir el escenario **2** preparar el terreno

scenery /'siːnəri/ *n* [U] **1** paisaje **NOTA** Scenery tiene un fuerte matiz positivo; suele usarse con adjetivos como *beautiful, dramatic*, etc. y se refiere fundamentalmente a paisajes naturales. **Landscape** suele usarse para paisajes construidos por el hombre: *an urban landscape* ◇ *Hedges are typical of the British landscape.* **2** (*Teat*) decorado

scenic /'siːnɪk/ *adj* pintoresco

scent /sent/ *n* **1** olor (*agradable*) **2** perfume **3** rastro, pista **scented** *adj* perfumado

sceptic (*GB*) = SKEPTIC

schedule /'skedʒuːl; 'ʃedjuːl *GB*/ *n* **1** programa: *be a month ahead of/behind ~* llevar un mes de adelanto/retraso según lo previsto ◇ *arrive on ~* llegar a la hora prevista **2** (*USA*) horario ● *vt* programar: *scheduled flight* vuelo regular

scheme /skiːm/ *n* **1** conspiración **2** (*GB*) plan, proyecto **3** *colour ~* combinación de colores ● *vi* conspirar

schizophrenia /ˌskɪtsə'friːniə/ *n* esquizofrenia **schizophrenic** /ˌskɪtsə'frenɪk/ *adj*, *n* esquizofrénico/a

scholar /'skɑːlər/ *n* **1** becario/a **2** erudito/a **scholarship** *n* **1** beca **2** erudición

school /skuːl/ *n* **1** colegio, escuela: *~ age/uniform* edad/uniforme escolar **NOTA** School, church, hospital, etc. se usan sin artículo cuando alguien va al colegio como alumno o profesor, a la iglesia para rezar, o al hospital como paciente: *I enjoyed being at ~.* ◇ *We go to church on Sunday.* ◇ *She's in hospital.* Se utiliza el artículo cuando se refiere a estos sitios por algún otro motivo: *I'm going to the ~ to talk to John's teacher.* ◇ *She works at the hospital.* **2** (USA) universidad **3** clases: *School begins at nine.* Las clases empiezan a las nueve. **4** facultad: *law ~* facultad de derecho **5** (*Arte*) escuela ▸ **school of thought** escuela de pensamiento

schoolboy, schoolgirl /'sku:lbɔɪ/-gɜːrl/ (*tb* **schoolchild** /'sku:ltʃaɪld/) *n* colegial/a

schooling /'sku:lɪŋ/ *n* educación, estudios

school-leaver *n* (GB) joven que termina el colegio

schoolmaster /'sku:lmæstər/ -mɑːs- GB/ *n* (*antic*) maestro

schoolmistress /'sku:lmɪstrəs/ *n* (*antic*) maestra

schoolteacher /'sku:lti:tʃər/ *n* profesor/a

science /'saɪəns/ *n* ciencia **scientific** /saɪən'tɪfɪk/ *adj* científico

science fiction (*coloq* **sci-fi** /'saɪ faɪ/) *n* ciencia ficción

scientist /'saɪəntɪst/ *n* científico/a

scissors /'sɪzərz/ *n* [pl] tijeras: *a pair of ~* unas tijeras →PAIR

scoff /skɒf; skɔf GB/ *vi* ~ (**at sth/sb**) mofarse (de algo/algn)

scold /skəʊld/ *vt* regañar

scoop /sku:p/ *n* **1** pala: *ice cream ~* cuchara para servir el helado **2** cucharada: *a ~ of ice cream* una bola de helado **3** (*Period*) primicia ● *vt* ~ **sth** (**up/out**) cavar, sacar algo (con pala, mano, cuchara)

scooter /'sku:tər/ *n* **1** Vespa®, motoneta (And) **2** patineta, patín del diablo (Mx)

scope /skəʊp/ *n* **1** potencial **2** ámbito, alcance

scorch /skɔːrtʃ/ *vt, vi* chamuscar(se), quemar(se) **scorching** *adj* abrasador

score /skɔːr/ *n* **1** tanteo: *keep the ~* llevar la cuenta de los tantos ◇ *the final ~* el resultado final **2** (*Educ*) puntuación **3** scores [pl] montones **4** (*Mús*) partitura **5** veintena ▸ **on that score** en ese sentido ● *vt, vi* **1** (*tb* vi) (*Dep*) marcar **2** *vt* (*Educ*) sacar **scoreboard** /'skɔːrbɔːrd/ *n* marcador

scorn /skɔːrn/ *n* ~ (**for sth/sb**) desdén (hacia algo/algn) ● *vt* desdeñar **scornful** *adj* desdeñoso

Scorpio /'skɔːrpiəʊ/ *n* (pl **-s**) Escorpio

scorpion /'skɔːrpiən/ *n* escorpión, alacrán

Scotch /skɒtʃ/ *n* whisky escocés

Scotch tape® *n* (USA) durex® (Mx), cinta pegante (And)

scour /'skaʊər/ *vt* **1** fregar, restregar **2** ~ **sth** (**for sth/sb**) registrar, recorrer algo (en busca de algo/algn)

scourge /skɜːrdʒ/ *n* azote

scout /skaʊt/ *n* **1** (*tb* (**Boy/Girl**) **Scout**) scout **2** (*Mil*) explorador

scowl /skaʊl/ *n* ceño fruncido ● *vi* mirar con el ceño fruncido

scrabble /'skræbl/ *vi* ~ (**about/around**) (**for sth**) escarbar (en busca de algo)

scramble /'skræmbl/ *vi* **1** trepar **2** ~ (**for sth**) pelearse (por algo) ● *n* [sing] barullo

scrambled eggs *n* [pl] huevos revueltos/pericos (And)

scrap /skræp/ *n* **1** pedazo: *~s* (**of food**) sobras **2** [U] chatarra: *~ paper* papel para apuntes **3** [sing] pizca **4** (*coloq*) pelea ● (**-pp-**) **1** *vt* desechar **2** *vi* (*coloq*) pelearse

scrapbook /'skræpbʊk/ *n* álbum de recortes

scrape /skreɪp/ **1** *vt* raspar: ~ **sth** *away/off* quitar algo raspando **2** *vi* rozar ■ **scrape in**; **scrape into sth** conseguir algo a duras penas: *~ into college* entrar en la universidad a duras penas **scrape through** (**sth**) aprobar (algo) a duras penas **scrape sth together/up** reunir algo a duras penas ● *n* raspadura

scratch /skrætʃ/ **1** *vt, vi* arañar(se) **2** *vt, vi* rascarse: ~ **sth** *away/off* quitar algo de algo raspándolo **3** *vt* rayar ● *n* **1** arañazo **2** [sing] rascada ▸ **from scratch** de cero **up to scratch** a la altura

scrawl /skrɔːl/ **1** *vt* garabatear **2** *vi* hacer garabatos ● *n* [sing] garabato

scream /skri:m/ **1** *vi* gritar **2** *vi* chillar ● *n* **1** chillido, grito **2** [sing] (*coloq*) algo/algn divertidísimo

screech /skri:tʃ/ *vi* chillar, chirriar ● *n* [sing] chillido, chirrido

screen /skri:n/ *n* **1** pantalla **2** biombo

screen saver *n* protector de pantalla, salvapantallas

screw /skru:/ *n* tornillo ● *vt* **1** atornillar, fijar con tornillos **2** enroscar ■ **screw sth up 1** (*papel*) hacer una pelota con algo **2** (*cara*) torcer algo **3** (*coloq*) estropear algo

screwdriver /'skru:draɪvər/ n destornillador, desarmador (Mx)

scribble /'skrɪbl/ 1 vt garabatear 2 vi hacer garabatos ● n [U] garabatos

script /skrɪpt/ n 1 guión 2 letra 3 escritura ● vt escribir el guión para

scripture /'skrɪptʃər/ (tb the Scriptures) n las Sagradas Escrituras

scroll /skrəʊl/ n 1 pergamino 2 rollo de papel ● vi (Comp) ~ down/up desplazar de arriba a abajo (por el documento)

scrounge /skraʊndʒ/ vt, vi ~ (sth) (off sb) (coloq) gorronear, gorrear (algo) (a algn)

scrub /skrʌb/ vt (-bb-) 1 restregar, tallar (Mx) ● 1 give sb a good ~ restregar/tallarse bien algo 2 [U] matorrales

scruff /skrʌf/ n ▶ by the scruff of the neck por el pescuezo

scruffy /'skrʌfi/ adj (-ier/-iest) (coloq) desaliñado

scrum /skrʌm/ n melé (rugby)

scruples /'skru:plz/ n [pl] escrúpulos **scrupulous** /'skru:pjələs/ adj escrupuloso

scrutiny /'skru:təni/ n (fml) 1 examen 2 (Pol) escrutinio **scrutinize** (tb fml) examinar

scuba-diving /'sku:bə daɪvɪŋ/ n buceo (con equipo)

scuff /skʌf/ vt rayarse

scuffle /'skʌfl/ n 1 enfrentamiento 2 forcejeo

sculpture /'skʌlptʃər/ n escultura **sculptor** /'skʌlptər/ n escultor/a

scum /skʌm/ n 1 espuma 2 (coloq) escoria

scurry /'skʌri/ vi (pt/pp -ied) ir apresuradamente: ~ about/around trajinar/corretear

scuttle /'skʌtl/ vi ir a toda prisa: ~ away/off escabullirse

scythe /saɪð/ n guadaña

sea /si:/ n 1 mar: at ~ en el mar ◇ heavy/rough ~s marejada ◇ ~ air/creatures brisa marina/animales marinos ◇ ~ port puerto marítimo →MAR 2 ~ of sth multitud de algo ▶ all at sea en medio de un mar de dudas

seafood /'si:fu:d/ n [U] mariscos

seagull /'si:gʌl/ n gaviota

seal /si:l/ n 1 foca 2 sello ● vt 1 sellar 2 lacrar 3 (sobre) cerrar ■ seal sth off acordonar algo

sea level n nivel del mar

seam /si:m/ n 1 costura 2 veta

search /sɜ:rtʃ/ 1 vt, vi ~ (for sth); ~ (sth for sth) buscar (algo) (en algo) 2 vt ~ sth/sb (for sth) registrar, catear (Mx) algo/a algn (en busca de algo) ● n 1 ~ (for sth/sb) búsqueda (de algo/algn) 2 (policial) registro, cateo (Mx) **searching** adj penetrante

search engine n (Comp) buscador

searchlight /'sɜ:rtʃlaɪt/ n (foco) reflector

seashell /'si:ʃel/ n concha marina

seashore /'si:ʃɔ:r/ n orilla (mar)

seasick /'si:sɪk/ adj mareado

seaside /'si:saɪd/ n 1 playa 2 costa

season¹ /'si:zn/ n 1 estación 2 temporada: ~ ticket abono de temporada ▶ in/out of season en/fuera de temporada **seasonal** adj 1 propio de la estación 2 (trabajo) de temporada

season² /'si:zn/ vt sazonar **seasoned** adj 1 condimentado 2 (persona) con mucha experiencia **seasoning** n condimento

seat /si:t/ n 1 asiento 2 (parque) banco 3 (Teat) butaca 4 (Pol) curul 5 (Pol) circunscripción electoral ● vt tener cabida para

seat belt n cinturón de seguridad

seating /'si:tɪŋ/ n [U] asientos

seaweed /'si:wi:d/ n [U] alga

secluded /sɪ'klu:dɪd/ adj 1 (lugar) apartado 2 (vida) retirado **seclusion** n 1 aislamiento 2 soledad

second¹ /'sekənd/ (abrev 2nd) adj, adv, pron segundo ▶ **second thoughts**: have ~ thoughts reconsiderar ◇ On ~ thoughts... Pensándolo bien, ... ● n 1 the second el (día) dos 2 (tb ~ gear) segunda 3 (tiempo) segundo: the ~ hand el segundero ● vt secundar

secondary /'sekənderi; -dri GB/ adj secundario: ~ school (GB) escuela secundaria

second-best adj 1 segundo mejor 2 inferior

second class n 1 segunda (clase) 2 correo de franqueo normal ● adv en segunda (clase): send sth ~ mandar algo por correo normal **second-class** adj de segunda (clase/categoría): a ~ stamp una estampilla/un timbre de franqueo normal

second-hand adj, adv de segunda mano

secondly /'sekəndli/ adv en segundo lugar

second-rate adj de segunda categoría

secret /'si:krət/ adj, n secreto **secrecy** n 1 secretismo 2 confidencialidad **secretive** adj reservado **secretly** adv en secreto

secretary /'sekrətəri/ -rətri GB/ n (pl -ies) 1 secretario/a 2 (GB, Pol) secretario/a, ministro/a

secretarial /ˌsekrə'teəriəl/ adj 1 (personal) administrativo 2 (trabajo) de secretario/a

Secretary of State n 1 (USA) Secretario/a de Estado 2 (GB) secretario/a, ministro/a

secrete /sɪ'kri:t/ vt 1 segregar 2 (fml) ocultar **secretion** n secreción

sect /sekt/ n secta

sectarian /sek'teəriən/ adj sectario

section /'sekʃn/ n 1 sección, parte 2 (carretera) tramo 3 (sociedad) sector 4 (Jur) artículo

sector /'sektər/ n sector

secular /'sekjələr/ adj laico

secure /sɪ'kjʊər/ adj 1 seguro 2 (prisión) de alta seguridad ● vt 1 fijar 2 (acuerdo, etc.) conseguir **securely** adv firmemente

security /sɪ'kjʊərəti/ n (pl -ies) 1 seguridad 2 (préstamo) fianza

security guard n guardia de seguridad

sedan /sɪ'dæn/ n (USA) automóvil de cuatro/cinco puertas

sedate /sɪ'deɪt/ adj reposado, calmado ● vt sedar **sedation** n sedación: under ~ bajo los efectos de calmantes **sedative** /'sedətɪv/ adj, n sedante

sedentary /'sednteri/ -tri GB/ adj sedentario

sediment /'sedɪmənt/ n sedimento

sedition /sɪ'dɪʃn/ n (fml) sedición

seduce /sɪ'dju:s; sɪ'dju:s GB/ vt seducir **seduction** /sɪ'dʌkʃn/ n seducción **seductive** adj seductor

see /si:/ (pt saw pp seen) 1 vt, vi ver: I'm seeing Sue tonight. Quedé de ver a Sue esta noche. → HEAR 2 vt acompañar 3 vi encargarse: I'll ~ that it's done. Ya me encargaré de que se lleve a cabo. 4 vt, vi comprender ▶ seeing that... en vista de que... **see you (around/later)** (coloq) hasta luego NOTA Para otras expresiones, ver el sustantivo, adjetivo, etc., p.ej. **see sense** en SENSE. ■ **see about sth** encargarse de algo **see sb off** 1 ir a despedir a algn 2 (GB) echar a algn **see through sth/sb** calar algo/a algn **see to sth** ocuparse de algo

seed /si:d/ n 1 semilla, simiente 2 (Dep) cabeza de serie

seedy /'si:di/ adj (-ier/-iest) sórdido

seek /si:k/ (pt/pp sought) (fml) 1 vt, vi ~ (after/for) sth/sb buscar algo/a algn 2 vi ~ to do sth intentar hacer algo ■ **seek sth/sb out** buscar y encontrar algo/a algn

seem /si:m/ vi parecer **NOTA** No se usa en tiempos continuos. **seemingly** adv aparentemente

seen /si:n/ pp de SEE

seep /si:p/ vi filtrarse

seething /'si:ðɪŋ/ adj ~ (with sth) abarrotado (de algo)

see-through adj transparente

segment /'segmənt/ n 1 segmento 2 (de naranja, etc.) gajo

segregate /'segrɪgeɪt/ vt segregar

seize /si:z/ vt 1 agarrar: ~ hold of sth agarrar algo ◊ I was seized by panic. El pánico se apoderó de mí. 2 (drogas, etc.) incautarse de 3 capturar 4 (bienes) embargar 5 (control) hacerse con 6 (oportunidad, etc.) aprovechar: ~ the initiative tomar la iniciativa ■ **seize on/upon sth** aprovecharse de algo **seize up** agarrotarse, atascarse **seizure** /'si:ʒər/ n 1 (drogas, etc.) incautación 2 captura 3 (Med) ataque

seldom /'seldəm/ adv rara vez →ALWAYS

select /sɪ'lekt/ vt elegir ● adj selecto **selection** n selección **selective** adj selectivo

self /self/ n (pl **selves**) el mismo: be your old ~ again volver a ser el mismo de siempre

self-centered (-centred GB) adj egocéntrico

self-confident adj seguro de sí mismo

self-conscious adj inseguro

self-contained adj (GB, vivienda) con baño y cocina

self-control n autocontrol

self-defense (-defence GB) n defensa propia

self-determination n autodeterminación

self-employed adj (trabajador) autónomo

self-interest n interés propio

selfish /'selfɪʃ/ adj egoísta

self-pity n autocompasión

self-portrait n autorretrato

self-respect n dignidad

self-rising flour (**self-raising flour** GB) n harina con levadura

self-satisfied adj excesivamente satisfecho de sí mismo

self-service adj de autoservicio

sell /sel/ *vt, vi* (*pp, pt* **sold**) ~ **(at/ for sth)** vender(se) (a algo) ▪ **sell sth off** vender algo a bajo precio **sell out** agotarse: *be sold out of sth* haber agotado las existencias de algo **seller** *n* vendedor/a **selling** *n* venta

sell-by date *n* (GB) fecha límite de venta

Sellotape® /'seləteɪp/ (GB) *Ver* SCOTCH TAPE®

selves /selvz/ *pl de* SELF

semi /'semi/ *n* (*pl* -**s**) (GB, coloq) casa pareada

semicircle /'semɪsɜːrkl/ *n* 1 semicírculo 2 semicircunferencia

semicolon /'semɪkoʊlən; ˌsemiˈkəʊlən GB/ *n* punto y coma

semi-detached *adj* (GB, casa) pareado

semi-final *n* semifinal

seminar /'semɪnɑːr/ *n* seminario (*clase*)

Senate /'senət/ *n* 1 (Pol) senado 2 (*universidad*) junta de gobierno **senator** /'senətər/ *n* (*abrev* **Sen.**) senador/a

send /send/ *vt* (*pt/pp* **sent**) 1 enviar, mandar 2 hacer (que): ~ *sb to sleep* hacer dormir a algn: *The idea sent shivers down my spine.* La idea me dio escalofríos. ◇ ~ *sb crazy* volver loco a algn ▪ **send for sb** llamar, mandar buscar a algn **send (off) for sth** pedir, encargar algo **send sb in** enviar a algn (*tropas, policía, etc.*) **send sth in** enviar algo **send sb off** (GB, Dep) expulsar a algn **send sth off** 1 mandar algo por correo 2 despachar algo **send sth out** 1 enviar algo 2 emitir algo **send sth/sb up** (GB, coloq) parodiar algo/a algn **sender** *n* remitente

senile /'siːnaɪl/ *adj* senil **senility** /sə'nɪləti/ *n* senilidad

senior /'siːniər/ *adj* 1 superior: ~ *partner* socio mayoritario 2 (*abrev* **Sr.**) padre: *Jim Brown Sr.* Jim Brown, padre ● *n* 1 mayor: *She is two years my ~.* Me lleva dos años. 2 (USA) jubilado/a **seniority** /ˌsiːni'ɔːrəti; -'ɒr- GB/ *n* antigüedad (*rango, años, etc.*)

senior citizen *n* ciudadano/a de la tercera edad

sensation /sen'seɪʃn/ *n* sensación **sensational** *adj* 1 sensacional 2 sensacionalista

sense /sens/ *n* 1 sentido: ~ *of smell/touch/taste* olfato/tacto/ gusto ◇ ~ *of humor* sentido del humor ◇ *It gives him a ~ of security.* Le hace sentirse seguro. 2 juicio, sensatez: *come to your*

~*s* recobrar el juicio ▸ **in a sense** en cierto sentido **make sense** tener sentido **make sense of sth** descifrar algo **see sense** entrar en razón ● *vt* 1 sentir, ser consciente de 2 detectar **senseless** *adj* 1 insensato 2 sin sentido (*inconsciente*)

sensibility /ˌsensə'bɪləti/ *n* sensibilidad

sensible /'sensəbl/ *adj* 1 sensato **NOTA** La palabra española "sensible" se traduce por **sensitive**. 2 (*decisión*) acertado **sensibly** *adv* 1 con prudencia 2 (*vestirse*) adecuadamente

sensitive /'sensətɪv/ *adj* 1 sensible **NOTA** La palabra inglesa **sensible** se traduce por "sensato". *be* ~ *to criticism* ser susceptible a la crítica 2 (*asunto, piel*) delicado: ~ *documents* documentos confidenciales **sensitivity** /ˌsensə'tɪvəti/ *n* 1 sensibilidad 2 susceptibilidad 3 (*asunto, piel*) delicadeza

sensual /'senʃuəl/ *adj* sensual **sensuality** /ˌsenʃu'æləti/ *n* sensualidad

sensuous /'senʃuəs/ *adj* sensual

sent /sent/ *pt, pp de* SEND

sentence /'sentəns/ *n* 1 frase, oración 2 sentencia: *a life* ~ cadena perpetua ● *vt* condenar

sentiment /'sentɪmənt/ *n* 1 sentimentalismo 2 sentimiento **sentimental** /ˌsentɪ'mentl/ *adj* 1 sentimental 2 sensiblero **sentimentality** /ˌsentɪmen'tæləti/ *n* 1 sentimentalismo, sensiblería

sentry /'sentri/ *n* (*pl* -**ies**) centinela

separate /'seprət/ *adj* 1 separado 2 distinto /'sepərət/ 1 *vt, vi* separar(se) 2 *vt* dividir **separately** *adv* por separado **separation** *n* separación

September /sep'tembər/ *n* (*abrev* **Sept.**) se(p)tiembre →JUNE

sequel /'siːkwəl/ *n* 1 secuela 2 (*Cine, etc.*) continuación

sequence /'siːkwəns/ *n* sucesión, serie

serene /sə'riːn/ *adj* sereno

sergeant /'sɑːrdʒənt/ *n* sargento

serial /'sɪəriəl/ *n* serie →SERIES

series /'sɪəriːz/ *n* (*pl* **series**) 1 serie 2 sucesión **NOTA** **Series** es una serie que trata una historia diferente en cada episodio, y **serial** una sola historia dividida en capítulos.

serious /'sɪəriəs/ *adj* 1 serio: *be* ~ *about sb* andar en serio con algn 2 grave **seriously** *adv* 1 en serio 2 gravemente **seriousness** n 1 seriedad 2 gravedad

sermon /'sɜːrmən/ n sermón

servant /'sɜːrvənt/ n criado/a

serve /sɜːrv/ 1 vt ~ sth (up) servir algo: a serving spoon una cuchara de servir 2 vi servir: ~ with the army servir en el ejército 3 vt (cliente) atender 4 vt, vi (disputa) resolver 5 vt, vi sth; cumplir 5 vt, vi (tenis, etc.) sacar ▸ serve sb right: It ~s him right. Se lo merece. ■ serve sth out 1 servir algo 2 distribuir algo ● n saque

server /'sɜːrvər/ n 1 (Comp) servidor 2 (tenis, etc.) jugador/a que tiene el saque 3 (Cocina) cubierto de servir

service /'sɜːrvɪs/ n 1 servicio 2 misa 3 (tenis, etc.) saque ● vt hacerle un servicio a

service charge n servicio: There's a 15% ~. Se cobra un 15% de servicio.

serviceman, servicewoman /'sɜːrvɪsmæn/-wʊmən/ n (pl -men/ -women) militar

service station n estación de servicio

serviette /ˌsɜːrviˈet/ n (GB) servilleta

session /'seʃn/ n sesión

set /set/ adj 1 situado ▸ be all set estar preparado ● n 1 juego: a ~ of saucepans una batería de cocina 2 (personas) círculo 3 (Elec) aparato 4 (tenis) set 5 (Teat) decorado 6 (Cine) escenario 7 a shampoo and ~ lavar y rizar ● (-tt-) (pt/pp set) 1 vt poner: ~ the alarm clock/VCR poner el despertador/programar el video ◇ ~ the prisoners free poner en libertad a los prisioneros ◇ It ~ me thinking. Me puso a pensar. ◇ She ~ us a lot of homework. Nos puso muchas tareas. 2 vt colocar 3 vt (Cine, etc.): The film is ~ in Peru. La película se desarrolla en Perú. 4 vt establecer: They haven't ~ a date for their wedding yet. No han fijado la fecha del matrimonio todavía. 5 vi (sol) ponerse 6 vi cuajar, endurecerse 7 vt (pelo) rizar 8 vt engarzar **NOTA** Para expresiones, ver el sustantivo, adjetivo, etc., p.ej. **set light to sth** en LIGHT. ■ **set about (doing) sth** ponerse a hacer algo **set off** salir: ~ off on a journey salir de viaje **set sth off** hacer explotar algo 2 ocasionar algo **set out** 1 emprender un viaje 2 salir (de viaje) **set out to do sth** proponerse hacer algo **set sth up** 1 levantar algo 2 montar algo

setback /'setbæk/ n revés

settee /se'tiː/ n (GB) sofá

setting /'setɪŋ/ n 1 montura 2 ambientación 3 (sol) puesta

settle /'setl/ 1 vi establecerse, quedarse a vivir 2 vi posarse 3 vt (estómago) asentar 4 vt (disputa) resolver 5 vt, vi sth; ~ (up) pagar algo; liquidar las cuentas 6 vi (sedimento) depositarse ■ **settle down** sentar cabeza **settle for sth** aceptar algo **settle in/into sth** adaptar(se) a algo **settle on sth** decidirse por algo **settled** adj estable **settlement** n 1 acuerdo 2 poblado 3 colonización **settler** /'setlər/ n poblador/a

seven /'sevn/ adj, n, pron siete **seventh** (abrev 7th) adj, n, pron séptimo

seventeen /ˌsevn'tiːn/ adj, n, pron diecisiete **seventeenth** 1 adj, pron decimoséptimo 2 n diecisieteavo

seventy /'sevnti/ adj, n, pron setenta **seventieth** 1 adj, pron septuagésimo 2 n setentavo

sever /'sevər/ vt (fml) 1 cortar 2 (relaciones) romper

several /'sevrəl/ adj, pron varios/as

severe /sɪ'vɪər/ adj (-er/-est) 1 severo 2 (tormenta, dolor, etc.) fuerte

sew /soʊ/ vt, vi (pt sewed pp sewed/sewn /soʊn/) coser ■ **sew sth up** coser algo: ~ up a hole remendar un agujero **sewing** n costura: ~ machine máquina de coser

sewer /'suːər/ n alcantarilla **sewage** n [U] aguas residuales/negras

sex /seks/ n 1 sexo 2 relaciones sexuales **sexual** /'sekʃuəl/ adj sexual **sexuality** /ˌsekʃuˈæləti/ n sexualidad **sexy** adj (-ier/-iest) 1 sexy 2 erótico

sexism /'seksɪzəm/ n sexismo **sexist** adj, n sexista

shabby /'ʃæbi/ adj (-ier/-iest) 1 (ropa) raído 2 en mal estado 3 (persona) desharrapado 4 (comportamiento) mezquino

shack /ʃæk/ n choza

shade /ʃeɪd/ n 1 sombra 2 pantalla (lámpara) 3 (USA) persiana 4 (color) tono 5 (significado) matiz ● vt dar sombra a **shady** adj (-ier/-iest) sombreado

shadow /'ʃædoʊ/ n 1 sombra 2 shadows tinieblas ● vt seguir y vigilar secretamente a ● adj (GB, Pol) de la oposición

shadowy /adj 1 (lugar) oscuro 2 indefinido

shaft /ʃæft/ n 1 dardo 2 mango largo 3 fuste 4 eje 5 pozo: *the elevator ~* el hueco del ascensor 6 (luz) rayo

shaggy /ˈʃægi/ adj peludo: *~ hair* pelo desgreñado

shake /ʃeɪk/ n sacudida: *a ~ of the head* una negación con la cabeza ● (pt **shook** pp **shaken** /ˈʃeɪkən/) 1 vt ~ sth/sb (about/around) sacudir, agitar algo/a algn 2 vi temblar 3 vt ~ sb (up) perturbar a algn ▸ **shake sb's hand/shake hands (with sb)/shake sb by the hand** dar la mano a algn **shake your head** negar con la cabeza ◼ **shake sb off** quitarse a algn de encima **shake sb up** dar una sacudida a algn **shake sb up** agitar algo **shaky** adj (**-ier/-iest**) 1 tembloroso 2 poco firme

shall /ʃəl, ʃæl/ (contracción **'ll** neg **shall not/shan't**) v aux (esp GB) futuro: *I ~ tell her tomorrow.* Se lo diré mañana. **NOTA** Shall y **will** se usan para formar el futuro. Shall se usa con I y we, y will con las demás personas. En inglés hablado, will (o **'ll**) es cada vez más común. ● v modal **NOTA** Shall es un verbo modal al que sigue un infinitivo sin **to**, y que no usa el auxiliar **do** en interrogaciones y negaciones. 1 (fml) (determinación): *He ~ be given a fair trial.* Tendrá un juicio justo. ◊ *I shan't go.* No iré. **NOTA** En este sentido, shall es más formal que **will**. 2 (GB, oferta, petición): *Shall I pick you up?* ¿Te voy a buscar? **NOTA** En EE.UU., se usa **should** en este sentido.

shallow /ˈʃæloʊ/ adj (**-er/-est**) 1 (agua) poco profundo 2 (persona) superficial

shambles /ˈʃæmblz/ n [sing] (coloq) desastre: *in a ~* hecho un desastre

shame /ʃeɪm/ n 1 vergüenza, pena 2 deshonra 3 **a shame** una lástima ▸ **put sth/sb to shame** superar a algn por mucho ● vt (fml) 1 avergonzar 2 deshonrar **shameful** adj vergonzoso **shameless** adj sinvergüenza

shampoo /ʃæmˈpuː/ n champú ● vt (pt/pp **-ooed** pt pres **-ooing**) lavar (con champú)

shan't /ʃænt; ʃɑːnt GB/ = SHALL NOT

shanty town /ˈʃænti taʊn/ n ciudad perdida (Mx), barrio de invasión (And)

shape /ʃeɪp/ n 1 forma 2 figura ▸ **give shape to sth** (fml) plasmar algo in **any shape (or form)** (coloq) de cualquier tipo in **shape** en forma out of **shape** 1 deformado 2 en mal estado (físico) **take shape** ir cobrando forma ● vt 1 ~ sth (into sth) dar forma (de algo) a algo 2 forjar **shapeless** adj amorfo

share /ʃeər/ n 1 parte 2 (Fin) acción ▸ vt 1 ~ sth (out) repartir algo 2 vt, vi compartir

shareholder /ˈʃeərhoʊldər/ n accionista

shark /ʃɑːrk/ n tiburón

sharp /ʃɑːrp/ adj (**-er/-est**) 1 afilado 2 (curva) cerrado 3 (subida) pronunciado 4 nítido 5 (sonido, dolor) agudo 6 (sabor) ácido 7 (olor) acre 8 (viento) cortante 9 (poco) escrupuloso 10 (Mús) sostenido ● n sostenido ● adv (hora) en punto **sharpen** vt, vi afilar

shatter /ˈʃætər/ 1 vt, vi hacer(se) añicos 2 vt destruir **shattering** adj demoledor

shave /ʃeɪv/ vt, vi afeitar(se)

she /ʃiː/ pron ella **NOTA** El pron pers no puede omitirse en inglés. ● n hembra: *Is it a he or a ~?* ¿Es macho o hembra?

shear /ʃɪər/ vt (pt **-ed** pp **-ed/shorn**) 1 (oveja) trasquilar 2 cortar **shears** n tijeras (de podar)

sheath /ʃiːθ/ n vaina, estuche

she'd /ʃiːd/ 1 = SHE HAD 2 = SHE WOULD

shed /ʃed/ n cobertizo ● vt (**-dd-**) (pt/pp **shed**) 1 (hojas) perder 2 (piel) mudar 3 (fml) (sangre, lágrimas) derramar 4 (luz) arrojar

sheep /ʃiːp/ n (pl **sheep**) oveja → CARNE **sheepish** adj tímido, avergonzado

sheer /ʃɪər/ adj 1 (absoluto) puro 2 (tela) diáfano 3 escarpado

sheet /ʃiːt/ n 1 sábana 2 (papel) hoja 3 (vidrio, metal) lámina

sheikh /ʃeɪk/ n jeque

shelf /ʃelf/ n (pl **shelves**) estante, repisa

she'll /ʃiːl/ = SHE WILL

shell /ʃel/ n 1 concha (huevo, nuez) cáscara →PEEL 3 caparazón 4 obús 5 (barco) casco 6 (edificio) armazón ● vt bombardear

shellfish /ˈʃelfɪʃ/ n (pl **shellfish**) 1 (Zool) crustáceo 2 marisco

shelter /ˈʃeltər/ n 1 abrigo, resguardo: *take ~* refugiarse 2 (lugar) refugio ● 1 vt resguardar, abrigar 2 vi refugiarse, ponerse al abrigo **sheltered** adj **1** abrigado **2** protegido

shelve /ʃelv/ vt archivar

shelves /ʃelvz/ pl de SHELF

shelving /ˈʃelvɪŋ/ n [U] estantería(s)

shepherd /ˈʃepəd/ n pastor

sherry /ˈʃeri/ n (pl -ies) jerez

she's /ʃiːz/ **1** = SHE IS **2** = SHE HAS

shied /ʃaɪd/ pt, pp de SHY

shield /ʃiːld/ n escudo ● vt proteger

shift /ʃɪft/ vt, vi mover(se), cambiar (de sitio) ● n **1** cambio **2** (trabajo) turno **3** (Comp) (tb ~ key) tecla de mayúsculas

shifty /ˈʃɪfti/ adj sospechoso

shilling /ˈʃɪlɪŋ/ n chelín

shimmer /ˈʃɪmər/ vi **1** brillar **2** resplandecer **3** (luz en agua) relucir

shin /ʃɪn/ n **1** espinilla (de la pierna) **2** (tb ~ bone) tibia

shine /ʃaɪn/ (pt/pp shone) **1** vi brillar: The sun was shining. Hacía sol. ◊ His face shone with happiness. Su cara irradiaba felicidad. ◊ She's always shone at languages. Siempre ha sido muy buena para los idiomas. **2** vt (linterna, etc.) dirigir ● n brillo

shiny /ˈʃaɪni/ adj (-ier/-iest) brillante, reluciente

shingle /ˈʃɪŋgl/ n [U] guijarros

ship /ʃɪp/ n barco, buque ➤ BOAT ● vt (-pp-) enviar (por mar)

shipbuilding /ˈʃɪpbɪldɪŋ/ n construcción naval

shipment /ˈʃɪpmənt/ n cargamento

shipping /ˈʃɪpɪŋ/ n [U] embarcaciones, buques: ~ lane vía de navegación

shipwreck /ˈʃɪprek/ n naufragio ● vt: be shipwrecked naufragar

shirt /ʃɜːt/ n camisa

shiver /ˈʃɪvər/ vi **1** temblar **2** estremecerse ● n escalofrío

shoal /ʃəʊl/ n banco (de peces)

shock /ʃɒk/ n **1** susto, conmoción **2** (tb electric ~) descarga eléctrica **3** (Med) shock ● vt **1** trastornar **2** escandalizar **shocking** adj **1** escandaloso **2** espantoso **3** (coloq) malísimo

shoddy /ˈʃɒdi/ adj (-ier/-iest) **1** de baja calidad **2** mal hecho

shoe /ʃuː/ vt (pt/pp shod /ʃɒd/) herrar ● n **1** zapato: What size ~ do you wear? ¿Qué número de zapato usa? ◊ ~ shop zapatería **2** herradura

shoelace /ˈʃuːleɪs/ n cordón (de zapato), agujeta (Mx)

shoestring /ˈʃuːstrɪŋ/ n ▸ **on a shoestring** con escasos medios

shone /ʃɒn; ʃɒn GB/ pt, pp de SHINE

shook /ʃʊk/ pt de SHAKE

shoot /ʃuːt/ (pt/pp shot) **1** vt pegar un tiro a: ~ rabbits cazar conejos ◊ He was shot in the leg. Recibió un disparo en la pierna. ◊ ~ sb dead matar a algn (a tiros) **2** vi ~ (at sth/sb) disparar (a algo/contra algn) **3** vt fusilar **4** vt (mirada) lanzar **5** vt (Cine) rodar **6** vi ~ along, past, etc. ir, pasar, etc., volando **7** vi (Dep) disparar ■ **shoot sb down** matar a algn (a tiros) **shoot sth down** derribar algo (a tiros) **shoot up 1** crecer rápidamente **2** (precios) dispararse ● n brote

shop /ʃɒp/ n **1** tienda, almacén: go to the ~ ir de compras **2** (USA) taller ▸ **talk shop** (pey) hablar del trabajo ● vi (-pp-) ir de/hacer compras: ~ for sth buscar algo (en las tiendas) ■ **shop around** comparar precios **shopper** n comprador/a **shopping** n compras: ~ center/mall centro comercial

shop assistant n (GB) dependiente/a

shopkeeper /ˈʃɒpkiːpər/ n comerciante, tendero/a

shoplifting /ˈʃɒplɪftɪŋ/ n hurto, robo (en tienda) **shoplifter** n ladrón/ona ➤ THIEF

shore /ʃɔːr/ n **1** costa: go on ~ desembarcar **2** orilla (mar, etc.)

shorn /ʃɔːn/ pp de SHEAR

short /ʃɔːrt/ n (coloq) **1** cortocircuito **2** (Cine) corto ● adj (-er/-est) **1** corto: a ~ while un rato ◊ a ~ time ago hace poco **2** (persona) bajo **3** ~ of sth escaso de algo: I'm a bit ~ of time. Ando un poco justo de tiempo. **4** Water is ~. Hay escasez de agua. ◊ I'm $2 ~. Me faltan dos dólares. **5** ~ for sth: Ben is ~ for Benjamin. Ben es el diminutivo de Benjamin. ▸ **fall short of sth** no alcanzar algo **for short** para abreviar **in short** resumiendo

shortage /ˈʃɔːtɪdʒ/ n escasez

short circuit n cortocircuito ● **short-circuit 1** vi tener un cortocircuito **2** vt causar un cortocircuito en

shortcoming /ˈʃɔːtkʌmɪŋ/ n deficiencia, punto débil

short cut n atajo: take a ~ cortar camino

shorten /ˈʃɔːtn/ vt, vi acortar(se)

shorthand /ˈʃɔːthænd/ n taquigrafía

shortlist /ˈʃɔːtlɪst/ n lista final de candidatos

short-lived adj efímero

shortly /ˈʃɔːtli/ adv 1 dentro de poco 2 muy pronto: ~ *before* poco antes

shorts /ʃɔːts/ n [pl] 1 pantalón corto, shorts 2 (USA) calzoncillos →PAIR

short-sighted adj 1 miope 2 imprudente

short-term adj a corto plazo

shot /ʃɑt/ pt, pp de SHOOT ● n 1 disparo 2 intento: *have a* ~ *at sth* intentar algo 3 (Dep) golpe 4 the shot (tb the shot-put) (Dep) lanzamiento de bala 5 (Fot) foto 6 (Med, coloq) inyección

shotgun /ˈʃɑtɡʌn/ n escopeta

should /ʃəd, ʃʊd/ v (neg **should not/shouldn't** /ˈʃʊdnt/) NOTA Should es un verbo modal al que sigue un infinitivo sin to, y que no usa el auxiliar do en interrogaciones y negaciones. 1 (sugerencias, consejos) deber: *You shouldn't drink and drive.* No deberías manejar si has bebido. 2 (probabilidad) deber de: *He* ~ *be there by now.* Ya debe de haber llegado. 3 *How* ~ *I know?* ¿Y yo qué sé? 4 (USA, oferta, petición): *Should I pick you up?* ¿Te recojo?

shoulder /ˈʃəʊldər/ n hombro ● vt cargar con

shoulder blade n omoplato

shout /ʃaʊt/ n grito ● vt, vi ~ (**out**) (out) gritar (algo) NOTA Shout at sb quiere decir "regañar", y shout to sb tiene el sentido de "decir a gritos": *Don't* ~ *at him, he's only little.* No le grites, que es muy pequeño. ◊ *She shouted the number out to me.* Me gritó el número. ■ **shout sb down** callar a algn con abucheos

shove /ʃʌv/ 1 vt, vi empujar 2 vt (coloq) meter ● n empujón

shovel /ˈʃʌvl/ n pala ● vt (-l-, -ll-GB) (re)mover con una pala

show /ʃəʊ/ n 1 espectáculo, función: *a TV* ~ un programa de televisión 2 exposición, feria: *on* ~ expuesto 3 demostración, alarde ▸ **for show** para impresionar ● (pt **showed** pp **shown** /ʃəʊn/) 1 vt mostrar, enseñar 2 vi verse 3 vt demostrar 4 vt (Cine) proyectar 5 vt (Arte) exponer ■ **show off** (**to sb**) (coloq, pey) presumir (delante de algn) **show sth/sb off** 1 hacer resaltar algo/a algn 2 (pey) presumir de algo/algn **show sb up** (coloq) presentarse **show sb up** avergonzar a algn

show business n el mundo del espectáculo

showdown /ˈʃəʊdaʊn/ n enfrentamiento decisivo

shower /ˈʃaʊər/ n 1 chubasco, chaparrón 2 ~ (**of sth**) lluvia (de algo) 3 ducha: *take/have a* ~ bañarse ● 1 vi ducharse 2 vt ~ **sb with sth** colmar a algn de algo

showing /ˈʃəʊɪŋ/ n 1 (Cine) función 2 actuación

show-off n (pl -offs) (coloq, pey) fanfarrón/ona

showroom /ˈʃəʊruːm/ n sala de exposición (y ventas)

shrank /ʃræŋk/ pt de SHRINK

shrapnel /ˈʃræpnəl/ n metralla

shred /ʃred/ n 1 (verduras) tira 2 (tabaco) brizna 3 (tela) jirón 4 (fig) pizca ● vt (-dd-) hacer tiras, desmenuzar

shrewd /ʃruːd/ adj (-er/-est) 1 astuto 2 (decisión) inteligente

shriek /ʃriːk/ vt, vi ~ (**with sth**) gritar, chillar (de algo): ~ *with laughter* reírse a carcajadas ● n chillido

shrift /ʃrɪft/ n ▸ **get short shrift** ser despachado de plano

shrill /ʃrɪl/ adj (-er/-est) 1 chillón 2 (protesta, etc.) estridente

shrimp /ʃrɪmp/ n camarón

shrine /ʃraɪn/ n santuario

shrink /ʃrɪŋk/ vt, vi (pt **shrank/ shrunk** pp **shrunk**) encoger(se), reducir(se) ■ **shrink from sth** vacilar ante algo/en hacer algo

shrivel /ˈʃrɪvl/ vt, vi (-l-, -ll-GB) ~ (**sth**) (**up**) 1 secar(se) (algo) 2 arrugar(se) (algo)

shroud /ʃraʊd/ n 1 sudario 2 (fml) ~ (**of sth**) manto (de algo) ● vt envolver: *shrouded in secrecy* rodeado de secreto

Shrove Tuesday /ˌʃrəʊv ˈtuːzdeɪ; -tjuː- GB/ n martes de Carnaval (víspera de cuaresma)

shrub /ʃrʌb/ n arbusto

shrug /ʃrʌɡ/ vt, vi (-gg-) ~ (**your shoulders**) encogerse de hombros ■ **shrug sth off** no dar importancia a algo ● n encogimiento de hombros

shrunk /ʃrʌŋk/ pt, pp de SHRINK

shudder /ˈʃʌdər/ vi 1 estremecerse 2 dar sacudidas ● n 1 escalofrío 2 sacudida

shuffle /ˈʃʌfl/ 1 vt, vi (cartas) barajar →BARAJA 2 vt ~ **your feet** arrastrar los pies 3 vi ~ (**along**) caminar arrastrando los pies

shun /ʃʌn/ vt (-nn-) rehuir

shut /ʃʌt/ vt, vi (-tt-) (pt/pp **shut**) cerrar(se) ■ **shut sth/sb away**

encerrar algo/a algn **shut (sth) down** cerrar (algo) **shut sb in sth** machucar(se) algo con algo **shut sth off** cortar algo (suministro) **shut sth/sb off (from sth)** aislar algo/a algn (de algo) **shut sth/sb out** excluir algo/a algn **shut up** (coloq) callarse **shut sb up** (coloq) hacer callar a algn **shut sth up** cerrar algo **shut sth/sb up** (en algo) encerrar algo/a algn (en algo) ● adj [después del verbo] cerrado

shutter /'ʃʌtər/ n 1 contraventana 2 (Fot) obturador

shuttle /'ʃʌtl/ n 1 (tb space ~) transbordador espacial 2 puente (aéreo): ~ service servicio de enlace

shy /ʃaɪ/ adj (-er/-est) tímido: be ~ of sth tener miedo de algo ● vi (pt/pp **shied**) 1 ~ (at sth) (caballo) espantarse (de algo) 2 ~ **away (from sth)** asustarse (de algo) **shyness** n timidez

sick /sɪk/ adj (-er/-est) 1 enfermo →**ENFERMO** 2 mareado 3 ~ **of sth/ sb** (coloq) harto de algo/algn: ~ to death/~ and tired of sth hasta la coronilla/~ and tired de algo 4 (coloq) morboso ▸ be sick vomitar **make sb sick** poner a algn enfermo **out/off** (GB) **sick** con licencia por enfermedad/la incapacidad (Mx) ● n (GB, coloq) vómito **sicken** vt dar asco a **sickening** adj 1 repugnante 2 irritante **sickness** n 1 enfermedad 2 náuseas

sickly /'sɪkli/ adj 1 enfermizo 2 (gusto, olor) empalagoso

side /saɪd/ n 1 cara 2 lado: ~ by ~ uno al lado de otro 3 (persona, casa, etc.) costado: a ~ door/ street lado puerta/calle lateral 4 (animal) flanco 5 (montaña) ladera 6 (lago, río) orilla 7 parte: change ~s pasarse al otro bando ◇ be on our ~ ser de los nuestros ◇ Whose ~ are you on? ¿De qué lado estás tú? 8 (GB, Dep) equipo 9 aspecto ▸ get on the right/ wrong side of sb caerle bien/ mal a algn **on/from all sides/ every side** por/de todos lados **put sth on/to one side** dejar algo a un lado **take sides** tomar partido ■ side with sb ponerse del lado de algn

sideboard /'saɪdbɔːrd/ n aparador

side effect n efecto secundario

sidetrack /'saɪdtræk/ vt desviar

sidewalk /'saɪdwɔːk/ n (USA) acera, banqueta (Mx)

sideways /'saɪdweɪz/ adv, adj 1 de lado 2 de reojo

siege /siːdʒ/ n 1 sitio 2 cerco policial

sieve /sɪv/ n cedazo ● vt cernir, colar

sift /sɪft/ 1 vt cernir, colar 2 vt, vi ~ **(through)** sth examinar algo cuidadosamente

sigh /saɪ/ vi suspirar ● n suspiro

sight /saɪt/ n 1 vista: in ~ a la vista 2 the sights los lugares de interés ▸ at/on sight en el acto **lose sight of sth/sb** perder de vista a algn de vista: We mustn't lose ~ of the fact that... Hay que tener presente el hecho de que... **out of sight, out of mind** ojos que no ven, corazón que no siente

sightseeing /'saɪtsiːɪŋ/ n turismo

sign /saɪn/ vt, vi firmar ■ sign sb **up** 1 contratar a algn 2 (Dep) fichar a algn **sign up (for sth)** 1 inscribirse (en algo) 2 hacerse socio (de algo) ● n 1 signo 2 señal 3 indicio 4 (Med) síntoma

signal /'sɪɡnəl/ n señal ● vt, vi (-l-, -ll- GB) 1 hacer señas 2 mostrar, indicar

signature /'sɪɡnətʃər/ n firma

significant /sɪɡ'nɪfɪkənt/ adj significativo **significance** n 1 significado 2 trascendencia

signify /'sɪɡnɪfaɪ/ vt (pt/pp **-ied**) 1 significar 2 indicar

sign language n lenguaje por señas

signpost /'saɪnpoʊst/ n poste indicador

silence /'saɪləns/ n, interj silencio ● vt acallar **silent** adj 1 silencioso 2 callado 3 (Cine, letra) mudo

silhouette /ˌsɪluˈet/ n silueta ● vt perfilar

silk /sɪlk/ n seda **silky** adj sedoso

sill /sɪl/ n alféizar

silly /'sɪli/ adj (-ier/-iest) 1 tonto: That was a very ~ thing to say. Qué bobada la que dijiste. 2 ridículo

silver /'sɪlvər/ n 1 plata: silverplated con baño de plata 2 [U] monedas 3 (objetos de) plata ● adj 1 de plata 2 (color) plateado **silvery** adj plateado

similar /'sɪmələr/ adj parecido **similarity** /ˌsɪmə'lærəti/ n (pl -ies) semejanza **similarly** adv 1 de forma parecida 2 del mismo modo, igualmente

simile /'sɪməli/ n símil

simmer /'sɪmər/ vt, vi hervir a fuego lento

simple /'sɪmpl/ adj (-er/-est) 1 sencillo, simple 2 fácil 3 (persona) tonto ▸ simply adv 1 sencillamente, simplemente **2** modestamente **3** tan sólo

simplicity /sɪm'plɪsəti/ n sencillez

simplify /'sɪmplɪfaɪ/ vt (pt/pp -ied) simplificar

simplistic /sɪm'plɪstɪk/ adj simplista

simulate /'sɪmjuleɪt/ vt simular

simultaneous /ˌsaɪml'teɪniəs, ˌsɪm- GB/ adj simultáneo

sin /sɪn/ n pecado ● vi (-nn-) pecar

sinful adj **1** pecador **2** pecaminoso

since /sɪns/ conj **1** (desde) que: How long is it ~ I visited you? ¿Cuánto hace que no te visito? **2** puesto que ● prep desde que → NOTA Since y from se usan para especificar el punto de partida de la acción del verbo. Since se usa cuando la acción se extiende hasta el presente: She has been here ~ six. Está aquí desde las seis. From se usa cuando la acción ya terminó o no ha empezado todavía: I was there from one until two. Estuve allá desde la una hasta las dos. ◇ I'll be there from three. Voy a estar allí a partir de las tres. → FOR ● adv desde entonces

sincere /sɪn'sɪər/ adj sincero **sincerely** adv sinceramente **sincerity** /sɪn'serəti/ n sinceridad

sing /sɪŋ/ vt, vi (pt sang pp sung) cantar **singer** n cantante **singing** n canto, cantar

single /'sɪŋɡl/ adj **1** solo, único: every ~ day cada día **2** individual **3** soltero: ~ mother madre soltera ▸ in single file en fila india ● n **1** (GB) (tb ~ ticket) boleto/tiquete de ida **2** (disco) single, sencillo **3** singles (Dep) individuales ■ single sth/sb out elegir algo/a algn

single-handed adv sin ayuda

single-minded adj decidido

single-parent family n familia monoparental

singular /'sɪŋɡjələr/ adj, n singular

sinister /'sɪnɪstər/ adj siniestro

sink /sɪŋk/ n **1** (tb bathroom ~) (USA) lavabo, lavamanos **2** fregadero, lavaplatos ● (pt sank pp sunk) **1** vt, vi hundir(se) **2** vt bajar **3** vi (sol) ocultarse **4** vt ~ sth into sth clavar algo en algo **5** vt (coloq) (planes) echar a perder ■ sink in **1** absorberse **2** It still hasn't sunk in. Todavía no me he hecho a la idea. sink into sth **1** (líquido) penetrar en algo **2** sumirse en algo

sinus /'saɪnəs/ n seno (de hueso)

sip /sɪp/ vt, vi (-pp-) beber a sorbos ● n sorbo

sir /sɜːr/ n **1** señor: Dear Sir Estimado señor → ATENTAMENTE **2** Sir /sər/: Sir Paul McCartney

siren /'saɪrən/ n sirena (ruido)

sister /'sɪstər/ n **1** hermana **2** (GB, Med) enfermera jefe **3** ~ ship/ organization barco gemelo/organización hermana **sister-in-law** n (pl -ers-in-law) cuñada

sit /sɪt/ (-tt-) (pt/pp sat) **1** vi sentarse, estar sentado **2** vt ~ sb (down) (hacer) sentar a algn **3** vi (Arte) posar **4** vi (comité, etc.) reunirse **5** vi (objeto) estar **6** vt (GB, examen) presentarse a ■ sit around: ~ around doing nothing pasarse el día sin hacer nada sit back ponerse cómodo sit (yourself) down sentarse sit up **1** incorporarse **2** quedarse levantado

site /saɪt/ n **1** emplazamiento: building ~ obra (de construcción) **2** (de suceso) lugar **3** (Comp) sitio

sitting /'sɪtɪŋ/ n **1** sesión **2** (para comer) tanda

sitting room n (GB) sala

situation /ˌsɪtʃu'eɪʃn/ n **1** situación **2** (fml): ~s vacant ofertas de trabajo **situated** adj ubicado

six /sɪks/ adj, n, pron seis **sixth** (abrev 6th) adj, n, pron sexto

sixteen /ˌsɪks'tiːn/ adj, n, pron dieciséis **sixteenth** **1** adj, adv, pron decimosexto **2** n dieciseisavo

sixth form n (GB) dos últimos años de secundaria

sixty /'sɪksti/ adj, n, pron sesenta **sixtieth** **1** adj, pron sexagésimo **2** n sesentavo

size /saɪz/ n **1** tamaño **2** talla, número: I take ~ six. Calzo 36. ■ size sth/sb up (coloq) evaluar algo/a algn: She sized him up immediately. Adivinó sus intenciones enseguida. **siz(e)able** adj considerable

skate /skeɪt/ n patín ● vi patinar **skater** n patinador/a **skating** n patinaje

skateboard /'skeɪtbɔːrd/ n monopatín, patineta (Mx) **skateboarding** n deporte del monopatín/de la patineta

skeleton /'skelɪtn/ n esqueleto ● adj mínimo: ~ staff personal mínimo

skeptic (sceptic GB) /'skeptɪk/ n escéptico/a **skeptical** adj escéptico **skepticism** n escepticismo

sketch /sketʃ/ n **1** esbozo **2** (Teat) sketch ● vt, vi bosquejar **sketchy** adj (-ier/-iest) superficial, vago

ski /skiː/ *vi* (*pt/pp* **skied** *pt pres* **skiing**) esquiar ● *n* esquí **skier** *n* esquiador/a ● **skiing** *n* esquí

skid /skɪd/ *vi* (**-dd-**) 1 (*Aut*) derrapar, patinar 2 (*persona*) resbalar ● *n* patinada

skies /skaɪz/ *pl de* SKY

ski lift *n* telesquí

skill /skɪl/ *n* 1 ~ (**at/in sth**) habilidad (para algo) 2 destreza **skillful** (**skilful** *GB*) *adj* 1 ~ (**at/in sth**) hábil (para algo) 2 diestro **skilled** *adj* ~ (**at/in sth**) hábil (para algo), experto (en algo): ~ **worker** trabajador especializado

skim /skɪm/ (**-mm-**) 1 *vt* descremar 2 *vt* quitar la grasa de 3 *vt* pasar casi rozando 4 *vt, vi* ~ (**through/over**) **sth** leer algo por encima

skin /skɪn/ *n* 1 piel 2 (*fruta, etc.*) piel, cáscara →PEEL 3 (*leche*) nata ▸ **by the skin of your teeth** (*coloq*) por un pelo ● *vt* (**-nn-**) despellejar

skinhead /'skɪnhed/ *n* cabeza rapada

skinny /'skɪni/ *adj* (**-ier/-iest**) (*coloq, pey*) flaco →DELGADO

skip /skɪp/ (**-pp-**) 1 *vi* brincar 2 *vi* (*GB*) saltar la cuerda 3 *vt* saltarse ● *n* 1 brinco 2 (*GB*) contenedor (*para escombros*)

skipper /'skɪpər/ *n* capitán/ana

skirmish /'skɜːrmɪʃ/ *n* escaramuza

skirt /skɜːrt/ *n* 1 falda ● 1 *vt* bordear: *skirting (board)* (*GB*) rodapié/guardaescobas (*And*) 2 *vt, vi* ~ (**around**) sth eludir algo

skirting board *n* rodapié, zócalo

skive /skaɪv/ *vi* ~ (**off**) (*GB, coloq*) irse de pinta (*Mx*), capar clase/trabajo (*And*)

skull /skʌl/ *n* calavera, cráneo

skunk /skʌŋk/ *n* zorrillo

sky /skaɪ/ *n* (*pl* **skies**) cielo: *sky-high* por las nubes

skylight /'skaɪlaɪt/ *n* claraboya

skyline /'skaɪlaɪn/ *n* línea del horizonte (*en una ciudad*)

skyscraper /'skaɪskreɪpər/ *n* rascacielos

slab /slæb/ *n* 1 losa 2 (*concreto*) bloque 3 (*chocolate*) tableta

slack /slæk/ *adj* (**-er/-est**) 1 flojo 2 descuidado **slacken** *vt, vi* ~ (**sth**) (**off/up**) aflojar (algo)

slain /sleɪn/ *pp de* SLAY

slam /slæm/ (**-mm-**) 1 *vt, vi* cerrar(se) (*de golpe*) 2 *vt* arrojar, tirar: ~ *your brakes on* frenar de golpe 3 *vt* (*criticar*) vapulear

slander /'slændər; 'slɑːn- *GB*/ *n* calumnia ● *vt* calumniar

slang /slæŋ/ *n* argot

slant /slænt; slɑːnt *GB*/ 1 *vt, vi* inclinar(se) 2 *vt* presentar de forma subjetiva ● *n* 1 inclinación 2 (*fig*) sesgo

slap /slæp/ *vt* (**-pp-**) 1 cachetear 2 (*espalda*) dar palmadas en 3 arrojar/tirar (con un golpe) ● *n* 1 bofetada, cachetada 2 (*espalda*) palmada ● *adv* (*coloq*): ~ **in the middle** justo en medio

slash /slæʃ/ *vt* 1 cortar 2 destrozar a navajazos 3 (*precios, etc.*) rebajar (*drásticamente*) ● *n* 1 navajazo 2 tajo, corte 3 (*Comp*) barra diagonal

slate /sleɪt/ *n* 1 pizarra 2 teja (*de pizarra*)

slaughter /'slɔːtər/ *n* matanza ● *vt* 1 matar (*en matadero*) 2 masacrar 3 (*coloq*) (*Dep*) darle una paliza a

slave /sleɪv/ *n* esclavo/a ● *vi* ~ (**away**) matarse trabajando **slavery** *n* esclavitud

slay /sleɪ/ *vt* (*pt* **slew** *pp* **slain**) matar (*violentamente*)

sleazy /'sliːzi/ *adj* (**-ier/-iest**) (*coloq*) sórdido

sled /sled/ (**sledge** /sledʒ/ *GB*) *n* trineo (*de nieve*)

sleek /sliːk/ *adj* (**-er/-est**) lustroso

sleep /sliːp/ *n* sueño: *go to* ~ dormirse ● (*pt/pp* **slept**) 1 *vi* dormir: *sleeping pill* pastilla para dormir 2 *vt* albergar, tener camas para ■ **sleep in** (*USA*) quedarse en la cama **sleep sth off** dormir para recuperarse de algo **sleep on sth** (*coloq*) consultar algo con la almohada **sleep through sth** no ser despertado por algo: ~ *through the film* dormir durante toda la película **sleep with sb** acostarse con algn **sleepless** *adj* en vela **sleepy** *adj* (**-ier/-iest**) 1 somnoliento: *be* ~ tener sueño 2 (*lugar*) tranquilo

sleeper /'sliːpər/ *n* 1 durmiente: *be a heavy/light* ~ tener el sueño pesado/ligero 2 (*en las vías del tren*) durmiente 3 tren con coches cama

sleeping bag *n* saco de dormir

sleepwalker /'sliːpwɔːkər/ *n* sonámbulo/a

sleet /sliːt/ *n* aguanieve

sleeve /sliːv/ *n* 1 manga 2 (*disco*) cubierta, carátula ▸ **have/keep sth up your sleeve** tener algo guardado en la manga **sleeveless** *adj* sin mangas

sleigh /sleɪ/ *n* trineo (*caballos*)

slender /'slendər/ *adj* (**-er/-est**) 1 delgado 2 escaso

slept /slept/ *pt, pp de* SLEEP

slew /slu:/ *pt de* SLAY

slice /slaɪs/ *n* 1 rebanada 2 (*fruta*) rodaja 3 (*carne*) pedazo 4 (*coloq*) porción ● *vt* 1 ~ **sth** (**up**) cortar algo (*en rebanadas, etc*) 2 ~ **through/into sth** cortar algo limpiamente

slick /slɪk/ *adj* (**-er/-est**) 1 (*representación*) logrado 2 astuto ● *n* (*tb oil* ~) mancha de petróleo

slide /slaɪd/ *n* 1 resbaladilla (*Mx*), rodadero (*And*) 2 diapositiva 3 (*microscopio*) portaobjetos 4 deslizamiento ● *vt/pp de* **slide** /slɪd/) 1 *vi* resbalar, deslizarse 2 *vt* deslizar

sliding door *n* puerta corrediza

slight /slaɪt/ *adj* (**-er/-est**) 1 mínimo, ligero: *without the slightest difficulty* sin la menor dificultad 2 (*persona*) delgado, frágil ▸ **not in the slightest** ni lo más mínimo

slightly *adv* ligeramente, un poco

slim /slɪm/ *adj* (**slimmer, -est**) 1 delgado →DELGADO 2 (*oportunidad*) escaso 3 (*esperanza*) ligero ● *vi* (**-mm-**) ~ (**down**) adelgazar

slime /slaɪm/ *n* 1 cieno 2 baba **slimy** *adj* (**-ier/-iest**) baboso

sling /slɪŋ/ *n* cabestrillo ● *vt* (*pt/pp* **slung**) 1 (*coloq*) lanzar (*con fuerza*) 2 colgar

slink /slɪŋk/ *vi* (*pt/pp* **slunk**) deslizarse (*sigilosamente*): ~ *away* largarse furtivamente

slip /slɪp/ *n* 1 resbalón 2 error 3 (*ropa*) fondo, enagua 4 papelito ▸ **give sb the slip** (*coloq*) escaparse de algn ● (**-pp-**) 1 *vi* resbalar, deslizar(se) 2 ~ **from/out of/through sth** escurrirse de/entre algo 3 *vt* ~ **sth** (**from/off sb**) soltar algo (de algo) ▸ **let slip sth** dejar escapar algo (*secreto*) **slip your mind**: *It slipped my mind.* Se me olvidó. ■ **slip away** escabullirse **slip on/off** ponerse/quitarse algo **slip out** 1 salir un momento 2 escabullirse 3 *It just slipped out.* Se me salió. **slip up** (*coloq*) equivocarse

slipper /ˈslɪpər/ *n* zapatilla, pantufla

slippery /ˈslɪpəri/ *adj* resbaladizo 2 escurridizo

slit /slɪt/ *n* 1 ranura 2 (*en falda*) abertura 3 corte 4 rendija ● *vt* (**-tt-**) (*pt/pp* **slit**) cortar: ~ *sb's throat* degollar a algn ◇ ~ *sth open* abrir algo con un cuchillo

slither /ˈslɪðər/ *vi* 1 deslizarse 2 resbalar, patinar

sliver /ˈslɪvər/ *n* 1 astilla 2 esquirla 3 rodaja fina

slob /slɑb/ *n* (*coloq*) 1 vago 2 fachoso (*Mx*), dejado (*And*)

slog /slɑg/ *vi* (*coloq*) (**-gg-**) 1 ~ (**through sth**), ~ (**away**) (**at sth**) trabajar como un loco con algo/haciendo algo 2 caminar trabajosamente

slogan /ˈsloʊgən/ *n* eslogan

slop /slɑp/ (**-pp-**) 1 *vt* echar descuidadamente 2 *vt, vi* derramar(se)

slope /sloʊp/ *n* 1 pendiente 2 (*esquí*) pista ● *vi* tener pendiente

sloppy /ˈslɑpi/ *adj* (**-ier/-iest**) 1 descuidado, mal hecho 2 desaliñado 3 (*coloq*) sensiblero

slot /slɑt/ *n* 1 ranura 2 puesto: *a ten-minute ~ on TV* un espacio de diez minutos en la tele ● *vt* (**-tt-**) 1 *vt* ~ **sth** (**in**) introducir, meter algo 2 *vi* (**in**) encajar, meter algo

slot machine *n* máquina de monedas

slow /sloʊ/ (**-er/-est**) *adj* 1 lento: *make ~ progress* avanzar lentamente 2 torpe: *He's a bit ~.* Le cuesta entender las cosas. 3 (*reloj*) atrasado ▸ **be slow to do sth/ in doing sth** tardar en hacer algo **in slow motion** en cámara lenta ● *adv* despacio ● *vt, vi* ~ (**sth**) (**up/down**) reducir la velocidad (de algo): ~ *down growth* frenar el crecimiento ◇ *Production has slowed.* La producción disminuyó. **slowly** *adv* 1 despacio 2 poco a poco

slowdown /ˈsloʊdaʊn/ *n* (*USA*) huelga pasiva, operación tortuga (*And*)

sludge /slʌdʒ/ *n* 1 fango 2 sedimento

slug /slʌg/ *n* babosa **sluggish** *adj* 1 lento 2 aletargado 3 (*Econ*) flojo

slum /slʌm/ *n* 1 barrio pobre/de tugurios 2 (*fig*) pocilga

slump /slʌmp/ *vi* 1 ~ (**down**) desplomarse 2 (*Com*) sufrir un bajón ● *n* depresión, bajón

slung /slʌŋ/ *pt, pp de* SLING

slunk /slʌŋk/ *pt, pp de* SLINK

slur /slɜːr/ *vt* (**-rr-**) articular mal ● *n* calumnia

slush /slʌʃ/ *n* nieve derretida y sucia

sly /slaɪ/ *adj* 1 astuto 2 (*mirada*) furtivo

smack /smæk/ *n* palmada, nalgada ● *vt* dar una palmada a ■ **smack of sth** oler a algo (*fig*)

small /smɔːl/ *adj* (**-er/-est**) 1 pequeño: *a ~ number of people* unas pocas personas ◇ ~ *change* dinero suelto ◇ *in the ~ hours*

(GB) de madrugada ◊ **make ~ talk** hablar de cosas sin importancia **2** (letra) minúscula ▸ **a small fortune** un dineral it's **a small world** el mundo es un pañuelo **the fine/small** (GB) **print** la letra pequeña (en contrato) NOTA Small suele usarse con el opuesto de **big/large** y puede ser modificado por adverbios: *Our house is smaller than yours.* ◊ *I have a fairly ~ income.* **Little** no se usa con adverbios y suele ir detrás de otro adjetivo: *a horrid little man* ◊ *What a lovely little house!*

smallpox /'smɔːlpɒks/ n viruela

small-scale adj a pequeña escala

smart /smɑːt/ adj (-er/-est) **1** astuto, vivo **2** elegante ● vi arder

smarten vt, vi **~ (sth/yourself) up** arreglar(se) (algo)

smash /smæʃ/ **1** vt **~ sth (up)** romper, destrozar algo **2** vi hacerse trizas **3** vt, vi **~ (sth) against, into, etc. sth** estrellar(se) (algo) contra algo ● n **1** estrépito **2** (GB, Aut) accidente **3** (tb → **hit**) exitazo

smashing /'smæʃɪŋ/ adj (GB, coloq) estupendo

smear /smɪər/ vt **1** untar **2** manchar

smell /smel/ (pt/pp **smelled** o GB **smelt** /smelt/ → DREAM) vt, vi **1** **~ (of sth)** oler (a algo): *What does it ~ like?* ¿A qué huele? → HEAR olfatear ● n **1** olor **2** (tb **sense of ~**) olfato **smelly** adj (-ier/-iest) (coloq) apestoso: *It's ~ in here.* Huele mal aquí.

smile /smaɪl/ n sonrisa: *give sb a ~* sonreírle a algn ▸ **bring a smile to sb's face** hacerle sonreír a algn ● vi sonreír

smirk /smɜːrk/ n sonrisa socarrona/de satisfacción ● vi sonreír con burla

smock /smɒk/ n **1** (pintor) delantal **2** (mujer) blusón

smog /smɒg/ n smog

smoke /smoʊk/ **1** vt, vi fumar **2** vi echar humo **3** vt ahumar ● n **1** humo **2** (coloq): *have a ~* fumar **smoker** n fumador/a **smoking** n fumar: *"No Smoking"* "Prohibido fumar" **smoky** adj (-ier/-iest) **1** lleno de humo **2** humeante **3** (sabor, color, etc.) ahumado

smolder (**smoulder** GB) /'smoʊldər/ vi arder (sin llama)

smooth /smuːð/ adj (-er/-est) **1** liso **2** (piel, vino, etc.) suave **3** (periodo, etc.) sin problemas **4** (salsa, etc.) sin grumos **5** (pey) (persona) zalamero ● vt alisar ■

smooth sth over allanar algo (dificultades) **smoothly** adv: *go ~* ir sobre ruedas

smother /'smʌðər/ vt **1** asfixiar **2** **~ sth/sb with/in sth** cubrir algo/a algn de algo **3** (llamas) sofocar

smudge /smʌdʒ/ n borrón, manchón ● vt, vi emborronar(se)

smug /smʌg/ adj engreído

smuggle /'smʌgl/ vt **1** pasar de contrabando **2** **~ sth/sb in/out** meter/sacar algo/a algn clandestinamente **smuggler** n contrabandista **smuggling** n contrabando

snack /snæk/ n tentempié: **~ bar** cafetería ◊ **have a ~** comer algo ligero ● vi picar

snag /snæg/ n obstáculo

snail /sneɪl/ n caracol

snake /sneɪk/ n serpiente, culebra ● vi serpentear

snap /snæp/ (-pp-) **1** vt, vi chasquear **2** vt, vi romper(se) en dos **3** vi **~ (at sb)** hablar bruscamente (a algn) ● n **1** (ruido seco) chasquido **2** (tb **snapshot** /'snæpʃɒt/) foto ● adj (coloq) repentino (decisión)

snapper /'snæpər/ (tb **red ~**) n (pez) pargo, huachinango (Mx)

snare /sneər/ n trampa ● vt atrapar

snarl /snɑːrl/ n gruñido ● vi gruñir

snatch /snætʃ/ vt **1** arrebatar, arrancar de un tirón **2** robar con un tirón **3** vt raptar **4** vi **~ at sth** tirar de algo, agarrar algo bruscamente **5** vt, vi **~ (at)** sth (oportunidad) aprovechar algo ● n **1** (conversación, etc.) fragmento **2** robo

sneak /sniːk/ **1** vi: **~ in/out** entrar/salir a hurtadillas ◊ **~ into/out of** sth entrar/salir de algo a hurtadillas **2** vt: **~ a look at sth/sb** mirar algo/a algn a hurtadillas ● n (GB, coloq) soplón/ona

sneaker /'sniːkər/ n (USA) tenis (zapato)

sneer /snɪər/ n **1** sonrisa sarcástica **2** comentario desdeñoso ● vi **~ (at sth/sb)** reírse con desprecio (de algo/algn)

sneeze /sniːz/ n estornudo ● vi estornudar

snicker /'snɪkər/ (**snigger** /'snɪgər/ GB) n risita sarcástica ● vi **~ (at sth/sb)** reírse (con sarcasmo) (de algo/algn)

sniff /snɪf/ **1** vi sorber (nariz) **2** vi husmear **3** vt olfatear **4** vt inhalar ● n inhalación

snip /snɪp/ vt (-pp-) cortar con tijeras: **~ sth off** recortar algo

sniper /'snaɪpər/ n francotirador/a

snob /snɑb/ n esnob **snobbery** n esnobismo **snobbish** adj esnob

snoop /snuːp/ (coloq) vi ~ (around) fisgonear ■ n 1 have a ~ about/around reconocer el terreno ◇ have a ~ around sth fisgonear algo 2 fisgón/ona

snore /snɔːr/ vi roncar ● n ronquido

snorkel /ˈsnɔːrkl/ n esnórquel

snort /snɔːrt/ vi bufar ● n bufido

snout /snaʊt/ n hocico

snow /snoʊ/ n nieve ● vi nevar
▸ **snowed in/up** aislado por la nieve **snowed under (with sth)** inundado (de algo) (trabajo)

snowball /ˈsnoʊbɔːl/ n bola de nieve ● vi multiplicarse (rápidamente)

snowboarding /ˈsnoʊbɔːrdɪŋ/ n snowboard: go ~ hacer snowboard

snowdrift /ˈsnoʊdrɪft/ n montón de nieve (acumulada durante una ventisca)

snowdrop /ˈsnoʊdrɑp/ n campanilla blanca (flor)

snowfall /ˈsnoʊfɔːl/ n nevada

snowflake /ˈsnoʊfleɪk/ n copo de nieve

snowman /ˈsnoʊmæn/ n (pl -men) muñeco de nieve

snowplow (-plough GB) /ˈsnoʊplaʊ/ n quitanieves

snowy /ˈsnoʊi/ adj 1 cubierto de nieve 2 (día, etc.) de nieve

snub /snʌb/ vt (-bb-) hacer un desaire a

snug /snʌg/ adj cómodo y agradable

snuggle /ˈsnʌgl/ vi ~ down; ~ up to sb acurrucarse (junto a algn)

so /soʊ/ adv, conj 1 tan: It's so late! ¡Está tardísimo! ◇ I'm so sorry ¡Lo siento! ◇ I'm so sorry ¡Cuánto lo siento! 2 así: It's about so big. Es así de grande. ◇ If so,... Si es así,... 3 I think/hope so. Creo/espero que sí. 4 (para expresar acuerdo): "I'm hungry." "So am I." —Tengo hambre. —Yo también. **NOTA** En este caso el pronombre o sustantivo va detrás del verbo. 5 (sorpresa): "Jo's gone home." "So she has!" —Jo se fue a casa. —¡Es verdad! 6 (énfasis): He's as good as you, maybe more so. Es tan bueno como tú, puede que aún más. ◇ She has complained, and rightly so. Se quejó, y con razón. 7 así que: The store was closed so I didn't get any milk. La tienda estaba cerrada, así que no compré leche. 8 entonces ▸ **and so on (and so forth)** etcétera, etcétera **is that so?** no

me digas **so (what)?** (coloq) ¿y qué? **so as to do sth** para hacer algo **so much/many** tanto(s) **so that** para que

soak /soʊk/ 1 vt remojar, empapar: get soaked (through) empaparse 2 vi estar en remojo ■ **soak into sth** ser absorbido por algo **soak through** penetrar (líquido) **soak sth up 1** absorber algo **2** (fig) empaparse de algo **soaked** adj empapado

soap /soʊp/ n [U] jabón **soapy** adj jabonoso

soap opera n telenovela

soar /sɔːr/ vi 1 (avión) remontarse 2 (precios) dispararse 3 (ave) planear

sob /sɑb/ vi (-bb-) sollozar ● n sollozo **sobbing** n [U] sollozos

sober /ˈsoʊbər/ adj 1 sobrio 2 serio

so-called adj (mal) llamado

soccer /ˈsɑkər/ n fútbol, futbol (Mx)

sociable /ˈsoʊʃəbl/ adj sociable

social /ˈsoʊʃl/ adj social **socialize** vi relacionarse: I don't ~ much. No salgo mucho.

socialism /ˈsoʊʃəlɪzəm/ n socialismo **socialist** n socialista

social security n (GB) seguridad social

social work n trabajo social **social worker** n asistente/a social, trabajador/a social

society /səˈsaɪəti/ n (pl -ies) 1 sociedad 2 (fml) compañía: polite ~ la gente bien 3 asociación

sociological /ˌsoʊsiəˈlɑdʒɪkl/ adj sociológico

sociology /ˌsoʊsiˈɑlədʒi/ n sociología **sociologist** n sociólogo/a

sock /sɑk/ n calcetín, media (corta) ▸ **pull your socks up** (GB, coloq) esforzarse por mejorar

socket /ˈsɑkɪt/ n 1 (ojo) órbita 2 enchufe (en la pared)

soda /ˈsoʊdə/ n 1 soda 2 (USA, coloq) refresco

sodden /ˈsɑdn/ adj empapado

sodium /ˈsoʊdiəm/ n sodio

sofa /ˈsoʊfə/ n sofá

soft /sɔːft; sʌft GB/ adj (-er/-est) 1 blando: ~ option opción fácil 2 suave 3 (voz) bajo ▸ **have a soft spot for sth/sb** (coloq) tener debilidad por algo/algn **soften** /ˈsɔːfn; ˈsʌfn GB/ vt, vi 1 ablandar(se) 2 suavizar(se) **softly** adv suavemente

soft drink n bebida no alcohólica

soft-spoken adj de voz suave

software /'sɔːftweər; 'sɒft- GB/ n [U] software

soggy /'sɒgi/ adj (-ier/-iest) 1 empapado (pan, etc.) correoso

soil /sɔɪl/ n tierra ● vt (fml) 1 ensuciar 2 (reputación) manchar

solace /'sɒləs/ n (fml) consuelo

solar /'səʊlər/ adj solar

sold /səʊld/ pt, pp de SELL

soldier /'səʊldʒər/ n soldado

sole /səʊl/ adj 1 único 2 exclusivo ● n 1 (pie) planta 2 suela 3 (pl sole) (pez) lenguado

solemn /'sɒləm/ adj 1 serio 2 solemne **solemnity** /sə'lemnəti/ n solemnidad

solicitor /sə'lɪsɪtər/ n (GB) 1 abogado/a 2 notario/a →ABOGADO

solid /'sɒlɪd/ adj 1 sólido 2 compacto 3 seguido: *sleep for ten hours* – dormir diez horas seguidas ● n 1 **solids** alimentos sólidos 2 (Geom) figura de tres dimensiones **solidly** adv 1 sólidamente 2 sin interrupción

solidarity /ˌsɒlɪ'dærəti/ n solidaridad

solidity /sə'lɪdəti/ n solidez **solidify** vi (pt/pp -ied) solidificarse

solitary /'sɒləteri; -tri GB/ adj 1 solitario 2 (lugar) apartado 3 solo

solitude /'sɒlətuːd; -tjuːd GB/ n soledad

solo /'səʊləʊ/ n (pl -s) solo ● adj, adv a solas **soloist** n solista

soluble /'sɒljəbl/ adj soluble

solution /sə'luːʃn/ n solución

solve /sɒlv/ vt resolver

solvent /'sɒlvənt/ n disolvente

somber (**sombre** GB) /'sɒmbər/ adj 1 sombrío 2 (color) oscuro 3 (persona) melancólico

some /sʌm/ adj, pron 1 algo: *There's* – *food here.* Hay comida aquí. ◇ *Would you like* –? ¿Quieres un poco? 2 unos (cuantos), algunos: *Do you want* – *chips?* ¿Quieres papas fritas? NOTA Some y any se usan con sustantivos incontables y en plural, y aunque muchas veces no se traducen en español, en inglés no pueden omitirse. Some se suele usar en afirmaciones y any en interrogaciones y negaciones: *I have* – *money.* ◇ *Do you have any children?* ◇ *I don't want any candy now.* Sin embargo, some se puede usar en interrogaciones cuando se espera una respuesta afirmativa, p. ej., para ofrecer o pedir algo: *Would you like* – *tea?* ◇ *Can I have*

– *bread, please?* Cuando any se usa en afirmaciones significa "cualquiera": *Any parent would have worried.*

somebody /'sʌmbədi/ (tb **someone** /'sʌmwʌn/) pron alguien: – *else* otra persona NOTA La diferencia entre **somebody** o **anybody**, o **someone** y **anyone**, es la misma que entre **some** y **any**. →SOME

somehow /'sʌmhaʊ/ adv 1 de algún modo 2 por alguna razón: *I* – *get the feeling I've been here before.* No sé por qué, me da la impresión de que ya he estado aquí.

someplace /'sʌmpleɪs/ (USA) Ver SOMEWHERE

somersault /'sʌmərsɔːlt/ n 1 voltereta 2 (acróbata) salto mortal 3 (Aut) vuelta de campana

something /'sʌmθɪŋ/ pron algo: – *else* otra cosa NOTA La diferencia entre **something** y **anything** es la misma que entre **some** y **any**. →SOME

sometime /'sʌmtaɪm/ adv 1 algún/un día: – *or other* un día de estos 2 en algún momento

sometimes /'sʌmtaɪmz/ adv a veces, de vez en cuando →ALWAYS

someway /'sʌmweɪ/ (tb **someways**) (USA, coloq) Ver SOMEHOW (1)

somewhat /'sʌmwɒt/ adv 1 algo, un tanto 2 bastante

somewhere /'sʌmweər/ adv a/en/por algún sitio: – *else* en algún otro lugar ● pron: *have* – *to go* tener adonde ir NOTA La diferencia entre **somewhere** y **anywhere** es la misma que entre **some** y **any**. →SOME

son /sʌn/ n hijo **son-in-law** (pl **sons-in-law**) yerno

song /sɔːŋ; sɒŋ GB/ n 1 canción 2 canto

songwriter /'sɔːŋraɪtər; sɒŋ- GB/ n compositor (de canciones)

soon /suːn/ adv (-er ►-est) pronto, dentro de poco ► **as soon as** apenas, en cuanto: *as* – *as possible* en cuanto sea posible (just) as soon do sth (as do sth): *I'd as* – *stay at home as go out.* Lo mismo me da quedarme en casa que salir. **sooner or later** tarde o temprano **the sooner the better** cuanto antes mejor

soot /sʊt/ n hollín

soothe /suːð/ vt 1 calmar 2 (dolor, etc.) aliviar

sophisticated /sə'fɪstɪkeɪtɪd/ *adj* sofisticado **sophistication** *n* sofisticación

sophomore /'sɒfəmɔː(r)/ /'sɑːfəmɔːr/ *n* (*USA*) estudiante de segundo año (*universidad*)

soppy /'sɒpi/ (*GB*) = SAPPY

sordid /'sɔːrdɪd/ *adj* 1 sórdido 2 (*comportamiento*) vil

sore /sɔːr/ *n* llaga ● *adj* dolorido: *a ~ throat* dolor de garganta ◇ *I have ~ eyes.* Me duelen los ojos. ▶ **a sore point** un asunto delicado **sorely** *adv: She will be ~ missed.* Se la echará de menos enormemente. ◇ *I was ~ tempted to do it.* Estuve muy tentado de hacerlo.

sorrow /'sɒrəʊ/ *n* pesar

sorry /'sɒri/ *interj* 1 perdón → EXCUSE **sorry?** ¿qué dijo? ● *adj* 1 *I'm ~ I'm late.* Siento llegar tarde. ◇ *I'm so ~!* ¡Lo siento mucho! ◇ *say you're ~* disculparse 2 arrepentido: *You'll be ~!* ¡Te vas a arrepentir! ◇ *Stop feeling ~ for yourself!* ● *adj* (-ier/-iest) (*estado*) lastimoso ▶ **feel sorry for sb/yourself** sentir lástima de algn/de uno mismo: *I felt ~ for her.* Me dio lástima (de ella).

sort /sɔːrt/ *n* 1 tipo, clase 2 (*coloq*) persona ▶ **a sort of:** *It's a ~ of novel.* Es una especie de novela. **sort of** (*coloq*): *I feel ~ of uneasy.* Me siento como inquieto. ● *vt* clasificar ■ **sort sth out** arreglar, solucionar algo **sort through sth** ordenar algo

so-so /adj, adv (coloq) regular

sought /sɔːt/ *pt, pp de* SEEK

sought after *adj* codiciado

soul /səʊl/ *n* alma: *Poor ~!* ¡El pobre!

sound /saʊnd/ *n* 1 sonido: *~ waves* ondas sonoras 2 ruido 3 **the sound of** el volumen ● *vi* 1 sonar 2 *vt* (*trompeta, etc.*) tocar 3 *vt* (*alarma*) hacer sonar 4 *vt* pronunciar 5 *vi* parecer 6 *vt* (*mar*) sondear ■ **sound sb out** tantear a algn ● *adj* (-er/-est) 1 sano 2 (*estructura*) sólido 3 (*creencia*) firme 4 (*consejo, etc.*) bueno ● *adv* ▶ **sound asleep** profundamente dormido

soundproof /'saʊndpruːf/ *adj* con aislamiento acústico ● *vt* insonorizar

soundtrack /'saʊndtræk/ *n* banda sonora

soup /suːp/ *n* sopa, caldo

sour /saʊər/ *adj* 1 agrio: *go/turn ~* agriarse/dañarse 2 (*leche*) cortado

source /sɔːrs/ *n* 1 (*información*) fuente 2 (*río*) nacimiento

south /saʊθ/ *n* (*abrev* **S**) sur ● *adj* (del) sur ● *adv* al sur

southbound /'saʊθbaʊnd/ *adj* en/con dirección sur

south-east *n* (*abrev* **SE**) sureste ● (*tb* **south-eastern**) *adj* (del) sureste ● *adv* al sureste

southern /'sʌðərn/ (*tb* **southern**) *adj* (del) sur **southerner** *n* sureño/a

southwards /'saʊθwərdz/ (*tb* **southward**) *adv* hacia el sur

south-west *n* (*abrev* **SW**) suroeste ● *adj* (*tb* **south-western**) (del) suroeste ● *adv* al suroeste

souvenir /ˌsuːvə'nɪər/ *n* recuerdo (*objeto*)

sovereign /'sɒvrən/ *adj, n* soberano/a **sovereignty** *n* soberanía

sow[1] /saʊ/ *n* marrana → CERDO

sow[2] /səʊ/ *vt* (*pt* **sowed** *pp* **sowed/sown** /səʊn/) sembrar

soy /sɔɪ/ (**soya** /'sɔɪə/ *GB*) *n* soya

spa /spɑː/ *n* balneario, spa

space /speɪs/ *n* espacio, sitio: *Leave some ~ for the dogs.* Deja espacio para los perros. ◇ *a ~ flight* un vuelo espacial ◇ *stare into ~* mirar al vacío ● *vt* ■ **space sth out** espaciar algo

spacecraft /'speɪskræft, -krɑːft *GB*/ *n* (*pl* **spacecraft**) (*tb* **spaceship** /'speɪsʃɪp/) nave espacial

spacious /'speɪʃəs/ *adj* amplio

spade /speɪd/ *n* 1 pala 2 **spades** (*cartas*) picas → BARAJA

spaghetti /spə'geti/ *n* [*U*] espagueti(s)

span /spæn/ *n* 1 (*puente*) luz 2 (*tiempo*) lapso, duración ● *vt* (-nn-) 1 (*puente*) cruzar 2 abarcar

spank /spæŋk/ *vt* dar una palmada a (*en las nalgas*)

spanner /'spænər/ *n* (*GB*) llave inglesa (*herramienta*)

spare /speər/ *adj* 1 sobrante, de sobra: *There are no ~ seats.* No quedan asientos. ◇ *the ~ room* el cuarto de visitas 2 de repuesto, de reserva 3 (*tiempo*) libre, de ocio ● *n* (*pieza de*) repuesto ● *vt* 1 (*tiempo, dinero, etc.*) tener 2 (*vida*) perdonar 3 escatimar: *No expense was spared.* No repararon en gastos. 4 ahorrar ▶ **to**

spare de sobra: *with a minute to ~* faltando un minuto **sparing** *adj* ~ *with sth* mesurado con algo

spark /spɑːk/ *n* chispa ● *vt* ~ **(off)** provocar algo

sparkle /spɑːkl/ *vi* centellear, destellar ● *n* centelleo **sparkling** *adj* 1 (*tb* **sparkly**) centelleante 2 (*vino, etc.*) espumoso

sparrow /spærəʊ/ *n* gorrión

sparse /spɑːs/ *adj* 1 escaso 2 disperso 3 (*pelo*) ralo

spartan /spɑːtn/ *adj* espartano

spasm /spæzəm/ *n* espasmo

spat /spæt/ *pt, pp* de SPIT

spate /speɪt/ *n* racha, ola

spatial /speɪʃl/ *adj* (*fml*) del espacio (*como dimensión*)

spatter /spætər/ *vt* ~ **sb** (**with sth**); ~ **sth** (**on sb**) rociar algo (sobre algn), salpicar a algn (de algo)

speak /spiːk/ (*pt* **spoke** *pp* **spoken**) 1 *vt, vi* ~ **(to sb)** hablar (con algn): ~ *the truth* decir la verdad ◇ *Her success ~s for itself.* Su éxito habla por sí solo. →HABLAR 2 *vi* dar una conferencia ▸ *generally, etc.* **speaking** en términos generales, etc. so to **speak** por así decirlo **speak your mind** hablar sin rodeos ■ **speak for sb** hablar en favor de algn **speak up** hablar más alto

speaker /spiːkər/ *n* 1 hablante: *Spanish* ~ hispanohablante 2 orador/a, conferencista 3 altavoz

spear /spɪər/ *n* 1 lanza 2 arpón

special /speʃl/ *adj* 1 especial 2 particular 3 (*reunión, etc.*) extraordinario ● *n* 1 especial 2 (*USA, colog*) oferta especial **specialist** *n* especialista **specially** *adv* 1 especialmente, expresamente **NOTA** Specially se usa fundamentalmente con participios y **especially** con conector entre frases: ~ *designed for schools* ◇ *He likes dogs, especially poodles.* 2 particularmente, sobre todo

specialize /speʃəlaɪz/ *vi* especializarse **specialization** *n* especialización **specialized** *adj* especializado

specialty /speʃəlti/ (**speciality** /ˌspeʃiˈæləti/ *GB*) *n* (*pl* -ies) especialidad

species /spiːʃiːz/ *n* (*pl* **species**) especie

specific /spəˈsɪfɪk/ *adj* específico, preciso **specifically** *adv* específicamente, especialmente

specify /spesɪfaɪ/ *vt* (*pt/pp* -**ied**) especificar, precisar **specification** *n* especificación

specimen /spesɪmən/ *n* espécimen, ejemplar, muestra

speck /spek/ *n* 1 (*suciedad*) manchita 2 (*polvo*) mota 3 *a ~ on the horizon* un punto en el horizonte

spectacle /spektəkl/ *n* espectáculo

spectacles /spektəklz/ *n* (*abrev* **specs**) [*pl*] (*fml*) gafas, lentes **NOTA** Es más común **glasses**. →PAIR

spectacular /spekˈtækjələr/ *adj* espectacular

spectator /spekˈteɪtər; spekˈteɪtə(r) *GB*/ *n* espectador/a

specter (**spectre** *GB*) /spektər/ *n* espectro, fantasma

spectrum /spektrəm/ *n* (*pl* -**tra** /-trə/) 1 espectro 2 (*fml*) gama

speculate /spekjuleɪt/ *vi* especular **speculation** *n* especulación **speculative** /spekjələtɪv/ *adj* especulativo **speculator** *n* especulador/a

sped /sped/ *pt, pp* de SPEED

speech /spiːtʃ/ *n* 1 habla: *freedom of* ~ libertad de expresión 2 discurso 3 lenguaje: ~ *therapy* terapia del lenguaje 4 (*Teat*) parlamento **speechless** *adj* sin habla, mudo

speed /spiːd/ *n* velocidad: *at (full)* ~ a toda velocidad ● *vt* (*pt/pp* **speeded**) acelerar ■ **speed** (**sth**) **up** apurarse, acelerar algo ● *vi* (*pt/pp* **sped**) ir a toda velocidad: *I was fined for speeding.* Me pusieron una multa por exceso de velocidad.

speedboat /spiːdbəʊt/ *n* lancha rápida

speedometer /spiːˈdɑːmɪtər/ *n* velocímetro

speedy /spiːdi/ *adj* (-**ier**/-**iest**) pronto, rápido

spell /spel/ *n* 1 hechizo 2 temporada, racha 3 turno ● (*pt/pp* **spelled**/**spelt** /spelt/) → DREAM 1 *vt, vi* deletrear, escribir 2 *vt* significar algo ■ **spell sth out** explicar algo claramente **spelling** *n* ortografía

spellchecker /speltʃekər/ *n* corrector ortográfico

sperm /spɜːrm/ *n* (*pl* **sperm**) esperma

sphere /sfɪər/ *n* esfera

sphinx /sfɪŋks/ *n* esfinge

spice /spaɪs/ n 1 especia(s) 2 interés: *add ~ to a situation* dar sabor a una situación ● vt sazonar ■ **spice sth up** (*fig*) dar más sabor a algo **spicy** adj (**-ier/-iest**) condimentado, picante

spider /'spaɪdər/ n araña

spied /spaɪd/ *pt, pp de* SPY

spike /spaɪk/ n 1 púa, clavo 2 punta **spiky** adj erizado de púas, puntiagudo

spill /spɪl/ vt, vi (*pt/pp* **spilled** *o* **spilt** /spɪlt/ *GB*) derramar(se) → DROP ■ **spill over** rebosar ● n (*tb* **spillage** /'spɪlɪdʒ/ *fml*) 1 derramamiento 2 derrame

spin /spɪn/ (**-nn-**) (*pt/pp* **spun**) 1 vt, vi ~ (**sth**) (**around**) (hacer) girar (algo), dar vueltas (a algo) 2 vt, vi centrifugar 3 vt hilar ■ **spin sth out** alargar algo ● n 1 vuelta, giro 2 (*coloq*) (*Aut*): *go for a ~* dar una vuelta

spinach /'spɪnɪtʃ/ n [U] espinaca(s)

spine /spaɪn/ n 1 columna vertebral 2 (*Bot*) espina 3 (*Zool*) púa 4 (*libro*) lomo **spinal** adj espinal: *~ column* columna vertebral

spinster /'spɪnstər/ n solterona

spiral /'spaɪrəl/ n espiral ● adj (en) espiral: *a ~ staircase* una escalera de caracol

spire /'spaɪər/ n aguja (*iglesia*)

spirit /'spɪrɪt/ n 1 espíritu, alma 2 fantasma 3 brío, ánimo 4 temple 5 **spirits** [*pl*] licor 6 **spirits** [*pl*] estado de ánimo: *in high ~s* de muy buen humor **spirited** adj brioso

spiritual /'spɪrɪtʃuəl/ adj espiritual

spit /spɪt/ (**-tt-**) (*pt/pp* **spat** *tb* **spit** *USA*) 1 vt, vi ~ (**sth**) (**out**) escupir (algo) 2 vt (*insulto, etc.*) soltar 3 vi (*fuego, etc.*) chisporrotear ● n 1 saliva 2 punta (*de tierra*) 3 asador (*giratorio*)

spite /spaɪt/ n despecho ▶ **in spite of** a pesar de ● vt fastidiar **spiteful** adj rencoroso

splash /splæʃ/ n 1 chapoteo 2 salpicadura 3 (*color*) mancha ▶ **make a splash** (*coloq*) causar sensación ● n 1 vi chapotear 2 vt salpicar ■ **splash out (on sth)** (*GB, coloq*) derrochar dinero (en algo), darse el lujo (de comprar algo)

splatter /'splætər/ vt salpicar

splendid /splɛndɪd/ adj espléndido **splendor** (**-our** *GB*) n esplendor

splint /splɪnt/ n (*Med*) tablilla

splinter /'splɪntər/ n astilla ● vt, vi 1 astillar(se) 2 dividir(se)

split /splɪt/ (**-tt-**) (*pt/pp* **split**) 1 vt, vi partir(se) 2 vt, vi dividir(se) 3 vt repartir ● vi rajarse ■ **split up (with sb)** separarse (de algn) ● n 1 división, ruptura 2 abertura 3 **the splits** [*pl*] split (*gimnasia*) ● adj partido, dividido

splutter /'splʌtər/ 1 vt, vi farfullar, balbucear 2 vi (*fuego, etc.*) chisporrotear ● n chisporroteo

spoil /spɔɪl/ (*pt/pp* **spoiled** *o* **spoilt** /spɔɪlt/ *GB*) → DREAM 1 vt, vi dañar(se), arruinar(se) 2 vt (*niño*) consentir

spoils /spɔɪlz/ n [*pl*] botín (*de robo, guerra, etc.*)

spoilsport /'spɔɪlspɔːrt/ n (*coloq*) aguafiestas

spoke /spoʊk/ pt de SPEAK ● n radio, rayo (*de una rueda*)

spoken /'spoʊkən/ pp de SPEAK

spokesman, spokeswoman /'spoʊksmən-wʊmən/ n (*pl* **-men/-women**) portavoz → CHAIRMAN

sponge /spʌndʒ/ n 1 esponja 2 (*tb ~ cake*) pastel, ponqué (*And*) ■ **sponge off/on sb** (*coloq*) vivir a costillas de algn

sponsor /'spɑnsər/ n patrocinador/a ● vt patrocinar **sponsorship** n patrocinio

spontaneous /spɑn'teɪniəs/ adj espontáneo **spontaneity** /,spɑntə'neɪəti/ n espontaneidad

spooky /'spuːki/ adj (**-ier/-iest**) (*coloq*) 1 de aspecto embrujado, que da miedo 2 misterioso

spoon /spuːn/ n 1 cuchara 2 (*tb* **spoonful**) cucharada ● vt sacar (*con cuchara*)

sporadic /spə'rædɪk/ adj esporádico

sport /spɔːrt/ n 1 deporte: *~s center/facilities* centro deportivo/instalaciones deportivas 2 (*coloq*) buen(a) chico/a: *a good/bad ~* un buen/mal perdedor **sporting** adj deportivo **sporty** adj (**-ier/-iest**) (*coloq*) deportista (*Aut, ropa*) deportivo

sports car n carro deportivo

sportsman, sportswoman /'spɔːrtsmən-wʊmən/ n (*pl* **-men/-women**) deportista → CHAIRMAN **sportsmanlike** adj deportivo (*justo*) **sportsmanship** n deportividad

spot /spɑt/ vt (**-tt-**) 1 divisar 2 encontrar, notar ● n 1 punto: *a skirt with red ~s on it* una falda con puntitos rojos 2 (*en animales, etc.*) mancha 3 (*Med*) grano 4 lugar 5 **a ~ of sth** (*GB, coloq*): *How about a ~ to eat?* ¿Quieres comer un poco? ◇ *You seem to be having a ~ of bother.* Parece que tienes problemas. **spotless** *adj* 1 inmaculado 2 (*reputación*) intachable **spotted** *adj* 1 (*animal*) con manchas 2 (*ropa*) con puntos **spotty** *adj* (*GB*) con muchos granos

spotlight /'spɒtlaɪt/ *n* 1 (*tb* **spot**) reflector 2 **be in the ~** ser el centro de la atención

spouse /spaʊs/ *n* (*fml*) cónyuge

spout /spaʊt/ *n* 1 (*tetera*) pico 2 (*de agua*) caño, bajante ● *vi* 1 **~ (out/up)**, **~ (out of/from sth)** salir a chorros (de algo) 2 *vt* **~ sth (out/up)** echar algo a chorros 3 (*coloq, pey*) recitar 4 (*coloq, pey*) perorar

sprain /spreɪn/ *vt* (*tobillo*) torcer ● *n* torcedura, esguince

sprang /spræŋ/ *pt de* SPRING

sprawl /sprɔːl/ *vi* 1 tumbarse, desparramarse 2 (*ciudad, etc.*) extenderse (*con desorden*)

spray /spreɪ/ *n* 1 rociada 2 (*mar*) espuma 3 atomizador, spray ● 1 *vt* **~ sth on/over sth/sb**; **~ sth/sb with** rociar algo/a algn de algo 2 *vi* **~ (over, across, etc. sth/sb)** salpicar (algo/a algn)

spread /spred/ (*pt/pp* **spread**) 1 *vt* **~ sth (out)** extender, desplegar algo 2 *vt* **~ sth with** cubrir algo de/con algo 3 *vt, vi* untar(se) 4 *vt, vi* propagar(se) 5 *vt, vi* (*noticia*) divulgar(se) 6 *vt* distribuir ● *n* 1 extensión 2 (*alas*) envergadura 3 difusión 4 paté, queso, etc. para untar

spreadsheet /'spredʃiːt/ *n* hoja de cálculo

spree /spriː/ *n*: **go on a spending ~** salir a gastar dinero

spring /sprɪŋ/ *n* 1 (*tb* **springtime** /'sprɪŋtaɪm/) primavera: *~ clean* limpieza general 2 salto 3 manantial 4 resorte 5 elasticidad ● (*pt* **sprang** *pp* **sprung**) 1 *vi* saltar: **~ into action** ponerse en acción 2 *vi* (*líquido*) brotar 3 *vt* **~ sth on sb** sorprender a algn con algo ■ **spring back** rebotar **spring from sth** (*fml*) provenir de algo

springboard /'sprɪŋbɔːrd/ *n* trampolín

sprinkle /'sprɪŋkl/ *vt* rociar, salpicar **sprinkling** *n* un poquito, unos cuantos

sprint /sprɪnt/ *vi* 1 correr a toda velocidad 2 (*Dep*) hacer un sprint ● *n* 1 carrera de velocidad 2 sprint

sprout /spraʊt/ 1 *vi* **~ (out/up)** brotar, aparecer 2 *vt* (*Bot*) echar (*flores, brotes, etc.*) ● *n* 1 brote:

bean ~s brotes de soya 2 (*tb* **Brussels ~**) col de Bruselas

sprung /sprʌŋ/ *pp de* SPRING

spun /spʌn/ *pt, pp de* SPIN

spur /spɜːr/ *n* 1 espuela 2 **a ~ (to sth)** un aliciente (para algo) ▶ **on the spur of the moment** impulsivamente ● *vt* (**-rr-**) **~ sth/sb (on)** incitar algo/a algn

spurn /spɜːrn/ *vt* (*fml*) rechazar

spurt /spɜːrt/ *vi* **~ (out)** salir a chorros ● *n* 1 chorro 2 arranque

sputter /'spʌtər/ *Ver* SPLUTTER (2)

spy /spaɪ/ *n* (*pl* **spies**) espía: *~ thriller* novela de espionaje ● *vi* (*pt/pp* **spied**) **~ (on sth/sb)** espiar (algo/a algn)

squabble /'skwɒbl/ *vi* **~ (about/ over sth)** reñir, pelearse (por algo) ● *n* riña, disputa

squad /skwɒd/ *n* 1 (*tb* **squadron** /'skwɒdrən/) (*Mil*) escuadrón 2 (*policía*) brigada 3 (*Dep*) plantel

squalid /'skwɒlɪd/ *adj* sórdido **squalor** *n* miseria

squander /'skwɒndər/ *vt* desp+ilfarrar

square /skweər/ *adj* cuadrado ▶ **a square meal** una buena comida **be (all) square (with sb)** quedar en paz (con algn) ● *n* 1 (*Mat*) cuadrado 2 cuadro 3 (*en tablero*) casilla 4 (*abrev* **Sq**) plaza ■ **square up (with sb)** pagar una deuda (a algn) **squarely** *adv* directamente

square root *n* raíz cuadrada

squash /skwɒʃ/ *vt, vi* aplastar(se) ● *n* 1 (*Dep*) squash 2 (*GB*) concentrado de frutas para refresco 3 (*coloq*): *What a ~!* ¡Qué apretujón!

squat /skwɒt/ *vi* (**-tt-**) **~ (down)** 1 ponerse en cuclillas 2 agazaparse ● *adj* (**squatter**, **-est**) rechoncho **squatter** *n* ocupante ilegal, paracaidista (*Mx*)

squawk /skwɔːk/ *vi* graznar, chillar ● *n* graznido, chillido

squeak /skwiːk/ *n* 1 chillido 2 (*gozne, etc.*) chirrido ● *vi* 1 chillar 2 (*gozne*) chirriar **squeaky** *adj* (**-ier/-iest**) 1 (*voz*) chillón 2 que chirría

squeal /skwiːl/ *n* alarido, chillido ● *vt, vi* chillar

squeamish /'skwiːmɪʃ/ *adj* delicado, remilgado

squeeze /skwiːz/ 1 *vt* apretar 2 *vt* exprimir 3 *vt, vi* **~ (sth/sb) into, past, through, etc. (sth)**: *Can you ~ past/by?* ¿Puedes pasar? ◇ *Can you ~ anything else into that case?* ¿Puedes meter algo más en esa maleta? ● *n* 1 apretón: *a*

~ *of lemon* un chorrito de limón 2 apretura 3 (*Fin*) recortes

squid /skwɪd/ *n* (*pl* squid) calamar

squint /skwɪnt/ *vi* 1 ~ (at/through sth) mirar (algo/a través de algo) con ojos entrecerrados 2 bizquear ● *n* estrabismo

squirm /skwɜːrm/ *vi* 1 retorcerse 2 sentir mucha verguenza

squirrel /skwɜːrəl; 'skwɪrəl *GB*/ *n* ardilla

squirt /skwɜːrt/ 1 *vt* echar un chorro de: ~ *sb with sth* cubrir a algn con un chorro de algo 2 *vi* salir a chorros ● *n* chorro

stab /stæb/ *vt* (-bb-) 1 apuñalar 2 punzar ● *n* puñalada ▶ **have a stab at sth** (*coloq*) intentar algo **stabbing** *adj* punzante **stabbing** *n* apuñalamiento

stability /stə'bɪləti/ *n* estabilidad

stable /'steɪbl/ *n* 1 establo 2 cuadra, caballeriza ● *adj* 1 estable 2 equilibrado **stabilize** *vt, vi* estabilizar(se)

stack /stæk/ *n* 1 pila (*libros, leña, etc.*) 2 a ~ **of sth** (*coloq*) un montón de algo ● *vt* ~ **sth (up)** amontonar algo

stadium /'steɪdiəm/ *n* estadio

staff /stæf; stɑːf *GB*/ *n* personal: *teaching* ~ cuerpo docente →JURADO ● *vt* dotar de personal

stag /stæg/ *n* ciervo →CIERVO

stage /steɪdʒ/ *n* 1 escenario 2 the **stage** el teatro (*profesión*): *go on the* ~ hacerse actor/actriz 3 etapa: *in* ~s por etapas ◇ *at this* ~ a estas alturas ◇ *~ by* ~ paso a paso ● *vt* 1 poner en escena 2 montar 3 organizar

stagger /'stægər/ 1 *vi* tambalearse: ~ *back home/to your feet* volver a casa/pararse tambaleando 2 *vt* dejar atónito 3 *vt* (*viaje, etc.*) escalonar ● *n* tambaleo **staggering** *adj* asombroso

stagnant /'stægnənt/ *adj* estancado

stagnate /'stægneɪt; stæg'neɪt *GB*/ *vi* estancarse **stagnation** *n* estancamiento

stag night (*tb* **stag party**) *n* (*GB*) despedida de soltero

stain /stem/ *n* 1 mancha 2 tintura (*para madera*) ● 1 *vt, vi* manchar(se) 2 *vt* teñir

stained glass *n*: *stained glass window* vitral

stainless steel /ˌstemləs 'stiːl/ *n* acero inoxidable

stair /steər/ *n* 1 **stairs** [*pl*] escalera →ESCALERA 2 peldaño

staircase /'steərkeɪs/ (*tb* **stairway** /'steərweɪ/) *n* escalera (*parte de edificio*) →ESCALERA

stake /steɪk/ *n* 1 estaca 2 **the stake** la hoguera 3 apuesta 4 (*Com*) participación ▶ **at stake** en juego ● *vt* 1 ~ **sth (on sth)** apostar algo (a algo) 2 apuntalar ▶ **stake (out) a/your claim (to sth/ sb)** reclamar un derecho (sobre algo/algn)

stale /steɪl/ *adj* 1 (*pan*) duro 2 (*comida*) pasado 3 (*aire*) viciado 4 (*persona*) anquilosado

stalemate /'steɪlmeɪt/ *n* 1 punto muerto (*ajedrez*) 2 tablas

stalk /stɔːk/ *n* 1 tallo 2 (*fruta*) palito ● *vt* 1 acechar 2 *vi* ~ **off** irse de manera indignada

stall /stɔːl/ *n* 1 (*mercado*) puesto 2 (*establo*) casilla 3 **stalls** [*pl*] (*GB, Teat*) platea ● 1 *vt, vi* (*motor*) parar(se) 2 *vi* buscar evasivas

stallion /'stæliən/ *n* semental (*caballo*)

stalwart /'stɔːlwərt/ *adj, n* incondicional

stamina /'stæminə/ *n* resistencia

stammer /'stæmər/ 1 *vi* tartamudear 2 *vt* ~ **sth (out)** decir algo tartamudeando ● *n* tartamudeo

stamp /stæmp/ *n* 1 estampilla, timbre, sello 2 (*Mx*) (*instrumento*) timbre, sello 3 (*con el pie*) patada ● 1 *vt, vi* patear, dar zapatazos 2 *vi* (*baile*) zapatear 3 *vt* (*carta*) franquear 4 *vt* imprimir, sellar ■ **stamp sth out** erradicar algo

stamp collecting *n* filatelia

stampede /stæm'piːd/ *n* estampida ● *vi* desbandarse

stance /stæns; stɑːns *GB*/ *n* 1 postura 2 ~ (**on sth**) actitud (hacia algo)

stand /stænd/ *n* 1 ~ (**on sth**) actitud (hacia algo) 2 pie, soporte: *music* ~ atril 3 puesto, quiosco 4 (*Dep*) grada 5 (*Jur*) estrado ▶ **make a stand (against sth/sb)** oponer resistencia (a algo/algn) **take a stand** adoptar una postura ● (*pt/pp* **stood**) 1 *vi* estar de pie/parado: *Stand still.* Estate quieto. 2 *vi* ~ (**up**) pararse 3 *vt* colocar 4 *vt* medir 5 *vi* encontrarse: *A house once stood here.* Antes había una casa acá. 6 *vi* (*oferta, etc.*) seguir en pie 7 *vi* estar: *as things* ~ tal como están las cosas 8 *vt* aguantar: *I can't ~ him.* No (me) lo aguanto. 9 *vi* ~ (**for sth**) (*Pol*) postularse (a algo) ▶ **it/that stands to reason** es lógico **stand a chance** tener posibilidades ■ **stand by sb** apoyar a algn **stand**

for sth 1 significar, representar algo **2** apoyar algo **3** tolerar algo **stand in** (for sb) sustituir a algn **stand out** destacarse **stand sb up** (coloq) dejar plantado a algn **stand up for sth/sb** defender algo/a algn **stand up to sb** hacer frente a algn

standard /'stændərd/ n nivel: *be up to ~* ser del nivel requerido ● adj **1** estándar **2** oficial **standardize** vt estandarizar

standard of living n nivel de vida

standby /'stændbaɪ/ n (pl -bys) **1** (cosa) recurso **2** (persona) reserva **3** lista de espera ▶ **be on standby 1** preparado para salir, ayudar, etc. **2** en lista de espera

stand-in n (pl -ins) sustituto/a, suplente

standing /'stændɪŋ/ n **1** prestigio **2** (de long) ~ duradero ● adj permanente

standing order n orden de debito bancario

standpoint /'stændpɔɪnt/ n punto de vista

standstill /'stændstɪl/ n: *be at/come to a ~* estar paralizado/paralizarse

stank /stæŋk/ pt de STINK

staple /'steɪpl/ adj principal ● n grapa ● vt (en)grapar **stapler** n grapadora

star /stɑːr/ n **1** estrella **2** (coloq) tesoro: *Thanks for helping me — you're a ~!* Gracias por ayudarme, ¡eres un amor! **3 stars** [pl] horóscopo ● vi (-rr-) ~ (**in** sth) protagonizar algo **stardom** n estrellato

starboard /'stɑːbərd/ n estribor

starch /stɑːtʃ/ n **1** almidón **2** fécula **starched** adj almidonado

stare /steər/ vi ~ (**at** sth/sb) mirar fijamente (algo/a algn) →MIRAR

stark /stɑːk/ adj (-er/-est) **1** desolador **2** crudo **3** (contraste) manifiesto

starry /'stɑːri/ adj estrellado

star sign n signo del zodíaco

start /stɑːt/ n **1** principio **2 the start** (Dep) la salida ▶ **a false start 1** (Dep) salida en falso **2** un intento fallido **for a start** (coloq) para empezar **get off to a good, bad, etc. start** tener un buen, mal, etc. comienzo ● **1** vt, vi empezar →BEGIN **2** vt, vi (motor) arrancar **3** vt (rumor) iniciar ▶ **to start with** para empezar ■ **start off** salir **start out** empezar **start (sth) up 1** (motor) arrancar, encender algo **2** (negocio) montar algo

starter /'stɑːtər/ n **1** entrada, entremés **2** motor de arranque

starting point n punto de partida

startle /'stɑːtl/ vt asustar **startling** adj asombroso

starve /stɑːv/ **1** vi pasar hambre: ~ (**to death**) morir de hambre **2** vt matar de hambre, hacer pasar hambre **3** vt (fig) privar ▶ **be starving** (coloq) morirse de hambre **starvation** n hambre →HAMBRE

state /steɪt/ vt **1** manifestar, afirmar: *State your name.* Haga constar su nombre. **2** establecer ● n **1** estado: ~ *of mind* estado mental ◊ *in a fit* ~ *to drive* en condiciones para manejar **2 the States** [sing] (coloq) los Estados Unidos ▶ **state of affairs** situación ● adj estatal: *a* ~ *visit* una visita oficial ◊ ~ *school* (GB) colegio público

stately /'steɪtli/ adj majestuoso: ~ *home* casa señorial

statement /'steɪtmənt/ n declaración

statesman /'steɪtsmən/ n (pl -men) estadista

static /'stætɪk/ adj estático ● n [U] **1** (Radio) interferencias ● (tb ~ **electricity**) electricidad estática

station /'steɪʃn/ vt destinar ● n **1** estación: *bus* ~ terminal de autobuses ◊ *TV/radio* ~ canal/estación de radio ◊ *police* ~ delegación/estación de policía ◊ *fire* ~ estación de bomberos ◊ *gas* ~ gasolinera ◊ *power* ~ central (de energía)

stationary /'steɪʃəneri; -nri GB/ adj parado, estacionario

stationery /'steɪʃəneri; -nri GB/ n artículos de papelería **stationer** n dueño/a de papelería **stationer's** n papelería

station wagon n (USA) camioneta

statistics /stə'tɪstɪks/ n estadística

statue /'stætʃuː/ n estatua

stature /'stætʃər/ n **1** estatura **2** (fig) talla

status /'steɪtəs; 'steɪtəs GB/ n posición: ~ *symbol* símbolo de posición social ◊ *marital* ~ estado civil

statute /'stætʃuːt/ n estatuto: ~ *book* código **statutory** /'stætʃətɔːri; -tri GB/ adj estatutario

staunch /stɔːntʃ/ adj (-er/-est) incondicional

stave /steɪv/ vt ~ **sth off 1** (crisis) evitar algo **2** (ataque) rechazar algo

stay /steɪ/ n estancia, estadía ● vi quedarse: ~ in/~ (at) home quedarse en casa ◇ What time are you staying at? ¿En qué hotel te alojas? ◇ ~ away permanecer alejado ■ **stay behind** quedarse atrás **stay on (at...)** quedarse (en...) **stay up** no acostarse: ~ up late acostarse tarde

steady /'stedi/ adj (-ier/-iest) 1 firme: hold sth ~ sostener algo con firmeza 2 constante, regular: a ~ boyfriend un novio en serio ◇ a ~ job un trabajo fijo ● (pt/pp -ied) 1 vi estabilizarse 2 vt ~ yourself recuperar el equilibrio

steak /steɪk/ n filete

steal /stiːl/ (pt stole pp stolen) 1 vt, vi ~ (sth) (from sth/sb) robar (algo) (a algo/algn) → ROB 2 vi ~ in, out, away, etc.: ~ into the room entrar en la habitación sigilosamente ◇ She stole away. Salió furtivamente. ◇ ~ up on sb acercarse a algn sin hacer ruido

stealth /stelθ/ n sigilo: by ~ sigilosamente **stealthy** adj sigiloso

steam /stiːm/ n vapor ■ **let off steam** (coloq) desahogarse **run out of steam** (coloq) perder el ímpetu ● 1 vi echar vapor: steaming hot humeante 2 vt cocinar al vapor ▶ **get (all) steamed up (about/over sth)** (GB, coloq) exaltarse/ponerse furioso por algo ■ **steam up** empañarse

steamer /'stiːmər/ n buque de vapor

steamroller /'stiːmroʊlər/ n aplanadora

steel /stiːl/ n acero ● vt ~ yourself (against sth) armarse de valor (para algo)

steep /stiːp/ adj (-er/-est) 1 empinado 2 (coloq) excesivo **steeply** adv con mucha pendiente: The plane climbed ~. El avión ascendió vertiginosamente. ◇ Share prices fell ~. Las acciones cayeron en picada.

steer /stɪər/ vt, vi 1 conducir: ~ north seguir rumbo al norte ◇ ~ by the stars guiarse por las estrellas ◇ He steered the discussion away from the subject. Llevó la conversación hacia otro tema. 2 (auto) steering n dirección

steering wheel n volante, timón (Auto)

stem /stem/ n tallo ● vt (-mm-) contener ■ **stem from sth** tener el origen en algo

stench /stentʃ/ n hedor

step /step/ vi (-pp-) dar un paso: ~ on/over sth pisar algo/pasar por encima de algo ■ **step down**

retirarse **step in** intervenir **step sth up** incrementar algo ● n 1 paso: ~ by ~ paso a paso 2 peldaño 3 steps escaleras ▶ **be in/out of step** (with sth/sb) 1 (no) llevar el paso (a algo/algn) 2 estar de acuerdo/en desacuerdo (con algo/algn) **take steps to do sth** tomar medidas para hacer algo **watch your step** tener cuidado

stepbrother /'stepbrʌðər/ n hermanastro

stepchild /'steptʃaɪld/ n (pl -children) hijastro/a

stepdaughter /'stepdɔːtər/ n hijastra

stepfather /'stepfɑːðər/ n padrastro

stepladder /'steplædər/ n escalera de tijera

stepmother /'stepmʌðər/ n madrastra

step-parent n padrastro, madrastra

stepsister /'stepsɪstər/ n hermanastra

stepson /'stepsʌn/ n hijastro

stereo /'sterioʊ/ n (pl -s) estéreo

stereotype /'steriətaɪp/ n estereotipo

sterile /'sterəl; 'steraɪl GB/ adj estéril **sterility** /stə'rɪləti/ n esterilidad **sterilize** /'sterəlaɪz/ vt esterilizar

sterling /'stɜːrlɪŋ/ adj 1 (plata) de ley 2 excelente ● (tb **pound ~**) n libra esterlina (=£)

stern /stɜːrn/ n popa ● adj (-er/-est) severo, duro

stew /stuː; stjuː GB/ vt, vi cocinar, guisar ● n guiso, cocido

steward /'stuːərd; 'stjuːəd GB/ n 1 (fem **stewardess** /'stuːərdəs; 'stjuː- GB/) (avión) auxiliar de vuelo, sobrecargo 2 (barco) camarero/a

stick /stɪk/ n 1 palo, vara 2 bastón 3 barra: a ~ of celery un tallo de apio ◇ a ~ of dynamite un cartucho de dinamita ● (pt/pp stuck) 1 vt clavar, hincar 2 vt, vi pegar(se) 3 vt (coloq) poner: ~ a pencil behind your ear ponerse un lápiz detrás de la oreja 4 vt atascarse 5 vt (GB, coloq) aguantar 6 vi ~ at sth seguir trabajando, persistir en algo 7 vi ~ by sb apoyar a algn 8 vi ~ to sth atenerse a algo ■ **stick around** (coloq) quedarse cerca **stick out** salir: His ears ~ out. Tiene las orejas muy salidas. **stick it/sth out** (coloq) aguantar algo **stick sth out 1** (mano, etc.) sacar algo 2 (cabeza) asomar algo **stick together** mantenerse unidos **stick up** sobresalir **stick up for sth/sb** defender algo/a algn

sticker /'stɪkər/ n calcomanía

sticky /'stɪki/ adj (**-ier/-iest**) **1** pegajoso: ~ tape (GB) durex®/cinta pegante **2** (coloq) (situación) difícil

stiff /stɪf/ adj (**-er/-est**) **1** rígido, duro **2** (Med) agarrotado **3** sólido **4** difícil **5** (persona) tieso **6** (brisa, bebida alcohólica) fuerte ● adv (coloq) extremadamente: bored/scared ~ muerto de aburrimiento/miedo **stiffen 1** vt ponerse rígido/tieso **2** vi (Med) agarrotarse

stifle /'staɪfl/ **1** vt, vi ahogar(se) **2** vt reprimir **stifling** adj sofocante

stigma /'stɪgmə/ n estigma

still /stɪl/ adv **1** todavía, aún **NOTA** Still se usa en afirmativo e interrogativo y va detrás de los verbos auxiliares o modales y delante de los demás verbos: He ~ talks about her. ◇ Are you ~ here? Yet se usa en negativo y va al final de la frase: Aren't they here yet? ◇ He hasn't done it yet. Sin embargo, **still** se puede usar en negaciones para dar énfasis a la frase. En este caso siempre se coloca delante del verbo, aunque sea auxiliar o modal: He ~ hasn't done it. ◇ He ~ can't do it. **2** aún así, sin embargo: Still, it didn't turn out badly. A pesar de todo, no salió del todo mal. ● adj **1** quieto: Stand ~! ¡No te muevas! **2** (agua, etc.) tranquilo **3** (GB, bebida) sin gas **stillness** n calma

still life n naturaleza muerta

stilt /stɪlt/ n **1** zanco **2** pilote

stilted /'stɪltɪd/ adj forzado, rebuscado

stimulate /'stɪmjuleɪt/ vt estimular **stimulant** n estimulante **stimulating** adj **1** estimulante **2** interesante

stimulus /'stɪmjələs/ n (pl **-li** /-laɪ/) estímulo, incentivo

sting /stɪŋ/ n **1** aguijón **2** picadura, piquete (Mx) [pret **stung**] **1** vt, vi picar **2** vi arder, escocer **3** vt (fig) herir

stingy /'stɪndʒi/ adj (coloq) tacaño

stink /stɪŋk/ vi [pret **stank/stunk** o **stunk**] (coloq) **1** ~ (of sth) apestar (a algo) **2** ~ (of sth) (fig) oler (a algo) ■ **stink sth out** hacer oler mal algo ● n (coloq) hedor, peste **stinking** adj maldito

stint /stɪnt/ n período

stipulate /'stɪpjuleɪt/ vt (fml) estipular

stir /stɜːr/ (**-rr-**) **1** vt revolver **2** vt, vi mover(se) **3** vt (imaginación, etc.) despertar ■ **stir sth up** provocar algo ● n **1** give sth a ~ revolver algo **2** alboroto **stirring** adj emocionante

stirrup /'stɪrəp/ n estribo

stitch /stɪtʃ/ n **1** (costura) puntada **2** (tejido) punto **3** dolor de caballo, bazo ▸ **in stitches** (coloq) muerto de risa ● vt, vi coser **stitching** n costura

stock /stɒk/ n **1** existencias **2** surtido, reserva **3** ganado **4** (Fin) acción **5** (empresa) capital social **6** (Cocina) caldo ▸ **out of/in stock** agotado/en existencia **take stock** hacer balance ● adj: gastado (frase, etc.) ● vt tener (existencias de) ■ **stock up (on/with sth)** abastecerse (de algo)

stockbroker /'stɒkbrəʊkər/ n corredor/a de bolsa

stock exchange (tb stock market) n bolsa

stocking /'stɒkɪŋ/ n media (de mujer)

stocktaking /'stɒkteɪkɪŋ/ n inventario (acción)

stocky /'stɒki/ adj (**-ier/-iest**) bajo y fornido

stodgy /'stɒdʒi/ adj (coloq) pesado (comida, literatura)

stoke /stəʊk/ vt ~ **sth (up) (with sth)** echar algo (a algo), avivar algo (con algo)

stole /stəʊl/ pt de STEAL

stolen /'stəʊlən/ pp de STEAL

stolid /'stɒlɪd/ adj impasible

stomach /'stʌmək/ n **1** estómago **2** vientre **3** ~ **for sth** ganas de algo ● vt aguantar

stone /stəʊn/ n **1** piedra **2** (fruta) hueso, pepa (And) **3** (GB) (pl stone) 6,356 kg ◇ Ver pág. 222 ● vt apedrear **stoned** adj (coloq) **1** atizado (Mx), trabado (And) (con droga) **2** borracho **stony** adj (**-ier/-iest**) **1** cubierto de piedras **2** (mirada) frío **3** (silencio) sepulcral

stood /stʊd/ pt, pp de STAND

stool /stuːl/ n taburete, butaca

stoop /stuːp/ vi ~ **(down)** agacharse ▸ **stoop so low (as to do sth)** (fml) llegar tan bajo (como para hacer algo) ● n: walk with/have a ~ andar encorvado

stop /stɒp/ (**-pp-**) **1** vt, vi parar(se), detener(se) **2** vt (proceso) interrumpir **3** vt acabar con **4** vt ~ **sth** dejar (de hacer) algo: Stop it! ¡No más! **5** vt ~ **sth/sb (from)**

doing sth impedir que algo/algn haga algo: ~ *yourself doing sth* hacer un esfuerzo por no hacer algo **6** vt cancelar **7** vt (*pago*) suspender **8** vt (*cheque*) dar orden de no pagar **9** (*GB, coloq*) quedarse ▶ **stop dead/short** pararse en seco **stop short of sth** no llegar a algo ■ **stop off (at/in...)** pasar (por...) ● n **1** parada, alto: *come to a* ~ parar(se) **2** (*tren, autobús, etc.*) parada, paradero **stoppage** n paro

stopgap /'stɑːpgæp/ n **1** sustituto/a **2** recurso provisional

stopover /'stɑːpoʊvər/ n escala (*en un viaje*)

stopper /'stɑːpər/ n tapón

stopwatch /'stɑːpwɑːtʃ/ n cronómetro

store /stɔːr/ n **1** tienda, almacén **2** provisión, reserva **3 stores** víveres ▶ **be in store for sb; have sth in store for sb** (*sorpresa, etc.*) aguardarle a algn ● vt ~ **sth (up/away)** guardar, acumular algo **storage** n **1** almacenamiento: ~ *space* sitio para guardar cosas **2** bodega

storekeeper /'stɔːrkiːpər/ n (*USA*) comerciante, tendero/a

storeroom /'stɔːruːm/ n depósito, despensa

stork /stɔːrk/ n cigüeña

storm /stɔːrm/ n tormenta, tempestad: *a* ~ *of criticism* fuertes críticas ● vi ~ **in/off/out** entrar/irse/salir furioso **2** vt (*edificio*) asaltar **stormy** adj (-**ier/-iest**) **1** tormentoso **2** (*debate*) acalorado **3** (*relación*) turbulento

story /'stɔːri/ n (pl -**ies**) **1** historia **2** cuento **3** (*Period*) noticia **4** (*USA*) (*storey GB*) piso

stout /staʊt/ adj **1** fuerte **2** gordo

stove /stoʊv/ n **1** estufa **2** calentador

stow /stoʊ/ vt ~ **sth (away)** guardar algo

straddle /'strædl/ vt poner una pierna a cada lado de

straggle /'strægl/ vi **1** desparramarse **2** (*persona*) rezagarse **straggler** n rezagado/a **straggly** adj (-**ier/-iest**) desordenado, desgreñado

straight /streɪt/ adj (-**er/-est**) **1** recto: ~ *hair* pelo liso/lacio **2** en orden **3** derecho **4** honesto ▶ **get sth straight** dejar algo claro **keep a straight face** no reírse ● adv **1** derecho **2** en línea recta: *Look* ~ *ahead.* Mira hacia delante. **2** (*sentarse*) derecho **3** (*pensar*) claramente **4** (*irse*)

directamente ▶ **straight off/out** (*coloq*) sin vacilar

straightaway /ˌstreɪtə'weɪ/ adv inmediatamente

straighten /'streɪtn/ **1** vi volverse recto **2** vt, vi ~ **(sth) (up)** enderezar(se) (algo) **3** vt (*ropa*) arreglar ■ **straighten sth out** desenredar algo

straightforward /ˌstreɪt'fɔːrwərd/ adj **1** honrado **2** franco **3** (*estilo*) sencillo

strain /streɪn/ **1** vi esforzarse **2** vt (*cuerda*) tensar **3** vt (*oído, vista*) aguzar **4** vt (*músculo, etc.*) torcer **5** vt (*vista, voz, corazón*) forzar **6** vt colar ● n **1** tensión **2** torcedura: *eye* ~ fatiga visual **strained** adj (*risa, etc.*) forzado **2** preocupado **strainer** n colador

straitjacket /'streɪtdʒækɪt/ n camisa de fuerza

straits /streɪts/ n [pl] **1** estrecho **2** *in dire* ~ en una situación desesperada

strand /strænd/ n **1** hebra, hilo **2** mechón

stranded /'strændɪd/ adj abandonado: *be left* ~ quedarse colgado/botado (*And*)

strange /streɪndʒ/ adj (-**er/-est**) **1** desconocido **2** raro, extraño: *I find it* ~ *that...* Me extraña que... **stranger** n **1** desconocido/a **2** forastero/a

strangle /'stræŋgl/ vt estrangular, ahogar

strap /stræp/ n **1** correa, tira **2** (*vestido*) tirante ● vt (-**pp-**) **1** ~ **sth (up)** vendar algo **2** ~ **sb in** ponerle el cinturón de seguridad a algn **3 sth on** amarrar algo (*con correas*)

strategy /'strætədʒi/ n (pl -**ies**) estrategia **strategic** /strə'tiːdʒɪk/ adj estratégico

straw /strɔː/ n paja ▶ **the last/final straw** la gota que colma el vaso/rebosa la copa

strawberry /'strɔːberi; -bəri GB/ n (pl -**ies**) fresa

stray /streɪ/ vi **1** extraviarse **2** apartarse ● adj **1** extraviado: *a* ~ *dog* un perro callejero **2** aislado: *a* ~ *bullet* una bala perdida

streak /striːk/ n **1** veta **2** rasgo, vena **3** racha: *be on a winning/losing* ~ tener una racha de suerte/mala suerte ● v **1** vt rayar, vetear **2** vi correr como un rayo

stream /striːm/ n **1** arroyo, quebrada **2** (*líquido, palabras*) torrente **3** (*gente*) oleada **4** (*tráfico*) caravana ● vi **1** (*líquido*) manar **2** (*lágrimas*) correr **3** (*luz*) entrar/salir a raudales **4** derramar

streamer /'stri:mər/ n serpentina

streamline /'stri:mlaɪn/ vt 1 hacer más aerodinámico 2 racionalizar

street /stri:t/ n (abrev **St**) calle **NOTA** Cuando las palabras **street**, **road**, etc. van precedidas por el nombre de la calle, se escriben con mayúscula: *Main Street.* ▸ **be streets ahead (of sth/sb)** llevar mucha ventaja a algo/algn **(right) up your street** (GB, coloq) ideal para ti

streetcar /'stri:tkɑr/ n (USA) tranvía

strength /streŋθ/ n 1 fuerza 2 resistencia 3 (luz, emoción) intensidad 4 punto fuerte ▸ **on the strength of sth** fundándose, confiando en algo **strengthen** vt, vi fortalecer(se), reforzar(se)

strenuous /'strenjuəs/ adj 1 agotador 2 vigoroso

stress /stres/ n 1 estrés 2 énfasis 3 (Mús, palabra) acento 4 (Mec) tensión ● vt recalcar **stressful** adj estresante

stretch /stretʃ/ 1 vt, vi estirar(se), alargar(se) 2 vi desperezarse 3 vt (terreno, etc.) extenderse 4 vt (persona) exigirle el máximo esfuerzo a ▸ **stretch (yourself) out** tenderse ● n 1 have a ~ estirarse 2 elasticidad 3 (terreno) trecho 4 (tiempo) período ▸ **at a stretch** sin interrupción, seguido

stretcher /'stretʃər/ n camilla

strewn /stru:n/ adj 1 ~ (all) over sth desparramado por algo 2 ~ with sth cubierto de algo

stricken /'strɪkən/ adj afligido: *drought-stricken* afectado por la sequía

strict /strɪkt/ adj (-er/-est) 1 severo 2 estricto, preciso: *in strictest confidence* con la más absoluta reserva **strictly** adv 1 severamente 2 estrictamente: *~ prohibited* terminantemente prohibido ▸ **strictly speaking** estrictamente hablando

stride /straɪd/ vi (pt strode) 1 andar a pasos largos 2 ~ **up to sth/sb** acercarse resueltamente a algo/algn ● n 1 zancada 2 (modo de andar) paso ▸ **take sth in your, etc. stride** tomarlo con calma

strident /'straɪdnt/ adj estridente

strife /straɪf/ n [U] lucha, conflicto

strike /straɪk/ n 1 huelga: *go on ~* declararse en huelga 2 (Mil) ataque ● (pt/pp struck) 1 vt golpear, pegar 2 vt atropellar 3 vt chocar contra 4 vi atacar 5 vt, vi (reloj) dar (la hora) 6 vt (oro, etc.) hallar 7 vt (fósforo/cerillo) encender 8 vt: *It ~s me that...* Se me ocurre que... 9 vt impresionar, llamar la atención a ■ **strike back (at sth/sb)** devolver el golpe a (algo/algn) **strike up (sth)** empezar a tocar (algo) **strike up sth 1** (conversación) entablar algo 2 (amistad) trabar algo

striker /'straɪkər/ n 1 huelguista 2 (Dep) delantero/a

striking /'straɪkɪŋ/ adj llamativo

string /strɪŋ/ n 1 cordel, mecate 2 (perlas, etc.) sarta ▸ **pull strings (for sb)** (coloq) mover palancas (para algn) **(with) no strings attached** sin condiciones ● vt (pt/pp strung) ~ **sth (up)** colgar algo (con cordel, etc.) ■ **string sth out** extender algo **string sth together** hilar algo

stringent /'strɪndʒənt/ adj (fml) riguroso

strip /strɪp/ n 1 (papel, metal, etc.) tira 2 (tierra, etc.) franja ● (-pp-) 1 vt quitar 2 vt (máquina) desmantelar 3 vt ~ **sth of sth** despojar a algo de algo 4 vt ~ **sb of sth** quitarle algo a algn 5 vt, vi ~ **(off)** desnudar(se)

stripe /straɪp/ n raya **striped** adj de rayas

strive /straɪv/ vi (pt strove pp striven /'strɪvn/) ~ **for/after sth** (fml) esforzarse (por alcanzar algo)

strode /stroʊd/ pt de STRIDE

stroke /stroʊk/ vt acariciar ● n 1 golpe: *a ~ of luck* una chiripa 2 (Dep) brazada 3 trazo (de lápiz) 4 campanada 5 (Med) derrame cerebral ▸ **at a stroke** de (un) golpe **not do a stroke (of work)** no hacer absolutamente nada

stroll /stroʊl/ n paseo: *go for a ~* dar un paseo ● vi caminar

stroller /'stroʊlər/ n (USA) coche (de niño), carreola (Mx)

strong /strɔ:ŋ, strɒŋ GB/ adj (-er/-est) fuerte ▸ **be going strong** (coloq) estar muy fuerte **sb's strong point/suit** el fuerte de uno/algn

strong-minded adj decidido

strove /stroʊv/ pt de STRIVE

struck /strʌk/ pt, pp de STRIKE

structure /'strʌktʃər/ n 1 estructura 2 construcción ● vt estructurar

struggle /'strʌgl/ vi 1 luchar 2 forcejear ● n 1 lucha 2 esfuerzo

strung /strʌŋ/ pt de STRING

strut /strʌt/ n puntal ● vi (-tt-) ~ **(about/along)** pavonearse

stub /stʌb/ n 1 cabo 2 (*cigarrillo*) colilla 3 (*cheque*) talón

stubble /'stʌbl/ n 1 rastrojo 2 barba (incipiente)

stubborn /'stʌbərn/ adj 1 terco 2 (*mancha, tos*) rebelde

stuck /stʌk/ pt, pp de STICK ● adj 1 atascado: get ~ atascarse 2 (*coloq*): be/get ~ with sth/sb tener que cargar con algo/algn

stuck-up adj (*coloq*) engreído

stud /stʌd/ n 1 tachuela 2 (*zapato*) taco 3 caballo semental 4 (*tb* ~ **farm**) criadero de caballos

student /'stu:dnt; 'stju:- GB/ n 1 estudiante (*de universidad*) 2 alumno/a → ALUMNO

studied /'stʌdid/ adj deliberado

studio /'stu:diou; 'stju:- GB/ n (*pl* -s) 1 taller 2 (*Cine, TV*) estudio

studious /'stu:diəs; 'stju:- GB/ adj 1 estudioso 2 deliberado

study /'stʌdi/ n (*pl* -ies) estudio ● vt, vi (*pt/pp* -ied) estudiar

stuff /stʌf/ n (*coloq*) 1 material, sustancia 2 cosas ● vt 1 rellenar 2 ~ **sth in**, ~ **sth into sth** meter algo a la fuerza (en algo) 3 ~ **yourself** (*with sth*) atiborrarse (de algo) 4 disecar ► **get stuffed!** (*GB, coloq*) ¡vete al carajo! **stuffing** n relleno

stuffy /'stʌfi/ adj (-ier/-iest) 1 (*ambiente*) sofocante (*coloq*) 2 (*persona*) estirado

stumble /'stʌmbl/ vi 1 dar un traspié 2 atrancarse ► **stumble across/on sth/sb** encontrarse con algo/algn

stumbling block n obstáculo

stump /stʌmp/ n 1 (*árbol*) tocón 2 (*extremidad*) muñón

stun /stʌn/ vt (-nn-) 1 asombrar 2 aturdir **stunning** adj asombroso

stung /stʌŋ/ pt, pp de STING

stunk /stʌŋk/ pt, pp de STINK

stunt /stʌnt/ n 1 truco 2 acrobacia ● vt atrofiar

stuntman, stuntwoman /'stʌntmæn/-wumən/ n (*pl* -men/-women) doble (*en películas*)

stupendous /stu:'pendəs; stju:- GB/ adj formidable

stupid /'stu:pɪd; 'stju:- GB/ adj (-er/-est) tonto, estúpido **stupidity** /stu:'pɪdəti; stju:- GB/ n estupidez

stupor /'stu:pər; 'stju:- GB/ n estupor: in a drunken ~ atontado por la bebida

sturdy /'stɜ:rdi/ adj (-ier/-iest) fuerte

stutter /'stʌtər/ vi tartamudear ● n tartamudeo

sty /staɪ/ n (*pl* sties) 1 pocilga 2 (*tb* stye) orzuelo

style /staɪl/ n 1 estilo 2 modo 3 distinción 4 modelo: the latest ~ la última moda **stylish** adj elegante

suave /swɑːv/ adj con buenas maneras (*excesivo a veces*)

subconscious /,sʌb'kɑnʃəs/ adj, n subconsciente

subdivide /'sʌbdɪvaɪd/ vt, vi subdividir(se)

subdue /səb'du:; -'dju: GB/ vt someter **subdued** adj 1 (*voz*) bajo 2 (*luz, color*) suave 3 (*persona*) abatido

sub-heading n subtítulo

subject /'sʌbdʒɪkt/ n 1 tema 2 asignatura, materia 3 (*Gram*) sujeto 4 súbdito ● adj ~ **to sth** /səb'dʒekt/ vt someter **subjection** n (*fml*) sometimiento

subject matter n tema

subjective /səb'dʒektɪv/ adj subjetivo

subjunctive /səb'dʒʌŋktɪv/ n subjuntivo

sublime /sə'blaɪm/ adj sublime

submarine /'sʌbməriːn; ,sʌbmə-'riːn GB/ adj, n submarino

submerge /səb'mɜːrdʒ/ vt, vi sumergir(se)

submission /səb'mɪʃn/ n 1 sumisión 2 (*documento, etc.*) presentación **submissive** adj sumiso

submit /səb'mɪt/ (-tt-) 1 vi someterse, rendirse 2 vt presentar: Applications must be submitted today. El plazo de entrega de solicitudes vence hoy.

subordinate /sə'bɔːrdmət/ adj, n subordinado/a ● /sə'bɔːrdmeɪt/ vt subordinar

subscribe /səb'skraɪb/ vi suscribirse ► **subscribe to sth** (*fml*) suscribir algo (*opinión*) **subscriber** n 1 suscriptor/a 2 abonado/a **subscription** n 1 suscripción 2 cuota

subsequent /'sʌbsɪkwənt/ adj [*antes de sustantivo*] posterior

subside /səb'saɪd/ vi 1 hundirse 2 (*agua*) bajar 3 (*viento*) amainar 4 (*emoción*) calmarse **subsidence** n hundimiento

subsidiary /səb'sɪdieri; -diəri GB/ adj secundario ● n (*pl* -ies) filial

subsidy /'sʌbsədi/ n (*pl* -ies) subvención, subsidio **subsidize** vt subvencionar

subsist /səb'sɪst/ vi ~ (**on sth**) subsistir (a base de algo) **subsistence** n subsistencia

substance /'sʌbstəns/ n 1 sustancia 2 esencia

substantial /səb'stænʃl/ *adj*
1 considerable **2** *(construcción)*
sólido **substantially** *adv* **1** considerablemente **2** esencialmente

substitute /'sʌbstɪtuːt; -tjuːt GB/
n **1** sustituto **2** sustitutivo **3** *(Dep)*
suplente ● *vt, vi* sustituir

subtitle /'sʌbtaɪtl/ *n* subtítulo ● *vt*
subtitular

subtle /'sʌtl/ *adj* **(-er/-est)** **1** sutil
2 *(sabor)* delicado **3** *(persona)*
perspicaz **4** *(olor, color)* suave
subtlety *n* *(pl -ies)* sutileza

subtract /səb'trækt/ *vt, vi* restar
subtraction *n* resta

suburb /'sʌbɜːb/ *n* barrio/colonia residencial de las afueras
suburban /sə'bɜːrbən/ *adj* suburbano

subversive /sʌb'vɜːrsɪv/ *adj* subversivo

subway /'sʌbweɪ/ *n* **1** *(USA)* metro **2** *(GB)* paso subterráneo

succeed /sək'siːd/ **1** *vi* tener
éxito, triunfar: ~ *in doing sth*
lograr hacer algo **2** *vt, vi* ~ *(sb)*
suceder *(a algn)* **3** *vi* ~ *to sth*
heredar algo: ~ *to the throne*
subir al trono

success /sək'ses/ *n* éxito: *be a* ~
tener éxito **successful** *adj* exitoso: *the* ~ *candidate* el candidato
elegido ◊ *be* ~ *in doing sth* lograr
hacer algo con éxito

succession /sək'seʃn/ *n* sucesión: *three times in quick* ~ tres
veces seguidas **2** serie

successor /sək'sesər/ *n* sucesor/a

succumb /sə'kʌm/ *vi* sucumbir

such /sʌtʃ/ *adj, pron* **1** semejante,
tal: *in* ~ *a way that...* de tal
manera que... ◊ *There's no*
~ *thing as ghosts.* Los fantasmas
no existen. **2** *(énfasis)* tan, tanto:
I had a wonderful time. La pasé
tan bien. ◊ *I'm in a hurry.*
Tengo muchísima prisa.
NOTA Such se usa con adjetivos
que acompañan a un sustantivo
y so con adjetivos solos: *The food
was so good.* ◊ *We had* ~ *good
food.* ◊ *You're so intelligent/* ~ *an
intelligent man.* → TAL ▶ **as such**
como tal: *It's not a promotion as*
~. No es un ascenso propiamente dicho. **such as** por ejemplo

suck /sʌk/ *vt, vi* **1** chupar
2 *(bomba)* succionar **sucker** *n*
1 *(coloq)* bobo/a **2** ventosa

sudden /'sʌdn/ *adj* repentino ▶ **all
of a sudden** de pronto **suddenly**
adv de pronto

suds /sʌdz/ *n [pl]* espuma

sue /suː/ *vt, vi* demandar

suede /sweɪd/ *n* ante, gamuza

suffer /'sʌfər/ **1** *vi* padecer **2** *vt, vi*
sufrir **3** *vi* salir perjudicado **suffering** *n* sufrimiento

sufficient /sə'fɪʃnt/ *adj* suficiente

suffix /'sʌfɪks/ *n* sufijo

suffocate /'sʌfəkeɪt/ **1** *vi, vi* asfixiar(se) **2** *vt* ahogarse **suffocating** *adj* sofocante **suffocation** *n*
asfixia

sugar /'ʃʊɡər/ *n* azúcar: ~ *bowl*
azucarera

suggest /sə'dʒest/ *vt* **1** proponer,
sugerir: *I* ~ *you go to the doctor.*
Te aconsejo que vayas al médico.
2 indicar **3** insinuar **suggestion** *n*
1 sugerencia **2** indicio **3** insinuación **suggestive** *adj* **1** indicativo
2 insinuante

suicide /'suːɪsaɪd/ *n* **1** suicidio:
commit ~ suicidarse **2** suicida
suicidal /ˌsuːɪ'saɪdl/ *adj*
2 a punto de suicidarse

suit /suːt/ *n* **1** traje *(cartas)* palo
→ BARAJA ● *vt* **1** quedar bien
2 convenir **3** sentar bien

suitable /'suːtəbl/ *adj* **1** adecuado
2 conveniente **suitability** /ˌsuːtə'bɪləti/ *n* idoneidad **suitably** *adv*
debidamente

suitcase /'suːtkeɪs/ *n* maleta

suite /swiːt/ *n* **1** *(hotel)* suite
2 juego: *a bathroom* ~ un juego
de baño

suited /'suːtɪd/ *adj* adecuado:
They're well ~ *(to each other)*.
Están hechos el uno para el otro.

sulfur **(sulphur** GB**)** /'sʌlfər/ *n*
azufre

sulk /sʌlk/ *vi* estar de mal genio,
enfurruñarse **sulky** *adj* **(-ier/
-iest)** enfurruñado, de mal genio

sullen /'sʌlən/ *adj* huraño

sultan /'sʌltən/ *n* sultán

sultana /sʌl'tænə; -ɑːnə GB/ *n*
(GB) (uva) pasa *(sin semilla)*

sultry /'sʌltri/ *adj* **1** sofocante
2 sensual

sum /sʌm/ *n* suma: *be good at* ~s
ser bueno en aritmética ● *v*
(-mm-) ▶ **sum (sth) up** resumir
(algo): *to* ~ *up...* en resumen...
sum sth/sb up hacerse una idea
de algo/algn

summary /'sʌməri/ *n* *(pl -ies)*
resumen **summarize** *vt, vi* resumir

summer /'sʌmər/ *n* *(tb* summertime /'sʌmərtaɪm/) verano
summery *adj* veraniego

summit /'sʌmɪt/ *n* cumbre:
~ *meeting* cumbre

summon /'sʌmən/ *vt* **1** convocar,
llamar: ~ *help* pedir ayuda
2 ~ *sth (up)* *(valor, etc.)* armarse
de algo: *I can't* ~ *up the energy.*

No tengo la energía. **3 ~ sth up** evocar algo

summons /'sʌmənz/ n (pl **-es**) (Jur) citación

sun /sʌn/ n sol ● vt (**-nn-**) **~ yourself** asolearse

sunbathe /'sʌnbeɪð/ vi tomar el sol

sunbeam /'sʌnbiːm/ n rayo de sol

sunburn /'sʌnbɜːrn/ n [U] quemadura de sol: get ~ quemarse **sunburnt** adj quemado por el sol

sundae /'sʌndeɪ/ n copa de helado

Sunday /'sʌndeɪ, -di/ n (abrev **Sun.**) domingo

sundry /'sʌndri/ adj varios, diversos ▸ **all and sundry** (coloq) todos y cada uno

sunflower /'sʌnflaʊər/ n girasol

sung /sʌŋ/ pp de SING

sunglasses /'sʌnglæsɪz, -glɑːsɪz GB/ n [pl] gafas/lentes de sol →PAIR

sunk /sʌŋk/ pp de SINK ▸ **sunk in sth** sumido en algo

sunken /'sʌŋkən/ adj hundido

sunlight /'sʌnlaɪt/ n luz solar

sunlit /'sʌnlɪt/ adj iluminado por el sol

sunny /'sʌni/ adj (**-ier/-iest**) **1** soleado: It's ~. Hace sol. **2** (carácter) alegre

sunrise /'sʌnraɪz/ n salida del sol

sunset /'sʌnset/ n puesta del sol

sunshine /'sʌnʃaɪn/ n sol

sunstroke /'sʌnstroʊk/ n insolación

suntan /'sʌntæn/ n bronceado: get a ~ broncearse **suntanned** adj bronceado

super /'suːpər/ adj estupendo

superb /suː'pɜːrb/ adj magnífico **superbly** adv de maravilla: ~ situated en un sitio magnífico

superficial /ˌsuːpər'fɪʃl/ adj superficial **superficiality** /ˌsuːpər-ˌfɪʃɪ'æləti/ n superficialidad **superficially** adv superficialmente

superfluous /suː'pɜːrfluəs/ adj superfluo: be ~ estar de más

superhuman /ˌsuːpər'hjuːmən/ adj sobrehumano

superimpose /ˌsuːpərɪm'poʊz/ vt superponer

superintendent /ˌsuːpərɪn'tendənt/ n **1** inspector/a (policía) **2** encargado/a, superintendente

superior /suː'pɪəriər/ adj **1** superior **2** (actitud) soberbio ● n superior **superiority** /suːˌpɪəri-'ɒrəti/ n superioridad

superlative /suː'pɜːrlətɪv/ adj, n superlativo

supermarket /'suːpərmɑːrkɪt/ n supermercado

supernatural /ˌsuːpər'nætʃrəl/ adj, n sobrenatural

superpower /'suːpərpaʊər/ n superpotencia

supersede /ˌsuːpər'siːd/ vt reemplazar, sustituir

supersonic /ˌsuːpər'sɑːnɪk/ adj supersónico

superstition /ˌsuːpər'stɪʃn/ n superstición **superstitious** adj supersticioso

superstore /'suːpərstɔːr/ n hipermercado

supervise /'suːpərvaɪz/ vt supervisar **supervision** /ˌsuːpər'vɪʒn/ n supervisión **supervisor** /'suː-pərvaɪzər/ n supervisor/a

supper /'sʌpər/ n cena: have ~ cenar/comer (And) →DINNER

supple /'sʌpl/ adj flexible

supplement /'sʌplɪmənt/ n **1** suplemento **2** (libro) apéndice ● vt complementar **supplementary** adj adicional

supply /sə'plaɪ/ vt (pt/pp **-ied**) **1** proveer **2** proporcionar, facilitar ● n (pl **-ies**) **1** suministro **2** supplies víveres **3** supplies (Mil) pertrechos **4** ~ and demand la oferta y la demanda **supplier** n proveedor/a

support /sə'pɔːrt/ vt **1** (peso) soportar **2** (causa) apoyar: a supporting role un papel secundario **3** (GB, Dep) seguir: Which team do you ~? ¿De qué equipo eres hincha? **4** (persona) mantener ● n **1** apoyo **2** soporte **supporter** n seguidor/a **supportive** adj que ayuda: be ~ apoyar

suppose /sə'poʊz/ vt **1** suponer, imaginarse **2** (sugerencia): Suppose we change the subject? ¿Qué le parece si cambiamos de tema? ▸ **be supposed to do sth** tener que hacer algo **supposed** adj supuesto **supposing** (tb ~ that) conj y si, en el caso de que

suppress /sə'pres/ vt **1** reprimir **2** (información) ocultar

supreme /suː'priːm/ adj sumo, supremo **supremacy** /suː-'preməsi/ n supremacía

surcharge /'sɜːrtʃɑːrdʒ/ n recargo

sure /ʃʊər/ adj (**-er/-est**) **1** seguro, cierto: He's ~ to be elected. Es seguro que lo van a elegir. **2** estable, firme ▸ **be sure to do sth** no dejar de hacer algo **for sure** (coloq) con seguridad **make sure (of sth)** asegurarse (de algo): Make ~ you're home by ten. Que

no se te olvide de estar en la casa
a las diez. ● *adv* (*coloq*) claro
▶ **sure enough** efectivamente

surely /'ʃʊəli; 'ʃʊrli *GB*/ *adv*
1 ciertamente, seguramente
2 (*sorpresa*): *You don't agree, ~?*
¿No estarás de acuerdo?

surf /sɜːrf/ *n* **1** oleaje, olas
2 espuma (*de mar*) ● **1** *vi* hacer
surf, surfear **2** *vt, vi* (*Comp*)
navegar (en/por): ~ *the Net* navegar en internet **surfer** *n* surfista **surfing** surf

surface /'sɜːrfɪs/ *n* **1** superficie:
~ *mail* correo terrestre o marítimo ◇ *a ~ wound* una herida
superficial **2** cara ● **1** *vt* recubrir
2 *vi* salir a la superficie

surfboard /'sɜːrfbɔːrd/ *n* tabla de surf(ing), tabla

surge /sɜːrdʒ/ *vi*: *They surged into
the stadium.* Entraron en tropel
en el estadio. ● *n* oleada

surgeon /'sɜːrdʒən/ *n* cirujano/a **surgery** *n* (*pl* **-ies**) **1** cirugía: *brain
~ neurocirugía* ◇ *undergo ~ someterse a una operación quirúrgica* **2** (*GB, Med*) consultorio: ~ *hours* horas de consulta **surgical** *adj* quirúrgico

surly /'sɜːrli/ *adj* arisco

surmount /sər'maʊnt/ *vt* (*fml*)
superar

surname /'sɜːrneɪm/ *n* apellido
NOTA En los países de habla
inglesa sólo se tiene un apellido
(**surname** o **family/last name**),
y suele ser el del padre.

surpass /sər'pæs; -'pɑːs *GB*/ *vt*
(*fml*) superar

surplus /'sɜːrpləs/ *n* excedente ●
adj sobrante

surprise /sər'praɪz/ *n* sorpresa:
take sth/sb by ~ tomar algo/a
algn por sorpresa ● *vt* sorprender **surprised** *adj* ~ (**at sth/sb**)
sorprendido (por algo/con algn):
I'm not ~! ¡No me extraña!

surrender /sə'rendər/ **1** *vi* rendirse **2** *vt* (*fml*) entregar ● *n*
1 rendición **2** entrega

surreptitious /ˌsʌrəp'tɪʃəs/ *adj*
subrepticio, furtivo

surrogate /'sʌrəgət/ *n* sustituto/a: ~ *mother* madre sustituta

surround /sə'raʊnd/ *vt* rodear
surrounding *adj* circundante:
the ~ area la zona de alrededor
surroundings *n* alrededores

surveillance /sɜːr'veɪləns/ *n* vigilancia

survey /sər'veɪ/ *vt* **1** contemplar
2 (*Geog*) medir, levantar un plano de **3** (*GB*) hacer una inspección de (*casa, etc.*) **4** /'sɜːrveɪ/
encuestar ● /'sɜːrveɪ/ *n* **1** en-

cuesta **2** (*GB*) inspección (*casa,
etc.*) **3** panorama **surveyor**
/sər'veɪər/ *n* **1** inspector que
avalúa edificios **2** topógrafo/a

survive /sər'vaɪv/ **1** *vt, vi* sobrevivir (a) **2** *vi* ~ (**on sth**) subsistir
(a base de algo) **survival** *n* supervivencia **survivor** *n* sobreviviente

susceptible /sə'septəbl/ *adj*
1 *He's very ~ to flattery.* Es fácil
de convencer con halagos. **2** propenso **3** susceptible

suspect /sə'spekt/ *vt* **1** ~ (**sb**) (**of
sth**) sospechar (de algn)(que
algn ha hecho algo) **2** (*motivo,
etc.*) desconfiar de ● /'sʌspekt/
adj, n sospechoso/a

suspend /sə'spend/ *vt* **1** colgar
NOTA Es más común **hang**.
2 suspender: *suspended sentence*
pena que no se cumple a menos
que se cometa otro crimen **suspension** *n* suspensión: ~ *bridge*
puente colgante

suspender /sə'spendər/ *n* **1** **suspenders** (*USA*) tirantes, cargaderas (*And*) **2** (*GB*) liga (*para
medias*)

suspense /sə'spens/ *n* suspenso,
tensión

suspicion /sə'spɪʃn/ *n* sospecha,
desconfianza **suspicious** *adj*
1 receloso: *be ~ of sb* sospechar
de algn **2** sospechoso

sustain /sə'steɪn/ *vt* **1** mantener
2 sostener **3** (*fml*) (*lesión, pérdida, etc.*) sufrir

swagger /'swægər/ *vi* andar con
aire orgulloso, pavonearse

swallow /'swɒloʊ/ *n* **1** golondrina
2 trago ● *vt, vi* tragar(se)

swam /swæm/ *pt de* swim

swamp /swɒmp/ *n* pantano ● *vt*
inundar

swan /swɒn/ *n* cisne

swap /swɒp/ *vt, vi* (**-pp-**) cambiar,
intercambiar: ~ *sth around* cambiar algo de lugar

swarm /swɔːrm/ *n* **1** enjambre
2 (*moscas*) nube **3** (*gente*) multitud: ~*s of people* un mar de gente
● *vi* **1** ~ (**in/out**) entrar/salir en
manada **2** ~ **with sth** ser un
hormiguero de algo

swat /swɒt/ *vt* (**-tt-**) aplastar

sway /sweɪ/ **1** *vt, vi* mecer(se) **2** *vi*
tambalearse **3** *vt* influir en ● *n*
1 balanceo **2** (*fml*) dominio

swear /swear/ (*pt* **swore** *pp*
sworn) **1** *vt* decir groserías **2** *vt,
vi* jurar ■ **swear by sth/sb** confiar
plenamente en algo/algn **swear
sb in** tomar juramento a algn

swear word *n* grosería

S

sweat /swet/ *n* sudor ● *vi* sudar
▸ **sweat it out** (*coloq*) aguantarse

sweaty *adj* (**-ier**/**-iest**) sudado,
que hace sudar

sweater /'swetər/ *n* suéter
NOTA En EE.UU. un **sweater**
puede ser abierto o cerrado, y un
pullover es siempre cerrado. En
Gran Bretaña ambos son cerrados
(y **jumper** también), y un
suéter abierto se dice **cardigan**.

sweats /swets/ *n* [*pl*] (*tb* **sweat-
suit** /'swetsuːt/) (*USA*) **pants**
(*Mx*), sudadera (*And*)

sweatshirt /'swetʃɜːrt/ *n* sudadera, suéter deportivo

sweep /swiːp/ (*pt/pp* **swept**) **1** *vt,
vi* ~ (**sth**) (**away/up**) barrer (algo)
2 *vt* (*chimenea*) deshollinar **3** *vt*
arrastrar **4** *vi* extenderse **5** *vi*:
~ **out of the room** salir de la
habitación con paso majestuoso
6 *vt, vi* ~ (**through, over, across,
etc.**) **sth** recorrer, extenderse por
algo ▸ **sweep sb off their feet**
robarle el corazón a algn ● *n*
1 barrida **2** gesto (*amplio*) **3** extensión **4** (*policía*) redada
sweeping *adj* **1** radical **2** (*afirmación*) tajante

sweet /swiːt/ *adj* (**-er**/**-est**) **1** dulce
2 (*olor*) fragante **3** (*sonido*) melodioso **4** (*coloq*) mono, cuco
(*And*) **5** encantador ▸ **have a
sweet tooth** (*coloq*) ser goloso
● *n* **1** (*GB*) dulce **2** (*GB*) postre
sweeten *vt* **1** endulzar **2** ~ **sb (up)**
(*coloq*) ablandar a algn **sweet-
ener** *n* edulcorante **sweetness** *n*
dulzura

sweetcorn /'swiːtkɔːrn/ *n* (*GB*)
maíz tierno, elote (*Mx*)

sweetheart /'swiːthɑːrt/ *n* **1** (*tratamiento*) (mi) amor **2** novio/a

sweet pea *n* guisante de olor

sweet potato *n* (*pl* **-es**) camote

swell /swel/ *vt, vi* (*pt* **swelled** *pp*
swelled/swollen) hinchar(se)
swelling *n* hinchazón

swept /swept/ *pt, pp* de **SWEEP**

swerve /swɜːrv/ *vt, vi* dar un
viraje brusco

swift /swift/ *adj* (**-er**/**-est**) rápido,
pronto

swill /swɪl/ *vt* ~ **sth** (**out/down**)
enjuagar algo

swim /swɪm/ (**-mm-**) (*pt* **swam** *pp*
swum) **1** *vt, vi* nadar: ~ **across a
river** atravesar un río a nado **2** *vi*
(*cabeza*) dar vueltas ● *n*: **go for a
~** ir a nadar **swimmer** *n* nada-
dor/a **swimming** *n* natación

swimming pool *n* piscina, alberca (*Mx*)

swimsuit /'swɪmsuːt/ *n* (*tb* **swimming costume** *GB*) traje/vestido
de baño (*esp de mujer*)

swindle /'swɪndl/ *vt* estafar ● *n*
1 estafa **2** engaño **swindler** *n*
estafador/a

swing /swɪŋ/ (*pt/pp* **swung**) **1** *vt,
vi* balancear(se) **2** *vt, vi* columpiar(se) **3** *vi* [*con adverbio*]:
~ **around** girar(se) (*algo*) **4** *vi*
(*cambio*): ~ (*se dar(se) media misma:
The door swung open.* La puerta
se abrió. ● *n* **1** balanceo **2** columpio **3** cambio: *mood* ~**s** cambios
bruscos de humor ▸ **in full swing**
en plena actividad

swirl /swɜːrl/ *vt, vi* arremolinar(se)

switch /swɪtʃ/ *n* **1** interruptor
2 cambio ● *vt, vi* (*inter*)cambiar
▸ **switch (sth)** on encender(se)
(algo) **switch (sth) off** apagar(se)
(algo)

switchboard /'swɪtʃbɔːrd/ *n* conmutador

swivel /'swɪvl/ *vt, vi* (**-l-**, **-ll-** *GB*)
~ (**sth**) around girar(se) (algo)

swollen /'swəʊlən/ *pp* de **SWELL**

swoop /swuːp/ *vi* ~ (**down**) descender en picada ● *n* redada

swop = **SWAP**

sword /sɔːrd/ *n* espada

swore /swɔːr/ *pt* de **SWEAR**

sworn /swɔːrn/ *pp* de **SWEAR**

swum /swʌm/ *pp* de **SWIM**

swung /swʌŋ/ *pt, pp* de **SWING**

syllable /'sɪləbl/ *n* sílaba

syllabus /'sɪləbəs/ *n* programa
(de estudios)

symbol /'sɪmbl/ *n* símbolo **symbolism** *n* simbolismo **symbolize**
vt simbolizar

symbolic /sɪm'bɑlɪk/ *adj* simbólico

symmetry /'sɪmətri/ *n* simetría
symmetric /sɪ'metrɪk/ *adj* simétrico

sympathetic /ˌsɪmpə'θetɪk/ *adj*
1 ~ (**to/towards sb**) comprensivo,
compasivo (con algn) **NOTA**
"Simpático" se dice **nice** o
friendly. **2** ~ (**to sth/sb**) con buena disposición (hacia algo/algn):
lawyers ~ *to the cause* abogados
que apoyan la causa

sympathy /'sɪmpəθi/ *n* (*pl* **-ies**)
1 compasión **2** condolencia **sympathize** *vi* **1** ~ (**with sth/sb**) **1** compadecerse (de algo/algn) **2** estar
de acuerdo (con algo/algn)

symphony /'sɪmfəni/ *n* (*pl* **-ies**)
sinfonía

symptom /'sɪmptəm/ *n* síntoma

synagogue /'sɪnəgɑg/ *n* sinagoga

synchronize /'sɪŋkrənaɪz/ *vt, vi*
sincronizar

syndicate /'sɪndɪkət/ n sindicato

syndrome /'sɪndrəʊm/ n síndrome

synonym /'sɪnənɪm/ n sinónimo **synonymous** /sɪ'nɒnɪməs/ adj ~ (with sth) sinónimo (de algo)

syntax /'sɪntæks/ n sintaxis

synthesizer /'sɪnθəsaɪzər/ n sintetizador

synthetic /sɪn'θetɪk/ adj 1 sintético 2 (pey) artificial

syringe /sɪ'rɪndʒ/ n jeringa

syrup /'sɪrəp/ n 1 almíbar 2 jarabe (para la tos)

system /'sɪstəm/ n sistema ▸ **get sth out of your system** (coloq) desahogarse de algo **systematic** /ˌsɪstə'mætɪk/ adj 1 sistemático 2 metódico

---

T t

T, t /tiː/ n (pl T's, t's) T, t

ta /tɑː/ interj (GB, coloq) gracias

tab /tæb/ n 1 etiqueta 2 (USA, en lata) anilla 3 cuenta

table /'teɪbl/ n 1 mesa: lay/set the ~ poner la mesa ◇ bedside ~ mesita de noche 2 tabla: ~ of contents índice de materias

tablecloth /'teɪblklɒːθ; -klɒθ GB/ n mantel

tablespoon /'teɪblspuːn/ n 1 cuchara (grande) 2 (tb tablespoonful) cucharada

tablet /'tæblət/ n pastilla

table tennis n ping-pong®

tabloid /'tæblɔɪd/ n: the ~ press la prensa sensacionalista

taboo /tə'buː/ adj, n tabú

tacit /'tæsɪt/ adj tácito

tack /tæk/ n tachuela ● vt clavar (con tachuelas) ■ **tack sth on** (to sth) (coloq) añadir algo (a algo)

tackle /'tækl/ n 1 [U] equipo: fishing ~ equipo de pesca 2 (Dep) entrada ● vt 1 hacer frente a algn 2 abordar 3 (fútbol, etc.) hacerle una entrada a

tacky /'tæki/ adj 1 (coloq) de mal gusto 2 pegajoso

tact /tækt/ n tacto **tactful** adj diplomático **tactless** adj poco diplomático, indiscreto

tactic /'tæktɪk/ n táctica **tactical** adj táctico 2 estratégico

tadpole /'tædpəʊl/ n renacuajo

tag /tæg/ n etiqueta ● vt (-gg-) etiquetar ■ **tag along** (behind/ with sb) acompañar a algn, pegarse (a algn)

tail /teɪl/ n 1 rabo, cola 2 **tails** [pl] frac 3 **tails** [pl] (moneda) sol (Mx), sello (And) ● vt perseguir ■ **tail away/off 1** disminuir 2 (ruido, etc.) apagarse

tailor /'teɪlər/ n sastre/a ● vt adaptar

tailor-made adj 1 a la medida 2 (fig) a la medida de sus necesidades

taint /teɪnt/ vt 1 contaminar 2 (reputación) manchar

take /teɪk/ vt (pt **took** pp **taken** /'teɪkən/) 1 tomar: ~ a photo tomar una foto 2 llevar(se): Take the dog with you. Llévate el perro. 3 ~ **sth from/out of sth** sacar algo de algo 4 ~ **sth from sb** quitar algo (a algn) 5 aceptar 6 soportar 7 (tiempo) tardar, demorar: It won't ~ long. No lleva mucho tiempo. 8 (cualidad) hacer falta 9 (talla) usar: What size shoes do you ~? ¿Qué número calzas? ▸ **take it (that...)** suponer (que...) **take some/a lot of doing** (coloq) no ser fácil **NOTA** Para otras expresiones, ver el sustantivo, adjetivo, etc., p. ej. **take place** en PLACE. ■ **take after sb** parecerse a algn **take sth apart** desarmar algo **take sth/sb away (from sth/sb)** quitar algo/a algn (de algo/algn) **take sth back** 1 devolver algo (a una tienda) 2 retractarse de algo **take sth down** 1 bajar algo 2 desmontar algo 3 anotar algo **take sb in** 1 acoger, alojar a algn 2 engañar a algn **take sth in** entender algo **take off** despegar **take sth off** 1 (ropa) quitarse algo 2 ~ the day off tomarse el día libre **take sb off** contratar a algn **take sth on** aceptar algo (trabajo) **take it/ sth out on sb** desquitarse de algo con algn **take sb out** invitar a algn a salir **take sth out** sacar, extraer algo **take over from sb** sustituir a algn (en algo) **take sth over 1** adquirir algo (empresa) 2 hacerse cargo de algo **take to sth/sb**: I took to his father immediately. Su padre me cayó bien inmediatamente. **take sb up on sth** (coloq) aceptar algo de algn (oferta) **take sth up** empezar algo (hobby) **take sth up with sb** plantear algo a algn **take up sth** ocupar algo (espacio, tiempo)

take-off n (pl -offs) despegue

takeout /'teɪkaʊt/ (**takeaway** /'teɪkəweɪ/ GB) n 1 restaurante que vende comida para llevar 2 comida para llevar

takeover /'teɪkoʊvər/ n 1 (Com) adquisición 2 (Mil) toma del poder

takings /'teɪkɪŋz/ n [pl] recaudación, ganancias

talc /tælk/ (tb **talcum powder** /'tælkəm paʊdər/) n talco

tale /teɪl/ n 1 cuento 2 chisme

talent /'tælənt/ n talento **talented** adj talentoso, de talento

talk /tɔːk/ n 1 conversación, charla 2 **talks** negociaciones ● v 1 vi hablar, platicar ▸ HABLAR 2 vi hablar de: ~ business hablar de negocios ▸ **talk your way out of sth** librarse de algo con pura labia ■ **talk down to sb** hablar a algn como si fuera tonto **talk sb into/out of doing sth** persuadir a algn para que haga/no haga algo **talkative** adj hablador

tall /tɔːl/ adj (**-er/-est**) alto: How ~ is he? ¿Cuánto mide? ◊ I'm six feet ~. Mido 1.80. ▸ALTO

tambourine /ˌtæmbə'riːn/ n pandereta

tame /teɪm/ adj (**-er/-est**) 1 domesticado 2 manso 3 (fiesta, etc.) insulso ● vt domar

tamper /'tæmpər/ v ■ **tamper with sth** alterar algo

tampon /'tæmpɒn/ n tampón

tan /tæn/ vt, vi (**-nn-**) broncear(se) ● n bronceado: get a ~ broncearse ● adj (color) canela

tangent /'tændʒənt/ n tangente ▸ **go off on/at** (GB) **a tangent** salirse por la tangente

tangerine /ˌtændʒə'riːn; 'tændʒə'riːn GB/ n mandarina ● adj (color) naranja oscuro

tangle /'tæŋɡl/ n 1 enredo 2 lío: get into a ~ armarse un lío ● vt, vi ~ (sth) (up) enredar(se) (algo) **tangled** adj enredado

tank /tæŋk/ n 1 tanque 2 depósito

tanker /'tæŋkər/ n 1 (tb oil ~) petrolero 2 camión cisterna

tanned /tænd/ adj bronceado

tantalize /'tæntəlaɪz/ vt atormentar **tantalizing** adj tentador

tantrum /'tæntrəm/ n berrinche: throw/have a ~ hacer berrinche

tap /tæp/ n 1 golpecito 2 (GB) llave (de agua) ● (**-pp-**) 1 vt ~ sth (against/on sth) dar golpecitos con algo en algo 2 vt ~ sth/sb (on sth) (with sth) darle golpecitos a algo/algn (en algo) (con algo): ~ sb on the back darle una palmadita a algn en la espalda 3 vt, vi ~ (into) explotar algo 4 vt (teléfono) intervenir

tape /teɪp/ n 1 cinta 2 cassette ● v 1 ~ sth (up) sujetar algo con cinta adhesiva 2 grabar

tape measure n cinta métrica

tape recorder n grabadora

tapestry /'tæpəstri/ n (pl **-ies**) tapiz

tar /tɑr/ n alquitrán

target /'tɑrɡɪt/ n 1 blanco 2 objetivo ● vt dirigir(se) a (un público)

tariff /'tærɪf/ n 1 tarifa 2 arancel

Tarmac® /'tɑrmæk/ n 1 asfalto 2 tarmac pista (aeropuerto)

tarnish /'tɑrnɪʃ/ 1 vt, vi deslucir(se) 2 vt desacreditar

tart /tɑrt/ n pay (dulce) →PIE

tartan /'tɑrtn/ n tela escocesa

task /tæsk; tɑːsk GB/ n tarea

taste /teɪst/ n 1 sabor 2 gusto 3 (comida, bebida) poquito 4 muestra: her first ~ of city life su primera experiencia de la vida de ciudad ● 1 vt, vi encontrarle el sabor (a): I can't ~ anything. No me sabe a nada. → HEAR 2 vi ~ (of sth) saber (a algo) 3 vt probar 4 vt experimentar **tasteful** adj de buen gusto **tasteless** adj 1 insípido 2 de mal gusto **tasty** adj (**-ier/-iest**) sabroso

tatters /'tætərz/ n [pl] harapos ▸ **in tatters** hecho jirones/pedazos **tattered** adj hecho jirones

tattoo /tæ'tuː; tə'tuː GB/ n tatuaje ● vt tatuar

tatty /'tæti/ adj (GB, coloq) en mal estado

taught /tɔːt/ pt, pp de TEACH

taunt /tɔːnt/ vt burlarse de ● n burla

Taurus /'tɔːrəs/ n Tauro

taut /tɔːt/ adj estirado, tenso

tavern /'tævərn/ n taberna

tax /tæks/ n impuesto: ~ return declaración de (la) renta ● vt 1 gravar con un impuesto 2 (persona) imponer contribuciones a 3 (paciencia, etc.) poner a prueba **taxable** adj gravable **taxation** n (recaudación de) impuestos **taxing** adj extenuante

tax-free adj libre de impuestos

taxi /'tæksi/ n (tb **taxicab** /'tæksikæb/) taxi: ~ driver taxista ● vi (pt/pp **-ied** pt pres **taxiing**) carretear (avión)

taxpayer /'tækspeɪər/ n contribuyente

tea /tiː/ n 1 té 2 merienda, onces (And) 3 (GB) cena, comida (And) →DINNER

teach /tiːtʃ/ (pt/pp **taught**) 1 vt enseñar 2 vt, vi dar clases (de) ▸ **teach sb a lesson** darle a algn una lección (como castigo) **teaching** n enseñanza: ~ materials materiales didácticos

teacher /ˈtiːtʃər/ n profesor/a

teacup /ˈtiːkʌp/ n taza para té

team /tiːm/ n equipo →JURADO ▶ **team up** formar equipo

teamwork /ˈtiːmwɜːrk/ n trabajo en equipo

teapot /ˈtiːpɒt/ n tetera

tear¹ /tɪər/ n lágrima: *be in ~s* estar llorando ▶ **bring tears to sb's eyes** hacerle llorar a algn **tearful** adj lloroso

tear² /teər/ (pt **tore** pp **torn**) **1** vt, vi rasgar(se) **2** vt ~ **sth up** hacer algo pedazos **3** vt ~ **sth out** arrancar algo **4** vi ~ **along/past** ir/pasar a toda velocidad ▶ **be torn between A and B** no poder decidirse entre A y B **tear sth down** derribar algo ● n desgarrón

tea room (tb **tea shop**) n (GB) salón de té

tease /tiːz/ vt tomarle el pelo a

teaspoon /ˈtiːspuːn/ n **1** cucharita **2** (tb **teaspoonful**) cucharadita

teatime /ˈtiːtaɪm/ n hora del té

technical /ˈteknɪkl/ adj **1** técnico **2** según la ley: *a ~ point* una cuestión de forma **technicality** /ˌteknɪˈkæləti/ n (pl **-ies**) **1** detalle técnico **2** formalismo **technically** adv **1** técnicamente **2** estrictamente

technician /tekˈnɪʃn/ n técnico/a

technique /tekˈniːk/ n técnica

technology /tekˈnɒlədʒi/ n (pl **-ies**) tecnología **technological** /ˌteknəˈlɒdʒɪkl/ adj tecnológico

teddy bear /ˈtedi beər/ n osito de peluche/felpa

tedious /ˈtiːdiəs/ adj tedioso **tedium** n tedio

teem /tiːm/ vi ~ **with sth** estar repleto de algo

teenage /ˈtiːneɪdʒ/ adj adolescente, de adolescentes **teenager** n adolescente

teens /tiːnz/ n [pl] adolescencia

tee shirt = T-SHIRT

teeth /tiːθ/ pl de TOOTH

teethe /tiːð/ vi salírsele los dientes (niño) ▶ **teething problems/ troubles** problemas iniciales

telecommunications /ˌtelɪkəˌmjuːnɪˈkeɪʃnz/ n [pl] telecomunicaciones

teleconference /ˈtelɪkɒnfərəns/ n teleconferencia

telegraph /ˈtelɪɡræf; -ɡrɑːf GB/ n telégrafo

telephone /ˈtelɪfəʊn/ n teléfono: *~ book* directorio (telefónico) ◊ *~ call* llamada ▶ **be on the telephone 1** estar hablando por teléfono **2** (GB) tener teléfono ● vt, vi llamar por teléfono

telephone box n (GB) cabina/caseta (telefónica)

telescope /ˈtelɪskəʊp/ n telescopio

television /ˈtelɪvɪʒn/ (abrev **TV**) (tb **telly** /ˈteli/ GB, coloq) n **1** televisión **2** (tb ~ **set**) televisor **televise** /ˈtelɪvaɪz/ vt televisar

tell /tel/ (pt/pp **told**) **1** vt decir: *~ the truth* decir la verdad **NOTA** En estilo indirecto **tell** suele ir seguido de un objeto directo de persona: *Tell him to wait.* Dile que espere. ◊ *She told him to come.* Le dijo que viniera. →SAY, ORDER **2** vt contar **3** vt, vi saber: *You never can ~.* Nunca se sabe. ◊ *You can ~ she's French.* Se nota que es francesa. **4** vt ~ **A from B** distinguir A de B ▶ **I told you (so)** (coloq) te lo dije **tell time (the time** GB) decir la hora **there's no telling** es imposible saberlo **you're telling me!** (coloq) ¡me lo vas a decir a mí! ■ **tell sb off** (for sth) (coloq) regañar a algn (por algo) **tell on sb** (coloq) soplarle a algn sobre algn

telling /ˈtelɪŋ/ adj significativo

telling-off n (pl **tellings-off**) (GB) regaño, bronca

temp /temp/ n empleado/a temporal

temper /ˈtempər/ vt templar ● n humor, genio: *in a bad ~* de mal genio ▶ **have a short temper** tener mal genio **keep/lose your temper** dominarse/perder los estribos

temperament /ˈtemprəmənt/ n temperamento **temperamental** /ˌtemprəˈmentl/ adj temperamental

temperate /ˈtempərət/ adj (clima) templado

temperature /ˈtemprətʃər/ n **1** temperatura **2** (Med) fiebre

template /ˈtemplət/ n plantilla

temple /ˈtempl/ n **1** (Rel) templo **2** (Anat) sien

tempo /ˈtempəʊ/ n **1** (Mús) (pl **tempi** /-piː/) tiempo **2** (pl **-s**) ritmo

temporary /ˈtempəreri; -prəri GB/ adj temporal, provisional

tempt /tempt/ vt tentar **temptation** n tentación **tempting** adj tentador

ten /ten/ adj, n, pron diez **tenner** n (coloq) (billete de) diez libras

tenacious /təˈneɪʃəs/ adj tenaz **tenacity** /təˈnæsəti/ n tenacidad

tenant /'tenənt/ n inquilino/a **tenancy** n (pl -ies) arrendamiento

tend /tend/ **1** vt cuidar, atender **2** vi ~ **to (do sth)** tender a (hacer algo) **tendency** n (pl -ies) tendencia

tender /'tendər/ adj **1** tierno **2** (herida) adolorido **tenderness** n ternura

tendon /'tendən/ n tendón

tenement /'tenəmənt/ n: a ~ block un edificio de apartamentos

tenner /'tenər/ n (GB, coloq) (billete de) diez libras

tennis /'tenɪs/ n tenis

tenor /'tenər/ n tenor

tense /tens/ adj tenso ● n (Gram) tiempo **tension** n tensión

tent /tent/ n tienda, carpa (And)

tentacle /'tentəkl/ n tentáculo

tentative /'tentətɪv/ adj **1** provisional **2** cauteloso

tenth (abrev **10th**) adj, adv, n, pron décimo

tenuous /'tenjuəs/ adj tenue

tenure /'tenjər/ n (puesto) titularidad **2** (propiedad) tenencia

tepid /'tepɪd/ adj tibio

term /tɜːrm/ n **1** período, plazo: ~ of office mandato (de un gobierno) **2** trimestre **3** término ▶ **in the long/short term** a largo/corto plazo ● vt (fml) calificar de

terminal /'tɜːrmɪnl/ adj, n terminal

terminate /'tɜːrmɪneɪt/ (fml) **1** vt, vi terminar **2** vt (contrato, etc.) rescindir

terminology /ˌtɜːrmɪ'nɑlədʒi/ n (pl -ies) terminología

terminus /'tɜːrmɪnəs/ n (pl -ni /-naɪ/ ~es) (estación) terminal

terms /tɜːrmz/ n [pl] **1** condiciones **2** términos ▶ **be on good, bad, etc. terms (with sb)** tener buenas, malas, etc. relaciones con algn **come to terms with sth/sb** aceptar algo/a algn

terrace /'terəs/ n **1** terraza **2** **the terraces** (Dep) las gradas **3** (GB) hilera de casas adosadas: terraced house casa adosada

terrain /tə'reɪn/ n terreno

terrible /'terəbl/ adj terrible **terribly** adv terriblemente: I'm ~ sorry. Lo siento muchísimo.

terrific /tə'rɪfɪk/ adj (coloq) **1** tremendo **2** fabuloso: It was ~ value. Fue baratísimo.

terrify /'terɪfaɪ/ vt (pt/pp -ied) aterrorizar **terrified** adj aterrorizado: She's ~ of flying. Le aterra volar. **terrifying** adj aterrador

territory /'terətɔːri; -tri GB/ n (pl -ies) territorio **territorial** /ˌterə-'tɔːriəl/ adj territorial

terror /'terər/ n terror **terrorize** vt aterrorizar

terrorism /'terərɪzəm/ n terrorismo **terrorist** n terrorista

terse /tɜːrs/ adj lacónico, seco

test /test/ n **1** prueba: blood ~ análisis de sangre **2** (Educ) examen, prueba ● vt **1** probar, poner a prueba **2** ~ **sth for sth** someter algo a pruebas de algo **3** ~ **sb (on sth)** (Educ) examinar a algn (en/sobre algo)

testament /'testəmənt/ n (fml) **1** testimonio **2** testamento

testicle /'testɪkl/ n testículo

testify /'testɪfaɪ/ vt, vi (pt/pp -ied) declarar

testimony /'testɪmouni; -məni GB/ n (pl -ies) testimonio

test tube n tubo de ensayo: test-tube baby bebé probeta

tether /'teðər/ vt (animal) amarrar ▶ n ▶ **be at the end of your tether** no poder más

text /tekst/ n texto: ~ (GB) lectura obligatoria ● vt mandar un mensaje de texto a

textbook /'tekstbʊk/ n libro de texto

textile /'tekstaɪl/ n textil

text message n mensaje (de texto)

texture /'tekstʃər/ n textura

than /ðən/ conj, prep **1** (+ comparativo) que: faster ~ ever más rápido que nunca **2** (seguido de número, etc.) de: more ~ an hour más de una hora

thank /θæŋk/ vt ~ **sb (for sth)** dar las gracias a algn (por algo), agradecerle algo a algn ▶ **thank you** (coloq **thanks**) gracias **thankful** adj agradecido

thanksgiving /ˌθæŋks'gɪvɪŋ/ n acción de gracias: Thanksgiving (Day) día de Acción de Gracias **NOTA** Thanksgiving se celebra en EE.UU. el cuarto jueves de noviembre. Es tradicional comer pavo asado (**turkey**) y pay/pastel de calabaza (**pumpkin pie**).

that /ðæt/ adj, pron (pl **those**) ese/a, eso, aquel/la, aquello ▶ **that is (to say)** es decir **that's right/it** eso es ● adv tan: It's ~ long. Es así de largo. ◇ ~ much worse tanto peor ● pron rel que: the horse ~ won el caballo que ganó ◇ the job ~ I applied for el trabajo que solicité ◇ the year ~ he died el año en que murió →QUE[1] ● /ðət/ conj que: I told him he should wait. Le dije que debía esperar.

thatch /θætʃ/ vt poner un techo de paja **thatched** adj con techo de paja

thaw /θɔː/ vt, vi descongelar(se) ● n deshielo

the /ðə/ **NOTA** Antes de vocal se pronuncia /ði/. **art def** el/la/lo, los/las ▸ **the more/less... the more/less...** cuanto más/menos...más/menos... **NOTA El artículo definido en inglés:**

1 No se usa con sustantivos contables en plural al hablar en general: *Books are expensive.* ◊ *Children learn fast.*

2 Se omite con sustantivos incontables al referirse a una sustancia o idea en general: *I like cheese/pop music.*

3 Suele omitirse con nombres propios y con los que indican relaciones familiares: *Mrs. Smith* ◊ *Ana's mother* ◊ *Grandma came yesterday.*

4 Con las partes del cuerpo y los objetos personales se suele usar el posesivo en vez del artículo: *Give me your hand.* ◊ *He put his tie on.*

5 *Hospital*, *school* y *church* pueden usarse con artículo o sin él, pero el significado es distinto. →SCHOOL

theater (*theatre* GB) /ˈθiːətər/ n teatro **theatrical** /θiˈætrɪkl/ adj teatral, de teatro

theft /θeft/ n robo →THIEF

their /ðeər/ adj su(s) (de ellos) →MY, THEY

theirs /ðeərz/ pron suyo (de ellos)

them /ðəm, ðem/ pron **1** [*objeto directo*] los, las **2** [*objeto indirecto*] les **3** [*después de prep o verbo be*] ellos/ellas →THEY

theme /θiːm/ n tema

theme park n parque temático/de diversiones

themselves /ðəmˈselvz/ pron **1** [*reflexivo*] se: *They enjoyed ~ a lot.* Se divirtieron mucho. **2** [*después de prep*] sí (mismos/as) **3** [*énfasis*] ellos/as mismos/as ▸ **(all) by themselves** solos/as

then /ðen/ adv **1** entonces **2** en aquella época **3** luego, después **4** en ese caso, pues: *You're not coming, ~?* ¿Así que no vienes?

theology /θiˈɒlədʒi/ n teología **theological** /ˌθiːəˈlɒdʒɪkl/ adj teológico

theory /ˈθɪəri/ n (pl -ies) teoría **theoretical** /ˌθɪəˈretɪkl/ adj teórico

therapeutic /ˌθerəˈpjuːtɪk/ adj terapéutico

therapy /ˈθerəpi/ n (pl -ies) terapia **therapist** n terapeuta

there /ðeər/ adv ahí, allí, allá ▸ **there and then** en el acto, ahí mismo ● pron ▸ **there + be**: *How many are ~?* ¿Cuántos hay? ◊ *There was an accident yesterday.* Hubo un accidente ayer. → HABER **there + v modal + be**: *There might be rain later.* Podría haber chubascos más tarde. ◊ *There shouldn't be any problems.* No debería haber ningún problema. **NOTA** Se usa también con *seem* y *appear*: *There seem/appear to be two possible approaches.*

thereafter /ˌðeərˈæftər; -ˈɑːf- GB/ adv (fml) a partir de entonces

thereby /ˌðeərˈbaɪ/ adv (fml) **1** por eso/ello **2** de este modo

therefore /ˈðeərfɔːr/ adv por (lo) tanto, por consiguiente

thermal /ˈθɜːrml/ adj **1** térmico **2** (*fuente*) termal

thermometer /θərˈmɒmɪtər/ n termómetro

thermostat /ˈθɜːrməstæt/ n termostato

these /ðiːz/ adj, pron [pl] estos/as

thesis /ˈθiːsɪs/ n (pl theses /-siːz/) tesis

they /ðeɪ/ pron ellos/ellas **NOTA** *They*, *their* y *them* también se usan para referirse a una sola persona cuando no se sabe o no se especifica el sexo: *If one of Tim's friends calls, tell them he's not well.* El pron pers no puede omitirse en inglés.

they'd /ðeɪd/ **1** = THEY HAD **2** = THEY WOULD

they'll /ðeɪl/ = THEY WILL

they're /ðeər/ = THEY ARE

they've /ðeɪv/ = THEY HAVE

thick /θɪk/ adj (-er/-est) **1** grueso: *The ice was an inch ~.* El hielo tenía dos centímetros de grosor. **2** espeso **3** (*barba*) poblado **4** (*acento*) marcado **5** (GB, coloq) estúpido ● adj (tb thickly) espeso: *Don't spread the butter too ~.* No te pongas demasiada mantequilla. ● n ▸ **in the thick of sth** en medio de algo ▸ **through thick and thin** contra viento y marea **thicken** vt, vi espesar(se) **thickly** adv **1** espesamente **2** (*poblado*) densamente **thickness** n espesor, grosor

thief /θiːf/ n (pl thieves /θiːvz/) ladrón/ona **NOTA** *Thief* es el término general para un ladrón que roba cosas, generalmente sin que nadie lo vea y sin violencia. Un **robber** roba bancos, tiendas, etc., a menudo con violencia o amenazas, un **burglar** roba en una casa o tienda cuando no hay nadie, y un **shoplifter** se lleva cosas de una tienda sin pagarlas. Los delitos se llaman **theft, robbery, burglary** y **shoplifting**.

thigh /θaɪ/ n muslo

thimble /'θɪmbl/ n dedal

thin /θɪn/ (**thinner, -est**) adj 1 (persona) delgado, flaco → DELGADO 2 fino 3 (sopa) aguado ▸ **thin on the ground** escaso **vanish, etc. into thin air** desaparecer sin dejar rastro ● adv (tb **thinly**) fino ● vt, vi (**-nn-**) (**sth**) (**out**) hacer(se) (algo) menos denso

thing /θɪŋ/ n 1 cosa: Put your ~s there. Pon tus cosas allá. ◊ What's that ~? ¿Qué es eso? ◊ I can't see a ~. No veo nada. ◊ the first/main ~ lo primero/más importante ◊ Forget the whole ~. Olvídate del asunto. ◊ The way ~s are going... Tal como está la situación... 2 Poor (little) ~! ¡Pobrecito! 3 **the thing**: Just the ~ for students. Justo lo que necesitan los estudiantes. ▸ **be a good thing (that)...** menos mal que(...). **first/last thing** a primera/última hora **for one thing** para empezar **the thing is...** (coloq) la cosa es que...

thingummy /'θɪŋəmi/ (tb **thingy** /'θɪŋi/) n (pl **-ies** o **-ies**) 1 chisme (Mx), vaina (And) 2 Is ~ going? Do you know who I mean? ¿Va a estar aquél? ¿Sabes a quién me refiero?

think /θɪŋk/ (pt/pp **thought**) 1 vt, vi pensar: Who'd have thought it? ¿Quién lo hubiera pensado? ◊ Just ~! ¡Imagínate! 2 vi reflexionar 3 vt creer: I (don't) ~ so. Creo que sí/no. ◊ What do you ~? ¿Qué opinas? ◊ It's nice, don't you ~? Está bien, ¿no te parece? ▸ **I should think so!** ¡no faltaría más! **think the world of sb** tener a algn en alta estima ■ **think about sth/sb** 1 pensar en algo/algn 2 recordar algo/a algn 3 tener algo/a algn en cuenta **think about (doing)** pensar en (hacer) algo **think of sth** 1 pensar en algo 2 imaginar algo 3 recordar algo **think sth out:** a well thought out plan un plan bien pensado **think sth over** reflexionar sobre algo **think sth up** (coloq) inventar, pensar algo **thinker** n pensador/a

thinking /'θɪŋkɪŋ/ n [U] forma de pensar: Quick ~! ¡Bien pensado!

● adj [antes de sustantivo] inteligente

third /θɜːd/ (abrev **3rd**) adj, adv, pron tercero ● n 1 tercio 2 **the third** el (día) tres 3 (tb ~ **gear**) tercera **thirdly** adv en tercer lugar (en enumeración)

third party n tercera persona

the Third World n el Tercer Mundo

thirst /θɜːst/ n ~ (**for sth**) sed (de algo) **thirsty** adj (**-ier/-iest**) sediento: be ~ tener sed

thirteen /ˌθɜː'tiːn/ adj, pron, n trece **thirteenth** 1 adj, adv, pron decimotercero 2 n treceavo

thirty /'θɜːti/ adj, pron, n treinta **thirtieth** 1 adj, pron trigésimo 2 n treintavo

this /ðɪs/ adj, pron (pl **these**) este/a, esto ● adv: ~ high así de alto ◊ ~ far tan lejos

thistle /'θɪsl/ n cardo

thorn /θɔːn/ n espina (rosal, etc.) **thorny** adj (**-ier/-iest**) espinoso

thorough /'θʌrə; 'θɜːrə GB/ adj 1 a fondo 2 (persona) meticuloso **thoroughly** adv 1 a conciencia 2 enormemente

those /ðəʊz/ adj, pron [pl] aquellos/as, esos/as

though /ðəʊ/ conj aunque, pero → AUNQUE ● adv de todas formas

thought /θɔːt/ pt, pp de THINK ● n 1 pensamiento 2 ~ (**of sth**) idea (de algo) **thoughtful** adj 1 pensativo 2 atento: It was very ~ of you. Fue todo un detalle de tu parte. **thoughtless** adj desconsiderado

thousand /'θaʊznd/ adj, pron, n mil → MIL **thousandth** 1 adj milésimo 2 n milésima parte

thrash /θræʃ/ vt dar una paliza a **thrashing** n paliza

thread /θred/ n hilo ● vt 1 ensartar 2 (cuerda, etc.) pasar

threat /θret/ n amenaza **threaten** vt ~ (**to do sth**) amenazar (con hacer algo) **threatening** adj amenazador

three /θriː/ adj, pron, n tres

three-dimensional (tb **3-D** /ˌθriː 'diː/) adj tridimensional

threshold /'θreʃhəʊld/ n umbral

threw /θruː/ pt de THROW

thrill /θrɪl/ n 1 emoción 2 escalofrío **thrilled** adj entusiasmado **thriller** n obra de suspenso **thrilling** adj emocionante

thrive /θraɪv/ vi ~ (**on sth**) prosperar, crecer (con algo): a thriving industry una industria floreciente

throat /θrəʊt/ n garganta

throb /θrɒb/ vi (-bb-) vibrar, palpitar ● n vibración, palpitación

throne /θroʊn/ n trono

through (tb thru USA, coloq) /θruː/ adj (tren, etc.) directo: No ~ road Callejón sin salida ● prep **1** a través de, por **2** durante, a lo largo de: I'm halfway ~ the book. Ya voy por la mitad del libro. **3** por (culpa de): ~ carelessness por descuido **4** por (medio de): I got the job ~ Dan. Conseguí el trabajo por medio de Dan. **5** (USA) hasta... inclusive: Monday ~ Friday de lunes a viernes **NOTA** Para el uso de through en PHRASAL VERBS ver el verbo, p.ej. break through en BREAK. ● adv **1** de un lado a otro: Can you get ~? ¿Puedes pasar al otro lado? **2** de principio a fin: I read the poem ~ once. Me leí el poema entero una vez. ◇ ~ all night ~ durante toda la noche

throughout /θruːˈaʊt/ prep **1** por, durante todo ● adv **1** por todas partes **2** todo el tiempo

throw /θroʊ/ n **1** lanzamiento **2** tiro: It's your ~. Te toca a ti. ● vt (pt threw pp thrown) **1** ~ sth (to sb) tirar algo (a algn) **2** ~ sth (at sb/sth) tirar, lanzar algo (a algo/algn) (con intención de darle a un objeto/hacerle daño a una persona) **3** [+ adv] echar: ~ back your head echar la cabeza atrás ◇ ~ up your hands in horror levantar los brazos horrorizado **4** (caballo, etc.) arrojar **5** (coloq) desconcertar **6** dejar (de cierta forma): We were thrown into confusion by the news. La noticia nos dejó confusos. ◇ be thrown out of work quedarse sin trabajo **7** (luz, etc.) proyectar ● **throw a wobbly** (GB, coloq) armar un escándalo ■ **throw sth about/around** desparramar algo **throw sth out** expulsar a algn **throw sth out** (tb ~ sth away) tirar algo (a la basura) **2** (propuesta, etc.) rechazar **throw (sth) up** vomitar (algo)

thrust /θrʌst/ (pt/pp thrust) vt **1** meter, clavar **2** ~ sth at sb lanzar algo a algn (de malas maneras) ■ **thrust sth/sb on/upon sth** obligar a algn a aceptar algo/algn ● n **1** empujón **2** (espada) estocada **3** ~ (of sth) idea fundamental (sobre algo)

thud /θʌd/ n ruido, golpe (sordo) ● vi (-dd-) **1** caer con un ruido sordo: ~ against/into sth chocar contra algo con un ruido sordo **2** (corazón) latir con fuerza

thug /θʌɡ/ n matón

thumb /θʌm/ n pulgar ● vi ~ **through sth** hojear algo ▸ **thumb a lift** pedir aventón, echar dedo

thumbtack /ˈθʌmtæk/ n (USA) chinche

thump /θʌmp/ vt golpear **2** vi (corazón) latir con fuerza ● n **1** puñetazo, golpazo **2** ruido sordo

thunder /ˈθʌndər/ n [U] trueno ● vi **1** tronar **2** retumbar

thunderstorm /ˈθʌndərstɔːrm/ n tormenta (eléctrica)

Thursday /ˈθɜːrzdeɪ, -di/ n (abrev Thur(s).) jueves

thus /ðʌs/ adv (fml) **1** así, de esta manera **2** por (lo) tanto

thwart /θwɔːrt/ vt frustrar

tick /tɪk/ n **1** (reloj, etc.) tictac **2** (marca) visto bueno, tic, palomita (Mx) ● vi **1** (reloj, etc.) hacer tictac **2** vt (GB) marcar (con tic/señal) ■ **tick away/by** pasar (tiempo) **tick sth/sb off** (GB) tachar algo a algn (de una lista) **tick over** (GB) **1** (motor) estar andando **2** (Com) mantenerse a flote

ticket /ˈtɪkɪt/ n **1** (tren, etc.) boleto, tiquete **2** (Teat, Cine) entrada, boleta (And) **3** (GB, biblioteca) tarjeta, carné **4** etiqueta

tickle /ˈtɪkl/ vt, vi hacer cosquillas (a) ● n cosquilleo, picor **ticklish** adj: be ~ tener cosquillas

tic-tac-toe /ˌtɪk tæk ˈtoʊ/ n (USA) gato (Mx), tres en línea (And)

tide /taɪd/ n **1** marea: high/low ~ marea alta/baja **2** (fig) corriente **tidal** adj (de la) marea: ~ wave maremoto

tidy /ˈtaɪdi/ adj (-ier/-iest) **1** ordenado **2** pulcro, aseado ● vt, vi (pt/pp -ied) ~ (sth) (up) arreglar, ordenar (algo): ~ sth away (GB) poner algo en su sitio

tie /taɪ/ n **1** corbata **2** lazo **3** (Dep) empate ● vt, vi (pt/pp tied pt pres tying) **1** ~ (sth/sb) (up) amarrar(se) (algo a algo/algn) **2** anudar(se) **3** (Dep) empatar ■ **tie sb/yourself down** atar(se) (algn): Having children ~s you down. Tener niños ata muchísimo.

tier /tɪər/ n grada, fila, piso

tiger /ˈtaɪɡər/ n tigre

tight /taɪt/ (-er/-est) adj **1** apretado, ajustado **2** tirante **3** (control) riguroso ● adv (tb tightly) bien, fuertemente: Hold ~! ¡Agárrese bien! **tighten** vt, vi ~ (sth) (up) apretar(se) (algo): ~ security hacer más rigurosa la seguridad

tightrope /'taɪtroʊp/ n cuerda floja

tights /taɪts/ n [pl] **1** (GB) pantimedia, medias (pantalón) (And) **2** (ballet, etc.) mallas →PAIR

tile /taɪl/ n **1** teja **2** azulejo **3** baldosa ● vt **1** tejar **2** revestir de azulejos **3** embaldosar

till conj, prep hasta (que) ● n (GB) caja (registradora)

tilt /tɪlt/ vt, vi inclinar(se), ladear(se) ● n inclinación, ladeo

timber /'tɪmbər/ n **1** madera **2** árboles (madereros) **3** madero, viga

time /taɪm/ n **1** tiempo: all the ~ todo el tiempo ◇ You've been a long ~! ¡Tardaste mucho! **2** hora: What ~ is it?/What's the ~? ¿Qué hora es? ◇ It's ~ we were going/~ for us to go. Es hora de que nos vayamos. ◇ by the ~ I reached home para cuando llegué a la casa ◇ (by) this ~ next year para esta época el año entrante ◇ at the present ~ actualmente **3** vez, ocasión: every ~ cada vez **4** época: at one ~ en cierta época ▶ (any) about time (too) (coloq) ya era hora at all times en todo momento at a time a la vez: one at a ~ de uno en uno at the same time en aquel momento at times a veces for a time durante algún tiempo for the time being por el momento from time to time de vez en cuando have a good time pasarla bien have the time of your life (coloq) pasarla de maravilla in good time temprano, con tiempo in time con el tiempo in time (for sth) a tiempo (para algo) on time a tiempo, puntual →PUNTUAL take your time (over sth) tomarse sin su tiempo (para algo) time after time; time and (time) again una y otra vez ● vt **1** programar, prever **2** ~ sth well/badly escoger un momento oportuno/inoportuno para algo ◇ cronometrar **timer** n reloj automático **timing** n coordinación: the ~ of the election la fecha escogida para las elecciones **2** cronometraje

time-consuming adj que exige mucho tiempo

timely /'taɪmli/ adj oportuno

times /taɪmz/ prep (multiplicado) por: Three ~ four is twelve. Cuatro por tres son doce.

timetable /'taɪmteɪbl/ n horario

timid /'tɪmɪd/ adj tímido

tin /tɪn/ n **1** estaño: ~ foil papel de aluminio **2** lata **tinned** adj (GB) enlatado

tinge /tɪndʒ/ vt ~ sth (with sth) teñir algo (de algo) ● n matiz

tingle /'tɪŋgl/ vi **1** hormiguear **2** ~ with sth estremecerse de algo

tinker /'tɪŋkər/ vi juguetear (intentando arreglar algo)

tin-opener n (GB) abrelatas

tinsel /'tɪnsl/ n oropel, guirnalda dorada o plateada

tint /tɪnt/ n **1** matiz **2** (pelo) tintura **tinted** adj **1** (pelo) teñido **2** (lentes) ahumado

tiny /'taɪni/ adj (-ier/-iest) diminuto, minúsculo

tip /tɪp/ n **1** punta **2** (GB, lugar) basurero **3** propina **4** consejo ● (-pp-) **1** vt, vi ~ (sth) (up) inclinar(se) (algo) **2** vt tirar, botar **3** vt dar (una) propina (a) ■ **tip sth off** (coloq) avisar a algn **tip (sth) over** volcar(se) (algo)

tiptoe /'tɪptoʊ/ n ▶ on tiptoe de puntillas ● vi: ~ in/out entrar/salir de puntillas

tire /'taɪər/ n **1** llanta ● vt, vi cansar(se) ■ **tire sb/yourself out** agotar(se) (a algn)

tired /'taɪərd/ adj cansado → BE ▶ (sick and) tired of sth/sb harto/jarto de algo/algn **tired out** agotado

tireless /'taɪərləs/ adj incansable

tiresome /'taɪərsəm/ adj **1** (tarea) tedioso **2** (persona) pesado

tiring /'taɪrɪŋ/ adj cansado, cansador (And) →BE

tissue /'tɪʃuː/ n **1** (Biol) tejido **2** pañuelo de papel, Kleenex® **3** (tb ~ paper) papel de seda/china

tit /tɪt/ n **1** (coloq) teta **2** (pájaro) herrerillo ▶ tit for tat ojo por ojo, diente por diente

title /'taɪtl/ n **1** título: ~ role papel principal ◇ ~ page portada **2** título nobiliario **3** tratamiento **4** ~ (to sth) (Jur) derecho a (algo): ~ deed título de propiedad

titter /'tɪtər/ n risita ● vi reírse disimuladamente

to /tə, tuː/ prep **1** (dirección) a: the road to York la carretera a York **2** (con objeto indirecto) a: He gave it to Bob. Se lo dio a Bob. **3** hacia **4** hasta **5** (duración): It lasts two to three hours. Dura entre dos y tres horas. **6** (hora): ten to one diez para la una **7** de: the key to the door la llave de la puerta **8** (comparación) a: I prefer cycling to climbing. Prefiero el ciclismo al alpinismo. **9** (proporción) por: How many kilometers does it do to the liter? ¿Cuántos kilómetros hace por litro?

10 (*propósito*): go to sb's aid ir en ayuda de algn **11** para: *to my surprise* para mi sorpresa **12** (*opinión*) a, para: *It looks red to me.* A mí me parece rojo. **NOTA** To se usa para formar el infinitivo: *to go* ◇ *I came to see you.* Vine para/a verte. ◇ *I don't know what to do.* No sé qué hacer. ◇ *It's for you to decide.* Tiene que decidirlo usted.

toad /toʊd/ n sapo

toadstool /ˈtoʊdstuːl/ n hongo no comestible

toast /toʊst/ n **1** [U] pan tostado **2** brindis ● vt **1** tostar **2** brindar por **toaster** n tostador(a)

tobacco /təˈbækoʊ/ n (*pl* -s) tabaco **tobacconist's** n tabaquería

toboggan /təˈbɑɡən/ n trineo

today /təˈdeɪ/ *adv, n* hoy (en día)

toddler /ˈtɑdlər/ n niño/a (que acaba de aprender a caminar)

toe /toʊ/ n **1** dedo (*del pie*): *big ~* dedo gordo **2** (*calcetín/media*) punta **3** (*zapato*) puntera ▸ **to be on your toes** alerta ● vt (*pt/pp* toed *pt pres* toeing) ▸ **to toe the line** conformarse

toenail /ˈtoʊneɪl/ n uña del pie

toffee /ˈtɔːfi; ˈtɒfi GB/ n caramelo

together /təˈɡeðər/ *adv* **1** juntos **2** a la vez ▸ **together with** junto con, además de **NOTA** Para el uso de **together** en PHRASAL VERBS ver el verbo, p. ej. **go together** en GO. **togetherness** n unidad, armonía

toil /tɔɪl/ (*fml*) vi trabajar duramente ● n trabajo, esfuerzo

toilet /ˈtɔɪlət/ n inodoro, baño, excusado: *~ paper* papel higiénico **NOTA** En EE.UU. el baño de las casas particulares se dice **bathroom**, y el de los edificios públicos es **bathroom** o **restroom**. En Gran Bretaña se dice **toilet** o **loo** (*coloq*) para una casa particular, y **the Gents/the Ladies**, **the toilets**, o **the cloakroom** para los lugares públicos. **toiletries** n productos de tocador

token /ˈtoʊkən/ n **1** señal, muestra **2** ficha **3** vale ● *adj* [*antes de sustantivo*] simbólico

told /toʊld/ *pt, pp* de TELL

tolerate /ˈtɑləreɪt/ vt tolerar **tolerance** n tolerancia **tolerant** *adj* tolerante

toll /toʊl/ n **1** peaje **2** número de víctimas ▸ **take its toll (on sth)** hacerse sentir (en algo)

tomato /təˈmeɪtoʊ; təˈmɑːtoʊ GB/ n (*pl* -es) tomate, jitomate (*Mx*)

tomb /tuːm/ n tumba

tombstone /ˈtuːmstoʊn/ n lápida

tomcat /ˈtɑmkæt/ (*tb* tom) n gato (macho) →GATO

tomorrow /təˈmɑroʊ/ *adv, n* mañana: *~ morning* mañana en la mañana ◇ *a week ~* dentro de ocho días

ton /tʌn/ n **1** tonelada (*907 kg, 1.016 kg GB*) →Ver pág. 222 **2 tons** (*coloq*) montones

tone /toʊn/ n **1** tono **2** tonalidad ■ **tone sth down** suavizar (el tono de) algo

tongs /tɑŋz/ n [*pl*] tenazas →PAIR

tongue /tʌŋ/ n **1** lengua: *stick your ~ out* sacar la lengua **2** (*fml*) idioma: *mother ~* lengua materna ▸ **(with) tongue in cheek** irónicamente

tonic /ˈtɑnɪk/ n **1** tónico **2** (*tb ~ water*) tónica, agua quina (*Mx*)

tonight /təˈnaɪt/ *adv, n* esta noche

tonne /tʌn/ n tonelada (métrica)

tonsil /ˈtɑnsl/ n amígdala **tonsillitis** /ˌtɑnsəˈlaɪtɪs/ n amigdalitis

too /tuː/ *adv* **1** también →TAMBIÉN **2** demasiado **3** para colmo, encima **4** muy: *I'm not ~ sure.* No estoy muy segura. ▸ **too much/many** demasiado(s)

took /tʊk/ *pt* de TAKE

tool /tuːl/ n herramienta

toolbar /ˈtuːlbɑːr/ n barra de herramientas

tooth /tuːθ/ n (*pl* teeth) diente, muela: *false teeth* dentadura postiza ▸ **tooth and nail** a brazo partido

toothache /ˈtuːθeɪk/ n dolor de muelas

toothbrush /ˈtuːθbrʌʃ/ n cepillo de dientes

toothpaste /ˈtuːθpeɪst/ n pasta de dientes

toothpick /ˈtuːθpɪk/ n palillo

top /tɑp/ n **1** lo más alto, la parte de arriba: *the ~ of the page* la parte de arriba de la página **2** (*colina*) cumbre **3** (*lista*) cabeza **4** tapón **5** blusa, camiseta, top **6** trompo ▸ **at the top of your voice** a gritos de (*sth*) dominar (algo) **off the top of your head** (*coloq*) sin pensarlo **on top** encima **on top of sth/sb 1** sobre algo/algn **2** además de algo/algn: *On ~ of all that...* Y para colmo... ● *adj* **1** superior: *~ floor* el piso de arriba ◇ *the ~ jobs* los mejores empleos ◇ *a ~ scientist* un científico de primera categoría **2** máximo ● vt (-pp-) rematar: *coffee topped with cream* café con crema por encima ■ **top sth up** rellenar algo

top hat (tb **topper**) /'tɒpər/ n sombrero de copa

topic /'tɒpɪk/ n tema **topical** adj actual

topple /'tɒpl/ vt, vi ~ (sth) (over) caerse, hacer caer algo

top secret adj reservado, secreto

torch /tɔːtʃ/ n 1 (GB) linterna 2 antorcha

tore /tɔːr/ pt de TEAR²

torment /'tɔːrment/ n (fml) tormento ● /tɔːr'ment/ vt 1 (fml) atormentar 2 martirizar

torn /tɔːrn/ pp de TEAR²

tornado /tɔːr'neɪdoʊ/ n (pl -es) tornado

torpedo /tɔːr'piːdoʊ/ n (pl -es) torpedo ● vt (pt/pp -oed pt pres -oing) torpedear

tortoise /'tɔːrtəs/ n tortuga (de tierra)

torture /'tɔːtʃər/ n tortura ● vt torturar **torturer** n torturador/a

Tory /'tɔːri/ adj, n (pl -ies) (coloq) conservador/a (en Gran Bretaña)

toss /tɔːs/ 1 vt, vi tirar, echar (descuidadamente) 2 vt (cabeza) sacudir 3 vi agitarse: ~ and turn dar vueltas (en la cama) 4 vt (moneda) tirar a cara o cruz: ~ sb for sth jugarle algo a algn a cara o cruz 5 vi: ~ (up) for sth sortear algo con una moneda ● n 1 (cabeza) sacudida 2 (moneda) tirada: win the ~ ganar al tirar la moneda

total /'toʊtl/ adj, n total ● vt (-ll-, tb -l- USA) 1 sumar 2 ascender a **totally** adv totalmente

totter /'tɒtər/ vi 1 titubear 2 tambalearse

touch /tʌtʃ/ 1 vt, vi tocar(se) 2 vt rozar 3 vt [frases negativas] probar (comida) 4 vt conmover 5 vt igualar ▶ **touch wood** (GB) tocar madera ● **touch down** aterrizar **touch on/upon sth** hablar de pasada de algo ● n 1 toque: put the finishing touches to sth dar el toque final a algo 2 roce 3 (tb sense of ~) tacto 4 a ~ (of sth) una pizca, un poco (de algo) 5 maña: lose your ~ perder facultades ▶ **be in/out of touch with sb** estar/no estar al corriente de algo **get/keep in touch with sb** ponerse/mantenerse en contacto con algn **in/out of touch (with sb)** en/fuera de contacto (con algn)

touched /tʌtʃt/ adj conmovido **touching** adj conmovedor

touchy /'tʌtʃi/ adj (-ier/-iest) 1 susceptible 2 (tema) delicado

tough /tʌf/ adj (-er/-est) 1 duro: get ~ with sb ponerse duro con algn 2 fuerte, sólido 3 tenaz 4 (medida) severo 5 (decisión, etc.) difícil: have a ~ time pasarla muy mal 6 (coloq): Tough luck! ¡Mala suerte! ▶ **(as) tough as old boots** (coloq) duro, resistente **toughen** vt, vi ~ (sth) (up) endurecer(se) (algo) **toughness** n 1 dureza, resistencia 2 firmeza

tour /tʊər/ n 1 excursión 2 visita 3 gira →VIAJE 1 vt recorrer 2 vi viajar 3 vt, vi efectuar una gira (en)

tourism /'tʊərɪzəm/ n turismo **tourist** n turista: ~ attraction/ guide lugar de interés turístico/ guía turística

tournament /'tʊərnəmənt/ n torneo

tow /toʊ/ vt remolcar: ~ sth away llevarse algo a remolque ● n remolque ▶ **in tow** (coloq): He had his family in ~. Iba con la familia detrás.

towards /tɔːrdz; tə'wɔːdz GB/ (tb **toward**) prep 1 hacia: ~ the end of the movie casi al final de la película 2 con, respecto a: be friendly ~ sb ser amable con algn 3 (propósito) para

towel /'taʊəl/ n toalla

tower /'taʊər/ n torre: ~ block (GB) bloque alto de apartamentos ■ **tower above/over sth/sb** alzarse por encima de algo/algn

town /taʊn/ n 1 ciudad →CIUDAD 2 centro: go into ~ ir al centro ▶ **go to town** (coloq) tirar la casa por la ventana (out) **on the town** (coloq) de parranda

town hall n ayuntamiento, alcaldía

toxic /'tɒksɪk/ adj tóxico

toy /tɔɪ/ n juguete ■ **toy with sth** 1 juguetear con algo 2 ~ with the idea of doing sth considerar la idea de hacer algo

trace /treɪs/ n rastro, huella ● vt 1 seguir la pista de 2 ~ sth/sb (to sth) dar con algo/algn (en algo) 3 remontar(se) 4 ~ sth (out) delinear, trazar algo 5 calcar

track /træk/ n 1 huella (animal, rueda, etc.): be on sb's ~ seguir la pista a algn 2 camino 3 (Dep) pista, circuito 4 (tren) vía 5 (Mús) canción ▶ **keep/lose track of sth/ sb** seguir/perder la pista de algo/algn: ~ lose ~ of time perder la noción del tiempo **make tracks (for...)** (coloq) irse (a...) **off track** fuera de rumbo en **the right/ wrong track** por buen/mal camino ● vt seguir la pista/las huellas de ■ **track sth/sb down** localizar algo/a algn

tracksuit /'træksuːt/ n (GB) pants (Mx), sudadera (And)

tractor /'træktər/ n tractor

trade /treɪd/ n 1 comercio 2 industria: ~ union (GB) sindicato (laboral) 3 oficio →WORK ● 1 vi comerciar 2 vi ~ (sb) sth for sth cambiar (a algn) algo por otro ■ **trade sth in (for sth)** dar algo en parte de pago (de algo) **trader** n comerciante **tradesman** n (pl -men) 1 proveedor: tradesmen's entrance entrada de servicio 2 comerciante **trading** n comercio

trademark /'treɪdmɑrk/ n marca registrada

tradition /trə'dɪʃn/ n tradición **traditional** adj tradicional

traffic /'træfɪk/ n tránsito, tráfico: ~ jam embotellamiento ● vi (-ck-) ~ (in sth) traficar (con algo) **trafficker** n traficante

traffic circle n (USA) glorieta

traffic light (tb traffic lights [pl]) n semáforo

tragedy /'trædʒədi/ n (pl -ies) tragedia **tragic** adj trágico

trail /treɪl/ n 1 (humo) estela 2 (sangre) reguero 3 senda 4 rastro (de animal) 5 be on sb's ~ seguirle la pista a algn ● 1 vt, vi arrastrar: ~ your hand in the water dejar deslizar la mano por el agua 2 vi ~ along behind (sth/sb) caminar despacio detrás (de algo/algn) 3 vi ir perdiendo, estar atrasado

trailer /'treɪlər/ n 1 (USA) tráiler, casa rodante 2 remolque 3 (Cine) avance, cortos (And)

train /treɪn/ n 1 tren: ~ station estación de ferrocarril 2 serie ▸ **train of thought** hilo de ideas ● 1 vi estudiar, formarse 2 vt capacitar, preparar 3 vt adiestrar 4 vt, vi (Dep) entrenar(se) 5 vt ~ sth on sth/sb apuntar a algo/algn con algo **trainee** /treɪ'niː/ n aprendiz/a **trainer** n 1 (Dep) entrenador/a 2 (animales) domador/a 3 (GB) tenis (zapato) **training** n 1 (Dep) entrenamiento 2 capacitación

trait /treɪt/ n rasgo (carácter)

traitor /'treɪtər/ n traidor/a

tram /træm/ n (GB) tranvía

tramp /træmp/ n 1 vi caminar pesadamente 2 vt patear ● n vagabundo/a

trample /'træmpl/ vt, vi ~ sth/sb (down); ~ on sth/sb pisotear algo/a algn

trampoline /'træmpəliːn/ n (gimnasia) cama elástica, catre elástico

tranquilize /'træŋkwəlaɪz/ vt tranquilizar (esp por medio de sedantes) **tranquilizer** n tranquilizante: be on ~s tomar sedantes

transfer /træns'fɜːr/ (-rr-) 1 vt, vi trasladar(se) 2 vt transferir 3 vi hacer transbordo ● /'trænsfɜːr/ n 1 transferencia, traslado 2 (Dep) traspaso 3 transbordo 4 (GB) calcomanía

transform /træns'fɔːrm/ vt transformar **transformation** n transformación **transformer** n (Elec) transformador

translate /træns'leɪt/ vt, vi traducir(se) →INTERPRET **translation** n traducción: Borges in ~ Borges traducido **translator** n traductor/a

transmit /træns'mɪt/ vt (-tt-) transmitir **transmitter** n (Elec) transmisor, emisora

transparent /træns'pærənt/ adj 1 transparente 2 evidente

transplant /træns'plænt; -'plɑːnt GB/ vt trasplantar ● /'trænsplænt; -plɑːnt GB/ n trasplante

transport /træn'spɔːrt/ vt transportar **transportation** n (transport /'trænspɔːt/ GB) transporte

transvestite /træns'vestaɪt/ n travesti

trap /træp/ n trampa ● vt (-pp-) 1 atrapar 2 engañar

trapdoor /'træpdɔːr/ n trampilla

trapeze /træ'piːz; trə- GB/ n trapecio (circo)

trash /træʃ/ n (esp USA) [U] 1 basura: ~ can bote/caneca de basura ◊ It's ~. No vale para nada. **NOTA** En inglés británico trash sólo se usa en sentido figurado. 2 (coloq) gentuza **trashy** adj (coloq) malo

trauma /'trɔːmə; 'trɔːmə GB/ n trauma **traumatic** /trɑ'mætɪk; 'trɔː- GB/ adj traumático

travel /'trævl/ n 1 [U] los viajes, viajar 2 travels [pl]: on your ~s de viaje →VIAJE ● (-l-, -ll- GB) 1 vi viajar 2 vt recorrer **traveler** (-ll- GB) n viajero/a

travel agency n (pl -ies) agencia de viajes **travel agent** n empleado de agencia de viajes

tray /treɪ/ n bandeja, charola

treachery /'tretʃəri/ n traición **treacherous** adj traicionero, pérfido

tread /tred/ (pt trod pp trodden/ trod) 1 vi ~ (on/in sth) pisar (algo) 2 vt pisotear ▸ tread

carefully andar con pies de plomo ● n [sing] paso

treason /'tri:zn/ n alta traición **NOTA** Treason es un acto de traición hacia el propio país.

treasure /'treʒər/ n tesoro: art ~s joyas de arte ● vt apreciar muchísimo: her most treasured possession su posesión más preciada **treasurer** n tesorero/a

the Treasury /'treʒəri/ n Ministerio de Hacienda y Crédito Público

treat /tri:t/ vt tratar: ~ sth as a joke tomar algo en broma 2 ~ sb (to sth) invitar a algn en algo 3 ~ yourself (to sth) darse el lujo/gusto (de algo) ▶ treat sb like dirt (coloq) tratar a algn como basura ● n 1 placer, gusto: as a special ~ como algo muy especial ◇ give yourself a ~ permitirse un lujo 2 This is my ~. Invito yo. ▶ a treat (GB, coloq) a las mil maravillas **treatment** n 1 tratamiento 2 trato

treaty /'tri:ti/ n (pl -ies) tratado

treble /'trebl/ n 1 (Mús) tiple 2 (Mús) [U] agudos 3 (GB) triple ● adj (de soprano): ~ clef clave de sol ● vt, vi triplicar(se)

tree /tri:/ n árbol

trek /trek/ n caminata ● vi (-kk-) caminar (penosamente): go trekking hacer senderismo (esp en la montaña) **trekking** n senderismo (esp en la montaña)

tremble /'trembl/ vi temblar

trembling /'tremblɪŋ/ adj tembloroso ● n temblor

tremendous /trə'mendəs/ adj 1 enorme 2 estupendo

tremor /'tremər/ n temblor

trench /trentʃ/ n 1 (Mil) trinchera 2 zanja

trend /trend/ n tendencia: set a ~ poner una moda

trendy /'trendi/ adj (coloq) de moda, en la onda

trespass /'trespəs/ vi entrar sin derecho: No trespassing. Prohibido el paso. **trespasser** n intruso/a

trial /'traɪəl/ n 1 juicio, proceso: be on/go on/stand ~ ser procesado 2 prueba 3 (Dep) preselección ▶ trial and error: learn by ~ and error aprender a base de cometer errores

triangle /'traɪæŋgl/ n triángulo **triangular** /traɪ'æŋgjələr/ adj triangular

tribe /traɪb/ n tribu

tribute /'trɪbju:t/ n 1 homenaje 2 a ~ (to sth): That's a ~ to his skill. Eso acredita su habilidad.

trick /trɪk/ n 1 engaño, trampa: play a ~ on sb hacerle una broma a algn ◇ a dirty ~ una mala pasada ◇ a ~ question una pregunta capciosa 2 truco: a ~ of the light un efecto de la luz 3 (magia): conjuring/card ~s juegos de manos/trucos con cartas ▶ every trick in the book: try every ~ in the book intentarlo todo **the tricks of the trade** los trucos del oficio ● vt engañar: ~ sb out of sth quitarle algo a algn mediante engaño ◇ ~ sb into (doing) sth embaucar a algn para que haga algo **trickery** n [U] engaño

trickle /'trɪkl/ vi salir en un chorro fino, gotear ● n 1 (líquido) hilo 2 (fig) goteo

tricky /'trɪki/ adj (-ier/-iest) complicado, difícil

tried /traɪd/ pt, pp de TRY

trifle /'traɪfl/ n 1 a trifle (fml) algo, un poco 2 (GB) postre hecho a base de capas de bizcocho, fruta, y crema ● vi ~ with sth/sb jugar con algo/algn

trigger /'trɪgər/ n gatillo ● vt ~ sth (off) 1 provocar algo 2 (alarma, etc.) accionar algo

trillion /'trɪljən/ adj, n billón →BILLION

trim /trɪm/ adj (trimmer, -est) 1 bien cuidado, aseado 2 esbelto ● vt (-mm-) 1 recortar 2 ~ sth off (sth) quitarle algo a (algo) 3 (vestido, etc.) adornar ● n 1 corte: have a ~ hacerse cortar el pelo un poco 2 adorno **trimming** n 1 adorno 2 trimmings [pl] (comida) guarnición

trip /trɪp/ n viaje, excursión →VIAJE ● vi (-pp-) 1 ~ (over/up) (on sth) tropezar (con algo) 2 vt ~ sb (up) poner zancadilla a algn ■ trip (sb) up confundir(se) (a algn)

triple /'trɪpl/ adj, n triple ● vt, vi triplicar(se)

triplet /'trɪplət/ n trillizo/a

triumph /'traɪʌmf/ n triunfo: return in ~ regresar triunfalmente ◇ a shout of ~ un grito de júbilo ● vi triunfar **triumphal** /traɪ'ʌmfl/ adj triunfal **triumphant** adj 1 triunfante 2 jubiloso

trivial /'trɪviəl/ adj trivial, insignificante **triviality** /ˌtrɪvi'æləti/ n (pl -ies) trivialidad

trod /trɒd/ pt de TREAD

trodden /'trɒdn/ pp de TREAD

trolley /'trɒli/ n 1 carrito 2 (USA) tranvía

troop /tru:p/ n 1 tropel, manada 2 troops tropas ● vi ~ in, out, etc. entrar, salir, etc. en tropel

trophy /'troufi/ n (pl -ies) trofeo

tropic /'trɒpɪk/ n 1 trópico 2 **the tropics** [pl] el trópico **tropical** adj tropical

trot /trɒt/ vi (-tt-) trotar, ir al trote ● n trote ▸ **on the trot** (GB, coloq) seguidos

trouble /'trʌbl/ n 1 [U] problemas: The ~ is (that)... Lo malo es que... ◇ What's the ~? ¿Qué pasa? 2 dificultades 3 [U] molestia, esfuerzo: go to a lot of ~ tomarse muchas molestias: It's not worth the ~. No vale la pena. 4 [U] disturbios, conflicto 5 [U] (Med) dolencia: back ~ problemas de espalda ▸ **be in trouble** tener problemas, estar en un aprieto: If I don't get home by ten, I'll be in ~. Si no llego a la casa antes de las diez, me matan. **get into trouble** meterse en un lío ● vt 1 molestar 2 preocupar **troubled** adj 1 preocupado, afligido 2 (periodo) agitado **troublesome** adj molesto

trouble-free adj sin problemas

troublemaker /'trʌblmeɪkər/ n alborotador/a, buscapleitos

trough /trɒf; trɔf GB/ n 1 abrevadero 2 comedero 3 canal 4 (clima) depresión

trousers /'traʊzərz/ n [pl] (GB) pantalón, pantalones → PANTALÓN **trouser** adj: ~ leg/pocket pierna/bolsillo del pantalón

trout /traʊt/ n (pl trout) trucha

truant /'truːənt/ n alumno/a que falta a clases ▸ **play truant** (GB) irse de pinta (Mx), capar clase (And)

truce /truːs/ n tregua

truck /trʌk/ n 1 camión (de carga) 2 (GB, tren) vagón

true /truː/ adj (truer, -est) 1 cierto, verdad 2 verídico 3 verdadero, real 4 fiel: be ~ to your word cumplir lo prometido ▸ **come true** hacerse realidad **true to life** realista **truly** adv 1 sinceramente 2 realmente

trump /trʌmp/ n triunfo: Hearts are ~s. Triunfan corazones.

trumpet /'trʌmpɪt/ n trompeta

trundle /'trʌndl/ 1 vi rodar lentamente 2 vt arrastrar 3 vt empujar

trunk /trʌŋk/ n 1 tronco 2 (USA, Aut) baúl (Mx), cajuela (And) 3 baúl 4 (elefante) trompa 5 **trunks** [pl] traje de baño (de hombre) → PAIR

trust /trʌst/ n 1 confianza 2 responsabilidad 3 fideicomiso 4 fundación ● vt 1 fiarse de 2 ~ **sb with sth** confiar algo a

align 3 ~ **to sth** confiar en algo **trusted** adj de confianza **trusting** adj confiado

trustee /trʌˈstiː/ n 1 fideicomisario/a 2 administrador/a

trustworthy /'trʌstwɜːrði/ adj digno de confianza

truth /truːθ/ n verdad **truthful** adj 1 sincero: be ~ decir la verdad

try /traɪ/ (pt/pp tried) 1 vi intentar **NOTA** Se puede decir **try to** o **try and** con el infinitivo: I'll ~ to/and finish it. Try and es más coloquial. 2 vt probar 3 vt (Jur, caso) ver 4 vt (Jur, persona) juzgar ▸ **try sb's patience** poner a prueba la paciencia de algn ▸ **try sth on** medirse algo (ropa, etc.) ● n (pl tries) 1 intento: have a ~ intentar algo 2 (rugby) ensayo **trying** adj difícil

T-shirt n camiseta, playera (Mx)

tub /tʌb/ n 1 cuba, platón (And) 2 envase (gen de plástico) 3 tina

tube /tuːb; tjuːb GB/ n 1 tubo 2 **the tube** (GB, coloq) el metro

tuck /tʌk/ vt 1 ~ **sth in**; ~ **sth into sth** meter algo (en algo) 2 ~ **sth around sth/sb** arropar algo/a algn con algo ■ **be tucked away** 1 (dinero) estar guardado 2 (lugar) estar escondido **tuck sb up** meter a algn (en cama)

Tuesday /'tuːzdeɪ, -di; 'tjuː- GB/ n (abrev **Tue(s).**) martes

tuft /tʌft/ n 1 (pelo) mechón 2 (plumas) penacho 3 (pasto) manojo

tug /tʌg/ (-gg-) 1 vi ~ (**at sth**) tirar (con fuerza) (de algo), dar un tirón/jalón a algo 2 vt arrastrar ● n 1 tirón, jalón 2 (tb **tugboat** /'tʌgbɒt/) remolcador

tuition /tuˈɪʃn; tjuˈ- GB/ n 1 (fml) instrucción, clases 2 ~ **fees** matrícula, colegiatura (Mx)

tulip /'tuːlɪp; 'tjuː- GB/ n tulipán

tumble /'tʌmbl/ vi caer(se): ~ **down** venirse abajo ● n caída

tumble-dryer (tb **tumble-drier**) n (GB) secadora

tumbler /'tʌmblər/ n vaso

tummy /'tʌmi/ n (pl -ies) (coloq) barriga

tumor (**-our** GB) /'tuːmər; 'tjuː- GB/ n tumor

tuna /'tuːnə/ n (tb ~ **fish**) n atún

tune /tuːn; tjuːn GB/ n 1 melodía 2 canción ▸ **in/out of tune** afinado/desafinado **in/out of tune** (**with sth/sb**) de acuerdo/en desacuerdo (con algo/algn) ● vt, vi ~ (**sth**) (**up**) (Mús) afinar (algo) ■ **tune in** (**to sth**) sintonizar (algo) **tuneful** adj melodioso

tunic /'tuːnɪk; 'tjuː- GB/ n túnica

tunnel /'tʌnl/ n 1 túnel 2 galería ● (-l-, -ll- GB) 1 vi abrir un túnel 2 vt, vi excavar

turban /'tɜːbən/ n turbante

turbulence /'tɜːbjələns/ n [U] turbulencia **turbulent** adj 1 turbulento 2 alborotado

turf /tɜːf/ n [U] pasto ● vt poner pasto a ■ **turf sth out** (GB, coloq) echar algo-a algn

turkey /'tɜːki/ n pavo, guajolote

turmoil /'tɜːmɔɪl/ n alboroto

turn /tɜːn/ 1 vi girar, dar vuelta(s): ~ right doblar/voltear a la derecha 2 vt hacer girar, dar (la) vuelta a, volver 3 vt, vi volver(se), voltear(se): ~ your back on sb dar la espalda a algn 4 vt (página) pasar 5 vi ponerse, volverse 6 vt, vi convertir(se) 7 vt: ~ forty cumplir los 40 ■ **turn around** girar, voltear(se) **turn sth/sb around** dar la vuelta a algo/algn **turn away** apartar la vista **turn sb away** negarse a ayudar a algn **turn sb away from sth** cerrar a algn de algo-a algn **turn back** volverse hacia atrás, hacer voltear a algn **turn sth/sb down** rechazar algo-a algn **turn sth down** bajar algo (volumen) **turn off** desviarse **turn sb off** desanimar/quitarle las ganas a algn **turn sth off 1** apagar algo (llave) **2** cerrar algo **3** desconectar algo **turn sb on** (coloq) excitar a algn **turn sth on 1** encender algo **2** (llave) abrir algo **turn out 1** asistir **2** resultar, salir **turn sb out** echar a algn **turn sth out** apagar algo (luz) **turn over** (motor) estar andando **turn (sth/sb) over** dar la vuelta (a algo/algn), voltear (algo/a algn) **turn to sb** acudir a algn **turn sth up** presentarse, aparecer **turn sth up** subir algo (volumen) ● **turn 1** vuelta **2** (cabeza) movimiento **3** giro, vuelta: take a wrong ~ tomar un camino equivocado **4** curva **5** (circunstancias) cambio: take a ~ for the better/worse empezar a mejorar/empeorar **6** turno: It's your ~. Te toca a ti. **7** (coloq) susto **8** (coloq) ataque, desmayo ▶ **a turn of phrase** un giro (de lenguaje) **do sb a good turn** hacer un favor a algn in turn sucesivamente, uno tras otro **take turns** turnarse

turning /'tɜːnɪŋ/ n bocacalle

turning point n momento crítico, punto decisivo

turnip /'tɜːnɪp/ n nabo

turnout /'tɜːnaʊt/ n asistencia, concurrencia

turnover /'tɜːnəʊvər/ n 1 (negocio) facturación 2 (personal, mercancías) movimiento

turntable /'tɜːnteɪbl/ n tornamesa

turpentine /'tɜːpəntaɪn/ (coloq **turps** /tɜːps/) n aguarrás

turquoise /'tɜːkwɔɪz/ adj, n turquesa

turret /'tʌrət/ n torreón, torre

turtle /'tɜːtl/ n 1 (tb **sea** ~ USA) tortuga (marina) 2 (USA) tortuga (de tierra)

turtleneck /'tɜːtlnek/ n (USA) (suéter de) cuello alto

tusk /tʌsk/ n colmillo

tutor /'tuːtər; 'tjuː- GB/ n 1 profesor/a particular 2 (universidad) profesor/a

tutorial /tuːtɔːriəl; tjuː- GB/ adj de tutor ● n seminario (clase)

TV /ˌtiː 'viː/ n tele

twang /twæŋ/ n 1 punteado (vibrante) 2 (voz) gangueo

tweezers /'twiːzəz/ n [pl] pinzas (de depilar) →PAIR

twelve /twelv/ adj, n, pron doce **twelfth 1** adj, pron duodécimo **2** n doceavo

twenty /'twenti/ adj, n, pron veinte **twentieth 1** adj, pron vigésimo **2** n veinteavo

twice /twaɪs/ adv dos veces: ~ as much/many el doble

twiddle /'twɪdl/ vt, vi ~ (with) sth jugar con algo, (hacer) girar algo ▶ **twiddle your thumbs** estar sin hacer nada

twig /twɪg/ n ramita

twilight /'twaɪlaɪt/ n crepúsculo

twin /twɪn/ n 1 mellizo/a, gemelo/a, cuate/a (Mx) 2 (de un par) gemelo, doble: twin-bedded room habitación de dos camas

twinge /twɪndʒ/ n punzada

twinkle /'twɪŋkl/ vi 1 centellear, destellar 2 (ojos) brillar

twirl /twɜːl/ vt, vi 1 (hacer) girar, dar vueltas (a) 2 retorcer(se)

twist /twɪst/ 1 vt torcer(se), retorcer(se) 2 vt, vi enrollar(se), enroscar(se) 3 vt (hilo, etc.) serpentear 4 vt tergiversar ● n 1 torsión, torcedura 2 (río, etc.) curva 3 (limón, papel) pedacito 4 (cambio) giro

twit /twɪt/ n (GB, coloq) tonto/a

twitch /twɪtʃ/ n 1 movimiento repentino 2 tic 3 tirón ● vt, vi 1 crispar(se), moverse (nerviosamente) 2 ~ (at) sth dar un tirón a algo

twitter /'twɪtər/ vi gorjear

two /tuː/ adj, n, pron dos ▶ **put two and two together** atar cabos

two-faced adj (coloq) falso

two-way adj **1** (proceso) doble **2** (comunicación) recíproco

tycoon /taɪ'kuːn/ n magnate

tying Ver TIE

type /taɪp/ n tipo, clase: She's not the artistic ~. No tiene mucha afición por lo artístico. ● vt, vi ~ (sth) (out/up) escribir (algo) (a máquina)

typescript /'taɪpskrɪpt/ n texto mecanografiado

typewriter /'taɪpraɪtər/ n máquina de escribir

typhoid /'taɪfɔɪd/ (tb ~ fever) n fiebre tifoidea

typhoon /taɪ'fuːn/ n tifón

typical /'tɪpɪkl/ adj típico **typically** adv **1** típicamente **2** por regla general

typify /'tɪpɪfaɪ/ vt (pt/pp -ied) tipificar, ser ejemplo de

typist /'taɪpɪst/ n mecanógrafo/a **typing** n mecanografía

tyranny /'tɪrəni/ n tiranía

tyrant /'taɪrənt/ n tirano/a

tyre (GB) = TIRE

U u

U, u /juː/ n (pl U's, u's) U, u

ubiquitous /juː'bɪkwɪtəs/ adj (fml) ubicuo

UFO (tb ufo) /juː 'ef 'əʊ, 'juːfəʊ/ n (pl -s) ovni

ugh /ɜː/ interj uf, puf

ugly /'ʌgli/ adj (-ier/-iest) **1** feo **2** siniestro, peligroso

ulcer /'ʌlsər/ n úlcera

ultimate /'ʌltɪmət/ adj **1** último, final **2** mayor **3** principal **ultimately** adv **1** al final **2** fundamentalmente

umbrella /ʌm'brelə/ n paraguas

umpire /'ʌmpaɪər/ n árbitro/a (tenis, beisbol)

U.N. /juː 'en/ abrev de United Nations ONU

unable /ʌn'eɪbl/ adj incapaz

unacceptable /ˌʌnək'septəbl/ adj inaceptable

unaccustomed /ˌʌnə'kʌstəmd/ adj **1** be ~ to sth no estar acostumbrado a algo **2** insólito

unambiguous /ˌʌnæm'bɪgjuəs/ adj inequívoco

unanimous /juː'nænɪməs/ adj unánime

unarmed /ʌn'ɑːrmd/ adj **1** desarmado, sin armas **2** inerme

unattractive /ˌʌnə'træktɪv/ adj poco atractivo

unavailable /ˌʌnə'veɪləbl/ adj no disponible

unavoidable /ˌʌnə'vɔɪdəbl/ adj inevitable

unaware /ˌʌnə'weər/ adj no consciente: be ~ of sth ignorar algo

unbearable /ʌn'beərəbl/ adj insoportable

unbeatable /ʌn'biːtəbl/ adj invencible, inigualable

unbeaten /ʌn'biːtn/ adj (Dep) nunca superado, invicto

unbelievable /ˌʌnbɪ'liːvəbl/ adj increíble

unbroken /ʌn'brəʊkən/ adj **1** intacto **2** ininterrumpido **3** (récord) imbatido **4** (espíritu) indómito

uncanny /ʌn'kæni/ adj misterioso **2** asombroso

uncertain /ʌn'sɜːrtn/ adj **1** indeciso, dudoso **2** incierto: It is ~ whether... No se sabe si... **3** variable **uncertainty** n (pl -ies) incertidumbre, duda

unchanged /ʌn'tʃeɪndʒd/ adj igual

uncle /'ʌŋkl/ n tío

unclear /ˌʌn'klɪər/ adj poco claro

uncomfortable /ʌn'kʌmfərtəbl; -ft- GB/ adj incómodo **uncomfortably** adv incómodamente: The exams are getting ~ close. Los exámenes se acercan de manera preocupante.

uncommon /ʌn'kɒmən/ adj poco común, insólito

uncompromising /ʌn'kɒmprəmaɪzɪŋ/ adj inflexible, firme

unconcerned /ˌʌnkən'sɜːrnd/ adj **1** ~ (about/by sth) indiferente (a algo) **2** despreocupado

unconditional /ˌʌnkən'dɪʃənl/ adj incondicional

unconscious /ʌn'kɒnʃəs/ adj, n inconsciente: be ~ of sth no darse cuenta de algo

uncontrollable /ˌʌnkən'trəʊləbl/ adj incontrolable

unconventional /ˌʌnkən'venʃənl/ adj poco convencional

unconvincing /ˌʌnkən'vɪnsɪŋ/ adj poco convincente

uncouth /ʌn'kuːθ/ adj grosero

uncover /ʌn'kʌvər/ vt **1** destapar **2** (fig) descubrir

undecided /ˌʌndɪ'saɪdɪd/ adj **1** sin resolver **2** indeciso

undeniable /ˌʌndɪ'naɪəbl/ adj innegable, indiscutible **undeniably** adv indudablemente

under /'ʌndər/ prep **1** debajo de **2** (edad) menor de **3** (cantidad) menos de **4** (*gobierno, etc.*) bajo **5** (*Jur*) según (*una ley, etc.*) **6** ~ **construction** en construcción

under- *pref* **1** insuficientemente: *Women are under-represented.* Las mujeres tienen una representación demasiado pequeña. ◊ *under-used* infrautilizado **2** (*edad*) menor de: *the under-fives* los menores de cinco años ◊ *under-age drinking* el consumo de bebidas alcohólicas por menores de edad

undercover /ˌʌndər'kʌvər/ *adj* secreto

underestimate /ˌʌndər'estɪmeɪt/ *vt* subestimar

undergo /ˌʌndər'goʊ/ *vt* (*pt* **-went** /-'went/ *pp* **-gone** /-'gɔːn, -'gɑːn *GB*/) **1** experimentar, sufrir **2** (*prueba*) pasar **3** (*curso*) seguir **4** (*Med*) someterse a

undergraduate /ˌʌndər'grædʒuət/ *n* estudiante no licenciado/graduado

underground /ˌʌndər'graʊnd/ *n* **1** (*GB*) metro **2** movimiento clandestino ● *adj* **1** subterráneo **2** clandestino ● /ˌʌndər'graʊnd/ *adv* **1** bajo tierra **2** en la clandestinidad

undergrowth /ˌʌndərgroʊθ/ *n* maleza

underlie /ˌʌndər'laɪ/ *vt* (*pt* **-lay** /-'leɪ/ *pp* **-lain** /-'leɪn/ *pt pres* **-lying**) (*fml*) estar detrás de

underline /ˌʌndər'laɪn/ (*tb* **underscore** /ˌʌndər'skɔːr/) *vt* subrayar

undermine /ˌʌndər'maɪn/ *vt* socavar, debilitar

underneath /ˌʌndər'niːθ/ *prep* debajo de ● *adv* (por) debajo ● **the underneath** *n* [*U*] la parte inferior

underpants /'ʌndərpænts/ (*coloq* **pants**) *n* (*GB*) [*pl*] calzoncillos →PAIR

underprivileged /ˌʌndər'prɪvəlɪdʒd/ *adj* marginado

undershirt /ˈʌndərʃɜːrt/ *n* (*USA*) camiseta (*interior*)

underside /'ʌndərsaɪd/ *n* parte de abajo, costado inferior

understand /ˌʌndər'stænd/ (*pt/pp* **-stood** /-'stʊd/) **1** *vt*, *vi* entender **2** *vt* explicarse **3** (*fml*) tener entendido **understandable** *adj* comprensible **understandably** *adv* naturalmente

understanding /ˌʌndər'stændɪŋ/ *adj* comprensivo ● *n* **1** comprensión **2** conocimiento **3** acuerdo (*informal*) **4** interpretación

understatement /ˈʌndərsteɪtmənt/ *n*: *To say he's sad would be an* ~. Decir que está triste

sería poco. **understate** *vt* decir que algo es más pequeño o menos importante de lo que es

undertake /ˌʌndər'teɪk/ *vt* (*pt* **-took** /-'tʊk/ *pp* **-taken** /-'teɪkən/) (*fml*) **1** emprender **2** comprometerse **undertaking** *n* **1** (*fml*) empresa **2** (*Com*) empresa

undertaker /ˈʌndərteɪkər/ *n* director/a (*de pompas fúnebres*) **undertaker's** *n* funeraria

underwater /ˌʌndər'wɔːtər/ *adj* submarino ● *adv* debajo del agua

underwear /ˈʌndərwear/ *n* ropa interior

underwent /ˌʌndər'went/ *pt* de UNDERGO

the underworld /ˈʌndərwɜːrld/ *n* **1** el hampa **2** el infierno

undesirable /ˌʌndɪ'zaɪərəbl/ *adj, n* indeseable

undisputed /ˌʌndɪ'spjuːtɪd/ *adj* indiscutible

undisturbed /ˌʌndɪ'stɜːrbd/ *adj* **1** sin tocar **2** (*persona*) tranquilo

undo /ʌn'duː/ *vt* (*pt* undid /ʌn'dɪd/ *pp* undone /ʌn'dʌn/) **1** deshacer **2** desabrochar **3** desamarrar **4** (*envoltura*) quitar **5** anular: ~ *the damage* reparar el daño **undone** *adj* **1** desabrochado, desamarrado: *come* ~ desabrocharse/desamarrarse **2** sin acabar

undoubtedly /ʌn'daʊtɪdli/ *adv* indudablemente

undress /ʌn'dres/ *vt*, *vi* desvestir(se) **NOTA** Es más común **get undressed**. **undressed** *adj* desvestido

undue /ˌʌn'duː; -'djuː *GB*/ *adj* [*antes de sustantivo*] (*fml*) excesivo **unduly** *adv* (*fml*) excesivamente

unearth /ʌn'ɜːrθ/ *vt* desenterrar

uneasy /ʌn'iːzi/ *adj* **1** inquieto **2** (*silencio*) incómodo **unease** *n* malestar

uneducated /ʌn'edʒukeɪtɪd/ *adj* inculto, ignorante

unemployed /ˌʌnɪm'plɔɪd/ *adj* desempleado ● **the unemployed** *n* [*pl*] los desempleados **unemployment** *n* desempleo

unequal /ʌn'iːkwəl/ *adj* **1** desigual **2** (*fml*): *feel* ~ *to sth* no sentirse a la altura de algo

uneven /ʌn'iːvn/ *adj* **1** desigual **2** (*pulso*) irregular **3** (*suelo*) desnivelado, disparejo

uneventful /ˌʌnɪ'ventfl/ *adj* sin incidentes, tranquilo

unexpected /ˌʌnɪk'spektɪd/ *adj* inesperado, imprevisto

unfair /ˌʌn'feər/ *adj* **1** ~ **(to/on sb)** injusto (con algn) **2**

(*competencia*) desleal 3 (*despido*) improcedente

unfaithful /ʌnˈfeɪθfl/ *adj* infiel

unfamiliar /ˌʌnfəˈmɪliər/ *adj* 1 poco familiar 2 (*cara, etc.*) desconocido 3 **~ with sth** poco familiarizado con algo

unfashionable /ʌnˈfæʃnəbl/ *adj* pasado de moda

unfasten /ʌnˈfæsn; ʌnˈfɑːsn *GB*/ *vt* 1 desabrochar, desamarrar 2 abrir 3 soltar

unfavorable (**-our-** *GB*) /ʌnˈfeɪvərəbl/ *adj* 1 desfavorable 2 poco propicio

unfinished /ʌnˈfɪnɪʃt/ *adj* sin terminar: **~ business** asuntos pendientes

unfit /ʌnˈfɪt/ *adj* 1 **~ (for sth/to do sth)** no apto (para hacer algo), incapaz (de hacer algo) 2 fuera de forma

unfold /ʌnˈfoʊld/ 1 *vt* extender, desdoblar 2 *vt, vi* revelar(se)

unforeseen /ˌʌnfɔːrˈsiːn/ *adj* imprevisto

unforgettable /ˌʌnfərˈgetəbl/ *adj* inolvidable

unforgivable /ˌʌnfərˈgɪvəbl/ *adj* imperdonable

unfortunate /ʌnˈfɔːrtʃənət/ *adj* 1 desafortunado 2 lamentable: *It is ~ (that)...* Es de lamentar que... 3 (*comentario*) inoportuno **unfortunately** *adv* por desgracia

unfriendly /ʌnˈfrendli/ *adj* **~ (to/ towards sb)** antipático (con algn)

ungrateful /ʌnˈgreɪtfl/ *adj* 1 desagradecido 2 ingrato

unhappy /ʌnˈhæpi/ *adj* (**-ier/-iest**) 1 triste 2 **~ (about/at sth)** preocupado, disgustado (por algo) **unhappiness** *n* infelicidad

unhealthy /ʌnˈhelθi/ *adj* 1 enfermizo 2 insalubre (*dieta, clima*) poco saludable 4 (*interés*) morboso

unheard-of *adj* sin precedentes

unhelpful /ʌnˈhelpfl/ *adj* poco servicial

unhurt /ʌnˈhɜːrt/ (*tb* **unharmed** /ʌnˈhɑːrmd/) *adj* ileso

uniform /ˈjuːnɪfɔːrm/ *adj, n* uniforme: *in ~* de uniforme

unify /ˈjuːnɪfaɪ/ *vt* (*pt/pp* **-ied**) unificar

unimportant /ˌʌnɪmˈpɔːrtnt/ *adj* sin importancia

uninhabited /ˌʌnɪnˈhæbɪtɪd/ *adj* deshabitado, despoblado

unintentionally /ˌʌnɪnˈtenʃənəli/ *adv* sin querer

uninterested /ʌnˈɪntrəstɪd/ *adj* **~ (in sth/sb)** indiferente (a algo/ algn)

union /ˈjuːniən/ *n* 1 unión: *the Union Jack* la bandera del Reino Unido 2 (*tb* **labor ~, trade ~** *GB*) sindicato

unique /juˈniːk/ *adj* 1 único 2 **~ to sth/sb** exclusivo de algo/algn 3 extraordinario

unison /ˈjuːnɪsn/ *n* ▶ **in unison** al unísono

unit /ˈjuːnɪt/ *n* 1 unidad 2 (*mobiliario*) módulo: *kitchen ~* mueble de cocina

unite /juˈnaɪt/ *vt, vi* unir(se) **unity** /ˈjuːnəti/ *n* 1 unidad 2 armonía

universal /ˌjuːnɪˈvɜːrsl/ *adj* universal, general

universe /ˈjuːnɪvɜːrs/ *n* universo

university /ˌjuːnɪˈvɜːrsəti/ *n* (*pl* **-ies**) universidad →SCHOOL

unjust /ˌʌnˈdʒʌst/ *adj* injusto

unkempt /ˌʌnˈkempt/ *adj* 1 descuidado 2 despeinado

unkind /ʌnˈkaɪnd/ *adj* 1 poco amable 2 cruel

unknown /ˌʌnˈnoʊn/ *adj* **~ (to sb)** desconocido (para algn)

unlawful /ʌnˈlɔːfl/ *adj* ilegal, ilícito

unleaded /ˌʌnˈledɪd/ *adj* sin plomo

unleash /ʌnˈliːʃ/ *vt* 1 (*animal*) soltar 2 desencadenar

unless /ənˈles/ *conj* a menos que

unlike /ˌʌnˈlaɪk/ *prep* 1 distinto de 2 no típico de: *It's ~ him to be late.* Es muy raro que llegue tarde. 3 a diferencia de ● *adj* distinto

unlikely /ʌnˈlaɪkli/ *adj* (**-ier/-iest**) 1 improbable 2 inverosímil

unlimited /ʌnˈlɪmɪtɪd/ *adj* ilimitado, sin límite

unload /ˌʌnˈloʊd/ *vt, vi* descargar

unlock /ˌʌnˈlɑːk/ *vt, vi* abrir(se) (*con llave*)

unlucky /ʌnˈlʌki/ *adj* 1 desafortunado: *be ~* tener mala suerte 2 que trae mala suerte

unmarried /ˌʌnˈmærid/ *adj* soltero

unmistakable /ˌʌnmɪˈsteɪkəbl/ *adj* inconfundible

unmoved /ˌʌnˈmuːvd/ *adj* impasible

unnatural /ʌnˈnætʃrəl/ *adj* 1 anormal 2 contra natura 3 afectado, poco natural

unnecessary /ʌnˈnesəseri; -səri *GB*/ *adj* 1 innecesario 2 (*comentario*) gratuito

unnoticed /ˌʌnˈnoʊtɪst/ *adj* desapercibido, inadvertido

unobtrusive /ˌʌnəbˈtruːsɪv/ *adj* discreto

unofficial /ˌʌnəˈfɪʃl/ adj no oficial, extraoficial

unorthodox /ˌʌnˈɔːrθədɑks/ adj poco ortodoxo

unpack /ˌʌnˈpæk/ 1 vt, vi desempacar (las maletas) 2 vt desembalar, desempaquetar

unpaid /ˌʌnˈpeɪd/ adj 1 no pagado 2 (trabajo, etc.) no retribuido

unpleasant /ˌʌnˈpleznt/ adj 1 desagradable 2 antipático

unplug /ˌʌnˈplʌɡ/ vt (-gg-) desenchufar

unpopular /ˌʌnˈpɑpjələr/ adj impopular, poco popular

unprecedented /ʌnˈpresɪdentɪd/ adj sin precedentes

unpredictable /ˌʌnprɪˈdɪktəbl/ adj imprevisible

unqualified /ˌʌnˈkwɑlɪfaɪd/ adj 1 sin título, no calificado 2 no competente

unravel /ʌnˈrævl/ vt, vi (-l-, -ll-GB) desenredar(se)

unreal /ˌʌnˈrɪəl/ adj irreal

unrealistic /ˌʌnriːəˈlɪstɪk/ adj poco realista

unreasonable /ʌnˈriːznəbl/ adj 1 poco razonable 2 excesivo

unreliable /ˌʌnrɪˈlaɪəbl/ adj 1 poco fiable 2 incumplido

unrest /ʌnˈrest/ n 1 malestar 2 (Pol) disturbios

unroll /ˌʌnˈroʊl/ vt, vi desenrollar(se)

unruly /ʌnˈruːli/ adj indisciplinado, revoltoso

unsafe /ʌnˈseɪf/ adj peligroso

unsatisfactory /ˌʌnˌsætɪsˈfæktəri/ adj inaceptable

unsavory (-oury GB) /ʌnˈseɪvəri/ adj desagradable

unscathed /ʌnˈskeɪðd/ adj 1 ileso 2 indemne

unscrew /ˌʌnˈskruː/ vt, vi 1 desatornillar(se) 2 desenroscar(se)

unscrupulous /ʌnˈskruːpjələs/ adj sin escrúpulos

unseen /ˌʌnˈsiːn/ adj invisible, inadvertido, no visto

unsettle /ʌnˈsetl/ vt perturbar **unsettled** adj 1 (persona) incómodo 2 inestable 3 variable 4 (asunto) pendiente **unsettling** adj inquietante

unshaven /ʌnˈʃeɪvn/ adj sin afeitar/rasurar

unsightly /ʌnˈsaɪtli/ adj feo

unskilled /ˌʌnˈskɪld/ adj 1 (trabajador) no calificado 2 (trabajo) no especializado

unspoiled /ˌʌnˈspɔɪld/ (tb unspoilt GB) adj intacto

unspoken /ʌnˈspoʊkən/ adj tácito, no expresado

unstable /ʌnˈsteɪbl/ adj inestable

unsteady /ʌnˈstedi/ adj 1 inseguro, vacilante 2 tembloroso

unstuck /ʌnˈstʌk/ adj despegado ▸ **come unstuck** 1 despegarse 2 (GB, coloq) fracasar

unsuccessful /ˌʌnsəkˈsesfl/ adj infructuoso: be ~ in doing sth no lograr hacer algo **unsuccessfully** adv sin éxito

unsuitable /ʌnˈsuːtəbl/ adj 1 no apto, inapropiado 2 inoportuno

unsure /ʌnˈʃʊər/ adj 1 inseguro 2 be ~ (about/of sth) no estar seguro (de algo)

unsuspecting /ˌʌnsəˈspektɪŋ/ adj confiado

unsympathetic /ˌʌnˌsɪmpəˈθetɪk/ adj 1 poco comprensivo 2 antipático

untangle /ʌnˈtæŋɡl/ vt desenredar

unthinkable /ʌnˈθɪŋkəbl/ adj impensable, inconcebible

untidy /ʌnˈtaɪdi/ adj 1 desordenado 2 (apariencia) descuidado 3 despeinado

untie /ʌnˈtaɪ/ vt (pt/pp -ied pt pres untying) desamarrar

until /ənˈtɪl/ conj, prep hasta (que) ➞ HASTA

untouched /ʌnˈtʌtʃt/ adj 1 intacto 2 (comida) sin probar 3 ~ (by sth) insensible a (algo) 4 no afectado 5 indemne

untrue /ʌnˈtruː/ adj falso

unused adj 1 /ˌʌnˈjuːzd/ sin usar 2 /ˌʌnˈjuːst/ no acostumbrado

unusual /ʌnˈjuːʒuəl/ adj 1 inusual 2 raro 3 distintivo **unusually** adv extraordinariamente: ~ talented de un talento poco común

unveil /ʌnˈveɪl/ vt 1 quitar el velo a 2 descubrir 3 revelar

unwanted /ʌnˈwɑntɪd/ adj 1 no deseado: feel ~ sentirse rechazado 2 superfluo

unwarranted /ʌnˈwɔːrəntɪd; -ˈwɒr- GB/ adj injustificado

unwelcome /ʌnˈwelkəm/ adj inoportuno, molesto: feel ~ sentirse de sobra

unwell /ʌnˈwel/ adj indispuesto

unwilling /ʌnˈwɪlɪŋ/ adj no dispuesto **unwillingness** n falta de voluntad

unwind /ˌʌnˈwaɪnd/ (pt/pp unwound /-ˈwaʊnd/) 1 vt, vi desenrollar(se) 2 vi relajarse

unwise /ˌʌnˈwaɪz/ adj imprudente

unwittingly /ʌnˈwɪtɪŋli/ adv inconscientemente

unwrap /ʌnˈræp/ vt (-pp-) desenvolver

unzip /ˌʌn'zɪp/ vt (-pp-) bajar el cierre/ziper de

up /ʌp/ adv **1** levantado: *Is he up yet?* ¿Ya se levantó? **2** más alto, más arriba: *Pull your trousers up.* Súbete el pantalón. **3** up (to sth/sb): *He came up (to me).* Se (me) acercó. **4** en trozos: *tear sth up* romper algo en pedazos **5** *lock sth up* guardar/encerrar algo bajo llave **6** *Your time is up.* Se le acabó el tiempo. **7** en su sitio, colocado ▸ **be up to sth** depender de, ser decisión de algn: *It's up to you.* Usted decide. **be up (with sb)** (coloq): *What's up with you?* ¿Qué te pasa? **not be up to much** (GB) no valer mucho **up and down 1** de arriba a abajo ◇ *jump up and down* dar saltos **up to sth 1** (tb *up until sth*) hasta algo **2** capaz de, a la altura de **3** (coloq): *What are you up to?* ¿Qué haces? ◇ *be up to no good* estar tramando algo **NOTA** Para el uso de **up** en PHRASAL VERBS ver el verbo, p.ej. **go up** en GO[1]. ● *prep* arriba ▸ **up and down sth** de un lado a otro de algo ● *n* ▸ **ups and downs** altibajos

upbringing /'ʌpbrɪŋɪŋ/ n crianza, educación (en la casa)

update /ˌʌp'deɪt/ vt **1** actualizar **2** ~ **sb** (on **sth**) poner al día a algn (de algo) ● /'ʌpdeɪt/ n **1** (tb *updating*) actualización **2** información actualizada

upgrade /ˌʌp'greɪd/ vt **1** mejorar, actualizar **2** (persona) ascender ● /'ʌpgreɪd/ n actualización

upheaval /ʌp'hi:vl/ n trastorno

uphill /ˌʌp'hɪl/ adj, adv cuesta arriba: *an ~ struggle* una lucha difícil

uphold /ʌp'hoʊld/ vt (pt/pp up-**held** /ʌp'held/) **1** (decisión) sostener **2** (tradición) mantener

upholstered /ˌʌp'hoʊlstərd/ adj tapizado **upholstery** n [U] tapicería, tapiz (Mx)

upkeep /'ʌpki:p/ n mantenimiento

uplifting /ˌʌp'lɪftɪŋ/ adj edificante

upon /ə'pɑn/ prep (fml) Ver ON

upper /'ʌpər/ adj **1** superior, de arriba: ~ *case* mayúsculas ◇ ~ *limit* tope **2** alto ▸ **gain, get, etc. the upper hand** conseguir, ganar, etc. ventaja

upper class n clase alta **upper-class** adj de clase alta

uppermost /'ʌpərmoʊst/ adj más alto (posición) ▸ **be uppermost in sb's mind** ser lo que más preocupa a algn

upright /'ʌpraɪt/ adj **1** (posición) vertical **2** (persona) honrado ● adv derecho, en posición vertical

uprising /'ʌpraɪzɪŋ/ n rebelión

uproar /'ʌprɔːr/ n [U] alboroto

uproot /ˌʌp'ruːt/ vt **1** arrancar (con raíces) **2** desarraigar

upset /ʌp'set/ vt (pt/pp **upset**) **1** disgustar, afectar **2** (plan, etc.) desbaratar **3** (recipiente) volcar, voltear ● adj **NOTA** Se pronuncia /ʌp'set/ antes de sustantivo. **1** molesto, disgustado **2** (estómago) revuelto ● /'ʌpset/ n trastorno, disgusto

upshot /'ʌpʃɑt/ n resultado final

upside down /ˌʌpsaɪd 'daʊn/ adj, adv **1** al revés, boca abajo **2** (coloq) patas arriba

upstairs /ˌʌp'steərz/ adv (en el piso de) arriba: *go* ~ subir las escaleras ● adj en/del piso de arriba ● n [sing] piso de arriba

upstream /ˌʌp'striːm/ adv río arriba, contra corriente

upsurge /'ʌpsɜːrdʒ/ n aumento

up to date adj **1** moderno: ~ *methods* los métodos más modernos **2** actualizado, al día ▸ **bring sth/sb up to date** actualizar algo/poner a algn al día

upturn /'ʌptɜːrn/ n mejora, aumento

upturned /ˌʌp'tɜːrnd/ adj **1** volcado, volteado **2** (nariz) respingado

upward /'ʌpwərd/ adj ascendente: *an ~ trend* una tendencia al alza ● adv (tb *upwards*) hacia arriba **upwards of** prep más de (cierto número)

uranium /ju'reɪniəm/ n uranio

Uranus /'jʊərənəs, jʊ'reɪnəs/ n Urano

urban /'ɜːrbən/ adj urbano

urge /ɜːrdʒ/ vt animar ■ **urge sb on** animar a algn ● n deseo, impulso

urgent /'ɜːrdʒənt/ adj **1** urgente: *be in ~ need of sth* necesitar algo urgentemente **2** apremiante **urgency** n apremio, urgencia

urine /'jʊərən/ n orina

us /əs, ʌs/ pron **1** [objeto] nos ➔LET **2** [después de prep o verbo be] nosotros/as

usage /'juːsɪdʒ/ n uso

use /juːz/ vt (pt/pp **used** /juːzd/) **1** utilizar, usar **2** aprovecharse de **3** gastar ■ **use sth up** agotar, acabar algo ● /juːs/ n **1** uso: *in ~* en uso ◇ *have the ~ of sth* poder usar algo ◇ *find a ~ for sth* encontrarle alguna utilidad a algo **2** *What's the ~ of crying?*

¿De qué sirve llorar? ◇ *What's the ~?* ¿Para qué? ◇ *What's the use of sth* aprovechar algo

used *adj* **1** /juːzd/ usado **2** /juːst/ acostumbrado: *get ~ to sth* acostumbrarse a algo

used to /'juːst tə, 'juːst tu/ *v*
NOTA Used to + infinitivo describe hábitos y situaciones que ocurrían en el pasado y que ya no ocurren: *I ~ live here.* Antes vivía acá. La forma interrogativa y negativa se suelen formar con **did**: *He didn't use to be fat.* ◇ *You ~ smoke, didn't you?*

useful /'juːsfl/ *adj* útil, provechoso **usefulness** *n* utilidad

useless /'juːsləs/ *adj* **1** inútil, inservible **2** (*coloq*) inepto

user /'juːzər/ *n* usuario/a: *user-friendly* fácil de manejar

usual /'juːʒuəl/ *adj* habitual, normal: *more than ~* más que de costumbre ◇ *the ~* lo de siempre ▸ **as usual** como siempre **usually** *adv* normalmente ▸ ALWAYS

utensil /juː'tensl/ *n* utensilio

utility /juː'tɪləti/ *n* (*pl* -ies) **1** utilidad **2** *the public utilities* **1** utilidad **2** *the public utilities* las empresas de servicios públicos

utmost /'ʌtmoʊst/ *adj* mayor: *with the ~ care* con sumo cuidado ● *n*: *do your ~* hacer todo lo posible

utter /'ʌtər/ *vt* pronunciar ● *adj* total **utterly** *adv* totalmente

V v

V, v /viː/ *n* (*pl* **V's, v's**) **1** V, v **2** *V-neck* (con) cuello en V ◇ *V-shaped* en forma de V

vacant /'veɪkənt/ *adj* **1** vacante **2** (*mirada*) distraído **vacancy** *n* (*pl* -ies) **1** vacante **2** habitación disponible

vacate /'veɪkeɪt; və'keɪt *GB*/ *vt* (*fml*) **1** desocupar **2** dejar vacío

vacation /və'keɪʃn/ *n* vacaciones
NOTA En Gran Bretaña **vacation** se usa para las vacaciones universitarias y de los tribunales de justicia. Es más común **holiday**. **vacationer** *n* (*USA*) turista

vaccine /væk'siːn; 'væksiːn *GB*/ *n* vacuna **vaccination** /ˌvæksɪ'neɪʃn/ *n* **1** vacunación **2** vacuna

vacuum /'vækjuːəm/ *n* **1** vacío **2** (*tb* ~ *cleaner*) aspiradora ▸ *in a vacuum* aislado (*de otras per-*sonas, eventos) ● *vt, vi* pasar la aspiradora (a/por)

vagina /və'dʒaɪnə/ *n* vagina

vague /veɪg/ *adj* (**-er/-est**) **1** vago **2** (*persona*) indeciso **3** (*gesto*) distraído **vaguely** *adv* **1** vagamente **2** aproximadamente **3** distraídamente

vain /veɪn/ *adj* **1** vanidoso **2** vano ▸ **in vain** en vano

valentine /'væləntam/ (*tb* ~ *card*) *n* tarjeta de San Valentín: *Valentine's Day* día de San Valentín

valiant /'væliənt/ *adj* valeroso

valid /'vælɪd/ *adj* válido **validity** /və'lɪdəti/ *n* validez

valley /'væli/ *n* valle

valuable /'væljuəbl/ *adj* valioso **valuables** *n* objetos de valor

value /'væljuː/ *n* **1** valor **2** *values* (*moral*) valores ▸ **good value** muy bien de precio ● *vt* **1** valorar, avaluar **2** apreciar **valuation** *n* tasación, avalúo

valve /vælv/ *n* válvula

vampire /'væmpaɪər/ *n* vampiro

van /væn/ *n* camioneta

vandal /'vændl/ *n* vándalo/a **vandalism** *n* vandalismo **vandalize** *vt* destrozar (*con intención*)

the vanguard /'væŋgɑːrd/ *n* la vanguardia

vanilla /və'nɪlə/ *n* vainilla

vanish /'vænɪʃ/ *vi* desaparecer

vanity /'vænəti/ *n* vanidad

vantage point /'væntɪdʒ pɔɪnt; 'vɑːn- *GB*/ *n* posición estratégica

vapor (*-our GB*) /'veɪpər/ *n* vapor

variable /'veəriəbl/ *adj, n* variable

variance /'veəriəns/ *n* (*fml*) discrepancia: *at ~ with sth* en desacuerdo con algo

variant /'veəriənt/ *n* variante

variation /ˌveəri'eɪʃn/ *n* variante

variety /və'raɪəti/ *n* (*pl* -ies) variedad: *a ~ of subjects* varios temas

various /'veəriəs/ *adj* varios

varnish /'vɑːrnɪʃ/ *n* barniz ● *vt* barnizar

vary /'veəri/ *vt, vi* (*pt/pp* -ied) variar **varied** *adj* variado **varying** *adj* variable

vase /veɪs; vɑːz *GB*/ *n* jarrón, florero

vast /væst; vɑːst *GB*/ *adj* vasto, inmenso **vastly** *adv* considerablemente

VAT /ˌviː eɪ 'tiː/ *n* (*abrev de* value added tax) (*GB*) IVA

vat /væt/ *n* tinaja, tanque

vault /vɔːlt/ n **1** bóveda **2** cripta **3** salto ● vt, vi ~ (over) (sth) saltar (algo) (*apoyándose en algo*)

VCR /ˌviː siː ˈɑːr/ n (*abrev de* **video cassette recorder**) (aparato de) video

VDU /ˌviː diː ˈjuː/ n (*abrev de* **visual display unit**) (*Comp*) monitor

veal /viːl/ n ternera →CARNE

veer /vɪər/ vi **1** virar, desviarse: ~ off course salirse del rumbo **2** (*viento*) cambiar (de dirección)

veg /vedʒ/ n (pl veg) (GB, coloq) verdura ● vi (-gg-) ■ **veg out** (coloq) vegetar

vegetable /ˈvedʒtəbl/ n **1** verdura **2** (*persona*) vegetal

vegetarian /ˌvedʒəˈteəriən/ adj, n vegetariano/a

vegetation /ˌvedʒəˈteɪʃn/ n vegetación

vehement /ˈviːəmənt/ adj vehemente, apasionado

vehicle /ˈviːəkl/ n vehículo

veil /veɪl/ n **1** velo ● vt disimular, encubrir **veiled** adj velado: veiled in secrecy rodeado de secreto

vein /veɪn/ n **1** vena **2** (*Geol*) veta **3** tono, estilo

velocity /vəˈlɒsəti/ n (pl -ies) velocidad **NOTA** Es más común **speed**.

velvet /ˈvelvɪt/ n terciopelo

vending machine /ˈvendɪŋ məˌʃiːn/ n máquina expendedora

vendor /ˈvendər/ n vendedor/a

veneer /vəˈnɪər/ n **1** (*madera, etc.*) chapa, enchapado **2** (*fig*) apariencia

vengeance /ˈvendʒəns/ n venganza: take ~ on sb vengarse de algn ► **with a vengeance** de verdad

venison /ˈvenɪsn/ n (carne de) venado →CARNE

venom /ˈvenəm/ n veneno **venomous** adj venenoso

vent /vent/ n **1** respiradero: air ~ rejilla de ventilación **2** (*ropa*) abertura ► **give (full) vent to sth** (*fml*) dar rienda suelta a algo ● vt (*fml*) descargar

ventilator /ˈventɪleɪtər/ n ventilador

venture /ˈventʃər/ n proyecto, empresa ● **1** vi aventurarse **2** vt (*fml*) (*opinión, etc.*) aventurar

venue /ˈvenjuː/ n **1** lugar (*de reunión*) **2** local (*para música*) **3** campo (*para un partido*)

Venus /ˈviːnəs/ n Venus

verb /vɜːrb/ n verbo **verbal** adj verbal

verdict /ˈvɜːrdɪkt/ n veredicto

verge /vɜːrdʒ/ n (GB) borde de hierba (*camino, etc.*) ► **on the verge of sth** a punto de algo ■ **verge on sth** rayar en algo

verify /ˈverɪfaɪ/ vt (pt/pp -ied) **1** (*detalles, etc.*) verificar **2** (*versión de los hechos*) confirmar **verification** n **1** verificación **2** ratificación

veritable /ˈverɪtəbl/ adj (*fml*) verdadero

versatile /ˈvɜːrsətl; -taɪl GB/ adj versátil, polifacético

verse /vɜːrs/ n **1** poesía **2** estrofa **3** versículo

versed /vɜːrst/ adj versado

version /ˈvɜːrʒn; -ʃn GB/ n versión

versus /ˈvɜːrsəs/ prep (*Dep*) contra

vertebra /ˈvɜːrtɪbrə/ n (pl -brae /-briː/) vértebra

vertical /ˈvɜːrtɪkl/ adj, n vertical

verve /vɜːrv/ n brío, entusiasmo

very /ˈveri/ adv **1** muy: I'm ~ sorry. Lo siento mucho. **2** the ~ best lo mejor posible ◇ at the ~ latest a más tardar ◇ your ~ own pony un poni sólo para ti **3** mismo: the ~ next day justo al día siguiente ● adj **1** at that ~ moment en ese mismísimo momento ◇ You're the ~ man I need. Eres precisamente el hombre que necesito. **2** at the ~ end justo al final **3** the ~ idea/thought of... la simple idea.../de sólo pensar en...

vessel /ˈvesl/ n **1** (*fml*) barco **2** (*fml*) vasija **3** conducto

vest /vest/ n **1** (USA) chaleco **2** (GB) camiseta

vested interest n intereses creados

vestige /ˈvestɪdʒ/ n vestigio

vet /vet/ vt (-tt-) (GB) investigar ● n **1** veterinario/a **2** (USA, coloq) (tb veteran) ex-combatiente

veteran /ˈvetərən/ adj, n veterano/a

veterinarian /ˌvetərɪˈneəriən; -neər- GB/ n veterinario/a

veto /ˈviːtoʊ/ n (pl -es) veto ● vt (pt pres ~ing) vetar

via /ˈvaɪə/ prep por, vía

viable /ˈvaɪəbl/ adj viable

vibrate /ˈvaɪbreɪt; vaɪˈbreɪt GB/ vt, vi (hacer) vibrar **vibration** n vibración

vicar /ˈvɪkər/ n párroco anglicano → PRIEST **vicarage** /ˈvɪkərɪdʒ/ n (GB) casa del párroco

vice /vaɪs/ n **1** vicio **2** (GB) = VISE

vice- pref vice-

vice versa /ˌvaɪs ˈvɜːrsə/ *adv* viceversa

vicinity /vəˈsɪnəti/ *n* (*fml*): *in the ~* en las inmediaciones

vicious /ˈvɪʃəs/ *adj* 1 cruel 2 (*perro*) bravo ▸ **a vicious circle** un círculo vicioso

victim /ˈvɪktɪm/ *n* víctima ▸ **fall victim to sth** ser víctima de algo
victimize *vt* 1 tratar injustamente 2 tiranizar

victory /ˈvɪktəri/ *n* (*pl* **-ies**) victoria **victor** *n* (*fml*) vencedor/a **victorious** /vɪkˈtɔːriəs/ *adj* 1 victorioso 2 (*equipo*) vencedor 3 **be ~ (over sth/sb)** triunfar (sobre algo/algn)

video /ˈvɪdiəʊ/ *n* (*pl* **-s**) vídeo: *~ game/camera* videojuego/videocámara 1 (*GB*) Ver VCR ● *vt* (*pt/pp* **videoed** *pt pres* **videoing**) grabar (*en vídeo*) **videotape** /ˈvɪdiəʊteɪp/ *n* cinta de vídeo

view /vju:/ *n* 1 vista (*tb* **viewing**) sesión 3 opinión, parecer 4 criterio 5 (*imagen*) equipo ▸ **in view of sth** en vista de algo **with a view to sth** con miras a algo ● *vt* 1 mirar, ver 2 considerar 3 (*Comp*) visualizar **viewer** *n* 1 telespectador/a 2 espectador/a 3 (*aparato*) visor **viewpoint** /ˈvju:pɔɪnt/ *n* punto de vista

vigil /ˈvɪdʒɪl/ *n* vela, vigilia

vigilant /ˈvɪdʒɪlənt/ *adj* alerta

vigorous /ˈvɪɡərəs/ *adj* enérgico

vile /vaɪl/ *adj* (**viler**, **-est**) (*coloq*) repugnante, asqueroso

villa /ˈvɪlə/ *n* (*GB*) casa de campo, finca *de vacaciones*)

village /ˈvɪlɪdʒ/ *n* 1 pueblo 2 aldea **villager** *n* habitante (*de un pueblo*)

villain /ˈvɪlən/ *n* 1 (*Teat, etc.*) malo/a 2 (*GB, coloq*) delincuente

vindicate /ˈvɪndɪkeɪt/ *vt* (*fml*) 1 rehabilitar 2 justificar

vine /vaɪn/ *n* 1 vid 2 enredadera

vinegar /ˈvɪnɪɡər/ *n* vinagre

vineyard /ˈvɪnjərd/ *n* viña, viñedo

vintage /ˈvɪntɪdʒ/ *n* 1 cosecha 2 vendimia ● *adj* 1 (*vino*) añejo 2 clásico 3 (*GB, Aut*) antiguo

vinyl /ˈvaɪnl/ *n* vinilo

violate /ˈvaɪəleɪt/ *vt* violar (*ley, normas*) **NOTA** En el sentido sexual de "violar", se dice **rape**. 2 (*confianza*) quebrantar 3 (*intimidad*) invadir

violent /ˈvaɪələnt/ *adj* violento **violence** *n* violencia

violet /ˈvaɪələt/ *n* violeta

violin /ˌvaɪəˈlɪn/ *n* violín

virgin /ˈvɜːrdʒɪn/ *adj, n* virgen

Virgo /ˈvɜːrɡəʊ/ *n* (*pl* **-s**) Virgo

virile /ˈvɪrəl; ˈvɪraɪl *GB*/ *adj* viril

virtual /ˈvɜːrtʃuəl/ *adj* virtual

virtue /ˈvɜːrtʃu:/ *n* 1 virtud 2 ventaja ▸ **by virtue of sth** (*fml*) en virtud de algo **virtuous** *adj* virtuoso

virtuoso /ˌvɜːtʃuˈəʊsəʊ/ *n* (*pl* **-os** o **virtuosi** /-siː, -ziː/) virtuoso (*artista, etc.*)

virus /ˈvaɪrəs/ *n* virus

visa /ˈviːzə/ *n* visa

vis-à-vis /ˌviːz ɑː ˈviː/ *prep* (*fml*) 1 con relación a 2 en comparación con

vise /vaɪs/ *n* tornillo de banco (*de carpintero*)

visible /ˈvɪzəbl/ *adj* 1 visible 2 patente

vision /ˈvɪʒn/ *n* 1 vista 2 visión

visit /ˈvɪzɪt/ 1 *vt, vi* visitar 2 *vt* (*país*) ir a ● *n* visita: *pay sb a ~* visitar a algn **visiting** *adj* visitante (*equipo, etc.*): *~ hours* horas de visita **visitor** *n* 1 visitante, visita 2 turista

vista /ˈvɪstə/ *n* (*fml*) 1 vista, panorámica 2 perspectiva

visual /ˈvɪʒuəl/ *adj* visual **visualize** *vt* 1 ver 2 prever

vital /ˈvaɪtl/ *adj* vital **vitally** *adv*: *~ important* de vital importancia

vitamin /ˈvaɪtəmɪn; ˈvɪt- *GB*/ *n* vitamina

vivacious /vɪˈveɪʃəs/ *adj* animado

vivid /ˈvɪvɪd/ *adj* vivo (*colores, imaginación, etc.*)

vocabulary /vəˈkæbjələri; -ləri *GB*/ *n* (*pl* **-ies**) (*coloq* **vocab** /ˈvəʊkæb/) vocabulario

vocal /ˈvəʊkl/ *adj* 1 vocal 2 ruidoso ● *n*: *be on ~s* ser el cantante **vocalist** *n* vocalista

vocation /vəʊˈkeɪʃn/ *n* vocación **vocational** *adj* técnico: *~ training* formación profesional

vociferous /vəʊˈsɪfərəs; və- *GB*/ *adj* vociferante

vogue /vəʊɡ/ *n* **~ (for sth)** moda (*de algo*): *in ~* en boga

voice /vɔɪs/ *n* voz: *have no ~ in the matter* no tener voz en el asunto ▸ **make your voice heard** expresar uno su opinión ● *vt* expresar

voicemail /ˈvɔɪsmeɪl/ *n* buzón de voz

void /vɔɪd/ *n* (*fml*) vacío ● *adj* (*fml*) anulado: *make sth ~* anular algo

volatile /ˈvɒlətl; -taɪl *GB*/ *adj* 1 (*persona*) voluble 2 inestable

volcano /vɒlˈkeɪnəʊ/ *n* (*pl* **-es**) volcán

W

volition /və'lɪʃn/ n (fml): of your own ~ por voluntad propia

volley /'vɒli/ n 1 (Dep) volea 2 (balas, preguntas etc.) lluvia

volleyball /'vɒlibɔːl/ n voleibol

volt /vəʊlt/ n voltio **voltage** /'vəʊltɪdʒ/ n voltaje: high ~ alta tensión

volume /'vɒljuːm/ n volumen **voluminous** /və'luːmɪnəs/ adj (fml) 1 amplio 2 copioso

voluntary /'vɒləntri; -tri GB/ adj voluntario

volunteer /ˌvɒlən'tɪər/ n voluntario/a ● 1 vi ofrecerse (voluntario) 2 vt ofrecer (información)

vomit /'vɒmɪt/ vt, vi vomitar ● n vómito **vomiting** /n vómitos

voracious /və'reɪʃəs/ adj voraz

vote /vəʊt/ n 1 voto 2 votación: take a ~ on sth/put sth to the ~ someter algo a votación 3 **the vote** el derecho al voto ▶ **vote of no confidence** voto de censura **vote of thanks** palabras de agradecimiento ● 1 vt, vi votar 2 vt ~ (that...) proponer que... **voter** n votante **voting** n votación

vouch /vaʊtʃ/ vi 1 ~ for sth/sb responder por algo/algn 2 ~ for sth confirmar algo

voucher /'vaʊtʃər/ n (GB) vale

vow /vaʊ/ n voto, promesa solemne ● vt jurar

vowel /'vaʊəl/ n vocal

voyage /'vɔɪɪdʒ/ n viaje →VIAJE

vulgar /'vʌlɡər/ adj 1 vulgar 2 (chiste, etc.) grosero

vulnerable /'vʌlnərəbl/ adj vulnerable

vulture /'vʌltʃər/ n buitre

W w

W, w /'dʌblju:/ n (pl W's, w's) W, w

wade /weɪd/ 1 vi caminar con dificultad por agua, lodo, etc. 2 vt, vi (riachuelo) vadear

wafer /'weɪfər/ n 1 galleta (tipo barquillo) 2 oblea

wag /wæɡ/ vt, vi (-gg-) 1 mover(se) (de un lado a otro) 2 (cola) menear(se)

wage /weɪdʒ/ n sueldo (semanal) ● vt ~ sth (against/on sth/sb) librar algo (contra algo/algn)

wagon /'wæɡən/ n 1 (tren) vagón 2 (tb waggon GB) carreta

wail /weɪl/ vi 1 gemir 2 (sirena) aullar ● n gemido, aullido

waist /weɪst/ n cintura

waistband /'weɪstbænd/ n cinturilla

waistcoat /'weskət; 'weɪskəʊt GB/ n (GB) chaleco

waistline /'weɪstlaɪn/ n cintura, talle

wait /weɪt/ n espera ● vt, vi ~ (for sth/sb) esperar (algo/a algn): keep sb waiting hacer esperar a algn ◊ I can't ~ to... No veo la hora de... →ESPERAR ■ **wait on sb** servir a algn **wait up (for sb)** esperar levantado (a algn) ● n espera: I had a two-hour ~. Me tocó esperar dos horas.

waiter /'weɪtər/ n (fem **waitress** /'weɪtrəs/) n mesero/a

waive /weɪv/ vt 1 (pago) renunciar a 2 (norma) pasar por alto

wake /weɪk/ vt, vi (pt woke pp woken) 1 ~ (sb) (up) 1 despertar(se) (a algn) 2 (fig) despabilar(se) (a algn) ■ **wake up to sth** darse cuenta de algo ● n 1 velatorio 2 (Náut) estela ▶ **in the wake of sth** después de algo

walk /wɔːk/ 1 vt, vi caminar 2 vi pasear: I'll ~ you home. Te acompaño a la casa. 3 vt recorrer (a pie) ■ **walk away/off** irse **walk into sth/sb** chocar(se) contra algo/con algn **walk out** 1 (coloq) declararse en huelga 2 (tb ~ out (of sth)) largarse (de algo) ● n 1 paseo, caminata: go for a ~ dar una vuelta ◊ It's a ten-minute ~. Está a diez minutos a pie. 2 andar ▶ **a walk of life**: people of all ~s of life gente de todos los tipos o profesiones **walker** n caminante **walking** n caminar

walking stick n bastón

Walkman® /'wɔːkmən/ n (pl -s) walkman®

walkout /'wɔːkaʊt/ n huelga

wall /wɔːl/ n 1 muro, pared 2 muralla **walled** adj 1 amurallado 2 cercado

wallet /'wɒlɪt/ n cartera, billetera

wallpaper /'wɔːlpeɪpər/ n papel tapiz/de colgadura

walnut /'wɔːlnʌt/ n 1 nuez (de castilla) 2 (árbol, madera) nogal

waltz /wɔːlts; wɔːls GB/ n vals ● vi bailar el vals

wand /wɒnd/ n vara, varita

wander /'wɒndər/ 1 vi deambular **NOTA** Wander se usa con around, about y otras preposiciones o adverbios, y se traduce por distintos verbos en español, con la idea de "distraídamente, sin propósito": to ~ in entrar distraídamente ◊ ~ across the road cruzar la calle distraídamente ◊

~ *away/off* alejarse/extraviarse **2** *vi* (*pensamientos*) vagar **3** *vi* (*mirada*) pasear **4** *vt* vagar por

wane /weɪn/ (*tb* **be on the ~**) *vi* (*fml*) menguar, disminuir

wanna /ˈwɒnə/ (*coloq*) **1** = WANT TO **2** = WANT A

want /wɒnt; wɒnt *GB*/ **1** *vt* querer **NOTA** *Would like* también significa "querer". Es más cortés que **want** y se usa para ofrecer algo o para invitar a alguien: *Would you like to come to dinner?* ◊ *Would you like something to eat?* **2** *vt* (*coloq*) necesitar: *It ~s fixing.* Hay que arreglarlo. ◊ *You're wanted upstairs/on the phone.* Lo buscan arriba./Lo llaman al teléfono. ● *n* **1** necesidad, deseo **2** ~ **of sth** falta de algo: *for ~ of* por falta de ◊ *not for ~ of trying* no por no intentarlo **3** (*fml*) pobreza **wanting** *adj* ~ (**in sth**) (*fml*) falto de algo

war /wɔːr/ *n* **1** guerra: *make/wage ~ on sth/sb* hacerle la guerra a algo/algn **2** lucha

ward /wɔːrd/ *n* **1** sala (*hospital*) ■ **ward sth off 1** ahuyentar algo **2** (*ataque*) rechazar algo **3** (*peligro*) prevenir algo

warden /ˈwɔːrdn/ *n* guardia

wardrobe /ˈwɔːrdroub/ *n* **1** clóset, armario **2** vestuario

warehouse /ˈweərhaus/ *n* bodega

wares /weərz/ *n* [*pl*] mercancías

warfare /ˈwɔːrfeər/ *n* guerra

warlike /ˈwɔːrlaɪk/ *adj* belicoso

warm /wɔːrm/ *adj* (**-er/-est**) **1** (*clima*) templado: *be ~* hacer calor ◊ *~* FRÍO **2** (*cosa*) caliente **3** (*persona*): *be/get ~* tener calor/calentarse **4** (*ropa*) abrigador **5** cordial ● *vt*, *vi* ~ (**sth/yourself**) (**up**) calentar(se) (algo) ■ **warm sth up** recalentar algo (*comida*) **warming** *n*: *global ~* calentamiento global **warmly** *adv* **1** calurosamente **2** ~ *dressed* bien abrigado **warmth** *n* **1** calor **2** simpatía, entusiasmo

warn /wɔːrn/ *vt* **1** ~ **sb** (**about/of sth**) advertir a algn (de algo), prevenir a algn (contra algo) **2** ~ **sb against doing sth** advertir a algn que no haga algo: *She warned me against going.* Me advirtió que no fuera. **3** ~ **sb** (**not**) **to do sth** ordenar a algn que (no) haga algo (*bajo amenaza*) **warning** *n* aviso, advertencia

warp /wɔːrp/ *vt*, *vi* combar(se) **warped** *adj* retorcido (*mente*)

warrant /ˈwɔːrənt; ˈwɒr- *GB*/ *n* (*Jur*) orden ● *vt* (*fml*) justificar

warranty /ˈwɔːrənti; ˈwɒr- *GB*/ *n* (*pl* **-ies**) garantía

warren /ˈwɔːrən; ˈwɒrən *GB*/ *n* **1** madriguera **2** laberinto

warrior /ˈwɔːriər; ˈwɒr- *GB*/ *n* guerrero/a

warship /ˈwɔːrʃɪp/ *n* buque de guerra

wart /wɔːrt/ *n* verruga

wartime /ˈwɔːrtaɪm/ *n* (tiempo de) guerra

wary /ˈweəri/ *adj* (**-ier/-iest**): *be ~ of sth* desconfiar de algo

was /wəz, wʌz, wɒz *GB*/ *pt de* BE

wash /wɒʃ/ *n* **1** lavado: *have a ~* lavarse **2** *the wash* [*sing*]: *All my clothes are in the ~.* Toda mi ropa se está lavando. **3** (*Náut*) estela ● **1** *vt*, *vi* lavar(se): *~ yourself* lavarse **2** *vi*: *Water washed over the deck.* El agua bañaba la cubierta. **3** *vt* ~ **sth/sb** (**away**) llevar, arrastrar algo/a algn: *be washed overboard* ser arrastrado por la borda por las olas ■ **wash sth off** quitarse, quitar algo (*lavando*) **wash sth out** lavar algo (*lavando*) **wash over sb** (*fml*) invadir a algn **wash up 1** (*USA*) lavarse (*manos y cara*) **2** (*GB*) lavar los platos/trastes (*Mx*) **wash sth up 1** (*GB*, *platos*) lavar algo **2** (*mar*) llevar algo a la playa **washable** *adj* lavable

washbasin /ˈwɒʃbeɪsn/ (*tb* **washbowl** /ˈwɒʃboul/ *USA*) *n* lavabo, lavamanos

washing /ˈwɒʃɪŋ; ˈwɒ- *GB*/ *n* **1** lavado **2** ropa sucia **3** ropa lavada

washing machine *n* lavadora

washing powder *n* (*GB*) detergente (de lavadora)

washing-up (*GB*) platos (para lavar): *do the ~* lavar los platos/trastes (*Mx*): *~ liquid* jabón para platos

washroom /ˈwɒʃruːm/ *n* (*USA*) (cuarto de) baño →TOILET

wasn't /ˈwʌznt/ = WAS NOT

wasp /wɒsp/ *n* avispa

waste /weɪst/ *adj* **1** ~ *material/ products* desechos **2** baldío (*terreno*) ● *vt* **1** malgastar **2** (*tiempo*, *ocasión*) perder ■ **waste away** consumirse ● *n* **1** pérdida **2** (*acción*) despilfarro **3** [*U*] desperdicios, desechos: *nuclear ~* residuos nucleares ▶ *a waste of space* (*coloq*) un inútil: *He's a complete ~ of space.* No sirve absolutamente para nada. *go/run to waste* desperdiciarse **wasted** *adj* inútil (*viaje*, *esfuerzo*) **wasteful** *adj* **1** derrochador **2** antieconómico

wastebasket /'weɪstbæskɪt; -bɑːs- GB/ (**waste paper basket** GB) n papelera, cesto de los papeles

wasteland /'weɪstlænd/ n tierra baldía

watch /wɒtʃ/ n 1 reloj (de pulsera) 2 (turno de) guardia: keep ~ over sth vigilar algo 3 (personas) guardia ● 1 vt, vi observar, mirar →MIRAR 2 vt, vi vigilar 3 vt (TV, etc.) ver 4 vt, vi ~ (over) sth/sb cuidar (algo/a algn) 5 vi ~ for sth esperar algo 6 vt tener cuidado con: Watch your language. No digas groserías. ▸ **watch out!** ¡cuidado! watch out tener cuidado ■ **watch out for sth** estar atento a algo **watchful** adj

watchdog /'wɒtʃdɒɡ; -dɔːɡ GB/ n organismo de control/vigilancia

water /'wɔːtər/ n agua: ~ sports deportes acuáticos ● 1 vt regar 2 vi (ojos) llorar 3 vi (boca) hacerse agua ■ **water sth down** 1 diluir algo con agua 2 suavizar algo

watercolor (-our GB) /'wɔːtər-kʌlər/ n acuarela

watercress /'wɔːtərkres/ n [U] berro

waterfall /'wɔːtərfɔːl/ n cascada

watermelon /'wɔːtərmelən/ n sandía

waterproof /'wɔːtərpruːf/ adj, n impermeable

watershed /'wɔːtərʃed/ n momento decisivo/crítico

waterskiing /'wɔːtərskiːɪŋ/ n esquí acuático

watertight /'wɔːtərtaɪt/ adj 1 hermético 2 irrefutable

waterway /'wɔːtərweɪ/ n vía fluvial, canal

watery /'wɔːtəri/ adj 1 aguado 2 (color) pálido 3 (ojos) lloroso

watt /wɒt/ n vatio, watt

wave /weɪv/ 1 vt, vi agitar(se) 2 vi ondear 3 vi hacer señas con la mano 4 vt, vi (pelo, etc.) ondular(se) ■ **wave sth aside** rechazar algo (protesta) ● n 1 ola 2 oleada 3 seña (con la mano) 4 onda **wavy** adj 1 ondulado 2 ondulante

wavelength /'weɪvleŋθ/ n longitud de onda

waver /'weɪvər/ vi 1 flaquear 2 (voz) temblar 3 vacilar

wax /wæks/ n cera

way /weɪ/ n 1 camino: ask/tell sb the ~ preguntar/indicar a algn por dónde se va ◇ ~ across/over the ~ al frente/al otro lado de la calle ◇ ~ out salida ◇ a long ~ (away) lejos →FAR 2 Way (en nombres) vía 3 paso: Get out of my ~! ¡Quítate de en medio! 4 dirección: "Which ~?" "That ~." —¡Por dónde? —Por ahí. 5 forma, manera 6 [gen pl] costumbre ▸ **by the way** a propósito divide, split, etc. sth two, three, etc. ways dividir algo entre dos, tres, etc. feel your way ir a tientas get/have your own way salirse con la suya give way to sth dejarse dominar por algo give way (to sth/sb) 1 ceder (ante algo/algn) 2 ceder el paso (a algo/algn) go out of your way (to do sth) tomarse la molestia (de hacer algo) in a/one way; in some ways en cierto modo make way (for sth/sb) dar paso (a algo/algn) make your way (to/towards sth) irse (a/hacia algo) no way! (coloq) ¡ni hablar! one way or another como sea on the way in (el) camino the other way around 1 al revés 2 por el otro lado under way en marcha way of life estilo de vida ways and means medios ● adv muy: ~ ahead muy por delante ▸ **way back** hace mucho: ~ back in the sixties allá por los años sesenta

WC /ˌdʌbljuː 'siː/ n (GB) baño (público) →TOILET

we /wiː/ pron nosotros **NOTA** El pron pers no puede omitirse en inglés.

weak /wiːk/ adj (-er/-est) 1 débil 2 (Med) delicado **weaken** 1 vt, vi debilitar(se) 2 vi ceder **weakness** n 1 debilidad 2 flaqueza

wealth /welθ/ n 1 [U] riqueza 2 a ~ of sth una abundancia de algo **wealthy** adj (-ier/-iest) rico

weapon /'wepən/ n arma

wear /weər/ (pt wore pp worn) 1 vt (ropa, etc.) llevar (puesto) 2 vt (expresión) tener 3 vt, vi desgastar(se) 4 vt (agujero, etc.) hacer 5 vi durar ■ **wear (sth) away/down/out** desgastar(se) (algo) **wear sb down/out** agotar a algn **wear sth down** minar algo **wear off** desaparecer (novedad, etc.) **NOTA** Wear se usa para referirse a ropa, calzado, accesorios, perfumes y lentes. Se usa **carry** al referirse a objetos que llevamos con nosotros, especialmente en las manos o en los brazos: She wasn't wearing her coat, she was carrying it over her arm. No llevaba puesto el abrigo, lo tenía en el brazo. ● n 1 desgaste 2 uso 3 ropa: ladies' ~ ropa de señora ▸ **wear and tear** desgaste por el uso

weary /'wɪəri/ adj (-ier/-iest) 1 agotado 2 hastiado

weather /'weðər/ n tiempo ▸ **under the weather** (coloq) decaído ● vt superar (crisis)

weave /wiːv/ (pt **wove** /wəʊv/ pp **woven**) 1 vt ~ sth (out of/from sth) tejer algo (con algo) 2 vt ~ sth into sth incluir algo en algo 3 vi (pt/pp **weaved**) serpentear

web /web/ n 1 (tb spider's ~) telaraña 2 red 3 (engaños) maraña 4 the Web la red: ~ page página web

webcam /'webkæm/ n webcam

website /'websaɪt/ n sitio web

we'd /wiːd/ 1 = WE HAD 2 = WE WOULD

wedding /'wedɪŋ/ n boda: golden ~ bodas de oro →MATRIMONIO

wedge /wedʒ/ n 1 cuña 2 (pastel, queso) pedazo (grande) 3 (limón) gajo ● vt 1 ~ sth open/shut mantener algo abierto/cerrado con cuña 2 ~ itself/get wedged atascarse 3 (esp personas) apretujar

Wednesday /'wenzdeɪ, -diː/ n (abrev Wed.) miércoles

wee /wiː/ adj (coloq) 1 (Esc) pequeño 2 poquito: a ~ bit un poquito

weed /wiːd/ n 1 maleza 2 [U] (en agua) algas 3 (GB, coloq) enclenque 4 (GB, coloq) persona sin carácter ● vt escardar ■ **weed sth/sb out** eliminar algo/a algn

weedkiller /'wiːdkɪlər/ n herbicida

week /wiːk/ n semana ▸ **a week from Monday** (tb a week on Monday/Monday week GB) del lunes en ocho días ▸ **a week today/tomorrow** de hoy/mañana en ocho días **weekday** /'wiːkdeɪ/ n día laborable

weekend /'wiːkend, ,wiːk'end/ GB/ n fin de semana NOTA En EE.UU. se dice **on the weekend**, pero en Gran Bretaña es **at the weekend**.

weekly /'wiːkli/ adj semanal ● adv semanalmente ● n (pl -ies) semanario

weep /wiːp/ vi (pt/pp **wept** /wept/ fml) llorar **weeping** n llanto

weigh /weɪ/ vt, vi pesar 2 vt ~ sth (up) sopesar algo 3 vi ~ (against sth/sb) influir en contra de algo/algn) ▸ **weigh anchor** levar anclas ■ **weigh sth/sb down**: weighed down with bags muy cargado de bolsas

weight /weɪt/ n 1 peso: by ~ a peso ◇ lose/put on ~ adelgazar/engordar 2 pesa, peso ▸ **pull your weight** poner todo tu esfuerzo ●

vt 1 poner peso/pesas en 2 ~ sth (down) sujetar algo **weighting** n 1 (GB) London ~ complemento salarial por trabajar en Londres 2 importancia **weightless** adj ingrávido **weighty** adj (-ier/-iest) 1 importante 2 pesado

weightlifting /'weɪtlɪftɪŋ/ n levantamiento de pesas

weir /wɪər/ n presa (en la corriente de un río)

weird /wɪərd/ adj (-er/-est) 1 raro 2 (fml) misterioso

welcome /'welkəm/ adj 1 bienvenido 2 agradable 3 be ~ to (do) sth: You're ~ to use my house/to stay. Mi casa está a tu disposición./Se puede quedar con toda confianza. ▸ **you're welcome** de nada, a la orden ● n bienvenida ● vt 1 dar la bienvenida a 2 agradecer 3 acoger **welcoming** adj acogedor

weld /weld/ vt, vi soldar(se)

welfare /'welfeər/ n 1 bienestar: the Welfare State el Estado del bienestar 2 asistencia 3 (USA) seguridad social

we'll /wiːl/ 1 = WE SHALL 2 = WE WILL

well[1] /wel/ (comp **better** superl **best**) adj bien: be/get ~ estar bien/mejorarse ● adv 1 bien: a well-dressed woman una mujer bien vestida NOTA Los adjetivos formados por **well** más otra palabra se usan separados cuando se usan detrás del verbo: He's always well behaved., y con guión cuando van seguidos de un sustantivo: well-behaved children. 2 [después de can, could, may, might]: I can ~ believe it. Lo creo totalmente. ◇ I can't very ~ leave. No puedo irme más. ▸ **as well** también → TAMBIÉN **as well as** además de **do well** 1 progresar 2 recuperarse **may/might (just) as well do sth**: You may as ~ go home. Más vale que te vayas para la casa. **well and truly** (coloq) completamente ● interj 1 (asombro) vaya: Well, look who's here! ¡Vaya, vaya! Mire quién está aquí. 2 (resignación) bueno 3 (interrogación) ¿y entonces? 4 (duda) pues: Well, I don't know... Pues, no sé...

well[2] /wel/ n pozo ● vi ~ (up) brotar

well behaved adj bien educado/portado (Mx): be ~ portarse bien → WELL[1]

well-being n bienestar

well earned adj merecido → WELL[1]

wellington /'welɪŋtən/ (tb ~ **boot**) n (GB) bota de hule/caucho

well kept adj 1 cuidado, bien conservado 2 (secreto) bien guardado →WELL¹

well known adj muy conocido, famoso: It's a well-known fact that... Es sabido que... →WELL¹

well meaning adj bienintencionado →WELL¹

well off (tb **well-to-do**) adj rico →WELL¹

welly /'weli/ n (pl **-ies**) (GB, coloq) Ver WELLINGTON

went /went/ pt de GO¹

wept /wept/ pt, pp de WEEP

we're /wɪər/ = WE ARE

were /wər, wɜːr/ pt de BE

weren't /'wɜːrnt/ = WERE NOT

west /west/ n 1 (abrev **W**) oeste 2 **the West** (el) Occidente ● adj (del) oeste, occidental ● adv al oeste

westbound /'westbaʊnd/ adj en/con dirección oeste

western /'westərn/ adj (del) oeste, occidental ● n película/novela del oeste **westerner** n occidental

westwards /'westwərdz/ (tb **westward**) adv hacia el oeste

wet /wet/ adj 1 mojado: get ~ mojarse 2 húmedo 3 lluvioso 4 (pintura, etc.) fresco 5 (GB, coloq, pey) (persona) timorato ● n 1 **the wet** la lluvia 2 humedad ● (-tt-) (pt/pp **wet/wetted**) vt 1 mojar, humedecer 2 ~ **yourself** orinarse: ~ the bed orinarse en la cama

we've /wiːv/ = WE HAVE

whack /wæk/ vt (coloq) dar un buen golpe a ● n golpe (duro)

whale /weɪl/ n ballena

wharf /wɔːrf/ n (pl **-s** o **wharves** /wɔːrvz/) muelle

what /wɑt/ adj/adv: What color is it? ¿De qué color es? ◇ What a pity! ¡Qué lástima! ◇ ~ money I have (todo) el dinero que tenga ● pron qué, lo que: What did you say? ¿Qué dijiste? ◇ I know ~ you're thinking. Sé lo que estás pensando. ◇ What's her number? ¿Cómo es su número? ◇ What's your name? ¿Cómo te llamas? **NOTA** Which se refiere a uno o más miembros de un grupo limitado: Which is your car, this one or that one? **What** se usa cuando el grupo no es tan limitado: What are your favorite books? ► **what about...?** 1 ¿qué te parece si...? 2 What about the money you owe me? ¿Y qué hay del dinero que me debes? **what**

if...? ¿y (qué pasa) si...?: What if it rains? ¿Y si llueve? ● interj ¡qué!, ¿cómo?

whatever /wɑt'evər/ pron 1 (todo) lo que ~ happens pase lo que pase ► **or whatever** (coloq) o el/la/lo que sea ● adj cualquier ● pron qué: Whatever can it be? ¿Qué demonios puede ser? ● adv (tb **whatsoever** /,wɑtsoʊ'evər/) en absoluto

wheat /wiːt/ n trigo

wheel /wiːl/ n 1 rueda 2 volante, timón ● 1 vt (bicicleta, etc.) empujar 2 vi (pájaro) revolotear 3 vi ~ (around) voltearse

wheelbarrow /'wiːlbæroʊ/ n carretilla, carreta (de mano)

wheelchair /'wiːltʃeər/ n silla de ruedas

wheeze /wiːz/ vi respirar con dificultad, resollar

when /wen/ conj cuando ● adv en (el/la/los/las) que: There are times when... Hay veces en que...

whenever /wen'evər/ conj 1 cuando 2 siempre que

where /weər/ adv, conj dónde, donde: Where are you going? ¿Adónde vas? ◇ the town ~ I was born el pueblo donde nací

whereabouts /,weərə'baʊts/ adv dónde ● /'weərəbaʊts/ n paradero

whereas /,weər'æz/ conj mientras que

whereby /weər'baɪ/ adv (fml) según cual, por el/la/lo cual

whereupon /,weərə'pɑn/ conj (fml) tras lo cual

wherever /weər'evər/ conj dondequiera que: ~ you like donde quieras ● adv dónde (demonios)

whet /wet/ vt (-tt-): ~ sb's appetite abrir el apetito a algn

whether /'weðər/ conj si ► **whether or not**: ~ or not it rains/~ it rains or not tanto si llueve como si no

which /wɪtʃ/ pron cuál ● adj 1 qué, cuál →WHAT 2 [relativo] que: the book ~ is on the table el libro que está sobre la mesa ◇ the article ~ I read yesterday el artículo que leí ayer 3 (fml) [después de prep] el/la/lo cual: in ~ case en cuyo caso ◇ the bag in ~ I put it la bolsa en la que lo puse **NOTA** Es más normal decir: the bag ~ I put it in.

whichever /wɪtʃ'evər/ adj, pron 1 el/la que: ~ you like el que quieras 2 cualquiera: It's the same, ~ way you go. No importa la ruta que elijas.

whiff /wɪf/ n **1** aroma, tufo **2** (fig) soplo

while /waɪl/ n [sing] tiempo, rato ▸ **once in a while** de vez en cuando ● conj (tb **whilst** /waɪlst/) **1** mientras (que): ~ you're at it ya que estás, vas, etc. **2** aunque ■ **while sth away** pasar algo: ~ the day away pasar el día

whim /wɪm/ n capricho, antojo

whimper /ˈwɪmpər/ vi lloriquear ● n lloriqueo

whine /waɪn/ **1** vt, vi gemir, gimotear **2** vi quejarse ● n gemido

whip /wɪp/ n **1** látigo, gimotear **2** (Pol) diputado/a encargado/a de la disciplina de su grupo parlamentario ● vt (-pp-) **1** azotar **2** ~ **sth (up) (into sth)** (Cocina) batir algo (hasta obtener algo): whipped cream crema batida ■ **whip sth up 1** provocar algo **2** preparar algo rápidamente

whir (tb **whirr** GB) /wɜːr/ n zumbido ● vi zumbar

whirl /wɜːrl/ **1** vt, vi (hacer) girar **2** vi (hojas) arremolinarse **3** vi (cabeza) dar vueltas ● n [sing] **1** giro **2** remolino **3** torbellino: My head is in a ~. La cabeza me da vueltas.

whirlpool /ˈwɜːrlpuːl/ n remolino

whirlwind /ˈwɜːrlwɪnd/ n torbellino ● adj (muy rápido) relámpago

whisk /wɪsk/ n batidor, batidora (eléctrica) ● vt **1** (Cocina) batir **2** ~ **sth/sb away/off** llevarse algo/a algn volando

whiskers /ˈwɪskərz/ n [pl] (animal) bigotes

whiskey (**whisky** GB (pl -ies)) /ˈwɪski/ n whisky

whisper /ˈwɪspər/ **1** vi susurrar **2** vi cuchichear **3** vt decir en voz baja ● n **1** cuchicheo **2** susurro

whistle /ˈwɪsl/ n **1** silbido **2** silbato, pito ● vt, vi silbar, pitar

white /waɪt/ adj (-er/-est) **1** blanco: ~ coffee café con leche **2** ~ **(with sth)** pálido (de algo) ● n **1** blanco **2** clara (de huevo) **whiteness** n blancura

white-collar adj de oficina: ~ workers oficinistas

White Paper n (GB) libro blanco (propuesta del gobierno)

whitewash /ˈwaɪtwɒʃ/ n lechada de cal ● vt **1** pintar con cal **2** (fig) encubrir

who /huː/ pron **1** quién(es) **2** que: people ~ eat garlic gente que come ajo ◊ the man ~ I spoke to el hombre con el que hablé
→WHOM

whoever /huːˈevər/ pron **1** quien **2** quienquiera que

whole /hoʊl/ adj **1** entero **2** todo ● n todo: the ~ of May todo mayo ▸ **on the whole** en general

wholehearted /ˌhoʊlˈhɑːrtɪd/ adj incondicional **wholeheartedly** adv sin reservas

wholemeal /ˈhoʊlmiːl/ (tb **wholewheat** /ˈhoʊlwiːt/) adj integral

wholesale /ˈhoʊlseɪl/ adj, adv **1** al por mayor **2** total

wholesome /ˈhoʊlsəm/ adj sano

wholly /ˈhoʊlli/ adv (fml) totalmente

whom /huːm/ pron (fml) **1** a quién: Whom did you meet? ¿Con quién te encontraste? **2** the investors, some of ~ bought shares los inversores, algunos de los cuales compraron acciones ◊ the person to ~ the letter was addressed la persona a quien iba dirigida la carta **NOTA** Es más normal decir: Who did you meet there? ◊ the person this letter was addressed to.

whoops /wʊps/ (tb **oops** /uːps/) interj ay

whose /huːz/ adj, pron de quién ● adj cuyo/a, cuyos/as: the woman ~ house I stayed in la mujer en cuya casa estuve

why /waɪ/ adv por qué: Why not? ¿Por qué no?

wicked /ˈwɪkɪd/ adj (-er/-est) **1** malvado **2** malicioso **3** (coloq) genial **wickedness** n maldad

wicker /ˈwɪkər/ n mimbre

wicket /ˈwɪkɪt/ (críquet) n **1** meta, palos **2** terreno

wide /waɪd/ adj (-er/-est) **1** ancho: How ~ is it? ¿Cuánto tiene de ancho? → BROAD **2** amplio **3** extenso ● adv muy: ~ awake/open completamente despierto/abierto de par en par **widely** adv extensamente, mucho: ~ used muy utilizado **widen** vt, vi ensanchar(se), ampliar(se)

wide-ranging adj de gran alcance, muy diverso

widespread /ˈwaɪdspred/ adj general, difundido

widow /ˈwɪdoʊ/ n viuda **widowed** adj viudo **widower** n viudo

width /wɪdθ/ n anchura, ancho

wield /wiːld/ vt **1** (arma, etc.) empuñar **2** (poder) ejercer

wife /waɪf/ n (pl **wives**) esposa

wig /wɪg/ n peluca

wiggle /ˈwɪɡl/ vt, vi (coloq) menear(se)

wild /waɪld/ adj (-er/-est) **1** salvaje **2** (planta) silvestre **3** (paisaje) agreste **4** (*tiempo*) tempestuoso **5** desenfrenado **6** furioso **7** (*coloq*) ~ (**about sth/sb**) loco (por algo/algn): *go* ~ *ponerse como loco* ● *n* **1** **the wild** [*sing*]: *in the* ~ *en estado salvaje* **2** **the wilds** (las) *tierras remotas* **wildly** *adv* **1** *locamente* **2** *violentamente*

wilderness /ˈwɪldənəs/ *n* **1** *tierra no cultivada* **2** (*fig*) *selva*

wildlife /ˈwaɪldlaɪf/ *n* *fauna*

will /wɪl/ (*contracción* **'ll** *neg* **will not/won't**) *v aux* [*para formar el futuro*]: *He'll come, won't he ?* Vendrá, ¿verdad? ◇ *I hope it won't rain.* Espero que no llueva. ◇ *That'll be the postman.* Ese será el cartero. ● **NOTA Will** es también un verbo modal al que sigue un infinitivo sin **to**. En interrogaciones y negaciones no se usa el auxiliar **do**. **1** *voluntad*: *She won't go.* No quiere ir. → SHALL **2** (*oferta, petición*): *Will you stay for tea ?* ¿Quiere quedarse a tomar té? ◇ *Will you help me ?* ¿Puedes ayudarme? **3** (*regla general*): *Oil ~ float on water.* El aceite flota en el agua. ● *n* **1** *voluntad* **2** *deseo* **3** *testamento* ▸ **at will** *libremente*

willful (**wilful** *GB*) /ˈwɪlfl/ *adj* (*pey*) **1** *voluntario* **2** (*delito*) premeditado **3** (*persona*) testarudo

willing /ˈwɪlɪŋ/ *adj* **1** *bien dispuesto* **2** *dispuesto* **3** (*apoyo, etc.*) *espontáneo* **willingly** *adv* *voluntariamente, de buena gana* **willingness** *n* (*buena*) *voluntad*

willow /ˈwɪloʊ/ *n* *sauce*

will power *n* *fuerza de voluntad*

wilt /wɪlt/ *vi* **1** *marchitarse* **2** *decaer*

win /wɪn/ (-**nn**-) (*pt/pp* **won**) **1** *vi, vt* *ganar* **2** (*victoria*) *lograr* **3** *vt* (*apoyo, amigos*) *ganarse* ■ **win sth/sb back** *recuperar algo/a algn* **win sb over/around** (**to sth**) *convencer a algn* (*de que haga algo*) ● *n* *victoria*

wince /wɪns/ *vi* **1** *hacer una mueca de dolor* **2** *hacer un gesto de disgusto*

wind¹ /wɪnd/ *n* **1** *viento* **2** *aliento* **3** (*GB*) [*U*] *gases* ▸ **get wind of sth** *enterarse de algo*

wind² /waɪnd/ (*pt/pp* **wound**) **1** *vi* *serpentear* **2** *vt* *enrollar* **3** *vt* ~ **sth** (**up**) *dar cuerda a algo* ■ **wind down** **1** *relajarse* **2** *llegar a su fin* **wind sb up** (*GB, coloq*) *darle cuerda a algn* **2** *provocar a algn* **wind** (**sth**) **up** *terminar* (*algo*) **wind sth up** (*Com*) *liquidar algo* **winding** *adj* *tortuoso* (*escalera*) *de caracol*

windfall /ˈwɪndfɔːl/ *n* **1** *sorpresa* *caída del cielo* **2** *fruta caída*

windmill /ˈwɪndmɪl/ *n* *molino de viento*

window /ˈwɪndoʊ/ *n* **1** *ventana* **2** *ventanilla* **3** (*tb* **windowpane** /ˈwɪndoʊpeɪn/) *vidrio* **4** *vitrina, aparador* (*Mx*)

window-shopping *n*: *go* ~ *mirar vitrinas*

window sill (*tb* **window ledge**) *n* *alféizar*

windshield /ˈwɪndʃiːld/ (**windscreen** /ˈwɪndskriːn/ *GB*) *n* *parabrisas*

windsurfing /ˈwɪndsɜːrfɪŋ/ *n* *windsurf*

windy /ˈwɪndi/ *adj* (-**ier/-iest**) **1** *de mucho viento* **2** *expuesto al viento*

wine /waɪn/ *n* *vino*

wing /wɪŋ/ *n* **1** *ala* **2** (*GB, carro*) *aleta* **the wings** (*Teat*) *bastidores*

wink /wɪŋk/ **1** *vt, vi* *guiñar* (*el ojo*) **2** *vi* (*luz*) *titilar* ● *n* *guiño*

winner /ˈwɪnər/ *n* *ganador/a*

winning /ˈwɪnɪŋ/ *adj* **1** *ganador* **2** (*persona, etc.*) *encantador* **winnings** *n* *ganancias*

winter /ˈwɪntər/ (*tb* **wintertime** /ˈwɪntərtaɪm/) *n* *invierno* ● *vi* *invernar, pasar el invierno* **wintry** *adj* *invernal*

wipe /waɪp/ *vt* **1** ~ **sth** (**away/off/up**); ~ **sth** (**from/off sth**) *limpiar* (*se*), *secar(se*) (*algo*) (*de algo*) **2** ~ **sth** (**from/off sth**) *borrar algo* (*de algo*) **3** ~ **sth across, onto, over, etc. sth** *pasar algo por algo* ■ **wipe sth out 1** *destruir algo* **2** *erradicar algo* **wiper** *n* *limpiaparabrisas*

wire /ˈwaɪər/ *n* **1** *alambre* **2** (*Elec*) *cable* **3** [*U*] *alambrado* ● *vt* **1** ~ **sth** (**up**) *hacer la instalación eléctrica de algo* **2** ~ **sth** (**up**) **to sth** *conectar algo a algo* **wiring** *n* [*U*] **1** *instalación eléctrica* **2** *cables*

wisdom /ˈwɪzdəm/ *n* **1** *sabiduría*: ~ *tooth muela cordal* **2** *cordura*

wise /waɪz/ *adj* (-**er/-iest**) **1** *sabio* **2** *acertado, prudente* ▸ **be none the wiser; not be any the wiser** *seguir sin entender nada*

wish /wɪʃ/ **1** *vt, vi* ~ **sb sth**; ~ **for sth** *desear algo* (*a algn*) **2** (*fml*) *querer* **3** *vt* (*que no se puede realizar*): *I* ~ *he'd go away.* ¡Ojalá se fuera! ◇ *She wished she had gone.* Se arrepintió de no haber ido. **NOTA** El uso de **were**, y no **was**, con **I**, **he** o **she** se considera más correcto: *I* ~ *I were rich!* **4** *vi* *pedir un* deseo ● n 1 ~ (for sth/to do sth) deseo (de algo/de hacer algo): *against my wishes* contra mi voluntad 2 wishes [pl]: (*with*) *best wishes, Tom* saludos, Tom **wishful** adj ▸ **wishful thinking**: *It's ~ thinking on my part.* Me estoy haciendo ilusiones.

wistful /'wɪstfl/ adj melancólico

wit /wɪt/ n 1 ingenio 2 (*persona*) persona ingeniosa 3 **wits** [pl] inteligencia, juicio ▸ **be at your wits' end** estar para volverse loco **frightened, scared, etc. out of your wits** muerto de miedo

witch /wɪtʃ/ n bruja

witchcraft /'wɪtʃkræft; GB -krɑːft/ n [U] brujería

witch-hunt n caza de brujas

with /wɪð/ prep 1 con: *He's ~ BP.* Trabaja en BP. 2 (*descripciones*) de, con: *the man ~ the scar* el hombre de la cicatriz ◇ *a house ~ a garden* una casa con jardín 3 de: *Fill the glass ~ water.* Llene el vaso de agua. 4 (*apoyo, etc.*) (de acuerdo) con 5 (*a causa de*) de: *tremble ~ fear* temblar de miedo ▸ **be with sb** (*coloq*) seguir lo que algn dice: *I'm not ~ you.* No te entiendo. **with it** (*coloq*) 1 al día 2 de moda 3 *He's not ~ it.* Está como ausente. **NOTA** Para el uso de **with** en PHRASAL VERBS ver el verbo, p.ej. **bear with** en BEAR.

withdraw /wɪð'drɔː/ (*pt* withdrew /-'druː/ *pp* withdrawn /-'drɔːn/) 1 vt, vi retirar(se) 2 vt (*fml*) (*palabras*) retractarse (de) **withdrawal** /wɪð'drɔːəl/ n 1 retirada, retiro 2 (*Med*): ~ *symptoms* síndrome de abstinencia **withdrawn** adj introvertido

wither /'wɪðə(r)/ vt, vi ~ (**away/up**) (**sth**) marchitarse, marchitar algo

withhold /wɪð'həʊld/ vt (*pt/pp* withheld /-'held/) (*fml*) 1 retener 2 (*información*) ocultar 3 (*consentimiento*) negar

within /wɪ'ðɪn/ prep 1 en el plazo de: ~ *a month of having left* al mes de haberse ido 2 (*distancia*) a menos de 3 al alcance de: *It's ~ walking distance.* Se puede ir a pie. 4 (*fml*) dentro de ● adv (*fml*) dentro

without /wɪ'ðaʊt/ prep sin

withstand /wɪð'stænd/ vt (*pt/pp* withstood /-'stʊd/) (*fml*) resistir

witness /'wɪtnəs/ n ~ (**to sth**) testigo (de algo) ● vt 1 presenciar 2 ser testigo de

witness stand (**witness box** GB) n estrado

witty /'wɪti/ adj (-ier/-iest) chistoso, ingenioso

wives /waɪvz/ pl de WIFE

wizard /'wɪzəd/ n mago

wobble /'wɒbl/ 1 vi tambalearse 2 vi (*silla*) cojear 3 vi (*gelatina*) temblar 4 vt mover **wobbly** adj (*coloq*) 1 que se tambalea 2 cojo

woe /wəʊ/ n (*fml*) desgracia ▸ **woe betide sb**: *Woe betide me if I forget!* ¡Ay de mí si se me olvida!

wok /wɒk/ n sartén china

woke /wəʊk/ *pt de* WAKE

woken /'wəʊkən/ *pp de* WAKE

wolf /wʊlf/ n (*pl* wolves /wʊlvz/) lobo

woman /'wʊmən/ n (*pl* women /'wɪmɪn/) mujer

womb /wuːm/ n útero

won /wʌn/ *pt, pp de* WIN

wonder /'wʌndə(r)/ 1 vt, vi preguntarse: *It makes you ~.* Te da que pensar. 2 vi ~ (**at sth**) admirarse (de algo) ● n 1 asombro 2 maravilla ▸ **it's a wonder** (**that...**) es un milagro (que...) **no wonder** (**that...**) no es de extrañar (que...) **work wonders** hacer milagros **wonderful** adj maravilloso

won't /wəʊnt/ = WILL NOT

wood /wʊd/ n 1 madera 2 leña 3 bosque → FOREST **wooded** adj arbolado **wooden** adj 1 de madera 2 (*pierna*) de palo

woodland /'wʊdlənd/ n bosque

woodwind /'wʊdwɪnd/ n instrumentos de viento (*de madera*)

woodwork /'wʊdwɜːk/ n 1 molduras 2 carpintería

wool /wʊl/ n lana **woolen** (**-ll-** GB) (*tb* **woolly**) adj de lana

word /wɜːd/ n 1 palabra 2 **words** [pl] (*canción*) letra ▸ **give sb your word** dar su palabra a algn **have a word** (**with sb**) hablar (con algn) **have the last word** tener la última palabra **in other words** en otras palabras, es decir **keep/break your word** cumplir/faltar a su palabra **put in a** (**good**) **word for sb** recomendar a algn, interceder por algn **take sb's word for it** (**that...**) creer a algn (cuando dice que...) **without a word** sin decir nada **words to that effect**: *He told me to go, or ~s to that effect.* Me dijo que me fuera, o algo parecido. ● vt expresar **wording** n términos, texto

word processor n procesador de textos **word processing** n procesamiento de textos

wore /wɔːr/ *pt de* WEAR

work /wɜːrk/ n 1 [U] trabajo: get (down)/go/set to ~ ponerse a trabajar ◇ ~ experience experiencia laboral/profesional 2 obra: the complete ~s of Borges las obras completas de Borges ◇ Is this your own ~? ¿Lo hizo usted sola? 3 **works** obras **NOTA** La palabra work es incontable, pero **job** es contable: I've found work/a new job. **Employment** es más formal, y se refiere a la condición de los que tienen empleo: Many women are in part-time employment. **Occupation** se usa en los impresos oficiales: Occupation: student, y **profession** se refiere a los trabajos que requieren una carrera universitaria: the medical profession. **Trade** designa los oficios que requieren una formación especial: He's a carpenter by trade. ● 1 vi trabajar: ~ on the assumption that... basarse en la suposición de que... 2 vi ~ **for sth** esforzarse por algo 3 vi (Mec) funcionar 4 vi surtir efecto: It will never ~. No va a ser factible. 5 vt (máquina, etc.) manejar 6 vt (persona) hacer trabajar 7 vt (mina, etc.) explotar 8 vt (tierra) cultivar ► **work free, loose, etc.** soltar(se), aflojar(se) ■ **work out** 1 resultar, salir 2 hacer ejercicio **work sth out** 1 calcular algo 2 solucionar algo 3 idear algo **work sb/yourself up** 1 entusiasmar(se) (a algn): get worked up exaltarse 2 poner(se) nervioso (a algn) **work sth up** 1 desarrollar algo 2 ~ **up an appetite** abrir el apetito **workable** adj factible

workaholic /ˌwɜːrkəˈhɒlɪk/ n (coloq) adicto/a al trabajo **NOTA** Workaholic es un derivado humorístico formado por la palabra **work** y el sufijo **-holic**, usado en **alcoholic**. Otras palabras nuevas similares son **chocaholic** (adicto al chocolate) y **shopaholic** (adicto a ir de compras).

workforce /ˈwɜːrkfɔːrs/ n mano de obra

working /ˈwɜːrkɪŋ/ adj 1 activo 2 de trabajo 3 laboral 4 que funciona 5 (conocimiento) básico ● n **workings** [pl] funcionamiento

working class n clase obrera • **working-class** adj de clase obrera

workload /ˈwɜːrkloʊd/ n cantidad de trabajo

workman /ˈwɜːrkmən/ n (pl -men) obrero **workmanship** n 1 (de persona) arte 2 (de producto) fabricación

workmate /ˈwɜːrkmeɪt/ n compañero/a de trabajo

workout /ˈwɜːrkaʊt/ n sesión de ejercicio físico

workplace /ˈwɜːrkpleɪs/ n lugar de trabajo

workshop /ˈwɜːrkʃɒp/ n taller

workstation /ˈwɜːrksteɪʃn/ n estación de trabajo (en oficina)

worktop /ˈwɜːrktɒp/ n (GB) superficie para trabajo (cocina)

world /wɜːrld/ n mundo: all over the ~/the ~ over por todo el mundo ◇ world-famous famoso en todo el mundo ◇ the ~ population la población mundial ► **how, what, why, etc. in the world** (coloq) ¿cómo, qué, por qué, etc. demonios? **worldly** adj 1 mundano 2 (bienes) terrenal 3 de mundo

worldwide /ˈwɜːrldwaɪd/ adj mundial, universal • /ˌwɜːrld-ˈwaɪd/ adv por todo el mundo

the World Wide Web (abrev **WWW**) (tb **the Web**) n la red mundial

worm /wɜːrm/ n 1 gusano 2 lombriz

worn /wɔːrn/ pp de WEAR

worn out adj 1 gastado 2 (persona) agotado

worry /ˈwʌri/ (pt/pp -ied) vt, vi ~ (yourself) (about sth/sb) preocupar(se) (por algo/algn) ● n (pl -ies) 1 [U] intranquilidad 2 preocupación: a ~ worried adj ~ (about sth/sb) preocupado (por algo/algn): I'm ~ he might get lost. Me preocupa que se pueda perder. **worrying** adj preocupante

worse /wɜːrs/ adj, adv peor: get ~ empeorar ► **make matters/things worse** para colmo (de desgracias) ● n lo peor: take a turn for the ~ empeorar **worsen** vt, vi empeorar

worship /ˈwɜːrʃɪp/ n 1 veneración 2 ~ (of sth/sb) (Rel) culto (a algo/algn) ● (-pp- tb -p- USA) 1 vt, vi adorar 2 vt rendir culto a **worshipper** n devoto/a

worst /wɜːrst/ adj, adv peor: My ~ fears were confirmed. Pasó lo que más me temía. ◇ the ~ hit areas las áreas más afectadas ● **the worst** n lo peor ► **at (the) worst; if the worst comes to the worst** en el peor de los casos

worth /wɜːrθ/ adj 1 con un valor de, que vale: be ~ five dollars valer $5 2 It's ~ reading. Vale la pena leerlo. ► **be worth it**; **be worth sb's while** valer la pena **get your money's worth** hacer rendir el dinero ● *n* **1** valor **2** (*dinero*): **ten dollars ~ of** gasolina **3** (*tiempo*): **a year's ~ of supplies** suministros para un año **worthless** *adj* **1** sin valor **2** (*persona*) despreciable

worthwhile /ˌwɜːθˈwaɪl/ *adj* que vale la pena

worthy /ˈwɜːði/ *adj* (**-ier/-iest**) **1** digno **2** (*causa*) noble **3** (*persona*) respetable

would /wəd, wʊd/ (contracción **'d** *neg* **would not/wouldn't** /ˈwʊdnt/) *v aux* (*condicional*): *Would you do it if I paid you?* ¿Lo harías si te pagara? ◇ *He said he ~ come.* Dijo que vendría.
● **NOTA Would** es un verbo modal al que sigue un infinitivo sin **to**, y que no usa el auxiliar **do** en interrogaciones y negaciones. **1** (*oferta, petición*): *Would you like a drink?* ¿Quiere tomar algo? ◇ *Would you come this way?* ¿Quiere venir por acá? **2** (*propósito*): *I left a note so (that) he'd call me.* Dejé una nota para que me llamara. **3** (*voluntad*): *He wouldn't shake my hand.* No quería darme la mano.

wound¹ /wuːnd/ *n* herida ● *vt* herir → **HERIDA** **the wounded** *n* [*pl*] los heridos

wound² /waʊnd/ *pt, pp* de **WIND** ²

wove /wəʊv/ *pt* de **WEAVE**

woven /ˈwəʊvn/ *pp* de **WEAVE**

wow /waʊ/ *interj* (*coloq*) guau

wrangle /ˈræŋgl/ *n* disputa ● *vi* discutir

wrap /ræp/ *vt* (**-pp-**) **1 ~ sth/sb (up)** envolver algo/a algn **2 ~ sth around sth/sb** atar algo alrededor de algo/algn ► **wrapped up in sth/sb** entregado a algo/algn, absorto en algo/algn ■ **wrap (sb/yourself) up** abrigar(se) a algn **wrap sth up** (*coloq*) concluir algo ● *n* chal **wrapper** *n* envoltura **wrapping** *n* envoltura

wrapping paper *n* papel de regalo/envolver

wrath /ræθ; *USA* ræθ *GB*/ *n* (*fml*) ira

wreath /riːθ/ *n* (*pl* **-s** /riːðz/) corona (*de flores, de Navidad*)

wreck /rek/ *n* **1** naufragio **2** (*coloq*) ruina **3** carcacha ● *vt* destrozar **wreckage** /ˈrekɪdʒ/ *n* restos (*accidente, etc.*)

wrench /rentʃ/ *vt* **1 ~ sth off** (*algo*) (*de un tirón*) **2 ~ sth out of sth** sacar algo (*de algo*) (*de un tirón*) ● *n*

1 (*USA*) llave inglesa **2** tirón, jalón **3** (*fig*) golpe

wrestle /ˈresl/ *vi* luchar **wrestler** *n* luchador/a **wrestling** *n* lucha libre

wretch /retʃ/ *n* desgraciado/a

wretched /ˈretʃɪd/ *adj* **1** desgraciado **2** maldito

wriggle /ˈrɪgl/ *vt, vi* **1 ~ (sth) (about)** moverse, mover algo **2** retorcer(se): **~ free** lograr soltarse

wring /rɪŋ/ *vt* (*pt, pp* **wrung**) **1 ~ sth (out)** estrujar, escurrir algo **2 ~ sth out of/from sb** sacarle algo a algn ► **wring sb's neck** retorcerle el pescuezo a algn

wrinkle /ˈrɪŋkl/ *n* arruga ● *vt* **1** arrugar(se) **2** *vt* (*ceño*) fruncir

wrist /rɪst/ *n* muñeca

write /raɪt/ *vt, vi* (*pt* **wrote** *pp* **written**) escribir ■ **write back (to sb)** contestar (a algn) (*por escrito*) **write sth down** anotar algo **write off/away for sth** escribir pidiendo algo **write sth off 1** (*deuda, etc.*) anular algo **2** dar algo por perdido **3** (*GB*) destrozar algo **write sth/sb off (as sth)** desechar algo/a algn (*por inútil*) **write sth out 1** escribir algo (*en limpio*) **2** copiar algo **write sth up** redactar algo **writer** *n* escritor/a

write-off *n* desastre: *The motorcycle was a ~.* A la moto la declararon siniestro total.

writhe /raɪð/ *vi* retorcerse

writing /ˈraɪtɪŋ/ *n* **1** escritura, escrito: **~ paper** papel de carta **2** escrito: **in ~** por escrito **3** estilo de redacción **4** letra **5 writings** obras

written /ˈrɪtn/ *pp* de **WRITE** ● *adj* por escrito

wrong /rɒŋ; rɔːŋ *GB*/ *adj* **1** malo, injusto: *It is ~ to...* No está bien... ◇ *He was ~ to say that.* Hizo mal en decir eso. **2** equivocado, falso: **be ~/get sth ~** equivocarse (en algo) **3** inoportuno: *the ~ way up/round* boca abajo/al revés **4** *What's ~?* ¿Qué pasa? ● *adv* mal, incorrectamente ► **get sb wrong** (*coloq*) malinterpretar a algn **go wrong 1** equivocarse **2** (*máquina*) descomponerse **3** salir/ir mal **wrongly** *adv* equivocadamente, incorrectamente

wrote /rəʊt/ *pt* de **WRITE**

wrought iron /ˌrɔːt ˈaɪərn/ *n* hierro forjado

wrung /rʌŋ/ *pt, pp* de **WRING**

X x

X, x /eks/ *n* (*pl* **X's, x's** /'eksɪz/) X, x

Xmas /'krɪsməs, 'eksməs/ *n* (*coloq*) Navidad

X-ray *n* 1 radiografía 2 **X-rays** rayos X ● *vt* hacer una radiografía de

xylophone /'zaɪləfoʊn/ *n* xilófono

Y y

Y, y /waɪ/ *n* (*pl* **Y's, y's**) Y, y

yacht /jɑt/ *n* yate **yachting** *n* navegación en yate

Yank /jæŋk/ (*tb* **Yankee**) *n* (*coloq*) yanqui

yank /jæŋk/ (*coloq*) 1 *vt, vi* dar un tirón brusco (a) 2 *vt* ~ **sth off/out** quitar, sacar algo de un tirón

yard /jɑrd/ *n* 1 (*USA*) jardín 2 (*GB*) patio 3 (*abrev* **yd**) yarda (0,9144 m) →*Ver pág. 222*

yardstick /'jɑrdstɪk/ *n* criterio

yarn /jɑrn/ *n* 1 hilo 2 cuento

yawn /jɔn/ *vi* bostezar ● *n* bostezo **yawning** *adj* enorme

yeah /jeə/ *interj* (*coloq*) sí

year /jɪr/ *n* año: *a two-year-old* (*child*) un niño de dos años ◊ *I am ten* (*~s old*). Tengo diez años. →OLD

yearly /'jɪrli/ *adj* anual ● *adv* anualmente, cada año

yearn /jɜrn/ *vi* (*fml*) 1 ~ (**for sth/ sb**) suspirar (por algo/algn) 2 ~ (**to do sth**) anhelar (hacer algo) **yearning** *n* 1 ~ (**for sth**) anhelo, añoranza (de algo) 2 ~ (**to do sth**) ansia (por/de hacer algo)

yeast /jist/ *n* levadura

yell /jel/ *vt, vi* ~ (**sth**) (**out**) gritar (algo) ● *n* grito

yellow /'jeloʊ/ *adj, n* amarillo **yellowish** *adj* amarillento

yelp /jelp/ *vi* 1 (*animal*) gemir 2 (*persona*) gritar

yes /jes/ *interj, n* sí

yesterday /'jestərdeɪ, -di/ *adv, n* ayer

yet /jet/ *adv* 1 [*frases negativas*] todavía, aún → STILL 2 [*frases interrogativas*] ya **NOTA** *Yet* sólo se usa en interrogaciones y siempre va al final de la frase:

Have you finished it ~? **Already** se usa en afirmaciones e interrogaciones y suele ir detrás de verbos auxiliares o modales y delante de los demás verbos: *Have you finished already?* ◊ *He already knew her.* Cuando **already** indica sorpresa por una acción realizada antes de lo esperado, puede ir al final de la frase: *He has found a job already!* ◊ *Is it there already? That was quick!* 3 [*después de superl*]: *her best novel* ~ su mejor novela hasta la fecha 4 [*antes de comp*] incluso: ~ *more work* aún más trabajo ► **yet again** una vez más ● *conj* aun así: *It's amazing* ~ *true.* Es increíble pero cierto.

yew /ju/ (*tb* ~ **tree**) *n* (*Bot*) tejo

yield /jild/ 1 *vt* producir, dar 2 *vt* (*Fin*) rendir 3 *vi* ~ (**to sth/sb**) rendirse (a algo/algn), ceder (ante algo/algn) **NOTA** Es más común **give in**. ● *n* 1 producción 2 cosecha 3 (*Fin*) rendimiento **yielding** *adj* 1 flexible 2 sumiso

yogurt (*tb* **yoghurt**) /'joʊgərt; 'jɒgət *GB*/ *n* yogur(t)

yoke /joʊk/ *n* yugo

yolk /joʊk/ *n* yema

you /ju; *pron* jə/ *pron* 1 [*sujeto*] tú, usted, ustedes **NOTA** El *pron pers* no puede omitirse en inglés. 2 [*frases impersonales*]: *You can't smoke here.* No se puede fumar aquí. **NOTA** En las frases impersonales se puede usar **one** en vez de **you**, pero es mucho más formal. 3 [*objeto directo*] te, lo, la, los, las 4 [*objeto indirecto*] te, le, les 5 [*después de prep*] ti, usted, ustedes

you'd /jud/ 1 = YOU HAD 2 = YOU WOULD

you'll /jul/ = YOU WILL

young /jʌŋ/ *adj* (-er /-ər/ -est /-ɪst/) joven: *people young* ~ nes ◊ *He's a year younger than me.* Es un año menor que yo. ● *n* [*pl*] 1 (*animales*) crías 2 **the young** los jóvenes

youngster /'jʌŋstər/ *n* joven

your /jɔr; *adj* jər/ tu, su: *break* ~ *arm* romperse el brazo →MY

you're /jʊər/ = YOU ARE

yours /jɜrz, jɔrz/ *pron* tuyo/a, -os/as, suyo/a, -os/as: *a friend of* ~ una amiga tuya/suya ► **Yours faithfully/sincerely** Lo/la saluda atentamente →ATENTAMENTE

yourself /jər'self; jɔr'self *GB*/ *pron* (*pl* **-selves**) 1 [*reflexivo*] te, se: *Enjoy yourselves!* ¡Pásenla bien! 2 [*después de prep*] ti (mismo/a), usted (mismo/a), ustedes (mismos/as) 3 [*énfasis*] tú mismo/a, usted mismo/a, ustedes mismos/as ▸ **(all) by yourself/ yourselves** solo(s) **be yourself/ yourselves** ser natural: *Just be ~*. Simplemente sé tú mismo.

youth /juːθ/ *n* **1** [U] juventud: *In my youth...* Cuando yo era joven... ◇ *~ club/hostel* club para jóvenes/albergue juvenil **2** (*frec pej*) joven **youthful** *adj* juvenil

you've /juːv/ = YOU HAVE

Yo Yo® (*tb* **yo-yo**) /ˈjoʊ joʊ/ *n* (*pl -s*) yo-yo

yuck (**yuk** *GB*) /jʌk/ *interj* guácala

Z z

Z, z /ziː; zed *GB*/ *n* (*pl* **Z's, z's**) Z, z

zeal /ziːl/ *n* entusiasmo, fervor **zealous** /ˈzeləs/ *adj* entusiasta

zebra /ˈziːbrə, ˈzebrə/ *n* cebra

zebra crossing *n* (*GB*) paso de cebra

zenith /ˈzenɪθ/ *n* cenit

zero /ˈzɪəroʊ/ *adj, n, pron* (*pl -s*) cero

zest /zest/ *n* entusiasmo, pasión

zigzag /ˈzɪgzæg/ *adj* en zigzag ● *n* zigzag

zinc /zɪŋk/ *n* zinc, cinc

zip /zɪp/ *n* (*GB*) cierre, zíper ● (**-pp-**) **1** *vt ~ sth* (**up**) cerrar (el zíper de) algo **2** *vi ~* (**up**) cerrarse (con zíper)

ZIP code *n* (*USA*) código postal

zipper /ˈzɪpər/ *n* cierre, zíper

zodiac /ˈzoʊdiæk/ *n* zodíaco

zone /zoʊn/ *n* zona

zoo /zuː/ (*pl -s*) *n* zoo, (parque) zoológico

zoology /zuːˈɑlədʒi/ *n* zoología **zoologist** *n* zoólogo/a

zoom /zuːm/ *vi* **1** ir muy deprisa: *~ past* pasar zumbando **2** *~ in* (**on sth/sb**) enfocar (algo/a algn) (*con zoom*) ● (*tb* ~ **lens**) *n* zoom

zucchini /zuˈkiːni/ *n* calabacín, calabacita (*Mx*)

Verbos irregulares

En los casos en que se incluyen dos formas, la forma regular suele ser más común en EE.UU. En los casos marcados con asterisco (*), consulte la entrada.

Infinitivo	Pasado	Participio
arise	arose	arisen
awake	awoke	awoken
babysit	babysat	babysat
be	was/were	been
bear	bore	borne
beat	beat	beaten
become	became	become
begin	began	begun
bend	bent	bent
bet	bet	bet
bid	bid	bid
bind	bound	bound
bite	bit	bitten
bleed	bled	bled
blow	blew	blown
break	broke	broken
breed	bred	bred
bring	brought	brought
broadcast	broadcast	broadcast
build	built	built
burn	burned, burnt	burned, burnt
burst	burst	burst
bust	busted, bust	busted, bust
buy	bought	bought
cast	cast	cast
catch	caught	caught
choose	chose	chosen
cling	clung	clung
come	came	come
cost	cost, costed*	cost, costed*
creep	crept	crept
cut	cut	cut
deal	dealt	dealt
dig	dug	dug
dive	dove, dived (GB)	dived
do²	did	done
draw	drew	drawn
dream	dreamed, dreamt	dreamed, dreamt
drink	drank	drunk
drive	drove	driven
dwell	dwelled, dwelt	dwelled, dwelt
eat	ate	eaten
fall	fell	fallen
feed	fed	fed
feel	felt	felt
fight	fought	fought

Infinitivo	Pasado	Participio
find	found	found
flee	fled	fled
fling	flung	flung
fly	flew	flown
forbid	forbade	forbidden
forecast	forecast, forecasted	forecast, forecasted
forget	forgot	forgotten
forgive	forgave	forgiven
forsake	forsook	forsaken
freeze	froze	frozen
get	got	gotten, got (GB)
give	gave	given
go	went	gone
grind	ground	ground
grow	grew	grown
hang	hung, hanged*	hung, hanged*
have	had	had
hear	heard	heard
hide	hid	hidden
hit	hit	hit
hold	held	held
hurt	hurt	hurt
keep	kept	kept
kneel	knelt	knelt
know	knew	known
lay¹	laid	laid
lead¹	led	led
lean	leaned, tb leant (GB)	leaned, tb leant (GB)
leap	leaped, leapt	leaped, leapt
learn	learned, learnt	learned, learnt
leave	left	left
lend	lent	lent
let	let	let
lie²	lay	lain
light	lit, lighted*	lit, lighted*
lose	lost	lost
make	made	made
mean	meant	meant
meet	met	met
mislay	mislaid	mislaid
mislead	misled	misled
mistake	mistook	mistaken
mow	mowed	mowed, mown
outdo	outdid	outdone

Infinitivo	Pasado	Participio	Infinitivo	Pasado	Participio
overcome	overcame	overcome	spell	spelled,	spelled,
outgrow	outgrew	outgrown		spelt	spelt
overdo	overdid	overdone	spend	spent	spent
override	overrode	overridden	spill	spilled,	spilled,
overtake	overtook	overtaken		*tb* spilt	*tb* spilt
pay	paid	paid		(GB)	(GB)
plead	pleaded,	pleaded,	spin	spun	spun
	tb pled	*tb* pled	spit	spat	spat
	(USA)	(USA)	split	split	split
put	put	put	spoil	spoiled,	spoiled,
quit	quit,	quit,		*tb* spoilt	*tb* spoilt
	tb quitted	*tb* quitted		(GB)	(GB)
	(GB)	(GB)	spread	spread	spread
read	read	read	spring	sprang	sprung
rewind	rewound	rewound	stand	stood	stood
rid	rid	rid	steal	stole	stolen
ride	rode	ridden	stick	stuck	stuck
ring²	rang	rung	sting	stang	stung
rise	rose	risen	stink	stank,	stunk
run	ran	run		stunk	
saw	sawed	sawn,	stride	strode	___
		tb sawed	strike	struck	struck
		(USA)	string	strung	strung
say	said	said	strive	strove	striven
see	saw	seen	swear	swore	sworn
seek	sought	sought	sweep	swept	swept
sell	sold	sold	swell	swelled	swollen
send	sent	sent	swim	swam	swum
set	set	set	swing	swung	swung
sew	sewed	sewed,	take	took	taken
		sewn	teach	taught	taught
shake	shook	shaken	tear	tore	torn
shear	sheared	sheared,	tell	told	told
		shorn	think	thought	thought
shed	shed	shed	throw	threw	thrown
shine	shone	shone	tread	trod	trodden
shoe	shod	shod	undergo	underwent	undergone
shoot	shot	shot	understand	understood	understood
show	showed	shown	undertake	undertook	undertaken
shrink	shrank	shrunk	undo	undid	undone
shut	shut	shut	unwind	unwound	unwound
sing	sang	sung	upset	upset	upset
sink	sank	sunk	wake	woke	woken
sit	sat	sat	wear	wore	worn
slay	slew	slain	weave	wove	woven
sleep	slept	slept	weep	wept	wept
slide	slid	slid	wet	wet	wet
sling	slung	slung	win	won	won
slit	slit	slit	wind	wound	wound
smell	smelled,	smelled,	withdraw	withdrew	withdrawn
	tb smelt	*tb* smelt	withhold	withheld	withheld
	(GB)	(GB)	withstand	withstood	withstood
sow	sowed,	sown	wring	wrung	wrung
	sowed		write	wrote	written
speak	spoke	spoken			
speed	sped,	sped,			
	speeded*	speeded*			

Pronunciación

Hay palabras que tienen más de una pronunciación posible. En el *Oxford Pocket* se incluyen las más comunes, ordenadas por su frecuencia de uso:

    either /'iːðər; 'aɪðər/

Si la pronunciación de la palabra cambia mucho en inglés británico, se indica mediante la abreviatura *GB*:

    address /'ædres; əˈdres GB /

/'/ indica el acento principal de la palabra:

    formal /'fɔːrml/ lleva el acento en la primera sílaba.

/ˌ/ indica el acento secundario de la palabra:

    pronunciation /prəˌnʌnsiˈeɪʃn/ lleva el acento secundario en la segunda sílaba /ˌnʌn/, y el principal en la sílaba /'eɪ/.

r En inglés americano siempre se pronuncia la r final, pero en inglés británico solamente se pronuncia la **r** final cuando la palabra siguiente empieza con una vocal.

    La **r** no se pronuncia en la frase *His car broke down*, pero sí en *His car is brand new*.

Formas tónicas y átonas

Algunas palabras de uso frecuente (**an, are, as, was,** etc.) tienen dos pronunciaciones posibles, una tónica y otra átona. De las dos, la forma átona es más común.

La preposición **from**, por ejemplo, normalmente se pronuncia /frəm/ en frases como:
He comes from Mexico.

Si aparece al final de la oración, en cambio, o si se le quiere dar un énfasis especial, se utiliza la pronunciación tónica /frʌm/, como en el caso de:
The ˌpresent's not 'from John, it's 'for him.

Palabras derivadas

En muchas ocasiones, la pronunciación de una palabra derivada es la suma de la pronunciación de sus elementos. En estos casos, no se incluye la transcripción fonética, ya que es predecible:

    slowly /'sloʊli/ = **slow** /sloʊ/ + **-ly** /li/

Pero a veces el acento de la palabra cambia al añadirle las desinencias, y en estos casos se indica la pronunciación:

    photograph /'foʊtəɡræf/
    photographic /ˌfoʊtəˈɡræfɪk/
    photography /fəˈtɒɡrəfi/

En el caso de las palabras derivadas terminadas en **–tion**, no se incluye la pronunciación, ya que la norma consiste en que el acento recae sobre la penúltima sílaba:

    alter /'ɔːltər/
    alteration /ˌɔːltəˈreɪʃn/